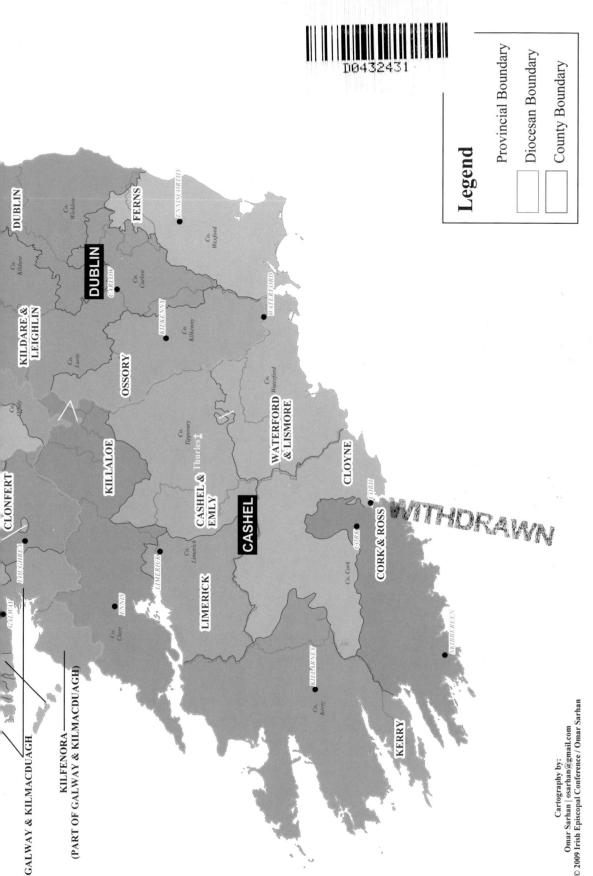

Legend

Provincial Boundary
Diocesan Boundary
County Boundary

DUBLIN

Co. Wicklow

FERNS

ENNISCORTHY

Co. Wexford

Co. Kildare

DUBLIN

KILDARE & LEIGHLIN

CARLOW

Co. Carlow

WATERFORD

KILKENNY

Co. Kilkenny

OSSORY

Co. Laois

Co. Offaly

Co. Waterford

WATERFORD & LISMORE

CLONFERT

KILLALOE

Co. Tipperary

Thurles

CASHEL & EMLY

CLOYNE

COBH

CASHEL

CORK & ROSS

CORK

Co. Cork

WITHDRAWN

LOUGHREA

GALWAY

ENNIS

Co. Clare

Co. Limerick

LIMERICK

LIMERICK

SKIBBEREEN

KILLARNEY

Co. Kerry

KERRY

GALWAY & KILMACDUAGH

KILFENORA
(PART OF GALWAY & KILMACDUAGH)

Cartography by:
Omar Sarhan | osarhan@gmail.com
© 2009 Irish Episcopal Conference / Omar Sarhan

IRISH CATHOLIC DIRECTORY 2010

BENEDICT XVI
BISHOP OF ROME
Vicar of Jesus Christ

Successor of the Prince of the Apostles, Supreme Pontiff of the Universal Church, Primate of Italy, Archbishop and Metropolitan of the Roman Province, Sovereign of the State of the Vatican City.

Servant of the Servants of God, Joseph Ratzinger, born at Marktl am Inn, Germany on 16 April 1927; ordained priest on 29 June 1951, ordained Archbishop of Munich and Freising on 25 March 1977; created Cardinal on 27 June 1977. He was elected Pope on 19 April 2005 and inaugurated on 24 April.

IRISH
CATHOLIC
DIRECTORY
2010

PUBLISHED BY AUTHORITY
FOR THE HIERARCHY OF IRELAND

This publication
has been supported
by the generous
sponsorship
of

VERITAS

Published for the Hierarchy by
Veritas Publications
7–8 Lower Abbey Street
Dublin 1
Ireland
Email publications@veritas.ie
Website www.veritas.ie

The publishers are not responsible for any
errors or omissions.

ISBN 978 1 84730 208 3

Cover design: Paula Ryan
Design & Typesetting: Colette Dower, Veritas Publications
Printed in the Republic of Ireland
by Hudson Killeen Ltd, Dublin

Veritas books are printed on paper made from the wood pulp of managed forests.
For every tree felled, at least one tree is planted, thereby renewing natural resources.

FOREWORD

This is the twentieth edition of the *Irish Catholic Directory*. Information for this edition was collected between August 2009 and November 2009. In general, all information comes from the organisation or community concerned.

Veritas has continued in its substantial effort to meticulously check information received and is confident that this year's *Irish Catholic Directory* will once again prove an accurate and useful resource.

We would like to express our gratitude to all the bishops, diocesan secretaries, priests, brothers, sisters and lay people who have over the years supplied information, answered queries, chased details and checked proofs.

We are also indebted to the advertisers and sponsors, without whose support this publication could not appear.

Finally, it may be appropriate to remind readers that the *Directory* is simply an orderly listing of personnel in the Church and related organisations. Our task is to make this listing as easy to use as possible. The *Directory* is not a statement of Church policy, nor an expression of precedence, and should not be taken as such.

CONTENTS

ALL IRELAND STD DIALLING

All STD numbers in this *Directory* are listed with both the number and the local area code.

Callers from the Irish Republic to Northern Ireland simply **need to dial 048 followed by the 8-digit local number**.

Every effort has been made to ensure the accuracy and completeness of the information in the *Directory*. However, this information can only be as good as that supplied to us by the individuals concerned.

REVIEW OF THE 2009 PASTORAL ACTIVITIES
OF THE IRISH EPISCOPAL CONFERENCE

The 2009 review of the pastoral initiatives undertaken by members of the Irish Bishops' Conference, and the commissions, angencies and offices of the Conference, reveals a particularly busy, challenging and exciting year. The following highlights some of these activities:

JANUARY

The theme of the message of His Holiness, Pope Benedict XVI, for the World Day of Prayer for Peace on 1 January was 'Fighting Poverty To Build Peace'. Speaking at a Mass in St Joseph's Church in Limerick, Bishop Donal Murray, Bishop of Limerick, said: 'Violence is once again raging in the land where Jesus and Mary lived. This year's Day of Prayer for Peace falls at a time when there is bloodshed and fear in the Holy Land. World leaders have called for an immediate end to the hostilities and the terrible loss of life that is occurring. At this time, when we are celebrating the birth of the Prince of Peace we should pray especially for the Holy Land, and we should look to the European Union and to all political leaders to do everything they can to bring about a ceasefire. We should long and pray that, in the coming year, peace may at last come to the people of that region who have experienced violence and fear for so long.'

On 2 January, Cardinal Seán Brady, Archbishop of Armagh and Primate of all Ireland, addressed the important role which is being undertaken by the National Board for Safeguarding Children in the Catholic Church. The NBSCCC was established as an independent body in 2006. Cardinal Brady said of the NBSC: 'The findings of the recent report of the National Board into the handling of allegations by the Diocese of Cloyne have brought further anxiety to victims of abuse … [the NBSC] has demonstrated an ability to investigate rigorously, report courageously and, crucially, to have its recommendations accepted. Everyone is entitled to know that in all Church activities, children will be safe.' Cardinal Brady continued: 'At all times the welfare of children must be the paramount consideration. This is a Gospel value as well as a core principle of safeguarding policy.'

On 12 January, the death took place of the former Bishop of Waterford and Lismore, Bishop Michael Russell (88). Bishop Russell was bishop of the diocese from 1965 to 1993. Bishop William Lee, Bishop of Waterford and Lismore, said: 'I am deeply saddened by the news of the death of Bishop Michael Russell, my predecessor as Bishop of Waterford and Lismore and great friend. Since becoming bishop of this diocese in July 1993 I have enjoyed and greatly valued his wisdom and support. Bishop Michael was loved and admired by the people and priests of Waterford and Lismore. He will be greatly missed by all. Bishop Michael will be remembered especially for his great love of the Church, his deep faith, his prayerfulness, his devotion to Our Lady, his humility, warmth and approachability.'

The Coordination of Episcopal Conferences in support of the Church in the Holy Land, which represents Catholic Bishops' Conferences of Europe and North America and was formed in Jurusalem in 1998 at the request of the Holy See, visited the Holy Land during January. Bishop Raymond Field, Auxiliary Bishop of Dublin, was the representative of the Irish bishops. The group called for prayers 'for the welfare of the Mother Church and the peace of Jurusalem'.

On 19 January, the Irish Commission for Justice and Social Affairs (ICJSA) launched a position paper, *In the Wake of the Celtic Tiger: Poverty in Contemporary Ireland,* at the Saint Vincent de Paul National Office on Sean McDermott Street, Dublin. Speaking at the launch of the position paper, ICJSA Chair Bishop Raymond Field said: 'In his World Day of Peace message Pope Benedict said that "every form of externally imposed poverty has at its root a lack of respect for the transcendent dignity of the human person". In addition to addressing world peace and the impact of globalisation, Pope Benedict also acknowledged the many forms of poverty that exist in "advanced, wealthy societies", warning us that "sooner or later, the distortions produced by unjust systems have to be paid for by everyone". Last June the ICJSA

published a position paper entitled *Violence in Irish Society: Towards an Ecology of Peace,* which highlights the connection between violence and social exclusion in Irish communities. At that time the ICJSA undertook to further research the issue of poverty. Today's paper, *In the Wake of the Celtic Tiger: Poverty in Contemporary Ireland,* is a deeper exploration of this problem and its consequences, not only for the individuals and families affected, but for our society as a whole.'

On 23 January, in advance of the Feast of Saint Francis de Sales, patron saint of journalists, Pope Benedict XVI published his message for the 43rd World Day of Communications (WDC). The theme for the 2009 WDC was 'New Technologies, New Relationships: Promoting a Culture of Respect, Dialogue and Friendship'.

The Bishops' Conference held a special meeting on 23 January on the subject of safeguarding children. Representatives of the National Board for Safeguarding Children in the Catholic Church addressed the meeting on policies and procedures for best practice in safeguarding children. Bishops discussed their pastoral responsibilities towards safeguarding children in the Church. Issues arising from the NBSCCC's *Report on the Management of Two Child Protection Cases in the Diocese of Cloyne,* published by the diocese on 19 December 2008, the *Reports of the HSE Audit of Catholic Church Dioceses* and the statement by the Minister for Children, Mr Barry Andrews TD, both published on 7 January, were discussed in detail.

On 24 January, Minister Barry Andrews held a meeting with Cardinal Brady and Archbishop Martin to discuss the issue of safeguarding children and the whole of society's responsibility to this criticially important issue.

The first all-island Catholic Schools Week took place from 26 January to 1 February and was themed 'Catholic Schools – A Vision for Life'. Catholic

Schools Week opened with seminars in Dublin and Belfast on education and the role of Catholic Schools. Key speakers included Archbishop Diarmuid Martin, Archbishop of Dublin, and Bishop Noel Treanor, Bishop of Down and Connor. According to Bishop Leo O'Reilly, Chair of the Bishops' Commission for Education: 'Catholic schools provide young people with the moral, intellectual and spiritual foundation to contribute to the common good. This special week is also a celebration of the indispensable role of teachers in the life of the school and parish through their committed service to the education of the young.'

FEBRUARY

The focus for the Year of Vocation for the month of February was 'religious life'. A weekend conference was held in the Stillorgan Park Hotel, Dublin, from 13 to 15 February. The conference was entitled 'Disturbed by the Spirit – Called to be Sent' and it focused on religious life, discipleship and vocations culture. The keynote speakers at the conference were Anthony J. Gittins, CSSp, Professor of Mission and Culture at the Catholic Theological Union in Chicago, and Mr John Waters, journalist and columnist.

On 11 February, Pope Benedict's message for the 17th World Day of the Sick focused particularly on sick and suffering children.

Bishop John Fleming, Bishop of Killala and President of CURA, addressed the 32nd Annual Conference of CURA. The weekend conference was held in Athlone, Co Westmeath, and was attended by CURA delegates from around the country. The theme for the conference was 'Volunteering in our Time'.

On 24 February, Cardinal Seán Brady and Archbishop Diarmuid Martin welcomed the publication by the National Board for Safeguarding Children in the Catholic Church, *Safeguarding Children – Standards and Guidance for the Catholic Church in Ireland* and its *Annual Report 2008*. Cardinal Brady said that it 'will be of great help in guiding those who are implementing safeguarding policy and procedures throughout Church life and I look forward to its implementation in

every parish and diocese in Ireland. I wish to thank the National Board for providing this essential reference on best practice … Today's publication is an indication of the Church's resolve to safeguard children at all times.'

MARCH

The 39th Annual Conferece of ACCORD, the Catholic Marriage Care Service, took place in Ballybrit, Co Galway, its theme was 'Leadership, Creation and Vocation'. Bishop Willie Walsh, Bishop of Killaloe and President of ACCORD, addressed the conference on the value and importance of the special vocation of married couples.

On 7 March, Pope Benedict XVI appointed the Archbishop of Cashel and Emly, the Most Reverend Dermot Clifford DD, as Apostolic Administrator, *sede plena* and *ad nutum Sanctae Sedis*, of the Diocese of Cloyne.

The Spring General Meeting of the Irish Bishops' Conference concluded in Maynooth on 11 March and addressed: Pope Benedict's and the bishops' statements on Northern Ireland, safeguarding children, preparation for Easter, Trócaire's 2009 Lenten Campaign, the Solemnity of Saint Patrick, ACCORD – Catholic Marriage Care Service, support for the Holy Land, Charities Act 2009, National Famine Memorial Day, keeping Sunday sacred, Day for Life 2009, Eucharistic Congress in Dublin in 2012, Year of Vocation and the Report on the 6th World Meeting of Families held in Mexico. At the press conference concluding the spring meeting, Bishop Christopher Jones, Bishop of Elphin and Chair of the Bishops' Committee on the Family, addressed the fear experienced by many families concerning home repossessions during the recession.

Bishop Jones said: 'I am proposing that family homes which are at risk would not be repossessed. This is not a blank cheque proposal. Each case would have to be appropriately assessed by a competent authority. In essence I am suggesting that the terms and conditions of a mortgage agreement could be renegotiated to enable a family to repay at a level appropriate to their current circumstances. This could be regularly reviewed. Why am I making this proposal? In Ireland the ownership

of the family home has always been considered important. Disruption of families and family life should be avoided where at all possible. I am therefore asking the State today, as it is obliged to do under the Constitution, "to protect the family … as the necessary basis of social order and as indispensable to the welfare of the Nation and the State" (Article 41,1,2). There is a lot of fear around. We must do all that we can do to remove the unnecessary fear from families that a sudden loss of income may bring. This will often include the trauma of displacement and all the negative consequences that result, especially for children.'

On 26 March, the Irish Bishops' Drugs Initiative (IBDI) hosted a seminar for parish representatives in St Patrick's College, Maynooth. Bishop Éamonn Walsh, Vice-Chair of the IBDI, opened the meeting, which was also addressed by Ms Marion Rackard, HSE Project Manager, Alcohol Initiatives. Ms Rackard focused on the benefits which accrue from community mobilisation in order to reduce the harm caused by alcohol and drug use in our parishes. Ms Rackard expressed strong support for the work of IBDI parish projects, which were first established in 2006. At the seminar, parish representatives discussed a draft handbook, *How Parishes can Respond to Alcohol and Drug Prevention*, which will be published in 2010. Information was also shared regarding parish events which were recently organised in order to change community attitudes towards alcohol and other drug misuse. Bishop Walsh said: 'Our target audience is the local community. Our work attempts to address, and prevent, the damage that alcohol inflicts on local communities – therefore our efforts to improve our local quality of life starts with parishes themselves. We need to educate children that alcohol is a drug which, if misused, detrimentally affects the way we think, feel and behave.'

APRIL

On 5 April, Cardinal Seán Brady celebrated the annual Mass for the Disappeared in St Patrick's Cathedral, Armagh. During his homily, Cardinal Brady said: 'Once again in this Mass I repeat the call to anyone who has any information which could help locate the bodies of the disappeared.

I beg them to pass that information on to the Commission for the Location of Victims.'

On 24 April, Bishop Leo O'Reilly, Bishop of Kilmore and Chair of the Bishops' Commission for Education, addressed the annual conference of the Catholic Primary Schools Management Association. At the conference, which took place in Dublin, Bishop O'Reilly said: 'The vision for Catholic Education today is rooted in faith as it has always been. It takes its inspiration from the person and the teaching of Christ.'

MAY

A weekend of events was held to mark the conclusion of the Year of Vocation. It began on 1 May with a special Year of Vocation concert in St Mary's Pro-Cathedral in Dublin with Fr Liam Lawton and the St John of God Choir. On 2 May, a series of vigils took place at monastic sites around Ireland. Finally, on Vocations Sunday, 3 May, Cardinal Seán Brady presided at the closing Mass for the Year of Vocation in St Patrick's Cathedral, Armagh. Following the Mass a new vocations DVD was launched in the Synod Hall of the Cathedral entitled *You Will Be My Witnesses*.

On 11 May, Cardinal Seán Brady addressed the Trinity Monday Service of Thanksgiving and Commemoration in the college chapel of Trinity College, Dublin. This was the first time that a Catholic Archbishop of Armagh preached in the chapel for this service. Cardinal Brady said: 'I thank God for the immense progress we have made on the journey of mutual respect and Christian solidarity between the Christians of Ireland.'

Bishops published a statement welcoming the first National Famine Commemoration Day, which took place on Sunday, 17 May. The Bishops' statement addressed the past and reflects on hunger and famine today. The statement was made available as part of a special Famine Commemoration feature on *www.catholicbishops.ie*. Liturgy notes, information for parishes and the 1995 pastoral letter, *Remembering the Irish Famine,* also formed part of this web feature.

On 20 May, Cardinal Seán Brady responded to the publication of the *Report of the Commission to Inquire into Child Abuse (Ryan Report).* Cardinal Brady said: 'Today's publication … throws light on a dark period of the past. The publication of this comprehensive report and analysis is a welcome and important step in establishing the truth, giving justice to victims and ensuring such abuse does not happen again. This Report makes it clear that great wrong and hurt were caused to some of the most vulnerable children in our society. It documents a shameful catalogue of cruelty: neglect, physical, sexual and emotional abuse, perpetrated against children. I am profoundly sorry and deeply ashamed that children suffered in such awful ways in these institutions. Children deserved better and especially from those caring for them in the name of Jesus Christ. I hope the publication of today's Report will help to heal the hurts of victims and to address the wrongs of the past. The Catholic Church remains determined to do all that is necessary to make the Church a safe, life-giving and joyful place for children.' In the aftermath of its publication, bishops also responded to issues raised by the *Ryan Report* in their dioceses and in the media.

On 30 May, up to one hundred young people from across Ireland attended the launch in Maynooth of a new framework document on youth ministry in Ireland entitled, *Called Together: Making the Difference.* Speaking at the launch, Bishop Donal McKeown, Auxiliary Bishop of Down and Connor, said: 'When we were seeking a date for the launch of this document, various factors were considered – availability of people, appropriate date and, of course, a desire not to be caught in the wake of other events. The theme of the 2008 World Youth Day in Sydney had been "You Will Be My Witnesses", and the Vigil of Pentecost seemed to be a good time to take up that theme. However, as we know, the *Ryan Report* has caused huge shock waves around the country and abroad and is a major part of the context in which this launch takes place. So before saying what this document is, it is important to say what it is not. This is not some claim by the Church that we are entitled to privileges in working with young people. This is not a pastoral plan for how to get more young people into active involvement in the various ways in which we are Church. This is not a structure that will replace the quiet – and not so quiet – work done in so many ways up and down this country.'

Bishop McKeown continued: 'So what is it [the new framework document on youth ministry]? It was conceived a couple of years ago and its proud parents were – and still are – two bodies set up by the Episcopal Conference whose work overlapped in this area. The two are: The National Committee of Diocesan Youth Directors (currently with Fr Gerry Kearns as Secretary) and The Youth Ministry Sub-Committee of the Episcopal Commission for Pastoral Renewal and Adult Faith Development (and the Resource Person for that Commission is Sr Anne Codd). Its purpose was to sketch out a framework that would set a context, priorities and methodology for youth ministry in this country.'

JUNE

On 5 June, Cardinal Seán Brady and Archbishop Diarmuid Martin met with Pope Benedict XVI to discuss a number of issues regarding the Irish Church, including the impact of the *Ryan Report.*

On 8 June, Bishop Éamonn Walsh launched a new expanded version of the Bishops' Council for Emigrants' document, *What the Bible says about the Stranger*. The launch took place at the Vincentian Refugee Centre in Phibsboro, Dublin. Speaking at the launch, Bishop Walsh said: 'While the composition of the Irish population was beginning to change in 1999 when the first edition of *What the Bible says about the Stranger* was published, few of us could have foreseen the changes which have taken place in the past decade. Changes which have resulted in our living in a country where over 160 languages are spoken by people coming from countries as distant from us, and from one another, as Croatia is from China and Estonia from Ecuador. At this time, in the face of the challenges which we face both globally and nationally, I am delighted to launch this publication. May it be widely distributed and, especially, widely used, and may 'Wet Paint' and every sign in our society, whatever its medium, be in a language that recognises, values and welcomes the stranger.'

The Summer General Meeting of the Bishops' Conference concluded in Maynooth on 10 June with a press conference and a statement addressing the following issues: discussion on the *Commission to Inquire into Child Abuse Report*, meetings of Cardinal Brady and Archbishop Martin in the Holy See, 50th Eucharistic Congress in Ireland in 2012, Pastoral response in a time of recession, Catholic schools, Northern Ireland Human Rights Commission, New rules on work permits for non-EU workers in Ireland and the impact of government cuts to its overseas aid budget.

On 12 June, Archbishop Diarmuid Martin launched *Who is my Neighbour?*, a new publication from the ICJSA. The publication was based on the papers delivered at the conference of the same name, organised by the ICJSA on 18 February 2008.

On 26 June, new statistics released by ACCORD, the Catholic Marriage Care Service, showed that problems around internet usage and time spent in 'cyberspace' are cited by a growing number of couples as a source of marital conflict. While this issue has been recorded by ACCORD for the past three years, it has now become statistically significant, with 7% of clients seen in the first half of 2009 citing it as their primary problem. Commenting on the increase, John Farrelly, Director of Counselling with ACCORD, said: 'The key areas which are causing conflict are internet gambling, infidelity and one partner spending too much time online rather than with their spouse and family.' The half yearly statistics from ACCORD also evidenced the continuing increasing trend in the number of couples attending marriage counselling as a result of financial pressures.

JULY

On 5 July, Cardinal Seán Brady and Archbishop Diarmuid Martin celebrated the festival day of St Oliver Plunkett by participating in a procession and Mass in Drogheda.

On 7 July, bishops welcomed the publication of the new Encyclical Letter, *Caritas In Veritate (Love In Truth),* by the Holy Father, Benedict XVI, to the bishops, priests and deacons, men and women religious,

the lay faithful and all people of good will, on integral human development in charity and truth. Globalisation is a key theme of *Caritas in Veritate*, which revisits the teachings on 'integral human development' expounded by Pope Paul VI in his landmark 1967 Encyclical Letter *Populorum Progressio*, seeking to apply them to the contemporary world.

On 25 July, Archbishop Michael Neary, Archbishop of Tuam, led up to 20,000 people for the annual Croagh Patrick Reek Sunday pilgrimage. In his homily on the summit, Archbishop Neary said: 'Christian hope proves to be a strength that enables us courageously and perseveringly to accept the present with all its imperfections, its sufferings, sin and selfishess.'

AUGUST

The first ever live broadcast of Mass from Lough Derg was aired by RTÉ on Sunday, 2 August. Lough Derg lies four miles north of the village of Pettigo in Co Donegal in the Diocese of Clogher. Station Island, the location of the pilgrimage, is often referred to as St Patrick's Purgatory. Welcoming the televised Mass, Bishop Joseph Duffy, Bishop of Clogher, said: 'Lough Derg is a special place of peace and personal challenge, renowned in Irish Christian tradition since the time of St Patrick. In former times the emphasis of the Lough Derg pilgrimage was more on physical penance and hardship. Today pilgrims see it as a grace-filled opportunity away from the stress and busyness of modern life. Lough Derg identifies itself with the universal mission of the Church in our divided society, while remaining very much part of our society. The Lough Derg experience exemplifies the healing and liberating work of the Church which we all agree is very much needed at the present time. As a pilgrimage, Lough Derg reminds us that we are all members of a community, searching for peace and reconciliation in our lives.'

On 23 August, 36 new seminarians commenced priesthood studies for Irish dioceses: 26 will be based in the national seminary of St Patrick's College, Maynooth; 7 will study at St Malachy's College, Belfast; 2 will study in the Beda College in Rome; whilst 1 candidate is entering the

pre-seminary discernment year (propaedeutic year) in Valladolid, Spain. The new seminarians range in age from eighteen to mid-forties and come from a wide variety of education and employment backgrounds. Welcoming the new candidates for the priesthood, their families and friends to Maynooth, the President of the College, Monsignor Hugh Connolly, said: 'You have responded in your hearts to the Lord's call. Our thoughts and prayers accompany you as you take the first step along the road to ordained ministry and to placing your lives at the service of Christ and of His people. It is truly wonderful to witness the generosity of spirit of our new seminarians as, at this time, the Church in Ireland has completed a 'Year of Vocation' and we begin, together with all the faithful throughout the world, the Year for Priests.'

SEPTEMBER

On 6 September, a special web feature went live on *www.catholicbishops.ie* to commemorate the pilgrimage to Ireland of the late Pope John Paul II thirty years ago. This feature includes a video reflection by Bishop Michael Smith, Bishop of Meath. Bishop Smith was secretary to the committee of Irish Bishops supervising the arrangements for the 1979 papal visit and this committee was chaired by Cardinal Tomás Ó Fiaich. The feature also includes live audio recordings of the Mass celebrated by Pope John Paul II in the Phoenix Park, Dublin; his homily in Drogheda on 29 September 1979; homilies from the Masses celebrated in Knock and Galway on 30 September 1979; Pope John Paul's address to clergy and religious in Maynooth and his homily in Limerick on 1 October 1979. Also available as part of this web feature is the publication, *The Pope in Ireland – Addresses and Homilies,* which includes the text versions of the above homilies as well as Pope John Paul II's address on his arrival at Dublin airport, his addresses to the President of Ireland, the Diplomatic Corps, the Government of Ireland, the visiting bishops, the Ecumenical Meeting, journalists, the sick, his address at Clonmacnois, to the Bishops of Ireland and upon his departure from Shannon.

On 12 September, Cardinal Brady was in Knock for the third National Grandparents Pilgrimage where he presided at Mass in the Basilica and preached the homily. In his homily, Cardinal Brady said: 'We salute with gratitude the Christian vocation of being a grandparent ... So I say, tell your grandchildren all you know about God. [Your] role in Irish families has always been cherished ... it is one of the things which made our society strong, especially in the most challenging economic times in our history.'

On 17 September, Pope Benedict XVI accepted the resignation of Bishop Fiachra Ó Ceallaigh. Commenting on the announcement, Archbishop Martin said that his years of dedicated service and unique charism had enriched the diocese: 'Bishop Ó Ceallaigh, particularly as he struggled with illness in recent years, was an outstanding witness to the motto he took on his Episcopal appointment *"Dia Ár Misneach"* (God is our courage).'

On 21 September, the Standing Committee of the Bishops' Conference issued a statement on the Lisbon Treaty. It stated: 'The Lisbon Treaty is of the greatest importance, not only for us here in Ireland but also for the future shape of the European project. Although the situation has changed since the June 2008 referendum with the addition of legal assurances to respond to the worries expressed at that time, our 2008 pastoral reflection, *Fostering a Community of Values*, remains relevant. In it we highlighted the distinctive roles of politics and religion. While we do not seek to align ourselves with either side of the referendum debate, we wish to make it clear that a Catholic can, in good conscience, vote YES or NO. We urge all Christians to consider carefully the contents of the Treaty; we also wish to stress the responsibility on all of us to vote and to do so with regard not just for our own personal or group interest, but for the good of every citizen and the whole community.'

On 22 September, the Pontifical Committee for International Eucharistic Congresses announced the theme for the next International Eucharistic Congress as 'The Eucharist: Communion with Christ and with one another'. The next Eucharistic Congress, the 50th of the series, will take place from 10 to 17 June 2012 in Dublin.

On 25 September, the ICJSA hosted a seminar in Mater Dei Institute, Dublin, inspired by its 2008 position paper *Violence in Irish Society: Towards an Ecology of Peace*. The seminar aimed to promote a multi-dimensional, community-based response to the problem of violence. The event was attended by a wide range of community and voluntary organisations working to address aspects of the problem of violence in our society. Opening the seminar, Bishop Éamonn Walsh stated: 'There is a clear need for all of us to actively engage with this problem. The Government and the Gardaí cannot by themselves alone remove violence from our midst. As a society we need to replace a culture of violence with a renewed sense of justice, responsibility and community.' Expert speakers and media commentators contributed to the seminar basing their responses to issues raised by *Violence in Irish Society: Towards an Ecology of Peace*.

On 29 September, Bishop Joseph Duffy, Chair of the Communications Commission of the Irish Bishops' Conference, welcomed the announcement by Pope Benedict XVI of the theme for World Day of Social Communications in 2010, which was 'The priest and pastoral ministry in a digital world: new media at the service of the Word'. Bishop Duffy said: 'The Holy Father's dedication of next year's World Communications Day is wholly consistent with this being the Year for Priests. Pope Benedict's theme invites us to reflect on the role of the priest and his ministry today but within the context of communications. A major difference between undertaking priestly ministry nowadays compared to previous generations is the extent and influence of communications in our everyday lives. Today's digital age is exemplified by the omnipresence and continuing diversification of new media technology. We must remain alert and continue to grow within this new media environment while being ever-mindful that it must be managed responsibly.'

OCTOBER
The Catholic Church in Ireland celebrated the Day for Life 2009 on Sunday, 4 October. The theme for the 2009 Day for Life was suicide, which built on the 2008 focus on mental health. On behalf of the Bishops' Conference, Bishop John Fleming, Bishop of Killala, launched the Day for Life Pastoral Letter, '*You are Precious in my Sight*' (Isaiah 43:3). Bishop Fleming said: '"You are precious in my sight" is the theme for this year's Day for Life – the day dedicated to raising awareness about the meaning and value of human life at every stage and in every condition. Day for Life 2009 focuses on suicide and in particular on the pastoral dimensions of this difficult and sensitive subject. It highlights why the Church believes that life is worth living and looks at some of the reasons why people may contemplate suicide. In particular, we reflect on the issue of mental illness, the stigma which tends to surround it and the resources which are available to those who suffer from it, as well the need for the promotion of positive mental health in our society.'

The Autumn General Meeting of the Bishops' Conference concluded in Maynooth on 7 October by addressing the following issues: meeting with survivors of institutional abuse, prayers for abducted GOAL workers in Darfur, prayers for victims of Indonesian earthquake and support for Trócaire aid appeal, Mr Brian McKeown RIP, recommendations on swine flu, Mission Sunday 18 October 2009, Fr Aengus Finucane RIP, Year for Priests, Permanent Diaconate and retirement of Bishop Fiachra Ó Ceallaigh.

On 9 October, Archbishop Diarmuid Martin delivered the opening address at the First Social Days Conference on Catholic Social Teaching in Gdansk, Poland. The theme of the conference was 'Solidarity – The Challenge for Europe'. In his address, Archbishop Martin said: 'Our Social Days have as their aim the encouragement of a new generation of young Europeans to be inspired by such a vision. The icons of the formation of modern Europe need not be just the well-known names of Schuman, de Gasperi and Adenauer, but of many smaller names, often totally forgotten and unjustly unrecognised, who through their lives have been inspired by noble ideals and have witnessed to the truth. Those who emerged on the world scene here in Gdansk twenty years ago were young and unknown and we need now a new generation of Europeans on that world scene.'

NOVEMBER

On 2 November, the Four Church Leaders, Cardinal Seán Brady, Archbishop Alan Harper, Reverend Donald Ker and Reverend Dr Stafford Carson, met with the recently appointed Police Service of Northern Ireland Chief Constable, Mr Matt Baggott. The meeting took place in Cardinal Brady's home in Armagh and lasted for one and a half hours. Areas covered by the meeting included the importance of developing community policing, the current security situation and anti-social behaviour in our society. Cardinal Brady said: 'We asked for today's introductory meeting with Chief Constable Baggott to welcome him in his new role as Chief Constable of the PSNI and to discuss some of the significant issues currently facing our society. Today's meeting gave us an opportunity to discuss ways to improve cooperation between local communities and the PSNI. We believe that the common good is best served by such a positive working relationship and we call on everyone to support the police service.'

On 10 November, Archbishop Dermot Clifford, Archbishop of Cashel and Emly, launched *The Cry of the Earth*, a pastoral reflection on climate change from the Irish Catholic Bishops' Conference. The launch took place in St Francis of Assisi Primary School in Belmayne, Dublin, beside Father Collins Park, Ireland's first wholly sustainable park. Launching *The Cry of the Earth,* Archbishop Clifford said: 'We are all stewards of God's creation. As political leaders from around the globe meet in Copenhagen next month for the UN Framework Conference on Climate Change to decide on a new global climate change deal, the Bishops of Ireland wish to raise awareness of our vital responsibility toward sustaining the environment. We need to protect the environment today and on behalf of future generations. Our response needs to be at an individual, community and governmental level. *The Cry of the Earth*, with an accompanying DVD, has been sent to all parishes and is available on *www.catholicbishops.ie*. It reflects on our Christian responsibility towards the environment and outlines the scientific analysis of climate change, the theological and ethical principles as to why we as Christians have a duty to respond, and practical advice as to how we can act now to sustain the environment.'

On 16 November, Bishop Noel Treanor, Bishop of Down and Connor, launched *Alcohol/Drugs Handbook, How to Form a Parish Response to Alcohol/Drug Issues* at a seminar in Drumalis Retreat and Conference Centre, Larne, Co Antrim. The seminar was organised by the Irish Bishops' Drugs and Alcohol Initiative and speakers included Bishop Éamonn Walsh, Vice-Chairperson of the IBDI, representatives from parishes, public health authorities, police service, Forum Against Substance Abuse, the Family Support Network, Inter-Church Addiction Project and the IBDI.

Bishop Treanor said: 'Today's seminar is a statement of Christian hope in the face of addiction. We bring together women and men of both practical and scientific experience in responding to and treating addiction to alcohol and drugs … [our] speakers have empowered community groups and individual addicts to conquer and manage addiction. The contributors did not spare us the harsh reality of the extent, complexity and challenge of addiction that we know only too well in the parishes that we serve.'

DECEMBER

The Winter General Meeting of the Bishops' Conference took place in Maynooth on 9 and 10 December. The normal business of the General Meeting was suspended. Bishops gave their full attention to the *Commission of Investigation Report into the Catholic Archdiocese of Dublin (Murphy Report)*, which was published on 26 November. Bishops said: 'We, as bishops, apologise to all those who were abused by priests as children, their families and to all people who feel rightly outraged and let down by the failure of moral leadership and accountability that emerges from the Report. We are deeply shocked by the scale and depravity of abuse as described in the Report. We are shamed by the extent to which child sexual abuse was covered up in the Archdiocese of Dublin and recognise that this indicates a culture that was widespread in the Church. The avoidance of scandal, the preservation of the reputations of individuals and of the Church, took precedence over the safety and welfare of children. This should never have happened and must never be allowed to happen again. We humbly ask for forgiveness. The Report raises very important issues for the Church in Ireland, including the functioning of the Bishops' Conference and how the lay faithful can be more effectively involved in the life of the Church. We will give further detailed consideration to these issues. We humbly ask that you continue to pray for all those who suffer due to child abuse.' In the aftermath of its publication, bishops also responded to issues raised by the *Murphy Report* in their dioceses and in the media.

On 11 December, Cardinal Seán Brady and Archbishop Diarmuid Martin met with Pope Benedict XVI in the Vatican. After their meeting, the Vatican Press Office issued the following statement: 'Today the Holy Father held a meeting with senior Irish Bishops and high-ranking members of the Roman Curia. He listened to their concerns and discussed with them the traumatic events that were presented in the *Irish Commission of Investigation's Report into the Catholic Archdiocese of Dublin*. After careful study of the Report, the Holy Father was deeply disturbed and distressed by its contents. He wishes once more to express his profound regret at the actions of some members of the clergy who have betrayed their solemn promises to God, as well as the trust placed in them by the victims and their families, and by society at large. The Holy Father shares the outrage, betrayal and shame felt by so many of the faithful in Ireland, and he is united with them in prayer at this difficult time in the life of the Church. His Holiness asks Catholics in Ireland and throughout the world to join him in praying for the victims, their families and all those affected by these heinous crimes. He assures all concerned that the Church will continue to follow this grave matter with the closest attention in order to understand better how these shameful events came to pass and how best to develop effective and secure strategies to prevent any recurrence. The Holy See takes very seriously the central issues raised by

Allianz ⑪

the Report, including questions concerning the governance of local Church leaders with ultimate responsibility for the pastoral care of children. The Holy Father intends to address a Pastoral Letter to the faithful of Ireland in which he will clearly indicate the initiatives that are to be taken in response to the situation. Finally, His Holiness encourages all those who have dedicated their lives in generous service to children to persevere in their good works in imitation of Christ the Good Shepherd.'

On 13 December, Cardinal Seán Brady issued the following statement on the killing of Fr Jeremiah Roche in Kenya: 'I was very saddened to hear the news of the vicious killing of Father Jeremiah Roche in Kericho, Kenya. I deeply sympathise with Father Roche's family and his confrers in the St Patrick's Missionary Society (Kiltegan Fathers) at this very difficult time. The gruesome circumstances surrounding Father Roche's death have also shocked all those who loved and admired him in his parish in Kericho and in his home parish of Athea, Co Limerick, where he planned to retire next year having spent over forty years working as a missionary priest. Father Roche's death is a reminder to us of the great sacrifice of those who risk their lives answering God's call to bring the Good News to the poorest of the poor around the world. I pray especially for the safety of our religious and lay missionaries who work under the threat of violence in their communities.'

On 17 December, the Vatican announced that Pope Benedict XVI had accepted the resignation of Bishop Donal Murray as Bishop of Limerick. Commenting on the resignation, Cardinal Seán Brady said: 'I acknowledge and respect the decision of Bishop Murray to resign

as Bishop of Limerick, as was announced earlier today. As Bishop Murray said in his statement this morning, the survivors of abuse must have first place in our thoughts and prayers. I apologise again to all who were abused as children by priests, who were betrayed and who feel outraged by the failure of Church leadership in responding to their abuse. Their suffering must always be the primary consideration in any assessment of past failings, as a Church and as individuals. I wish to acknowledge and thank Bishop Murray for his contribution to the work of the Irish Bishops' Conference. He is in my prayers at this time.'

On 23 December, Bishop James Moriarty, Bishop of Kildare and Leighlin, offered his resignation to Pope Benedict XVI.

On 24 December, Auxiliary Bishops of Dublin, Bishop Éamonn Walsh and Bishop Raymond Field, offered their resignations to Pope Benedict XVI.

Amongst the issues addressed by Cardinal Seán Brady's 2009 Christmas message to the people of Ireland for 25 December, Cardinal Brady reminded the faithful of the eternal hope offered by the birth of Our Saviour: 'That famous prophesy from the prophet Isaiah foretold the coming of Christ. When I hear it read at Midnight Mass every Christmas Eve – it never fails to lift my heart. We all need at times to see a great light – especially when we find ourselves in darkness – the darkness of doom and gloom, the darkness of despondency and despair. Christ is our light – He breaks through the gloom, dispels the deepest darkness and enables us to understand the meaning and value of our own lives and indeed of all of history. Down through the centuries the New Born King has brought comfort and

consolation to generations of people all over the world. Seeing the Baby Jesus in the Crib has given us strength through good times and bad – especially the bad times – for in the fullness of difficult times Jesus was born and continues to be born. His gaze of love, outstretched arms of welcome and disarming innocence bring us to our knees. In Ireland this Christmas, many are experiencing the fullness of difficulties with the economic recession, the unprecedented flooding and the horrendous scandal of child abuse. And yet, it is precisely into this agonising, here and now of our world, our country and our Church, that Jesus comes with His blessing. He comes to tell us the outstanding Good News of God's healing love and mercy, for He is God's word of ever-faithful love, coming to bring us fresh joy and hope. We believe that God's mercy and God's healing love are without end. So this Christmas, we remember all those who live in darkness and confusion and doubt. We pray that they may be led into the light of the truth, which is Jesus Christ.'

On 31 December, the former Primate of All Ireland and Archbishop Emeritus of Armagh, Cardinal Cahal Daly, passed away in Belfast aged ninety-two years. Cardinal Brady said of his predecessor: 'It is difficult to do full justice to the significance and achievements of his long, full and happy life but I believe, when fully assessed and appreciated, the legacy of Cardinal Cahal Daly to the ecclesiastical and civil history of Ireland will be seen as immense.'

Please see the website of the Irish Bishops' Conference **www.catholicbishops.ie** *for greater detail on all the foregoing as well as other initiatives and statements.*

THE ROMAN CURIA

SECRETARIAT OF STATE

Secretary of State:
Cardinal Tarcisio Bertone (SDB)

First Section: General Affairs
Sostituto:
Archbishop Fernando Filoni
Palazzo Apostolico Vaticano
Tel 66988-3913 Fax 66988-5255

Second Section: Relations with States
Secretary:
Archbishop Dominique Mamberti
Palazzo Apostolico Vaticano
Tel 66988-3913 Fax 66988-5255

CONGREGATIONS

Congregation for the Doctrine of the Faith
Prefect: Cardinal William J. Levada
Secretary:
Luis Francisco Ladaria Ferrer (SJ)
Piazza del S. Uffizio 11, Roma 00193
Tel 66988-3357/3413
Fax 66988-3409

Congregation for the Oriental Churches
Prefect:
Cardinal Leonardo Sandri
Secretary:
Archbishop Cyril Vasil (SJ)
Via della Conciliazione 34, 00193 Roma
Tel 66988-4282 Fax 66988-4300

Congregation for Divine Worship and the Discipline of the Sacraments
Prefect:
Cardinal Antionio Cañizares Llovera
Secretary: Archbishop Joseph Augustine Di Noia (OP)
Piazza Pio XII 10, 00193 Roma
Tel 66988-4316/4318
Fax 66988-3499

Congregation for the Causes of Saints
Prefect: Cardinal Angelo Amato (SDB)
Secretary: Archbishop Michele di Ruberto
Piazza Pio XII 10, 00193 Roma
Tel 66988-4247 Fax 66988-1935

Congregation for Bishops
Prefect: Cardinal Giovanni Battista Re
Secretary:
Archbishop Manuel Monteiro de Castro
Piazza Pio XII 10, 00193 Roma
Tel 66988-4217 Fax 66988-5303

Pontifical Commission for Latin America
President:
Cardinal Giovanni Battista Re
Vice President:
Archbishop José Octavio Ruiz Arenas
Palazzo di San Paolo, Via della Conciliazione 1, 00193 Roma
Tel 66988-3131/3500 Fax 66988-4260

Congregation for the Clergy
Prefect:
Cardinal Cláudio Hummes (OFM)
Secretary: Archbishop Mauro Piacenza
Palazzo delle Congregazioni,
00193 Roma
Tel 66988-4151 Fax 66988-4845

Congregation for the Evangelisation of Peoples
Prefect: Cardinal Ivan Dias
Secretary: Archbishop Robert Sarah
SAC Official:
Archbishop Pierguiseppe Volcchelli
Palazzo di Propaganda Fide, Piazza di Spagna 48, 00187 Roma
Tel 66987-9299 Fax 66988-0118

Congregation for the Institutes of Consecrated Life and for Societies of Apostolic Life
Prefect: Cardinal Franc Rodé
Secretary: Archbishop Gianfranco Agostino Gardin (OFM)
Palazzo delle Congregazioni,
Piazza Pio XII 3, 00193 Roma
Tel 6988-4128 Fax 6988-4526

Congregation for Catholic Education
Prefect: Cardinal Zenon Grocholewski
Secretary:
Archbishop Jean-Louis Bruguès (OP)
Palazzo delle Congregazioni, Piazza Pio XII 3, 00193 Roma
Tel 66988-4167 Fax 66988-4172

TRIBUNALS

Apostolic Penitentiary
Major Penitentiary:
Archbishop Fortunato Baldelli
Official:
Bishop Gianfranco Girotti (OFM Conv)
Palazzo della Cancelleria Apostolica,
Piazza della Cancelleria 1, 00186 Roma
Tel 66988-7526/7523 Fax 66988-7557

Supreme Tribunal of the Apostolic Signatura
Prefect: Raymond Leo Burke
Secretary:
Bishop Frans Daneels (OPraem)
Palazzo della Cancelleria Apostolica,
Piazza della Cancelleria 1, 00186 Roma
Tel 66988-7520 Fax 66988-7553

Tribunal of the Roman Rota
Dean:
Bishop Antoni Stankiewicz
Palazzo della Cancelleria Apostolica,
Piazza della Cancelleria 1, 00186 Roma
Tel 66988-7502 Fax 66988-7554

PONTIFICAL COUNCILS

Pontifical Council for the Laity
President: Archbishop Stanislaw Rylko
Secretary: Bishop Josef Clemens
Piazza S. Calisto 16, 00120 Città del Vaticano, 00153 Roma
Tel 66988-7322/7141 Fax 66988-7214

Pontifical Council for Promoting Christian Unity
President: Cardinal Walter Kasper
Secretary: Bishop Brian Farrell (LC)
Via dell'Erba 1, 00193 Roma
Tel 66988-3072/4271
Fax 66988-5365

Pontifical Council for the Family
President: Cardinal Ennio Antonelli
Secretary: Bishop Jean Laffitte
Piazza S. Calisto 16, 00153 Roma
Tel 66988-7243 Fax 66988-7272

Pontifical Council for Justice and Peace
President: Cardinal Peter Kodwo Appiah Turkson
Secretary: Bishop Mario Toso (SDB)
Piazza S. Calisto 16, 00120 Città del Vaticano, 00153 Roma
Tel 66987-9911 Fax 66988-7205

Pontifical Council 'Cor Unum'
President: Archbishop Paul Josef Cordes
Piazza S. Calisto 16, 00120 Città del Vaticano, 00153 Roma
Tel 66988-9411 Fax 66988-7301

Allianz (ll)

Pontifical Council for the Pastoral Care of Migrants and Itinerant People
President:
Archbishop Antonio Maria Vegliò
Secretary: Archbishop Agostino Marchetto
Piazza S. Calisto 16, 00120 Città del Vaticano
Tel 66988-7193/7242 Fax 66988-7111

Pontifical Council for Pastoral Assistance to Healthcare Workers
President:
Archbishop Zygmunt Zimowski
Secretary:
Bishop José Luis Redrado Marchite (OH)
Via della Conciliazione 3, 00193 Roma
Tel 66889-4720/3138 Fax 66889-3139

Pontifical Council for Legislative Texts
President:
Archbishop Francesco Coccopalmerio
Vice-President: Bishop Bruno Bertagna
Secretary: Juan Ignacio Arrieta Ochoa de Chinchetru
Palazzo della Congregazioni, Piazza Pio XII 10, 00193 Roma
Tel 66988-4008 Fax 66988-4710

Pontifical Council for Inter-Religious Dialogue
President:
Cardinal Jean-Louis Pierre Tauran
Secretary: Archbishop Pier Luigi Celata
Via dell'Erba 1, 00193 Roma
Tel 66988-4321/5745
Fax 66988-4494

Pontifical Council for Culture
President:
Archbishop Gianfranco Ravasi
Secretary:
Cardinal Paul Joseph Jean Poupard
Piazza S. Calisto, 16,
00120 Città del Vaticano
Tel 66989-3811 Fax 66988-7368

Pontifical Council for Social Communications
President:
Archbishop Claudio Maria Celli
Secretary Emeritus:
Bishop Pierfranco Pastore
Palazzo S. Carlo,
00120 Città del Vaticano
Tel 66989-1800 Fax 66989-1840

OFFICES

Apostolic Chamber
Chamberlain of the Holy Church:
Cardinal Tarcisio Bertone (SDB)
Vice-Chamberlain: Archbishop Paolo Sardi
Palazzo Apostolico,
00120 Citta del Vaticano
Tel 66988-3554

Administration of the Patrimony of the Apostolic See
President: Cardinal Attilio Nicora
Secretary:
Archbishop Domenico Calcagno
Palazzo Apostolico,
00120 Citta del Vaticano
Tel 66989-3403 Fax 66988-3141

Prefecture for the Economic Affairs of the Holy See
President: Velasio De Paolis (CS)
Secretary: Bishop Vincenzo Di Mauro
Palazzo delle Congregazioni,
Largo del Colonnato 3, 00193 Roma
Tel 66988-4263 Fax 66988-5011

Synod of Bishops
President: His Holiness Pope Benedict XVI
Secretary-General:
Archbishop Nikola Eterovic
Palazzo del Bramante, 00193 Roma
Tel 66988-4821/4324 Fax 66988-3392

Prefecture of the Papal Household
Prefect: Archbishop James M. Harvey
Official: Paolo De Nicolò
Palazzo Apostolico,
00120 Città del Vaticano
Tel 6988-3114 Fax 6988-5863

Office of Papal Charities
Almoner of His Holiness:
Archbishop Félix de Blanco Prieto
00120 Città del Vaticano
Tel 6988-3135 Fax 6988-3132

International Theological Commission
President:
Cardinal William Joseph Levada
Palazzo della Congr. per la Dottrina della Fede, 00193 Roma,
Piazza del S. Uffizio, 11
Tel 66988-4638

Pontifical Ecclesiastical Academy
President: Archbishop Beniamino Stella,
00186 Roma, Piazza della Minerva, 74
Tel 06688201 Fax 066880-1274

Vatican Library
Librarian: Cardinal Raffaele Farina (SDB)
Cortile del Belvedere,
00120 Citta del Vaticano
Tel 66987-9411 Fax 66988-4795

Vatican Secret Archives
Prefect: Bishop Sergio Pagano
Archivist: Cardinal Raffaele Farina (SDB)
00120 Città del Vaticano
Tel 66988-3314 Fax 66988-5574

COMMISSIONS AND COMMITTEES

Pontifical Commission for the Cultural Heritage of the Church
President:
Archbishop Gianfranco Ravasi
Palazzo della Cancelleria Apostolica,
Piazza della Cancelleria n. 1,
00186 Roma, Italy
Tel 6988-7517/7556 Fax 6988-7556

Pontifical Commission 'Ecclesia Dei'
President:
Cardinal William Joseph Levada
Piazza del S. Ufficio, 11,
00193 Roma, Italy
Tel 6988-5213/8494 Fax 6988-3412

Pontifical Biblical Commission
President:
Cardinal William Joseph Levada
Palazzo della Congr. per la Dottrina della Fede, 00193 Roma, Piazza del S. Uffizio, 11
Tel 66988-4682

Pontifical Commission for Sacred Arachaeology
President: Archbishop Gianfranco Ravasi
Palazzo del Pontificio Istituto di Archeologia Cristiana, in via Napoleone III, 1 - 00185 Roma
Tel 6446-5610/7601 Fax 6446-7625

Pontifical Committee for International Eucharistic Congresses
President: Archbishop Piero Marini
00120 Città del Vaticano,
Palazzo San Calisto
Tel 66988-7366 Fax 66988-7154

INSTITUTIONS CONNECTED WITH HOLY SEE

L'Osservatore Romano
Editor-in-Chief: Giovanni Maria Vian
00120 Citta del Vaticano
Tel 66989-9390 Fax 66988-3252
Email ornet@ossrom.va

APOSTOLIC NUNCIATURE

Address: The Apostolic Nunciature, 183 Navan Road, Dublin 7
Tel 01-8380577 Fax 01-8380276

Papal Nuncio: His Excellency Most Reverend Dr Giuseppe Leanza, Titular Archbishop of Lilybaeum
Born in Cesarò (Messina), Italy, on 2 January 1943,
Ordained priest 17 July 1966, appointed Titular Archbishop of Lilybaeum 3 July 1990,
Episcopal Ordination 22 September 1990, appointed Apostolic Nuncio to Ireland 22 February 2008.

Secretary: Reverend Juan Antonio Cruz Serrano

THE IRISH EPISCOPATE

THE HIERARCHY

Archbishops

His Eminence Seán Cardinal Brady DCL, DD
Archbishop of Armagh
Primate of All Ireland
Ara Coeli, Armagh BT61 7QY
Tel 028-37522045 Fax 028-37526182
Email admin@aracoeli.com

Most Rev Diarmuid Martin DD
Archbishop of Dublin and Primate of
Ireland, Archbishop's House,
Drumcondra, Dublin 9
Tel 01-8373732 Fax 01-8369796

Most Rev Dermot Clifford DD
Archbishop of Cashel and Emly
Archbishop's House, Thurles,
Co Tipperary
Tel 0504-21512 Fax 0504-22680
Email office@cashel-emly.ie

Most Rev Michael Neary DD
Archbishop of Tuam
Archbishop's House,
Tuam, Co Galway
Tel 093-24166 Fax 093-28070
Email archdiocesetuam@eircom.net

Retired Archbishops

His Eminence Desmond Cardinal Connell DD
Retired Archbishop of Dublin
29 Iona Road, Glasnevin,
Dublin 9
Tel 01-8373732 Fax 01-8369796

Most Rev Joseph Cassidy DD
Retired Archbishop of Tuam
The Presbytery, Moore,
Ballydangan, Athlone,
Co Roscommon
Tel/Fax 0905-73539

Bishops

Most Rev Philip Boyce DD
Bishop of Raphoe
Ard Adhamhnáin, Letterkenny,
Co Donegal
Tel 074-9121208 Fax 074-9124872
Email raphoediocese@eircom.net

Most Rev Denis Brennan DD
Bishop of Ferns
Bishop's House, Summerhill,
Wexford
Tel 053-22177 Fax 053-23436
Email adm@ferns.ie

Most Rev John Buckley DD
Bishop of Cork and Ross,
Diocesan Office, Bishop's House,
Redemption Road, Cork
Tel 021-4301717 Fax 021-4301557
Email secretary@corkandross.org

Most Rev Gerard Clifford DD
Titular Bishop of Geron and Auxiliary
Bishop of Armagh
Annaskeagh, Ravensdale,
Dundalk, Co Louth
Tel 042-9371012 Fax 042-9371013
Email gcliffrd@indigo.ie

Most Rev Martin Drennan DD
Bishop of Galway
Mount St Mary's,
Taylor's Hill, Galway
Tel 091-563566 Fax 091-528536
Email galwaydiocese@eircom.net

Most Rev Joseph Duffy DD
Bishop of Clogher
Bishop's House, Monaghan
Tel 047-81019 Fax 047-84773
Email cloghdiocoffmon@eircom.net

Most Rev Anthony Farquhar DD
Titular Bishop of Ermiana, Auxiliary
Bishop of Down and Connor
24 Fruithill Park, Belfast BT11 8GE
Tel 028-90624252
Email ajf@downandconnor.org

Most Rev Raymond Field DD
Titular Bishop of Ard Mor and
Auxiliary Bishop of Dublin
3 Castleknock Road,
Blanchardstown, Dublin 15
Tel 01-8209191 Fax 01-8209191
Email rf6275@eircom.net

Most Rev John Fleming DD, DCL
Bishop of Killala
Bishop's House, Ballina, Co Mayo
Tel 096-21518 Fax 096-70344
Email bishop@killaladiocese.org

Most Rev Séamus Freeman (SAC) DD
Bishop of Ossory
Sion House, Kilkenny
Tel 056-7762448 Fax 056-7763753
Email bishop@ossory.ie

Most Rev Seamus Hegarty DD
Bishop of Derry
Bishop's House, St Eugene's Cathedral,
Derry BT48 9AP
Tel 028-71262302 Fax 028-71371960
Email office@derrydiocese.org

Most Rev Christopher Jones DD
Bishop of Elphin,
St Mary's, Sligo
Tel 071-62670/62769 Fax 071-62414
Email elphindo@eircom.net

Most Rev Brendan Kelly DD
Bishop of Achonry; Bishop's House,
Ballaghaderreen, Edmondstown,
Co Roscommon
Tel 094-9860021 Fax 094-9860921
Email bishop@achonrydiocese.org

Most Rev John Kirby DD
Bishop of Clonfert
St Brendan's, Coorheen, Loughrea,
Co Galway
Tel 091-841560 Fax 091-841818
Email clonfert@iol.ie

Most Rev Francis Lagan DD
Titular Bishop of Sidnascestre and
Auxiliary Bishop of Derry
9 Glen Road, Strabane,
Co Tyrone BT82 8BX
Tel 028-71884533 Fax 028-71884551
Email fblagan@gotadse.co.uk

Most Rev William Lee, DD, DCL
Bishop of Waterford and Lismore
Bishop's House,
John's Hill, Waterford
Tel 051-874463 Fax 051-852703
Email waterfordlismore@eircom.net

Most Rev John McAreavey DD, DCL
Bishop of Dromore
Bishop's House,
44 Armagh Road, Newry,
Co Down BT35 6PN
Tel 028-30262444 Fax 028-30260496
Email bishopofdromore@btinternet.com

Most Rev Donal McKeown DD
Titular Bishop of Killossy and Auxiliary
Bishop of Down and Connor,
73 Somerton Road, Belfast BT15 4DE
Tel 028-90776185 Fax 028-90779377

Most Rev John Magee DD
Bishop of Cloyne
Cloyne Diocesan Centre,
Cobh, Co Cork
Tel 021-4811430 Fax 021-4811026
Email cloyne@indigo.ie

Most Rev James Moriarty DD,
Bishop of Kildare and Leighlin,
Bishop's House, Carlow
Tel 059-9176725 Fax 059-9176850
Email bishop@kandle.ie

Most Rev William Murphy DD
Bishop of Kerry
Bishop's House, Killarney, Co Kerry
Tel 064-31168 Fax 064-31364
Email bishopshouse@eircom.net

Most Rev Colm O'Reilly DD
Bishop of Ardagh and Clonmacnois
St Michael's, Longford, Co Longford
Tel 043-46432 Fax 043-46833
Email ardaghdi@iol.ie

Most Rev Leo O'Reilly DD
Bishop of Kilmore, Bishop's House,
Cullies, Co Cavan
Tel 049-4331496 Fax 049-4361796
Email bishop@kilmorediocese.ie

Most Rev Michael Smith DD, DCL
Bishop of Meath
Bishop's House, Dublin Road, Mullingar,
Co Westmeath
Tel 044-9348841/9342038
Fax 044-9343020
Email bishop@dioceseofmeath.ie

Most Rev Noel Treanor DD
Bishop of Down and Connor
Lisbreen, 73 Somerton Road,
Belfast, Co Antrim BT15 4DE
Tel 028-90776185 Fax 028-90779377
Email dccuria@downandconnor.org

Most Rev Eamonn Walsh DD, VG
Titular Bishop of Elmham and
Auxiliary Bishop of Dublin
Naomh Brid, Blessington Road,
Tallaght, Dublin 24
Tel/Fax 01-4598032
Email elmham@eircom.net

Most Rev William Walsh DD
Bishop of Killaloe, Westbourne,
Ennis, Co Clare
Tel 065-6828638 Fax 065-6842538
Email cildalua@iol.ie

Retired Bishops
Most Rev Eamonn Casey DD
Retired Bishop of Galway
Beagh, Co Galway

Most Rev Brendan Comiskey DD
Retired Bishop of Ferns
PO Box 40, Summerhill, Wexford

Most Rev Edward Daly DD
Retired Bishop of Derry, Gurteen,
9 Steelstown Road, Derry BT48 8EU

Most Rev Thomas A. Finnegan DD
Retired Bishop of Killala
Carrowmore-Lacken,
Ballina, Co Mayo
Tel 096-34966

Most Rev Thomas Flynn DD
Retired Bishop of Achonry
St Michael's, Cathedral Grounds,
Ballaghaderreen, Co Roscommon
Tel 094-9877808
Email bishopflynn@achonrydiocese.org

Most Rev Laurence Forristal DD
Retired Bishop of Ossory
Molassy, Freshford Road, Kilkenny

Most Rev Donal Murray DD
Retired Bishop of Limerick,
Kilmoyle, North Circular Road, Limerick
Tel 061-315856 Fax 061-310186
Email office@ldo.ie

Most Rev Fiachra Ó Ceallaigh DD
Titular Bishop of Tre Taverne &
Retired Auxiliary Bishop of Dublin,
19 St Anthony's Road, Rialto, Dublin 8
Tel 01-4537495 Fax 01-4544966
Email diaarmisneach@eircom.net

Most Rev Dermot O'Mahony DD
Titular Bishop of Tiava and Retired
Auxiliary Bishop of Dublin
19 Longlands, Swords, Co Dublin
Tel 01-8401596 Fax 01-8403950

Most Rev Patrick J. Walsh DD
Retired Bishop of Down and Connor
6 Waterloo Park North, Belfast BT15
5HW
Tel 028-90778182

MITRED ABBOTS

Rt Rev Dom Mark Patrick Hederman
(OSB)
Glenstal Abbey, Murroe, Co Limerick
Tel 061-386103

Rt Rev Dom Eamon Fitzgerald (OCSO)
Mount Melleray Abbey,
Cappoquin, Co Waterford
Tel 058-54404

Rt Rev Dom Eoin Waldron (de
Bhaldraithe) (OCSO)
Bolton Abbey, Moone, Athy, Co Kildare
Tel 0507-24102

Rt Rev Dom Celsus Kelly (OCSO)
Our Lady of Bethlehem Abbey,
11 Ballymena Road, Portglenone,
Ballymena, Co Antrim BT44 8BL
Tel 0266-821211 Fax 0286-822310

Rt Rev Dom Richard Purcell (OCSO)
Mount St Joseph Abbey, Roscrea,
Co Tipperary
Tel 0505-21711

Rt Rev Dom Bernard Boyle (OCSO)
Mellifont Abbey, Collon, Co Louth
Tel 041-26103

Rt Rev Charles J. White (CRL)
Apartment 3, 52 Castle Avenue,
Clontarf, Dublin 3
Tel 01-8333229

THE IRISH EPISCOPAL CONFERENCE

*Full details of membership, Commissions
and Agencies can be found on
www.catholicbishops.ie*

Executive Secretary
Rev Eamon Martin
Columba Centre,
Maynooth, Co Kildare
Tel 01-5053000 Fax 01-6292360
Email ex.sec@iecon.ie

Communications Director
Mr Martin Long
Columba Centre,
Maynooth, Co Kildare
Tel 01-5053000 Fax 01-6016401
Email mlong@catholicbishops.ie

*Executive Administrator of the
Commissions & Agencies of the Episcopal
Conference:* Mr Harry Casey
Columba Centre,
Maynooth, Co Kildare
Tel 01-5053000 Fax 01-6016401
Email harry.casey@iecon.ie

ARCHDIOCESES AND DIOCESES OF IRELAND

Ireland is divided into four provinces: Armagh, Dublin, Cashel and Tuam, named from metropolitan sees. The areas covered by each province and diocese are described at the beginning of the entry for each diocese; a map of the ecclesiastical areas is printed on the front endpaper of this directory.

For ease of reference, the four archdioceses appear at the beginning of this section in the traditional order, but the individual dioceses appear in full alphabetical order regardless of province. Thus Achonry, from the Province of Tuam, starts the section, followed by Ardagh and Clonmacnois from the Province of Ardagh and so on.

The provinces and their suffragan sees are as follows:

Province of Armagh
Metropolitan See: Armagh
Suffragan Sees: Dioceses of Ardagh & Clonmacnois, Clogher, Derry, Down & Connor, Dromore, Kilmore, Meath, Raphoe.

The Archbishop of Armagh is Primate of All Ireland.

Province of Dublin
Metropolitan See: Dublin
Suffragan Sees: Dioceses of Ferns, Kildare & Leighlin, Ossory.

The Archbishop of Dublin is Primate of Ireland.

Province of Cashel
Metropolitan See: Cashel
Suffragan Sees: Dioceses of Cloyne, Cork & Ross, Kerry, Killaloe, Limerick, Waterford & Lismore.

Province of Tuam
Metropolitan See: Tuam
Suffragan Sees: Dioceses of Achonry, Clonfert, Elphin, Galway & Kilmacduagh with Kilfenora*, Killala.

*Kilfenora is in the Province of Cashel, but the Bishop of Galway and Kilmacduagh is its Apostolic Administrator.

ARCHDIOCESE OF ARMAGH

PATRONS OF THE ARCH DIOCESE
ST MALACHY, 3 NOVEMBER; ST PATRICK, 17 MARCH;
ST OLIVER PLUNKETT, 1 JULY

SUFFRAGFEN SEES: ARDAGH AND CLONMACNOIS, CLOGHER, DERRY,
DOWN AND CONNOR, DROMORE, KILMORE, MEATH, RAPHOE

INCLUDES ALMOST ALL OF COUNTIES ARMAGH AND LOUTH
APPROX HALF OF COUNTY TYRONE
AND PARTS OF COUNTIES DERRY AND MEATH

His Eminence Cardinal Seán Brady DCL, DD
Archbishop of Armagh;
Primate of All Ireland;
born 1939; ordained priest
22 February 1964; ordained
Coadjutor Archbishop 19
February 1995; installed
Archbishop of Armagh 3
November 1996; created
Cardinal 24 November 2007.

Residence
Ara Coeli, Armagh BT61 7QY
Tel 028-37522045 Fax 028-37526182
Email admin@aracoeli.com
Website
www.archdioceseofarmagh.com

ST PATRICK'S CATHEDRAL, ARMAGH

The building of the new St Patrick's Cathedral lasted from St Patrick's Day 1840, when the foundation stone was laid, until its solemn consecration in 1904. There were occasional intermissions of the work, and one of the longest gaps occurred because of the Great Famine. Primate Crolly, who had initiated the building, became a victim of famine cholera, and, at his own wish, his body was laid to rest under the sanctuary of the unfinished cathedral.

For five years the low outline of the bare walls remained, but with the translation of Dr Paul Cullen to the See of Dublin, work was resumed under Primate Dixon. On Easter Monday 1854, tarpaulins and canvas covers were drawn from wall to wall to allow Mass to be celebrated in the unfinished building.

During the Famine cessation the original architect, Thomas J. Duff, died. The architect to take over from Duff's original Perpen-dicular Gothic design was J. J. McCarthy, destined to become one of the famous architects of the nineteenth century. In his anxiety to achieve a greater degree of classical purity, McCarthy drew up a continuation design in the old fourteenth-century Decorated Gothic. While critics may debate the wisdom of such a radical change when the building had reached a relatively advanced stage, the effect was undoubtedly to create an overall impression of massive grandeur.

The final impetus to complete the building came when Dr McGettigan was appointed (1870) to Armagh, and the solemn dedication took place in 1873.

Dr Logue, following Primate McGettigan's death, was to achieve the splendid interior decoration and the addition of the Synod Hall. He travelled to Rome and Carrara in search of precious marble for the reredos, pulpit and altar, and it was he also who achieved the decoration of the interior with mosaic. Under him, stained-glass windows were commissioned from Meyer in Germany. Cardinal Vanutelli represented Pope Pius X at the solemn consecration in 1904. A grand carillon was installed in 1924.

Vatican II's decree on Sacred Liturgy stressed the participation of the laity and hence greater visibility had to be afforded to the congregation. For this reason all the architects who submitted designs based their plans on the removal of the 1904 marble screens, which hindered visibility of the sanctuary from the sides. By raising, enlarging and opening the sanctuary area, the cathedral has, to a large extent, been restored to its original form.

With the removal of the rood screen, a new crucifix had to be placed at the sanctuary, and a specially commissioned 'Cross of Life' by Imogen Stuart was affixed to the right of the sanctuary.

The rededication took place in 1982, and a portion of St Malachy's relics from France, together with a relic of St Oliver Plunkett, was placed in the new altar. And so, the mortal remains of two of Armagh's most celebrated *comharbaí Phádraig* were carried back to the scene of their labours in more troubled times.

A unique, but now also an historical feature of the primatial cathedral, is the Cardinals' Hats. They are no longer

conferred on new Cardinals. They were hung here and went deliberately untended so that their decay would represent the end of all earthly glory. The most recently hung (and last to be presented) is that of Cardinal Conway. Beside it are Cardinal Logue's and Cardinal O'Donnell's, while on the opposite side are the hats of Cardinals D'Alton and MacRory.

Most Rev Gerard Clifford DD
Titular Bishop of Geron and Auxiliary
Bishop to the Archbishop of Armagh;
born 1941; ordained priest 18 June 1967;
ordained Bishop 21 April 1991
Residence: Annaskeagh, Ravensdale,
Dundalk, Co Louth
Tel 042-9371012 Fax 042-9371013
Email gcliffrd@indigo.ie

CHAPTER

Dean: Very Rev Colum Curry VG
Archdeacon: Rt Rev Francis Donnelly
Canons: Most Rev Gerard Clifford VG
Rt Rev Liam McEntegart VG
Very Rev John Donaghy
Very Rev Tomás Ó Sabhaois
Very Rev Michael Ward
Very Rev Patrick McDonnell
Rt Rev Christopher O'Byrne
Rt Rev Raymond Murray
Very Rev James Clyne
Very Rev Michael Crawley
Very Rev James Carroll

ADMINISTRATION

Vicars General
Most Rev Gerard Clifford DD
Annaskeagh, Ravensdale, Dundalk,
Co Louth
Tel 042-9371012 Fax 042-9371013
Email gcliffrd@indigo.ie
Rt Rev Liam McEntegart PE
10 Killymeal Road, Dungannon,
Co Tyrone BT71 6DP
Tel 028-87722906
Very Rev Dean Colum Curry PP
4 Circular Road, Dungannon,
Co Tyrone BT71 6BE
Tel 028-87722775

Vicars Forane
Very Rev Gerard Campbell Adm,
St Patrick's, Dundalk
Very Rev James Carroll PP, Drogheda
Very Rev Paul Clayton-Lea PP,
Clogherhead
Very Rev Malachy Conlon PP, Kilkerley
Very Rev Kevin Cullen PP, Cullyhanna
Very Rev Dean Colum Curry PP, VG,
Dungannon
Very Rev Benedict Fee PP, Clonoe
Very Rev John Gates PP, Magherafelt
Very Rev Patick Hannigan PP, Killeeshil
Very Rev Patrick McEnroe PP,
Darver & Dromiskin
Very Rev Peter McParland PP, Cooley
Very Rev Dermot Maloney PP, Dromintee
Very Rev Peter Murphy PP, Ardee & Collon
Very Rev Richard Naughton PP,
Cloghogue
Very Rev Michael O'Dwyer PP, Portadown
Rev Seán O'Neill PP, Termonmaguirc
Very Rev Eugene Sweeney Adm, Armagh
Very Rev Gerard Tremer PP, Cookstown

Chancellor
Vacant

Diocesan Curia
Rev John Connolly, Diocesan Secretary
Email jconnolly@aracoeli.com
Ara Coeli, Armagh BT61 7QY
Tel 028-37522045 Fax 028-37526182
Email admin@aracoeli.com
Mr John McVey
Financial Administrator
Email jmcvey@aracoeli.com

Archives
Acting Librarian: Mr Joe Canning
Cardinal Tomás Ó Fiaich Memorial Library
and Archive,
15 Moy Road, Armagh BT61 7LY
Tel 028-37522981 Fax 028-37511944
Email eolas@ofiaich.ie

CATECHETICS EDUCATION

**Catholic Primary School Managers'
Association**
Secretary: Very Rev Malachy Conlon PP, VF
Parochial House, Kilkerley,
Dundalk, Co Louth
Tel 042-9333482
Email malachykilkerley@eircom.net

Council for Catholic Maintained Schools
Senior Management Officer
Mr Stephen Walsh
1 Killyman Road, Dungannon
Co Tyrone BT71 6DE
Tel 028-87752116 Fax 028-87752783
Email stephen.walsh@ccmsschools.com

Diocesan Advisers for Religious Education
Primary Schools
Rev Eugene O'Neill
Email freoneill@btopenworld.com
4 Ballymacnab Road, Armagh BT60 2QS
Tel/Fax 028-37531620
Post-Primary Schools
Rev Declan O'Loughlin
Parochial House, 30 Newline,
Killeavy, Newry, Co Down BT35 8TA
Tel 028-30889609
Email decoloughlin@yahoo.co.uk

PASTORAL

Accord
Drogheda Chairperson
Mrs Anne Brogan
Verona, Cross Lane, Drogheda, Co Louth
Tel 041-9843860
Email accorddrogheda@eircom.net

Armagh Chairperson
Mr Denis Bradley
1 Tavanagh Avenue, Portadown,
Co Armagh BT62 3AJ
Tel 028-38334781
Email armagh@accordni.com

Dundalk Chairperson
Mr Seamus Corrigan
St Patrick's, Roden Place,
Dundalk, Co Louth
Tel 042-9331731
Email accorddundalk@eircom.net

Apostolic Work Society
Diocesan President: Ms Jean Hanratty
13 College Street, Armagh BT61 9BT
Tel 028-37522781

Armagh Diocesan Pastoral Centre
Director: Sr Rhoda Curran (RSM)
The Magnet, The Demesne,
Dundalk, Co Louth
Tel 042-9336393 Fax 042-9336432

Charismatic Renewal
Very Rev Dean Colum Curry PP, VG
Parochial House, 4 Circular Road,
Dungannon, Co Tyrone BT71 6BE
Tel 028-87722775

Chokmah
Co-ordinator: Rev Thomas Hamill
'Shekinah', 25 Wynnes Terrace,
Dundalk, Co Louth
Tel 042-9331023
Email tomhamill@eircom.net

Communications
Diocesan Officer: Vacant

CURA
17 Jocelyn Street, Dundalk, Co Louth
Tel 042-9337533
Co-ordinator: Ms Betty McNally

Deaf – Ministry to
Chaplain: Rev Garrett Campbell CC
Parochial House, 3 Convent Road,
Cookstown, Co Tyrone BT80 8QA
Tel 028-86763293 Fax 028-86763490

Ecumenism
Very Rev Pádraig Murphy PP
Email pplordship@live.ie
Parochial House, Ravensdale,
Dundalk, Co Louth
Tel 042-9371327 Fax 042-9371327
Rev Seán Dooley CC
Email seandooleyfriesian@btconnect.com
Parochial House, 42 Abbey Street,
Co Armagh BT61 7D2
Tel 028-37522802 Fax 028-37522245

Family Ministry & Pastoral Renewal
Directors: Rev Andrew McNally
Email andy@parishandfamily.ie
Dr Tony Hanna
Email tonyhann@indigo.ie
Armagh Diocesan Pastoral Centre,
The Magnet, The Demesne,
Dundalk, Co Louth
Tel 042-9336649

Fr Mathew Union
Diocesan Chairman
Very Rev Seamus Rice PE, AP
Parochial House, 89 Derrynoose Road,
Derrynoose, Co Armagh BT60 3EZ
Tel 028-37531222
Email seamusrice@live.co.uk

Allianz (ii)

Armagh Diocesan Pastoral Council
Chairperson: Mr Liam McCallion
4 The Links, Blackrock, Co Louth
Tel 042-9321317
Secretary: Mrs Sheila McEneaney
Ashridge, Brackley, Markethill,
Co Armagh BT60 1SE
Tel 028-37552056
Email sheila.mceneaney@hotmail.com

Historic Churches Advisory Committee
(Armagh, Clogher and Kilmore)
Chair: Most Rev Gerard Clifford VG
Annaskeagh, Ravensdale,
Dundalk, Co Louth
Tel 042-9371012 Fax 042-9371013
Email gcliffrd@indigo.ie

Knock Pilgrimage
Director: Rev Benedict Fee PP, VF
Parochial House, Magheralanfield,
140 Mountjoy Road, Coalisland,
Co Tyrone BT71 5DY
Tel 028-87738381
Email frbennyfee@hotmail.com

Legion of Mary
Armagh Curia President
Margaret McManus
Newry Road, Armagh
Tel 077-99867714
Drogheda Curia President
Elizabeth Molony
194 Meadow View, Drogheda, Co Louth
Tel 041-9830617
Dundalk Curia President
Maureen Murphy
81 Seafield Lawns, Avenue Road,
Dundalk, Co Louth
Tel 042-9335360

Liturgy Commission
Chair: Rev Peter McAnenly CC
Parochial House, 6 Circular Road,
Dungannon, Co Tyrone BT71 6BE
Tel 028-87722831 Fax 028-87726893

LMFM Community Radio
Very Rev Canon James Carroll PP, VF
Parochial House, 9 Fair Street,
Drogheda, Co Louth

Lourdes Pilgrimage
Director: Very Rev Gerard Tremer PP, VF
Parochial House, 1 Convent Road,
Cookstown, Co Tyrone BT80 8QA
Tel 028-86763370

Marriage Tribunal
(See Marriage Tribunals section.)

Pioneer Total Abstinence Association
Diocesan Director
Very Rev Seamus Rice PE, AP
Parochial House, 89 Derrynoose Road,
Derrynoose, Co Armagh BT60 3EZ
Tel 028-37531222

Polish Chaplaincy
Rev Stanislaw Kowalski (SChr) CC
Parochial House, 6 Circular Road,
Dungannon, Co Tyrone BT71 6BE
Tel 028-87722631

Pontifical Mission Societies
Diocesan Director
Very Rev Vincent Darragh PE
81 Mullinahoe Road, Ardboe,
Dungannon, Co Tyrone BT71 5AU
Tel 028-86735774
Email vdarragh@aol.com

Safeguarding Children
Chairperson: Sr Loretto McKeown (RSM)
Convent of Mercy, Catherine Street,
Newry, Co Down BT35 6JG
Tel 028-30257095
Designated Officers
Kate Acton Tel 087-9374070
Aileen Oates Tel 078-95460797

Seminarian Liaison
Very Rev Joseph McKeever PP
9 Newry Road, Crossmaglen, Newry,
Co Down BT35 9HH
Tel 028-30861208
Email jmckeever02@googlemail.com

Senate of Priests
Chairman
Very Rev Dean Colum Curry PP, VG
Parochial House, 4 Circular Road,
Dungannon, Co Tyrone BT71 6BE
Tel 028-87722775
Email ccurry@btinternet.com

SPRED
Co-ordinator: Ms Patricia Lennon
19 The Glen, Newry, Co Down BT35 8BS
Tel 028-30265353

Travellers
Co-ordinator: Rev Aloysius MacCourt CC
Parochial House, 55 West Street,
Stewartstown, Dungannon,
Co Tyrone BT71 5HT
Tel 028-87738252

Vocations Commission
Vocations Director: Rev Patrick Rushe CC
Holy Redeemer Parochial House,
Ard Easmuinn, Dundalk, Co Louth
Tel 042-9334259
Email revpicard1@eircom.net

Youth Commission (ADYC)
Chairperson: Rev Brian White CC
Portadown
Director: Ms Kate Acton
Archdiocese of Armagh,
Cathedral Road, Armagh BT61 7QY
Tel 028-37525592
Email kate@armaghyouth.com

PARISHES

*Mensal parishes are listed first. Other
parishes follow alphabetically. Historical
names are given in parentheses. Church
titulars are in italics.*

ARMAGH
St Patrick's Cathedral, St Malachy, Irish
Street, *St Colmcille's,* Knockaconey
Immaculate Conception, Tullysaran
Very Rev Eugene Sweeney Adm, VF
Email esweeney64@btconnect.com
Rev Seán Dooley CC
Email seandooleyfriesian@btconnect.com
Rev Rory Coyle CC
Email rory_coyle@hotmail.com
Rev John McKeever CC
Email john_mckeever@yahoo.com
Parochial House, 42 Abbey Street,
Armagh BT61 7DZ
Tel 028-37522802 Fax 028-37522245
Rev Kevin Donaghy *(Priest in residence)*
Parochial House, 86 Maydown Road,
Artasooley, Tullysaran, Benburb,
Co Armagh BT71 7LN
Tel 028-37548210

DUNDALK, ST PATRICK'S
St Patrick's, Roden Place
St Nicholas's, Church Street
www.stpatricksparishdundalk.org
Very Rev Gerard Campbell Adm, VF
Email wgcampbell@eircom.net
Rev Séamus Dobbin CC
Rev Mark O'Hagan CC
Email ohagan.mark@gmail.com
Rev Michael Sheehan CC
Email frmichaelpsheehan@eircom.net
Rev John Anih (MSP) CC
St Patrick's Presbytery, Roden Place,
Dundalk, Co Louth
Tel 042-9334648 Fax 042-9336355
Email mensalparish@eircom.net

DUNDALK, HOLY REDEEMER
Holy Redeemer
www.redeemerparish.ie
Very Rev Pádraig Keenan Adm
Email pkredeemer@eircom.net
Rev Patrick Rushe CC
Email revpicard1@eircom.net
Ard Easmuinn, Dundalk, Co Louth
Tel 042-9334259 Fax 042-9329073
Email holyredeemer@eircom.net

DUNDALK, ST JOSEPH'S
St Joseph's
Very Rev Richard Delahunty (CSsR) Adm
Email richard.del@bol.com.br
Rev Eamon Hoey (CSsR) CC
Email nedhoey@gofree.indigo.ie
Rev William McGettrick (CSsR) CC
St Joseph's, St Alphonsus Road,
Dundalk, Co Louth
Tel 042-9334042 Fax 042-9330893
Email redsdalk@iol.ie

DUNDALK, HOLY FAMILY
Holy Family
Very Rev James O'Connell (SM) Adm
Rev Patrick Stanley (SM) CC
Rev Francis Corry (SM) CC
Holy Family Parish,
Dundalk, Co Louth
Tel 042-9336301 Fax 042-9336350
Email theholyfamily@eircom.net

DROGHEDA

St Peter's, West Street
Our Lady of Lourdes, Hardman's Gardens
www.saintpetersdrogheda.ie
Email stpetersadmin1@eircom.net
Very Rev Canon James Carroll PP, VF
Parochial House, 9 Fair Street, Drogheda,
Co Louth
Tel 041-9838537 Fax 041-9841351
Email jcarlpp@eircom.net
Very Rev Canon Patrick McDonnell PE, AP
Tel 041-9831899
Rev John McAlinden (CSsR) CC
Tel 041-9831899
Rev Francis Coll CC
Email francis.coll@nuim.ie
Our Lady of Lourdes Presbytery,
Hardman's Gardens, Drogheda, Co Louth
Rev Piotr Delimat CC
Email pieetro@wp.pl
Rev Sean Ryan (SMA) CC
St Peter's Presbytery, 10 Fair Street,
Drogheda, Co Louth
Tel 041-9838239

DUNGANNON (DRUMGLASS, KILLYMAN AND TULLYNISKIN)

St Patrick's, Dungannon,
St Malachy's Edendork,
St Brigid's, Killyman,
Sacred Heart, Clonmore
www. parishofdungannon.com
Very Rev Dean Colum Curry PP, VG
4 Circular Road, Dungannon,
Co Tyrone BT71 6BE
Tel 028-87722775
Email ccurry@btinternet.com
Rev Aidan Dunne CC
Email fadunne@googlemail.com
Rev Peter McAnenly CC
Email p.mcanenly@btopenworld.com
Rev Séamus White CC
Rev Stanislaw Kowalski (SChr) CC
Parochial House, 6 Circular Road,
Dungannon, Co Tyrone BT71 6BE
Tel 028-87722631
Parish Office: 4 Killyman Road,
Dungannon, Co Tyrone BT71 6DH
Tel/Fax 028-87726893
Email parishofdungannon@lycos.com

ARDBOE

Blessed Sacrament, Mullinahoe
Immaculate Conception, Moortown
Very Rev Séamus McGinley PP
Email smginley01@btinternet.com
Parochial House, Moortown, Cookstown,
Co Tyrone BT80 0HT
Tel 028-86737236
Very Rev Vincent Darragh PE
81 Mullinahoe Road, Ardboe,
Dungannon, Co Tyrone BT71 5AU
Tel 028-86735774

ARDEE & COLLON

Nativity of Our Lady, Ardee
St Catherine's, Ballapousta
Mary Immaculate, Collon
Website www.ardeeparish.com
Email ardee.collon@net1.ie
Very Rev Peter Murphy PP, VF
Tel 041-6850920 Fax 041-6850922
Very Rev Thomas McGeough PE, AP
Tel 041-6850920 Fax 041-6850922

Rev Anselm Emechebe (MSP) CC
Tel 041-6860080
Parochial House, Hale Street,
Ardee, Co Louth
Rev William Mulvihill CC
Parochial House, Collon, Co Louth
Tel 041-9826106

AUGHNACLOY (AGHALOO)

St Mary's, Aughnacloy,
St Brigid's, Killens,
St Joseph's, Caledon
Very Rev Seán McEvoy PP
Parochial House, 19 Caledon Road
Aughnacloy, Co Tyrone BT69 6HX
Tel 028-85557212 Fax 028-85557074
Rev John McGoldrick (in residence)
Parochial House, 56 Minterburn Road,
Laireakean, Caledon, Co Tyrone BT68 4XH
Tel 028-37568288

BALLINDERRY

St Patrick's
Very Rev Peter Donnelly PP
Parochial House,
130 Ballinderry Bridge Road, Coagh,
Cookstown, Co Tyrone BT80 0AY
Tel 028-79418244

BALLYGAWLEY (ERRIGAL KIERAN)

St Matthew's, Garvaghy, St Mary's,
Dunmoyle, Immaculate Conception,
Ballygawley, St Malachy's, Ballymacilroy
Very Rev Michael Seery PP
Parochial House, 115 Omagh Road,
Ballygawley, Co Tyrone BT70 2AG
Tel 028-85568208
Email errigalciarog@aol.com
Very Rev Brian Hackett PE, AP
Parochial House, 31 Church Street,
Ballygawley, Co Tyrone BT70 2HA
Tel 028-85568219

BERAGH

Immaculate Conception, Beragh,
St Malachy's, Seskinore,
St Patrick's, Drumduff
Very Rev Arthur McAnerney PP
Parochial House, Beragh, Omagh,
Co Tyrone BT79 0SY
Tel 028-80758206
Email arthur.mcanerney@btinternet.com

BESSBROOK (KILLEAVY LOWER)

SS Peter and Paul, Bessbrook,
St Malachy, Camlough, Sacred Heart, Lislea,
Immaculate Conception, Lissummon Road,
Newry, Good Shepherd, Cloughreagh
Rev Seán Larkin PP
Parochial House, 11 Chapel Road,
Bessbrook, Newry, Co Down BT35 7AU
Tel 028-30830206 Fax 028-30838154
Rev Phelim McKeown CC
Email frphelim@eircom.net
Tel 028-30830272
Parochial House, 9 Chapel Road,
Bessbrook, Newry, Co Down BT35 7AU
Very Rev Robert McKenna PE, AP
Parochial House, 26 Newtown Road,
Camlough, Newry, Co Down BT35 7JJ
Tel 028-30830237 Fax 028-30837273
Email robert.mckenna3@btinternet.com

CARLINGFORD AND CLOGHERNY

St Michael's, Carlingford
St Lawrence's, Omeath
www.carlinnparish.com
Very Rev Brian MacRaois PP
Parochial House, Chapel Hill,
Carlingford, Co Louth
Tel 042-9373111 Fax 042 9373131
Email cairlinnparish@eircom.net
Very Rev James Shevlin PE, AP
Parochial House, Omeath, Co Louth
Tel 042-9375198
Email jamesshevlin@eircom.net

CLOGHERHEAD

St Michael's, Clogherhead,
SS Peter and Paul, Walshestown
www.clogherhead.com
Very Rev Paul Clayton-Lea PP, VF
Tel 041-9822438
Email clogherheadparish@hotmail.com
Very Rev William Murtagh PE, AP
Tel 041-9822224
Parochial House, Clogherhead,
Drogheda, Co Louth

CLOGHOGUE (KILLEAVY UPPER)

Sacred Heart, Cloghogue, St Joseph's,
Meigh, St Michael's, Killean
Very Rev Richard Naughton PP, VF
Mountain Lodge, 132 Dublin Road,
Newry, Co Down BT35 8QT
Tel 028-30262174 Fax 028-30262174
Very Rev S. James Clyne PE, AP
Email clyne@eircom.net
Mountain Lodge, 134 Dublin Road,
Newry, Co Down BT35 8QT
Tel 028-30262053
Rev Andrew McNally (in residence)
24 Chapel Road, Killeavy, Newry,
Co Down BT35 8JY
Tel 028-30848222
Email andymacs@mac.com

CLONOE

St Patrick's, Clonoe, St Columcille's,
Kingsland, St Brigid's, Brockagh
Email clonoeparish@tiscali.co.uk
Very Rev Benedict Fee PP, VF
Parochial House, Magheralanfield,
140 Mountjoy Road, Coalisland,
Co Tyrone BT71 5DY
Tel 028-87738381 Fax 028-87738048
Email frbennyfee@hotmail.com
Very Rev Kieran MacKeone PE, AP
Parochial House, 132 Washing Bay Road,
Coalisland, Dungannon,
Co Tyrone BT71 4QZ
Tel 028-87740376
Email kieran.mckeone@btinternet.com
Rev John McCallion CC
Parochial House, 18 Annaghmore Road,
Coalisland, Dungannon,
Co Tyrone BT71 4QZ
Email revtrad@btinternet.com

COAGH

Our Lady's, Coagh
SS Joseph and Malachy, Drummullan
Very Rev Oliver Breslan PP
Parochial House, Hanover Square,
Coagh, Cookstown, Co Tyrone BT80 0EF
Tel 028-86737212
Email coaghparish@aol.com

COALISLAND

*Holy Family, Coalisland
St Mary & St Joseph, Coalisland,
St Mary's, Stewartstown*
Email coalislandparish@yahoo.co.uk
Very Rev Paul Byrne PP
Parochial House, 31 Brackaville Road,
Coalisland, Co Tyrone BT71 4NH
Tel 028-87740221 Fax 028-87746449
Email pauldbyrne@yahoo.co.uk
Rev John Burns CC
5 Plater's Hill, Coalisland,
Co Tyrone BT71 4JZ
Tel 028-87740302
Email frjohnnyburns@btinternet.com
Rev Aloysius McCourt CC
55 West Street, Stewartstown,
Dungannon, Co Tyrone BT71 5HT
Tel 028-87738252

COOKSTOWN (DESERTCREIGHT AND DERRYLORAN)

*Holy Trinity, Cookstown, Sacred Heart,
Tullydonnell, St John's, Slatequarry,
St Laurán's, Cookstown*
Very Rev Gerard Tremer PP, VF
Parochial House, 1 Convent Road,
Cookstown, Co Tyrone BT80 8QA
Tel 028-86763370 Fax 028-86763370
Email gerardtremer@btinternet.com
Rev Garrett Campbell CC
Parochial House, 3 Convent Road,
Cookstown, Co Tyrone BT80 8QA
Tel 028-86763293 Fax 028-86763490
Email garrett.campbell@btinternet.com
Rev John Flanagan (SPS) CC
Parochial House, 6 Tullydonnell Road,
Dungannon, Co Tyrone BT70 3JE
Tel 028-87758224

COOLEY

*St James's, Grange
Our Lady, Star of the Sea, Boher
St Anne's, Mullaghbuoy*
Very Rev Peter McParland PP, VF
Top Rath, Cooley, Carlingford, Co Louth
Tel 042-9376105 Fax 042-9376075
Email pjmcparland@eircom.net
Rev Thomas McNulty CC
Parochial House, Grange,
Carlingford, Co Louth
Tel 042-9376577
Email tommymcnulty37@gmail.com

CROSSMAGLEN (CREGGAN UPPER)

*St Patrick's, Crossmaglen,
St Brigid's, Glassdrummond,
Sacred Heart, Shelagh*
Email uppercreggan@googlemail.com
Very Rev Joseph McKeever PP
9 Newry Road, Crossmaglen,
Newry, Co Down BT35 9HH
Tel 028-30861208 Fax 028-30860163
Email jmckeever02@googlemail.com
Rev Liam McKinney CC
Parochial House, 9a Newry Road,
Crossmaglen, Newry, Co Down BT35 9HH
Tel 028-30868698 Fax 028-30860163
Email ltpmckinney@yahoo.com
Rev Bernard King (SM) CC
Parochial House, Glassdrummond,
Crossmaglen, Newry, Co Down BT35 9DY
Tel 028-30861270
Email baking@btinternet.com

CULLYHANNA (CREGGAN LOWER)

*St Patrick's, Cullyhanna
St Michael's, Newtownhamilton
St Oliver Plunkett's, Dorsey*
Very Rev Kevin Cullen PP, VF
Parochial House, Tullinavall Road,
Cullyhanna, Newry, Co Down BT35 OPZ
Tel 028-30861235
Very Rev Patrick McGuckin PE, AP
Parochial House, 80 Dundalk Street,
Newtownhamilton,
Newry, Co Down BT35 OPE
Tel 028-30878232

DARVER AND DROMISKIN

St Peter's, Dromiskin, St Michael's, Darver
Very Rev Patrick McEnroe PP, VF
Darver, Readypenny, Dundalk, Co Louth
Tel 042-9379147
Email patrickmmcenroe@eircom.net
Very Rev Liam Pentony CC
Parochial House, Dromiskin,
Dundalk, Co Louth
Tel 042-9382877
Email frliampentony@gmail.com

DONAGHMORE

*St Patrick's, Donaghmore
St John's, Galbally*
Very Rev Gerard McAleer PP
Parochial House, 63 Castlecaulfield Road,
Donaghmore, Dungannon,
Co Tyrone BT70 3HF
Tel 028-87761327

DROMINTEE

*St Patrick's, Dromintee
Sacred Heart, Jonesboro*
Very Rev Dermot Maloney PP
Parochial House, 40 The Village,
Jonesboro, Newry, Co Down BT35 8HP
Tel 028-30849345
Email drominteeparish@btinternet.com

DUNLEER

*St Brigid's, Dunleer,
St Finians's Dromin,
St Kevin's, Philipstown*
www.dunleerparish.ie
Very Rev G. Michael Murtagh PP
Parochial House, Old Chapel Lane,
Dunleer, Co Louth
Tel 041-6851278
Email gmmurtagh@eircom.net
Rev Emlyn McGinn
Parochial House, Barn Road,
Dunleer, Co Louth
Tel 041-6863822
Email emlynmcginn@yahoo.com

EGLISH

St Patrick's
Very Rev Patrick Breslan PP
Parochial House, 124 Eglish Road,
Dungannon, Co Tyrone BT70 1LB
Tel 028-37548289

FAUGHART

*St Brigid's, Kilcurry,
Most Holy Rosary, Brid-a-Crinn,
St Joseph's, Castletown*
Very Rev Christopher McElwee (IC) PP
Rev Bernard Hughes (IC) CC
St Brigid's, Kilcurry, Dundalk, Co Louth
Tel 042-9334410/9333235

HAGGARDSTOWN AND BLACKROCK

*St Fursey's Haggardstown
St Oliver Plunkett's, Blackrock*
Very Rev Oliver Brennan PP
Parochial House, Grianán Mhuire,
Main Street, Blackrock, Dundalk, Co Louth
Tel 042-9321621
Email olivervbrennan@eircom.net
Rev Paul Montague CC
6 Ard na Mara, Blackrock,
Dundalk, Co Louth
Tel 042-9322244 Fax 042-9322244
Email revpaulmontague@eircom.net

KEADY (DERRYNOOSE)

*St Patrick's, Keady, St Joseph's,
Derrynoose, St Joseph's, Madden*
Very Rev Canon Michael Crawley PP
Parochial House, 34 Madden Row, Keady,
Co Armagh BT60 3RW
Tel 028-37531242 Fax 028-37539627
Email parishofkeady@btinternet.com
Rev Sean McCartan CC
Parochial House, St Patrick Street, Keady,
Co Armagh BT60 3TQ
Tel 028-37531246 Fax 028-37530850
Email sean.westend@talk21.com
Very Rev Séamus Rice PE, AP
Parochial House, 89 Derrynoose Road,
Derrynoose, Keady, Co Armagh BT60 3EZ
Tel 028-37531222 Fax 028-37539397
Email seamusrice@live.co.uk

KILDRESS

*St Joseph's, Killeenan
St Mary's, Dunamore*
Very Rev Patrick Hughes PP
Parochial House, 10 Cloughfin Road,
Kildress, Cookstown, Co Tyrone BT80 9JB
Tel 028-86751206

KILKERLEY

Immaculate Conception
Very Rev Malachy Conlon PP, VF
Parochial House, Kilkerley,
Dundalk, Co Louth
Tel 042-9333482
Email malachykilkerley@eircom.net

KILLCLUNEY

*St Patrick's, Baile Mhic an Aba,
St Michael's, Cladaí Móra,
St Mary's, Grainseach Mhór*
Very Rev Peter Kerr PP
Parochial House, Ballymacnab,
Armagh BT60 2QT
Tel/Fax 028-37531641

KILLEESHIL

*Assumption, Killeeshil, St Patrick's,
Aughnagar, St Joseph's, Ackenduff*
Very Rev Patrick Hannigan PP, VF
Parochial House, 65 Tullyallen Road,
Dungannon, Co Tyrone BT70 3AF
Tel 028-87761211
Email killeeshilparish@yahoo.co.uk

KILMORE

*Immaculate Conception, Mullavilly,
St Patrick's, Stonebridge*
www.parishofkilmore.com
Very Rev Michael Toner PP
Parochial House, 114 Battlehill Road,
Richhill, Co Armagh BT61 8QJ
Tel 028-38871661
Email parishofkilmore@googlemail.com

KILSARAN
St Mary's, Kilsaran
St Nicholas, Stabannon
Very Rev Eamon Treanor PP
Parochial House, Kilsaran,
Castlebellingham, Dundalk, Co Louth
Tel 042-9372255
Email treanoret@eircom.net

KNOCKBRIDGE
St Mary's, Knockbridge
Very Rev Gerard McGinnity PP
Parochial House, Knockbridge,
Dundalk, Co Louth
Tel 042-9374125

LISSAN
St Michael's
Very Rev Seán Hegarty PP
Parochial House, 2 Tullynure Road,
Cookstown, Co Tyrone BT80 9XH
Tel 028-86763674
Email dshegarty@utvinternet.com

LORDSHIP (AND BALLYMASCANLON)
St Mary's, Ravensdale
St Mary's, Lordship
Our Lady of the Wayside, Jenkinstown
www.lordship-ballymascanlon.org
Very Rev Pádraig Murphy PP
Parochial House, Ravensdale,
Dundalk, Co Louth
Tel/Fax 042-9371327
Email pplordship@live.ie
Very Rev Patrick Larkin, PE, AP
Parochial House, Jenkinstown,
Dundalk, Co Louth
Tel 042-9371328

LOUGHGALL
Our Lady of Peace, Maghery
St Peter's, Collegeland
St Patrick's, Loughgall
St John's, Tartaraghan
Very Rev Eamonn McCamley PP
Parochial House, 17 Eagralougher Road,
Loughgall, Co Armagh BT61 8LA
Tel 028-38891231 Fax 028-38891827
Email loughgall@gmail.com

LOUTH
Our Lady of Immaculate Conception, Louth
Our Lady of the Snows, Stonetown
Very Rev Seán Quinn PP
Parochial House, Louth Village, Dundalk,
Co Louth
Tel 042-9374285
Email louthparish@dna.ie

MAGHERAFELT AND ARDTREA NORTH
Assumption, Magherafelt
St John's, Milltown
St Patrick's Castledawson
Email magherafeltparish@btinternet.com
www.magherafeltparish.org
Very Rev John Gates PP, VF
Parochial House, 30 King Street,
Magherafelt, Co Derry BT45 6AS
Tel 028-79632439
Email jgatesbrack@btconnect.com
Rt Rev Mgr Canon Christopher O'Byrne PE, AP
Parochial House, 12 Aughrim Road,
Magherafelt, Co Derry BT45 6AY
Tel 028-79634038

Rev David Moore CC
Parochial House, 10 Aughrim Road,
Magherafelt, Co Derry BT45 6AY
Tel 028-79632351
Email d.moore2323@btinternet.com

MELL
St Joseph's
Very Rev Martin Kenny PP
Parochial House, Slane Road, Mell,
Drogheda, Co Louth
Tel 041-9838278

MELLIFONT
Our Lady of the Assumption, Tullyallen
Very Rev Laurence Caraher PP
Parochial House, Tullyallen,
Drogheda, Co Louth
Tel 041-9838520
Email lac@mellifont.com

MIDDLE KILLEAVY
St Mary's, Dromalane,
St Malachy's, Carnagat
www.middlekilleavy.com
Very Rev Lawrence Boyle PP
'Glenshee', Dublin Road,
Newry, Co Down BT35 8DA
Tel 028-30262376
Email lorcanboyle@gmail.com
Rev Gregory Carvill CC
Parochial House, 17 Carnmore Drive,
Newry, Co Down BT35 8SB
Tel 028-30269047
Email greg.carvill@gmail.com

MIDDLETOWN (TYNAN)
St John's, Middletown
St Joseph's, Tynan
Very Rev Seán Moore PP
Parochial House, 290 Monaghan Road,
Middletown, Co Armagh BT60 4HS
Tel 028-37568406

MONASTERBOICE
Immaculate Conception, Tenure,
Nativity of Our Lady, Fieldstown
Very Rev Stephen Duffy PP
Parochial House, Monasterboice,
Drogheda, Co Louth
Tel 041-9822839
Email fatherduffy@eircom.net
Rev Michael Hickey (CSSp) CC
Parochial House, Tenure,
Dunleer, Co Louth
Tel 041-6851281
Email michaelhickey01@eircom.net

MONEYMORE (ARDTREA)
SS John and Trea, Moneymore
St Patrick, Loup
Very Rev Martin McArdle PP
Parochial House, 10 Springhill Road,
Moneymore, Magherafelt,
Co Derry BT45 7NG
Tel 028-86748242
Email ardtrea@btinternet.com
Rev Harry Coyle *(in residence)*
Lisieux, 99 Loup Road,
Ballynenagh, Moneymore,
Co Derry BT45 7ST
Tel 028-79418235

MOY (CLONFEACLE)
St John the Baptist, Moy
St Jarlath's, Clonfeacle
www.clonfeacleparish.com
Very Rev Gabriel Bannon (OSM) PP
Parochial House, 11 Benburb Road, Moy,
Dungannon, Co Tyrone BT71 7SQ
Tel 028-87784262
Very Rev John Hughes PE, CC
Parochial House, Benburb Road, Moy,
Dungannon, Co Tyrone BT71 7SQ
Rev John Connolly *(in residence)*
75 Clontrecle Road, Blackwatertown,
Dungannon, Co Tyrone BT71 7HP
Tel 028-37548919

MULLAGHBAWN (FORKHILL)
St Mary's, Mullaghbawn
Our Lady, Queen of Peace, Aughanduff
St Oliver Plunkett, Forkhill
Very Rev John Heagney PP
Parochial House, Mullaghbawn,
Newry, Co Down BT35 9XN
Tel 028-30888286 Fax 028-30888370
Email heagneyjh@aol.com

NEWBRIDGE
St James, Newbridge
Very Rev John Fox PP
Parochial House, 153 Aughrim Road,
Toomebridge, Antrim BT41 3SH
Tel 028-79468277 Fax 028-79468277
Email newbridgechurch@googlemail.com

POMEROY
Assumption, Pomeroy,
Immaculate Conception, Altmore
www.pomeroyparish.homestead.com
Very Rev Martin McVeigh PP
Parochial House,
9 Cavanakeeran Road, Pomeroy,
Dungannon, Co Tyrone BT70 2RD
Tel 028-87758329
Email pomeroyparish@hotmail.com

PORTADOWN (DRUMCREE)
St John the Baptist's, Garvaghy Road
St Patrick's, William Street
www.drumcreeparish.com
Very Rev Michael O'Dwyer PP, VF
Parochial House, 15 Moy Road,
Portadown, Co Armagh BT62 1QL
Tel 028-38350610
Email modppvf@fsmail.net
Rev Brian White CC
Parochial House, 11 Moy Road,
Portadown, Co Armagh BT62 1QL
Tel 028-38332218
Email roadbowler@hotmail.com

TALLANSTOWN
St Malachy's, Reaghstown,
St Medoc's, Clonkeen,
SS Peter and Paul, Tallanstown
Very Rev Peter Clarke PP
Parochial House, Tallanstown,
Dundalk, Co Louth
Tel 042-9374197
Email tallanstownparish@eircom.net

TANDRAGEE (BALLYMORE AND MULLAGHBRAC)

St James's, Tandragee
St Patrick's, Ballyargan
St Joseph's, Poyntzpass
St James's, Markethill
Very Rev Michael Woods PP
Parochial House, 40 Market Street,
Tandagree, Co Armagh BT62 2BW
Tel 028-38840442
Email parishofbandm@aol.com

TERMONFECHIN

Immaculate Conception, Termonfechin
The Assumption, Sandpit
Very Rev Aidan Murphy PP
Parochial House, Termonfechin,
Drogheda, Co Louth
Tel 041-9822121
Email termonfechinparish@eircom.net

TERMONMAGUIRC (CARRICKMORE, LOUGHMACRORY & CREGGAN)

St Colmcille's, Carrickmore
St Oliver Plunkett, Creggan
St Mary's, Loughmacrory
Email termonmaguircparish@gmail.com
Rev Sean O'Neill PP, VF
Parochial House, 1 Rockstown Road,
Carrickmore, Omagh,
Co Tyrone BT79 9BE
Tel 028-80761207 Fax 028-80760938
Email oneillsean@btinternet.com
Rev Malachy Murphy CC
1a Rockstown Road, Carrickmore,
Omagh, Co Tyrone BT79 9BE
Tel 028-80760853
Email malomurphy@googlemail.com
Very Rev Thomas Mallon PE, AP
Parochial House, 170 Loughmacrory Road,
Omagh, Co Tyrone BT79 9LG
Tel 028-80761230 Fax 028-80761131

TOGHER

St Columcille, Togher
St Finnian, Dillonstown
St Borchill, Dysart
St Mary's, Drumcar
http://homepage.eircom.net
/~togherparish/
Very Rev Thomas Daly PP
Parochial House, Boicetown, Togher,
Drogheda, Co Louth
Tel 041-6852110
Very Rev Sean Quinn PE, AP
Parochial House, Dillonstown,
Dunleer, Co Louth
Tel 041-6863570

WHITECROSS (LOUGHILLY)

St Teresa's, Tullyherron
St Malachy's, Ballymoyer
St Brigid's, Carrickananney
St Laurence O'Toole, Belleeks
Very Rev Michael Rogers PP
Parochial House, 25 Priestbush Road,
Whitecross, Co Armagh BT60 2TP
Tel 028-37507214
Email rogers228@freeuk.com

INSTITUTIONS AND CHAPLAINCY SERVICES

Aiken Military Barracks
Barrack Street, Dundalk, Co Louth
Rev Bernard McCay-Morrissey OP
Tel 042-9332295

Community School
Ardee, Co Louth
Mr Seán Moran
Tel 041-6853313

Cuan Mhuire
Armagh Road, Newry, Co Down
Tel 028-30262429
(Bessbrook Parish Clergy)

Dundalk Institute of Technology
Dundalk, Co Louth
Rev Emlyn McGinn
Dundalk Institute of Technology,
Dublin Road, Dundalk, Co Louth
Tel 042-9370224

Our Lady of Lourdes Hospital
Drogheda, Co Louth
Rev Thomas Hogan CSsR
Rev Richard Goode OSA
Our Lady of Lourdes Hospital,
Drogheda, Co Louth
Tel 041-9837601

St Paul's High School
Bessbrook, Co Armagh
Very Rev Dermot Maloney PP, VF
Parochial House, 40 The Village,
Jonesboro, Newry, Co Down BT35 8HP
Tel 028-3084945 (H) 028-30830309 (S)
Email maloney750@btinternet.com

The following hospitals are served by parochial clergy:
Armagh Community Hospital
Armagh
Tel 028-37522802 (Chaplain)
Longstone Special Care Hospital
Armagh
Tel 028-37522802 (Chaplain)
Louth County Hospital
Dundalk, Co Louth
Tel 042-9334648 (Chaplain)
Mid-Ulster Hospital
Magherafelt, Co Derry
Tel 028-79632351
Mullinure Geriatric Hospital
Armagh
Tel 028-37522802 (Chaplain)
St Brigid's Hospital
Ardee, Co Louth
Tel 041-6850920 (Chaplain)
St Joseph's Hospital
Ardee, Co Louth
Tel 041-6853313 (Chaplain)
St Luke's Psychiatric Hospital, Armagh
Armagh
Tel 028-37522802 (Chaplain)
St Oliver Plunkett's Hospital
Dundalk, Co Louth
Tel 042-9334259 (Chaplain)
South Tyrone Hospital
Dungannon, Co Tyrone
Tel 028-87722631 (Chaplain)

PRIESTS OF THE DIOCESE ELSEWHERE

Rev Dominic Mallon
13 Richview Heights, Keady,
Co Armagh BT60 3SW
Very Rev John O'Leary
175 Adams Street, 11E Brooklyn,
NY 11208 USA
Tel 718-5107111
Email jpolear7@aol.com

RETIRED PRIESTS

Very Rev John Bradley PE
8 Killymeal Road, Dungannon,
Co Tyrone BT71 6BE
Tel 028-87722183
Very Rev Joseph Campbell PE
17 Lough Road, Mullaghbawn, Newry,
Co Down BT35 9XP
Rev Desmond Corrigan
c/o Ara Coeli, Armagh BT61 7QY
Very Rev James Crowley PE
Parochial House, 60 Aughnagar Road,
Ballygawley, Dungannon,
Co Tyrone BT70 2HP
Tel 028-85568399
Very Rev Canon John Donaghy PE
Ashbrook Private Nursing Home,
50 Moor Road, Coalisland,
Co Tyrone BT71 4QB
Rt Rev Archdeacon Francis Donnelly PE
64 Meadow Grove, Dundalk, Co Louth
Tel/Fax 042-9353264
Very Rev John Finn PE
Parochial House, Grange,
Knockbridge, Dundalk, Co Louth
Tel 042-9374792
Very Rev James Grimes PE
61 Castlecaulfield Road,
Donaghmore, Co Tyrone BT70 3HF
Tel 028-87767727
Very Rev Terence Kelly PE
3 Cranagh, Ballinderry Bridge Road,
Coagh, Cookstown, Co Tyrone BT80 0AS
Very Rev Kieran MacOscar PE
Parochial House, 10 Mullavilly Road,
Tandragee, Co Armagh BT62 2LX
Tel 028-38840840
Email revmacoscar@btinternet.com
Very Rev Patrick J. McCrory PE
Parochial House, Sixemilecross,
Omagh, Co Tyrone BT79 9NF
Tel 028-80758344
Rt Rev Mgr Canon Liam McEntegart PE, VG
10 Killymeal Road, Dungannon,
Co Tyrone BT71 6DP
Tel 028-87722906
Email lmcentegart@btinternet.com
Very Rev Brendan McHugh PE
Parochial House, Mullanhoe, Ardboe,
Dungannon, Co Tyrone BT71 5AU
Tel 028-86737338
Very Rev Brendan McNally PE
Parochial House, Reaghstown,
Ardee, Co Louth
Tel 041-6855117
Very Rev James McNally PE
14 Derrygarve Road, Castledawson,
Co Derry BT45 8HA
Tel 028-79469998
Email sainttrea@aol.com

Allianz (Ⅱ)

Very Rev John Murphy PE
30 Moorehall Village, Hale Street,
Ardee, Co Louth,
Tel 041-6871942
Rt Rev Mgr Raymond Murray PE
60 Glen Mhacaha, Cathedral Road,
Armagh BT61 8AS
Tel 028-37510821
Email raylmurray@tiscali.co.uk
Very Rev Christopher O'Brien PE
Haroldstown, Tobinstown,
Tullow, Co Carlow
Tel 059-9161633
Very Rev Owen O'Donnell PE
Parochial House, Dunamore,
Cookstown, Co Tyrone
Tel 028-86751216
Very Rev Canon Tomás Ó Sabhaois PE
Avila Nursing Home, Convent Hill,
Bessbrook, Newry,
Co Down BT35 7AW
Very Rev Canon Michael Ward PE
6 Augherainey Close,
Donaghmore, Dungannon,
Co Tyrone BT70 3HF
Tel 028-87761847

RELIGIOUS ORDERS AND CONGREGATIONS

PRIESTS

AUGUSTINIANS
St Augustine's Priory, Shop Street,
Drogheda, Co Louth
Tel 041-9838409 Fax 041-9831847
Prior: Rev Richard Goode (OSA)
Email focal@eircom.net

CISTERCIANS
Mellifont Abbey, Collon, Co Louth
Tel 041-9826103 Fax 041-9826713
Email mellifontabbey@eircom.net
Abbot: Rt Rev Augustine McGregor
Prior: Rev Laurence McDermott

DOMINICANS
St Magdalen's, Drogheda, Co Louth
Tel 041-9838271
Prior: Very Rev Ronan Cusack (OP)

St Malachy's Priory, Dundalk, Co Louth
Tel 042-9334179/9333714
Prior: Very Rev Bede McGregor (OP)

JESUITS
Iona, 211 Churchill Park,
Portadown, Co Armagh BT62 1EU
Tel 028-38330366 Fax 028-38338334
Superior: Vacant
Email iona@jesuit.ie

MARISTS
Cerdon, Marist Fathers,
St Mary's Road, Dundalk, Co Louth
Tel 042-9334019
Superior: Rev Kevin Cooney (SM)

St Mary's College, Dundalk, Co Louth
Tel 042-9339984
Principal: Mr Con McGinley

(See also under parishes – Dundalk,
Holy Family)

REDEMPTORISTS
St Joseph's,
Dundalk, Co Louth
Tel 042-9334042/9334762
Fax 042-9330893
Superior
Very Rev Richard Delahunty (CSsR) PP
Email redsdalk@iol.ie
Vicar-Superor: Rev Eamonn Hoey (CSsR)

(See also under parishes – Dundalk,
St Joseph's)

ROSMINIANS
See under parishes – Faughart

SERVITES
Servite Priory,
Benburb, Co Tyrone
Tel 028-37548241
Retreat, conference and youth centre
Prior: Very Rev Christ O'Brien (OSM)

BROTHERS

DE LA SALLE BROTHERS
Dundalk, Co Louth
Tel 042-9334439 Fax 042-9330870
Superior: Br Raymond McKeever
Community: 4

De La Salle College,
Dundalk, Co Louth
Tel 042-9331179 Fax 042-9330870
Principal: Mr Martin Brennan

ST JOHN OF GOD BROTHERS
St Mary's, Drumcar, Dunleer, Co Louth
Tel 041-6851211 Fax 041-6851529
Email admin.northeast@sjog.ie
Director: Mrs Bernadette Shevlin
Community Superior
Br Barry Larkin (OH)
Community: 2
School Principal: Mr Kevin Toale
Residential and day services for children
and adults with varying degrees of
learning disability. Administrative centre
for Domus Services (Tel 041-9873044)
Drumcar Park Enterprises
Tel 041-6851112

St John of God Day Centre,
Hilltop, Dundalk, Co Louth
Tel 042-9334663

SISTERS

CONGREGATION OF THE SISTERS OF MERCY
Mill Street, Dundalk, Co Louth
Tel 042-9334200
Leader: Sr Regina McGeown
Community: 15

Mile End, Avenue Road,
Dundalk, Co Louth
Tel 042-9330410
Community: 4

Bethany, 34 Point Road,
Dundalk, Co Louth
Tel 042-9331602

15 Cypress Gardens, Bay Estate,
Dundalk, Co Louth
Tel 042-9329315

6 Newry Road, Dundalk, Co Louth
Tel 042-9339285

Convent of Mercy,
Ardee, Co Louth
Tel 041-6853359
Community: 12

Dun Mhuire, 29 Convent Hill, Bessbrook,
Newry, Co Down BT35 7AW
Tel 028-30830258
Leader: Sr Kathleen O'Connor
Community: 5

58 Fairhill Road, Cookstown,
Co Tyrone BT80 8AG
Tel 028-86763363
Community: 6

Convent of Mercy, Dungannon,
Co Tyrone BT71 6AR
Tel 028-87722623
Leader: Sr Bríd Brady
Community: 6

Sisters of Mercy,
90 Church View, Bessbrook,
Newry, Co Down BT35 78T
Tel 028-30837140

65 Mullaghmarget Road,
Aghakinsallagh, Glebe, Bush,
Dungannon, Co Tyrone BT71 6QX
Tel 028-87740156

115 Oaklawns,
Dundalk, Co Louth
Tel 042-9334569

Convent Lodge, Ein Karim,
Hale Street, Ardee

Teach Suaimhis, Callystown,
Clogherhead, Co Louth
Tel 041-9883609

DAUGHTERS OF CHARITY OF ST VINCENT DE PAUL
St Vincent's, 5 Fair Street House,
Fair Street, Drogheda, Co Louth
Tel 041-9838204
and
St Vincent's Retreat and Holiday Centre
Termonfeckin, Drogheda, Co Louth
Tel 041-9822115
Superior: Sr Louise Coughlan
Community: 6
Pastoral work, Retreat & Holiday Centre

DOMINICAN CONTEMPLATIVES
Monastery of St Catherine of Siena,
The Twenties, Drogheda, Co Louth
Tel 041-9838524
Email siena@eircom.net
www.dominicans.ie/siena and
www.dominicannuns.ie
Prioress: Sr Mairéad Mullen (OP)
Community: 21

FRANCISCAN MISSIONARIES OF THE DIVINE MOTHERHOOD
Franciscan Friary, Laurence Street,
Droghega, Co Louth
Tel 041-9838554
Fax 041-9832535
Community: 3

FRANCISCAN MISSIONARY SISTERS FOR AFRICA
Franciscan Convent, Mount Oliver,
Dundalk, Co Louth (Motherhouse)
Tel 042-9371123 Fax 042-9371159
Email fmsamto@gofree.indigo.ie
Sister-in-Charge
Sr Patricia McConvey (FMSA)
Community: 38

HOLY FAMILY OF BORDEAUX SISTERS
1-2 Wesleyan Mews, Church Street,
Magherafelt, Co Derry BT45 6NZ
Tel 028-79632529
Contact: The Superior
Community: 2
Parish and pastoral work

MARIST SISTERS
15 Martin's Lane, Carnagat,
Newry, Co Down BT35 8PJ
Tel 028-30262376
Community: 3
Parish ministry

MEDICAL MISSIONARIES OF MARY
Motherhouse, Beechgrove,
Drogheda, Co Louth
Tel 041-9837512 Fax 041-9839219
Email beechgroveadm@eircom.net
Leader: Sr Bernadette Freyne

MMM Nursing Facility
Áras Mhuire, Beechgrove,
Drogheda, Co Louth
Tel 041-9842222
Email arasmhuire@eircom.net

Greenbank, Mell, Drogheda, Co Louth
Tel 041-9831028
Email mmmgreenbankmell@eircom.net
Community: 5

13-14 Ashleigh Heights,
Drogheda, Co Louth
Tel 041-9830779/041-9830778
Email mmmashleigh@eircom.net
Community: 6

MISSIONARIES OF CHARITY
19A Cathedral Road, Armagh BT61 7QX
Tel 04837-528654
Superior: Sr Marija Crucis
Community: 4
Hostel for men

NOTRE DAME DES MISSIONS (OUR LADY OF THE MISSIONS)
Pine Cottage, Dublin Road,
Dundalk, Co Louth
Community: 4
Pastoral work

5 Sandymount Square, Blackrock,
Dundalk, Co Louth
Community: 3
Pastoral work

PRESENTATION SISTERS
Greenhills, Drogheda, Co Louth
Tel 041-9831420
Community: 7
School ministry
Our Lady's College, Greenhills
Tel 041-9831786 Fax 041-9832809
Email greenhillsconvent@yahoo.com

Primary Convent Primary School,
Ballymakenny Road,
Drogheda, Co Louth
Tel 041-9837119
Fax 041-9839425
Email presdrogheda.ias@eircom.net

103 Thomas Street, Portadown,
Co Armagh BT62 3AH
Tel 028-38332220
Email presentation103@hotmail.com
Community: 4
Cross community, pastoral ministry

28 Garvaghy Park,
Portadown, Co Armagh BT62 1HB
Tel 028-38335964
Email evetere1234@yahoo.com
Community: 3
School and pastoral ministry

SACRED HEART SOCIETY
Linked with 2 Convent Road,
Gate Lodge, 4 Convent Road
Armagh BT60 4BG
Email nora.smyth@virgin.net
Pastoral work and writing

2B Callan Crescent,
Armagh BT61 7RH
Community: 2
Tel/Fax 028-37528473
Email nandolo21@hotmail.com
Neighbourhood projects

SISTERS OF ST CLARE
St Clare's Convent, Keady, Co Armagh
Tel 028-37531252
Contact Person
Sr Dominic Savio Ward
Community: 8

St Clare's Convent,
4 The Brambles, Stewartstown Road,
Coalisland, Co Tyrone
Tel 028-37746418
Community: 3

ST JOHN OF GOD SISTERS
3 Tudor Grove, Mullaharlin Road,
Dundalk, Co Louth
Tel 042-9336422
Community: 1

ST LOUIS SISTERS
Middletown, Co Armagh
Tel 028-37568498
Community: 11

Dún Lughaidh,
Dundalk, Co Louth
Tel 042-9335786
Community: 14
Dún Lughaidh Post-Primary School
Tel 042-9334474
Pupils: 700

137 Cedarwood Park,
Cox's Demesne,
Dundalk, Co Louth
Tel 042-9339816
Community: 2

2 Mill Road,
Dundalk, Co Louth
Tel 042-9335773
Community: 4

EDUCATIONAL INSTITUTIONS

Coláiste Rís
Chapel Street, Dundalk, Co Louth
Tel 042-9334336 Fax 042-9338380
Headmaster: Mr Kevin Wynne

St Patrick's Academy
37 Killymeal Road, Dungannon,
Co Tyrone BT71 6DS
Tel 028-87722668
Fax 028-87722745
Principal: Mrs Margaret Connolly

St Patrick's Grammar School, Armagh
Tel 028-37522018
Fax 028-37525930
Headmaster: Rev Kevin Donaghy
Priests on Staff
Rev John McGoldrick
Tel 028-37568288

St Joseph's Convent Grammar School
58 Castlecaulfied, Donaghmore,
Co Tyrone BT70 3HF
Tel 028-87761227
Principal: Mr Enda Cullen

EDMUND RICE SCHOOLS TRUST
St Joseph's Secondary School,
Newfoundwell, Drogheda, Co Louth
Tel 041-9837232
Principal: Ms Mary Adamson

St Joseph's Primary School,
Sunday's Gate, Drogheda, Co Louth
Tel 041-9833620
Principal: Mr Frank Bradley

EDMUND RICE SCHOOLS TRUST NORTHERN IRELAND
Christian Brothers' Primary School,
Greenpark, Keady Road,
Armagh BT60 4AB
Tel 028-37524354
Fax 028-37522308
Principal: Mr Nial P. Smyth

CHARITABLE AND OTHER SOCIETIES

Aras Mhuire
Shambles Lane, Dungannon,
Co Tyrone BT70 1BW
Tel 028-87726852
Oratory and bookshop

Avila Nursing Home
Convent of Mercy, Convent Hill,
Bessbrook, Co Armagh BT35 7AW
Tel 028-30838969

Armagh Diocesan Family Care Society
Under the patronage and immediate direction of the Archbishop and clergy executive committee.
Secretary: Mr John McVey
Ara Coeli, Armagh BT61 7QB
Tel 028-37522045

Cuan Mhuire
132 Armagh Road, Newry, Co Down
Tel 028-30269121
Alcohol counselling

Family of God Community
The Oratory, Carroll's Village,
Dundalk, Co Louth
Tel 042-9335851 Fax 042-9335566

Pioneer Shop
30 Thomas Street, Armagh BT61 7QB
Tel 028-37523586

also

Holy Family Church, Coalisland,
Co Tyrone BT71 4LS
Tel 028-87749046

St Mary's Drumcar
Residential and Day Training Centre for Mentally Handicapped
St Mary's, Drumcar, Co Louth
Tel 041-6851211/6851264

SOS Prayer
The Oratory, Carroll's Village,
Dundalk, Co Louth
Tel 042-9339888

ARCHDIOCESE OF DUBLIN

PATRONS OF THE ARCHDIOCESE
ST KEVIN, 3 JUNE; ST LAURENCE O'TOOLE, 14 NOVEMBER

SUFFRAGEN SEES: KILDARE AND LEIGHLIN, FERNS, OSSORY

INCLUDES CITY AND COUNTY OF DUBLIN, NEARLY ALL OF COUNTY WICKLOW
AND PORTIONS OF COUNTIES CARLOW, KILDARE, LAOIS AND WEXFORD

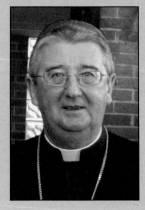

Most Rev Diarmuid Martin DD
Archbishop of Dublin and
Primate of Ireland
Born 8 April 1945; ordained priest
25 May 1969; ordained bishop by
Pope John Paul II 6 January 1999;
elevation to Dignity of
Archbishop and Apostolic Nuncio
March 2001; appointed Coadjutor
Archdiocese of Dublin 3 May
2003; Canonical/Liturgical
Reception as Coadjutor 30 August
2003; succeeded as Archbishop of
Dublin 26 April 2004
Residence: Archbishop's House,
Drumcondra, Dublin 9
Tel 01-8373732 Fax 01-8369796

ST MARYS PRO-CATHEDRAL, DUBLIN

Though Catholic Dublin has not possessed a cathedral since the Reformation, for almost two hundred years now St Mary's Pro-Cathedral has served as the Mother Church of the Dublin arch-diocese. In that time it has won a special place in the hearts of the Dublin people, to whom it is known affectionately as 'The Pro'.

The Pro-Cathedral was born of the vision of Archbishop John Thomas Troy and brought to fruition thanks to the unstinting labours of its second administrator, Archdeacon John Hamilton. The parish of Saint Mary's, straddling the Liffey, was established in 1707 and a chapel dedicated to St Mary was opened in 1729. In 1797 Archbishop Troy successfully petitioned the Holy See to allow him take St Mary's as his *mensal* parish. He thereupon set about raising funds to build a 'dignified, spacious church' in a central location in the parish.

The site chosen was a building on Marlborough Street, opposite Tyrone House. Formerly the town house of the Earl of Annesley, it was purchased for £5,100 and a deposit was paid in 1803. However, it was not until 1814 that designs were publicly invited for the new church. A design of uncertain authorship, marked only with the letter 'P', for a church in the form of a Grecian Doric temple, was chosen as the winner. The only substantial alteration to the design was the erection of a dome.

The foundation stone was laid by Archbishop Troy in 1815. On the feast of St Laurence O'Toole in 1825, Archbishop Murray celebrated High Mass, to mark the dedication of the church to the 'Conception of the Virgin Mary', to a packed congregation, which included Daniel O'Connell. After the dedication, the interior embellishment of the church continued. Highlights included the alto relief representation of the Ascension by John Smyth; the high

altar carved by Peter Turnerelli, and the marble statues of Archbishops Murray and Cullen by Thomas Farrell. Stained-glass windows, depicting Our Lady flanked by St Laurence O'Toole and St Kevin, were installed behind the

sanctuary in 1886. The high point of liturgical embellishment was the generous benefaction by Edward Martyn, who endowed the Palestrina choir for male voices in 1902.

Emeritus Archbishop
His Eminence Desmond Cardinal Connell
born in Dublin 24 March 1926; ordained
priest 19 May 1951; ordained Archbishop
of Dublin 6 March 1988; created Cardinal
21 February 2001
Address: Archbishop's House,
Drumcondra, Dublin 9
Tel 01-8373732 Fax 01 8369796

Most Rev Eamonn Walsh DD, VG
Titular Bishop of Elmham;
Auxiliary Bishop of Dublin; Apostolic
ordained Bishop 22 April 1990
Residence: Naomh Brid,
Blessington Road, Tallaght, Dublin 24
Tel/Fax 01-4598032

Most Rev Raymond Field DD, VG
Titular Bishop of Ard Mor;
Auxiliary Bishop of Dublin; ordained
Bishop 21 September 1997
Residence: 3 Castleknock Road,
Blanchardstown, Dublin 15
Tel/Fax 01-8209191

Most Rev Dermot O'Mahony DD
Titular Bishop of Tiava; former Auxiliary
Bishop of Dublin; ordained Bishop
13 April 1975
Residence: 19 Longlands,
Swords, Co Dublin
Tel 01-8401596 Fax 01-8403950

Most Rev Fiachra Ó Ceallaigh DD, VG
Titular Bishop of Tre Taverne; former
Auxiliary Bishop of Dublin; ordained
Bishop 17 September 1994
Residence: 19 St Anthony's Road, Rialto,
Dublin 8
Tel 01-4537495 Fax 01-4544966

**Episcopal Vicar with responsibility for
the deaneries of Howth, Fingal South
East and Fingal South West**
Rt Rev Mgr John Fitzpatrick PP
3 Glencarraig, Church Road,
Sutton, Co Dublin
Tel 01-8323147

**Episcopal Vicar with responsibility for
the deaneries of Bray, Donnybrook, Dun
Laoghaire and Wicklow**
Rt Rev Mgr Enda Lloyd PP
The Presbytery, Herbert Road,
Bray, Co Wicklow

Vicar for Priests
Rev John Hughes (OSA)
Archbishop's House, Dublin 9
Tel 01-8379253

Vicar for Evangelisation
Rev Ciarán O'Carroll
Diocesan Offices,
Archbishop's House, Dublin 9
Tel 01-8373732

CHAPTER

Dean: Most Rev Dermot O'Mahony DD
Precentor: Most Rev Eamon O. Walsh VG
Chancellor: Rt Rev Mgr James Ardle
Canon MacMahon

Treasurer:
Rt Rev Mgr Owen Canon Sweeney
Archdeacon of Dublin:
Ven Archdeacon Macarten Brady PE
Archdeacon of Glendalough:
Ven Archdeacon Kevin Lyon PE
Prebendaries:
Cullen: Very Rev Sean Canon Battelle PE
14 Pine Valley, Grange Road, Dublin 16
Kilmactalway: Vacant
Swords: Very Rev Patrick Canon Rice PE
Holy Family Residence, Roebuck Road,
Dundrum, Dublin 14
Yago: Very Rev James Canon Loughran PE
Parochial House, Esker, Lucan, Co Dublin
St Audoen's:
Very Rev Bernard Canon Brady
61 Glasnevin Hill, Dublin 9
Clonmethan:
Very Rev Walter Canon Harris PE
151 Clonsilla Road, Blanchardstown,
Dublin 15
Wicklow:
Very Rev Erill D. Canon O'Connor
167 Charlemont, Griffith Avenue, Dublin 9
Timothan: Very Rev Patrick Canon Fagan PE
The Presbytery, Ballyboughal, Co Dublin
Malahidert:
Very Rev Raymond T. Canon Molony
Presbytery No. 2, Thormanby Road,
Howth, Co Dublin
Castleknock: Vacant
Tipper: Rev John Canon Piert PC
The Presbytery, Johnstown,
Arklow, Co Widklow
Tassagard:
Very Rev Maurice Canon O'Moore PE
6 Richmond Avenue,
Monkstown, Co Dublin
Dunlavin: Rev Patrick Canon Dowling
Holy Family Residence, Roebuck Road,
Dundrum, Dublin 14
Maynooth:
Very Rev Patrick Canon Fitzsimons PE
Holy Family Residence, Roebuck Road,
Dundrum, Dublin 14
Howth: Very Rev John Canon Flaherty Adm
Cathedral House,
83 Marlborough Street, Dublin 1
Rathmichael:
Very Rev Brendan Canon Carbery
5 Griffith Avenue, Marino, Dublin 5
Monmahenock:
Rt Rev Mgr Andrew P. Canon Boland PE
13 Griffith Avenue, Dublin 9
Stagonilly: Vacant
Tipperkevin, 1a pars:
Very Rev John Canon Fitzgibbon PE
The Presbytery, Chapel Road,
Lusk, Co Dublin
Tipperkevin, 2a pars:
Very Rev James A. Canon Randles PE
5 St Margaret's Road, Malahide, Co Dublin
Donaghmore, 1a pars:
Very Rev John Canon MacMahon PE
Holy Family Residence, Roebuck Road,
Dundrum, Dublin 14
Donaghmore, 2a pars:
Very Rev Michael D. Canon
Supple, Apartment 8, Giltown Lodge,
Kilcullen, Co Kildare

Deaneries and Vicars Forane
Bray: Very Rev Liam Belton PP, VF
Parochial House, Kilquade, Co Wicklow
Tel 01-2819252
Dun Laoghaire:
Rt Rev Mgr Dan O'Connor PP, VF
3 Eblana Avenue, Dun Laoghaire, Co Dublin
Tel 01-2801505
Wicklow: Very Rev Kevin Rowan Adm, VF
Parochial House, Ashford, Co Wicklow
Tel 0404-40540
Donnybrook: Very Rev Richard Behan VF
Presbytery No. 1,
Ballinteer Avenue, Dublin 16
South City Centre:
Very Rev John Gilligan Adm, VF
47 Westland Row, Dublin 2
Tel 01-6765517
North City Centre:
Very Rev John Canon Flaherty Adm
Pro-Cathedral House,
83 Marlborough Street, Dublin 1
Tel 01-8745441
Cullenswood:
Very Rev Richard Sheehy PP, VF
54 Lower Rathmines Road,
Rathmines, Dublin 6
Tel 01-4969049
South Dublin: Very Rev Patrick Madden PP, VF
Presbytery No. 1, Ballycullen Avenue,
Firhouse, Dublin 24
Tel 01-4599855
Tallaght: Very Rev Ben Moran (OP) PP, VF
St Aengus' Presbytery, Balrothery,
Tallaght, Dublin 24
Tel 01-4513757
Blessington: Very Rev Francis McEvoy PP, VF
Parochial House, Crookstown, Athy,
Co Kildare
Tel 059-8623154
Fingal North:
Very Rev John McNamara PP, VF
Parochial House, Brackenstown Road,
Swords, Co Dublin
Tel 01-8401661
Finglas: Vacant
Maynooth: Rev John Hassett CC, VF
127 Castlegate Way, Adamstown,
Lucan, Co Dublin
Fingal South-East:
Very Rev Peter Finnerty PP, VF
2 Maypark, Malahide Road, Dublin 5
Tel 01-8313722
Fingal South-West:
Very Rev John Delaney PP, VF
137 Ballymun Road, Dublin 9
Tel 01-8376347
Howth: Very Rev Miceál Comer PP, VF
St Anne's Strand Road,
Portmarnock, Co Dublin
Tel 01-8461081

College of Consultors
Most Rev Eamonn Walsh DD
Most Rev Raymond Field DD
Rt Rev Mgr John Dolan, Chancellor
Rt Rev Mgr John Fitzpatrick, Episcopal Vicar
Rt Rev Mgr Enda Lloyd, Episcopal Vicar
Very Rev Eoin McCrystal PP
Very Rev Benedict Moran (OP) PP
Rt Rev Mgr Lorcan O'Brien, Moderator of
the Curia
Very Rev Gerard Tanham PP

ADMINISTRATION

Chancellor
Rt Rev Mgr John Dolan LCL
The Chancellery,
Archbishop's House, Dublin 9
Tel 01-8379253 Fax 8571650

Ecclesiastical Censor
Rt Rev Mgr John Dolan
The Chancellery, Archbishop's House,
Dublin 9
Tel 01-8379253

Diocesan Archivist
Ms Noelle Dowling
Diocesan Offices, Archbishop's House,
Dublin 9
Tel 01-8379253

Vicar for Religious
Sr Elizabeth Cotter
Archbishop's House, Dublin 9
Tel 01-8379253

Financial Administrator
Mr Kieran O'Farrell
Finance Secretariat, Archbishop's House,
Drumcondra, Dublin 9
Tel 01-8379253 Fax 01-8368393

Master of Ceremonies to the Archbishop
Rev Damian McNeice
Diocesan Liturgical Resource Centre,
Holy Cross College, Clonliffe, Dublin 3
Tel 01-8379253 Ext 238

Moderator of the Curia
Rt Rev Mgr Lorcan O'Brien VG
Office of the Moderator,
Holy Cross College, Clonliffe, Dublin 3
Tel 01-8379347

Archbishop's Secretary
Very Rev Mgr Paul Callan
Archbishop's House, Drumcondra, Dublin 9
Tel 01-8373732 Fax 01-8369796

SECRETARIATS

Diocesan Offices,
Archbishop's House, Dublin 9
Moderator of the Curia
Rt Rev Mgr Lorcan O'Brien VG
Tel 01-8379253
Vicar for Evangelisation
Rev Ciarán O'Carroll
Diocesan Offices, Archbishop's House,
Dublin 9
Tel 01-8373732
Child Protection Service
Tel 01-8360314 Fax 01-8842599
Email cps@dublindiocese.ie
Website www.cps.dublindiocese.ie
Director: Mr Philip Garland
Tel 01-8842590
Victim Support Person:
Mr Joseph McDonagh
Tel 01-8842591
Priest Delegate: Appointment Pending
Child Protection Training Coordinator
Rev Paddy Boyle
Email p.boyle@dublindiocese.ie

Communications Office
Director: Ms Annette O'Donnell
Tel 01-8360723 Fax 01-8360793
Email annetteodonell@dublindiocese.ie
Website www.dublindiocese.ie
Diocesan Office for Public Affairs
Director: Vacant
Education
Director: Ms Anne McDonagh
Tel 01-8379253 Fax 01-8368393
Email amcdonagh@dubcated.org
Senior Education Specialists:
Ms Catherine Hennessy
Email chennessy@abhouse.org
Mr Bill Lowe
Email blowe@dubcated.org
Finance
Mr Kieran O'Farrell
Email k.ofarrell@abfinance.org
Mr Raymond Hogan BCL
Email r.hogan@abfinance.org
Ms Ide Finnegan ACMA
Email i.finnegan@abfinance.org
Mr James Frain
Email james.frain@abfinance.org
Diocesan Liturgical Resource Centre
Director: Rev Pat O'Donoghue
Email pod@dublindiocese.ie
50th International Eucharistic Congress
President: Most Rev Diarmuid Martin
Secretary General: Rev Kevin Doran
Secretary: Ms Eithne Merins
Holy Cross Diocesan Centre,
Clonliffe Road, Dublin 3
Tel 01-8087531 (English language)
01-8087532 (Gaeilge, Francais, Italiano)
Eail info@iec2012.ie

DIOCESAN COMMITTEES

Clerical Fund Society
Diocesan Offices, Archbishop's House,
Dublin 9
Tel 01-8379253
President: The Archbishop of Dublin
Vice-Presidents: The Vicars General

Standing Committee
Chairman: Most Rev Eamonn Walsh DD
Secretary: Mr Kieran O'Farrell

Commission on Parish Boundaries
c/o Archbishop's House,
Drumcondra, Dublin 9
Tel 01-8379253
Chairman: Mr Willie Soffe
Secretary: Ms Anne Donnellan

Common Fund Executive Committee
Diocesan Offices,
Archbishop's House, Dublin 9
Tel 01-8379253
Chairman: Very Rev Anthony Reilly
Secretary: Mr Kieran O'Farrell

Finance Committee
Diocesan Offices,
Archbishop's House, Dublin 9
Tel 01-8379253
Chairman: Mr Leo O'Donnell
Joint Secretaries:
Mr Raymond Hogan BCL
Mr Kieran O'Farrell

CATECHETICS EDUCATION

Diocesan Advisers for Religious Education in Primary Schools
Education Secretariat,
Archbishop's House, Drumcondra, Dublin 9
Tel 01-8379253 Fax 01-8368393
Ms Cathy Burke, Ms Fiona Crotty, Ms
Elaine Mahon, Ms Sonya Murray
All at the Education Secretariat

Diocesan Advisors for Religious Education in Post Primary Schools:
Ms Brigid Gilligan

LITURGY

Liturgy Commission
Chairperson
Rt Rev Mgr Brendan Houlihan PP
Executive Secretary: Mrs Grainne Clinton
Mrs Monica Carr, Rev Peter Conaty (CSSp),
Ms Colette Furlong, Rev David Halpin, Sr
Patricia Holden, Rev Patrick Jones, Rev
Damian McNeice, Rev Pat O'Donoghue,
Rev Liam Tracey (OSM), Ms Ciara Walsh

Commission for Sacred Music
Chairperson: Professor Gerard Gillen
Executive Secretary: Mrs Grainne Clinton
Mr Ian Callanan, Mr David Connolly, Very
Rev Derek Farrell, Mr Gerard Gallagher,
Very Rev Paul Kenny, Ms Una Markey, Mrs
Goretti Newell, Rev Patrick O'Donoghue,
Mrs Anne O'Leary, Sr Louise O'Sullivan
(IBVB), Mr Michael Quinn, Ms Paula
Sweeney, Very Rev Paul Ward

Commission for Sacred Art and Architecture
Chairperson: Dr Richard Hurley
Secretary: Ms Anne Donnellan
Ms Marie Carroll, Mr Peter Cassidy, Mr
Ray Hogan, Rev Paddy Jones, Dr Eileen
Kane, Sr Elaine McDonald (IBVM), Very
Rev Frank McDonnell, Very Rev Barry
Murphy, Rev Paul Taylor, Mr Paul O'Daly,
Mr Eddie O'Shea

Historical Churches Advisory Commission
Chairperson: Mr Blaise Treacy
Secretary: Ms Anne Donnellan
Rev Paddy Finn, Rev Colm Gallagher PP,
Mr Ray Hogan, Dr Richard Hurley, Rev
Paddy Jones, Rev Damian McNeice,
Professor John Turpin

PASTORAL

Accord
Ms Barbara Gilroy (Dublin Director)
35 Harcourt Street, Dublin 2
Tel 01-4780866 Fax 01-4750462
Email admin@dublin.accord.ie

Catholic Guides of Ireland
Diocesan Chaplain: Vacant

CROSSCARE
Catholic Social Service Conference
Director: Mr Conor Hickey
Holy Cross College, Clonliffe, Dublin 3
Tel 01-8360011/5

Catholic Young Men's Society
National Chaplain: Rev Finbarr Mullane
The Presbytery, Vevay Road, Bray,
Co Wicklow
Tel 01-2867303

Catholic Youth Care
Director: Rev Jim Caffrey
20/23 Arran Quay, Dublin 7
Tel 01-8725055 Fax 01-8725010

Chaplaincy for Deaf People
Chaplain: Rev Gerard Tyrrell
40 Lower Drumcondra Road, Dublin 9
Tel 01-8305744 Fax 01-8600284
Email office@ncdp.ie
Website www.ncdp.ie

Committee for the Continuing Formation of Priests
c/o Archbishop's House, Dublin 9
Tel 01-8375107
Email john@abhouse.org

Council of Priests
President: Most Rev Diarmuid Martin DD
Chairman: Very Rev Joseph Mullan PP
Secretary: Very Rev Peter O'Reilly Adm

CÚNAMH
30 South Anne Street, Dublin 2
Tel 01-6710598

Emigrants
Contact: Yvonne Fleming
1A Cathedral Street, Dublin 1
Tel 01-8732844/8726171
Fax 01-8727003
Email info @emigrantadvice.ie
Website www.emigrantadvice.ie

Ecumenism
Chairman and Secretary:
Rev Brendan Leahy
St Patrick's College, Maynooth, Co Kildare

Hospital Chaplains Conference
Chairman of Committee
Rev Gerard Byrne
Chaplain, Blackrock Clinic
Tel 01-2832222

Knock Diocesan Pilgrimage
Director: Very Rev David Lumsden PP
83 Tonlegee Drive,
Edenmore, Dublin 5
Tel 01-8480917

Legion of Mary
Diocesan Chaplain: Vacant

Lourdes Diocesan Pilgrimage
Director: Rev John Gilligan
Lourdes Pilgrimage Office,
Holy Cross College, Clonliffe, Dublin 3
Tel 01-8376820

Marriage Tribunal
(See Marriage Tribunals section)

Pontifical Mission Societies
Diocesan Director
Very Rev Patrick Carroll PP
124 New Cabra Road, Dublin 7
Tel 01-8385244

Social Service Centre
Crosscare Housing and Welfare
Tel 01-8726775 Fax 01-8727003
Crosscare Migrant Project
Tel 01-8732844 Fax 01-8727003
1 Cathedral Street, Dublin 1

Travellers
Ministry to the Travelling People (Dublin Diocese): Very Rev Derek Farrell PP
Office: St Laurence House,
6 New Cabra Road,
Phibsboro, Dublin 7
Tel 01-8388874/087-2573857 Fax 01-8388901
Email partravs@iol.ie

Vocations
Co-ordinator: Rev Eamonn Bourke
Holy Cross College, Clonliffe, Dublin 3
Tel 01-8379253

PARISHES

Mensal parishes are listed first. Other parishes follow alphabetically. Church titulars are in italics.

PRO-CATHEDRAL
St Mary's (Immaculate Conception)
Marlborough Street, Dublin 1
Very Rev John Canon Flaherty Adm
Rev Patrick O'Donoghue CC
Rev Damian O'Reilly CC
Rev Denis Laverty PC
Parish Sister: Sr Angela Garahy (DC)
Pro-Cathedral House,
83 Marlborough Street, Dublin 1
Tel 01-8745441 Fax 01-8742406
Email procath@dublindiocese.ie
Website www.procathedral.ie

WESTLAND ROW
St Andrew's, Westland Row, Dublin 2
Tel 01-6761270
Rev John Gilligan Adm
Email john.gilligan@dcu.ie
Rev Anthony Asare PC
Tel 01-6765517 Fax 01-6763544
Email westlandrow@dublindiocese.ie
Website www.standrewsparish.ie

CITY QUAY
Immaculate Heart of Mary, Dublin 2
Very Rev Paul St John (SVD) Adm
Tel 01-6673073
Rev Rudy Montades (SVD) CC
Tel 01-6773706
The Presbytery, City Quay, Dublin 2
Parish Brother: Br Michael Ancheta
(6773073)
Parish Sister: Sr Goretti (6713130)

SEAN MCDERMOTT STREET
Our Lady of Lourdes,
Sean MacDermott Street, Dublin 1
Very Rev Michael Casey (SDB) Adm
Rev Tomasz Grzegorzewski (SDB) PC
24 Killarney Street, Dublin 1
Tel 01-8363554/086-8382631
Email seanmcdermott@dublindiocese.ie

ARDLEA
St John Vianney, Ardlea Road,
Artane, Dublin 5
Tel 01-8474123
Very Rev Robert Mann (SCJ) Moderator
Rev David Marsden (SCJ)
Rev Liam Rooney (SCJ)
Rev Marian Szalwa (SCJ)
Parochial House, St John Vianney,
Ardlea Road, Dublin 5
Tel 01-8474173/8474123
Email st.jvianney@yahoo.ie

ARKLOW
SS Mary and Peter, Arklow, Co Wicklow
Chapel of Ease: St David's, Johnstown,
Co Wicklow
Very Rev Martin Cosgrove PP
Parochial House, Arklow, Co Wicklow
Tel 0402-32294
Rev Paul O'Driscoll CC
The Presbytery, 2 St Mary's Terrace,
Arklow, Co Wicklow
Tel 0402-32196
Rev Jim Kenny CC
The Presbytery, 5 St Mary's Terrace,
Arklow, Co Wicklow
Tel 0402-32483
Very Rev John Canon Piert PC
The Presbytery, Johnstown, Co Wicklow
Tel 0402-31112

ARTANE
Our Lady of Mercy,
Brookwood Grove, Dublin 5
Very Rev Peter O'Connor PP
12 Brookwood Grove, Artane, Dublin 5
Tel 01-8312390
Rev James Sheeran CC
16 Brookwood Grove, Artane, Dublin 5
Tel 01-8187908

ASHFORD
Church of the Most Holy Rosary,
Co Wicklow
Rev Kevin Rowan Adm
Parochial House, Ashford, Co Wicklow
Tel 0404-40540
Very Rev William Farrell
St Joseph's, Glasthule, Co Dublin
Tel 01-2801226
Email farrellw@eircom.net
Rev Edward Barry CC
The Presbytery, Ashford, Co Wicklow
Tel 0404-40224

ATHY
St Michael's, Co Kildare
Very Rev Michael Murtagh PP
Parochial House, Athy, Co Kildare
Tel 059-8631781
Rev John McDonald CC
3 Stanhope Place, Athy, Co Kildare
Tel 059-8631698

AUGHRIM
The Most Sacred Heart, Co Wicklow
Very Rev Jerry O'Brien PP
Parochial House, Aughrim, Co Wicklow
Tel 0402-36298

AUGHRIM STREET
The Holy Family, Dublin 7
Very Rev Mgr Dermot Clarke PP
Parochial House,
34 Aughrim Street, Dublin 7
Tel 01-8386571
Email frdermot@eircom.net
Rev Pat O'Rourke CC
Presbytery No 2,
St Joseph's Road, Dublin 7
Tel 01-8386231
Email pat4263@eircom.net
Rev Michael Gilton CC
Rev Seán Quigley PC
48 Aughrim Street, Dublin 7
Tel 01-8386176

AVOCA
SS Mary and Patrick, Co Wicklow
Very Rev Eamonn Crosson PP
Parochial House, Avoca, Co Wicklow
Tel 0402-35156
Rev Thomas Coughlan (Assistant priest)
The Presbytery, Avoca, Co Wicklow
Tel 0402-35204

AYRFIELD
St Paul's, Dublin 13
Very Rev Tom Colreavy PP
28 Glentworth Park,
Ard na Gréine, Dublin 13
Tel/Fax 01-8484836
Email tomcolreavy@eircom.net
Rev Tom Clowe (SDB) CC
8 Slademore Close, Ard na Gréine,
Dublin 13
Email tomclowe@eircom.net

BALALLY
*Church of the Ascension of The Lord,
Dublin 16*
Email balally@catholic.org
Website http://gofree.indigo.ie/~balally/
Very Rev Dermot A. Lane PP
162 Sandyford Road, Dublin 16
Tel 01-2956165 Fax 01-2956068
Email dalane@eircom.net
Rev Paddy Moran CC
Presbytery No 1, Church of the
Ascension, Balally, Dublin 16
Tel 01-2952869
Email padmoran@gmail.com

BALBRIGGAN
SS Peter and Paul, Ballbriggan, Co Dublin
Very Rev Eugene Taaffe PP
Parochial House, Balbriggan, Co Dublin
Tel 01-8412116
Rev Gerard Moore CC
Tel 01-8412116
Rev Padraig O'Sullivan CC
Tel 01-8412116
The Presbytery, Dublin Road,
Balbriggan, Co Dublin
Email balbrigganparishoffice@gmail.com
Rev Aloysius Zuribo
16 Ashfield Drive, Balbriggan, Co Dublin
Tel 01-8020602
Parish Pastoral Worker: Niamh Morris
Tel 01-8412116

BALCURRIS
St Joseph's, Ballymun
Rev Val Kyne (SSC) PP
Very Rev John Chute (SSC) CC
Rev Gerry French (SSC)
The Presbytery, St Joseph's,
Balcurris, Ballymun, Dublin 11
Tel 01-8423865

BALDOYLE
SS Peter and Paul, Dublin 13
Very Rev Francis D. Dooley PP
The Presbytery, Baldoyle, Dublin 13
Tel 01-8322060

BALLINTEER
*St John the Evangelist, Ballinteer
Avenue, Dublin 16*
Very Rev Richard M. Behan
Presbytery No 1, Ballinteer Avenue,
Dublin 16
Tel 01-4944448
Email rmfb@eircom.net
Very Rev Patrick Battelle PE
14 Pine Valley, Grange Road,
Rathfarnham, Dublin 16
Tel 01-4935962

BALLYBODEN
Our Lady of Good Counsel, Dublin 16
Very Rev Pádraig Daly (OSA) PP
Rev Michael Brennock (OSA) CC
St Augustine's, Taylors Lane,
Ballyboden, Dublin 16
Tel 01-4944966

BALLYBRACK-KILLINEY
SS Alphonsus and Columba, Co Dublin
Very Rev Alex Conlan PP
Parochial House, Ballybrack, Co Dublin
Tel 01-2826404
Rev James Tormey CC
130 Churchview Road,
Ballybrack, Co Dublin
Tel 01-2851919

BALLYFERMOT
Our Lady of the Assumption, Dublin 10
Rev Michael O'Kelly *(Moderator)*
Tel 01-6264789
Rev Fergus McGlynn *(Team member)*
Tel 01-6264881
197 Kylemore Road,
Ballyfermot, Dublin 10
Rev Patrick Sweeney *(Team member)*
77 Colepark Drive, Dublin 10
Tel 01-6264639

BALLYFERMOT UPPER
St Matthew, Blackditch Road, Dublin 10
Very Rev Seamus Ryan PP
No 1 Presbytery, Blackditch Road,
Dublin 10
Tel 01-6265695
Rev Joseph Ryan CC
11 Palmerstown Court, Dublin 20
Tel 01-6268772

BALLYGALL
*Our Mother of Divine Grace,
Ballygall Road East, Dublin 11*
Very Rev Brendan Quinlan PP
41 Cremore Heights, St Canice's Road,
Ballygall, Dublin 11
Tel 01-8573776
Email bquinlan@indigo.ie
Rev Tony Power CC
112 Ballygall Road East, Glasnevin,
Dublin 11
Tel 01-8342248
Email ringo11@eircom.net
Parish office: Tel 01-8369291
Email omdgballygallchurch@eircom.net
Website www.ballygallparish.ie

BALLYMORE EUSTACE
Immaculate Conception, Naas, Co Kildare
Very Rev Sean Breen PP
The Presbytery, Ballymore Eustace, Naas,
Co Kildare
Tel 045-864114
Rev James Prendiville CC
The Presbytery, Hollywood (via Naas),
Co Wicklow
Tel 045-864206 Fax 01-8621031

BALLYMUN
*Church of the Virgin Mary, Ballymun,
Dublin 9*
Rev Frank Brady (SJ) PC
Rev Gerard Corcoran CC, Moderator
Rev Brian McKittrick CC
The Presbytery, Shangan Road,
Ballymun, Dublin 9
Tel 01-8421551

BALLYMUN ROAD
*Our Lady of Victories, Ballymun Road,
Dublin 9*
Very Rev John Delany PP
137 Ballymun Road, Dublin 11
Tel 01-8376347
Email johnamdelany@eircom.net
Rev Kevin Doherty CC
97 Ballymun Road, Dublin 11
Tel 01-8375440

BALLYROAN
*Church of the Holy Spirit, Marian Road,
Dublin 14*
Very Rev Brendan Madden PP
67 Anne Devlin Park, Ballyroan, Dublin 14
Tel 01-4947303

BALLYWALTRIM
St Fergal's, Bray, Co Wicklow
Rev John O'Brien PP
Tel 01-2768191
Rev Hugh O'Donnell (OFM)
Parish Chaplain
Tel 01-2768192
Parochial House, St Fergal's,
Killarney Road, Bray, Co Wicklow
Parish office: Tel 01-2860980
Email stfergal@iol.ie
Website www.stfergalsbray.ie

BAWNOGUE
Church of the Transfiguration,
Bawnogue, Clondalkin, Dublin 22
Very Rev Joseph Beere (CSSp) PP
Rev Marino Nguekam (CSSp) CC
Presbytery, Bawnogue, Clondalkin,
Dublin 22
Tel 01-4592273/4519810
Email transtig2000@yahoo.com

BAYSIDE
Church of the Resurrection, Bayside, Dublin 13
Tel 01-8323083
Very Rev Paul Ward PP
Parochial House, Bayside Square North,
Sutton, Dublin 13
Tel 01-8323150
Email wardp@iol.ie
Rev Joe Kelly CC
5 Bayside Square East, Sutton, Dublin 13
Tel 01-8322305
Email gradyjoe1@eircom.net

BEAUMONT
Church of Nativity of Our Lord, Dublin 5
Rev Frank O'Gara (OCarm) PP
Rev Donal Byrne (OCarm) CC
Rev Brian McKay (OCarm)
Rev Martin Parokkaran (OCarm)
Presbytery, Montrose Park,
Beaumont, Dublin 5
Tel 01-8477740/8476359
Fax 01-8473209 Mobile 086-8134445

BEECHWOOD AVENUE
Church of the Holy Name, Dublin 6
Rev Bernard Kennedy MA, MSc, Adm
67 Edenvale Road, Dublin 6
Tel 01-4972165
Email b.kennedy@esatclear.ie
Rev Paul Freeney PE
Parochial House,
43 Upper Beechwood Avenue, Dublin 6
Tel 01-4972687
Rev Pat Mangan (in residence)
44 Upper Beechwood Avenue, Dublin 6
Tel 01-4975180

BERKELEY ROAD
St Joseph's, Dublin 7
Very Rev Christopher Clarke (OCD) PP
Rev Patrick Keenan (OCD) CC
Rev Peter Cryan (OCD) CC
The Presbytery, Berkeley Road, Dublin 7
Tel 01-8306356/8306336
Fax 01-8304681

BLACKROCK
St John the Baptist, Blackrock, Co Dublin
Parish Office: 01-2882104
Email johnthebaptist@eircom.net
Very Rev Edward Conway PP
1 Maretimo Gardens West, Blackrock,
Co Dublin
Tel 01-2882248
Rev Philip O'Driscoll CC
23 Barclay Court, Blackrock, Co Dublin
Tel 01-2883329
Rev Michael Collins CC
24 Barclay Court, Blackrock, Co Dublin
Tel 01-2832302
Email michaelcollins3000@yahoo.com

BLAKESTOWN
St Mary of the Servants, Dublin 15
Very Rev Liam Ó Cuív PP
Blakestown, Clonsilla, Dublin 15
Tel 01-8210874/8216800
Email blakestownparish@dublindiocese.ie

BLANCHARDSTOWN
St Brigid's
Very Rev John Jones PP
Parochial House, Blanchardstown,
Dublin 15
Tel 01-8213660
Email jj36297@hotmail.com
Rev John Casey (CSsR)
28 Broadway Road, Blanchardstown,
Dublin 15
Tel 01-8213716
Email johnffcasey@eircom.net
Rev Patrick Guckian CC
44 Woodview Grove, Blanchardstown,
Dublin 15
Tel 01-8262799
Rev Thaddeus Mhamwa PC
128 Roselawn Road, Blanchardstown,
Dublin 15
Tel 01-8219014

BLESSINGTON
Church of Our Lady
Very Rev Tim Murphy PP
The Presbytery, Main Street,
Blessington, Co Wicklow
Tel 045-865442
Email office@blessington.info
Our Lady of Mercy, Crosschapel
Rev Kevin Lyon CC
Archdeacon of Glendalough,
Parochial House, Crosschapel,
Blessington, Co Wicklow
Tel 045-865215
Email lyonk@indigo.ie
St Brigid's Church, Manor Kilbride
Rev Padraic McDermott CC
The Presbytery, Manor Kilbride,
Blessington, Co Wicklow

BLUEBELL
Our Lady of the Wayside, Dublin 12
Very Rev Patrick Carolan (OMI)
Tel 01-4501040/087-2900468
Rev Dermot Mills (OMI)
Parochial House, 118 Naas Road, Dublin 8
Tel 01-4501040

BOHERNABREENA
St Anne's, Dublin 24
Very Rev David Brough PP
Parochial House, Bohernabreena,
Tallaght, Dublin 24
Tel/Fax 01-4627080
Email david.brough@ucd.ie
Rev Colm Mathews CC
47 Old Court Manor, Dublin 24
Tel 01-4525624
Rev David Fleming
Parochial House, Bohernabreena,
Tallaght, Dublin 24
Tel/Fax 01-4510986
Email davg@eircom.net

BONNYBROOK
St Joseph's, Dublin 17
Very Rev Kevin Moore, Moderator
122 Greencastle Road, Coolock, Dublin 17
Tel 01-8487657
Rev Frank Duggan, Parish Team Priest
Parochial House No 2,
124 Greencastle Road, Dublin 17
Tel 01-8485194
St Joseph the Artisan Church,
Bonnybrook, Dublin 17
Parish Office: 01-8485262

BOOTERSTOWN
Church of the Assumption
Rt Rev Mgr Seamus Conway PP
Parochial House, Booterstown, Co Dublin
Tel 01-2882889
Rev Laurence Behan CC
Tel 01-2882162
The Presbytery, 52 Booterstown Avenue,
Blackrock, Co Dublin
Email info@booterstownparish.ie

BRACKENSTOWN
St Cronan's
Very Rev John McNamara PP, VF
Parochial House, Brackenstown Road,
Swords, Co Dublin
Tel 01-8401661
Email cronanc@gofree.indigo.ie
Rev Tony Pazhayakalam (CST) PC
The Presbytery, Brackenstown Road,
Swords, Co Dublin
Tel 01-8408926
Parish Office: 01-8401188
www.brackenstown.dublindiocese.ie

BRAY
Holy Redeemer, Main Street,
Bray, Co Wicklow
Very Rev John O'Connell DD, PP
Tel 01-2867309
Email 2johnoconnell@eircom.net
Rev George Begley CC
Tel 01-2868413 (w)/2862955 (h)
The Presbytery, Herbert Road, Bray,
Co Wicklow

BRAY, PUTLAND ROAD
Our Lady Queen of Peace
Very Rev Laurence White PP
Parochial House, Putland Road, Bray,
Co Wicklow
Tel 01-2862346
Email secretary@queenofpeace.ie
Parish Office: 01-2745497
Villa Pacis – Parish Centre: 01-2760045

BRAY, ST PETER'S
St Peter's, Little Bray, Co Wicklow
Very Rev Ben Mulligan PP
42 Corke Abbey, Little Bray, Co Wicklow
Tel 01-2822204

BROOKFIELD
St Aidan's, Brookfield Road
Very Rev Hugh Kavanagh PP
No 1 Presbytery, Brookfield Road,
Tallaght, Dublin 24
Tel 01-4525370
Email aodh@eircom.net

CABINTEELY

St Brigid's, Dublin 18
Rev Arthur O'Neill
1B Willow Court, Druid Valley,
Cabinteely, Dublin 18
Tel 01-2814435/087-2597520
Very Rev Thomas O'Keeffe
20 Glen Avenue, The Park,
Cabinteely, Dublin 18
Tel 01-2853643/086-2646270

CABRA

Christ the King, Dublin 7
Very Rev Gregory O'Brien PP
124 New Cabra Road, Dublin 7
Tel 01-8385244
Rev Tom O'Shaughnessy CC
73 Annamoe Road, Dublin 7
Tel 01-8685626

CABRA WEST

*Church of the Most Precious Blood,
Dublin 7*
Very Rev John Greene PP
No 3 Presbytery, Dunmanus Court,
Cabra West, Dublin 7
Tel 01-8384325
Rev Finbarr Neylon CC
No 4 Presbytery, Dunmanus Court,
Cabra West, Dublin 7
Tel 01-8380181

CASTLEDERMOT

The Assumption, Castledermot, Co Kildare
Very Rev Brendan Cantwell PP
Parochial House, Castledermot,
Co Kildare
Tel 059-9144164/086-2528545
Parish Office: Tel/Fax 059-9144888

CASTLEKNOCK

*Our Lady Mother of the Church
Castleknock, Dublin 15*
Very Rev Maurice O'Shea PP
6 Beechpark Lawn, Castleknock,
Dublin 15
Tel 01-8212967
Email ciaranos@eircom.net
Rev Denis O'Connor CC
32 Auburn Drive, Dublin 15
Tel 01-8214003

CASTLETOWN

St Patrick's, Castletown, Co Wexford
Very Rev Eugene McCarney PP
Parochial House, Castletown, Gorey,
Co Wexford
Tel 0402-37115

CASTLEVIEW

St Kilian's, Ballymount Road, Dublin 24
Very Rev Philip Curran PP
See Kilnamanagh Parish for details
Rev David Halpin
43 Chestnut Grove, Dublin 24
Tel 01-4415001/087-2048898

CELBRIDGE

St Patrick's, Celbridge, Co Kildare
Very Rev Patrick Carmody PP
Parochial House, Main Street,
Celbridge, Co Kildare
Tel 01-6288827

Rev Paul Taylor CC
The Presbytery, Main Street,
Celbridge, Co Kildare
Tel 01-6275874/086-3524530
Rev Innocent Uwah
The Presbytery, 12 Coarse Moore Park,
Straffan, Co Kildare
Tel 01-6012197/085-1404355

CHAPELIZOD

Navity of the BVM, Chapelizod, Dublin 20
Very Rev Martin Daly PP
Parochial House, Chapelizod, Dublin 20
Tel 01-6264645
Rev James Somers (SDB) CC
The Presbytery, Chapelizod, Dublin 20
Tel 01-6264656

CHERRY ORCHARD

Most Holy Sacrament
Parish Team: Rev Patrick Reynolds (CSsR)
Rev John Birmingham (CSsR)
The Presbytery,
103 Cherry Orchard Avenue, Dublin 10
Tel 01-6267930
Rev Gerry O'Connor (CSsR) PC
52 Elmdale Park, Dublin 10
Tel 01-6263813
Parish sisters: Sr Cora McCullogh (OP)
Sr Elizabeth Healy (OP)
2 Croftwood Crescent
Tel 01-6231127

CHURCHTOWN

The Good Shepherd
Very Rev Dermot Nestor
Parochial House, Nutgrove Avenue,
Dublin 14
Tel 01-2985916
Rev Gerard Young CC
23 Oakdown Road, Dublin 14
Tel 01-2981744
Email info@goodshepherdchurchtown.ie
www.goodshepherdchurchtown.ie

CLOGHER ROAD

St Bernadette's
Rev Melvyn Mullins Adm
192 Sundrive Road, Dublin 12
Tel 01-4540811
Email mullins.melvin@gmail.com

CLONDALKIN

Immaculate Conception, Dublin 22
Website www.clondalkin.dublindiocese.ie
Very Rev John Wall PP
St Columba Parish House, New Road,
Clondalkin, Dublin 22
Tel 01-4640441
Email johnwall@gofree.indigo.ie
Rev Damian Farnon CC
St Cecilia's, New Road,
Clondalkin, Dublin 22
Tel 01-4592665

Clonburris, Our Lady Queen of the Apostles
Rev Shan O'Cuiv PC
The Presbytery, Clonburris,
Clondalkin, Dublin 22

Knockmitten
Rev Des Byrne (CSSp) CC
45 Woodford Drive, Monastery Road,
Clondalkin, Dublin 22
Tel 01-4592323
Rev James McCaffrey (CSSp) CC
The Presbytery, St Mary's, New Road,
Clondalkin, Dublin 22
Tel 01-4592311

CLONSKEAGH

*Immaculate Virgin Mary of the Miraculous
Medal, Bird Avenue, Dublin 14*
Sacristy Tel/Fax 01-2837948
Website www.clonskeagh.org
Email parishoffice@clonskeagh.org
Very Rev John Murphy PP
14 Rosemount Crescent,
Roebuck Road, Clonskeagh, Dublin 14
Tel 01-2697754
Rev Paul Hampson PC
3 Beechmount Drive, Clonskeagh,
Dublin 14
Tel 01-2697797
Email apaul@shawcable.com

CLONTARF, ST ANTHONY'S

St Anthony, Dublin 3
Very Rev Cormac McIlraith PP
186 Clontarf Road, Dublin 3
Tel 01-8333394

CLONTARF, ST JOHN'S

*St John the Baptist, Clontarf Road,
Dublin 3*
Rev Cormac McIlraith
186 Clontarf Road, Dublin 3
Tel 01-8333394
Rev Martin Hogan
187 Clontarf Road, Clontarf, Dublin 3
Tel 01-8338575

CONFEY

St Charles Borromeo, Leixlip, Co Kildare
Very Rev Philip Corcoran PP
73 Newtown Park, Leixlip, Co Kildare
Tel 01-6244637
Rev Peter Clancy CC
75 Newtown Park, Leixlip, Co Kildare
Tel 01-6243533

COOLOCK

St Brendan's, Coolock Village, Dublin 5
Rev John Hand (SM) Moderator
Email johnhand@eircom.net
Rev John Harrington (SM) PC
Rev Pat Byrne (SM) PC
Rev Kieran Butler (SM) AP
The Presbytery, Coolock Village, Dublin 5
Tel 01-8484799
Parish mobile 087-2269887
Email malachy@stbrendanscoolock.org
Website www.stbrendanscoolock.org

CORDUFF

*St Patrick's, Corduff, Blanchardstown,
Dublin 15*
Very Rev Liam McClarey (SAC) PP
Parochial House, Corduff
Blanchardstown, Dublin 15
Tel/Fax 01-8213596
Rev Joseph McLoughlin (SAC) CC
The Presbytery, Corduff,
Blanchardstown, Dublin 15
Tel 01-8215930

CRUMLIN
St Agnes
Very Rev Mgr John Deasy, Moderator
55 St Agnes' Road, Crumlin, Dublin 12
Tel 01-4550955
Rev Michael Kelly Co-PP
94 Old County Road, Crumlin Dublin 12
Tel 01-4542308
Rev Peter Coffey (SDB) Co-PP
Rev Patrick Brewster (SDB) CC
Rev John Foster (SDB) CC
Tel 01-4555605
Salesian House, St Teresa's Road
Crumlin, Dublin 12
Tel 01-4555368 Fax 01-4652500
Parish Pastoral Worker: Gráinne Prior
Email crumlinparish@eirccom.net

DALKEY
Assumption of BVM
Very Rev John McDonagh PP
No 1 Presbytery, Castle Street,
Dalkey, Co Dublin
Tel 01-2857773
Email johnmcdo@eircom.net
Rev Peter J. Sinnott CC
No 3 Presbytery, Castle Street,
Dalkey, Co Dublin
Tel 01-2859212
Email pjsinnott@eircom.net
Declan Gallagher CC
No 2 Presbytery, Castle Street,
Dalkey, Co Dublin
Tel 01-2859212
Email office@dalkeyparish.org

DARNDALE
Our Lady Immaculate, Dublin 17
Very Rev Terence Murray (OMI) PP
The Presbytery, Darndale, Dublin 17
Tel 01-8474547 Fax 01-8474599
Rev Peter Daly (OMI) CC
The Presbytery, Darndale, Dublin 17
Tel/Fax 01-8474547

DEANSRATH
Very Rev Daithi Kenneally (CSSp) PP
St Ronan's Presbytery, Deansrath,
Clondalkin, Dublin 22
Tel 01-4570380
Email stronansdeansrath@hotmail.com

DOLLYMOUNT
St Gabriel's, St Gabriel's Road, Dublin 3
Very Rev Míceál Hastings PP
103 Mount Prospect Drive,
Clontarf, Dublin 3
Tel 01-8335255/087-2358634
Rev Gareth Byrne PC
107 Mount Prospect Avenue,
Clontarf, Dublin 3
Tel 01-8339301
Rev Dermot Mansfield (SJ) PC
Maressa House, Dollymount, Dublin 3
Tel 01-8339666

DOLPHIN'S BARN
Our Lady of Dolours, Dublin 8
Very Rev Gerard Fleming (SAC) CC
437 South Circular Road, Dublin 8
Tel 01-4533490
Email dolphinsbarn@dublindiocese.ie
Rev Diarmuid Byrne Adm
18 St Anthony's Road, Dublin 8
Tel 01-4534469

Parish Chaplin: Fr Josephat Mandi
287 South Circular Road, Dublin 8
Tel 01-4533490
The above are also priests of the Rialto
parish

DOMINICK STREET
St Saviour's, Dublin 1
Very Rev Adrian Farrelly (OP) PP
Tel 01-8897612
Email adrianfarrelly@hotmail.com
Rev Marek Grubka (OP) CC
Tel 01-8897610
St Saviour's, Dominick Street, Dublin 1

DONABATE
St Patrick's
Very Rev Patrick O'Byrne PP
Parochial House, Donabate, Co Dublin
Tel 01-8436011
Rev Patrick Reilly (OPraem) CC
Tel 01-8436099
Rev Patrick Hannon PC
Tel 01-8434604
Parish office: 01-8434574 (9.30-12.00 noon)

DONAGHMEDE – CLONGRIFFIN – BALGRIFFIN
Church of the Holy Trinity
Very Rev Eoin McCrystal PP
12 Grangemore Grove, Dublin 13
Tel 01-8474652
Email epmcc@eircom.net
Rev Gary Darby (OS Cam) CC
41 Grangemore Grove, Donaghmede,
Dublin 13
Tel 01-8476392
Email garydarby@eircom.net

DONNYBROOK
Church of the Sacred Heart, Dublin 4
Very Rev Martin Clarke PP
Tel 01-2838311
Rev Julius Shibanada CC
Tel 01-2692052
No 1 Presbytery, Stillorgan Road, Dublin 4
Rt Rev Mgr Richard Sherry DD, PE
No 2 Presbytery, Stillorgan Road, Dublin 4
Tel 01-2692102

DONNYCARNEY
Our Lady of Consolation, Dublin 5
Email info@donnycarneyparish.ie
Website www.donnycarneyparish.ie
Very Rev Peter Finnerty PP
2 Maypark, Malahide Road, Dublin 5
Tel 01-8313722
Very Rev Noel Madden PE
3 Rosemount, Malahide Road, Dublin 5
Tel 01-8315207
Rev Patrick McKinley CC
1 Maypark, Malahide Road, Dublin 5
Tel 01-8313033
Rev Padraig Gleeson
3 Maypark, Malahide Road, Dublin 5
Tel 01-8329598

DONORE AVENUE
St Teresa of the Child Jesus, Dublin 8
Very Rev Edwin McCallion (SM) PP
Very Rev Sean McArdle (SM) CC
Rev Robert Kelly (SM) CC
The Presbytery, Donore Avenue, Dublin 8
Tel 01-4542425 Fax 01-4530364

DRUMCONDRA
Corpus Christi, Home Farm Road, Dublin 9
Rev William King PP
23 Clare Road, Drumcondra, Dublin 9
Tel 01-8378552
Rev Lorcan O'Brien PC
Moderator of the Curia
Archbishop's House, Dublin 9
Tel 01-8379253
Email obrienlorcan@eircom.net

DUBLIN AIRPORT *see* **SWORDS**

DUNDRUM
Holy Cross, Dublin 14
Website www.holycrossdundrum.org
Rev Kieran McDermott
'Emmaus', Holy Cross, Main Street,
Dundrum, Dublin 14
Tel 01-2984348
Email kieranjmcdermott@gmail.com
Rev Peter Healy
3 Sweetmount Drive, Dundrum, Dublin 14
Tel 01-2983557
Very Rev Mgr Donal O'Doherty PE
Holy Cross, Upper Kilmacud Road,
Dundrum, Dublin 14
Tel 01-2985264
Email 32donalodoherty@eircomm.net

DUN LAOGHAIRE
St Michael's, Co Dublin
Rt Rev Mgr Dan O'Connor PP
St Michael's Parochial House, 4 Eblana
Avenue, Dun Laoghaire, Co Dublin
Tel 01-2804969
Parish Office: 01-2804969
Rev Patrick Monahan CC
'Renvyle', Corrig Avenue,
Dun Laoghaire, Co Dublin
Tel 01-2802100
Rev Aidan Carroll CC
'Carraig Donn', 23 Glenageary Woods,
Dun Laoghaire, Co Dublin
Tel 01-2807223

DUNLAVIN
St Nicholas of Myra, Dunlavin, Co Wicklow
Very Rev Alex Conlan PP
The Presbytery, Littlemore,
Dunlavin, Co Wicklow
Tel 045-401227
Rev Eamonn McCarthy CC
The Presbytery, Donard, Co Wicklow
Tel 045-404614

EADESTOWN
*The Immaculate Conception,
Naas, Co Kildare*
Very Rev Patrick Ryan PP
The Presbytery, Eadestown, Naas, Co Kildare
Tel 045-862187

EAST WALL
St Joseph's, Church Road, Dublin 3
Very Rev Peter Reilly PP
Parochial House, East Wall, Dublin 3
Tel 01-8742320
Email pjreilly@eircom.net

EDENMORE
St Monica's, Dublin 5
Very Rev David Lumsden PP
83 Tonlegee Drive, Raheny, Dublin 5
Tel 01-8480917/087-2569873

Rev Paddy Boyle CC
29 Glenayle Road, Edenmore, Dublin 5
Tel 01-8481160/086-1011415
Rev Paul Dunne
60 Grange Park Grove, Dublin 5
Tel 01-8771466/087-6902246

ENNISKERRY
Immaculate Heart of Mary, Enniskerry,
Co Wicklow
Very Rev John Sinnott PP
Parochial House, Enniskerry, Co Wicklow
Tel 01-2863506
Email jmpsinnott@eircom.net
Rev Owen Lynch CC
The Presbytery, Kilmacanogue,
Bray, Co Wicklow
Tel 01-2862110
Mrs Margaret Blackbyrne
Parish Office, Enniskerry
Tel 01-2760030 (10 am-1 pm, Mon-Fri)
Email stmarysparishoffice@eircom.net
Joyce Townsend
Parish Office, Kilmacanogue
Tel 01-2021882 (10 am-1 pm, Mon-Fri)
Email stmochonogs@eircom.net

ESKER-DODDSBORO-ADAMSTOWN
St Patrick's
Rev John Hassett, Moderator
125 Castlegate Way, Adamstown, Co Dublin
Tel 01-6812088
Rev Denis Carroll, semi-retired
85 Hillcrest Drive, Lucan, Co Dublin
Tel 01-6280948
Rev Michael Drumm, Chaplain
47 Westbury Drive, Lucan, Co Dublin
Tel 01-5031106

FAIRVIEW
Church of the Visitation of BVM, Dublin 3
Very Rev Joseph Connick (OFM Conv) PP
Rev Patrick Griffin (OFM Conv) CC
Rev Antony Nallukunnel (OFM Conv) CC
Rev Ciprian Budau (OFM Conv) CC
Friary of the Visitation,
Fairview Strand, Dublin 3
Tel 01-8376000 Fax 01-8376021

FINGLAS
St Canice's, Dublin 11
Parish Office/Sacristy: 01-8343110
Email stcanices2@eircom.net
Very Rev Pádraig O'Cochláin PP
The Presbytery, 5 The Lawn,
Finglas, Dublin 11
Tel 01-8341894
Rev Gabriel O'Dowd CC
The Presbytery, St Margaret's,
Finglas, Dublin 11
Tel 01-8341009
Rev Colm Kenny CC
The Presbytery, 2 St Canice's Church,
Finglas, Dublin 11
Tel 01-8341051
Email colken@iol.ie

FINGLAS WEST
Church of the Annunciation, Dublin 11
Very Rev Joseph Connolly PP
7 Cardiffcastle Road, Finglas West, Dublin 11
Tel 01-8343928
Rev Piaras MacLochlainn CC
10 Finglaswood Road, Finglas West,
Dublin 11
Tel 01-8347041

Rev Ray Hannon CC
10 Farnham Drive, Finglas West, Dublin 11
Tel 01-8341284
Rev Corry Brennan PE
4 The Lawn, Finglas, Dublin 11
Tel 01-8341000

FIRHOUSE
Our Lady of Mount Carmel, Dublin 24
Parish Office: 01-4524702
ourladyofmountcarmelchurch@eircom.net
Sacristy: 01-4524702
Very Rev Patrick Madden PP
Presbytery No 1, Ballycullen Avenue,
Firhouse, Dublin 24
Tel 01-4599855
Rev Padraig Coleman PC
Presbytery No 2, Ballycullen Avenue,
Firhouse, Dublin 24
Tel 01-4599899

FOXROCK
Our Lady of Perpetual Succour
Website www.foxrockparish.ie
Parish Office: 01-2893492
Secretary: Evelyn Healy
Email secretary@foxrockparish.ie
Sacristy: 01-2898879
(all certs available 10.30 am–11.30 am)
Very Rev Ciarán Holahan PP
Parochial House, Foxrock, Dublin 18
Tel 01-2893229
Email cholahan@eircom.net
Rev John Bracken CC
11 Foxrock Court, Foxrock, Dublin 18
Tel 01-2895780
Email padrejb@gmail.com
Rev Derek Smyth CC
2 Kill Lane, Foxrock, Dublin 18
Tel 01-2894734
Parish Pastoral Worker: Maeve Davidson
Tel 087-6904814
Email maevedavidson1@gmail.com

FRANCIS STREET
St Nicholas of Myra, Dublin 8
Very Rev Michael Shields Adm
Parochial House, Francis Street, Dublin 8
Tel 01-4542109
Rev Martin Dolan CC
The Presbytery, Francis Street, Dublin 8
Tel 01-4544861

GARDINER STREET
St Francis Xavier, Dublin 1
Very Rev Donal Neary (SJ) PP
Rev William Reynolds (SJ) CC
Presbytery, Upper Gardiner Street, Dublin 1
Tel 01-8363411 Fax 01-8555624

GARRISTOWN
Church of the Assumption, Co Dublin
Very Rev Brendan McAleer PP
Parochial House, Garristown, Co Dublin
Tel/Fax 01-8354138

GLASNEVIN
Our Lady of Dolours, Dublin 9
Very Rev Sean Mundow PP
77 Botanic Avenue, Dublin 9
Tel 01-8373455
Rev Eamonn Bourke PC
Tel 086-8346071

GLASTHULE
St Joseph's, Glasthule, Co Dublin
Very Rev William Farrell PP
Parochial House, St Joseph's,
Glasthule, Co Dublin
Tel 01-2801226
Rev Denis Kennedy (CSSp) CC
Tel 01-2800403
St Joseph's Presbytery, Glasthule, Co Dublin

GLENDALOUGH
St Kevin's, Co Wicklow
Very Rev Oliver Crotty Adm
Parochial House, Glendalough, Co Wicklow
Tel 0404-45140
Email glendalough2007@eircom.net

GRANGE PARK
St Benedict's, Grange Park View,
Dublin 5
Very Rev David Lumsden PP
83 Tonlegee Drive, Raheny, Dublin 5
Tel 01-8480917
Rev Paul Dunne
60 Grange Park Grove, Raheny, Dublin 5
Tel 01-8480647
Very Rev Joseph Drumgoole PE
35 Grange Park Avenue, Raheny, Dublin 5
Tel 01-8480244

GREENHILLS
Church of the Holy Spirit, Dublin 12
Very Rev Myles Healy (CSSp) PP
55 Fernhill Road, Greenhills, Dublin 12
Tel 01-4504040
Rev Roddy Curran (CSSp) CC
104 St Joseph's Road, Greenhills, Dublin 12
Tel 01-4506617

GREYSTONES
Church of the Holy Rosary, Co Wicklow
Very Rev Paul Kenny PP
Parochial House, La Touche Road,
Greystones, Co Wicklow
Tel 01-2874278
Rev Denis Quinn CC
The Presbytery, Kimberley Road,
Greystones, Co Wicklow
Tel 01-2877025
Rev Dan AnNguyen CC
The Presbytery, Blacklion,
Greystones, Co Wicklow
Tel 01-2877036

HADDINGTON ROAD
St Mary's, Dublin 4
Very Rev Mgr Patrick Finn PP
St Mary's, Haddington Road, Dublin 4
Tel 01-6643295/086-3848432
Email frpfinn@stmaryshaddingtonroad.ie
Rev Eoin Cassidy PC
Rev Paul Tyrrell CC
The Presbytery, Haddington Road,
Dublin 4
Tel 01-6600075

HALSTON STREET AND ARRAN QUAY
St Michan's, Halston Street, Dublin 7
Very Rev Desmond McNaboe (OFMCap) PP
Capuchin Parochial Friary,
Church Street, Dublin 7
Tel 01-8730599

Very Rev Richard Hendrick (OFMCap) CC
Capuchin Parochial Friary, Church Street,
Dublin 7
Tel 01-8730599

HAROLD'S CROSS
Our Lady of the Rosary, Dublin 6W
Very Rev Gerry Kane PP
213B Harold's Cross Road, Dublin 6W
Tel 01-4972816/086-8220956
Very Rev Ronald Neville PE
213A Harold's Cross Road, Dublin 6W
Tel 01-4974044

HARRINGTON STREET
St Kevin's, Dublin 8
Very Rev Gerard Deighan Adm
Latin Mass Chaplain, The Parochial House,
Harrington Street, Dublin 8
Tel 01-4751506
Rev Michael G. Nevin PC
The Presbytery, Harrington Street,
Dublin 8
Tel 01-4751506

HARTSTOWN
St Ciaran's, Dublin 15
Very Rev Liam Hickey PP
St Ciaran's, 1 Cherryfield Park,
Hartstown, Dublin 15
Tel 01-8214863
Email hickeyliamj@eircom.net

HOWTH
*Church of the Assumption
Howth, Co Dublin*
Right Rev Mgr Brendan Houlihan PP
Parochial House, Mount Saint Mary's,
Howth, Co Dublin
Tel 01-8322036
Rev Michael Cooney CC
Presbytery No 1, Thormanby Road,
Howth, Co Dublin
Tel 01-8323193
Rev Raymond Canon Molony
(retired priest in residence)
Presbytery No 2, Thormanby Road,
Howth, Co Dublin
Tel 01-8222092

HUNTSTOWN
Sacred Heart of Jesus, Dublin 15
Very Rev Joseph Coyne, Moderator
Rev George P. Begley Co-PP

INCHICORE, MARY IMMACULATE
*Mary Immaculate, Tyrconnell Road,
Dublin 8*
Very Rev Michael O'Connor (OMI)
Moderator
Rev Michael Guckian (OMI) CC
Br Frank Flanegan (OMI)
Ms Joanne Lanigan *(Faith Development
Worker)*
Oblate Fathers, House of Retreat,
Inchicore, Dublin 8
Tel 01-454111 Fax 01-4543466

INCHICORE, ST MICHAEL'S
St Michael's, Emmet Road, Dublin 8
www.oblateparishesindublin.ie
Very Rev Ray Warren (OMI) PP
52a/52b Bulfin Road, Dublin 8
Tel 01-4531660

IONA ROAD
St Columba's, Dublin 9
Very Rev James Caffrey PP
'Marmion', 87 Iona Road, Dublin 9
Tel 01-8308257
Rev Peter Kilroy CC
74 Iona Road, Dublin 9
Tel 01-8305698

JAMES'S STREET
St James's Church, Dublin 8
Moderator: Very Rev John Collins
The Presbytery, James' Street, Dublin 8
Tel 01-4531143

JOBSTOWN
St Thomas the Apostle
Very Rev Valentine Martin PP
Rev John Ennis CC
The Presbytery, Jobstown, Tallaght,
Dublin 24
Tel 01-4523595/4610277

JOHNSTOWN-KILLINEY
*Our Lady of Good Counsel, Killiney,
Co Dublin*
Very Rev Peadar Murney PP
56 Auburn Road, Killiney, Co Dublin
Tel/Fax 01-2856660
Rev Aidan Kieran CC
59 Auburn Road, Dun Laoghaire, Co Dublin
Tel 01-2852509

KILBARRACK-FOXFIELD
*St John the Evangelist, Greendale Road,
Kilbarrack, Dublin 5*
www.kilbarrackfoxfieldparish.ie
Rev Declan Doyle Adm
56 Foxfield Saint John, Dublin 5
Tel 01-8325871
Email dec_doyle@eircom.net
Very Rev Cathal Price CC
54 Foxfield St John, Dublin 5
Tel 01-8323683

KILBRIDE AND BARNDARRIG
St Mary's, Barndarrig, Co Wicklow
Very Rev Michael V. Dempsey PP
Parochial House, Barndarrig, Co Wicklow
Tel 0404-48130
Very Rev Patrick B. Moore PE
Brittas Bay, Co Wicklow
Tel 0404-47177

KILCULLEN
Sacred Heart and St Brigid, Kilcullen
Very Rev Michael Murphy PP
Parochial House, Kilcullen, Co Kildare
Tel 045-481230
Email mclm@eircom.net
Rev Patrick Ryan (CSSp) CC
The Presbytery, Kilcullen, Co Kildare
Tel 045-481222
Email patricksryan@eircom.net
Parish office: Tel 045-480727
Email kilcullenparish@eircom.net

KILLESTER
St Brigid's, Howth Road, Dublin 5
Rt Rev Mgr Alex Stenson PP
126 Furry Park Road, Dublin 5
Tel/Fax 01-8333793
Rev Michael Simpson CC
264 Howth Road, Dublin 5
Tel 01-8339177

KILLINARDEN
*Church of the Sacred Heart, Killinarden,
Tallaght, Dublin 24*
Very Rev Thomas Plower (MSC) PP
Rev Desmond Farren (MSC) CC
The Presbytery, Killinarden, Tallaght,
Dublin 24
Tel 01-4522251 Fax 01-4527183
Email dfarren@02.ie
Parish email sacredheartparish@eircom.net

KILL-O'-THE-GRANGE
*Holy Family, Kill Avenue,
Dun Laoghaire, Co Dublin*
Very Rev John D. Killeen PP
20 Abbey Court, Abbey Road,
Blackrock, Co Dublin
Tel 01-2802533
Rev Michael O'Connor (CSSp) CC
Presbytery No 2, Church Grounds,
Kill Avenue, Dun Laoghaire, Co Dublin
Tel 01-2140863
Rev Henry Regan
Presbytery No 1, Church Grounds,
Kill Avenue, Dun Laoghaire, Co Dublin
Tel 01-2800901

KILMACANOGUE see ENNISKERRY

KILMACUD-STILLORGAN
St Laurence, Co Dublin
Very Rev Liam Lacey PP
6 Allen Park Road, Stillorgan, Co Dublin
Tel 01-2880545
Rev Joseph Doran CC
Presbytery No 1, Church Grounds, Lower
Kilmacud Road, Kilmacud, Co Dublin
Tel 01-2880595
Rev Martin Harte CC
Presbytery No 2, Church Grounds,
Lower Kilmacud Road, Kilmacud,
Co Dublin
Tel 01-2882257

KILMORE ROAD WEST
St Luke the Evangelist, Dublin 5
Rev Patrick Littleton CC
Tel 01-8486806/087-2408188
Very Rev Douglas Malone Adm
Tel 01-8475898
St Luke's, Kilbarron Road,
Kilmore West, Dublin 5

KILNAMANAGH
St Kevin's, Dublin 24
Very Rev Philip Curran PP
Presbytery No 1, Kilnamanagh,
Tallaght, Dublin 24
Tel 01-4523805/086-2408188
Email philipcurran@dublindiocese.ie
Rev David Halpin
43 Chestnut Grove, Tallaght, Dublin 24
Tel 01-4415001/087-2048898
Email dpm.halpin@gmail.com

KILQUADE
St Patrick's, Kilquade, Co Wicklow
Parish Office: 01-2819658
Email kilquadeparish@eircom.net
Website www.kilquadeparish.com
Very Rev Liam Belton PP
Parochial House, Kilquade, Co Wicklow
Tel/Fax 01-2819252

Rev Eamonn Clarke CC
The Presbytery, Kilcoole, Co Wicklow
Tel 01-2876207
Rev Sean Smith CC
The Presbytery,
Newtownmountkennedy, Co Wicklow
Tel 01-2819253

KIMMAGE MANOR
Church of the Holy Spirit, Kimmage Manor,
Whitehall Road, Dublin 12
Very Rev Patrick Doody (CSSp) PP
66 Rockfield Avenue, Dublin 12
Tel 01-4558316
Rev Austin Healy (CSSp) CC
Shanahan House, Kimmage Manor,
Whitehall Road, Dublin 12
Tel 01-4928583
Parish Office: Tel 01-4064377

KINSEALY
St Nicholas of Myra,
Malahide Road, Co Dublin
Very Rev Martin O'Farrell PP
Aghadoe, Kinsaley Lane,
Malahide, Co Dublin
Tel 01-8461767
Secretary/Sacristan: Ms Carmel Maguire
Tel 01-8460028 (after 10 am Mass)

KNOCKLYON
St Colmcille, Idrone Avenue, Dublin 16
Very Rev Jimmy Murray (OCarm) PP
Rev Michael Morrissey (OCarm) CC
Rev Sean MacGiollarnáth (OCarm) CC
Carmelite Presbytery, Idrone Avenue,
Knocklyon, Dublin 16
Tel 01-4941204 Fax 01-4946842
Email presbytery@knocklyonparish.com

LARKHILL-WHITEHALL-SANTRY
Holy Child, Thatch Road, Dublin 9
Parish Office: 01-8375274
Very Rev Michael Carey Adm
151 Swords Road, Whitehall, Dublin 9
Tel 01-8374387
Rev Aidan D'Arcy CC
2 Knightswood, Coolock Lane,
Santry, Dublin 9
Tel 01-8428283
Rev Thomas Kearney CC
137 Shantalla Road, Whitehall, Dublin 9
Tel 01-8420260
Rev Damian McNeice, Parish Chaplain
149 Swords Road, Whitehall, Dublin 9
Tel 01-8372521
Chapel of Ease: Blessed Margaret Ball,
Oak Park, Santry, Dublin 9
Tel 01-8375274/8620792
Parish Pastoral Council Tel 01-8374887
Chairperson: Una Kearns
Secretary: Anne Flanagan

LAUREL LODGE-CARPENTERSTOWN
St Thomas the Apostle, Castleknock,
Dublin 15
Very Rev Michael Cullen PP
The Presbytery, Church Grounds,
Castleknock, Dublin 15
Tel 01-8208144

LEIXLIP
Our Lady's Nativity, Co Kildare
Very Rev Michael Hurley PP
Parochial House, Old Hill,
Leixlip, Co Kildare
Tel 01-6245597
Email hurleymichael@eircom.net
Rev Noel Watson CC
No 1 Presbytery, 4 Old Hill,
Leixlip, Co Kildare
Tel 01-6243718

LITTLE BRAY see BRAY, ST PETER'S

LOUGHLINSTOWN
St Columbanus, Dun Laoghaire
Very Rev Edward Griffin PP
10 The Oaks, Loughlinstown Drive,
Dun Laoghaire, Co Dublin
Tel 086-2395706

LUCAN
St Mary's, Lucan, Co Dublin
Very Rev Peter O'Reilly Co-PP, VF
231 Beech Park, Lucan, Co Dublin
Tel 01-6281756
Very Rev Thomas Kennedy Co-PP
14 Roselawn, Lucan, Co Dublin
Tel 01-6280205
Very Rev Denis Henry Co-PP
1A Ballydowd Grove, Lucan, Co Dublin
Tel 01-2955541
Email frhenry@sandyfordparish.org

LUCAN SOUTH
Church of Divine Mercy, Balgaddy
Very Rev Donal Roche PP
Parochial House, Foxdene Avenue,
Lucan, Co Dublin
Tel 01-4056858
Email donalroche@oceanfree.net

LUSK
St MacCullin's, Lusk, Co Dublin
Very Rev Joseph Mullan PP
Tel 087-2326254 (texts only)
Email jmullan39@eircom.net
Very Rev Canon John Fitzgibbon PE
Tel 01-8438023
Parish Secretary: Yvonne Duignam
Mon, Wed, Fri: 9.30am-12.30pm

MALAHIDE
St Sylvester's, Malahide, Co Dublin
Very Rev Gerard Tanham PP
12 The Warren, Malahide, Co Dublin
Tel 01-8457950/087-2311947
Email gerardtenham@eircom.net
Rev Paul Thornton CC
Tel 087-7404729

MARINO
St Vincent de Paul, Griffith Avenue,
Dublin 9
Very Rev Thomas Noone PP
69 Griffith Avenue, Dublin 9
Tel 01-83322864
Rev Michael Shiels CC
c/o The Sacristy, St Vincent de Paul,
Griffith Avenue, Dublin 9
Tel 01-8339756

MARLEY GRANGE
The Divine Word, 25/27 Hermitage Downs,
Rathfarnham, Dublin 16
Rev Colm McGlynn (OSM) PP
Rev Camillus McGrane (OSM) CC
25/27 Hermitage Downs,
Marley Grange, Rathfarnham, Dublin 16
Tel 01-4944295 Fax 01-4941056
Email divine_word@ireland.com

MAYNOOTH
St Mary's, Maynooth, Co Kildare
Very Rev Liam Rigney PP
St Mary's, Maynooth, Co Kildare
Tel 01-6286220
Email liamrigney@eircom.net
Rev Paul Coyle CC
The Presbytery, Maynooth, Co Kildare
Tel 01-6290553

MEADOWBROOK
St Attracta's Oratory, Dublin 16
Very Rev Joseph Whelan Adm
75 Ludford Drive, Dublin 16
Tel 01-2988746

MEATH STREET
St Catherine of Alexandria, Dublin 8
Rev Declan Brennan (OSA) PP
Rev Niall Coghlan (OSA) CC
St Catherine's, Meath Street, Dublin 8
Tel 01-4543356

MERCHANT'S QUAY
Church of the Immaculate Conception
(popularly known as Adam and Eve's)
4 Merchant's Quay, Dublin 8
Very Rev Ulic Troy (OFM) Guardian
Adam and Eve's, Merchant's Quay,
Dublin 8
Tel 01-6771128 Fax 01-6771000

MERRION ROAD
Our Lady Queen of Peace, Dublin 4
Very Rev Fergus O'Connor (Opus Dei) PP
Rev Charles Connolly (Opus Dei) CC
31 Herbert Avenue, Dublin 4
Tel 01-2692001
Very Rev Seamus Moore PE
8 Herbert Avenue, Dublin 4
Tel 01-2692501

MILLTOWN
SS Columbanus and Gall, Dublin 6
Rev Gerard Deegan
67 Ramleh Park, Milltown, Dublin 6
Tel 01-2196600
Rev Alan Mowbray (SJ)
Tel 01-2196740
Rt Rev Mgr Tom Stack
Tel 01-2697613

MONKSTOWN
St Patrick's, Carrickbrennan Road
Very Rev Michael Coady PP
Parochial House, Carrickbrennan Road,
Monkstown, Co Dublin
Tel 01-2802130
Email mclarke@monkstownparish.ie
Very Rev Maurice Canon O'Moore PE
6 Richmond Avenue,
Monkstown, Co Dublin
Tel 01-2802186

Rev Cornelius Dowling CC
St Anthony's, 13 Richmond Grove,
Monkstown, Co Dublin
Tel 01-2800789
Email dowcpb@eircom.net

MOONE
Church of the Blessed Trinity
Very Rev Frank McEvoy Adm
Parochial House, Moone, Athy, Co Kildare
Tel 059-8624109

MOUNT ARGUS
St Paul of the Cross, Harold's Cross,
Dublin 6W
Very Rev Frank Keerins (CP) PP
Rev Kenneth Brady (CP) AP
St Paul's Retreat,
Mount Argus, Dublin 6W
Tel 01-4992000

MOUNT MERRION
St Therese, Mount Merrion, Co Dublin
Very Rev Tony Coote Adm
79 The Rise, Mount Merrion, Co Dublin
Tel 01-2889879
Rev Andrew O'Sullivan CC
83 The Rise, Mount Merrion, Co Dublin
Tel 01-2882556
Parish office: Tel 01-2881271
Email
mountmerrionparishoffice@eircom.net
Website www.mountmerrionparish.ie

MOUNTVIEW
St Philip the Apostle, Blanchardstown,
Dublin 15
Very Rev Liam O'Cuív Adm
The Presbytery, Blakestown, Dublin 15
Tel 01-8210874/086-2342170
Rev Patrick O'Byrne CC
The Presbytery, Mountview,
Blanchardstown, Dublin 15
Tel 01-8216380

MOURNE ROAD
Our Lady of Good Counsel, Dublin 12
Rev Declan Blake
Parochial House, Sperrin Road, Dublin 12
Tel 01-4556103
Rev Denis Robinson CC
Tel 01-4556199
The Presbytery, Mourne Road, Dublin 12

MULHUDDART
Very Rev Eugene McCarthy (CP) PP
24 The Court, Mulhuddart Wood,
Mulhuddart, Dublin 15
Tel 01-8202544
Email sle@connect.ie
Website www.mulhuddartparish.com

NARRAGHMORE
SS Mary and Laurence, Co Kildare
www.narraghmoreparish.org
Very Rev Francis McEvoy PP
Parochial House, Crookstown,
Athy, Co Kildare
Tel 059-8623154
Email mcevoy@eircom.net
Rev Colm R. Ó Siochrú CC
The Presbytery, Kilmead, Athy, Co Kildare
Tel 059-8626117
Email kilmeadnarraghmore@eircom.net

NAUL
St Canice's, Damastown, Co Dublin
The Nativity of BVM, Naul
The Assumption of BVM, Ballyboughal
Very Rev Denis M. Delaney, Moderator
Parochial House, Naul, Co Dublin
Tel 01-8412932

NAVAN ROAD
Our Lady Help of Christians, Dublin 7
Very Rev Seamus Cassidy PP
Parochial House, 199 Navan Road, Dublin 7
Tel 01-8389482
Rev Harry Gaynor CC
194 Navan Road, Dublin 7
Tel 01-8383313
Rev John Moran CC
192 Navan Road, Dublin 7
Tel 01-8387902

NEILSTOWN
St Peter the Apostle, Dublin 22
Very Rev Donal Toal (SMA) PP
Rev Paul Monahan (SMA) CC
The Presbytery, Neilstown,
Clondalkin, Dublin 22
Tel 01-4573546

NEWCASTLE
St Finian's, Co Dublin
Very Rev Patrick Shiel PP
1 The Glebe, Peamount Road, Newcastle,
Co Dublin
Tel 01-4589230

NEWTOWNPARK
The Guardian Angels, Blackrock, Co Dublin
Very Rev Dermot Leycock PP
64 Newtownpark Avenue,
Blackrock, Co Dublin
Tel 01-2784860
Very Rev J. Anthony Gaughan PE
56 Newtownpark Avenue,
Blackrock, Co Dublin
Tel 01-2833897
Rev Seamus Toohey CC
7 Avondale Court, Blackrock, Co Dublin
Tel 01-2884043
Rev William Fortune CC
32 Newtownpark Avenue,
Blackrock, Co Dublin
Tel 01-2100337

NORTH WALL-SEVILLE PLACE
St Laurence O'Toole's (North Wall), Dublin 1
Rev Declan Blake Adm
Parochial House, 49 Seville Place, Dublin 1
Tel 01-8741625
Rev Fergus Farrell PC
St Laurence O'Toole's Presbytery,
49 Seville Place, Dublin 1
Tel 01-8740796

NORTH WILLIAM STREET
St Agatha's, Dublin 1
Very Rev Brian Lawless Adm
Presbytery, 46 North William Street,
Dublin 1
Tel 01-8556474
Rev Tony Scully CC
89 Ballybough Road, Dublin 3
Tel 01-8363451
Rev Patrick Devitt PC
128 Clonliffe Road, Dublin 3
Tel 01-8373869
Email paddy.devitt@materdei.dcu.ie

OLD BAWN (*see* TALLAGHT, OLDBAWN)

PALMERSTOWN
St Philomena's, Dublin 20
Very Rev Anthony Reilly PP
Parochial House, Palmerstown, Dublin 20
Tel 01-6266254
Rev Flor Lynch (CSSp) Assistant Priest
37 Palmerstown Drive,
Palmerstown, Dublin 20
Tel 01-6264642

PHIBSBORO
St Peter's, Dublin 7
Very Rev Paschal Scallon (CM) PP
Rev Eamon Devlin (CM) CC
St Peter's, Phibsboro, Dublin 7
Tel 01-8389708 Fax 01-8389950
Email info@stpetersphibsboro.ie
Website www.stpetersphibsboro.ie

PORTERSTOWN-CLONSILLA
St Mochta's, Porterstown, Dublin 15
Very Rev John Daly PP
St Mochta's, Porterstown, Dublin 15
Tel 01-8213218 Fax 01-8213516
frjohn@stmochtasparish.ie
Parish Pastoral Worker: Mary Greene Byrne
Email pastoralcare@stmochtasparish.ie
secretary@stmochtasparish.ie
Website www.stmochtasparish.ie

PORTMARNOCK
St Anne's, Portmarnock, Co Dublin
Very Rev Micheál Comer PP
St Anne's, Strand Road,
Portmarnock, Co Dublin
Tel/Fax 01-8461081
Rev Niall McDermott CC
12 Blackberry Rise
Tel 01-8461398
Rev Bryan Nolan PC
21 Wheatfield Grove

PRIORSWOOD
St Francis of Assisi, Dublin 17
Very Rev Angelus O'Neill (OFMCap) PP
Guardian
Rev Patrick Flynn (OFMCap) CC
Rev Dan Joe O'Mahony (OFMCap)
Chaplain, The Oratory,
Blanchardstown Shopping Centre
Rev Bryan Shortall (OFMCap)
Chaplain, Beaumont Hospital
Rev Bill Ryan (OFMCap)
Chaplain, Bon Secours Hospital
Capuchin Parochial Friary,
Clonshaugh Drive, Priorswood, Dublin 17
Tel 01-8474469/8474538 Fax 01-8487296

RAHENY
Our Lady Mother of Divine Grace,
Howth Road, Dublin 5
Rt Rev Mgr Martin O'Shea PP
5 St Assam's Road West, Raheny, Dublin 5
Tel 01-8313806
Rev Pat O'Rourke CC
24 Watermill Road, Raheny, Dublin 5
Tel 01-8316219

RATHDRUM
SS Mary and Michael, Co Wicklow
Very Rev Brian O'Reilly PP
Parochial House, Rathdrum, Co Wicklow
Tel 0404-46229
Website www.rathdrumparish.com

RATHFARNHAM

The Annunciation, Dublin 14
Very Rev Martin Noone PP, Moderator
St Mary's, Willbrook Road,
Rathfarnham, Dublin 14
Tel 01-4954554
Very Rev Joseph Hanlon, Assistant Priest
St Mary's Presbytery, Willbrook Road,
Rathfarnham, Dublin 14
Tel 01-4932390
Email rathfarnhamparish1@eircom.net

RATHGAR

Church of the Three Patrons,
Rathgar Road, Dublin 6
Very Rev Paul Lavelle PP
49 Rathgar Road, Dublin 6
Tel 01-4971058
Rev Liam O'Connell (CSsR) PC
Marianella, 75 Orwell Road,
Rathgar, Dublin 6
Tel 01-4067212
Rev Frank Sammon (SJ) CC
156 Rathgar Road, Dublin 6
Tel 01-4966042

RATHMINES

Mary Immaculate, Refuge of Sinners,
Rathmines, Dublin 6
Very Rev Richard Sheehy PP
52 Lower Rathmines Road, Dublin 6
Tel 01-4969049
Rev John Galvin CC
60 Mountpleasant Avenue, Dublin 6
Tel 01-4968969
Rev Patrick McCafferty CC
52 Lower Rathmines Road, Dublin 6
Tel 01-4976148

RIALTO

Our Lady of the Holy Rosary of Fatima,
Rialto, Dublin 8
Very Rev Gerard Fleming (SAC) PP
437 South Circular Road, Dublin 8
Tel 01-4533490
Email dolphinsbarn@dublindiocese.ie
Rev Diarmuid Byrne CC
18 St Anthony's Road Dublin 8
Tel 01-4534469
Parish Chaplin: Fr Josephat Mandi
287 South Circular Road, Dublin 8
Tel 01-4533490
The above are also priests of the
Dolphins Barn parish

RINGSEND

St Patrick's, Dublin 4
Very Rev Ivan Tonge PP
St Patrick's, 2 Cambridge Road, Dublin 4
Tel 01-6684192
Rev Fergal MacDonagh CC
St Mary's, Irishtown Road, Dublin 4
Tel 01-6689854

RIVERMOUNT

St Oliver Plunkett, St Helena's Drive,
Dublin 11
Very Rev Seamus Ahearne (OSA) PP
The Presbytery, 60 Glenties Park,
Finglas South, Dublin 11
Tel 01-8343722/087-6782746

Rev Noel Hession (OSA) CC
Rev Paddy O'Reilly (OSA) CC
The Presbytery, St Oliver Plunkett's,
St Helena's Drive, Finglas South, Dublin 11
Tel 01-8343444

RIVER VALLEY

St Finian's, Swords, Co Dublin
Very Rev Niall Mackey PP
Parochial House, 1 River Valley Heights,
Swords, Co Dublin
Tel 01-8403400
Email mackeyniall@mac.com
Rev Peter McCarron CC
The Presbytery, 2 River Valley Heights,
Swords, Co Dublin
Tel 01-8404162
Email peteremccarron@eircom.net

ROLESTOWN–OLDTOWN

St Brigid's, Rolestown, Co Dublin
Very Rev John Keegan PP
Parochial House, Rolestown,
Swords, Co Dublin
Tel 01-8401514
Rev John Carey CC
The Presbytery, Oldtown, Co Dublin
Tel 01-8433133

ROUNDWOOD

St Laurence O'Toole, Co Wicklow
Very Rev Paul Kelly PP
Parochial House,
Roundwood, Co Wicklow
Tel 01-2818149
Email roundwoodparish@eircom.net
Parish office: Tel 01-2818384 (mornings)
Parish Pastoral Council
Chairperson: Mr Paddy O'Brien
Mullinaveigue, Roundwood

ROWLAGH

Immaculate Heart of Mary, Clondalkin,
Dublin 22
Rev John Dunphy Adm
30 Wheatfields Close, Clondalkin,
Dublin 22
Tel 01-6263920/087-6165666
Parish Office: Tel/Fax 01-6261010

RUSH

St Maur's, Rush, Co Dublin
Very Rev Kieran Coghlan PP
The Presbytery, Chapel Green,
Rush, Co Dublin
Tel 01-8437208
Email kcoghlan@eircom.net
Rev Rossa Doyle CC
3 Hoskyn Bank, Bawn Road,
Rush, Co Dublin
Tel 01-8430973
Email rossadoyle@hotmail.com

SAGGART

Nativity of the BVM, Co Dublin
Tel 01-4589209
Rev Michael Shortall *(in residence)*
Tel 087-2861765

Very Rev Enda Cunningham
Nativity of BVM Parochial House,
Saggart, Co Dublin
Tel 087-1380695
Rev Michael McGowan PC
7 St Patrick's Crescent, Rathcoole, Co Dublin
Tel 01-4589210

SALLYNOGGIN

Our Lady of Victories, Co Dublin
Very Rev Liam Talbot (SDS) PP
Rev Eric Powell (SDS) CC
St Kevin's Presbytery, Pearse Street,
Sallynoggin, Co Dublin
Tel 01-2854667 Fax 01-2847024

SANDYFORD

St Mary's, Dublin 18
Very Rev Éamann Cahill PP
Parochial House, Sandyford Village,
Dublin 18
Tel 01-2956317
Rv Brian Edwards
10 Bearna Park, Sandyford, Dublin 18
Tel 01-2956916
Rev Robert Colclough CC
St Mary's, Sandyford Village, Dublin 18
Tel 01-2958933
Pastoral Worker: Sr Angela O'Connor
St Mary's, Sandyford Village, Dublin 18
Tel 01-2956367

SANDYMOUNT

St Mary's Star of the Sea, Dublin 4
Rt Rev Mgr Peter Briscoe PP
Stella Maris, Oswald Road,
Sandymount, Dublin 4
Tel 01-6684265
Rev Peter O'Connor CC
10 Cranfield Place, Sandymount, Dublin 4
Tel 01-6676438

SHANKILL

St Anne's, Co Dublin
Very Rev John O'Connor (SAC) PP
Rev Michael O'Dwyer (SAC) CC
Rev Rory Hanly (SAC) CC
St Benin's, Dublin Road,
Shankill, Co Dublin
Tel 01-2824425

SILLOGE

Holy Spirit, Silloge Road, Dublin 11
Virgin Mary, Shangan Road, Dublin 9
Rev Gerard Corcoran, Moderator
Rev Brian McKittrick
The Presbytery, Shangan Road,
Ballymun, Dublin 9
Tel 01-8421551
Rev Patrick McKinley
Parish House, Silloge Road, Dublin 11
Tel 01-8421551

SKERRIES

St Patrick's, Co Dublin
Very Rev Richard Hyland PP
42 Strand Street, Skerries, Co Dublin
Tel 01-8491250
Rev Richard Shannon CC
42A Strand Street, Skerries, Co Dublin
Tel 01-8494033

SPRINGFIELD
St Mark's, Maplewood Road,
Tallaght, Dublin 24
Email stmarkspringfield@irishchurch.net
http://stmarkspringfield.irishchurch.net
Very Rev Frank Herron PP
68 Maplewood Road, Springfield,
Tallaght, Dublin 24
Tel 01-4513109
Rev Gerard Doyle CC
Tel 01-2859212

SRULEEN
Sacred Heart, St John's Drive, Dublin 22
Rev Patrick Bradley (SSCC) PP
Rev Eamon Aylward (SSCC) CC
Sacred Hearts Presbytery,
St Johns Drive, Sruleen, Dublin 22
Tel 01-4570032

SUTTON
St Fintan's, Greenfield Road, Dublin 13
Rt Rev Mgr John V. Fitzpatrick PP, Area
Episcopal Vicar
Parochial House, 3 Glencarraig,
Church Road, Sutton, Dublin 13
Tel 01-8323147
Email jvf@eircom.net
Rev Kevin Bartley CC
8 Greenfield Road, Sutton, Dublin 13
Tel 01-8322396

SWORDS
St Colmcille's, Co Dublin
(Dublin Airport Church, Our Lady Queen
of Heaven, is in this parish)
Website www.swordsparish.com
Very Rev Cyril Mangan PP
5 Lissenhall Park, Seatown Road,
Swords, Co Dublin
Tel 01-8403378
Rev John Ferris CC *(priest in charge, Church*
of Our Lady of the Visitation, Drynam)
The Presbytery, 18 Aspen Road,
Kinsealy Court
Tel 01-8405948
Email jcferris@eircom.net
Rev Des Doyle CC
Chaplain's Residence,
Dublin Airport, Co Dublin
Tel 01-8144340
Mass times: Saturday: Vigil Mass 7.00 pm
Sunday: 10.00 am, 11.30 am

TALLAGHT, DODDER
St Dominic's, Dublin 24
Very Rev Laurence Collins (OP) Adm
Rev Declan Corish (OP) CC
Presbytery, St Dominic's Road,
Tallaght, Dublin 24
Tel 01-4510620 Fax 01-4623223

TALLAGHT, OLDBAWN
St Martin de Porres, Dublin 24
Very Rev David Brough PP
85 Tymon Crescent, Old Bawn, Dublin 24
Tel 01-4627080
Email davidj08@eircom.net
Rev David Fleming CC
Parochial House, Bohernabreena,
Tallaght, Dublin 24
Tel 01-4510986
Email davg@eircom.net

TALLAGHT, ST MARY'S
St Mary's, Tallaght Village, Dublin 24
Rev Dermot J. Brennan (OP) Adm
St Mary's Priory, Tallaght, Dublin 24
Tel 01-4048100 (Priory)

TALLAGHT, TYMON NORTH
St Aengus's, Castletymon Road, Dublin 24
Very Rev Benedict Moran (OP) PP
Email benmoran@indigo.ie
Rev Albert Leonard (OP) CC
Email aldleonard@yahoo.com
Presbytery, St Aengus's, Balrothery,
Tallaght, Dublin 24
Tel 01-4513757 Fax 01-4624038

TEMPLEOGUE
St Pius X, College Drive, Dublin 6W
Tel 01-4905284
www.stpiusx.ie
Very Rev Aquinas T. Duffy PP
22 Wainsfort Park, Terenure, Dublin 6W
Tel 01-4908288
Rev Karl Fortune CC
55 Wainsfort Manor Crescent,
Templeogue, Dublin 6W
Tel 01-4928651

TERENURE
St Joseph's, Dublin 6
Very Rev Francis McDonnell PP
Parochial House, 83 Terenure Road East,
Dublin 6
Tel 01-4905520
Rev Tom Dooley (SM) CC
4 Greenmount Road, Dublin 6
Tel 01-4904959

TRAVELLING PEOPLE
Chapel of Ease, St Oliver's Park,
Clondalkin, Dublin 22
Very Rev Derek Farrell PP
6 New Cabra Road, Phibsboro, Dublin 7
Tel 087-2573857
Email derek@ptrav.ie
Parish Office: St Laurence House,
6 New Cabra Road, Phibsboro, Dublin 7
Tel 01-8388874 Fax 01-8388901
Urgent messages: 087-2573875
Email into@ptrav.ie
Website www.ptrav.ie
Secretarial: Ms Geraldine McDonnell, Ms
Pauline McDonnell, Ms Louise McDonnell
Baptisms and Marriages by appointment
Catechists: Ms Cairenn Bryson,
Ms May Nyhan DC
Crosscare Traveller Project
Manager: Colin Thomson
Tel 01-8388874
Email cthomson@crosscare.ie
Naitonal Traveller Suicide Prevention
Tel 01-8388874
Email ntspo@crosscare.ie

UNIVERSITY CHURCH
Our Lady, Seat of Wisdom,
St Stephen's Green, Dublin 2
Very Rev Pearse Walsh PP
87A St Stephen's Green, Dublin 2
Tel 01-4780616

VALLEYMOUNT
St Joseph's, Valleymount
Our Lady of Mount Carmel, Lacken
Very Rev Tim Murphy PP
The Presbytery, Main Street,
Blessington, Co Wicklow
Tel 045-865442
Rev Teddy Downes CC
The Presbytery, Cross,
Vallymount, Co Wicklow
Tel 045-867151

WALKINSTOWN
Assumption of the BVM, Dublin 12
Very Rev John Jacob Adm
12 Walkinstown Road, Dublin 12
Tel 01-4502541
Rev P. J. Healy (SDB) CC
162 Walkinstown Road, Dublin 12
Tel 01-4501372
Very Rev Denis Foley PE
32 Walkinstown Road, Dublin 12
Tel 01-4501350

WHITEFRIAR STREET
Our Lady of Mount Carmel,
Whitefriar Street, Dublin 2
Very Rev Charles Hoey (OCarm) PP
Rev Desmond Kelly (OCarm) CC
Carmelite Priory,
56 Aungier Street, Dublin 2
Tel 01-4758821

WICKLOW
St Patrick's, Wicklow, Co Wicklow
Email wicklowparish@eircom.net
Rev Denis Nolan CC
The Presbytery, Rathnew, Co Wicklow
Tel 0404-67488/087-2389594
Email drnolan@eircom.net
Rev Peter O'Reilly CC
The Presbytery, Wicklow
Tel 0404-67133

WILLINGTON
St Jude the Apostle, Orwell Park,
Dublin 6W
Very Rev Denis Ryan PP, VF
Parochial House,
1 Rossmore Road, Dublin 6W
Tel 01-4500785
Rev James Norman PC
Dun Bhríd, 64 Orwell Park Rise, Dublin 6W
Tel 01-8376027 (w)/4507879 (h)
Email jamesnorman@dcu.ie
Rev Gregory O'Brien CC
2 Rossmore Road, Dublin 6W
Tel 01-4508432

YELLOW WALLS
Sacred Heart Church, Eastuary Road,
Malahide, Co Dublin
Email yellowwallsparish@gmail.com
www.yellowwallsparish.ie
Very Rev G. Tanham PP
12 The Warren, Malahide, Co Dublin
Tel 01-8457950
Ref Frank Reburn CC
11 Millview Court, Malahide, Co Dublin
Tel 01-8451902
Rev Paul Thornton CC
146 Seapark, Malahide, Co Dublin
Tel 01-8454172

INSTITUTIONS AND THEIR CHAPLAINS

COLLEGES

Coláiste Mhuire Marino
Griffith Avenue, Dublin 9
Chaplain: Vacant

Dublin Institute of Technology
Co-ordinator of Chaplaincy Team at DIT:
Sr Mary Flanagan
Office: 143-149 Rathmines Road, Dublin 6
Tel 01-4023307 Fax 01-4023449
Email mary.flangan@dit.ie

Dublin Institute of Technology
at Bolton Street
Tel 01-4023000 Fax 01-4023999
Chaplain: Rev Padraig Gleeson
Office Tel 01-4023618

Dublin Institute of Technology
at Kevin Street
Ms Fionnuala Walsh
Tel 01-4024568 Fax 01-4024999
Email fionnuala.walsh@dit.ie

Dublin Institute of Technology
at Mounjoy Square
Tel 01-4023000 Fax 01-4024298
Contact Co-ordinator of Chaplaincy

Dublin Institute of Technology
at Cathal Brugha Street
Tel 01-4023000 Fax 01-4024499
Chaplain: Mr Finbarr O'Leary
Tel 01-4024308

Dublin Institute of Technology
at Aungier Street
Tel 01-4023000 Fax 01-4023003
Chaplain: Sr Mary Flanagan
Office Tel 01-4023050
Email mary.flanagan@dit.ie
Residence: 14 Heather Lawn,
Marlay Wood, Dublin 16
Tel 01-4942324

Dublin Institute of Technology
at Rathmines Road
Tel 01-4023000 Fax 01-4023499
Contact Co-ordinator of Chaplaincy

Dublin Institute of Technology
at Adelaide Road
Tel 01-4023000
Contact Co-ordinator of Chaplaincy

Dublin City University
Rev Joe Jones
InterFaith Centre, Dublin 9
Tel 01-7005268 Fax 01-7005663
Residence: 30 Willow Park Crescent
Glasnevin, Dublin 11
Email joe.jones@dcu.ie

Institute of Technology
Tallaght, Dublin 24
Tel 01-4042000
Sr Bernadette Purcell

Mater Dei Institute of Education
Tel 01-8376027
Mr Barry McEntee

National College of Art and Design
100 Thomas Street, Dublin 8
Chaplain: Vacant

St Patrick's College, Drumcondra
Dublin 9
Tel 01-8842000
Rev Sean Farrell (CM)

National University of Ireland,
Maynooth (NUIM)
Chaplaincy Service,
NUI Maynooth, Co Kildare
Tel 01-7083588
Chaplains: Sr Margaret McConalogue RSM
Tel 01-7083469
Email margaret.mcconalogue@nuim.ie
Mr Shay Claffey
Tel 01-7083588
Email seamus.claffey@nuim.ie
Executive Assistant: Ms Susan Caldwell
Tel 01-7083320
Email susan.caldwell@nuim.ie

Trinity College, Dublin 2
Rev Patrick Gleeson
Tel 01-6081260
48 Westland Row, Dublin 2
Rev Peter Sexton (SJ)
House 27 Trinity College, Dublin 2
Tel 01-8961260

University College, Dublin
Chaplains' Room, UCD, Belfield, Dublin 4
Tel 01-7068317
Rev John McNerney Tel 01-2600715
Rev David Brough Tel 01-2605582
Rev John Callanan (SJ) Tel 01-7167408
Rev Tony Coote Tel 01-7162100/2839290
Rev Leon Ó Giollain (SJ)
Chaplains' Residence: St Stephen's, UCD
Belfield, Dublin 4 Tel 01-7161971

DEFENCE FORCES

Department of Defence
Colaiste Caoimhin, Glasnevin, Dublin 9
Tel 01-8379911 ext 3197 Fax 01-8379928

Head Chaplain
Rt Rev Mgr Eoin Thynne HCF
Tel 01-8042270
Administrative Secretary: Sgt John Kellett

McKee Barracks
Dublin 7
Tel 01-8388614
Rev Patrick Mernagh

McKee Barracks and St Bricin's Hospital
Dublin 7
Tel 01-6778502
Rt Rev Mgr Eoin Thynne HCF

Cathal Brugha Barracks
Rathmines, Dublin 6
Tel 01-8046493
Rev David Tyndall

Casement Aerodrome
Baldonnel, Co Dublin
Tel 01-4592497
Rev Jerry Carroll

International Military Pilgrimage to
Lourdes
(Pelerinage Militaire Internationale)
Director: Defence Forces HQ, Dublin 9
Tel 01-8042271

KFOR
Irish Transport Company, KFOR
BSPO 559, London, England

HOSPITALS

Adelaide and Meath Hospital
(incorporating National Children's Hospital)
Tallaght, Dublin 24
Tel 01-4142000/4142480
Chaplains: Rev Peter Murphy, Rev John
Kelly, Rev Michael Browne (SDB), Sr Joan
Smith, Sr Margaret Deegan, Ms Eden
dela Cruz, Sr Rose Gallagher, Sr Jennie
O'Connell, Ms Catherine Shirley

Baggot Street Hospital
Baggot Street, Dublin 4
Vacant

Beaumont Hospital
Beaumont Road, Dublin 9
Tel 01-8377755
Direct Line: 01-8092815/8093229
Rev Eoin Hughes Tel 01-8477573
Rev Denis Sandham (OSCam)
Rev Bryan Shortall (OFMCap)
Sr Brenda Swan (MMM)

Beaumont Convalescent Home
Tel 8379186
Vacant

Blackrock Clinic
Blackrock, Co Dublin
Tel 01-2832222
Rev Gerard Byrne

Blackrock Hospice
Sweetman's Avenue, Blackrock, Co Dublin
Tel 01-2064000
Ms Margo McKay
Tel 01-2064024

Bloomfield
Donnybrook, Dublin 4
Tel 01-4950021
Carmelite Fathers, Avila,
Morehampton Road, Dublin 4
Tel 01-6683155/6683091

Bon Secours Hospital
Glasnevin, Dublin 9
Tel 01-8065300
Rev William Ryan (OFMCap), Sr Goretti
Spillane, Ms Fionnuala Prunty, Ms
Patricia Nolan, Sr Anne Marie Fahey

Central Mental Hospital
Dundrum
Tel 01-2989266
Rev Desmond O'Grady (SJ)

Cherry Orchard Hospital
Ballyfermot
Tel 01-6264702
Rev Seamus Fleming (CSSp)
St Mary's Presbytery, Lucan, Co Dublin
Tel 086-8903864

Children's Hospital
Temple Street
Tel 01-8748763
Sr Julie Buckley, Sr Mary McWeeney

Clonskeagh Hospital
Vergemount, Dublin 6
Tel 01-2697877
Appointment pending

Coombe Women's Hospital
Dolphin's Barn, Dublin 8
Tel 01-4085200
Sr Margaret Nolan

Connolly Hospital
Blanchardstown, Dublin 15
Tel 01-8213844
Rev Martin Geraghty (OSCam)
Rev Anthony O'Riordan (SVD)
Tel 01-6465168
Ms Caroline Mullen

Hermitage Medical Centre
Old Lucan Road, Lucan, Co Dublin
Tel 01-6459000
Rev Vincent O'Connell (CSSp)
Kimmage Tel 01-4928561

Mater Hospital
Eccles Street, Dublin 7
Tel 01-8301122
Rev Vincent Xavier Kakkadampallil
(OSCam), Sr Maura Irwin, Ms Catherine
Ingoldsby, Ms Maire Breathnach, Sr Mary
Flynn, Sr Margaret Sleator

Mater Private Hospital
Dublin 7
Tel 01-8858888
Rev Seamus O'Brien

Mount Carmel Hospital
Tel 01-4922211
Rev Stan Mellett (CSsR)
Marianella, 75 Orwell Road, Rathgar,
Dublin 6
Tel 01-4922688

National Maternity Hospital
Holles Street, Dublin 2
Tel 01-6373100
Ms Jo Young Lee
Sr Marion Ryan

National Rehabilitation Hospital
Rochestown Avenue,
Dun Laoghaire, Co Dublin
Tel 01-2854777
Rev Michael Kennedy (CSSp)
Sr Catherine O'Neill

Newcastle Hospital
Tel 01-2819001
Rev Sean Smith CC
The Presbytery, Newtownmountkennedy,
Co Wicklow
Tel 01-2819253

Orthopaedic Hospital
Castle Avenue, Clontarf
Tel 01-8332521
Vacant

Our Lady's Hospice
Harold's Cross
Tel 01-4972101
Rev Brendan McKeever CP
Sr Rita Deegan
Ms Elizabeth Coyle

Our Lady's Children's Hospital
Crumlin, Dublin 12
Tel 01-4096100
Rev Fintan Brennan Whitmore (OH)
Ms Katherine McElwee

Peamount Hospital
Newcastle, Co Dublin
Tel 01-6010300
Rev Jim Byrnes (CSSp)

Rotunda Hospital
Parnell Street, Dublin 1
Tel 01-8730700
Ms Anne Charlton
Tel 01-8745441

Royal Hospital Donnybrook
Morehampton Road, Dublin 4
Tel 01-4972844
Rev Enda Watters (CSSp)
Tel 01-2888681

Royal Victoria Eye and Ear Hospital
Adelaide Road, Dublin 12
Tel 01-6785500
Chaplain: Vacant

St Brendan's Hospital
Upper Grangegorman, Dublin 7
Tel 01-8385844
Rev Piaras Ó Duill (OFMCap)
Tel 01-8730599

St Columcille's Hospital
Loughlinstown, Co Dublin
Tel 01-2825800
Rev John McCarthy (MSC)
Ms Marianne Quinn
Ms Rita McAuley

St Francis Hospice
Raheny, Dublin 5
Tel 01-8327535
Rev Eustace McScweeney (OFMCap)
Capuchin Friary, Raheny, Dublin 5
Tel 01-8313886
Sr Marian Gribbin, St Ita's, Portrane
Tel 01-8436337
Very Rev Patrick O'Byrne PP
Parochial House, Donabate, Co Dublin
Tel 01-8436011

St James's Hospital
James's Street, Dublin 8
Tel 01-4103000
Direct Line 01-4103659/4162023
Rev Brian Gough, Rev Anthony Darragh
(CSSp), Rev Jim Stapleton (CSSp), Sr Joyce
Cullinane, Sr Anne Kelly

St John of God Hospital
Stillorgan, Co Dublin
Tel 01-2881781
Rev Hugh Gillan (OH)

St Joseph's Hospital
Clonsilla
Tel 01-8217177
Chaplain: Vacant

St Joseph's Hospital
Springdale Road, Raheny, Dublin 5
Tel 01-8478433
Rev Sean Donohoe (OFMCap)

St Loman's Hospital
Ballyowen, Palmerstown, Dublin 20
Tel 01-6264077
Rev Jeremiah Lambe (CSSp)

St Luke's Hospital
Highfield Road, Rathgar, Dublin 6
Rev Patrick O'Brien (OSCam)
Tel 01-4065000 Res 01-2882873

St Mary's Hospital
Phoenix Park, Dublin 20
Tel 01-6778132
Rev James Hannon

St Mary's Orthopaedic Hospital
Cappagh, Dublin 11
Tel 01-8341211
Rev Christopher O'Brien (CSSp)

St Michael's Hospital
Lower George's Street,
Dun Laoghaire, Co Dublin
Tel 01-2806901
Rev Thomas McDonald (CSSp)
Sr Margaret Hilliard

St Patrick's Hospital
James Street, Dublin 8
Tel 01-6775423
Chaplain: Vacant

St Vincent's Hospital
Athy, Co Kildare
Tel 0507-31614
Rev Ross McAuley (OP)

St Vincent's University Hospital
Elm Park, Dublin 4
Tel 01-2694533
Direct Line 01-2094325
Rev Anthony Conlan, Rev Jim
MacDonnell (CSSp), Rev Liam Cuffe, Sr
Rosaleen Heslin, Sr Daphne O'Gorman

St Vincent's Private Hospital
Tel 01-2695622
Rev John O'Keeffe (SJ), Rev Brendan
Staunton (SJ), Ms Phil O'Neill, Sr Sheila
Wall, Sr Jacinta Forde

St Vincent's, Fairview
Tel 01-8375101
Mr Jim Owens

PRISONS

Arbour Hill Prison
Ard na Gaoithe, Arbour Hill, Dublin 7
Rev Ciaran Enright
Tel 01-6770901
Email ccenright@irishprisons.ie
Prison General Office 01-6719333

Clover Hill Remand Centre
Cloverhill Road, Clondalkin, Dublin 22
Rev John O'Sullivan (MSC)
Tel 01-6304606
Email jjosullivan@irishprisons.ie
Sr Carmel Miley (CP)
Tel 01-6304585
Email cjmiley@irishprisons.ie
Sr Margaret O'Doovan (DC)
Tel 01-6304584
Email mmodonovan@irishprisons.ie
Prison General Office Tel 01-6304531/2

Dóchas Centre Mountjoy Women's Prison
North Circular Road, Dublin 7
Sr Mary Mullins Tel 01-8858920
Email mtmullins@irishprisons.ie
Prison General Office 01-8858987

Mountjoy Prison
North Circular Road, Dublin 7
Sr Ruth Breen
Tel 01-8062876
Email rabreen@irishprisons.ie
Sr Eithne Corcoran (IBVM)
Tel 01-8062843
Email emcorcoran@irishprisons.ie
Sr Gráinne Haslam (RSM)
Tel 01-8062846
Prison General Office 01-8062800

Saint Patrick's Institution
North Circular Road, Dublin 7
Tel 01-8062894
Miss Ruth Comerford
Email rmcomerford@irishprisons.ie
Sr Eileen Crowley (SHC) (part-time)
Email eccrowley@irishprisons.ie
General Office Tel 01-8062906

Shelton Abbey
Arklow, Co Wicklow
Sr Patricia Egan (RSCJ)
Tel 0402-32140 ext 44
General Office Tel 0402-32140

Training Unit
Glengariff Parade, Dublin 7
Sr Mairead Gahan LCM
Tel 01-8309612
Email gahanmairead@eircom.net
Prison General Office 01-8062881

Wheatfield Prison
Cloverhill Road, Clondalkin, Dublin 22
Sr Esther Murphy (RSC) Tel 01-6209447
Email esmurphy@irishprisons.ie
Sr Imelda Wickham (PBVM)
Tel 01-6209466
Email imwickham@irishprisons.ie
Sr Joan Kane (OSU) Tel 01-6209446
Email jakane@irishprisons.ie
Sr Kathleen Cunningham (DC)
Tel 01-6209466/7
Prison General Office 01-6209400

PRIESTS ELSEWHERE IN THE DIOCESE

Rev Patrick Desmond
Apostolic Nunciature, *Res:* The Lodge,
Mount Sackville, Chapelizod, Dublin 20
Tel 01-8214004
Rev Patrick Jones, Director
National Centre for Liturgy,
St Patrick's College, Maynooth, Co Kildare
Tel 01-7083478
Rev Brendan Leahy
St Patrick's College, Maynooth, Co Kildare
Rev Dermod McCarthy
RTÉ, Donnybrook, Dublin 4
Tel 01-2083237/087-2499719 Fax 01-2083974
Email mccartd@rte.ie
Rev Peter Murphy
Accord Catholic Marriage Care Service,
Columba Centre, Maynooth, Co Kildare

PRIESTS WORKING OUTSIDE THE DIOCESE

Rev Seamus Connell
c/o St Columban's, Dalgan Park,
Navan, Co Meath
Rev Adrian Crowley
Instituto de Idiomas Maryknoll Padres,
Casilla 550, Cochabamba, Bolivia
Rev Derek Doyle
c/o St Columban's, Dalgan Park,
Navan, Co Meath
Rev Ian Evans
Chaplain, England
Rev John Kennedy (Congregation for the
Doctrine of the Faith)
Via del Mascherino 12, 00193 Roma, Italy
Rev Aidan Larkin
c/o St Columban's, Dalgan Park,
Navan, Co Meath
Rev Eoin Murphy
St Joseph's Church, 109 Linden Street,
Saint John's, MI48879, USA
Rev Seamus O'Brien
(address not available at time of going
to print)
Rev Desmond O'Reilly
St Charles Borromeo Parish,
7584 Center Parkway, Sacramento,
California 95823, USA
Rt Rev Mgr Paul Tighe
Secretary of the Pontifical Council for
Social Communications, Vatican City

PRIESTS STUDYING ABROAD

Rev Desmond Hayden
Pontificio Collegio Teutonico,
Via della Sagrestia 17,
00120 Rome, Vatican City

RETIRED PRIESTS

Very Rev John Canon Battelle PE
14 Pine Valley, Grange Road, Dublin 16
Very Rev Denis T. Bergin
76 Trintonville Road,
Sandymount, Dublin 4
Rt Rev Mgr Andrew P. Canon Boland PE
13 Griffith Avenue, Dublin 9
Very Rev Bernard Canon Brady
61 Glasnevin Hill, Dublin 9
Ven Archdeacon Macarten Brady PE,
Sacred Heart Residence, Sybil Hill Road,
Killester, Dublin 5
Very Rev Daniel Breen
2 St Mary's Court, Arklow, Co Wicklow
Rev Noel Campbell
Ballysmutlan, Manor Kilbride,
Blessington, Co Wicklow
Rev Gerald T. Canning
35 Dun Emer Green, Lusk, Co Dublin
Very Rev Brendan F. Canon Carbery
5 Griffith Avenue, Marino, Dublin 9
Rev Myles Christy
c/o Elmhurst Nursing Home,
Hampstead Avenue, Glasnevin, Dublin 9
Rev Denis Carroll
85 Hillcrest Drive, Esker, Lucan, Co Dublin
Rev Martin G. Colleran
Our Lady's Manor, Bulloch Castle,
Dalkey, Co Dublin

Rev Diarmuid Connolly
4 Summerfield Lawn, Blanchardstown,
Dubin 15
Rev Michael Connolly
54 Wyattville Park,
Loughlinstown, Co Dublin
Rev Morgan Costelloe
21 Cullenswood Gardens, Dublin 6
Tel 01-4975201
Rev Edward Corry
Presbytery No. 2, Treepark Road,
Kilnamanagh, Dublin 24
Very Rev Patrick J. Culhane
138 Lucan Road, Chapelizod, Dublin 20
Rev Seamus Cullen
2 Ceol na Mara, Lower Main Street,
Rush, Co Dublin
Rt Rev Mgr Jerome Curtin PE
Holy Family Residence, Roebuck,
Dundrum, Dublin 14
Very Rev Hugh Daly PE
St Mary's, 50 Cremore Road,
Glasnevin, Dublin 11
Rev Philip Dennehy
4 Stanhope Place, Athy, Co Kildare
Rev Cornelius Dowling
St Anthony's, 13 Richmond Grove,
Monkstown, Co Dublin
Rev Patrick Dowling
Holy Family Residence, Roebuck,
Dundrum, Dublin 14
Very Rev Joseph Drumgoole PE
35 Grange Park Avenue,
Raheny, Dublin 5
Rev Thomas Early
23 Estuary Road, Malahide, Co Dublin
Very Rev Patrick Fagan PE
The Presbytery, Ballyboughal, Co Dublin
Rt Rev Mgr G. Thomas Fehily PE
Hampstead Hospital, Glasnevin, Dublin 11
Rev James Fingleton
279 Howth Road, Raheny, Dublin 5
Very Rev John Canon Fitzgibbon PE
The Presbytery, Chapel Road,
Lusk, Co Dublin
Very Rev Patrick Canon Fitzsimons
Holy Family Residence, Roebuck,
Dundrum, Dublin 14
Very Rev Denis Foley
32 Walkinstown Road, Dublin 12
Very Rev Desmond Forristal
St Joseph's Centre, Crinken Lane,
Shankill, Co Dublin
Very Rev Paul Freeney PE
Parochial House,
43 Upper Beechwood Avenue,
Ranelagh, Dublin 6
Very Rev Mgr Colm Gallagher
594 Howth Road, Raheny, Dublin 5
Very Rev J. Anthony Gaughan
56 Newtownpark Avenue, Blackrock,
Co Dublin
Rev Michael Geaney
3 Hillview Cross, Douglas Road, Cork
Rev Oliver Hanratty
The Bungalow, Crescent Road,
Rogerstown, Rush, Co Dublin
Rev Francis Hardy
58 Shelmartin Avenue, Marino, Dublin 9
Very Rev Walter Canon Harris PE
151 Clonsilla Road, Blanchardstown,
Dublin 15

Very Rev Míceál Hastings
103 Mount Prospect Drive, Dollymount, Dublin 3
Very Rev Liam Hickey
St Ciaran's, 1 Cherryfield Park, Hartstown, Dublin 15
Rev Anthony Johnston CC
8 Corrig Park, Dun Laoghaire, Co Dublin
Tel 01-2805594
Rev Gilbert Kelly
Ballycarron House, Golden, Co Tipperary
Very Rev James J. Kelly PE
Parochial House, Clogher Road, Dublin 12
Very Rev Thomas V. Kelly
Castlebar Road, Westport, Co Mayo
Rev Eugene Kennedy
7 Riverwood Vale, Carpenterstown, Castleknock, Dublin 15
Very Rev Patrick J. Kett
27 Huntsgrove, Ashbourne, Co Meath
Very Rev James Canon Loughran PE
Parochial House, Esker, Lucan, Co Dublin
Rev John Lynch
2 Cooleen Avenue, Beaumont, Dublin 9
Rt Rev Mgr James Ardle Canon MacMahon
Queen of Peace Centre,
6 Garville Avenue, Rathgar, Dublin 6
Very Rev John Canon MacMahon PE
Holy Family Residence, Roebuck, Dundrum, Dublin 14
Rev Christopher J. Madden, Lisieux
196 Oakcourt Avenue, Palmerstown, Dublin 20
Very Rev Noel Madden PE
3 Rosemount, Malahide Road, Dublin 5
Very Rev Patrick J. Mangan
Dun Mhuire, 44 Upper Beechwood Avenue, Ranelagh, Dublin 6
Very Rev Eugene McCarney
Parochial House, Castletown, Gorey, Co Wexford
Rev Cornelius McGillicuddy
33 Gracepark Road, Drumcondra, Dublin 9
Rt Rev Mgr John J. Moloney PE
50 Rathgar Road, Dublin 6
Very Rev Raymond T. Moloney
Presbytery No 2, Thormanby Road, Howth, Co Dublin
Very Rev Patrick B. Moore PE
The Presbytery, Brittas Bay, Co Wicklow
Very Rev Seamus Moore
8 Herbert Avenue, Dublin 4
Very Rev Patrick Mulvey
25 Thomastown Road, Dun Laoghaire, Co Dublin
Rev James Murray
9 Hillcrest Manor, Templeogue, Dublin 6W
Very Rev Liam Murtagh
167 Charlemont, Griffith Avenue, Dublin 9
Tel 087-2408416
Very Rev Ronald Neville PE
213a Harold's Cross Road, Dublin 6
Rt Rev Mgr J. Michael Nolan
26 Harmony Avenue, Donnybrook, Dublin 4
Rev Sean Noone
The Presbytery, Pollathomas, Co Mayo
Rev James O'Brien
Sacred Heart Residence, Sybil Hill Road, Killester, Dublin 5

Rev Peadar O'Ciarain
Sons of Divine Providence, Orione House, 13 Lower Teddington Road, Hampton, Wick, Kingston-upon-Thames KT1 4EU
Very Rev John O'Connell PE
Cluain Mhuire, Killarney Road, Bray, Co Wicklow
Very Rev Erill D. Canon O'Connor
14 Clare Road, Drumcondra, Dublin 9
Very Rev Donal O'Doherty PE
Holy Cross, Upper Kilmacud Road, Dundrum, Dublin 14
Very Rev Thomas O'Keeffe
20 Glen Avenue, The Park, Cabinteely, Dublin 18
Very Rev Maurice O'Moore PE
6 Richmond Avenue, Monkstown, Co Dublin
Very Rev Sean O'Neill PE
'Iona', 3 St Colmcille's Park, Swords, Co Dublin
Rev Sean O'Rourke
15 Seaview Park, Shankill, Co Dublin
Rev Padraig O'Saorai
12 Ashville, Athy, Co Kildare
Rev Brian O'Sullivan
The Cottage, Glengara Park, Glenageary, Dun Laoghaire, Co Dublin
Rev John K. O'Sullivan
97 Kincora Avenue, Clontarf, Dublin 3
Rev Sean O'Toole
The Presbytery, Sea Road, Arklow, Co Wicklow
Very Rev Leo Quinlan
42A Strand Street, Skerries, Co Dublin
Very Rev James A. Canon Randles PE
5 St Margaret's Road, Malahide, Co Dublin
Rev Henry Regan
Presbytery No. 1, Church Grounds, Kill Avenue, Dun Laoghaire, Co Dublin
Very Rev Patrick Canon Rice PE
Little Sisters of the Poor, Holy Family Residence, Roebuck Road, Dundrum, Dublin 14
Rt Rev Mgr Richard Sherry PE
Presbytery No 2, Stillorgan Road, Donnybrook, Dublin 4
Very Rev Mgr Thomas Stack PE
Apt 4, Maple Hall (adjoining church), SS Columbanus and Gall, Milltown, Dublin 6
Very Rev John Stokes
44 Carlton Court, Swords, Co Dublin
Rev Michael D. Supple
Apartment 8, Giltown Lodge, Kilcullen, Co Kildare
Rt Rev Mgr Owen Sweeney
54 Seabury, Sydney Parade Avenue, Dublin 4
Rev Jeremiah Threadgold
Sacred Heart Residence, Sybill Hill Road, Raheny, Dublin 5
Rev Martin Tierney
Ballycotton North, Liscannor, Co Clare
Tel 087-2780496
Rev John M. Ward
1 Chestnut Grove, Ballymount Road, Dublin 24
Rev Michael Wall
Sacred Heart Residence, Sybill Hill Road, Raheny, Dublin 5

PERSONAL PRELATURE

OPUS DEI
Harvieston, Cunningham Road, Dalkey, Co Dublin
Tel 01-2859877 Fax 01-2305059
Vicar for Ireland:
Rt Rev Robert Bucciarelli DD

RELIGIOUS ORDERS AND CONGREGATIONS

PRIESTS

AUGUSTINIANS
St Augustine's, Taylor's Lane, Ballyboden, Dublin 16
Tel 01-4241000 Fax 01-4939915
Email www.augustinians.ie
Provincial: Rev Gerry Horan (OSA)
Prior: Rev John Lyng (OSA)

St John's Priory, Thomas Street, Dublin 8
Tel 01-6770393/6770415/6770601
Fax 01-6713102/6770423
Prior: Rev Tony Egan (OSA)

Orlagh Retreat Centre
Old Court Road, Dublin 16
Tel 01-4930932/4933315/4931163
Fax 01-4930987
Email orlagh@augustinians.ie
Prior: Rev John Byrne (OSA)
Bursar: Rev Columba Higgins (OSA)

(See also under parishes – Ballyboden, Meath Street and Rivermount)

BLESSED SACRAMENT CONGREGATION
Blessed Sacrament Chapel,
20 Bachelor's Walk, Dublin 1
Tel 01-8724597 Fax 01-8724724
Email sssdublin@eircom.net
Superior: Rev James Campbell (SSS)

CAMILLIANS
St Camillus, South Hill Avenue, Blackrock, Co Dublin
Tel 01-2882873 Fax 01-2833380
Superior: Rev Denis Sandham

CAPUCHINS
St Mary of the Angels, Church Street, Dublin 7
Tel Parish 01-8730925
Tel Friary 01-8730599/Fax 01-8730250
Guardian
Rev Desmond McNaboe (OFMCap)

Capuchin Friary (Immaculate Heart of Mary), Raheny, Dublin 5
Tel 01-8313886/8312805
Guardian and Definitor
Rev Sean Donohoe (OFMCap)

(See also under parishes – Halston Street and Priorswood)

CARMELITES (OCARM)
Provincial Office, Gort Muire,
Ballinteer, Dublin 16
Tel 01-2984014 Fax 01-2987221
Provincial: Rev Martin Kilmurray (OCarm)

Whitefriar Street Church,
56 Aungier Street, Dublin 2
Tel 01-4758821 Fax 01-4758825
Email whitefriars@eircom.net
Prior: Rev David Weakliam (OCarm)
Parish Priest: Rev Charles Hoey (OCarm)

Terenure College, Terenure, Dublin 6W
Tel 01-4904621 Fax 01-4902403
Email admin@terenurecollege.ie
Prior/Manager: Rev Michael Troy (OCarm)
Sub-Prior: Rev Eoin Moore (OCarm)
Principal (Senior School):
Rev Eanna Ó hÓbáin (OCarm)
Principal (Junior School):
Rev Michael Troy (OCarm)

(See also under parishes – Beaumont,
Knocklyon and Whitefriar Street)

CARMELITES (OCD)
53 Marlborough Road, Donnybrook,
Dublin 4
Tel 01-6617163 Fax 01-6683752
Email jnoonan@ocd.ie
Website www.ocd.ie
Provincial: Rev James Noonan (OCD)

St Teresa's, Clarendon Street, Dublin 2
Tel 01-6718466/6718127
Prior: Rev David Donnellan (OCD)

Avila, Bloomfield Avenue,
Morehampton Road, Dublin 4
Tel 01-6430200 Fax 01-6430281
Email avila@ocd.ie
Prior: Rev Michael MacLaifeartaigh (OCD)

Karmel Vocation Centre,
53/55 Marlborough Road, Dublin 4
Tel 01-6601832
Prior: Rev Herman Doolan (OCD)

St Joseph's, Berkeley Road, Dublin 7
Tel 01-8306356/8306336
Prior: Rev Christopher Clarke (OCD) PP

CISTERCIANS
Bolton Abbey, Moone, Co Kildare
Tel 059-8624102 Fax 059-8624309
Email info@boltonabbey.ie
Website www.boltonabbey.ie
Abbot: Rt Rev Dom Peter Garvey (OCSO)

COMBONI MISSIONARIES
8 Clontarf Road, Dublin 3
Tel/Fax 01-8330051
Email combonimission@eircom.net
Superior: Awaiting Appointment

CONGREGATION OF THE PRIESTS OF THE SACRED HEART OF JESUS
Fairfield, 66 Inchicore Road, Dublin 8
Tel 01-4538655
Email scjdublin@eircom.net
House of Formation
Superior and Formation Director:
Rev John Kelly (SCJ)

(See also under parishes – Ardlea)

CONGREGATION OF THE SACRED HEARTS OF JESUS AND MARY (SACRED HEARTS COMMUNITY)
Provincialate: Coudrin House,
27 Northbrook Road, Dublin 6
Tel 01-6604898
Email ssccdublin@eircom.net
Website www.sacredhearts.ie
Community 01-6671513 Fax 01-6608341
Provincial: Very Rev Michael Ruddy (SSCC)

Sacred Heart Presbytery,
St John's Drive, Clondalkin, Dublin 22
Tel 01-4570032

(See also under parishes – Sruleen)

DIVINE WORD MISSIONARIES
3 Pembroke Road, Dublin 4
Tel 01-6680904
Praeses: Rev Albert Escoto
Email albert_escoto2000@yahoo.com

133 North Circular Road, Dublin 7
Tel 01-8386743 Fax 01-8686257
Email provincial@svdireland.com
Provincial: Rev Brian O'Reilly
Praeses: Rev John Feighery

Maynooth, Co Kildare
Tel 01-6286391/2 Fax 01-6289184
Email rector@svdireland.com
Rector: Rev Peter Madden

(See also under parishes – City Quay)

DOMINICANS
Provincial Office, St Mary's,
Tallaght, Dublin 24
Tel 01-4048118/4048115 Fax 01-4515584
Email provincialop@eircom.net
Provincial: Very Rev Pat Lucey (OP)

St Mary's Priory, Tallaght, Dublin 24
Tel 01-4048100 Fax 01-4596784
Parish 01-4048188
Prior: Very Rev Gerard Norton (OP)
Email gerard.norton@dominicanstallaght.org

St Saviour's, Upper Dorset Street, Dublin 1
Tel 01-8897610 Fax 01-8734003
Email stsaviours@eircom.net
Prior: Very Rev Anthony Morris (OP)

St Dominic's, Athy, Co Kildare
Tel 0507-31573
Prior: Very Rev Joseph O'Brien (OP)

Dominican Community,
47 Leeson Park, Dublin 6
Tel 01-6602427
Superior: Very Rev Bernard Treacy (OP)

(See also under parishes – Dominick
Street and three of the Tallaght parishes)

FRANCISCANS (OFM)
Adam and Eve's, Merchant's Quay,
Dublin 8
Tel 01-6771128 Fax 01-6771000
Guardian: Rev Ulic Troy (OFM)

Franciscan House of Studies, Dún Mhuire,
Seafield Road, Killiney, Co Dublin
Tel 01-2826760 Fax 01-2826993
Email dmkilliney@eircom.net
Guardian: Rev Kieran Cronin (OFM)

(See also under parishes – Merchant's Quay)

FRANCISCANS: ORDER OF FRIARS MINOR
Conventual (Greyfriars) (OFMConv)
The Friary of the Visitation of the BVM,
Fairview Strand, Fairview, Dublin 3
Tel 01-8376000 Fax 01-8376021

(See also under parishes – Fairview)

HOLY GHOST CONGREGATION
Spiritan Provincialate, Temple Park,
Richmond Avenue South, Dublin 6
Tel 01-4977230/4975127 Fax 01-4975399
Email secretaryspiritan@irishspiritans.ie
Provincial Superior
Rev Brian Starken (CSSp)

Spiritan Missionary College,
Kimmage Manor, Dublin 12
Tel 01-4064300 Fax 01-4920062
Superior: Rev Michael Kilkenny (CSSp)
Development Studies Centre
Tel 01-4064386 Fax 01-4064388
Director: Mr Patrick Reilly

Spiritan House – SPIRASI Project,
Spiritan Asylum Services Initiative,
213 North Circular Road, Dublin 7
Tel 01-8389664
Director: Mr Michael McMahon

Blackrock College, Blackrock, Co Dublin
Tel 01-2888681 Fax 01-2834267
Email info@blackrockcollege.com
Superior: Rev Tom Nash (CSSp)
Principal: Alan MacGinty

Willow Park
Tel 01-2881651 Fax 01-2783353
Email admin@willowparkschool.ie
Principal Senior School: Donal Brennan
Principal Junior School: Jim Casey

St Mary's College, Rathmines, Dublin 6
Tel 01-4062160 Fax 01-4972621
Junior School Tel 01-4062121
Email junsec@stmarys.ie
Senior School Tel 4062100 Fax 01-4972574
Email sensec@stmarys.ie
Superior: Rev Patrick B. Cleary (CSSp)
Principal: Liam Naughton
Principal Junior School: Mary O'Donnell

St Michael's College,
Ailesbury Road, Dublin 4
Tel 01-2189400 Fax 01-2698862
Email stmcoll@indigo.ie
Superior: Rev Patrick Dundon (CSSp)
Principal: Tim Kelleher
Principal Junior School: Lorna Heslin

Templeogue College,
Templeogue, Dublin 6W
Tel 01-4903909 Fax 01-4920903
Superior: Rev John Byrne (CSSp)
Principal: Ms Aoife O'Donnell
Info@templeoguecollege.ie

(See also under parishes – Bawnogue,
Greenhills and Kimmage)

JESUITS

Jesuit Provincial Curia,
IMI Centre, Sandyford Road, Dublin 16
Tel 01-2932820 Fax 01-2934923
Email curia@jesuit.ie
Provincial: Rev John Dardis (SJ)
Assistant Provincial: Rev Noel Barber (SJ)

Jesuit Curia Community,
33 Sandford Road, Ranelagh, Dublin 6
Tel 01-4988004/5
Superior: Rev Noel Barber (SJ)

Belvedere College, Dublin 1
Tel 01-8586600 Fax 01-8744374
Rector: Rev Derek Cassidy (SJ)
Secondary day school
Headmaster: Gerard Foley

Milltown Park, Sandford Road, Dublin 6
Tel 01-2698411/2698113 Fax 01-2600371
Email milltown@jesuit.ie
Rector: Rev Kevin O'Rourke (SJ)

Milltown Institute of Theology and
Philosophy, Milltown Park, Dublin 6
Tel 01-2776300 Fax 01-2692528
Email info@milltown-institute.ie
Acting President
Rev Cornelius Casey (CSsR)

Lay Retreat Association of St Ignatius,
Milltown Park, Dublin 6
Tel 01-2951856
Spiritual Director: Rev Fergus O'Keefe (SJ)

25 Croftwood Park,
Cherry Orchard, Dublin 10
Tel 01-6267413
Superior: Rev William Toner (SJ)

Gonzaga College,
Sandford Road, Dublin 6
Community Tel 01-4972943
Email gonzaga@s-j.ie
(College) Tel 01-4972931 Fax 01-4967769
Email (College) office@gonzaga.ie
Fax (Community) 01-4960849
Email (Community) gonzaga@jesuit.ie
Rector: Rev Myles O'Reilly (SJ)
Headmaster: Mr Kevin Whirdy

Manresa House, Dollymount, Dublin 3
Tel 01-8331352 Fax 01-8331002
Email manresa@jesuit.ie
Rector: Rev Joseph Dargan (SJ)

Dominic Collins' House, Residence,
129 Morehampton Road, Dublin 4
Tel 01-2693075 Fax 01-2698462
Acting Superior: Rev David Coghlan (SJ)

John Sullivan House, 56/56a Mulvey Park,
Dundrum, Dublin 14
Tel 01-2983978
Email sullivan@jesuit.ie
Rector: Rev Fergus O'Keefe (SJ)

35 Lower Leeson Street, Dublin 2
Tel 01-6761248 Fax 01-7758598
Superior: Rev Brian Grogan (SJ)

Jesuit Communication Centre
36 Lower Leeson Street, Dublin 2
Tel 01-6768408 Fax 01-6629292
Email jcc@jesuit.ie
Manager: Ms Pat Coyle
Tel 01-7758514

Campion House, Residence,
28 Lower Hatch Street, Dublin 2
Tel 01-6383990 Fax 01-6762805
Email campion@s-j.ie
Superior: Rev John O'Keeffe (SJ)

John Austin House,
135 North Circular Road, Dublin 7
Tel 01-8386768
Email mosullivan@jesuit.ie
Superior: Rev Neil O'Driscoll (SJ)

Arrupe Community, 127 Shangan Road,
Ballymun, Dublin 9
Tel/Fax 01-8625345
Email ballymun@jesuit.ie
Superior: Rev Proinsias Mac Bradaigh (SJ)

27 Leinster Road, Rathmines, Dublin 6
Tel 01-4970250
Email leinster@jesuit.ie
Superior: Rev James Corkery (SJ)

(See also under parishes – Ballymun,
and Gardiner Street)

LEGIONARIES OF CHRIST

Leopardstown Road, Foxrock, Dublin 18
Tel 01-2955985/2955902
Email ireland@legionaries.org
Superior & Novice Master
Rev Matthew Brackett (LC)

Clonlost Retreat and Youth Centre
Killiney Road, Killiney, Co Dublin
Tel 01-2350064

Dublin Oak Academy
Kilcroney, Bray, Co Wicklow
Tel 01-2863290 Fax 01-2865315
Email dublinoaksecretariat@arcol.org
Chaplain: Rev Francisco Cepeda (LC)

Woodlands Academy
Wingfield House, Bray, Co Wicklow
Tel 01-2866323 Fax 01-2864918

John Paul II Centre, Dal Riada House,
Avoca Avenue, Blackrock, Co Dublin
Tel 01-2889317
Director: Rev Michael Mullan (LC)

MARIANISTS

St Columba's, Church Avenue,
Ballybrack, Co Dublin
Tel 01-2858301
Director: Br James Contadino (SM)

St Laurence College, Loughlinstown,
Shankill PO, Co Dublin
Tel 01-2826930 Fax 01-2821878
Principal: Mr John Carr

MARISTS

Mount St Mary's, Milltown, Dublin 14
Regional Superior: Rev David Corrigan (SM)
Tel 01-2698100
Superior: Rev Brendan Bradshaw (SM)
Tel 01-2697322 (Residence)

Catholic University School,
89 Lower Leeson Street, Dublin 2
Tel 01-6762586/6760247
Superior: Rev Brian Keenan (SM)

Chanel College, Coolock, Dublin 5
Tel 01-8480896/8480655
Superior: Rev Kieran Butler (SM)

(See also under parishes – Coolock and
Donore Avenue)

MILL HILL MISSIONARIES

St Joseph's House, 50 Orwell Park,
Rathgar, Dublin 6
Tel 01-4127700 Fax 01-4127781
Email josephmhm@eircom.net
Regional Superior
Rev Maurice McGill (MHM)
Rector: Rev Patrick Molloy (MHM)
Vice Rector: Rev Patrick O'Connell (MHM)
Bursar: Rev Patrick Murray
Email millhill@iol.ie

MISSIONARIES OF AFRICA

Provincialate, Cypress Grove Road,
Templeogue, Dublin 6W
Tel 01-4992346
Email provirl@indigo.ie
Delegate Superior
Rev Ian Buckmaster (MAfr)

Cypress Grove, Templeogue, Dublin 6W
Tel 01-4055263/4055264
Email provirl@indigo.ie
Superior: Rev Andre Filion (MAfr)

MISSIONARIES OF THE SACRED HEART

Provincialate,
65 Terenure Road West, Dublin 6W
Tel 01-4906622 Fax 01-4920148
Provincial Leader
Rev Patrick Courtney (MSC)

Woodview House, Mount Merrion
Avenue, Blackrock, Co Dublin
Tel 01-2881644
Leader: Rev David Smith (MSC)

(See also under parishes – Killinarden
and Mount Merrion)

OBLATES OF MARY IMMACULATE

Provincial Residence,
Oblates of Mary Immaculate House of
Retreat, Tyrconnell Road,
Inchicore, Dublin 8
Email omisec@eircom.net
Provincial
Very Rev William Fitzpatrick (OMI)

Oblate House of Retreat,
Inchicore, Dublin 8
Tel 01-4534408 Fax 01-4543466
Superior: Rev Anthony Clancy (OMI)

Oblate Scholasticate, St Anne's,
Goldenbridge Walk, Inchicore, Dublin 8
Tel 01-4540841 Fax 01-4731903
Superior: Rev Michael Hughes (OMI)

(See also under parishes – Bluebell,
Darndale and the two Inchicore parishes)

PALLOTTINES
Provincial House, 'Homestead',
Sandyford Road, Dundrum, Dublin 16
Tel 01-2956180
Provincial: Rev Eamonn Monson (SAC)
Rector: Rev John Kelly (SAC)
Email pallotti@eircom.net

(See also under parishes – Corduff and St Anne's)

PASSIONISTS
St Paul's Retreat, Mount Argus, Dublin 6W
Tel 01-4992000 Fax 01-4992001
Email passionistsmtargus@eircom.net
Provincial: Rev Pat Duffy (CP)

(See also under parish – Mount Argus)

REDEMPTORISTS
Liguori House, 75 Orwell Road, Dublin 6
Tel 01-4067100 Fax 01-4922654
Email provlig@eircom.net
Provincial: Rev Michael G. Kelleher (CSsR)

Marianella, 75 Orwell Road, Dublin 6
Tel 01-4067100 Fax 01-4929635
Superior: Rev Peter Burns (CSsR)

(See also under parishes – Cherry Orchard)

ROSMINIANS
1 Grace Park Gardens,
Drumcondra, Dublin 9
Tel 01-8378314 Fax 01-8368726
Provincial: Rev Joseph O'Reilly (IC)

Clonturk House, Ormond Road,
Drumcondra, Dublin 9
Tel 01-8378314

Cottrell Lodge, 16A Ormond Road,
Drumcondra, Dublin 9
Tel 01-8572234

ST COLUMBANS MISSIONARY SOCIETY
St Columban's, Grange Road,
Donaghmede, Dublin 13
Tel 01-8476647
Contact Person: Rev Patrick Crowley (SSC)

House of Studies: St Columban's,
67-68 Castle Dawson, Rathcoffey Road,
Maynooth, Co Kildare
Tel 01-6286036
Priest-in-Charge: Rev William Curry (SSC)

(See also under parishes – Balcurris)

ST PATRICK'S MISSIONARY SOCIETY
21 Leeson Park, Dublin 6
Tel 01-4977897 Fax 01-4962812
House Leader: Rev Peter Coyle (SPS)

SALESIANS
Provincialate: Salesian House,
45 St Teresa's Road, Crumlin, Dublin 12
Tel 01-4555787 Fax 01-4558781
Email (secretary) tsdun@gofree.indigo.ie
Provincial: Very Rev John Horan (SDB)
Email ruanet@indigo.ie
Novitiate: Tel 01-4555605
Rector: Rev Michael Ross (SDB)

Salesian College, Maynooth Road,
Celbridge, Co Kildare
Tel 01-6275058/6275060 Fax 01-6272208
Rector: Rev Patrick Hennessy (SDB)
Secondary School Tel 01-6272166/6272200

Don Bosco Houses
57 Lower Drumcondra Road, Dublin 1
Tel 01-8360696/8373449
12 Clontarf Road, Dublin 3
Tel 01-8336009/8337045
Rev Val Collier *(Priest-in-charge)*
Students' Residence

Rinaldi House
72 Seán Mac Dermott Street, Dublin 1
Tel 01-8363358 Fax 01-8552320
Rector: Rev Hugh O'Donnell (SDB)

(See also under parishes – Sean McDermott Street)

SALVATORIANS
Our Lady of Victories,
Sallynoggin, Dun Laoghaire, Co Dublin
Tel 01-2854667 Fax 01-2847024
Email sallynogginparish@eircom.net
Superior: Rev Liam Talbot (SDS)

SERVITES
Servite Priory, St Peregrine,
Kiltipper Road, Tallaght, Dublin 24
Tel 01-4517115
Prior: Rev Tim Flynn (OSM)

Servite Oratory,
Rathfarnham Shopping Centre,
Dublin 14
Tel 01-4936300
Director: Rev Timothy M. Flynn (OSM)

Divine Word, Marley Grange,
25-27 Hermitage Downs, Rathfarnham,
Dublin 16
Tel 01-4944295
Prior: Rev Liam Tracey (OSM)

SOCIETY OF AFRICAN MISSIONS
SMA House,
82 Ranelagh Road,
Ranelagh, Dublin 6
Tel 01-4968162/3 Fax 01-4968164
Rector: Rev John O'Brien (SMA)

(See also under parishes – Neilstown)

SOCIETY OF ST PAUL
St Paul's House,
Moyglare Road,
Maynooth, Co Kildare
Tel 01-6285933 Fax 01-6289330
Email book@stpauls.ie
Superior & Rector of Scholasticate
Rev Pius Nechikattil (SSP)

SONS OF DIVINE PROVIDENCE
Sarsfield House, Sarsfield Road,
Ballyfermot, Dublin 10
Tel 01-6266233/6266193
Email don-orion@clubi.ie
Superior: Rev Michael Moss (FDP)

VINCENTIANS
Provincial Office: St Paul's, Sybill Hill,
Raheny, Dublin 5
Tel 01-8510840/8510842 Fax 01-8510846
Email cmdublin@iol.ie
Provincial: Very Rev Brian Moore (CM)

11 Iona Drive, Glasnevin, Dublin 9
Tel 01-8305238
Superior
Very Rev Stephen Monaghan (CM)

St Joseph's, 44 Stillorgan Park,
Blackrock, Co Dublin
Tel 01-2886961
Superior
Very Rev Joseph Cunningham (CM)

All Hallows Institute for Mission and
Ministry, Drumcondra, Dublin 9
Tel 01-8373745/6 Fax 01-8377642
Email info@allhallows.ie
President: Very Rev Mark Noonan (CM)
Superior: Very Rev Joseph McCann (CM)
Ministry to Priests,
Missions and Retreat: Tel 01-8373745

St Vincent's College,
Castleknock, Co Dublin
Tel 01-8213051
President/Superior
Very Rev Peter Slevin (CM)

St Paul's College, Raheny, Dublin 5
Tel 01-8314011/2 Fax 01-8316387
Email rmccm@eircom.net
Tel 01-8318113 (Community)
Superior: Very Rev Eamon Flanagan (CM)

(See also under parishes – Phibsboro)

BROTHERS

ALEXIAN BROTHERS
47 Upper Drumcondra Road, Dublin 9
Tel 01-8375973
Contact: Br Vianney Kerr
Community: 3

CHRISTIAN BROTHERS
Province Centre, Marino,
Griffith Avenue, Dublin 9
Tel 01-8073300 Fax 01-8073366
Email cbprov@edmundrice.ie
Province Leader: Br J. K. Mullan
Community: 9

St Helen's, York Road,
Dun Laoghaire, Co Dublin
Tel 01-2801214/2841656 Fax 01-2841657
Community Leader: Br Paul Tobin
Community: 8

Christian Brothers' House,
Woodbrook, Bray, Co Wicklow
Tel 01-2821510
Community Leader: Br Pat Gaffney
Community: 6

Christian Brothers' House,
Drimnagh Castle, Walkinstown, Dublin 12
Tel 01-4501567 Fax 01-4508930
Community Leader: Br T. A. Earley
Community: 10

Christian Brothers' House, Oatlands,
Mount Merrion, Co Dublin
Tel 01-2889510 Fax 01-2109511
Community Leader: Br John Hearne
Community: 15

Christian Brothers; House,
Synge Street, Dublin 8
Tel 01-4751292/4755/98 Fax 01-4761015
Community Leader: Br Declan Power
Community: 10

Community Education Centre
D8CEC, 108 James' Street,
Digital Hub, Dublin 8
Tel 01-5424130
Email info@d8cec.com
Director: Marie Mulvihil

Christian Brothers' House,
46 Westland Row, Dublin 2
Tel 01-6762112
Community Leader: Br Seamus Nolan
Community: 7

Christian Brothers' House,
10 Rosmeen Gardens, Dun Laoghaire,
Co Dublin
Tel 01-2802105
Community Leader: Br T. L. Nevin
Community: 10

42 Glasnevin Avenue, Dublin 11
Tel 01-8623564
Community: 3

Christian Brothers' Residence,
St David's Park, Artane, Dublin 5
Tel 01-8317833
Community Leader: Br John Ledwidge
Community: 5

Artane School of Music
Tel 01-8318929
Administrator: Joe Edge
Musical Director: Ronan O'Reilly
Email artaneschooofmusic@eircom.net

Oratory of the Resurrection,
Artane, Dublin 5
Tel 01-8327168
Director: Br John Ledwidge

St Patrick's, Baldoyle, Dublin 13
Tel 01-8391287
Retirement home for brothers
Community Leader: Br Pat Bowler
Community: 40

Christian Brothers' Monastery,
St Declan's, Nephin Road, Dublin 7
Tel 01-8389560
Community Leader: Br F. Donnelly
Community: 5

Clareville, 89A Finglas Road,
Finglas, Dublin 11
Tel 01-8309811
Community: 5

Marino Institute of Education,
Griffith Avenue, Dublin 9
Tel 01-8057700 Fax 01-8335290
President: Dr Anne O'Gara

Christian Brothers, St Joseph's Community,
Marino Institute of Education,
Griffith Avenue, Marino, Dublin 9
Tel 01-8057790
Community Leader: Br Chris Glavey
Community: 8

242 North Circular Road, Dublin 7
Tel 01-8680454
Community Leader: Br Paddy McShane
Community: 6

Edmund Rice House,
North Richmond Street, Dublin 1
Tel 01-8556258 Fax 01-8555243
Community Leader: Br Leo Judge
Community: 4

The Allen Library, Christian Brothers,
Edmund Rice House,
North Richmond Street, Dublin 1
Tel 01-8551077 Fax 01-8555243
Curator: Br Tom Connoll
Email allenlib@connect.ie

Emmaus Retreat Centre, Lissenhall,
Swords, Co Dublin
Tel 01-8401399/8402450 Fax 01-8408248
Community Leader: Br D. D. Young
Community: 4
Retreat Centre with Holy Faith Sisters
and Oblate Fathers

Mainistir Aodhain,
Collins Avenue West, Whitehall, Dublin 9
Tel 01-8379953
Community Leader: Br Kieran Walsh
Community: 6

Christian Brothers, Navan Road,
Cabra, Dublin 7
Community: 6
Tel 01-8684926

Christian Brothers, 8 Croftwood Grove,
Cherry Orchard, Ballyfermot, Dublin 10
Community: 2
Tel 01-6208920

Education Inclusion Initiative,
17 Synge Street, Dublin 8
Tel 01-4053868
Co-ordinator: Br Michael Murray
Email mmurray32@hotmail.com

The Life Centre,
57 Pearse Square, Dublin 2
Tel 01-6718894 Fax 01-6709179
Email lifecentre@dna.ie
Director: Br Paul Hendrick

Cherry Orchard Life Centre, 61 Elmdale
Crescent, Cherry Orchard, Ballyfermot,
Dublin 10
Tel 01-6235832
Director: Br Ger O'Connell
Email oconnell_gervase@hotmail.com

DE LA SALLE BROTHERS
Provincialate, 121 Howth Road, Dublin 3
Tel 01-8331815 Fax 01-8339130
Email province@iol.ie
Superior: Br Pius McCarthy
Community: 5

Beneavin College, Beneavin Road,
Finglas East, Dublin 11
Tel 01-8341410
Headmaster: Mr Joe Twomey

Mount La Salle, Ballyfermot, Dublin 10
Tel 01-6264408
Superior: Br Christopher Commins
Community: 9
Scoil Iosagain Mhuire
Principal: Mr Patrick Deeley
Scoil Mhuire Sheosaimh
Principal: Ms Naomi Plant
Tel 01-6267527 Schools
Tel 01-6262696 Staff Room
Tel 01-6234829 Home/School Liaison
Fax 01-6236021

Ard Scoil La Salle,
Raheny Road, Dublin 5
Tel 01-8480055 Fax 01-8480082
Principal: Mr Gerard Lynch

Benildus House,
160A Upper Kilmacud Road, Dublin 14
Tel 01-2981110
Superior: Br Ciarán Creedon
Community: 4

Benildus Pastoral Centre,
160A Upper Kilmacud Road, Dublin 14
Tel 01-2694195 Fax 01-2694168
Director: Ms Michelle Sinnott

St Benildus College, Upper Kilmacud
Road, Blackrock Co Dublin
Tel 01-2986539 Fax 01-2962710
Headmaster: Mr Sean Mulvihill

Hazelwood House,
160 Upper Kilmacud Road, Dublin 14
Tel 01-2985670
Superior: Br Gregory Ferguson
Community: 5

St John's Monastery,
Le Fanu Road, Dublin 10
Tel 01-6260867
Superior: Br Martin Breen
Community: 4
Secondary School
Principal: Ms Ann Marie Leonard
Tel/Fax 01-6264943

De La Salle College, Wicklow Town
Tel 0404-67581 Fax 0404-66661
Headmaster: Ms Marie Carroll

FRANCISCAN BROTHERS
49 Laurleen Estate,
Stillorgan, Co Dublin
Email franciscanbrs@eircom.net

MARIST BROTHERS
Marian College, Lansdowne Road,
Ballsbridge, Dublin 4
Tel 01-6683740
Superior: Br John Hyland
Community: 5
Secondary School

Moyle Park College,
Clondalkin, Dublin 22
Tel 01-4574837
Superior: Br Nicholas Smith
Community: 4
Secondary School

PATRICIAN BROTHERS
Patrician College, 35 Cardiffcastle Road,
Finglas West, Dublin 11
Tel 01-8342811
Superior: Br Dermot Dunne
Community: 2

PRESENTATION BROTHERS
Provincial House, Glasthule, Co Dublin
Tel 01-2842228
Contact: Br Andrew Hickey
Community: 6

ST JOHN OF GOD BROTHERS
Provincial Curia,
Granada, Stillorgan, Co Dublin
Tel 01-2771495 Fax 01-2831274
Email provincial@sjog.ie

St John of God Hospital,
Stillorgan, Co Dublin
Tel 01-2771400 Fax 01-2881034
Superior: Br Kilian Keaney (OH)
Director: Ms Monica Mooney
Community: 8
Private psychiatric hospital

Cluain Mhuire,
Community Mental Health Services,
Newtownpark Avenue,
Blackrock, Co Dublin
Tel 01-2172100 Fax 01-2833886
Email cms@sjog.ie
Director: Br Gregory McCrory (OH)

St John of God Kildare Services,
St Raphael's, Celbridge, Co Kildare
Tel 01-6288161 Fax 01-6273614
Email admin.kildare@sjog.ie
Superior: Br Charles Somers (OH)
Director: Ms Claire Dempsey (OH)
School Principal: Mrs Kathy Waldron
Community: 2
Residential and day centre for children
and adults with varying degrees of
learning disability

St John of God, Carmona Services,
Dunmore House,
111 Upper Glenageary Road,
Dun Laoghaire, Co Dublin
Tel 01-2852900 Fax 01-2851713
email admin.carmona@sjog.ie
Director: Ms Philomena Gray
School Principal: Ann Campbell
Incorporating residential, day &
enterprise services.

St Augustine's School, Obelisk Park,
Carysfort Avenue, Blackrock, Co Dublin
Tel 01-2881771 Fax 01-2834117
Email staugustines@sjog.ie
Director: Ms Deirdre Reece
Principal: Mr John Kingston
Special School

St John of God Lucena Clinic Services,
59 Orwell Road, Rathgar, Dublin 6
Tel 01-4923596 Fax 01-4928388
Email admin.lucena@sjog.ie
Superior: Br Gregory McCrory (OH)
Director: Mr Patrick Conroy
School Principal: Mr John Condon
Community: 3
Psychiatric service

St John of God Menni Services,
St John of God Centre,
Island Bridge, Dublin 8
Tel 01-6741500 Fax 01-6703829
Email admin.menni@sjog.ie
Director: Mrs Anna Plunkett
School Principal: Ms Marian Coughlan
Incorporating Menni Day Services
(Islandbridge Tel 01-6774022)
Menni Residential Services (Menni House
Tel 01-4731474) and Menni Enterprises
(Bluebell Tel 01-4569320)

Suzanne House, 6 Main Road,
Tallaght, Dublin 24
Tel 01-4521966 Fax 01-4525504
Email laurance.kearns@sjog.ie
Director: Mr Andrew Heffernan
Respite service for multiple handicapped
and sick children

STEP Enterprises, Sandyford Enterprise
Centre, 30 Carmanhall Road, Sandyford
Industrial Estate, Dublin 18
Tel 01-2952379 Fax 01-2952371
Email step@sjog.ie
Director: Ms Deirdre Reece
Training centre and supported
employment

St Joseph's Centre,
Crinken Lane, Shankill, Co Dublin
Tel 01-2823000 Fax 01-2823119
email stjosephs@sjog.ie
Director: Mrs Monica Mooney
Residential day service for elderly people

Granada Institute, Crinken House,
Crinken Lane, Shankill, Co Dublin
Tel 01-2721030 Fax 01-2720129
Email granadainstitute@sjog.ie
Director: Mrs Monica Mooney
Assessment and treatment for people
who have sexually abused and services
for people who have suffered or been
affected by abuse.

City Gate, 30 Charmanhall Road,
Sandyford Industrial Estate, Dublin 18
Tel 01-2952379 Fax 01-2952371
Email citygate@sjog.ie
Director: Ms Deirdre Reece
Housing Service

Genil Community,
17 Laurleen, Blackrock, Co Dublin
Community: 2

SISTERS

BLESSED SACRAMENT SISTERS
91 Seabury Crescent, Malahide, Co Dublin
Tel 01-8451878
Community: 3

BON SECOURS SISTERS (PARIS)
Sisters of Bon Secours, Sacre Coeur,
1 Beechmount, Glasnevin Hill, Dublin 9
Tel 01-8065353
Community: 2
Hospital Ministry

Bon Secours Convent,
Glasnevin, Dublin 9
Co-ordinator: Sr Margaret O'Shea
Tel 01-8375111 Fax 01-8571020
Community: 10
Hospital Ministry, Outreach Ministry

'Le Chéile', 9 St David's Terrace,
Glasnevin, Dublin 9
Tel 01-8370018
Community: 4
Hospital Ministry

Sisters of Bon Secours, 9 Abbeyvale,
215 Botanic Avenue, Drumcondra,
Dublin 9
Tel 01-8373209
Community: 2
Hospital Ministry, Outreach Ministries

Sisters of Bon Secours,
119 Esker Lawns, Lucan, Co Dublin
Tel 01-6217158
Community: 1
Parish Ministries

Sisters of Bon Secours,
2 Northumberland Court,
Haddington Road, Ballsbridge, Dublin 4
Tel 01-660825
Community: 1
Ministry: Holles Row

BRIGIDINE SISTERS
5 Sycamore Drive, Dundrum, Dublin 16
Tel 01-2988130
Contact: Sr Theresa Kilmurray
Community: 2
Clinical Pastoral Education

7 Sycamore Drive, Dublin 16
Tel 01-2966449
Community: 1
Contact: Sr Loretto Ryan

2 Dartmouth Road, Dublin 6
Tel 01-6603027
Community: 4
Pastoral Work, Spiritual Direction

15 Gortmore Drive, Rivermount,
Finglas, Dublin 11
Tel 01-8642440
Contact: Sr Rita Minehan
Community: 1
Parish, Counselling

94 Moyville, Ballyboden, Dublin 16
Tel 01-7941596
Contact: Sr Anna Hennessy
Community: 1

163 Park Drive Avenue, Castlenock,
Dublin 15
Tel 01-8200482
Contact: Sr Mary Slattery
Community: 1

Allianz (ⅲ)

CARMELITES

Carmelite Monastery of the Immaculate
Heart of Mary, Delgany, Greystones,
Co Wicklow
Email
prioress@carmelitemonasterydelgany.ie
Prioress: Sr Monica Lawless
Community: 18
Contemplatives, altar breads

Carmelite Monastery of St Joseph,
Upper Kilmacud Road, Stillorgan, Co Dublin
Email contact@kilmacudcarmel.ie
Prioress: Sr Carmel Breen
Community: 11
Contemplatives, altar breads

Carmelite Monastery of the Incarnation,
Hampton, Grace Park Road,
Drumcondra, Dublin 9
Email carmeliteshampton@eircom.net
Prioress: Sr Brigid Murphy
Community: 11

Carmelite Monastery of St Joseph,
Seapark, Malahide, Co Dublin
Email malahidecarmelites@eircom.net
Prioress: Sr Rosalie Burke
Community: 11
Contemplatives

Carmelite Monastery of the Assumption,
Firhouse, Dublin 24
Tel 01-4526320
Email firhousecarmel@oceanfree.net
Prioress: Sr John Cunningham
Community: 8
Contemplatives, mortuary habits, scapulars

Carmelite Monastery of the Immaculate
Conception, Roebuck, Dublin 14
Tel 01-2884732 Fax 01-2870145
Altar Breads Fax 01-2835037
www.roebuckcarmel.com
Email carmel@roebuckcarmel.com
Prioress: Sr Teresa Whelan
Community: 7
Contemplatives; altar breads supplied

CARMELITE SISTERS FOR THE AGED AND INFIRM

Our Lady's Manor, Bullock Castle,
Dalkey, Co Dublin
Tel 01-2806993 Fax 01-2844802
Email ourladysmanor1@eircom.net
Superior: Sr Therese Eileen Mulvaney
Email sistereileen@eircom.net
Administrator: Sr Bernadette Murphy
Community: 8

CHARITY OF JESUS AND MARY SISTERS

11 Mount Shannon Road,
Kilmainham, Dublin 8
Tel 01-4531503

CHARITY OF NEVERS SISTERS

91 Cherrywood, Loughlinstown Drive,
Dun Laoghaire, Co Dublin
Tel 01-2824204
Email scnmkelly@eircom.net
Parish work

66 Verschoyle Court, Dublin
Tel 01-6624815

17 Stephen's Place, Dublin
Tel 01-6768159

29 Hazelgrove Court,
Tallaght, Dublin 24
Contact person: Sr Rosaleen Cullen
Email rosaleencullen@upcmail.ie

CHARITY OF ST PAUL THE APOSTLE SISTERS

St Paul's Convent, Greenhills, Dublin 12
Tel 01-4505358 Fax 01-4505132
Email marylyons446@hotmail.com
Contact: Sr Mary Lyons
Community: 11
Education Office: Tel/Fax 01-4567016
Primary and secondary schools; parish
work; chaplaincy

CLARISSAN MISSIONARY SISTERS OF THE BLESSED SACRAMENT

Our Lady of Guadalupe Residence for
Students, 28 Waltersland Road,
Stillorgan, Co Dublin
Tel/Fax 01-2886600
Email misclaridub@hotmail.com
www.guadaluperesidence.com
Superior: Sr Francisca Riera

CONGREGATION OF THE SISTERS OF MERCY

'Rachamim', 13/14 Moyle Park,
Convent Road, Clondalkin, Dublin 22
Tel 01-4673737 Fax 01-4673749
Email mercy@csm.ie
Website www.sistersofmercy.ie
Congregational Leader: Sr Coirle McCarthy

Mercy International Centre
64A Lower Baggot Street, Dublin 2
Tel 01-6618061
Email caitlinconneely@mercyintenational.ie
Director: Sr Caitlín Conneely
Heritage tours, school tours, conference
facilities and pilgrimages to the tomb of
Ven. Catherine McAuley

South Central Province

St Mary's Convent, Arklow, Co Wicklow
Tel 0402-32422 Fax 0402-32675
Non-resident Leader: Sr Luarena McCormick
Community: 2
Primary School, St Mary's Secondary
School, Pastoral ministry

1 & 2 Church Crescent, Athy, Co Kildare
Tel 059-8631361 Fax 059-8638180
Non-resident Leader: Sr Dolores Fitzgerald
Community: 10
St Michael's Primary School
St Mary's Secondary School
Pastoral ministry

2 Oak Lawn, Carlow Road,
Athy, Co Kildare
Tel 059-8638209
Non-resident Leader: Sr Nancy McLoughlin
Community: 2

12 Park Avenue, Athy, Co Kildare
Tel 059-8634220 Fax 059-8634221
Non-resident Leader: Sr Dolores Fitzgerald
Community: 4

21 Shamrock Drive, Athy, Co Kildare
Tel 059-8632908 Fax 059-8633071
Non-resident Leader: Sr Dolores Fitzgerald
Community: 2

101/102 Rockfield Green,
Maynooth, Co Kildare
Tel 01-6291992 Fax 01-6016896
Non-resident Leader
Sr Maureen Ryan
Community: 5

Mercy Convent, Beaumont, Dublin 9
Tel 01-8376741/8379186
Fax 01-8372770
Non-resident Leader: Sr Basil Gaffney
Community: 17

Our Lady of Mercy Secondary School
Tel 01-8371478
St Paul's Hospital and Primary School for
Autistic Children, Convalescent Home,
McAuley Centre

18 Beverley Crescent,
Knocklyon, Dublin 16
Tel 01-4941232
Community: 2
Non-resident Leader: Sr Agnes Coll
Teaching and parish ministry

St Ann's, Booterstown, Co Dublin
Tel 01-2882140 Fax 01-2782047
Non-resident Leader: Sr Sheila Cronin
Community: 13
Primary schools
All Irish Secondary School
Tel 01-2884028
Pastoral and spiritual ministry

Flat 339 St Teresa's Gardens,
Donore Avenue, Dublin 8
Tel 01-4530498 Fax 01-4530498
Non-resident Leader: Sr Sheila Cronin
Community: 2
Family Resource Centre

St Brendan's Drive, Coolock, Dublin 5
Tel 01-8486420
Non-resident Leader: Sr Mary McKeever
Community: 9
Scoil Caitriona primary and secondary
schools; pastoral work

26 Myrtle Park, Dun Laoghaire,
Co Dublin
Tel 01-2803181 Fax 01-2300040
Non-resident Leader
Sr Luarena McCormick
Community: 4

Our Lady of Lourdes Hospital,
Rochestown Avenue, Dun Laoghaire,
Co Dublin
Tel 01-2851804 Fax 01-2854663
Non-resident Leader: Sr Caitriona O'Hara
Community: 13
National Medical Rehabilitation Centre

23-26 The Paddocks,
Kilmainham, Dublin 8
Tel 01-4737234 Fax 01-4546299
Non-resident Leader: Sr Agnes Coll
Community: 9

81 Mackintosh Park,
Dun Laoghaire, Co Dublin
Tel-2851707
Non-resident Leader
Sr Luarena McCormick
Community: 4

13 Emmet Crescent, Inchicore, Dublin 8
Tel 01-4163275
Non-resident Leader: Sr Agnes Coll
Community: 2

19 Emmet Crescent, Inchicore, Dublin 8
Tel 01-4163890
Non-resident Leader: Sr Agnes Coll
Community: 2

49 Emmet Crescent, Inchicore, Dublin 8
Tel 01-4538196
Non-resident Leader: Sr Sheila Cronin
Community: 1
Family Resource Centre; pastoral work

Mater Misericordiae,
Eccles Street, Dublin 7
Tel 01-8301122 Fax 01-8309070
Resident Leader: Sr Moira Lynam
Community: 25
Hospital; school of nursing; school of
physiotherapy

8-9 Leo Street, Dublin 7
Tel 01-8858593 Fax 01-8300464
Non-resident Leader: Sr Mary McKeever
Community: 2

1 Oatfield Grove, Rowlagh, Clondalkin,
Dublin 22
Tel 01-6261114
Non-resident Leader: Sr Ann Scully
Community: 4
House of prayer

Stella Maris, Convent Lane, Rush,
Co Dublin
Tel/Fax 01-8437347
Non-resident Leader: Sr Mary McKeever
Community: 4
Secondary school; visitation

St Michael's, Dun Laoghaire, Co Dublin
Tel 01-2805557 Fax 01-2805470
Resident Leader: Sr Margaret Reid
Community: 21
General hospital, schools of
nursing; pastoral ministry

1 Rossfield Grove, Brookfield, Tallaght,
Dublin 24
Tel 01-4510444
Non-resident Leader: Sr Agnes Coll
Community: 2
Pastoral ministry

40 Hillcourt Road, Glenageary, Co Dublin
Tel 01-2854729
Non-resident Leader: Sr Sheila Cronin
Community: 3
Teaching, pastoral care, art therapy

14 Coolatree Close, Beaumont, Dublin 9
Tel/Fax 01-8377023
Resident Leader: Sr Mary McKeever
Community: 3

12 Cremore Lawn, Glasnevin, Dublin 11
Tel 01-8644045
Non-resident Leader: Sr Mary McKeever
Community: 3
Health care; social/pastoral, teaching

63 Kenilworth Park, Harolds Cross,
Dublin 6W
Tel/Fax 01-4928191
Non-resident Leader: Sr Margaret Corkery
Community: 3

65 Kenilworth Park, Harolds Cross,
Dublin 6W
Tel/Fax 01-4929414
Non-resident Leader: Sr Sheila Cronin
Community: 3
Chaplaincy; social work; education

Glencree, 60 Knocklyon Road,
Templeogue, Dublin 16
Tel/Fax 01-4933027
Non-resident Leader: Sr Margaret Corkery
Community: 4
Teaching; pastoral work

90/91 The Park, Beaumont Woods,
Dublin 9
Tel 01-8570741 Fax 01-7979966
Non-resident Leader: Sr Ann Scully
Community: 4

McAuley House, Beaumont, Dublin 9
Tel 01-8379186 Fax 01-8373503
Non-resident Leader: Sr Nuala Kennedy
Community: 22

Catherine McAuley Centre,
23 Herbert Street, Dublin 2
Tel 01-6387600 Fax 01-6387611

82/83 Silloge Road, Ballymun, Dublin 11
Tel/Fax 01-8429885
Non-resident Leader: Sr Ann Scully
Community: 3

6 Butterfield Avenue, Rathfarnham,
Dublin 16
Tel 01-4943169 Fax 01-4947234
Non-resident Leader
Sr Margaret Corkery
Community: 3

40 Gilford Road, Sandymount, Dublin 4
Tel/Fax 01-2601081
Resident Leader: Sr Sheila Cronin
Community: 3

Sisters of Mercy, 14 Walnut Avenue,
Courtlands, Drumcondra, Dublin 9
Tel 01-8377602 Fax 01-8570684
Non-resident Leader: Sr Ann Scully
Community: 4

Sisters of Mercy,
1 Charlemont, Griffith Avenue, Dublin 9
Tel 01-8571246 Fax 01-8368149
Non-resident Leader: Sr Mary McKeever
Community: 3

Sisters of Mercy, 25 Cork Street, Dublin 8
Tel 01-4533262
Non-resident Leader: Sr Margaret Corkery
Community: 6

11 Grangemore Road, Donaghmede,
Dublin 13
Tel 01-8482242
Non-resident Leader: Sr Ann Scully
Community: 2

2 Charlemont, Griffith Avenue, Dublin 9
Tel 01-8571248
Non-resident Leader: Sr Ann Scully
Community: 2

Cuan Mhuire, Athy, Co Kildare
Tel 059-8631493
Non-resident Leader: Sr Dolores Fitzgerald
Community: 2

Sunnybank, Laragh East,
Glendalough, Co Wicklow
Tel 0404-45791
Non-resident Leader
Sr Luarena McCormick
Community: 2

CROSS AND PASSION CONGREGATION
Cross and Passion Sisters,
3-5 Carberry Road, Glandore Road,
Dublin 9
Tel 01-8377256
Community: 4
Education, pastoral ministry

Cross and Passion Convent
22 Griffith Avenue, Marino, Dublin 9
Tel 01-8336381
Sister in Charge: Sr Nora Horan
Community: 17
Nursing, pastoral ministry, care of elderly

Cross and Passion Convent,
41 Alderwood Green, Springfield,
Tallaght, Dublin 24
Tel 01-4511850 Fax 01-4624416
Community: 4
Pastoral ministry, prison chaplaincy,
retreat work

Cross and Passion Convent,
13 Clare Road, Drumcondra, Dublin 9
Tel 01-8375511 Fax 01-8375500
Community: 4
Community development, pastoral
ministry, formation

25 Stanford, Harlech Grove,
Clonskeagh, Dublin 14
Tel 01-2104833
Parish work

DAUGHTERS OF CHARITY OF ST VINCENT DE PAUL
Provincialate, St Catherine's Provincial House, Dunardagh, Blackrock, Co Dublin
Tel 01-2882669/2882896 Fax 01-2834485
Local Superior: Sr Carmel McArdle
Community: 25
Administration; retreats and missions

Rickard House, Dunardagh, Blackrock, Co Dublin
Tel 01-2833900/2833933
Superior: Sr Kathleen McErlean
Community: 24
House for retired sisters

St Vincent's Centre, Navan Road, Dublin 7
Tel 01-8384304
Superior: Sr Marian Harte
Community: 6
Care, training and education of intellectually disabled people

St Vincent's, North William Street, Dublin 1 Tel 01-8552998
Superior: Sr Bridget O'Connor
Community: 6
Primary schools, parish and social work
Social Housing Project, Rendu Apartments

77 Kilbarron Park, Kilmore West, Dublin 5
Tel 01-8470648
Superior: Sr Anna Kennedy
Community: 6
Social and pastoral ministry

3 St Assam's Drive, Raheny, Dublin 5
Tel 01-8312859
Superior: Sr Marie Gribbon
Community: 3
St Francis Hospice and Home Care

St Louise's, Drumfinn Road, Ballyfermot, Dublin 10
Tel 01-6264921
Superior: Sr Claire Sweeney
Community: 7
Education and parish work

St Joseph's Hospital, Clonsilla, Co Dublin
Tel 01-8217177
Superior: Sr Zoe Kileen
Community: 13
Care and training of intellectually disabled adult women, placements for nurses training at DCU for services for persons with intellectual disability

St Louise's, Glenmaroon, Chapelizod, Dublin 20
Tel 01-8216166 Fax 01-8211991
Residential centre for girls with intellectual disability.

St Michael's School for girls and boys with learning difficulties.
Glen College Training Centre
Horticulture, Catering and Accomodation Services
Tel 01-8215866/8217169 Fax 01-8211991

10 Henrietta Street, Dublin 1
Tel 01-8732771
Superior: Sr Clare Hurley
Community: 23
House of residence

St Vincent's Trust, 8/9 Henrietta Street, Dublin 1
(Specialised second chance education for young people ad adults)
Tel 01-8874100 Fax 01-8723486

109 Mount Prospect Avenue, Clontarf, Dublin 3
Tel 01-8338508
Superior: Sr Angela Doyle
Community: 17
House for retired sisters; parish work

3 Shanliss Drive, Santry, Dublin 9
Tel 01-8423951
Superior: Sr Patricia Walsh
Community: 3
Parish work

St Teresa's, Temple Hill, Blackrock, Co Dublin
Tel 01-2788205 Fax 01-2886915
Superior: Sr Bernadette McGinn
Community: 8
Residential centre for persons with intellectual disability, Day care and Respite Centre for persons with Alzheimer's Disease

St Rosalie's, Portmarnock, Co Dublin
Tel 01-8460132
Residential centre for intellectually disabled people

St Catherine's, Knockmore Avenue, Killinarden, Tallaght, Dublin 24
Tel 01-4516320
Superior: Sr Louise O'Connell
Community: 4
Teaching; parish and social work

Seton House, 25 Northbrook Road, Dublin 6
Tel 01-6687300
Superior: Sr Bridget Callaghan
Community: 7
House of residence, After care services

7 Belvedere Road, Dublin 1
Tel 01-8556719
Superior: Sr Nuala Dolan
Community: 3
Pastoral care, child and family services

166 Navan Road, Dublin 7
Tel 01-8383801
Superior: Sr Margaret Joyce
Community: 3
House of residence, pastoral work

St Louise's, 16 Dalymount, Phibsboro, Dublin 7
Tel 01-8680308
Superior: Sr Aine Cahalan
Community: 5
Parish work, work with refugees and homeless people

25 Killarney Street, Dublin 1
Tel 01-8366487
Superior: Sr Patrica Lynch
Community: 5
Parish work

DAUGHTERS OF THE CROSS OF LIÈGE
Beech Park, Stillorgan, Co Dublin
Tel 01-2887401/2887315 Fax 01-2881499
Email beech@eircom.net
Superior: Sr Anne Kelly
Community: 18

DAUGHTERS OF THE HEART OF MARY
St Joseph's, Tivoli Road, Dun Laoghaire, Co Dublin
Tel 01-2801204. Community: 8
Email heartofmary@eircom.net
Parish work; teaching; social work, prayer groups
St Joseph's Primary School
Principal's Office: Tel 01-2803504

32 Brackenbush Road, Killiney, Co Dublin
Tel 01-2750917

DAUGHTERS OF THE HOLY SPIRIT
88 Foxfield Road, Raheny, Dublin 5
Tel 01-8312795
Community: 2
Contact person: Sr Teresa Buckley DHSp
Email tbuckley1929@eircom.net

9 Walnut Park, Drumcondra, Dublin 9
Tel 01-8371825
Community: 3
Pastoral ministry

DAUGHTERS OF JESUS
133 St Declans Road, Marino, Dublin 3
Tel 01-8335530
Contact: Sr Elizabeth Fox

DAUGHTERS OF MARY AND JOSEPH
65 Iona Road, Glasnevin, Dublin 11
Tel 01-8305640
Community: 6
Pastoral, education, Refugee project, Counselling

142 Chapelgate, St Alphonsus' Road, Dublin 9
Tel 01-8827740
Contact person: Sr Brigid Devane
Community: 1
Pastoral

37 Bancroft Road, Tallaght, Dublin 24
Tel 01-4515321
Community: 4
Pastoral

2 Moynihan Court, Tallaght, Dublin 24
Tel 01-4627923
Contact person: Sr Cathleen Calvey
Community: 1
Education

10 Moynihan Court, Tallaght, Dublin 24
Tel 087-7549313
Contact person: Sr Mary Doyle
Community: 1
Pastoral

Flat 7, 116 North Circular Road, Dublin 7
Tel 01-8380525
Contact person: Sr Peggy McArdle
Community: 1
Community Development

109 Botanic Avenue, Dublin 9
Tel 01-8367107
Contact person: Sr M. Fintan Curran
Community: 1
Pastoral

DAUGHTERS OF OUR LADY OF THE SACRED HEART
Provincial House,
14 Rossmore Avenue, Templeogue,
Dublin 6W
Tel 01-4903200 Tel/Fax 01-4903113
Email olshprov@eircom.net
Provincial: Sr Vianney Murray
Community: 4

50 Maplewood Road, Springfield,
Tallaght, Dublin 24
Tel 01-4512183
Superior: Sr Juliana O'Donoghue
Community: 2

DISCIPLES OF THE DIVINE MASTER
Divine Master Convent, Newtownpark
Avenue, Blackrock, Co Dublin
Tel 01-2114949 *(community)*
01-2886414 *(Liturgical Centre)*
Fax 01-2836935
Email pddmdublin@eircom.net
Sister in Charge: Sr Kathryn Williams
Community: 6
Contemplative-apostolic, perpetual
adoration, Liturgical apostolate,
distributors and producers of high-
quality Liturgical art, vestments, church
goods, private retreats, prayer groups.

DOMINICAN SISTERS
Generalate, 5 Westfield Road, Dublin 6
Tel 01-4055570/1/2/3 Fax 01-4055682
Email domgen@eircom.net
Congregation Prioress: Sr Helen Mary Harmey
Community: 5
Congregaton Bursar: Sr Kathleen Crowley
Congregation Archivist: Sr Mary O'Byrne

Regional House, Mary Bellew House,
Navan Road, Cabra, Dublin 7
Tel 01-8383716 Fax 01-8387828
Email dominica@indigo.ie
Region Prioress in capite
Sr Marie Cunningham
Community: 3

Novitiate, 71 Bancroft Park,
Tallaght, Dublin 24
Tel 01-4515130
Email domban@eircom.net
Prioress: Sr Margaret Mary Ryder
Community: 5

Dominican Convent, 9 Elgin Road,
Ballsbridge, Dublin 4
Tel 01-6601757
Email dominicanelginrd@eircom.net
Prioress: Sr Blanaid Gallagher
Community: 3

St Mary's, Rectory Green,
Riverston Abbey, Cabra, Dublin 7
Tel 01-8683041
Email domcab1@eircom.net
Prioress: Sr Mary Kehoe
Community: 8

St Mary's, Cabra, Dublin 7
Tel 01-8380567 Fax 01-8682050
Email domcabra@eircom.net
Prioress: Sr Odhran Flavin
Community: 19
Secondary School
Tel 01-8385282 Fax 01-8683003
Primary and secondary schools, Schools
for hearing-impaired, blind/deaf girls
and boys (day and boarding) Special
schools for emotionally disturbed
children. Parish work

Dominican Convent,
Sion Hill, Blackrock, Co Dublin
Tel 01-2886831/2/3
Email siondoms2002@yahoo.com
Prioress: Sr Darina Hosey
Community: 22
Froebel. Tel 01-2888520
Secondary School. Tel 01-2886791

St Mary's, 47 Mount Merrion Avenue,
Blackrock, Co Dublin
Tel 01-2888551
Email stmarysblackrock@yahoo.ie
Community: 6
Education and parish work

Matt Talbot Community, 'Cana'
40 St Laurence Road, Chapelizod, Dublin 20
Tel 01-6202769
Email scmhndom@indigo.ie
Community: 1
Adult education

Dominican Convent, Convent Road,
Dun Laoghaire, Co Dublin
Tel 01-2801379 Fax 01-2302209
Email dldoms@eircom.net
Prioress: Sr Dympna O'Shaughnessy
Community: 11
Primary School. Tel 01-2809011
Education, pastoral ministry

Dominican Convent,
204 Griffith Avenue, Dublin 9
Tel 01-8379550 Fax 01-8571802
Email dsisters@gofree.indigo.ie
Prioress: Sr Mary Daly
Secondary School. Tel 01-8376080
Community: 16

Dominican Sisters, 52 Newtownpark Ave,
Blackrock, Co Dublin
Tel 01-2833964
Email galldoms@eircom.net
Community: 1

Dominican Convent, Muckross Park,
Donnybrook, Dublin 4
Tel 01-2693018/2693707 Fax 01-2604041
Email muckrossconvent@eircom.net
Prioress: Sr Teresita Hetherton
Community: 19
Secondary school. Tel 01-2691096
Hostel for university students
Tel 01-2694179

St Catherine's, 2 Heather View Road,
Aylesbury, Tallaght, Dublin 24
Tel 01-4523462 Fax 01-4625636
Email domabury2@eircom.net
Community: 5
Education; pastoral ministry

Dominican Convent,
461 Griffith Avenue, Dublin 6
Tel 01-8374523 Fax 01-8360544
Email mairemkealy@eircom.net
Community: 6
Education

1 Avonbeg Road, Tallaght, Dublin 24
Tel 01-4514627
Email avonbeg@dominicansisters.com
Community: 2
Pastoral

2 Croftwood Crescent, Cherry Orchard,
Ballyfermot, Dublin 10
Tel 01-6231127
Email miriammar@hotmail.com
Community: 3
Education, pastoral ministry

93 Nephin Road, Cabra, Dublin 7
Tel 01-8682054
Email domsis@gofree.indigo.ie
Community: 4
Education

Dominican Sisters,
Santa Sabina House, Cabra, Dublin 7
Tel 01-8682666 Fax 01-8682667
Email santasabina@dominicansisters.com
Prioress: Sr Joan Looby
Community: 29

St Dominic's, St Mantan's Road, Wicklow
Tel 0404-67148
Email opwicklow@eircom.net
Community: 6
Education

An Clochán Retreat Centre,
Glendalough, Co Wicklow
Tel 0404-45137 Fax 0404-45962
Email anclochan@eircom.net
Community: 1

Dominican Sisters,
St Mary's Convent, Wicklow
Tel 0404-67328 Fax 0404-65054
Email ecenw@eircom.net
Community: 4

Dominican Sisters, St Mary's,
63 Annamor Road, Phibsboro, Dublin 7
Tel 01-8385541
Email annamoe63@eircom.net
Community: 3

Dominican Sisters, 62 Ashington Avenue,
Navan Road, Dublin 7
Tel 01-8386304
Community: 3

FAITHFUL COMPANIONS OF JESUS
11 Priory Walk, Whitehall Road, Dublin 12
Tel 01-4924075
Leader: Sr Maria Dunne
Community: 3
Administration, primary teaching,
university ministry

310 Wedgewood, Sandyford Road,
Ballaly, Dublin 16
Tel 01-2952372
Leader: Sr Catherine Toomey
Community: 3
Spirituality, family therapy, parish,
community school

FRANCISCAN MISSIONARIES OF THE DIVINE MOTHERHOOD
Arus Mhuire, 185 Swords Road,
Whitehall, Dublin 9
Tel 01-8570844
Community: 4

Emohruo, 2 Fonthill Abbey,
Ballyboden Road, Rathfarnham, Dublin 14
Tel/Fax 01-4934275
Community: 3

St Francis Convent, 3/4 Fonthill Abbey,
Ballyboden Road, Rathfarnham, Dublin 14
Tel 01-4932537 Fax 01-4954846
Community: 4

FRANCISCAN MISSIONARIES OF MARY
St Francis Convent, The Cloisters,
Mount Tallant Avenue, Terenure,
Dublin 6W
Tel 01-4908549
Email fmmecloisters@eircom.net
Superior: Sr Josephine McGlynn
Community: 8
House of formation

Assisi, 36 Grange Abbey Drive,
Donaghmede, Dublin 13
Tel 01-8470591
Superior: Sr Mary Dunne
Community: 4
Social, pastoral and educational work

97 St Lawrence Road, Clontarf, Dublin 3
Tel 01-8332683/8332181
Email fmmclontarf@yahoo.co.uk
Superior: Sr Ann Condon
Community: 8
Pastoral; teaching; hospitality for
missionary sisters

St Joseph's Convent, Old Road,
Rush, Co Dublin
Tel 01-8439308
Superior: Sr Declan O'Connor
Community: 23
Care of elderly sisters

FHM, 4 Muckross Drive,
Perrystown, Dublin 12
Tel 01-4562028
Email fmmctmargaret@hotmail.co.uk
Community 5

FRANCISCAN MISSIONARIES OF ST JOSEPH
St Joseph's, 16 Innismore,
Crumlin Village, Dublin 12
Tel 01-4563445
Superior: Sr Johanna Kelly
Community: 4

FRANCISCAN MISSIONARY SISTERS FOR AFRICA
Generalate, 34A Gilford Road,
Sandymount, Dublin 4
Tel 01-2838376 Fax 01-2602049
Email fmsagen@iol.ie
Congregational Leader
Sr Miriam Duqqan (FMSA)
Community: 5

34 Gilford Road, Sandymount, Dublin 4
Tel 01-2691923
Contact person: Sr Maurita Kennedy (FMSA)
Community: 8

Regional House
142 Raheny Road, Raheny, Dublin 5
Tel 01-8473140 Fax 01-8481428
Email fmsanar@iol.ie
Contact person Regional
Sr Jeanette Watters (FMSA)
Community: 5

FRANCISCAN SISTERS
6 Collinstown Grove, Neilstown, Dublin 22
Tel 01-4573049
Email angela_oconnell@eircom.net
Community: 3

3 St Andrew's Fairway, Lucan, Co Dublin
Tel 01-6108756
Email citaearls@yahoo.com
Community: 2

FRANCISCAN SISTERS OF THE IMMACULATE CONCEPTION
Franciscan Sisters, 97/99 Riverside Park,
Clonshaugh, Dublin 17
Tel 01-8771778/8474214 Fax 01-8771731
Co-ordinator: Sr M. Patricia Coyle
Email pcoylefran@eircom.net
Community: 4
Administration, pastoral ministry,
nursing

FRANCISCAN SISTERS MINORESS
St Anthony's Convent,
1 Cabra Grove, Dublin 7
Tel 01-8380185
Superior: Sr Barbara Flynn
Community: 4
Pastoral ministry

GOOD SHEPHERD SISTERS
245 Lower Kilmacud Road, Goatstown,
Dublin 14
Tel 01-2982699 Fax 01-2989033
Email rgsdublin@eircom.net
Community: 3
Provincialate

65 Taney Crescent,
Goatstown, Dublin 14
Tel 01-2960235
Email rgstaney@iolfree.ie
Community: 4
Social work, apostolate

HANDMAIDS OF THE SACRED HEART OF JESUS
St Raphaela's, Upper Kilmacud Road,
Stillorgan, Co Dublin
Tel 01-2889963 Fax 01-2889536
Superior: Sr Mary Corr
Email secretary@straphaelasns.ie
Community: 8
Primary School. Tel 01-2886878
Secondary School. Tel 01-2888730
Students' residence. Tel 01-2887159
Fax 01-2889536

HOLY CHILD JESUS, SOCIETY OF THE
1 Stable Lane, Off Harcourt Street,
Dublin 2
Tel 01-4754053
Email stablelane@shcj.org
Community: 10

21 Grange Park Avenue, Raheny, Dublin 5
Tel 01-8488961
Email shcjdub@gofree.indigo.ie
Community: 2

Convent of the Holy Child Jesus,
Kilmuire, Military Road, Killiney,
Co Dublin
Tel 01-2823089
Email kilmuire@gofree.indigo.ie
Community: 4
Secondary School. Tel 01-2823120

Holy Child Community School,
Sallynoggin, Co Dublin
Tel 01-2855334

HOLY FAITH SISTERS
Generalate, Aylward House,
Glasnevin, Dublin 11
Tel 01-8371426 Fax 01-8377474
Email aylward@eircom.net
Superior General: Sr Margo Delaney

Regional Superior: Sr Evelyn Greene
68 Iona Road, Dublin 9
Tel 01-8301404 Fax 01-8303530
Email ionahfs@eircom.net

Main Street, Celbridge, Co Kildare
Tel 01-6288267
Community: 4
Ministries, Primary school

25 Clare Road, Drumcondra, Dublin 9
Tel 01-8373569
Community: 5
Social work, prayer ministry

183 Clontarf Road, Dublin 3
Tel 01-8336076
Community: 6
Holy Faith Secondary School
Tel 01-8332754
Principal: Ms Deirdre Gogarty
Parish ministry

Star of the Sea,
182 Clontarf Road, Dublin 3
Community: 5
Social work, faith development, prison
ministry

The Coombe, Dublin 8
Tel 01-4540244. Community: 13
Primary and Secondary Education, Parish
Centre, Pastoral, Miltown Institute, NUI
Maynooth, Counselling
St Brigid's Orphanage
Tel 01-4542917
Sister-in-Charge: Sr M. Benignus McDonagh
St Brigid's Primary School
Tel 01-4547734
Principal: Ms Deirdre Early
Home-school link; Parish Centre;
Counselling; Parish sister, Whitefriar
Street

11 Drumcairn Green, Fettercairn,
Tallaght, Dublin 24
Tel 01-4513951
Community: 1
Counselling, parish work

12 Finglaswood Road, Dublin 11
Tel 01-8641551
Community: 2
Counselling

13/14 Wellmount Parade, Dublin 11
Tel 01-8640874
Community: 4
Congregational house; prayer ministry,
justice work

St Michael's Secondary School
Tel 01-8341767
Principal: Mr John Barry
St Brigid's School
Senior School. Tel 01-8342416
Principal: Ms Martha Savage
Infant School. Tel 01-8342416
Principal: Mrs Carmel Lillis

Holy Faith Sisters,
144 Cappagh Road, Finglas, Dublin 11
Tel 01-8643205
Community: 1
Ministry to Travellers

Glasnevin, Dublin 11
Tel 01-8373427
Resident Co-ordinator: Sr Maura Keogh
Community: 36
St Mary's Secondary School Tel 01-8374413
Principal: Mrs Margaret Lennon
St Brigid's Primary School Tel 01-8376653
Principal: Mrs Evelyn O'Brien
Mother of Divine Grace Primary School
Tel 01-8344000
Principal: Ms Alice Bermingham
Pastoral ministries; social work;
secondary and primary education
Marian House Centre for Sick
Tel 01-8376165
Care Team: Sr Eileen Holton &
Sr Maureen Ferguson

Greystones, Co Wicklow
Tel 01-2874081
Community: 5
Prayer, parish ministry
St David's Co-educational Secondary
School Tel 01-2874800/2874802
Principal: Mary O'Doherty
St Brigid's Primary School. Tel 01-2876113
Principal: Sr Kathleen Lyng

Credo, 2 Fairways Grove,
Griffith Road, Dublin 11
Tel 01-8348015
Community: 2
St John's Education Centre,
Mater Dei lecturer

Regional House, 68 Iona Road, Dublin 9
Tel 01-8301404/8305668
Regional Leader: Sr Evelyn Greene
Community: 2
Regional administration

Kilcoole, Co Wicklow
Tel 01-2874229
Community: 5
Parish ministry, faith development,
Justice, Luisne Spirituality Centre
Primary Schools
Tel 01-2874649

St Brigid's Road, Killester, Dublin 5
Tel 01-8310009
Community: 7
Primary school, library work, pastoral
work

6 St Mary's Road, Dublin 4
Tel 01-6681124
Community: 7
Parish ministry, prayer ministry
St Brigid's Primary School
Tel 01-6681155
Principal: Ms Ann-Marie Hogan

18 Church Street, Skerries, Co Dublin
Tel 01-8491203
Community: 5
Pastoral work, Emmaus Retreat Centre

14 Main Road, Tallaght, Dublin 24
Tel 01-4515904
Community: 2
Spiritual direction, faith development,
retreat ministry

81 Naas Road, Dublin 12
Tel 01-4551142
Community: 2
Parish work and administration

11 Aylward Green, Finglas, Dublin 11
Tel 01-8646401
Community: 2
Parish work, club for people with disabilities

11 Johnstown Park, Ballygall Road East,
Dublin 11
Tel 01-864640
Commun ity: 5
Parish ministry; Chaplaincy to St
Wolstan's Community School

178-180 Clontarf Road, Dublin 3
Community: 9
Secondary education, Spiritual Direction,
pastoral, healing remedies, prayer
network, congregational website, art
therapy, social justice, St John's
Education Support Centre, Third-level
education

5 Dargan Court, Meath Road,
Bray, Co Wicklow
Counselling, pastoral

Joseph's Cottage, Kippure East,
Manor Kilbride, Co Wicklow
Tel 0404-4507
Conservation work, parish work

18 St Joseph's Square, Clontarf, Dublin 3
Art Therapy

105 Tyrconnel Park, Inchicore, Dublin 8
Pastoral work

HOLY FAMILY OF BORDEAUX SISTERS
11 Arran Road, Drumcondra, Dublin 9
Tel 01-8370922
Contact person: Sr Colette Keegan
Community: 3
Hospitality and pastoral work

Irishtown, Clane, Co Kildare
Tel 01-6288459
Contact person: The Superior
Community: 4
House for retired sisters; parish work

INFANT JESUS SISTERS
Provincial House, 56 St Lawrence Road,
Clontarf, Dublin 3
Tel 01-8338930 Fax 01-8530857
Provincial: Sr Rosemary Barter
Email rbarterijs@eircom.net
Tel 01-8339577
Community: 2

121 Tonlegee Road, Dublin 5
Tel 01-8472926
Community: 2
Pastoral ministry

140 Carrickhill Rise, Portmarnock,
Co Dublin
Tel 01-8461647
Community: 2
Pastoral ministry

211 Clontarf Road, Dublin 3
Tel 01-8331700
Community: 6
Pastoral ministry

16 Ard na Meala, Ballymun, Dublin 11
Tel 01-8426534
Pastoral ministry, youth ministry, social
work

2 Carrig Close, Poppintree,
Ballymun, Dublin 11

1 Eccles Court, Dublin 7
Tel 01-8309004
Pastoral ministry

JESUS AND MARY, CONGREGATION OF
Provincialate, 'Errew House',
110 Goatstown Road, Dublin 14
Tel 01-2993130
Provincial Superior: Sr Mary Mulrooney
Email mulrooney.mary@gmail.com
Local superior: Sr Pauline Caffrey
Community: 5

Our Lady's Grove Community,
110 Goatstown Road, Dublin 14
Community: 7
Convent. Tel 01-2966104
Primary School. Pupils: 383
Secondary School. Pupils: 377

Home Farm Community, 'Errew House',
110 Goatstown Road, Dublin 14
Tel 01-2993130
Superior: Sr Mary Langan
Community: 4

LA RETRAITE SISTERS
77 Grove Park, Rathmines, Dublin 6
Tel 01-4911771
Contact: Sr Barbara Stafford
Email barbarastaffordlr@eircom.net
Community: 3

LA SAGESSE (DAUGHTERS OF WISDOM)
20 Grace Park Meadows,
Drumcondra, Dublin 9
Tel 01-8316508
Community: 2

LA SAINTE UNION DES SACRES COEURS
Teallach Mhuire, 41 Broadway Road,
Blanchardstown, Dublin 15
Tel 01-8214459
Community: 4
Pastoral work, student counsellor, group
facilitation consultation

9 Tandy's Hill, Lucan, Co Dublin
Tel 01-6218863
Contact: Sr Rosemarie Madden
Parish work

126 Malahide Road, Clontarf, Dublin 3
Tel 01-8332778
Community: 3
Pastoral work, literacy

14 Glenshane Grove,
Brookfield, Tallaght, Dublin 24
Tel 01-4527684
Community: 2
Teaching, pastoral work, travellers,
counselling

LITTLE COMPANY OF MARY
Provincialate, Cnoc Mhuire,
29 Woodpark, Ballinteer Avenue,
Dublin 16
Tel 01-2987040 Fax 01-2961936
Province Leader: Sr Celine Bourke

40 Braemor Park, Churchtown, Dublin 14
Tel 01-4904755/4904692/4904794/
4904795
Community: 22

14 Heather Lawn,
Marlay Wood, Dublin 16
Tel 01-4942324
Apostolic Community: 1
Province Resource Centre

16 Heather Lawn,
Marlay Wood, Dublin 16
Tel 01-4947205
Apostolic Community: 1

Little Company of Mary,
81 Mountain View Park,
Churchtown, Dublin 14
Tel 01-2986854
Apostolic Community: 1

Little Company of Mary,
12 The Avenue, Grange Manor,
Lucan, Co Dublin
Tel 01-6109360
Apostolic Community: 1

Little Company of Mary
2 Esker Wood Grove, Lucan, Co Dublin
Tel 01-6210474
Apostolic Community: 1

Little Company of Mary,
64 Templeroan Avenue, Knocklyon,
Dublin 16
Tel 01-4957130
Apostolic Community: 1

Little Company of Mary, 45 Priory Way,
Kimmage, Dublin 12
Tel 01-4907763
Community: 1

Little Company of Mary,
62 West Priory, Navan Road, Dublin 7
Tel 01-8386325
Community: 1

LITTLE SISTERS OF THE ASSUMPTION
Provincial House, 42 Rathfarnham Road,
Terenure, Dublin 6W
Tel 01-4909850 Fax 01-4925740
Email pernet42@eircom.net
Provincial: Sr Mary Keenan
Sisters work in nursing, social work and
family care, and with local community
development groups

12 Convent Lawns, Ballyfermot,
Dublin 10
Tel 01-6230898

155 Swords Road, Whitehall, Dublin 9
Tel 01-8374894
Email lsas.155@gmail.com

11 The Covert, Woodfarm Acres,
Palmerstown, Dublin 20
Tel 01-6268556
Email littlesisters@eircom.net

8 Owendore Crescent,
Rathfarnham, Dublin 14
Tel 01-4931147

Patrickswell Place, Finglas, Dublin 11
Tel 01-8342592
Email fagefinglas@yahoo.co.uk

Mount Argus, Assumption Convent,
Mount Argus Road, Dublin 6W
Tel 01-4977038

4 Oakdale, Oakton Park,
Ballybrack, Co Dublin
Tel 01-2821143

5-6 Grange Crescent, (off Pottery Road),
Dun Laoghaire, Co Dublin
Tel 01-2853961

41 Liscarne Court, Rowlagh,
Clondalkin, Dublin 22
Tel 01-6263077
Email lsarow@gofree.indigo.ie

14 Forestwood Avenue, Santry Avenue,
Dublin 9
Tel 01-8428016
Email lsacomm@oceanfree.net

LITTLE SISTERS OF THE POOR
Sacred Heart Residence,
Sybil Hill Road, Raheny, Dublin 5
Tel 01-8332308
Provincial: Sr Christine Devlin
Superior: Sr Monica
Email msraheny@eircom.net
Community: 25
Nursing home for the elderly

Holy Family Residence,
Roebuck Road, Dublin 14
Tel 01-2832455
Superior: Sr Bridget
Community: 20
Nursing home for the elderly

St Brigid's Novitiate,
Roebuck Road, Dublin 14
Tel 01-2832536

LORETO (IBVM)
Provincialate, Loreto House,
Beaufort, Dublin 14
Tel 01-4933827
Email lorprovbeaufort@eircom.net
Provincial: Sr Teresa MacPaul
Community: 2

Loreto Abbey House, Loreto Terrace,
Grange Road, Rathfarnham, Dublin 14
Tel 01-4932807
Superior: Sr Marie Carr
Community: 32
Primary School, Secondary Day School,
pastoral work

Loreto College and Junior School,
53 St Stephen's Green, Dublin 2
Tel 01-6618179/6618181

Loreto Community,
Nos 3, 6, 9 Fort Ostman,
Old County Road, Crumlin, Dublin 12
Community: 3
Superior: Sr Mary O'Dwyer
Loreto Secondary School. Tel 01-4542380
Senior Primary School. Tel 01-4541669
Junior Primary School. Tel 01-4541746
Loreto Centre Apartments, Crumlin Road
Tel 01-4541078
Email loretoc@gofree.indigo.ie
Community: 7
Personal and community development

Loreto Community,
Bray, Co Wicklow
Tel 01-2862021
Email loretoconventbray@eircom.net
Superior: Sr Miriam Doran
Community: 12
Primary and secondary schools;
pastoral work

Nos 29/30 The Courtyard
Vevay Crescent
Superior: Sr Josephine Keegan
Community: 4

Loreto Abbey, Dalkey, Co Dublin
Tel 01-2804331/2804416
Email lorcomdalkey@eircom.net
Superior: Sr Kathleen Fitzgerald
Community: 9
Primary and secondary schools;
pastoral work

Teach Muire, Leslie Avenue,
Dalkey, Co Dublin
Tel 01-2800495
Email lorlesliedalkey@eircom.net
Superior: Sr Kathleen Fitzgerald
Community: 5
Educational and pastoral work

Loreto Community,
Balbriggan, Co Dublin
Tel 01-8412796
Superior: Sr Cora Grimes
Community: 21
Secondary school; pastoral work

Loreto Education Trust,
Foxrock, Dublin 18
Tel 01-2899956
Education and offices

Loreto Hall, 77 St Stephen's Green,
Dublin 2
Tel 01-4781816
Superior: Sr Eileen Cullen
Community: 15
Pastoral work

Loreto, 13 Carrigmore Place, City West,
Saggart, Co Dublin
Tel/Fax 01-4589918
Also, 15 Carrigmore Place, City West,
Saggart, Co Dublin
Tel 01-4580780

Loreto, 22 Brookdale Drive,
River Valley, Swords, Co Dublin
Superior: Sr Josephine Keegan
Community: 5
Tel 01-8405982
Secondary School, River Valley, Swords
Social and pastoral work

Loreto, 5 Greenville Road, Blackrock,
Co Dublin
Tel 01-2843171
Superior: Sr Josephine Keegan
Community: 4
Education, social and pastoral work

Loreto, 20 Herberton Park,
Rialto, Dublin 8
Tel 01-4535048
Email lorialto@hotmail.com
Superior: Sr Mary O'Dwyer
Community: 3
Social and pastoral work

265 Sundrive Road, Dublin 12
Tel 01-4541509
Superior: Sr Mary O'Dwyer
Community: 4
Education and pastoral work

7/8/9/10 Stonepark Orchard,
Stonepark Abbey
Tel 01-4952110/4952111/4951444/4950155
Community: 10
Education and pastoral work

175, 176, 178, 184, 185 Prior's Gate,
Greenhills Road, Tallaght, Dublin 24

9, 11, 50, 52 New Bancrost Hall,
Tallaght Main Street, Dubin 24

64, 66, 68 Griffith Hall,
Glandore Road, Dublin 9

MARIE AUXILIATRICE SISTERS
7 Florence Street, Portobello, Dublin 8
Tel 01-4537622
Contact Person: Sr Máire Nally
Community: 4
Spiritual direction, social outreach,
education

Marie Auxiliatrice Sisters
130 Upper Glenageary Road,
Dun Laoghaire, Co Dublin
Tel 01-2857389
Contact Person: Sr Eileen Cartin
Email eileencartin@marieaux.org
Community: 4
Spiritual direction, social outreach,
counselling, prison ministry

MARIE REPARATRICE SISTERS
Regional House, 29 Brackenstown
Village, Swords,Co Dublin
Tel 01-8406321
Email smrbtown@eircom.net
Regional Superior: Sr Eileen Carroll
Community: 4
Hospital chaplaincy, spiritual direction/
retreats, house of welcome to parish
groups

9 St Andrew's Grove, Malahide,
Co Dublin
Tel 01-8455113
Email smrmal@eircom.net
Superior: Sr Elizabeth Dunne
Community: 3
Parish ministry, spiritual direction/
retreats

MARIST SISTERS
Provincialate, 51 Kenilworth Square,
Rathgar, Dublin 6
Tel 01-4972196
Leader – Ireland: Sr Brigid M. McGuinness
Community: 3

10 Cambridge Terrace,
Dartmouth Square, Dublin 6
Tel 01-6605332
Community: 4
Justice, education

Sundrive Road, Crumlin, Dublin 12
Tel 01-4540778
Superior: Sr Georgina Cawley
Community: 17
Primary school
Social work, youth work, health care,
adult education, Marist laity

185 Killarney Park, Bray, Co Wicklow
Tel 01-2863396
Community: 4
Education, social work, parish ministry,
retreat work

27 Grange Park Grove, Raheny, Dublin 5
Tel 01-8480232
Superior: Sr Maria Gratia Gormley
Community: 5
Education, chaplaincy

MEDICAL MISSIONARIES OF MARY
Congregational Centre,
Rosemount, Rosemount Terrace,
Booterstown, Co Dublin
Tel 01-2882722 Fax 01-2834626
Email rcsmmm@eircom.net

MMM Communications Department,
Rosemount Terrace, Booterstown,
Co Dublin
Tel 01-2887180/087-9701891
Fax 01-2834626
Email mmm@iol.ie

Réalt na Mara, 11 Rosemount Terrace,
Booterstown, Co Dublin
Tel 01-2832247
Email mmmrealtnamara@eircom.net
Community: 6

26 Malahide Road, Artane, Dublin 5
Tel 01-8310427
Email mmmartane@eircom.net
Community: 8

52 St Agnes Road, Crumlin, Dublin 12
Tel 01-4552692
Email mmmcrumlin@eircom.net
Community: 4

33 Templeville Drive
Templeogue, Dublin 6W
Tel 01-4991803
Email mmm.templeogue@iol.ie
Contact Person: Sr Doreen McEvoy
Community: 3

177 Philipsburgh Avenue,
Marino, Dublin 3
Tel 01-8376336
Email mmmmarino@eircom.net
Community: 3

1 The Grange, Laurel Place,
Terenure Road West, Dublin 6W
Tel 01-4925263
Email mmmtv@gofree.indigo.ie
Community: 6

The Lodge, 1A School Avenue,
Killester, Dublin 5
Tel 01-8187552
Email mmmkillester@gmail.com

Hillview, St Margaret's Avenue,
Raheny, Dubin 5
Tel 01-8324221
Email mmmraheny@eircom.net

MISSIONARY FRANCISCAN SISTERS OF THE IMMACULATE CONCEPTION
Assisi House, Navan Road, Dublin 7
Tel 01-8682216
Community: 3
Contact: Sr Philomena Conroy

MISSIONARY SISTERS OF THE HOLY ROSARY
Generalate, 23 Cross Avenue,
Blackrock, Co Dublin
Tel 01-2881708/9 Fax 01-2836308
Email mshrgen@indigo.ie
Superior General: Sr Maureen O'Malley
Community: 7

Regional House, Drumullac,
42 Westpark, Artane, Dublin 5
Tel 01-8510010 Fax 01-8187494
Email mshrreg@eircom.net
Regional Superior: Sr Conchita McDonnell
Community: 3

Holy Rosary Convent, Brookville,
Westpark, Artane, Dublin 5
Tel 01-8480603/8481216
Superior: Sr Leonie Horgan
House for sisters on leave from mission.
Pastoral, health care
Community: 4

Holy Rosary Convent, 48 Temple Road,
Dartry, Dublin 6
Tel 01-4971918/4971094
Superior: Sr Mary Neville
Pastoral, education, care of the elderly
Community: 38

Holy Rosary Sisters, Glankeen,
9 Richmond Avenue South, Dartry,
Dublin 6
Tel 01-4977277
Pastoral, health care, care of elderly
Community: 9

Holy Rosary Sisters (Community)
11 Dalymount, Phibsboro, Dublin 7
Tel 01-8680381
Pastoral, educational, health care
Community: 7

Holy Rosary Sisters, 2 Grange Abbey
Cresent, Baldoyle Dublin 13
Tel 01-8476219
Pastoral, health care, education
Community: 4

Holy Rosary Sisters, 72 Grange Park,
Baldoyle, Dublin 13
Tel 01-8390291
Regional administration, counselling
Community: 3

Holy Rosary Sisters,
140 Brookwood Avenue, Artane, Dublin 5
Tel 01-8187672
Community: 4

Holy Rosary Sisters, Greenfields,
Greenfield Road, Sutton, Dublin 13
Tel 01-8392005/8392070 Fax 01-8392025
Superior: Sr Angela Morgan
Regional administration, pastoral
Community: 19

Holy Rosary Sisters, The Hermitage,
Roebuck Road, Dublin 14
Community: 4

Holy Rosary Sisters, 'Greenacres',
Upper Kilmacud Road, Dublin 14
Superior: Sr Brenda Kelly
Community: 11

Holy Rosary Sisters,
25/26 Rathfarnham Wood,
Rathfarnham, Dublin 14
Community: 6

MISSIONARY SISTERS OF OUR LADY OF APOSTLES
70b Shellbourne Road,
Ballsbridge, Dublin 4
Tel 01-6685796
Email olasrsdub@eircom.net
No. of sisters: 5
House of studies

MISSIONARY SISTERS OF ST COLUMBAN
St Columban's Convent,
Magheramore, Wicklow
Tel 0404-67348 Fax 0404-67002
Email colsrsww@eircom.net
Community Leader: Sr Ita McElwain
Community: 44
Motherhouse, congregational nursing
home for sick and retired members

22 Woodview, Ashford, Co Wicklow
Tel 0404-49101
Community: 2
Parish ministry

St Agnes Road, Crumlin, Dublin 12
Tel 01-4555435
Community: 9
Mission awareness

85 Eglinton Road, Donnybrook, Dublin 4
Tel 01-2695936
Community: 7
House of studies

Apt C14, Killarney Street, Dublin 1
Tel 01-6577339
Community: 2
Parish ministry, work with migrants

2 Seskin View Park, Tallaght, Dublin 24
Tel 01-4940392
Community: 3
Hospital ministry and Parish ministry

Columban Sisters,
Parish House No. 1, Holy Spirit Parish,
Silloge, Ballymun, Dublin 11
Tel 01-8423696

Contact Person for above six houses
Sr Patricia McGuinness
85 Eglinton Road, Donnybrook, Dublin 4

MISSIONARY SISTERS OF ST PETER CLAVER
Our Lady of the Angels
81 Bushy Park Road/PO Box 228,
Terenure, Dublin 6
Tel 01-4909360 Fax 01-4920918
Superior: Sr Sr Lucyna Wisniowska
Email claver4@hotmail.com
Community: 4
Assist needy missions, especially those in
Africa

MISSIONARY SISTERS SERVANTS OF THE HOLY SPIRIT
Regional House,
143 Philipsburgh Avenue,
Fairview, Dublin 3
Tel 01-8369383 Fax 01-8369912
Email sspsfairview@yahoo.com
Community Leader: Sr Carmen Lee
Comunity: 4

98 Foxfield Road,
Raheny, Dublin 5
Tel 01-8319011
Community Leader: Sr Renata Sistemich
Community: 2

NOTRE DAME DES MISSIONS
Upper Churchtown Road, Dublin 14
Tel 01-2983308
Email ntrdame@hotmail.com
Leader: Sr Carmel Looby
Email mlooby1@hotmail.com
Community: 23
Education and parish work

Sisters of Our Lady of the Missions
5 Griffeen Glen Park, Griffeen Valley,
Lucan South, Co Dublin
Tel 01-6219088
Shared Leadership
Community: 2
Education, pastoral work

OBLATES OF THE ASSUMPTION
1 Churchview Avenue, Johnstown,
Killiney, Co Dublin
Tel 01-2854572
Sister-in-Charge: Sr Monica
Liturgical, pastoral, educational and
social work; 'Communauté d'acceuil' for
young people

OUR LADY OF THE CENACLE
3 Churchview Drive,
Killiney, Co Dublin
Tel/Fax 01-2840175
Email cenacledublin@eircom.net
Contact: Cenacle Sisters
Community: 3
Retreats, spiritual direction, hospital
chaplain, facilitation days/ evenings of
prayer, pastoral work

OUR LADY OF CHARITY SISTERS
Regional House,
63 Lower Sean MacDermott Street,
Dublin 1
Tel 01-8711109 Fax 01-8366526
Residential hostel for women, varied
ministries

Beechlawn Complex, High Park,
Grace Park Road, Drumcondra, Dublin 9
Services to women, the elderly and
various ministries
Nursing Home Tel 01-8369622
House No. 3 (Community)
Tel 01-8368828

St Anne's, Kilmacud, Stillorgan, Co Dublin
Tel 01-2889843
Varied ministries

72 Clonshaugh Road, Dublin 17
Tel 01-8479088
Varied ministries

206 Grace Park Road, Dublin 9
Tel 01-8572677
Varied ministries

OUR LADY OF SION SISTERS
127 Griffith Avenue,
Drumcondra, Dublin 9
Tel 01-8573130 Fax 01-8573189
Website www.sistersofsion.org

POOR CLARES
St Damian's, Simmonscourt Road,
Ballsbridge, Dublin 4
Fax 01-6685464
Email pccdamians@mac.com
Website www.pccdamians.ie
Abbess/Contact: Sr M. Brigid
Community: 10
Contemplatives
Public exposition of the Blessed
Sacrament on Sundays 1.00-4.30 pm and
First Fridays 8.00 am-4.30 pm
Usually ending with Evening Prayer and
Benediction

POOR SERVANTS OF THE MOTHER OF GOD
St Mary's Convent, Manor House,
Raheny, Dublin 5
Tel/Fax 01-8317626

St Mary's Convent, Castledermot,
Athy, Co Kildare
Tel 059-9144152
Community: 3

St Mary's Convent, Manor House,
Raheny, Dublin 5
Tel 01-8313652 Fax 01-8313299
Community: 10
Education, pastoral work

Maryfield Convent, Chapelizod,
Dublin 20
Tel 01-6264684/6265402 Fax 01-6233673
Community: 10
Home for elderly

Teach Muire,
217 Tonlegee Road, Dublin 5
Tel 01-8470633
Community: 3
Pastoral ministry; Care of elderly

216 Tonlegee Road, Dublin 5
Tel 01-8478566
Community: 3
Care of the elderly, pastoral ministry

Ardeevin, 67 Lucan Road,
Chapelizod, Dublin 20
Tel 01-6267731
Community: 2
Work with elderly in Maryfield, pastoral

Providence, 2 Creighton Street, Dublin 2
Tel 01-6713130
Community: 2
Pastoral Ministry

Croí Mhuire, 120 Lucan Road,
Chapelizod, Dublin 20
Fax/Tel 01-6233734
Community: 3
Elderly and pastoral work

St Gabriel's Home, Glenayle Road,
Cameron Park, Dublin 5
Tel 01-8474339 Fax 01-8486610
Community: 4
Home for elderly and community care
service

39 Glenayle Road, Dublin 5
Tel 01-8770700
Community: 4
Pastoral Ministry

CONGREGATION OF THE SISTERS OF NAZARETH
Nazareth House,
Malahide Road, Dublin 3
Tel 01-8338205 Fax 01-8330813
Email nazarethdublin@eircom.net
Superior: Sr Hannah O'Connor
Community: 15
Regional Superior: Sr Cataldus Courtney
Tel 01-8332024 Fax 01-8334988
Home for elderly. Beds: 85

PRESENTATION SISTERS
Lucan, Co Dublin
Tel 01-6280305
Home for missionaries on home leave
Mission Office
Tel/Fax 01-6282467
Contact: Sr Regina Campbell
Email pbvmmo@gofree.indigo.ie

69 Fortlawn Drive, Mountview,
Blanchardstown, Dublin 15
Tel 01-8119430
Contact: Sr Mary Byrne
Interprovincial Community: 3
School and pastoral work

Northern Province:
George's Hill, Dublin 7
Tel 01-8746914
Community: 8
Presentation Convent Primary School
Tel/Fax 01-8733061
Email presghill@eircom.net
School and pastoral ministry

2/3 Castlebridge Estate,
Maynooth, Co Kildare
Tel 01-6289952
Community Leader: Sr Eithne Cunniffe
Community: 7
Schoi Mhuire Primary School
Tel 01-6280056 Fax 01-6282611
School and pastoral ministry

South-East Province:
Provincialate, 27 Wainsfort Drive,
Terenure, Dublin 6W
Tel 01-4929588 Fax 01-4929590
Email presse@iol.ie
Provincial: Sr Frances Murphy
Community: 3

Presentation Convent of the Immaculate
Conception, Clondalkin, Dublin 22
Tel 01-4592656
Local Leader: Sr Concepta O'Brien
Community: 17
Scoil Mhuire Primary School,
Convent Road, Clondalkin, Dublin 22
Tel 01-4592986
Scoil Ide Primary School,
New Road, Clondalkin, Dublin 22
Tel 01-4592973
Scoil Aine Primary School
Tel 01-4591645
Coláiste Bríde Secondary School,
New Road, Clondalkin, Dublin 22
Tel 01-4592900

Presentation Convent,
Warrenmount, Dublin 8
Tel 01-4543358
Local Leader: Sr Teresa Ryan
Community: 15
Primary. Tel 01-8788852
Post Primary. Tel 01-4547520
Community and Adult Education Centre
Tel 01-4542622

7B Oliver Bond House, Dublin 8
Tel 01-6776702
Contact Person: Sr Brigid Phelan
Community: 2

17A South Earl Street, Dublin 8
Contact: Sr Clare O'Dwyer
Tel 01-4532239
Community: 3

41 O'Curry Road, Dublin 8
Tel 01-4542806
Contact: Sr Carmel Daly
Community: 3

335 Dolphin House,
Dolphin's Barn, Dublin 8
Contact: Sr Mary Flynn
Tel 01-4540499
Community: 2

5 Foxdene Green, Balgaddy,
Lucan, Co Dublin
Tel 01-4574533
Community: 3

2 The Weavers, Meath Place, Dublin 8
Contact: Sr Bernadette Flanagan
Community: 1

62 Mayfield Park, Watery Lane, Dublin 22
Tel 01-4037316
Contact: Sr Kathleen Barrett
Community: 1

Block G, 176 The Tramyard,
Spa Road, Inchicore, Dublin 8
Contact: Sr Bernadette Purcell
Community: 1

13 Temple Hill,
Terenure Road West, Dublin 6
Tel 01-4067706
Contact: Sr Una Trant
Community: 1

REDEMPTORISTINES
Monastery of St Alphonsus,
St Alphonsus Road, Dublin 9
Tel 01-8305723 Fax 01-8309129
Superior: Sr Gabrielle
Email gabrielle.fox@redemptorists.ie
Community: 14
Contemplatives

RELIGIOUS OF CHRISTIAN EDUCATION
Provincial Office, 3 Bushy Park House,
Templeogue Road, Dublin 6W
Tel 01-4901668 Fax 01-4901101
Provincial leader: Sr Rosemary O'Looney

Community Residence,
4/5 Bushy Park House,
Templeogue Road, Dublin 6W
Tel 01-4905516
Superior: Sr Rosemary Looney

13 Oriel Street Lower, Dublin 1
Tel 087-6359057
Counselling

Our Lady's School,
Templeogue Road, Dublin 6W
Secondary School. Tel 01-4903241
Principal: Ms Gráinne Friel

RELIGIOUS OF SACRED HEART OF MARY
Cormaria, 7 Bancroft Road,
Tallaght, Dublin 24
Tel 01-4515674
Community: 5
Ministry in local area

13/14 Huntstown Wood,
Mulhuddart, Dublin 15
Tel 01-8214888
Community: 4
Pastoral ministry, addiction, HIV
counselling

70 Upper Drumcondra Road,
Dublin 9
Tel 01-8379898
Community: 4
Education, pastoral

72 Upper Drumcondra Road,
Dublin 9
Tel 01-8368331
Community: 4
Spiritual direction, ministry in local area

RELIGIOUS SISTERS OF CHARITY
Generalate, Caritas, 15 Gilford Road,
Sandymount, Dublin 4
Tel 01-2697833/2697935

Provincialate, Provincial House,
Our Lady's Mount, Harold's Cross,
Dublin 6W
Tel 01-4973177

Marmion House, St Mary's,
185 Merrion Road, Dublin 4
Tel 01-2027223
Various Apostolic Ministries

Overseas Office, Naomh Bríd,
28/38 Belvedere Place, Dublin 1
Tel/Fax 01-8553206

St Anne's, 29 Thornville Drive,
Kilbarrack East, Dublin 5
Tel 01-8321112/8321114
Various Apostolic Ministries

St Mary's, Stanhope Street, Dublin 7
Tel 01-6779183
Various Apostolic Ministries

Stanhope Lodge,
Stanhope Green, Dublin 7
Tel 01-6704016
Various Apostolic Ministries

Sisters of Charity, 30 Clonard Road,
Dundrum, Dublin 16
Tel 01-2955251
Various Apostolic Ministries

Convent of the Assumption,
76 Upper Gardiner Street, Dublin 1
Tel 01-8746431
Various Apostolic Ministries

Sisters of Charity, 3C Liberty House,
Railway Street, Dublin 1
Tel 01-8364269
Various Apostolic Ministries

St Monica's, Belvedere Place, Dublin 1
Tel (Community) 01-8552317
Various Apostolic Ministries

Naomh Bríd Community,
28/38 Belvedere Place, Dublin 1
Tel 01-8557647
Various Apostolic Ministries

Our Lady of the Nativity, Lakelands,
Sandymount, Dublin 4
Tel 01-2692076/2603362
Various Apostolic Ministries

St Mary's, Donnybrook, Dublin 4
Tel 01-2600315/2600818
Various Apostolic Ministries

Mary Aikenhead House, St Mary's,
Donnybrook, Dublin 4
Tel 01-2693258
Various Apostolic Ministries

Sisters of Charity, Our Lady's Mount,
Harold's Cross, Dublin 6W
Ard Mhuire Community
Tel 01-4961488
Maranatha Community
Tel 01-4961423
St Michael's Community
Tel 01-4972158
Shandon community
Tel 01-4982614
Various Apostolic Ministries

4 Telford House, St Mary's,
Merrion Road, Dublin 4
Tel 01-2605495
Various Apostolic Ministries

Stella Maris Convent, Baily, Co Dublin
Tel 01-8322228 Fax 01-8063469
Various Apostolic Ministries

St Joseph's, 11 Dublin Road,
Bray, Co Wicklow
Tel 01-2820599
Various Apostolic Ministries

St Agnes' Convent, Armagh Road,
Crumlin, Dublin 12
Tel 01-4555591
Various Apostolic Ministries

Our Lady Queen of Ireland,
Walkinstown, Dublin 12
Tel 01-4503491
Various Apostolic Ministries

Sisters of Charity,
Seville Place, Dublin 1
Tel 01-8744179
Various Apostolic Ministries

Sisters of Charity, 95/97 Richmond Road,
Fairview, Dublin 3
Tel 01-8376874
Various Apostolic Ministries

Sisters of Charity,
1 Temple Street, Dublin 1
Tel 01-8745778/8745779

Presbytery 2, Dunmanus Road,
Cabra West, Dublin 7
Tel 01-8687231
Various Apostolic Ministries

26 Park Avenue, Sandymount, Dublin 4
Tel 01-2604659
Various Apostolic Ministries

28 Park Avenue, Sandymount, Dublin 4
Tel 01-2604654
Various Apostolic Ministries

Providence,
St Mary's, Merrion Road, Dublin 4
Tel 01-2693450
Various Apostolic Ministries

Shalom
St Mary's, Merrion Road, Dublin 4
Tel 01-2602775
Various Apostolic Ministries

386 Clogher Road, Crumlin, Dublin 12
Tel 01-4169016/4169622
Various Apostolic Ministries

ROSMINIANS (SISTERS OF PROVIDENCE)
104a Griffith Court, Fairview, Dublin 3
Tel 01-8375021
Email teresamolloy@eircom.net
Contact Person: Sr Teresa Molloy
Community: 2

SACRED HEART SOCIETY
76 Home Farm Road,
Drumcondra, Dublin 9
Tel 01-8375412 Fax 01-8375542
Email rscj@eircom.net
Provincial Superior: Sr Aideen Kinlen
Email aideenkinlen@eircom.net

6 Achill Road, Drumcondra, Dublin 9
Tel 01-8360866 Fax 01-8360112
Email 6achill@eircom.net
Community: 4. Administration;
Adult education and pastoral work;
youth and pastoral ministry.

Linked with Achill Road:
49 Philipsburgh Terrace, Marino, Dublin 3
Tel 01-8554018
Email lawlesse@hotmail.com

9 Clonshaugh Drive, Priorswood, Dublin 17
Tel 01-8474244 Fax 01-8488940
Email tdeasy@eircom.net
Community: 3
Parish work

10 Walnut Rise, Dublin 9
Fax 01-8844547
Email laughlinc@eircom.net
Community: 3
Literacy tutor to immigrants; pastoral
ministry

7 Merrion View Avenue, Dublin 4
Tel 01-2602533
Email dairne@eircom.net
almcs@eircom.net
Community: 3
Facilitation; English teaching; refugees
and asylum seekers; Religious Formation
Ministry Programme

Linked with Merrion View Avenue:
5 Redcourt Oaks, Seafield Road East,
Clontarf, Dublin 3
Engaged in Educational Trusteeships and
voluntary work

23 Castlelands Grove, Dalkey, Co Dublin
Historical research; part-time university
teaching

Sacred Heart Schools Network Ltd
Mount Anville Day Secondary
School 658 pupils. Tel 01-2885313/4
Mount Anville Junior and Montessori
School 468 pupils. Tel 01-2885313/4
Mount Anville Primary School,
Lower Kilmacud Road,
Stillorgan, Co Dublin
Pupils: 414
Tel 01-2831148 Fax 01-2836395

Cedar House, Provincial Infirmary,
35 Mount Anville Park, Dublin 14
Tel 01-2831024/5 Fax 01-2831348
Superior: Sr Eleanor Dorgan
Email emdorgan@eircom.net
Community: 21

36 Mount Anville Park, Dublin 14
Tel 01-2880739 Fax 01-2104826
Community: 3
Work in Ceder House

37/38 Mount Anville Park,
Dublin 14
Tel 01-2880708 Fax 01-2780673
Community: 6
Work in Mount Anville and parish;
translation

96 Mount Anville Wood,
Lower Kilmacud Road, Dublin 14
Tel 01-2880786 Fax 01-2789119
Email sshdublin@eircom.net
Community: 6
Work in Mount Anville and othe schools;
administration' spiritual ministry; prison
chaplaincy; research

201 Lower Kilmacud Road,
Stillorgan, Co Dublin
Tel 01-2834832 Fax 01-2104825
Community: 3
Work in Mount Anville, Cedar House and
parish

107 Beechwood Lawn, Rochestown
Avenue, Dun Laoghaire, Co Dublin
Tel 01-2354933
Community: 2
Email silemac@eircom.net
Pastoral Ministry

67 Clonard Park,
Sandyford, Dubin 16
Tel 01-2999989
Email rbk@eircom.net
Pastoral ministry

5 South Hill Avenue,
Blackrock, Co Dublin
Tel 01-2789308
Email dairne@eircom.net
almcs@eircom.net
Community: 2
Facilitation work and adult education

SACRED HEARTS OF JESUS AND MARY (PICPUS) SISTERS
Sector House, 11 Northbrook Road,
Ranelagh, Dublin 6
Tel 01-4910173 Fax 01-4965551
Community: 5
Contact: Mary McCloskey (SSCC)
Tel 01-4974831 (Community)

Aymer House, 11 Northbrook Lane,
Ranelagh, Dublin 6
Tel 01-4975614
Community: 2

SALESIAN SISTERS OF ST JOHN BOSCO
Provincialate, 203 Lower Kilmacud Road,
Stillorgan, Co Dublin
Tel 01-2985188 Fax 01-2951572
Provincial Superior: Sr Nora Ryan
Convent Tel 01-2985908
Superior: Sr Moira O'Sullivan
Community: 7
Parish ministry, provincial administration

38-40 Morehampton Road,
Donnybrook, Dublin 4
Tel 01-6684643
Community: 7
Mission promotion, hospital ministry,
working in resource centre, art therapy

91-95 Ashwood Road, Bawnoge,
Clondalkin, Dublin 22
Tel 01-4571792
Superior: Sr Mary McCormack
Community: 6
Teaching and related activities

36 Glenties Park, Finglas South, Dublin 11
Tel 01-8345777
Community: 4
Social and parish work, co-ordinator of
Youth Reach

28 Hazelwood Crescent, Greenpark,
Clondalkin, Dublin 22
Tel 01-4123928
Community: 4
Teaching and related activities, parish
work

SISTERS OF ST CLARE
St Clare's Convent, 63 Harold's Cross,
Dublin 6W
Contact: Sr Carmela Farrelly
Community: 11
Primary School

ST JOHN OF GOD SISTERS
34 Dornden Park, Booterstown, Co Dublin
Tel 01-2698898
Community: 4
Community Project residence

39 St David's Wood, Malahide Road,
Artane, Dublin 5
Community: 2

SISTERS OF ST JOSEPH OF CHAMBERY
St Joseph's Convent,
Springdale Road, Raheny, Dublin 5
Tel 01-8478351 Fax 01-8485764
Superior: Sr Mary Peter Raleigh
Email mpraleigh@eircom.net
Community: 5
Care of the sick and pastoral activity

St Joseph's Convent, 5 Kincora Grove,
Clontarf, Dublin 3
Tel 01-8337866
Regional Superior: Sr Eileen Silke
Email esilke10@eircom.net
Tel 01-8337866
Community: 4

SISTERS OF ST JOSEPH OF CLUNY
Mount Sackville Convent,
Chapelizod, Dublin 20
Tel 01-8213134
Email clunyprov@sjc.ie
Website www.sjc.ie
Provincial Superior: Sr Maeve Guinan
Tel 01-8213134
Superior: Sr Louis Marie O'Connor
Tel 01-8213134
Community: 42
Primary school; secondary day school;
nursing home

St Joseph of Cluny Convent,
Ballinclea Road, Killiney, Co Dublin
Tel 01-2851038
Superior: Sr Clare Little
Community: 14
Junior and secondary schools

Cluny House, 1 Beechwood Park,
Rathmines, Dublin 6
Tel 01-4971641
Superior: Sr Peggy McLoughlin
Community: 4

Parslickstown Drive,
Mulhuddart, Dublin 15
Tel 01-8217339
Superior: Sr Ignatius Davis
Community: 4
Education and pastoral ministry

SISTERS OF ST JOSEPH OF LYON
8-10 Kilbarrack Road,
Sutton, Dublin 5
Tel 01-8325896
Email sistersofjoseph@oceanfree.net
Contact Person: Sr Marcelle
Community: 4

ST JOSEPH OF PEACE SISTERS
Peace House, 43 Kenilworth Park,
Harold's Cross, Dublin 6
Tel 01-4922011
Nursing; Care of the homeless;
Promotion of peace through prayer and
action

ST JOSEPH OF THE SACRED HEART SISTERS
St Joseph's Convent, 6 Farmleigh Avenue,
Stillorgan, Co Dublin
Tel 01-2781228 Fax 01-2782139

Sisters of St Joseph of the Sacred Heart,
25 Nutley Square, Donnybrook, Dublin 4
Tel 01-2602306

Sisters of St Joseph of the Sacred Heart,
27 Castlerosse View, Baldoyle, Dublin
Tel 01-8324508

Sisters of St Joseph, 11 The Courtyard,
Vevay Crescent, Bray, Co Wicklow
Tel 01-2761288

Sisters of St Joseph, 48 Seatown Villas,
Swords, Co Dublin
Tel 01-8907345

ST LOUIS SISTERS
St Louis Generalate, 3 Beech Court,
Ballinclea Road, Killiney, Dublin
Tel 01-2350304/2350309 Fax 01-2350345
Institute Leader: Sr Donna Hansen

St Louis Convent,
Charleville Road, Dublin 6
Tel 01-4975467
Community: 30
St Louis High School, Rathmines
Tel 01-4975458. Pupils: 750
St Louis Primary School, Rathmines
Tel 01-4976098. Pupils: 400
St Louis Infant School, Rathmines
Tel 01-4972188. Pupils: 300

Blakestown Road,
Mulhuddart, Dublin 15
Tel 01-8217432
Community: 7
Varied apostolates

7 Grosvenor Road, Rathgar, Dublin 6
Tel 01-4965485
Community: 7
Varied apostolates

8 Grosvenor Road, Rathgar, Dublin 6
Tel 01-4966631
Community: 7
Varied apostolates

St Louis Mission House,
1 Grosvenor Road, Rathgar, Dublin 6
Tel 01-4960538
Community: 3

38 Bushy Park Road, Terenure, Dublin 6
Tel 01-4900043
Community: 3
Varied apostolates

130 Beaufort Downs,
Rathfarnham, Dublin 16
Tel 01-4934194
Community: 4
Varied apostolates

17 Kilclare Crescent, Jobstown,
Tallaght, Dublin 24
Tel 01-4526344
Community: 1
Education

49 Moynihan Court,
Main Road, Tallaght Village, Dublin 24
Tel 01-4628386
Community: 6
Varied apostolates

37 Beresford Street, Dublin 7
Tel 01-8724093
Community: 1
Community work

ST MARY MADELEINE POSTEL SISTERS
35 Charlemont, Griffith
Avenue, Dublin 9
Regional Superior: Sr M. Luke Minogue
Tel 01-8373931
Community: 1

ST PAUL DE CHARTRES SISTERS
Queen of Peace Centre, Garville Avenue,
Rathgar, Dublin 6
Tel 01-4975381/4972366 Fax 01-4964084
Email spcqueen@eircom.net
Regional Superior
Sr Rose Margaret Nuval
Community: 6
Residences for the elderly

URSULINES
Generalate, 17 Trimleston Drive,
Booterstown, Co Dublin
Tel 01-2693503
Congregational Leader
Sr Kitty Kelly

Ursuline Sisters, 24 Shrewsbury Wood,
Cabinteely, Dublin 18
Tel 01-2853706
Email urscab@eircom.net
Community: 4

St Ursula's, Sandyford, Dublin 18
Tel 01-2956881
Contact Person: Sr Finbarr Muckley
Community: 4
Pastoral ministry

URSULINES OF JESUS
26 The Drive, Seatown Park,
Swords, Co Dublin
Tel 01-8404323
Email ujswords@eircom.net
Contact Person: Sr Mary McLoughney
Community: 3
Parish ministry, reflexology and
aromatherapy.

EDUCATIONAL INSTITUTIONS

Holy Cross College,
Clonliffe, Dublin 3
Tel 01-8375103/4 Fax 01-8371474

All Hallows College
Drumcondra, Dublin 9
Tel 01-8373745/8373746 Fax 01-8377642
President
Rev Mark Noonan (CM) BA, BD
(See Seminaries and Houses of Study
section)

Kimmage Mission Institute at Milltown
Milltown Institute, Dublin 6
Tel 01-2698388 Fax 01-4928506
Department Head
Rev Patrick Roe (CSSp)

Marino Institute of Education
Griffith Avenue, Dublin 9
Tel 01-8057700
Director: Mr Pat Diggins

Mater Dei Institute of Education
Clonliffe Road, Dublin 3
Tel 01-8376027/8/9 Fax 01-8370776
Email info@materdei.deu.ie
Website www.materdei.ie
President: Very Rev Dermot Lane
Director: Dr Andrew McGrady PhD

The Milltown Institute of Theology and Philosophy
Milltown Park, Dublin 6
Tel 01-2698388
President: Rev Brian Grogan (SJ)
(See Seminaries and Houses of Study section)

St Patrick's College
Drumcondra, Dublin 9
Tel 01-8376191
President: Dr Padraic Travers

St Patrick's College
Maynooth, Co Kildare
Tel 01-6285222 Fax 01-7083959
President: Rt Rev Mgr Hugh Connolly
(See Seminaries and Houses of Study section)

EDMUND RICE SCHOOLS TRUST
Ardscoil Chaoimhin,
Christian Brothers Secondary School,
Coolgreaney Road, Arklow, Co Wicklow
Tel 0402-32564/39176 Fax 0402-32565
Principal: Mr Peter Somers

St Brendan's College, Woodbrook, Bray,
Co Wicklow
Tel 01-2822317 (Principal)
Tel 01-2822800 (Staff) Fax 01-2822616
Email stbrendanscollege@hotmail.com
Principal: Mr John Taylor

Colaiste Eanna, Ballyroan, Dublin 16
Tel 01-4931767 Fax 01-4933489
Staff Tel 01-4932821
Email secretary@colaiste.enna.ie
Principal: Mr John O'Sullivan

Clonkeen College, Clonkeen Road,
Blackrock, Co Dublin
Tel 01-2892709/2892790 Fax 01-2898260
Email clonkeenrec@eircom.net
Principal: Mr Neil O'Toole

Edmund Rice Schools Trust
Meadow Vale, Clonkeen Road,
Blackrock, Co Dublin
Tel 01-2897511
CEO: Mr Gerry Bennett

Christian Brothers Primary School,
Armagh Road, Crumlin, Dublin 12
Tel 01-4562622 Fax 01-4550766
Email scoilcolm.ias@eircom.net
Principal: Mr B. Sheedy

Christian Brothers Primary School,
Drimnagh Castle, Walkinstown,
Dublin 12
Tel 01-4552066 (Principal)
Tel 01-4516049 (Staff)
Email drimnaghcastle.ias@eircom.net
Principal: Mr Eugene Duffy

Meánscoil Iognáid Rís, Drimnagh Castle,
Walkinstown, Dublin 12
Tel 01-4518316 (Principal)
Tel 01-4500805 (Staff) Fax 01-4505401
Email dch@eircom.met
Principal: Mr Ray Walsh

Scoil San Séamus,
Basin Lane, Dublin 8
Tel 01-4534321 Fax 01-4730382
Email jamesst@eircom.net
Principal: Mr Joe Tulie

Christian Brothers Secondary School,
James's Street, Dublin 8
Tel 01-4547756 Fax 01-4547856
Acting Principal: Mr William O'Brien
Email willieobrien@dublin.ie
Website www.jambo.com

Scoil Mhuire Primary School,
Oatlands, Mount Merrion, Co Dublin
Tel 01-2887108
Email oatlandsprimary@eircom.net
Principal: Ms Ber O'Sullivan

Oatlands College,
Mount Merrion, Co Dublin
Tel 01-2888533/2880662
Email oatlands@iol.ie
Principal: Mr Keith Ryan

Coláiste Eoin, Bóthar Stigh Lorgan,
Baile an Bhóthair, Carraig Dubh,
Co Atha Cliath
Tel 01-2884002/2884029 Fax 01-2836896
Email coleoin@iol.ie
Principal: Finian Martin

Coláiste Íosagáin, Stillorgan Road,
Booterstown, Co Dublin
Tel 01-2884028
Principal: Maedhbh Uí Chiagáin

Scoil Iosagáin, Aughavannagh Road,
Dublin 12
Tel 01-4541821 Fax 01-4169930
Principal: Mr Denis Costello

St Teresa's Primary School,
Donore Avenue, Dublin 8
Tel 01-4541899
Email scoiltreasa@hotmail.com
Principal: Ms Annmarie Spillane

Bunscoil Sancta Maria,
Synge Street, Dublin 8
Tel 01-4784316 Staff Tel 01-4781705
Fax 01-4784316
Email bscoilsynge.eircom.net
Website www.syngestreet.com
Acting Principal: Pádraig Ó Néill

St Paul's Secondary School,
Synge Street, Dublin 8
Tel 01-4783998 Staff Tel 01-4782327
Fax 01-4784154
Email syngestoffice@eircom.net
Website www.syngestreet.com
Principal: Mr Michael Minnock

Christian Brothers Primary School,
Francis Street, Dublin 8
Tel 01-4531800
Email francisstcbs.ias@eircom.net
Acting Principal: Ms Fiona Collins

Christian Brothers Secondary School,
Cumberland Street, Dublin 2
Tel 01-6614143 Fax 01-6763653
Email westlandcbs@eircom.net
Principal: Ms Kate Byrne

CBC Junior School, Monkstown Park, Dun
Laoghaire, Co Dublin
Tel 01-2805854 Fax 01-2805907
Email cbcadmin@indigo.ie
Principal: Mr D. Molloy

Christian Brothers College,
Monkstown Park, Dun Laoghaire,
Co Dublin
Tel 01-2805854/2809314 Fax 01-2805907
Email cbcadmin@indigo.ie
Principal: Dr Gerard Berry

Coláiste Phádraig, Ballydowd, Lucan,
Co Dublin
Tel 01-6282299 Fax 01-6282713
Email lucancbs@iol.ie
Principal: Mr Brian Murtagh

St David's Secondary School
Tel 01-8315322
Principal: Mr Padraic Kavanagh

Scoil Chiaráin Primary School,
Collins Avenue East, Dublin 5
Tel 01-8313072
Principal: Mr Martin Troy

St Fintan's High School,
Sutton, Dublin 13
Tel 01-8324632/8324595
Principal: Mr Ray Quinn

Pobal Scoil Neasain, Bayside,
Sutton, Dublin 13
Tel 01-8063092/8063093
Acting Principal: Mr Pat McKenna

St Kevin's College,
Ballygall Road East, Dublin 11
Tel 01-8371423/8375318
Principal: Mr Ciaran O'Hare

St Declan's Secondary School,
Nephin Road, Dublin 7
Tel 01-8381531
Principal: Ms Miriam Marsh

Gaelscoil Choláiste Mhuire,
4 Cearnóg Pharnell, Baile Átha Cliath 1
Tel 01-8729131
Príomhoide: An tUas S. Feiritéar

Coláiste Mhuire,
Bothar Ráth Tó, Baile Átha Cliath 7
Tel 01-8688996 Fax 01-8688998
Príomhoide: Tomás O'Mhurchú (Acting)

St Vincent's Primary School,
Glasnevin, Dublin 11
Tel 01-8302328
Principal: Mr Peter Molumby

St Vincent's Secondary School,
Glasnevin, Dublin 11
Tel 01-8304375/8304748
Principal: Mr John Horan (Acting)

Scoil Mhuire, Griffith Avenue, Dublin 9
Tel 01-8338294/8336421
Principal: Mr Ben Dorner

Scoil Iosef, Fairview, Dublin 3
Tel 01-8336127
Principal: An tUsal P. Ó Fainín

St Joseph's Secondary School,
Fairview, Dublin 3
Tel 01-8339779
Principal: Mr Brian O'Dwyer

Ard Scoil Ris, Griffith Avenue,
Marino, Dublin 9
Tel 01-8332633/8332172
Acting Principal: Mr Daithi O'Broin

St Paul's Primary School,
North Brunswick Street, Dublin 7
Tel 01-8722167
Principal: Mr Donal Ó Suibhne

St Paul's Secondary School,
North Brunswick Street, Dublin 7
Tel 01-8720781/8722472
Principal: Mr Michael Blanchfield

O'Connell Primary School,
North Richmond Street, Dublin 1
Tel 01-8557517
Principal: Mr Patsy O'Keeffe

O'Connell Secondary School,
North Richmond Street, Dublin 1
Tel 01-8748307
Principal: Mr Gerry Duffy

St Laurence O'Toole Primary School,
Seville Place, Dublin 1
Tel 01-8363490
Principal: Mr Mark Candon

Coláiste Choilm,
Swords, Co Dublin
Tel 01-8401420
Principal: Mr David Neville

St Aidan's Secondary School,
Collins Avenue West, Dublin 9
Tel 01-8377587/8379869
Principal: Mr James Reynolds

CHARITABLE AND OTHER SOCIETIES

Adoption Societies

CÚNAMH
30 South Anne Street, Dublin 2
Tel 01-6779664
Administrative Secretary: Mr Jim Dwan
Senior Social Worker: Ms Julie Kerins

St Brigid's Orphanage
Holy Faith Convent, The Coombe,
Dublin 8
Tel 01-4542917/4540244
Sister in Charge
Sr M. Benignus McDonagh

St Louise Adoption Society
Park House, North Circular Road, Dublin 7
Tel 01-8387122

St Patrick's Guild
203 Merrion Road, Dublin 4
Tel 01-2196551
Director: Sr Francis Fahy

Travellers Family Care

Derralossary House
Roundwood, Co Wicklow
Tel 01-2818355
Residential home for girls
Ballyowen Meadows
Tel 01-6235735
Exchange House Youth Service
61 Great Strand Street, Dublin 1
Tel 01-4546488
Training and employment programme
and youth work

Hostels

**CROSSCARE The Catholic Social Service
Conference, Boys' Hostel**
49 Percy Place, Dublin 4

Don Bosco House
57 Lower Drumcondra Road, Dublin 9
Tel 01-8360696
Salesian hostel for homeless boys.
Priest in Charge: Rev V. Collier (SDB)
Homeless Girls' Hostel
Sherrard House,
19 Upper Sherrard Street, Dublin 1
Tel 01-8743742

Iveagh Hostel
Bride Road, Dublin 8
Tel 01-4540182

Home Again
22 Newtown Avenue, Blackrock,
Co Dublin
Tel 01-2882295
Director: Mr John Molloy
Residential home for boys

Morning Star Hostel
Morning Star Avenue,
Brunswick Street, Dublin 7
Tel 01-8723401

Echlin House
666 South Circular Road, Dublin 8
Tel 01-4539008

Regina Coeli Hostel
Morning Star Avenue,
Brunswick Street, Dublin 7
Tel 01-8723142

St Brigid's Hostel
8/9/10 Henrietta Street, Dublin 1
For girls
Tel 01-8732580/8727469

St Vincent de Paul Night Shelter
Back Lane, Dublin 8
Tel 01-4542181

Housing

Catholic Housing Aid Society
Grenville Street, Dublin 1
Tel 01-8741020
Secretary: Mrs Valerie Power
Flats for the aged

**Mother Mary Aikenhead Social Services
Centre**
Mount St Anne's, Milltown, Dublin 6
Tel 01-2698995
Provides flats at a nominal rent for
young married couples

Threshold
21 Stoneybatter, Dublin 7
Tel 01-6353600/6786090
Website www.threshold.ie

Other

**CROSSCARE Catholic Social Service
Conference**
Holy Cross College, Clonliffe, Dublin 3
Tel 01-8360011
Chairman: Mr Frank O'Connell
Director: Mr Conor Hickey

Conference of St Philip Neri (SVP)
91-92 Sean McDermott Street, Dublin 1
Tel 01-8550022
Prison visitation and aid to discharged
prisoners

Cuan Mhuire
Athy, Co Kildare
Tel 059-8631493 Fax 059-8638765
Rehabilitation centre for alcoholics and
those with allied problems

Our Lady's Choral Society
(The Archdiocesan Choir)
Director: Rev Paul Ward
Hon Secretary: Lois Jarvis
Tel 01-2819363

Society of St Vincent de Paul
Dublin Office,
91-92 Sean McDermott Street, Dublin 1
Tel 01-8550022 Fax 01-8559168

ARCHDIOCESE OF CASHEL AND EMLY

PATRON OF THE ARCHDIOCESE
ST AILBE, 12 SEPTEMBER

SUFFRAGEN SEES: CLOYNE, CORK AND ROSS, KERRY, KILLALOE, LIMERICK, WATERFORD AND LISMORE

INCLUDES MOST OF COUNTY TIPPERARY AND PARTS OF COUNTY LIMERICK

Most Rev Dermot Clifford PhD, DD
Archbishop of Cashel and Emly; born 1939; ordained priest 22 February 1964; ordained Coadjutor Archbishop 9 March 1986; installed Archbishop of Cashel and Emly 12 September 1988; appointed Apostolic Administrator of Cloyne 7 March 2009

Residence: Archbishop's House, Thurles, Co Tipperary
Tel 0504-21512 Fax 0504-22680
Email office@cashel-emly.ie
Website www.cashel-emly.ie

CATHEDRAL OF THE ASSUMPTION, THURLES

The Cathedral of the Assumption stands on the site of earlier chapels. The first church on this site was part of the Carmelite priory, which dates from the early fourteenth century.

Some time before 1730 George Mathew, Catholic proprietor of the Thurles Estate, built a chapel for the Catholics of Thurles beside the ruins of the Carmelite priory. It was known as the Mathew Chapel. In 1810 Archbishop Bray consecrated the new 'Big Chapel', which was more spacious and ornate than its humble predecessor.

Soon after his appointment as archbishop in 1857, Dr Patrick Leahy revealed his plan to replace the Big Chapel with 'a cathedral worthy of the archdiocese'. Building commenced in 1865, and the impressive Romanesque cathedral, with its façade modelled on that of Pisa, was consecrated by Archbishop Croke on 21 June 1879. The architect was J. J. McCarthy. Barry McMullen was the main builder, and J. C. Ashlin was responsible for the enclosing walls, railing and much of the finished work.

The cathedral has many beautiful features, including an impressive rose window, a free-standing baptistry and a magnificent altar. The prize possession of the cathedral is its exquisite tabernacle, the work of Giacomo dello Porta (1537–1602), a pupil of Michelangelo. This tabernacle, which belonged to the Gesú (Jesuit) Church in Rome, was purchased by Archbishop Leahy and transported to Thurles.

The cathedral was extensively renovated and the sanctuary sympathetically remodelled on the occasion of its first centenary in 1979.

The most recent extensive conservation and renewal of the Cathedral, during 2001–2003, has restored the building to its original splendour.

CHAPTER

Dean
Rt Rev Mgr Christy O'Dwyer VG
Archdeacon
Venerable Matthew McGrath VG
Tipperary
Chancellor: Very Rev Denis Talbot
Galbally
Precentor: Vacant
Treasurer: Vacant
Penitentiary: Very Rev Conor Ryan
Hospital
Theologian: Very Rev Liam McNamara
Ballybricken, Grange,
Kilmallock, Co Limerick
Prebendaries
Newchapel: Very Rev Canon Thomas J.
Ryan, Murroe
Lattin: Vacant
Killennellick: Very Rev Canon Liam Ryan
Killenaule

ADMINISTRATION

College of Consultors
Rt Rev Mgr Christy O'Dwyer PP, VG
Venerable Matthew McGrath PP, VG
Rev Nicholas J. Irwin
Very Rev John J. O'Rourke PP
Rev Celsus Tierney

Vicars General
Rt Rev Mgr Christy O'Dwyer PP, VG
Cashel, Co Tipperary
Tel 062-61127
Venerable Matthew McGrath PP, VG
St Michael Street, Tipperary Town
Tel 062-51536

Vicars Forane
Very Rev Canon Thomas J. Ryan
Very Rev Canon Denis Talbot
Very Rev Canon Conor Ryan
Very Rev Canon Liam Ryan
Very Rev Canon Thomas F. Breen
Very Rev Canon Eugene Everard

Diocesan Planning Finance Committee
Secretary
Venerable Matthew McGrath PP, VG
Tel 062-51536
Very Rev George Bourke PP
Tel 0504-44227
Very Rev Conor Hayes PP
Parochial House, Kilteely, Co Limerick
Tel 061-384213
Rev Nicholas J. Irwin CC
Borrisoleigh, Thurles, Co Tipperary
Tel 0504-51230
Rev John O'Keefe CC
Birdhill, Killaloe, Co Tipperary
Tel 061-379172

Diocesan Archivist
Rt Rev Mgr Christy O'Dwyer PP, VG
Cashel, Co Tipperary
Tel 062-61127

Diocesan Secretary/Chancellor
Rev Nicholas J. Irwin
Archbishop's House, Thurles, Co Tipperary
Tel 0504-21512

CATECHETICS EDUCATION

Adult Religious Education
Rev Thomas Dunne CC
Templemore, Co Tipperary
Tel 0504-32890

Catechetics
Director: Rev Patrick Coffey
Lisgaugh, Doon, Co Limerick
Tel 061-380247
Assistant Director
Very Rev Michael Kennedy PP
The Parochial House, New Inn,
Cashel, Co Tipperary
Tel 052-62395

Boards of Management of Primary Schools
Secretary: Rev John O'Keefe CC
Birdhill, Killaloe, Co Tipperary
Tel 061-379172/087-2421678

LITURGY

Liturgical Commission
Secretary
Very Rev Canon Eugene Everard PP
The Parochial House, Templemore,
Co Tipperary
Tel 0504-31684

PASTORAL

Accord
Accord House, Cathedral Street,
Thurles, Co Tipperary
Tel 0504-22279
Diocesan Director: Rev Patrick Coffey CC
Doon, Co Limerick
Tel 061-380247

Adoption Society
Director: Rev Celsus Tierney
Holy Cross Abbey, Holy Cross,
Thurles, Co Tipperary
Tel 0504-43118

Charismatic Renewal
Adviser
Very Rev Canon Denis Talbot PP, VF
Galbally, Co Tipperary
Tel 062-37922

Child Protection Delegate
Rev Michael Mullaney
Tel 087-7914517

Cura
Cura Centre, 20A Liberty Square,
Thurles, Co Tipperary
Tel 0504-26226

Communications
Diocesan Counsellor
Rev Nicholas J. Irwin
Borrisoleigh, Thurles
Tel 0504-51230

Council of Priests
Chairman
Rt Rev Mgr Christy O'Dwyer PP, VG
Cashel, Co Tipperary
Tel 062-61127
Secretary: Rev Michael Mullaney
Ballycahill, Thurles, Co Tipperary
Tel 0504-26080

Ecumenism
Archbishop's House, Thurles,
Co Tipperary
Tel 0504-21512

Emigrant Commission
Rev Loughlin Brennan CC
Upperchurch, Thurles, Co Tipperary
Tel 0504-54492

Marriage Tribunal
(See Marriage Tribunals section.)

Parish Renewal
Director: Rev Pat Burns CC
Pallasgreen, Co Limerick
Tel 061-384114

Pilgrimages
Director: Rev Thomas Hearne CC
Brittas, Boher, Co Limerick
Tel 061-352223

Pioneer Total Abstinence Association
Diocesan Director
Very Rev William Hennessy PP
Knocklong, Co Limerick
Tel 062-53114

Pontifical Mission Societies
Diocesan Director
Very Rev Canon Eugene Everard PP
The Parochial House, Templemore,
Co Tipperary
Tel 0504-31684

Social Services
Director: Rev Gerard Hennessy CC
Cathedral Prestybery, Thurles,
Co Tipperary
Tel 0504-22229/22779

Travellers
Chaplain
Rev Daniel O'Gorman CC
Herbertstown, Hospital, Co Limerick
Tel 061-385104

Vocations
Director: Rev Patrick Coffey
Lisgaugh, Doon, Co Limerick
Tel 061-380247
Email piusix@eircom.net

PARISHES

Mensal parishes are listed first. Other parishes follow alphabetically. Church titulars are in italic.

THURLES, CATHEDRAL OF THE ASSUMPTION
Very Rev Martin Hayes Adm
Rev Gerard Hennessy CC
Rev Tomás O'Connell CC
Cathedral Presbytery, Thurles,
Co Tipperary
Tel 0504-22229/22779

THURLES, SS JOSEPH AND BRIGID
Rev James Donnelly
Rev Thomas Lanigan-Ryan CC
Bóthar na Naomh Presbytery,
Thurles, Co Tipperary
Tel 0504-22042/22688

ANACARTY
St Brigid's, Anacarty
Immaculate Conception, Donohill
Very Rev John Beatty PP
Anacarty, Co Tipperary
Tel 062-71104

BALLINA
Our Lady and St Lua, Ballina,
Mary, Mother of the Church, Boher
Very Rev Edmond V. O'Rahelly PP
Tel 061-376178
Rev Enda Brady CC
Tel 061-376430
Ballina, Co Tipperary

BALLINAHINCH
St Joseph's, Ballinahinch,
Sacred Heart, Killoscully
Very Rev Robert Fletcher PP
Déalginis, Garraun Upper, Ballinahinch,
Birdhill, via Killaloe, Co Clare
Tel 086-1927455/061-379862
Very Rev Francis Gallagher AP
Ballinahinch, Birdhill, Co Limerick
Tel 061-379111

BALLINGARRY
Assumption
Very Rev Thomas O. Breen PP
Ballingarry, Thurles, Co Tipperary
Tel 052-9154115

BALLYBRICKEN
St Ailbe's, Ballybricken,
Immaculate Heart of Mary, Bohermore
Very Rev Liam Canon McNamara PP
Ballybricken, Grange, Kilmallock,
Co Limerick
Tel 061-351158

BALLYLANDERS
Assumption of BVM
Very Rev John O'Neill PP
Ballylanders, Kilmallock,
Co Limerick
Tel 062-46705

BANSHA AND KILMOYLER
Annunciation, Our Lady of the
Assumption, Kilmoyler
Very Rev Michael Hickey PP
Bansha, Co Tipperary
Tel 062-54132

BOHERLAHAN AND DUALLA
Immaculate Conception, Boherlahan
Our Lady of Fatima, Dualla
Very Rev Joseph Egan PP
Boherlahan, Cashel, Co Tipperary
Tel 0504-41114
Rev Peter Brennan CC
Tel 0504-41215
Ballinree, Boherlahan,
Cashel, Co Tipperary

BORRISOLEIGH
Sacred Heart, Borrisoleigh
Very Rev Liam Everard PP
Tel 0504-51259
Rev Nicholas J. Irwin CC
Tel 0504-51230
Rev Michael Barry CC
Tel 0504-51275
Borrisoleigh, Thurles, Co Tipperary

CAHERCONLISH
Our Lady, Mother of the Church
Arch. O'Hurley Mem., Caherline
Very Rev Patrick Currivan PP
Tel 061-351248
Rev Roy Donovan CC
Tel 061-351213
Caherconlish, Co Limerick

CAPPAMORE
St Michael's
Very Rev Richard Browne PP
Cappamore, Co Limerick
Tel 061-381288

CAPPAWHITE
Our Lady of Fatima
Very Rev Tadgh Furlong PP
Cappawhite, Co Tipperary
Tel 062-75427

CASHEL
St John the Baptist, Cashel
St Thomas the Apostle, Rosegreen
Rt Rev Mgr Christy O'Dwyer PP, VG
Tel 062-61127
Rt Rev Mgr James Ryan AP
Tel 062-61353
Rev James O'Donnell CC
Bohermore, Cashel, Co Tipperary
Tel 062-61409
Rev James Purcell CC
Rosegreen, Cashel, Co Tipperary
Tel 062-61713
Rev Bernard Moloney
Cahir Road, Cashel, Co Tipperary
Tel 062-61443

CLERIHAN
St Michael's
Very Rev Ailbe O'Bric PP
Clerihan, Clonmel, Co Tipperary
Tel 052-6135118

CLONOULTY
Church of St John the Baptist, Clonoulty
Church of Jesus Christ Our Saviour,
Rossmore
Very Rev James Fogarty PP
Tel 0504-42388
Very Rev Thomas F. Egan AP
Tel 0504-42494
Clonoulty, Cashel,
Co Tipperary

DOON
St Patrick's
Very Rev Anthony Ryan PP
Parochial House, Church Grounds,
Doon, Co Limerick
Tel 061-380165
Rev Patrick Coffey
Lisgaugh, Doon, Co Limerick
Tel 061-380165

DRANGAN
Immaculate Conception, Visitation,
Cloneen
Very Rev Tony Lambe PP
Drangan, Thurles, Co Tipperary
Tel 052-52103

DROM AND INCH
St Mary's, Drom,
St Laurence O'Toole, Inch
Very Rev Martin Murphy PP
Drom, Thurles, Co Tipperary
Tel 0504-51196

EMLY
St Ailbe's
Very Rev Seamus Rochford PP
Tel 062-57103
Rev Sean Kennedy CC
Tel 062-57111
Emly, Co Tipperary

FETHARD
Holy Trinity, Fethard
Sacred Heart, Killusty
Very Rev Thomas F. Breen PP
Tel 052-6131178
Rev Anthony McSweeney CC
Tel 052-6131187
Fethard, Co Tipperary

GALBALLY
Christ the King, Galbally
Sacred Heart, Lisvernane
Very Rev Canon Denis Talbot PP, VF
Galbally, Co Tipperary
Tel 062-37929
Rev Derry Quirke CC
Lisvernane, Aherlow, Co Tipperary
Tel 062-56155

GOLDEN
Blessed Sacrament, Golden
St Patrick's, Kilfeade
Very Rev Patrick O'Gorman PP
Golden, Co Tipperary
Tel 062-72146

GORTNAHOE
Sacred Heart, Gortnahoe
SS Patrick & Brigid, Glengoole
Very Rev John O'Rourke PP
Tel 056-8834128
Rev Joseph Walsh CC
Tel 056-8834867
Crabb, Gortnahoe, Thurles, Co Tipperary

HOLY CROSS
Holy Cross Abbey, St Cataldus, Ballycahill
Very Rev Thomas J. Breen PP
Holy Cross, Thurles, Co Tipperary
Tel 0504-43124
Rev Celsus Tierney CC
Holy Cross Abbey, Thurles, Co Tipperary
Tel 0504-43118

HOSPITAL
St John the Baptist, Hospital
Sacred Heart, Herbertstown
Very Rev Canon Conor Ryan PP, VF
Castlefarm, Hospital, Co Limerick
Tel 061-383108
Rev Danny O'Gorman CC
Herbertstown, Hospital, Co Limerick
Tel 061-385104

KILBEHENNY
St Joseph's, Kilbehenny,
St Patrick's, Anglesboro
Very Rev Richard Kelly PP
Kilbehenny, Mitchelstown, Co Cork
Tel 025-24040

KILCOMMON
St Patrick's, Kilcommon
St Joseph's, Hollyford
Our Lady of the Visitation, Rearcross
Very Rev Daniel Woods PP
Kilcommon, Thurles, Co Limerick
Tel 062-78103
Rev James O'Donoghue CC
Hollyford, Co Tipperary
Tel 062-71104

KILLENAULE
St Mary's, Killenaule
St Joseph the Worker, Moyglass
Very Rev Canon Liam Ryan PP, VF
Tel 052-9156244
Rev Francis McCarthy CC
Holycross House, Moyglass,
Fethard, Co Tipperary
Tel 052-6131343

KILTEELY
SS Patrick & Brigid, Kilteely
St Bridget's, Dromkeen
Very Rev Conor Hayes PP
Parochial House, Killeely, Co Limerick
Tel 061-384213

KNOCKAINEY
Our Lady, Knockainey
St Patrick's, Patrickswell
Very Rev Liam Holmes PP
Knockainey, Hospital, Co Limerick
Tel 061-383127
Rev Sean Fennelly
Barrysfarm, Hospital, Co Limerick
Tel 061-383565

KNOCKAVILLA
Assumption, Knockavilla
St Bridget's, Donaskeigh
Very Rev James Egan PP
Knockavilla, Dundrum,
Co Tipperary
Tel 062-71168

KNOCKLONG
St Joseph's, Knocklong
St Patrick's, Glenbrohane
Very Rev William Hennessy PP
Knocklong, Co Limerick
Tel 062-53114
Very Rev John J. Ryan AP
Garryspillane, Kilmallock,
Co Limerick
Tel 062-53189

LATTIN AND CULLEN
Assumption, Lattin, St Patrick's, Cullen
Very Rev John Egan PP
Lattin, Co Tipperary
Tel 062-55240

LOUGHMORE
Nativity of Our Lady, Loughmore
St John the Baptist, Castleiney
Very Rev Padraig Corbett PP
Parochial House, Castleiney,
Templemore, Co Tipperary
Tel 0504-31392
Very Rev Monsignor Maurice Dooley AP
Loughmore, Templemore, Co Tipperary
Tel 0504-31375

MOYCARKEY
St Peter's, Moycarkey
St James's, Two-Mile-Borris
Our Lady & St Kevin, Littleton
Very Rev George Bourke PP
Moycarkey, Thurles, Co Tipperary
Tel 0504-44227
Rev Joseph Tynan CC
Ballydavid, Littleton,
Thurles, Co Tipperary
Tel 0504-44317

MULLINAHONE
St Michael's
Very Rev John McGrath PP
Mullinahone, Co Tipperary
Tel 052-53152

MURROE AND BOHER
Holy Rosary, Murroe
St Patrick's, Boher
Very Rev Canon Thomas J. Ryan PP, VF
Liscreagh, Murroe, Co Limerick
Tel 061-386227
Rev Thomas Hearne CC
Murroe, Co Limerick
Tel 061-352223

NEW INN
Our Lady Queen, New Inn,
St Bartholomew's, Knockgrafton
Very Rev Michael Kennedy PP
New Inn, Cashel, Co Tipperary
Tel 052-7462395

NEWPORT
Most Holy Redeemer, Newport
Our Lady of the Wayside, Birdhill
Our Lady of Lourdes, Toor
Very Rev Joseph Delaney PP
Tel 061-378126
Clonbealy, Newport, Co Tipperary
Rev John O'Keeffe CC
Birdhill, Killaloe, Co Tipperary
Tel 061-379172

PALLASGREEN
St John the Baptist, Pallasgreen
St Brigid's, Templebraden
Very Rev James Holloway PP
Moymore, Pallasgreen, Co Limerick
Tel 061-384111
Rev Pat Burns CC
Pallasgreen, Co Limerick
Tel 061-384114

SOLOHEAD
Sacred Heart, Oola
Very Rev John Morris PP
Solohead, Co Limerick
Tel 062-47614

TEMPLEMORE
Sacred Heart, Templemore
St Anne's, Clonmore
St James's, Killea
Very Rev Canon Eugene Everard PP
Tel 0504-31684
Very Rev Canon William Noonan AP
Tel 0504-31492
Rev James Walton CC
Tel 0504-31225
Rev Thomas Dunne CC
Tel 0504-32890
Templemore, Co Tipperary

TEMPLETUOHY
Sacred Heart, Templetuohy
St Mary's, Moyne
Very Rev Patrick Murphy PP
Templetuohy, Thurles, Co Tipperary
Tel 0504-53114
Very Rev John O'Connell AP
Moyne, Thurles, Co Tipperary
Tel 0504-45129

TIPPERARY
St Michael's
Venerable Matthew McGrath PP, VG
Tel 062-51536
Rev James Kennedy CC
Tel 062-51114
Rev James Foley CC
Tel 062-51283
St Michael's Street, Tipperary Town
Rev Edward Cleary CC
Knockinrawley, Tipperary
Tel 062-51242

UPPERCHURCH
Sacred Heart, Upperchurch
St Mary's, Drombane
Very Rev Donal Cunningham PP
Tel 0504-54181
Rev Loughlin Brennan
Tel 0504-54492
Upperchurch, Thurles, Co Tipperary

INSTITUTIONS AND THEIR CHAPLAINS

Cashel Community School
Tel 062-61167
Rev Bernard Moloney

Hospital Community School
Tel 061-383565
Rev Sean Fennelly

Tipperary Institue, Thurles
Tel 062-71252
Rev James O'Donnell

Vocational School, Thurles
Tel 0504-22042
Rev Thomas Lanigan-Ryan

Vocational School, Tipperary Town
Tel 062-51242
Rev James Kennedy

PRIESTS OF THE DIOCESE ELSEWHERE

Rev Joseph Browne
The Presbytery, St Mellitus Church,
Tollington Park, London N4 3AG
Tel 0171-2723415
Rev John Littleton
The Priory Institute,
Tallaght Village, Dublin 24
Rev Daniel J. Ryan
c/o Archbishop's House,
Thurles, Co Tipperary
Rev Joseph Ryan CC
St Matthew's,
11 Palmerstown Court,
Dublin 20
Tel 01-6268772
Very Rev Seamus Ryan PP
No 1 Presbytery,
Blackditch Road, Dublin 10
Tel 01-6265695

RETIRED PRIESTS

Very Rev James Feehan
1 Castle Court, Thurles,
Co Tipperary
Tel 0504-24935
Very Rev Canon Denis O'Meara
Millbrae Lodge Nursing Home,
Newport, Co Tipperary
Very Rev Liam Ryan DD
Cappamore, Co Tipperary

RELIGIOUS ORDERS AND CONGREGATIONS

PRIESTS

AUGUSTINIANS
The Abbey, Fethard,
Co Tipperary
Tel 052-31273
Prior: Rev Martin Crean (OSA)

BENEDICTINES
Glenstal Abbey,
Murroe, Co Limerick
Tel 061-8386103 Fax 061-8386328
Email abbot@glenstal.org
Abbot
Rt Rev Dom Mark Patrick Hederman (OSB)

HOLY SPIRIT CONGREGATION
Rockwell College,
Cashel, Co Tipperary
Tel 062-61444 Fax 062-61661
www.rockwell-college.ie
Superior: Rev John Meade (CSSp)
Secondary Residential and Day Boys
School; Agricultural College

PALLOTTINES
Pallottine College, Thurles, Co Tipperary
Tel 0504-21202
Rector: Very Rev Phil Barry (SCA)

BROTHERS

CHRISTIAN BROTHERS
Christian Brothers Cowper Care,
Monastery Close, Templemore Road,
Thurles, Co Tipperary
Tel 0504-91152
Community: 8

SISTERS

CONGREGATION OF THE SISTERS OF MERCY
Sisters of Mercy, 28 Spafield Crescent,
Cashel, Co Tipperary
Tel 062-61402
Non-resident Leader: Sr Monica Twomey
Community: 1

Convent of Mercy, New Inn, Cashel,
Co Tipperary
Tel 052-62205 Fax 052-62315
Non-resident Leader: Sr Monica Twomey
Community: 6

Convent of Mercy, Newport,
Co Tipperary
Tel 061-378145 Fax 061-378809
Non-resident Leader: Sr Frances Minahan
Community: 8

Convent of Mercy, Templemore,
Co Tipperary
Tel 0504-31427 Fax 0504-31164
Non-resident Leader
Sr Helena Blackwell
Community: 12

1 Church Street,
Templemore, Co Tipperary
Tel 0504-32019 Fax 0504-32019
Non-resident Leader: Sr Helena Blackwell
Community: 2

Sisters of Mercy, 1 Parkview Drive,
Thurles, Co Tipperary
Tel/Fax 0504-21137
Non-resident Leader: Sr Monica Twomey
Community: 2

Sisters of Mercy, Stanwix House,
Dublin Road, Thurles, Co Tipperary
Tel/Fax 0504-22320
Non-resident Leader: Sr Monica Twomey
Community: 3

Convent of Mercy, Tipperary Town
Tel 062-51218 Fax 062-52277
Leader: Sr Martina Fox
Community: 17

Convent of Mercy,
Knockinrawley, Tipperary Town
Tel/Fax 062-51120
Non-resident Leader: Sr Martina Fox
Community: 5

Convent of Mercy, Cappamore,
Co Limerick
Tel/Fax 061-381268
Non-resident Leader: Sr Nora Hartigan
Community: 5

Sisters of Mercy, Clonbealy,
Newport, Co Tipperary
Tel/Fax 061-378072
Non-resident Leader: Sr Frances Minahan
Community: 3

Convent of Mercy,
Doon, Co Limerick
Tel 061-380660 Fax 061-380263
Non-resident Leader: Sr Nora Hartigan
Community: 14

PRESENTATION SISTERS
Presentation Convent, Thurles,
Co Tipperary
Tel 0504-21250
Local leader: Sr Fidelis Purcell
Community: 25
Scoil Mhuire Primary School
Tel 0504-22331
Sacred Heart Secondary School
Tel 0504-21783

Presentation Sisters,
The Commons, Thurles, Co Tipperary

Presentation Convent, Hospital,
Co Limerick
Tel 061-383141
Local Leader: Sr Claude Meagher
Community: 9
Primary School, Secondary
St John The Baptist Community School
Tel 061-383283
Primary
Tel 061-383197

Presentation Sisters,
14 Assumption Terrace, Ballingarry,
Thurles, Co Tipperary
Tel 052-54118
Contact: Sr Patricia Wall
Community: 2
Secondary Coeducational School
Tel 052-54104

Presentation Convent, Fethard,
Co Tipperary
Tel 052-31225
Local Leader: Sr Maureen Power
Community: 10
Primary School
Tel 052-31493
Secondary Patrician
Tel 052-31572

Child care at St Bernard's group homes,
Rocklow Road, Fethard,
Co Tipperary
Director: Awaiting appointment
Tel 052-31141/31305/31392

16/17 Greenane Drive, Tipperary
Tel 062-31797
Contact: Sr Rosarii Treacy
Community: 3

20 Ard Alaínn, Killenaule Road,
Fethard, Co Tipperary
Contact: Sr Winnie Kirwan

URSULINES
Ursuline Convent, Thurles, Co Tipperary
Tel 0504-21561
Email ursulinethurles@eircom.net
Local Leader: Sr Cecelia O'Dwyer
Community: 12
Scoil Aingeal Naofa Primary School
Tel 0504-22561 Fax 0504-20763
Email scoilangela@unison.ie
Secondary School
Tel 0504-22147 Fax 0504-22737
Email sec.uct@oceanfree.net
Website www.uct.ie

EDUCATIONAL INSTITUTIONS

St Patrick's College
Thurles, Co Tipperary
Tel 0504-21201 Fax 0504-23735
Email luceat@eircom.net
President: Very Rev Thomas Fogarty
Registrar: Ms Paula Hourigan

EDMUND RICE SCHOOLS TRUST
Christian Brothers Primary School,
Doon, Co Limerick
Tel 061-380239 Fax 061-380060
Email nineco,ias@eircom.net
Principal: Br J. Dormer

Christian Brothers Secondary School,
Doon, Co Limerick
Tel 061-380388 Fax 061-380060
Email stfintandoon@eircom.net
Principal: Mr Eddie Bourke

Scoil Ailbhe Primary School,
Parnell Street, Thurles, Co Tipperary
Tel 0504-21448 Fax 0504-26094
Email scoilailbhecbs@eircom.net
Principal: Mr F. Quigney

Christian Brothers Secondary School,
Thurles, Co Tipperary
Tel 0504-22054/22171 Fax 0504-23645
Email thurlescbs@eircom.net
Principal: Mr Martin Quirke

The Abbey Secondary School,
Tipperary Town
Tel 062-52299/51624 Fax 062-52511
Email abbeyoffice@eircom.net
Principal: Mr J. Heffernan

CHARITABLE AND OTHER SOCIETIES

Apostolic Work Society
Thurles Parish Centre, Cathedral Street,
Thurles, Co Tipperary
Tel 0504-22229 Fax 0504-22415
Email parishcentre@thurlesparish.ie
President: Mrs Anne Minihan
Secretary: Mrs Anna Maher

Community Social Services Centres
Rossa Street, Thurles, Co Tipperary
Tel 0504-22169

St Michael's Street,Tipperary Town
Tel 062-51622

Templemore, Co Tipperary
Tel 0504-31244
Sr Catherine Gannon

Cashel, Co Tipperary
Tel 062-61395

ARCHDIOCESE OF TUAM

PATRON OF THE ARCHDIOCESE
ST JARLATH, 6 JUNE

SUFFRAGEN SEES: ACHONRY, CLONFERT, ELPHIN, KILLALA,
UNITED DIOCESES OF GALWAY AND KILMACDUAGH

INCLUDES HALF OF COUNTY MAYO, HALF OF COUNTY GALWAY
AND PART OF COUNTY ROSCOMMON

Most Rev Michael Neary DD
Archbishop of Tuam;
born 15 April 1946;
ordained priest 20 June 1971;
ordained bishop 13 September
1992; installed Archbishop of
Tuam 5 March 1995.

Residence: Archbishop's House,
Tuam, Co Galway
Tel 093-24166 Fax 093-28070
Email
archdiocesetuam@gmail.com
Website
www.tuamarchdiocese.org

CATHEDRAL OF THE ASSUMPTION, TUAM

The Cathedral of the Assumption is the metropolitan cathedral of the Western Province.

Archbishop Oliver Kelly (1815–34) laid the foundation stone on 30 April 1827 – before Catholic Emancipation. The cathedral was dedicated on 18 August 1836 by Archbishop John MacHale (1834–81). It cost £14,204.

The cathedral is English-decorated Gothic in style, is cruciform in shape and has a three-stage West Tower. It was designed by architect Dominick Madden. Nineteen windows light the cathedral. It has seating capacity for 1,100 people.

Among the cathedral's notable features are its superbly cut Galway and Mayo limestone, its plaster-vaulted ceiling with heads and bosses, and its cantilevered oak organ loft. Its huge Oriel window has eighty-two compartments, is forty-two feet high and eighteen feet wide; it is the work of Michael O'Connor and was made in Dublin in 1832. Four large windows from the Harry Clarke studio also grace the cathedral. It has a very fine Compton organ with 1,200 pipes, a unique set of early nineteenth-century Stations of the Cross, recently restored, and a seventeenth-century painting of the Assumption by Carlo Maratta.

The sanctuary, as shown above, was completely redesigned in 1991 under the direction of the late Ray Carroll. The altar is Wicklow granite, and all the timberwork is by local craftsman Tom Dowd.

Most Rev Joseph Cassidy DD, PP
Retired Archbishop of Tuam; born 1933; ordained priest 1959; ordained Coadjutor Bishop of Clonfert 23 September 1979; succeeded 1 May 1982; translated to Tuam September 1987; resigned 28 June 1994; Apostolic Administrator until 5 March 1995; PP Moore 13 July 1995.
Residence: 1 Kilgarve Court, Creagh, Ballinasloe, Co Galway

CHAPTER

Dean: Rt Rev Mgr Dermot Moloney VG
Prebendaries
Very Rev Joseph Cooney PP
Ballyhaunis
Very Rev John Cosgrove PP
Castlebar
Very Rev Conal Eustace PP
The Parochial House, Ballinrobe, Co Mayo
Very Rev Michael Flannery PP
An Cnoc, Indreabhán
Very Rev Anthony King PP
Athenry
Very Rev Oliver Hughes PP
Cummer, Tuam
Very Rev Thomas Mannion PP
Claremorris
Rt Rev Mgr John O'Boyle
Diocesan Resource Office, Tuam
Very Rev Padraig O'Connor PP
Mountbellew
Very Rev James Ronayne PP, VF
Clifden
Very Rev Kieran Waldron PP
Killererin
Very Rev Brendan Kilcoyne
President, St Jarlath's College
Very Rev Peter Waldron PP
Keelogues, Ballyvary, Castlebar
Very Rev James Walsh PP
Kilmeena, Westport
Very Rev Des Grogan PP
Partry, Claremorris

Honorary Canons
Very Rev Eamon Concannon PE, Knock
Very Rev John Fitzgerald PE, Tuam
Very Rev John D. Flannery PE, Milltown
Very Rev Colm Kilcoyne PE, Castlebar
Very Rev Seán Blake, Clonberne
Very Rev Patrick Costello, Mountbellew
Very Rev Seamus Cunnane
Grove House, Tuam
Very Rev Arthur Devine PE, Castlebar
Very Rev Martin Gleeson AP, Belclare
Very Rev Michael Goaley PE
Glenamaddy
Very Rev James Kelly AP, Tooreen
Very Rev Liam Kitt
Cleveland, Ohio
Very Rev Joseph Moloney PP, Tuam
Very Rev Joseph Moran
Abbeybreaffy Nursing Home, Castlebar
Very Rev Martin Newell AP, Claran

Very Rev Colm Ó Ceannahbáin AP
An Tulach, Baile na hAbhann
Very Rev Tadhg Ó Móráin AP
Cornamona
Rt Rev Mgr Michael Walsh, Aghamore
Venerable Patrick Williams PE
Tulla, Co Clare

ADMINISTRATION

Vicar General
Rt Rev Mgr Dermot Moloney PP, VG
Crossboyne, Claremorris, Co Mayo
Tel 094-9371824

Episcopal Vicar for Knock
Rt Rev Mgr Joseph Quinn PP
Knock

Chancellor
Rt Rev Mgr Dermot Moloney PP, VG
Crossboyne, Claremorris, Co Mayo
Tel 094-9371824

Vicars Forane
Very Rev Anthony King
Very Rev Conal Eustace
Very Rev Thomas Mannion
Very Rev James Ronayne
Very Rev Kieran Waldron
Very Rev Francis Mitchell
Very Rev John Cosgrove
Very Rev John Kenny

Judicial Collegium for Non-Matrimonial Cases
Rev Michael Carragher (OP) JCD
Angelicum University, Rome
Rt Rev Mgr Michael Quinlan JCD, VG
Diocese of Salford, England
Rev Kevin Cahill JCD
Diocese of Ferns
Rev Paul Churchhill JCD
Archdiocese of Dublin
Rev Patrick Connolly JCD
Diocese of Clogher

Diocesan Secretary
Rev Fintan Monahan
Archbishop's House, Tuam, Co Galway
Tel 093-24166

CATECHETICS EDUCATION

Director of Adult Religious Education
Rev Tod Nolan
Diocesan Resource Centre,
Bishop Street, Tuam, Co Galway
Tel 093-52284

Post-Primary Education
Director: Rt Rev Mgr John O'Boyle
Diocesan Resource Centre,
Bishop Street, Tuam, Co Galway
Tel 093-52284
Assistant Director: Sr Margaret Buckley
Sisters of the Christian Retreat and
Sr Mary McDonagh, Presentation Sister
Diocesan Resource Centre,
Bishop Street, Tuam, Co Galway
Tel 093-52284

Post-Primary School Retreats and Promotion of Universal Catechism
Director: Rev Benny McHale CC
The Presbytery, Ballyhaunis, Co Mayo
Tel 094-9630095

Primary Catechetics
Director: Rev John Kenny PP
Dunmore, Co Galway
Tel 095-42251
Assistant Director: Sr Nancy Clarke
Diocesan Resource Centre,
Bishop Street, Tuam, Co Galway

Primary Education
Director: Rt Rev Mgr John O'Boyle
Diocesan Resource Centre,
Bishop Street, Tuam, Co Galway
Tel 093-52284

Child Protection Office
Director: Rt Rev Mgr John O'Boyle
Diocesan Resource Centre,
Bishop Street, Tuam, Co Galway
Tel 093-52284

LITURGY

Liturgical Commission, Sacred Art and Sacred Music
Chairman: Rt Rev Mgr Joseph Quinn PP
Knock, Co Mayo
Tel 094-9388100
Secretary: Very Rev Michael Molloy PP
The Presbytery, Moor, Ballydangan,
Athlone, Co Westmeath
Tel 090-9673539

Diocesan Liturgical Resource Person
Ms Mary Connolly
Diocesan Resource Centre,
Bishop Street, Tuam, Co Galway
Tel 093-52284

PASTORAL

Accord
Diocesan Directors
Rev Conal Eustace PP
Ballinrobe, Co Mayo Tel 093-24342
Rev James Ronayne PP
Clifden, Co Galway Tel 095-21251
Rev Francis Mitchell Adm
Westport, Co Mayo Tel 098-28871

Ecumenism
Contact: Rev Francis Mitchell
The Presbytery, Westport, Co Mayo
Tel 098-28871

Emigrants
Director: Very Rev Gerard Burns PP
The Presbytery, Letterfrack, Co Galway
Tel 095-41053

Family Ministry
Director: Mr Cathal Kearney
The Family Centre, Castle Street,
Castlebar, Co Mayo Tel 094-9025900

Family Prayer Apostolate
Director: Mr Cathal Kearney
The Family Centre, Chapel Street,
Castlebar, Co Mayo Tel 094-9025900

Allianz ⓘ

GMIT, Castlebar
Chaplain: Rev Pat Farragher
Castlebar, Co Mayo
Tel 094-9035748

Implementation Body for the Diocesan Assembly
Rev Tod Nolan
Tel 093-52284

Knock Marriage Bureau
Canon Joe Cooney
Tel 094-9630006

L'Arche
National Chaplain: Rev Fergal Cunnane CC
Castlebar
Tel 094-9021844

Laity Commission
Diocesan Representative
Ms Eileen Gildea
Riverview, Dunmore, Co Galway

Marriage Tribunal
(See Marriage Tribunals section.)

Our Lady's School of Evangelisation
Knock, Co Mayo
Mr Johnny McCarthy
Tel 094-9388245

Pastoral Councils Resource Person
Director: Rev Patrick Farragher
Curradrish Road, Castlebar, Co Mayo
Tel 094-9035748

Pilgrimage Director
Mr John McLoughlin
St Jarlath's College, Tuam
Tel 093-24342

Pioneer Total Abstinence Association
Director: Rev Seán Cunningham
The Presbytery, Tuam, Co Galway
Tel 093-24250

Polish Chaplain
Rev Krzysztof Sikora (SVD)
Knock Shrine, Co Mayo
Tel 094-9388100/087-3230382

Pontifical Mission Societies
Diocesan Director
Very Rev Patrick Mooney PP
The Parochial House, Glenamaddy
Tel 094-9659017

Travellers
Chaplain
Very Rev Stephen Farragher Adm
Tuam, Co Galway
Tel 093-24250

World Youth Day
Contact: Rev Tod Nolan, Tuam
Tel 093-52284
Rev Charles McDonnell
Tel 091-844227

Vocations Committee
Contact: Rev Fintan Monahan
Archbishop's House, Tuam, Co Galway
Tel 093-24166

Youth
Director: Rev Charles McDonnell
The Presbytery, Athenry, Co Galway
Tel 091-844227

PARISHES

Mensal parishes are listed first. Other parishes follow alphabetically. Historical names are in parentheses.

TUAM (CATHEDRAL OF THE ASSUMPTION)
Rev Stephen Farragher Adm
Rev Seán Cunningham CC
Rev Raymond Flaherty CC
Tuam, Co Galway
Tel 093-24250

WESTPORT (AUGHAVAL)
Rev Francis Mitchell Adm
Rev Mícheál Mannion CC
Westport, Co Mayo
Tel 098-28871 Fax 098-26900
Very Rev Patrick Gill AP
Lecanvey, Westport, Co Mayo
Tel 098-64808

ABBEYKNOCKMOY
Very Rev Joseph O'Brien PP
Abbey, Tuam, Co Galway
Tel 093-43510
Rev Enda Howley CC
Parochial House, Ryehill,
Monivea, Co Galway
Tel 091-849019

ACHILL
Very Rev Michael Gormally PP
Achill Sound, Achill, Co Mayo
Tel 098-45288
Rev Ronnie Boyle CC
Achill Sound, Achill, Co Mayo
Tel 098-45109
Rev Thomas Kearney, SMA, CC
Keel, Achill, Co Mayo
Tel 098-43123

AGHAMORE
Very Rev John Walsh PP
Aghamore, Ballyhaunis, Co Mayo
Tel 094-9367024
Rev James Canon Kelly AP
Tooreen, Ballyhaunis, Co Mayo
Tel 094-9649002

ARAN ISLANDS
Very Rev Kieran Blake PP
Kilronan, Aran Islands, Co Galway
Tel 099-61221
Rev Joseph Jennings (SM) CC
Inishere, Aran Islands, Co Galway
Tel 099-75003

ATHENRY
Very Rev Anthony Canon King PP, VF
Tel 091-844076
Rev Charles McDonnell CC
Tel 091-844169

AUGHAGOWER
Very Rev Jackie Conroy PP
Aughagower, Westport, Co Mayo
Tel 098-25057

BALLA AND MANULLA
Very Rev Denis Carney PP
Balla, Co Mayo
Tel 094-9365025

BALLINDINE (KILVINE)
Very Rev Martin O'Connor PP
Ballindine, Co Mayo
Tel 094-9364423

BALLINLOUGH (KILTULLAGH)
Very Rev Joseph Feeney PP
Ballinlough, Co Roscommon
Tel 094-9640155

BALLINROBE
Very Rev Conal Canon Eustace PP, VF
Ballinrobe, Co Mayo
Tel 094-9541085/9541784

BALLYHAUNIS (ANNAGH)
Very Rev Joseph Canon Cooney PP
Tel 094-9630006
Rev Benny McHale CC
Tel 094-9630095
Ballyhaunis, Co Mayo

BEKAN
Very Rev Patrick Mullins PP
Bekan, Claremorris, Co Mayo
Tel 094-9380203

BURRISCARRA AND BALLINTUBBER
Very Rev John Garvey PP
Carnacon, Claremorris, Co Mayo
Tel 094-9360205
Rev Francis Fahey CC
Ballintubber Abbey,
Claremorris, Co Mayo
Tel 094-9030934

CAHERLISTRANE (DONAGHPATRICK AND KILCOONA)
Very Rev Pat O'Brien PP
Caherlistrane, Co Galway
Tel 093-55428

CARNA (MOYRUS)
Very Rev Peter Connolly PP
Tel 095-32232
Carna, Co Galway
Rev Séamus Ó Dúill (SDS) CC
Cill Chiaráin
Tel 095-33403

CARRAROE (KILEEN)
Very Rev Padraic Audley PP
Carraroe, Co Galway
Tel 091-595452
Rev Eamon Ó Conghaile CC
Tiernea, Lettermore, Co Galway
Tel 091-551133

CASTLEBAR (AGLISH, BALLYHEANE AND BREAGHWY)
Very Rev John Canon Cosgrove PP, VF
Tel 094-9021274
Rev Michael Farragher CC
Rev Fergal Cunnane CC
Rev John Murray CC
Tel 094-9021253/21844
Castlebar, Co Mayo
Rev Patrick Burke, hospital chaplain
Rev John McCormack (SMA) CC
Breaffy, Castlebar, Co Mayo
Tel 094-9022799
Parish Coordinator: Mrs Mary Connell
The Monastery, Castlebar, Co Mayo
Tel 094-9028473

CLARE ISLAND/INISHTURK
Pastoral Care
Rev Micheál Mannion and priests of
Westport Deanery
Tel 098-28871

CLAREMORRIS (KILCOLMAN)
Very Rev Thomas Canon Mannion PP
Rev Peter Gannon CC
The Presbytery, Claremorris, Co Mayo
Tel 094-9362477
Very Rev Colm Burke AP
Barnacarroll, Claremorris, Co Mayo
Tel 094-9388189

CLIFDEN (OMEY AND BALLINDOON)
Very Rev James Canon Ronayne PP
Clifden, Co Galway
Tel 095-21251
Rev John Dunleavy CC
Ballyconneely, Co Galway
Tel 095-23541
Rev Anthony Neville CC
Claddaghduff, Co Galway
Tel 095-44668

CLONBUR (ROSS)
Very Rev William Reilly PP
Clonbur, via Claremorris, Co Galway
Tel 094-9546304

CONG AND NEALE
Very Rev Patrick Gilligan PP
Cong, Co Mayo
Tel 094-9546030

CORRANDULLA (ANNAGHDOWN)
Very Rev Hughie Loftus PP
Corrandulla, Co Galway
Tel 091-791125
Rev Oliver McNamara CC
Annaghdown, Co Galway
Tel 091-791142

CROSSBOYNE AND TAUGHEEN
Rt Rev Msgr Dermot Moloney PP, VG
Crossboyne, Claremorris, Co Mayo
Tel 094-9371824
Rev James Quinn CC
Taugheen, Claremorris, Co Mayo
Tel 094-9362500

CUMMER (KILMOYLAN AND CUMMER)
Very Rev Oliver Canon Hughes PP
Cummer, Tuam, Co Galway
Tel 093-41427
Very Rev Martin Gleeson AP
Belclare, Tuam, Co Galway
Tel 093-55429

DUNMORE
Very Rev John Kenny PP, VF
Dunmore, Co Galway
Tel 093-38124

GLENAMADDY (BOYOUNAGH)
Very Rev Patrick Mooney PP
Glenamaddy, Co Galway
Tel 094-9659017

HEADFORD (KILLURSA AND KILLOWER)
Very Rev James O'Grady PP
Headford, Co Galway
Tel 093-35448
Very Rev Martin Canon Newell AP
Claran
Tel 093-35436

INISHBOFIN
Rev Anthony Neville CC
Claddaghduff, Co Galway
Tel 095-44668

ISLANDEADY
Very Rev Patrick Donnellan PP
Islandeady, Castlebar, Co Mayo
Tel 094-9024125
Rev Martin O'Keefe CC
Glenisland, Castlebar, Co Mayo
Tel 094-9024161

KEELOGUES
Very Rev Peter Canon Waldron PP
Keelogues, Ballyvary, Co Mayo
Tel 094-9031009

KILCONLY AND KILBANNON
Very Rev Michael Kenny PP
Kilconly, Tuam, Co Galway
Tel 093-47613

KILKERRIN AND CLONBERNE
Very Rev Thomas Commins PP
Kilkerrin, Ballinasloe, Co Galway
Tel 094-9659212
Very Rev Seán Canon Blake AP
Clonberne, Ballinasloe, Co Galway
Tel 093-45797

KILLERERIN
Very Rev Kieran Canon Waldron PP, VF
Killererin, Barnderg,
Tuam, Co Galway
Tel 093-49222

KILMAINE
Very Rev John Fallon PP
Kilmaine, Co Galway
Tel 093-33378

KILMEEN
Rev Declan Kelly Adm
Killoran, Ballinasloe, Co Galway
Tel 090-9627120

KILMEENA
Very Rev James Walsh PP
Kilmeena, Westport, Co Mayo
Tel 098-41270

KNOCK
Rt Rev Mgr Joseph Quinn, PP
Tel 094-9388100
Rev Richard Gibbons CC
Tel 094-9388100

LACKAGH
Very Rev Des Walsh PP
Turloughmore, Co Galway
Tel 091-797114
Rev Bernard Shaughnessy CC
Coolarne, Turloughmore, Co Galway
Tel 091-797626

LEENANE (KILBRIDE)
Very Rev Kieran Burke PP
Leenane, Co Galway
Tel 095-42251

LETTERFRACK (BALLINAKILL)
Very Rev Gerry Burns PP
The Parochial House, Letterfrack,
Connemara, Co Galway
Tel 095-41053/087-2408171

LOUISBURGH (KILGEEVER)
Very Rev Martin Long PP
Louisburgh, Co Mayo
Tel 098-66198

MAYO ABBEY (MAYO AND ROSSLEA)
Very Rev Austin Fergus PP
Mayo Abbey, Claremorris, Co Mayo
Tel 094-9365086

MENLOUGH (KILLASCOBE)
Very Rev John O'Gorman PP
Menlough, Ballinasloe, Co Galway
Tel 090-9684818

MILLTOWN (ADDERGOLE AND LISKEEVEY)
Very Rev J. J. Cribben PP
Milltown, Co Galway
Tel 093-51609

MOORE
Very Rev Michael Molloy PP
Ballydangan, Athlone,
Co Roscommon
Tel 090-9673539
Very Rev Seán Kilbane (SMA), AP
Clonfad, Oldtown, Athlone,
Co Roscommon
Tel 090-9673527

MOYLOUGH AND MOUNTBELLEW
Very Rev Padraig Canon O'Connor PP
Mountbellew, Ballinasloe, Co Galway
Tel 090-9679235
Rev Michael Nohilly (SMA) CC
Moylough, Ballinasloe, Co Galway
Tel 090-9679262

NEWPORT (BURRISHOOLE)
Very Rev Declan Carroll CC
Newport, Co Mayo
Tel 098-41123

PARKE (TURLOUGH)
Very Rev Karl Burns Adm
Parke, Castlebar, Co Mayo
Tel 094-9031314

PARTRY (BALLYOVEY)
Very Rev Desmond Canon Grogan PP
Partry, Claremorris, Co Mayo
Tel 094-9543013
Rev Pádraic Standún CC
Tourmakeady,
Claremorris, Co Mayo
Tel 094-9544037

ROBEEN
Rev Paddy Sheridan CC
Robeen, Hollymount, Co Mayo
Tel 094-9540026

ROUNDFORT (KILCOMMON)
Very Rev Michael Murphy PP
Roundfort, Hollymount, Co Mayo
Tel 094-9540934

ROUNDSTONE
Very Rev John McCarthy PP
Roundstone, Co Galway
Tel 095-35846
Rev Patrick Breen CC
Recess, Co Galway
Tel 095-34605

SPIDDAL/KNOCK
Very Rev Michael Canon Flannery PP
Knock, Inverin, Co Galway
Tel 091-593122
Very Rev Colm Canon Canavan AP
Tully, Ballinahown, Co Galway
Tel 091-593142

WILLIAMSTOWN (TEMPLETOHER)
Very Rev Brendan McGuinness PP
Williamstown, Co Galway
Tel 094-9643007

PRIESTS OF THE DIOCESE ELSEWHERE

Rev Eamon Conway
Mary Immaculate College,
University of Limerick,
South Circular Road, Limerick
Tel 061-204353
Very Rev Seamus Cunnane
Grove House, Tuam, Co Galway
Rev Denis Gallagher
'Shraheens', Achill South,
Achill, Co Mayo
Rev Thomas Gallagher
Cloughmore, Achill, Co Mayo
Rev John Gavin
c/o Archbishop's House, Tuam
Rev Jarlath Heraty
Hillside, Westport, Co Mayo
Rev Michael Keane
Claremount Nursing Home,
Claremorris, Co Mayo

Rev Michael O'Malley
c/o Archbishop's House, Tuam
Rev Michael Whelan
c/o Archbishop's House, Tuam

RETIRED PRIESTS

Very Rev Seamus Carter
Abbeybreaffey Nursing Home,
Dublin Road, Castlebar, Co Mayo
Most Rev Dr Joseph Cassidy
1 Kilgarve Court, Creagh,
Ballinasloe, Co Galway
Very Rev Eamon Canon Concannon
Ballyhowley, Knock, Co Mayo
Very Rev Patrick Costello
51 Ashgrove, Mountbellew,
Co Galway
Very Rev Arthur Devine PE
Rathbawn Road, Castlebar, Co Mayo
Very Rev John Canon Fitzgerald
7 Cunnane Place, The Gleve,
Tuam, Co Galway
Very Rev John D. Canon Flannery
Cartron, Milltown, Co Galway
Very Rev Michael Canon Goaley
Glenamaddy, Co Galway
Rev Paul Keane
Ballycrodick, Dunhill, Co Waterford
Very Rev Colm Canon Kilcoyne
20 Rathbawn Drive, Castlebar, Co Mayo
Rev Christopher Kilkelly
c/o Archbishop's House, Tuam,
Co Galway
Rev Dr Enda Lyons
Bermingham Road, Tuam, Co Galway
Rev Enda McDonagh
St Patrick's College,
Maynooth, Co Kildare
Tel 01-6285222
Very Rev Francis McMyler
Chapel Street, Louisburgh, Co Mayo
Very Rev Joseph Moloney
Grove House, Vicar Street,
Tuam, Co Galway
Very Rev Joseph Canon Moran
Abbeybreaffey Nursing Home,
Dublin Road, Castlebar, Co Mayo
Very Rev Máirtín Ó Lainn
Carraroe, Co Galway
Very Rev Tadhg Ó Morain PE
Cornamona, Claremorris, Co Galway
Tel 094-9548003
Rt Rev Mgr Michael Walsh
Aghamore, Ballyhaunis, Co Mayo
Venerable Archdeacon Patrick Williams
Caherlohan, Tulla, Co Clare

PERSONAL PRELATURE

OPUS DEI
Ballyglunin Park Conference Centre,
Tuam, Co Galway
Tel 093-41423
Rev Walter Macken, Chaplain

RELIGIOUS ORDERS AND CONGREGATIONS

PRIESTS

OBLATES OF MARY IMMACULATE
Robeen, Hollymount, Co Mayo
Tel 094-9540026
Email patsheri@eircom.net

The Presbytery, Glenisland,
Castlebar, Co Mayo
Tel 085-1086639
Email glenislandcc@eircom.net

**ST PATRICK'S MISSIONARY SOCIETY
(KILTEGAN FATHERS)**
Main Street, Knock, Co Mayo
Tel 094-9388661
House Leader
Rev Donald McDonagh (SPS)

BROTHERS

DE LA SALLE BROTHERS
St Gerald's College
Tel 094-9021383 Fax 094-9026157
Headmaster: Mr Bernard Keeley

FRANCISCAN BROTHERS
Franciscan Brothers Generalate
Newtown, Mountbellew,
Co Galway
Tel 090-9679295 Fax 090-9679687
Email franciscanbrs@eircom.net
Minister General: Br Peter Roddy (OSF)

Corrandulla, Co Galway
Tel 091-791127
Local Minister: Br Conal Thomas (OSF)
Community: 2

Clifden, Co Galway
Tel 095-21195
Local Minister: Br James Mungovan (OSF)
Community: 5

Franciscan Brothers, Newtown,
Mountbellew, Co Galway
Tel 090-9679906
Local Minister: Br Denis Lawlor (OSF)
Community: 9

Franciscan Brothers Agricultural College,
Mountbellew, Co Galway
Tel 090-9679205 Fax 090-9679276
Commmunity: 2

ST JOHN OF GOD BROTHERS
St Joseph's at the Shrine,
Knock, Co Mayo
Tel 094-9388215 Fax 094-9375980
Email stjosephs.knock@sjog.ie
Prior: Br Ronan Lennon (OH)
Director: Ms Monica Mooney
Community: 1

SISTERS

BENEDICTINE NUNS
Kylemore Abbey,
Kylemore, Connemara, Co Galway
Tel 095-41146
Email info@kylemoreabbey.ie
Administrator
Sr Máire Hickey (OSB)
Community: 16
Abbey, Gothic Church, Craft Shop,
Restaurant, Pottery Studio and 6-acre
Victorian Walled Garden open to visitors
Website www.kylemoreabbey.com

BON SECOURS SISTERS (PARIS)
Sisters of Bon Secours, Drum,
Ballyhaunis Road, Knock, Co Mayo
Tel 094-9388439
Contact: Sr Felicitas O'Mahony
Community: 4
Prayer Ministry

99 Kilane View, Edenderry, Co Offaly
Tel 0405-33382
Community: 1
Health Ministry

CARMELITES
Carmelite Monastery,
Tranquilla, Knock, Co Mayo
Email tranquillacarmel@eircom.net
Prioress: Sr Catherine
Community: 16
Hidden life of prayer in the service of the
Church

CHRISTIAN RETREAT SISTERS
Holy Rosary Convent,
Mountbellew, Ballinasloe, Co Galway
Tel 090-9679311
Sister-in-Charge: Sr Margaret Buckley
Community: 5

Holy Rosary College Coeducational
Secondary School
Tel 090-9679222
Pupils: 547
Catechetical and pastoral ministry

CONGREGATION OF THE SISTERS OF MERCY
Sisters of Mercy, The Glebe,
Tuam, Co Galway
Tel 090-9625045
Community: 3

Convent of Mercy, Knock Road,
Ballyhaunis, Co Mayo
Tel 094-9630108
Community: 3

Cuan Chaitríona,
The Lawn, Castlebar, Co Mayo
Tel 094-9021171 Fax 094-9022031
Community: 20
Nursing Home: 21

Teach Mhuire,
The Lawn, Castlebar, Co Mayo
Tel 094-9022141 Fax 094-9025266
Community: 4

Ard Bhride,
The Lawn, Castlebar, Co Mayo
Tel 094-9286410 Fax 094 9286404
Community: 32

Pontoon Road, Castlebar, Co Mayo
Tel 094-9025463 Fax 094-9026695
Community: 5

7 Chapel Street, Castlebar, Co Mayo
Tel 094-9021734
Community: 3

6 Riverdale Court, Castlebar, Co Mayo
Tel/Fax 094-9023622
Community: 2

Manor Court, Westport Road,
Castlebar, Co Mayo
Community: 4

1 Clareville, Claremorris, Co Mayo
Tel 094-9372654
Community: 2

Bethany, Dalton Street,
Claremorris, Co Mayo
Tel 094-9362198
Community: 3

Convent of Mercy,
Dunmore, Co Galway
Tel 093-38141 Fax 093-38567
Community: 4

Sisters of Mercy,
37, 38, 39, 40 St Jarlath's Court,
The Glebe, Tuam, Co Galway
Community: 4

Sisters of Mercy,
18 The Beeches, Louisburgh, Co Mayo
Tel 098-66325
Community: 2

Apartment 4, St Dominic's Estate,
Barrack Hill, Newport, Co Mayo
Tel 098-41157
Community: 1

Convent of Mercy, Tuam, Co Galway
Tel 093-24363 Fax 093-25242
Community: 23

Sisters of Mercy,
Ruah, Cappanraheen,
Craughwell, Co Galway
Tel 091-876646
Community: 3

37 Michael Davitt Park,
Westport, Co Mayo
Tel 098-27137
Community: 2

DAUGHTERS OF CHARITY OF ST VINCENT DE PAUL
St Mary's Hostel, Knock, Co Mayo
Tel 094-9388119
Superior: Sr Caitriona MacSweeney
Community: 8
Hostel for pilgrims

FRANCISCAN SISTERS OF LITTLEHAMPTON
Eden, Knock, Co Mayo
Tel 094-9388302
Leader: Sr Stanislaus
Community: 5

MISSIONARY SISTERS OF OUR LADY OF APOSTLES
52 Elm Park, Claremorris, Co Mayo
Tel 094-9373569
Community: 8

PRESENTATION SISTERS
Presentation Convent, St Joseph's, Tuam,
Co Galway
Tel 093-24111 Fax 093-25584
Email presjos@eircom.net
Community Leader: Sr Philomena Noone
Community: 37
Care of sick and elderly sisters, school
and pastoral ministry
Presentation Primary School
Tel 093-28324
Email clochard.ias@eircom.net

Presentation Convent, Athenry,
Co Galway
Tel 091-844077
Community Leader: Sr Marie Ward
Community: 11
School and pastoral ministry
Scoil Chroí Naofa Primary School
Tel 091-844510
Presentation College
Tel 091-844144 Fax 091-850862
Email pcathenry@hotmail.com

ST JOSEPH OF THE SACRED HEART SISTERS
Sisters of St Joseph of Sacred Heart
Apt 2, Old Ground House,
Knock, Co Mayo
Tel 094-9375975

ST LUCY FILIPPINI SISTERS
Mother of the Church Convent,
Newport, Co Mayo
Tel 098-41248 Fax 098-41092
Superior: Sr Joan Henry
Community: 3
Playgroup for pre-school children.
Weekends given for girls interested in
the religious life

ST MARY MADELEINE POSTEL SISTERS
'Fatima House', Kilkelly Road,
Knock, Co Mayo
Apply: Sister-in-charge
Tel 094-9388719
Community: 3

URSULINES
Ard Chiaráin Prayer Centre,
Shannonbridge, Co Roscommon
Tel 090-9674305/9674194
Email usac@eircom.net
Community: 2

EDUCATIONAL INSTITUTIONS

St Colman's College
Claremorris, Co Mayo
Tel 094-9371442
Principal: Daniel McHugh
Chaplain: Rev Peter Gannon CC
Claremorris

St Jarlath's College
Tuam, Co Galway
Tel 093-24342
President:
Very Rev Brendan Canon Kilcoyne
Tel 093-24248
Chaplain: Rev Fintan Monahan
Tel 093-24166
Rev Raymond Flaherty
Tel 093-24250

EDMUND RICE SCHOOLS TRUST
St Patrick's Primary School,
Newport Road, Westport, Co Mayo
Tel 098-26450
Principal: Mr Stiofán Ó Moráin

Rice College, Castlebar Road,
Westport, Co Mayo
Tel 098-25698 Fax 098-26154
Principal: Ms Patricia Atkins

CHARITABLE AND OTHER SOCIETIES

ACCORD
Shrine House, No 6 Bishop Street,
Tuam, Co Galway
Tel 093-24900/24776
Contacts: Rev Conal Eustace
Ms Anne Maguire
Mr Christopher Kelly
Castle Street, Castlebar
Tel 094-9022214
Contact: Rev Michael Murphy

Apostolic Work Society
Branches at:
Abbeyknockmoy, Athenry, Achill,
Ballinrobe, Ballyhaunis, Barnaderg, Balla,
Belcarra, Brickens, Bekan, Castlebar,
Claremorris, Carnacon, Claran, Clifden,
Clonberne, Cortoon, Corofin,
Caherlistrane, Dunmore, Glenamaddy,
Headford, Kilkerrin, Knock, Kilconly,
Lavally, Leenane, Louisburgh, Monivea,
Mountbellew, Moylough, Newport,
Tooreen, Westport, Robeen, Roundfort,
Tuam, Tiernaul

Flats for Newly Weds
Tuam Community Council

Homes for the Elderly
Conference of St Vincent de Paul,
Castlebar

Information Centres
Tuam, Ballinrobe, Claremorris,
Glenamaddy, Castlebar, Westport

Social Services Centres
Dublin Road, Tuam
Tel 093-24577
Contact: Sr Loreto

Community Centre, Westport, Co Mayo
Tel 098-25669
Contact: Sr Agnes

Castle Street, Castlebar, Co Mayo
Tel 094-9021880
Contact: Sr Dolores

Society of St Vincent de Paul
Conferences at: Castlebar, Tuam,
Athenry, Westport, Dunmore,
Claremorris, Ballyhaunis, Ballinrobe,
Ballinlough, Headford, Monivea.

DIOCESE OF ACHONRY

Most Rev Brendan Kelly DD
Bishop of Achonry;
born 20 May 1946;
ordained priest 20 June 1971;
ordained Bishop of Achonry
27 January 2008

Residence: Bishop's House,
Edmondstown,
Ballaghaderreen,
Co Roscommon
Tel 094-9860021
Fax 094-9860921
Email
bishop@achonrydiocese.org
Website www.achonrydiocese.org

PATRONS OF THE DIOCESE
ST NATHY, 9 AUGUST; AT ATTRACTA, 11 AUGUST

INCLUDES PARTS OF COUNTIES MAYO, ROSCOMMON AND SLIGO

CATHEDRAL OF THE ANNUNCIATION AND ST NATHY, BALLAGHADERREEN

The building of the cathedral was begun in 1855 by Bishop Durcan. The architects were Messrs Hadfield & Goldie of Sheffield, while the Clerk of Works was Mr Charles Barker. It was completed in 1860.

The style is simple Gothic, known as Early English, of the Gothic Revival. The original intention was to have the roof fan-vaulted in wood and plaster, but it was abandoned owing to cost, and was finished in open timbers. The plan for a spire also had to be abandoned. This, however, was built in 1905 by Bishop Lyster, and a carillon of bells was installed.

The organ was built with continental pipes by Chestnutt of Waterford in 1925. The sanctuary was reconstructed to conform to the liturgical reforms of Vatican II in 1972. The baptistry in the left-hand Side Chapel was donated by Lydia Viscountess Dillon in memory of Charles Henry Viscount Dillon who died on 18 November 1865. The Apostles' Creed is carved on the baptistry lid.

There are commemorative plaques to former bishops of Achonry in the left-hand side Chapel: Bishops McNicholas, Durcan, Lyster and Morrisroe.

The window in the Lady Chapel has the inscription: 'This window to the Glory of God and Honour of the Blessed Virgin Mary was erected by united subscription of the Bishop, Clergy and 19 inhabitants of the Parish and neighbourhood to commemorate their respect and esteem for Charles Strickland and his wife Maria of Loughglynn and their zealous assistance in the erection of the Cathedral Church in 1860.' Charles Strickland was agent for Lord Dillon and was associated with the building of the neighbouring town of Charlestown and its church.

Most Rev Thomas Flynn DD
Bishop Emeritus of Achonry;
born 8 July 1931;
ordained priest 17 June 1956; ordained
Bishop of Achonry 20 February 1977;
retired 20 November 2007

Residence: St Michael's,
Cathedral Grounds,
Ballaghaderreen, Co Roscommon
Tel 094-9877808
Email bishopflynn@achonrydiocese.org

CHAPTER

Dean
Very Rev Michael Canon Joyce PP, Bohola
Archdeacon
Very Rev Patrick Canon Kilcoyne PP,
Kiltimagh

Rt Rev Mgr Thomas Johnston PP,
Charlestown
Very Rev James Canon Finan PP,
Keash
Very Rev Patrick Canon Peyton PP,
Collooney

ADMINISTRATION

Vicar General
Rt Rev Mgr Thomas Johnston PP
Charlestown, Co Mayo
Tel 094-9254315

Chancellor
Rev Ronan Murtagh
Bishop's House, Edmondstown,
Ballaghaderreen, Co Roscommon
Tel 094-9860021

College of Consultors
Rt Rev Mgr Thomas Johnston
Very Rev Padraig Costello
Very Rev Thomas Towey
Very Rev Dermot Meehan

Finance Committee
Chairman: Mr Pat O'Connor
Secretary: Very Rev Martin Convey

Vicars Forane
Very Rev Michael Canon Joyce PP
Very Rev Gregory Hannan PP
Very Rev Patrick Lynch PP

Church Property Advisory Commission
Very Rev Michael Canon Joyce
Bohola, Claremorris, Co Mayo
Tel 094-9384115

Church Building Advisory Commission
Rt Rev Mgr Thomas Johnston PP
Charlestown, Co Mayo
Very Rev Joseph Caulfield PP
Gurteen, Co Sligo
Mr John Halligan
Charlestown, Co Mayo

Historic Churches Advisory Committee
Chair
Very Rev Patrick Canon Peyton PP
Tel 071-9167235
Very Rev Dermot Meehan
Tel 094-9252952

Diocesan Secretary
Rev Ronan Murtagh
Bishop's House, Edmondstown,
Ballaghaderreen, Co Roscommon
Tel 094-9860021
Email rmurtagh@achonrydiocese.org

Diocesan Communications Officer
Very Rev Vincent Sherlock
Kilmovee, Ballaghaderreen, Co Mayo
Tel 094-9649137
Email vsherlock@achonrydiocese.org

CATECHETICS EDUCATION

Post-Primary Education
Secretary
Very Rev Martin Convey BSc, MLitt, PhD
St Nathy's College, Ballaghaderreen,
Co Roscommon
Tel 094-9260010

Primary Education
Secretary
Very Rev Patrick Canon Peyton PP
Collooney, Co Sligo
Tel 071-9167235

Advisory Committee for Catholic Education
Contact
Very Rev Martin Convey BSc, MLitt, PhD
St Nathy's College, Ballaghaderreen,
Co Roscommon
Tel 094-9860010

Religious Education in Schools
Diocesan Religious Adviser
Primary: Sr Regina Lydon
Tel 071-9183350
Rev John Maloney
Kikelly, Co Mayo
Tel 094-9367031

LITURGY

Chairman
Very Rev Patrick Lynch PP
Tubbercurry, Co Sligo
Tel 071-9185049
Secretary
Very Rev Thomas Towey PP
Ballisodare, Co Sligo
Tel 071-9167467

PASTORAL

Accord
Director
Very Rev Joseph Caulfield PP
Gurteen, Co Sligo
Tel 071-9182551

Council of Priests
Chairman
Very Rev Thomas Towey PP
Ballisodare, Co Sligo
Tel 071-9167467
Secretary
Very Rev Dermot Meehan PP
Swinford, Co Mayo
Tel 094-9252952

Ecumenism
Director
Very Rev Dermot Burns PP
Straide, Foxford, Co Mayo
Tel 094-9031029

Emigrants
Director
Very Rev Vincent Sherlock PP
Kilmovee, Ballaghaderreen, Co Mayo
Tel 094-9649137

Laity Commission
Diocesan Representative
Mr Gabriel Ó Laimhin
Boherhalla, Foxford, Co Mayo
Tel 094-9256670

Marriage Tribunal
(See Marriage Tribunals section)

Pastoral Centre
Rt Rev Mgr Thomas Johnston
St Nathy's Pastoral Centre,
Charlestown, Co Mayo
Tel 094-9254173

Pioneer Total Abstinence Association
Spiritual Director
Very Rev Joseph Gavigan PP
Ballaghaderreen, Co Roscommon
Tel 094-9860011

Pontifical Mission Society
Diocesan Director
Very Rev Thomas Mulligan PP
Attymass, Ballina, Co Mayo

Travellers
Chaplain
Very Rev Patrick Canon Peyton PP
Collooney, Co Sligo
Tel 071-9167235

Vocations
Director: Rev Gabriel Murphy CC
Kiltimagh, Co Mayo
Tel 094-9381492

Youth
Rev Derek Gormley CC
Swinford, Co Mayo
Tel 094-9251143

PARISHES

The mensal parish is listed first. Other parishes follow alphabetically. Historical names are in parentheses. Church titulars are in italics.

BALLAGHADERREEN (CASTLEMORE AND KILCOLMAN)
Cathedral of The Annunciation & St Nathy
St Aidan, Monasteraden
SS John the Baptist & Colman, Derrinacartha
Sacred Heart, Brusna
Very Rev Joseph Gavigan PP
Rev Martin Henry CC
The Presbytery, Ballaghaderreen,
Co Roscommon
Tel 094-9860011 Fax 094-9860350

ACHONRY
SS Nathy and Brigid, Achonry, Ballymote
Sacred Heart, Mullinabreena, Ballymote
Very Rev Peter Gallagher PP
Lavagh, Ballymote, Co Sligo
Tel 071-9184002

ATTYMASS
St Joseph's
Very Rev Thomas Mulligan PP
Attymass, Ballina, Co Mayo
Tel 096-45095 Fax 096-45375

BALLISODARE
St Brigid
Very Rev Thomas Towey PP
Ballisodare, Co Sligo
Tel 071-9167467

BALLYMOTE (EMLEFAD AND KILMORGAN)
Immaculate Conception, Ballymote
St Joseph's, Doo
Very Rev Greg Hannan PP
Tel 071-9183361
Rev James McDonagh CC
Tel 071-9189778
Ballymote, Co Sligo

BOHOLA
Immaculate Conception & St Joseph
Very Rev Michael Joyce PP
Bohola, Claremorris, Co Mayo
Tel 094-9384115

BONNICONLON (KILGARVAN)
Immaculate Heart of Mary
Very Rev John Geelan PP
Parochial House, Bonniconlon,
Ballina, Co Mayo
Tel 096-45016

BUNNINADDEN (KILSHALVEY, KILTURRA AND CLOONOGHILL)
Sacred Heart, Bunninadden
Immaculate Heart of Mary, Killavil
Very Rev Michael Reilly PP
Bunninadden,
Ballymote, Co Sligo
Tel 071-9183232
Fax 071-9189167

CARRACASTLE
St James', Carracastle
St Joseph's, Rooskey
Very Rev Michael Quinn PP
Carracastle, Ballaghaderreen,
Co Mayo
Tel 094-9254301

CHARLESTOWN (KILBEAGH)
St James', Charlestown
St Patrick's, Bushfield
Rt Rev Mgr Thomas Johnston PP
Charlestown, Co Mayo
Tel 094-9254173

COLLOONEY (KILVARNET)
Assumption, Collooney
SS Fechin & Lassara, Ballinacarrow
Very Rev Patrick Peyton PP
Collooney, Co Sligo
Tel 071-9167235

COOLANEY (KILLORAN)
Church of the Sacred Heart & St Joseph, Coolaney
Very Rev Patrick Holleran PP
Coolaney, Co Sligo
Tel 071-9167235

CURRY
Immaculate Conception, Curry
St Patrick's, Moylough
Very Rev Martin Jennings PP
Curry, Ballymote, Co Sligo
Tel 094-9254508
Rev Seamus Collery
Curry, Ballymote, Co Sligo
Chaplain, St Attracta's Secondary School,
Tubbercurry, Co Sligo

FOXFORD (TOOMORE)
St Michael's
Very Rev Padraig Costello PP
Tel 094-9256131
Rev Gerard Davey CC
Tel 094-9256401
Foxford, Co Mayo

GURTEEN (KILFREE AND KILLARAGHT)
St Patrick's, Gurteen
St Joseph's, Cloonloo
St Attracta's, Killaraght
Very Rev Joseph Caulfield PP
Gurteen, Ballymote, Co Sligo
Tel 071-9182551 Fax 071-9182762
Rev Ronan Murtagh CC
Cloonloo, Boyle, Co Sligo
Tel 071-9662111

KEASH (DRUMRAT)
St Kevin
Our Lady of the Rosary, Culfadda
Very Rev James Canon Finan PP
Keash, Ballymote, Co Sligo
Tel 071-9183334

KILLASSER
All Saints, Killasser
St Thomas', Callow
Very Rev John Durkan PP
Killasser, Swinford, Co Mayo
Tel 094-9251431

KILMOVEE
Immaculate Conception, Kilmovee
St Joseph's, Orlar
Very Rev Vincent Sherlock PP
Kilmovee, Ballaghaderreen, Co Mayo
Tel 094-9649137
St Celsus, Kilkelly
St Patrick's, Glann
Rev John Maloney CC
Kilkelly, Co Mayo
Tel 094-9367031

KILTIMAGH (KILLEDAN)
Holy Family, Souls in Purgatory &
St Aidan
Very Rev Patrick Canon Kilcoyne PP
Tel 094-9381198
Rev Gabriel Murphy CC
Tel 094-9381492
Rev Stephen O'Mahony
Chaplain to school
Tel 094-9381261
Kiltimagh, Co Mayo

STRAIDE (TEMPLEMORE)
SS Peter & Paul
Very Rev Dermot Burns PP
Straide, Foxford, Co Mayo
Tel 094-9031029

SWINFORD (KILCONDUFF AND MEELICK)
Our Lady Help of Christians, Swinford
St Luke's, Meelick
St Joseph's, Midfield
Very Rev Dermot Meehan PP
Tel 094-9252952
Rev Derek Gormley CC
Tel 094-9253338
Swinford, Co Mayo

TOURLESTRANE (KILMACTIGUE)
St Attracta's, Tourlestrane
Our Lady of the Rosary, Kilmactigue
Sacred Heart, Loch Talt
Very Rev John Glynn PP
Tourlestrane, Ballymote, Co Sligo
Tel 071-9181105

TUBBERCURRY (CLOONACOOL)
St John, Evangelist, Tubbercurry
Very Rev Patrick Lynch PP
Tubbercurry, Co Sligo
Tel 071-9185049
St Michael's, Cloonacool
Rev Dan O'Mahony CC
Cloonacool, Tubbercurry, Co Sligo
Tel 071-9185156

PRIESTS OF THE DIOCESE ELSEWHERE

Rev Eugene Duffy DD
Mary Immaculate College,
South Circular Road, Limerick
Tel 061-204968
Rev Michael Maloney
c/o Parochial House,
Charlestown, Co Mayo
Rev Adrian McHugh
Diocese of Rockville Centre, St Patrick's,
Huntington, New York NY11743
Tel +1-631-3853311
Rev Tómas Surlis
Pontificio Collegio Irlandese,
Via dei SS Quattro 1, 00184, Roma
Very Rev Liam Swords, Dublin
Tel 01-4972503

RETIRED PRIESTS

Very Rev Farrell Cawley
Ballinacarrow, Co Sligo
Tel 086-0864347
Rt Rev Mgr John Doherty
Priest-in-residence,
Charlestown, Co Mayo
Tel 094-9255793
Very Rev Dean Robert Flynn
Ballymote, Co Sligo
Tel 071-9183312
Very Rev Andrew Canon Johnston
c/o Sonas Care Centre, Cloghanboy,
Ballymahon Road, Athlone,
Co Westmeath
Very Rev Christopher Canon McLoughlin
Kilmactigue, Aclare, Co Sligo
Tel 071-9181007
(Priest in residence, Tourlestrane Parish)
Rt Rev Mgr Joseph Spelman
Collooney, Co Sligo
Tel 071-9167109
(Priest in residence, Collooney Parish)
Rev Paul Surlis
1684 Albermarle Drive, Crofton,
Maryland 21114, USA
Tel 001-410-4511459

RELIGIOUS ORDERS AND CONGREGATIONS

BROTHERS

ALEXIAN BOTHERS
Regional Residence
Churchfield, Knock, Co Mayo
Tel 094-9376996
Email alexianbros@eircom.net
Regional Leader: Br Barry Butler (CFA)
Community: 3

SISTERS

CONGREGATION OF THE SISTERS OF MERCY
Convent of Mercy,
Collooney, Co Sligo
Tel/Fax 071-9167153
Community: 6

Tabor
Swinford, Co Mayo
Tel 094-9252197
Community: 3

Convent of Mercy,
Ballymote, Co Sligo
Tel 071-9183350 Fax 071-9189177
Community: 6

Convent of Mercy,
Ballisodare, Co Sligo
Tel 071-9167279 Fax 071-9130538
Community: 6

Mercyville,
Ballaghaderren, Co Roscommon
Tel 094-9861193
Community: 5

Belgarrow, Sisters of Mercy,
Foxford, Co Mayo
Tel 094-9256573 Fax 094-9256064
Community: 2

MARIST SISTERS
Marist Convent,
Tubbercurry, Co Sligo
Tel 071-9185018
Superior: Sr Angela Durkin
Community: 13
Primary school, parish visiting,
Marist laity
Day care centre (for HSE – Western Region)

Marist Convent,
Charlestown, Co Mayo
Tel 094-9254133
St Joseph's Secondary School
Tel 094-9254133
Community: 4
Teaching in secondary school, parish ministry, Marist laity

ST JOHN OF GOD SISTERS
Dun Bhríd,
Ballymote, Co Sligo
Tel 071-9183196/9183973
Leader: Sr Vitalis Kilroy
Community: 10

ST JOSEPH OF THE SACRED HEART SISTERS
Sisters of St Joseph of Sacred Heart,
Killasser, Swinford, Co Mayo
Tel 094-9251265

ST LOUIS SISTERS
'Louisville', Cordarragh,
Kiltimagh, Co Mayo
Tel 094-9381205
Community: 9
Varied apostolates

St Louis Community School
Tel 094-9381228
Pupils: 570

Brooklodge,
Ballyhaunis Road, Knock, Co Mayo
Tel 094-9388020
Community: 1
Prayer ministry

EDUCATIONAL INSTITUTIONS

St Nathy's College
Ballaghaderreen,
Co Roscommon
Tel 094-9860010 Fax 094-9860891
President
Very Rev Martin Convey BSc, MLitt, PhD
Priests on Staff
Rev Andrew Finan BA, HDE
Rev Leo Henry BA, HDE

CHARITABLE AND OTHER SOCIETIES

Cloonmahon Residential Centre
Cloonamahon,
Collooney, Co Sligo
North Western Health Board

Hope House
Foxford, Co Mayo
Tel 094-9256888 Fax 094-9256865
Counsellors: Sr Attracta Canny,
Sr Dolores Duggan
Treatment centre for addiction problems

Fr Patrick Peyton Centre
Attymass, Co Mayo
Tel 096-45374 Fax 096-45376

Society of St Vincent de Paul
Contact: Mr Liam McKibben
Swinford, Co Mayo
Tel 087-2522616

The Family Institute of Achonry
Family Centre, Ballaghaderreen
Tel 094-9861000
Counsellor: Sr Ethna O'Grady

DIOCESE OF ARDAGH AND CLONMACNOIS

PATRON OF THE DIOCESE
ST MEL, 7 FEBRUARY

INCLUDES NEARLY ALL OF COUNTY LONGFORD,
THE GREATER PART OF COUNTY LEITRIM
AND PARTS OF COUNTIES CAVAN, OFFALY, ROSCOMMON,
SLIGO AND WESTMEATH

Most Rev Colm O'Reilly DD
Bishop of Ardagh and
Clonmacnois;
born 11 January 1935;
ordained priest 19 June 1960;
ordained Bishop of Ardagh and
Clonmacnois 10 April 1983

Residence:
St Michael's, Longford,
Co Longford
Tel 043-3346432
Fax 043-3346833
Email ardaghdi@iol.ie

ST MEL'S CATHEDRAL, LONGFORD

On 19 May 1840, Bishop William O'Higgins laid the foundation stone of a new cathedral for the Diocese of Ardagh and Clonmacnois. The foundation stone was taken from the original Cathedral of St Mel at Ardagh. The preacher at that ceremony was the Archbishop of Tuam, Archbishop John MacHale. Four other bishops, one hundred and twenty priests and an estimated forty thousand people were present.

The architect of the cathedral was Mr John Benjamin Keane. The magnificent portico was not included in the original design. This was the work of another architect, Mr George Ashlin, and was not erected until 1883. Without any doubt Bishop O'Higgins influenced the original design, which reflected some of his own life experience, having been educated in Paris, Rome and having lived for a time in Vienna. The cathedral owes something in its design to the Madeleine in Paris, and the Pantheon and the Basilica of St John Lateran in Rome. Certainly something of the Lateran is to be seen in the attempt that was made to incorporate the bishop's house at the rear of the sanctuary.

Raising the money necessary to build the cathedral was an enormous challenge in poverty-stricken Ireland in the 1840s. Bishop O'Higgins travelled the length and breadth of the diocese and his appeals for help went well beyond the diocesan boundaries. He received great help, especially from the Dioceses of Elphin, Tuam and Meath, and contributions came from as far away as Belfast. A priest of the diocese toured North America and Canada to raise funds there.

By 1846 the walls, pillars and entire masonry were completed and the roof was the next stage in the building programme. Then the potato blight came and the Great Hunger. Work had to be suspended. Bishop O'Higgins would never see the great cathedral completed. He died in 1853.

Bishop John Kilduff, successor of Bishop O'Higgins, resumed work on the cathedral. It was opened for worship in September 1856. Though the work was not complete, it was a time of great rejoicing. Present on that special day were Archbishop Dixon of Armagh and Archbishop Cullen of Dublin, and fourteen other bishops.

It was Bishop Bartholomew Woodlock who commissioned the erection of the impressive portico, with its huge Ionic columns. He was still bishop of the diocese in 1893 when the cathedral was consecrated on 19 May.

Since 1893 much additional work has been done. Bishop Hoare, successor of Bishop Woodlock, added a pipe organ and bell chimes. Later still, two beautiful stained-glass windows, the work of the Harry Clarke Studios in Dublin, were installed in the transepts. In the 1970s a major restyling of the sanctuary was undertaken.

CHAPTER

Trustee of St Mel's Diocesan Trust
Very Reverend Jeremiah Macaulay
Archdeacon
Right Rev Mgr Patrick Earley
Very Rev Brian Brennan
Very Rev Padraig McGowan
Very Rev George Balfe
Very Rev Francis Gray
Very Rev Owen Devaney
Very Rev Peter Brady
Very Rev Aidan Ryan
Very Rev Bernard Hogan
Rt Rev Mgr Bernard Noonan
Very Rev Peter Burke
Very Rev Liam Murray
Honorary Members:
Very Rev Sean O'Rourke

ADMINISTRATION

Vicars General
Rt Rev Mgr Patrick Earley PP, VG
Rt Rev Mgr Bernard Noonan PP, VG

Diocesan Chancellor
Very Rev Michael Bannon PP
St Mary's, Drumlish, Co Longford
Tel 043-3324132

College of Consultors
Rt Rev Mgr Patrick Earley PP, VG
Rt Rev Mgr Bernard Noonan PP, VG
Rev Eamonn Corkery
Rev Francis Garvey
Rev Bernard Hogan
Rev Pat Murphy
Rev Tom Murray

Vicars Forane
Rt Rev Mgr Bernard Noonan PP, VG
Very Rev Francis Garvey PP
Very Rev Patrick Murphy PP
Very Rev Simon Cadam PP

Financial Administrator
Rev Tom Murray
Diocesan Office, St Michael's, Longford
Tel 043-3346432 Fax 043-3346833

Finance Committee
Chairman: Very Rev Brian Brennan PP
Ballinalee, Co Longford
Tel 043-3323110
Members
Mr Frank Gearty, Solicitor
Mr Des Mooney, Accountant
Mr Brian Loughran
Mr Eddie Cowan
Mr Michael Glennon
Rev Michael Bannon
Rev Tom Murray

Diocesan Archivist
Rev Tom Murray
Diocesan Office, St Michael's, Longford
Tel 043-3346432 Fax 043-3346833

Diocesan Secretary
Rev Tom Murray
Diocesan Office, St Michael's, Longford
Tel 043-3346432 Fax 043-3346833
Email ardaghdi@iol.ie

CATECHETICS EDUCATION

Pastoral Renewal and Faith Development
Rev James MacKiernan CC
Boher, Ballycumber, Co Offaly
Tel 057-9336119
Sr Anna Burke
31 Templemichael Glebe, Longford
Tel 043-3345255/3348240 (office)

Religious Education in Schools
Diocesan Advisers
Primary: Rev Michael McGrath CC
Carrick-on-Shannon, Co Leitrim
Tel 071-9620347
Sr Rose Moron
26 Castlepark, Newtownforbes,
Co Longford
Tel 043-3348021
Post-Primary: Rev Tom Murray
Diocesan Office, St Michael's, Longford
Tel 043-3346432

Diocesan Council of Catholic Primary School Managers' Association
Secretary: Mrs Eileen Ward
Diocesan Office, St Michael's, Longford
Tel 043-3346432

LITURGY

Church Music
Director: Rev Turlough Baxter CC
St Mary's, Carrick-on-Shannon,
Co Leitrim
Tel 071-9620054

Liturgy Commission
Secretary: Rev Turlough Baxter CC
St Mary's, Carrick-on-Shannon,
Co Leitrim
Tel 071-9620054

Sacred Art and Architecture Commission
Secretary: Rev Sean Casey PP
Killoe, Co Longford
Tel 043-3323119

PASTORAL

Accord
Director: Rev Patrick Murphy PP
St Mary's, Edgeworthstown,
Co Longford
Tel 043-6671046/043-3347222

Committee for Special Marriage Preparation Procedures
Rev Cathal Faughnan PP
Keadue, Boyle, Co Roscommon
Tel 071-9647212
Rev Thomas Healy Adm
The Presbytery, Longford
Tel 043-3346465
Very Rev Michael Bannon PP
St Mary's, Drumlish, Co Longford
Tel 043-3324132

Communications
Diocesan Counsellor
Very Rev Patrick Murphy PP
St Mary's, Edgeworthstown, Co Longford
Tel 043-6671046

Council of Priests
Chairman: Rev Patrick Murphy PP
St Mary's, Edgeworthstown, Co Longford
Tel 043-6671046
Secretary: Rev Tom Murray
Diocesan Office, St Michael's, Longford
Tel 043-3346432

CURA
Tel 0902-74272 (Centre)/1850-626260

Ecumenism
Rev Padraig Kelliher CC
The Presbytery, Longford
Tel 043-3346465

Family Ministry
Rev Patrick Murphy PP
St Mary's, Edgeworthstown, Co Longford
Tel 043-6671046
Sr Angela Clarkson
Teallach Iosa, St Mel's Road, Longford
Tel 043-3346827

Marriage Tribunal
(See Marriage Tribunals section.)

Pilgrimage (Lourdes)
Director
Rt Rev Mgr Bernard Noonan PP, VG

Pioneer Total Abstinence Association
Diocesan Director
Very Rev Michael Campbell PP
Abbeylara, Co Longford
Tel 043-6686270

Pontifical Mission Societies
Diocesan Director
Very Rev Aidan Ryan PP
Ballinahown, Athlone, Co Westmeath
Tel 090-6430124

Spirituality Committee
Very Rev Jeremiah Macaulay AP
Edgeworthstown, Co Longford
Tel 043-6671159

Travellers
Chaplain: Rev Nigel Charles CC
The Presbytery, Longford
Tel 043-3346465
Rev Patsy McDermott CC
St Mary's Athlone, Co Westmeath
Tel 090-6472088

Trócaire
Diocesan Director
Very Rev Bernard Hogan PP
Mohill, Co Leitrim
Tel 071-9631024

Vocations
Director: Very Rev Simon Cadam PP, VF
St Mary's, Granard, Co Longford
Tel 043-6686550

Youth Commission
Diocesan Director: Rev Patsy McDermott
St Mary's, Athlone, Co Westmeath
Tel 090-6472088/6473358

PARISHES

Mensal parishes are listed first. Other parishes follow alphabetically. Historical names are given in parentheses. Church titulars are in italics.

LONGFORD (TEMPLEMICHAEL, BALLYMACORMACK AND KILLASHEE)
St Mel's Cathedral; St Anne's, Curry, St Michael's, Shroid, St Patrick's, Killashee St Brendan's, Clondra
Rev Thomas Healy Adm
Rev Merlyn Kenny CC
Rev Nigel Charles CC
Rev Brendan O'Sullivan CC
Rev Padraig Kelliher CC
The Presbytery, Longford
Tel 043-3346432

ATHLONE
St Mary's, Athlone
Our Lady Queen of Peace, Coosan
Rev Liam Murray Adm
Rev Patrick McDermott CC
Rev Declan Shannon CC
Rev Charles Healy CC
Rev Mark Bennett CC
Rev Marek Kosciolek *(Polish Chaplaincy)*
St Mary's, Athlone, Co Westmeath
Tel 090-6472088

ABBEYLARA
St Bernard's, Abbeylara
St Mary's, Carra
Very Rev Michael Campbell PP
Carra, Granard, Co Longford
Tel 043-6686270

ANNADUFF
Immaculate Conception, Annaduff
Immaculate Conception, Drumsna
Very Rev John Wall PP
Annaduff, Carrick-on-Shannon,
Co Leitrim
Tel 071-9624093

ARDAGH AND MOYDOW
St Brigid's, Ardagh; Our Lady's, Moydow
Very Rev George Balfe PP (on sick leave)
Rev Pat Lennon, Parish Administrator
Ardagh, Co Longford
Tel 043-6675006

AUGHAVAS AND CLOONE
St Joseph's, Aughavas
St Stephen's, Rossan
St Mary's, Cloone
Very Rev Samuel Holmes PP
Cloone, Co Leitrim
Tel 071-9636016

BALLINAHOWN, BOHER AND POLLOUGH (LEMANAGHAN)
St Colmcille's, Ballinahown
St Manchain's, Ballycumber
St Mary's, Pollough
Very Rev Aidan Ryan PP
Ballinahown, Athlone,
Co Westmeath
Tel 090-6430124
Rev James MacKiernan CC
Boher, Ballycumber, Co Offaly
Tel 057-9336119

BALLYMAHON (SHRULE)
St Matthew's, Ballymahon
Very Rev Padraig MacGowan PP
Ballymahon, Co Longford
Tel 090-6432253

BORNACOOLA
St Michael's, Bornacoola
St Joseph's, Clonturk
Very Rev Gerard O'Brien PP
Bornacoola, Carrick-on-Shannon,
Co Leitrim
Tel 071-9638229

CARRICKEDMOND AND ABBEYSHRULE
(Taghshiney, Taghshinod & Abbeyshrule)
Sacred Heart, Carrickedmond
Our Lady of Lourdes, Abbeyshrule
Very Rev Peter Tiernan PP
Carrickedmond, Colehill, Co Longford
Tel 044-9357442

CARRICK-FINEA (DRUMLUMMAN SOUTH AND BALLYMACHUGH)
St Mary's, Carrick
St Mary's, Ballynarry
Very Rev Francis Gray PP
Carrick, Finea, Mullingar,
Co Westmeath
Tel 043-6681129

CARRICK-ON-SHANNON (KILTOGHERT)
St Mary of the Assumption
Carrick-on-Shannon
Sacred Heart, Jamestown
St Patrick's, Gowel
St Joseph's, Leitrim
Very Rev Francis Garvey PP, VF
Carrick-on-Shannon, Co Leitrim
Tel 071-9620118
Rev Michael McGrath CC
Tel 071-9620347
Rev Turlough Baxter CC
Tel 071-9620054
St Mary's, Carrick-on-Shannon,
Co Leitrim

CLOGHAN AND BANAGHER (GALLEN AND REYNAGH)
St Mary's, Cloghan
St Rynagh's Banagher
Very Rev Michael Scanlon PP
Cloghan, Birr, Co Offaly
Tel 090-6457122
Rev Pierre Pepper CC
Banagher, Co Offaly
Tel 057-9151338

CLONBRONEY
St James, Clonbroney
Holy Trinity, Ballinalee
Very Rev Brian Brennan PP
Ballinalee, Co Longford
Tel 043-3323110

CLOONE (CLOONE-CONMAICNE)
St Mary's, Cloone
See Aughavas & Cloone

COLMCILLE
St Colmcille's, Aughnacliffe
St Joseph's, Purth
Very Rev Seamus McKeon PP
Aughnacliffe, Co Longford
Tel 043-6684118

DROMARD
St Mary's, Legga; St Mary's, Moyne
Very Rev Eamonn Corkery PP
Dromard, Moyne, Co Longford
Tel 049-4335248

DRUMLISH
St Mary's, Drumlish
St Patrick's, Ballinamuck
Very Rev Michael Bannon PP
Drumlish, Co Longford
Tel 043-3324132
Rev Jim Sorahan CC
Ballinamuck, Co Longford
Tel 043-3324110

DRUMSHANBO (MURHAUN)
St Patrick's, Drumshanbo
Very Rev Peter Burke PP
Drumshanbo, Co Leitrim
Tel 071-9641010

EDGEWORTHSTOWN (MOSTRIM)
St Mary of the Immaculate Conception
Very Rev Patrick Murphy PP, VF
St Mary's, Mostrim,
Co Longford
Tel 043-6671046
Rev Canon Jeremiah Macaulay AP
Edgeworthstown, Co Longford
Tel 043-6671159

FENAGH
St Mary's, Foxfield
See Mohill Parish

FERBANE HIGH STREET AND BOORA (TISARAN AND FUITHRE)
Immaculate Conception, Ferbane
SS Patrick and Saran, Belmont
St Oliver Plunkett, Boora
Very Rev Francis Murray PP
Tel 090-6454380
Rev Tom Cox CC
Tel 090-6454309
Ferbane, Co Offaly

GORTLETTERAGH
St Mary's, Gortletteragh
St Thomas', Fairglass
St Joseph's, Cornageetha
Very Rev John Quinn PP
Gortletteragh,
Carrick-on-Shannon, Co Leitrim
Tel 071-9631074

GRANARD
St Mary's
Very Rev Simon Cadam PP
St Mary's, Granard, Co Longford
Tel 043-6686550
Rev Thomas Flynn CC
Granard, Co Longford
Tel 043-6686591

KEADUE, ARIGNA AND BALLYFARNON (KILRONAN)
Nativity of the Blessed Virgin, Keadue
Immaculate Conception, Arigna
St Patrick's, Ballyfarnon
Very Rev Cathal Faughnan PP
Keadue, Boyle, Co Roscommon
Tel 071-9647212

KILCOMMOC (KENAGH)
St Dominic's
Rev Thomas Barden PIC
Kenagh, Co Longford
Tel 043-3322127

KILLASHEE
St Patrick's, Killashee
St Brendan's, Clondra
See Longford (Templemichael &
Ballmacormack)

KILLENUMMERY AND BALLINTOGHER (KILLENUMMERY AND KILLERY)
St Mary's, Killenummery
St Michael's, Killavoggy
St Teresa's, Ballintogher
Rev Vincent Connoughton Adm
Killenummery, Dromahair,
via Sligo, Co Leitrim
Tel 071-9164125
Rev Sean Burke CC
Ballintogher, Co Sligo
Tel 071-9164154

KILLOE
St Mary's, Ennybegs
St Oliver Plunkett's, Cullyfad
Very Rev Sean Casey PP
Ennybegs, Longford
Tel 043-3323119

KILTUBRID
St Brigid's, Drumcong
St Joseph's, Rantogue
Very Rev Tomás Flynn PP
Drumcong, Carrick-on-Shannon
Co Leitrim
Tel 071-9642021

LANESBORO (RATHCLINE)
St Mary's, Lanesboro
Very Rev Michael Reilly PP
Lanesboro, Co Longford
Tel 043-3321166

LEGAN AND BALLYCLOGHAN (KILGLASS AND RATHREAGH)
Nativity of the Blessed Virgin Mary, Lenamore
St Ann's, Ballycloghan
Very Rev Peter Brady PP
Lenamore, Co Longford
Tel 044-9357404

LOUGH GOWNA AND MULLINALAGHTA (SCRABBY AND COLMCILLE EAST)
Holy Family, Lough Gowna
St Columba's, Mullinalaghta
Very Rev PJ Fitzpatrick PP
Gowna, Co Cavan
Tel 043-6683120

MOATE AND MOUNT TEMPLE (KILCLEAGH AND BALLYLOUGHLOE)
St Patrick's, Moate; St Ciaran's, Castledaly
Corpus Christi, Mount Temple
Rt Rev Mgr Bernard Noonan PP, VG
Tel 090-6481180
Rev Liam Farrell CC
Tel 090-6481189
Moate, Co Westmeath
Rev Patrick Kiernan CC
Mount Temple, Moate,
Co Westmeath
Tel 090-6481239

MOHILL (MOHILL-MANACHAIN)
St Patrick's, Mohill
St Joseph's, Gorvagh
St Mary's, Eslin Bridge
St Mary's, Foxfield
Very Rev Bernard Hogan PP
Tel 071-9631024
Rev Sean Connaughton (SSC) CC
Tel 071-9631097
Mohill, Co Leitrim

MULLAHORAN AND LOUGHDUFF (DRUMLUMMAN NORTH)
Our Lady of Lourdes, Mullahoran
St Joseph's, Loughduff
Very Rev Owen Devaney PP
Mullahoran, Kilcogy via Longford,
Co Cavan
Tel 043-6683141

NEWTOWNCASHEL (CASHEL)
The Blessed Virgin
Very Rev Gerard Brady PP
Newtowncashel, Co Longford
Tel 043-3325112

NEWTOWNFORBES (CLONGUISH)
St Mary's
Very Rev Ciaran McGovern PP
Newtownforbes, Co Longford
Tel 043-3346805

RATHOWEN (RATHASPIC, RUSSAGH & STREETE)
St Mary's, Rathowen
Rt Rev Mgr Patrick Earley VG
Rathowen, Mullingar,
Co Westmeath
Tel 043-6676044

SHANNONBRIDGE (CLONMACNOIS)
St Ciaran's, Shannonbridge
St Ciaran's, Clonfanlough
Very Rev Francis O'Hanlon PP
Shannonbridge,
Athlone, Co Westmeath
Tel 090-9674125

STREETE
St Mary's
See Rathown (Rathaspic and Rossagh)
Rev Joseph McGrath
Chaplain, Parochial House, Boherquill,
Lismacaffney, Mullingar, Co Westmeath

HOSPITALS AND THEIR CHAPLAINS

St Joseph's and Mount Carmel Hospitals, Longford
Chaplain's Residence,
Dublin Road, Longford
Tel 043-3346211

St Vincent's Hospital
Athlone, Co Westmeath
Very Rev Liam Murray Adm
Tel 090-6472323; 6478318 (H)

PRIESTS OF THE DIOCESE ELSEWHERE

Rev Colman Carrigy
Clonee, Killoe, Co Longford
Rev Gerard Carroll
Ballinalee Road, Longford
Rev Liam Cuffe
Chaplaincy, St Vincent's Hospital, Dublin 4
Rev Christy Stapleton
Rev Hugh Turbitt
c/o Diocesan Office, St Michael's,
Longford
Rev P. J. Hughes
On mission to Equador

RETIRED PRIESTS

Very Rev Peter Beglan PE
12 Pairc na-hAbhainn,
Edgeworthstown, Co Longford
Rev Michael Killian
Mulross Nursing Home,
Carrick-on-Shannon, Co Leitrim
Rev Dominic Lynch
Gallen Nursing Home,
Ferbane, Co Offaly
Very Rev James O'Beirne
Moate, Co Westmeath
Very Rev Canon Seán O'Rourke
Retreat Nursing Home, Athlone,
Co Westmeath
Very Rev Sean Tynan
Laurel Lodge Nursing Home,
Longford

Allianz (il)

RELIGIOUS ORDERS AND CONGREGATIONS

PRIESTS

FRANCISCANS
Franciscan Friary,
Athlone, Co Westmeath
Tel 090-6472095 Fax 090-6424713
Email athlonefriary@eircom.net
Guardian
Very Rev Michael Nicholas (OFM)

BROTHERS

MARIST BROTHERS
Champagnat House, Athlone,
Co Westmeath
Tel 090-6472336
Superior: Br Gerard Cahill
Community: 5

Marist College,
Athlone, Co Westmeath
Tel 090-6474491
Secondary pupils: 510

SISTERS

CONGREGATION OF THE SISTERS OF MERCY
Villa Maria, Ardagh, Co Longford
Tel 043-75080
Community: 1

Convent of Mercy,
St Joseph's, Longford
Tel 043-46435 Fax 043-48392
Community: 20

Bracklin
Edgeworthstown, Co Longford
Tel/Fax 043-71015
Community: 3

Sisters of Mercy,
Shalom, Edgeworthstown, Co Longford
Tel 043-71852 Fax 043-72989
Community: 8

Sisters of Mercy,
Manor Lodge, Edgeworthstown,
Co Longford
Tel 043-71102
Community: 2

Upper Main Street, Ballymahon,
Co Longford
Tel 090-6432532 Fax 090-6432848
Community: 5

Convent of Mercy,
Lanesboro, Co Longford
Tel 043-21105 Fax 043-21436
Community: 7

Convent of Mercy, 2 Cnoc na Greine
Granard, Co Longford
Tel/Fax 043-86633
Community: 3

Sisters of Mercy, 61 Cnoc na Greine,
Granard, Co Longford
Tel 043-86563
Community: 2

Mount Carmel, Station Road,
Moate, Co Westmeath
Tel 090-6481912 Fax 090-6482803
Community: 5

Gort Mhuire, Knockdomney,
Moate, Co Westmeath
Tel/Fax 090-6482265
Community: 2

Shannagh Grove,
Mohill, Co Leitrim
Tel 071-9631064
Community: 2

St Michele, Curryline,
Newtownforbes, Co Longford
Tel 043-46326
Community: 2

20 Annaly Gardens, Longford
Tel 043-41407
Community: 2

19 Midara Gardens, Longford
Tel/Fax 043-46702
Community: 1

6 Curryline, Newtownforbes,
Co Longford
Tel 043-41826
Community: 3

Sisters of Mercy,
31 Templemichael Glebe, Longford
Tel 043-45255
Community: 2

Sisters of Mercy, The Lodge,
Drumshanbo, Co Leitrim
Tel 071-9641308
Community: 3

7 Ard Michael Park,
Ballinalee Road, Longford
Tel 043-34248
Community: 3

LA SAINTE UNION DES SACRES COEURS
Our Lady's Bower,
Our Lady's Bower, Athlone,
Co Westmeath
Tel 090-6472061/6472092
Fax 090-6474853
Co-ordinato
 Sr Christopher Mary Callan
Community: 17

Secondary School (boarding and day)
Pupils: 650
Principal: Sr Denise O'Brien
Tel 090-6474777/6475524
Fax 090-6476356
Email bower@iol.ie &
srdenise@eircom.net
Web www.ourladysbower.com
St Mary's National School (Parish)
Headmistress: Mrs Margaret Naughton
Tel 090-6472321

Mont Vista, House of the Sick,
Retreat Road, Athlone
Tel 090-6472887
Sister in Charge
Sr Mary Thecla Garvey
Sick and frail elderly, province ministry,
healthcare
Community: 12

Banagher, Co Offaly
Tel 0509-51319
Email lsu1@eircom.net
Community: 13
Teaching, Parish care of the Sick and Frail
Secondary School (day pupils)
Tel 0509-51406 Fax 0509 51439
Principal: Mr Tom McGlacken
Pupils: 450

MARIST SISTERS
Marist Convent
Carrick-on-Shannon, Co Leitrim
Tel 071-9620010
Superior: Sr Eva Horkin
Community: 10

6/7 Summerhill Grove,
Carrick-on- Shannon, Co Leitrim
Tel 071-9621396
Community: 3
Health care ministry in St Patrick's
Hospital, pastoral ministry in St Patrick's
Hospital, Marist laity

MISSIONARY SISTERS OF THE HOLY ROSARY
Pullagh, Tullamore, Co Offaly
Tel 0506-36050
Community: 1

POOR CLARES
Poor Clare Monastery of Perpetual
Adoration, Drumshanbo, Co Leitrim
Abbess: Mother M. Angela McCabe
Community: 10
Contemplatives
Perpetual adoration of the Blessed
Sacrament
Small self-catering private retreat house
attached
Tel 071-9641308 Fax 071-9640789

PRESENTATION SISTERS
Presentation Sisters Provincialate,
Garden Vale, Athlone, Co Westmeath
Tel 090-6472186 Fax 090-6477617
Email presnpro@iol.ie
Administration of Northern Province of
Presentation Sisters
Provincial Superior: Sr Elizabeth Maxwell
Community: 6

ST JOSEPH OF CLUNY SISTERS
St Joseph's Convent,
Main Street, Ferbane, Co Offaly
Tel 090-6454324
Email stjf@eircom.net
Superior: Sr Helena Egan
Community: 9
Pastoral Ministry

Gallen Priory,
Ferbane, Co Offaly
Tel 090-6454416
Superior: Sr Brigid Moore
Community: 15

EDUCATIONAL INSTITUTIONS

St Mel's College, Longford
Tel 043-3346469
Principal: Mr Damian Cunningham
Priests on Teaching Staff:
Rev Joe McGrath
Chaplain: Rev Joe McGrath

Athlone Institute of Technology
Athlone, Co Westmeath
Chaplain: Rev Seamus Casey
Tel 090-6424400
Res: 11 Auburn Heights, Athlone,
Co Westmeath
Tel 090-6478318

CHARITABLE AND OTHER SOCIETIES

Apostolic Work Society
Mrs Nuala Claffey
Ferbane, Co Offaly

Knights of St Columbanus
St Mary's Square,
Athlone, Co Westmeath

Legion of Mary
Centres at Longford, Athlone,
Carrick-on-Shannon, Granard, Mohill

Our Lady's Nursing Home
Edgeworthstown, Co Longford
Tel 043-6671007

St Christopher's
Battery Road, Longford
School for mentally handicapped

St Hilda's
Grace Park Road,
Athlone, Co Westmeath
School for mentally handicapped

Social Service Council, Longford
Tel 043-3346452
Mr Padraig Gearty

Society of St Vincent de Paul
Longford:
Mrs Anne Kane
Athlone:
Mr Eugene Lee
Carrick-on-Shannon:
Mr Patrick Keaney
Mohill:
Mr Sean McGuinness
Drumshanbo:
Mrs Bea Cullen
Ferbane:
Mrs Breda Connolly

DIOCESE OF CLOGHER

PATRON OF THE DIOCESE
ST MACARTAN, 24 MARCH

INCLUDES COUNTY MONAGHAN, MOST OF COUNTY FERMANAGH
AND PORTIONS OF COUNTIES TYRONE, DONEGAL, LOUTH AND CAVAN

Most Rev Joseph Duffy DD
Bishop of Clogher;
born 3 February 1934;
ordained priest 22 June 1958;
ordained Bishop of Clogher
2 September 1979

Residence:
Bishop's House, Monaghan
Tel 047-81019 Fax 047-84773
Email diocesanoffice
@clogherdiocese.ie
Website www.clogherdiocese.ie

ST MACARTAN'S CATHEDRAL, MONAGHAN

On Sunday, 3 January 1858, at a meeting of the Catholic inhabitants of the parish and vicinity of Monaghan, with the Bishop of Clogher, Dr Charles MacNally, presiding, it was formally resolved that a new Catholic church at Monaghan was urgently required. An eight-acre site was purchased by the bishop from Humphrey Jones of Clontibret for £800, and an architect, James Joseph McCarthy of Dublin, was employed to draw a design.

The style is French Gothic of the fourteenth century. In June 1861 the foundation stone was laid, and the work got underway the following year. Dr MacNally died in 1864, and work resumed under his successor, Dr James Donnelly, in 1865. The architect died in 1882 and was succeeded by William Hague, a Cavan man, who was responsible for the design of the spire and the gate-lodge. The work was completed in 1892, and the cathedral was solemnly dedicated on 21 August of that year.

Under the direction of the present bishop, Dr Joseph Duffy, a radical rearrangement and refurbishing of the interior of the cathedral was begun in 1982 to meet the requirements of the revised liturgy. The artist responsible for the general scheme was Michael Biggs of Dublin, in consultation with local architect Gerald MacCann. The altar is carved from a single piece of granite from south County Dublin. The sanctuary steps are in solid Travertine marble. The sanctuary crucifix is by Richard Enda King; the cross is of Irish oak and the figure of Christ is cast in bronze. The Lady Chapel has a bronze Pietà by Nell Murphy, and the lettering of the Magnificat is by Michael Biggs. The tabernacle, made of silver-plated sheet bronze and mounted on a granite pillar, has the form of a tent and was designed and made by Richard Enda King. In the chapel of the Holy Oils the aumbry was designed by Michael Biggs, while the miniature bronze gates were executed by Martin Leonard. The five great tapestries on the east walls of the cathedral are a striking feature of the renovation; they were designed by Frances Biggs and woven by Terry Dunne, both of Dublin.

CHAPTER

Dean: Rt Rev Mgr Seán Cahill
Archdeacon
Rt Rev Mgr Vincent Connolly
Members
Very Rev Macartan McQuaid
Very Rev Joseph Mullin
Very Rev John McKenna
Very Rev Laurence Dawson
Very Rev John Finnegan
Rt Rev Mgr Joseph McGuinness
Very Rev John McCabe
Rt Rev Mgr Liam S. MacDaid
Very Rev Larry Duffy

ADMINISTRATION

Vicars General
Rt Rev Mgr Seán Cahill VG
6 Boyhill Road, Maguiresbridge,
Enniskillen, Co Fermanagh BT94 4LN
Tel 028-67721258
Rt Rev Mgr Vincent Connolly PP, VG
St Joseph's, Carrickmacross,
Co Monaghan
Tel 042-9663200

Chancellor
Rt Rev Mgr Liam S. MacDaid, Adm
Tyholland, Monaghan
Tel 047-85385 Fax 047-85051
Email diocesanoffice@clogherdiocese.ie

Vicars Forane
Very Rev Canon Larry Duffy
Very Rev Canon Joseph Mullin
Very Rev Canon John McCabe

Council of Administration
Rt Rev Mgr Seán Cahill
Rt Rev Mgr Vincent Connolly
Rt Rev Mgr Joseph McGuinness

Finance Committee
Chairman: Most Rev Joseph Duffy
Members
Rt Rev Mgr Sean Cahill
Rt Rev Mgr Vincent Connolly
Rt Rev Mgr Joseph McGuinness
Rt Rev Mgr Liam S. MacDaid
Mr Desmond McKenna
Financial Administrator
Mr Joseph Berwick
Bishop's House, Monaghan
Tel 047-81019 Fax 047-84773
Email diocesanoffice@clogherdiocese.ie

Diocesan Secretary
Rt Rev Mgr Liam S. MacDaid, Adm
Tyholland, Monaghan
Tel 047-85385 Fax 047-85051
Email diocesanoffice@clogherdiocese.ie

**Communications Office & Co-ordinator
of Diocesan Website**
Rev Noel McConnell CC
Shantonagh, Castleblayney,
Co Monaghan
Tel 042-9745015
Email ntmcconnell@yahoo.co.uk

CATECHETICS EDUCATION

Adult Faith Development
Diocesan Adviser
Very Rev Canon Macartan McQuaid
St Michael's College, Enniskillen,
Co Fermanagh BT74 6DE
Tel 028-66322935 Fax 028-66325128
Email mmcquaid@saintmichaels.org.uk

**Catholic Primary School Managers'
Association (RI)**
Diocesan Council Secretary
Very Rev Peter O'Reilly PP
Parochial House, Roslea,
Co Fermanagh BT92 7LA
Tel/Fax 028-67751227
Email rosleaparish@btinternet.com

Diocesan Education (NI)
Administrator: Ms Suzette Bracken
Clogher Diocesan Education Office,
8 Darling Street, Enniskillen,
Co Fermanagh BT74 7DP
Tel 028-66322709 Fax 028-66327939

Religious Education
Diocesan Advisers
Primary: Rev John Flanagan CC
Roslea, Enniskillen,
Co Fermanagh BT92 7LA
Tel 028-67751393
Post-Primary: Rev Noel McConnell
St Macartan's College, Monaghan
(ROI Schools)
Tel 047-72795 Fax 047-83341
Email ntmcconnell@yahoo.co.uk
Mrs Eileen Gallagher
St Michael's College,
Enniskillen, Co Fermanagh
(NI Schools) (Friday 9.00am-5.00pm)
Tel 028-66328210
Email egallagher@stmichaels.org.uk

LITURGY

Church Music
Director
Rt Rev Mgr Joseph McGuinness
1 Darling Street, Enniskillen,
Co Fermanagh BT74 7DP
Tel 028-66322627

Diocesan Liturgy Commission
Chairman
Rt Rev Mgr Joseph McGuinness
1 Darling Street, Enniskillen,
Co Fermanagh BT74 7DP
Tel 028-66322627
Secretary
Very Rev Owen J. McEneaney Adm
The Presbytery, Park Street, Monaghan
Tel 047-81220 Fax 047-84004
Email
parishoffice@stjosephspresbytery.com

PASTORAL

Accord
Diocesan Directors: Rev John Chester
St Joseph's Presbytery,
Park Street, Monaghan
Tel 047-81220 Fax 047-84004
Email
parishoffice@stjosephspresbytery.com
Rev Noel McGahan CC
4 Darling Street, Enniskillen,
Co Fermanagh BT74 7DP
Tel 028-66322075
Fax 028-66322248

Asylum Network Liaison Group
Chairperson: Very Rev Brian Early PP
Scotstown, Co Monaghan
Tel 047-89204 Fax 047-79772
Email bearly@eircom.net

Council of Priests
Chairman: Very Rev Peter O'Reilly PP
Parochial House, Roslea,
Co Fermanagh BT92 7LA
Tel/Fax 028-67751227
Email rosleaparish@btinternet.com
Secretary: Rev John Flanagan CC
Roslea, Enniskillen,
Co Fermanagh BT92 7LA
Tel 028-67751393

Ecumenism
Director
Rt Rev Mgr Vincent Connolly PP, VG
St Joseph's, Carrickmacross,
Co Monaghan
Tel 042-9663200
Email stjosephscarrickmacross@eircom.net

Emigrants
Director: Very Rev Lorcan Lynch PP
Derrygonnelly, Enniskillen,
Co Fermanagh BT93 6HW
Tel 028-68641207

Lourdes Pilgrimage
Director
Very Rev Canon Joseph Mullin PP, VF
Lisoneill, Lisnaskea, Enniskillen,
Co Fermanagh BT92 0JE
Tel 028-67721342

Marriage Tribunal
*Clogher Office of Armagh Regional
Marriage Tribunal*
Sr Elizabeth Fee
St Michael's Parish Centre,
28 Church Street, Enniskillen,
Co Fermanagh BT74 7EJ
Tel 028-66347860

Pioneer Total Abstinence Association
Directors: Rev James McPhillips CC
Killanny, Carrickmacross, Co Monaghan
Tel 042-9661452
Email jimmymcp@eircom.net
Rev Ian Fee CC
Lisnaskea, Enniskillen,
Co Fermanagh BT92 0JE
Tel 028-67721324
Email ianfee@aol.com

Pontifical Mission Societies
Diocesan Director
Very Rev Canon John McCabe PP, VF
Castleblayney, Co Monaghan
Tel 042-9740051

Travellers
Chaplain: Rev Michael Jordan CC
St Joseph's, Carrickmacross, Co Monaghan
Tel 042-9661231
Email michaeljordan@eircom.net

Vocations
*Director and Chairman of Vocations
Committee:* Rt Rev Mgr Seán Cahill VG
6 Boyhill Road, Maguiresbridge,
Enniskillen, Co Fermanagh BT94 4LN
Tel 028-67721258

Youth Ministry Co-ordinator
Mr Matthew McFadden
Clogher don Óige,
St Macartan's College, Monaghan
Tel 047-72784
Email info@clogherdonoige.com
Website www.clogherdonoige.com

PARISHES

*The mensal parish is listed first. Other
parishes follow alphabetically. In each
case the postal name is given first,
except where inappropriate, and the
official name in parentheses. Church
titulars are in italics.*

MONAGHAN
*St Macartan's Cathedral, St Joseph's,
St Michael's*
Email parishoffice@stjosephspresbytery.com
Very Rev Owen J. McEneaney Adm
Rev Patrick McGinn CC
Rev John Chester CC
Email jchester@stjosephspresbytery.com
St Joseph's Presbytery, Park Street,
Monaghan
Tel 047-81220 Fax 047-84004

ARNEY (CLEENISH)
*St Mary's, Arney
St Patrick's, Holywell
St Joseph's, Mullaghdun*
Very Rev Canon John Finnegan PP
Arney, Enniskillen,
Co Fermanagh BT92 2AB
Tel 028-66348217

AUGHNAMULLEN EAST
*Sacred Heart, Lough Egish
St Mary's, Carrickatee*
Very Rev Thomas Quigley PP
Latton, Castleblayney, Co Monaghan
Tel 042-9742212
Rev Noel McConnell CC
Shantonagh, Castleblayney, Co Monaghan
Tel 042-9745015
Email ntmcconnell@yahoo.co.uk

BALLYBAY (TULLYCORBET)
*St Patrick's, Ballybay
Holy Rosary, Tullycorbet
Our Lady of Knock, Ballintra*
Very Rev Laurence Flynn PP
Tel/Fax 042-9741032
Email lajflynn@eircom.net
Rt Rev Mgr Gerard McSorley PE
Tel/Fax 042-9741031
Ballybay, Co Monaghan

**BELLEEK-GARRISON (INIS MUIGHE
SAMH)**
*Our Lady, Queen of Peace, Garrison
St John the Baptist, Toura
St Joseph's, Cashelnadrea
St Patrick's, Belleek
St Michael's, Mulleek*
Very Rev Tiernach Beggan PP
Belleek, Enniskillen,
Co Fermanagh BT93 3FJ
Tel 028-68658229
Rev Joseph McVeigh CC
Loughside Road, Garrison, Enniskillen,
Co Fermanagh BT93 4AE
Tel 028-68659747
Very Rev Canon Patrick Lonergan PE
Garrison, Enniskillen,
Co Fermanagh BT93 4AE
Tel 028-68658234

BROOKEBORO (AGHAVEA-AGHINTAINE)
*St Mary's, Brookeboro
St Joseph's, Coonian
St Mary's, Fivemiletown*
Very Rev Denis Dolan PP
Fivemiletown,
Co Tyrone, BT75 OQP
Tel 028-89521291

BUNDORAN (MAGH ENE)
*Our Lady, Star of the Sea, Bundoran
St Joseph's, The Rock, Ballyshannon*
Very Rev Ramon Munster PP
Bundoran, Co Donegal
Tel 071-9841290 Fax 071-9841596
Email ppbundoran@eircom.net
Rev Frank McManus CC
The Rock, Ballyshannon, Co Donegal
Tel 071-9851221
Email stjrock@eircom.net

CARRICKMACROSS (MACHAIRE ROIS)
*St Joseph's, Carrickmacross
St Michael's, Corduff
St John the Evangelist, Raferagh*
Rt Rev Mgr Vincent Connolly PP, VG
Tel 042-9663200
Email stjosephscarrickmacross@eircom.net
Rev Michael Jordan CC
Email michaeljordan@eircom.net
Rev Padraig McKenna CC
Tel 042-9661231
St Joseph's, Carrickmacross,
Co Monaghan
Rev Brendan McCague CC
Corduff, Carrickmacross, Co Monaghan
Tel 042-9669456

CASTLEBLAYNEY (MUCKNO)
*St Mary's, Castleblayney
St Patrick's, Oram*
Very Rev Canon John McCabe PP, VF
Tel 042-9740051
Email mucknoparish@eircom.net
Rev Kevin Duffy CC
Rev Adrian Walshe CC
Email ad-walshe@eircom.net
Tel 042-9740027
Castleblayney, Co Monaghan

CLOGHER
St Patrick's, St Macartan's
Very Rev Canon Laurence Dawson PP
Clogher, Co Tyrone BT76 0TQ
Tel 028-85548600
Email dawson829@btinternet.com
Rev John F. McKenna CC
19 Ballagh Road, Clogher,
Co Tyrone BT76 0TQ
Tel 028-85548525
Email jmckenna420@live.ie

CLONES
*Sacred Heart, Clones
St Macartan's, Aghadrumsee
St Alphonsus, Connons*
Very Rev Canon Larry Duffy PP, VF
Clones, Co Monaghan
Tel 047-51048
Email clonesparish@eircom.net
Rev John Kearns CC
Priests' House, Clones, Co Monaghan
Tel/Fax 047-51064
Email jkearnzie@hotmail.com
Rev Owen Gorman CC
Aghadrumsee, Roslea, Enniskillen,
Co Fermanagh BT92 7NQ
Tel 028-67751231

CLONTIBRET
*St Michael's, Annyalla
St Mary's, Clontibret
All Saints, Doohamlet*
Very Rev Paudge McDonnell PP
Annyalla, Castleblayney, Co Monaghan
Tel 042-9740121
Email ppclontibretparish@eircom.net
Rev Michael Gilsenan (SSCC) CC
Clontibret, Co Monaghan
Tel 047-80631
Email gilsenaeve@eircom.net
Very Rev Canon Philip Connolly PE
Doohamlet Castleblayney, Co Monaghan
Tel 042-9741239

**CORCAGHAN (KILMORE AND
DRUMSNAT)**
*St Michael's, Corcaghan
St Mary's, Threemilehouse*
Very Rev Joseph McCluskey PP
Threemilehouse, Monaghan
Tel 047-81501
Very Rev Thomas Coffey PE
Corcaghan, Monaghan
Tel 042-9744806

DERRYGONNELLY (BOTHA)
St Patrick's, Derrygonnelly
Sacred Heart, Boho
Immaculate Conception, Monea
Very Rev Lorcan Lynch PP
Derrygonnelly, Enniskillen,
Co Fermanagh BT93 6HW
Tel 028-68641207

DONAGH
St Mary's, Glennan
St Patrick's, Corracrin
Very Rev Hubert Martin PP
Glaslough, Monaghan
Tel 047-88120
Email donaghparish@emyvale.eu
Rev Cathal Deery CC
Emyvale, Monaghan
Tel 047-87221
Email cathaldeery@utvinternet.com

DONAGHMOYNE
St Lastra's, Donaghmoyne
St Patrick's, Broomfield
St Mary's, Lisdoonan
Very Rev Michael Daly PP
Broomfield, Castleblayney,
Co Monaghan
Tel 042-9743617
Email dalyml@eircom.net

DROMORE
St Davog's
Very Rev Patrick MacEntee PP
Shanmullagh, Dromore, Omagh,
Co Tyrone BT78 3DZ
Tel 028-82898641
Email pmacentee@tiscali.co.uk
Very Rev Canon Thomas Breen PE
37 Esker Road, Dromore, Omagh,
Co Tyrone BT78 3LE
Tel 028-82898216

EDERNEY (CÚL MÁINE)
St Joseph's, Ederney
St Patrick's, Montiagh
Very Rev Brendan Gallagher PP
Ederney, Enniskillen,
Co Fermanagh BT93 0DG
Tel 028-68631315
Email beegeeb@hotmail.com

ENNISKILLEN
St Michael's, Enniskillen
St Mary's, Lisbellaw
Rt Rev Mgr Joseph McGuinness PP
1 Darling Street, Enniskillen,
Co Fermanagh BT74 7DP
Tel 028-66322627
Email parishcentre@st-michaels.net
Rev Noel McGahan CC
Rev Martin O'Reilly CC
4 Darling Street, Enniskillen,
Co Fermanagh BT74 7DP
Tel 028-66322075
Fax 028-66322248

ERRIGAL TRUAGH
Holy Family, Ballyoisin
St Patrick's, Clara
Sacred Heart, Carrickroe
Very Rev Seán Nolan PP
St Joseph's, Emyvale, Monaghan
Tel/Fax 047-87152
Email tru@tinet.ie
Rev Cathal Deery CC
Emyvale, Monaghan
Tel 047-87221
Email cathaldeery@utvinternet.com

ESKRA
St Patrick's
Very Rev Terence Connolly PP
178 Newtownsaville Road,
Omagh, Co Tyrone BT78 2RJ
Tel 028-82841306

FINTONA (DONACAVEY)
St Laurence's
Very Rev James Moore PP
Tel 028-82841907
Email frjlm@hotmail.com
Very Rev Canon Patrick Marron PE
Tel 028-82841239 Fax 028-82840302
Email fintonaparish@hotmail.com
Fintona, Omagh, Co Tyrone BT78 2NS

INNISKEEN
Mary, Mother of Mercy
Very Rev Martin Treanor PP
Inniskeen, Dundalk, Co Louth
Tel 042-9378105
Email martintreanor@eircom.net
Rev Noel Conlon CC
Inniskeen, Dundalk, Co Louth
Tel 042-9378678

IRVINESTOWN (DEVENISH)
Sacred Heart, Irvinestown
St Molaise, Whitehill
Very Rev Michael McGourty PP
Irvinestown, Enniskillen,
Co Fermanagh BT94 1EY
Tel 028-68628600
Very Rev Canon Gerald Timoney PE
Irvinestown, Enniskillen,
Co Fermanagh BT94 1GD
Tel 028-68621329

KILLANNY
St Enda's
Very Rev Martin Treanor PP
Inniskeen, Dundalk, Co Louth
Tel 042-9378105
Email martintreanor@eircom.net
Rev James McPhillips CC
Killanny, Carrickmacross, Co Monaghan
Tel 042-9661452
Email jimmymcp@eircom.net

KILLEEVAN (CURRIN, KILLEEVAN AND AGHABOG)
St Livinus', Killeevan, St Mary's, Ture
Immaculate Conception, Scotshouse
St Mary's, Latnamard
Very Rev Peter Corrigan PP
Shanco, Newbliss, Co Monaghan
Tel 047-54011
Email pocorragine@eircom.net

Rev Seamus Quinn CC
Scotshouse, Clones, Co Monaghan
Tel 047-56016
Email ocoinne@iol.ie
Very Rev Hugh McCaughey PE
St Mary's, Latnamard,
Smithboro, Co Monaghan
Tel 042-9744976

LATTON (AUGHNAMULLEN WEST)
St Mary's, Latton, St Patrick's, Bawn
Very Rev Thomas Quigley PP
Latton, Castleblayney, Co Monaghan
Tel 042-9742212

LISNASKEA (AGHALURCHER)
Holy Cross, Lisnaskea
St Mary's, Maguiresbridge
Very Rev Canon Joseph Mullin PP, VF
Tel 028-67721342
Rev Ian Fee CC
Tel 028-67721324
Email ianfee@aol.com
Lisnaskea, Enniskillen,
Co Fermanagh BT92 0JE
Rt Rev Mgr Seán Cahill VG
6 Boyhill Road, Maguiresbridge,
Enniskillen, Co Fermanagh BT94 4LN
Tel 028-67721258

MAGHERACLOONE
St Patrick's (The Rock Chapel), Carrickasedge
SS Peter and Paul, Drumgossatt
Very Rev Thomas Finnegan PP
Liscarnan, Magheracloone,
Carrickmacross, Co Monaghan
Tel 042-9663500
Email magheraclooneparish@eircom.net
Rev Philip Crowe (CSSp) CC
Drumgossatt, Carrickmacross,
Co Monaghan
Tel 042-9661388

NEWTOWNBUTLER (GALLOON)
St Mary's, Newtownbutler
St Patrick's, Donagh, Lisnaskea
Very Rev Michael King PP
Tel 028-67738229
Very Rev Canon Edward Murphy PE
Tel 028-67738640
Newtownbutler, Enniskillen,
Co Fermanagh BT92 8JJ

PETTIGO
St Mary's, Pettigo
St Patrick's, Lettercran
Rt Rev Mgr Richard Mohan Adm
Pettigo, Co Donegal
Tel 071-9861666
Lough Derg (see Charitable Societies)
Tel/Fax 071-9861518
Email pettigoparish@loughderg.org

ROCKCORRY (EMATRIS)
Holy Trinity, St Mary's, Corrawacan
Very Rev Thomas Quigley PP
Latton, Castleblayney, Co Monaghan
Tel 042-9742212
Very Rev Canon Gerard Ferguson PE
Rockcorry, Monaghan
Tel 042-9742243

ROSLEA
St Tierney's, Roslea
St Mary's, Magherarney
Very Rev Peter O'Reilly PP
Parochial House, Roslea,
Co Fermanagh BT92 7LA
Tel/Fax 028-67751227
Email rosleaparish@btinternet.com
Rev John Flanagan CC
Roslea, Enniskillen,
Co Fermanagh BT92 7LA
Tel 028-67751393

TEMPO (POBAL)
Immaculate Conception, Tempo
St Joseph's, Cradien
Very Rev John Halton PP
Tempo, Enniskillen,
Co Fermanagh BT94 3LY
Tel 028-89541344
Email johnhalton19@btinternet.com

TRILLICK (KILSKEERY)
St Macartan's, Trillick
St Mary's, Coa
Very Rev Canon John McKenna PP
Trillick, Omagh, Co Tyrone BT78 3RD
Tel 028-89561350
Very Rev Canon Thomas Marron PE
Trillick, Omagh, Co Tyrone BT78 3RD
Tel 028-89561217

TYDAVNET
St Dympna's, Tydavnet
St Mary's, Urbleshanny
St Joseph's, Knockatallon
Very Rev Brian Early PP
Scotstown, Co Monaghan
Tel 047-89204 Fax 047-79772
Email bearly@eircom.net
Very Rev Canon Sean Clerkin PE
Tydavnet, Co Monaghan
Tel/Fax 047-89402
Email sclerkin@utvinternet.com

TYHOLLAND
St Patrick's
Rt Rev Mgr Liam S. MacDaid Adm
Tyholland, Monaghan
Tel 047-85385 Fax 047-85051
Email diocesanoffice@clogherdiocese.ie

INSTITUTIONS AND THEIR CHAPLAINS

Daughters of Our Lady of the Sacred Heart Convent
Ballybay, Co Monaghan
Rev Gerard Jennings
Tel 042-9741524

Erne Hospital, Enniskillen
Curates of Enniskillen parish
Tel 028-66322075 Fax 028-66322248

Finner Army Camp
Ballyshannon, Co Donegal
Rev Alan Ward CF
Tel 071-9842294

Monaghan General Hospital
Curates of Monaghan parish
Tel 047-81220 Fax 047-84004

St Davnet's Hospital, Monaghan
Curates of Monaghan parish
Tel 047-81220 Fax 047-84004

St Mary's Hospital
Castleblayney, Co Monaghan
Curates of Castleblayney parish
Tel 042-9740027

PRIESTS OF THE DIOCESE ELSEWHERE

Rev Dr Patrick Connolly
Theology Department,
Mary Immaculate College,
South Circular Road, Limerick
Tel 061-204575 Fax 061-313632
Email patrick.connolly@mic.ul.ie
Rev Patrick McHugh
Western Theological Institute,
1 The Mall, Knock, Co Mayo
Tel 094-9376664
Email pat@theologywest.ie
Rev Jeremiah Carroll
Archdiocese of Dublin/Defence Forces
Study leave/contact addresses
Rev Benedict Hughes
Kellystown, Coolderry Road,
Carrickmacross, Co Monaghan
Tel 086-3864907
Rev Terence McElvaney
Church Square, Monaghan
Tel 047-82255

RETIRED PRIESTS

Very Rev Liam Hughes PE
Inniskeen, Dundalk, Co Louth
Tel 042-9378338 Fax 042-9378988
Very Rev Canon Brian McCluskey PE
Apt 2, 2 Danesfort Park North,
Stranmillis Road, Belfast BT9 5RB
Tel 028-90683544
Very Rev Edmond Maguire PE
Donaghmoyne, Carrickmacross,
Co Monaghan
Tel 042-9661586
Rev Joseph McKenna
(Birmingham Diocese)
1 St Joseph's Villas, Church Road,
Bundoran, Co Donegal
Tel 071-9841756
Very Rev Canon Gerard McGreevy PE
Magherarney, Smithboro,
Co Monaghan
Tel 047-57011
Very Rev Canon Peter McGuinness PE
3 Castleross Retirement Village,
Carrickmacross, Co Monaghan
Tel 042-9690013

RELIGIOUS ORDERS AND CONGREGATIONS

PRIESTS

PASSIONISTS
St Gabriel's Retreat,
The Graan, Enniskillen, Co Fermanagh
Tel 028-66322272
Fax 028-66325201
Superior: Rev Brian D'Arcy (CP)
Email crccp@aol.com

SACRED HEARTS COMMUNITY
Cootehill, Co Cavan
Tel 049-5552188
Br Harry O'Gara (SSCC)

St Mary's,
Clontibret, Co Monaghan
Tel 047-80631
Rev Michael Gilsenan
Email gilsenaeve@eircom.net

BROTHERS

PATRICIAN BROTHERS
Kilmactrasna,
Carrickmacross, Co Monaghan
Tel 042-9662462
Superior: Br Gregory Fox
Community: 2

SISTERS

CONGREGATION OF THE SISTERS OF MERCY
Northern Province, Provincial House,
74 Main Street, Clogher,
Co Tyrone BT76 0AA
Tel 028-85548127 Fax 028-85549459
Provincial Leader: Sr Nellie McLaughlin

11 Castlehill Gardens, Augher,
Co Tyrone BT77 0HA
Tel 028-85548157

Castleblayney, Co Monaghan
Tel 042-9740069
Contact: Sr Margaret McQuaid
Community: 12

St Brigid's, 2 Ballagh Road, Clogher,
Co Tyrone BT76 0HE
Tel 028-85548015

Convent of Mercy, 6 Belmore Street,
Enniskillen, Co Fermanagh
Tel 028-66322561
Leader: Sr Maureen McGurren
Community: 20

55 Carrowshee Park, Lisnaskea,
Co Fermanagh BT92 0FR
Tel 028-67721955

Gate House, 72 Main Street, Clogher,
Co Tyrone BT76 0AA
Tel 028-85549545

Sisters of Mercy, 6 Gorminish Park,
Garrison, Co Fermanagh BT93 4GP
Tel 028-68659742

No. 16 The Grange,
Presentation Walk, Monaghan
Tel 047-84569

Buíochas, 29 The Commons, Bellanaleck,
Enniskillen, Co Fermanagh BT92 2BD
Tel 028-66349722

6 Ferndale,
Clogher, Co Tyrone BT76 0AS
Tel 028-85548163

16 Featherbed Glade, Enniskillen,
Co Fermanagh BT74 7HW
Tel 028-66320792

St Faber's, 8 Castlecourt, Monea,
Co Fermanagh BT93 7AR
Tel 028-66341197

73 Scaffog Avenue, Sligo Road,
Enniskillen, Co Fermanagh BT74 7JJ
Tel 028-66327474

100A Drungoon Road, Maguiresbridge,
Co Fermanagh BT94 4QX
Tel 028-66385056

1 Castle View Court, Sligo Road,
Enniskillen, Co Fermanagh BT74

DAUGHTERS OF OUR LADY OF THE SACRED HEART
Ballybay, Co Monaghan
Tel 042-9741068
Superior: Sr Aloysius O'Rourke
Community: 5
St Joseph's Nursing Home
Superior: Sr Kathleen McQuillan
Tel 042-9741141. Beds: 26
Community: 19

ST LOUIS SISTERS
St Louis Convent,
Louisville, Monaghan
Tel 047-81411
Leader: Sr Miriam Brady
Community: 27
Varied apostolates
Post-Primary School. Tel 047-81422
Pupils: 820
Primary School. Tel 047-81305
Pupils: 237
Infant School. Tel 047-82913
Pupils: 278

Our Lady's Community,
Louisville, Monaghan
Tel 047-82006
Community: 5
Varied apostolates

5 Lakeview, Monaghan
Tel 047-84122
Community: 3
Varied apostolates

St Raphael,
3 Lakeview, Monaghan
Tel 047-84719
Community: 2
Varied apostolates

173 Mullaghmatt, Monaghan
Tel 047-84110
Community: 3
Varied apostolates

Rowan Tree Court,
24 Mullach Glas Close, Monaghan
Tel 047-38685
Community: 1

Carrickmacross, Co Monaghan
Tel 042-9661247
Community: 18
Varied apostolates
Secondary. Tel 042-9661587/9661467
Pupils: 600

Iona House, Farney Street
Carrickmacross, Co Monaghan
Tel 042-9663326
Community: 3
Varied apostolates

Clondergole, Clones, Co Monaghan
Tel 047-51136
Community: 1
Parish work

4 White Maple Drive,
Bundoran, Co Donegal
Tel 071-9829505
Community: 3
Varied apostolates

5 White Maple Drive,
Bundoran, Co Donegal
Tel 071-9841330
Community: 2
Varied apostolates

EDUCATIONAL INSTITUTIONS

St Macartan's College
Monaghan, Co Monaghan
Tel 047-81642/83365/83367
Fax 047-83341
Email admin@stmacartanscollege.ie
Manager
Very Rev Shane McCaughey BD
Principal
Mr Raymond McHugh BA, HDipEd, MSc
Chaplain
Rev Stephen Joyce
Email joyces@eircom.net

St Michael's College
Enniskillen, Co Fermanagh BT74 6DE
Tel 028-66322935
Fax 028-66325128
Email office@saintmichaels.org.uk
Principal: Mr Eugene McCullough
Chaplain
Very Rev Canon Macartan McQuaid
Email mmcquaid@stmichaels.org.uk

CHARITABLE AND OTHER SOCIETIES

ACCORD
St Macartan's College, Monaghan
Tel 047-83359
(10am-1pm Mon-Fri)

Ros Erne House,
8 Darling Street, Enniskillen,
Co Fermanagh BT74 7EW
Tel 028-66325696
(9am-5pm Mon-Fri)

CURA
7 The Grange, Plantation Walk,
Monaghan
Tel 047-83600
Contact person: Sr Brenda McCrudden

Lough Derg, St Patrick's Purgatory
Pettigo, Co Donegal
Tel/Fax 071-9861518
Email info@loughderg.org
Prior: Rt Rev Mgr Richard Mohan
Manager: Ms Deborah Maxwell
Email manager@loughderg.org
Pilgrimage season, 1 June-15 August.
No advance booking or notice required.
Pilgrims arrive daily before 3 pm, having
fasted from midnight, and remain on the
island for two complete days of prayer
and penance.
One-day retreats before and after main
pilgrimage season.
School retreats also offered.
Tel for details and reservations.

Veritas Bookshop & Christian Art Gallery
Park Street, Monaghan
Manager: Ms Mary Flynn
Tel 047-84077

DIOCESE OF CLONFERT

PATRON OF THE DIOCESE
ST BRENDAN, 16 MAY

INCLUDES PORTIONS OF COUNTIES GALWAY, OFFALY AND ROSCOMMON

Most Rev John Kirby DD
Bishop of Clonfert;
born October 1938;
ordained priest 23 June 1963;
ordained Bishop of Clonfert
9 April 1988

Residence:
Coorheen, Loughrea,
Co Galway
Tel 091-841560
Fax 091-841818
Email clonfert@iol.ie

ST BRENDAN'S CATHEDRAL, LOUGHREA

St Brendan's Cathedral stands at the western extremity of the Diocese of Clonfert on the main highway from Dublin to Galway. The foundation stone of the cathedral was laid on 10 October 1897, and the fabric was completed in 1902. Plans were drawn by the Dublin architect William Byrne for a building in the neo-Gothic style, having a nave and an aspidal sanctuary, lean-to aisles and shallow transepts, with a graceful spire at the western end. Its dimensions were determined by the needs of the parish of Loughrea. While not impressive, its proportions are good, and despite a departure from the original plan by curtailment of the sanctuary, the overall effect is pleasing. The simplicity of the exterior, however, hardly prepares the visitor for the riches within.

It was due to two fortuitous circumstances that St Brendan's became a veritable treasure house of the Celtic Revival in sculpture, stained glass, woodcarving, metalwork and textiles.

The first circumstance was that the building of a Catholic cathedral was delayed for various reasons until close to the turn of the last century. The Irish Literary Renaissance was by then well advanced. When the building was completed in 1902, the Arts and Crafts movement was having effect.

The second circumstance was that of Edward Martyn's birth at the home of his maternal grandfather, James Smyth, in the parish of Loughrea. Martyn was an ascetic man and devoted his time and fortune to the development of every phase of the Irish revival, the Gaelic League, Sinn Féin, the Irish Literary Theatre, Irish music, church music and church art. With innate business acumen, he insured by personal donation and the financial support of the Smyth family that the new cathedral would reflect his views. The bishop, Dr John Healy, who was sensitive to the prevailing trend, accepted the challenge and assigned the project to the supervision of a young

curate in the parish, Fr Jeremiah O'Donovan, who was himself actively engaged in propaganda for Revival.

John Hughes was the foremost sculptor in the country at the time, and Bishop Healy commissioned him to do the modelling and carving. His work is found in the bronze figure of Christ on the reredos of the high altar and in the magnificent marble statue of the Virgin and Child. Michael Shortall, a student of Hughes in the Metropolitan School of Art, did the carvings on the corbels and executed the statue of St Brendan on the wall of the tower. His connection with the cathedral continued over twenty years, and he was responsible for carvings of incidents from the life and voyage of St Brendan carved on the capitals of the pillars.

The Yeats sisters, Lily and Elizabeth, along with their friend Evelyn Gleeson, set up the Dun Emer guild. They embroidered twenty-four banners of Irish saints for use in the cathedral. Jack B. Yeats and his wife Mary designed

these banners. With an economy of detail and richness of colour, they almost achieve the effect of stained glass. Mass vestments, embroidered with silk on poplin, also came from the same studio.

More than anything else, St Brendan's is famous for its stained glass. Martyn was particularly concerned about the quality of stained glass then available in Ireland. He was eager to set up an Irish stained-glass industry. He succeeded in having Alfred E. Childe appointed to the Metropolitan School of Art, and he later persuaded Sarah Purser to open a co-operative studio, where young artists could be trained in the technique of stained glass. This new studio, An Túr Gloinne, opened in January 1903, with Childe as manager, and so began the work of the Loughrea stained-glass windows. Over the next forty years, Childe, Purser and Michael Healy executed almost all the stained-glass windows in the cathedral, and it is these windows that have given St Brendan's its place in the Irish Artistic Revival.

ADMINISTRATION

Vicars General
Rt Rev Mgr Cathal Geraghty VG
St Brendan's Cathedral, Barrack Street,
Loughrea, Co Galway
Tel 091-841212

Vicars Forane
Very Rev Michael Finneran PP
Very Rev Ciaran Kitching PP
Very Rev Martin McNamara PP

Bishop's Secretary
Mrs Geraldine Dowling
Coorheen, Loughrea, Co Galway
Tel 091-841560 Fax 091-841818
Email clonfert@iol.ie

Diocesan Secretary
Vacant

Chancellor
Rt Rev Mgr Cathal Geraghty VG
St Brendan's Cathedral, Barrack Street,
Loughrea, Co Galway
Tel 091-841212

College of Consultors
Very Rev Michael Finneran PP, VF
Very Rev Ciaran Kitching PP
Very Rev John Garvey Adm
Very Rev Cathal Geraghty Adm
Very Rev Martin McNamara PP

Diocesan Finance Committe
Most Rev John Kirby DD
Very Rev Cathal Geraghty VG
Very Rev Martin McNamara PP
Mr Gerard McInerney
Mrs Nancy O'Gorman
Mr Patrick McDonagh

Diocesan Council of Priests
Chairman
Very Rev Seamus Bohan PP
Tynagh, Loughrea, Co Galway
Tel 090-9745113
Secretary: Very Rev P. J. Bracken PP
Fahy, Eyrecourt, Ballinasloe, Co Galway
Tel 090-9675116
Members
Most Rev John Kirby DD
Right Rev Mgr Ned Stankard PP
Very Rev Michael Finneran PP, VF
Very Rev Ciaran Kitching PP
Very Rev John Garvey Adm
Very Rev Cathal Geraghty Adm
Rev Bernard Costello
Rev Iomar Daniels
Rev Declan Kelly
Rev Thomas Shanahan (ODC)

Diocesan Archivist
Rev Declan Kelly Adm
St Andrew's Church, Leitrim,
Loughrea, Co Galway
Tel 091-841758

CATECHETICS EDUCATION

Adult Education
Very Rev Ciaran Kitching PP
Killimor, Ballinasloe, Co Galway
Tel 090-9676151

Catholic Primary School Managers' Association
Secretary: Very Rev P. J. Bracken PP
Fahy, Eyrecourt,
Ballinasloe, Co Galway
Tel 090-9675116

Primary Schools
Diocesan Adviser
Rev Declan McInerney
Our Lady of Lourdes, Creagh,
Ballinasloe, Co Galway
Tel 090-9645080

PASTORAL

Accord
Director: Rev John Garvey Adm
St Michael's,
Ballinasloe, Co Galway
Tel 090-9643916

Legion of Mary
Diocesan Director
Very Rev Patrick Conroy PP
Ballinakill, Loughrea, Co Galway
Tel 090-9745021

Marriage Tribunal
(See Marriage Tribunals section)

Mixed Marriages
Counsellor
Rt Rev Mgr Edward Stankard PP
Cappatagle, Ballinasloe, Co Galway
Tel 091-843017

Pilgrimages
Diocesan Director: Rev Pat Conroy PP
Ballinakill, Loughrea, Co Galway
Tel 090-9745021

Pioneer Total Abstinence Association
Diocesan Director
Very Rev John Naughton PP
Eyrecourt, Ballinasloe, Co Galway
Tel 090-9675148

Pontifical Mission Societies
Diocesan Director
Very Rev Brendan Lawless PP
Dunkellin Terrace,
Portumna, Co Galway
Tel 090-9741092

Travellers
Chaplain: Very Rev John Naughton PP
Eyrecourt, Ballinasloe, Co Galway
Tel 090-9675148

Trócaire
Very Rev Brendan Lawless PP
Dunkellin Terrace, Portumna, Co Galway
Tel 090-9741092

Vocations
Director: Rev Iomar Daniels
Chaplaincy Department, NUIG,
St Declan's, Distillery Road, Galway
Tel 091-492168 ext 2168

PARISHES

Mensal parishes are listed first. Other parishes follow alphabetically. Historical names are given in parentheses. Church titulars are in italics.

LOUGHREA, ST BRENDAN'S CATHEDRAL
Very Rev Cathal Geraghty Adm, VG
Rev Sean Egan CC
Rev Aidan Costello CC
The Presbytery, Loughrea, Co Galway
Tel 091-841212

BALLINASLOE, CREAGH AND KILCLOONEY
St Michael's, Ballinasloe
Very Rev John Garvey Adm
Rev Dan O'Donovan
Tel 090-9643916
Our Lady of Lourdes, Creagh
Rev Declan McInerney CC
Creagh, Ballinasloe, Co Galway
Tel 090-9645080

AUGHRIM AND KILCONNELL
St Catherine's, Aughrim
Sacred Heart, Kilconnell
Very Rev Gerard Geraghty PP
Aughrim, Ballinasloe, Co Galway
Tel 090-9673724/ 090-9686614

BALLINAKILL
St Joseph's, Ballinakill
St Patrick's, Derrybrien
Very Rev Pat Conroy PP
Ballinakill, Loughrea, Co Galway
Tel 090-9745021

BALLYMACWARD AND GURTEEN (BALLYMACWARD AND CLONKEENKERRIL)
SS Peter and Paul
Very Rev Sean Slattery PP
Ballymacward, Ballinasloe, Co Galway
Tel 090-9687614
St Michael's

CAPPATAGLE AND KILRICKLE (KILLALAGHTAN AND KILRICKILL)
Our Lady of Lourdes
St Michael's
Rt Rev Mgr Edward Stankard PP
Cappatagle, Ballinasloe, Co Galway
Tel 091-843017

CLONTUSKERT
St Augustine's
Very Rev Michael Finneran PP, VF
Clontuskert, Ballinasloe, Co Galway
Tel 090-9642256

**CLOSTOKEN AND KILCONIERAN
(KILCONICKNY, KILCONIERAN AND
LICKERRIG)**
Holy Family, Immaculate Conception
Very Rev Benny Flanagan PP
Carrabane, Athenry, Co Galway
Tel 091-841103

**DUNIRY AND ABBEY (DUNIRY AND
KILNELEHAN)**
Holy Family
Very Rev Seán Lyons PP
Duniry, Loughrea, Co Galway
Tel 090-9745125
Assumption
Rev John Hickey CC
Abbey, Loughrea, Co Galway
Tel 090-9745217

**EYRECOURT, CLONFERT AND MEELICK
(CLONFERT, DONANAGHTA AND
MEELICK)**
St Brendan's
Very Rev John Naughton PP
Eyrecourt, Ballinasloe, Co Galway
Tel 090-9675148

**FAHY AND QUANSBORO (FAHY AND
KILQUAIN)**
Consoler of the Afficted, Christ the King
Very Rev P. J. Bracken PP
Fahy, Eyrecourt, Ballinasloe,
Co Galway
Tel 090-9675116

**FOHENAGH AND KILLURE (FOHENAGH
AND KILGERRILL)**
St Patrick's
Rev Christy McCormack
Fohenagh, Ahascragh,
Ballinasloe, Co Galway
Tel 090-9688623

**KILLIMOR AND TIRANASCRAGH
(KILLIMORBOLOGUE AND
TIRANASCRAGH)**
St Joseph's
Very Rev Ciaran Kitching PP
Killimor, Ballinasloe, Co Galway
Tel 090-9676151
Rev Noel Lynch CC
Tiranascragh, Ballinasloe, Co Galway
Tel 090-9675238

**KILNADEEMA AND AILLE (KILNADEEMA
AND KILTESKILL)**
St Dympna's, St Mary's, Aille, Loughrea
Very Rev Joseph Clarke PP
Kilnadeema, Loughrea, Co Galway
Tel 091-841201

**KILTULLA AND ATTYMON
(KILLIMORDALY AND KILLTULAGH)**
*SS Peter & Paul, Kiltulla,
St Mary's, Cloncagh,
St Iomar's, Killimordaly*
Very Rev Martin McNamara PP
Kiltulla, Athenry, Co Galway
Tel 091-848021
Rev Richard McMahon (CSsR) CC
Tel 091-848208

**LAWRENCETOWN AND KILTORMER
(KILTORMER AND OGHILL)**
St Mary's, St Patrick's
Very Rev Christopher O'Byrne PP
Lawrencetown, Ballinasloe, Co Galway
Tel 090-9685613

**LEITRIM AND BALLYDUGGAN
(KILCOOLEY AND LEITRIM)**
St Andrew's, St Jarlath's, Ballyduggan
Rev Declan Kelly Adm
St Andrew's Church, Leitrim,
Loughrea, Co Galway
Tel 091-841758

LUSMAGH
St Cronan's
Very Rev Phil Hearty (CSsR) Adm
Lusmagh, Banagher, Co Offaly
Tel 0509-51358

**MULLAGH AND KILLORAN
(ABBEYGORMICAN AND KILLORAN)**
St Brendan's
Very Rev Vivian Twohig PP
Mullagh, Loughrea, Co Galway
Tel 091-843119
Our Lady of the Assumption
Rev John Mannion CC
Killoran, Ballinasloe, Co Galway
Tel 090-9627120

**NEW INN AND BULLAUN (BULLAUN,
GRANGE AND KILLAAN)**
*St Killian's, New Inn
St Patrick's, Bullaun*
Very Rev Pat Kenny PP
St Killian Church, Newinn,
Ballinasloe, Co Galway
Tel 090-9675819

**PORTUMNA (KILMALINOGUE AND
LICKMOLASSEY)**
St Brigid's, SS Peter & Paul, Ascension
Very Rev Brendan Lawless PP
Dunkellin Terrace, Portumna, Co Galway
Tel 090-9741092

TAGHMACONNELL
St Ronan's
Very Rev Sean Neylon PP
Taghmaconnell, Ballinasloe, Co Galway
Tel 090-9683929

TYNAGH
St Lawrence's, Sacred Heart
Very Rev Seamus Bohan PP
Tynagh, Loughrea, Co Galway
Tel 090-9745113

WOODFORD
St John the Baptist, St Brendan's
Very Rev Kieran O'Rourke PP
Looscaun, Woodford, Co Galway
Tel 090-9749100

INSTITUTIONS AND THEIR CHAPLAINS

Emmanuel House of Providence
Clonfert, Ballinasloe, Co Galway
Director: Mr Eddie Stones
Chaplain: Fr Michael Kennedy
Tel 057-9151552

Portiuncula Hospital
Ballinasloe, Co Galway
Tel 090-9642140
Rev Bernard Costello

St Brendan's Home
Loughrea, Co Galway
Tel 091-841122
Rt Rev Mgr Cathal Geraghty Adm
Tel 091-841212

St Brigid's Hospital
Ballinasloe, Co Galway
Tel 090-9642117
Rev Bernard Costello

Vocational School
Loughrea, Co Galway
Tel 091-841919
Rev Declan Kelly Adm
Tel 090-9675819

Vocational School
New Inn, Co Galway
Tel 090-9675811
Very Rev Pat Kenny PP
Tel 091-841081

PRIESTS OF THE DIOCESE ELSEWHERE

Rev Martin Hough, England
Rev Cathal Stanley, Portumna

PRIESTS WORKING OUTSIDE THE DIOCESE

Rev Michael Byrnes
Galway Marriage Tribunal
Rev T. J. O'Connell
Kent, England
Rev Iomar Daniels
Chaplain, NUIG

RETIRED PRIESTS

Rev Anthony Cummins
Ballinderry NH, Kilconnell,
Ballinasloe, Co Galway
Rev John Higgins
Arus Vianney, Ard Mhuire,
Ballinasloe, Co Galway
Tel 090-9631076
Rev Patrick Naughten
Woodford, Co Galway
Tel 090-9749010

RELIGIOUS ORDERS AND CONGREGATIONS

PRIESTS

CARMELITES (OCD)
The Abbey,
Loughrea, Co Galway
Tel 091-841209
Fax 091-842343
Prior: Rev Liam Finnerty (OCD)

REDEMPTORISTS
St Patrick's, Esker,
Athenry, Co Galway
Tel 091-844549
Fax 091-845698
Superior
Rev John Doherty (CSsR)
Vicar Superior
Rev Michael Cusack (CSsR)

SISTERS

CARMELITES
St Joseph's Monastery,
Mount Carmel, Loughrea, Co Galway
Prioress: Sr M. Catharina Murphy
Community: 11
Contemplative order, primitive
observance

**CONGREGATION OF THE
SISTERS OF MERCY**
Convent of Mercy, Loughrea, Co Galway
Tel 091-841354 Fax 091-847271
Community: 17

St Laurence's Fields,
Loughrea, Co Galway
Tel 091-842989
Community: 3

Sisters of Mercy,
Lake Road, Loughrea, Co Galway
Tel/Fax 091-847715
Community: 7

Beech Haven, Church Street,
Ballinasloe, Co Galway
Tel 090-9642191
Community: 4

Mount Pleasant, Ballinasloe, Co Galway
Tel 090-9631695
Community: 4

'Cana', Garbally Drive,
Ballinasloe, Co Galway
Tel 090-9644570 Fax 090-9644834
Community: 4

20 Hymany Park, Ballinasloe, Co Galway
Tel 090-9643716
Community: 2

17 Hawthorn Crescent,
Ballinasloe, Co Galway
Tel 090-9644171
Community: 2

An Gairdín, Portumna, Co Galway
Tel 090-9741689
Community: 3

Shannon Road,
Portumna, Co Galway
Tel 090-9741035
Community: 2

St Brendan's Convent of Mercy,
Eyrecourt, Co Galway
Tel 090-9675123
Community: 2

St Ann's Convent of Mercy,
Woodford, Co Galway
Tel 090-9749007
Community: 1

**FRANCISCAN MISSIONARIES OF THE
DIVINE MOTHERHOOD**
Regional House,
Assisi, Harbour Road,
Ballinasloe, Co Galway
Tel 090-9648952
Community: 4

Franciscan Convent, Garbally Drive,
Ballinasloe, Co Galway
Tel 090-9642314/9648548
Local Leader: Sr Madeleine de Cruz
Community: 26

St Joseph's, 21 Garbally Oaks,
Ballinasloe, Co Galway
Tel 090-9645767
Community: 3

La Verna, Brackernagh,
Ballinasloe, Co Galway
Tel 090-9643679
Community: 3

St Clare's, Brackernagh,
Ballinasloe, Co Galway
Tel 090-9643986 Fax 090-9631757
Community: 3

Bethany, Brackernagh,
Ballinasloe, Co Galway
Tel 090-9643499
Community: 2

EDUCATIONAL INSTITUTIONS

Portumna Community School
Portumna, Co Galway
Chairman, BOM
Very Rev P. J. Bracken BSc, HDE
Tel 090-9675116
Chaplain: Rev Abe Kennedy
St Molaise's, Portumna, Co Galway
Tel 090-9741188 (H)
Tel 090-9741053 (S)

St Joseph's College
Garbally Park, Ballinasloe, Co Galway
Tel 090-9642504/9642254
President
Very Rev Colm Allman BA, HDE
Vice-President
Rev Niall Foley BSc, BD, HDE

DIOCESE OF CLOYNE

PATRON OF THE DIOCESE
ST COLMAN, 24 NOVEMBER

COVERS MOST OF COUNTY CORK

Most Rev John Magee DD
Bishop of Cloyne;
born 24 September 1936;
ordained priest 17 March 1962;
ordained Bishop of Cloyne 17
March 1987

Residence: Cloyne Diocesan
Centre, Cobh, Co Cork
Tel 021-4811430
Fax 021-4811026
Email cloyne@indigo.ie

ST COLMAN'S CATHEDRAL, COBH

St Colman's Cathedral, overlooking Cobh, enshrines within its walls the traditions of thirteen centuries of the Diocese of Cloyne.

Built in the form of a Latin cross, its exterior is of Dalkey granite, with dressings of Mallow limestone. The style of architecture is French Gothic. The architects were Pugin (the Younger), Ashlin and Coleman.

The cathedral took forty-seven years to build (1868–1915). The total cost was £235,000. Of this, £90,000 was raised by the people of Cobh, with the remainder coming from the diocese and from collections in America and Australia.

The spire was completed in 1915 and the famous carillon and the clock were installed in 1916. The carillon – the largest in Britain and Ireland – has forty-nine bells and is tuned to the accuracy of a single vibration. This unusual instrument covers a range of four octaves and is played from a console located in the belfry, consisting of a keyboard and pedalboard. Inside, the cathedral has all the hallmarks of Gothic grandeur: the massive marble pillars, the beautiful arches, the capitals with their delicate carving of foliage, the shamrock design on the Bath Stone, and mellow, delicate lighting.

The carved panels over the nave arches give a history of the Church in Ireland from the time of St Patrick. The stained-glass windows in the northern aisle depict the parables of Christ, while those in the southern aisle depict the miracles of Christ. Overhead, in the clerestory, are forty-six windows, each having the patron of one of the forty-six parishes of the diocese. The high altar and its surround was designed by Ashlin. The pulpit is of Austrian oak. Towards the rear of the cathedral is the magnificent rose window, which depicts St John's vision of the throne of God. The organ was built by Telford and Telford, and has a total of 2,468 pipes.

Allianz ⑪

CHAPTER

Dean: Rt Rev Mgr Eamonn Goold PP, VG
Midleton
Archdeacon: Vacant
Chancellor: Very Rev Seán Cotter PP
Charleville
Prebendaries
Aghulter: Very Rev Timothy O'Leary PE,
CC, VF, Mitchelstown
Ballyhea: Rt Rev Mgr Denis O'Callaghan
PC, Mallow
Buttevant: Vacant
Cahirulton: Very Rev Michael Harrington
PP, Buttevant
Coole: Very Rev Finbar Kelleher CC *(pro tem)*
Glanworth and Ballindangan
Cooline: Very Rev Patrick Twomey PP
Kildorrery
Glanworth: Very Rev Gerard Casey PP, VF
Doneraile
Inniscarra: Very Rev Michael O'Brien PE
Buttevant
Kilmaclenine: Rt Rev Mgr James
O'Donnell AP, Macroom
Killenemer: Vacant
Subulter: Very Rev John Terry PE
Kanturk
Brigown: Very Rev Mgr Denis Reidy PP,
Carrigtwohill
Kilmacdonogh
Very Rev Vincent O'Donohue PE
Blarney
Donoughmore
Very Rev Michael O'Connell PE,
Doneraile
Laken
Very Rev Patrick T. McSweeney PE,
Glantane
Honorary Canons
Very Rev John Aherne PE
Aghada
Very Rev Colman O'Donovan PE
Inniscarra
Very Rev Tom Browne PP
Youghal
Very Rev Donal O'Mahony PP
Cloyne
Very Rev Jackie Corkery PP, VF
Kanturk

ADMINISTRATION

College of Consultors
Secretary
Very Rev Canon Gerard Casey PP VF
Doneraile, Co Cork
Tel 022-24156

Vicar General
Very Rev Dean Eamonn Goold PP, VG
Midleton, Co Cork
Tel 021-4631750

Vicars Forane
Rt Rev Mgr Eamonn Goold
Very Rev Canon Gerard Casey
Very Rev Canon Jackie Corkery
Very Rev Canon Timothy O'Leary
Very Rev Donal Roberts

Finance Council
Financial Administrator
Rt Rev Mgr Eamonn Goold PP, VG
Midleton
Tel 021-4631750
Accountants: Messrs Deloitte & Touche
6 Lapp's Quay, Cork

Diocesan Administration
Diocesan Secretary for Primary Education
Very Rev Donal O'Brien PP
Tel 026-45042
*Diocesan Secretary for Second-level
Education*
Vacant
Diocesan Secretary for Canonical Affairs
Very Rev William O'Donovan PP
Tel 058-59138

Religious Education
Education Commission Secretary:
Vacant
Adult Religious Education
Sr Emmanuel Leonard
5 Ashgrove, Cluain Ard, Cobh, Co Cork
Tel 021-4815305
Diocesan Advisers
Rev Gerard Condon CC
Shanballymore, Doneraile, Co Cork
Tel 022-25197
Rev Paul Bennett CC
2 Church Cross, Coolmona,
Donoughmore, Co Cork
Tel 021-7437728
Sr Claire Fox
Darchno, Castleredmond,
Midleton, Co Cork
Tel 021-4631912

Pastoral Coordinator
Rev Jim Killeen
Cloyne Diocesan Centre,
Cobh, Co Cork
Tel 021-4811430

Administrative Secretary
Mrs Eileen Greaney
Cloyne Diocesan Centre,
Cobh, Co Cork
Tel 021-4811430
Email cloyne@indigo.ie

Diocesan Archivist
Vacant

LITURGY

Diocesan Director of Liturgy
Rev Daniel Murphy
Castlelyons, Co Cork
Tel 025-36196

Cathedral Master of Ceremonies
Rev Robin Morrissey CC
1 Cathedral Terrace,
Cobh, Co Cork
Tel 021-4813951

Liturgical Commission
Secretary: Miss Anne Cox
Castletownroche

Church Music
Director: Very Rev Gerard Coleman PP
Castlelyons, Co Cork
Tel 025-36372

PASTORAL

Accord
Diocesan Director
Very Rev Stephen O'Mahony PP
Liscarroll
Tel 022-48128
Assistant Director: Rev James Moore CC
Jamesbrook, Midleton, Co Cork
Tel 021-4652456

Communications
Diocesan Director: Rev James Killeen
3 Cathedral Terrace, Cobh, Co Cork
Tel 021-4813601

Cura
Diocesan Director
Very Rev Francis O'Neill PP
Ballyclough, Mallow, Co Cork
Tel 022-27650

Diocesan Youth Services
Chairman: Mr Noel O'Connor
Director: Mr Brian Williams
Mallow Community Youth Centre,
New Road, Mallow, Co Cork
Tel 022-53526

Ecumenism
Secretary
Very Rev Canon Tom Browne PP
South Abbey, Youghal, Co Cork
Tel 024-92336

Emigrant Apostolate
Diocesan Director
Very Rev William O'Donovan PP
Conna, Co Cork
Tel 058-59138

Diocesan Chaplaincy to the Deaf
Very Rev Joseph McGuane
St Mary's, Church Street,
Youghal, Co Cork
Tel 024-93392

Diocesan Lay Ministry
Director: Mrs Kay Hyden
Cloyne Diocesan Centre,
Cobh, Co Cork
Tel 021-4811430/087-2696143

Immigrant Apostolate
Diocesan Director: Rev Andrew Carvill CC
Feermoy, Co Cork
Tel 025-32212

Marriage Tribunal
(See also Marriage Tribunals section)
Cork Regional Marriage Tribunal:
Officialis:
Very Rev Gerard Garrett VJ

Perpetual Eucharistic Adoration
Diocesan Director: Rev Patrick Winkle CC
Youghal, Co Cork
Tel 024-92270

Pilgrimage Director
Rev Tobias Bluitt, CC
Mallow, Co Cork
Tel 022-21259

Pioneer Total Abstinence Association
Dicoesan Director
Rev Eamonn McCarthy CC
Coachford, Co Cork
Tel 021-7334059

Pontifical Mission Societies
Diocesan Director
Very Rev Donal Coakley PP
Inniscarra, Co Cork
Tel 021-4385311

Prayer and Retreat Ministries
Facilitator: Rev Eamonn Barry
St Colman's College, Fermoy, Co Cork
Tel 025-31622 Fax 025-31634

Prayer Groups
Co-ordinator
Very Rev Michael Fitzgerald PP
Mitchelstown, Co Cork
Tel 025-84090

Travellers
Chaplain: Very Rev Padraig Keogh PP
Milford, Co Cork
Tel 063-80038

Trócaire
Rev Tom McDermott CC
Churchtown, Mallow, Co Cork
Tel 022-41916

Vicar for Religious
Very Rev Canon Sean Cotter PP
Charleville, Co Cork
Tel 063-81319

Vocations
Director: Rev Patrick Relihan CC
Youghal, Co Cork
Tel 024-92456
Assistant Director: Rev Jim Moore CC
Jamesbrook, Midleton, Co Cork
Tel 021-4652456

Ongoing Formation of the Clergy
Director: Very Rev Patrick Buckley PP
Dromahane, Mallow, Co Cork
Tel 022-21244

PARISHES

Mensal parishes are listed first. Other parishes follow alphabetically. Historical names are given in parentheses.

COBH, ST COLMAN'S CATHEDRAL
Sacred Heart, Rushbrooke
Sacred Heart, Rallymore
Very Rev Michael Leamy Adm
Rushbrooke, Cobh, Co Cork
Tel 021-4813144
Rev Robin Morrissey CC
Tel 021-4813951
Rev John McCarthy CC
Tel 021-4815619
Rev James Killeen CC
Tel 021-4813601
Rev Peter O'Farrell CC
Tel 021-4855983
Cobh, Co Cork

FERMOY
St Patrick's
Very Rev Aquin Casey Adm
The Presbytery, Ravenswood,
Fermoy, Co Cork
Tel 025-31414
Rev Eugene Baker CC
Greenhill, Fermoy, Co Cork
Tel 025-33507
Rev P. J. O'Driscoll CC
Tel 087-6490381
Rev Andrew Carvill CC
Tel 025-32212
Monument Hill, Fermoy, Co Cork

AGHABULLOGUE
St John's, Aghabullogue
St Patrick's, Coachford
St Olan's, Rylane
Very Rev Peadar Murphy PP
Aghabullogue, Co Cork
Tel 021-7334035
Rev Eamonn McCarthy CC
Coachford, Co Cork
Tel 021-7334059

AGHADA
St Erasmus, Aghada
St Mary's, Saleen
St Mary's, Ballinrostig
Very Rev Denis Kelleher PP
Church Road, Aghada, Co Cork
Tel 021-4661298
Rev James Moore CC
Jamesbrook, Midleton, Co Cork
Tel 021-4652456

AGHINAGH
St John the Baptist, Bealnamorrive,
Rusheen, Ballinagree
Very Rev Michael Corkery PP
Aghinagh, Coachford, Co Cork
Tel 026-48037

BALLYCLOUGH
St John the Baptist, Ballyclough, Kilbrin
Very Rev Francis O'Neill PP
Ballyclough, Mallow, Co Cork
Tel 022-27650
Rev Michael Campbell CC
Kilbrin, Kanturk, Co Cork
Tel 022-48169

BALLYHEA
St Mary's
Very Rev Mortimer Downing PP
Tel 063-81470

BALLYMACODA AND LADYSBRIDGE
St Mary's, Ladysbridge
St Peter in Chains, Ballymacoda
Very Rev David O'Riordan PP
Ladysbridge, Co Cork
Tel 021-4667173
Rev Kevin Mulcahy CC
Ballymacoda, Co Cork
Tel 024-98110

BALLYVOURNEY
St Gobnait, Ballyvourney
Séipéal Ghobnatan, Cúil Aodha
Very Rev Donal O'Brien PP
Tel 026-45042

BANTEER (CLONMEEN)
St Fursey's, Banteer
St Nicholas', Kilcorney
St Joseph's, Lyre
Very Rev William Winter PP
Banteer, Co Cork
Tel 029-56010

BLARNEY
Immaculate Conception, Blarney
St Patrick's, Whitechurch
St Mary's, Waterloo
Very Rev William Bermingham PP
Tel 021-4385105
Rev Timothy Hazelwood CC
Tel 021-4385229
Blarney, Co Cork
Rev Tadhg O'Donovan CC
Whitechurch, Co Cork
Tel 021-4884111

BUTTEVANT
St Mary's, Buttevant
St Mary's, Lisgriffin
Very Rev Canon Michael Harrington PP
Tel 022-23195
Rev Joseph O'Mahony CC
Tel 022-23716
Buttevant, Co Cork

CARRIGTWOHILL
St Mary's
Very Rev Mgr Denis Reidy PP
Tel 021-4883236
Rev Denis O'Hanlon CC
Tel 021-4883867
Carrigtwohill, Co Cork

CASTLELYONS
St Nicholas', Castlelyons
St Mary's, Coolagown
Very Rev Gerard Coleman PP
Tel/Fax 025-36372
Rev Daniel Murphy *(priest in residence)*
Tel 025-36196
Castlelyons, Fermoy, Co Cork

CASTLEMAGNER
St Mary's
Very Rev Michael Dorgan PP
Tel 022-27600
Castlemagner, Mallow, Co Cork

CASTLETOWNROCHE
Immaculate Conception,
Castletownroche
Nativity of Our Lady, Ballyhooly
Very Rev Patrick Scanlan PP
Castletownroche, Co Cork
Tel 022-26188
Rev Brian Boyle
Ballyhooly, Co Cork
Tel 022-39148

CHARLEVILLE
Holy Cross
Very Rev Canon Seán Cotter PP
Tel/Fax 063-81319
Rev Michael Fitzgerald CC
Tel 063-81437
Charleville, Co Cork

CHURCHTOWN (LISCARROLL)
St Nicholas', Churchtown
St Joseph's, Liscarroll
Very Rev Stephen O'Mahony PP
Liscarroll, Mallow, Co Cork
Tel 022-48128
Rev Thomas McDermott CC
Churchtown, Mallow, Co Cork
Tel 022-41916

CLONDROHID
St Abina's, Clondrohid
St John the Baptist, Carriganimma
Very Rev Anthony Wickham PP
Clondrohid, Macroom, Co Cork
Tel 026-41014
Rev Bartholomew Desmond CC
Carriganimma, Macroom, Co Cork
Tel 026-44027

CLOYNE
St Colman's, Cloyne
Star of the Sea, Ballycotton
Immaculate Conception, Shanagarry
St Colmcille's, Churchtown South
Very Rev Canon Donal O'Mahony PP
Cloyne, Midleton, Co Cork
Tel 021-4652597
Rev Aidan Crowley CC
Ballycotton, Midleton, Co Cork
Tel 021-4646726

CONNA
St Catherine's, Conna
St Catherine's, Ballynoe
St Mary's, Glengoura
Very Rev William O'Donovan PP
Conna, Mallow, Co Cork
Tel 058-59138
Rev Joseph O'Keeffe CC
Ballynoe, Mallow, Co Cork
Tel 058-59269

DONERAILE
The Nativity of the Blessed Virgin Mary,
Doneraile
Christ the King, Shanballymore
St Joseph the Worker, Hazelwood
Very Rev Canon Gerard Casey PP, VF
Tel 022-24156
Rev Anthony Sheehan CC
Tel 022-24120
Doneraile, Co Cork
Rev Gerard Condon CC
Shanballymore, Mallow, Co Cork
Tel 022-25197

DONOUGHMORE
St Lachteen's, Stuake
St Joseph's, Fornaught
Very Rev Jeremiah O'Riordan PP
Donoughmore, Co Cork
Tel 021-7337023
Rev Paul Bennett CC
2 Church Cross, Coolmona,
Donoughmore, Co Cork
Tel 021-7437728

GLANTANE
St Peter the Apostle, Dromahane
St John the Evangelist, Glantane
St Columba, Bweeng
Very Rev Patrick Buckley PP
Dromahane, Mallow, Co Cork
Tel 022-21244
Very Rev Micheál Cogan PE,CC
Glantane, Mallow, Co Cork
Tel 022-47158
Rev Chris Donlon CC
Dromore, Mallow, Co Cork
Tel 022-21198

GLANWORTH AND BALLINDANGAN
Holy Cross, Glanworth
Immaculate Conception, Ballindangan
Holy Family, Curraghagulla
Very Rev Donal Broderick PP
Glanworth, Co Cork
Tel 025-38123
Very Rev Canon Finbar Kelleher CC
(Pro tem)
Ballindangan, Mitchelstown, Co Cork
Tel 025-85563

GRENAGH
St Lachteen's, Grenagh
St Joseph's, Courtbrack
Very Rev Liam Kelleher PP
Grenagh, Co Cork
Tel 021-4886128

IMOGEELA (CASTLEMARTYR)
Sacred Heart, Mogeely
St Joseph's, Castlemartyr
St Peter's, Dungourney
St Lawrence's, Clonmult
Very Rev John Cogan PP
Castlemartyr, Co Cork
Tel 021-4667133
Rev Finbarr O'Flynn CC
Dungourney, Co Cork
Tel 021-4668406

INNISCARRA
St Senan's, Cloghroe
St Mary's, Berrings
St Joseph's, Matehy
Very Rev Donal Coakley PP
4 Upper Woodlands, Cloghroe, Co Cork
Tel 021-4385311
Rev Michael Lomasney CC
Cloghroe, Blarney, Co Cork
Tel 021-4385163
Rev Gerard Coleman CC
Berrings, Co Cork
Tel 021-7332155

KANTURK
Immaculate Conception, Kanturk
St Joseph's, Lismire
Very Rev Canon Jackie Corkery PP, VF
Tel 029-50192
Rev Patrick Linehan CC
Tel 029-50061
Kanturk, Co Cork

KILDORRERY
St Bartholomew's, Kildorrery
St Molaga's, Sraharla
Very Rev Canon Patrick Twomey PP
Tel 022-25174
Rev Liam Foley CC
Tel 022-25110
Kildorrery, Co Cork

KILLAVULLEN
St Nicholas', Kilavullen
St Crannacht's, Anakissa
Very Rev Daniel Gould PP
Ballygriffin, Mallow, Co Cork
Tel 022-26153
Very Rev Richard Hegarty PE, CC
Killavullen, Co Cork
Tel 022-26125

KILLEAGH
St John the Baptist, Killeagh
St Patrick's, Inch
Very Rev John Broderick PP
Killeagh, Co Cork
Tel 024-95133
Rev Patrick Corkery CC
Inch, Killeagh, Co Cork
Tel 024-95148

KILNAMARTYRA
St Lachtaín's, Kinamartyra, Renaniree
Very Rev Richard Browne PP
Kilnamartyra, Macroom, Co Cork
Tel 026-40013

KILWORTH
St Martin's, Kilworth
Immaculate Conception, Araglin
Very Rev Donal Leahy PP
Kilworth, Co Cork
Tel 025-27186

LISGOOLD
St John the Baptist, Lisgoold
Sacred Heart, Leamlara
Very Rev Anthony O'Brien PP
Tel 021-4642363

Allianz ⑪

MACROOM
St Colman's, Macroom
St John the Baptist, Caum
Very Rev Donal Roberts PP, VF
Rt Rev Mgr James O'Donnell AP
Tel 026-41042
Rev Francis Manning CC
Tel 026-41092
Rev Gabriel Burke CC
Tel 026-41247
Macroom, Co Cork

MALLOW
St Mary's, Mallow
Resurrection, Mallow
Very Rev Declan Hennessy PP
Tel 022-21149
Rt Rev Mgr Denis O'Callaghan PC
Tel 022-21112
Rev Micheál Leader CC
Tel 022-21382
Rev Tobias Bluitt CC
Tel 022-21259
Rev Patrick McCarthy CC
Tel 086-3831621
Rev Brendan Mallon
Tel 022-20792
Mallow, Co Cork

MIDLETON
Holy Rosary, Midleton
St Colman's, Ballintotas
Rt Rev Mgr Eamonn Goold PP, VG
Tel 021-4631750
Rev Micheál Ó Loingsigh CC
Tel 021-4631354
Rev Eamonn Kelleher CC
Tel 021-4631094
Rev Tom Naughton CC
Tel 021-4636704
Rev Marek Pecak CC *(in residence)*
Tel 021-4634027
Midleton, Co Cork

MILFORD
Assumption of BVM, Milford
St Michael's, Freemount
St Berchert's, Tullylease
Very Rev Pádraig Keogh PP
Milford, Charleville, Co Cork
Tel 063-80038
Rev John Ryan CC
Freemount, Charleville, Co Cork
Tel 022-28788

MITCHELSTOWN
Our Lady Conceived Without Sin,
Mitchelstown
Holy Family, Ballygiblin, Killacluig
Very Rev Michael Fitzgerald PP
Tel 025-84090
Very Rev Canon Timothy O'Leary CC, VF
Tel 025-84088
Rev James Greene CC
Tel 025-84077
Mitchelstown, Co Cork

MOURNE ABBEY
St Michael the Archangel, Analeentha
St John the Baptist, Burnfort
Very Rev Peadar O'Callaghan PP
Burnfort, Mallow, Co Cork
Tel 086-8054040

NEWMARKET
Immaculate Conception, Newmarket
Holy Spirit, Taur
Very Rev David Herlihy PP
Newmarket, Co Cork
Tel 029-60999

RATHCORMAC
Immaculate Conception, Rathcormac
St Bartholomew's, Bartlemy
Very Rev Cornelius O'Donnell PP
Tel 025-36286
Rev Joseph Rohan CC
Tel 025-36858
Rathcormac, Fermoy, Co Cork

ROCKCHAPEL AND MEELIN
St Joseph's, Meelin
St Peter's, Rockchapel
Very Rev Denis Stritch PP
Meelin, Newmarket, Co Cork
Tel 029-68007

SHANDRUM
St Joseph's, Shandrum
St Peter & Paul's, Dromina
Very Rev Patrick Lawton PP
Shandrum, Charleville, Co Cork
Tel 063-70016
Very Rev David Buckley PE, CC
Very Rev Canon Seán Cotter
Dromina, Charleville, Co Cork
Tel 063-70207

YOUGHAL
St Mary's, Our Lady of Lourdes, Holy
Family, Youghal; St Ita's, Gortroe
Very Rev Canon Thomas Browne PP
Tel 024-93199
Rev Patrick Winkle CC
Tel 024-92270
Rev Michael Murphy CC
Tel 024-92336
Rev Patrick Relihan CC
Tel 024-92456
Youghal, Co Cork

PRIESTS OF THE DIOCESE ELSEWHERE

Rev Sean Corkery
St Patrick's College, Maynooth,
Co Kildare
Tel 01-7084700
Rev Gerard Cremin
Pontifical Irish College,
Via dei SS Quattro 1, 00184 Roma, Italy
Tel 003906-772631
Rt Rev Mgr Michael Crotty DD
Secretariat of State, Vatican City

Rev Mark Hehir
North Cathedral Presbytery,
Roman Street, Cork
Tel 021-4304325
Rev John Keane
c/o Cloyne Diocesan Centre,
Cobh, Co Cork
Tel 021-4811430
Rev Thomas Lane
Mount Saint Mary's Seminary,
16300 Old Emmitsburg Road,
Emmitsburg,
Maryland 21727-7797, USA
Rev Daniel McCarthy CF
Office of the Chaplain,
James Stephen's Barracks, Kilkenny City
Very Rev Mgr Joseph Murphy
Secretariat of State, (Section for
Relations with States),
00120 Vatican City
Tel 0039-0669883193
Rev Declan O'Brien
c/o Cloyne Diocesan Centre,
Cobh, Co Cork
Tel 021-4811430
Rt Rev Mgr James O'Brien
Congregation for Divine Worship and
the Discipline of the Sacraments,
Vatican City 00120, Italy
Tel 003906-69884551
Fax 003906-69883499
Rev Donal O'Callaghan
Monacreigh Cottage,
Garryvoe, Co Cork
Tel 021-4623911

RETIRED PRIESTS

Very Rev Canon John Aherne PE
Aghada, Co Cork
Tel 021-4661239
Very Rev Anthony Cronin PE
Newmarket, Co Cork
Tel 029-60605
Very Rev Robert Forde PE
Fermoy, Co Cork
Tel 025-34022
Rev James Hannon
Sandhill Road, Ballybunion, Co Kerry
Dr Patrick Hannon
Emeritus Professor of Theology,
St Patrick's College, Maynooth,
Co Kildare
Tel 01-6285222
Very Rev Michael Madden PE
Ballycrennane, Ballymacoda, Co Cork
Tel 024-98840
Very Rev Canon P. T. McSweeney PE
Nazareth House, Mallow, Co Cork
Tel 022-21561
Very Rev Canon Michael O'Brien PE
Buttevant, Co Cork
Tel 022-23014
Very Rev Canon Michael O'Connell PE
Buttevant, Co Cork

Very Rev Canon Vincent O'Donoghue PE
18 Kilcrea Park, Magazine Road, Cork
Very Rev Canon Colman O'Donovan PE
1 Youghal Road, Midleton, Co Cork
Tel 021-4621617
Very Rev Con O'Donovan PE
16 Deer Park Avenue,
St Joseph's Road, Mallow, Co Cork
Tel 022-51948
Very Rev Philip O'Keeffe PE
Kiliphilbeen, Ballynoe, Mallow, Co Cork
Tel 058-59526
Rev Martin O'Riordan
Lisgoold, Co Cork
Tel 021-4642343
Very Rev Liam Ryan PE
Mondaniel, Fermoy, Co Cork
Very Rev Canon John Terry PE
Terriville, Ballylanders, Cloyne, Co Cork
Tel 021-4646779
Rev Denis Vaughan
45 The Oaks, Maryborough Ridge,
Douglas, Cork

RELIGIOUS ORDERS AND CONGREGATIONS

BROTHERS

PRESENTATION BROTHERS
Presentation Monastery,
Cobh, Co Cork
Tel 021-4811218
Contact: Br Walter Hurley
Community: 3

SISTERS

ADORERS OF THE SACRED HEART OF JESUS OF MONTMARTRE, OSB
St Benedict's Priory,
The Mount, Cobh, Co Cork
Tel 021-4811354
Prioress: Mother Mary Vianney
Community: 6
Contemplative Benedictines
Residential retreats
Contact person: Guest Mistress

BON SECOURS SISTERS (PARIS)
38 Norwood Park, Cobh, Co Cork
Tel 021-4815350
Co-ordinator: Sr Ursula O'Neill
Community: 5
Parish Ministry, Care of Elderly

Sisters of Bon Secours,
Bon Secours Convent, Cobh, Co Cork
Tel 021-4811346
Community: 2
Parish Ministry

CONGREGATION OF THE SISTERS OF MERCY
'Trócaire', 6 Castleowen,
Blarney, Co Cork
Tel 021-4381745
Contact: Sr Nora Murphy

Buttevant, Co Cork
Tel 022-23113 Fax 022-23634
Contact: Emmanuel Sherlock
Primary School Tel 022-23506
Mercy Day Care Centre Tel 022-23507

Charleville, Co Cork
Tel 063-81276 Fax 063-81830
St Joseph's Infant School Tel 063-89467
St Ann's Primary School Tel 063-89451

St Mary's Primary School
Cobh, Co Cork
Tel 021-4812038

Kanturk, Co Cork
Tel 029-50068 Fax 029-50332
Contact: Sr Philomena Sweetman &
Sr de Lourdes Flynn
Primary School. Tel 029-50021
Mercy House Day Centre. Tel 029-51161

Dan Corkery Place, Macroom, Co Cork
Tel 026-42673
Contact: Sr Loyola O'Donovan

Macroom, Co Cork
Tel 026-41068 Fax 026-42535
Contact: Sr Consilio O'Hea
Primary School. Tel 026-41847

Fairy Hill, Kennell Hill,
Mallow, Co Cork
Tel 022-21395 Fax 022-43168
Contact: Sr Sr Ursula Sheehan &
Sr Ita Looney
Scoil Iosagáin Infants' School
Primary School. Tel 022-42211
Anchor – Outpatients Addiction Therapy
Centre. Tel 022-42559

Holy Spirit Convent,
Bank Place, Mallow, Co Cork
Tel 022-21780

3 Beechwood Grove, Cluain Ard, Cobh,
Co Cork
Tel 021-4815062
Contact: Sr Mary Cashman

5 Ashgrove, Cluain Ard, Cobh, Co Cork
Tel 021-4815305

16 Meadow Grove,
Summerhill, Mallow, Co Cork
Tel 022-43624
Contact: Sr Paul Murphy

Sirona, 57 Rockbrook Lawn,
Mallow, Co Cork
Tel 022-20769
Contact: Sr Nora Ann Lombard

41 Ivy Gardens, Mallow, Co Cork
Tel 022-58036
Contact: Sr Norma Landy

Convent Bungalow,
Bathview, Mallow, Co Cork
Tel 022-31905
Contact: Sr Noreen Foley

Billkit, Hume's Terrace,
Mallow, Co Cork
Tel 022-21414
Contact: Sr Patricia Walsh

Island Road, Longacre,
Newmarket, Co Cork
Tel 063-81877
Contact: Sr Margaret O'Keeffe

17 Bromley Court, Midleton, Co Cork
Tel 021-4632732

Rushbrooke, Co Cork
Tel 021-4811453 Fax 021-4813836
Contact: Sr Margaret Daly
Primary School. Tel 021-4811019

INFANT JESUS SISTERS
Bellevue, Mallow, Co Cork
Tel 022-43085
Community: 10
Retired sisters

LITTLE COMPANY OF MARY
Convent of the Maternal Heart,
Monument Hill, Fermoy, Co Cork
Tel 025-31679
Community: 4
Pastoral ministry, with special emphasis
on bereavement counselling

LORETO (IBVM)
Loreto Community,
Fermoy, Co Cork
Tel 025-31207
Community Leader
Sr Veronica O'Donoghue
Community: 13
Secondary School
Tel 025-32124

Loreto Sisters, Copperton,
Corrin View Estate, Fermoy, Co Cork
Tel 025-33693
Community: 3
Secondary school, pastoral work

Greenlawn, Summerfield,
Youghal, Co Cork
Community: 6

8 Dún na Mara, Youghal, Co Cork
Community: 3

MISSIONARIES OF CHARITY
St Helen's Convent, Blarney, Co Cork
Tel 021-4382041
Superior: Sr M. Cleopha
Community: 4
Residential Treatment Centre

POOR SERVANTS OF THE MOTHER OF GOD
St Aloysius' Convent,
Carriqtwohill, Co Cork
Tel 021-4883237 Fax 021-4883955
Community: 4
St Aloysius' Secondary School
Pastoral

CONGREGATION OF THE SISTERS OF NAZARETH
Nazareth House,
Mallow, Co Cork
Tel 022-21561 Fax 022-21147
Email nazarethmallow@eircom.net
Superior: Sr Victoire Mulligan
Community: 12
Home for elderly. Beds: 84

PRESENTATION SISTERS
Presentation Convent, Midleton, Co Cork
Tel 021-4631892
Team Leadership
Community: 12
Primary School Tel 021-4631593
St Mary's Secondary School
Tel 021-4631973

Presentation Primary School,
Doneraile, Co Cork
Tel 022-24512

Nagle Rice Secondary School,
Doneraile, Co Cork
Tel 022-24500

Presentation Convent,
Fermoy, Co Cork
Tel 025-31248
Leader: Sr Rosarii Shinnick
Community: 13
Primary School. Tel 025-31550

Presentation Lodge, College Road,
Fermoy, Co Cork
Tel 025-49928
Community: 1

Presentation Convent,
Front Strand, Youghal, Co Cork
Tel 024-93039
Non-resident Leader
Sr Mary John Staunton
Community: 6
Primary School. Tel 024-92700

Presentation Sisters, 'Darchno',
Castleredmond, Midleton, Co Cork
Tel 021-4631912
Community: 2

Presentation Primary School,
Mitchelstown, Co Cork
Tel 025-24264
Presentation Secondary School
Mitchelstown, Co Cork
Tel 025-24394

Nano Nagle Centre,
Presentation Sisters,
Ballygriffin, Mallow, Co Cork
Tel 022-26411 Fax 022-26953
Email nanonaglecentre@eircom.net
Community: 4

ST JOSEPH OF THE SACRED HEART SISTERS
Sisters of St Joseph of Sacred Heart,
Penola, 25B Harrison Place,
Charleville, Co Cork

Sisters of St Joseph of Sacred Heart,
No. 8 Ozanam Court, Casement Street,
Clonakilty, Co Cork

EDUCATIONAL INSTITUTIONS

St Colman's College (Diocesan College)
Fermoy, Co Cork
Tel 025-31622 Fax 025-31634
Email stcolmansfermoy@eircom.net
Priests on Staff
Rev Martin Heffernan BA, BD, HDE
Tel 025-31622
Rev Eamonn Barry, Facilitator for Prayer
and Retreat Ministries (in residence)
Tel 025-31622/086-8157952

EDMUND RICE SCHOOLS TRUST
Midleton, Co Cork Secondary School
Tel 021-4631555 Fax 021-4631917
Email cbssecmidleton@eircom.net
Principal: Mr Pat Hurley

Primary School, Baker's Road,
Charleville, Co Cork
Tel 063-89544
Principal: Mr. Jerry Murray

Secondary School, Baker's Road,
Charleville, Co Cork
Tel/Fax 063-81789 Staff 063-81669
Email rathluirccbs.ias@tinet.ie
Principal: Mr Patrick Walsh

Christian Brothers Secondary School,
Mitchelstown, Co Cork
Tel 025-24104 Fax 025-85153
Email donnchac@eircom.net
Principal: Mr Donncha Crowley

Nagle Rice Secondary School,
Doneraile, Co Cork
Tel 022-24500 Fax 022-24586
Email horseclose.ie@eircom.net
Principal: Ms Bríd Lysaght

CHARITABLE AND OTHER SOCIETIES

St Mary's District Hospital
Youghal, Co Cork

County Hospital
Mallow, Co Cork

Society of St Vincent de Paul
Conferences at: Ballyvourney,
Castlemartyr, Cobh, Fermoy, Doneraile,
Kanturk, Macroom, Mallow, Midleton,
Mitchelstown, Youghal, Carrigtwohill,
Lisgoold, Aghada, Charleville

DIOCESE OF CORK AND ROSS

PATRON OF THE DIOCESE OF CORK
ST FINBARR, 25 SEPTEMBER

PATRON OF THE DIOCESE OF ROSS
ST FACHTNA, 14 AUGUST

INCLUDES CORK CITY AND PART OF COUNTY CORK

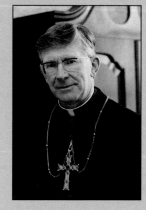

Most Rev John Buckley DD
Bishop of Cork and Ross;
born 1939;
ordained priest 1965;
ordained Titular Bishop of
Leptis Magna 29 April 1984 and
installed 6 February 1998

Address:
Cork and Ross Offices,
Redemption Road, Cork
Tel 021-4301717
Fax 021-4301557

CATHEDRAL OF ST MARY AND ST ANNE, CORK

The first cathedral on the site of the present Cathedral of St Mary and St Anne was the vision of Bishop Francis Moylan, who was Bishop of Cork from 1786 to 1815. The foundation stone was laid in 1799 and the cathedral was opened in 1808 as the parish church of the single parish then on the northside of the city – hence its local, popular name: the North Chapel. But in June 1820, the heat of the political climate struck the North Chapel when it was maliciously burned during the night.

Bishop John Murphy, one of the famous brewing family, wasted no time in calling a meeting to help restore the cathedral. The people of Cork generously rallied to the call.

The task of rebuilding was given to architect George Pain, who later designed Blackrock Castle, the court house and St Patrick's Church. The interior of the present-day cathedral, including the ornate ceiling, owes much to his creative gifts.

The next major alteration to the cathedral was undertaken in the 1870s when Canon Foley set about building the tower and the great Western Door – now the main door of the cathedral. The tower is higher than that of its more famous neighbour: St Anne's Church, Shandon, home of the much-played bells.

Almost a hundred years later, after the Second Vatican Council, Cornelius Lucey, then Bishop of Cork and Ross, added a further major extension at the other end of the cathedral. This included a completely new sanctuary and a smaller tower, and added capacity to the church, which served an area with a rapidly increasing population.

In 1994, major problems were discovered in the roof and other fabric of the building, which led to the closing of the cathedral for major refurbishment. The bishop, Michael Murphy, decided it was

time to renovate the interior of the cathedral too. The task was entrusted to architect Richard Hurley, whose plan for the new interior saw a greater unity being achieved between the sanctuary and the rest of the floor area, and the

new altar occupying the central place of prominence. The reordering and renovation was completed in 1996 at a cost of £2.5m and Bishop Murphy presided over its rededication – his last public function before he died a week later.

CHAPTER

Dean: Very Rev Denis O'Connor
Archdeacon:
Very Rev Kerry Murphy O'Connor
Precentor: Canon Jim O'Donovan
Treasurer: Canon Ted O'Sullivan
Prebendaries
Kilbritain: Very Rev Micheál O Dálaigh
Desertmore: Very Rev Tadhg Ó Mathúna
Kilnaglory: Very Rev Dan Crowley
Holy Trinity: Very Rev Thomas Kelleher
Kilbrogan: Very Rev Kevin O'Callaghan
Caherlag: Very Rev Donal Linehan
Kilanully: Very Rev John K. O'Mahony
Killaspugmullane: Rev Michael Murphy
Liscleary: Very Rev Liam O'Regan
St Michael: Very Rev Michael Riordan
Inniskenny: Canon Vincent Hodnett
Drimoleague: Very Rev Liam O'Driscoll

Honorary Canons
Very Rev Diarmuid Linehan
Very Rev Liam Leader
Very Rev Denis Forde
Very Rev Michael Crowley
Very Rev Michael G. O'Brien
Very Rev Michael Crowley

ADMINISTRATION

Vicars General
Rt Rev Mgr Kevin O'Callaghan PP, VG
Ballineaspaig, Cork
Tel 021-4346818
Rt Rev Mgr Leonard O'Brien PP, VG
Clonakilty, Co Cork
Tel 023-8833165

Vicars Forane
Very Rev Canon John K. O'Mahony
Rt Rev Mgr Kevin O'Callaghan
Very Rev Declan Mansfield
Very Rev Patrick Walsh

Diocesan Secretary
Rev Thomas Deenihan
Cork & Ross Offices,
Redemption Road, Cork
Tel 021-4301717
Email secretary@corkandross.org

PASTORAL

Catechetics
Primary: Sr Geraldine Howard
North Presentation Convent, Cork
Tel 087-6115672
Second-level: Marie Murphy
Cork and Ross Offices,
Redemption Road, Cork
Tel 021-4301717
Email catechetics@corkandross.org

Child Protection
Diocesan Director: Canon Liam O'Driscoll
Diocesan Offices, Redemption Road, Cork
Tel 021-4301717

CMCC Marriage Counselling
Director: Dr Colm O'Connor
34 Paul Street, Cork
Tel 021-4275678 Fax 021-4270932
ACCORD, 5 Main Street,
Bantry, Co Cork
Tel 027-50272

CURA
Adm. Secretary: Mrs Anne Murphy
Tel 021-4277544

Diocesan Education Office
Cork and Ross Offices,
Redemption Road, Cork
Tel 021-4301717 Fax 021-4301557
Secretary for Education
Rev Dr Tom Deenihan
Secretary: Ms Clare O'Leary
Email clare.oleary@corkandross.org

Immigrants
Cois Tine, St Mary's, Pope's Quay, Cork
Tel 021-4557760
Email coistine@sma.ie
Diocesan Chaplain to Polish Community
Rev Piotr Galus
c/o St Augustine's,
Washington Street, Cork
Tel 021-4275390

Marriage Tribunal
(See Marriage Tribunals section)

Parish Pastoral Development
1 The Presbytery, Friar's Walk,
Ballyphehane, Cork
Tel 021-4537472
Email ppo@corkandross.org
Director: Rev Tom Hayes
Email tom.hayes@corkandross.org
Co-ordinator: Sr Karen Kent
Email karen.kent@corkandross.org
Co-ordinator of Liturgy:
Rev Christopher Fitzgerald
Email liturgy@corkandross.org
*Co-ordinator of Adult Religious
Education:* Rev Seán O'Sullivan
Email are@corkandross.org

Pilgrimages
Director
Rt Rev Mgr Kevin O'Callaghan PP, VG
Tel 021-4346818

Pontifical Mission Society
Rev John O'Callaghan
The Presbytery, Drimoleague, Co Cork
Tel 028-31133

PARISHES

*The mensal parishes are listed first. Other
names follow alphabetically. Historical
names are given in parentheses.*

CATHEDRAL OF ST MARY & ST ANNE
Very Rev Declan Mansfield Adm
Rev Mark Hehir CC
Cathedral Presbytery, Cork
Tel 021-4304325 Fax 021-4304204

ST PATRICK'S CATHEDRAL, SKIBBEREEN
Very Rev Donal Cotter Adm
Tel 028-22877
Rev Martin O'Driscoll CC
Skibbereen, Co Cork
Tel 028-22878
Rev Kevin O'Regan CC
The Hill, Baltimore, Co Cork
Tel 028-20283

ARDFIELD AND RATHBARRY
Very Rev Patrick J. McCarthy Adm
Ardfield, Clonakilty, Co Cork
Tel 023-8840649

AUGHADOWN
Very Rev Donal Cahill Adm
Lisheen, Skibbereen, Co Cork
Tel 028-38111

BALLINCOLLIG
Very Rev George O'Mahony PP
Tel 021-4871206
Ballincollig, Co Cork
Rev James MacSweeney CC
64 Westcourt, Ballincollig, Co Cork
Tel 021-4870434
Rev Michael O'Mahony CC
8 The Meadows, Classis Lake,
Ballincollig, Co Cork
Tel 021-4877161
Also in residence: Rev Billy O'Sullivan
c/o Parochial House, Ballincollig, Co Cork
Tel 021-4371206

BALLINEASPAIG
Rt Rev Mgr Kevin O'Callaghan PP, VG
Tel/Fax 021-4346818
Very Rev Dean Denis O'Connor PE
Tel 021-4542972
Very Rev Tom Clancy AP
Tel 021-4348588
Woodlawn, Model Farm Road,
Ballineaspaig, Cork

BALLINHASSIG
Very Rev Kieron O'Driscoll PP
Barrett's Hill, Ballinhassig, Co Cork
Tel 021-4885104
Rev Pearse Timoney
The Presbytery,
Ballygarvan, Co Cork
Tel 021-4888971

BALLINLOUGH
Very Rev Canon James O'Donovan PP
Tel 021-4292296
Very Rev Canon Michael Crowley PE
Tel 021-4292684
Ballinlough, Cork

BALLINORA
Very Rev Canon Donal Linehan PP
Ballinora, Waterfall, near Cork
Tel 021-4873448

BALLYPHEHANE
Very Rev Canon Michael Murphy PP
Tel 021-4965560
Rev Sean O'Driscoll
Tel 021-4310835

BANDON
Very Rev Denis J. O'Leary PP
Tel 023-8841278
Rev Myles McSweeney CC
Tel 023-8865067
Rev Paul O'Donoghue CC
Bandon, Co Cork

BANTRY
Very Rev Robert Brophy PP
The Presbytery, Bantry, Co Cork
Tel 027-50096
Most Rev Patrick O'Donoghue AP
The Presbytery, Bantry, Co Cork
Tel 027-50082
Rev Anthony O'Mahony CC
The Presbytery, Bantry, Co Cork
Tel 027-50193

BARRYROE
Very Rev Eoin Whooley PP
Lislevane, Bandon, Co Cork
Tel 023-8846171 Fax 023-8846914

BLACKPOOL/THE GLEN
Very Rev John O'Donovan PP
Hattons Alley, Blackpool, Cork
Tel 021-4501022
Rev Christopher Harrington CC
1 Kilmorna Heights,
Ballyvolane, Cork
Tel 021-4550425

BLACKROCK
Canon Tadhg Ó Mathúna SP
2 Parochial House, Blackrock, Cork
Tel 021-4358025
Rev Damian O'Mahony CC
1 Parochial House, Blackrock, Cork
Tel 021-4358381

CAHERAGH
Rev Daniel Pyburn PP
The Presbytery, Dromore,
Bantry, Co Cork
Very Rev Michael O'Donovan AP
The Presbytery, Caheragh, Co Cork
Tel 028-31126

CARRAIG NA BHFEAR
Very Rev John Collins PP
Carraig na bhFear, Co Cork
Tel 021-4884119

CARRIGALINE
Very Rev Bartholomew O'Mahony PP
Tel 021-4371684
Rev Aidan Cremin CC
Tel 021-4372229
Rev Charles Nyhan CC
Cork Road, Carrigaline, Co Cork
Tel 021-4371860

CASTLEHAVEN
Very Rev Christopher Coleman (MSC) PP
Parish House, Union Hall,
Skibbereen, Co Cork
Tel 028-34940

CLOGHEEN (KERRY PIKE)
Canon Liam O'Driscoll Adm
Rev Johnson Chalissery CC
Church of the Most Precious Blood,
Clogheen, Co Cork
Tel 021-4392122

CLONAKILTY AND DARRARA
Right Rev Mgr Leonard O'Brien PP, VG
Tel 023-33165
Rev Edward J. Collins CC
Tel 023-33100
The Presbytery, Clonakilty, Co Cork

CLONTEAD
An tAth Tomás Ó Murchú Adm
Riverstick, Kinsale, Co Cork
Tel 021-4771332
Rev Daniel Burns PE
Belgooly, Co Cork

COURCEYS
Very Rev Canon Thomas Kelleher PP
Ballinspittle, Co Cork
Tel 021-4778055

CROSSHAVEN
Most Rev Patrick Coveney AP
Crosshaven, Co Cork
Tel 021-4831218

CURRAHEEN ROAD
Very Rev Canon Micheál Ó Dálaigh PP
Rev Cristoír MacDonald CC
The Presbytery, Curraheen Road, Cork
Tel 021-4343535

DOUGLAS
Very Rev Canon Teddy O'Sullivan PP
Parochial House, Douglas, Cork
Tel 021-4891265
Very Rev Canon Liam O'Regan AP
'Carraigin', Moneygourney,
Douglas, Cork
Tel 021-4363998
St Patrick's, Rochestown:
Rev Michael Keohane PIC
St Patrick's Presbytery,
Rochestown Road, Cork
Tel 021-4892363

DRIMOLEAGUE
Very Rev John O'Callaghan PP
Drimoleague, Co Cork
Tel 028-31133

DUNMANWAY
Very Rev Timothy Collins PP
Rev John O'Donovan CC
The Presbytery, Dunmanway, Co Cork
Tel 023-8845000

ENNISKEANE AND DESERTSERGES
Very Rev Martin Keohane PP
Parochial House, Enniskeane, Co Cork
Tel 023-8847769

FARRANREE
Very Rev Kieran Twomey PP
The Presbytery, Farranree, Cork
Tel 021-4393815/4210111

FRANKFIELD-GRANGE
Rev John Walsh PP
Tel 021-4361711
Rev Colin Doocey CC
Tel 021-4362377
The Presbytery, Frankfield, Cork

GLANMIRE
Very Rev Dr Noel O'Sullivan PP
Glanmire, Co Cork
Tel 021-4866307
Rev Ted Sheehan
Springhill, Glanmire, Co Cork
Tel 021-4866306

GLOUNTHAUNE
Very Rev Liam Ó h-Ici PP
Tel 021-4353195
Rev Gregory Howard (OSA) CC
Tel 021-4353078
Glounthaune, Co Cork

GOLEEN
Ver Rev Pat Stevenson PP
The Presbytery, Goleen, Co Cork
Tel 028-35188
Rev Alan O'Leary
The Presbytery, Schull, Co Cork

GURRANABRAHER
Very Rev Kieran Shorten (OFMCap) PP
Rev John Manley (OFMCap) CC
Rev Kevin Kiernan (OFMCap) CC
Ascension Presbytery,
Gurranabraher, Cork
Tel 021-4303655

INNISHANNON
Very Rev John Kingston PP
Innishannon, Co Cork
Tel 021-4775348

KILBRITTAIN
Very Rev Thomas Riordan PP
Kilbrittain, Co Cork
Tel 023-8849637

KILMACABEA
Very Rev Patrick O'Sullivan (MSC) Adm
Leap, Co Cork
Tel 028-33177

KILMEEN AND CASTLEVENTRY
Very Rev Agustine Keating PP
Rossmore, Clonakilty, Co Cork
Tel 023-8838630

KILMICHAEL
Very Rev Jeremiah Cremin PP
Parochial House, Tirelton,
Macroom, Co Cork
Tel 026-46012/086-2578065

KILMURRY
Very Rev Bernard Donovan PP
Cloughdubh, Crookstown, Co Cork
Tel 021-7336053
Rev Seán O'Sullivan AP
Lissarda, Crookstown, Co Cork
Tel 021-7336053

KINSALE
Very Rev Robert Young PP
Tel 021-4774019
Very Rev Canon John K. O'Mahony AP
Tel 021-4773700 Fax 021-4773821
The Presbytery, Kinsale, Co Cork

KNOCKNAHEENY/HOLLYHILL
Very Rev Pat Fogarty PP
The Presbytery, Knocknaheeny, Cork
Tel 021-4392459
Tel 021-4392459 (Parish Office)

THE LOUGH
Very Rev Canon Vincent Hodnett PP
Tel 021-4273821
Very Rev Canon Michael Crowley AP
Tel 021-4322633
Rev David O'Connell CC
Tel 021-4322633
The Lough Presbytery,
St Finbarr's West, Cork

MAHON
Very Rev Michael Kelleher PP
1 The Presbytery,
Holy Cross Church, Mahon, Cork
Tel 021-4357394
Rev Kaz Nawalaniec
2 The Presbytery, Mahon, Cork
Tel 021-4357665

MONKSTOWN
Very Rev John Newman PP
Rev Pat O'Donovan CC
Monkstown, Co Cork
Tel 021-4863267
Rev John Galvin AP
Passage West, Co Cork

MUINTIR BHÁIRE
Very Rev Gerard Galvin PP
Durrus, Co Cork
Tel 027-61013

MURRAGH AND TEMPLEMARTIN
Fr Finbarr Crowley Adm
Farnivane, Bandon, Co Cork
Tel 023-8820861

OVENS
Very Rev Patrick Keating PP
Ovens, Co Cork
Tel 021-4871180

PASSAGE WEST
Very Rev John Newman Adm
Tel 021-4863267
Rev John Galvin AP
Tel 021-4841267
Rev Pat O'Donovan CC
Passage West, Co Cork

RATH AND THE ISLANDS
Very Rev Donal Cotter Adm
Tel 028-22877
Rev Martin O'Driscoll CC
North Street, Skibbereen
Tel 028-22878
Rev Kevin O'Regan CC
The Hill, Baltimore
Tel 028-20283
Rev Peter Queally AP
Oiléan Cléire, Baltimore, Co Cork
Tel 028-39103

ROSSCARBERY AND LISSAVAIRD
Very Rev John McCarthy PP
Rosscarbery, Co Cork
Tel 023-8848168
Rev Chris O'Donovan AP
Lissavaird, Rosscarbery, Co Cork
Tel 023-8834334

SACRED HEART
Very Rev John Fitzgerald (MSC) PP
Sacred Heart Parish, Western Road, Cork
Tel 021-4804120 Fax 021-4543823

ST FINBARR'S SOUTH
Very Rev Richard Hurley PP
South Presbytery, Dunbar Street, Cork
Tel 021-4272989

ST JOSEPH'S (MAYFIELD)
Very Rev John Paul Hegarty PP
St Joseph's Presbytery, Mayfield, Cork
Tel 021-4501861

ST JOSEPH'S (BLACKROCK ROAD)
Very Rev Thomas Wade (SMA) PP
Rev Eugene McLoughlin (SMA) CC
St Joseph's, Blackrock Road, Cork
Tel 021-4292871

ST PATRICK'S
Very Rev Canon Dan Crowley PP
The Presbytery, Lower Road, Cork
Tel 021-4502696
Very Rev John Cotter PE
Tel 021-4551503
Very Rev Canon Liam Leader AP
Tel 021-4500282
The Presbytery, Lower Road, Cork

ST VINCENT'S, SUNDAY'S WELL
Very Rev Colm McAdam (CM) PP
122 Sunday's Well Road, Cork
Tel 021-4304070 Fax 021-4300103

SS PETER'S AND PAUL'S
Very Rev Patrick A. McCarthy PP
Tel 021-4276573
Rev John L. O'Sullivan (CSSp) CC
Tel 021-4276575
35 Paul Street, Cork

SCHULL
Very Rev Alan O'Leary PP
The Presbytery, Schull
Tel 028-28171
Rev Joseph Spillane (SPS) CC
Ballydehob, Co Cork
Tel 028-3711

TIMOLEAGUE AND CLOGAGH
Very Rev Patrick Hickey Adm
The Presbytery, Clogagh,
Timoleague, Co Cork
Tel 023-8839114

TOGHER
Very Rev Michael Riordan PP
Tel 021-4316700
Rev Martin O'Hare (SMA) CC
Tel 021-4316800
The Presbytery, Togher, Cork
Parish Office: 021-4318899

TRACTON ABBEY
Very Rev George Murphy PP
Tel 021-4887105
Minane Bridge, Co Cork

TURNER'S CROSS
Ven Archdeacon Kerry Murphy O'Connor PP
Tel 021-4312466
Rev Charles Kiely CC
Tel 021-4313103
The Presbytery, Turner's Cross, Cork

UIBH LAOIRE
Very Rev Bernard Cotter PP
Ballingeary, Co Cork
Tel 086-3684164

UPPER MAYFIELD
Very Rev Aidan O'Driscoll PP
Tel 021-4503116
Rev Pat O'Mahony (SMA) CC
Tel 021-4500828
The Presbytery, Upper Mayfield, Cork

WATERGRASSHILL
Very Rev Denis Cashman PP
Parochial House, Watergrasshill, Co Cork
Tel 021-4889103

WILTON, ST JOSEPH'S
Ver Rev Cormac Breathnach (SMA) PP
Rev Denis Collins (SMA) CC
St Joseph's, Wilton, Cork
Tel 021-4341362 Fax 021-4343940

INSTITUTIONS AND THEIR CHAPLAINS

THIRD LEVEL COLLEGES

Cork Institute of Technology
Chaplaincy Office: 021-4326225
Chaplaincy Base: 3 Elton Lawn,
Rossa Avenue, Bishopstown, Cork
Tel 021-4326256
Full-time chaplains
Rev Dr David McAuliffe
Tel 021-4346244
Ms Edel Dullea
Tel 021-4326778

University College, Cork
Chaplaincy Office: Iona,
College Road, Cork
Tel 021-4902459
Chaplains: Rev Seosamh Ó Cochláin
Tel 021-4902703
Rev David McAuliffe
Tel 021-4902704
Sr Bride Given (PBVM)
Tel 021-4902700

HOSPITALS

Bandon District Hospital
Bandon, Co Cork
Tel 023-8841403
Chaplain: Parish clergy, Bandon

Bantry Hospital
Bantry, Co Cork
Tel 027-50133
Chaplain: Parish clergy, Bantry

Bon Secours Hospital
College Road, Cork
Tel 021-4542807
Chaplain: Rev Aidan Vaughan (OFMCap)
Tel 021-4546682
Mrs Pat Healy
Sr Claire O'Driscoll
Ms Anne Bermingham
Ms Catherine O'Regan

Cork South Infirmary
Victoria Hospital Ltd
Old Blackrock Road, Cork
Tel 021-4926100
Chaplains
Sr Catherine Quane
Tel 021-4926100
Rev Francis Kelleher
Tel 021-4966555

Cork University Hospital
Wilton, Cork
Tel 021-4546400
Chaplains
Fr Ray Riordan (CSsR)
Tel 021-4546400
Rev Thomas Lyons
Tel 021-4546400/4922391
Sr Maura Farrell
Tel 021-4546400

District Hospital
Skibbereen, Co Cork
Tel 028-21677
Chaplain: Parish Clergy

Mercy University Hospital, Cork
Tel 021-4271971
Chaplains
Rev Michael Regan
Rev Pierce Cormac

Mount Carmel Hospital
Clonakilty, Co Cork
Tel 023-8833205
Chaplain: Parish Clergy

Sacred Heart Hospital
Kinsale, Co Cork
Tel 021-4772202
Chaplain: Parish clergy, Kinsale

St Anne's Hospital
Shanakiel, Cork
Tel 021-4541901
Chaplain: Rev Mil Whelan (MSC)

St Anthony's Hospital
Dunmanway, Co Cork
Tel 023-8845102
Chaplain: Parish clergy, Dunmanway

St Finbarr's Hospital
Douglas Road, Cork
Tel 021-4966555
Chaplains: Rev Francis Kelleher
Tel 021-4966555
Sr Eleanor Redican
Tel 021-4966553

St Gabriel's Hospital
Schull, Co Cork
Tel 028-28120
Chaplain: Parish clergy, Schull

St Joseph's Hospital
Mount Desert, Lee Road, Cork
Tel 021-4541765

St Mary's Orthopaedic Hospital
Baker's Road, Cork
Tel 021-4303264
Chaplains: Parish clergy, Gurranabraher
Tel 021-4303655

St Patrick's Hospital
Wellington Road, Cork
Tel 021-4501201
Chaplains: Rev Robert Talty (OP)
Rev Martin McCarthy (OP)
Sr Nan O'Mahony

St Stephen's Hospital
Glanmire, Co Cork
Tel 021-4821411
Chaplain: Rev Liam O'Callaghan (MSC)

Shanakiel Hospital
Shanakiel, Cork
Tel 021-4396955
Chaplain: Parish clergy, Clogheen
Tel 021-4392122

Port

Port Chaplaincy
Rev Desmond Campion (SDB)
Tel 021-4378046

PRISONS

Cork Prison
Chaplain: Fr Michael Kidney (SMA)
Tel 021-4518820/087-6836567

PRIESTS OF THE DIOCESE ELSEWHERE

Rev Dr Pádraig Corkery
St Patrick's College,
Maynooth, Co Kildare
Tel 01-7083639
Most Rev Patrick Coveney
Athenai, 154 52 Paleo Psychico,
Odos Mavili, 2, Greece
Rev Dr Gearóid Dullea
St Patrick's College, Maynooth,
Co Kildare
Rev Joseph O'Leary
1-38-16 Ekoda, Nakanoku, Tokyo,
16J0022 Japan

RETIRED PRIESTS

Rev James Good
Park View, Church Street,
Douglas, Cork
Tel 021-4363913
Rev Edmund Keohan
The Bungalow, Turners Cross, Cork
Tel 021-4320592
Ven Archdeacon Michael O'Brien
Nazareth House, Mallow, Co Cork
Rev Michael O'Driscoll
Bushmount, Clonakilty, Co Cork
Tel 023-33991
Very Rev Canon Diarmuid Linehan
2 Maglin View, Ballincollig, Co Cork
Tel 021-4875857
Very Rev Cornelius White
Nazareth Home, Dromahane,
Mallow, Co Cork
Tel 022-50486
Rev John Hurley
St Paul's, Bushmount,
Clonakilty, Co Cork
Very Rev Dan Burns
St Paul's, Bushmount,
Clonakilty, Co Cork
Tel 023-33991
Very Rev Jeremiah Hyde
The Presbytery, Kinsale, Co Cork
Very Rev Denis O'Connor
2 Woodlawn, Model Farm Road, Cork
Rev Pat Walsh
Priests House, Aliohill,
Enniskeane, Co Cork

RELIGIOUS ORDERS AND CONGREGATIONS

PRIESTS

AUGUSTINIANS
St Augustine's Priory,
Washington Street, Cork
Tel 021-4275398/4270410 Fax 021-4275381
Prior: Rev Pat Moran (OSA)

CAPUCHINS
Holy Trinity, Father Mathew Quay, Cork
Tel 021-4270827 Fax 021-4270829
Guardian: Rev Dermot Lynch (OFMCap)
Vicar: Rev Silvester O'Flynn (OFMCap)

Capuchin Community,
Monastery Road, Rochestown, Co Cork
Tel 021-4896244 Fax 021-4895915
Guardian: Rev Paul O'Donovan (OFMCap)

St Francis Capuchin Franciscan College,
Rochestown, Co Cork
Tel 021-4891417 Fax 021-4361254

The Presbytery, Gurranabraher, Cork
Tel 021-4303655/4303606
Fax 021-4303658
Guardian: Rev John Manley (OFMCap)
Vicar: Rev Kevin Kiernan (OFMCap)

CARMELITES (OCARM)
Carmelite Friary, Kinsale, Co Cork
Tel 021-4772138
Email kinsale@irishcarmelites.com
Prior: Very Rev Míceál O'Neill (OCarm)

DOMINICANS
St Mary's, Pope Quay, Cork
Tel 021-4502267 Fax 021-4502307
Prior: Very Rev Edward Conway (OP)

St Dominic's Retreat House,
Montenotte, Cork
Tel 021-4502520 Fax 021-4502712
Prior: Very Rev Benedict Hegarty (OP)

FRANCISCANS
Franciscan Friary, Liberty Street, Cork
Tel 021-4270302 Fax 021-4271841
Guardian: Rev Eugene Barrett (OFM)

MISSIONARIES OF THE SACRED HEART
Western Road, Cork
Tel 021-4804120 Fax 021-4543823
Leader: Rev Dan O'Connor
Parish Priest
Very Rev John Fitzgerald (MSC) PP

MSC Mission Support Centre,
PO Box 23, Western Road, Cork
Tel 021-4545704 Fax 021-4343587
Director: Rev Michael O'Connell (MSC)
www.mscireland.com

Coláiste an Chroí Naofa
Carraig na Bhfear, Co chorcaí
Tel 021-4884104

Myross Wood House,
Leap, Skibbereen, Co Cork
Tel 028-33793 Fax 028-33793
Director & Leader
Rev Michael Curran (MSC)

REDEMPTORISTS
Scala, Bessboro, Blackrock, Cork
Tel 021-4358800 Fax 021-4359696
Superior: Rev Noel Kehoe (CSsR)

ROSMINIANS
Upton, Innishannon, Cork
Tel 021-4776268/4776923 Fax 021-4776268
Rector: Rev Seamus McKenna (IC)
Residential services for adults with
learning disabilities

ST COLUMBAN'S MISSIONARY SOCIETY
No. 2 Presbytery,
Our Lady Crowned Church,
Mayfield Upper, Cork
Tel 021-4508610
Rev Patrick O'Herlihy (SSC)

ST PATRICK'S MISSIONARY SOCIETY
Kiltegan House, 11 Douglas Road, Cork
Tel 021-4969371
House Leader: Rev Jim Barry (SPS)

SOCIETY OF AFRICAN MISSIONS
St Joseph's Provincial House, Feltrim,
Blackrock Road, Cork
Tel 021-4292871 Fax 021-4292873
Email provincial@sma.ie
Provincial: Rev Fachtna O'Driscoll (SMA)
Superior: Rev Colum P. O'Shea (SMA)

Wilton College, Cork
Tel/Fax 021-4541069
Superior: Rev Daniel Cashman (SMA)

VINCENTIANS
St Vincent's,
122 Sunday's Well Road, Cork
Tel 021-4304070/4304529 Fax 021-4300103
Superior: Very Rev Jack Harris (CM) PP

BROTHERS

BROTHERS OF CHARITY
Our Lady of Good Counsel, Lota,
Glanmire, Co Cork
Tel 021-4821012 Fax 021-4821711
Chaplain: Fr Paul Thettayil (IC)

CHRISTIAN BROTHERS
Christian Brothers House,
Ard Mhuire, Fair Hill, Cork
Tel 021-4300879
Community Leader: Br Gary O'Shea
Community: 6

Christian Brothers, 36 Beechwood Grove,
Onslow Gardens, Commons Road, Cork
Tel 021-2393119
Community: 2

Churchfield Community Trust,
109 Knockfree Avenue, Cork
Tel 021-4210348
Email cyct109@hotmail.com
Director: Eileen O'Brien

Sunday's Well Life Centre,
6 Winter's Hill, Sunday's Well, Cork
Tel 021-4304391
Email thelifecentrecork@eircom.net
Director: Don O'Leary

PRESENTATION BROTHERS
2/3 Heatherton Park,
South Douglas Road, Cork
Tel 021-4364288
Contact: Br De Paul Hennessy
Community: 3

'Callan', 4 Lynbrook, Glasheen Road, Cork
Tel 021-4346765 Fax 021-4346770
Contact: Br Donatus Brazil
Email callanpb@iol.ie

Westcourt Community,
Mardyke House, Cork
Tel 021-4272239
Community: 4
Contact: Br Stephen O'Gorman

Maiville, Turner's Cross, Cork
Tel 021-4272649
Community: 14
Contact: Br Aidan McHugh
Email presbrosmaiville@eircom.net

Mount St Joseph, Blarney Street, Cork
Tel 021-4392160
Community: 7
Contact: Br Bede Minehane

SISTERS

BON SECOURS SISTERS (PARIS)
Provincial House, College Road, Cork
Tel 021-4542416 Fax 021-4542533
Provincial: Sr Margaret Mary Hanafin
Co-ordinator: Sr Angela Leamy
Provincialate and novitiate
Email mhanafin@province.bonsecours.ie
Community: 23
Parish and hospital ministry

Soilse Community
Mount Finbarr, Glasheen Road, Cork
Tel 021-4964804
Contact: Sr Columbanus Byrne
Community: 4

Cnoc Mhuire, Fernhurst,
College Road, Cork
Tel 021-4345410 Fax 021-4345491
Co-ordinator: Sr Norrie Finan
Community: 41
Pastoral, community, nursing and
hospital ministry, care of sick and poor in
their own homes

Casa Maria, Fernhurst, College Road, Cork
Tel 021-4345411
Contact: Sr Maureen Condon
Community: 2
Pastoral and hospital ministry

3 Brookfield Villas, College Road, Cork
Tel 021-4545018
Community: 1

1 Aylsbury Lawn, Ballincollig, Co Cork
Tel 021-4872978
Community: 4

CONGREGATION OF THE SISTERS OF MERCY
Provincial Offices, Bishop Street, Cork
Tel 021-4975380 Fax 021-4915220
Email provincialoffice@mercysouth.ie
Provincial: Sr Liz Murphy

13 Kempton Park, Ballyvolane, Cork
Tel 021-4551375
Contact: Sr Bernie Ryan

14 Kempton Park, Ballyvolane, Cork
Tel 021-4551371

49 Hollymount, Blarney Road, Cork
Tel 021-4302123

13 Ronayn's Court, Rochestown Road,
Cork
Contact: Sr Kate O'Connor

2 Rowan Hill, Mount Oval Village,
Rochestown, Cork
Tel 021-4366611
Contact: Sr Veronica Mangan

19 Sheraton Court, Glasheen Road, Cork
Contact: Sr Eileen O'Connell

144 Dun Eoin, Ballinrea Road,
Carrigaline, Co Cork
Tel 021-4919748
Contact: Sr Liz Murphy

2 Woodbrook Grove,
Bishopstown, Cork
Tel 021-4342286
Contact: Sr Anna Holden

St Columba's, Convent,
Bishopstown Avenue West, Cork
Tel 021-4545549
Leader: Sr Marcella Nagle

St Marie's of the Isle,
Sharman Crawford Street, Cork
Tel 021-4316029
Leader: Sr Rita Twomey &
Sr Catherine Harrington
St Joseph's Primary School
Tel 021-4963994

38 Sheares Street, Cork
Tel 021-4272982
Contact: Sr Imelda O'Shaughnessy

St Catherine's Convent,
Bishopstown Avenue, Cork
Tel 021-4541376
St Catherine's Primary School
Tel 021-4546868

1 Kinloch Court, Bishopstown Avenue,
Model Farm Road, Cork
Tel 021-4345332
Contact: Sr Agnes Daly

23 Wentworth Gardens, Wilton, Cork
Tel 021-4347833
Contact: Sr Lucy O'Sullivan

St Maries Bungalow, Convent Place,
Crosses Green, Cork
Tel 021-4318628
Contact: Sr Xavier O'Leary

Mercy Hospital, Grenville Place, Cork
Tel 021-4271971

Convent of Our Lady Crowned,
Boherboy Road, Mayfield, Cork
Tel 021-4500080 Fax 021-4552267
Primary school. Tel 021-503003

'Lorg Dé', 27 St Joseph's Park,
Boherboy Road, Mayfield, Cork
Tel 021-4508519

56 Glenamoy Lawn, Mayfield, Cork
Tel 021-4509410
Contact: Sr Mary B. Williams

1 Sandymount Drive, Glasheen Road,
Cork
Tel 021-4541613
Contact: Sr Hilary McCarthy

Cuan na Trócaire, 23 Benvoirlich Estate,
Bishopstown, Cork
Tel 021-4343371

Wellsprings, Wandesford Quay, Cork
Tel 021-4313953

Convent of Mercy, Winter's Hill, Kinsale,
Co Cork
Tel 021-4772165
St Joseph's Primary School
Tel 021-4774294

Avila, Ard na Gaoithe Mór,
Bantry, Co Cork
Tel 027-50035

The Bungalow, Balindeasig,
Belgooly, Co Cork
Tel 021-4887954
Contact: Sr Eileen O'Sullivan

Casa Maria Seskin, Bantry, Co Cork
Tel 027-51198
Primary School.Tel 027-50590

Schull, Co Cork
Tel 028-28189
Primary School Tel 028-28400

'Tigh Amos', South Terrace,
Schull, Co Cork
Contact: Sr Sheila Minehane

1 Park View, Church Hill,
Passage West, Co Cork
Tel 021-4863121
Primary School. Tel 021-842072

Arus Muire, McCurtain Hill, Scartagh,
Clonakilty, Co Cork
Tel 023-8833391
Leader: Sr Genevieve Hurley &
Sr Baptist Lombard
St Joseph's Primary School
Tel 023-8833050

Mount Carmel Convent,
Clonakilty, Co Cork
Tel 023-8833072

St Joseph's Primary School
Skibbereen, Co Cork
Tel 028-21804

Pairc-a-Tobair, Rosscarbery, Co Cork
Tel 023-8848963

Apt 1, Arus Muire, McCurtain Hill,
Scartagh, Clonakilty, Co Cork
Contact : Sr Lily O'Byrne

Apt 2, Arus Muire, McCurtain Hill,
Scartagh, Clonakilty, Co Cork
Contact: Sr Eilis McGrath

Apt 3, Arus Muire, McCurtain Hill,
Scartagh, Clonakilty, Co Cork
Contact: Sr Eileen McSweeney

Apt 4, Arus Muire, McCurtain Hill,
Scartagh, Clonakilty, Co Cork
Contact: Sr Martina Kearney

2 The Drive, Priory Court,
Watergrasshill, Co Cork
Tel 021-4513949

DAUGHTERS OF CHARITY OF ST VINCENT DE PAUL
St Louise's, Hollyhill House,
Harbour View Road, Knocknaheeny, Cork
Tel 021-4392762
Superior: Sr Mary Connaire
Community: 7
Teaching, parish and social work
AND
Labouré House,
Mount Nebo, Blarney Street, Cork
Tel 021-4304207
Sister's residence, Pastoral work

FRANCISCAN MISSIONARIES OF ST JOSEPH
Convent of St Francis,
Blackrock Road, Cork
Tel 021-4317059
Superior: Sr Margaret Quinn
Community: 11

GOOD SHEPHERD SISTERS
Baile an Aoire, Leycester Lane,
Montenotte, Cork
Tel 021-4551200 Fax 021-4551202
Email rgsbaile@eircom.net
Leader: Sr Jo Horgan
Community: 8

Edel House, Residential Centre,
Grattan Street, Cork
Tel 021-4274240 Fax 021-4274160
Email gsscork@eircom.net

Bruac, Henry Street, Cork
Tel 021-4273890 Fax 021-4222977
Email gsscork@eircom.net

Riverview, 3 North Mall, Cork
Tel/Fax 021-4304205
Email gsscork@eircom.net

'The Well', Sunday's Well, Cork
Tel 021-4303216 Fax 021-4305250
Email rgsthewell@eircom.net
Leader: Sr Jennifer McAleer
Community: 2

17 Killiney Heights, Knockaheeny, Cork
Tel 021-4302660
Email janebmurphy@eircom.net
Leader: Sr Jane Murphy
Community: 2

INFANT JESUS SISTERS
10 Willow Drive, Muskerry Estate,
Ballincollig, Co Cork
Tel 021-4870625
Community: 3
Pastoral work

19 Cherry Walk,
Ballincollig, Co Cork
Tel 021-4873599
Community: 3

St Joseph's,
Model Farm Road, Cork
Tel 021-4342348
Community: 14
House for elderly sisters

LA RETRAITE SISTERS
22 Salmon Weir, Hanover Street, Cork
Tel 021-4251100/4276789
Contact. Sr Bridget Dunne
Email bridgetdunne@eircom.net

LITTLE SISTERS OF THE ASSUMPTION
32 St Francis Gardens,
Thomas Davis Street, Blackpool, Cork
Tel 021-4391407

1 Ballinure Crescent, Mahon,
Blackrock, Cork
Tel 021-4358372
Contact: Sr Thérèse Farrell
Email lsamahck@eircom.net
Professional services to the family

2-3 College View,
Old Youghal Road, Cork
Tel 021-4500023

MARIE REPARATRICE SISTERS
7 Knockrea Lawn, Ballinlough Road, Cork
Tel 021-4313429
Community: 5
Email smrknock@eircom.net
Superior: Sr Catherine Corry
Parish ministry

4 Ashwood, South Douglas Road, Cork
Tel 021-4365909
Email pauline@smr.org
Superior: Sr Pauline Clarke
Community: 3

MISSIONARY SISTERS OF THE HOLY ROSARY
7 The Circle, Broadale, Douglas, Cork
Tel 021-4362424
Healthcare, work with refugees
Community: 3

MISSIONARY SISTERS OF OUR LADY OF APOSTLES
Ardfoyle Convent, Ballintemple, Cork
Tel 021-4291851 Fax 021-4291105
Email prov@eircom.net
Provincial: Sr Mary Crowley
Sister-in-Charge: Sr Mary Barron
Community: 65

OUR LADY OF THE CENACLE
16 Mervue Lawn, Ballyvolane, Cork
Tel 021-4508059
Email cenacle@iol.ie
Contact: Cenacle Sisters
Community: 2

POOR CLARES
Poor Clare Colettine Monastery,
College Road, Cork
Abbess: Sr Miriam Buckley
Community: 8
Contemplatives
Eucharistic Adoration: Daily 7am-6pm
Mass Times: Daily 10.00 am
Rosary: Monday-Saturday 5.30 pm
Sunday Rosary, Evening Prayer and
Benediction: 5.00 pm

PRESENTATION SISTERS
Presentation Provincial Office,
Evergreen Street, Cork
Tel 021-4975190 Fax 021-4975192
Email swpres@iol.ie
Provincial Leader: Sr Mary Hoare

54 Hollymount,
Blarney Road, Cork
Tel 021-4309262
Community: 2

South Presentation Convent,
Douglas Street, Cork
Tel 021-4975042
Leader: Sr Patricia O'Shea
Community: 13

115 Cathedral Road, Cork
Tel 021-4393086
Community: 2

Christ King Convent,
Turner's Cross, Cork
Tel 021-4966552
Leader: Sr Mary Dineen
Community: 10
Primary School. Tel 021-4963695
Christ King Girls' Secondary School
Tel 021-4961448

Presentation Convent,
Ballyphehane, Cork
Non-resident Leader
Sr Mary Jane Donaldson
Tel 021-4321606
Community: 9
Primary School (Junior). Tel 021-4315857
Primary School (Senior). Tel 021-4315724
Secondary School. Tel 021-4961765

18 The Orchards,
Montenotte, Cork
Tel 021-4501456
Community: 2

North Presentation Convent,
Gerald Griffin Street, Cork
Tel 021-4302878
Team Leadership
Community: 20
Primary School Tel 021-4307132
An Gleann Primary School
Tel 021-4504877

Regina Coeli Convent,
Farranree, Cork
Tel 021-4302770
Non-resident Leader: Sr Grace McKernan
Community: 10
Aiséirí Chríost Primary School
Tel 021-4301383
Secondary School
Tel 021-4303330

25 Rosbarra, Deerpark,
Friar's Walk, Cork
Tel 021-4323321
Community: 2

Presentation Convent, Bandon, Co Cork
Tel 023-8841476
Non-resident Leader: Sr Marie Wall
Community: 15
Primary School Tel. 023-8841809
Secondary School. Tel 023-8841814

Presentation Convent,
Crosshaven, Co Cork
Tel 021-4831189
Non-resident Leader
Sr Goretti O'Callaghan
Community: 11
Primary School. Tel 021-4831646
Coláiste Mhuire Secondary School
Tel 021-4831604

Ardán Mhuire, Togher Road, Cork
Tel 021-4961471
Community: 2

7 Churchfield Terrace West,
Gurranabraher, Cork
Tel 021-4306640
Community: 3

7 Old Waterpark, Carrigaline, Co Cork
Tel 021-4372718
Community: 2

20 Fairhill Drive, Fairhill, Cork
Tel 021-4399760
Community: 2

7 Avoca Crescent, The Glen, Cork
Tel 021-4504025
Community: 1

Dóchas, 21 Ashdene,
South Douglas Road, Cork
Tel 021-4897597
Community: 3

Presentation Centre,
Evergreen Street, Cork
Tel 021-4314255
Community: 4

44 Castlemeadows,
Mahon, Cork
Tel 021-4515944
Community: 2

44 Ashbrook Heights, Lehenaghmore,
Togher, Cork
Tel 021-4320006
Community: 2

78 Grange Way, Douglas, Cork
Tel 021-4899704
Community: 1

5 Abbey View, Nano Nagle Walk,
Douglas Street, Cork
Tel 021-4322097
Community: 1

18 Convent View, Nano Nagle Walk,
Douglas Street, Cork
Tel 021-4915380
Community: 1

RELIGIOUS SISTERS OF CHARITY
St Vincent's Convent,
St Mary's Road, Cork
Tel 021-4211176/4211238
Various apostolic ministries

St Anthony's Convent, Vincent's Avenue,
St Mary's Road, Cork
Tel 021-4308162

SACRED HEARTS OF JESUS AND MARY
Blackrock, Cork
Tel 021-4357841
Community Leader: Sr Alexander

URSULINES
Ursuline Convent,
Blackrock, Cork
Tel 021-4358663 Fax 021-4356077
Email corckucb@eircom.net
Community: 12
Local Leader: Sr Jean Browne
Primary School
Tel 021-4358476 Fax 021-4359073
Secondary School
Tel 021-4358012 Fax 021-4358012

58 Meadowgrove,
Blackrock, Cork
Tel 021-4357249
Community: 2

EDUCATIONAL INSTITUTIONS

Christ the King Secondary School
South Douglas Road, Cork
Tel 021-4961448 Fax 021-4314563

Christian Brothers College, Cork
Tel 021-4501653 Fax 021-4504113

Coláiste Chríost Rí, Cork
Tel 021-4274904 Fax 021-4964784

Coláiste an Spioraid Naoimh
Bishopstown, Cork
Tel 021-4543790 Fax 021-4543625

Deerpark CBS
St Patrick's Road, Cork
Tel 021-4962025 Fax 021-4311792

EDMUND RICE SCHOOLS TRUST
Scoil Mhuire Fatima
North Monastery, Cork
Tel 021-4305340 Fax 01-4305011
Principal: Mr C. Higgins

Christian Brothers Secondary School,
North Monastery, Cork
Tel 021-4301318 Fax 021-4307994
Staff Tel 021-4301247
Careers Tel 021-4309330
Email northmonastery.ias@eircom.net
Principal: Mr Patrick Mulcahy

Gael Choláiste Mhuire,
An Mhainistir Thuaidh, Corcaigh
Tel 021-4307579 Fax 021-4288011
Email gaelcholaistemhuireag@eircom.net
Principal: Dónal Ó Gráda

Scoil Cholmcille, Blarney Street, Cork
Tel/Fax 021-4397000
Email colmcillecbs.ias@eircom.net
Principal: Mr Billy Lynch

Coláiste Iognáid Rís,
St Patrick's Road, Cork
Tel 021-4963265 Fax 021-4311792
Email deerparkcbs@eircom.net
Principal: Mr Mike O'Floinn

Christian Brothers Junior School,
Sidney Hill, Wellington Road, Cork
Tel 021-4501653 Fax 021-4504113
Email christianscork@eircom.net
education@cbccork.ie
In Charge: Mrs S. Hayes

Christian Brothers College,
Sidney Hill, Wellington Road, Cork
Tel 021-4501653 Fax 021-4504113
Email christianscork@eircom.net
Principal: Dr L. Jordan

Mercy Heights Secondary School
Skibbereen, Co Cork
Tel 028-21550 Fax 028-21451

Mercy Sisters Secondary School
Roscarbery, Co Cork
Tel 023-8848114 Fax 023-8848520

Mount Mercy College
Model Farm Road, Cork
Tel 021-4542366 Fax 021-4542709

North Monastery,
Our Lady's Mount, Cork
Tel 021-4301318 Fax 021-4309891

Presentation College, Cork
Tel 021-4272743 Fax 021-4273147

Presentation Convent
Bandon, Co Cork
Tel 023-8841814 Fax 023-8841385

Presentation Convent Secondary School
Crosshaven, Co Cork
Tel/Fax 021-4831604

Presentation Secondary School
Ballyphehane, Cork
Tel 021-4961765/4961767
Fax 021-4312864

Regina Coeli Convent Secondary School
Farranree, Cork
Tel 021-4303330 Fax 021-4303411

Sacred Heart College
Carrig na bhFear, Co Cork
Tel 021-4884104 Fax 021-4884442

Sacred Heart Secondary School
Clonakilty, Co Cork
Tel 023-8833737 Fax 023-8833908

St Aloysius School, Cork
Tel 021-4316017 Fax 021-4316007

St Angela's College, Cork
Tel 021-4500059 Fax 021-4504515

St Fachtna's Secondary School
Skibbereen, Co Cork
Tel 028-21454 Fax 028-21256

St Francis Capuchin College,
Rochestown, Co Cork
Tel 021-4891417 Fax 021-4361254

St Vincent's Secondary School, Cork
Tel 021-4307730 Fax 021-4307252

Ursuline Convent Secondary School
Blackrock, Cork
Tel/Fax 021-435801

DIOCESE OF DERRY

PATRONS OF THE DIOCESE
ST EUGENE, 23 AUGUST; ST COLUMBA, 9 JUNE

INCLUDES ALMOST ALL OF COUNTY DERRY,
PARTS OF COUNTIES DONEGAL AND TYRONE
AND A VERY SMALL AREA ACROSS THE RIVER BANN IN COUNTY ANTRIM

Most Rev Seamus Hegarty DD
Bishop of Derry;
born 1940;
ordained priest 19 June 1966;
ordained Bishop of Raphoe
28 March 1982;
appointed Bishop of Derry
1 October 1994;
installed 6 November 1994

Office: PO Box 227, Bishop's
House, Derry BT48 9YG
Tel 028-71262302
Fax 028-71371960
Email office@derrydiocese.org

ST EUGENE'S CATHEDRAL, DERRY

In the 1830s, following the Catholic Emancipation Act of 1829, the Catholic community of Derry was able to contemplate building a cathedral. In the summer of 1838, a number of Catholics of the city met with the then Bishop of Derry, Peter McLaughlin, to consider such a project. Over the next thirteen years a weekly collection was made in the city and eventually, on 26 July 1851, the foundation stone was laid by Bishop Francis Kelly.

The construction of the cathedral was sporadic as the funds became available over twenty-five years, and owing to the difficulty in raising money, it was agreed to postpone the building of the tower, belfry and spire until a later date. Due to the lack of funds in the diocese, the windows were initially all of plain glass, and it was only in later years that the stained glass was installed.

J. J. McCarthy (1817–1882) was the architect commissioned to design St Eugene's Cathedral. He was one of the most outstanding church architects in Ireland in his time and he designed many churches and convents all over the country, including St Patrick's Cathedral, Armagh, St Macartan's Cathedral, Monaghan and the Cathedral of the Assumption, Thurles.

The actual construction work took twenty-two years to complete, at a cost of £40,000. It was not until 1873 that the building was brought to a stage where it could be dedicated and used for liturgical celebrations. The cathedral was dedicated by Bishop Francis Kelly on 4 May 1873.

In 1899 it was decided to add a spire to the tower, which was estimated to cost £15,000. The spire was completed on 19 June 1903, and on 27 June the eight-foot-high granite cross was put in position by Fathers John Doherty and Lawrence Hegarty. The full complement of stained-glass windows was achieved in the Spring and Autumn of 1896 at a cost of £2,270. The ten bells of the cathedral first rang out on Christmas Eve, 1902.

St Eugene's was solemnly consecrated on 21 April 1936, the seventh cathedral in Ireland to be consecrated, and the event is celebrated annually on 21 April.

Most Rev Francis Lagan DD
Titular Bishop of Sidnacestre and
Auxiliary Bishop of Derry; born 1934;
ordained priest 19 June 1960; ordained
Bishop 20 March 1988
Residence: 9 Glen Road, Strabane,
Co Tyrone BT82 8BX
Tel 028-71884533 Fax 028-71884551
Email fblagan@gotadsl.co.uk

Most Rev Edward Daly DD
Retired Bishop of Derry: born 1933;
ordained priest 16 March 1957; ordained
Bishop of Derry 31 March 1974; retired
as Bishop of Derry 26 October 1993
Residence: 9 Steelstown Road,
Derry BT48 8EU
Tel 028-71359809 Fax 028-71357098
Email Edward.Daly@btinternet.com

ADMINISTRATION

Vicars General
Most Rev Francis Lagan DD
9 Glen Road, Strabane,
Co Tyrone BT82 8BX
Tel 028-71884533 Fax 028-71884551
Email fblagan@gotadsl.co.uk
Rt Rev Mgr Bryan M. Canny PP, VG
St Patrick's Presbytery, Buncrana Road,
Derry BT48 7QL
Tel 028-71262360

College of Consultors
Most Rev Francis Lagan DD, VG
Rt Rev Mgr Bryan McCanny PP, VG
Very Rev Kieran Devlin PEm
Very Rev John Farren PP
Very Rev Seamus O'Connell PP, VF
Very Rev Brian Donnelly PP
Very Rev Patrick McGoldrick CC
Very Rev Eamon Martin
Very Rev Paul McCafferty

Episcopal Vicars
Episcopal Vicar for Family Ministry:
Very Rev Seamus O'Connell PP, VF
159 Glen Road, Maghera,
Co Derry BT46 5JN
Tel 028-75642496
Episcopal Vicar for Religious:
Very Rev Colum Clerkin PP
55 St Patrick's Street, Draperstown,
Magherafelt, Co Derry BT45 7AJ
Tel 028-79628248

Vicars Forane
Derry City Deanery
Very Rev Seamus Kelly PP, VF
Co Derry Deanery
Very Rev Seamus O'Connell PP, VF
Co Tyrone Deanery
Rt Rev Mgr Joseph Donnelly PP, VF
Inishowen Deanery
Rev James McGonagle PP

Diocesan Archives
Archivists: Most Rev Edward Daly DD
Rev Kieran Devlin PEm
9 Steelstown Road, Derry BT48 8EU
Tel 028-71359809
Email edward.daly@btinternet.com

Diocesan Finance Committee
PO Box 227, Bishop's House,
Derry BT48 9YG
Tel 028-71262302 Fax 028-71371960
Email office@derrydiocese.org
Administrator: Ms Teresa McMenamin

Diocesan Office
Moderator of the Diocesan Curia
Rev Paul McCafferty
Administrative & Financial Secretary
Ms Teresa McMenamin
PO Box 227, Bishop's House,
Derry BT48 9YG
Tel 028-71262302 Fax 028-71371960
Email office@derrydiocese.org
Bishop Lagan's Office
Secretary: Ms Breedge Conway
9 Glen Road, Strabane,
Co Tyrone BT82 8BX
Tel 028-71884533
Email fblagan@gotadsl.co.uk

Diocesan Notaries
Rev Kevin McElhennon CC
Rev Francis Bradley
Rev Colum Clerkin PP
Rev Eamonn Graham PP

Priest Penitentiary
Rev Kieran O'Doherty PP
34 Moneysharvin Road, Swatragh
Co Derry BT46 5PY
Tel 028-79401236

CATECHETICS EDUCATION

**Adult Religious Education and Faith
Formation**
Director: Rev Kevin McElhennon CC
The Gate Lodge, 2 Francis Street,
Derry BT48 9DS
Tel 028-71264087 Fax 028-71269090
Email adulteducation@derrydiocese.org

Catechetical Centre
Director: Rev Paul Farren
Derry Diocesan Catechetical Centre,
The Gate Lodge, 2 Francis Street,
Derry BT48 9DS
Tel 028-71264087 Fax 028-71269090
Email ddcc@derrydiocese.org

**Catholic Primary School Managers'
Association**
Contact: Rev Peter Devlin PP
Orchard Park, Murlog,
Lifford, Co Donegal
Tel 074-9142022

Religious Education
Derry Diocesan Catechetical Centre,
The Gate Lodge, 2 Francis Street,
Derry BT48 9DS
Tel 028-71264087 Fax 028-71269090
Email ddcc@derrydiocese.org
Director: Rev Paul Farren
Adviser: Miss Thérèse Ferry

LITURGY

Diocesan Master of Ceremonies
Rev Francis Bradley
Diocesan Pastoral Centre,
164 Bishop Street, Derry BT48 6UJ
Tel 028-71362475

PASTORAL

Accord
Derry Centre: Diocesan Pastoral Centre,
164 Bishop Street, Derry BT48 6UJ
Tel 028-71362475 Fax 028-71260970
Omagh Centre: Mount St Columba
Pastoral Centre, 48 Brook Street, Omagh,
Co Tyrone BT78 5HD
Tel 028-82242439
Maghera Centre: Pastoral Centre,
159 Glen Road, Maghera
Tel 028-79642983
Inishowen Centre: Pastoral Centre
Church Road, Carndonagh, Co Donegal
Tel 074-9374103

Chaplain to the Deaf
Rev Eamon Graham PP
42 Glenedra Road, Feeny,
Dungiven, Co Derry BT47 4TW
Tel 028-77781223

Charismatic Renewal
Director: Very Rev Seamus Kelly PP, VF
23 Thornhill Park, Culmore,
Derry BT48 4PB
Tel 028-71358519

Columba Community
Chaplain: Rev Neal Carlin
St Anthony's, Dundrean,
Burnfoot, Co Donegal
Tel 074-9368370
Email sarced@eircom.net
Columba House, 11 Queen Street,
Derry BT48 7E6
Tel 028-71262407

Communications
Media Liaison Person:
Rev Michael Canny Adm
PO Box 227, Bishop's House,
Derry BT48 9YG
Tel 028-71262302 Fax 028-71371960
Email steugenes@btconnect.com

Ecumenism
Director: Rev Eamon McDevitt PP
78 Lisnaragh Road, Dunamanagh,
Strabane, Co Tyrone BT82 0QN
Tel 028-71398212

Family Care Society (NI)
Colmcille House, 1A Millar Street,
Derry BT48 6SU
Tel 028-71368592

Family Ministry
Episcopal Vicar for Family Ministry
Very Rev Seamus O'Connell PP, VF
159 Glen Road, Maghera,
Co Derry BT46 5JN
Tel 028-79642496

Library/Museum
Curators: Rev John R. Walsh PP
Buncrana
Rev Brian McGoldrick PP
Doneyloop
Very Rev Kieran Devlin PP, Gortin

Marriage Tribunal
(See Marriage Tribunals section)

Migrants and Asylum Seekers
Rev Pat O'Hagan CC
41 Melmount Road, Strabane,
Co Tyrone BT82 9EF
Tel 028-71882651

NEST – New Existence for Survivors of Trauma
Ministry to adult victims of abuse of all kinds.
Centre: Pastoral Centre,
Maghera BT46 5JN
Tel 028-79642983
Email nest.int@btconnect.com

Pastoral Centres
Diocesan Pastoral Centre
164 Bishop Street,
Derry BT48 6UJ
Tel 028-71362475 Fax 028-71260970
Director: Rev Francis Bradley

Inishowen Pastoral Centre
Carndonagh, Co Donegal
Tel 074-9374103
Director: Rev Con McLaughlin PP

Maghera Pastoral Centre
159 Glen Road, Maghera, Co Derry
Tel 028-79642983
Director
Very Rev Seamus O'Connell PP

Omagh Pastoral Centre
Mount St Columba Pastoral Centre,
48 Brooke Street, Omagh,
Co Tyrone BT78 5HD
Tel 028-82242439
Director: Rev John McDevitt CC

Pilgrimages
Lourdes and Marian:
Sr Perpetua McNulty
Thornhill Centre, Culmore Road,
Derry BT48 5JA
Tel 028-71351233

Pioneer Total Abstinence Association
Director: Rev John Downey CC
36 Moneyneena Road, Draperstown,
Magherafelt, Co Derry BT45 7DZ
Tel 028-79628375

Travellers
Chaplain: Very Rev Brian Donnelly PP
16 Castefin Road, Castlederg,
Co Tyrone BT81 7EB

Trócaire
Diocesan Representative:
Rev Colm O'Doherty CC
7 Cloonty Road, Drumquin,
Omagh, Co Tyrone
Tel 028-81661475

Vocations
Directors: Rev Colm O'Doherty CC
7 Cloonty Road, Drumquin,
Omagh, Co Tyrone
Tel 028-81661475
Rev Paul Farren
21 Derry Road, Strabane,
Co Tyrone BT82 8DX
Tel 028-71883247

PARISHES

Mensal parishes are listed first, followed by other Derry city parishes. Other parishes follow alphabetically. Historical names are in parentheses. Church titulars are in italics.

DERRY CITY
St Eugene's Cathedral (Templemore)
Rev Michael Canny Adm
Rev Peter Raftery CC
Rev Daniel McFaul CC
Parochial House, St Eugene's Cathedral,
Derry BT48 9AP
Tel 028-71262894/71365712
Fax 028-71377494
Email steugenes@btconnect.com

ST COLUMBA'S, LONG TOWER (TEMPLEMORE)
Rev Roland Colhoun Adm
Email frroland@hmcolhoun.freeserve.co.uk
Rev Gerard Mongan CC
St Columba's Presbytery,
6 Victoria Place, Derry BT48 6TJ
Tel 028-71262301
Fax 028-71372973
Email longtowerparish@aol.com

THE THREE PATRONS
Rt Rev Mgr Bryan McCanny PP, VG
St Patrick's, Buncrana Road, Pennyburn,
Derry BT48 7QL
Tel 028-71262360
Rev Dermott Harkin CC
St Brigid's, Carnhill, Derry BT48 8HJ
Tel 028-71351261
Rev Dermot McGirr CC
St Joseph's, Fairview Road, Galliagh,
Derry BT48 8NJ
Tel 028-71352351

ST MARY'S, CREGGAN
Rev Stephen McLaughlin PP
Rev Gerald Hasson CC
Parochial House, St Mary's, Creggan,
Derry BT48 9QE
Tel 028-71263152
Fax 028-71264390
Email cregganchapel@aol.com

OUR LADY OF LOURDES, STEELSTOWN
Rev John Cargan PP
Rev Francis Bradley *(priest in residence)*
The Presbytery, 11 Steelstown Road,
Derry BT48 8EU
Tel 028-71351718 Fax 028-71357810
Email steelstown@aol.com

HOLY FAMILY, BALLYMAGROARTY
Rev Francis Lynch CC
1 Aileach Road, Ballymagroarty,
Derry BT48 0AZ
Tel 028-71267070 Fax 028-71308687

AGHYARAN (TERMONAMONGAN)
St Patrick's
Rev John Gilmore PP
11 Church Road, Aghyaran,
Castlederg, Co Tyrone BT81 7XZ
Tel 028-81670728
Email moregilj@enterprise.net

ARDMORE
St Mary's
Rev Neil Farren PP
Parochial House, 49 Ardmore Road,
Derry BT47 3QP
Tel 028-71349490
Rt Rev Mgr Ignatius McQuillan *(priest in residence)*
60 Glenmore Park, Belt Road,
Derry BT47 2JZ
Tel 028-91291758

BALLINASCREEN (DRAPERSTOWN)
St Columba's
Very Rev Colum Clerkin PP
55 St Patrick's Street, Draperstown,
Magherafelt, Co Derry BT45 7AJ
Tel 028-79628248
Email cclerkinpp@aol.com
Rev John Downey CC
36 Moneyneena Road,
Draperstown, Magherafelt,
Co Derry BT45 7DZ
Tel 028-79628375

BANAGHER
St Joseph's, Fincairn
Rev Eamon Graham PP
42 Glenedra Road, Feeny,
Co Derry BT47 4TW
Tel 028-77781223
Rev Arthur P. O'Reilly CC
285 Foreglan Road, Dungiven,
Co Derry BT47 4PJ
Tel 028-71338261

BELLAGHY (BALLYSCULLION)
St Mary's
Rev Andrew Dolan PP
25 Ballynease Road, Bellaghy,
Magherafelt, Co Derry BT45 8JS
Tel 028-79386259
Email frdolan@bellaghyparish.com

BUNCRANA (DESERTEGNEY AND LOWER FAHAN)
St Mary's, Cockhill
Rev John Walsh PP
Parochial House, Buncrana, Co Donegal
Tel 074-9361393 Fax 074-9361637

Allianz (ⁱⁱⁱ)

Rev Edward McGuinness CC
Cockhill, Buncrana, Co Donegal
Tel 074-9363768
Rev George Doherty CC
Glebe, Linsfort, Buncrana, Co Donegal
Tel 074-9361126
Rev Rafal Januszewski
2 Gortaugher, Lisnakelly,
Buncrana, Co Donegal
Tal 074-9363455
Parish Office: Tel 074-9361253
Fax 074-9361637
Email buncranaparish@eircom.net

CARNDONAGH (DONAGH)
Sacred Heart
Rev Con McLaughlin PP
Barrack Hill, Carndonagh,
Lifford, Co Donegal
Tel 074-9374104

CASTLEDERG (ARDSTRAW WEST AND CASTLEDERG)
St Eugene's
Very Rev Brian Donnelly PP
16 Castlefin Road, Castlederg,
Co Tyrone BT81 7EB
Tel 028-81671393 Fax 028-81679199
Rev Colm O'Doherty
7 Cloonty Road, Drumquin, Omagh,
Co Tyrone BT78 7TG
Tel 028-81661475

CLAUDY (CUMBER UPPER AND LEARMOUNT)
St Patrick's
Rev David O'Kane PP
9 Church Street, Claudy,
Co Derry BT47 4AA
Tel 028-71337727 Fax 028-71338236

CLONMANY
St Mary's
Rev Fintan Diggin PP
Parochial House, Cleagh,
Clonmany, Co Donegal
Tel 074-9376264

COLERAINE (DUNBOE, MACOSQUIN AND AGHADOWEY)
St John's
Rev Charles Keaney PP
Chapelfield, 59 Laurel Hill,
Coleraine, Co Derry BT51 3AY
Tel 028-70343130

CULDAFF
St Mary's, Bocan
Rev James McGonagle PP
Parochial House, Culdaff, Co Donegal
Tel 074-9379107
Email caz_derg_1@compuserve.com

CULMORE
Assumption
Very Rev Seamus Kelly PP, VF
23 Thornhill Park, Culmore,
Derry BT48 4PB
Tel 028-71358519 Fax 028-71353161
Email info@culmore.com
Website www.culmore.com

DESERTMARTIN (DESERTMARTIN AND KILCRONAGHAN)
St Mary's, Coolcalm
Rev Peter Madden PP
50 Tobermore Road, Desertmartin,
Magherafelt, Co Derry BT45 5LE
Tel 028-79632196 Fax 028-79300051
Email desertmartin@aol.com

DONEYLOOP (URNEY AND CASTLEFINN)
St Columba's
Rev Brian McGoldrick PP
Doneyloop, Castlefin,
Lifford, Co Donegal
Tel 074-9146183
Email bfmcfgoldrick@eircom.net
Rev Desmond Polke CC
Parochial House, Castlefin,
Lifford, Co Donegal
Tel 074-9146251

DRUMQUIN (LANGFIELD)
St Patrick's
Fr Kevin Mullan PP
257 Dooish Road, Drumquin,
Omagh, Co Tyrone BT78 4RA
Tel 028-82831225

DUNAMANAGH (DONAGHEADY)
St Patrick's
Rev Eamon McDevitt PP
78 Lisnaragh Road, Dunamanagh,
Strabane, Co Tyrone BT82 0QN
Tel 028-71398212

DUNGIVEN
St Patrick's
Rev Aidan Mullan PP
19 Chapel Road, Dungiven,
Co Derry BT47 4RT
Tel 028-77741219 Fax 028-77742633
Email dungivenparish@aol.com
Rev Joseph Gormley CC
2 Station Road, Dungiven,
Co Derry BT47 4LN
Tel 028-77741256 Fax 028-77742953
Rev Michael Mullan CC
300 Drumsurn Road, Limavady,
Co Derry BT49 0PX
Tel 028-77762165

FAHAN (BURT, INCH AND FAHAN)
St Mura's
Rev Neil McGoldrick PP
Parochial House, Fahan,
Lifford,Co Donegal
Tel 074-9360151
Rev Michael Porter CC
Parochial House, Burt,
Lifford, Co Donegal
Tel 074-9368155

FAUGHANVALE (FAUGHANVALE AND LOWER CUMBER)
Star of the Sea
Rev Patrick Mullan PP
Stella Maris House, Eglinton,
Co Derry BT47 3EA
Tel 028-71810240

Rev Michael Keaveny
53 Brisland Road, Eglinton,
Co Derry BT47 3EA
Tel 028-71810234 Fax 028-71812358
Rev Noel McDermott CC
91 Ervey Road, Eglinton,
Co Derry BT47 3AU
Tel 028-71810235

GARVAGH (ERRIGAL)
St Mary's, Ballerin
Rev Brian Brady PP
78 Ballerin Road, Garvagh,
Co Derry BT51 5EQ
Tel 028-29558251
Rev Karl Haan CC
33 Glen Road, Garvagh,
Co Derry BT51 5DB
Tel 028-29558342

GORTIN (BADONEY LOWER)
St Patrick's
Very Rev John Forbes PP
Parochial House, Gortin, Omagh,
Co Tyrone BT79 8PU
Tel 028-81648203

GREENCASTLE
St Patrick's
Rev Eugene Hasson PP
164 Greencastle Road, Omagh,
Co Tyrone BT79 7RU
Tel 028-81648474 Fax 028-81647829
Email smacridire@hotmail.com

GREENLOUGH (TAMLAGHT O'CRILLY)
St Mary's
Rev Oliver Crilly PP
230b Mayogall Road,
Clady, Portglenone,
Co Derry BT44 8NN
Tel 028-25821190

ISKAHEEN (ISKAHEEN AND UPPER MOVILLE)
St Mary's
Very Rev John Farren PP
Muff, Co Donegal
Tel 074-9384037 Fax 074-9384029
Rev Anthony Mailey CC
Parochial House
Quigley's Point, Co Donegal
Tel 074-9383008

KILLYCLOGHER (CAPPAGH)
St Mary's
Rev Eugene Boland PP
14 Killyclogher Road, Omagh,
Co Tyrone BT79 0AX
Tel 028-82243375 Fax 028-82251881
Email eugene@cappaghparish.com
Rev Francis Murray CC
46 Knockmoyle Road, Omagh,
Co Tyrone BT79 7TB
Tel 028-82242793
Rev Kevin McElhennon CC
5 Strathroy Road, Omagh,
Co Tyrone BT79 7DW
Tel 028-82251055

KILLYGORDON (DONAGHMORE)

St Patrick's
Rev Patrick Arkinson PP
Sessiaghoneill, Ballybofey, Co Donegal
Tel 074-9131149
Rev Robert Devine *(priest in residence)*
Crossroads, Killygordon, Co Donegal
Tel 074-9149194

KILREA (KILREA AND DESERTOGHILL)

St Mary's, Drumagarner
Rev Brendan Doherty PP
4 Garvagh Road, Kilrea,
Co Derry BT51 5QP
Tel 028-29540343
Rev Charles Logue CC
91 Drumgarner Road, Kilrea,
Co Derry BT51 5TE
Tel 028-29540528

LAVEY (TERMONEENY AND PART OF MAGHERA)

St Mary's
Rev Brian O'Donnell PP
Tel 028-79642458
Rev Patrick McLaughlin CC
Tel 028-79642435
65 Mayogall Road, Knockloughrim,
Magherafelt, Co Derry BT45 8PG

LECKPATRICK (LECKPATRICK AND PART OF DONAGHEADY)

St Mary's, Cloughcor
Rev John Doherty PP
Parochial House, 447 Victoria Road,
Ballymagorry, Strabane,
Co Tyrone BT82 0AT
Tel 028-718802274 Fax 028-71884353
Rev Paul Farren *(priest in residence)*
21 Derry Road, Strabane,
Co Tyrone BT82 8DX
Tel 028-71883247

LIFFORD (CLONLEIGH)

St Patrick's, Murlog
Rev Edward Kilpatrick PP
Murlog, Lifford, Co Donegal
Tel 074-9142022
Parish Office: St Patrick's Church, Murlog,
Lifford, Co Donegal
Tel/Fax 074-9142001

LIMAVADY (DRUMACHOSE, TAMLAGHT, FINLAGAN AND PART OF AGHANLOO)

St Mary's, Irish Green Street
Rev Michael Collins PP
119 Irish Green Street, Limavady,
Co Derry BT49 9AB
Tel 028-77765649 Fax 028-77765290
Rev Edward Gallagher CC
4 Scroggy Road, Limavady,
Co Derry BT49 0NA
Tel 028-77763944
Rev Liam Donnelly CC
20 Loughermore Road, Ogill, Ballykelly,
Co Derry BT49 9PD
Tel 028-77762721

MAGHERA

St Patrick's, Glen
Very Rev Seamus O'Connell PP, VF
159 Glen Road, Maghera,
Co Derry BT46 5JN
Tel 028-79642496 Fax 028-79644593
Email seamus.oconnell@btinternet.com
Rev Patrick Baker CC
157 Glen Road, Maghera,
Co Derry BT46 5JN
Tel 028-79642359
Parish Office: 159A Glen Road,
Maghera, Co Derry BT46 5JN
Tel 028-79642983

MAGILLIGAN

St Aidan's
Rev Francis O'Hagan PP
71 Duncrun Road, Bellarena,
Limavady, Co Derry BT49 0JD
Tel 028-77750226

MALIN (CLONCA)

St Patrick's, Aghaclay
Rev Peter Devlin PP
Malin, Co Donegal
Tel 074-9370615
Rev Brendan Crowley CC
Malin Head, Co Donegal
Tel 074-9370134

MELMOUNT (MOURNE)

St Mary's, Melmount, Strabane
Rev Michael Doherty PP
39 Melmount Road, Strabane,
Co Tyrone BT82 9EF
Tel 028-71882648
Rev Patrick O'Hagan CC
41 Melmount Road, Strabane,
Co Tyrone BT82 9EF
Tel 028-71882651
Email ohaganp@aol.com
Parish Office: Melmount Parish Centre,
Melmount Road, Strabane,
Co Tyrone BT82 9EF
Tel 028-71383777 Fax 028-71886469
Email melparish@aol.com

MOVILLE (MOVILLE LOWER)

St Mary's, Ballybrack
Rev Patrick O'Kane PP
Tel 074-9382057
Rev Patrick McGoldrick CC
Tel 074-9382102
Parochial House,
Moville, Co Donegal

NEWTOWNSTEWART (ARDSTRAW EAST)

St Eugene's, Glenock
Rev Stephen Kearney PP
41 Moyle Road, Newtownstewart,
Co Tyrone BT78 4AP
Tel 028-81661445 Fax 028-81662462
Email ardstraw@btinternet.com

OMAGH (DRUMRAGH)

St Mary's, Drumragh
Rt Rev Mgr Joseph Donnelly PP, VF
52 Brook Street, Omagh,
Co Tyrone BT78 5HE
Tel 028-82243011 Fax 028-82252149
Email jopd@drumraghparish.com

Rev John McDevitt CC
Rev Thomas Canning CC
50 Brook Street, Omagh,
Co Tyrone BT78 5HE
Tel 028-82242092
Parish Office: 48 Brook Street,
Omagh, Co Tyrone BT78 5HE
Tel 028-82442092 Fax 028-82252149

PLUMBRIDGE (BADONEY UPPER)

Sacred Heart
Rev Joseph O'Connor PP
Parochial House, Plumbridge,
Omagh, Co Tyrone BT79 8EF
Tel 028-81648283

SION MILLS

St Theresa's
Rev Peter McLaughlin PP
143 Melmount Road, Sion Mills,
Strabane, Co Tyrone BT82 9EX
Tel 028-81658264

STRABANE (CAMUS)

Immaculate Conception
Rev Declan Boland PP
44 Barrack Street, Strabane,
Co Tyrone BT82 8HD
Tel 028-71883293 Fax 028-71882615
Email declan.boland@virgin.net
Rev John McCullagh
Parochial House, 46 Barrack Street,
Strabane, Co Tyrone BT82 8HD
Tel 028-71882215 Fax 028-71882615

STRATHFOYLE (STRATHFOYLE, ENAGH LOUGH)

St Oliver Plunkett
Served by the Parish of Glendermot
Parochial House, Parkmore Drive,
Strathfoyle, Co Derry BT47 1XA
Tel 028-71342303

SWATRAGH

St John the Baptist
Very Rev Kieran O'Doherty PP
34 Moneysharvin Road, Swatragh,
Maghera, Co Derry BT46 5PY
Tel 028-79401236

WATERSIDE (GLENDERMOTT)

St Columb's
Rev Patrick Doherty PP
Rev Michael McCaughey CC
Rev Chris Ferguson CC
Parochial House, 32 Chapel Road,
Waterside, Derry BT47 2BB
Tel 028-71342303 Fax 028-71345495
Rev Gerard Sweeney CC
The Presbytery, 10b Trench Road,
Waterside, Derry BT47 3UB
Tel 028-71348856
Website www.watersideparish.org

INSTITUTIONS AND THEIR CHAPLAINS

Altnagelvin Hospital, Derry
Waterside General Hospital
Rev Neil Farren PP
Rev Chris Ferguson CC
Parochial House, 32 Chapel Road,
Waterside, Derry BT47 2BB
Tel 028-71342303

Community Hospital, Lifford
Rev Edward Kilpatrick PP
Townparks, Lifford,
Co Donegal
Tel 074-9142001

District Hospital, Carndonagh
Rev Con McLaughlin PP
Parochial House,
Carndonagh
Tel 074-9174104

Foyle Hospice
Most Rev Edward Daly DD
9 Steelstown Road, Derry BT48 8EU
Tel 028-71359809

Gransha Hospital, Derry
Rev Neil Farren PP
Rev Chris Ferguson CC
Parochial House, 32 Chapel Road,
Waterside, Derry BT47 2BB
Tel 028-71342303

Magilligan Prison
Point Road, Magilligan,
Limavady BT49 OLR, Co Derry
Rev Francis O'Hagan PP
Tel 028-77763311

Nazareth House
Bishop Street, Derry BT48 6UN
Rev John Irwin
Tel 028-71261425/71262180

Nazareth House
Fahan, Co Donegal
Rev Neil McGoldrick PP
Tel 074-9360151

Tyrone County Hospital, Omagh
Rev Eugene Boland PP

Tyrone and Fermanagh Hospital, Omagh
Rev Eugene Boland PP

University of Ulster
Magee College, Derry
Rev Paul Farren
Derry Diocesan Catechetical Centre,
Gate Lodge, Francis Street, Derry BT48 9AP
Tel 028-71264087

PRIESTS OF THE DIOCESE ELSEWHERE

Rev Manus Bradley
St Ignatius of Loyola, 4455 West Broadway,
Montreal, Quebec H4B 2A7

Rt Rev Mgr Brendan Devlin MA, DD
St Patrick's College, Maynooth,
Co Kildare
Tel 01-6285222
Very Rev Eamon Martin
Exective Secretary, Irish Bishops'
Conference Secretariat,
Columba Centre, Maynooth, Co Kildare
Tel 00353-1-5053000
Rev James McGrory
Armagh Regional Marriage Tribunal,
15 College Street, Armagh BT61 9BT
Tel 028-37524537
Rev Peter O'Kane
Pontificio Collegio Irlandese,
Via Dei SS Auattro 1, 00184 Roma, Italy
Rev Seamus O'Kane
12 Gortinure Road, Maghera,
Co Derry BT46 5RB
Tel 07989-946344
Email sokane@maghera.fsnet.co.uk

RETIRED PRIESTS

Rev Bernard Bryson PEm
Anniscliff House, 141 Moneysharvin Road,
Maghera, Co Derry
Rev Walter Carolan PEm
100 Altinure Road Park, Claudy,
Co Derry BY47 4DE
Rev Kieran Devlin PEm
Collon House, 21 Buncrana Road,
Derry BY48 8LA
Rev Joseph Doherty PEm
Clarcarricknagun, Donegal Town
Co Donegal
Tel 073-21259
Rev T. Phil Donnelly PEm
Nazareth House, Fahan, Co Donegal
Rt Rev Mgr Austin Duffy PEm
28 Glenroe Park, Dungiven,
Co Derry BT47 4PE
Tel 028-77741811
Rev John Farrell PEm
5 Ballyreagh Road, Portrush, Co Antrim
Rev James McCrory PEm
124 Carrigans Road, Knockmoyle,
Omagh, Co Tyrone BT79 7TW
Rev James McGlinchey PEm
'Mellifont', Grianan Park,
Buncrana, Co Donegal
Tel 074-9361465
Rev Kevin McKenna PEm
24 Glenroe Park, Dungiven,
Co Derry BT47 4PE
Tel 028-77743857
Rev George McLaughlin
Chez Nous, Drumawier,
Greencastle, Co Donegal
Rev Colm Morris PEm
Muff, Co Donegal
Tel 074-9384407
Rev John Ryder PEm
16 Whitehouse Park,
Duncrana Road, Derry

RELIGIOUS ORDERS AND CONGREGATIONS

PRIESTS

CARMELITES (OCD)
St Joseph's Retreat House,
Termonbacca, Derry BT48 9XE
Tel 028-71262512 Fax 028-71373589
Prior: Rev Jeremiah Fitzpatrick (OCD)
Community: 5

BROTHERS

CHRISTIAN BROTHERS
20 Kevlin Road, Omagh,
Co Tyrone BT78 2LD
Tel 028-82242103
Community Leader: Br Tom Gough
Community: 4

SISTERS

CONGREGATION OF THE SISTERS OF MERCY
Thornhill Centre,
121 Culmore Road, Derry BT48 8JF
Tel 028-71351233
Sisters involved in prayer and retreat
ministry

St Catherine's, Thornhill,
123 Culmore Road, Derry BT48 8JF
Tel 028-71354082
Community: 7
Nursing care unit for sick and aged
sisters

3 Steelstown Road,
Derry BT48 8EU
Tel 028-71351432
Community: 4

4 School House Mews,
Eglinton, Co Derry BT47 3WA
Tel 028-71811464

22 Newtownkennedy Street,
Strabane, Co Tyrone BT82 8HT
Tel 028-71882269
Shared leadership: Sr Carmel Fanning
Community: 7

Buncrana, Co Donegal
Tel 074-9361054
Community: 5

8A Sheelin Park, Ballymagroarty,
Derry BT48 0PD
Tel 028-71260398
Community: 5

6 Ballycolman Road, Melmount,
Strabane, Co Tyrone BT82 9PH
Tel 028-71885913
Community: 3

60 Steelstown,
Derry BT48 8JA
Tel 028-71352300

North Gate Lodge,
125 Culmore Road, Derry BT48 8JF
Tel 028-71350014

1 Lawrence Hill,
Derry BT48 7NJ
Tel 028-71269854
Community: 5

103 Elmvale,
Culmore, Derry BT48 8SL
Tel 028-71358507
Contact: Sr Frances O'Kane
Investing in excellence

3 Milestone Way,
Fintona Road, Tattyreagh,
Omagh, Co Tyrone BT78 2LY
Sr Mary Daly RSM
Sr Maura Twohig PBVM

44 Ballynagard Crescent,
Culmore, Derry BT48 8JR
Tel 028-71355776

17 Garvaghy Mews,
Rarogan Road,
Dungannon, Co Tyrone BT70 2DP

31 Belmont Crescent,
Derry BT48 7RR
Tel 028-71358758

16 Papworth Avenue,
Derry BT48 8PT
Tel 028-71358827
Community: 3

CONGREGATION OF ST JOHN
Sisters of St John
10 Belvoir Park, Culmore, Derry
Tel 028-71353414
Prioress: Sr Mary Magdalen

GOOD SHEPHERD SISTERS
Dungiven Road, Waterside,
Derry BT47 2AL
Tel 028-71342429 Fax 028-71341711
Email rgsderry@hotmail.com
Superior: Sr Clare Kenny
Community: 9

44/45 Virginia Court,
Gobnascale, Waterside, Derry BT47 2DX
Tel 028-71345127
Email vircourt@yahoo.com
Community: 3
Social work apostolate

HOLY FAMILY OF BORDEAUX SISTERS
Holy Family Convent,
2a The High Street, Draperstown,
Co Derry BT45 7AA
Tel 028-79628030
Contact: Sr Rose Devlin
Community: 1
Pastoral work, urban and rural
community development, community
relations work, religious education of
both able-bodied and disabled adults.

**CONGREGATION OF THE SISTERS OF
NAZARETH**
Nazareth House, Bishop Street,
Derry BT48 6UN
Tel 028-71262180 Fax 028-71263254
Superior: Sr Anastasia Marie Lenihan
Community: 8
Residential home for elderly
Primary School
Principal: Sr M. Paul O'Hea
Tel 028-71280212
Pupils: 400

Nazareth House, Fahan,
Lifford, Co Donegal
Tel 074-9360113 Fax 074-9360561
Superior: Sr Alice Kirwan
Community: 8
Home for aged. Residents: 48

LORETO (IBVM)
Convent Grammar, Omagh BT78 1DL
Tel 028-82243633
Primary School,
Brookmount Road, Omagh
Tel 028-82243551

Loreto Community, Coleraine,
Co Derry BT51 3JZ
Tel 028-70344426
Superior: Sr Mary Jo Corcoran
Community: 10
Loreto College, Coleraine BT51 3JZ
Tel 028-70343611

Loreto Sisters, 30 Buskin Way, Coleraine,
Co Derry BT51 3BD
Tel 028-70358065
Community: 2
Educational and pastoral work

Loreto Community,
Linsfort, Buncrana, Co Donegal
Tel 074-9362204
Superior: Sr Eveleen Hallahan
Retreat and pastoral work

PRESENTATION SISTERS
Inter Congregational Community,
3 Milestone Way, Tattyreagh,
Omagh BT78 2OY, Co Tyrone
Tel 028-82840893
Community: 2 (1 Presentation Sister and
1 Mercy Sister)
Counselling ministry

Tara Counselling Centre,
11 Holmview Terrace,
Omagh BT97 OAH,
Co Tyrone
Tel 028-82250024 Fax 028-82250023

SACRED HEART OF JESUS SISTERS
119 Irish Green Street,
Limavady, Co Derry BT49 9AB
Tel 015047-68357
Superior: Sr Eileen McElhone
Community: 2
Pastoral ministry

EDUCATIONAL INSTITUTIONS

**EDMUND RICE SCHOOLS TRUST
NORTHERN IRELAND**
Christian Brothers Grammar School,
Kevlin Road, Omagh BT78 1LD
Tel 028-82243567 Fax 028-82240656
Principal: Mr Paul Brannigan

CHARITABLE SOCIETIES

St Vincent de Paul Diocesan Centre
Ozanam House,
22 Bridge Street, Derry
Tel 028-71265489

DIOCESE OF
DOWN AND CONNOR

PATRONS OF THE DIOCESE
ST MALACHY, 3 NOVEMBER; ST MACNISSI, 4 SEPTEMBER

INCLUDES COUNTY ANTRIM, THE GREATER PART OF COUNTY DOWN
AND PART OF COUNTY DERRY

Most Rev Noel Treanor DD
Bishop of Down and Connor;
ordained priest 13 June 1976;
ordained Bishop of Down and
Connor 29 June 2008

Residence: Lisbreen,
73 Somerton Road,
Belfast, Co Antrim BT15 4DE
Tel 028-90776185
Fax 028-90779377
Email
dccuria@downandconnor.org

ST PETER'S CATHEDRAL, BELFAST

Several bishops in Ireland began the building of cathedrals in their dioceses in the 1830s and 1840s. They usually chose the largest and most central town as the site of their episcopal administration, and their cathedrals were generally larger and more ornate than the churches that were then being built in other towns.

Belfast had been chosen by Bishop William Crolly in 1825 as the seat of episcopal governance for Down and Connor. Ten years later he was transferred to Armagh before he could make any arrangements to build a cathedral. A third church was required for the growing Catholic population, and Bishop Crolly's successor, Bishop Cornelius Denvir, gave some thought to making the new church, St Malachy's, which was blessed in 1844, his cathedral. But paucity of resources forced him to reduce the size of his plan,

and the project of erecting a cathedral was abandoned.

With the big increase in the Catholic population in the 1850s, another church was needed in Belfast. A site was acquired in 1858, and the foundation stone of the church, dedicated to St Peter, was laid in 1860. It was designed by Jeremiah Ryan McAuley, a Belfast architect, who, two years previously, had become a priest. Built in the Gothic style, it cost £16,000. Among the many bishops who attended the opening ceremony in 1866 was Cardinal Cullen, who had received the red hat a short time previously, and the preacher on the occasion was the Bishop of Birmingham, William Ullathorne. Since then, many alterations have been made to St Peter's. An organ was installed at a cost of £1,400 in 1883, together with a carillon of bells costing £1,500, and the spires were completed in 1885 at a cost of £5,000.

St Peter's and St Patrick's churches were both used as pro-cathedrals by the Bishops of Down and Connor since the 1860s until St Peter's was raised to the status of Cathedral in 1986.

In 2003 Bishop Patrick Walsh undertook a major refurbishment of the exterior and interior of the Cathedral to restore it to its neo-Gothic splendour. It was re-opened on 5 February 2005. To mark this occasion, as a gesture of the unity of the Church in Down and Connor with the universal Church, Pope John Paul II sent the gift of a chalice for use in the Cathedral. Subsequent to the opening the Cathedral Organ was restored by Kenneth Jones. The diocese has since appointed a full-time music director and now has a Schola of over forty boys' voices and ten organ pupils, both for the Cathedral and for other parishes in the diocese. This Cathedral is regarded as one of the finest Victorian buildings in Belfast.

Most Rev Anthony Farquhar DD
Titular Bishop of Ermiana and Auxiliary Bishop of Down and Connor; ordained priest 13 March 1965; ordained Bishop 15 May 1983
Office: 73 Somerton Road,
Belfast BT15 4DE Tel 028-90776185
Residence: 24 Fruithill Park,
Belfast BT11 8GE Tel 028-90624252

Most Rev Donal McKeown DD
Titular Bishop of Killossy and Auxiliary Bishop of Down and Connor; ordained priest 3 July 1977; ordained Bishop 29 April 2001
Office: 73 Somerton Road,
Belfast BT15 4DE Tel 028-90776185
Residence: 96 Downview Park West,
Belfast BT15 5HZ Tel 028-90781642

Most Rev Patrick J. Walsh DD
Bishop Emeritus of Down and Connor; ordained priest 25 February 1956; ordained Titular Bishop of Ros Cré 15 May 1983; installed Bishop of Down and Connor 28 April 1991
Residence: 6 Waterloo Park North,
Belfast BT15 5HW
Tel 028-90778182

CHAPTER

Dean: Rt Rev Brendan McGee
Archdeacon: Venerable Kevin Donnelly
Members
Very Rev Dominic McHugh
Very Rev Bernard Magee
Very Rev Noel Conway
Very Rev Hugh Starkey
Very Rev Robert Fullerton
Very Rev Malachy Murphy
Very Rev Brendan Murray
Very Rev George O'Hanlon
Very Rev Alex McMullan
Very Rev Sean Rogan

Honorary Canons
Very Rev Joseph Cunningham
Rt Rev Mgr Sean Connolly

ADMINISTRATION

Chancellor
Very Rev John McManus
Lisbreen, 73 Somerton Road,
Belfast BT15 4DE
Tel 028-90776185 Fax 028-90779377

Vicar General
Rt Rev Mgr Sean Connolly VG
2/4 Broughshane Road, Ballymena,
Co Antrim BT43 7DX
Tel 028-25641515

Vicar for Religious
Rev Tom Layden SJ
Assistants: Sr Majella, Dominican Sister
Sr Francis, Mercy Sister
Br Christopher, De La Salle Brother

Consultors
Most Rev Anthony J. Farquhar
Most Rev Donal McKeown
Rt Rev Mgr Sean Connolly
Very Rev Brian Daly
Very Rev John McManus
Very Rev Sean Emerson
Very Rev John Forsythe
Very Rev Canon Sean Rogan
Very Rev Patrick Delargy
Very Rev Michael Spence

Episcopal Vicar for Sick & Retired Priests
Very Rev Canon Alex McMullan PP

Council of Priests
Chairman: Very Rev John Forsythe PP
81 Lagmore Grove,
Belfast BT17 0TD
Tel 028-90309011
Secretary: Very Rev Joseph Rooney
45 Ballyholme Esplanade, Bangor,
Co Down BT20 5NJ
Tel 028-91465425

Judicial Vicar for Diocese of Down and Connor
Very Rev Eugene O'Hagan JCL
The Good Shepherd Centre,
511 Ormeau Road, Belfast BT7 3GS
Tel 028-90491990 Fax 028-90491440

Finance Committee
Chairman: Most Rev Noel Treanor
Members: Most Rev Anthony Farquhar
Most Rev Donal McKeown
Very Rev John McManus
Rev John O'Connor
Mr John B. McGuckian
Mr Brian Finegan
Mr Anthony Harbinson
Mr Daniel Harvey
Mr Tom Cahill
Ms Alice Quinn
Financial Administrators
Rev Joseph M. Glover, Ms Maria Morgan
73 Somerton Road, Belfast BT15 4DE
Tel 028-90776185 Fax 028-90779377

Diocesan Building Committee
Chairman: Very Rev John McManus
Secretary: Ms Maria Morgan
73 Somerton Road, Belfast BT15 4DE
Tel 028-90776185 Fax 028-90779377

Seminary Fund Committee
Chairman: Most Rev Noel Treanor
Secretary: Very Rev Michael Spence
St Malachy's College,
36 Antrim Road, Belfast BT15 2AE
Tel 028-90748285

Media Liaison Officer
Rev Edward McGee
St Malachy's College, 36 Antrim Road,
Belfast BT15 2AE
Tel 078-11144268

Diocesan Archivist
Very Rev Canon George O'Hanlon
62 Coolkeeran Road, Armoy,
Ballymoney, Co Antrim BT53 8XN

Diocesan Secretary
Rev Joseph M. Glover
Lisbreen, 73 Somerton Road,
Belfast BT15 4DE
Tel 028-90776185 Fax 028-90779377

CATECHETICS EDUCATION

Trustees Support Service
Director: Mr Gerard Lundy
c/o Ara Coeli, Armagh BT61 7QY
Tel 028-37522045

Diocesan Education Committee
Administrator: Ms Susan Sullivan
193-195 Donegall Street,
Belfast BT1 2FL
Tel 028-90327875 Fax 028-90327866

Diocesan Advisers in Religious Education
Very Rev John McManus
Mr Frank Donnelly
Mrs Kathleen Hagan
Miss Catherine McGinnity
511 Ormeau Road, Belfast BT7 3GS
Tel 028-90491886 Fax 028-90491440

LITURGY

Diocesan Commission on Liturgy
Chairman
Very Rev Canon Robert Fullerton
501 Ormeau Road, Belfast BT7 3GR
Tel 028-90641064
Secretary: Rev Edward McGee
St Malachy's College, 36 Antrim Road,
Belfast BT15 2AE
Tel 028-90748285

PASTORAL

Accord
Belfast
Curran House, Twin Spires,
Northumberland Street, Belfast BT13 2JF
Tel 028-90339944
Ballymena
All Saints Parish Centre, 9 Cushendall Road,
Ballymena, Co Antrim
Tel 028-25644072
Downpatrick
Priest Director: Very Rev Colm McGrady
Appointments Secretary
Mrs Sheila McPoland
32 English Street, Downpatrick,
Co Down BT30 6AB
Tel 028-44613435

Office of the Armagh Regional Marriage Tribunal
511 Ormeau Road, Belfast BT7 3GS
Tel 028-90491990 Fax 028-90491440
Administrator
Very Rev Eugene O'Hagan JCL
Notary: Rev Joseph Rooney JCL

Allianz (ⅲ)

Ecumenism (Diocesan Committee)
Secretary: Rev Colin Grant
St Malachy's College, Antrim Road,
Belfast BT15 2AE
Tel 028-90748285

Pioneer Total Abstinence Association
Diocesan Director
Rev Raymond McCullagh
1 Seafield Park South,
Portstewart BT55 7LH
Tel 028-70832066

Pontifical Mission Societies
Diocesan Director
Very Rev Colm McGrady PP
Parochial House, 8 Shore Road,
Strangford, Co Down BT30 7NL
Tel 028-44881206

Vocations
Director: Very Rev John Murray PP
St Luke's Presbytery, Twinbrook Road,
Dunmurry, BT17 0RP
Tel 028-90619459
Assistant Director: Rev Kevin McGuckien
St Patrick's Presbytery,
199 Donegall Street, Belfast BT1 2FL
Tel 028-90324597

Diocesan Family Commission
Director: Rev Michael McGinnity
Family Ministry Office,
Good Shepherd Centre,
511 Ormeau Road, Belfast BT7 3GS
Tel 028-90492777
Fax 028-90491779

Diocesan Social Affairs Commission
Secretary: Rev Timothy Bartlett
92 Somerton Road, Belfast BT15 4DE
Also: Irish Bishops' Conference, Columba
Centre, St Patrick's College, Maynooth,
Co Kildare
Tel 01-5053000

Diocesan Care Home
Our Lady's Home,
68 Ard Na Va Road, Belfast BT12 6FF
Director: Very Rev John C. O'Connor
Tel 028-90325731/90242429
Fax 028-90249596

Children's Home
Glenmona Resource Centre
Glen Road, Belfast BT11 8BX
Tel 028-90301100
Director: Mr Liam Dumigan

Diocesan Youth Commission
68 Berry Street, Belfast BT1 1FJ
Tel 028-90232432
Fax 028-90239598
Chairman: Mr Brian Gibson
Director: Mr Brian McKee

Youth Link Training Offices
143 University Street, Belfast BT7 1HP
Tel 028-90323217
Fax 028-90323247
Training and Development Officer
Rev Patrick White

PARISHES

Mensal parishes are listed first. Other parishes follow alphabetically, city parishes first. Historical names are in parentheses.

THE CATHEDRAL (ST PETER'S)
Very Rev Hugh Kennedy Adm
Rev Stephen Quinn CC
St Peter's Square, Belfast BT12 4BU
Tel 028-90327573

ST MARY'S
Very Rev James A. Boyle (MHM) Adm
Rev James O'Donoghue (MHM) CC
St Mary's, Marquis Street, Belfast BT1 1JJ
Tel 028-90320482

ST PATRICK'S
Very Rev Michael Sheehan Adm
Dean Brendan McGee
Rev Kevin McGuckien CC
St Patrick's Presbytery,
199 Donegall Street, Belfast BT1 2FL
Tel 028-90324597

HOLY FAMILY
Very Rev Gerard McCloskey Adm
Holy Family Presbytery,
Newington Avenue, Belfast BT15 2HP
Tel 028-90743119
Rev Colin Crossey CC
120 Cavehill Road, Belfast BT15 5BU
Tel 028-90714892
Very Rev Canon Brendan Murray
St Thérèse's Presbytery,
71 Somerton Road, Belfast BT15 4DE
Tel 028-90205041

ST COLMCILLE'S
Very Rev Ciaran Feeney Adm
191 Upper Newtownards Road,
Belfast BT4 3JB
Tel 028-90654157

CITY PARISHES

CHRIST THE REDEEMER, LAGMORE
Very Rev John Forsythe PP, VF
81 Lagmore Grove, Dunmurry,
Belfast BT17 0TD
Tel 028-90309011

CORPUS CHRISTI
Very Rev Jim Crudden PP
Corpus Christi Presbytery,
4-6 Springhill Grove, Belfast BT12 7SL
Tel 028-90246857
Very Rev Aidan Denny
10 New Barnsley Green, New Barnsley,
Belfast BT12 7HS
Tel 028-90328877

DERRIAGHY
Very Rev Fergal McGrady PP
111 Queensway, Lambeg, Lisburn BT27 4QS
Tel 028-92662896

GREENCASTLE
Very Rev Anthony Alexander PP
824 Shore Road, Newtownabbey,
Co Antrim BT36 7DG
Tel 028-90370845

HOLY CROSS
Very Rev Gary Donegan (CP) PP
Rev Casimir Haran (CP) CC
Rev Myles Kavanagh (CP) CC
Rev John Craven (CP) CC
Holy Cross Retreat, 432 Crumlin Road,
Ardoyne, Belfast BT14 7GE
Tel 028-90748231/2

HOLY ROSARY
Very Rev Patrick McKenna PP, VF
503 Ormeau Road, Belfast BT7 3GR
Tel 028-90642446
Very Rev Canon Robert Fullerton CC
Holy Rosary Presbytery,
501 Ormeau Road, Belfast BT7 3GR
Tel 028-90641064

HOLY TRINITY
Very Rev Matthew Wallace PP
Holy Trinity Presbytery,
26 Norglen Gardens, Belfast BT11 8EL
Tel 028-90590985/6

THE NATIVITY
Very Rev Patrick Sheehan PP
Rev Vincent Cushnahan CC
The Presbytery, Bell Steel Road,
Poleglass, Belfast BT17 0PB
Tel 028-90625739

OUR LADY QUEEN OF PEACE, KILWEE
Very Rev Colm McBride PP
Netherley Lodge, 130 Upper Dunmurry
Lane, Belfast BT17 0EW
Tel 028-90616300

SACRED HEART
Very Rev Ciaran Dallat PP
Sacred Heart Presbytery,
1 Glenview Street, Belfast BT14 7DP
Tel 028-90351851
Rev Ciaran Hegarty
The Presbytery, 30A Deanby Gardens,
Belfast BT14 6NN
Tel 028-90745140

ST AGNES'
Very Rev Peter Owens PP
143 Andersonstown Road,
Belfast BT11 9BW
Tel 028-90615702/90603951
Rev Robert Markuszewski CC
139 Andersonstown Road,
Belfast BT11 9 BW
Tel 028-90613724

ST ANNE'S
Very Rev Edward O'Donnell PP
St Anne's Parochial House,
Kingsway, Finaghy, Belfast BT10 0NE
Tel 028-90610112

ST ANTHONY'S
Very Rev Stephen McBrearty PP
St Anthony's Presbytery, 4 Willowfield
Crescent, Belfast BT6 8HP
Tel 028-90458158

ST BERNADETTE'S
Very Rev Paul Armstrong PP
28 Willowbank Park, Belfast BT6 0LL
Tel 028-90793023

ST BRIGID'S
Rt Rev Mgr Ambrose MacAulay PP
42 Derryvolgie Avenue, Belfast BT9 6FP
Tel 028-90668053
Rev Eugene O'Neill CC
40 Derryvolgie Avenue, Belfast BT9 6FP
Tel 028-90665409

ST GERARD'S
Redemptorist Fathers
Very Rev Gerard Cassidy (CSsR) PP and
Rector
Rev Patrick McLoughlin (CSsR) CC
Rev Patrick Cunning (CSsR) CC
Rev Brendan Mulhall (CSsR) CC
722 Antrim Road, Newtownabbey,
Co Antrim BT36 7PG
Tel 028-90774833/4

ST JOHN'S
Very Rev Paul Strain PP
470 Falls Road, Belfast BT12 6EN
Tel 028-90321511
Rev Mariusz Dabrowski CC
Very Rev Anthony McLaverty (priest in
residence)
470 Falls Road, Belfast BT12 6EN
Tel 028-90321102

ST LUKE'S
Very Rev John Murray PP
Rev Darach MacGiolla Catháin CC
St Luke's Presbytery, Twinbrook Road,
Dunmurry, Co Antrim BT17 0RP
Tel 028-90619459

ST MALACHY'S
Very Rev Anthony Curran PP, VF
Rev Martin Graham CC
St Malachy's Presbytery,
24 Alfred Street, Belfast BT2 8EN
Tel 028-90321713

ST MARY'S ON THE HILL
Very Rev Daniel Whyte PP, VF
Elmfield, 165 Antrim Road, Glengormley,
Newtownabbey, Co Antrim BT36 7QR
Tel 028-90832979
Rev Paul Byrne CC
142 Carnmoney Road, Newtownabbey,
Co Antrim BT36 6JU
Tel 028-90832488
Very Rev Brendan Beagon CC
1 Christine Road, Newtownabbey,
Co Antrim BT36 6TG
Tel 028-90841507

ST MATTHEW'S
Very Rev Aidan Keenan PP
St Matthew's Presbytery, Bryson Street,
Newtownards Road, Belfast BT5 4ES
Tel 028-90457626

ST MICHAEL'S
Very Rev Peter Carlin PP
St Michael's Presbytery,
206 Finaghy Road North, Belfast BT11 9EG
Tel 028-90913761

ST OLIVER PLUNKETT
Very Rev Martin Magill PP
27 Glenveagh Drive, Belfast BT11 9HX
Tel 028-90618180
Rev Andrzej Koxaczkowski (SCHR)
27 Glenveagh Drive, Belfast BT11 9HX
Tel 028-90615702

ST PAUL'S
Very Rev Anthony Devlin PP
Rev Brian McCann CC
St Paul's Presbytery, 125 Falls Road,
Belfast BT12 6AB
Tel 028-90325034
Assistant Priest
Rev Patrick Horgan (CSsR)
Clonard Monastery, Clonard Gardens,
Belfast BT13 2RL

ST TERESA'S
Very Rev Brendan Hickland PP
St Teresa's Presbytery, Glen Road,
Belfast BT11 8BL
Tel 028-90612855
Rt Rev Mgr Thomas Toner
43b Glen Road, Belfast BT11 8BB
Tel 028-90613949

ST VINCENT DE PAUL
Very Rev Paul Alexander PP
St Vincent de Paul Presbytery,
169 Ligoniel Road, Belfast BT14 8DP
Tel 028-90713401

WHITEABBEY (ST JAMES'S)
Very Rev Anthony Alexander PP
824 Shore Road,
Newtownabbey BT36 7DG
Very Rev Samuel Kerr (priest in
residence)
463 Shore Road, Whiteabbey,
Newtownabbey, Co Antrim BT37 0AE
Tel 028-90365773

WHITEHOUSE
Very Rev Anthony Alexander PP
824 Shore Road,
Newtownabbey BT36 7DG
Rev Joseph Glover (priest in residence)
Star of the Sea Presbytery,
305 Shore Road, Whitehouse,
Newtownabbey, Co Antrim BT37 9RY
Tel 028-90365142

COUNTRY PARISHES

AGHAGALLON AND BALLINDERRY
Very Rev Laurence McElhill PP
Parochial House, 5 Aghalee Road,
Aghagallon, Craigavon,
Co Armagh BT67 0AR
Tel 028-92651214

AHOGHILL
Very Rev Hugh J O'Hagan PP
Parochial House, 31 Ballynafie Road,
Ahoghill BT42 1LF
Tel 028-25871351

ANTRIM, ST COMGALL'S
Very Rev Sean Emerson PP
Parochial House, 3 Oriel Road,
Antrim BT41 4HP
Tel 028-94428016

Very Rev Felix McGuckin
5 Oriel Road, Antrim BT41 4HP
Tel 028-94428086

ANTRIM, ST JOSEPH'S
Very Rev Sean Emerson PP
3 Oriel Road, Antrim BT41 4HP
Very Rev Canon Malachy Murphy (priest
in residence)
56 Greystone Road, Antrim BT41 1JZ
Tel 028-94429103

ARDGLASS (DUNSFORD)
Very Rev Robert Fleck PP
Parochial House, Ardglass,
Co Down BT30 7TU
Tel 028-44841208

ARMOY
Very Rev Christopher Nellis PP
Parochial House, Armoy,
Ballymoney, Co Antrim BT53 8RL
Tel 028-20751205

BALLINTOY
Very Rev Maurice Henry Adm
Rev Hugh O'Kane (SMA) CC (priest in
residence)
53 Ballinlea Road, Ballycastle,
Co Antrim BT54 6JL
Tel 028-20762498

BALLYCASTLE (RAMOAN)
Very Rev Maurice Henry PP
Parochial House, 15 Moyle Road,
Ballycastle, Co Antrim BT54 6LB
Tel 028-20762223
Rev Hugh O'Kane (SMA) CC
53 Ballinlea Road,
Ballycastle, Co Antrim BT54 6JL
Tel 028-20762498
Rev Barney McCahery (CSsR) CC
6 Market Street,
Ballycastle, Co Antrim BT54 6DP
Tel 028-20762202

BALLYCLARE AND BALLYGOWAN
Very Rev Eugene O'Hagan Adm
Parochial House, 69 Doagh Road,
Ballyclare, Co Antrim BT39 9BG
Tel 028-93342226

BALLYGALGET
Very Rev Patrick Mulholland PP
Very Rev John McManus (priest in
residence)
Parochial House, 9 Ballygalget Road,
Portaferry, Co Down BT22 1NE
Tel 028-42771212

BALLYMENA (KIRKINRIOLA)
Very Rev Patrick Delargy PP
Venerable Archdeacon Kevin Donnelly
Rev Paul Symonds CC
Rev Aidan McCaughan (priest in
residence)
Parochial House, 4 Broughshane Road,
Ballymena, Co Antrim BT43 7DX
Tel 028-25641515 Fax 028-25631493
Rev Liam Toland CC
Parochial House, 189 Carnlough Road,
Broughshane BT43 7DX
Tel 028-25684211

BALLYMONEY AND DERRYKEIGHAN
Very Rev Francis O'Brien PP
81 Castle Street, Ballymoney,
Co Antrim BT53 6JT
Tel 028-27662003
Very Rev Canon Dominic McHugh
79 Castle Street, Ballymoney,
Co Antrim BT53 6JT
Tel 028-27662259

BANGOR
Very Rev Joseph Gunn PP, VF
St Comgall's Presbytery,
27 Brunswick Road, Bangor,
Co Down BT20 3DS
Tel 028-91465522
Rev Joseph Rooney (priest in residence)
45 Ballyholme Esplanade, Bangor,
Co Down BT20 5NJ
Tel 028-91465425

BRAID
Very Rev Patrick Delargy Adm
Rev Liam Toland CC
189 Carnlough Road,
Broughshane, Co Antrim BT43 7JW
Tel 028-25684211

CARNLOUGH
Very Rev Peter Forde PP
51 Bay Road, Carnlough,
Ballymena, Co Antrim BT44 0HJ
Tel 028-28885220

CARRICKFERGUS
Very Rev Sean Dillon PP
Parochial House, 8 Minorca Place,
Carrickfergus, Co Antrim BT38 8AU
Tel 028-93363269

CASTLEWELLAN (KILMEGAN)
Very Rev Sean Cahill PP
Parochial House, 91 Main Street,
Castlewellan, Co Down BT31 9DH
Tel 028-43778259
Very Rev Canon Bernard Magee
41 Lower Square,
Castlewellan BT31 9DN
Tel 028-43770377

COLERAINE
Very Rev Gregory Cormican PP
72 Nursery Avenue, Coleraine,
Co Derry BT52 1LR
Tel 028-70343156

CROSSGAR (KILMORE)
Very Rev Kevin McMullan PP
Parochial House, Crossgar,
Downpatrick, Co Down BT30 9EA
Tel 028-44830229
Rev Patrick McKenna CC
2 Drumnaconagher Road,
Crossgar BT30 9AN
Tel 028-44830342

CULFEIGHTRIN
Very Rev James O'Kane PP
87 Cushendall Road, Ballyvoy,
Ballycastle, Co Antrim BT54 6QY
Tel 028-20762248

CUSHENDALL
Very Rev Brian Daly PP, VF
Parochial House,
28 Chapel Road, Cushendall,
Ballymena BT44 0RS
Tel 028-21771240

CUSHENDUN
Very Rev Brian Daly PP
Parochial House, 28 Chapel Road,
Cushendall, Ballymena,
Co Antrim BT44 0RS
Tel 028-21771240
Very Rev Canon Alex McMullan (priest in residence)
21 Knocknacarry Avenue,
Cushenden, Co Antrim BT44 0NX
Tel 028-21761269

DOWNPATRICK
Very Rev Canon Sean Rogan PP, VF
Tel 028-44612443
Rev Eamon McCreave (OSM)
Tel 028-44612443
Parochial House,
54 St Patrick's Avenue,
Downpatrick, Co Down BT30 6DN
Rev Patrick Devlin CC
Priest's House, 29 Killough Road,
Downpatrick, Co Down BT30 6PX
Tel 028-44613430
Very Rev Finbar Glavin
Parochial House, 16 Ballykilbeg Road,
Downpatrick, Co Down BT30 8HJ
Tel 028-44613203
Very Rev Canon Noel Conway (priest in residence)
23 Rathkeltair Road, Downpatrick,
Co Down BT30 6NL
Tel 028-44614777

DRUMAROAD AND CLANVARAGHAN
Very Rev Peter Donnelly PP
Parochial House,
15 Drumaroad Hill,
Castlewellan, Co Down BT31 9PD
Tel 028-44811474

DRUMBO
Very Rev Martin Kelly PP
Parochial House,
546 Saintfield Road, Carryduff,
Belfast BT8 8EU
Tel 028-90812238
Rev Brian Watters CC
79 Ivanhoe Avenue, Carryduff,
Belfast BT8 8BW
Tel 028-90817410

DUNDRUM AND TYRELLA
Very Rev Gerard Patton PP
Parochial House, Dundrum,
Newcastle, Co Down BT33 0LU
Tel 028-43751212
Very Rev Canon Hugh Starkey
Parochial House,
26 Tyrella Road,
Ballykinlar, Downpatrick BT30 8DF
Tel 028-44851221

DUNEANE
Very Rev Patrick McWilliams PP
103 Roguery Road, Moneyglass,
Toomebridge, Co Antrim BT41 3PT
Tel 028-79650225
Very Rev Francis McCorry
212 Staffordstown Road,
Cargin, Toomebridge,
Co Antrim BT41 3QT
Tel 028-79650079

DUNLOY AND CLOUGHMILLS
Very Rev Aidan Brankin PP
7 Culcrum Road, Cloughmills BT44 9NH
Tel 028-27638267

GLENARIFFE
Very Rev David White PP
Parochial House, 182 Garron Road,
Glenariffe, Co Antrim BT44 0RA
Tel 028-21771249

GLENARM (TICKMACREEVAN)
Very Rev Aidan Kerr PP
Parochial House, 1 The Cloney, Glenarm,
Co Antrim BT44 0AB
Tel 028-28841246

GLENAVY AND KILLEAD
Very Rev Luke McWilliams PP
Parochial House, 59 Chapel Road,
Glenavy, Crumlin, Co Antrim BT29 4LY
Tel 028-94422262
Rev Brendan Smyth CC
Parochial House, Glenavy Road,
Crumlin, Co Antrim BT29 4LA
Tel 028-94422278

GLENRAVEL (SKERRY)
Very Rev Gabriel Lyons PP
119 Glenravel Road, Martinstown,
Ballymena, Co Antrim BT43 6QL
Tel 028-21758217

HANNAHSTOWN
Very Rev David Delargy PP
Parochial House,
23 Hannahstown Hill,
Belfast BT17 0LT
Tel 028-90614567
Rt Rev Mgr John Murphy (priest in residence)
18 Rock Road, Lisburn,
Co Antrim BT28 3SU
Tel 028-92648244

HOLYWOOD
Very Rev Peter O'Kane PP
2A My Lady's Mile, Holywood,
Co Down BT18 9EW
Tel 028-90422167

KILCLIEF AND STRANGFORD
Very Rev Colm McGrady PP
Parochial House, Strangford,
Co Down BT30 7NL
Tel 028-44881206

KILCOO
Very Rev Denis McKinlay PP
Parochial House, 121 Dublin Road,
Kilcoo, Co Down BT34 5HP
Tel 028-40630314

KILKEEL (UPPER MOURNE)
Very Rev Michael Murray PP
Parochial House, Greencastle Road,
Kilkeel, Co Down BT34 4DE
Tel 028-41762242
Rev Anthony Fitzsimons CC
Curates' Residence, Massforth,
152 Newry Road, Kilkeel,
Co Down BT34 4ET
Tel 028-41762257

KILLOUGH (BRIGHT)
Very Rev Peter O'Hare PP
Parochial House, 22 Castle Street,
Killough, Co Down BT30 7QQ
Tel 028-44841221

KILLYLEAGH
Very Rev Colum Curran PP
4 Irish Street, Killyleagh,
Co Down BT30 9QS
Tel 028-44828211

KIRCUBBIN (ARDKEEN)
Very Rev Patrick Neeson PP
46 Blackstaff Road, Ballycranbeg,
Kircubbin, Newtownards,
Co Down BT22 1AG
Tel 028-42738294

LARNE
Very Rev Dermot McKay PP
Rev Mariusz Uranowski (SCHR)
Parochial House, 51 Victoria Road, Larne,
Co Antrim BT40 1LY
Tel 028-28273230/28273053
Rev John Burns CC
Parochial House, Ballycraigy Road,
Craigyhill, Larne, Co Antrim BT40 2LE
Tel 028-28260130

LISBURN (BLARIS)
Very Rev Dermot McCaughan PP
St Patrick's Presbytery, 29 Chapel Hill,
Lisburn, Co Antrim BT28 1EP
Tel 028-92662341
Rev Eamon Magorian CC
Tel 028-92660206
Parochial House, 27 Chapel Hill, Lisburn,
Co Antrim BT28 1EP

LOUGHGUILE
Very Rev Robert Butler PP
Parochial House, 44 Lough Road,
Loughguile, Ballymena,
Co Antrim BT44 9JN
Tel 028-27641206
Very Rev Canon George O'Hanlon (priest in residence)
62 Coolkeeran Road, Armoy,
Ballymoney, Co Antrim BT53 8XN

LOUGHINISLAND
Very Rev Kieran Whiteford PP
Parochial House, Loughinisland,
Downpatrick, Co Down BT30 8QH
Tel 028-44811661

LOWER MOURNE
Very Rev Sean Gilmore PP
Parochial House, 284 Glassdrumman Road,
Annalong, Newry, Co Down BT34 4QN
Tel 028-43768208

NEWCASTLE (MAGHERA)
Very Rev Albert McNally PP, VF
Rev Declan Mulligan CC
24 Downs Road, Newcastle,
Co Down BT33 0AG
Tel 028-43722401

NEWTOWNARDS
Very Rev Martin O'Hagan PP
71 North Street, Newtownards,
Co Down BT23 4JD
Tel 028-91812137

PORTAFERRY (BALLYPHILIP)
Very Rev Patrick Mulholland PP
Parochial House, Portaferry,
Co Down BT22 1RH
Tel 028-42728234

PORTGLENONE
Very Rev Henry McCann PP
St Mary's Presbytery, 12 Ballymena Road,
Portglenone, Co Antrim BT44 8BL
Tel 028-25821218

PORTRUSH
Very Rev Rory Sheehan PP
Parochial House,
111 Causeway Street,
Portrush, Co Antrim BT56 8JE
Tel 028-70823388

PORTSTEWART
Very Rev Austin McGirr PP, VF
Parochial House, 4 The Crescent,
Portstewart, Co Derry BT55 7AB
Tel 028-70832534
Rev Raymond McCullagh (priest in residence)
1 Seafield Park South,
Portstewart BT55 7LH
Tel 028-70832066

RANDALSTOWN
Very Rev Con Boyle PP
Parochial House, 1 Craigstown Road,
Randalstown, Co Antrim BT41 2AF
Tel 028-94472640

RASHARKIN
Very Rev John Murray PP
Parochial House, 9 Gortahor Road,
Rasharkin, Ballymena,
Co Antrim BT44 8SB
Tel 028-29571212

SAINTFIELD AND CARRICKMANNON
Very Rev Anthony McHugh PP
Parochial House, 33 Crossgar Road,
Saintfield, Ballynahinch,
Co Down BT24 7JE
Tel 028-97510237

SAUL AND BALLEE
Very Rev Raymond Fulton PP
10 St Patrick's Road, Saul, Downpatrick,
Co Down BT30 7JG
Tel 028-44612525
Rev Anthony Meaney CC
Parochial House, Ballycruttle Road,
Downpatrick, Co Down BT30 7EL
Tel 028-44841213

INSTITUTIONS AND THEIR CHAPLAINS

HOSPITALS

City Group of Hospitals, Belfast
Tel 028-90329241
Rev Gerard Fox
201 Donegall Street, Belfast BT1 2FL
Tel 028-90263473 (chaplain's office)

Mater Hospital, Belfast
Tel 028-90741211
Rev Kevin McGuckien
St Patrick's Presbytery,
199 Donegall Street, Belfast BT1 2FL
Tel 028-90324597

Musgrave Park Hospital, Belfast
Tel 028-90669501
Rev Adrian Eastwood (CM)
99 Cliftonville Road, Belfast BT14 6JQ
Tel 028-90751771

Royal Victoria Hospital, Belfast
Tel 028-90240503
Rev Thomas McGlynn
The Cathedral Presbytery,
St Peter's Square, Belfast BT12 4BU

PENAL INSTITUTIONS

Maghaberry Prison
Old Road, Ballinderry Upper, Lisburn,
Co Antrim BT28 2TP
Pastoral Team: Rev Michael Bingham
Sr Angela Burke
Sr Rosaleen McMahon
Tel 028-92614825
Prison General Office: 028-92611888

Young Offenders' Detention Centre
Hydebank Wood, Hospital Road,
Belfast BT8 8NA
Very Rev Stephen McBrearty
Tel 028-90253666
Sr Oona, Sisters of Nazareth (Women Prisoners)

UNIVERSITIES

Queen's University, Belfast
Rev Gary Toman
The Chaplaincy, 28 Elmwood Avenue,
Belfast BT9 6AY
Tel 028-90669737

University of Ulster, Coleraine
Rev Raymond McCullagh
1 Seafield Park South, Portstewart,
Co Derry BT55 7LH
Tel 028-70832066

University of Ulster, Jordanstown
Rev Alan McGuckian (SJ)
Peter Faber House,
28 Brookvale Avenue,
Belfast BT14 6BW
Tel 028-90757615

PRIESTS OF THE DIOCESE ELSEWHERE

Rev Martin Henry
Rev Oliver Treanor
St Patrick's College,
Maynooth, Co Kildare
Tel 01-6285222 Fax 01-6289063
Rev Gerard McFlynn
18 Maresfield Gardens,
London NW3 5SX
Rev Patrick McCafferty
52 Lower Rathmines Road, Dublin 6
Rev Timothy Bartlett
Columba Centre, St Patrick's College,
Maynooth, Co Kildare
Tel 01-5053000
Rev Gerard Magee
Cistercian Monastery, Portglenone

RETIRED PRIESTS

Rev Conleth Byrne
c/o 73 Somerton Road, Belfast BT15 4DE
Rev Colm Campbell
20 Continental Avenue, Apt 4D,
Forest Hills, New York 11375, USA
Tel 001-7185443304
Very Rev Harry Carlin
5 Fortwilliam Court, Belfast BT15 4DS
Tel 028-90772376
Rt Rev Mgr Sean Connolly VG
7 Tullyview, Loughguile,
Co Antrim BT44 9JY
Very Rev Canon Joseph Cunningham
Our Lady's Home, 68 Ardnava Road,
Belfast BT12 6FF
Very Rev Christopher Dallat
Leabank Nursing Home,
1 Beechwood Avenue,
Ballycastle BT54 6BL
Very Rev John Fitzpatrick
116 Strangford Road, Ardglass, BT30 7SS
Very Rev Gerald Forrester
62 Rathgannon, Warrenpoint BT34 3TU
Very Rev Padraic Gallinagh
'Polperro', 8 Beverley Close,
Newtownards BT23 7FN
Very Rev Frank Harper
32 Bryansford Avenue,
Newcastle BT33 0EQ
Very Rev John Hutton
Apt 2, Ceara Court, Windsor Avenue,
Belfast BT9 6EJ
Tel 028-90683002
Very Rev Donal Kelly
7 Knocksinna Park, Bray Road,
Foxrock, Dublin 18
Tel 01-2894170
Rev Oliver P. Kennedy
68 Shore Road, Toomebridge,
Co Antrim BT41 3NW
Tel 028-79650213/79650618
Very Rev Sean McCartney
25 Alt-Min Avenue, Belfast BT8 6NJ
Very Rev Joseph MacGurnaghan
14 Presbytery Lane,
Dunloy, Ballymena,
Co Antrim BT44 9DZ
Tel 028-27657223

Rev Gerard McAteer
124 Staffordstown Road, Randalstown,
Co Antrim BT41 3LH
Tel 028-94478373
Very Rev Gerard McConville
68 Main Street, Portglenone BT44 8HS
Rev Hugh McIldowney
7 Riverdale Close, Belfast BT11 9DH
Tel 028-90603042
Rev Gordon McKinstry
12 The Meadows, Randalstown,
Co Antrim BT41 2JB
Very Rev Brendan McMullan
26 Willowbank Park, Belfast BT6 0LL
Very Rev George McLaverty
518 Donegall Road,
Belfast BT12 6DY
Very Rev Patrick McVeigh
3 Broughshane Road, Ballymena,
Co Antrim BT43 7DX
Very Rev John Moley
24 Mallard Road, Downpatrick,
Co Down BT30 6DY
Very Rev Eamon O'Brien
No. 5 Hopecroft, Main Street,
Glenavy BT29 4LN
Very Rev Prof Martin O'Callaghan
c/o 73 Somerton Road, Belfast BT15 4DE
Very Rev Kevin O'Leary
1 Clarmont Court, Castlewellan,
Co Down BT31 9SE
Very Rev John O'Sullivan
6 Ferngrove Avenue, Aghagallon,
Craigavon BT67 0HA
Very Rev Cyril Reilly
18 Whitehall Avenue, Ballycastle,
Co Antrim BT54 6WA
Very Rev Jim Sheppard
189 Carrigenagh Road, Ballymartin,
Kilkeel, Co Down BT34 4GA
Very Rev John Stewart
27F Windsor Avenue,
Belfast BT9 6EE
Rev Desmond Wilson
6 Springhill Close, Belfast BT12 7SE
Tel 028-90326722

RELIGIOUS ORDERS AND CONGREGATIONS

PRIESTS

CISTERCIANS
Our Lady of Bethlehem Abbey,
11 Ballymena Road, Portglenone,
Ballymena, Co Antrim BT44 8BL
Tel 028-25821211 Fax 028-25822795
Website www.bethlehem-abbey.org.uk
Abbot
Rt Rev Dom Celsus Kelly (OCSO)

JESUITS
Peter Faber House, 28 Brookvale Avenue,
Belfast BT14 6BW
Tel/Fax 028-90747615
Email peter_faber@lineone.net
Superior: Rev Alan McGuckian (SJ)

MILL HILL MISSIONARIES
St Mary's Parish, 25 Marquis Street,
Belfast BT1 1JJ
Tel 028-90320482
Rev James A. Boyle (MHM) Adm
Rev Jim O'Donoghue (MHM) CC

PASSIONISTS
Holy Cross Retreat, Ardoyne,
Crumlin Road, Belfast BT14 7GE
Tel 028-90748231 Fax 028-90740340
Superior: Rev Gary Donegan (CP) PP

Passionist Retreat Centre, Tobar Mhuire,
Crossgar, Downpatrick,
Co Down BT30 9EA
Tel 028-44830242 Fax 028-44831382
Superior: Rev John Friel (CP)

Passionist Community,
108 Salisbury Avenue, Belfast BT15 5ED
Tel 028-90288306 Fax 01-90294085

REDEMPTORISTS
Clonard Monastery, 1 Clonard Gardens,
Belfast BT13 2RL
Tel 028-90445950 Fax 028-90445988
Superior: Rev Michael Murtagh (CSsR)

St Gerard's Parish,
722 Antrim Road, Newtownabbey,
Co Antrim BT36 7PG
Tel 028-90774833
Fax 028-90770923
Superior & PP: Rev Gerry Cassidy (CSsR)

ST PATRICK'S MISSIONARY SOCIETY (KILTEGAN FATHERS)
St Patricks, 21 Old Cavehill Road,
Belfast BT15 5GT
Tel 028-90778696

VINCENTIANS
99 Cliftonville Road, Belfast BT14 6JQ
Tel 028-90751771 Fax 028-90740547
Email cmbelfast@ntlworld.co.uk
Superior: Very Rev Peter Gildea (CM)

BROTHERS

CHRISTIAN BROTHERS
An Dúnán, 210 Glen Road,
Belfast BT11 8BW
Tel 028-90611343
Community Leader: Br Tim Monaghan
Community: 5

Christian Brothers
1 Jubilee Avenue, Belfast 14
Tel 028-90751141
Community: 3

The Open Doors Learning Centre
Barrack Street, Belfast BT12 4AH
Tel 028-90325867 Fax 028-90241013

Westcourt Centre
Barrack Street, Belfast BT12 4AH
Tel 028-90323009

681 Crumlin Road, Belfast BT14 7GD
Community: 5
Tel 028-90717694

DE LA SALLE BROTHERS
La Salle Secondary School,
Edenmore Drive, Belfast BT11 8LT
Tel 028-90508800
Headmaster: Mr Paul Barry

De La Salle Brothers, Glanaulin,
141 Glen Road, Belfast BT11 8BP
Tel 028-90614848
Superior: Br Ailbe Mangan
Community: 5

La Salle Pastoral Retreat Centre,
Glanaulin, 141 Glen Road,
Belfast BT11 8BP
Tel 028-90501932 Tax 028-90501932

La Salle House, 4 Stream Street,
Downpatrick, Co Down BT30 6DD
Tel 028-44612996
Superior: Br Mark Jordan
Community: 6

Miguel Pastoral Centre, 4 Stream Street,
Downpatrick, Co Down BT30 6DD
Tel 028-44615877

St Patrick's Grammar School,
Downpatrick, Co Down BT30 6NJ
Tel 028-44619722
Headmaster: Mr Sean Sloan

Secondary School, Struell Road,
Downpatrick, Co Down BT30 6JR
Tel 028-44612520
Headmaster: Mr Barry Sharvin

Primary School, St Dillon's Avenue,
Downpatrick, Co Down BT30 6HZ
Tel 028-44612787
Headmaster: Mr Hugh Kelly

ST JOHN OF GOD ASSOCIATION
Colcha Suite, 129 Ormeau Road,
Belfast BT7 1SH
Tel 028-90320909 Fax 028-90320907
Email association@sjoga.org
Director Br Finnian Gallagher (OH)
Residential service for people with
learning disabilities.

'Iona', 7 Firmount, Fortwilliam, Belfast,
Co Antrim BT15 4HZ
Tel 028-90779808 Fax 028-90775925
Superior: Br Finnian Gallagher (OH)
Community: 1

SISTERS

BON SECOURS SISTERS (PARIS)
52A Tullymore Gardens,
Belfast BT11 8ND
Tel 028-90625757
Community: 1
Pastoral ministry

**CONGREGATION OF THE SISTERS OF
MERCY**
Convent of Mercy, 2A Fruithill Park,
Belfast BT11 8GD
Tel 028-90616399

Convent of Mercy, Beechmount,
Ard Na Va Road, Belfast BT12 6FF
Tel 028-90319496
Leader: Sr Josephine McAteer
Community: 8

Convent of Mercy, Downpatrick,
Co Down BT30 6DT
Tel 028-44612200
Leader: Sr Vianney McVeigh
Community: 6

27a Glenveagh Drive,
Belfast BT11 9HX
Tel 028-90602175
Community: 3

Mercy Convent, Whiteabbey,
453 Shore Road, Newtownabbey,
Co Antrim BT37 9SE
Tel 028-90863128
Leader: Sr Claire Loughran
Community: 3

Convent of Mercy,
252 Limestone Road, Belfast BT15 3AR
Tel 028-90748830

Sisters of Mercy
616 Crumlin Road, Belfast BT14 7GL
Tel 028-90717112
Community: 3

Sisters of Mercy, 2-3 The Glen,
Limestone Road, Belfast,
Co Antrim BT15 3AT
Tel 028-90740430
Community: 6

Sisters of Mercy, 24 Floral Park,
Glengormley, Co Antrim BT36 7RU
Tel 028-90878384

Sisters of Mercy, 2 Lever Street,
Ligoniel, Belfast BT14 8EF
Tel 028-90710529

Sisters of Mercy, Ballysillan House,
614 Crumlin Road, Belfast BT14 7GL
Tel 028-90715758
Community: 6

27 Wheatfield Gardens,
Belfast BT14 7HU
Tel 028-90715478

Apt 8, Luxembourg Court,
Antrim Road, Belfast BT15 5AR
Tel 028-90582742

**CONGREGATION OF THE SISTERS OF
NAZARETH**
Nazareth House Care Village,
516 Ravenhill Road,
Belfast BT6 0BX
Tel 028-90690600 Fax 028-90690601
Superior: Sr Teresa Walsh
Community: 12
Home for the elderly. Beds: 70

Bethlehem Nursery School,
516 Ravenhill Road, Belfast BT6 0BW
Tel 028-90640406
Pupils: 50
St Michael's Primary,
516 Ravenhill Road, Belfast BT6 0BW
Tel 028-90491529. Pupils: 400

**CONGREGATION OF THE SISTERS OF
SION**
547 Ormeau Road, Belfast BT7 3JA
Tel 028-90643208
Email sionbelfast@hotmail.co.uk
Community: 3
Education, spirituality, counselling

CROSS AND PASSION CONGREGATION
6 Lisbon Street, Belfast BT5 4DA
Tel 028-90597914
Community: 3
Parish visitation and pastoral centre,
SPRED

4 Innisfayle Road, Belfast BT15 4ER
Tel 028-90774238
Community: 3
Adult education, ecumenical work,
healing ministries

St Teresa's Convent, 78 Glen Road,
Belfast BT11 8BH
Tel 028-90613955
Community: 4
Hospital chaplaincy and pastoral care,
ecumenical work, bereavement
counselling

Villa Pacis, 78A Glen Road,
Belfast BT11 8BH
Tel 028-90621766
Superior: Sr Mary Sloan
Community: 13
Care of sick and elderly

Cross and Passion Convent, Drumalis,
Glenarm Road, Larne, Co Antrim BT40 1DT
Tel 028-28272196
Community: 3
Retreat work

Drumalis Retreat Centre,
Larne, Co Antrim
Tel 028-28276455/28272196
Fax 028-28277999
Email drumalis@btconnect.com

Cross and Passion Convent
120 B Drains Bay, Larne, Co Antrim
Tel 028-28279428
Community: 3
Prayer and Retreat work

Cross and Passion Convent,
3 Gort an Chlochair, Ballycastle,
Co Antrim BT54 6NU
Tel 028-20762228
Community: 2
Parish ministry, education

Cross and Passion College,
Ballycastle, Co Antrim BT54 6LA
Tel 028-20762473. Pupils: 600
Co-educational

Cloona House, 31 Colin Road,
Poleglass, Belfast BT17 0LG
Tel 028-90626221
Community: 2
Parish ministry, education, prayer
ministry

5c Easton Avenue, Cliftonville road,
Belfast BT14 6LL
Tel 028-90749507
Community: 2
Retreat work, Bosnia project, counselling
and facilitation

DAUGHTERS OF CHARITY OF ST VINCENT DE PAUL
23 Glen Road, Belfast BT11 8BA
Tel 028-9023052
Superior: Sr Rosaleen MacMahon
Community: 3

St Louise's Comprehensive College,
468 Falls Road, Belfast BT 6EN
Tel 028-90325631

Moyard House,
Moyard Park,Belfast BT12 7FR
Tel 028-90331562
Temporary accommodation for homeless
and parish work
Superior: Sr Mary Hayden
Community: 5

1c Grainne House
(for families in transition)
Newlodge, Belfast BT 2LA

DAUGHTERS OF JESUS
Ard Mhuire, 12 Shorelands, Greenisland,
Co Antrim BT38 8FB
Tel 02890-864759
Community: 4
Superior: Sr Teresa McMenamin

DOMINICAN SISTERS
Dominican Convent, Falls Road,
Belfast BT12 6AE
Tel 028-90327056
Email opfalls@dominicansisters.com
Prioress: Sr Lucina Montague
Community: 14
Grammar School. Tel 028-90320081
St Rose's High School. Tel 028-90240937

Lecceto, 9 Wynchurch Park,
Belfast BT6 0JL
Tel 028-90645068
Email brighdevalley@btinternet.com
Community: 2

St Martin's Dominican Convent,
22 Gransha Rise, Belfast BT11 8ES
Tel 028-90619395
Community: 4

Dominican Convent,
Fortwilliam Park, Belfast BT15 4AP
Tel 028-90370008
Email ionahouse@btinternet.com
Prioress: Sr Aine Killen
Community: 8
Grammar School
Tel 028-90370298

FAMILY OF ADORATION
63 Falls Road,
Belfast BT12 4PD
Tel 01232-325668
Email adorationsisters@utv.net
Superior: Sr Molly Caldwell
Community: 3
A contemplative community with mission
of adoration, altar breads

GOOD SHEPHERD SISTERS
25 Rossmore Drive,
Belfast BT7 3LA
Tel 028-90641346 Fax 028-90646353
Email rossmoredrive@yahoo.co.uk
Superior: Sr Noeleen Bowen
Community: 19

Good Shepherd Contemplative Sisters,
Lysmarie, 19 Rossmore Drive,
Belfast BT7 3LA
Tel 028-90491346/820
Fax 028-90493565
Email lysmariesisters@yahoo.com
Superior: Sr Evelyn Fitzsimmons
Community: 12

Summerhill Road, Twinbrook,
Dunmurry, Belfast BT17 0RL
Tel 028-90618987
Fax 028-90302863
Community: 4
Sisters engaged in community services

Good Shepherd Sisters,
80 Glenholm Park, Four Winds,
Belfast BT8 6LR
Tel 028-90582391
Email gsglenholm@yahoo.co.uk
Community: 1
Counselling, spiritual direction and youth
work

Good Shepherd Sisters,
49 Knockbreda Park, Rosetta,
Belfast BT6 0HD
Tel 028-90224236
Email peggetty@yahoo.com
Community: 2
Parish work

MARIST SISTERS
22 St Peter's Place,
Belfast BT12 4SB
Tel 028-90246238
Community: 3
Parish ministry

Grosvenor House,
259 Grosvenor Road,
Belfast BT12 4LL
Tel 028-90310383
Community: 2
Hostel for the Homeless

MISSIONARY SISTERS OF THE HOLY CROSS
86 Glen Road, Belfast BT11 8BH
Tel 028-90614631 Fax 028-90614631
Email mary@thcross.freeserve.co.uk
Superior: Sr M. Brigid McGuigan
Community: 4

NOTRE DAME DES MISSIONS (OUR LADY OF THE MISSIONS SISTERS)
125 Maghera Lane Road,
Randalstown,
Co Antrim BT41 2PD
Tel 028-94478594
Community: 2
Parish ministry

442 Falls Road, Belfast BT12 6EN
Tel 01232-329776
Community: 3
Pastoral ministry

POOR CLARES
120 Cliftonville Road,
Belfast BT14 6LA
Superior: Sr Immaculata Enderez OSC
Community: 6
Contemplatives
St Clare's Prayer Centre
Tel 028-90744064
Email poor.clare@btconnect.com
Private retreats, or quiet days.
Accommodation for four retreatants,
self-catering

RELIGIOUS OF SACRED HEART OF MARY
100 Hillsborough Road, Lisburn,
Co Antrim BT28 1JU
Tel 01846-678501
Community: 4
Ministry in local area

28 Upper Green, Dunmurry,
Belfast BT17 0EL
Tel 01232-600792
Community 5
Ministry in local area and education

Sacred Heart of Mary Grammar School
for Boys and Girls,
Rathmore, Finaghy, Belfast BT10 0LF
Pupils: 1,350
Tel 01232-610115
Email
userid.rathmore@schools.class-ni.org.uk.

ROSMINIANS (SISTERS OF PROVIDENCE)
6 Churchview Court, Belfast BT14 7RE
Tel 01232-756664
Contact Person: Sr M. Fabian Barden
Community: 2
Pastoral work

SACRED HEARTS OF JESUS AND MARY
The Curragh Community,
2 Workman Avenue, Belfast BT13 3SB
Tel 028-90312658

ST CLARE SISTERS
Shalom, 43 Rosetta Park,
Lower Ormeau Road, Belfast BT6 0DL
Tel 028-90694108
Community: 3

ST LOUIS SISTERS
St Louis Grammar School, Kilkeel
Tel 016937-62747
Pupils: 573

Allianz (ⅠⅠ)

St Louis Grammar School
Cullybackey Road, Ballymena,
Co Antrim BT43 5DW
Tel 01266-49534
Pupils: 989

14 Carndale Meadows, Carniny Road,
Ballymena BT43 5NX
Tel 028-25651683
Community: 2

21 Glenbawn Square, Poleglass,
Dunmurry, Belfast BT17 0TT
Tel 028-90225236
Community: 2

7 Riverdale Park Avenue, Belfast BT11 9BP
Tel 028-90209074
Community: 1

22 Riverdale Park North, Belfast BT11 9DL
Tel 028-90619375
Community: 1

24 Riverdale Park North, Belfast BT11 9PS
Tel 028-90202608
Community: 2

Apartment 2 Hollycroft,
1-3 Inver Avenue, Belfast BT15 5DG
Tel 028-90721037
Community: 1

91 Hillhead Crescent,
Stewartstown Road, Belfast BT11 9FW
Tel 028-90621900
Community: 6
Varied Apostolates

49 Bracken Avenue, Castlewellan Road,
Newcastle, Co Down BT33 0HG
Tel 028-43726282
Community: 1

EDUCATIONAL INSTITUTIONS

Aquinas College
518 Ravenhill Road, Belfast BT6 0BY
Tel 028-90643939
Principal: Ms Diana Press
Priest on staff
Rev Colin Grant MA, STL, PGCE

Our Lady and St Patrick's College
Knock, Belfast BT5 7DQ
Tel 028-90401184
Principal: Mr Dermot G. Mullan MA, PGCE

St MacNissi's College
Garron Tower, Carnlough,
Co Antrim BT44 0JS
Tel 028-28885202/28885214
Principal
Mrs Eileen O'Loan BEd, MSc

St Malachy's College
Antrim Road, Belfast BT15 2AE
Tel 028-90748285
Principal
Dr John PK Morrin BEd, MSc, PhD
Priest on Staff
Very Rev Michael Spence BA, STL
Resident Priests
Rev Prof James McEvoy (Queen's University)
Rev Edward McGee (St Mary's University College)
Rev Colin Grant (Aquinas College)

St Mary's University College
A College of Queen's University Belfast
191 Falls Road,
Belfast 12 6FE
Tel 028-90327678
Principal
Professor Peter Finn BA MSSc
Priest Lecturers
Rev Feidhlimidh Magennis MA, BD, LSS (Dromore)
Rev Edward McGee BA, BD
Rev Paul Fleming BA, BD, STL
Rev Niall Coll BA, BD (Raphoe)

EDMUND RICE SCHOOLS TRUST NORTHERN IRELAND

St Mary's Grammar School,
Glen Road, Belfast BT11 8NR
Tel 028-90294000 Fax 028-90294009
Principal: Mr Jim Sheerin

Christian Brothers' Secondary School,
Glen Road, Belfast BT11 8BW
Tel 028-90808050 Fax 028-90808055
Principal: Mr Tommy Armstrong

Edmund Rice College,
96-100 Hightown Road, Glengormley,
Newtownabbey, Belfast BT36 7AU
Tel 028-90848433/90840566
Fax 028-90844924
Principal: Mr Kevin Gough

Edmund Rice Primary School,
Pim Street, Belfast BT15 2BN
Tel 028-90351206 Fax 028-90747192
Principal: Mr John Devine

St Aidan's Primary School,
Whiterock Road, Belfast BT12 7FW
Tel/Fax 028-90320565
Principal: Mr Raymond Hunter

CHARITABLE AND OTHER SOCIETIES

Apostolic Work Society
Xavier House,
156 Cliftonpark Avenue,
Belfast BT14 6DT
Tel 028-90351912
Email apostolic.work@btinternet.com
Office hours:
Monday-Wednesday 9.00 am-2.30 pm
Society for lay women
President: Mrs Anne Donaghy

Legion of Mary
14 Cliftonville Road,
Belfast BT14 6JX
Tel 028-90746626
President: Mr Joe Drew

Morning Star House
2-12 Divis Street, Belfast
Tel 028-90333500

Regina Coeli Hostel
8-10 Lake Glen Avenue,
Belfast BT11 8FE
Tel 028-90612473
Night shelter for destitute and homeless women. Under the care of the Legion of Mary

Society of St Vincent de Paul
196-200 Antrim Road,
Belfast BT15 2AJ
Tel 028-90351561
Regional Administrator
Ms Aileen Coney

St Joseph's Centre for the Deaf
321 Grosvenor Road,
Belfast BT12 4LP
Tel 028-90448211
The Centre provides a wide range of facilities for the deaf.
Co-ordinator: Rev Paul Strain
Northern Diocesan Lay Chaplain:
Ms Denise Flack
Tel 078-77643961

DIOCESE OF DROMORE

PATRONS OF THE DIOCESE
ST PATRICK, 17 MARCH; ST COLMAN, 7 JUNE

INCLUDES PORTIONS OF COUNTIES ANTRIM, ARMAGH AND DOWN

Most Rev John McAreavey DD
Bishop of Dromore; born 1949;
ordained priest 10 June 1973;
ordained Bishop of Dromore
19 September 1999

Residence:
Bishop's House,
44 Armagh Road,
Newry, Co Down BT35 6PN
Tel 028-30262444
Fax 028-30260496
Email
bishopofdromore@btinternet.com
Website dromorediocese.org

ST PATRICK AND ST COLMAN'S CATHEDRAL, NEWRY

Newry cathedral was founded in 1825, at the centre of a growing and prosperous town. It symbolised, in many ways, the increasing confidence of the local Catholic population of the day, especially the newly emerging Catholic middle class.

The cathedral was designed by Thomas J. Duff, a prominent architect in the northern part of Ireland at the turn of the century. The building was dedicated in May 1829 by the then Irish Primate, Dr Curtis. It was believed to be the first major dedication ceremony in Ireland following the granting of Catholic Emancipation.

Originally, the cathedral was sparsely furnished, and it received its first significant interior decoration in 1851. The building was developed considerably between 1888 and 1891. During these years, its two transepts were added and a handsome bell tower erected. From 1904 to 1909, Bishop Henry O'Neill oversaw a further major phase of building. The main body of the church was extended in length by some forty feet and a new sanctuary was added. Much of the internal fabric of the cathedral, as we know it today, belongs to this period. Rich interior mosaic decoration was undertaken, side chapels were constructed and the cathedral's tubular organ was installed. The cathedral was solemnly consecrated in July 1925 – a century after its foundation! It enjoys the joint patronage of Ss Patrick and Colman.

Interior renovation was necessary in the wake of the Second Vatican Council. This work of extending and refurbishing the sanctuary area was undertaken by

Bishop Francis Gerard Brooks from 1989 to 1990. It included the construction of the present marble altar, the rebuilding of the reredos of the former high altar, now in three parts, and the relocation of the bishop's chair to the front of the sanctuary. This work of renovation has earned widespread praise in the field of contemporary ecclesiastical architecture.

Most Rev Francis Gerard Brooks DD
Retired Bishop of Dromore; born 1924;
ordained priest 19 June 1949; ordained
Bishop of Dromore 25 January 1976
Residence:
Drumiller House, 14 Drumiller Road,
Jerrettspass, Newry, Co Down
Tel 028-30821508

CHAPTER

Dean: Vacant
Archdeacon: Vacant
Prebendaries
Saint Colman and Lann
Very Rev Canon Cathal Jordon PP
Seagoe
Drumeragh
Very Rev Canon Francis Boyle, Saval
Lanronan
Rt Rev Mgr Aidan Hamill PP, VG
Shankill, St Peter's
Aghaderg
Very Rev Canon Liam Stevenson PP, VF
Seapatrick
Clondallon
Very Rev Canon Michael Hackett PP
Kilbroney (Rostrevor)
Kilmycon
Very Rev Canon John Kearney Adm, VF
Warrenpoint
Canon Penitentiary
Very Rev Canon Francis Brown Adm,
Newry
Downaclone
Very Rev Canon Gerard McCrory PP
Magheradroll, Canon Theologian
Retired Members, Honorary Canons:
Very Rev Liam Boyle
Very Rev Arthur Byrne
Very Rev Anthony Davies
Very Rev Desmond Knowles
Very Rev Patrick McAnuff
Very Rev Joseph O'Hagan

ADMINISTRATION

Vicar General
Rt Rev Mgr Aidan Hamill PP, VG
Parochial House, 70 North Street,
Lurgan, Co Armagh
Tel 028-38326949

Chancellor/Diocesan Secretary
Very Rev Gerald Powell PP
Parochial House, 4 Holymount Road
Laurencetown, Craigavon BT63 6AT
Co Armagh
Tel 028-40624236 Fax 028-40625440
Email gpowellpp@aol.com

Council of Priests
Chairman
Very Rev Canon John Kearney Adm, VF
Riverfields, Warrenpoint,
Co Down BT34 3PU
Tel 028-41754684 Fax 028-41754685
Secretary: Very Rev Martin McAlinden PP
The Presbytery, 11 Tullygally Road,
Legahory, Craigavon BT65 5B
Tel 028-38341901
Email martinmcalinden@hotmail.com

Finance Council
Administrator and Secretary
Rev Feidlimidh Magennis
St Mary's University College, Belfast

Bishop's Secretary
Miss Agatha Larkin
Bishop's House, Newry, Co Down
Tel 028-30262444

CATECHETICS EDUCATION

Diocesan Advisers for Religious Education
Primary Schools: Sr Attracta Devlin
Post-Primary Schools:
Mrs Elizabeth McNeice
Lismore Comprehensive School,
Craigavon

Diocesan Education Committee
Chairman: Rt Rev Mgr Aidan Hamill
70 North Street, Lurgan,
Co Armagh BT67 9AH
Tel 028-38326949
Senior Management Officer
Mr Martin Cromie
CCMS Office, 56 Armagh Road,
Newry, Co Down BT35 6DN
Tel 028-30262423

LITURGY

Music
Director: Very Rev Terence Rafferty PP
10 Barr Hill, Newry
Tel 028-30821252
Email terryrafferty@hotmail.com

PASTORAL

Accord
Director: Rev Niall Sheehan
Cathedral Presbytery, Newry
Tel 028-30262586

Adult Faith Development
Very Rev Martin McAlinden PP, VF
The Presbytery, 11 Tullygally Road,
Craigavon
Tel 028-38341901
Email martinmcalinden@hotmail.com

Chaplaincy to Deaf People
Contact: Fr Colum Wright
10 Oaklands, Loughbrickland, Co Down
Email colum.wright@btinternet.com

Communications
Press Officer: c/o Bishops' House,
Newry, Co Down

Dromore Clerical Provident Society
Contact: Very Rev Jarlath Cushenan PP
17 Castlewellan Road, Hilltown,
Newry BT34 5UY
Tel 028-4063026

Ecumenism
Director: Rev Andrew McMahon CC
St Paul's Presbytery, Old Portadown Road,
Lurgan, Co Armagh BT66 8RG

Emigrant Services
Director: Very Rev Patrick J. Murray PP
Maypole Hill, Dromore,
Co Down BT25 1BQ
Tel 028-40623264

Immigrant Services
Rev Stanislaw Hajkowski
Cathedral Presbytery, Newry
Tel 028-30262586

Knock Diocesan Pilgrimage
Director: Very Rev Jarlath Cushenan PP
17 Castlewellan Road, Hilltown,
Newry BT34 5UY
Tel 028-4063026

Lourdes Diocesan Pilgrimage
Director: Very Rev Jarlath Cushenan PP
17 Castlewellan Road, Hilltown, Newry,
Co Down BT34 5UY
Tel 028-40630206

Marriage Tribunal
Rev Peter C. McNeill
Diocesan Office, 44 Armagh Road,
Newry, Co Down BT35 6PN
Tel 028-30269836

Pastoral Planning
Director:
Very Rev Martin McAlinden PP, VF
The Presbytery, Tullygally Road, Craigavon
Tel 028-38341901

Permanent Diaconate
Rev John Byrne CC
Cathedral Presbytery, 38 Hill Street,
Newry BT34 1AT
Tel 028-30262586

Pioneer Total Abstinence Association
Diocesan Director: Rt Rev Dean A. Davies
17 Castlewellan Road, Hilltown,
Newry, Co Down

**Pontifical Mission Societies and
Dromore/Lodwar Mission Project**
Diocesan Director: Rev Desmond Mooney
13 Tullygally Road, Legahory, Craigavon
Tel 028-38343297
Email mooneydesmond@hotmail.com

Special Needs Committee – Reachout
Mrs Anne Loughlin
22 Dallan Hill, Warrenpoint
Tel 077-34330336

Travellers
Chaplain: Rev Niall Sheehan CC
Cathedral Presbytery, Hill Street, Newry,
Co Down BT34 1AT
Tel 028-30262586

Vocations
Director: Very Rev Patrick J. Murray PP
Maypole Hill, Dromore
Tel 028-92692218
Assistant Director: Rev Brendan Kearns

Youth
Very Rev Canon Francis Brown
St Colman's College, Violet Hill, Newry
Tel 028-30262451

Youth Ministry
Ms Anita Ryan
Pastoral Centre, The Mall, Newry
Tel 028-30833898

PARISHES

Mensal parishes are listed first. Other parishes follow alphabetically. Historical names are given in parentheses.

NEWRY
Very Rev Canon Francis Brown Adm
Rev John Byrne CC
Rev Niall Sheehan CC
Rev Conor McConville CC
Rev Stanislaw Hajkowski (SC) CC
Cathedral Presbytery, 38 Hill Street,
Newry BT34 1AT
Tel 028-30262586 Fax 028-30267505
Email newrycathedral@lineone.net

CLONALLON, ST PETER'S (WARRENPOINT)
Very Rev Canon John Kearney Adm, VF
Riverfields, Warrenpoint,
Co Down, BT34 3PU
Tel 028-41754684 Fax 028-41754685
Rev Brendan Kearns CC
14 Great George's Street, Warrenpoint,
Co Down BT34 3PU
Tel 028-41772201
Email stpetersclonallon@hotmail.com
Parish Office: Tel 028-41759981
Fax 028-41759980

AGHADERG
Very Rev Colum Wright PP
10 Oaklands, Loughbrickland,
Co Down BT32 3NH
Tel 028-40623264 Fax 028-41759980
Email colum.wright@btinternet.com

ANNACLONE
Very Rev Francis Kearney PP
17 Monteith Road, Annaclone,
Banbridge, Co Down BT32 5AQ
Tel 028-40671201

CLONALLON, ST MARY'S (BURREN)
Very Rev Charles Byrne
84 Milltown Street, Burren, Warrenpoint,
Co Down BT34 3PU
Tel 028-41772200
Rev Tom McAteer
15 Chapel Hill, Mayobridge, Newry,
Co Down BT34 2EX
Tel 028-30851225 Fax 028-30851607

CLONALLON, ST PATRICK'S (MAYOBRIDGE)
Very Rev Charles Byrne
84 Milltown Street, Burren, Warrenpoint,
Co Down BT34 3PU
Tel 028-41772200
Rev Tom McAteer
15 Chapel Hill, Mayobridge, Newry,
Co Down BT34 2EX
Tel 028-30851225 Fax 028-30851607

CLONDUFF (HILLTOWN)
Very Rev Jarlath Cushenan PP
17 Castlewellan Road, Hilltown,
Newry, Co Down BT34 5UY
Tel/Fax 028-40630206

DONAGHMORE
Very Rev Terence Rafferty PP
10 Barr Hill, Newry, Co Down BT34 1SY
Tel 028-30821252
Email terryrafferty@hotmail.com

DROMORE
Very Rev P. J. Murray PP
Maypole Hill, Dromore,
Co Down BT25 1BQ
Tel 028-92692218

DRUMGATH (RATHFRILAND)
Very Rev Stephen Ferris PP
91 Newry Road, Barnmeen,
Rathfriland, Co Down BT34 5AP
Tel 028-40630306 Fax 028-40631205

DRUMGOOLAND LOWER (GARGORY)
Rev Peter C. McNeill Adm
58 Ballydrumman Road,
Castlewellan, Co Down BT31 9UG
Tel 028-40650207 Fax 028-40650205
Very Rev Archdeacon Liam Boyle PE
9 Gargory Road, Ballyward, Castlewellan,
Co Down BT31 9RN
Tel 028-40650234

DRUMGOOLAND UPPER (LEITRIM)
Rev Peter C. McNeill Adm
58 Ballydrumman Road,
Castlewellan, Co Down BT31 9UG
Tel 028-40650207 Fax 028-40650205

DROMARA
Rev Peter C. McNeill Adm
58 Ballydrumman Road,
Castlewellan, Co Down BT31 9UG
Tel 028-40650207 Fax 028-40650205

KILBRONEY (ROSTREVOR)
Very Rev Canon Michael Hackett PP
44 Church Street, Rostrevor,
Co Down BT34 3BB
Tel 028-41738277 Fax 028-41738315
Office: Tel 028-41739495

MAGHERADROLL (BALLYNAHINCH)
Very Rev Canon Gerard McCrory PP
Church Street, Ballynahinch,
Co Down BT24 8LP
Tel/Fax 028-97562410
Rev Desmond Loughran CC
Drumaness, Ballynahinch,
Co Down BT24 8NG
Tel 028-97561432
Parish Office: 028-97565429

MAGHERALIN
Very Rev Brian Brown PP
25 Bottier Road, Moira, Craigavon,
Co Armagh BT67 0PE
Tel 028-92611347
Parish Office: 028-92617435

MOYRAVERTY (CRAIGAVON)
Very Rev Martin McAlinden PP, VF
The Presbytery, 11 Tullygally Road,
Legahory, Craigavon BT65 5BL
Tel 028-38341901
Email martinmcalinden@hotmail.com

Rev Desmond Mooney CC
The Presbytery, 13 Tullygally Road,
Legahory, Craigavon BT65 5BY
Tel 028-38343297
Email mooneydesmond@hotmail.com
Rev Krzysztof Olejnik (SC) CC
12 Tullygally Road,
Legahory, Craigavon BT65 5BL
Tel 028-38311872
Parish Office: Moyraverty,
10 Tullygally Road
Tel 028-38343013

SAVAL
Very Rev Canon Francis Boyle PP
4 Shinn School Road, Newry,
Co Down BT34 1PA
Tel/Fax 028-40630276

SEAGOE (DERRYMACASH)
Very Rev Canon Cathal Jordan PP
6 Derrymacash Road, Lurgan,
Co Armagh BT66 6LG
Tel 028-38341356

SEAPATRICK (BANBRIDGE)
Very Rev Canon Liam Stevenson PP, VF
6 Scarva Road, Banbridge,
Co Down BT32 3AR
Tel 028-40662136
Rev Anthony Corr CC
100 Dromore Street, Banbridge,
Co Down BT32 4DW
Tel 028-40622274 Fax 028-40622847
Parish Office
Tel 028-40624950 Fax 028-40626547
Email parishseapatrick@btconnect.com

SHANKILL, ST PAUL'S (LURGAN)
Very Rev Michael Maginn PP
Lisadell, 54 Francis Street,
Lurgan, Co Armagh BT66 6DL
Tel 028-38327173 Fax 028-38317974
Rev Andrew McMahon CC
St Paul's Presbytery, Old Portadown
Road, Lurgan, Co Armagh BT66 8RG
Tel 028-38326883 Fax 028-38321289
St Paul's Parish Office: Tel 028-38321289
Email parishsecretary@btinternet.com

SHANKILL, ST PETER'S (LURGAN)
Rt Rev Mgr Aidan Hamill PP, VG
70 North Street, Lurgan,
Co Armagh BT67 9AH
Tel 028-38323161
Rev Stephen Crossan CC
68 North Street, Lurgan,
Co Armagh BT67 9AH
Tel 028-38323161 Fax 028-38347927

TULLYLISH
Very Rev Gerald Powell PP
4 Holymount Road, Gilford, Craigavon
Co Armagh BT63 6AT
Tel 028-40624236 Fax 028-40625440
Email gpowell@aol.com
Rev Martin McDonagh (CSSp) CC
Hunter's Hill, Gilford, Co Armagh BT63 6AJ
Tel 028-38831256
Parish Office: Tel 028-40624236
Email tullylish.dromore@btinternet.com
Website www.tullylish.com

HOSPITALS AND THEIR CHAPLAINS

Craigavon Area Hospital
Co Armagh
Chaplains: Rev Martin McDonagh
Sr Fiona Galligan

District Hospital
Lurgan and Portadown, Co Armagh
Chaplain: Very Rev Michael Maginn PP

Hospice
Southern Area Hospice Services,
St John's House, Courtenay Hill, Newry,
Co Down BT34 2EB
Tel 028-30267711 Fax 028-30268492
Chaplain: Very Rev Jarlath Cushenan

PRIESTS OF THE DIOCESE ELSEWHERE

Rt Rev Mgr Hugh Connolly BA, DD
President, St Patrick's College,
Maynooth, Co Kildare
Rev Matthew McConville
c/o Bishop's House
Rev Feidlimidh Magennis LSS
St Mary's University College, Belfast

RETIRED PRIESTS

Very Rev Liam Boyle
9 Gargory road, Ballyward, Castlewellan,
Co Down BT31 9RN
Very Rev Arthur Byrne
Castor's Bay Road, Lurgan
Very Rev P. G. Conway
Warrenpoint Road, Newry, Co Down
Very Rev John Joe Cunningham
Newcastle, Co Down
Very Rev Canon Anthony Davies
Killowen, Rostrevor
Rev Gerard Green
c/o Bishop's House
Rev Charles Kelly, Lurgan
Very Rev Canon Desmond Knowles
Newry, Co Down
Very Rev Brendan McAteer
Warrenpoint, Co Down
Very Rev Arthur MacNeill
14 Ballyholland Road, Newry, Co Down
Very Rev Canon Patrick McAnuff
58 Armagh Road, Newry, Co Down
Very Rev John McCauley
40 Rathmore, Clonallon Road,
Warrenpoint, Co Down
Rev T. J. McGuinness
South Africa
Very Rev Francis Molloy
Lurgan, Co Armagh
Very Rev Oliver Mooney
Newry, Co Down
Rev John Murtagh, Warrenpoint
Very Rev Canon Joseph O'Hagan
Cabra, Hilltown
Very Rev James Poland
Rostrevor, Co Down

RELIGIOUS ORDERS AND CONGREGATIONS

PRIESTS

BENEDICTINES
Holy Cross Monastery, 119 Kilbroney Road,
Rostrevor, Co Down BT34 3BN
Tel 028-41739979 Fax 028-41739978
Superior
Dom Mark-Ephrem M. Nolan OSB
Email benedictinemonks@btinternet.com
Website www.benedictinemonks.co.uk

DOMINICANS
St Catherine's, Newry,
Co Down BT35 8BN
Tel 028-30262178 Fax 028-30252188
Prior: Very Rev Maurice Fearon (OP)

SOCIETY OF AFRICAN MISSIONS
Dromantine, Newry,
Co Down BT34 1RH
Tel 028-30821224 Fax 028-30821704
Superior: Rev Noel O'Leary (SMA)

Dromantine Retreat and Conference
Centre
Newry, Co Down BT34 1RH
Tel 028-30821964 Fax 028-30821963
Email admin@dromantineconference.com
Website www.dromantineconference.com
Director: Rev Desmond Corrigan (SMA)

SISTERS

CARMELITES
Carmelite Monastery of Mary
Immaculate and St Therese,
42 Glenvale Road, Newry,
Co Down BT34 2RD
Fax 028/048-30252778
Email nuns@carmelitesglenvale.org
Prioress: Sr M. Carmel Clarke
Community: 4

CONGREGATION OF THE SISTERS OF MERCY
'Stillpoint' Providence House,
Lurgan, Co Armagh BT67 9JN
Tel 028-38322300
Leader: Sr Carmel McNally
Community: 3

Convent of Mercy, Catherine Street,
Newry, Co Down BT34 6JG
Tel 028-30262065/30264964
Contact: Sr Perpetua McArdle
Community: 11

1 Home Avenue,
Newry, Co Down BT34 2DL
Community: 4
Tel 028-30267141

Sisters of Mercy, Arbour House,
16 Great George's Street South,
Warrenpoint, Co Down BT34 3HR
Tel 028-41774181
Services to people with learning
difficulties

Convent of Mercy, 3 Glenashley,
Rostrevor, Co Down BT34 3FW
Tel 028-41738356
Community: 3

14 Victoria Place, Lurgan,
Co Armagh BT67 9DL
Tel 028-38348602

89 North Street, Lurgan,
Co Armagh BT67 9AH
Tel 028-38347858

Convent of Mercy, 9 Queen Street,
Warrenpoint, Co Down BT34 3HZ
Tel 028-41752221
Community: 3

12 Cloghogue Heights, Newry,
Co Down BT35 8BA
Tel 028-30261628

Sisters of Mercy, Edward Street,
Lurgan, Co Armagh BT66 6DG
Tel 028-38322635
Community: 8

No 4 Ummericam Road, Silverbridge,
Newry, Co Down BT35 9PB
Tel 028-30860441

33 Church Street,
Warrenpoint, Co Down BT34 3HN

8 The Woodlands,
Lower Dromore Road,
Warrenpoint, Co Down BT34 6WL
Tel 028-41752383

17 Oakleigh Grove, Lurgan,
Co Armagh BT67 9AY
Tel 028-38347984

Convent of Mercy,
42 Antrim Road,
Lurgan, Co Armagh BT67 9BW
Tel 028-38347415

Sisters of Mercy, 6 Portadown Road,
Lurgan, Co Armagh BT66 8QW
Tel 028-38327956

204 Drumglass, Craigavon,
Co Armagh BT65 5BB
Tel 028-38343266

8 Parkhead Crescent, Newry,
Co Down BT35 8PE
Tel 028-30264615

16 Oakleigh Fold, North Street,
Lurgan, Co Armagh BT67 9BS
Tel 028-38348852

Sisters of Mercy, 49 Ardfreelan,
Rathfriland Road, Newry,
Co Down BT34 1CD
Tel 028-30250951

Sisters of Mercy, 2 Carrickree,
Bridle Loanan, Co Down BT34 3FA
Tel 028-41752347

Allianz (ⅼⅼⅼ)

27 Catherine Street, Newry,
Co Down, BT35 6JG
Tel 028-30833641

Rose Cottage,
14 Drumbanagher Wall Road,
Drumbanagher, Newry,
Co Down BT35 6LR
Tel 028-30821425

78 Chapel Street,
Newry, Co Down BT34 2DN
Tel 028-30265342

76 Chapel Street,
Newry, Co Down BT34 2DN
Tel 028-30266309

80 Chapel Street,
Newry, Co Down
Tel 028-30265184

15 Bracken Grove, Armagh Road,
Newry, Co Down BT35 4PG
Tel 028-30250630

MISSIONARY FRACISCAN SISTERS OF THE IMMACLATE CONCEPTION
28 Hawtorn Avenue,
Lurgan, Co Armagh BT66 6DU
Tel 028-38316958
Email elisegorman@btinternet.com

MISSIONARY SISTERS OF THE ASSUMPTION
Assumption Convent,
34 Crossgar Road, Ballynahinch,
Co Down BT24 8EN
Tel 028-97561765 Fax 028-97565754
Email mail@assumption.org
Superior: Sr Ursula Hinchion
Email srursula@msassumption.org
Community: 11
Assumption Grammar School
Tel 028-97562250
Pupils: 880

MISSIONARY SISTERS OF OUR LADY OF APOSTLES
Rostrevor, Newry, Co Down
Tel 028-41737653 Fax 028-417377656
Community: 4
Email olagreendale@hotmail.com
1 Greendale Crescent, Greenpark Road,
Rostrevor, Newry, Co Down BT34 3HF

SISTERS OF ST CLARE
St Clare's Convent, Ashgrove, Newry,
Co Down BT34 1PR
Contact: Sr Tarcsius Traynor
Community: 33
St Clare's Primary School, High Street,
Newry, Co Down BT34 1HD
Tel 028-30264909. Pupils: 665

St Clare's Convent,
75 Upper Damolly Road,
Newry, Co Down BT34 1QW
Tel 028-30268471. Community: 4
Sacred Heart Grammar School,
10 Ashgrove Avenue, Newry, Co Down
Tel 028-30264632. Pupils: 875

ST JOHN OF GOD SISTERS
Southern Area Hospice Services,
St John's House, Courtenay Hill,
Newry, Co Down
Tel 028-30267711

EDUCATIONAL INSTITUTIONS

St Colman's College (Diocesan College)
Violet Hill,
Newry, Co Down
Tel 028-30262451
President: Very Rev Canon Francis Brown
Vice Principals: Mr Aidan Henry,
Mr Barry Kelly, Mr Michael Doyle

EDMUND RICE SCHOOLS TRUST NORTHERN IRELAND
St Colman's Abbey Primary School,
Courtenay Hill, Newry, Co Down BT34 2ED
Tel 028-30262175
Fax 028-30250648
Principal: Mr Eddie Sweeney

Abbey Christian Brothers' Grammar
School, Courtenay Hill,
Newry, Co Down BT34 2ED
Tel 028-30263142 Fax 028-30262514
Principal: Mr D. McGovern

CHARITABLE AND OTHER SOCIETIES

Accord
Cana House,
Newry Parish Pastoral Centre, The Mall,
Newry, Co Down
Tel 028-30263577

Society of St Vincent de Paul
Conferences at:
Ballynahinch (St Patrick's)
Banbridge (St Patrick's)
Craigavon (St Anthony's)
Dromore (St Colman's)
Gilford (St John's)
Hilltown (St John's)
Laurencetown (St Patrick's)
Lurgan (St Peter's)
Newry (Cathedral)
Newry (St Brigid's)
Rathfriland (St Marys)
Rostrevor (St Bronach's)
Warrenpoint (St Patrick's)

DIOCESE OF ELPHIN

PATRONS OF THE DIOCESE
ST ASICUS, 27 APRIL; IMMACULATE CONCEPTION, 8 DECEMBER

INCLUDES PORTIONS OF COUNTIES ROSCOMMON, SLIGO,
WESTMEATH AND GALWAY

Most Rev Christopher Jones DD
Bishop of Elphin;
born 1936;
ordained priest 21 June 1962;
ordained Bishop of Elphin
15 August 1994

Residence: St Mary's, Sligo
Tel 071-9162670/9162769
Fax 071-9162414
Email elphindo@eircom.net

CATHEDRAL OF THE IMMACULATE CONCEPTION, SLIGO

The 125-year-old cathedral church dominates the skyline of Sligo town. It was erected during the episcopate of Bishop Laurence Gillooly (1858–1895), whose knowledge of ecclesiastical architecture is imprinted on every stone.

The foundation stone was laid on 6 October 1868. It was designed by a renowned English architect, George Goldie, and was modelled on Normano-Romano-Byzantine style. It was acclaimed by an eminent architect as a 'poem in stone'. It is 275 feet long, with transepts and nave, and can accommodate 4,000 people. A square tower incorporating the main entrance to the cathedral is surmounted by a four-sided pyramidal spire which reaches a height of 210 feet. The stained-glass windows and the original high altar are magnificent works of art.

Although the cathedral was open for public worship in 1874, it wasn't until 1882 that all construction work was completed. The cathedral was finally consecrated on 1 July 1897 and dedicated in honour of the Immaculate Conception of the Blessed Virgin Mary.

The cathedral has undergone extensive renovations on two occasions since it was erected, including the remodelling of the sanctuary to comply with liturgical norms in 1970.

CHAPTER

Castlerea: Very Rev Joseph Fitzgerald
Athlone: Very Rev Liam Devine
Roscommon
Very Rev Eugene McLoughlin
Boyle: Very Rev Gerard Hanly
Strandhill: Very Rev Niall Ahern
Frenchpark: Very Rev Kevin Early
Strokestown: Very Rev Ciaran Whitney
Knockcroghery: Very Rev Peadar Lavin
Sligo: Very Rev Thomas Hever

ADMINISTRATION

Vicar General
Right Rev Mgr Gerard Dolan PP, VG
Rosses Point, Co Sligo
Tel 071-9177133

Vicars Forane
Very Rev Canon Eugene McLoughlin
Very Rev Canon Thomas Hever
Very Rev Canon Joseph Fitzgerald
Very Rev Canon Ciaran Whitney
Very Rev Canon Gerard Hanly
Very Rev Canon Liam Devine

Finance Committee
Secretary
Rt Rev Mgr Gerard Dolan VG
St Mary's, Sligo

Building Committee
Chairman
Very Rev Canon P. Lavin PP
Knockcroghery, Co Roscommon

Diocesan Secretary
Rt Rev Mgr Gerard Dolan VG
St Mary's, Sligo
Tel 071-9162670/9162769
Email elphindo@eircom.net

Assistant Diocesan Secretary
Rev Michael Duignan SThD
St Mary's, Sligo
Tel 071-9162670/9162679

CATECHETICS EDUCATION

Education (Post-Primary)
Secretary
Very Rev Canon Peadar Lavin PP
Knockcroghery, Co Roscommon
Tel 090-6661127

Education (Primary)
Secretary
Very Rev Austin McKeon PP
Tulsk, Castlerea, Co Roscommon
Tel 071-9639005

Religious Instruction (Primary Schools)
Diocesan Director
Sr Annette Duignan
Sisters of Mercy,
No. 1 St Patrick's Avenue, Sligo
Tel 071-9142731

LITURGY

Liturgical Music
Adviser Church Organ Music:
Mr Charles O'Connor
Maugheraboy, Sligo
Tel 071-9145722

Diocesan Liturgical Commission
Rev Ian Kennedy
The Parochial House, Ballinafad,
Boyle, Co Roscommon
Tel 071-9666006

Diocesan Magazine
The Angelus, St Mary's, Sligo
Tel 071-9162670
Editor: Very Rev A. B. O'Shea PP
Sooey, via Boyle, Co Sligo
Tel 071-9165144
Email aboshea@eircom.net

PASTORAL

Accord
Director: Rev James Murray CC
Carraroe, Sligo
Tel 071-9162136

Adoption Society
Director: Very Rev Thomas Hever VF
Sligo Social Services,
Charles Street, Sligo
Tel 071-9145682

Council of Priests
Chairman: Very Rev Michael Breslin PP
Ballygar, Co Galway
Tel 090-6624637
Secretary: Rev Ian Kennedy
Ballinafad, Co Sligo
Tel 071-9666006

CURA
Co-ordinator: Ms Grace Clarke
Sligo Social Services,
Charles Street, Sligo
Tel 071-9145682

Diocesan Pastoral Council
Secretary: Ms Marion McGowan
St Anne's, Sligo
Tel 071-9145028

Ecumenism
Rev Pat Lombard CC
St Mary's, Sligo
Tel 071-9162670

Family Ministry
Director: Very Rev Brian Conlon
Family Life Centre, Boyle, Co Roscommon
Tel 071-9633000

Laity Commission
Diocesan Representative
Miss Mary T. McLoughlin
Caltra, Ballinasloe, Co Galway
Tel 090-9678125

Marriage Tribunal
(See Marriage Tribunals section)
Pastoral Development
Diocesan Director: Dr Justin Harkin
Pastoral Development Office,
Church Grounds, Elphin Street,
Strokestown, Co Roscommon
Tel 071-9634960

Pilgrimage Directors (Lourdes)
Rev Hugh McGonagle CC
7 Elm Park, Ballinode, Sligo
Tel 071-9143430
Rev Raymond Milton CC
Drum, Athlone
Tel 090-6437125

Pioneer Total Abstinence Association
Diocesan Director
Very Rev Canon Liam Devine PP, VF
SS Peter and Paul, Athlone
Tel 090-6492171

Pontifical Mission Societies
Diocesan Director
Very Rev Ciaran Whitney PP, VF
Strokestown, Co Roscommon
Tel 071-9633027

Social Services
Director: Ms Christine McTaggart
Sligo Social Services, Charles Street, Sligo
Tel 071-9145682

Travellers
Chaplain: Rev John Carroll (SPS)
Cregg House, Rosses Point, Co Sligo
Tel 071-9177241

Vocations to the Permanent Diaconate
Director: Rev Michael Duignan
St Mary's, Sligo, Co Sligo
Tel 071-9162670

Vocations to the Priesthood
Directors: Rev James Murray
Carraroe, Sligo, Co Sligo
Tel 071-9162136
Rev John Coughlin
Deerpark Road, Athlone, Co Westmeath
Tel 090-6490575

Youth Ministry and Safeguarding Children
Diocesan Director: Mr Frank McGuinness
St Mary's, Sligo, Co Sligo
Tel 087-9880690

PARISHES

Mensal parishes are listed first. Other parishes follow alphabetically. Historical names are given in parentheses.

SLIGO, ST MARY'S
Very Rev Canon Thomas Hever Adm, VF
Rev Patrick Lombard CC
In Residence: Rev Gerard Cryan
St Mary's, Sligo
Tel 071-9162670/9162769

SLIGO, CALRY ST JOSEPH'S
Very Rev Noel Rooney PP
279 Sunset Drive, Cartron Point, Sligo
Tel 071-9142422
Rev Hugh McGonagle CC
7 Elm Park, Ballinode, Sligo
Tel 071-9143430

SLIGO, ST ANNE'S
Very Rev Dominic Gillooly PP
Tel 071-9145028
Rev Stephen Walshe (CSSp) CC
Tel 071-9145028
St Anne's, Sligo
Rev James Murray CC
Carraroe, Co Sligo
Tel 071-9162136

AHASCRAGH (AHASCRAGH AND CALTRA)
Rev Kevin Reynolds (MHM) PC
Ahascragh, Ballinasloe, Co Galway
Tel 090-9688617
Rev Mícheál Donnelly CC
Caltra, Ballinasloe, Co Galway
Tel 090-9678125

ATHLEAGUE (ATHLEAGUE AND FUERTY)
Very Rev John Leogue PP
Athleague, Co Roscommon
Tel 090-6663338

ATHLONE, SS PETER AND PAUL'S
Very Rev Canon Liam Devine PP, VF
SS Peter and Paul's, Athlone
Tel 090-6492171
Rev John McManus (SPS) CC
10 Ashford, Monksland,
Athlone, Co Westmeath
Tel 090-6493262
Rev John Coughlan CC
Deerpark Road, Athlone,
Co Westmeath
Tel 090-6490575
Rev Raymond Milton CC
Drum, Athlone, Co Westmeath
Tel 090-6437125

AUGHRIM (AUGHRIM AND KILMORE)
Very Rev Edward Moore PP
Aughrim, Hillstreet,
Carrick-on-Shannon, Co Roscommon
Tel 071-9637010

BALLAGH (CLOONTUSKERT, KILGEFIN AND CURRAGHROE)
Very Rev Raymond A. Browne PP
Kilrooskey, Roscommon
Tel 090-6626273
Rev Larry Shine (CSSp) CC
Ballyleague, Lanesboro, Co Longford
Tel 043-21171

BALLINAFAD (AGHANAGH)
Very Rev Ian Kennedy PC
Ballinafad, Boyle,
Co Roscommon
Tel 071-9666006

BALLINAMEEN (KILNAMANAGH AND ESTERSNOW)
Very Rev Francis McGauran PP
Ballinameen, Boyle, Co Roscommon
Tel 071-9668104

BALLINTUBBER (BALLINTOBER AND BALLYMOE)
Very Rev Oliver McDonagh PP
Ballintubber, Castlerea, Co Roscommon
Tel 094-9655226

BALLYFORAN (DYSART AND TISRARA)
Very Rev Francis Beirne PP
Four Roads, Roscommon
Tel 090-6623313

BALLYGAR (KILLIAN AND KILLERORAN)
Very Rev Michael Breslin PP
Ballygar, Co Galway
Tel 090-6624637
Very Rev Thomas Beirne CC
Newbridge, Ballinasloe, Co Galway
Tel 090-6660018

BOYLE
Very Rev Canon Gerard Hanly PP, VF
Tel 071-9662218
Rev Alan Conway CC
Tel 071-9662012
Boyle, Co Roscommon

CASTLEREA (KILKEEVAN)
Very Rev Canon Joseph Fitzgerald PP, VF
Tel 094-9620040
Rev Michael McManus CC
Tel 094-9620039
Castlerea, Co Roscommon

CLIFFONEY (AHAMLISH)
Very Rev Christopher McHugh PP
Grange, Co Sligo
Tel 071-9163100
Rev Padraig Flanagan (SPS) CC
Cliffoney, Co Sligo
Tel 071-9166133

CLOVERHILL (ORAN)
Very Rev Francis Glennon PP
Cams, Roscommon
Tel 090-6626275
Rev Thomas Leahy (SPS) CC
Ballinaheglish, Co Roscommon
Tel 090-6662229

COOTEHALL (ARDCARNE)
Very Rev Brian Conlon PC
Cootehall, Boyle,
Co Roscommon
Tel 071-9667004

CREGGS (GLINSK AND KILBEGNET)
Very Rev Gerard McCarthy (SVD)
Donamon Castle, Co Roscommon
Tel 090-6662222

CROGHAN (KILLUKIN AND KILLUMMOD)
Very Rev Martin Mulvaney PP
Drumlion, Carrick-on-Shannon,
Co Roscommon
Tel 071-9620415

DRUMCLIFF/MAUGHEROW
Very Rev Michael Donnelly PP
Drumcliff, Sligo
Tel 071-9142779

ELPHIN (ELPHIN AND CREEVE)
Very Rev John J Gannon PP
Elphin, Co Roscommon
Tel 071-9635058
Very Rev James Tighe CC
Elphin, Co Roscommon
Tel 071-9635131

FAIRYMOUNT (TIBOHINE)
Very Rev James Creaton PC
Fairymount, Castlerea,
Co Roscommon
Tel 094-9870243

FOURMILEHOUSE (KILBRIDE)
Very Rev Raymond Browne PP
Fourmilehouse, Roscommon
Tel 090-6629518

FRENCHPARK (KILCORKEY AND FRENCHPARK)
Very Rev Canon Kevin Early PP
Frenchpark, Castlerea, Co Roscommon
Tel 094-9870105
Rev Brendan Sherry CC
Ballinagare, Castlerea, Co Roscommon
Tel 094-9870410

GEEVAGH
Very Rev Laurence Cullen PP
Geevagh, Boyle,
Co Roscommon
Tel 071-9647107

KILGLASS (KILGLASS AND ROOSKEY)
Rev Eamonn Conaty (SSC) CC
Rooskey, Carrick-on-Shannon,
Co Roscommon
Tel 071-9638014
Rev Edmund Prendergast (MHM) CC
Kilglass, Co Roscommon
Tel 071-9638162

KILTOOM (KILTOOM AND CAM)
Very Rev John Cullen PP
Kiltoom, Athlone, Co Roscommon
Tel 090-6489105
Rev Hugh Lee (MHM) CC
Curraghboy, Athlone, Co Roscommon
Tel 090-6488143

KNOCKCROGHERY (ST JOHN'S)
Very Rev Canon Peadar Lavin PP
Knockcroghery, Roscommon
Tel 090-6661127
Rev Donal Morris CC
St John's, Lecarrow, Roscommon
Tel 090-6661115

LOUGHGLYNN (LOUGHGLYNN AND LISACUL)
Very Rev John O'Rourke PP
Loughglynn, Castlerea, Co Roscommon
Tel 094-9880007
Rev Brendan McDonagh (SPS) CC
Lisacul, Castlerea, Co Roscommon
Tel 094-9880068

RIVERSTOWN
Very Rev A. B. O'Shea PP
Sooey, Coola, via Boyle, Co Sligo
Tel 071-9165144
Email aboshea@eircom.net

ROSCOMMON
Very Rev Canon Eugene McLoughlin PP, VF
Parochial House, Roscommon
Tel 090-6626298
Rt Rev Mgr Charles Travers CC
1 Convent Court, Roscommon
Tel 090-6628917
Rev Kevin Fallon CC
Curate's Residence, Roscommon
Tel 090-6626189
Rev Sean Beirne CC
Kilteevan, Roscommon
Tel 090-6626374
Rev James Heneghan (CSSp)
(Chaplain to Brazilian Community)
12 Abbeyville, Roscommon
Tel 090-6627978

ROSSES POINT
Rt Rev Mgr Gerard Dolan PP, VG
St Columba's, Rosses Point, Co Sligo
Tel 071-9177133

STRANDHILL/RANSBORO
Very Rev Canon Niall Ahern PP
Strandhill, Co Sligo
Tel 071-9168147
Rev Christopher McCrann (LC) CC
Knocknahur, Sligo
Tel 071-9128470

STROKESTOWN (KILTRUSTAN, LISSONUFFY AND CLOONFINLOUGH)
Very Rev Ciaran Whitney PP, VF
Strokestown, Co Roscommon
Tel 071-9633027

TARMONBARRY
Very Rev Eamonn O'Connor PP
Tarmonbarry, Longford
Tel 043-26020

TULSK (OGULLA AND BASLIC)
Very Rev Austin McKeon PP
Tulsk, Castlerea, Co Roscommon
Tel 071-9639005
Rev Peter Gillooly (SPS) CC
Kilmurray, Castlerea, Co Roscommon
Tel 094-9651018

INSTITUTIONS AND THEIR CHAPLAINS

Ballinode Vocational School
Sligo
Tel 071-9147111
Very Rev Noel Rooney PP

Castlerea Prison
Tel 094-9625278
Email chaplaincastlereaprison@eircom.net
Prison General Office: 094-9625213

Christian Brothers School,
Roscommon
Tel 090-6626189
Rev Kevin Fallon CC

Convent of Mercy
Mullaghmore, Co Sligo
Tel 071-9166345
Rev Michael Glynn

Coola Vocational School
Riverstown, Boyle, Co Roscommon
Tel 071-9165144
Very Rev A. B. O'Shea PP

Cregg House, Sligo
Tel 071-9177241
Rev John Carroll (SPS)

Custume Barracks
Athlone, Co Westmeath
Tel 090-6421277
Rev Gerard Dowd CF

Grange Vocational School, Sligo
Tel 071-9163100
Very Rev Christopher McHugh PP

Nazareth House, Sligo
Tel 071-9162278
Chaplain: Vacant

Plunkett Home
Boyle, Co Roscommon
Tel 071-9662012
Rev Alan Conway CC

Post-Primary School, Elphin,
Co Roscommon
Tel 071-9635058
Very Rev John J Gannon PP

Post-Primary School, Strokestown
Co Roscommon
Tel 071-9633041
Very Rev Ciaran Whitney PP

Roscommon Hospital
Tel 090-6620039
Rev Seán Beirne CC

St Angela's College
Lough Gill, Co Sligo
Tel 071-9143580
Rev Michael Duignan SThD

St Cuan's College
Castleblakeney, Ballinasloe, Co Galway
Tel 090-9678127
Rev Michéal Donnelly CC

St Mary's Post-Primary School
Ballygar, Co Galway
Tel 090-664637
Very Rev Michael Breslin PP

Sligo General Hospital
St Columba's, St John's
Tel 071-9171111
Chaplains: Rev J. Carroll,
Rev B. Conway

Sligo Institute of Technology
Tel 071-9155215
Rev Declan Brady

Vocational School, Roscommon
Rev Kevin Fallon CC
Roscommon
Tel 090-6626189

PRIESTS OF THE DIOCESE ELSEWHERE
Rev Anthony Conry, Brazil
Rev Michael Drumm STL
Columba Centre, Maynooth, Co Kildare
Very Rev Joseph Gilmartin
Churchfield Presbytery, Knock, Co Mayo
Very Rev Brian Hanley
Ballyhard, Glenamaddy, Co Galway

RETIRED PRIESTS
Very Rev Seamus Cox
Ballyleague, Co Roscommon
Rev Thomas Garvey
Kilconnell, Ballinasloe
Very Rev Cyril Haran, Grange, Co Sligo
Rev Colm Hayes
15 St Patrick's Terrace, Sligo
Very Rev Canon Gerald Donnelly
Ballygar, Co Galway
Very Rev Canon Patrick Murray
27 Ardbrea Park, Baylough, Athlone
Very Rev Patrick McHugh
22 Rosehill, Sligo
Rev Liam Sharkey
Ballyweelin, Rosses Point, Co Sligo

RELIGIOUS ORDERS AND CONGREGATIONS

PRIESTS

DIVINE WORD MISSIONARIES
Donamon Castle,
Roscommon
Tel 090-6662222
Fax 090-6662511
Rector: Rev Gerard McCarthy (SVD)
Email gearoidmccarthy@o2.ie

DOMINICANS
Holy Cross, Sligo
Tel 071-9142700
Fax 071-9146533
Prior: Very Rev Timothy Mulcahy (OP)

SISTERS

CONGREGATION OF THE SISTERS OF MERCY
43 Battery Heights, Athlone,
Co Westmeath
Tel 090-6494748
Community: 3

Sisters of Mercy, 3 Newtown Terrace,
Athlone, Co Westmeath
Tel 090-6473944 Fax 090-6474134
Community: 4

Sisters of Mercy, Dún Mhuire,
Lyster Street, Athlone, Co Westmeath
Tel 090-6494166 Fax 090-6440079
Community: 23

Sisters of Mercy, Cois Abhann,
Lyster Street, Athlone, Co Westmeath
Community: 19

Sisters of Mercy, Bethany,
Chapel Hill, Sligo
Tel 071-9138498
Community: 5

Our Lady of Mercy,
3 St Patrick's Avenue, Sligo
Tel 071-9142731 Fax 071-9147090
Community: 12

Sisters of Mercy,
No 1 St Patrick's Avenue, Sligo
Tel 071-9142393
Community: 3

Sisters of Mercy,
No 2 St Patrick's Avenue, Sligo
Tel 071-9145755
Community: 3

Sisters of Mercy,
8 Cleveragh Road, Sligo
Tel 071-9162074
Community: 2

Sisters of Mercy,
1 Racecourt Manor,
Tonaphubble, Sligo
Tel 071-9154656
Community: 3

Convent of Mercy,
Mullaghmore, Co Sligo
Tel 071-9176722 Fax 071-9176710
Community: 3
Retreat house

McAuley House,
Roscommon
Tel 090-6627904 Fax 090-6627581
Community: 7

Sisters of Mercy, Knockaire,
Galway Road, Roscommon
Tel 090-6625897 Fax 090-6626065
Community: 3

Sisters of Mercy,
Crubyhill, Roscommon
Tel 090-6625725
Community: 3

Convent of Mercy,
St Catherine's, Roscommon
Tel 090-6626767
Community: 4

Convent of Mercy,
Castlerea, Co Roscommon
Tel 094-9620127 Fax 094-9621249
Community: 5

Convent of Mercy,
Boyle, Co Roscommon
Tel 071-9662144 Fax 071-9662745
Community: 8

Galilee Community,
Sisters of Mercy, Tintagh,
Boyle, Co Roscommon
Tel 071-9664101 Fax 071-9664684
Community: 3

Lisroyne,
Strokestown, Co Roscommon
Tel 071-9633056
Community: 4

Breedogue, Co Roscommon
Tel 094-9870020
Community: 1

CONGREGATION OF THE SISTERS OF NAZARETH
Nazareth House, Sligo
Tel 071-9162278 Public
Tel 071-9160664 Fax 071-9160344
Tel Convent 071-9154446
Superior: Sr Bernardine Hannon
Email bhannan@hotmail.co.uk
Community: 10
Home for the elderly. Beds 50
Nursing Home now managed by
Nazareth House Management
Committee Ltd, Sligo
Director of Service: Claire Reynolds
Tel 071-9180900

DISCIPLES OF THE DIVINE MASTER
8 Castle Street, Athlone, Co Westmeath
Tel 090-6498755 *(Community)*
090-6492278 *(Liturgical Centre)*
Fax 090-6492649
Email pddmathlone@gmail.com
liturgicalcentre@gmail.com
Sister-in-Charge: Sr Maria Sonia Cerdenia
Community: 5
Contemplative-apostolic, perpetual
adoration, Liturgical apostolate,
distributors and producers of high-
quality Liturgical art, vestments, church
goods, private retreats, prayer groups.

LA SAGESSE (DAUGHTERS OF WISDOM)
Cregg House, Rosses Point, Co Sligo
Tel 071-9177229 Fax 071-9177439
Community: 3
St Cecilia's Special School and Cregg
House Residential and Day Centre.
Care of adults and children with a
learning disability.
Number in care: 215

35 The Park,
Strandhill Road, Sligo
Tel 071-9154019
Community: 2

12 The Greenlands, Rosses Point, Sligo
Tel 071-91977607
Community: 2

Weatherly, Ballincar, Sligo
Tel 071-9194299
Co-ordinator: Sr Maureen Seddon DW
Community: 2

MISSIONARIES OF CHARITY
Temple Street, Sligo
Tel 071-9154843
Superior: Sr Joseph
Community: 6
Contemplative

PRESENTATION OF MARY SISTERS
4 Lower John Street, Sligo
Tel 071-9160740
Superior: Sr Elenita Baguio (PM)
Email elenitabaguio@yahoo.fr
Community: 5

SISTERS OF ST JOSEPH OF THE APPARITION
St Joseph's Convent, Garden Hill, Sligo
Tel 071-9162330 (Convent)
Fax 071-9152500
Email stjsligo@eircom.net
Contact: Sr Magdalen Ennis
Community: 12

URSULINES
Ursuline Convent, Temple Street, Sligo
Tel 071-9161538
Local Leader: Sr Fidelma McDermott
Community: 11
Primary School
Tel 071-9154573 Fax 071-9154573
Secondary School
Tel 071-9161653 Fax 071-9146141

St Angela's College of Education
Lough Gill, Sligo
Tel 071-9143580 Fax 071-9144585
Email ursulines@stacs.edu.ie
Website www.stacs.edu.ie
President: Anne Taheny
St Ursula's Community House
Tel 071-9147218/47238
Local Leader: Sr Moya Hegarty
Community: 6

Ursuline Sisters,
'Brescia', Ballytivnan, Sligo
Community: 2
Pastoral Ministry

EDUCATIONAL INSTITUTIONS

College of the Immaculate Conception
Summerhill, Sligo
Tel 071-9160311
Acting Principal: Mr Tommy McManus
Clerical Staff
Rev Gerard Cryan BA, HDE, STB, L Eccl Hist

St Aloysius College
Athlone, Co Westmeath
Tel 090-6494153
Principal: Mr Gearoid O'Conamha

St Joseph's College
Summerhill, Athlone, Co Roscommon
Tel 090-6492383
Principal: Mrs Mary Fahy

St Cuan's College
Castleblakeney,
Ballinasloe, Co Galway
Tel 090-9678127
Principal: Mr Martin Giblin

EDMUND RICE SCHOOLS TRUST
Meán Mhuire na mBráithre,
Roscommon Town
Tel 090-6626496/6626279
Principal: Mr Pat Hanlon

CHARITABLE AND OTHER SOCIETIES

Family Life Centres
St Michael's Family Life Centre
Church Hill, Sligo
Tel 071-9170329
Director: Ms Eileen Sheridan

Boyle Family Life Centre
Knocknashee, Boyle, Co Roscommon
Tel 071-9663000
Director: Very Rev Brian Conlon

Vita House
Roscommon
Tel 090-6625898
Director: Sr Mary Lee

Cuan Aire Family Centre
Castlerea, Co Roscommon
Tel 094-9620057

Legion of Mary
Assumpta House, John Street, Sligo

Social Services Centre
Charles Street, Sligo
Tel 071-9145682

Society of St Vincent de Paul
Conferences at Athlone, Boyle, Castlerea,
Roscommon, Sligo

DIOCESE OF FERNS

PATRON OF THE DIOCESE
ST AIDAN, 30 JANUARY

INCLUDES ALMOST ALL OF COUNTY WEXFORD
AND PART OF COUNTY WICKLOW

Most Rev Denis Brennan DD
Bishop of Ferns
Ordained Bishop 23 April 2006

Contact: Bishop's House,
Summerhill, Wexford
Tel 053-9122177
Fax 053-9123436

ST AIDAN'S CATHEDRAL, ENNISCORTHY

The foundation stone for St Aidan's Cathedral, Enniscorthy, was laid in 1843. The cathedral was designed by the architect Augustus Welby Northmore Pugin and is the largest church Pugin built in Ireland. The recent renovations of 1996 have restored to a great extent the original beautiful building as visualised by Pugin. The external stonework was executed by Irish stonemasons who were praised by Pugin. The restored stencilling of the interior gives some idea of what Pugin visualised for his churches.

Pugin, a Londoner, was as important an influence on the history of nineteenth-century English architecture as Frank Lloyd Wright was to be on American architecture. He was an extraordinarily gifted artist and designed ceramics, stained glass, wallpapers, textiles, memorial brasses, church plate, etc. His connection with the Diocese of Ferns came through the patronage of John, 16th Earl of Shrewsbury, Waterford and Wexford. Shrewsbury's wife was a native of Blackwater, Co Wexford. Her uncle, John Hyacinth Talbot, was the first Catholic MP for Co Wexford after Catholic Emancipation in 1829. A rich man through his marriage into the Redmond family, John Hyacinth Talbot introduced Pugin to Wexford, where through the patronage of the Talbot and Redmond family connections, he was to gain most of his Irish commissions.

Pugin was to die through overwork at the age of forty in 1852, but he has left a unique diocesan heritage to Ferns in his churches. His son and son-in-law, E.W. Pugin and George Ashlin, were to continue the building of Gothic Revival churches and monuments in Ireland.

Most Rev Brendan Comiskey DD
Retired Bishop of Ferns
PO Box 40, Summerhill, Wexford

CHAPTER

Right Rev Mgr Patrick Corish
Very Rev James B. Curtis
Right Rev Mgr Joseph L. Kehoe
Very Rev Seán McCarthy
Very Rev Nicholas Power
Very Rev Brendan Kirby
Very Rev James Finn
Very Rev Seamus De Val
Very Rev Thomas Curtis
Very Rev Felix Byrne
Very Rev Noel Hartley
Very Rev Lorenzo Cleary

ADMINISTRATION

College of Consultors
Right Rev Mgr Joseph L. Kehoe PA
Very Rev Denis Lennon
Very Rev Joseph McGrath
Very Rev Patrick Cushen
Very Rev James Hammel
Very Rev Noel Canon Hartley
Very Rev Anthony O'Connell
Very Rev Aidan Kavanagh
Very Rev James Byrne
Very Rev Richard Hayes
Very Rev Brian Broaders
Very Rev John Jordan

Vicar General
Very Rev Joseph McGrath VF, VG
New Ross, Co Wexford
Tel 051-421348

Vicars Forane
Very Rev Patrick Cushen
Very Rev Joseph McGrath
Very Rev Denis Lennon
Very Rev John Sweetman

Diocesan Finance Council
Very Rev Patrick Cushen VF
Very Rev James Fegan Adm
Very Rev William Howell PP
Mr Pat Kent
Mrs Catherine O'Gara
Mr Liam Gaynor
Mr John Murphy
Mr Patrick F. Dore
Ms Eleanor Furlong
Finance Officer and Chairman
Mr Eugene Doyle

Diocesan Archivist
Very Rev Seamus Canon De Val
1 Irish Street, Bunclody, Co Wexford
Tel 053-9376140

Bishop's Secretary
Miss Theresa Gleeson
Bishop's Office,
Summerhill, Wexford
Tel 053-9122177
Email adm@ferns.ie

Diocesan Secretary
Rev John Carroll
PO Box 40, Bishop's House,
Summerhill, Wexford
Tel 053-9124368
Email jc@ferns.ie

Chancellor
Rev Kevin Cahill
PO Box 40, Bishop's House,
Summerhill, Wexford
Tel 053-9165108
Email kcahill@ferns.ie

CATECHETICS EDUCATION

Catholic Primary School Management Association (CPSMA)
Rev Francis Murphy CC
Gorey, Co Wexford
Tel 053-9421117

Diocesan Adviser for Primary School Catechetics
Rev John Paul Sheridan CC
Blackwater, Enniscorthy, Co Wexford
Tel 053-9129288

Director of Religious Education
Sr Anna McDonagh
Ferns Diocesan Centre
Tel 053-9145511

PASTORAL

Apostolic Work Society
Diocesan Director
Very Rev Joseph Power PP
Kilrush, Bunclody, Co Wexford
Tel 053-9377262

Chaplain to Special Needs Groups
Very Rev Tom Dalton PP
Rathangan, Co Wexford
Tel 051-563104

CORI (Ferns Branch)
Secretary: Sr Anna McDonagh
Ferns Diocesan Centre
Tel 053-9145511

Diocesan Mission Commission
Chairman: Very Rev Denis Lennon PP
39 Beechlawn, Wexford
Tel 053-9124417

Ecumenism
Director: Very Rev Aidan G. Jones PP
Bunclody, Enniscorthy, Co Wexford
Tel 053-9377319

FDYS Youth Work Ireland
Director
Mr Kieran Donohoe,
Francis Street, Wexford
Tel 053-9123262

Fatima Pilgrimage
Director
Very Rev Thomas Doyle PP
Craanford, Gorey, Co Wexford
Tel 053-9428163

House of Mission
Rev Thaddeus Doyle
Shillelagh, Arklow, Co Wicklow
Tel 053-9429926

ISANDS
Contact Person: Jean Wafer
Wexford General Hospital
Tel 053-9142233
Chaplain: Rev Ken Quinn
General Hospital, Wexford
Tel 053-9142233

Knights of St Columbanus
Rev John Power (OSA)
St Augustine's Priory, New Ross,
Co Wexford
Tel 051-421237

Knock Pilgrimage
Director: Very Rev Oliver Sweeney PP
Poulfur, Fethard-on-Sea, New Ross,
Co Wexford
Tel 051-397048

Legion of Mary
(Northern Curia)
Very Rev Seamus De Val
1 Irish Street, Bunclody, Co Wexford
Tel 053-9376140 (Southern Curia)
Very Rev Brendan Nolan PP
Our Lady's Island, Co Wexford
Tel 053-9131167

Lourdes Pilgrimage
Director: Rev Richard Lawless CC
St Aidan's Cathedral,
Enniscorthy, Co Wexford
Tel 053-9235777

Marriage Tribunal
(See also Marriage Tribunals section)
Ferns Diocesan Auditor for Dublin Regional Marriage Tribunal
Rev Kevin Cahill (OCL) CC
Ballymitty, Wexford
Tel 051-561128/053-9165108

Our Lady's Island Pilgrimage
Director: Very Rev Brendan Nolan PP
Our Lady's Island, Broadway,
Co Wexford
Tel 053-9131167

Pioneer Total Abstinence Association
Diocesan Director
Rev Michael Byrne CC
Boolavogue, Ferns, Co Wexford
Tel 053-9233530

Pontifical Mission Societies
Diocesan Director
Very Rev Hugh O'Byrne PP
Blackwater, Co Wexford
Tel 053-9127118

St Aidan Retirement Fund
Chairman
Very Rev Joe Power PP
Kilrush, Bunclody, Co Wexford
Tel 053-9377262

St Joseph's Young Priests' Society
Diocesan Chaplain
Very Rev Joseph McGrath PP
New Ross, Co Wexford
Tel 051-421348

Travellers
Diocesan Co-ordinator
Rev Ken Quinn
Traveller Resource Centre,
Mary Street, New Ross,
Co Wexford
Tel 051-422272

Vocations
Director
Very Rev James Finn PP
Crossabeg, Co Wexford
Tel 053-9159015

PARISHES

Mensal parishes are listed first. Other parishes follow alphabetically.

ENNISCORTHY, CATHEDRAL OF ST AIDAN
Very Rev Denis Kelly Adm
Rev Patrick Sinnott CC
Rev Richard Lawless CC
St Aidan's, Enniscorthy, Co Wexford
Tel 053-9235777
Fax 053-9237700

WEXFORD
Very Rev James Fegan Adm
Rev Michael O'Shea CC
Rev Aodhan Marken CC
Rev Brian Whelan CC
The Presbytery,
12 School Street, Wexford
Tel 053-9122055 Fax 053-9121724

ADAMSTOWN
Very Rev Robert Nolan PP
Adamstown, Enniscorthy,
Co Wexford
Tel 053-9240512

ANNACURRA
Very Rev James Hammel PP
Annacurra, Aughrim, Co Wicklow
Tel 0402-36119

BALLINDAGGIN
Very Rev John Sinnott PP
Ballindaggin, Enniscorthy,
Co Wexford
Tel 053-9388559
Rev Fintan Morris CC
Kiltealy, Enniscorthy, Co Wexford
Tel 053-9255124

BALLYCULLANE
Very Rev Laurence O'Connor PP
Ballycullane, New Ross, Co Wexford
Tel 051-562123
Rev Patrick Banville CC
St Leonard's, Saltmills, New Ross,
Co Wexford
Tel 051-562135
Very Rev Sean Laffan CC
Gusserane, Co Wexford
Tel 051-562111

BALLYGARRETT
Very Rev James Butler PP
Ballygarrett, Gorey, Co Wexford
Tel 053-9427330

BALLYMORE AND MAYGLASS
Very Rev Martin Byrne PP
Ballymore, Killinick, Co Wexford
Tel 053-9158966

BANNOW
Very Rev James Kehoe PP
Carrig-on-Bannow,
Wellington Bridge, Co Wexford
Tel 051-561192
Rev Kevin Cahill (OCL) CC
Ballymitty, Co Wexford
Tel 051-561128

BLACKWATER
Very Rev Hugh O'Byrne PP
Tel 053-9127118
Rev John Paul Sheridan CC
Tel 053-9129288
Blackwater, Enniscorthy,
Co Wexford

BREE
Very Rev Aidan Kavanagh PP
Bree, Enniscorthy, Co Wexford
Tel 053-9247843
Rev Matthew Boggan CC
Galbally, Ballyhogue, Enniscorthy,
Co Wexford
Tel 053-9247814

BUNCLODY
(*Parish office:* Tel/Fax 054-76190)
Very Rev Aidan G. Jones PP
Tel 053-9377319
Rev James Doyle CC
Tel 053-9377264
Bunclody, Enniscorthy, Co Wexford
Rev Gabriel Barros IVE
Kilmyshall, Enniscorthy, Co Wexford
Tel 053-9377188

CAMOLIN
Very Rev Joseph Kavanagh PP
Camolin, Co Wexford
Tel 053-9383136
Rev Thomas Orr CC
Ballycanew, Gorey, Co Wexford
Tel 053-9427184

CARNEW
Very Rev Martin Casey PP
Woolgreen, Carnew, Co Wicklow
Tel 053-9426888
Rev William Byrne CC
Coolfancy, Tinahely, Co Wicklow
Tel 0402-34725

CASTLEBRIDGE
Very Rev Walter Forde PP
Castlebridge, Co Wexford
Tel 053-9159769 Fax 053-9159158
Rev James Fitzpatrick CC
Galbally, Curracloe, Co Wexford
Tel 053-9137140

CLONARD
(*Parish office:* Tel 053-9123672
Fax 053-9146699)
Very Rev Denis Lennon PP
39 Beechlawn, Wexford
Tel 053-9124417
Rev James Moynihan CC
6 Meadowvale, Coolcotts, Wexford
Tel 053-9143932
Rev Martin Doyle CC
1 Clonard Park, Wexford
Tel 053-9147686

CLONGEEN
Very Rev Colm Murphy PP
Clongeen, Foulksmills, Co Wexford
Tel 051-565610

CLOUGHBAWN
Very Rev Richard Hayes PP
Clonroche, Enniscorthy, Co Wexford
Tel 053-9244115
Rev Robert McGuire CC
Poulpeasty, Clonroche,
Enniscorthy, Co Wexford
Tel 053-9244116

CRAANFORD
Very Rev Thomas Doyle PP
Craanford, Gorey, Co Wexford
Tel 053-9228163
Very Rev Felix Canon Byrne CC
Monaseed, Gorey, Co Wexford
Tel 053-9428207

CROSSABEG AND BALLYMURN
Very Rev James Finn PP
Crossabeg, Co Wexford
Tel 053-9159015

CUSHINSTOWN
Very Rev Michael Byrne PP
Cushinstown, Foulksmills, Co Wexford
Tel 051-428347
Rev Odhran Furlong CC
Rathgarogue, New Ross, Co Wexford
Tel 051-424521

DAVIDSTOWN AND COURTNACUDDY
Very Rev James Nolan PP
Davidstown, Enniscorthy,
Co Wexford
Tel 053-9233382

DUNCANNON
Very Rev John P. Nolan PP
Duncannon, New Ross,
Co Wexford
Tel 051-389118

FERNS
Very Rev Patrick Cushen PP, VF
Ferns, Enniscorthy, Co Wexford
Tel 053-9366152
Rev Richard Redmond CC
(Ballyduff) The Square, Ferns,
Enniscorthy, Co Wexford
Tel 053-9366162

GLYNN
Very Rev Patrick Stafford PP
Glynn, Enniscorthy, Co Wexford
Tel 053-9128115
Rev John Carroll CC
(Diocesan Secretary)
Barntown, Co Wexford
Tel 053-9120853

GOREY
Very Rev William Howell PP
St Michael's, Gorey, Co Wexford
Tel 053-9421112
Rev Frank Murphy CC
Rev Thomas Conroy CC
Tel 053-9421117
St Patrick's, Gorey, Co Wexford

HORESWOOD
Very Rev Gerald O'Leary PP
Horeswood, Campile, Co Wexford
Tel 051-388129
Rt Rev Mgr Donald Kenny CC
Ballykelly, New Ross, Co Wexford
Tel 051-422729

KILANERIN
Very Rev Patrick O'Brien PP
Kilanerin, Gorey, Co Wexford
Tel/Fax 0402-37120
Rev Michael Doyle CC (Tyler, Texas)
Ballyfad, Gorey, Co Wexford
Tel 0402-37124

KILLAVENEY
Very Rev Raymond Gahan PP
Killaveney, Tinahely, Co Wicklow
Tel 0402-38188
Rev Donal Berney CC
St Kevin's, Tinahely, Co Wicklow
Tel 0402-38138

KILMORE
Very Rev Denis Doyle PP
Kilmore, Co Wexford
Tel 053-9135181
Rev James Cogley CC
Kilmore Quay, Co Wexford
Tel 053-9129638
Rev Patrick O'Conor (SSC) CC
Mulrankin, Co Wexford
Tel 053-9135166

KILMUCKRIDGE (LITTER)
Very Rev Seamus Larkin PP
Kilmuckridge, Gorey, Co Wexford
Tel 053-9130116
Rev John Byrne CC
Monamolin, Gorey, Co Wexford
Tel 053-9389223

KILRANE AND ST PATRICK'S
Very Rev Diarmuid Desmond PP
Kilrane, Co Wexford
Tel 053-9133128

KILRUSH AND ASKAMORE
Very Rev Joseph Power PP
Kilrush, Bunclody, Co Wexford
Tel 053-9377262

MARSHALLSTOWN
Very Rev Daniel McDonald PP
Marshallstown, Enniscorthy,
Co Wexford
Tel 053-9388521
Rev James Lennon CC (Hexham &
Newcastle)
Castledockrell, Ballycarney, Enniscorthy,
Co Wexford
Tel 053-9388569

MONAGEER
Very Rev William Cosgrave PP
Monageer, Ferns, Enniscorthy,
Co Wexford
Tel 053-9233530
Rev Michael Byrne CC
Boolavogue, Ferns, Wexford
Tel 053-9366282

NEWBAWN
Very Rev Thomas McGrath PP
Newbawn, Co Wexford
Tel 051-428227
Very Rev James Furlong CC
Raheen, Clonroche, Co Wexford
Tel 051-428328

NEW ROSS
Very Rev Joseph McGrath PP, VF
New Ross, Co Wexford
Tel 051-421348
Rev Tomás Kehoe CC
Rev Roger O'Neill CC
Tel 051-421214
New Ross, Co Wexford

OULART
Very Rev John Jordan PP
Oulart, Gorey, Co Wexford
Tel 053-9136139
Rev Dermot Gahan CC
The Ballagh, Wexford
Tel 053-9136200

OUR LADY'S ISLAND AND TACUMSHANE
Very Rev Brendan Nolan PP
Our Lady's Island, Broadway,
Co Wexford
Tel 053-9131167

OYLEGATE
Very Rev Tobias Kinsella PP
Oylegate, Co Wexford
Tel 053-9138163
Rev William Flynn CC
Glenbrien, Enniscorthy, Co Wexford
Tel 053-9138112

PIERCESTOWN AND MURRINTOWN
Very Rev John O'Reilly PP
Piercestown, Co Wexford
Tel 053-9158851

RAMSGRANGE
Very Rev Bernard Cushen PP
Ramsgrange, New Ross,
Co Wexford
Tel 051-389148

RATHANGAN AND CLEARIESTOWN
Very Rev Thomas Dalton PP
Rathangan, Duncormick,
Co Wexford
Tel 051-563104
Very Rev James Ryan (priest in residence)
Cleariestown, Co Wexford
Tel 053-9139110

RATHNURE AND TEMPLEUDIGAN
Very Rev Anthony O'Connell PP
Rathnure, Co Wexford
Tel 054-55122

THE RIVERCHAPEL, COURTOWN HARBOUR
Very Rev John Sweetman PP
The Riverchapel, Courtown Harbour,
Gorey, Co Wexford
Tel 053-9425241

ST SENAN'S, ENNISCORTHY
Parish office: Tel 053-9237611
Very Rev Brian Broaders Adm
Rev Patrick Browne CC
The Presbytery, Templeshannon,
Enniscorthy, Co Wexford
Tel 053-9237611

TAGHMON
Very Rev Seán Gorman PP
Taghmon, Co Wexford
Tel 053-9134123
Rev David Murphy CC
Caroreigh, Taghmon, Co Wexford
Tel 053-9134113

TAGOAT
Very Rev Matthias Glynn PP
Tagoat, Co Wexford
Tel 053-9131139
Rev James Murphy CC
St Brigid's, Rosslare, Co Wexford
Tel 053-9132118

TEMPLETOWN AND POULFUR
Very Rev Oliver Sweeney PP
Poulfur, Fethard-on-Sea,
New Ross, Co Wexford
Tel 051-397113

INSTITUTIONS AND THEIR CHAPLAINS

Community School
Gorey, Co Wexford
Tel 053-9421000
Chaplain: Rev Thomas Conroy

Loreto Convent, Wexford
Rev James Cashman
1 Pinewood, Wexford

Vocational College Wexford
Rev David Murphy CC
Caroreigh, Taghmon, Co Wexford
Tel 053-9134113

Wexford General Hospital
Tel 053-9142233
Chaplain: Rev Ken Quinn
General Hospital, Wexford
Tel 053-9142233

Community School
Ramsgrange
Tel 051-389211
Chaplain: Rt Rev Mgr Donald Kenny

St John of God Convent
Very Rev Sean Canon McCarthy
Loma, Newtown Road, Wexford

PRIESTS OF THE DIOCESE ELSEWHERE IN IRELAND

Right Rev Mgr Patrick Corish DD
St Patrick's College,
Maynooth, Co Kildare
Tel 01-6285222
Rev Patrick Mernagh CF
McKee Barracks,
Blackhorse Avenue, Dublin 7
Rev Peter O'Connor
10 Cranfield Place, Dublin 4

PRIESTS OF THE DIOCESE ABROAD

Rev Thomas Brennan, USA
Rev Denis Browne, Brazil
Rev Sean Devereux
The Gambia, West Africa
Rev Oliver Doyle
Diocese of Great Falls, Billings, Montana,
USA
Rev Chris Hayden
Pontifical Irish College,
Via de SS Quattro 1, Roma 00184, Italy
Rev Willam Swan
Pontifical Irish College,
Via de SS Quattro 1, Roma 00184, Italy

RETIRED PRIESTS

Very Rev James Byrne
Ballylannon, Wellingtonbridge,
Co Wexford
Very Rev Matthew L. Cleary
The Stables, Bridgetown, Co Wexford
Most Rev Brendan Comiskey (SSCC) DD
PO Box 40, Wexford

Very Rev James Curtis
3 Oldtown Court, Clongreen, Foulksmills,
New Ross, Co Wexford
Very Rev James B. Canon Curtis
Rathjarney, Drinagh, Co Wexford
Rev Thomas Canon Curtis
2 The Hollows, Lugduff, Tinahely,
Co Wicklow
Very Rev Seamus Canon De Val
1 Irish Streeet, Bunclody, Co Wexford
Very Rev Thomas Eustace
The Cools, Barntown, Wexford
Very Rev James Canon Finn
c/o 76 Corish Park, Wexford
Very Rev John French
Horeswood, New Ross, Co Wexford
Tel 051-593196
Very Rev Noel Canon Hartley
10 Donovan's Wharf, Crescent Quay,
Wexford
Very Rev Liam Jordan
c/o Bishop's House, Wexford
Rt Rev Mgr J.L. Kehoe VG, PA
13 Priory Court, Spawell Road, Wexford
Very Rev Brendan Canon Kirby
9 Kilmartin Hill, Wicklow,
Co Wicklow
Very Rev Sean Canon McCarthy
Loma, Newtown Road, Wexford
Rev John O'Brien
Elmfield Mews, Spawell Road,
Wexford
Very Rev Nicholas Canon Power
Moorfield, Rathaspeck, Co Wexford
Very Rev James Ryan
Cleariestown, Co Wexford

RELIGIOUS ORDERS AND CONGREGATIONS

PRIESTS

AUGUSTINIANS
St Augustine's Priory, New Ross,
Co Wexford
Tel 051-421237
Prior: Rev Michael Collender (OSA)
Community: 9

Good Counsel College,
New Ross, Co Wexford
Tel 051-421663/421909
Fax 051-421909

St Augustine's Priory,
Grantstown, New Ross, Co Wexford
Tel 051-561119
Superior: Rev Aidan O'Leary (OSA)
Community: 1

BROTHERS

CHRISTIAN BROTHERS
Christian Brothers' House,
Joseph Street, Wexford
Tel 053-45659
Community Leader: Br E. Kinsella
Community: 6

SISTERS

CARMELITES
Mount Carmel Monastery,
New Ross, Co Wexford
Prioress: Sr Margaret Mary Morris
Community: 11
Contemplatives
Altar breads

CONGREGATION OF THE SISTERS OF MERCY
Convent of Mercy,
Clonard Road, Wexford
Tel 053-23024
Contact: Sr Martina Hayes
Primary School,
St John's Road, Wexford

Sisters of Mercy,
52 Westlands, Wexford
Tel 053-42917
Contact: Sr Susan Kavanagh

Convent of Mercy, St Brigid's,
Rosslare Strand, Co Wexford
Tel 053-32104
Contact: Sr Mercy Kilroy
Primary School

Convent of Mercy, Templeshannon,
Enniscorthy, Co Wexford
Tel 054-33156/33940
Leader: Sr Monica Crowley

Sisters of Mercy, Lower South Knock,
New Ross, Co Wexford
Tel 051-425340
Contact: Sr Mary Hahesy
St Joseph's Primary School

'Misericordia', 1 Tower Grove,
New Ross, Co Wexford
Tel 051-422027
Contact: Cecilia McGinn

DAUGHTERS OF CHARITY OF ST VINCENT DE PAUL
Cluain Mhuire, Gorey Road, Carnew,
Arklow, Co Wicklow
Tel 053-9426371
Superior: Sr Mary Crosbie
Community: 4
Residential housing for elderly, day care
centre, parish work

FAITHFUL COMPANIONS OF JESUS
St Mary's Convent,
Bunclody, Co Wexford
Tel 053-9377117
Leader: Sr Beatrice Molyneux
Community: 3
Secondary School (Coeducational)
Counselling
FCJ Secondary School
Tel 053-9377308 Fax 053-9377981
Principal: Mrs Frances Threadgold

Allianz (ⅲ)

FAMILY OF ADORATION
St Aidan's Monastery of Adoration,
Ferns, Co Wexford
Tel 053-9366634
Email staidansferns@eircom.net
Superior: Sr Dolores O'Brien
Community: 3
Contemplative life with adoration of the
Eucharist. 6 hermitages for private
retreats. Icon reproduction workshop.
The Centre for Contemplative Outreach
Ireland – Facilitating Centering Prayer
Retreats
Email contemplativeoutreachireland@
gmail.com

MISSIONARY SISTERS OF THE HOLY
ROSARY
Parish House, Terrerath,
New Ross, Co Wexford
Tel 051-428313
Community: 3
Pastoral

LORETO (IBVM)
Loreto Community, Railway Road,
Gorey, Co Wexford
Tel 055-21257
Email lorqor@indigo.ie
Superior: Sr Helen O'Riordan
Community: 9
Primary School

Conabury,
11 Newtown Court, Wexford
Tel 053-43470
Superior: Sr Helen O'Riordan
Community: 3
Secondary School

NOTRE DAME DES MISSIONS (OUR LADY
OF THE MISSIONS SISTERS)
60 Pineridge,
Summerhill, Wexford
Tel 053-9143170
Contact: Sr Anna McDonagh
Community: 1
RE Adviser

PERPETUAL ADORATION SISTERS
Perpetual Adoration Convent,
Bride Street, Wexford Town,
Co Wexford
Tel 053-9124134
Email adoration44@eircom.net
Superior: Sr Peter Leech
Community: 12
Perpetual adoration of the Blessed
Sacrament
Altar breads, vestments, altar linen

PRESENTATION SISTERS
Presentation Convent, Wexford
Tel 053-22504
Superior: Sr Vera Dalton
Community: 11
Secondary School
Tel 053-24133/24138 Fax 053-24048

ST JOHN OF GOD SISTERS
St John of God Congregational Centre,
1 Summerhill Heights, Wexford
Tel 053-9142396 Fax 053-9141500
Email stjohnogoffice@eircom.net
Congregational Leader
Sr Bríd Ryan

St John of God Convent,
Newtown Road, Wexford
Tel 053-9142276
Resident Leader: Sr Anne Kenny
Community: 24
Primary School, The Faythe, Wexford
Tel 053-9123105

St John of God Sisters,
Kilpatrick, Kyle,
Crossabeg, Wexford
Tel 053-9128481
Community: 3
(Sisters of Ely Hospital)

St John of God Convent, Ballyvaloo,
Blackwater, Co Wexford
Tel 053-9137160
Community: 5
Holiday and retreat house

St John of God Sisters,
26 The Orchard, Bellefield,
Enniscorthy, Co Wexford
Tel 053-9233079
Community: 2

St John of God Sisters,
Moorefield House, Loreto Village,
Enniscorthy, Co Wexford
Community: 3
Sheltered home for the elderly

St John of God Sisters,
6 Parkside, Stoneybatter,
Wexford
Tel 053-9146058
Community: 3

St John of God Sisters,
Ard Coilm, 15 Millpark,
Castlebridge, Co Wexford
Tel 053-9159862
Community: 2

St John of God Sisters,
1 Beechville, Clonard, Wexford
Tel 053-9142601
Community: 2

St John of God Sisters,
26 Mansfield Drive,
Coolcots, Wexford
Tel 053-9144427
Community: 2

St John of God Sisters,
2 Farnogue Drive,
Newlands, Wexford
Tel 053-9146149
Community: 2

St John of God Sisters,
Caritas, Glenbrook,
Newtown Road, Wexford
Tel 053-9143752
Community: 3

St John of God Sisters,
9 Farnogue Drive,
Newlands, Wexford
Tel 053-9140537
Community: 2

ST LOUIS SISTERS
Convent of St Louis,
Ramsgrange,
Co Wexford
Tel 051-389119
Community: 6
Varied apostolates

EDUCATIONAL
INSTITUTIONS

St Peter's Diocesan College
Tel 053-9142071
Principal: Mr Pat Quigley
Chaplain/Counsellor
Rev Aodhan Marken

EDMUND RICE SCHOOLS TRUST
New Ross, Co Wexford
Secondary School
Tel 051-21384/22976
Fax 051-425961
Principal: Mr Pat Rossiter

Scoil na mBráithre (Primary School),
Green Street, Wexford
Tel 053-41324/22186
Email edmundusc.ias@eircom.net
Principal: Mr Jos Furlong

Coláiste Eamonn Rís,
Thomas Street, Wexford
Tel 053-41391/24067
Fax 053-46803
Email admin@wexfordcbs.org
Website www.wexfordcbs.org
Principal: Mr Michael McMahon

Christian Brothers Secondary School
Enniscorthy, Co Wexford
Tel 054-34330/35308 Fax 054-36424
Email cbsenniscorthy@eircom.net
Principal: Mr John Ryan

CHARITABLE AND OTHER
SOCIETIES

Aiseiri
Roxborough House, Wexford
Tel 053-9141818

Christian Media Trust
Tel 053-9145176

CURA
Tel 053-9122255

FDYS Youth Work Ireland
Wexford
Tel 053-9123262/9123358

Society of St Vincent de Paul
17 Conferences in the Diocese of Ferns
South Ferns President
Mrs Kitty Hynes
2 Mary Street, Wexford
Tel 053-9124989
North Ferns President
Mr D, Sheehan
Rafter Street, Enniscorthy,
Co Wexford
Tel 053-9233511

Traveller Resource Centre
Tel 051-422272

Special Schools
Our Lady of Fatima, Wexford
Tel 053-9123376
St John of God, Enniscorthy
Tel 053-9233419

St Patrick's, Enniscorthy
Tel 053-9233657
Dawn House, Wexford
Tel 053-9145351
Community Workshop
Enniscorthy Ltd
Tel 053-9233069
Community Workshop
New Ross Ltd
Tel 051-421956

DIOCESE OF GALWAY, KILMACDUAGH AND KILFENORA

PATRONS OF THE DIOCESE
GALWAY – OUR LADY ASSUMED INTO HEAVEN, 15 AUGUST
KILMACDUAGH – ST COLMAN, 29 OCTOBER
KILFENORA – ST FACHANAN, 20 DECEMBER

INCLUDES PORTIONS OF COUNTIES GALWAY, MAYO AND CLARE
KILFENORA IS IN THE PROVINCE OF CASHEL BUT THE BISHOP OF GALWAY AND
KILMACDUAGH IS ITS APOSTOLIC ADMINISTRATOR

Most Rev Martin Drennan DD
Bishop of Galway;
born 2 January 1944;
ordained priest 16 June 1968;
ordained Auxiliary Bishop of
Dublin 21 September 1997;
installed Bishop of Galway
3 July 2005

Residence: Mount Saint Mary's,
Taylor's Hill, Galway
Tel 091-563566
Fax 091-528536
Email
galwaydiocese@eircom.net
Website www.galwaydiocese.ie

CATHEDRAL OF OUR LADY ASSUMED INTO HEAVEN AND ST NICHOLAS, GALWAY

In 1484, the Church of St Nicholas in Galway became a collegiate church, with a warden and vicars. However, with the Reformation, after 1570, the Catholic people of Galway lost the right to practise their religion publicly. Mass was celebrated in private houses until the rigour of persecution moderated and a parish chapel was built in Middle Street about 1750. The Diocese of Galway was established in 1831, and the parish chapel became its pro-cathedral. A fund for the building of a more fitting cathedral was inaugurated in 1876 and was built up by successive bishops. In 1883 the Diocese of Kilmacduagh was joined with Galway, and the Bishop of Galway was made Apostolic Administrator of Kilfenora.

In 1941, Galway County Council handed over Galway Jail to Bishop Michael Browne as a site for the proposed new cathedral. The jail was demolished, and in 1949 John J. Robinson of Dublin was appointed architect for the new cathedral. Planning continued until 1957, when Pope Pius XII approved the plans submitted to him by Dr Browne. Cardinal D'Alton, the Archbishop of Armagh, blessed the site and the foundation stone on 27 October 1957. The construction, which began in February 1958, was undertaken by Messrs John Sisk Ltd of Dublin. The people of the diocese contributed to a weekly collection, and donations were received from home and abroad. The total cost, including furnishing, was almost one million pounds.

Pope Paul VI appointed Cardinal Richard Cushing, Archbishop of Boston, Pontifical Legate to dedicate the cathedral. The cathedral was dedicated on the Feast of the Assumption, 15 August 1965.

Most Rev Eamonn Casey DD
Born 1927; ordained priest June 1951;
ordained Bishop of Kerry 9 November
1969; translated to Galway 19 September
1976; resigned 6 May 1992.
Residence: Shanaglish, Gort, Co Galway

CHAPTER

Rt Rev Mgr Malachy Hallinan VG
Sacred Heart Church, Galway
Members
Rt Rev Mgr Seán O'Flaherty
The Cathedral
Very Rev Canon Noel Mullin,
Claregalway
Very Rev Canon Michael Kelly,
Craughwell
Very Rev Canon Patrick Considine,
Rosmuc
Very Rev Canon Eamonn Dermody
Clarinbridge
Very Rev Canon Richard Tarpey,
Ennistymon
Very Rev Canon John O'Dwyer,
Oranmore
Very Rev Canon Seán Manning
St Mary's College
Very Rev Canon Patrick Callanan,
Kilbeacanty
Very Rev Canon Francis Larkin,
Kinvara
Very Rev Canon Richard Higgins,
Ardrahan

ADMINISTRATION

Vicar General
Rt Rev Mgr Malachy Hallinan PP, VG
Church of the Sacred Heart,
Seamus Quirke Road, Galway
Tel 091-522713

Vicars Forane
Rt Rev Mgr Malachy Hallinan PP, VG
Rt Rev Mgr Séan O'Flaherty PP
Very Rev Canon Michael Kelly PP
Very Rev Peter Rabbitte PP
Very Rev Canon Noel Mullin PP

Consultors
Rt Rev Mgr Malachy Hallinan PP, VG
Rt Rev Mgr Seán O'Flaherty PP, VF
Very Rev Canon Noel Mullin PP, VF
Very Rev Peter Rabbitte PP, VF
Very Rev Martin Glynn PP
Rev Barry Horan

Finance Committee
Most Rev Martin Drennan, Chairman
Rt Rev Mgr Malachy Hallinan PP, VG
Rt Rev Mgr Sean O'Flaherty PP, VF
Mr John Rafferty
Miss Una Fleming
Rev Ian O'Neill
Mr Thomas Kilgarriff, Secretary

Financial Administrator
Mr Thomas Kilgarriff
Diocesan Office, The Cathedral, Galway
Tel 091-563566

Diocesan Development (Meitheal)
Director: Mr Thomas Kilgarriff,
Diocesan Office, The Cathedral, Galway
Tel 091-563566
Chairperson: Most Rev Martin Drennan
Members
Rt Rev Mgr Sean O'Flaherty PP, VF
Mr Frank Canavan
Mr Prionsias Ó Máille
Mrs Breda Ryan
Mrs Dairin Coen
Mr Pat McCambridge
Mr Cathal Nagle

Diocesan Secretary
Rev Ian O'Neill
Diocesan Office, The Cathedral, Galway
Tel 091-563566 Fax 091-568333
Email galwaydioceseion@eircom.net

CATECHETICS EDUCATION

Primary Education
Diocesan Adviser: Sr Breda Coyne (RJM)
Diocesan Pastoral Centre, Árus De Brún,
Newtownsmith, Galway
Tel 091-575050
Mr Tom O'Doherty (Irish schools)
Tel 091-565066

Post-Primary Education
Post-Primary Schools Religious Education
Co-ordinator: Margaret McCarrick
27 Devon Gardens, Salthill, Galway
Tel 087-2306831

LITURGY

Liturgical Committee
Chairperson: Rev Alan Burke
Chaplain, University Hospital Galway
Tel 091-524222
Members
Sr Breda Coyne,
Rev James Walsh Adm
Mr Ray O'Donnell

Sacred Music
Diocesan Director
Mr Raymond O'Donnell MA, HDE, LTCL
Tel 091-563577/087-2241365
Fax 091-534881
Email music@galwaycathedral.ie

PASTORAL

Accord
Árus de Brún, Newtownsmith, Galway
Tel 091-562331
Diocesan Director
Rev Murchadh Ó Madagáin CC
Renmore, Galway
Tel 091-757859

Apostolic Work Society
President: Mrs Ita Meehan
34 Rockbarton Road, Salthill, Galway
Tel 091-521890
Secretary: Mrs Eileen Flannery
102 Hazel Park, Newcastle, Galway
Tel 091-523845

Brazilian Community
Chaplain: Rev Kevin Keenan (SVD)
26 Cloonarkin Drive,
Oranmore, Co Galway
Tel 091-788823

**Catholic Primary School Managers'
Association**
Diocesan Education Office
Pastoral Centre, Árus de Brún,
Newtownsmith, Galway
Tel 091-565066
Co-ordinator: Mr P. J. Callanan

Child Protection Office
Tel 091-575051
Ms Ita O'Mahony
Diocesan Pastoral Centre,
Arús de Brún,
Newtownsmith, Galway

Communications Committee
Secretary: Rev Seán McHugh PP
Spiddal, Co Galway
Tel 091-533155
Email cilleinde@eircom.net

CURA
Pastoral Centre, Árus de Brún,
Newtownsmith, Galway
Tel 091-562558

Diocesan Archivist
Mr Tom Kilgarriff
Tel 091-563566
Email galwaydiocesetk@eircom.net

Diocesan Pastoral Centre
Árus de Brún,
Newtownsmith, Galway
Tel 091-565066
Acting Director: Mrs Eileen Kelly

Diocesan Pilgrimage Committee
Chairman
Rt Rev Mgr Seán O'Flaherty PP, VF
The Cathedral, Galway
Tel 091-563577
Chaplain to the Sick
Very Rev Des Forde PP
Ballyvaughan, Co Clare
Tel 065-7077045
Pilgrimage Director
Very Rev Martin Moran PP
Rosscahill, Co Galway
Tel 091-550106

Diocesan Youth Faith Development
Diocesan Pastoral Centre,
Árus de Brún, Newtownsmith,
Galway
Tel 091-565066

Drug Misuse Prevention
Contact Person
Rev David Cribbin, Chaplain
University Hospital, Galway
Tel 091-524222

Ecumenism
Rev Conor Cunningham CC
Galilee House, Monksfield,
Salthill, Galway
Tel 091-585693

Emigrants Committee
Director
Very Rev Gearóid Ó Griofa PP
Gort, Co Galway
Tel 091-631055
Secretary
Very Rev Michael Reilly PP
Castlegar, Galway
Tel 091-751548

Laity Commission
Chairman
Rt Rev Mgr Séan O'Flaherty PP, VF
The Cathedral, Galway
Tel 091-563577
Diocesan Representative
Mrs Grace Semple
c/o The Diocesan Office,
The Cathedral, Galway
Tel 091-563566

Legion of Mary
Annunciata House,
15 Fr Griffin Road, Galway
Tel 091-521871
Contact: Mr Bernard Finan
Chaplain: Rev Martin Keane
Tel 091-796106

Marriage Tribunal
Officials: Rev Michael Byrnes
Rev Barry Horan
(see also Marriage Tribunals section)

Missions Committee
Chairman
Very Rev Martin Downey PP
24 Presentation Road, Galway
Tel 091-562276
Secretary
Mrs Ita Meehan
Diocesan President, Apostolic Work,
c/o Diocesan Office,
The Cathedral, Galway

Diocesan Council of Priests
Most Rev Martin Drennan
Rt Rev Mgr Malachy Hallinan PP, VG
Rt Rev Mgr Sean O'Flaherty PP, VF
Very Rev Canon Noel Mullin PP, VF
Vry Rev Canon Michael Kelly PP, VF
Very Rev Peter Rabbitte PP, VF

Members
Very Rev Gerard Jennings
Rev Conor Cunningham *(Chairman)*
Very Rev Seán McHugh
Very Rev Joseph Roche
Very Rev Derek Feeney

Very Rev Barry Hogg
Very Rev Canon Edward Kelly PE
Rev Michael Screene (MSC)
Rev Alan Burke *(Secretary)*
Rev Barry Horan
Very Rev Michael McLoughlin
Very Rev Martin Downey
Very Rv Canon Eamonn Dermody

Pioneer Total Abstinence Association
Diocesan Director
Very Rev Canon Patrick Callanan PP
Kilbeacanty, Gort, Co Galway
Tel 091-631691

Pontifical Mission Societies
Diocesan Director
Rev Michael Connolly CC
Lakeview House, Barnacranny,
Bushypark, Galway
Tel 091-588622

St Joseph's Young Priests' Society
Diocesan Chaplain
Rev Sean Kilcoyne
Chaplain, Bon Secours Hospital,
Renmore, Galway
Tel 091-757711

Travellers
Rev Adrian McGrath
Chaplain, GMIT, Dublin Road, Galway
Tel 091-753161

Trócaire
Diocesan Director
Very Rev Martin Downey PP
24 Presentation Road, Galway
Tel 091-562276

Vocations Team
Director: Rev Diarmuid Hogan
Chaplain, NUI, Galway
Tel 091-495055
Email diarmuid.hogan@nuigalway.ie

Youth
Youth Office, Ozanam House,
St Augustine Street, Galway
Tel 091-562434/568483

PARISHES

Church titulars, if different from parish name, are in italics.

CATHEDRAL
Our Lady Assumed into Heaven and St Nicholas
Right Rev Mgr Séan O'Flaherty PP, VF
Tel 091-563577
Rev Martin Whelan CC
18 University Road, Galway
Tel 091-524875/563577
Email cathedralparishoffice@eircom.net

City Parishes

BALLYBANE
St Brigid
Very Rev John D. Keane
St Brigid's, Ballybane, Galway
Tel 091-755381

GOOD SHEPHERD
Very Rev Martin Glynn PP
129 Túr Uisce, Doughiska, Galway
Tel 091-756823
Email goodshepherdgalway@gmail.com
Website www.goodshepherdgalway.com

MERVUE
Holy Family
Very Rev William Cummins PP
Mervue, Galway
Tel 091-751721
Rev Robert McNamara (CSsR) CC
Curate's House, Walter Macken Road,
Mervue, Galway
Tel 091-771662

RENMORE
St Oliver Plunkett
Very Rev Michael Mulkerrins PP
Tel 091-751707
Rev Murchadh Ó Madagáin CC
Tel 091-757859
Renmore Avenue, Renmore, Galway

SACRED HEART CHURCH
Rt Rev Mgr Malachy Hallinan PP, VG
Tel 091-522713
Rev David Murphy CC
Tel 091-524751
Email davidmurphy2000@eircom.net
The Presbytery, Seamus Quirke Road,
Galway

ST AUGUSTINE'S
Very Rev Richard Lyng (OSA) PP
St Augustine's Priory,
St Augustine's Street, Galway
Tel 091-562524
Email rlyng@indigo.ie

ST FRANCIS
Very Rev Pádraig Breheny (OFM) PP
Rev Hilary Steblecki (OFM) CC
The Abbey, St Francis Street, Galway
Tel 091-562518

ST JOHN THE APOSTLE
Very Rev Tadhg Quinn PP
St John the Apostle,
Knocknacarra, Galway
Tel 091-590059
Rev Kevin Keenan (SVD) AP
26 Cloonarkin Drive,
Oranmore, Co Galway
Tel 087-9905755

ST JOSEPH'S
Very Rev Martin Downey PP
24 Presentation Road, Galway
Tel 091-562276
Rev Michael Connolly CC
Lakeview House, Barnacranny,
Bushypark, Galway
Tel 091-588622

ST MARY'S
PP to be appointed
Rev John O'Reilly (OP) CC
Rev Denis Murphy (OP) CC
St Mary's Priory, The Claddagh, Galway
Tel 091 582884

ST PATRICK'S
Very Rev Patrick Whelan PP
Tel 091-567994
Rev Ian O'Neill (In residence)
Tel 091-563813
St Patrick's Presbytery,
Forster Street, Galway

SALTHILL
Christ the King
Very Rev Gerard Jennings PP
Tel 091-523413
Rev Conor Cunningham CC
Tel 091-585693
Rev Michael Baily (OFM) CC
Tel 091-526006
Curate's House, Monksfield,
Salthill, Galway
Email salthillparish@eircom.net

TIRELLAN
Resurrection
Very Rev Augustine O'Brien (MSC) PP
Rev Gerard Thornton (MSC) CC
Church of the Resurrection,
Headford Road, Galway
Tel 091-762883
Email ballinfoyleparish@eircom.net

Country Parishes

ARDRAHAN
St Teresa's
Very Rev Joseph Roche (Adm)
Ardrahan, Co Galway
Tel 091-635164

BALLINDEREEN
St Colman's
Very Rev Anthony Minniter PP
Ballindereen, Kilcolgan, Co Galway
Tel 091-796118

BALLYVAUGHAN
St John the Baptist
Very Rev Desmond Forde PP
Ballyvaughan, Co Clare
Tel 065-7077045

BARNA
Mary Immaculate Queen
Very Rev Francis Lee PP
Barna, Galway
Tel 091-592173
Very Rev Dean Thomas Kyne AP
Réalt na Mara, Furbo, Co Galway
Tel 091-592457

CARRON AND NEW QUAY
St Columba's, Carron,
St Patrick's, New Quay
Very Rev Enda Glynn PP
Rev Colm Clinton (SPS) *(Adm protem)*
New Quay, Co Clare
Tel 065-7078026

CASTLEGAR
St Columba's
Very Rev Michael Reilly PP
Castlegar, Co Galway
Tel 091 751548
Email frmreilly@eircom.net

CLAREGALWAY
Assumption and St James
Very Rev Canon Noel Mullin PP, VF
Claregalway, Co Galway
Tel 091-798104
Email claregalwayparish@eircom.net

CLARINBRIDGE
Annunciation of the BVM
Very Rev Canon Eamonn Dermody PP
Clarinbridge, Co Galway
Tel 091-796208
Email ederm@eircom.net

CRAUGHWELL
St Colman's
Very Rev Canon Michael Kelly PP, VF
Craughwell, Co Galway
Tel 091-846057

ENNISTYMON
Our Lady and St Michael
Very Rev Derek Feeney PP
Tel 065-7071063
Very Rev Canon Richard Tarpey AP
Tel 065-7071346
Ennistymon, Co Clare

GORT/BEAGH
St Colman's and St Ann
Very Rev Thomas Marrinan PP
Tel 091-631220
Rev Gearóid Ó Griofa CC
Tel 091-631055
Gort, Co Galway

KILBEACANTY/PETERSWELL
St Columba and St Thomas Apostle
Very Rev Canon Patrick Callanan PP
Kilbeacanty, Gort, Co Galway
Tel 091-631691

KILCHREEST/CASTLEDALY
Nativity and Church of St Teresa
Very Rev Joseph Roche PP
Parochial House, Kilchreest,
Loughrea, Co Galway
Tel 091-840859

KILFENORA
St Fachanan's
Very Rev Edward Crosby PP
Kilfenora, Co Clare
Tel 065-7088006
Email kilfenoraparish@gmail.com

KINVARA
St Colman's
Very Rev Canon Francis Larkin PP
Tel 091-637154
Rev Edward Casey (SMA) CC
Tel 091-637283
Kinvara, Co Galway

LETTERMORE
Naomh Colmcille
Very Rev Michael Brennan PP
Lettermore, Co Galway
Tel 091-551169

LISCANNOR
St Brigid's
Very Rev Denis Crosby PP
Liscannor, Co Clare
Tel 065-7081248

LISDOONVARNA AND KILSHANNY
Corpus Christi
Very Rev Peter Rabbitte PP, VF
Lisdoonvarna, Co Clare
Tel 065-7074142

MOYCULLEN
Immaculate Conception
Very Rev Michael McLoughlin PP
Moycullen, Co Galway
Tel 091-555106
Email moycullenparish@eircom.net
Website www.moycullenparish.com

ORANMORE
Immaculate Conception
Very Rev Canon John O'Dwyer PP
Oranmore, Co Galway
Tel 091-794634
St Joseph's
Rev Peter Joyce CC
Maree, Oranmore, Co Galway
Tel 091-794113

OUGHTERARD
Immaculate Conception
Rev James Walsh Adm
Oughterard, Co Galway
Tel 091-552290

ROSMUC
Séipéal an Ioncolnaithe
Very Rev Canon Patrick Considine PP
Rosmuc, Co Galway
Tel 091-574130

ROSSCAHILL (KILLANIN)
Immaculate Heart of Mary
Very Rev Martin Moran PP
Rosscahill, Co Galway
Tel 091-550106

SHRULE
St Joseph's
Very Rev Michael Crosby PP
Shrule, Galway
Tel 093-31262

AN SPIDÉAL
Cill Éinne
An tAthair Seán MacAodh PP
Teach an Sagairt, An Spidéal,
Co na Gaillimhe
Tel 091-553155

INSTITUTIONS AND THEIR CHAPLAINS

Brothers of Charity
Kilcornan, Clarinbridge, Co Galway
Rev Martin Keane
Tel 091-796106

Dún Uí Mhaoilíosa
Renmore, Galway
Rev Thomas Brady CF
Tel 091-701055
Email bradt56@hotmail.com

Bon Secours Hospital
Renmore, Galway
Rev Seán Kilcoyne
Tel 091-751534/757711

Galway/Mayo Insititute of Technology
Dublin Road, Galway
Rev Adrian McGrath
Tel 091-753161/757298

Galway Clinic
Doughiska, Galway
Chaplain's Office
Rev Joe Delaney
Sr Goretti Bohan
Tel 091-785000

Gort Community School
Chaplain's Office
Tel 091-632163
Ms Orla Duggan

Merlin Park University Hospital
Chaplains Office
Tel 091-757631
Rev Robert McNamara (CSsR)
Mr Ray Gately

Moneenageisha Community College
Rev Martin Whelan
Tel 091-563577

NUI, Galway
Rev Diarmuid Hogan
Tel 091-524853/495055
Email diarmuid.hogan@nuigalway.ie
Rev Iomar Daniels
Tel 091-582719/495055
Email iomar.daniels@nuigalway.ie

St Enda's College
Threadneedle Road,
Salthill, Galway
Sr Pauline Uhlemann (RJM)
Tel 091-522458

St Joseph's Secondary College
Nun's Island, Galway
Chaplain to be appointed
Tel 091-565980

University Hospital
Chaplain's Office
Tel 091-524222
Rev David Cribbin
Email david.cribbin@mailn.hse.ie
Rev Alan Burke

PRIESTS OF THE DIOCESE ELSEWHERE

Rev Hugh Clifford
Pontifical Irish College,
Via dei Quattro 1, 00184 Rome, Italy
Tel 003906-77263301
Email hughclifford@eircom.net
Rev Patrick Connaughton
St Columban's, Dalgan Park,
Navan, Co Meath
Tel 046-21525
Rev Michael Conway
St Patrick's College,
Maynooth, Co Kildare
Tel 01-6285222
Rev Vivian Loughrey
St Gregory the Great Parish,
200 Nr University Drive,
Plantation, FL 33324, USA
Rev Thomas Lyons
Cork University Hospital, Wilton, Cork
Tel 021-4546109
Rev Michael O'Flaherty
School of Law, University of Nottingham,
University Park, Nottingham NG7 2RD,
England
Rev Gregory Raftery
An Der Tiefenriede 11, 3000,
Hanover 1, Germany
Rev Olan Rynn
c/o Diocesan Office, The Cathedral,
Galway
Tel 091-563566

RETIRED PRIESTS

Rev Michael Carney PE
c/o Diocesan Office, The Cathedral,
Galway
Tel 091-563566
Very Rev Bernard Duffy PE
20 Clonarkin Drive,
Oranmore, Co Galway
Tel 091-794552
Very Rev Canon Patrick Heneghan PE
5 Pine Grove, Moycullen, Co Galway
Tel 091-556698
Very Rev Canon Richard Higgins PE
c/o The Diocesan Office,
The Cathedral, Galway
Tel 091-563566
Rev Stephen Keane PE
7 Garrai Sheann, Roscam, Galway
Tel 091-767528
Very Rev Canon Edward Kelly PE
'Inchagill' Ballinamana Road,
Clarinbridge, Co Galway
Tel 091-796095
Very Rev Henry Keogh PE
The Presbytery, Bushypark, Galway
Tel 091-520300
Very Rev Canon Joseph Keogh PE
Cregclare, Ardrahan, Co Galway
Tel 091-635940
Rev Dr James Mitchell
11 St Mary's Terrace, Galway
Tel 091-524411
Very Rev Leo Morahan PE
2 The Beeches, Louisburg, Co Mayo
Tel 098-66869

Very Rev Dean Christopher O'Connor PE
Craughwell, Co Galway
Tel 091-846124
Very Rev Martin O'Connor PE
Coral Haven Nursing Home,
Headford Road, Galway
Tel 091-762800
Very Rev Canon J. A. O'Halloran PE
Creggana More, Oranmore, Co Galway
Tel 091-794116

PERSONAL PRELATURE

Opus Dei
Gort Ard University Residence,
Rockbarton North, Salthill, Galway
Tel 091-523846
Rev Walter Macken
Email watermacken@gmail.com
Rev Oliver Powell

RELIGIOUS ORDERS AND CONGREGATIONS

PRIESTS

AUGUSTINIANS
St Augustine's Priory, Galway
Tel 091-562524 Fax 091-564378
Prior: Rev Desmond Foley (OSA)

DOMINICANS
St Mary's, The Claddagh, Co Galway
Tel 091-582884 Fax 091-581252
Prior and Parish Priest
Very Rev Domhnall Mac Suibhne (OP)

FRANCISCANS
The Abbey, 8 Francis Street, Galway
Tel 091-562581 Fax 091-565663
Guardian: Rev Gabriel Kinahan (OFM)

JESUITS
St Ignatius Community & Church
27 Raleigh row, Salthill, Galway
Tel 091-523707
Email galway@jesuit.ie
Rector: Rev John O'Keeffe (SJ)

Coláiste Iognáid, 24 Sea Road, Galway
Tel 091-501500 Fax 091-501551
Email colaisteiognaid@eircom.net
Headmaster: Mr Bernard O'Connell

PASSIONISTS
Passionist Community,
35-36 Coill Tire, Doughiska, Galway

MISSIONARIES OF THE SACRED HEART
Croí Nua, Rosary Lane,
Taylor's Hill, Galway
Tel 091-520960 Fax 091-521168
Leader: Rev Michael Screene (MSC)

SOCIETY OF AFRICAN MISSIONS
Claregalway, Co Galway
Tel 091-798880 Fax 091-798879
Email smafathers@eircom.net
Superior: Rev Gerard Murray (SMA)

BROTHERS

BROTHERS OF CHARITY
Regional Office, Kilcornan Centre,
Clarinbridge, Co Galway
Tel 091-796389/796413
Regional Leader: Br Noel Corcoran
Chaplain: Rev Martin Keane
Community: 3

CHRISTIAN BROTHERS
Christian Brothers' House,
Mount St Joseph, Ennistymon, Co Clare
Tel 065-7071130

12 Oldfield, Kingston, Galway
Tel 091-526705
Community Leader: Br Christy O'Carroll
Community: 4

PATRICIAN BROTHERS
Manor Drive, Kingston, Galway
Tel 091-523267
Superior: Br David Byrne
Community: 7

St Patrick's Primary School,
Market Street, Galway
Tel 091-568707. Pupils: 616
Principal: Mr Noel Cunningham
Email sfoc@eircom.net

St Joseph's Patrician College,
Nun's Island, Galway
Tel 091-565980
Pupils: 775
Principal: Mr John O'Keeffe

SISTERS

BON SECOURS SISTERS (PARIS)
Sisters of Bon Secours,
5 Glenina Heights, Mervue, Galway
Tel 091-755979
Community: 3
Hospital Ministry

Sisters of Bon Secours,
Apartment 9, Pointe Boise,
107-109 Upper Salthill, Galway
Community: 1
Parish Ministry

BRIGIDINE SISTERS
27 Cuimín Mór,
Cappagh Road, Bearna, Co Galway
Tel 091-592234
Contact: Sr Margaret Coyle
Education

CONGREGATION OF THE SISTERS OF MERCY
Sisters of Mercy, Cnoc Mhuire,
Ballyloughaun Road, Renmore, Galway
Tel 091-753693 Fax 091-758502
Community: 2

Convent of Mercy,
St Vincent's, Newtownsmith, Galway
Tel 091-565519 Fax 091-564739
Community: 20

Convent of Mercy,
47 Forster Street, Galway
Tel 091-562356 Fax 091-561304
Community: 11

61 The Green,
College Road, Galway
Tel 091-564148
Community: 2

Convent of Mercy, St Joseph's,
Oughterard, Co Galway
Tel 091-552154
Community: 4

Convent of Mercy, Clochar Éinde,
An Spidéal, Gaillimh
Guthán 091-553288
Community: 6

Sisters of Mercy
12 Heather Grove, Ballybane, Galway
Tel 091-753543
Community: 2

Convent of Mercy,
Gort, Co Galway
Tel 091-631069 Fax 091-631482
Community: 9

Sisters of Mercy, Station Road,
Lahinch, Co Clare
Tel 065-7081906 Fax 065-7082069
Community: 4

30/31 Gleann Bhreandáin,
St Brendan's Road,
Lisdoonvarna, Co Clare
Tel 065-7074319
Community: 3

Aisling Court, Ballyloughaun Road,
Renmore, Galway
Community: 4

Sisters of Mercy 3 Greenview Heights,
Inishannagh Park, Newcastle, Galway
Tel 091-526126
Community: 2

Sisters of Mercy,
49 Monalee Heights, Knocknacarra,
Galway
Tel 091-590735
Community: 2

146 Seacrest Road,
Knocknacarra, Galway
Tel 091-591685
Community: 2

Sisters of Mercy, 13 Beech Park,
Oranmore, Galway
Tel 091-794635
Community: 1

Sisters of Mercy, McAuley House,
7A Francis Street, Galway
Community: 3

1 Na Cuilíní, Dr Mannix Road,
Salthill, Galway
Tel 091-584250
Community: 3

17 Newtownsmith, Galway
Apt 1 Tel 091-563297
Apt 2 Tel 091-563698
Community: 2

147 Seacrest, Knocknacarra, Galway
Tel 091-591598
Community: 2

DAUGHTERS OF CHARITY OF ST VINCENT DE PAUL
65 Shantalla Road, Galway
Tel 091-584410
Superior: Sr Christina Quinn
Community: 4
SVP Hostel, pastoral work

DOMINICAN SISTERS
Dominican Convent, Taylor's Hill, Galway
Tel 091-522124/523975
Email dominicancg@eircom.net
Prioress: Sr Padraigín McKenna
Community: 15
Primary School. Tel 091-521517
Pupils: 715
Secondary School. Tel 091-523171

FRANCISCAN MISSIONARIES OF MARY
16 Tirellan Heights, Headford Road,
Galway
Tel 091-768272
Superior: Sr Bernadette Maxwell
Email fmmgalway@irishbroadband.net
Community: 5
Sisters involved in pastoral and social work in parish

GOOD SHEPHERD SISTERS
101 Gleann Dara,
Bishop O'Donnell Road, Rahoon, Galway
Tel 091-861432
Email rgsgalway@eircom.net
Community: 2
Youth work and counselling

JESUS AND MARY, CONGREGATION OF
Convent of Jesus and Mary,
23 Lenaboy Gardens, Salthill, Galway
Tel 091-524277
Superior: Sr Maria O'Toole
Community: 8
Sisters on staff of primary and post-primary schools

St Ita's Primary School
Tel 091-522716. Pupils: 300
Salerno Post-Primary School
Tel 091-529500. Pupils: 522

Convent of Jesus and Mary,
229 Castlepark, Ballybane, Galway
Tel 091-764320
Superior: Sr Mary Xavier McNamara
Community: 4

LA RETRAITE SISTERS
2 Distillery Road, Galway
Tel 091-524548 Fax 091-581312
Contact: Sr Aileen Murphy
Email aileen@laretraite.ws
Community: 3

LITTLE SISTERS OF THE ASSUMPTION
25 Sea Road, Galway
Tel 091-583979
Email lsagalway@eircom.net
Community: 8
Professional services in the family,
nursing and social work

50 St Finbarr's Terrace,
Bohermore, Galway
Tel 091-568870
Community: 2
Professional services in the family, social
work

92 Currach Buí, Rahoon Park, Galway
Tel 091-588750
Community: 2
Professional services in the family, social
work

POOR CLARES
St Clare's Monastery,
Nuns' Island, Galway
www.poorclares.ie
Abbess: Sr. M. Colette Hayden
Community: 13
Contemplatives. Adoration of the
Blessed Sacrament. Altar breads

PRESENTATION SISTERS
Presentation Convent,
Presentation Road, Galway
Tel 091-561067 Fax 091-562384
Email presroad@eircom.net
Community Leader: Sr Anne Fox
Community: 20
School and pastoral ministry
Scoil Chroí Íosa, Primary School
Tel 091-525904
Pupils: 142
Presentation Secondary School
Tel 091-563495
Fax 091-561875
Email presgalpdp@eircom.net

Shantalla Road, Galway
Tel 091-522598
Email presshantalla@eircom.net
Community: 8
School and pastoral ministry
Scoil Bhride Primary School
Tel/Fax 091-525052
Email sns.ias@eircom.net

160 Corrib Park, Newcastle, Galway
Tel 091-522678
Community: 2
Counselling ministry

14 Crescent View,
Riverside, Galway
Tel 091-753639
Email presrside@eircom.net
Community: 2
Pastoral ministry

RELIGIOUS SISTERS OF CHARITY
Our Lady's Priory,
Clarinbridge, Co Galway
Tel 091-796254
Various apostolic ministries

ASSOCIATION OF THE FAITHFUL

FRATERNITY OF MARY IMMACULATE QUEEN
'Síol Dóchas', Ballard, Barna, Galway
Tel/Fax 091-592196
Email miq@eircom.net

EDUCATIONAL INSTITUTIONS

Coláiste Einde, Gaillimh
Tel 091-522458/524904
Principal: Mrs Siobháin Quinn
Chaplain's Office: Tel 091-522458/524904
Sr Pauline Uhlemann (RJM)

St Mary's College, Galway
Tel 091-522369/521984
President: Very Rev Barry Hogg BA, HDE
Principal: Mr Bartley Fannin
Chaplain: Canon Seán Manning
Email smcollege@eircom.net

EDMUND RICE SCHOOLS TRUST
Primary School,
Ennistymon, Co Clare
Tel 065-7071909
Email etyn.ias@eircom.net
Principal: Ms Helen Sheridan

Meanscoil na mBráithre,
Ennistymon, Co Clare
Tel 065-7072005
Email cbsennistymon.ias@tinet.ie
Principal: Ms Ann Tuohy

CHARITABLE AND OTHER SOCIETIES

COPE Galway
(Crisis Housing, Caring Support) Ltd
3-5 Calbro House,
Tuam Road, Galway
Tel 091-778750
Director: Jacquie Horan
Cope provides emergency
accommodation for homeless persons
and families and women and children
experiencing domestic violence. It also
provides a community catering service in
Galway City and runs a day centre for
older people in Mervue.

Society of St Vincent de Paul
Ozanam House,
St Augustine Street, Galway
Tel 091-563233/562254
Director: Mr Colm Noonan

DIOCESE OF KERRY

PATRON OF THE DIOCESE
ST BRENDAN, 16 MAY

INCLUDES COUNTY KERRY, EXCEPT KILMURRILY, AND PART OF COUNTY CORK

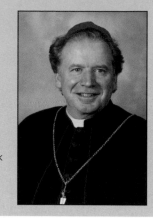

Most Rev William Murphy DD
Bishop of Kerry;
born 6 June 1936;
ordained priest 18 June 1961;
ordained Bishop of Kerry
10 September 1995

Residence:
Bishop's House, Killarney,
Co Kerry
Tel 064-6631168
Fax 064-6631364
Email bishopshouse@eircom.net

ST MARY'S CATHEDRAL, KERRY

The Cathedral of Our Lady of the Assumption, better known as St Mary's, was designed by Augustus Welby Pugin. The main part of the cathedral was built between 1842 and 1855. Work was suspended between 1848 and 1853 because of the Famine and the building was used as a shelter for victims of the Famine.

Between 1908 and 1912 the nave and side aisles were extended and the spire, sacristy and mortuary chapel were added.

In 1972/3 the cathedral was extensively renovated. The interior was reordered to meet the demands of the liturgical renewal that followed the Second Vatican Council.

CHAPTER

Dean Sean Hanafin PP, VF
Tralee
Rt Rev Mgr Daniel O'Riordan VG
Castleisland
Rt Rev Mgr Declan O'Connor PP, VG
Millstreet
Archdeacon: Venerable Thomas Crean
Kenmare
Very Rev William Crean, Cahirciveen
Very Rev Thomas Looney
Dingle
Very Rev James Linnane, Listowel
Very Rev Gearóid Walsh, Castletownbere
Very Rev Michael Fleming, Killorglin

Honorary Canons
Very Rev Larry Kelly, Rathmore
Very Rev Eoin Mangan, Knocknogoshel

Retired Members
Rt Rev Mgr Pádraig Ó Fiannachta
Very Rev Matthew Keane
Rt Rev Mgr Michael Leahy
Very Rev John McKenna
Very Rev Michael O'Doherty
Venerable Michael J. Murphy
Very Rev Denis O'Mahony
Very Rev Patrick Sheehan

Retired Honorary Members
Very Rev Patrick J. Horgan

ADMINISTRATION

College of Consultors
Rt Rev Mgr Daniel O'Riordan PP, VG, VF
Rt Rev Mgr Declan O'Connor PP, VG
Dean Sean Hanafin PP, VF
Very Rev Gearóid Godley
Very Rev Nicholas Flynn Adm, VF
Rev Niall Howard CC
Vry Rev George Hayes

Vicars General
Rt Rev Mgr Daniel O'Riordan PP, VG, VF
The Presbytery, Castleisland, Co Kerry
Tel 066-7141241 Fax 066-7141273
Rt Rev Mgr Declan O'Connor PP, VG
Millstreet, Co Cork
Tel 029-70043 Fax 029-70919

Vicars Forane
Venerable Thomas Crean
Very Rev William Canon Crean
Very Rev James Canon Linnane
Very Rev Gearóid Walsh
Very Rev Michael Canon Fleming
Very Rev Declan Canon O'Connor
Very Rev Thomas Canon Looney
Dean Sean Hanafin
Very Rev Liam Comer
Very Rev Jack Fitzgerald
Very Rev John Lawlor
Very Rev Nicholas Flynn

Finance Council
Rt Rev Mgr Daniel O'Riordan PP, VG, VF
Rev George Hayes, Mr Jim McMahon,
Mr Liam Chute, Ms Mary Harty,
Mr Dan Hourigan, Ms Mary McBride,
Mr Brian Durran, Rev Gearóid Godley,
Rev Bernard Healy

Foreign Missions Committee
Chairman: Rev Gearóid Godley
John Paul II Pastoral Centre,
Rock Road, Killarney, Co Kerry
Tel 064-6630535 Fax 064-6631170

Diocesan Archivist
Ms Margaret de Brún
Diocesan Office, Killarney, Co Kerry
Tel 064-6631168 Fax 064-6631364

Diocesan Secretary
Rev George Hayes
Bishop's House, Killarney, Co Kerry
Tel 064-6631168 Fax 064-6631364
Email bishopshouse@eircom.net

Diocesan Communications Officer
Ms Mary Fagan
Tel 087-1301555

Property Management Committee
Chairman: Very Rev M. Canon Fleming
Killorglin, Co Kerry
Tel 066-9761172
Secretary: Mr Willie Wixted
Diocesan Centre, Cathedral Walk,
Killarney, Co Kerry
Tel 064-6631168

CATECHETICS EDUCATION

Post-Primary Religious Education
Director: Ms Edwina Gottstein
John Paul II Pastoral Centre,
Rock Road, Killarney, Co Kerry
Tel 064-6632644 Fax 064-6631170

Primary Religious Education
Director: Sr Noreen Quilter
Assistant Director: Mr Joe Linnane
Mrs Jean McGearailt
c/o John Paul II Pastoral Centre,
Rock Road, Killarney, Co Kerry
Tel 064-6632644

Primary School Management
Secretary: Very Rev John Lawlor PP, VF
The Presbytery, Ballydonoghue,
Co Kerry
Tel 068-47103 Fax 068-47230

LITURGY

**Building Committee/Sacred Art and
Architecture Commission**
Chairman: Very Rev Canon Michael Fleming
The Presbytery, Killorglin, Co Kerry
Tel 066-9761172 Fax 066-9762302
Secretary: Rev George Hayes
Bishop's House, Killarney, Co Kerry
Tel 064-6631168 Fax 064-6631364

Liturgical Committee
Chairman:
Very Rev Canon Eoin Mangan PP
Diocesan Office, Bishop's House,
Killarney, Co Kerry
Tel 068-46107 Fax 068-46494

PASTORAL

Accord
Killarney Centre: John Paul II Pastoral
Centre, Killarney, Co Kerry
Tel 064-6632644 Fax 064-6631170
Email jp2centre@eircom.net
Director: Rev Joseph Begley
Tralee Centre: St John's Pastoral Centre,
Castle Street, Tralee, Co Kerry
Tel 066-7122280
Director: Very Rev Jack Fitzgerald

Council of Priests
Chairman: Dean Sean Hanafin
Secretary: Rev Niall Howard

CURA
Tel 066-7127355

Diocesan Pastoral Centre
Director: Rev Gearóid Godley
John Paul II Pastoral Centre,
Rock Road, Killarney, Co Kerry
Tel 064-6632644 Fax 064-6631170

Diocesan Pastoral Council
Chairman: Mr Tony Darmody
Kerry Parents & Friends Association, The
Old Monastery, Port Road, Killarney
Tel 064-6632742
Secretary: Ms Frances Rowland
John Paul II Pastoral Centre,
Rock Road, Killarney, Co Kerry
Tel 064-6630508

Diocesan Pastoral Strategic Plan
Co-ordinator: Rev Gearoid Godley
John Paul II Pastoral Centre,
Killarney, Co Kerry
Tel 064-6630535

**Diocesan Safeguarding Children
Committee**
Chairman: Very Rev G. Canon Walsh
Castletownbere, Co Cork
Tel 027-70849
Secretary: Very Rev George Hayes
Kilgarvan, Co Kerry
Tel 064-6685313
Designated Officer:
Very Rev Pádraig Walsh
Our Lady & St Brendan's,
Upper Rock Street, Tralee, Co Kerry
Tel 066-7125932/087-6362780
Deputy Designated Officer:
Rev John Quinlan
c/o Diocesan Office, Killarney, Co Kerry

Ecumenism
Secretary: Very Rev Pat Crean-Lynch
The Presbytery, Ballymacelligott,
Tralee, Co Kerry
Tel 066-7137118 Fax 066-7137137

Marriage Tribunal
(See Marriage Tribunals Section)

Pastoral Renewal Team
Rev Gearóid Godley
Ms Frances Rowland
Pastoral Centre, Killarney, Co Kerry
Tel 064-6632644

Pilgrimage Director
Very Rev William Radley PP
St Agatha's Parish Centre, Headford,
Killarney, Co Kerry
Tel 064-7754008 Fax 064-7754458

Pioneer Total Abstinence Association
Diocesan Director
Very Rev Noel Spring PP
The Presbytery, Firies, Co Kerry
Tel 066-9764122 Fax 066-9764046

Pontifical Mission Societies
Diocesan Director: Rev Gearóid Godley
John Paul II Pastoral Centre,
Killarney, Co Kerry
Tel 064-6630535 Fax 064-6631170

Retreat Centre
Ardfert, Co Kerry
Director: Rev Liam Lovell CC
Tel 066-7134276 Fax 066-7133169

Travellers
Chaplain: Very Rev Luke Roche PP
Castlemaine, Co Kerry
Tel 066-9767322 Fax 066-9767467

Vocations
Director: Rev Liam Lovell
Kilmoyley, Ardfert, Co Kerry
Tel 066-7133169
Assistant Director: Rev Michael Moynihan
The Presbytery, Castleisland, Co Kerry
Tel 066-7141241

Youth Director
Mr Tim O'Donoghue
Diocesan Youth Office, The Friary,
Killarney, Co Kerry
Tel 064-6631748 Fax 064-6636770

PARISHES

The mensal parish is listed first. Other parishes follow alphabetically Historical names are given in parentheses. Church titulars are in italics.

KILLARNEY
St Mary's Cathedral, Killarney
Holy Spirit, Muckross
Resurrection, Park Road
Very Rev Nicholas Flynn Adm, VF
Rev Kevin McNamara (MSC) CC *(pro-tem)*
Rev Gerard O'Leary CC
Very Rev Patrick Horgan *(in residence)*
Killarney, Co Kerry
Tel 064-6631014 Fax 064-6631148

ABBEYDORNEY
St Bernard's, Abbeydorney
Very Rev John Fitzgerald PP
Abbeydorney, Co Kerry
Tel 066-7135146 Fax 066-7135204
St Mary's, Kilflynn
Rev Kevin Sullivan *(in residence)*
Tel 066-7135236

ADRIGOLE
St Fachtna's
Very Rev Kieran O'Sullivan PP
Adrigole, Bantry, Co Cork
Tel 027-60006 Fax 027-60137

ALLIHIES
St Michael's, Allihies,
St Michael's, Cahermore
Rev Jim Lenihan Adm
Allihies, Bantry, Co Cork
Tel 027-73024 Fax 027-73024

ANNASCAUL
Sacred Heart, Annascaul
St Mary's, Camp
St Joseph's, Inch
Very Rev John Buckley PP
Annascaul, Co Kerry
Tel 066-9157103 Fax 066-9157221

ARDFERT
St Brendan's, Ardfert
Very Rev Denis Leahy PP
Ardfert, Co Kerry
Tel 066-7134131 Fax 066-7134148
Sacred Heart, Kilmoyley
Rev Liam Lovell CC
Kilmoyley, Ardfert, Co Kerry
Tel 066-7133169 Fax 066-7134148

BALLINSKELLIGS (PRIOR)
St Michael the Archangel, Ballinskelligs,
St Patrick's, Portmagee,
Sacred Heart and St Finan, The Glen
Very Rev Michael Hussey PP
St Michael's, Ballinskelligs, Co Kerry
Tel 066-9479108 Fax 066-9479193

BALLYBUNION
St John's
Very Rev Martin Hegarty PP
Ballybunion, Co Kerry
Tel 068-27102 Fax 068-27153

BALLYDESMOND
St Patrick's
Very Rev Pádraig MacCarthaigh PP
Ballydesmond, Mallow, Co Cork
Tel 064-51104 Fax 064-51154

BALLYDONOGHUE
St Teresa's
Very Rev John Lawlor PP
Ballydonoghue, Lisselton, Co Kerry
Tel 068-47103 Fax 068-47230

BALLYFERRITER
Uinseann Naofa, Baile an Fheitearaigh
Naomh Gobnait, Dún Chaoin
Séipéal na Carraige
Very Rev Eugene Kiely PP
Tel 066-9156131 Fax 066-9156440
Very Rev Tomás Ó hIceadha AP
Tel 066-9156499
Ballyferriter West, Tralee, Co Kerry

BALLYHEIGUE
St Mary's
Very Rev Thomas Leane PP
Ballyheigue, Tralee, Co Kerry
Tel 066-7133110 Fax 066-7133114

BALLYLONGFORD
St Michael the Archangel
Very Rev Philip O'Connell PP
Ballylongford, Co Kerry
Tel 068-43110 Fax 068-43187
St Mary's
Rev Joseph Tarrant CC
Asdee, Co Kerry
Tel 068-41152 Fax 068-41205

BALLYMACELLIGOTT
Immaculate Conception, Ballymacelligott
St Brendan's, Clogher
Very Rev Pat Crean-Lynch PP
Ballymacelligott, Co Kerry
Tel 066-7137118 Fax 066-7137137

BEAUFORT (TUOGH)
St Mary's, Beaufort
Our Lady of the Valley, The Valley
Very Rev Micheál Ó Dochartaigh PP
The Presbytery, Beaufort, Co Kerry
Tel 064-6644128 Fax 064-6644130

BOHERBUE/KISKEAM
Immaculate Conception, Boherbue
Sacred Heart, Kiskeam
Very Rev Séamus Kennelly PP
Boherbue, Mallow, Co Cork
Tel 029-76038 Fax 029-76201

BROSNA
St Carthage, Brosna
Our Lady of the Assumption, Knockaclarig
Very Rev Tadhg Fitzgerald PP
Brosna, Co Kerry
Tel 068-44112 Fax 068-44176

CAHIRCIVEEN
Holy Cross, O'Connell Memorial,
Immaculate Conception, Filemore;
St Joseph's, Aghatubrid
Very Rev Canon William Crean PP, VF
Rev Niall Howard CC
Cahirciveen, Co Kerry
Tel 066-9472210
Fax 066-9473130

CAHIRDANIEL
St Crohan's, Mary Immaculate, Lohar
Most Precious Blood, Castlecove
Very Rev Fergal Ryan PP
Cahirdaniel, Co Kerry
Tel 066-9475111 Fax 066-9475001

CASTLEGREGORY
St Mary's, Castlegregory
St Brendan's, Cloghane
Very Rev Tadhg Ó Dochartaigh PP
Assistant priest pro tem: Rev Seán Sheehy
Castlegregory, Co Kerry
Tel 066-7139145 Fax 066-7139136

CASTLEISLAND
SS Stephen and John
Rt Rev Mgr Dan O'Riordan PP
Rev Michael Moynihan CC
Castleisland, Co Kerry
Tel 066-7141241 Fax 066-7141273
Our Lady of Lourdes
Immaculate Conception, Cordal

CASTLEMAINE
St Gobnait, Keel
St Carthage, Kiltallagh
Very Rev Luke Roche PP
Castlemaine, Co Kerry
Tel 066-9767322 Fax 066-9767467

FRANCISCANS
Franciscan Friary, Killarney, Co Kerry
Tel 064-6631334/6631066
Fax 064-6637510
Email friary@eircom.net
Guardian: Rev Philip Forker

OBLATES OF MARY IMMACULATE
Department of Chaplaincy,
Tralee General Hospital, Co Kerry
Rev Edward Barrett
Tel 066-7126222

BROTHERS

PRESENTATION BROTHERS
Presentation Monastery, Killarney,
Co Kerry
Tel 064-31267
Contact: Br Terence Hurley
Community: 3

ST JOHN OF GOD KERRY SERVICES
Cloonanorig, Monavalley,
Tralee, Co Kerry
Tel 066-7124333 Fax 066-7126197
Email kerry@sjog.ie
Director: Mr Kevin Ryan
Training and supported employment
service with back-up residential service.
Community Superior: Br Martin Taylor
Community: 2

Teach Eoin, 2 Bóthar an Mhuillean,
Ballyard, Tralee, Co Kerry
Tel 066-7194786 Fax 066-7194474

SISTERS

BON SECOURS SISTERS (PARIS)
Bon Secours Hospital, Strand Street,
Tralee, Co Kerry
Tel 066-7149800 Fax 066-7129068
Co-ordinator: Sr Teresita Hoare
Community: 8
General hospital. Beds: 78
Pastoral ministry

1 Cahermoneen, Tralee, Co Kerry
Tel 066-7127600
Contact: Sr Katherine Therese Tierney
Community: 2
Pastoral parish ministry

5 Strand View Terrace, Tralee, Co Kerry
Tel 066-7181279
Community: 1
Hospital Ministry

6 Strand Street, Tralee, Co Kerry
Tel 066-7194647
Community: 1
Hospital Ministry

CONGREGATION OF THE SISTERS OF MERCY
Mercy Lodge, Balloonagh,
Tralee, Co Kerry
Tel 066-7126336 Fax 066-7125901
Contact: Sr Bernadette Smyth

St John's, Balloonagh, Tralee, Co Kerry
Tel 066-7121199/7122370
Apartment, Catherine McAuley Home
Tel 066-7127517
Contact: Sr Dorothea Foley
Primary School. Tel 066-21375

Holy Cross, Killarney, Co Kerry
Tel 064-31040/31916
Primary School. Tel 064-31241

Suaineas, Woodlawn Road,
Killarney, Co Kerry
Tel 064-6633660
Contact: Sr Columba Relihan

7 Arbutus Drive, Killarney, Co Kerry
Tel 064-6637484
Contact: Sr Julianne Sullivan

11 Holy Cross Gardens,
Killarney, Co Kerry
Tel 064-6620554
Contact: Sr Mary Lyne

21 The Grove, Mounthawk,
Tralee, Co Kerry
Tel 066-7189029
Primary School. Tel 066-24403

St Brigid's Convent, Greenville, Listowel,
Co Kerry
Tel 068-21557
Contact: Sr Margaret Flynn

Divine Providence, Castletownbere,
Co Cork
Tel 027-70061
Contact: Sr Mary O'Connor
Primary School. Tel 027-70325

'Mount St Michael', Rosscarbery,
Co Cork
Tel 023-8848116
Contact: Sr Brigid O'Flanagan
Primary School

14 Brandon Place, Basin Road,
Tralee, Co Kerry
Tel 066-7144997
Contact: Sr Maura O'Dowd

9-10 Carraig Lí, Killerisk,
Tralee, Co Kerry
Contact: Sr Casimir O'Carroll

Goodwin House, The Mall,
Dingle, Co Kerry
Contact: Sr Loyola Buckley

Mercy Sisters, Aoibhneas,
103 Gort na Sidhe, Mounthawk,
Tralee, Co Kerry
Tel 066-7128056
Contact: Sr Joan Curtin

62 The Marina, Tralee, Co Kerry
Tel 066-7129196
Contact: Sr Nora Flynn

Ardfert Retreat Centre,
Ardfert, Co Kerry
Tel 066-7134276

7 Woodview, Moyderwell,
Tralee, Co Kerry
Tel 066-7118027

DAUGHTERS OF MARY AND JOSEPH
Fairways, Killowen, Kenmare, Co Kerry
Tel 064-40755
Contact Person: Sr Helen Lane (DMJ)
Community: 1
Chaplaincy

DOMINICAN SISTERS (KING WILLIAM'S TOWN)
Oak Park, Tralee, Co Kerry
Tel 066-71256641
Community: 7
Our Lady of Fatima Retirement Home
Tel 066-7125900 Fax 066-7180834
Email info@fatimahome.com
Beds: 66
Siena Court for Active Retired:
Bungalows: 10
Contact Person: Sr Teresa McEvoy OP
Email teresamcevoy@fatimahome.com

Muire na nGael, 22 Manor Avenue,
Tralee, Co Kerry
Tel 066-7128083
Sr Audrey McNamee OP
Community: 1

FRANCISCAN MISSIONARIES OF THE DIVINE MOTHERHOOD
Sancta Chiara, 5 St Margaret's Road,
Killarney, Co Kerry
Tel 064-6626866 Fax 064-6626414
Community: 4

INFANT JESUS SISTERS
Killarney Road, Millstreet, Co Cork
Tel 029-70143
Community: 8
Retired sisters

Cluain Iosagáin, St Brendan's Road,
Tralee, Co Kerry
Tel 066-7121384
Pastoral work

20 Blackrock, St Brendan's Road,
Tralee, Co Kerry
Tel 066-7127974
Community: 4
Teaching and pastoral ministry

7 Blackrock, St Brendan's Road,
Tralee, Co Kerry
Tel 066-7124455
Pastoral ministry

LITTLE COMPANY OF MARY
Park Road, Killarney, Co Kerry
Tel 064-6671220 Fax 064-6671240
Community: 6

LORETO (IBVM)
Gortahoonig, Muckross,
Killarney, Co Kerry
Tel 064-31077
Sr Pauline Boyle

Allianz (ⅲ)

PRESENTATION SISTERS
Teach na Toirbhirte, Miltown, Co Kerry
Tel 066-9767387
Non-resident Leader: Sr Maureen Guerin
Community: 5
Primary School. Tel 066-9767626
Post-Primary School. Tel 066-9767168

Presentation Convent,
Killarney, Co Kerry
Tel 064-6631172
Non-resident Leader: Sr Kathleen Quinlan
Community: 12
Secondary School. Tel 064-6632209

Presentation Sisters,
25 Ballyspillane, Killarney, Co Kerry
Tel 064-6636389
Community: 2

Presentation Convent, Castle Street,
Tralee, Co Kerry
Tel 066-7122128
Team Leadership
Community: 18
Primary School. Tel 066-7123314
Secondary School. Tel 066-7122737

Presentation Convent, Dingle, Co Kerry
Tel 066-9151194
Community: 1
Primary School. Tel 066-9151154

Presentation Convent,
Cahirciveen, Co Kerry
Tel 066-9472005
Non-resident Leader
Sr Columbanus Quirke
Community: 3

Presentation Convent,
Castleisland, Co Kerry
Tel 066-7141256
Non-resident Leader
Sr Elizabeth McMahon
Community: 10
Primary School. Tel 066-7141147
Secondary School. Tel 066-7141178

Presentation Convent, Lixnaw, Co Kerry
Tel 066-7132138
Non-resident Leader: Sr Maureen Kane
Community: 6
Primary School. Tel 066-7132600

Presentation Convent,
Rathmore, Co Kerry
Tel 064-7758027
Non-resident Leader: Sr Margaret O'Brien
Community: 10
Primary School. Tel 064-7758499

Presentation Convent,
Millstreet, Co Cork
Tel 029-70067
Non-resident Leader: Sr Grace Foley
Community: 5
Primary School. Tel 029-70957

48 Hawley Park, Tralee, Co Kerry
Tel 066-7122111
Community: 2

'Tigh na Féile', Ballygologue Road,
Listowel, Co Kerry
Tel 068-21156
Community: 2
Primary School. Tel 068-22294
Secondary School. Tel 068-21452
Nano Nagle Special School. Tel 068-21942

9 Beech Grove, Cahirdown,
Listowel, Co Kerry
Tel 068-53951
Community: 1

Mail Road, Cahirdown,
Listowel, Co Kerry
Tel 068-22500
Community: 1

Presentation Sisters, 1 Glenard,
Mona Valley, Tralee, Co Kerry
Tel 066-7181318
Community: 3

7 Tamhnach Lí,
Monavalley, Tralee, Co Kerry
Tel 066-7180800
Community: 1

8 Tamhnach Lí,
Monavalley, Tralee, Co Kerry
Tel 066-7194174
Community: 1

9 Tamhnach Lí,
Monavalley, Tralee, Co Kerry
Tel 066-7195312
Community: 1

9 Woodbrooke Manor,
Monavalley, Tralee, Co Kerry
Tel 066-7185454
Community: 2

SISTERS OF ST CLARE
St Clare's Convent, Kenmare, Co Kerry
Tel 064-41385
Contact person: Sr Assumpta Hegarty
Community: 4
St Clare's Primary. Pupils: 151
Kenmare Community School
Tel 064-40846/7

ST JOSEPH OF ANNECY SISTERS
St Joseph's Convent, Killorglin, Co Kerry
Tel 066-9761809 Fax 066-9761127
Superior: Sr Helena Lyne
Email margaret.lyne@talk21.com
Community: 4

St Joseph's Home for the Aged,
Killorglin, Co Kerry
Tel 066-9761124 (H)
Tel 066-9761808 (Patients)
Beds: 40

ST JOSEPH OF THE SACRED HEART SISTERS
Sisters of St Joseph of Sacred Heart,
St Joseph's, Brosna Road,
Castleisland, Co Kerry
Tel 066-7141472

Sisters of St Joseph of Sacred Heart,
St Joseph's, 5 Allman's Terrace,
Killarney, Co Kerry
Tel 064-23528

EDUCATIONAL INSTITUTIONS

St Brendan's College (Diocesan College)
Killarney, Co Kerry
Tel 064-6631021
Principal: Mr Ed O'Neill

St Michael's College
Listowel, Co Kerry
Tel 068-21049
Principal: Mr John Mulvihill

EDMUND RICE SCHOOLS TRUST
Christian Brothers Primary School,
An Daingean, Co Kerry
Tel 066-9152157
Email iognaidris@eircom.net
Principal: Máire Bean Ní Fhlaighimh

Pobalscoil Chorca Dhuíbhne,
An Daingean, Co Kerry
Principal: An tUas Pádraig Feirtéar

Coláiste Scoil Mhuire na mBráithre
Críostaí Primary School, Clounalour,
Tralee, Co Kerry
Tel 066-7124029 Fax 066-7120522
Principal: Mr Denis Coleman

Christian Brothers Secondary School,
The Green, Tralee, Co Kerry
Tel 066-7145841/7145824
Fax 066-7129807
Principal: Mr Tony O'Keeffe
Email thegreen@eircom.net

CHARITABLE AND OTHER SOCIETIES

Legion of Mary
Ardfert, Ballyheigue, Ballymacelligott,
Castleisland, Castletownbere, Dingle,
Eyeries, Firies, Glenflesk, Kenmare,
Killeentierna, Listowel, Millstreet,
Rathmore, Sneem, Spa, Tuogh, Tralee

St Vincent de Paul
Conferences at: Ballybunion,
Caherciveen, Castleisland, Cloghane,
Dingle, Kenmare, Killarney, Killorglin,
Listowel, Lixnaw, Millstreet, Milltown,
Moyvane, Rathmore, Tralee

DIOCESE OF KILDARE AND LEIGHLIN

PATRONS OF THE DIOCESE
ST BRIGID, 1 FEBRUARY; ST CONLETH (KILDARE), 4 MAY;
ST LAZERIAN (LEIGHLIN) 18 APRIL

INCLUDES COUNTY CARLOW AND PARTS OF COUNTIES KILDARE, LAOIS,
OFFALY, KILKENNY, WICKLOW AND WEXFORD

Most Rev James Moriarty DD
Bishop of Kildare and Leighlin, born 1936;
ordained priest 1961;
ordained Bishop 22 September 1991;
installed as Bishop of Kildare and Leighlin on 31 August 2002

Residence:
Bishop's House, Carlow
Tel 059-9176725
Fax 059-9176850
Email bishop@kandle.ie

CATHEDRAL OF THE ASSUMPTION, CARLOW

The ancient cathedrals of the Diocese of Kildare and Leighlin passed into Protestant usage in the period of the Reformation. Thus the cathedrals of Kildare and Old Leighlin stand on the sites of the ancient monasteries of St Brigid and St Laserian. Even before the Catholic Emancipation Act passed through the Westminster Parliament (1829), Bishop James Doyle OSA was working on the building of the Cathedral of the Assumption, Carlow. It is built on the site of and incorporates parts of the previous parish church of Carlow, which had been built in the 1780s by Dean Henry Staunton.

Carlow cathedral is not particularly large, having more the dimensions of a big parish church. The architectural work was begun by Joseph Lynch, but the final building is stamped with the design of Thomas Cobden, who replaced Lynch in 1829. Cobden gave the cathedral quite an elaborate exterior, with the obvious influence of the Bruges Town Hall tower. The cost of the building work was about £9,000. At its opening in November 1833, the interior decoration was incomplete. In fact, many elements were integrated over the following hundred years, sometimes adding to the mixture of styles.

The cathedral was consecrated on the occasion of its centenary, on 29 November 1933. A thorough reordering of the interior was completed in 1997, giving a very bright, welcoming, prayerful location for both diocesan and parish liturgical celebrations. The most notable elements are: the baptistry, the aumbry, the bishop's and president's chairs, and the Hogan statue of James Doyle, former Bishop of Kildare and Leighlin popularly known as JKL.

Allianz (ⓘ)

ADMINISTRATION

Diocesan Website
www.kandle.ie

Vicars General
Rt Rev Mgr Thomas Coonan CC, VG
Geashill, Co Offaly
Tel 057-9343517
Rt Rev Mgr Brendan Byrne PP, VG
Tullow, Co Carlow
Tel 059-9152159

Vicars Forane
Rt Rev Mgr Brendan Byrne PP, VG
Tullow, Co Carlow
Tel 059-9152159
Rt Rev Mgr John Byrne PP
Dublin Road, Portlaoise, Co Laois
Tel 057-8621142
Very Rev Adrian Carbery PP
26 Beech Grove, Kildare
Tel 045-521900
Very Rev John Dunphy PP
Graiguecullen, Co Carlow
Tel 059-9141833
Very Rev Francis MacNamara PP
Mountmellick, Co Laois
Tel 057-8624198
Very Rev Declan Foley
Bagenalstown, Co Carlow
Tel 059-9721154
Very Rev William O'Byrne PP
Kill, Co Kildare
Tel 045-878008

Consultors
Rt Rev Mgr Brendan Byrne PP, VG
Rt Rev Mgr John Byrne PP, VF
Rt Rev Mgr Thomas Coonan CC, VG
Rev Bill Kemmy
Very Rev Francis MacNamara PP, VF
Rev Mícheál Murphy
Very Rev Pierce Murphy

Chancellor/Diocesan Secretary
Rev Bill Kemmy
Bishop's House, Carlow
Tel 059-9176725 Fax 059-9176850
Email chancellor@kandle.ie

Diocesan Communications Officer
Rev Mícheál Murphy
Knockbeg College, Carlow
Tel 059-9142127
Email communications@kandle.ie

Finance Committee
Chairperson: Mrs Anna-May McHugh
Fallaghmore, Ballylinan, Athy, Co Kildare
Secretary: Rev Bill Kemmy
Bishop's House, Carlow
Tel 059-9176725 Fax 059-9176850
Email chancellor@kandle.ie

Churches and Buildings Committee
Chairman: Very Rev Francis MacNamara PP
Mountmellick, Co Laois
Tel 057-8624198
Secretary: Very Rev Thomas McDonnell
Sallins Road, Naas, Co Kildare
Tel 045-897703

Child Protection – Delegate
Rt Rev Mgr John McDonald
Curragh Camp, Co Kildare
Tel 045-441369
Email cpi@kandle.ie

Archivist
Very Rev Thomas McDonnell
Bishop's House, Carlow
Tel 059-9176725 Fax 059-9176850

CATECHETICS EDUCATION

Faith Development Services
Cathedral Parish Centre, College Street,
Carlow Town
Tel 059-9164084 Fax 059-9164020
Email fds@kandle.ie
Primary Diocesan Advisor
Ms Maeve Mahon
Email maeve.mahon@kandle.ie
Post-Primary Diocesan Advisor
Sr Anne Holton
Email anne.holton@kandle.ie
Youth Ministry/Meitheal Co-ordinator
Mr Robert Norton
Email robert.norton@kandle.ie
Ms Yvonne Rooney
Email yvonne.rooney@kandle.ie
Pastoral Resource Person
Ms Julie Kavanagh
Email julie.kavanagh@kandle.ie

Church Music
Rev Liam Lawton
Crossneen, Carlow Tel 059-9134548
Email liam.lawton@ireland.com

Catholic Primary School Managers Association
Chairman: Very Rev Francis MacNamara PP
Mountmellick, Co Laois
Tel 057-8624198
Secretary: Br Camillus Regan
10 Hawthorne Drive, Tullow, Co Carlow
Tel 087-2244175
Email cpsma@kandle.ie

PASTORAL

ACCORD
Centre Directors
Carlow: Rev John Cummins Adm
The Presbytery, Dublin Road, Carlow
Tel 059-9131227
Portlaoise: Ms Carmel Kelly
Tel 045-431394
Accord, Parish Office, Portlaoise, Co Laois
Newbridge: Very Rev Joseph McDermott PP
St Conleth's, Newbridge, Co Kildare
Tel 045-431741

ALPHA
Very Rev James O'Connell PP
Stradbally, Co Laois
Tel 057-8625132

African Chaplaincy
Rev Peter Uzochukwu
Presbytery, Portlaoise, Co Laois
Tel 087-7850862

Conciliators
Rt Rev Mgr John McDonald PP
Curragh Camp, Co Kildare
Tel 045-441369

Very Rev William O'Byrne PP
Kill, Co Kildare
Tel 045-878008
Ms Breda Parker
9 Moorepark, Newbridge, Co Kildare
Tel 045-431462
Mr Brian O'Sullivan
Drumcooley, Edenderry, Co Offaly
Tel 046-9731522 (W) 046-31435 (H)

Council of Priests
Chairman: Very Rev Declan Foley PP
Muine Bheag, Co Carlow
Tel 059-9721154
Secretary: Rev William Byrne CC
Newbridge, Co Kildare
Tel 045-433979

Ecumenism
Director: Very Rev Tom Lalor PP
Leighlinbridge, Co Carlow
Tel 059-9721463
Rev Liam Morgan CC
Askea, Carlow
Tel 059-9143260
Very Rev Liam Merrigan PP
Drogheda Street, Monasterevin, Co Kildare
Tel 045-525346

Pioneer Total Abstinence Association
Diocesan Director: Rev Mark Townsend CC
Mountrath, Co Laois
Tel 057-8732234

Pontifical Mission Societies
Diocesan Director: Very Rev Thomas O'Reilly
Clonaslee, Co Laois
Tel 057-8648030

Polish Chaplaincy
Fr Tadeusz Durrajczyk
60 College Orchard, Newbridge, Co Kildare
Tel 086-2354320

Prisons
Contact Priest: Rev Eugene Drumm (SPS)
Portlaoise Prison, Portlaoise, Co Laois
Tel 057-8622549

Travellers
Chaplains
Very Rev Thomas Dooley PP
Portarlington, Co Laois
Tel 057-8643004
Rev John Brickley CC
Sallins Road, Naas, Co Kildare
Tel 045-897260

Vocations Committee
Chairman: Rev Ruairí Ó Domhnaill
Newbridge, Co Kildare
Tel 045-434069
Email vocations@kandle.ie

Youth Ministry
Chairman: Rev Liam Morgan
Holy Family Presbytery, Askea, Carlow
Tel 059-9143260
Meitheal Co-ordinator: Mr Robert Norton
Email robert.norton@kandle.ie
Ms Yvonne Rooney
Faith Development Services,
Cathedral Parish Centre,
College Street, Carlow
Tel 059-9164084 Fax 059-9164020

PARISHES

Mensal parishes are listed first. Other parishes follow alphabetically. Historical names are given in parentheses. Church titulars are in italics.

CATHEDRAL, CARLOW
Cathedral of the Assumption
Email info@carlowcathedral.ie
Website www.carlowcathedral.ie
Rev John Cummins Adm
Email johncummins@kandle.ie
Rev Padraig Shelley CC
Email pmshelley@eircom.net
The Presbytery, Carlow
Tel 059-9131227 Fax 059-9130805
Rev Rory Nolan CC
1 Green Road, Carlow
Tel 059-9142632
Cathedral/Parish Shop & Office
Tel 059-9164087

ASKEA
Holy Family
Email askeaparishcc@eircom.net
Very Rev Thomas Little Adm
Browneshill Avenue, Carlow
Tel 059-9131559
Email tomlittle@eircom.net
Rev Liam Morgan CC
Holy Family Presbytery, Askea, Carlow
Tel 059-9143260

ABBEYLEIX
Holy Rosary, Abbeyleix
St Patrick, Ballyroan
Very Rev Gerard Ahern PP
Tel 057-8731135
Email aherngerard@eircom.net
Very Rev Patrick Kehoe CC
Tel 057-8731181
Abbeyleix, Co Laois

ALLEN
Holy Trinity, Allen
St Brigid's, Milltown
Immaculate Conception, Allenwood
Very Rev Edward Moore PP
Allen, Kilmeague, Naas, Co Kildare
Tel 045-860135
Rev Brian Kavanagh CC
15 Lowtown Manor,
Robertstown, Naas, Co Kildare
Tel 045-890559
Email rbkav@gmail.com

ARLES
Sacred Heart, Arles, St Anne's, Ballylinan
St Abban's, Maganey
Very Rev Thomas O'Shea PE
Ballylinan, Athy, Co Kildare
Tel 059-8625261
Email tommieoshea1@eircom.net
Rev Bill Kemmy *(in residence)*
Arles, Ballickmoyler, Carlow
Tel 059-9147637
Email chancellor@kandle.ie

BALLINAKILL
St Brigid's, Ballinakill
St Lazarian's, Knock
Very Rev Seán Conlon PP
Ballinakill, Co Laois
Tel 057-8733336

BALLON
SS Peter and Paul, Ballon
St Patrick's, Rathoe
Very Rev Brendan Howard PP
Clonegal, Enniscorthy, Co Wexford
Tel 053-9377291
Rev Edward Whelan PE, CC
Ballon, Co Carlow
Tel 059-9159329

BALLYADAMS
St Joseph's, Ballyadams
St Mary's, Wolfhill
Holy Rosary, Luggacurren
Very Rev Daniel Dunne PP
Tullamoy, Stradbally, Co Laois
Tel 059-8627123

BALLYFIN
St Fintan's
Very Rev Pat Hennessy PP
Ballyfin, Portlaoise, Co Laois
Tel 057-8755227

BALTINGLASS
St Joseph's, Baltinglass
St Oliver's, Grange Con
St Mary's, Stratford
Very Rev Thomas Dillon PP
Tel 059-6482768
Email tfdb@eircom.net
Rev Sean Maher CC
Tel 059-6481123
Baltinglass, Co Wicklow

BALYNA
St Mary's, Broadford,
St Patrick's Johnstownbridge,
St Brigid's, Clogherinchoe
Email balynaparish@eircom.net
Website www.balynaparish.ie
Very Rev Gerard Breen PP
Broadford, Co Kildare
Tel 046-9551203

BENNEKERRY
St Mary's
Very Rev Thomas Little PP
St Mary's, Browneshill Avenue, Carlow
Tel 059-9131559
Email tomlittle@eircom.net

BORRIS
Sacred Heart, Borris
St Patrick's, Ballymurphy
St Forchan's, Rathanna
Rev John O'Brien PP
Tel 059-9773128
Email john51@eircom.net
Very Rev Pierce Murphy *(In residence)*
Borris, Co Carlow via Kilkenny
Tel 059-9773128

CARAGH
Our Lady and St Joseph, Caragh,
Email parishoffice@caragh.net
Very Rev John O'Connell PP
Caragh, Naas, Co Kildare
Tel 045-875602

CARBURY
Holy Trinity, Carbury
Holy Family, Derrinturn
Email carburyparish@eircom.net
Very Rev John Fitzpatrick PP
Carbury, Co Kildare
Tel 046-9553355

CLANE
SS Patrick and Brigid, Clane
Sacred Heart, Rathcoffey
Email claneparish@eircom.net
Website www.claneparish.com
Very Rev Paul O'Boyle PP
Tel 045-868249
Email oboylepaul@eircom.net
Very Rev Denis Harrington PE, CC
Tel 045-868224
Clane, Naas, Co Kildare

CLONASLEE
St Manman's
Very Rev Thomas O'Reilly PP
Clonaslee, Co Laois
Tel 057-8648030

CLONBULLOGUE
Sacred Heart, Clonbullogue
St Brochan's, Bracknagh,
Immaculate Conception, Walsh Island
Very Rev Patrick Gaynor PP
Walsh Island, Geashill, Co Offaly
Tel 057-8649510

CLONEGAL
St Brigid's, Clonegal
St Lasarian's, Kildavin
Very Rev Joseph Fleming Adm
Clonegal, Enniscorthy, Co Wexford
Tel 053-9377298

CLONMORE
St Mary's, Ballyconnell
St Finian's, Kilquiggan
Our Lady of the Wayside, Clonmore
St Finian's Oratory, Killinure
Very Rev James Gahan PP
Killinure, Tullow, Co Carlow
Tel 059-9156111
Email jkgahan@eircom.net

COOLERAGH AND STAPLESTOWN
Christ the King, Cooleragh,
St Benignus, Staplestown
Email standco@eircom.net
Very Rev Patrick Daly PP
Cooleragh, Coill Dubh,
Naas, Co Kildare
Tel 045-860281

CURRAGH CAMP
St Brigid's
Very Rev Mgr John McDonald PP
Tel 045-441369
Rev P. J. Somers
Tel 045-441277
Email spj40@hotmail.com
Curragh Camp, Co Kildare

DAINGEAN
Mary Mother of God, Daingean
SS Peter and Paul, Kilclonfert
St Francis of Assisi and St Brigid,
Ballycommon; Oratory of the Immaculate
Conception, Cappincur
Very Rev John Stapleton Adm
Email johnstapleton@eircom.net
Rev Michael Moloney
Tel 057-9362006
Rev Patrick O'Byrne PE, CC
Tel 057-9344161
Daingean, Co Offaly

DOONANE
St Abban's, Doonane
Blessed Virgin Mary, Mayo
Very Rev Denis Murphy PP
Tolerton, Ballickmoyler, Carlow
Tel 056-4442126

DROICHEAD NUA/NEWBRIDGE
St Conleth's, Newbridge
Cill Mhuire, Ballymany
St Eustace's, Dominican Church
Parish Office: 045-431394
Email parishoffice@newbridgeparish.ie
Website www.newbridgeparish.ie
Very Rev Joseph McDermott PP
Tel 045-431741
Email jmcder@eircom.net
Rev Willie Byrne CC
Tel 045-433979
Email wmby@eircom.net
Rev Pat Hughes CC
Tel 045-438036
St Conleth's, Chapel Lane,
Droichead Nua, Co Kildare
Rev Rúairí Ó Dómhnaill CC
The Presbytery, Ballymany,
Droichead Nua, Co Kildare
Tel 045-434069

EDENDERRY
St Mary's
Very Rev P.J. McEvoy PP
Francis Street, Edenderry, Co Offaly
Tel 046-9731296
Rev Gregory Corcoran CC
Rhode, Co Offaly
Tel 046-9737010

EMO
St Paul's, Emo; Sacred Heart, Rath
Very Rev Tom Dooley PP
Portarlington, Co Laois
Tel 057-8643004
Email frtomdooley@eircom.net
Rev Thomas O'Byrne CC *(in residence)*
Priest's House, Emo, Portlaoise, Co Laois
Tel 057-8646517
Email obyrneta@eircom.net

GRAIGNAMANAGH
Duiske Abbey, Graignamanagh
Our Lady of Lourdes,
Skeoughvosteen, Co Kilkenny
Email graicac@eircom.net
Very Rev Gerald Byrne PP
Parochial House,
Graignamanagh, Co Kilkenny
Tel 059-9724973
Abbey Centre: 059-9724238

GRAIGUECULLEN AND KILLESHIN
St Clare's, Graiguecullen
Holy Cross, Killeshin
Very Rev John Dunphy PP
Tel 059-9141833
Email dunphyj@iol.ie
Rev PJ Madden
Tel 059-9179855
Graiguecullen, Carlow

HACKETSTOWN
St Brigid's, Hacketstown
Our Lady, Killamoate
Rev James McCormack (MSC) Adm
Hacketstown, Co Carlow
Tel 059-6471257

KILCOCK
St Coca, Kilcock
Nativity of the BVM, Newtown
Email stcocasparish@eircom.net
Website www.kilcockparish.net
Very Rev P. J. Byrne PP
Kilcock, Co Kildare
Tel 01-6287448

KILDARE
St Brigid's
Our Lady of Victories, Kildangan
Sacred Heart, Nurney
Parish Office: 045-521352
Email arasbride@eircom.net
Website www.kildareparish.ie
Very Rev Adrian Carbery PP, VF
26 Beech Grove, Kildare
Tel 045-521900
Rev Gaspar Habara CC
St Brigid's, Kildare
Tel 045-520347

KILL
St Brigid's, Kill
St Anne's, Ardclough
Email killparish@eircom.net
Website www.killparish.ie
Very Rev William O'Byrne PP
Kill, Co Kildare
Tel 045-878008
Very Rev Matthew Kelly PE, CC
60 Hartwell Green, Kill, Naas, Co Kildare
Tel 045-877880

KILLEIGH
St Patrick's, Killeigh
St Joseph's, Ballinagar
St Mary's, Geashill
Email killeighparish@eircom.net
Website www.killeigh.com
Very Rev John Stapleton PP
Killeigh, Co Offaly
Tel 057-9344161
Email johnstapleton@eircom.net
Rt Rev Mgr Thomas Coonan CC, VG
Geashill, Co Offaly
Tel 057-9343517

LEIGHLIN
St Laserian's, Leighlin
St Fintan's, Ballinabranna
Very Rev Thomas Lalor PP
Leighlinbridge, Co Carlow
Tel 059-9721463

MONASTEREVAN
SS Peter and Paul, Monasterevan
Very Rev Liam Merrigan PP
Tougher Road, Monasterevan, Co Kildare
Tel 045-525346

MOUNTMELLICK
St Joseph's, Mountmellick
St Mary's, Clonaghadoo
Very Rev Francis MacNamara PP, VF
Tel 057-8624198
Rev Edward Kavanagh CC
Tel 057-8679302
Very Rev Noel Dunphy PE, CC
Tel 057-8624141
Mountmellick, Co Laois

MOUNTRATH
St Fintan, Mountrath
Sacred Heart, Hollow
Rev Patrick Hennessy PP
Ballyfin, Portlaoise, Co Laois
Tel 057-8755227
Rev Mark Townsend CC *(priest in residence)*
Mountrath, Co Laois
Tel 057-8732234

MUINEBHEAG/BAGENALSTOWN
St Andrew's, Bagenalstown
St Patrick's Newtown
St Laserian's, Ballinkillen
Email info@bagenalstownparish.ie
Website www.bagenalstownparish.ie
Very Rev Declan Foley PP
Tel 059-9721154
Email pdlfoley@gmail.com
Rev Patrick Byrne CC
Tel 059-9723886
Email pmlb@eircom.net
Rev Thomas Bambrick (SM)
Tel 059-9721154
Muinebheag, Co Carlow

MYSHALL
Exaltation of the Cross, Myshall
St Laserian's, Drumphea
Very Rev Philip O'Shea PP
Myshall, Co Carlow
Tel 059-9757635
Rev Brendan Howard CC
Curate's House, Clonegal,
Enniscorthy, Co Wexford
Tel 053-9377291

NAAS
Our Lady and St David, Naas
Irish Martyrs, Ballycane
Very Rev Thomas McDonnell PP
Tel 045-897703
Rev John Brickley CC
Tel 045-897260
Rev James Doyle
Tel 045-897150
Chapel Lane, Sallins Road,
Naas, Co Kildare
Rev Paul Dempsey CC
Two-Mile-House, Naas, Co Kildare
Tel 045-876160

PAULSTOWN
The Assumption, Paulstown
Holy Trinity, Goresbridge
Very Rev Laurence Malone PP
Goresbridge, Co Kilkenny
Tel 059-9775180

PORTARLINGTON
St Michael's, Portarlington
St John the Evangelist, Killenard
Very Rev Thomas Dooley PP
Portarlington, Co Laois
Tel 057-8643004
Email frtomdooley@eircom.net
Rev Thomas O'Byrne CC
Emo, Portlaoise, Co Laois
Tel 057-8646517

PORTLAOISE
SS Peter and Paul, Portlaoise
The Assumption, The Heath
The Holy Cross, Ratheniska
Email info@portlaoiseparish.ie
Website www.portlaoiseparish.ie
Rt Rev Mgr John Byrne PP, VF
Parochial House, Portlaoise, Co Laois
Tel 057-8692153
Email jmbyrne@eircom.net
Rev Paul Fitzpatrick CC
St Mary's, Tower Hill,
Portlaoise, Co Laois
Tel 057-8621671
Email paulfitzpatrick2@eircom.net
Rev Kevin Walsh CC
Dublin Road, Portlaoise, Co Laois
Tel 057-8622301
Email walshkev@hotmail.com
Rev Joe O'Neill CC
Ballyfin Road, Portlaoise, Co Laois
Tel 086-2354320

PROSPEROUS
Our Lady and St Joseph, Prosperous
Rev Pat O'Brien (SPS) CC
Curate's House, Prosperous, Co Kildare
Tel 045-868187

RAHEEN
St Fintan's, Raheen
St Brigid's, Shanahoe
Very Rev Jimmy Kelly PP
Raheen, Abbeyleix, Co Laois
Tel 057-8731182
Email jameskelly1@eircom.net

RATHANGAN
Assumption and St Patrick
Very Rev Gerard O'Byrne PP
Rathangan, Co Kildare
Tel 045-524316
Email gerobyrne@eircom.net

RATHVILLY
St Patrick's, Rathvilly
St Brigid's, Talbotstown
Blessed Virgin Mary, Tynock
Very Rev Michael Kelly PP
Rathvilly, Co Carlow
Tel 059-9161114
Rev Joseph Brophy CC
Kiltegan, Co Wicklow
Tel 059-6473211

RHODE
St Peter's, Rhode
St Anne's, Croghan
Website www.rhodeparish.ie
Very Rev P.J. McEvoy Adm
Francis Street, Edenderry, Co Offaly
Rev Gregory Corcoran CC
Rhode, Co Offaly
Tel 046-9737010

ROSENALLIS
St Brigid's
Email rosenallisparish@eircom.net
Website www.rosenallis.com
Very Rev Thomas Walshe PP
Rosenallis, Portlaoise, Co Laois
Tel 057-8628513

ST MULLINS
St Moling's, Glynn
St Brendan's, Drummond
Very Rev Edward Aughney PP
Glynn, St Mullins via Kilkenny
Tel 051-424563

SALLINS
Our Lady of the Rosary & Guardian Angels
Email sallinsparish@eircom.net
Very Rev Thomas McDonnell PP
Sallins Road, Naas, Co Kildare
Tel 045-897703
Rev James Doyle CC *(in residence)*
Chapel Lane, Sallins, Co Kildare
Tel 045-897150

STRADBALLY
Sacred Heart, Stradbally
Assumption, Vicarstown
St Michael, Timahoe
Very Rev James O'Connell PP
Very Rev Seán Kelly PE, CC
Stradbally, Co Laois
Tel 057-8625132/057-8625831

SUNCROFT
St Brigid's
Email suncroftparish@eircom.net
Very Rev Barry Larkin PP
Suncroft, Curragh, Co Kildare
Tel 045-441586

TINRYLAND
St Joseph's
Website www.tinryland.ie
Very Rev John McEvoy PP
Tinryland, Carlow
Tel 059-9131212
Email jmce51@gmail.com

TULLOW
Most Holy Rosary, Tullow
Immaculate Conception, Ardattin
Our Lady of the Wayside, Grange
Email tullowparish@eircom.net
Website www.tullowparish.com
Rt Rev Mgr Brendan Byrne PP, VG
Tullow, Co Carlow
Tel 059-9152159
Email frbrenby@eircom.net
Rev Andy Leahy CC
Tullow, Co Carlow
Tel 059-9180641
Email andyolaoithe@eircom.net

TWO-MILE-HOUSE
Very Rev Thomas McDonnell PP
Sallins Road, Naas, Co Kildare
Tel 045-897150
Rev Paul Dempsey CC *(in residence)*
Two-Mile-House, Naas, Co Kildare
Tel 045-876160

INSTITUTIONS AND THEIR CHAPLAINS

Abbeyleix District Hospital
Very Rev Gerard Ahern PP
Tel 057-8731135

Baltinglass District Hospital
Very Rev Thomas Dillon PP
Tel 059-6482768

County Hospital, Portlaoise
Very Rev John Byrne PP
Portlaoise, Co Laois
Tel 057-8621142

Curragh Camp
Rt Rev Mgr John McDonald
Tel 045-441369

Edenderry Hospital
Very Rev P. J. McEvoy
Tel 046-9731296

Institute of Technology, Carlow
Rev Rory Nolan CC
Tel 059-9142632

Midlands Prison
Rev Tom Sinnott
Tel 057-8672222
Ms Janet Mahon
Tel 057-8672222
Ms Vera McHugh
Tel 057-8672221

Portlaoise Prison
Rev Eugene Drumm (SPS)
Tel 057-8622549

Sacred Heart Hospital, Carlow
Very Rev John Cummins Adm
Tel 059-9131227

St Brigid's Hospital
Shaen, Portlaoise, Co Laois
Very Rev John Byrne PP
Tel 057-8621142

St Dympna's Hospital, Carlow
Very Rev John Cummins Adm
Tel 059-9131227

St Fintan's Hospital, Portlaoise
Very Rev John Byrne PP
Dublin Road, Portlaoise, Co Laois
Tel 057-8621142

St Vincent's Hospital, Mountmellick
Very Rev Francis MacNamara PP, VF
Mountmellick, Co Laois
Tel 057-8624198

PRIESTS OF THE DIOCESE ELSEWHERE

Very Rev Peter Cribbin
c/o Bishop's House, Dublin Road, Carlow
Very Rev Patrick Dunny
Wood Road, Graignamanagh, Co Kilkenny
Tel 059-9724518
Rev Paul McNamee
c/o Bishop's House, Dublin Road, Carlow

RETIRED PRIESTS

Very Rev Patrick Breen PE
Timahoe, Portlaoise, Co Laois
Tel 057-8627023
Very Rev Charles Byrne
Holy Family Convent,
Newbridge, Co Kildare
Rev Denis Doyle PE, CC
77 Lakelands, Naas, Co Kildare
Tel 045-897470
Very Rev John Fingleton PE
Graiguecullen, Carlow
Tel 059-9142132
Very Rev Laurence Fleming PE
Teach Moling, Oak Park, Carlow
Tel 059-9140944
Very Rev Edward Kelly PE
Rhode, Co Offaly
Tel 046-9737013
Very Rev Moling Lennon PE
364 Sundays Well, Naas, Co Kildare
Tel 045-888667
Very Rev Alphonsus Murphy PE
Carbury, Co Kildare
Tel 046-9553020
Very Rev Michael Noonan PE
Portarlington, Co Laois
Tel 057-8623431
Very Rev Sean O'Laoghaire PE
Paulstown, Gowran, Co Kilkenny
Tel 059-9726104
Very Rev Denis O'Sullivan PE
Monasterevin, Co Kildare
Tel 045-525351
Very Rev Pat Ramsbottom PE
Gorman's Cottage, Cooleragh, Co Kildare
Tel 045-890744
Very Rev Colum Swan PE
32 Cherrygrove, Naas, Co Kildare
Tel 045-856274
Very Rev John Walsh PE
Rath, Portlaoise, Co Laois
Tel 057-8626401

RELIGIOUS ORDERS AND CONGREGATIONS

PRIESTS

CAPUCHINS
Capuchin Friary, 43 Dublin Street, Carlow
Tel 0503-42543/41221 Fax 0503-42030
Guardian: Rev John Wright
Vicar: Rev Michael Duffy

CARMELITES (OCARM)
Carmelite Priory, White Abbey, Co Kildare
Tel 045-521391 Fax 045-522318
Email whiteabbey@eircom.net
Prior: Rev Anthony McDonald (OCarm)
Bursar: Rev Frederick Lally (OCarm)

DOMINICANS
Newbridge College,
Droichead Nua, Co Kildare
Tel 045-431248
Prior: Very Rev Stephen Hutchinson (OP)
Secondary School for Boys

JESUITS
Clongowes Wood College,
Naas, Co Kildare
Tel 045-868663/868202 Fax 045-861042
Email *(College)* reception@clongowes.ie
(Community) reception@clongowes.ie
Rector: Rev Bruce Bradley (SJ)
Headmaster: Rev Leonard Moloney (SJ)
Minister: Rev Michal Sheil (SJ)
Boarding School for Secondary Pupils

ST PATRICK'S MISSIONARY SOCIETY
St Patrick's, Kiltegan, Co Wicklow
Tel 059-6473600 Fax 059-6473622
Email spsoff@iol.ie (office)
Society Leader: Rev Seamus O'Neill (SPS)
Assistant Society Leader
Rev David Walsh (SPS)
Fax *(Society Leader & Council)*
059-6473644

BROTHERS

CHRISTIAN BROTHERS
Christian Brothers' House,
Friary's Road, Naas, Co Kildare
Tel 045-897884
Commuity Leader: Br P.J. McMahon
Community: 6

Christian Brothers' House,
Railway Street, Portlaoise, Co Laois
Tel 057-8621129
Community: 5

DE LA SALLE BROTHERS
St Joseph's Academy, Kildare Town
Tel 045-521788
Headmaster: Mr David Smyth

De La Salle Primary School, Kildare
Tel 045-521852
Headmaster: Mr Shay Nolan

PATRICIAN BROTHERS
Patrician Brothers General Secretariat,
Newbridge, Co Kildare
Tel 045-432357/087-2949504
Fax 045-432731
Email pbros@iol.ie
Superior General: Br Jerome Ellens

Delany House, Castledermot Road,
Tullow, Co Carlow
Tel 059-9151244 Fax 059-9152063
Email patbros@iol.ie
Superior: Br Bosco Mulhare
Community: 3

10 Hawthorn Drive, Tullow, Co Carlow
Tel 059-9181727 Fax 059-9181728
Provincial: Br Camillus Regan
Community: 2

Newbridge, Co Kildare
Tel 045-431475 Fax 045-431505
Superior: Br Cormac Commins
Community: 9
Monastery National School
Tel 045-432174
Patrician Secondary School
Tel 045-432410
Principal: Mr Peter O'Reilly

Rathmoyle, Abbeyleix, Co Laois
Tel 057-8731229
Community: 3
Scoil Mhuire Primary School
Superior: Br James Moran

Patrician Brothers, Cavansheath,
Mountrath, Co Laois
Tel 057-8755964
Superior: Br Gerard Reburn
Community: 2

Patrician Brothers
Shannon Road, Mountrath, Co Laois
Tel 057-8732260
Superior: Br Justin Madden
Community: 2

The Irish Province has seven houses
in Kenya
Regional Superior: Br Felim Ryan
Patrician Formation House,
PO Box 5064, via Eldoret, Kenya
Tel/Fax 0321-61134
Email pbroskam@africaonline.co.ke
Community: 9

SISTERS

AUGUSTINIAN SISTERS
'Villa Nova' Prayer House,
Grangecon, Co Wicklow
Tel 045-403874
Contact: Sr Mary Bernard (OSA)

BRIGIDINE SISTERS
Brigidine Provincialate,
42 The Downs, Portlaoise, Co Laois
Tel/Fax 057-8680280
Provincial Leader: Sr Eileen Deegan
Community: 1

16 Mount Clare, Graguecullen, Co Carlow
Tel 059-9135869
Contact: Sr Maureen O'Leary
Community: 1
Education

Brigidine Convent, Tullow, Co Carlow
Tel 059-9151308
Community Co-ordinator
Sr Thomasina Murphy
Community: 10
Education, Parish Work

Brigidine Sisters, Delany Court, New
Chapel Lane, Tullow, Co Carlow
Contact: Sr Elizabeth Mary McDonald

Teach Bhríde, Tullow, Co Carlow
Tel/Fax 059-9152465
Email teachbhride@eircom.net
Contact: Sr Carmel McEvoy
Brigidine Sisters
Community: 1
Holistic education centre

11 The Rise,
Ballymurphy Road, Tullow, Co Carlow
Tel 059-9152498
Contact: Sr Betty McDonald
Community: 1
Education

1 Salem House,
Chantiere Gate, Portlaoise, Co Laois
Tel 057-8665516
Contact: Sr Kathleen Campion
Community: 1

1 Melrose, Chantiere Gate,
Portlaoise, Co Laois
Tel 057-8682743
Contact: Sr Angela Phelan

Carlow Road, Abbeyleix, Co Laois
Tel 057-8731467
Community: 2
Contact: Sr Mary Hiney
Parish, education

Brigidine Convent, Castletown Road,
Mountrath, Co Laois
Tel 057-8732799
Local Leader: Sr Mary Sheedy
Community: 6

Kiln Lane, Mountrath, Co Laois
Tel 057-8732946
Contact: Sr Breda O'Neill
Community: 1

Brigidine Convent, Paulstown, Co Kilkenny
Tel 059-9726156
Contact: Sr Margaret Walsh
Community: 7

Solas Bhríde, 18 Dara Park, Kildare
Tel 045-522890 Fax 045-522212
Contact: Sr Mary Minehan
Community: 2
Education, spirituality centre

CHARITY OF JESUS AND MARY, SISTERS OF
Moore Abbey, Monasterevan, Co Kildare
Tel 045-525327
Superior: Sr Mary-Anna Lonergan
Email maryannal@eircom.net
Community: 12
Residential centre for mentally
handicapped people
Number in care: 164

CONGREGATION OF THE SISTERS OF MERCY
St Leo's Convent of Mercy, Carlow
Tel 059-9131158 Fax 059-9142226
Non-resident Leader
Sr Bernadette Sheerin
Community: 17

Holy Family Girls' Primary,
Askea, Carlow
Tel 059-9142343

St Leo's College Secondary School,
Dublin Road, Carlow
Tel 059-9131744

4 Pinewood Avenue, Rathnapish, Carlow
Tel/Fax 059-9140408
Non-resident Leader: Sr Bernadette Sheerin
Community: 3

Convent of Mercy,
Monasterevan, Co Kildare
Tel/Fax 045-525372
Non-resident Leader: Sr Dolores Fitzgerald
Community: 5
Primary Girls' School
Two sisters teach in parish secondary
school

St Helen's Convent of Mercy,
Naas, Co Kildare
Tel/Fax 045-897673
Non-resident Leader: Sr Maureen Ryan
Community: 5
Primary Girls' School
Secondary School, Abbeyfield,
Naas, Co Kildare
Tel 045-879634

Convent of Mercy, Rathangan, Co Kildare
Tel/Fax 045-524391
Non-resident Leader: Sr Maureen Ryan
Community: 4
Primary School
Sister teaches in vocational school

Convent of Mercy,
Leighlinbridge, Co Carlow
Tel 059-9721350 Fax 059-9721350
Non-resident Leader: Sr Nancy McLoughlin
Community: 4

4 Lacken View, Naas,
Co Kildare
Tel/Fax 045-874168
Leader: Sr Maureen Ryan
Community: 2

Parkmore, Baltinglass, Co Wicklow
Tel 059-6481561 Fax 059-6481561
Non-resident Leader: Sr Bernadette Sheerin
Community: 2

59 Fr Byrne Park, Graiguecullen, Carlow
Tel/Fax 059-9141479
Non-resident Leader: Sr Nancy McLoughlin
Community: 3

DAUGHTERS OF MARY AND JOSEPH
3/4 Sycamore Road, Connell Drive,
Newbridge, Co Kildare
Tel 045-431842
Community: 3
Parish work
ICJP Refugee Project – Refugees

HOLY FAMILY OF BORDEAUX SISTERS
Holy Family Convent,
Droichead Nua, Co Kildare
Tel 045-431268
Contact: Sr Catherine Moran
Community: 27
Retired sisters, parish work, teaching
English to non-nationals

'Sonas Chríost', Moorfield Park,
Droichead Nua, Co Kildare
Tel 045-431939
Contact: The Superior
Regional Superior: Sr Maureen Slamen
Tel/Fax 045-450125
Community: 5
Sisters involved in administration,
community and parish work

5 Glen Barrow, Ballyfin Road,
Portlaoise, Co Laois
Tel 057-8620365
Contact Person: The Superior
Community: 2
Pastoral care of the sick, nursing,
pastoral work and counselling

POOR CLARES
Poor Clare Colettine Monastery,
Graiguecullen, Carlow
Email poorclarescarlow@gmail.com
Abbess: Sr M. Francis O'Brien
Community: 9
Perpetual adoration, contemplatives

PRESENTATION SISTERS
Generalate, Monasterevin, Co Kildare
Tel 045-525335/525503 Fax 045-525209
Email adminpresevin@eircom.net
Website
www.presentationsistersunion.org
Congregational Leader
Sr Terry Abraham

Presentation Sisters,
Nagle Community (Inter Provincial)
55 Kirwan Park, Mountmellick, Co Laois
Tel 057-8644005 Fax 057-8644372
Email presnagle@jmin.iol.ie
Community: 3
Justice ministry

Mount St Anne's
Retreat and Conference Centre,
Killenard, Portarlington, Co Laois
Tel 057-8626153 Fax 057-8626700
Director: Sr Kathleen Kennedy
Email msannes@iol.ie
Community: 4
Facilities available for seminars,
conferences and meetings on request

St Michael's Primary School
Patrick Street, Portarlington, Co Laois
Tel 0502-23007
Coláiste Íosagáin Secondary School
Tel 0502-23407 Fax 0502-43423
Email
colaisteiosagainprincipla@eircom.net

Presentation Convent,
Ashbrook Gardens, Mountrath Road,
Portlaoise, Co Laois
Tel 057-8670877
School and counselling
Community: 10

Scoil Chroí Ró-Naofa Primary School
Tel/Fax 057-8621904
Scoil Mhuire Primary School
Tel 057-8621476
Scoil Chríost Rí Secondary School
Tel 057-8621441 Fax 057-8661437
Email scrport@eircom.net

17 Parnell Crescent, Knockmay,
Portlaoise, Co Laois
Tel 057-8620358
Community: 3
School and pastoral ministry

O'Moore Place, Portlaoise, Co Laois
Tel 057-8622919
Community: 2
School and pastoral ministry

Presentation Convent, Kildare Town
Tel 045-521481
Community: 15
Community Leader: Sr Bríd Kenny
School and pastoral ministry
Scoil Bhride Naofa Primary School
Tel 045-521799 Fax 045-530653
Email sbpp@eircom.net
Presentation Secondary School
Tel 045-521654 Fax 045-521090
Email psskprincipal@eircom.net

56 Oakley Park, Tullow Road, Carlow
Tel 059-9143103
Community: 4
School ministry
Scoil Mhuire gan Smal Primary School
Tel 059-9142705 Fax 059-9140645
Email officesmns@eircom.net
Presentation College, Askea, Carlow
Tel 059-9143927 Fax 059-9140645
Email presentationcollege@eircom.net

Presentation Convent,
Bagenalstown, Co Carlow
Tel 059-9721263
Email presbagenalstown@eircom.net
Community Leader: Sr Angela Maher
School and pastoral ministry
Community: 13
Queen of the Universe Primary School
Tel 059-9721075
Presentation/De La Salle Secondary
School
Tel 059-9721860 Fax 059-9722558
Email pdlsbc@eircom.net

Presentation/De La Salle College
Muinebheag, Co Carlow
Secondary
Tel 059-9121860
Principal: Mrs Anne Keating

Presentation Convent, Bridge Street,
Mountmellick, Co Laois
Tel 057-8624129
Community: 11
School and pastoral ministry
St Joseph's Primary School
Tel/Fax 057-8624540
Email stjosephsgns.ias@eircom.net
St Mary's Community School
Tel 057-8624220 Fax 057-8644126
Email mountmellick@eircom.net

Shalom, Kilcock, Co Kildare
Tel 01-6287018 Fax 01-6287316
Email culnacille@eircom.net
Community Leader
Sr Kathleen McDonagh
Community: 34
Care of sick and elderly sisters
Scoil Choca Naofa Primary School
Tel 01-6287967
Email scoilchoca.ias@eircomm.net
Scoil Dara Secondary School
Tel 01-6287258 Fax 01-6284075
Email scoildara@eircom.net

Presentation Convent,
27 Abbeyfield, Kilcock, Co Kildare
Tel 01-6284579
Community: 3
Faith development, counselling and
pastoral ministry

ST JOHN OF GOD SISTERS
49 Blundell Wood, Edenderry, Co Offaly
Tel 046-9731582
Community: 1
St Mary's Primary School
Tel 0405-31424. Pupils: 606

St John of God Sisters,
1 Churchview Heights,
Edenderry, Co Offaly
Tel 046-9772717
Community: 3

St John of God Sisters,
88 Lakelands, Naas, Co Kildare
Tel 045-897056
Community: 2

EDUCATIONAL INSTITUTIONS

Carlow College (founded 1785)
College Street, Carlow
Tel 059-9153200 Fax 059-9140258
Email info@carlowcollege.ie
Website www.carlowcollege.ie
President
Rt Rev Mgr Kevin O'Neill BA, MSc Ed
Vice-President and Bursar
Rev John McEvoy BA, STL
Chaplain
Rev Conn Ó Maoldhomhnaigh MA
Priests on Staff
Rev Fergus Ó Fearghaill DSS
Rev Liam Power STL
Rev Sean Maher LSS

St Mary's, Knockbeg College
Knockbeg, Carlow
Tel 059-9142127 Fax 059-9134437
Email knockbegcollege@eircom.net
Rector
Very Rev Mícheál Murphy
Headmaster
Mr Cyril Hughes
www.knockbegcollege.ie

EDMUND RICE SCHOOLS TRUST
St Mary's Academy, Station Road,
Carlow
Tel 0503-42419 Fax 0503-30922
Email principal@cbscarlow.net
Principal: Mr Leo Hogan

Meanscoil Iognáid Rís, Naas, Co Kildare
Tel 045-886402/045-879587
Fax 045-881580
Email admin@naascbs.ie
Website www.naascbs.ie
Principal: Mr N. Merrick

St Mary's Secondary School,
Tower Hill, Portlaoise, Co Laois
Tel 0502-22849/66749
Fax 0502-61292
Email omar2@eircom.net
Website www.portlaoisecbs.20m.com
Principal: Mr Tony Brady

CHARITABLE AND OTHER SOCIETIES

Apostolic Work Society
President: Mrs Carmel Shortt
Glendara, Dublin Road, Clane,
Co Kildare
Tel 045-8688420

Community Services
St Catherine's
Community Services Centre,
St Joseph's Road, Carlow
Tel 059-9131354

DIOCESE OF KILLALA

PATRON OF THE DIOCESE
ST MUREDACH, 12 AUGUST

INCLUDES PORTIONS OF COUNTIES MAYO AND SLIGO

Most Rev John Fleming DD, DCL
Bishop of Killala;
born 16 February 1948;
ordained priest 18 June 1972;
ordained Bishop of Killala
7 April 2002

Residence: Bishop's House,
Ballina, Co Mayo
Tel 096-21518
Fax 096-70344
Email deocilala@eircom.net

ST MUREDACH'S CATHEDRAL, BALLINA

In the lead-up to Catholic Emancipation and the erasing of restrictive laws on the building of Catholic places of worship, Killala diocese, one of the poorest in terms of resources and population, embarked on the massive project of building a new cathedral to replace the stone and thatch structure in Chapel Lane, which had served since 1740.

The project was first envisaged by the elderly Bishop Peter Waldron (1814–1835), but taken vigorously in hand by his coadjutor, Bishop John MacHale, who succeeded him for a short time before becoming Archbishop of Tuam.

In 1831 the first Mass was celebrated within the rough-hewn shell of the new cathedral. The architect was Dominick Madden, who designed Tuam cathedral. Because of financial restraints and the disruption caused by the Famine, several modifications of the design had to be made. It was not until 1853, some twenty-three years after the roofing of the main building, that work on the spire resumed. The entire work on the cathedral was completed in 1892.

The glory of the edifice is in the interior ceiling and overall design, modelled on the vaulting and ribbing of the Church of Santa Maria Sopra Minerva in Rome. The contract for the groining, plastering and stucco work was awarded to Arthur Canning, who undertook to have the bosses at the intersection of the rib mouldings, the centre over the intersections of the nave and transepts, the busts at the intersections of the groins of the naves and side aisles, and the crochets over the eastern windows 'executed by the first artists in the Kingdom'. How well he succeeded can be seen in the much-admired plasterwork of the cathedral ceiling, enhanced by the colour schemes and mosaics. The windows in the cathedral are the artistic treasures of the building, all being the work of the Meyer studios of Munich, whose premises were destroyed by the Allied bombings in World War II.

The cathedral was completely renovated and refurbished in 2000, as part of a diocesan millennium project.

Photo: David Farrell, *The Western People*, Ballina

CHAPTER

Dean: Vacant
Chancellor: Very Rev Canon Seán Killeen
Archdeacon: Very Rev Seán Durkan
Members
Very Rev Patrick Hegarty
Very Rev John McHale
Rt Rev Mgr Kevin Loftus
Rt Rev Mgr Seamus Heverin

Honorary Canons
Very Rev Thomas Finan
Very Rev John Flynn
Very Rev Mark Diamond
Very Rev Patrick Gallagher
Most Rev Thomas Finnegan DD,
Bishop Emeritus

ADMINISTRATION

Vicars General
Rt Rev Mgr Sean Killeen PP
Ballycastle, Co Mayo
Tel 096-43010
Rt Rev Mgr Kevin Loftus PP
Easkey, Co Sligo
Tel 096-49011

Vicars Forane
Very Rev Francis Judge
Very Rev Canon Seán Killeen
Very Rev Brendan Hoban
Very Rev Canon John George MacHale

College of Consultors
Most Rev John Fleming
Canon Sean Killeen
Canon John George MacHale
Very Rev Kevin Loftus
Very Rev Paddy Hoban
Very Rev Gerry O'Hora
Very Rev Brendan Hoban
Very Rev Kevin Hegarty
Rev Michael Gilroy
Rev Liam Reilly

Finance Secretary
Right Rev Mgr Seamus Heverin
Enniscrone, Co Sligo
Tel 096-37802

Diocesan Secretary
Mrs Anne Forbes
Bishop's House, Ballina, Co Mayo
Tel 096-21518 Fax 096-70344
Email secretary@killaladiocese.org

CATECHETICS EDUCATION

Diocesan Advisers for Religious Education
Primary: Sr Patricia Lynott
Convent of Jesus & Mary,
Gortnor Abbey, Crossmolina, Co Mayo
Tel 096-31395
Post-Primary: Vacant

Diocesan Education Council
Chairman: Mr John Cummins

LITURGY

Church Music
Director: Ms Regina Deacy
c/o The Pastoral Centre, Ballina, Co Mayo
Tel 096-70555

Diocesan Liturgy and Music Commission
Chairman: Very Rev Michael Flynn PP
Parochial House, Knockmore,
Ballina, Co Mayo
Tel 094-58108

PASTORAL

Accord
Director: Rev Gerard O'Hora
The Pastoral Centre, Ballina, Co Mayo
Tel 096-70555

Child Protection Committee
Chairperson: Mrs Carmel Jenkins

Communications
Directors: Rev Gerard O'Hora,
Rev Muredach Tuffy

Council of the Laity
Chairperson: Peter McLoughlin

Council of Priests
Chairperson: Very Rev Michael O'Horo PP
Skreen, Co Sligo
Tel 071-9166629
Secretary: Rev Gerard O'Hora CC
St Patrick's Presbytery, Ballina, Co Mayo
Tel 096-71360

Diocesan Finance Committee
Chairman: Bishop Fleming
Secretary: Rt Rev Mgr Seamus Heverin

Ecumenism
Director: Very Rev Anthony Gillespie PP
Moygownagh, Ballina, Co Mayo
Tel 096-31288

Emigrants
Advisors
Very Rev Michael Harrison PP
Binghamstown, Belmullet, Co Sligo
Tel 097-82350
Rev Gerard O'Donnell PP
Geesala, Bangor, Ballina, Co Mayo
Tel 097-86740

Immigrants
Diocesan Representative
Vacant

Legion of Mary
Rev Kieran Holmes
Tel 096-36164

Marriage Tribunal
(See Marriage Tribunals section)

Pilgrimages
Directors: Rev Kieran Holmes CC
Enniscrone, Co Sligo
Tel 096-36164

Pioneer Total Abstinence Association
Diocesan Director
Very Rev Patrick Munnelly PP
Ardagh, Ballina, Co Mayo
Tel 096-31144

Pontifical Mission Societies
Diocesan Director: Rev Edward Rogan
Inver, Ballina, Co Mayo
Tel 097-84598

Travellers
Chaplain: Rev Michael Reilly CC
Crossmolina, Co Mayo
Tel 096-31871

Trócaire
Secretary: Rev Michael Nallen
Aughoose, Ballina, Co Mayo
Tel 097-87990

Vocations
Director: Rev Muredach Tuffy
Newman Institute, Ballina, Co Mayo
Tel 096-72066

Youth Ministry
Co-ordinators: Rev Francis Judge,
Rev Muredach Tuffy

PARISHES

BALLINA (KILMOREMOY)
St Muredach's Cathedral, St Patrick's
Very Rev Brendan Hoban PP, VF
Cathedral Presbytery, Ballina, Co Mayo
Tel 096-71365
Rev Gabriel Rosbotham CC
Cathedral Close, Ballina, Co Mayo
Tel 096-71355
Rev Dr Michael Gilroy CC *(pro tem)*
Cathedral Close, Ballina, Co Mayo
Tel 096-21764
Rev Gerard O'Hora CC
St Patrick's Presbytery, Ballina, Co Mayo
Tel 096-71360
Parish Sister: Sr Maureen McDonnell
Tel 096-23066

BACKS
Christ the King
Very Rev Michael Flynn PP
Knockmore, Ballina, Co Mayo
Tel 094-58108
St Teresa's
Rev Muredach Tuffy CC
Rathduff, Ballina, Co Mayo
Tel 096-21596
Rev Alan Munnelly CC *(pro tem)*

ARDAGH
Very Rev Patrick Munnelly PP
Ardagh, Ballina, Co Mayo
Tel 096-31144

BALLYCASTLE (KILBRIDE AND DOONFEENY)
St Bridget's, St Teresa's
Rt Rev Mgr Seán Killeen PP, VF
Ballycastle, Co Mayo
Tel 096-43010

BALLYCROY
Holy Family
Very Rev Christopher Ginnelly PP
Parochial House, Ballycroy,
Westport, Co Mayo
Tel 098-49134

BALLYSOKEARY
Very Rev James Corcoran PP
Cooneal, Ballina, Co Mayo
Tel 096-32242

BELMULLET
Sacred Heart, Our Lady of Lourdes
Very Rev Francis Judge PP, VF
Belmullet, Co Mayo
Tel 097-81426
Rev John Loftus CC
Church Road, Belmullet, Co Mayo
Tel 097-81087

CASTLECONNOR
St Brendan's
Very Rev Desmond Kelly PP
Corballa, Ballina, Co Mayo
Tel 096-36266

CROSSMOLINA
St Tiernan's, Holy Souls,
Our Lady of Mercy, St Mary's
Very Rev Michael Conway PP
Tel 096-31677
Rev Michael Reilly CC
Tel 096-31344
Crossmolina, Ballina, Co Mayo
Rev Albert Slater CC
Keenagh, Ballina, Co Mayo
Tel 096-53018

DROMORE-WEST (KILMACSHALGAN)
Very Rev Gerard Gillespie PP
Dromore West, Co Sligo
Tel 096-47012

EASKEY
St James's
Rt Rev Mgr Kevin Loftus PP
Easkey, Co Sligo
Tel 096-49011

KILCOMMON-ERRIS
Very Rev Michael Nallen, Co-Pastor
Aughoose, Ballina, Co Mayo
Tel 097-87990
Very Rev Edward Rogan, Co-Pastor
Inver, Barnatra, Ballina
Tel 097-84598

KILFIAN
Sacred Heart
Very Rev Peter O'Brien PP
Kilfian, Killala, Co Mayo
Tel 096-32420

KILGLASS
Holy Family, Christ the King
Very Rev Canon John George MacHale PP
Kilglass, Enniscrone,
Ballina, Co Mayo
Tel 096-36191
Rev Kieran Holmes CC
Enniscrone, Ballina, Co Mayo
Tel 096-36164

KILLALA
St Patrick's
Very Rev Patrick Hoban PP
Killala, Co Mayo
Tel 096-32176

KILMORE-ERRIS
St Joseph's, Holy Family, Seven Dolours
Very Rev Michael Harrison
Binghamstown,
Belmullet, Co Mayo
Tel 097-82350
Rev Kevin Hegarty
Carne, Belmullet, Co Mayo
Tel 097-81011

KILTANE
Sacred Heart
Very Rev Brian Conlon, Co-Pastor
Bangor Erris, Ballina, Co Mayo
Tel 097-83466
St Pius X
Rev Gerard O'Donnell, Co-Pastor
Geesala, Ballina, Co Mayo
Tel 097-86740

LACKEN
St Patrick's
Very Rev Canon Patrick Hegarty PP
Carrowmore, Ballina, Co Mayo
Tel 096-34014

LAHARDANE (ADDERGOOLE)
St Patrick's
Very Rev John Reilly PP
Lahardane, Ballina, Co Mayo
Tel 096-51007
St Mary's
Rev James Cribbin CC
Glenhest, Newport, Co Mayo
Tel 098-41170

MOYGOWNAGH
St Cormac's
Very Rev Anthony Gillespie PP
Moygownagh,
Ballina, Co Mayo
Tel 096-31288

SKREEN AND DROMARD
St Adamnan's
Very Rev Michael O'Horo PP
Skreen, Co Sligo
Tel 071-9166629

TEMPLEBOY
Very Rev John Judge PP
Templeboy, Co Sligo
Tel 096-47103

INSTITUTIONS AND THEIR CHAPLAINS

An Coláiste
Rossport, Ballina, Co Mayo
Tel 097-88940

Convent of Mercy
Belmullet, Co Mayo
Tel 097-81044
Rev Kevin Hegarty

Convent of Jesus and Mary
Enniscrone, Ballina, Co Mayo
Tel 096-36151
Rev Kieran Holmes CC

Convent of Jesus and Mary
Crossmolina, Co Mayo
Tel 096-30876/30877
Very Rev Michael Conway PP

Distrist Hospital
Ballina, Co Mayo
Tel 096-21166
Very Rev Brendan Hoban

District Hospital
Belmullet, Co Mayo
Tel 097-81301
Very Rev Michael Harrison

St Mary's Secondary School
Ballina, Co Mayo
Tel 096-70333
Rev Gerard O'Hora CC

Vocational School
Easkey, Co Sligo
Tel 096-49021
Rt Rev Mgr Kevin Loftus

Vocational School
Ballina, Co Mayo
Tel 096-21472
Rev Gabriel Rosbotham

Vocational School
Crossmolina, Co Mayo
Tel 096-31236
Rev Michael Reilly CC

Vocational School
Belmullet, Co Mayo
Tel 097-81437
Rev Michael Nallen

Vocational School
Lacken Cross, Co Mayo
Tel 096-32177
Very Rev Canon Patrick Hegarty

PRIESTS OF THE DIOCESE ELSEWHERE

Rev Martin Barrett
Saint Paul University, 223 Main Street,
Ottawa, Ontario, Canada KIS 1CU
Rev Thomas Finan
St Patrick's College,
Maynooth, Co Kildare
Tel 01-6285222
Very Rev Martin Keveny
Paroquia Sao Sebastiao,
Caixa Postal 94, CEP 77760-000
Colinas Do Tocantins, Brazil
Tel 63-8311427
Rev Aidan O'Boyle
Loyola University, Chicago
Rev William Reilly
Casilla 09-01-5825, Guayaquil, Ecuador

RETIRED PRIESTS

Very Rev Michael Cawley
Sick leave
Very Rev Canon Mark Diamond
Cathedral Close, Ballina, Co Mayo
Very Rev Sean Durkan
79 The Glebe, Ballina, Co Mayo
Very Rev Canon J. Flynn
Mount Falcon, Knockmore,
Ballina, Co Mayo
Most Rev Thomas Finnegan DD
Carrowmore Lacken,
Ballina, Co Mayo
Right Rev Mgr Patrick Gallagher
Cathedral Close, Ballina
Rt Rev Mgr Seamus Heverin
Enniscrone, Co Sligo
Rev Sean McHugh
Bohernasup, Ballina, Co Mayo

Retired Priests (Other Dioceses)
Very Rev Joseph Cahill
Bohernasup, Ballina, Co Mayo
Rt Rev Mgr Patrick Fox
14 Amana Estate, Ballina, Co Mayo
Very Rev Tony Hannick
Ardnaree, Ballina, Co Mayo

RELIGIOUS ORDERS AND CONGREGATIONS

PRIESTS

SPIRITUAL LIFE INSTITUTE
Holy Hill Hermitage, Skreen, Co Sligo
Tel 071-66021
Superior: Rev Eric Haarer
Community: 8

BROTHERS

MARIST BROTHERS
Convent Hill, Ballina, Co Mayo
Tel 096-22342
Superior: Br Sebastian Davis
Community: 4

SISTERS

CONGREGATION OF THE SISTERS OF MERCY
Sisters of Mercy,
35 Amana Estate, Ballina, Co Mayo
Tel 096-76674 Fax 096-76675
Community: 2

Sisters of Mercy, 'Bethany',
8/9 Rockwell Estate, Killala Road,
Ballina, Co Mayo
Tel 096-23060/23066
Community: 7

Sisters of Mercy, 11 Drom Ard,
Church Road, Belmullet, Co Mayo
Tel 097-81044 Fax 097-20737
Community: 4

JESUS AND MARY, CONGREGATION OF
Convent of Jesus and Mary,
Mullinmore Road,
Crossmolina, Co Mayo
Tel 096-30876/30877
Superior: Sr Fionnuala Keveny
Headmistress: Tel 096-31194/096-31597
Community: 4
Post-Primary Coeducational Day School
Tel 096-31131
Pupils: 467

Convent of Jesus and Mary,
Enniscrone, Co Sligo
Tel 096-36151
Superior: Sr Goretti McGowan
Community: 6
Post-Primary, Coeducational School
Tel 096-36496
Pupils: 362

EDUCATIONAL INSTITUTIONS

St Muredach's College
Ballina, Co Mayo
Tel 096-21298
Principal: Mr Joseph Kenny
Post-Primary Pupils: 400
Rev Dr Michael Gilroy

Newman Institute Ireland
Centre for Pastoral Care,
Salmon Weir, Ballina, Co Mayo
Tel 096-72066
Chancellor
Most Rev John Fleming, DD, DCL
Director: Rev Muredach Tuffy
Academic Director: Rev Dr Michael Gilroy

CHARITABLE AND OTHER SOCIETIES

Council for the West
(Parish Renewal and Development)
Asahi Business Park, Killala, Co Mayo
Tel 096-32014

Society of St Vincent de Paul
Ozanam House, Teeling Street,
Ballina, Co Mayo
Tel 096-72905

St Joseph's Young Priests Society
c/o Pastoral Centre, Ballina, Co Mayo
Tel 096-70555

Legion of Mary
c/o Pastoral Centre, Ballina, Co Mayo
Tel 096-70555
Rev Kieran Holmes
Tel 096-36164

Accord
CMAC Centre
c/o Pastoral Centre, Ballina, Co Mayo
Tel 096-70555

DIOCESE OF KILLALOE

PATRON OF THE DIOCESE
ST FLANNAN, 18 DECEMBER

INCLUDES PORTIONS OF COUNTIES CLARE, LAOIS, LIMERICK,
OFFALY AND TIPPERARY

Most Rev William Walsh DD
Bishop of Killaloe;
born 1935;
ordained priest 21 February
1959;
ordained Bishop of Killaloe
2 October 1994

Residence:
Westbourne, Ennis, Co Clare
Tel 065-6828638
Fax 065-6842538
Email office@killaloediocese.ie
Website www.killaloediocese.ie

CATHEDRAL OF
SS PETER AND PAUL, ENNIS

The church that now serves as the cathedral of the Diocese of Killaloe was originally built to serve as the parish church of Ennis. The diocese had not had a permanent cathedral since the Reformation. In 1828, Francis Gore, a Protestant landowner, donated the site for the new Catholic church. Dominick Madden, who also designed the cathedrals in Ballina and Tuam, was chosen as the architect.

The construction of the new church was a protracted affair. Shortly after the work began, the project ran into financial difficulties and was suspended for three years. Aided by generous donations from local Protestants, including Sir Edward O'Brien of Dromoland and Vesey Fitzgerald, the work began again in 1831. Progress was slow throughout the 1830s and there were many problems. In September 1837 there was a serious accident on the site when the scaffolding collapsed, killing two and seriously injuring two more. Finally, in 1842, the roof was on and the parish priest, Dean O'Shaughnessy, was able to say the first Mass inside the still-unfinished building.

On 26 February 1843, the new church was blessed and placed under the patronage of Saints Peter and Paul, by Bishop Patrick Kennedy. Fr Matthew, 'The Apostle of Temperance', preached the sermon.

Much still remained to be done on the project, but the Great Famine brought the work to a halt. After the Famine, the work recommenced. J. J. McCarthy, one of the leading church architects in nineteenth-century Ireland, was commissioned to oversee the interior decoration of the building. Much of this is still visible, including the internal pillars and arches and the organ gallery.

A local committee decided in 1871 to complete the tower and spire, but owing to financial difficulties, it was not until 23 October 1874 that the final stone was put in place.

In 1889 Dr Thomas McRedmond was appointed coadjutor bishop and he was consecrated in 1890. He had full charge of the diocese, owing to the illness of Bishop Flannery. Though he was already Parish Priest of Killaloe, the new bishop chose to make Ennis his home, remaining there after he succeeded to the office of diocesan bishop, on the death of Dr Flannery. The Parish Church of Ss Peter and Paul was thus designated the pro-cathedral of the diocese.

Major renovations were carried out in 1894. The present main entrance under the tower was constructed, a task that necessitated breaking through a six-foot-thick wall. The building was also redecorated. The improvements were under the direction of Joshua Clarke, father of the stained-glass artist Harry Clarke. The large painting of the Ascension, which dominates the sanctuary, the work of the firm Nagle and Potts, was also installed at this time. The building remained largely unchanged for the next eighty years. A new sacristy and chapter room were added in the 1930s, as were the pipe organ and chapter stalls for the canons.

Another major renovation was carried out in 1973 to bring the building into line with the requirements of the Second Vatican Council. The architect for the work was Andrew Devane and the main contractors were Ryan Brothers, Ennis. The artistic adviser was Enda King. The building was reopened after six months in December 1973. The Clare

Champion reported: 'The main features of the renovation included new altar, ambo, new tabernacle on granite pillar, baptismal font located near sanctuary, new flooring. New heating system, new amplification system and complete reconstruction of the sanctuary.'

In 1990, 163 years after work on the building began, Bishop Harty named it his cathedral. The solemn dedication of the cathedral and the altar took place on 18 November 1990. A fire at a shrine in the cathedral in October 1995 caused serious internal damage. The sanctuary had to be rebuilt and the building redecorated. The restoration was celebrated with Solemn Evening Prayer in November 1996.

In 2006 major repair and refurbishment was completed on the Cathedral spire.

CHAPTER

Dean: Vacant
Archdeacon: Venerable John F. Hogan AP
Ballycommon, Nenagh, Co Tipperary
Chancellor: Very Rev Brendan
O'Donoghue, Shannon
Precentor: Very Rev Patrick O'Brien
Tuamgraney, Co Clare
Treasurer: Very Rev Patrick Taaffe, Ennis
Members
Very Rev Reuben Butler,
Newmarket-on-Fergus
Very Rev Caimin O'Carroll, Barefield
Very Rev Seamus Mullin, Miltown Malbay

COLLEGE OF CONSULTORS

Ven John F. Hogan AP
Ballycommon, Nenagh, Co Tipperary
Very Rev Caimin O'Carroll AP
Barefield, Co Clare
Very Rev Seamus Gardiner PP
Portroe, Co Tipperary
Very Rev Michael Sheedy PP
Kilrush, Co Clare
Very Rev Michael McLaughlin PP
Kilmaley, Co Clare
Very Rev Brian Geoghegan PP
Tubber, Co Clare
Rev Willie Teehan PP
Templederry, Co Tipperary
Rev Ger Nash
Crusheen, Co Clare
Rev Pat Treacy CC
Roscrea, Co Tipperary

ADMINISTRATION

Killaloe Diocesan Office
Diocesan Secretary (part-time)
Rev Ger Nash
Diocesan Finance Officer: Mr John Lillis
Diocesan Office Administrator
Ms Margaret Flynn
Secretarial: Ms Mary Brohan
Westbourne, Ennis, Co Clare
Tel 065-6828638 Fax 065-6842538
Email office@killaloediocese.ie
Education Secretary: Rev Gerry Kenny
Westbourne, Ennis, Co Clare
Tel 085-7858344
Sr Marie McNamara
Parish Pastoral Office,
c/o Westbourne, Ennis, Co Clare
Tel 065-6842235
Email kpastoral5@eircom.net

Vicars General
Very Rev Seamus Gardiner PP
Portroe, Nenagh, Co Tipperary
Tel 067-23105
Rev Michael Sheedy PP
Kilrush, Co Clare
Tel 065-9051093

Vicars Forane & Moderators of Clusters
Inish Chathaigh: Rev Michael Collins
Kilrush, Co Clare
Tel 065-9051016
South-East Clare: Rev Brendan Kyne PP
Castleconnell, Co Limerick
Tel 061-377170

Mid Clare: Very Rev Pat Larkin
Mullagh, Co Clare
Tel 065-7087012
Clare Central: Rev Tom Hogan
Cathedral, Ennis, Co Clare
Tel 065-6824043
Imeall Boirne: Rev Ger Nash
Crusheen, Co Clare
Tel 065-6827113
Ralahine: Rev Arnold Rosney
5 Drumgeely Avenue, Shannon, Co Clare
East Clare: Very Rev John Jones PP
Mountshannon, Co Clare
Tel 061-927213
Nenagh: Rev Brendan Moloney
Silvermines, Co Tipperary
Tel 067-25864
Birr/Roscrea: Rev Michael Harding
Templemore Road, Roscrea
Tel 0505-21218
Cois Deirge: Rev Michael Cooney
Terryglass, Co Tipperary
Tel 067-22017

Finance Committee
Chairman: Most Rev William Walsh DD
Secretary: Mr John Lillis
Mr David Williams
Rev Gerard Kenny
Teresa Fell

Killaloe Priests' Benevolent Fund
Secretary: Mr John Lillis
c/o Westbourne, Ennis, Co Clare
Tel 065-6828638

Killaloe Priests' Subsidy Fund
Secretary: Mr John Lillis
c/o Westbourne, Ennis, Co Clare
Tel 065-6828638

Killaloe Priests' Hospital Fund
Secretary: Mr John Lillis
c/o Westbourne, Ennis, Co Clare
Tel 065-6828638 Fax 065-6842538

Diocesan Archivist
c/o Diocesan Secretary
Westbourne, Ennis, Co Clare
Tel 065-6828638

Diocesan Secretary (part-time)
Rev Ger Nash
c/o Westbourne, Ennis, Co Clare
Tel 065-6828638

Episcopal Vicars for Retired Priests
Very Rev Tim O'Brien PP
Carrigatoher, Nenagh, Co Tipperary
Tel 067-31231
Very Rev Joe Hourigan PP
Lissycasey, Co Clare
Tel 065-6834145

CATECHETICS EDUCATION

Boards of Management
Primary Schools: St Senan's Education
Office, Limerick Diocesan Office, Social
Service Centre, Henry Street, Limerick
Tel 061-317743
Director: Vacant

Religious Education in Primary Schools
Directors: Sr Essie Hayes
Ashe Road, Nenagh, Co Tipperary
Tel 067-33835
Mr Joe Searson
Mullagh, Co Clare
Tel 065-7087875/087-6762023
Mr Gerald Cronin
La Salette, Clare Road, Ennis, Co Clare
Tel 087-2908412

Religious Education in Post-Primary Schools
Directors: Rev Tom Hogan Adm
The Cathedral Presbytery,
Ennis, Co Clare
Tel 065-6824043
Sr Marie McNamara
Pastoral Office, Westbourne,
Ennis, Co Clare
Tel 065-6842235/086-8373922

PASTORAL

Diocesan Pastoral Planning
Director: Rev Harry Bohan
Pastoral Planing Office,
Westgate Business Park,
Kilrush Road, Ennis, Co Clare
Tel 065-6824094
Parish Pastoral Office
c/o Westbourne, Ennis, Co Clare
Tel 065-6842235
Diocesan/Parish Resource Person
Sr Mary Nash
Feighroe, Connolly, Ennis, Co Clare
Tel 065-6839339

Pastoral Office and Biblical Ministry
Sr Marie McNamara
c/o Killaloe Diocesan Office,
Westbourne, Ennis, Co Clare
Tel 065-6842235
Email kpastoral5@eircom.net
Pastoral Worker – West Clare Parishes
Ms Maureen Kelly

Diocesan Pastoral Council
Chairperson: Mr Leonard Cleary
Ballyportry, Corofin, Co Clare
Secretary: Ms Margaret Flynn
Westbourne, Ennis, Co Clare

Accord
Director: Rev Tom Fitzpatrick
Ennis Accord Centre, c/o Clarecare,
Harmony Row, Ennis, Co Clare
Tel 1850-585000
Director: Very Rev W. Teehan
Nenagh Centre, Loretto House,
Kenyon Street, Nenagh, Co Tipperary
Tel 067-31272

CURA
Barrack Street, Ennis, Co Clare
Tel 065-6829905/1850-58-5000

Communications
Director: Rev Brendan Quinlivan
c/o Bishop's House, Westbourne,
Ennis, Co Clare
Tel 065-6828638/061-924035

Child Protection Committee
Chairperson: Rev Pat Malone
Killaloe, Co Clare
Delegates: Rev Pat Malone
Tel 086-8096074
Mrs Christina Lemass
Tel 086-8096027

Council of Priests
Chairperson: Very Rev Michael Sheedy PP
Kilrush, Co Clare
Tel 065-9051093
Secretary: Rev Pat Larkin
Mullagh, Co Clare
Tel 065-7087012

Ecumenism
Director: Very Rev Tom Corbett
Roscrea, Co Tipperary

Lourdes Pilgrimage
Director: Very Rev Tom Ryan PP
Shannon, Co Clare
Tel 061-361257

Marriage Tribunal
(See Marriage Tribunals section)

Pastoral Care of Immigrants
Sr Maureen Haugh
c/o Bishop's House, Westbourne, Ennis,
Co Clare
Tel 065-6828638

Pioneer Total Abstinence Association
Diocesan Director
Very Rev Michael McInerney AP
Quin, Co Clare
Tel 065-6825649

Polish Chaplain
Rev Tomasz Daukszewicz
Cathedral Presbytery, Ennis, Co Clare
Tel 087-0515788

Pontifical Mission Societies
Diocesan Director
Very Rev Tom O'Halloran
Borrisokane, Co Tipperary
Tel 067-27105

Ceifin, Centre for Values Led Change
Founder/Director
Rev Harry Bohan BA, MScEcon
Westgate Business Park, Ennis, Co Clare
Tel 065-6824094

Social Services
North Tipperary Community Services
Kenyon Street, Nenagh, Co Tipperary
Tel 067-31800
Clarecare
Harmony Row, Ennis, Co Clare
Tel 065-6828178

Travellers
Chaplain
c/o Bishops House, Westbourne,
Ennis, Co Clare
Tel 065-6828638

Vocations
Director: Rev Ignatius McCormack
St Flannan's College, Ennis, Co Clare
Tel 065-6828019/086-2777139

PARISHES

Parishes follow alphabetically. Historical names are given in parentheses. Church titulars are in italics.

ENNIS
Cathedral: SS Peter & Paul
Very Rev Tom Hogan Adm
Tel 087-6446410
Rev Fergal O'Neill
Tel 087-6615975
Rev Martin Blake CC
Tel 087-9033682
Rev Tomasz Daukszewicz
Tel 087-0515788
Cathedral Presbytery, Ennis, Co Clare
Tel 065-6824043 Fax 065-6842541
Email cathedralennis@eircom.net
Website www.ennisparish.com
St Joseph's, Lifford
Very Rev John McGovern
Tel 065-6822166/086-3221210
St Joseph's Presbytery, 52 Kincora Park,
Lifford, Ennis, Co Clare
Christ the King, Cloughleigh
Rev Tom O'Gorman
Tel 065-6840715/087-2285355
Christ the King, Cloughleigh,
Ennis, Co Clare
Tel 065-6840715
Rev Pat Taaffe AP
3 Cottage Garden, Station Road,
Ennis, Co Clare
Tel 065-6891983/086-1731070
Rev Paddy Conway AP
c/o Wesbourne, Ennis, Co Clare
Tel 087-6831992
Parish Sisters: Sr Ann Boland
Tel 065-6844742/087-1369517
Sr de Montfort
Tel 065-6828024/086-1993838

INIS CHATHAIGH PARISHES
Carrigaholt & Cross (Kilballyowen)
Blessed Virgin Mary, Carrigaholt
The Holy Spirit, Doonaha
Our Lady of Lourdes, Cross
St John the Baptist, Kilbaha
Very Rev Michael Casey PP
Cross, Co Clare
Tel 065-9058008/086-0842216
Very Rev Patrick Culligan AP
Carrigaholt, Co Clare
Tel/Fax 065-9058043 Tel 087-9863865

Doonbeg (Killard) & Kilkee
Our Lady Assumed into Heaven,
Doonbeg
St Senan, Bealaha
Our Lady Assumed into Heaven &
St Senan, Kilkee
St Flannan, Lisdeen
Very Rev Gerry Kenny PP
Circular Road, Kilkee, Co Clare
Tel 065-9056580/087-7858344
Fax 065-9056104

Very Rev Joe Haugh AP
Bealaha, Doonbeg, Co Clare
Tel/Fax 065-9055022
Tel 065-9051093/086-2603314

Killimer & Kilrush
St Senan, Knockerra
St Imy, Killimer
St Senan, Kilrush
Little Senan Church, Monmore
Very Rev Michael Sheedy PP
Toler Street, Kilrush, Co Clare
Tel 065-9051093/087-2623972 Fax 065-9052015
Rev Michael E. Collins CC and Moderator
O'Gorman Street, Kilrush, Co Clare
Tel 065-9051016/087-6389847

Cooraclare (Kilmacduane) & Kilmurry McMahon
St Senan, Cooraclare
St Mary, Cree
St Mary, Kilmurry McMahon
St Kerin, Labasheeda
Very Rev John Kelly PP
Labasheeda, Co Clare
Tel 065-6830126/087-2439273
Very Rev Patrick Carmody AP
Cooraclare, Co Clare
Tel 065-9059010/086-3017371
Very Rev Peter O'Loughlin AP
Kilmihil, Co Clare

Kilmihil
St Michael
Very Rev Peter O'Loughlin PP
Kilmihil, Co Clare
Tel 065-9050016/086-8250016

Pastoral Assistant, Inis Chathaigh
Ms Maureen Kelly
Pastoral Office, Youth Centre,
Kilrush, Co Clare
Tel 065-9062565/087-2890942

IMEALL BÓIRNE PARISHES
Corofin
St Brigid, Corofin
St Joseph, Kilnaboy
St Mary, Rath
Rev Damien Nolan
1a Laghtagoona, Corofin, Co Clare
Tel 065-6837178/086-8396636

Crusheen (Inchicronan)
St Cronan, Crusheen
The Immaculate Conception, Ballinruan
Rev Ger Nash
c/o Crusheen, Ennis, Clare
Tel 065-6827113/086-8576153
Fax 065-6827163

Dysart & Ruan
St Mary's, Ruan
St Tola, Dysart
Rev Pat O'Neill
Ruan, Co Clare
Tel 065-6827799/086-2612124

Tubber (Kilkeedy)
St Michael, Tubber
All Saints, Boston
Rev Brian Geoghegan
Tubber, Gort, Co Clare
Tel 091-633124/087-2387067

BALLYNACALLY (CLONDEGAD)
Our Lady of the Wayside, Lissycasey
Christ the King, Ballynacally
Very Rev Joseph Hourigan PP
Lissycasey, Ennis, Co Clare
Tel 065-6834145
Rev Tom O'Dea
Ballynacally, Co Clare
Tel 065-6838135/086-8107475

BIRR
St Brendan, Birr
Our Lady of the Annunciation, Carrig
Email info@stbrendansbirr.ie
Website www.stbrendansbirr.ie
Very Rev Anthony Cahir PP
Tel 057-9120097/086-2612121
Rev David Carroll
Tel 057-9120098/086-2367909
Rev Patrick Gilbert (Chaplain)
Tel 057-9120098/087-2431956
Birr, Co Offaly
Rev Michael Reddan (SVD)
5 Woodlands Park, Birr, Co Offaly
Tel 057-9121757/087-7599789

BODYKE (KILNOE AND TUAMGRANEY)
Our Lady Assumed into Heaven, Bodyke
Rev Maurice Harmon *(priest in residence)*
Bodyke, Co Clare
Tel 061-921060/087-6979773
St Joseph, Tuamgraney
Very Rev Canon Patrick O'Brien AP
Tuamgraney, Co Clare
Tel 061-921056

BORRISOKANE
SS Peter & Paul, Borrisokane
St Michael the Archangel, Eglish
Very Rev Tom O'Halloran PP
Tel 067-27105 Fax 067-27821
Rev J. J. Rodgers CC
Borrisokane, Co Tipperary
Tel 067-27140

BOURNEA (COURAGANEEN)
St Patrick, Bournea
St Brigid, Clonakenny
Very Rev Noel Kennedy PP
Bournea, Roscrea, Co Tipperary
Tel 0505-43211/086-3576775

BROADFORD
St Peter, Broadford
St Mary, Kilbane
St Joseph, Kilmore
Very Rev John Bane PP
Broadford, Co Clare
Tel 061-473123/086-8246555

CASTLECONNELL
St Joseph, Castleconnell
St Patrick, Ahane
Very Rev Brendan Kyne PP
Tel 061-377170/087-2025038
Very Rev James Minogue AP
Tel 061-377166/087-6228674
Rev Donal Dwyer CC
Tel 061-377126
Castleconnell, Co Limerick

CLARECASTLE (CLARE ABBEY)
SS Peter & Paul, Clarecastle
St John the Baptist, Ballyea
Very Rev Harry Brady PP
Parochial House, Clarecastle, Co Clare
Tel 065-6823011

CLONLARA (DOONAS AND TRUAGH)
St Senan, Clonlara
Mary, the Mother of God, Truagh
Very Rev Pat Greed PP
18 Churchfield, Clonlara, Co Clare
Tel 061-354594/086-6067003
Very Rev Brendan Cleary AP
17 Churchfield, Clonlara, Co Clare
Tel 061-354028/086-8484550

CLOUGHJORDAN
St Michael & St John, Cloughjordan
St Flannan's, Ardcroney
St Ruadhán, Kilruane
Rev Tom Hannon PP
Templemore Road, Cloughjordan,
Co Tipperary
Tel 0505-42266
Very Rev Enda Burke AP
Cloughjordan, Co Tipperary
Tel 0505-42120

COOLMEEN (KILFIDANE)
St Benedict, Coolmeen
St Mary, Cranny
Very Rev John O'Keeffe *(priest in residence)*
Cranny, Ennis, Co Clare
Tel 065-6832119

DOORA AND KILRAGHTIS
St Brecan, Doora
The Immaculate Conception, Barefield
Our Lady's Chapel
Rev Jerry Carey
3 The Woods, Cappahard, Tulla Road,
Ennis, Co Clare
Tel 065-6822225/086-2508444
Very Rev Caimin Canon O'Carroll AP
Barefield, Ennis, Co Clare
Tel 065-6821190/087-2521388
Fax 065-6841902

DUNKERRIN
SS Mary & Joseph, Dunkerrin
St Joseph, Moneygall
Sacred Heart, Barna
Very Rev Pat Mulcahy PP
Dunkerrin, Birr, Co Offaly
Tel 0505-45982/087-6329913

FEAKLE
St Mary, Feakle
St Joseph, Kilclarin
Very Rev Brendan Quinlivan Adm
(priest in residence)
Feakle, Co Clare
Tel 061-924035/087-2736310

INCH AND KILMALEY
St John the Baptist, Kilmaley
Our Lady of the Wayside, Inch
St Michael the Archangel, Connolly
Very Rev Michael McLaughlin PP
Airfield, Inch, Ennis, Co Clare
Tel 065-6839332

Assistant Priest
Rev Ignatius McCormack
St Flannan's College,
Ennis, Co Clare
Tel 086-2777139/065-6828019

KILBARRON AND TERRYGLASS
Immaculate Conception, Terryglass
St Barron, Kilbarron
Very Rev Michael Cooney PP
Terryglass, Nenagh, Co Tipperary
Tel 067-22017

KILCOLMAN
St Colman, Kilcolman
St Ita, Coolderry
St John, Ballybritt
Very Rev Kieran Blake PP
Kilcolman, Sharavogue,
Birr, Co Offaly
Tel 0509-20812/087-9302214

KILDYSART
St Michael
Very Rev Neil Dargan PP
Kildysart, Co Clare
Tel 065-6832155/087-7530209
Parish Office
c/o Community Centre,
Kildysart, Co Clare
Tel 065-6832838

KILLALOE
St Flannan, Killaloe
St Thomas, Bridgetown
Sacred Heart & St Lua, Garraunboy
Very Rev James Grace PP
Killaloe, Co Clare
Tel 061-376137/087-6843315
Rev Noel Hayes (SPS)
Bridgetown, Co Clare
Tel 061-377158

KILLANAVE AND TEMPLEDERRY
Immaculate Conception, Templederry
Our Lady of the Wayside, Killeen
Our Lady of the Wayside, Curreeney
Very Rev Willie Teehan PP
Tel 067-25140/087-2347927
Rev Leo Long
Tel 0504-52988/086-8353388
Templederry, Nenagh,
Co Tipperary

KILLANENA AND FLAGMOUNT
St Mary, Killanena
St Mary, Flagmount
Very Rev James O'Brien
Flagmount, Co Clare
Tel 061-925032/087-2665793
Very Rev Brendan Quinlivan
Feakle, Co Clare
Tel 061-924035

KILNAMONA (INAGH)
Immaculate Conception, Inagh
The Blessed Virgin Mary, Cloonanaha
St Joseph, Kilnamona
Very Rev Sean Sexton PP
Kilnamona, Ennis, Co Clare
Tel 065-6829507/087-2621884

KINNITTY
St Flannan, Kinnity
St Luna, Caddamstown
St Finan Cam, Longford
St Molua, Roscomroe
Very Rev Michael O'Meara PP
Kinnity, Birr, Co Offaly
Tel 0509-37021/087-7735977

KYLE AND KNOCK
St Molua, Ballaghmore
St Patrick, Knock
Service provided by priests of Roscrea
Parish

LORRHA AND DORRHA
St Ruadhan, Lorra
Our Lady Queen of Ireland, Rathcabbin
Redwood Church
Very Rev Joe Kennedy PP
Lorrha, Nenagh, Co Tipperary
Tel 090-9747009
Very Rev John Donnelly AP
Rathcabbin, Roscrea, Co Tipperary
Tel 0509-39072

MILTOWN MALBAY (KILFARBOY)
St Joseph, Miltown Malbay
St Mary, Moy
Very Rev Seán Murphy PP
Tel 065-7084129
Very Rev Canon Seamus Mullin AP
Tel 065-7084003
Miltown Malbay, Co Clare
Parish Office: Tel 065-7079829

MOUNTSHANNON (CLONRUSH)
St Caimin, Mountshannon
St Flannan, Whitegate
Very Rev John Jones PP
Mountshannon, Co Clare
Tel 061-927213/086-1933479
Very Rev Liam Murray AP
Whitegate, Co Clare
Tel 061-927009

MULLAGH (KILMURRAY-IBICKANE)
Our Lady, Star of the Sea, Quilty
St Mary, Mullagh
The Most Holy Redeemer, Coore
Very Rev Pat Larkin PP
Tel 065-7087012/087-2300627
Very Rev Timothy Tuohy AP
Tel 065-7087014
Mullagh, Co Clare

NENAGH
St Mary of the Rosary, Nenagh
St John the Baptist, Tyone
Sacristy: 067-37135
Parish Office: 067-37136
Fax: 067-37137
Priest on Duty: 087-2405762
Email stmarysnenagh@eircom.net
Very Rev Pat Malone PP
'Maryville', Church Street,
Nenagh, Co Tipperary
Tel 067-37130
Rev Tom Whelan CC
Tel 067-37131/087-2730299
Rev Dan Fitzgerald (SSC)
Tel 067-37132

Rev Anthony McMahon CC
Tel 067-37134/086-8243801
The Presbytery, Nenagh, Co Tipperary
Tel 067-31272
Very Rev Tom Seymour AP
Church Road, Nenagh, Co Tipperary
Tel 067-31381

NEWMARKET-ON-FERGUS
BVM of the Rosary, Newmarket-on-Fergus
Our Lady of the Wells
St Conaire, Carrygarry
Very Rev Tom Fitzpatrick PP
Tel 061-368127
Very Rev Reuben Canon Butler AP
Tel 061-368433 Fax 061-368808
Newmarket-on-Fergus, Co Clare

O'CALLAGHAN'S MILLS
St Patrick's, O'Callaghan's Mills
St Senan, Kilkishen
St Vincent de Paul, Oatfield
Very Rev Hugh O'Dowd PP
Parochial House
O'Callaghan's Mills, Co Clare
Tel 065-6835148
Rev Diarmuid McCormick CC
Kilkishen, Co Clare
Tel 061-367193

OGONNELLOE
St Molua, Ogonnelloe
St Mary, Ballybrohan
Priest in residence
Ballyheafey, Killaloe, Co Clare
Tel 061-376766

PORTROE (CASTLETOWN ARRHA)
Blessed Virgin Mary
Very Rev Seamus Gardiner
Portroe, Nenagh, Co Tipperary
Tel 067-23105/086-8392741

PUCKANE (CLOGHPRIOR AND MONSEA)
Our Lady & St Patrick, Puckane
St Mary's Church, Carrig
Very Rev John Slattery PP
Puckane, Nenagh, Co Tipperary
Tel 067-24105/087-2466078
Archdeacon John F. Hogan AP
Ballycommon, Nenagh, Co Tipperary
Tel 067-24153/087-7536526

QUIN
St Mary, Quin
St Stephen, Maghera
Pope John XXIII Memorial Church, Clooney
Very Rev Michael Collins PP
Tel 065-6825430/086-3475085
Very Rev Michael McInerney AP
Tel 065-6825649
Quin, Co Clare

ROSCREA
St Cronan, Roscrea
St John the Baptist, Camblin
Email rosrc@eircom.net
Very Rev Dr Tom Corbett PP
The Valley, Roscrea, Co Tipperary
Tel 0505-21108/086-8418570

Rev Michael Harding CC
Templemore Road, Roscrea, Co Tipperary
Tel 0505-21218/087-3223827
Rev Pat Treacy CC
Roscrea, Co Tipperary
Tel 0505-21370/087-9798643
Rev Lorcan Kenny, Chaplain
The Valley, Roscrea, Co Tipperary
Tel 0505-23637/087-6553402

SCARIFF AND MOYNOE
Sacred Heart, Scariff
St Mary, Clonusker
Very Rev Pat Sexton, *Priest in residence*
Scariff, Co Clare
Tel 061-921013/087-2477814

SHANNON
The Immaculate Mother of God, Shannon
SS John & Paul, Shannon
Very Rev Tom Ryan PP
4 Dun na Rí, Shannon, Co Clare
Tel 061-364133/087-2349816
Very Rev Canon Brendan O'Donoghue AP
12 Tullyglass Square,
Shannon, Co Clare
Tel 061-361257/086-8308153
Rev Arnold Rosney CC
5 Drumgeely Avenue,
Shannon, Co Clare
Tel 061-471513/087-8598710

SHINRONE
St Mary, Shinrone
St Patrick, The Pike
Very Rev Frank Meehan PP
Tel 0505-47167/087-2302413
Very Rev Francis Bergin AP
Tel 0505-47133
Shinrone, Co Offaly

SILVERMINES
Our Lady of Lourdes, Silvermines
Our Lady of the Wayside, Ballinaclough
Very Rev Brendan Moloney PP
Silvermines, Nenagh,
Co Tipperary
Tel 067-25864/087-2907705
Very Rev Manus Rodgers AP
Silvermines, Nenagh,
Co Tipperary
Tel 067-25131

SIXMILEBRIDGE
St Finaghta, Sixmilebridge
St Mary's, Kilmurry
Very Rev Harry Bohan PP
2 Oakwood, Sixmilebridge, Co Clare
Tel 061-369134/086-8223362
Parish Office: Sixmilebridge, Co Clare
Tel 061-713682

TOOMEVARA
St Joseph, Toomevara
St Joseph, Ballinree
St Joseph, Gortagarry
St Joseph, Grenanstown
Rev William McCormack PP
Tel 067-26023/087-4168855
Rev Pat Deely
Tel 067-26010/086-8330225
Toomevara, Co Tipperary

TULLA
SS Peter & Paul, Tulla
The Immaculate Conception,
Drumcharley
St James, Knockjames
Very Rev Martin O'Brien PP
Newline, Tulla, Co Clare
Tel 065-6835117/087-2504075
Rev Brendan Lawlor CC
2 Powerscourt, Tulla, Co Clare
Tel 065-6835284/087-9845417

YOUGHALARRA (BURGESS AND YOUGHAL)
Holy Spirit, Youghalarra
The Immaculate Conception, Ballywilliam
Very Rev Timothy O'Brien PP
Carrigatoher, Nenagh, Co Tipperary
Tel 067-31231/087-2623922
Very Rev Edmund Kennedy AP
Newtown, Nenagh, Co Tipperary
Tel 067-23103

INSTITUTIONS AND THEIR CHAPLAINS

Carrigoran House
Newmarket-on-Fergus, Co Clare
Tel 061-368100
Very Rev Tom Fitzpatrick
Tel 061-471406

Community Hospital
Kilrush, Co Clare
Tel 065-9051966
Very Rev Michael Sheedy PP, VG

General Hospital, Ennis
Acute Psychiatric Unit
Tel 065-6863218
Very Rev Tom Hogan Adm
Tel 065-6824043

Cahercalla Community Hospital and Hospice
Cahercalla, Ennis, Co Clare
Rev Tom Hogan
Tel 065-6824388

County Hospital, Nenagh
Co Tipperary
Tel 067-31491
Very Rev Pat Malone PP

District Hospital, Birr
Co Offaly
Tel 0509-20819
Very Rev Anthony Cahir PP

District Hospital, Raheen
Tuamgraney, Co Clare
Tel 061-923007
Rev Maurice Harmon

St Joseph's Hospital
Ennis, Co Clare
Tel 065-6840666
Very Rev John McGovern Adm

Welfare Home, Birr
Co Offaly
Tel 0509-20248
Very Rev Anthony Cahir PP

Welfare Home, Nenagh
Co Tipperary
Tel 067-31893
Very Rev Pat Malone PP

Welfare Home, Roscrea
Co Tipperary
Tel 0505-21389
Very Rev Tom Corbett PP

Regina House
Kilrush, Co Clare
Tel 065-9051209
Very Rev Michael Sheedy PP, VG

Community School, Roscrea
Co Tipperary
Tel 0505-21454
Rev Lorcan Kenny

St Anne's Community College
Killaloe, Co Clare
Tel 061-376257
Veronica Molloy

St Brendan's Community School
Birr, Co Offaly
Tel 0509-20510
Rev Patrick Gilbert

St Caimin's Community School
Shannon, Co Clare
Tel 061-364211
Cora Guinnane

Kilrush Community School
Tel 065-9051359
Sr Margaret Pepper

St Joseph's Community College
Kilkee, Co Clare
Tel 065-9056138
Mrs Ann Healy

St Patrick's Comprehensive School
Shannon, Co Clare
Tel 061-361428
Nuala Murray

Kiladysart Community College
Co Clare
Tel 065-6832300
Joanne O'Brien

PRIESTS OF THE DIOCESE ELSEWHERE

Rev Tony Casey
Padres de San Columbano,
Apartado 39-073/074, Lima 39, Peru
Rev Pat Cotter
c/o Killaloe Diocesan Office
Rev Des Hillery
Padres de San Columbano,
Apartado 39-073/074, Lima 39, Peru
Rev Capt Paschal Hanrahan
2/2 Paul Gehardt Strasse, Sennelager,
33104 Paderborn, Germany
Rev Colm Hogan
Casilla 09-01-5825, Guayaquil,
Ecuador, South America
Rev Michael Hogan
c/o Killaloe Diocesan Office

Rev Seamus Horgan
Apostolic Nunciature, En Suisse,
Thunstrasse 60, Case Postale 259,
3000 Berne 6, Switzerland
Rev Michael Leonard
6020 West Ardmore Avenue,
Chicago, IL 60646, USA
Tel 001-7736775341
Rev Albert McDonnell
Vice Rector, Irish College,
Via dei SS Quattro 1, 00184 Roma, Italy
Tel 00-3906-772631
Rev John Molloy
Casa Central Santiago Apostal,
Av. Pedro do Osma 428, Barranco,
Lima, Peru
Right Rev Mgr Eugene Nugent DCL
167 Argyle Street, Kowloon City,
Hong Kong
Rev John O'Donovan
PO Box 897, Oldsmar,
Florida 34677 USA
Rev Donagh O'Meara
St Kevin's Catholic Church,
550 Stanford Road, Windvogel,
Port Elizabeth 6059, South Africa
Rev Paul Ryan
c/o Killaloe Diocesan Office

RETIRED PRIESTS

Rev Tom Burke
Ruan, Co Clare *and* c/o Carrigoran House,
Newmarket-on-Fergus, Co Clare
Tel 061-368100
Rev Con Desmond
c/o Westbourne, Ennis, Co Clare
Very Rev Gerard Fitzpatrick
Cahercalla Community Hospital,
Ennis, Co Clare
Tel 065-6824388/086-2311923
Very Rev Paschal Flannery
Ballinderry, Nenagh, Co Tipperary
Tel 067-22916/086-2225099
Very Rev Paddy Lynch
Deerpark, Clarecastle
Tel 065-6822588
Very Rev Charles Navin
Tubber, Gort, Co Galway
Tel 091-63323
Very Rev Oliver O'Doherty
Church Road, Neenagh, Co Tipperary

RELIGIOUS ORDERS AND CONGREGATIONS

PRIESTS

CISTERCIANS
Mount Saint Joseph Abbey
Roscrea, Co Tipperary
Tel 0505-25600 Fax 0505-25610
Email community@msjroscrea.ie
Abbot: Rt Rev Dom Richard Purcell (OCSO)

FRANCISCANS
Franciscan Friary, Ennis, Co Clare
Tel 065-6828751 Fax 065-6822008
Email friars.ennis@eircom.net
Guardian: Rev Hugh McKenna (OFM)

Allianz ⑪

BROTHERS

CHRISTIAN BROTHERS
Christian Brothers' House,
New Road, Ennis, Co Clare
Tel 065-6821471/6828469 (office)
Community Leader: Br Liam Roche
Community: 6

Christian Brothers' House,
Nenagh, Co Tipperary
Tel 067-31557
Community Leader: Br John Dooley
Community: 7

PRESENTATION BROTHERS
Presentation Brothers,
Birr, Co Offaly
Tel 0509-20247
Contact: Br Ultan Rohan
Community: 4

SISTERS

CONGREGATION OF THE SISTERS OF MERCY
Mercy Sisters,
Garinis Clonroadmore, Ennis, Co Clare
Tel 065-6820768 Fax 065-6829174
Non-resident Leader: Sr Alice O'Gorman
Community: 2

St Xavier's, Ennis, Co Clare
Tel 065-6828024 Fax 065-6828776
Non-resident Leader: Sr Mairead Kelly
Community: 20
Primary education, social work, visitation

1 Corovorrin Crescent, Ennis, Co Clare
Tel 065-6841375
Non-resident Leader: Sr Teresa Browne
Community: 5
Social work, education

7 Shalee Drive,
Cloughleigh, Ennis, Co Clare
Tel 065-6828894 Fax 065-6828892
Non-resident Leader: Sr Betty O'Riordan
Community: 5
Spiritual direction, parish work,
addiction counselling

8/9 Greendale, Clonroad,
Ennis, Co Clare
Tel 065-6840385 Fax 065-6823869
Non-resident Leader: Sr Regina Roche
Community: 6
Education, pastoral and social work

5 & 6 Rosanore, Gort Road,
Ennis, Co Clare
Tel 065-6821554 Fax 065-6821558
Non-resident Leader: Sr Mairead Kelly
Community: 4
Education, social work, health care

Mercy Sisters, Killaloe, Co Clare
Tel061-376138 Fax 061-376153
Non-resident Leader: Sr Maureen Frawley
Community: 6
Education, social work and health care

West End, Milltown Road,
Kilkee, Co Clare
Tel 065-9056116 Fax 065-9056404
Non-resident Leader: Sr Teresa Browne
Community: 3
Education and Parish Ministry

Convent of Mercy,
Kilkee Road, Kilrush, Co Clare
Tel 065-9051068 Fax 065-9051622
Non-resident Leader: Sr Teresa Browne
Community: 11
Education, social work, health care

20 Sycamore Drive, Kilrush, Co Clare
Tel/Fax 065-9051957
Non-resident Leader: Sr Regina Roche
Community: 2
Education and social work

31 Shannon Heights, Kilrush, Co Clare
Tel 065-9052354
Non-resident Leader: Sr Regina Roche
Community: 2
Education, parish ministry

64 Shannon Heights, Kilrush, Co Clare
Tel 065-9052789
Resident Leader: Sr Teresa Browne
Community: 2
Education, parish ministry

Ashe Road, Nenagh, Co Tipperary
Tel 067-33835 Fax 067-34266
Non-resident Leader: Sr Maureen Frawley
Community: 8
Health care, teaching

5 Dromin Court, Neenagh, Co Tipperary
Tel/Fax 067-31591
Non-resident Leader: Sr Teresa O'Connell
Community: 2

Spanish Point, Miltown Malbay, Co Clare
Tel 065-7084005 Fax 065-7084865
Non-resident Leader: Sr Regina Roche
Community: 7
Education, social work

Tulla, Co Clare
Tel 065-6835118 Fax 065-6835002
Non-resident Leader: Sr Helen Kennedy
Community: 4
Education, health care, counselling

1/2 Fergus Drive, Shannon, Co Clare
Tel 061-471637
Resident Leader: Sr Helen Kennedy
Community: 5
Social work, education

St Mary's, Nenagh, Co Tipperary
Tel 067-31357 Fax 067-43586
Non-resident Leader:
Sr Teresa O'Connell
Community: 19
Education, health care, social work

33 Yewston Estate, Nenagh, Co Tipperary
Tel/Fax 067-32830
Non-resident Leader: Sr Frances Minahan
Community: 3
Education, health care

St John's, Riverside,
Birr, Co Offaly
Tel 057-9120891 Fax 057-9120597
Non-resident Leader
Sr Maureen Frawley
Community: 7

McAuley Drive,
Birr, Co Offaly
Tel 057-9121023 Fax 057-9121303
Non-resident Leader
Sr Helena Blackwell
Community: 4
Education, pastoral and social work

84 Aughanteeroe, Gort Road,
Ennis, Co Clare
Tel/Fax 065-6844533
Non-resident Leader: Sr Regina Roche
Community: 3

10/11 Ardlea Close,
Clare Road, Ennis, Co Clare
Tel 065-6842399 Fax 065-6842048
Non-resident Leader: Sr Helen Kennedy
Community: 7

DAUGHTERS OF CHARITY OF ST VINCENT DE PAUL
St Vincent's, Woodstown House,
Lisnagry, Co Limerick
Tel 061-501490/332577
Superior: Sr Sheila Ryan
Community: 8
St Vincent's Special School, day and
residential for people with moderate
intellectual disability. Training and
socialisation centre
Nursing and caring for moderately and
severely intellectually disabled people.
Placements for nurses training at
Limerick University for services for
persons with intellectual disability.

POOR CLARES
Poor Clare Monastery,
St Francis Street, Ennis, Co Clare
Abbess: Sr Bernardine Meskell
Email bernardinemeskell@eircom.net
Community: 12
Contemplative

SACRED HEART SOCIETY
Sacred Heart Primary School, Air Hill,
Roscrea, Co Tipperary
Tel 0505-21620
Pupils: 245

SACRED HEARTS OF JESUS AND MARY
St Anne's, Sean Ross Abbey, Roscrea,
Co Tipperary
Tel 0505-21629 Fax 0505-22525
School Principal: Mr James McMahon
Tel 0505-21002
Special school for children with
intellectual disabilities

St Mary's,
Corville Road, Roscrea, Co Tipperary
Tel 0505-31599

SISTERS OF CHARITY OF THE INCARNATE WORD
St Michael Convent, Carrigoran,
Newmarket-on-Fergus, Co Clare
Tel 061-368381
Community: 3
Carrigoran House, Retirement and
Convalescent Centre
Tel 061-368100 Fax 061-368170
Email carrigoranhouse@eircom.net

ST JOHN OF GOD SISTERS
St John of God Sisters,
19 Water Park View, Ennis Co Clare
Tel 065-6843579
Community: 1

ST JOSEPH OF THE SACRED HEART SISTERS
7 Woodlands, Kilrush Road,
Ennis, Co Clare
Tel 065-6844742
Regional Leader: Sr Anne Boland

57 Woodlands, Kilrush Road,
Ennis, Co Clare
Tel 065-6891178

Sisters of St Joseph,
24 Dun-an-Oir, Kilkee Housing Estate,
Kilkee, Co Clare

ST MARY MADELEINE POSTEL SISTERS
Mount Carmel Nursing Home, Parkmore
Convent, Abbey Street,
Roscrea, Co Tipperary
Tel 0505-21146 Fax 0505-21542
Apply: Matron
Contact: Sr Marie Keegan
Community: 14

EDUCATIONAL INSTITUTION

St Flannan's College (Diocesan College)
Ennis, Co Clare
Tel 065-6828019 Fax 065-6840644
President
Rev Joseph McMahon BA, BD, HDE
Rev Ignatius McCormack

EDMUND RICE SCHOOLS TRUST
Bunscoil na mBráithre,
New Road, Ennis, Co Clare
Tel 065-6822150 Fax 065-6823865
Email cbsennis@eircom.net
Principal: Br W. M. Roche

Rice College,
New Road, Ennis, Co Clare
Tel 065-6822105 Fax 065-6824755
Email ricecollegecbs@eircom.net
Website www.ricecollege.ennis.ie
Principal: Mr T. Clohessy

CBS Primary School, Summer Hill,
Nenagh, Co Tipperary
Tel 067-32748
Email cbsnenagh@eircom.net
Principal: Mr Gerry Ryan

St Joseph's CBS Secondary School,
Summer Hill, Nenagh, Co Tipperary
Tel 067-34789 Fax 067-34967
Email cbsnen.ias@eircom.net
Principal: Mr Ray Cowan

CHARITABLE AND OTHER SOCIETIES

Apostolic Work Society
Diocesan Headquarters at Maria
Assumpta Hall, Station Road, Ennis,
Co Clare

Birr Social Service Council
c/o 47 New Road, Birr, Co Offaly

Clarecare
Clarecare, Harmony Row,
Ennis, Co Clare
Tel 065-6828178

Clare Youth Advisory Service
Carmody Street, Ennis, Co Clare
Tel 065-684350

Geriatric Centre
Carrigoran House,
Newmarket-on-Fergus, Co Clare
Tel 061-368100

Legion of Mary
Headquarters at Maria Assumpta Hall,
Station Road, Ennis, Co Clare

Mount Carmel Nursing home
Parkmore, Abbey Street, Roscrea,
Co Tipperary
Tel 0505-21146

North Tipperary Community Services
Loreto House, Kenyon Street,
Nenagh, Co Tipperary
Tel 067-31800

North Tipperary Youth Advisory Service
c/o The Institute, Nenagh, Co Tipperary
Tel 067-32000

Roscrea Community Service Centre
Rosemary Street, Roscrea, Co Tipperary
Tel 0505-21498

Schools for children with Special Needs
St Vincent's, Woodstown House,
Lisnagry, Co Limerick
(Daughters of Charity)
Tel 061-501400

St Anne's, residential and day school,
Sean Ross Abbey,
Roscrea, Co Tipperary
Tel 0505-21187

St Clare's, day school,
Gort Road, Ennis, Co Clare
Tel 065-21899

St Anne's, day school,
Ennis, Co Clare
Tel 065-29072

Society of St Vincent de Paul
Conferences at: Birr, Castleconnell,
Clarecastle, Cloughjordan, Ennis, Kilrush,
Kilkee, Nenagh, Newmarket-on-Fergus,
Roscrea, Scariff/Tuamgraney and
Shannon

DIOCESE OF KILMORE

PATRONS OF THE DIOCESE
ST PATRICK, 17 MARCH; ST FELIM, 9 AUGUST

INCLUDES ALMOST ALL OF COUNTY CAVAN,
AND A PORTION OF COUNTIES LEITRIM, FERMANAGH, MEATH AND SLIGO

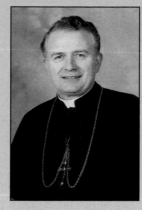

Most Rev Leo O'Reilly DD
Bishop of Kilmore;
born 1944;
ordained priest 15 June 1969;
ordained bishop 2 February
1997; installed as Bishop of
Kilmore 15 November 1998

Residence:
Bishop's House,
Cullies, Co Cavan
Tel 049-4331496
Fax 049-4361796
Email bishop@kilmorediocese.ie
Website www.kilmorediocese.ie

CATHEDRAL OF ST PATRICK AND ST FELIM, CAVAN

The original cathedral of the diocese was situated about four miles south of Cavan in the present parish of Kilmore. Some time in the sixth century, St Felim had established a church there. Bishop Andrew MacBrady (1445–1455) rebuilt the ancient church of St Felim and received permission from Pope Nicholas V to raise it to the status of a cathedral. After the confiscation of the Cathedral of St Felim at Kilmore, the diocese had no cathedral for three hundred years. Bishop James Browne extended Cavan parish church and erected it into a cathedral in 1862. It was replaced by the new Cathedral of St Patrick and St Felim, built by Bishop Patrick Lyons in the years 1938–1942. The architects were W. H. Byrne & Son and the contractors John Sisk & Son. The cathedral cost £209,000 and was opened and dedicated in 1942. It was consecrated in 1947.

The cathedral is neo-classical in style with a single spire rising to 230 feet. The portico consists of a tympanum supported by four massive columns of Portland stone with Corinthian caps. The tympanum figures of Christ, St Patrick and St Felim were executed by a Dublin sculptor, George Smith. The twenty-eight columns in the cathedral, the pulpit on the south side and all the statues are of Pavinazetto marble and came from the firm of Dinelli Figli of Pietrasanta in Italy.

The fine work of George Collie can be seen in the Stations of the Cross and in the mural of the Risen Christ on the wall of the apse. Directly above the mural are twelve small windows, showing the heads of the twelve apostles. The High Altar is of green Connemara marble and pink Middleton marble, while the altar rails are of white Carrara marble. The apse has two side-chapels on the north and two on the south. The Blessed Sacrament is now reserved in the south chapel closest to the altar. The six splendid stained-glass windows in the nave and one in the south transept came from the studios of Harry Clarke.

Allianz (ii)

ADMINISTRATION

College of Consultors
Rt Rev Mgr Michael Cooke
Very Rev Canon John Murphy
Very Rev Charles Heerey
Very Rev Raymond Brady
Very Rev Eamonn Lynch
Very Rev John Gilhooly
Rev Michael Router
Rev Ultan McGoohan
Rev Francis Duffy

Vicar General
Right Rev Mgr Michael Cooke
Manorhamilton, Co Leitrim
Tel 049-9522109

Council of Priests
Chairman: Very Rev Gerard Alwill PP
Drunkeerin, Co Leitrim
Tel 071-9648025
Secretary: Rev Francis Duffy

Vicars Forane
Very Rev Raymond Brady
Very Rev Oliver Kelly
Very Rev Charles Heerey
Very Rev John Murphy

Vicars for Clergy
Very Rev Eugene Dowd
Very Rev Eamonn Lynch
Very Rev Michéal Quinn
Rev Thomas McManus

Finance Committee
Rt Rev Mgr Michael Cooke VG
Very Rev Canon John Murphy PP, VF
Very Rev Anthony Fagan PP
Mr John V. Kelly
Mrs Helen O'Reilly
Mr Kevin O'Connor

Financial Administrator
Rev Francis Duffy

Chancellor/Diocesan Secretary
Rev Francis Duffy
Bishop's House, Cullies, Co Cavan
Tel 049-4331496 Fax 049-4361796
Email bishop@kilmorediocese.ie

Bishop's Secretary
Kathleen Conaty
Bishop's House, Cullies, Co Cavan
Tel 049-4331496 Fax 049-4361796
Email bishop@kilmorediocese.ie

Diocesan Archivist
Rev Francis Duffy
Bishop's House, Cullies, Co Cavan
Tel 049-4331496 Fax 049-4361796

CATECHETICS EDUCATION

**Catholic Primary School Managers'
Association**
Secretary: Mrs Nancy Shiels
Kilmore Diocesan Pastoral Centre,
Cullies, Cavan
Tel 049-4375004 (ext 4) Fax 049-4327497
Email edsec@kilmorediocese.ie

Diocesan Catechetical Advisers
Primary: Sr Anna Smith
Sisters of Mercy, 2 Dún na Bó,
Willowfield Road, Ballinamore, Co Leitrim
Tel 071-9645973
Second level: Rev Gabriel Kelly
Kinawley, Enniskillen, Co Fermanagh
Tel 028-66348250

LITURGY

Pastoral Team: Kilmore Diocesan Pastoral
Centre, Cullies, Cavan
Tel 049-4375004
Advisor: Very Rev Daniel Sheridan
Staghall, Belturbet, Co Cavan
Tel 049-9522140

Church Music
Kilmore Diocesan Pastoral Centre,
Cullies, Cavan
Tel 049-4375004

Art, Architecture and Buildings
Chairman: Very Rev Michéal Quinn

PASTORAL

Kilmore Diocesan Pastoral Centre
Cullies, Cavan
Director: Rev Gerard M. Kearns
Secretary: Ms Anne Clarke
Tel 049-4375004 Fax 049-3227497
Email pastoralcentre@kilmorediocese.ie

Accord
Kilmore Diocesan Pastoral Centre
Tel 049-4375004
Diocesan Director: Fr Kevin Donohoe
Magheranure, Cootehill, Co Cavan
Tel 049-5552155

Apostolic Society
Diocesan President: Mrs Anne Fitzpatrick
Killygarry, Co Cavan
Tel 049-4332297
Spiritual Director: Rev John McMahon CC
Tel 071-9856987

Communications
Diocesan Director: Rev Francis Duffy
Bishop's House, Cullies, Co Cavan
Tel 049-4331496 Fax 049-4361796

Diocesan Pastoral Council
Chairperson: Sr Suzie Duffy (IBVM)
Secretary: Mr Sean Coll
Tel 049-4375004

Ecumenism
Director: Rev Andrew Tully CC
The Presbytery, Cavan
Tel 049-4331404

Family Ministry
Rev Andrew Tully CC
The Presbytery, Cavan
Tel 049-4331404

Knock Pilgrimage
Director: Very Rev Anthony Fagan
Killinkere, Virginia, Co Cavan
Tel 049-8547307

Legion of Mary
Spiritual Director: Rev Pat Farrelly CC
Tel 049-9526252

Lourdes Pilgrimage
Director
Very Rev Canon Colm Hurley PP
Killeshandra, Co Cavan
Tel 049-4334155

Marriage Tribunal
*Kilmore Office of Armagh Regional
Marriage Tribunal*
Mrs Rosaleen Howard
Kilmore Diocesan Pastoral Centre,
Cullies, Cavan
Tel 049-4375004 Fax 049-4327497
Mobile 086-7319760
Email tribunal@kilmorediocese.ie

Adult Faith Formation
Director: Rev Michael Router
Kilmore Diocesan Pastoral Centre,
Cullies, Cavan
Tel 049-4375004

Safeguarding Children
Diocesan Committee
Chairperson: Ms Teresa Carroll
Co-ordinator: Sr Suzie Duffy
Kilmore Diocesan Pastoral Centre
Tel 049-4375004
Designated Persons
Very Rev Anthony Fagan
Killinkere, Virginia, Co Cavan
Tel 049-8547307
Rev Sean Mawn
Ballinaglera, Carrick-on-Shannon,
Co Leitrim
Tel 071-9643014

Permanent Diaconate
Director: Rev Gabriel Kelly
Kinawley, Enniskillen, Co Fermanagh
Tel 028-66348250

Pioneer Total Abstinence Association
Diocesan Director: Rev John Cusack
Virginia, Co Cavan
Tel 049-8547063

Pontifical Mission Societies
Diocesan Director: Rev John McMahon CC
Bridge Street, Manorhamilton, Co Leitrim
Tel 071-9856987

St Joseph's Young Priests Society
Chaplain: Very Rev Philip Brady PP
Laragh, Co Cavan
Tel 049-4330142
Diocesan President: Mr Pat Denning
Drumcave, Cavan
Tel 049-4331362

Travellers
Chaplain: Very Rev Tom McKiernan PP
Bawnboy, Co Cavan
Tel 049-9523103

Vocations
Director: Rev Noel Boylan
Knockraven, Enniskillen, Co Fermanagh
Tel 028-67748266

Youth Ministry Team
Director: Rev Gerard Kearns
Kilmore Diocesan Pastoral Centre,
Cullies, Cavan
Sr Suzie Duffy
Email youthministry@kilmorediocese.ie

PARISHES

Mensal parishes are listed first. Other parishes follow alphabetically. Historical names are given in parentheses. Church titulars appear in italics

CAVAN (URNEY AND ANNAGELLIFF)
Cathedral of SS Patrick and Felim, Cavan
St Clare's, Cavan
St Brigid's, Killygarry
St Aidan's, Butlersbridge
Rev John Gilhooly Adm
Gatehouse, St Patrick's College,
Cullies, Cavan
Tel 049-4371583
Rev Andrew Tully CC
Rev Ultan McGoohan CC
Rev Rafal Siwek CC
The Presbytery, Cavan
Tel 049-4331404/4332269
Fax 049-4332000
Information line 049-4371787
Email cavan@kilmorediocese.ie
Rev Tom Mannion CC
Butlersbridge, Co Cavan
Tel 049-4365266

BAILIEBORO (KILLANN)
St Anne's, Bailieboro; St Anne's, Killann
St Patrick's, Shercock
Very Rev Canon John Murphy PP, VF
Tel 042-9665117
Email bailieboro@kilmorediocese.ie
Rev Oliver O'Reilly CC
Tel 042-9665364
Email bailieboro2@kilmorediocese.ie
Bailieboro, Co Cavan
Rev Charles O'Gorman CC
Shercock, Co Cavan
Tel 042-9669127
Email shercock@kilmorediocese.ie

BALLAGHAMEEHAN
St Aidan's, Ballaghameehan
St Mary's, Rossinver
St Aidan's, Glenaniff
St Patrick's, Kiltyclogher
Very Rev John Phair PP
Rossinver, Co Leitrim
Tel 071-9854022
Email rossinver@kilmorediocese.ie

BALLINAGLERA
St Hugh's, Ballinaglera
St Columcill, Newbridge
Immaculate Conception, Doobally
Very Rev Sean Mawn PP
Ballinaglera, Carrick-on-Shannon,
Co Leitrim
Tel 071-9643014
Email ballinaglera@kilmorediocese.ie

BALLINAMORE (OUGHTERAGH)
St Patrick's Ballinamore,
St Mary's Aughnasheelin
Very Rev Charles Heerey PP
Tel 071-9644039
Email ballinamore@kilmorediocese.ie
Very Rev James Duffy VF
Tel 071-9644050
Ballinamore, Co Leitrim

BALLINTEMPLE
St Michael's, Potahee
St Mary's, Bruskey
St Patrick's, Aghaloora
Very Rev Peter McPartlan PP
Ballintemple, Ballinagh, Co Cavan
Tel 049-4337106
Email potahee@kilmorediocese.ie

BELTURBET (ANNAGH)
Immaculate Conception, Belturbet
St Patrick's, Drumalee
St Brigid's, Redhills
Very Rev Michael Cooke PP, VG
Bridge Street, Belturbet, Co Cavan
Tel 049-9522109
Email belturbet2@kilmorediocese.ie
Rev Canon Patrick J. Corrigan
Fairgreen, Belturbet, Co Cavan
Tel 049-9522151
Email belturbet@kilmorediocese.ie
Rev Gerard Kearns CC
Redhills, Co Cavan
Tel 047-55021
Email redhills@kilmorediocese.ie

CARRIGALLEN
St Mary's, Carrigallen
St Mary's, Drumeela
St Mary's, Drumreilly
Very Rev Denis Murray PP
Carrigallen, Co Leitrim, via Cavan
Tel 049-4339610
Email carrigallen@kilmorediocese.ie

CASTLERAHAN AND MUNTERCONNAUGHT
St Bartholomew's, Munterconnaught
St Mary's, Castlerahan
St Joseph's, Ballyjamesduff
Very Rev Francis Kelleher PP
Knocktemple, Virginia, Co Cavan
Tel 049-8547435
Email frfkelleher@eircom.net
Very Rev Felim Kelly CC
Castlerahan, Ballyjamesduff, Co Cavan
Tel 049-8544150
Email castlerahan@kilmorediocese.ie
Rev Donal Kilduff CC
Ballyjamesduff, Co Cavan
Tel 049-8544410
Email
ballyjamesduff@kilmorediocese.ie

CASTLETARA
St Mary's Ballyhaise,
St Patrick's, Castletara
Very Rev Raymond Brady PP
Ballyhaise, Co Cavan
Tel 049-4338121
Email ballyhaise@kilmorediocese.ie
Rev Michael Router
Castletara, Ballyhaise, Co Cavan
Tel 049-4338146
Email castletara@kilmorediocese.ie

COOTEHILL (DRUMGOON)
St Michael's, Cootehill
St Mary's, Middle Chapel
St Patrick's, Maudabawn
Very Rev Owen Collins PP
Tel 049-5552120
Email cootehill@kilmorediocese.ie
Rev Paul Casey CC
Tel 049-5552163
Cootehill, Co Cavan
Rev Edward Burns CC
Maudabawn, Cootehill, Co Cavan
Tel 049-5552508

CORLOUGH AND DRUMREILLY
St Patrick's, Corlough,
St Brigid's, Corraleehan,
St Patrick's, Aughawillan
Very Rev Thomas McManus PP
Corlough, Belturbet, Co Cavan
Tel 049-9523122
Email corlough@kilmorediocese.ie
Rev Laurence Kearney (SPS) *(in residence)*
Derradda, Ballinamore, Co Leitrim
Tel 071-9644067

CROSSERLOUGH
St Patrick's, Kilnaleck
St Mary's, Crosserlough
St Joseph's, Drumkilly
Very Rev Michael Quinn PP
Crosserlough, Co Cavan
Tel 049-4336122
Email crosserlough@kilmorediocese.ie
Rev Patrick V. Brady CC
Drumkilly, Co Cavan
Tel 049-4336120

DENN
St Matthew's, Crosskeys
St Matthew's, Drumavaddy
Email crosskeys@kilmorediocese.ie
Very Rev Liam Kelly PP
Tel 049-4336102
Rev Jason Murphy
Tel 049-4336563
Crosskeys, Co Cavan

DERRYLIN (KNOCKNINNY)
St Ninnidh's, Derrylin
St Mary's, Teemore
Very Rev Fintan McKiernan PP
56 Mary Street, Derrylin, Co Fermanagh
Tel 028-67748315
Email derrylin@kilmorediocese.ie
Rev Noel Boylan CC
Knockraven,
Enniskillen, Co Fermanagh
Tel 028-67748266
Email teemore@kilmorediocese.ie

DRUMAHAIRE AND KILLARGUE
St Patrick's, Drumahaire
St Mary's, Newtownmanor
St Brigid's, Killargue
Very Rev John McTiernan PP
Drumahaire, Co Leitrim
Tel 071-9164143
Email drumahaire@kilmorediocese.ie

DRUMKEERIN (INISHMAGRATH)
St Brigid's, Drumkeerin
St Patrick's, Termon
St Brigid's, Creevalea
Very Rev Gerard Alwill PP
Drumkeerin, Co Leitrim
Tel 071-9648025
Email drumkeerln@kilmorediocese.ie

DRUMLANE
St Mary's, Staghall
St Patrick's, Milltown
Very Rev Daniel Sheridan PP
Staghall, Belturbet, Co Cavan
Tel 049-9522140
Email staghall@kilmorediocese.ie

GLENFARNE
St Michael's, Glenfarne
St Mary's, Brockagh
Very Rev Thomas Woods PP
East Barrs, Glenfarne, Co Leitrim
Tel 071-9855134
Email glenfarne@kilmorediocese.ie

KILDALLAN AND TOMREGAN
Our Lady of Lourdes, Ballyconnell
St Dallan's, Kildallan
Very Rev Eamonn Lynch PP
Ballyconnell, Co Cavan
Tel 049-9526291
Email ballyconnell@kilmorediocese.ie
Rev Pat Farrelly CC
Kildallan, Ballyconnell, Co Cavan
Tel 049-9526252

KILLESHANDRA
St Brigid's, Killeshandra
Sacred Heart, Arva
Immaculate Conception, Coronea
Very Rev Canon Michael C. Hurley PP, VF
Tel 049-4334155
Killeshandra, Co Cavan
Email killeshandrans@eircom.net
Rev Eamonn Bredin CC
Arva, Co Cavan
Tel 049-4335246
Email arva@kilmorediocese.ie

KILLESHER
St Patrick's, Killesher
St Lasir's, Wheathill
Very Rev Canon Brian McNamara Adm
Derrylester, Enniskillen,
Co Fermanagh
Tel 028-66348224
Email killesher@kilmorediocese.ie

KILLINAGH AND GLANGEVLIN
St Patrick's, Killinagh
St Patrick's, Glangevlin
St Felim's, Gowlan
Very Rev John O'Donnell PP
Blacklion, Co Cavan
Tel 071-9853012
Email blacklion@kilmorediocese.ie
Rev Charles McPadden *(in residence)*
Glangevlin, Via Carrick-on-Shannon,
Co Leitrim
Tel 071-9643104

KILLINKERE
St Ultan's, Killinkere
St Mary's, Clanaphilip
Very Rev Anthony Fagan PP
Killinkere, Virginia, Co Cavan
Tel 049-8547307
Email killinkere@kilmorediocese.ie
Rev Darragh Connolly
Termon, Virginia, Co Cavan
Tel 049-8545737

KILMAINHAMWOOD AND MOYBOLOGUE
Sacred Heart
Very Rev John Cooney PP
Kilmainhamwood, Kells, Co Meath
Tel 046-9052129
Email
kilmainhamwood@kilmorediocese.ie
St Patrick's
Rev Brian Flynn *(in residence)*
Tierworker, via Kells,
Co Meath
Tel 042-9665374
Email tierworker@kilmorediocese.ie

KILMORE
St Felim's, Ballinagh
St Patrick's, Drumcor
Very Rev Peter Casey PP
Ballinagh, Co Cavan
Tel 049-4337232

KILSHERDANY AND DRUNG
Immaculate Conception, Drung
St Patrick's, Corick
St Mary's, Bunnoe
St Brigid's, Kill
Very Rev Patrick Bannon PP
Bunnoe, Co Cavan
Tel 049-5553035
Email drung@kilmorediocese.ie
Rev Gerard Comiskey CC
Kill, Cootehill, Co Cavan
Tel 049-5553218
Email kill@kilmorediocese.ie

KINLOUGH AND GLENADE
St Aidan's, Kinlough
St Patrick's, Tullaghan
St Michael's, Glenade
St Brigid's, Ballintrillick
Very Rev Thomas M. Keogan PP
Kinlough, Co Leitrim
Tel 071-9841428
Email kinlough@kilmorediocese.ie
Rev Maurice McMorrow CC
Glenade, Kinlough, Co Leitrim
Tel 071-9841461
Email glenade@kilmorediocese.ie

KNOCKBRIDE
St Brigid's, Tunnyduff
St Brigid's, East Knockbride
Very Rev Peter McKiernan PP
Knockbride, Bailieboro, Co Cavan
Tel 042-9660112
Email tunnyduff@kilmorediocese.ie

LARAGH
St Brigid's, Laragh
St Brigid's, Carrickallen
St Michael's, Clifferna
Very Rev Philip Brady
Laragh, Stradone, Co Cavan
Tel 049-4330142
Email laraghparish1@gmail.com
Rev Francis Duffy *(priest in residence)*
Clifferna, Stradone, Co Cavan
Tel 049-4330119

LAVEY
St Dympna's, Upper Lavey
St Dympna's, Lower Lavey
Very Rev Brian McElhinney PP
Lavey, Stradone, Co Cavan
Tel 049-4330125
Email lavey@kilmorediocese.ie
Rev Kevin Fay *(priest in residence)*
Lavey, Ballyjamesduff, Co Cavan
Tel 049-4330018
Email lavey1@kilmorediocese.ie

MANORHAMILTON (KILLASNETT)
St Clare's, Manorhamilton
Annunciation, Mullies
St Osnat's, Glencar
Very Rev Oliver Kelly PP, VF
Manorhamilton, Co Leitrim
Tel 071-9855042
Email manorhamilton@kilmorediocese.ie
Rev Patrick Sullivan CC
Glencar, Manorhamilton, Co Leitrim
Tel 071-9855433
Email glencar@kilmorediocese.ie
Rev John McMahon CC
Bridge Street, Manorhamilton, Co Leitrim
Tel 071-9856987
Email jmcmahon59@eircom.net

MULLAGH
St Kilian's, Mullagh
St Mary's, Cross
Very Rev John Quinn PP
Mullagh, via Kells, Co Meath
Tel 046-42208
Email mullagh@kilmorediocese.ie
Very Rev Bernard Maguire CC
Cross, Mullagh, Kells, Co Meath
Tel 049-8547024

SWANLINBAR (KINAWLEY)
St Mary's, Swanlinbar
St Naile's, Kinawley
Very Rev Donald Hannon PP, VF
Swanlinbar, Co Cavan
Tel 049-9521221/087-2830145
Email swanlinbar@kilmorediocese.ie
Rev Gabriel Kelly CC
Kinawley, Enniskillen, Co Fermanagh
Tel 028-66348250
Email kinawley@kilmorediocese.ie

TEMPLEPORT
St Patrick's, Kilnavart,
St Mogue's, Bawnboy
Very Rev Thomas McKiernan PP
Bawnboy, Co Cavan
Tel 049-9523103
Email bawnboy@kilmorediocese.ie

VIRGINIA (LURGAN)
Mary Immaculate, Virginia
St Patrick's, Lurgan
St Matthew's, Maghera
Very Rev John Cusack PP
Virginia, Co Cavan
Tel 049-8547063
Email virginia@kilmorediocese.ie
Rev Dermot Prior
Virginia, Co Cavan
Tel 049-8547015
Email priordermot@eircom.net

INSTITUTIONS AND THEIR CHAPLAINS

Bailieboro Community School,
Chaplain: Ms Mary Grimes
Tel 042-9665295

Breifne College
Cootehill Road, Cavan
Catechist: Rev Jason Murphy
Tel 049-4331735

Carrigallen Vocational School
Visiting Chaplain: Rev Denis Murray
Tel 049-4339640

Cavan General Hospital
Tel 049-4361399
Rev Martin Gilcreest

Cavan Institute
Cathedral Road, Cavan
Chaplain: Rev Gerard Comiskey
Tel 049-4332334

Cavan and Monaghan Defence Forces
Chaplain: Rev Sean McDermott
Dun Ui Neill, Cavan
Tel 049-4361631/087-8292333
Email jlmcdermott@eircom.net

Loreto College, Cavan
Tel 049-4331354
Visiting Chaplain: Rev Kevin Fay

Lough Allen College
Drumkeerin, Co Leitrim
Visiting Chaplain: Rev Gerard Alwill
Tel 071-9648017

Loughan House
Blacklion, Co Cavan
Rev John McMahon
General Office: 071-9853059

St Aidan's Comprehensive School
Cootehill, Co Cavan
Tel 049-5552161
Chaplain: Rev Kevin Donohoe

St Aidan's High School
Derrylin, Co Fermanagh
Visiting Chaplain: Rev Noel Boylan
Tel 028-67748337

St Bricin's Vocation School
Belturbet, Co Cavan
Visiting Chaplain: Rev Gerard Kearns
Tel 049-9522170

St Clare's College
Ballyjamesduff, Co Cavan
Visiting Chaplain: Rev Donal Kilduff
Tel 049-854451

St Clare's Comprehensive School, Manorhamilton
Chaplain: Rev John Sexton
Tel 071-9855060

St Mogue's College
Bawnboy, Co Cavan
Visiting Chaplain: Rev Tom McKiernan
Tel 049-9523112

St Patrick's College, Cavan
Chaplain: Rev Kevin Fay
Tel 049-4361888

Virginia College
Virginia, Co Cavan
Visiting Chaplain: Rev John Cusack
Tel 049-8547050

PRIESTS OF THE DIOCESE ELSEWHERE

Rev Bernard Fitzpatrick
Lagos, Nigeria
Rev P. J. Sexton
Mater Dei Institute
Rev Paul Prior
Director of Formation,
St Patrick's College, Maynooth, Co Kildare
Rev Brian Flynn
Administrator of the National Marriage
Appeal Tribunal, St Patrick's College,
Maynooth, Co Kildare
Rev Enda Murphy
Pontificio Collegio Irlandese, Rome, Italy
Rev Loughlain Carolan
15 Lisdarn Heights, Cavan
Rev Gerard Cassidy
Sabbatical

RETIRED PRIESTS

Rev Eugene Clarke
5 Brookside, Farnham Road, Cavan
Tel 049-4331755
Canon Eugene Dowd
51 Drumnavanagh,
Farnham Road, Cavan
Tel 049-4326821
Rev Bernard Doyle
Kiltyclogher, Co Leitrim
Tel 071-9854302
Very Rev Canon Thomas W. Gaffney
Derrylin Tel 028-66748921
Rev Laurence Kearney (SPS)
Derrada, Ballinamore, Co Leitrim
Tel 071-9644067
Very Rev Canon Michael J. Kelly
Church Street, Ballinamore, Co Leitrim
Tel 071-9644580
Rev Felim McGovern
The Presbytery, Cavan
Tel 049-4331404
Rt Rev Mgr Patrick J. McManus
Kilnaleck, Co Cavan
Tel 049-4336118

Very Rev Patrick Young
Billis, Cavan
Tel 049-4372386
Rev Patrick McHugh

RELIGIOUS ORDERS AND CONGREGATIONS

PRIESTS

NORBERTINE CANONS
Abbey of the Most Holy Trinity and
St Norbert, Kilnacrott Abbey,
Ballyjamesduff, Co Cavan
Tel 049-8544416
Fax 049-8544909
Email kilnacrottabbeytrust@eircom.net
Prior: Rt Rev Oliver Martin (OPraem)

SISTERS

CONGREGATION OF THE SISTERS OF MERCY
Church Street,
Belturbet, Co Cavan
Tel 049-9522110

Sisters of Mercy, Convent of Mercy,
Cootehill, Co Cavan
Tel 049-5552151
Community: 6

Sisters of Mercy,
2 Castle View, Manorhamilton,
Co Leitrim
Tel 071-9855401

No 2 Dun na Bo, Willowfield Road,
Ballinamore, Co Leitrim
Tel 071-9645973
Community: 4

No 16 Dun na Bo, Willowfield Road,
Ballinamore, Co Leitrim
Tel 071-9644006
Community: 4

FRANCISCAN SISTERS OF THE ATONEMENT
2 Clooneen Park,
Manorhamilton, Co Leitrim
Tel 071-9856785 Fax 071-9820821
Email fsoa@eircom.net
Superior: Sr Ita Flynn
Community: 3

LORETO (IBVM)
Loreto Post-Primary School
Tel 049-4331354

MISSIONARY SISTERS OF THE HOLY ROSARY
Cavan Town
Tel 049-4332735/4332733
Fax 049-4362077
Centre for mission education
co-ordination
Pastoral, care of the elderly
Community: 28

27 Cherrymount,
Keadue, Cavan Town
Tel 049-4372936
Pastoral, healthcare, regional
administration
Community: 2

SISTERS OF ST CLARE
St Clare's Convent, Cavan
Tel 049-4331134
Community: 3
Primary School. Pupils: 550
Tel 049-4332671

EDUCATIONAL INSTITUTIONS

St Clare's College
Ballyjamesduff, Co Cavan
Tel 049 8544551
Fax 049-8544081
Principal: Mr Séan Fegan

St Felim's and Fatima College
Ballinamore, Co Leitrim
Tel 071-9644049
Email felims.ias@eircom.net
Website www.ballinamorepps.ie
Principal: Mr Padraig Leyden

St Patrick's College
Cullies, Co Cavan
Tel 049-4361888
Email stpats@kilmorediocese.ie
Principal
Dr Liam McNiffe BA, HDip in ED, MA,
MSc in ED Mngt, PhD
Chaplain: Rev Kevin Fay

DIOCESE OF LIMERICK

PATRONS OF THE DIOCESE
ST MUNCHIN, 3 JANUARY; ST ITA, 15 JANUARY

INCLUDES THE GREATER PART OF COUNTY LIMERICK, PART OF COUNTY CLARE
AND ONE TOWNLAND IN COUNTY KERRY

Very Rev Anthony Mullins PP
Diocesan Administrator
Dromin, Kilmallock, Co Limerick
Tel 063-31962
Email
tonymullinsda@eircom.net

Diocesan Office: Social Service
Centre, Henry Street, Limerick
Tel 061-315856 Fax 061-310186
Email office@ldo.ie
Diocese of Limerick website
www.limerickdiocese.org

ST JOHN'S CATHEDRAL, LIMERICK

Since the twelfth century, a church dedicated to St John has stood in the area of Limerick city known as Garryowen. The earliest reference to the first church comes from the year 1205 when the Cathedral Chapter of the Diocese of Limerick was founded by Bishop Donatus O'Brien, Bishop of Limerick from 1195 to 1207. In the document of foundation, the revenues from the Church of St John were given to the Archdeacon of Limerick. This medieval church was replaced by a penal church, which in turn was supplanted by the parish church of St John in the middle of the eighteenth century. With an increase in population in the area around Garryowen, it was decided to build a new church to accommodate the estimated 15,000 parishioners of St John's. An appeal for funds was so well received that the decision was made to abandon the plans for a parish church and build a cathedral for the diocese instead.

Designed by Philip Charles Hardwick, a contemporary and associate of Pugin, St John's Cathedral is revival Gothic in the early English style. It was opened for worship in 1861 and consecrated in 1894 by Cardinal Logue. The spire, standing at 308 feet, 3 inches, is the tallest in Ireland and was built between 1878 and 1883.

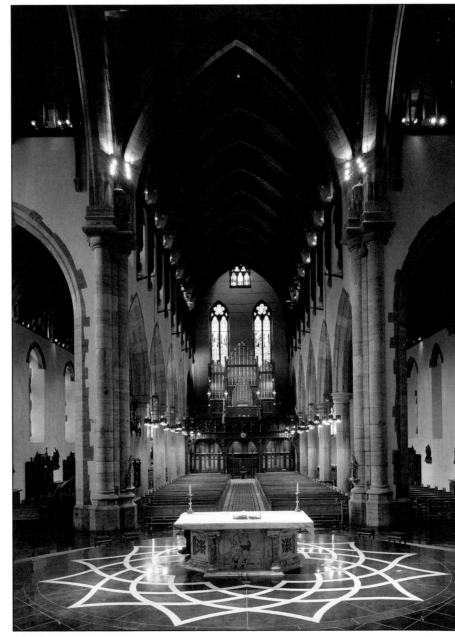

Allianz ⑪

Most Rev Donal Murray DD
Former Bishop of Limerick
born 29 May 1940; ordained priest 22
May 1966; ordained bishop 18 April
1982; installed as Bishop of Limerick 24
March 1996; retired December 2009

CHAPTER

Dean: Right Rev Michael Kelly
Archdeacon: Vacant
Theologian
Very Rev Donough Canon O'Malley
Penitentiary
Very Rev Garry Canon Bluett
Chancellor
Very Rev Frank Canon Duhig PP, VF
Precentor
Very Rev James Canon Ambrose PP
Prebendaries and Canons
Dysart: Very Rev John Canon O'Shea PP
Croagh: Very Rev James Canon Neville
Effin
Very Rev James Canon Costello PP, VF
Killeedy
Very Rev Donal Canon McNamara
Athnitt: Very Rev Denis Canon Browne
Tullybrackey
Very Rev Anthony Canon O'Keeffe PP, VF
Ardcanny: Very Rev Patrick Canon Kelly PE
St Munchin's
Rt Rev Mgr Michael Lane VG
Kilpeacon
Very Rev Joseph Canon Dempsey PP
Donaghmore
Rt Rev Mgr Daniel Neenan VG, PP
Ballycahane
Very Rev William Canon Fitzmaurice PP, VF

COLLEGE OF CONSULTORS

Rt Rev Mgr Michael Lane VG
Rt Rev Mgr Daniel Neenan PP, VG
Very Rev David Gibson Adm
Rev Chris O'Donnell
Very Rev Patrick O'Sullivan Adm
Very Rev Thomas Crawford PP
Rev Richard Keane CC
Rev Richard Davern CC
Rev Paul Finnerty

ADMINISTRATION

Vicars General
Rt Rev Mgr Michael Lane VG
2 Meadowvale, Raheen, Limerick
Tel 061-228761/087-2544450
Email mwlane@esatclear.ie
Rt Rev Mgr Daniel Neenan PP, VG
1 Trinity Court, Monaleen Road,
Monaleen, Limerick
Tel 061-330974/087-2208547
Email danneenan@eircom.net
Rt Rev Éamonn Fitzgibbon VG
Ballyduane, Clarina, Co Limerick
Tel 087-6921191
Email eamonn@ldo.ie

Vicars Forane
Very Rev Mícheál Canon Liston PP
Very Rev John Leonard PP
Very Rev Canon James Costello PP

Very Rev Canon Joseph Dempsey PP
Very Rev Canon Anthony O'Keeffe PP
Very Rev Canon William Fitzmaurice PP
Very Rev Thomas Carroll PP
Very Rev Canon Frank Duhig PP

Diocesan Secretary
Rev Paul Finnerty
Diocesan Office, Social Service Centre,
Henry Street, Limerick
Tel 061-315856 Fax 061-310186
Email office@ldo.ie or paul@ldo.ie
Website www.limerickdiocese.org
Finance Manager: Mr Tony Sadlier
Secretarial Staff: Margaret Dalton,
Gwen O'Sullivan, Linda Fleming
Diocesan Spokesperson
To be appointed

Diocesan Archivist
To be appointed
Diocesan Office, Social Service Centre,
Henry Street, Limerick
Tel 061-315856

DIOCESAN PASTORAL COUNCIL

Members: Most Rev Donal Murray DD,
Very Rev Joseph Shire, Sr Patricia
Coughlan, Ms Patricia Hannon, Mr John
Kernan, Ms Noirín Lynch, Rev John
Mockler, Mr Christy Murray, Very Rev
Michael Noonan, Mr Anthony O'Brien,
Mr Maurice O'Connor, Rev Chris
O'Donnell, Ms Mary O'Shaughnessy,
Very Rev John Canon O'Shea, Ms Mary
Ryan-Synott, Ms Aoife Walsh
c/o Diocesan Office, Social Service Centre,
Henry Street, Limerick

CATECHETICS EDUCATION

Primary Level Religious Education
Director: Rev Liam Enright
Church Road, Croom, Co Limerick
Tel 061-397986
Ms Nora Collins
Ms Fiona Dineen
Tel 061-315856

Second Level Religious Education
Adviser: Rev Frank O'Connor
c/o Limerick Diocesan Pastoral Centre,
St Michael's Courtyard,
Denmark Street, Limerick
Tel 061-400133

Primary Education Secretary
To be appointed
Diocesan Office, Social Service Centre,
Henry Street, Limerick
Tel 061-317742 Fax 061-310186
Email joe@ldo.ie
Ms Fiona Shanley
Tmail fiona@ldo.ie

LITURGY

Liturgical Music
Adviser: Rev Terence Loughran
Parochial House, Cappagh,
Askeaton, Co Limerick
Tel 087-7524439

PASTORAL

Accord
Limerick City Centre:
St Munchin's College, Corbally, Limerick
Email accordlimerick@eircom.net
www.accord.ie
Director: Rev Joseph Shire PP
Ballyagran, Kilmallock, Co Limerick
Tel 063-82028
Enquiries: Tel 061-343000 Fax 061-350000
Administrator: Ms Katrina Quilligan
Newcastle West Centre:
Parish Centre, Newcastle West,
Co Limerick
Contact: Helen Ahern
Tel 069-61000 (Mon-Fri 10.00am-1.00pm)
Spiritual Director
Very Rev Frank Duhig PP, VF
St Ita's Presbytery,
Newcastle West, Co Limerick
Tel 069-62141/087-6380299

Apostleship of the Sea, Foynes
Director and Port Chaplain
Very Rev Anthony Canon O'Keeffe PP, VF
Shanagolden, Co Limerick
Tel 069-60112

Charismatic Renewal Groups
Liaison Priest: Rev Damian Ryan PP
Lourdes House, Childers Road, Limerick
Tel 061-301047/087-2274412

Council of Priests
Chairman: Very Rev Noel Kirwan PP
St Michael's Courtyard,
Denmark Street, Limerick
Tel 061-400133/087-2616843
Email stmlslk@eircom.net

CURA
Helpline: Tel 061-318207
Administrator: Sr Anne McCarthy

Limerick Diocesan Pastoral Centre
St Michael's Courtyard,
Denmark Street, Limerick
Tel 061-400133 Fax 061-400601
Email ldpc@eircom.net
http://www.limerickdiocese.org/ldpc/
Director: Very Rev Noel Kirwan PP

Ecumenism
Director: Rev Frank O'Connor
c/o Limerick Diocesan Pastoral Centre,
Denmark Street, Limerick
Tel 061-400133

Emigrant Apostolate
Director
Very Rev William O'Gorman PP
Tournafulla, Co Limerick
Tel 069-81010/087-2580020

Apostolate of the Laity
Adviser: Very Rev Noel Kirwan PP
Limerick Diocesan Pastoral Centre,
St Michael's Courtyard,
Denmark Street, Limerick
Tel 061-400133 Fax 061-400601
Email ldpc@eircom.net

Allianz ⑪

Diocesan Representative on the National Council for the Laity
Diocesan Representative
Ms Mary Sadlier
Rockfield, Crecora, Co Limerick
Tel 061-301044

Marriage Encounter Movement
Very Rev Liam Enright PP
Cratloe, Co Clare
Tel 061-357196/087-2546335
Email leppcrat@iol.ie

Marriage Tribunal
Contact: Mrs Jean Ryan
Diocesan Offices, Social Service Centre,
Henry Street, Limerick
Office hours: Tuesday 2.00-5.00 pm
Thursday 9.00-5.00 pm
Tel 061-315856 Fax 061-310186
Email office@ldo.ie

Military Chaplain
Rev Seamus Madigan
Sarsfield Barracks, Limerick
Tel 061-316817

Pioneer Total Abstinence Association
Spiritual Director: Vacant

Pilgrimage
(Lourdes) Director
Very Rev Donal Canon McNamara PP
St Munchin's,
Clancy Strand, Limerick
Tel 061-455635/087-2402518
Email donalmcnamara@hotmail.com

Pre-Marriage Courses
Contact: ACCORD
Limerick City Centre
Tel 061-343000 Fax 061-350000
Newcastle West Parish Centre
Tel 069-61000

Pontifical Mission Societies
Diocesan Director
Very Rev Thomas Crawford PP
Glin, Co Limerick
Tel 068-23897/087-2218078
Email tdec@eircom.net

Social Communications
Director: Very Rev Francis Moriarty
Adare, Co Limerick
Tel 061-396177

Social Service Council
General Manager: Mr Brian Ryan
Henry Street, Limerick
Tel 061-314111/314213

Travelling Community
Diocesan Chaplain
Very Rev Joseph Shire
Ballyagran, Kilmallock, Co Limerick
Tel 063-82028/087-6924563
Email taylor@eircom.net

Trócaire
Director: Very Rev Thomas Carroll PP
Parteen, Co Clare
Tel 061-345613
Email thomascarroll@eircom.net

Vocations
Director: Very Rev Noel Kirwan
Limerick Diocesan Pastoral Centre,
St Michael's Courtyard, Denmark Street,
Limerick
Tel 061-400133/087-2616843
Email ldpc@eircom.net

Youth Apostolate
Director: Rev Chris O'Donnell
Limerick Diocesan Pastoral Centre,
St Michael's Courtyard,
Denmark Street, Limerick
Tel 061-400133 Fax 061-400601
Email codonnell@ldpc.ie

PARISHES

*Mensal and city parishes are listed first.
Other parishes follow alphabetically.
Church titulars are in italics.*

ST JOHN'S
St John's Cathedral
Very Rev Austin McNamara Adm
Rev Seán Harmon CC
Rev Leo McDonnell CC
Cathedral House,
Cathedral Place, Limerick
Tel 061-414624/087-2589279
Fax 061-316570
Email stjohnsparishlk@eircom.net

ST JOSEPH'S
St Joseph's
Sacristy: 061-313401 (10.00 am-1.00 pm)
Very Rev Thomas Mangan Adm
'Naomh Joseph', Lifford Avenue,
Limerick
Tel 061-303777/087-2376032

ST MICHAEL'S
St Michael's
Very Rev Noel Kirwan PP
St Michael's Church,
Denmark Street, Limerick
Tel 061-400133 (work)
061-413315 (church)/087-2616843
Email nkirwan@ldpc.ie

ST MARY'S
St Mary's
Sacristy: 061-416300
Very Rev Donough Canon O'Malley PP
Tel 061-414092
St Mary's, Athlunkard Street, Limerick
Very Rev Brendan Canon Connellan AP
Tel 061-417087

ST MUNCHIN'S AND ST LELIA'S
St Munchin's and St Lelia's
Sacristy: 061-455133
Email stmunchinspresbytery@eircom.net
St Lelia's, Ballynanty
Tel 061-328577
Very Rev Donal Canon McNamara PP
Clancy Strand, Limerick
Tel/Fax 061-455635
Email donalmcnamara@hotmail.com
Rev Richard Crowe CC
10 Mayorstone Park, Limerick
Tel 061-452952

Rev Patrick Seaver CC
4 Glenview Terrace,
Farranshone, Limerick
Tel 061-328838
Email patseaver@hotmail.com

ST PATRICK'S
St Patrick's & St Brigid's
Very Rev Edwin Irwin PP
St Patrick's, Dublin Road, Limerick
Tel 061-415397/087-2547707
Fax 061-417152
Rev Eamon Purcell CC
112 Hilltop, St Patrick's Road, Limerick
Tel 061-413734

ST PAUL'S
St Paul's
Very Rev John Leonard PP, VF
The Presbytery, 10 St Nessan's Park,
Dooradoyle, Limerick
Tel 061-302729
Rev Eugene Boyce CC
14 Springfield Drive, Dooradoyle
Tel 061-304508/086-2542517

ST SAVIOUR'S
St Saviour's
Very Rev James Donleavy (OP) PP
St Saviour's, Glentworth Street,
Limerick
Tel 061-412333 Fax 061-311728
Email oplimerick@eircom.net

OUR LADY QUEEN OF PEACE
Our Lady Queen of Peace
Sacristy: 061-467676
Very Rev Patrick O'Sullivan PP
'Elm View', Roxboro Road, Limerick
Tel 061-410846/087-2237501

OUR LADY OF LOURDES
Our Lady of Lourdes
Very Rev Damian Ryan PP
Lourdes House, Childers Road,
Limerick
Tel 061-467676
Email 4dlord@eircom.net

OUR LADY OF THE ROSARY
Holy Rosary
Very Rev William Walsh PP
8 Merval Crescent, Clareview, Limerick
Tel/Fax 061-453026
Very Rev Thomas Ryan CC
Gleneden, North Circular Road,
Limerick
Tel 061-329448
Parish mobile 087-2997733

HOLY FAMILY
Holy Family
Very Rev Patrick Hogan PP
334 O'Malley Park, Southill, Limerick
Tel 061-414248
Email pkfhogan@yahoo.co.uk
Pastoral Worker: Maggie Enright
Tel 061-437074

CHRIST THE KING
Christ the King
Very Rev Thomas Ryan PP
5 Derravaragh Road,
Caherdavin Park, Limerick
Tel 061-452790
Rev Richard Davern CC
17 Alderwood Avenue,
Caherdavin Heights, Limerick
Tel 061-453226

CORPUS CHRISTI
Corpus Christi
Very Rev Francis O'Dea PP
134 Cosgrave Park, Moyross, Limerick
Tel 061-451783/087-2443106
Email frankodea@eircom.net

OUR LADY HELP OF CHRISTIANS
Our Lady, Help of Christians
Very Rev John Campion (SDB) PP
Email johncampion00@eircom.net
Rev Robbie Swinburne (SDB) CC
Email robei2iq@eircom.net
Salesian House, Milford,
Castletroy, Limerick
Tel 061-330268

ST NICHOLAS
St Nicholas, St Munchin's College Chapel
Very Rev John Daly PP
St Nicholas' Presbytery, Westbury,
Limerick
Tel 061-340614/087-8180815
Email jgdalystnicholas@eircom.net

ABBEYFEALE
Our Lady of the Assumption
Very Rev John Canon O'Shea PP
Tel 068-31157/087-9708282
Very Rev Micheál Canon Liston,
Assistant Priest
Tel 087-2314804
Convent Street,
Abbeyfeale, Co Limerick
Email fealechurch@feale.com

ADARE
Holy Trinity Abbey
Very Rev Joseph Noonan PP
Adare, Co Limerick
Tel 061-396172/087-2400700

ARDAGH AND CARRICKERRY
St Molua, Ardagh
St Mary, Carrickerry
Very Rev Laurence Madden PP
Ardagh, Co Limerick
Tel 069-76121/087-2286450

ARDPATRICK
St Patrick
Very Rev Michael Hanley Adm
Kilfinane, Co Limerick
Tel 063-91016/086-8595733
Very Rev David Browne
Parochial House,
Ardpatrick, Co Limerick
Tel 063-91015
Email frdavidbrowne@hotmail.com

ASKEATON AND BALLYSTEEN
St Mary, Askeaton
St Patrick, Ballysteen
Very Rev Seán Ó Longaigh PP
Tel/Fax 061-392249
Email seanonlongaigh@eircom.net
Rev Senan Murray (CSSp) CC
Askeaton, Co Limerick
Tel 061-392131

ATHEA
St Bartholomew
Very Rev Patrick Bowen PP
Tel 068-42116/087-6532842
Email pbowen@eircom.net
Very Rev Patrick Canon Kelly PE
Tel 068-42107
Athea, Co Limerick

BALLINGARRY AND GRANAGH
Our Lady of the Immaculate Conception
St Joseph
Very Rev Daniel Lane PP
Ballingarry, Co Limerick
Tel/Fax 069-68141/087-2533030
Email danfl@eircom.net

BALLYAGRAN AND COLMANSWELL
St Michael/St Colman
Very Rev Joseph Shire PP
Ballyagran, Kilmallock, Co Limerick
Tel 063-82028/087-6924563
Email taylor@eircom.net

BANOGUE
Very Rev Joseph Kennedy Adm *(Pro-tem)*
Croom, Co Limerick
Tel 061-397231/087-9217622
Rev Eamonn O'Brien
Church Road, Croom, Co Limerick
Tel 061-397213
Email eamonfsanjose@aol.com

BRUFF/MEANUS/GRANGE
SS Peter & Paul (Bruff); St Mary (Meanus)
SS Patrick and Brigid (Grange)
SS Peter & Paul
Very Rev James Canon Costello PP, VF
Tel 061-382555
Very Rev Joseph Foley CC
Tel 061-382290/087-2618412
Bruff, Kilmallock, Co Limerick

BULGADEN/MARTINSTOWN
Our Lady of the Assumption
Very Rev Gerard McNamara PP
Bulgaden, Kilmallock, Co Limerick
Tel/Fax 063-88005/087-2408998
Email gmcn@iol.ie
Our Lady of the Assumption
Martinstown, Kilmallock, Co Limerick

CAPPAGH
St James
Very Rev Terry Loughran
Parochial House, Cappagh,
Askeaton, Co Limerick

COOLCAPPA
St Colman, Kilcolman
St Kieran, Coolcappa
Very Rev Denis Mullane PP
Kilcolman, Ardagh, Co Limerick
Tel 069-60126

CRATLOE
St John, Cratloe
St John, Sixmilebridge
Very Rev Liam Enright PP
Cratloe, Co Clare
Tel 061-357196/087-2546335
Fax 061-357230
Email leppcrat@iol.ie

CROAGH AND KILFINNY
St John the Baptist, Croagh
St Kieran, Kilfinny
Very Rev Anthony Mulvihill PP
Croagh, Rathkeale, Co Limerick
Tel 069-64185/087-9059348

CROOM
St Mary
Very Rev Joseph Kennedy PP
Croom, Co Limerick
Tel 061-397231/087-9217622
Rev Eamonn O'Brien
Church Road, Croom, Co Limerick
Tel 061-397213/087-0767521
Email eamonnofsanjose@aol.com

DONAGHMORE/KNOCKEA
St Patrick, Donaghmore
St Patrick, Knockea
Very Rev Oliver Plunkett PP
Email dkrchurches@eircom.net
Donaghmore, Co Limerick
Tel 061-313898/087-6593176

DROMCOLLOGHER/BROADFORD
St Bartholomew
Our Lady of the Snows
Very Rev James Canon Ambrose PP
Dromcollogher, Charleville, Co Limerick
Tel 087-7740753

DROMIN & ATHLACCA
St John the Baptist
Very Rev Anthony Mullins PP
Dromin, Kilmallock, Co Limerick
Tel 063-31962
Email tonymullinsda@eircom.net
Rev Patrick Howard
Athlacca, Kilmallock, Co Limerick
Tel 063-90540

EFFIN/GARRIENDERK
Our Lady, Queen of Peace (Effin)
St Patrick (Garrienderk)
Very Rev Thomas Coughlan PP
Effin, Kilmallock, Co Limerick
Tel 063-71314

FEDAMORE
St John the Baptist
Very Rev Michael Cussen PP
Fedamore, Kilmallock, Co Limerick
Tel 061-390112/087-1279015
Email mcuss@eircom.net

FEENAGH AND KILMEEDY
St Ita
Very Rev Brendan Murphy PP
Feenagh, Kilmallock, Co Limerick
Tel 063-85013/086-8094490

GLENROE AND BALLYORGAN
Our Lady of Ransom, Glenroe
St Joseph, Ballyorgan
Very Rev Timothy O'Leary PP
Glenroe, Kilmallock, Co Limerick
Tel 063-86040

GLIN
Immaculate Conception
Very Rev Thomas Crawford PP
Glin, Co Limerick
Tel 068-26897

KILCORNAN
St John the Baptist
Rev William Russell Adm
Enniscouch, Rathkeale, Co Limerick
Tel 069-63490/087-2272825
Rev Michael Irwin (SSC) *(Priest in residence)*
Kilcornan, Co Limerick
Tel 061-393113
Email mlirwin@iolfree.ie

KILDIMO AND PALLASKENRY
St Joseph, Kildimo
St Mary, Pallaskenry
Very Rev John Donworth PP
Kildimo, Co Limerick
Tel 061-394134/087-2237501
Fax 061-394280
Email johndonworth@hotmail.com

KILFINANE
St Andrew
Very Rev Michael Hanley PP
Kilfinane, Co Limerick
Tel 063-91016/086-8595733

KILLEEDY
St Ita's, Ashford; St Ita's, Killeedy
Very Rev John Keating PP
Raheenagh, Ballagh, Co Limerick
Tel 069-85014

KILMALLOCK
SS Peter & Paul, Kilmallock
St Mary, Ballingaddy
Very Rev William Canon Fitzmaurice PP, VF
Kilmallock, Co Limerick
Tel 063-98287/086-2423728
Email kilmallockchurch@eircom.net
Rev Joseph Cussen CC
Glenfield Road, Kilmallock,
Co Limerick
Tel 063-98061

KNOCKADERRY & CLONCAGH
St Mary, Cloncagh
St Munchin, Knockaderry
Very Rev Tony Kelleher PP
Cloncagh, Ballingarry, Co Limerick
Tel 069-83006

LOUGHILL/BALLYHAHILL
Our Lady of the Visitation (Ballyhahill)
Our Lady of the Wayside (Loughill)
Very Rev Gerard O'Leary Adm
Parochial House, Ballyhahill,
Co Limerick
Tel 069-82103/087-9378685
Email olearyg22@eircom.net

MAHOONAGH
St John the Baptist, Castlemahon
St Mary, Feohanagh
Very Rev John Duggan PP
Castlemahon, Co Limerick
Tel 069-72108/086-2600464

MANISTER
St Michael
Very Rev Garrett Canon Bluett PP
Manister, Croom, Co Limerick
Tel 061-397335

MONAGEA
Church of Visitation of BVM
Very Rev David Gibson Adm
'Brookhaven', Monagea,
Newcastle West, Co Limerick
Tel 069-72743/087-2528738
Email brookhaven@eircom.net

MONALEEN
St Mary Magdalene
Right Rev Mgr Daniel Neenan PP, VG
1 Trinity Court, Monaleen Road,
Monaleen, Limerick
Tel 061-330974/087-2208547
Email danneenan@eircom.net
Rev Michael O'Shea CC
9 Castletroy Heights, Monaleen,
Limerick
Tel 061-335764/087-9791432

MUNGRET/CRECORA
St Nessan, Raheen
St Oliver Plunkett, Mungret
SS Peter & Paul, Crecora
Very Rev Michael Noonan PP
The Presbytery, Raheen, Limerick
Tel 061-301112/087-6796217
Email mnmcraheen@oceanfree.net
Rev Jeremiah Brouder CC
Crecora, Patrickswell, Co Limerick
Tel 061-355148

NEWCASTLE WEST
Immaculate Conception of BVM
Very Rev Frank Canon Duhig PP
St Ita's Presbytery,
Newcastle West, Co Limerick
Tel 069-62141/087-6380299
Rev Patrick Bluett CC
Gortboy, Newcastle West, Co Limerick
Tel 069-61881
Rev Richard Keane CC
Gortboy, Newcastle West, Co Limerick
Tel 069-77090/087-9552729

PARTEEN/MEELICK
St Patrick, Parteen
St John the Baptist, Meelick
Very Rev Thomas Carroll PP
Parteen, Co Clare
Tel 061-345613
Email thomascarrollpp@eircom.net
Rev Fred McDonnell CC
The Presbytery, Meelick, Co Clare
Tel 061-325556/087-7706023

PATRICKSWELL/BALLYBROWN
Blessed Virgin Mary, Patrickswell
St Joseph, Ballybrown
Very Rev Muiris O'Connor PP
Ballybrown, Clarina,
Co Limerick
Tel 061-353711/086-6075628
Email muirisoc@eircom.net

RATHKEALE
St Mary
Very Rev Joseph Canon Dempsey PP, VF
Lower Main Street, Rathkeale,
Co Limerick
Tel 069-63133
Rev William Russell CC
Enniscouch, Rathkeale,
Co Limerick
Tel 069-63490/087-2272825

ROCKHILL/BRUREE
St Munchin, Rockhill
Immaculate Conception, Bruree
Very Rev John Fitzgerald PP
Parish Administrator
Very Rev Desmond McAuliffe Adm
Rockhill, Bruree, Co Limerick
Tel 063-90515/087-2336476

SHANAGOLDEN & FOYNES
St Senan, Shanagolden
St Senan, Foynes
St Senan, Robertstown
Very Rev Anthony Canon O'Keeffe PP, VF
Shanagolden, Co Limerick
Tel 069-60112/087-4163401

TEMPLEGLANTINE
Most Holy Trinity
Very Rev David Gibson Adm
'Brookhaven', Monagea,
Newcastle West, Co Limerick
Tel 069-72743/087-2528738
Very Rev Thomas Hurley
Templeglantine, Co Limerick
Tel 069-84021
Email thurley@eircom.net

TOURNAFULLA/MOUNTCOLLINS
St Patrick, Tournafulla
Our Lady of the Assumption, Mountcollins
Very Rev William O'Gorman PP
Tournafulla, Co Limerick
Tel 069-81010/087-2580020

Allianz (ⅱ)

INSTITUTIONS AND THEIR CHAPLAINS

Askeaton Community College
Coláiste Mhuire, Askeaton, Co Limerick
Ms Diane Brown
Tel 061-392368

Brothers of Charity Services
Bawnmore, Clonlong Road, Limerick
Rev Joseph Young
21 Marian Avenue, Janesboro, Limerick
Tel 061-405835

Castletroy Community College
Castletroy, Limerick
Tel 061-330785
Ms Brenda Cribben

Coláiste Iosaf, Kilmallock
Mr Eddie O'Carroll
Tel 063-98275

Coláiste Na Trócaire
Rathkeale, Co Limerick
Rev Tim Curtin
Tel 069-63432

County Prison, Limerick
Mulgrave Street, Limerick
Prison General Office: Tel 061-415111
Rev John Walsh
Mountdavid House,
North Circular Road, Limerick
Tel 061-452063/087-2433488

Croom County Hospital
Croom, Co Limerick
Very Rev Garrett Canon Bluett
Tel 061-397335

Regional Hospital
Dooradoyle, Limerick
Tel 061-301111
Rev Joseph O'Keeffe
42 Nessan Court, Church Road,
Raheen, Limerick
Tel 061-309151/086-3333539
Rev Robert Coffey
37 Gouldavoher Estate,
Dooradoyle, Limerick
Tel 061-482437/087-6540908

Regional Maternity Hospital
Ennis Road, Limerick
Parish clergy, Our Lady of the Rosary
087-2997733

St Camillus's Hospital
Shelbourne Road, Limerick
Rev Richard Crowe
Tel 061-452952

St Enda's Community School, Limerick
Old Cork Road, Limerick
Ms Maeve Hickey
Tel 061-419222

St Ita's Hospital
Newcastle West, Co Limerick
Tel 069-62311
Very Rev Frank Duhig PP
Tel 069-62141

St John's Hospital, Limerick
Pastoral Care Department
Tel 061-462111
Very Rev Austin McNamara Adm
Tel 087-2589279/061-414624
Ms Lourda O'Sullivan CHC
Ms Joyce O'Sullivan CHC

St Joseph's Hospital, Limerick
Tel 061-414624
Rev Sean Harmon

St Nessan's Community College
Moylish, Limerick
Tel 061-452422
Ms Maí Patton

St Paul's Home
Dooradoyle, Limerick
Tel 061-228209
Clergy of St Paul's Parish
Tel 061-302729/307508

Sarsfield Barracks, Limerick
Tel 061-316817
Rev Seamus Madigan

PRIESTS OF THE DIOCESE ELSEWHERE

Rev David Costello
c/o The Missionary Society of St James
the Apostle, 24 Clark Street,
Boston, MA 02109, USA
Email davidmpc@oceanfree.net
Rev Gerard Garrett
Cork Regional Marriage Tribunal,
The Lough, Cork
Tel 021-4963653
Email crmt@iol.ie
Rev Derek Leonard
c/o The Missionary Society of St James
the Apostle, 24 Clark Street,
Boston, MA 02109, USA
Email derekleonard@eircom.net
Rev John McCarthy
Irish Pastoral Centre, 953 Hancock Street,
Quincy, Massachusetts CO2170, USA
Tel 001-617479740
Rev Leslie McNamara
Columban Missionary Society, Dalgan Park,
Dublin Road, Navan, Co Meath
Rev Terry O'Connell
c/o Diocesan Office, Social Service Centre,
Henry Street, Limerick

PRIESTS ON STUDY LEAVE

Rev David Bracken
c/o Diocesan Office, Social Service Centre,
Henry Street, Limerick
Rev Brendan Fitzgerald
c/o Diocesan Office, Social Service Centre,
Henry Street, Limerick
Rev John Mockler
c/o Diocesan Office, Social Service Centre,
Henry Street, Limerick
Rev Gerard Slattery
c/o Diocesan Office, Social Service Centre,
Henry Street, Limerick

RETIRED PRIESTS

Rt Rev Liam Boyle
Knockaderry, Co Limerick
Very Rev David Browne
Ardpatrick, Kilmallock, Co Limerick
Very Rev Denis Canon Browne
Kilmallock, Co Limerick
Rev Cornelius Collins
Patrickswell, Co Limerick
Rev Sean Condon
Cathedral House, Cathedral Place,
Limerick
Tel 061-414624
Rev Maurice Costello
Main Street, Rathkeale, Co Limerick
Tel 069-63452
Very Rev Peadar de Burca
Kilmeedy, Co Limerick
Tel 063-87008
Very Rev William Doolan
c/o Diocesan Office, Social Service Centre,
Henry Street, Limerick
Very Rev Patrick Howard
Athlacca, Kilmallock, Co Limerick
Very Rev Thomas Hurley
Templeglantine, Co Limerick
Tel 068-84021
Right Rev Michael Dean Kelly
St Catherine's Nursing Home,
Newcastle West, Co Limerick
Very Rev David Kennedy
Clonlusk Doon, Co Limerick
Rt Rev Mgr Michael Lane PE, VG
2 Meadowvale, Raheen, Limerick
Tel 061-228761
Email mwlane@esatclear.ie
Very Rev Michael Lane
Shravokee, Clonlara, near Limerick
Very Rev Micheál Canon Liston
21 Sullane Crescent,
Raheen Heights, Limerick
Very Rev Martin Madigan
Hamilton's Terrace, Glin, Co Limerick
Tel 087-9418568
Very Rev Frank Moriarty
Adare, Co Limerick
Tel 061-396177
Very Rev James Canon Neville
Cedarville, Abbeyfeale, Co Limerick
Tel 068-32884
Rev P. J. O'Donnell
c/o Diocesan Office, Social Service Centre,
Henry Street, Limerick
Rev Charles O'Neill
Colmanswell, Charleville, Co Limerick
Tel 063-89459
Rev Antóin Ó Tuathaigh
c/o Diocesan Office, Social Service Centre,
Henry Street, Limerick
Very Rev Seamus Power PE
'Sheen Lodge', Ennis Road, Limerick
Tel 061-454841

PERSONAL PRELATURE

OPUS DEI
Rev Brian McCarthy
Castleville Study Centre,
Golf Links Road, Castletroy, Limerick
Tel 061-331223 Fax 061-331204
Email castleville@eircom.net

RELIGIOUS ORDERS AND CONGREGATIONS

PRIESTS

AUGUSTINIANS
St Augustine's Priory,
O'Connell Street, Limerick
Tel 061-415374
Prior: Rev Frank Sexton (OSA)

DOMINICANS
St Saviour's, Glentworth Street,
Limerick
Tel 061-412333 Fax 061-311728
Prior: Very Rev James Donleavy (OP)

JESUITS
Crescent College Comprehensive,
Dooradoyle, Limerick
Tel 061-480920 Fax 061-480928
Email dooradoyle@jesuit.ie
Superior: Rev Liam O'Connell (SJ)
Headmaster: Mr Nicholas Cuddihy
Tel 061-229655 Fax 061-229013
Email ccadmin.ias@eircom.net

REDEMPTORISTS
Mount St Alphonsus Mission House,
Limerick
Tel 061-315099 Fax 061-315303
Superior
Rev Adrian Egan (CSsR)

St Clement's College, Limerick
Tel 061-315878 Fax 061-316640
Email cssrlimerick@eircom.net
Secondary school for boys

SALESIANS
Salesian College, Pallaskenry, Co Limerick
Tel 061-393313 Fax 061-393021
Rector: Very Rev Martin Loftus (SDB)
Email salesian@indigo.ie
Secondary and agricultural schools

Salesian House, Milford,
Castletroy, Limerick
Tel 061-330268/330194
Rector: Rev Koenraad Van Gucht (SDB)
Parish Priest: Rev John Campion (SDB)
Student hostel and parish

BROTHERS

BROTHERS OF CHARITY
Bawnmore, Clonlong Road, Limerick
Tel 061-412288 Fax 061-412389
Chaplain: Rev Joe Young

CHRISTIAN BROTHERS
Christian Brothers, St Teresa's,
North Circular Road, Limerick
Tel 061-451811
Community Leader: Br M. S. Hynes
Community: 4

SISTERS

BON SECOURS SISTERS (TROYES)
St Paul's Home, Dooradoyle, Limerick
Tel 061-228209/227749
Community: 5
Home for the aged

SISTERS OF CHARITY OF OUR LADY MOTHER OF MERCY
St Andrew's, 3 Avonmore Road,
Raheen, Limerick
Tel 061-229935 Fax 061-229984
Superior: Sr Nora Hayes
Community: 3

CHARITY OF ST PAUL THE APOSTLE SISTERS
St Paul's Convent, Kilfinane, Co Limerick
Tel 063-91025 Fax 063-91639
Email stpaulstin@eircom.net
Contact: Sr Eileen Kelly
Community: 5
Secondary school day pupils

St Paul's, Glenfield Road,
Kilmallock, Co Limerick
Tel 063-98086
Email sisterskilm@eircom.net
Contact: Sr Teresa Murphy
Community: 4
Primary school, parish and social work

CONGREGATION OF THE SISTERS OF MERCY
Convent of Mercy, Westbourne,
Ashbourne Avenue, Limerick
Tel 061-229388/229605 Fax 061-304088
Non-resident Leader: Sr Alice O'Gorman
Community: 12
Primary and secondary education, school
for slow learners, youth work and other
community work, pastoral counselling,
prayer ministry, writing on social justice
issues, pastoral care, adult education,
radio, liturgy at national level

Mountmahon, Abbeyfeale, Co Limerick
Tel 068-31203 Fax 068-32783
Non-resident Leader: Sr Phyllis Moynihan
Community: 5
Primary and secondary education,
community work, prayer ministry

Mount St Vincent,
O'Connell Avenue, Limerick
Tel 061-314965 Fax 061-404175
Resident Leader: Sr Regina Kelly
Community: 20
Children in care. Day Care Centre.
Primary and secondary education,
community work, residential centre for
students, counselling, adult education,
youth ministry

Sisters of Mercy, St Mary's Convent,
Bishop Street, Limerick
Tel 061-317356 Fax 061-317361
Non-resident Leader: Sr Catherine Ryan
Community: 11

St Anne's Convent,
Thomas Street, Rathkeale, Co Limerick
Tel 069-64175 Fax 069-63155
Non-resident Leader: Sr Phyllis Moynihan
Community: 7
Primary and secondary education,
teenage training centre for travellers,
community work, orthopaedic nursing

7 Sullane Crescent, Raheen, Limerick
Tel/Fax 061-227436
Non-resident Leader: Sr Betty O'Riordan
Community: 3
Nursing in Regional Hospital with
attendant ministries, focusing, spiritual
direction, addiction counselling

16 Portland Estate, St Clare's, Newcastle
Tel/Fax 069-62373
Non-resident Leader: Sr Phyllis Moynihan
Community: 3
Geriatric nursing and administration of
hospital, prayer ministry

33 Danesfort, Corbally, Limerick
Tel 061-341214 Fax 061-342041
Non-resident Leader: Sr Catherine Ryan
Community: 3

34 Danesfort, Corbally, Limerick
Tel/Fax 061-349411
Non-resident Leader: Sr Betty O'Riordan
Community: 3

7 Fitzhaven Square,
Ashbourne Avenue, Limerick
Tel/Fax 061-304614
Non-resident Leader: Sr Alice O'Gorman
Community: 3

Corpus Christi, 129 Cosgrave Park,
Moyross, Limerick
Tel/Fax 061-452511
Non-resident Leader: Sr Nora Hartigan
Community: 4
Family care, home/hospital visitation,
adult education, home/school/
community liaison, prayer groups, youth
ministry

1 Greenfields, Rosbrien, Limerick
Tel/Fax 061-229773
Non-resident Leader: Sr Betty O'Riordan
Community: 3
Home visitation, community work,
primary education, community work,
campus ministry

Catherine McAuley House
Old Dominic Street, Limerick
Tel 061-315313/315384 Fax 061-315455
Non-resident Leader: Sr Margaret Hogan
Community: 26
Holistic care of sick and elderly sisters

136 Fortview Drive,
Ballinacurra Gardens, Limerick
Tel/Fax 061-304798
Non-resident Leader: Sr Frances Minahan
Community: 2

Allianz (ⓘ)

1 Mount Vincent Place,
O'Connell Avenue, Limerick
Tel 061-468448
Non-resident Leader: Sr Catherine Ryan
Community: 4

Emmanuel,
9 The Grange, Raheen, Limerick
Tel/Fax 061-301363
Non-resident Leader: Sr Catherine Ryan
Community: 2

22 Galtee Drive,
O'Malley Park, Southill, Limerick
Rel/Fax 061-416706
Non-resident Leader: Sr Betty O'Riordan
Community: 2

Cuan Mhuire, Bruree, Limerick
Non-resident Leader: Sr Phyllis Moynihan
Community: 1

FAITHFUL COMPANIONS OF JESUS
Maryville Residence FCJ,
Laurel Hill, Limerick
Tel 061-416009
Leader: Sr Beatrice Molyneux
Community: 12

4/5 Laurel Hill Court,
Summerville Avenue, Limerick
Tel 061-319916 Fax 061-311876
Leader: Sr Beatrice Molyneux
Community: 5
Care of elderly sisters
Laurel Hill Coláiste
Tel 061-313636 Fax 061-315373
Principal: Ms Ardín Ní Bhriain
Laurel Hill Secondary School
Tel 061-319383 Fax 061-316048
Principal: Mr Adrian Cantillon

Ballygrennan, Bruff, Co Limerick
Tel 061-382106
Leader: Sr Catherine Toomey
Community: 3
Secondary coeducational school
Chaplaincy, Parish
Principal: Mr Michael Clifford
Tel 061-382349 Fax 061-382511

FRANCISCAN MISSIONARIES OF MARY
Castle View Gardens,
Clancy Strand, Limerick
Tel 061-455320
Email limfmm1@yahoo.ie
Superior: Sr Carina Lee
Community: 9

GOOD SHEPHERD SISTERS
Good Shepherd Avenue,
12 Pennywell Road, Limerick
Tel 061-415178 Fax 061-415147
Email rgslim@eircom.net
Superior: Sr Dolores Madigan
Community: 19

Omega B, Roxboro Road,
Janesboro, Limerick
Tel 061-416676 Fax 061-418207
Email rgsroxboro@hotmail.com
Community: 3

Good Shepherd Sisters, 33 Salvia Court,
Keyes Park, Southill, Limerick
Tel 061-414918
Email rgsanna02@eircom.net
Community: 1
Assistance to people in difficulty and
alcoholics

INFANT JESUS SISTERS
Dromcollogher, Co Limerick
Tel 063-83407
Pastoral ministry

LITTLE COMPANY OF MARY
Milford House, Castletroy, Limerick
Tel 061-485800 Fax 061-330351
Community: 15
Milford Care Centre
Tel 061-485800 Fax 061-331181
Email milford@milfordcarecentre.ie
Hospice & nursing home and
convalescent beds
Manager of Nursing Services
Ms Marian Moriarty
Tel 061-485856 Fax 061-330142
Email m.moriarty@milfordcarecentre.ie

St Joseph's Convent, Plassey Park Road,
Castletroy, Limerick
Tel 061-331144 Fax 061-331188
Apostolic Community: 4

'Genazzano', 1 Shrewsbury Lawn,
Wesbtury, Corbally, Limerick
Tel 061-345656
Apostolic community: 1

1 Mary Potter Court, Plassey Park Road,
Castletroy, Limerick
Tel/Fax 061-332798
Community: 1

2 Mary Potter Court,
Plassey Park Road, Castletroy, Limerick
Tel 061-332777
Community: 1

3 Mary Potter Court,
Plassey Park Road, Castletroy, Limerick
Tel 061-332755
Community: 1

LITTLE SISTERS OF THE ASSUMPTION
12 Springfield Drive, Dooradoyle,
Limerick
Tel 061-304494

MARIE REPARATRICE SISTERS
Laurel Hill Avenue, Limerick
Tel 061-315045 Fax 061-312561
Email smrlim@eircom.net
Superior: Sr Bernadette O'Driscoll
Community: 14

POOR SERVANTS OF THE MOTHER OF GOD
39 Cluain Arra Estate,
Newcastle West, Co Limerick
Community: 2
Daycare Centre

PRESENTATION SISTERS
Presentation Sisters,
9-10 Butterfield Avenue,
Old Cork Road, Limerick
Tel 061-414812
Shared Leadership
Community: 3

Presentation Sisters,
8-9 Oakvale Drive,
Dooradoyle, Limerick
Tel 061-302011
Non-resident Leader
Sr Colette Hourigan
Community: 4
Sexton Street Primary School
Tel 061-412494
Secondary School. Tel 061-410390

Roxboro Road, Limerick
Tel 061-417204
Non-resident Leader
Sr Jennie Clifford
Community: 12
Janesboro Primary. Tel 061-311285
Galvone National School. Tel 061-311286

34 McDonagh Avenue,
Janesboro, Limerick
Tel 061-594777
Community: 2

Apartment A, 6 Sexton Street, Limerick
Tel 061-467866
Community: 1

Apartment B, 6 Sexton Street, Limerick
Tel 061-467867
Community: 1

SALESIAN SISTERS OF ST JOHN BOSCO
Salesian Convent, Fernbank,
North Circular Road, Limerick
Tel 061-455322
Superior: Sr Patricia Murtagh
Community: 13
Kindergarten and primary schools and
related activities

34 Bracken Crescent,
North Circular Road, Limerick
Tel 061-455132
Superior: Sr Mary McInerney
Community: 5
Teaching, related activities and
chiropody

Salesian Convent, Dun Ide,
Lower Shelbourne Road, Limerick
Tel 061-454511
Superior: Sr Frances Beggan
Community: 10
Secondary School. Tel 061-454699
Principal: Sr Bridget O'Connell

Salesian Convent, Ard Mhuire,
Caherdavin Heights, Limerick
Tel 061-451322
Superior: Sr Kay Meehan
Community: 12
Ministry to the elderly

Salesian Sisters, Cill Leala, New Road,
Thomondgate, Limerick
Tel 061-453099 Fax 061-455413
Community: 4
Involvement in Ballynanty Resource
Centre

Salesian Sisters, 14 Clonile,
Old Cratloe Road, Limerick
Tel 061-329673
Superior: Sr Maureen Mullen
Community: 4
Teaching and related activities; social
work

Salesian Sisters, 3 Oakton Road,
Westbury, Corbally, Limerick
Community: 3
Social work

ST JOSEPH OF THE SACRED HEART SISTERS

Granagh, Kilmallock, Co Limerick
Tel 061-399027
Regional Leader: Sr Margaret O'Sullivan
Email lmargaretosullivan@eircom.net

Sisters of St Joseph of Sacred Heart,
7 Plassey Grove, Castletroy, Limerick
Tel 061-335794

Sisters of St Joseph of Sacred Heart,
Mackillop House, Dromcollogher,
Co Limerick
Tel 063-83911

Sisters of St Joseph of Sacred Heart,
No. 2 St Ita's Centre, Convent Street,
Abbeyfeale, Co Limerick
Tel 068-51984

Sisters of St Joseph of Sacred Heart,
4 Clover Field, Glin, Co Limerick
Tel 068-26015

Sisters of St Joseph of Sacred Heart,
14 Court Villas, Rathkeale, Co Limerick
Tel 069-63682

Sisters of St Joseph, St Catherine's,
Bungalow 2, Bothar Buí, Newcastle West,
Co Limerick
Tel 069-62584

Sisters of St Joseph, Apt 15, Liosan Court,
Gort Boy, Newcastle West, Co Limerick
Tel 069-69603

Sisters of St Joseph, St Joseph's,
Banogue Cross, Croom, Co Limerick
Tel 061-600932

EDUCATIONAL INSTITUTIONS

Limerick Institute of Technology
Tel 061-327688
Chaplain: Rev Alphonsus Cullinan
142 Mayorstone Park, Limerick
Tel 061-327836/208302
Email alphonsus.cullinan@lit.ie

Mary Immaculate College of Education
Tel 061-204300
Chaplain: Rev Michael Wall
Tel 061-204331
Email michael.wall@mic.ul.ie
*Head of Department of Theology &
Religious Studies:* Rev Eamonn Conway
Tel 061-204353
Email eamonn.conway@mic.ul.ie

St Munchin's College (Diocesan College)
Corbally, Limerick
Tel 061-348922 Fax 061-340465
Email stmunchins@eircom.net
President: Very Rev Charles Irwin BD, HDE
Chaplain: Mr Oliver Joyce

University of Limerick
Chaplain: Rev Koenraad Van Gucht (SDB)
Salesian House, Milford,
Castletroy, Limerick
Tel 061-330268/202180
Email koenraad.vangucht@ul.ie

EDMUND RICE SCHOOLS TRUST
Scoil Iosagáin Primary School,
Sexton Street, Limerick
Tel 061-413950 Fax 061-416011
Email cbslk@eircom.net
Website www.cbslk.com
Principal: Mr. P. Hanley

Coláiste Mhichíl Secondary School,
Sexton Street, Limerick
Tel 061-416628/419261 Fax 061-416011
Email rice@iol.ie
Principal: Mr Noel Earlie

St Munchin's Primary School,
Shelbourne Road, Limerick
Tel 061-455180 Fax 061-455108
Email primarymun@eircom.net
Principal: Mr Michael Condon

Ardscoil Rís Secondary School,
North Circular Road, Limerick
Tel 061-453828/455251
Fax 061-325035
Email asroffice@eircom.net
Website www.ardscoil.com
Principal: Bríd de Brún

CHARITABLE AND OTHER SOCIETIES

Adapt
Adapt House, Rosbrien, Limerick
Tel 061-412354
Contact: Ms Monica McElvaney

Alcoholics Anonymous
(Also Al/Anon and Alateen)
Social Service Centre,
Henry Street, Limerick
Tel 061-314111
24 hour service Tel 061-311222

Apostolic Work Society
Contact: Mrs Brid Shine
Glenbrohane, Garryspillane,
Kilmallock, Co Limerick
Tel 062-46612
Email dirb@iol.ie

Catholic Housing Aid Society
Contact: Very Rev Donal McNamara PP
Tel 061-455635

Catholic Institute Athletic Club
Rosbrien, Limerick
President: Tel 061-455635
Secretary: Tel 061-452023

**Doras Luimní
(Development organisation for Refugees
and Asylum Seekers)**
Mount St Vincent, O'Connell Street,
Limerick
Tel 061-609960
Email dorasluimni@eircom.net

Knights of St Columbanus
Contact: Mr William Ryan
Tel 061-414173 (work)/061-227530 (home)

Legion of Mary
Assumpta House, Windmill Street,
Limerick
Tel 061-314071

Limerick Youth Service
5 Lower Glentworth Street, Limerick
Tel 061-412444/412545 Fax 061-412795
Director: Catherine Kelly
Email lys@limerickyouthservice.net

Order of Malta
7A Davis Street, Limerick
Tel/Fax 061-314250

Samaritans
20 Barrington Street, Limerick
Tel 061-412111/1850-609090

St John's Hospital
Limerick
Tel 061-415822

St Joseph's Young Priests' Society
Contact: Ms Una Nunan
10 Garravogue Road, Raheen, Limerick
Tel 061-227852

St Vincent de Paul Society
Ozanam House, Hartstonge Street,
Limerick
Tel 061-317327 Fax 061-310320
Email info@svpmw.com
Administrator: Ms Mary Leahy
Drop-In Centre
The Lane, Hartstonge Street, Limerick
Manager: Mr Tom Flynn
Tel 061-313557

DIOCESE OF MEATH

PATRON OF THE DIOCESE
ST FINIAN, 12 DECEMBER

INCLUDES THE GREATER PART OF COUNTIES MEATH, WESTMEATH AND OFFALY,
AND A PORTION OF COUNTIES LONGFORD, LOUTH, DUBLIN AND CAVAN

Most Rev Michael Smith DCL, DD
Bishop of Meath;
born 1940;
ordained priest 1963;
consecrated Bishop 29 January
1984; Co-adjutor Bishop of
Meath 10 October 1988;
succeeded 16 May 1990

Residence: Bishop's House,
Dublin Road,
Mullingar, Co Westmeath
Tel 044-9348841 Fax 044-9343020
Email bishop@dioceseofmeath.ie
Website www.dioceseofmeath.ie

CATHEDRAL OF
CHRIST THE KING, MULLINGAR

As the Penal Laws began to be relaxed, Bishop Patrick Plunkett was appointed Bishop of Meath in 1778. He was to spend the next forty-nine years of his life restoring and rebuilding the diocese. He had no cathedral, but providing one was not his immediate priority. Towards the end of his time as bishop, work began on the magnificent new Church of St Mary in Navan. This was opened in 1830 and was considered the Cathedral Church of the Diocese. In 1870 Bishop Thomas Nulty decided to locate the bishop's residence in Mullingar, and the parish church there was designated Cathedral Church of the Diocese. It had been built in 1828 but was quite small.

On his appointment as bishop in 1900, Matthew Gaffney called a public meeting to discuss the building of a cathedral for the Diocese of Meath. This meeting adopted the following resolution: 'The Diocese of Meath not having a cathedral nor the parish of Mullingar a suitable church, be it resolved that a church be built in Mullingar which will fulfil this double purpose.' A building fund was established, and £15,000 was subscribed at this first meeting – a very sizeable sum at that time. It was not until the day of his consecration as bishop in 1929 that Thomas Mulvany was able to announce the decision to proceed with the project. Ralph A. Byrne, chief architect with William H. Byrne & Son, Dublin, prepared plans, which were accepted. Work began in 1932, and the Cathedral of Christ the King was opened for worship in September 1936. It was consecrated on 30 August 1939, the debt having been cleared. In recent years, a major renovation, including the replacement of the roof, has been completed.

ADMINISTRATION

Diocesan website
www.dioceseofmeath.ie

Vicars General
Rt Rev Mgr Dermot Farrell PP, VG
Parochial House, Dunboyne, Co Meath
Tel 01-8255342 Fax 01-8252321
Rt Rev Mgr Seán Heaney PP, VG
Parochial House, Tullamore, Co Offaly
Tel 057-9321587 Fax 057-9351510

Vicars Forane
Very Rev John Byrne PP, VF
Parochial House, Kells, Co Meath
Tel 046-9240213 Fax 046-9293475
Very Rev Joseph Clavin PP, VF
Parochial House,
Dunshaughlin, Co Meath
Tel 01-8259114 Fax 01-8011614
Very Rev Richard Matthews PP, VF
Parochial House, Killucan, Co Westmeath
Tel 044-9374127
Very Rev Patrick Keary PP, VF
Parochial House, Clara, Co Offaly
Tel 057-9331170 Fax 057-9330100
Very Rev Patrick Moore PP, VF
Parochial House,
Castlepollard, Co Westmeath
Tel 044-9661126 Fax 044-9661881
Very Rev Andrew Doyle PP, VF
Parochial House, Bohermeen,
Navan, Co Meath
Tel/Fax 046-9021439
Very Rev Denis Nulty PP, VF
St Mary's, Drogheda, Co Louth
Tel 041-9834958 Fax 041-9845144
Very Rev Patrick O'Connor PP, VF
Parochial House, Athboy, Co Meath
Tel 046-9432184 Fax 046-9430021

College of Consultors
Most Rev Michael Smith DD, DCL
Rt Rev Mgr Seán Heaney PP, VG
Rt Rev Mgr Dermot Farrell PP, VG
Very Rev John Byrne PP, VF
Very Rev Joseph Clavin PP, VF
Very Rev Richard Matthews, PP, VF
Very Rev Patrick Keary PP, VF
Very Rev Patrick Moore PP, VF
Very Rev Andrew Doyle PP, VF
Very Rev Denis Nulty PP, VF
Very Rev Patrick O'Connor PP, VF
Rev Paul Crosbie CC

Diocesan Secretary
Rev Paul Crosbie
Bishop's House, Dublin Road, Mullingar,
Co Westmeath
Tel 044-9348841 Fax 044-9343020
Email paul@dioceseofmeath.ie

Secretary
Mrs Irene Connaughton
Bishop's House, Dublin Road, Mullingar,
Co Westmeath
Tel 044-9348841 Fax 044-9343020
Email secretary@dioceseofmeath.ie

CATECHETICS EDUCATION

Education
Diocesan Secretary
Rev Brendan Ludlow
St Mary's, Navan, Co Meath
Tel 046-9027518
Email cpsma@dioceseofmeath.ie

Post-Primary Catechetics
Diocesan Director: Mr Seán Wright
The Whinnies, Tierworker,
Kells, Co Meath
Tel 042-9665547 Fax 042-9666969
Email ppdd@eircom.net

Primary Religious Education
Diocesan Advisers
Rev Tony Gavin CC
Parochial House,
Rosemount, Co Westmeath
Tel 090-6436110
Rev Barry Condron CC
Parochial House, Dunshaughlin,
Co Meath
Tel 01-8259114
Rev Shane Crombie CC
Parochial House, Tullamore, Co Offaly
Tel 057-9321587
Rev Patrick Donnelly CC
Parochial House, Ratoath, Co Meath
Tel 01-8256207
Nuala Cosgrave
c/o Bishop's House, Dublin Road,
Mullingar, Co Westmeath
Tel 044-9348841

LITURGY

Liturgical Commission
Chairman: Very Rev Joseph McEvoy PP
Parochial House, Moynalty, Co Meath
Tel 046-9244305
Email josephus@indigo.ie
Secretary: Mr James Walsh
18 Beechgrove, Laytown, Co Meath

PASTORAL

Accord
Director, Mullingar Centre
Very Rev Stan Deegan PP
Parochial House, Rochfortbridge,
Co Westmeath
Tel 044-9222107
Chairperson, Navan Centre
Ms Lillie Mahon
St Anne's Resource Centre,
Navan, Co Meath
Director, Tullamore Centre
Very Rev Gerry Boyle PP
Multyfarnham, Co Westmeath
Tel 057-9321587
www.dioceseofmeath.ie/marriage

Apostolic Work Society
Mullingar Branch
Chaplain: Rev Colm Browne CC
Cathedral House, Mullingar, Co Westmeath
Tel 044-9348338

Navan Branch
Chaplain: Rev William Coleman CC
St Mary's, Navan, Co Meath
Tel 046-9027518

Council of Priests
Chairman: Very Rev Denis Nulty PP, VF
St Mary's Drogheda, Co Louth
Tel 041-9834958
Secretary: Rev William Coleman CC
St Mary's, Navan, Co Meath
Tel 046-9027518

Dowdstown House (Blowick Conference Centre)
Dowdstown House,
Navan, Co Meath
Tel 046-9021407 Fax 046-9073091
Director: Sr Elma Peppard
Family Ministry Co-ordinators
Sr Rose King, Sr Rose Sloan

Ecumenism
Secretary: Rev William Coleman CC
St Mary's, Navan, Co Meath
Tel 046-9027518 Fax 046-9071774

Fr Matthew Union
Secretary: Very Rev Seamus Houlihan PP
Parochial House,
Nobber, Co Meath
Tel 046-9052197 Fax 046-9052195

Knock Pilgrimage
Director: Very Rev Stan Deegan PP
Parochial House, Rochfortbridge,
Co Westmeath
Tel 044-9222107

Laity Commission
Diocesan Representative
Mrs Molly Buckley
Moylena, Clara Road,
Tullamore, Co Offaly
Tel 0506-41357

Lourdes Pilgrimage
Director
Very Rev Joseph Gallagher PP
Parochial House, Kilcormac, Co Offaly
Tel 0509-35013

Marriage Tribunal
(See Marriage Tribunals section)

Pioneer Total Abstinence Association
Very Rev Seamus Houlihan PP
Parochial House, Nobber,
Co Meath
Tel 046-9052197 Fax 046-9052195

Pontifical Mission Societies
Diocesan Director
Very Rev Gerard Stuart PP
Parochial House, Ratoath, Co Meath
Tel 01-8256207

Vocations

Director: Rev Mark English CC
Parochial House,
Dunboyne, Co Meath
Tel 01-8255342
Email mjpenglish@eircom.net

Youth Director

Rev Mark English CC
Parochial House,
Dunboyne, Co Meath
Tel 01-8255342
Email mjpenglish@eircom.net

PARISHES

*Mensal parishes are listed first. Other
parishes follow alphabetically.*

MULLINGAR,
Cathedral of Christ the King
St Paul's, Mullingar
Assumption, Walshestown
Immaculate Conception, Gainstown
*Little Flower and Our Lady of Good
Counsel, Brotenstown*
Very Rev Padraig McMahon Adm
Rev Colm Browne CC
Rev Paul Crosbie CC
Rev Michael Kilmartin CC
Cathedral House, Mullingar,
Co Westmeath
Tel 044-9348338/9340126
Fax 044-9340780
Email cathedral@dioceseofmeath.ie

NAVAN
St Mary's; St Oliver's
Very Rev Declan Hurley Adm
Rev William Coleman CC
Rev Dwayne Gavin CC
Rev Brendan Ludlow CC
St Mary's, Navan, Co Meath
Tel 046-9027518/9027414
Fax 046-9071774
Email stmarysnavan@eircom.net
Website www.navanparish.ie

ARDCATH
St Mary's, Ardcath
St John the Baptist, Clonalvy
Very Rev Philip Gaffney PP
Parochial House, Ardcath,
Garristown, Co Dublin
Tel 01-8354117

ASHBOURNE-DONAGHMORE
Immaculate Conception, Ashbourne
St Patrick, Donaghmore
Parish Office: Tel/Fax 01-8353149
Email ashdon@indigo.ie
Very Rev James Lynch PP
Parochial House, Ashbourne,
Co Meath
Tel 01-8350406
Rev Derek Darby CC
54 Brookville, Ashbourne, Co Meath
Tel 01-8350547

ATHBOY
St James', Athboy
St Lawrence, Rathmore
Naomh Pádraig, Rathcairn
Very Rev Patrick O'Connor PP, VF
Parochial House, Athboy, Co Meath
Tel 046-9432184 Fax 046-9430021

BALLINABRACKEY
Assumption, Ballinabrackey
Trinity, Castlejordan
Very Rev Martin Halpin PP
Parochial House, Ballinabrackey,
Kinnegad, Co Westmeath
Tel/Fax 046-9739015
Email mhalpin@eircom.net

BALLYNACARGY
The Nativity, Ballynacargy
St Michael, Sonna
Very Rev John Nally PP
Parochial House, Ballynacargy,
Co Westmeath
Tel 044-9373932

BALLIVOR
St Columbanus
Very Rev Oliver Devine PP
Parochial House, Ballivor,
Co Meath
Tel/Fax 046-9546488
Email ballivorkildalkeyparish@eircom.net

BALLYMORE
The Holy Redeemer, Ballymore
St Brigid's, Boher
Very Rev Philip Smith PP
Parochial House, Ballymore, Mullingar,
Co Westmeath
Tel 044-9356212

BEAUPARC
The Assumption, Beauparc
The Assumption, Kentstown
Very Rev Peter Farrelly PP
Parochial House, Beauparc,
Navan, Co Meath
Tel 046-9024114
Email peterfarrelly@eircom.net
Rev P.J. Coyne CC
Kentstown, Navan, Co Meath
Tel 041-9825276
Email kentstownparish@eircom.net

BOHERMEEN
St Ultan's, Bohermeen
St Cuthbert's, Boyerstown
Christ the King, Cortown
Very Rev Andrew Doyle PP, VF
Durhamstown, Bohermeen,
Navan, Co Meath
Tel 046-9073805
Very Rev Patrick A. Mackin PE
Parochial House, Bohermeen,
Kells, Co Meath
Tel 046-9240633
Email patmack@iolfree.ie

CARNAROSS
St Ciaran, Carnaross
Sacred Heart, Mullaghea
Rt Rev Mgr John Hanly PP
Parochial House, Carnaross,
Kells, Co Meath
Tel 046-9245904

CASTLEPOLLARD
St Michael's, Castlepollard
St Michael's, Castletown
St Mary's, Finea
Very Rev Patrick A. Moore PP, VF
Parochial House, Castlepollard,
Co Westmeath
Tel 044-9661126 Fax 044-9661881
Email moorep@eircom.net

CASTLETOWN-GEOGHEGAN
St Michael, Castletown-Geoghegan
St Stephen, Tyrrellspass
St Peter, Raheenmore
Very Rev Seamus Giles PP
Parochial House,
Castletown-Geoghegan, Co Westmeath
Tel 044-9226118
Rev Brendan Ferris CC
Tyrrellspass, Co Westmeath
Tel 044-9223115

CASTLETOWN-KILPATRICK
St Patrick's, Castletown-Kilpatrick
St Colmcille's, Fletcherstown
Very Rev Martin McErlean PP
Parochial House, Castletown-Kilpatrick,
Navan, Co Meath
Tel 046-9055789
Office: Tel 046-9054142

CLARA
St Brigid's, Clara
Sts Peter & Paul, Horseleap
Very Rev Patrick Keary PP, VF
Parochial House, Clara, Co Offaly
Tel 057-9331170 Fax 057-9330100

CLONMELLON
Sts Peter & Paul, Clonmellon
St Bartholomew, Killallon
Very Rev Sean Garland PP
Parochial House, Clonmellon
Navan, Co Meath
Tel 046-9433124

COLLINSTOWN
St Mary's, Collinstown
St Feichin's, Fore
Very Rev Michael Walsh PP
Parochial House, Collinstown,
Co Westmeath
Tel 044-9666326

COOLE (MAYNE)
Immaculate Conception, Coole
St John the Baptist, Whitehall
Very Rev Oliver Skelly PP
Parochial House, Coole, Co Westmeath
Tel 044-9661191

CURRAHA
St Andrew's
Very Rev Philip Gaffney PP
Parochial House, Curraha,
Ashbourne, Co Meath
Tel 01-8350136

DELVIN
Assumption, Delvin
St Livinius, Killulagh
Very Rev Seamus Heaney PP
Parochial House, Delvin, Co Westmeath
Tel 044-9664127 Fax 044-9664534
Email info@delvinparish.ie

DONORE
Nativity, Donore
Nativity, Rosnaree
Very Rev Michael Meade PP
Parochial House, Donore,
Drogheda, Co Louth
Tel 041-9823137

DROGHEDA, HOLY FAMILY
Very Rev David Bradley PP
The Presbytery, Ballsgrove,
Drogheda, Co Louth
Tel 041-9831991
Email holyfamilyballsgrove@eircom.net
Rev Anthony Gonoude CC
The Presbytery, Ballsgrove,
Drogheda, Co Louth
Tel 041-9836287 Fax 041-9836287

DROGHEDA, ST MARY'S
Very Rev Denis Nulty PP, VF
Email frdnulty@eircom.net
Rev Martin Carley CC
Rev John Hogan CC
St Mary's, Drogheda, Co Louth
Tel 041-9834958 Fax 041-9845144
Parish Office: Tel 041-9838347
Parish email
stmarysparishdheda@eircom.net

DRUMCONRATH
Sts Peter & Paul, Drumconrath
Sts Brigid & Patrick, Meath Hill
Very Rev Finian Connaughton PP
Parochial House, Drumconrath,
Navan, Co Meath
Tel 041-6854146

DRUMRANEY
Immaculate Conception, Drumraney
Immaculate Conception, Tang
Immaculate Conception, Forgney
Very Rev Joseph Brilley PP
Drumraney, Athlone, Co Westmeath
Tel 044-9356207
Rev Jerry Murphy CC
St Mary's, Tang,
Ballymahon, Co Longford
Tel 090-6432214

DULEEK
St Cianan, Duleek
St Thérèse, Bellewstown
Very Rev John Conlon PP
Parochial House, Duleek, Co Meath
Tel 041-9823205
www.duleek.net

DUNBOYNE
SS Peter & Paul, Dunboyne
St Brigid & Sacred Heart, Kilbride
Rt Rev Mgr Dermot Farrell PP, VG
Parochial House, Dunboyne, Co Meath
Tel 01-8255342 Fax 01-8252321
Rev Mark English CC
2 Orchard Court, Dunboyne, Co Meath
Rev Gabriel Flynn DD, PC
1 Orchard Court, Dunboyne, Co Meath
Tel 01-8255342
Email gabriel.flynn@materdei.dcu.ie

DUNDERRY
Assumption, Dunderry
Assumption, Robinstown
Assumption, Kilbride
Very Rev Noel Horneck PP
Parochial House, Dunderry,
Navan, Co Meath
Tel 046-9431433 Fax 046-9431474

DUNSHAUGHLIN
Sts Patrick & Seachnall, Dunshaughlin
St Martin, Culmullen
Very Rev Joseph Clavin PP, VF
Rev Barry Condron CC
Parochial House,
Dunshaughlin, Co Meath
Tel 01-8259114 Fax 01-8011614
Email dunshaughlinparish@eircom.net
Very Rev John Kerrane PE
'St Martin's', Culmullen,
Drumree, Co Meath
Tel 01-8241976

DYSART
St Patrick's, Dysart
Assumption, Loughanavalley
Very Rev Philip O'Connor PP
Parochial House, Dysart, Mullingar,
Co Westmeath
Tel 044-9226122

EGLISH
St James, Eglish
St John the Baptist, Rath
Very Rev John Moorhead PP
Parochial House, Eglish, Birr, Co Offaly
Tel 057-9133010

ENFIELD
St Michael, Rathmolyon
Assumption, Jordanstown
Very Rev Michael Whittaker PP
The Presbytery, Enfield, Co Meath
Tel 046-9541282
Very Rev Sean Fay PE
Parochial House,
Rathmolyon, Co Meath
Tel 046-9555212
Email frfay@eircom.net

GLASSON
Immaculate Conception, Tubberclaire
Very Rev Seamus Mulvany PP
Parochial House, Tubberclaire-Glasson,
Athlone, Co Westmeath
Tel 090-6485103

JOHNSTOWN
Nativity, Johnstown
Assumption, Walterstown
Very Rev Martin Mulvaney PP
Parochial House, Johnstown,
Navan, Co Meath
Tel 046-9021731
Email mjmul@eircom.net

KELLS
Columcille, Kells
Immaculate Conception, Girley
Very Rev John Byrne PP, VF
Email frjohnbyrne@eircom.net
Rev Liam Malone CC
Parochial House, Kells, Co Meath
Tel 046-9240213 Fax 046-9293475
Email info@kellsparish.ie
www.kellsparish.ie

KILBEG
Nativity of Our Lady, Kilbeg
St Michael, Staholmog
Very Rev Michael Cahill PP
Parochial House, Kilbeg,
Kells, Co Meath
Tel 046-9246604

KILBEGGAN
St James, Kilbeggan
St Hugh, Rahugh
Very Rev Brendan Corrigan PP
5 The Gallops, Kilbeggan,
Co Westmeath
Tel 057-9332155
Very Rev Lauri Halpin PE
Parochial House, Kilbeggan,
Co Westmeath
Tel 057-9332155

KILCLOON
St Oliver Plunkett, Kilcloon
The Assumption, Batterstown
Little Chapel of the Assumption, Kilcock
Very Rev Gerard Rice PP
Parochial House, Kilcloon, Co Meath
Tel 01-6286252 Fax 01-6106404
Email johngmrice@eircom.net
Rev John Cunningham (OP) CC
Batterstown, Dunboyne, Co Meath
Tel 01-8259267

KILCORMAC
Nativity, Kilcormac
St Brigid, Mountbolus
Very Rev Joseph Gallagher PP
Parochial House, Kilcormac, Co Offaly
Tel 057-9335013
Very Rev Edward Daly PE
Mount Bolus, Tullamore, Co Offaly
Tel 057-9354035 Fax 057-9354791

KILDALKEY
St Dympna's
Very Rev Oliver Devine Adm
Parochial House, Kildalkey, Co Meath
Tel 046-9435133

KILLUCAN
St Joseph's, Rathwire
St Brigid's, Raharney
Very Rev Richard Matthews PP, VF
Parochial House, Killucan,
Co Westmeath
Tel 044-9374127

KILMESSAN
Nativity, Kilmessan
Assumption, Dunsany
Very Rev Terence Toner PP
Parochial House, Kilmessan,
Co Meath
Tel 046-9025172

KILSKYRE
St Alphonsus Liguori, Kilskyre
Assumption, Ballinlough
Very Rev John Brogan PP
Parochial House, Kilskyre,
Kells, Co Meath
Tel 046-9243623

KINGSCOURT
Immaculate Conception, Kingscourt
St Joseph's, Corlea
Our Lady of Mount Carmel, Muff
Very Rev Gerard MacCormack PP
Parochial House, Kingscourt, Co Cavan
Tel 042-9667314 Fax 042-9668141
Email info@kingscourtparish.com

KINNEGAD
Assumption, Kinnegad
St Agnes, Coralstown
St Finian, Clonard
Very Rev Thomas Gilroy PP
Tel 044-9379170 Fax 044-9375373
Rt Rev Mgr Eamonn Marron PE
Parochial House, Raharney,
Co Westmeath
Tel 044-9374271
Email kinnegadparish@eircom.net
www.kinnegadparish.ie

LAYTOWN-MORNINGTON
Sacred Heart, Laytown
Star of the Sea, Mornington
Very Rev Denis McNelis PP
Parochial House, Laytown, Co Meath
Tel 041-9827258
Rt Rev Mgr William Cleary PE
Curate's Residence, Mornington,
Co Meath
Tel 041-9827384 Fax041-9827324
Email mgtparish@eircom.net

LOBINSTOWN
Holy Cross
Very Rev Michael Sheerin PP
Parochial House, Lobinstown,
Navan, Co Meath
Tel 046-9053155
Email frmlsheerin@eircom.net

LONGWOOD
Assumption, Longwood
Assumption, Killyon
Very Rev Patrick Kearney PP
Parochial House, Longwood, Co Meath
Tel 046-9555009

MILLTOWN
St Matthew, Milltown
St Matthew, Empor
St Patrick, Moyvore
Very Rev William Fitzsimons PP
Parochial House, Milltown,
Rathconrath, Co Westmeath
Tel 044-9355106

MOUNTNUGENT
St Brigid, Mountnugent
Sts Brigid & Fiach, Ballinacree
Very Rev Oliver J. Devine PP
Parochial House, Mountnugent,
Co Cavan
Tel 049-8540123
Email froliverdevine@eircom.net

MOYNALTY
Assumption, Moynalty
Assumption, Newcastle
Very Rev Joseph McEvoy PP
Parochial House, Moynalty,
Kells, Co Meath
Tel 046-9244305
Email moynaltyparish@eircom.net
Website www.moynaltyparish.ie

MOYNALVEY
Nativity, Moynalvey
Assumption, Kiltale
Rev David Brennan Adm
Parochial House, Moynalvey, Summerhill,
Co Meath
Tel 046-9557031

MULTYFARNHAM
St Nicholas, Multyfarnham
St Patrick's, Leney
Very Rev Gerry Boyle PP
Parochial House, Multyfarnham,
Co Westmeath
Tel 044-9371124

NOBBER
St John the Baptist
Very Rev Séamus Houlihan PP
Parochial House, Nobber,
Co Meath
Tel 046-9052197 Fax 046-9052195
Email nobberparish@eircom.net

OLDCASTLE
St Brigid, Oldcastle
St Mary, Moylough
Very Rev Ray Kelly PP
Parochial House, Oldcastle,
Co Meath
Tel 049-8541142 Fax 049-8542865

ORISTOWN
St Catherine, Oristown
St John the Baptist, Kilberry
Very Rev John O'Brien PP
Parochial House, Oristown,
Kells, Co Meath
Tel 046-9054124

RAHAN
St Carthage, Killina
St Patrick, The Island
St Colman, Mucklagh
Very Rev Séamus Dunican PP
Parochial House, Killina, Rahan,
Tullamore, Co Offaly
Tel/Fax 057-9355917
Rev John McEvoy (SSC) CC
Mucklagh, Tullamore, Co Offaly
Tel 057-9321892

RATHKENNY
Sts Louis & Mary, Rathkenny
Our Lady, Rushwee
Our Lady, Grangegeeth
Very Rev Gerard Stanley PP
Parochial House,
Rathkenny, Co Meath
Tel 046-9054138
Email jerrystan04@hotmail.com
Website www.rathkennyparish.ie

RATOATH
Holy Trinity
Very Rev Gerard Stuart PP
Rev Patrick Donnelly CC
Parochial House, Ratoath,
Co Meath
Tel 01-8256207 Fax 01-8256662
Parish email ratoathparish@eircom.net

ROCHFORTBRIDGE
Immaculate Conception, Rochfortbridge
Sacred Heart, Meedin
St Joseph, Milltownpass
Very Rev Stan Deegan PP
Email standeegan2@eircom.net
Very Rev Eamonn O'Brien PE
Parochial House, Rochfortbridge,
Co Westmeath
Tel 044-9222107
Parish email
rbridgeparish@eircom.net

SKRYNE
St Colmcille, Skryne
Immaculate Conception, Rathfeigh
Very Rev Thomas O'Mahony PP
Parochial House, Skryne,
Tara, Co Meath
Tel 046-9025152
Very Rev Joseph Gleeson PE
Rathfeigh, Tara, Co Meath
Tel/Fax 041-9825159

SLANE
St Patrick, Slane
Assumption, Monknewtown
Very Rev Joseph Deegan PP
Parochial House, Slane, Co Meath
Tel 041-9824249

STAMULLEN
St Patrick, Stamullen
St Mary's, Julianstown
Very Rev Declan Kelly PP
Preston Hill, Stamullen, Co Meath
Tel/Fax 01-8418066
Email prestonhill@eircom.net
Parish email secsj@eircom.net
www.stamullenparish.ie

Rev Robert McCabe CF
Gormanston Military Camp, Gormanston,
Co Meath
Tel 01-8413990
Email robertmccabe@dioceseofmeath.ie
www.militarychaplaincy.ie

SUMMERHILL
Our Lady of Lourdes, Dangan
Assumption, Coole
Very Rev Thomas P. Gavin PP
Parochial House, Summerhill,
Co Meath
Tel 046-9557021
Email gavant@eircom.net

TAGHMON
Assumption, Taghmon
St Joseph, Turin
Very Rev Declan Smith PP
Parochial House, Taghmon,
Mullingar, Co Westmeath
Tel 044-9372140

TRIM
St Patrick, Trim
St Brigid, Boardsmill
Very Rev Sean Henry PP
Very Rev Andrew Farrell PE
Rev Mark Mohan CC
Email mohan@ireland.com
Parochial House, Trim, Co Meath
Tel 046-9431251
Parish email spcctrim@eircom.net

TUBBER
Holy Family, Tubber
St Thomas the Apostle, Rosemount
Very Rev Michael Walsh PP
Springlawn, Tubber, Moate,
Co Westmeath
Tel 090-6481141
Rev Tony Gavin CC
Rosemount, Moate, Co Westmeath
Tel 090-6436110

TULLAMORE
Assumption, Tullamore
St Colmcille, Durrow
Rt Rev Mgr Seán Heaney PP, VG
Email heaneysean@eircom.net
Rev Shane Crombie CC
Email frshane@gmail.com
Rev Pádraig Corcoran CC
Tullamore, Co Offaly
Tel 057-9321587 Fax 057-9351510
Parish email tulmorch@iol.ie

INSTITUTIONS AND THEIR CHAPLAINS

St Francis Private Hospital
Ballinderry, Mullingar, Co Westmeath
Tel 044-9341605
Rev Stan Connolly (SSP)

St Loman's Hospital
Mullingar, Co Westmeath
Tel 044-9340191
Rev Colm Browne
Residence: Cathedral House, Mullingar
Tel 044-9348338

Longford & Westmeath General Hospital
Mullingar, Co Westmeath
Tel 044-9340221

Our Lady's Hospital
Navan, Co Meath
Tel 046-9021210

Tullamore General Hospital
Tullamore, Co Offaly
Tel 057-9321501
Rev Pádraig Corcoran
Residence: Parochial House,
Tullamore, Co Offaly
Tel 057-9321587

PRIESTS OF THE DIOCESE ELSEWHERE

Rev James Crofton
'Vinea Mea', Via S. Francesco, 4,
Lappiano, 50064 Incisa (FI), Italy
Rev Anthony Draper DD
All Hallows College,
Drumcondra, Dublin 9
Tel 01-373745
Email tdraper@allhallows.ie
Rev Ronan Drury
St Patrick's College, Maynooth, Co Kildare
Tel 01-6285222
Rev David Hanratty
Tierhogar, Portarlington, Co Laois
Tel 057-8645719
Rev Thomas O'Connor DD
St Patrick's College, Maynooth, Co Kildare
Tel 01-6285222
Rev David O'Hanlon
c/o Bishop's House, Mullingar

RETIRED PRIESTS

Very Rev Ray Brady
c/o Bishop's House, Mullingar
Very Rev Eamonn Butler
10 Lynn Heights, Mullingar,
Co Westmeath
Tel 044-9344008
Very Rev Patrick Casey
5 St Mary's Terrace, Bishopsgate Street,
Mullingar, Co Westmeath
Tel 044-9342746
Very Rev Michael V. Daly
35 Herbert Place, Navan, Co Meath
Tel 046-9093935
Very Rev Nicholas Dunican
Knightsbridge Nursing Home,
Trim, Co Meath
Rt Rev Mgr Edward Dunne
Ratoath, Co Meath
Very Rev Edward Flynn
Multyfarnham Retirement Village,
Co Westmeath
Very Rev Joseph Garvey PE
Kilbrew Nursing Home, Curaha,
Ashbourne, Co Meath
Very Rev Lauri Halpin
Parochial House,
Kilbeggan, Co Westmeath
Very Rev John Kiernan
Holy Trinity Abbey, Kilnacrot,
Ballyjamesduff, Co Cavan

Rev Barney Maxwell
Empor, Ballymacargy, Co Westmeath
Very Rev Frank McNamara
Portiuncula Nursing Home,
Multyfarnham, Co Westmeath
Very Rev Matthew Mollin
Maryfield Nursing Home, Chapelizod,
Co Dublin
Very Rev Michael Murchan PE
Knightsbridge Nursing Home,
Trim, Co Meath
Very Rev Colm Murtagh
Parochial House, Kildalkey, Co Meath
Tel 046-9546488
Very Rev F. X. O'Reilly
Portiuncula Nursing Home,
Multyfarnham, Co Westmeath
Rt Rev Mgr Thomas Woods DD
Newbrook Nursing Home,
Mullingar, Co Westmeath

PERSONAL PRELATURE

OPUS DEI
Lismullin Conference Centre
Navan, Co Meath
Tel 046-9026936
Rev James Gavigan, Chaplain

RELIGIOUS ORDERS AND CONGREGATIONS

PRIESTS

CAMILLIANS
St Camillus Community,
Killucan, Co Westmeath
Tel 044-74115
Superior: Rev Frank Monks (OSCam)
Nursing Centre
Tel 044-74196

CARMELITES (OCARM)
Carmelite Priory, Moate, Co Westmeath
Tel 090-6481160/6481398
Fax 090-6481879
Email carmelitemoate@eircom.net
Prior: Rev Martin Ryan (OCarm)

FRANCISCANS
Provincial Office, 'La Verna',
Gormanston, Co Meath
Tel 01-8020951 Fax 01-08020952
Provincial: Rev Caoimhín Ó Laoide (OFM)
Email caoimhinofm@eircom.net

Franciscan College,
Gormanston, Co Meath
Tel 01-8412203 Fax 01-8412685
Email friary@gormanstoncollege.ie
Guardian: Rev Malcolm Timothy (OFM)

Franciscan Abbey,
Multyfarnham, Co Westmeath
Tel 044-9371114/9371137 Fax 044-9371387
Guardian: Rev Joseph Walsh (OFM)

HOLY SPIRIT CONGREGATION
Spiritan Missionaries,
Ardbraccan, Navan, Co Meath
Tel 046-9021441
Superior: Br Conleth Tyrrell (CSSp)

ST COLUMBAN'S MISSIONARY SOCIETY
St Columban's, Dalgan Park,
Navan, Co Meath
Tel 046-9021525
Regional Director: Rev Donal Hogan (SSC)

St Columban's Retirement Home,
Dalgan Park, Navan, Co Meath
Tel 046-9021525
Director
Rev Bernard Mulkerins (SSC)

SALESIANS
Salesian House
Warrenstown, Drumree, Co Meath
Tel 01-8259761
Community 01-8259894
Fax 01-8240298
Rector: Rev P. J. Nyland (SDB)

SOCIETY OF ST PAUL
St Paul Book Centre
Castle Street, Athlone, Co Westmeath
Tel/Fax 090-6492882
Email saintpaul_books@yahoo.com

BROTHERS

CHRISTIAN BROTHERS
St Joseph's, Kells, Co Meath
Tel 046-9240239
Community Leader: Br John Devaney
Community: 4

Edmund Rice Centre
Bective Street, Kells, Co Meath
Tel 046-9240239

FRANCISCAN BROTHERS
The Monastery, Clara, Co Offaly
Tel 057-9331130
Local Minister: Br Charles Conway (OSF)
Community: 5

SISTERS

BLESSED SACRAMENT SISTERS
Marian Hostel, High Street,
Tullamore, Co Offaly
Tel 057-9321182
Community: 3
Hostel for women
Day centre for children with mental
handicap. Tel 057-9323774
Activation and resource centre for
people with mental handicap
Tel 057-9351629

CHARITY OF JESUS AND MARY SISTERS
St Mary's Convent, South Hill, Delvin,
Co Westmeath
Tel 044-64108/9 Fax 044-64488
Contact: Sr Kathleen O'Connor
Community: 10
Residential and day services for children
and adults with mental handicap
Number of residents: 80

Aisling, Mitchelstown,
Delvin, Co Westmeath
Tel 044-64379
Contact: Sr Kathleen O'Connor

CONGREGATION OF THE SISTERS OF MERCY
St Mary's Convent of Mercy, Athlumney,
Navan, Co Meath
Tel 046-9021271
Facilitator: Sr Consilio Rock
Community: 8

Sisters of Mercy,
6 Meadowlands, Athboy, Co Meath
Tel 046-9430085

Sisters of Mercy,
3 St Brigid's Court, Connaught Street,
Athboy, Co Meath
Tel 046-9430047

Convent of Mercy, Charlestown,
Clara, Co Offaly
Tel 057-9331184
Leader: Sr Francis O'Brien

St Mary's Convent of Mercy,
Drogheda, Co Louth
Tel 041-9838184
Leader: Sr Claire Nugent
Community: 6

202 Ballsgrove,
Drogheda, Co Louth
Tel 041-9830160

38 Congress Avenue,
Drogheda, Co Louth
Tel 041-9837876

Convent of Mercy, Kells, Co Meath
Tel 046-9240159
Leader: Sr Mary Clavin
Community: 10

Sisters of Mercy
1 Circular Road, Kells, Co Meath
Tel 046-9249381

Cill na Gréine, Convent of Mercy,
Kells, Co Meath
Tel 046-9252536

Sisters of Mercy,
13 Grand Priory, Kells, Co Meath
Tel 046-9249027

Convent of Mercy, Kilbeggan,
Co Westmeath
Tel 057-9332161
Leader: Sr Concepta Brennan
Community: 5

Convent of Mercy,
Kilcormac, Co Offaly
Tel 057-9335007
Community: 5

Sisters of Mercy, Ard Aoibhinn
Mount Bolus, Co Offaly
Tel 057-9354867

Convent of Mercy,
Laytown, Co Meath
Tel 041-9827271
Community: 3
Leader: Sr Anna Haughian

Sisters of Mercy, Loughcrew,
Laytown, Co Meath
Tel 041-9827432
Community: 3

29 Green Road,
Mullingar, Co Westmeath
Tel 044-9341680

10 College Court, College Street,
Mullingar, Co Westmeath
Tel 044-9341505

St Joseph's,
Leighsbrook, Navan, Co Meath
Tel 046-9071760
Community: 6

Sisters of Mercy,
Mount Carmel, 15 Aylesbury Lodge,
Navan, Co Meath
Tel 046-9071757
Community: 5

Sisters of Mercy, 4 Ferndale,
Navan, Co Meath
Tel 046-9023844

Sisters of Mercy, Sacre Coeur,
The Commons, Navan, Co Meath
Tel 046-9021970

Convent of Mercy,
Rochfortbridge, Co Westmeath
Tel 044-9322130
Leader: Sr Bridge Commins
Community: 6

Convent of Mercy, Trim, Co Meath
Tel 046-9431264
Leader: Sr Immaculata Phelan
Community: 11

Sisters of Mercy,
1 Mornington Way, Trim, Co Meath
Tel 046-9437025 Fax 046-9437025
Community: 5

Convent of Mercy,
St Joseph's, Tullamore, Co Offaly
Tel 057-9321221
Community: 30
Facilitator: Srs Mildred Lynam
and Cecilia Cadogan

Sisters of Mercy, 130 Arden Vale,
Tullamore, Co Offaly
Tel 057-9352733

Sisters of Mercy, 47 Tara Crescent,
Clonminch, Tullamore, Co Offaly
Tel 057-9322150

69 Carne Hill, Johnstown,
Navan, Co Meath
Tel 046-9091772

Allianz ⑪

42 Blackcastle Estate,
Navan, Co Meath
Tel 046-9073325

14 Limekiln Wood, Dublin Road,
Navan, Co Meath
Tel 046-9060679

Sisters of Mercy,
Blackfriary, Trim, Co Meath
Tel 046-9437759

Sisters of Mercy,
5 Headfort Road, Kells, Co Meath
Tel 046-9249775
Community: 3

6 Friars Park, Trim, Co Meath
Tel 046-9437037
Community: 3

Sisters of Mercy, 133 College Hill,
Irishtown, Mullingar, Co Westmeath
Tel 044-9335303

Mission House,
St Colmcille's, Laytown, Co Meath
Tel 041-9887904
Community: 3

20 The Crescent, Athlumney,
Navan, Co Meath
Tel 046-9088940

135 Droim Liath, Collins Lane,
Tullamore, Co Offaly
Tel 057-9361133

No. 2 Bishopsgate Street,
Mullingar, Co Westmeath
Tel 044-9396721

14 Roselawn, High Street,
Tullamore, Co Offaly
Tel 057-9320747

FRANCISCAN MISSIONARIES OF OUR LADY
St Francis private hospital
Ballinderry, Mullingar, Co Westmeath
Tel 044-48732
Superior: Sr Cecilia Cody
Email ccody@stfrancishospital.ie
Commmunity: 7
Medical, surgical and geriatric.
Beds: 120

HOLY FAITH SISTERS
5 Carin Court, Fairyhouse Road, Ratoath,
Co Meath
Tel 01-8254566
Music coordinator, retreat work

HOLY FAMILY OF ST EMILIE DE RODAT
Arden Road, Tullamore, Co Offaly
Tel 057-9321577
Superior: Sr Mary-Paul English
Email mpe1809@eircom.net
Community: 8

LORETO (IBVM)
Loreto Community,
St Michael's, Navan, Co Meath
Tel 046-9021740
Email loretonavan@eircom.net
Superior: Sr Maria Barry
Community: 13
Loreto Secondary School
Tel 046-9023830
Day Care Centre

Loreto Sisters, Athlumney Road,
Navan, Co Meath
Tel 046-9073423
Community: 2
Education

Loreto Community,
Mullingar, Co Westmeath
Tel 044-48976
Superior: Sr Maria Barry
Community: 7
Loreto Secondary School
Tel 044-40184

Anam Aras, Laytown, Co Meath
Tel 041-9828952
Superior: Sr Julie Clinton
Retreat centre

MEDICAL MISSIONARIES OF MARY
Bruach na Mara,
Bettystown, Co Meath
Tel 041-9827207
Email mmmeuro@iol.ie

MISSIONARY SISTERS OF THE HOLY ROSARY
Holy Rosary Convent,
Coast Road, Bettystown, Co Meath
Tel 041-9827362
Community: 6
Pastoral

PRESENTATION SISTERS
15 Central Park, Mullingar,
Co Westmeath
Tel 044-48402
Community: 6
School and pastoral ministry
Presentation Junior Primary School
Tel 044-42166
Scoil na Maighdine Muire Primary School
Tel 044-40933
Email pressnt.ias@eircom.net

17 Grange Crescent,
Mullingar, Co Westmeath
Tel 044-45422
Community: 3
Pastoral work

Killina, Rahan,
Tullamore, Co Offaly
Tel 0506-55920
Community Leader: Sr Marie Walsh
Community: 8
School and pastoral ministry
Scoil Naomh Seosamh Primary School
Tel 0506-55790
Presentation Secondary School
Tel 0506-55706

VISITATION SISTERS
Visitandines, Monastery of the Visitation,
Stamullen, Co Meath
Tel 01-8417142 Fax 01-8412768
Superior
Sr Paul Mary Supple
Email visitationstamullen@gmail.com
Community: 9
Altar Breads Tel 01-8412533

EDUCATIONAL INSTITUTIONS

Diocesan Office for Post-Primary Schools
Director: Mr Liam Murphy BA, HDE
Moatlands, Navan, Co Meath
Tel 046-9021847

St Finian's College
Mullingar, Co Westmeath
Tel 044-9348313 Fax 044-9345275
President: Rev Paul Connell PhD
Tel 044-9348672
Chaplain: Very Rev Gerry Boyle PP

St Mary's Diocesan School
Beamore Road,
Drogheda, Co Louth
Tel Office: 041-9837581
Staff: 041-9838001 Fax 041-9841151
Headmaster
Ms Caroline Clarke BA, HDE
Chaplain: Rev John Hogan CC

St Patrick's Classical School
Mount Rivers, Moatlands,
Navan, Co Meath
Tel 046-9021847
Principal: Mr Colm O'Rourke
Chaplain: Rev Dwayne Gavin CC

St Columba's College
Tullamore, Co Offaly
Tel 057-9351756
Headmaster: Mr Colin Roddy
Chaplain: Rev Pádraig Corcoran CC

Boyne Community School
Trim, Co Meath
Tel 046-9431358
Headmaster: Ms Cora Dunne
Chaplain: Ms Aoife Daly

Ashbourne Community School
Ashbourne, Co Meath
Tel 01-8353066
Headmaster: Mr Ciarán Flynn
Chaplain: Mr Ken Hogan

St Peter's College
Dunboyne, Co Meath
Tel 01-8252552
Headmaster: Mr Eamonn Gaffney
Chaplain: Mr John Tighe

Allianz (ιlι)

EDMUND RICE SCHOOLS TRUST
Pobalscoil Chiaráin, Kells, Co Meath
Tel 046-9241551
Principal: Mr Dermot Carney

Scoil Mhuire Primary School,
Mullingar, Co Westmeath
Tel 044-41517
Principal: Mr Fergus Oakes

Coláiste Mhuire Secondary School,
Mullingar
Tel 044-44743
Principal: Mr J. O'Meara

CHARITABLE AND OTHER SOCIETIES

Cathedral Social Services Centre
Mullingar, Co Westmeath
The Secretary, Bishopsgate Street,
Mullingar, Co Westmeath
Tel 044-9348707

Society of St Vincent de Paul
Ozanam Holiday Home, Mornington,
Co Meath
Tel 041-9827924

DIOCESE OF OSSORY

PATRON OF THE DIOCESE
ST KIERAN, 5 MARCH

INCLUDES MOST OF COUNTY KILKENNY
AND PORTIONS OF COUNTIES LAOIS AND OFFALY

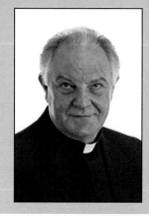

Most Rev Seamus Freeman (SAC) DD
Bishop of Ossory;
born 23 February 1944;
ordained priest 12 June 1971;
Consecrated Bishop of Ossory
2 December 2007

Residence:
Tilbury Place, James' Street,
Kilkenny
Tel 056-7762448
Fax 056-7763753
Email bishop@ossory.ie

ST MARY'S CATHEDRAL, KILKENNY

It was only in the last decade of the twelfth century, during the episcopate of Felix O'Dulany, that Kilkenny became the seat of the Bishop of Ossory. The new cathedral, dedicated to St Canice, was begun early in the thirteenth century by Bishop Hugh de Rous and took over half a century to complete. During the period of the Confederation, it was David Rothe's cathedral church, and it was here that the aged bishop formally received the Papal Nuncio, Archbishop Rinuccini, in November 1645. With the coming of Cromwell, St Canice's reverted to Protestant hands and the Catholics had no cathedral. A small chapel in St Mary's parish – St James's Chapel, built in 1700 just outside St James's Gate – functioned as a cathedral and was in use up to 1857.

It was William Kinsella, appointed Bishop of Ossory in 1829, who initiated the building of St Mary's. William Deane Butler, the architect for St Kieran's College and the parochial church of Ballyragget, was chosen to be the architect of St Mary's. His neo-Gothic style marked a new and ambitious phase in church architecture and reflected the newfound confidence of the Catholic community.

The site chosen was Burrell's Hall, which housed the first Catholic college founded in Ireland after the repeal of the law against Catholic schoolmasters in 1782. Subscribers from St Mary's parish pledged over £1,500, including £100 from Bishop Kinsella and £20 from Fr Theobald Matthew. Money was also raised from door and street collections, from the sale of site materials and from bank loans. Work was begun in April 1843. On 18 August the foundation stone was laid by Bishop Kinsella, assisted by the administrator, Fr Robert O'Shea, and others. When Bishop Kinsella died in December 1845, the walls were only seven feet high.

The new bishop, Edmond Walsh, aided by Robert O'Shea and a very active lay committee, continued the project. They kept it going right through the famine years, providing much-needed work locally. Collections were taken up in all the parishes of the diocese and bank loans were obtained on the securities of local merchants. The much-publicised sermon of Dr Patrick Murray of Maynooth also helped to raise funds. The cost of the original building is estimated at £25,000. The grand opening took place on 4 October 1857.

The cathedral was described as 'of pure Gothic design, built entirely of chiselled limestone and cruciform in shape'. The tower, originally designed for St Kieran's College, rises to a height of 186 feet. The high altar of Italian marble was purchased in Italy. The relics of Ss Cosmos and Damian and St Clement were brought from Rome. Those of St Victoria came later. A statue of Our Lady by Benzoni was commissioned by Bishop Walsh and stands in the remodelled sanctuary. The railings around the cathedral were added in 1862. During Bishop Brownrigg's time, a new sacristy and chapter room were added and many other improvements were made. The centre porch and organ gallery were remodelled, heating was installed and new statues purchased. James Pearse, the father of Patrick and Willie, completed the marble altar rails and erected the altar to the Sacred Heart. About £8,000 was expended and the refurbished cathedral was reopened on 9 April 1899 in the presence of Cardinal Logue, Archbishop Walsh of Dublin and many other dignitaries.

Less than thirty years later, Bishop Collier found it necessary to do further work on St Mary's. Turrets had to be repaired and a leaking roof overhauled. Mosaic work and painting were done on the sanctuary and side chapels, pitch pine seats were put in the aisles and transepts, an altar was erected to the Little Flower, the organ was remodelled at a cost of £2,500, and choir stalls introduced. The cost came to £28,000 and was raised by collections throughout the diocese.

During Bishop Birch's time, the cathedral was modernised to bring it into line with the requirements of Vatican II. Under the great tower was placed a new high altar of polished limestone surrounded by copper reliefs depicting scenes of Church life in Ossory. Many other changes were made, including a new tabernacle to facilitate exposition of the Blessed Sacrament and a new organ, constructed by a distinguished German organ-builder.

St Mary's Cathedral still dominates the landscape of Kilkenny. It stands as a reminder of the faith and growing confidence of a far-off generation.

Most Rev Laurence Forristal DD
Retired Bishop of Ossory
Born 5 June 1931; ordained priest
21 December 1955; ordained Titular
Bishop of Rotdon and Auxiliary Bishop
of Dublin 20 January 1980; installed
Bishop of Ossory 13 September 1981;
Retired 14 September 2007
Residence
Molassy, Freshford Road, Kilkenny
Tel/Fax 056-7777928/087-2330369
Email laurenceforristal@ossory.ie

CHAPTER

Dean: Very Rev Seamus McEvoy
Archdeacon
Venerable Archdeacon Patrick Grace
Members
Very Rev Patrick Dalton
Very Rev Patrick Duggan
Very Rev Laurence Dunphy
Very Rev Brian Flynn
Very Rev Peter Grant
Very Rev Seamus Henry
Very Rev Thomas Murphy
Very Rev Sean O'Doherty
Very Rev Richard Phelan
Rt Rev Mgr Michael Ryan
Honorary Members
Very Rev Patrick Brennan
Very Rev James Carrigan
Rt Rev Mgr Thomas Maher
Very Rev Robert Raftice

ADMINISTRATION

Chancellor
Rev William Dalton
c/o Diocesan Office, Sion Road, Kilkenny
Tel/Fax 056-7725287

College of Consultors
Rt Rev Mgr Michael Ryan PP, VG
Very Rev Dean Seamus McEvoy
Rt Rev Mgr Kieron Kennedy
Very Rev Joseph Delaney
Very Rev Daniel Carroll
Very Rev Oliver Maher
Very Rv Patrick Canon Dalton
Vey Very Anthony O'Connor

Vicars General
Rt Rev Mgr Michael Ryan PP, VG

Vicars Forane
Very Rev Thomas Canon Murphy PP
Very Rev Daniel Cavanagh PP
Very Rev Patrick Canon Dalton PP

Episcopal Vicars
Primary Education
Very Rev Patrick Canon Dalton
Family and Social Affairs
Rt Rev Mgr Kieron Kennedy
Retired Priests
Rev Thomas O'Toole

Diocesan Pastoral Co-Ordinator
Very Rev Daniel Bollard PP
Thomastown, Co Kilkenny
Tel 056-7724279/087-6644858
Email dbollard@eircom.net

Finance Committee
Chairman: Mr Geoffrey Meagher
Slievanon, Granges Road, Kilkenny
Tel 056-7762092
Secretary: Vacant at time of print
Diocesan Office, Sion Road, Kilkenny
Tel 056-7762448

Buildings and Properties Committee
Chairman: Mr John Norris
Rathpatrick, Slieverue, Co Kilkenny
Tel 051-832495
Secretary: Mrs Frances Lennon
Diocesan Office, Sion Road, Kilkenny
Tel 056-7762448

Diocesan Secretary
Mrs Frances Lennon
Diocesan Office, Sion Road, Kilkenny
Tel 056-7762448 Fax 056-7763753
Email admin@ossory.ie

Diocesan Finance
Mrs Sheila Walshe
Diocesan Office, Sion Road, Kilkenny

CATECHETICS EDUCATION

Diocesan Advisers for Religious Education
Primary Education: Rev Kieran O'Shea CC
Ballycallan, Co Kilkenny
Tel 056-7769564/086-8272828
Email kieranoshea@ossory.ie
Post Primary: Rev Sean O'Connor
St Kieran's College, Kilkenny
Tel 086-3895911

Catholic Primary School Managers Association
Chairperson: Mrs Maureen Daly
Granges Road, Kilkenny
Secretary
Very Rev Patrick Canon Dalton PP
Gowran, Co Kilkenny
Tel 056-7726128/086-8283478
Fax 056-7726134
Email pdalton@iolfree.ie

LITURGY

Liturgy Chairman
Rev Richard Scriven
St John's Presbytery, Dublin Road,
Kilkenny
Tel 056-7756889/087-2420033
Email rscriven@eircom.net

PASTORAL

Accord
St Mary's Centre,
James's Street, Kilkenny
Tel 056-7722674
Chaplain: Rev Kieran O'Shea
Tel 086-8272828

Adult Faith Formation
Director: Rev Dermot Ryan CC
Mooncoin, Co Kilkenny
Tel 086-6097483

Advisory Committee on Housing Elderly People
Chairman: Very Rev Liam Cassin PP
Hugginstown, Co Kilkenny
Tel 087-2312354/056-7768678

Chaplain to the Deaf
Very Rev Daniel Carroll
St Fiacre's Gardens, Bohernatoonish
Road, Loughboy, Kilkenny
Tel 056-7764400/087-9077769
Fax 056-7770173
Email dancarroll@ossory.ie

Chaplain to the Travelling Community
Rev Sean O'Connor
St Kieran's College, Kilkenny
Tel 056-7721086/086-3895911
Email seanoconnor@ossory.ie

Clerical Fund Society
Secretary: Very Rev Kieran Cantwell PP
Danesfort, Co Kilkenny
Tel 056-7727137/087-2661228

Communications
Director: Very Rev Daniel Carroll
St Fiacre's Gardens, Bohernatoonish
Road, Loughboy, Kilkenny
Tel 056-7764400 Fax 056-7770173
Email dancarroll@ossory.ie

Council of Priests
Chairman: Very Rev Daniel Carroll
Tel 056-7764400/087-9077769

CURA
Tel 056-7722739 Fax 056-7770240
Co Ordinator: Mrs Ann Coyne
Chaplain: Rev Sean O'Connor
Tel 086-3895911

Ecumenism
Very Rev James Murphy PP
St Canice's Presbytery, Dean Street,
Kilkenny
Tel 056-7752991/087-2609545
Email jimmurphy@ossory.ie

Emigrant Commission
Very Rev Laurence Wallace PP
Muckalee, Ballyfoyle, Co Kilkenny
Tel 056-4441271/087-2326807
Fax 056-4440007
Email muckalee@ossory.ie

Lourdes Pilgrimage
Director: Very Rev M. A. O'Connor PP
Glenmore, via Waterford, Co Kilkenny
Tel 051-880213/087-2517766

Marriage Tribunal
(See Marriage Tribunals section)

Ossory Adoption and Referral Services
Information and Guidance in all matters
in relation to adoption Tel 056-7721685
Ms Mary Curtin, Social Service Centre,
Waterford Road, Kilkenny
Tel 056-7721685

Ossory Priests' Society
Secretary: Rev Thomas O'Toole
Kilmacow, via Waterford, Co Kilkenny
Tel/Fax 051-88529/087-2240787

Ossory Youth
Desart Hall, New Street, Kilkenny
Tel 056-7761200 Fax 056-7752385
Chairman: Padraig Fleming
CEO: Ms Mary Mescal

Pioneer Total Abstinence Association
Diocesan Director
Very Rev Thomas Murphy PP
Ballyragget, Co Kilkenny
Tel 056-8833123/086-8130694

Pontifical Mission Societies
Diocesan Director
Very Rev James Crotty PP
Ferrybank, Waterford
Tel/Fax 051-832787/087-8317711
Email jimcrotty@ossory.ie

Vocations
Director: Rev William Purcell CC
Callan, Co Kilkenny
Tel 056-7725858/087-6286858

PARISHES

*Kilkenny city parishes are listed first.
Other parishes follow alphabetically.
Church titulars are in italics.*

ST MARY'S
St Mary's Cathedral
Very Rev Oliver Maher Adm
Tel 056-7721253 Ext 181/086-8323010
Fax 056-7770100
Email olmaher@ossory.ie
Rev Mark Condon CC
Tel 056-7721253 Ext 180/086-6005402
Email markcondon@ossory.ie
St Mary's Cathedral, Kilkenny

ST JOHN'S
*St John the Evangelist, Holy Trinity,
St John the Baptist*
Email stjohns@ossory.ie
Website www.stjohnskilkenny.com
Very Rev Francis Purcell
Tel 056-7721072/086-6010001
Fax 056-7722209
Email jfpurcell@eircom.net
Rev Richard Scriven
Tel 056-7756889/086-2420033
Fax 056-7722209
Email rscriven@eircom.net
St John's Presbytery, Kilkenny

ST CANICE'S
St Canice's
Very Rev James Murphy PP
St Canice's Presbytery, Dean Street,
Kilkenny
Tel 056-7752991/087-2609545
Fax 056-7721533
Email jimmurphy@ossory.ie
Rev James Forristal CC
Tel 056-7722150
Rev Martin Delaney CC
Tel 056-7752994/086-2444594
Email delaneymartin@eircom.net
St Canice's Presbytery, Granges Road,
Kilkenny
Parish Office: 056-7721533/087-9335663
Email stcanice@ossory.ie

ST PATRICK'S
St Patrick's, St Fiacre's, St Joseph's
Very Rev Daniel Carroll PP
Tel 087-9077769/056-7764400
Email dancarroll@ossory.ie
Rev Liam Taylor
Tel 056-7764400/086-8180954
Email liamtaylor@ossory.ie
Rev Roderick Whearty
Tel 056-7764400/086-8133661
St Fiacre's Gardens, Bohernatownish
Road, Loughboy, Kilkenny
Tel 056-7764400 Fax 056-7770173
Email stpatricksparish@ossory.ie
Website www.patricksparish.com

AGHABOE
Immaculate Conception, St Canice
Very Rev Noel Maher PP
Clough, Ballacolla, Portlaoise, Co Laois
Tel 057-878513 Fax 057-8738909
Email nmaher@eircom.net

AGHAVILLER
*St Brendan's, Stoneyford,
St Brendan's, Newmarket
Holy Trinity*
Very Rev Liam Cassin PP
Hugginstown, Co Kilkenny
Tel/Fax 056-7768693/087-2312354
Email liamcassin@ossory.ie
Very Rev Peter Hoyne PE
Newmarket, Hugginstown, Co Kilkenny
Tel/Fax 056-7768678

BALLYCALLAN
Queen of Peace, St Molua, St Brigid
Very Rev Richard Canon Phelan PP
Kilmanagh, Co Kilkenny
Tel 056-7769116/087-2843461
Fax 056-7769597
Email dickphelan@ossory.ie
Rev Kieran O'Shea CC
Ballycallan, Co Kilkenny
Tel 056-7769564/086-8272828
Email kieranoshea@ossory.ie
Parish email ballycallan@ossory.ie

BALLYHALE
*St Martin of Tours, Our Lady of the
Assumption, All Saints*
Very Rev Peter Kehoe (OCarm) PP
Ballyhale, Co Kilkenny
Tel/Fax 056-7768686/7768675/
086-8252093
Email knockcar@indigo.ie

BALLYRAGGET
St Patrick's, Assumption of BVM
Very Rev Thomas Murphy PP
Ballyragget, Co Kilkenny
Tel 056-8833123/086-8130694
Email tommurphy@ossory.ie

BORRIS-IN-OSSORY
St Canice, Assumption, St Kieran
Very Rev John Robinson PP
Borris-in-Ossory, Portlaoise, Co Laois
Tel/Fax 0505-41148/087-2431412
Email robjon@eircom.net

CALLAN
Assumption, All Saints, Nativity of BVM
Very Rev William Dalton PP
Callan, Co Kilkenny
Tel 056-7725287/086-8506215
Fax 056-7725287
Email williamdalton@ossory.ie
Rev William Purcell CC
Callan, Co Kilkenny
Tel 056-7725858/087-6286858
Fax 056-7725966
Email wpurcell@eircom.net
Website
www.callanparish@irishchurch.net

CAMROSS
St Fergal
Very Rev John Lalor PP
Camross, Portlaoise, Co Laois
Tel/Fax 0502-35122/087-6888711
Email johnflalor@eircom.net

CASTLECOMER
Immaculate Conception
Rt Rev Mgr Michael Ryan PP
Tel 056-4441262/086-3693863
Fax 056-4441969
Rev Thomas Corcoran CC
Tel/Fax 056-4441263/087-6886678
Email tjcor@eircom.net
Castlecomer, Co Kilkenny
Parish email castlecomer@ossory.ie

CASTLETOWN
St Edmund
Very Rev William Hennessy PP
Castletown, Portlaoise, Co Laois
Tel/Fax 0502-32622/087-8736155

CLARA
St Coleman
Very Rev Laurence O'Keeffe PP
Clifden Villa, Clifden, Co Kilkenny
Tel 056-7726560/087-2258443
Fax 056-7726558
Email larryokeeffe@ossory.ie
Parish email clara@ossory.ie

CLOGH
St Patrick's, Sacred Heart
Very Rev Martin Tobin PP
Clogh, Castlecomer, Co Kilkenny
Tel 056-4442135/086-2401278
Fax 056-4442135
Email martintobin@ossory.ie

CONAHY
St Coleman, Our Lady of Perpetual Help
Very Rev James Dollard PP
Conahy, Jenkinstown, Co Kilkenny
Tel 056-7767657 Fax 056-7767666
Email conahyparish@eircom.net

DANESFORT
*St Michael the Archangel, Holy Cross, Kells
Holy Cross, Cuffesgrange*
Very Rev Kieran Cantwell PP
Danesfort, Co Kilkenny
Tel/Fax 056-7727137/087-2661228
Email kierancantwell@eircom.net
Rev Denis Purcell CC
Cuffesgrange, Co Kilkenny
Tel 056-7729299/087-1356687

DUNAMAGGAN
St Leonard, St Eoghan
Very Rev Nicholas Flavin PP
Dunamaggan, Co Kilkenny
Tel/Fax 056-7728173/087-2257498
Email naflavin@eircom.net

DURROW
Holy Trinity, St Tighearnach
Very Rev Seán Canon O'Doherty PP
Durrow, Portlaoise, Co Laois
Tel 057-8736156
Rev Thomas McGree CC
Durrow, Portlaoise, Co Laois
Tel 057-8736155/087-7619235
Fax 057-8736226

FERRYBANK
Sacred Heart
Very Rev James Crotty PP
Tel/Fax 051-832787
Email jimcrotty@ossory.ie
Rev Raymond Dempsey CC
Tel/Fax 051-832577/087-2859682
Email raydempsey@ossory.ie
Ferrybank, Waterford
Website www.ferrybankparish.com

FRESHFORD
St Lachtain, St Nicholas
Very Rev Seamus Canon Henry PP
Tel/Fax 056-8832146/086-0879296
Email freshford@ossory.ie
Rev Joseph Campion (SAC) CC
Freshford, Co Kilkenny
Tel/Fax 056-8832461/086-1775172
Email josecampion@yahoo.co.uk

GALMOY
Immaculate Conception
Very Rev Thomas Coyle PP
Galmoy, Crosspatrick, via Thurles,
Co Kilkenny
Tel/Fax 056-8831227/087-7668969
Email tjcoyle@eircom.net

GLENMORE
St James
Very Rev Anthony O'Connor PP
Glenmore, via New Ross, Co Kilkenny
Tel/Fax 051-880213/087-2517766
Email maoci@eircom.net

GOWRAN
Assumption
Very Rev Patrick Canon Dalton PP
Gowran, Co Kilkenny
Tel 056-7726128/086-8283478
Fax 056-7726134
Email pdalton@iolfree.ie

INISTIOGE
St Columcille, Assumption, St Brendan
Very Rev Dean Seamus McEvoy PP
The Rower, Inistioge, Co Kilkenny
Tel/Fax 051-423619/086-2634093

JOHNSTOWN
St Kieran, St Michael
Very Rev Francis Maher PP
Johnstown via Thurles, Co Kilkenny
Tel 056-8831219/087-2402487
Email frankmaher@ossory.ie

KILMACOW
St Senan
Very Rev Brian Flynn PP
Tel 051-885122/087-2828391
Email brianflynn@ossory.ie
Email kilmacowparish@ossory.ie
Rev Thomas O'Toole CC
Tel/Fax 051-885269/087-2240787
Kilmacow, via Waterford, Co Kilkenny

LISDOWNEY
St Brigid, St Munchin, St Fiacre
Very Rev Patrick O'Farrell PP
Lisdowney, Ballyragget, Co Kilkenny
Tel 056-8833138/087-2353520
Fax 056-8833701
Email patofarrell@ossory.ie
Parish email lisdowney@ossory.ie

MOONCOIN
Assumption, St Kevin, St Kilgoue
Very Rev Eamon O'Gorman PP
Tel/Fax 051-895123/087-2236145
Email 1eamonnogorman@eircom.net
Rev Dermot Ryan CC
Tel 086-6097483
Email dermotryan@ossory.ie
Mooncoin, Co Kilkenny
Website www.mooncoinparish.com

MUCKALEE
St Brendan, St Brigid, St Joseph
Very Rev Laurence Wallace PP
Muckalee, Ballyfoyle, Co Kilkenny
Tel 056-4441271/087-2326807
Fax 056-4440007
Email wallace@eircom.net
Rev John Delaney CC
Coon, Carlow
Tel 056-4443116/086-8596321
Fax 056-4443283
Email jondel@eircom.net
Parish email muckalee@ossory.ie

MULLINAVAT
St Beacon, St Paul
Very Rev Liam Barron PP
Tel/Fax 051-898108/087-2722824
Mullinavat, via Waterford, Co Kilkenny
Email liambarron@ossory.ie

RATHDOWNEY
*Holy Trinity, Our Lady, Queen of the
Universe*
Very Rev Eamon Foley PP
Rathdowney, Portlaoise, Co Laois
Tel 0505-46282 Fax 0505-46213
Email rathdowney@ossory.ie
Rev Patrick Carey CC
Errill, Portlaoise, Co Laois
Tel 0505-44973/087-2599087
Email paddycarey@ossory.ie

ROSBERCON
Assumption, St David, St Aidan
Very Rev Daniel Cavanagh PP
Rosbercon, New Ross, Co Wexford
Tel 051-421515/087-2335432
Fax 051-425093
Email danieljcavanagh@eircom.net
Very Rev Michael Norton PE
Rosbercon, New Ross, Co Wexford
Tel/Fax 051-420333/087-2580496

SEIR KIERAN
St Kieran
Very Rev Peter Muldowney PP
Seir Kieran, Clareen,
Birr, Co Offaly
Tel/Fax 0509-31080/086-8265955
Email peter.muldowney@hotmail.com

SLIEVERUE
Assumption
Very Rev Patrick Comerford PP
Slieverue, via Waterford,
Co Kilkenny
Tel/Fax 051-832773/086-1038430
Email patcomerford@ossory.ie
Parish email slieverue@ossory.ie
Website www.slieverue.com

TEMPLEORUM
Assumption
Very Rev Paschal Moore PP
Piltown, Co Kilkenny
Tel 051-643112/087-2408078
Fax 051-644911
Email paschalmoore@eircom.net
Assumption
Rev John Condon CC
Templeorum, Piltown,
Co Kilkenny
Tel/Fax 051-643124/086-8394615

THOMASTOWN
Assumption
Very Rev Daniel Bollard PP
Thomastown, Co Kilkenny
Tel/Fax 056-7724279/087-6644858
Email dbollard@eircom.net
Parish Email thomastown@ossory.ie

TULLAHERIN
St Bennet, St Kieran
Very Rev Patrick Canon Duggan PP
Bennetsbridge, Co Kilkenny
Tel 056-7727140/087-6644858
Fax 056-7727755
Email patduggan@ossory.ie

TULLAROAN
Assumption
Very Rev Patrick Guilfoyle PP
Tullaroan, Co Kilkenny
Tel/Fax 056-7769141/087-6644858
Email guilfoylepat@eircom.net

URLINGFORD
Assumption, St Patrick
Very Rev Laurence Canon Dunphy PP
Urlingford, Co Kilkenny
Tel/Fax 056-8831121/087-2300849
Email urlingford@ossory.ie

WINDGAP
*St Nicholas, Windgap
St Nicholas, Tullahought*
Very Rev Martin Cleere PP
Windgap, Co Kilkenny
Tel/Fax 051-648111/087-2954010
Email mfcleere@eircom.net

Allianz ⑪

INSTITUTIONS AND THEIR CHAPLAINS

Aut Even Hospital
Aut Even, Kilkenny
Priests of St Canice's Parish
Tel 056-7721523/087-9335663

City Vocational School, Kilkenny
Rev Mark Condon CC
Tel 056-7721086 Ext 135/7722984/
7765058/087-2420033

Community School
Castlecomer, Co Kilkenny
Mrs Eithne McKenna
Tel 056-4441447

Abbey Community College
Ferrybank, Waterford
Ms Claire Bolger
Tel 051-832930

District Hospital
Castlecomer, Co Kilkenny
Rt Rev Mgr Michael Ryan
Tel 056-4441262/086-3034155

Orthopaedic Hospital
Kilcreene, Kilkenny
Priests of St Mary's Parish
Tel 056-7721253 Ext 180/181

St Canice's Hospital, Kilkenny
Priests of St John's Parish
Tel 056-7721072

St Columba's Hospital
Thomastown, Co Kilkenny
Very Rev Daniel Bollard
Tel 056-7724279/087-6644858

St Luke's Hospital, Kilkenny
Rev Lorcan Moran
Tel 056-7785000/7771815/086-8550521

Stephen Barracks, Kilkenny
Rev Daniel McCarthy
Tel 056-7761852

PRIESTS OF THE DIOCESE ELSEWHERE

In Ireland
Rt Rev Mgr James Cassin
St Patrick's College,
Maynooth, Co Kildare
Tel 01-6285222/086-2380984
Email jamescassin@ossory.ie
Rev Thomas Norris
St Patrick's College,
Maynooth, Co Kildare
Tel 01-7083627/087-9407282
Fax 01-7083441
Rev Fergus Farrell
Mater Dei Institute of Education,
Clonliffe Road, Dublin 3
Tel 01-8376027/086-0782066
Email fearghusof@materdei.ie/
sfofearghail@eircom.net
Most Rev Thomas White
6 Osborne Court, Seapoint Avenue,
Blackrock, Co Dublin
Tel 01-2806609

Abroad
Very Rev Liam Bergin, Rector,
Pontificio Collegio Irlandese,
via dei SS Quattro 1, 00184 Rome, Italy
Tel 003906-77263301
Fax 003906-77263323
Email www.irishcollege.org
Rev John Duggan
St John and Paul Church,
341 South Main Street,
Coventary RI R102816-5987, USA
Te 001-401-8275022

RETIRED PRIESTS

Very Rev Patrick Canon Brennan
Gathabawn, Via Thurles, Co Kilkenny
Tel 056-8832110
Very Rev James Canon Carrigan
Ballacolla, Portlaoise, Co Laois
Tel 0502-34016
Very Rev Joseph Delaney
St Kieran's College, Kilkenny
Tel 056-7721086/086-8206730
Very Rev Liam Dunne
The Forge, Martin's Lane,
Upper Main Street, Arklow, Co Wicklow
Tel 0402-32779
Venerable Archdeacon Patrick Grace
Inistioge, Co Kilkenny
Tel 056-7758429/086-8817628
Very Rev Patrick Canon Grant
Ballyragget, Co Kilkenny
Tel 056-8833120
Right Rev Mgr Thomas Maher
Archersrath Nursing Home, Kilkenny
Tel 056-7790137
Rev John O'Brien
'The Knock', Danville,
Bennettsbridge Road, Kilkenny
Tel 087-6430620
Very Rev Robert Canon Raftice
Mount Carmel, Callan, Co Kilkenny
Tel 056-7725301/7725553/086-0614682
Very Rev Edward Rhatigan
Castletown, Portlaoise, Co Laois
Tel 087-8732622
Very Rev Donal Walsh
Tinnahinch, Graiguenamanagh,
Co Kilkenny
Tel 059-9725550

RELIGIOUS ORDERS AND CONGREGATIONS

PRIESTS

CAPUCHINS
Capuchin Friary, Friary Street,
Kilkenny
Tel 056-7721439 Fax 056-7722025
Guardian: Rev Benignus Buckley (OFMCap)

CARMELITES (OCARM)
Carmelite Priory, Knocktopher,
Co Kilkenny
Tel 056-7768675
Email knockcar@indigo.ie
Prior: Rev Peter Kehoe (OCarm) PP

DOMINICANS
Black Abbey, Kilkenny, Co Kilkenny
Tel 056-7721279
Prior: Very Rev Louis Hughes (OP)

MILL HILL MISSIONARIES
St Joseph's, Freshford House,
Kilkenny
Tel 056-7721482 Fax 056-7751490
Rector: Rev Jim O'Connell (MHM)
Email jimocmhm@eircom.net

BROTHERS

BROTHERS OF CHARITY
St Vincent's Brothers' Community,
Ferrybank, Waterford
Tel 051-832180 Fax 051-833490
Community Leader: Br Joseph Killoran
Email
jkilloran@waterford.brothersofcharity.ie
Community: 7

CHRISTIAN BROTHERS
Christian Brothers, Edmund Rice House,
Westcourt, Callan, Co Kilkenny
Tel 056-7725141
Community Leader: Br M. J. Keane
Community: 6

Edmund Rice Centre,
Callan, Co Kilkenny
Tel 056-7725993

DE LA SALLE BROTHERS
De La Salle Monastery,
Castletown, Portlaoise, Co Laois
Tel 057-8732359 (residence)
Fax 057-8732925
Superior: Br Stephen Deignan
Community: 8

Miguel House, Castletown,
Portlaoise, Co Laois
Tel 057-8732136 Fax 057-8756648
Superior: Br David O'Riordan
Community: 19
House for retired brothers

La Salle Pastoral Centre, Castletown,
Portlaoise, Co Laois
Tel 057-8732442 Fax 057-872925
Director: Mr Derek Doherty
Retreat centre

SISTERS

CONGREGATION OF THE SISTERS OF MERCY
Convent of Mercy, Ballyragget,
Co Kilkenny
Tel 056-8833114
Contact: Mary Kenny
Primary School

Aislinn Adolescence Drug-free Addiction
Treatment Centre,
Ballyragget, Co Kilkenny
Tel 056-8833777 Fax 056-8833780

Convent of Mercy, Aras Muire,
Thomastown, Co Kilkenny
Tel 056-7724226

Convent of Mercy, Callan, Co Kilkenny
Tel 056-7725223
Contact: Sr Hannah Frisby

1 Mountain View, Borris-in-Ossory,
Portlaoise, Co Laois
Tel/Fax 0505-41964
Leader: Sr Regina Delaney
Primary School

Villa Maria, Talbot's Inch, Kilkenny
Tel 056-7765774

20 Archer's Court, Loughboy,
Kilkenny
Contact: Sr Frances Kennedy

DAUGHTERS OF MARY AND JOSEPH
Peace in Christ, Sion Road, Kilkenny
Tel 056-7721054 Fax 056-7770755
Director of Retreat House
Sr Margaret Moloney
Community: 4
Retreat work, parish work

FRANCISCAN MISSIONARIES OF ST JOSEPH
Prague House, Freshford, Co Kilkenny
Tel 056-8832281
Regional Superior: Sr Bridget Ann Lonergan
Community: 4
Residential care for elderly, general
social work

HOLY FAMILY OF BORDEAUX SISTERS
Holy Family Convent, Moneenroe,
Castlecomer, Co Kilkenny
Tel 056-4442147
Contact: The Superior
Community: 3
Sisters involved in community and social
work

LITTLE COMPANY OF MARY
Troy's Court, Kilkenny
Tel 056-7763117
Community: 5
Sheltered accommodation for older people

LORETO (IBVM)
Loreto Community, Freshford Road,
Kilkenny
Tel 056-7721187
Superior: Sr Brigid Tunney
Community: 11
Loreto Secondary School
Tel 056-7765131
Education and pastoral work

MEDICAL MISSIONARIES OF MARY
The Mews, Rosedale,
Kilmacow, via Waterford, Co Kilkenny
Tel 051-885931
Email mmmkilmacow@eircom.net

PRESENTATION SISTERS
Presentation Convent, Kilkenny
Tel 056-7721351
Local Leader: Sr Sheila Bowe
Community: 17
Primary School. Tel 056-7765598
Secondary School. Tel 056-7765684

Presentation Convent, Mooncoin,
Co Kilkenny
Tel 051-895114
Local Leader: Sr Mary Lenehan
Community: 12
Primary Girls' School
Tel 051-895503

Presentation Sisters, 8 Rosemount,
Newpark Drive, Kilkenny
Tel 056-7721693
Local Leader: Sr Maura Murphy
Community: 5
Pastoral work

RELIGIOUS OF SACRED HEART OF MARY
Ferrybank, Waterford
Tel 051-832592
Superior: Sr Philippa O'Sullivan
Community: 12
Primary School. Pupils: 200+
Secondary School. Pupils: 630

22 Castle Oaks, Rockshire Road,
Ferrybank, Waterford
Tel 051-851606
Community: 3
Education, pastoral work

37 Castle Oaks, Rockshire Road,
Ferrybank, Waterford
Tel 051-833996
Community: 3
Education, pastoral work

4 Briar Wood, Slieverue, Co Kilkenny
Community: 3
Pastoral

RELIGIOUS SISTERS OF CHARITY
St Patrick's Convent,
Kells Road, Kilkenny
Tel 056-7770580
Various apostolic ministries

ST JOHN OF GOD SISTERS
Provincialate,
College Road, Kilkenny
Tel 056-7722870 Fax 056-7751411
Email sjgprovincialate@eircom.net
Province Leader: Sr Teresa Byrne
Secretary: Sr Maeve Cregan
Convent. Tel 056-7721914

St John of God Sisters
College Road, Kilkenny
Resident Leader: Sr Anne Harpur
Community: 26
Primary School. Tel 056-7721290
Pupils: 424
Altar breads department
Tel 056-7762278

St John of God Sisters,
Galtrim, Waterford Road, Kilkenny
Tel 056-7775510
Community: 3

St John of God Sisters, Moorville,
Rathdowney, Co Laois
Tel 0505-46258
Community: 3
Primary School. Pupils: 166
Tel 0505-46183

St John of God Sisters, 'Villa Marie',
Mooreville, Rathdowney, Co Laois
Tel 0505-46940
Community: 2

St John of God Sisters (Social Services)
Cuan Bhríde, Rathdowney, Co Laois
Tel 0505-46521
Community: 3

St Columba's Hospital, 7 Maudlin Court,
Thomastown, Co Kilkenny
Tel 056-7724046
Community: 2
Hospital Tel 056-7724178

Lady Sue Ryder House, Owning,
Co Kilkenny
Tel 051-643136
Community: 3

St John of God Sisters,
11 Dean's Court,
Waterford Road, Kilkenny
Tel 056-7764576
Community: 1

St John of God House, College Road,
Kilkenny
Leader: Sr Brenda Gardiner
Tel 056-7756788
Community: 9

St John of God Sisters, 'Fermoyle',
Greenshill, Kilkenny
Tel 056-7751259
Community: 4

St John of God Sisters
Aut Even Convent, Kilkenny
Tel 056-7761451
Community: 4

EDUCATIONAL INSTITUTIONS

St Kieran's College
Kilkenny
Tel 056-7721086 Fax 056-7770001
Email skc1782@iol.ie
President
Rt Rev Mgr Kieron Kennedy Ext 118
Principal: Mr John Curtis
Tel 056-7721086 Ext 223/7761707
Chaplain: Rev Sean O'Connor Ext 134

Adult Educational Institute
Seville Lodge, Callan Road, Kilkenny
Tel/Fax 056-7721453
Business Manager: Mr Richard Curtin

EDMUND RICE SCHOOLS TRUST
Scoil McAuley Rice Primary School,
West Street, Callan, Co Kilkenny
Tel 056-7725572 Fax 056-7725572
Email cbsnscallan.ias@eircom.net
Principal: Mr John Moloney

Coláiste Eamonn Rís Secondary School,
Callan, Co Kilkenny
Principal: Mr Frank McKenna
Tel 056-7725340
Tel 056-7725355 (staff) Fax 056-7725721
Email coleamannris@eircom.net

Scoil Iognáid de Rís,
CBS Primary School, Kilkenny
Tel 056-7761739 Fax 056-7771982
Email cbskilkenny.ias@eircom.net
Principal: Mr D. O'Reilly

Secondary School, James's Street,
Kilkenny
Tel 056-7761225 Fax 056-7763652
Email cbskk@indigo.ie
Principal: Mr Tom Clarke

CHARITABLE AND OTHER SOCIETIES

Good Shepherd Centre
Administrator: Mr Seamus Roche
Hostel for transient homeless men
Tel 056-7722566

Homes for Elderly People
Kilkenny: Troy's Court
Tel 056-7763117
St Patrick's Parish: Tel 056-7764400
St Johns' Parish: Tel 056-7721072
Ballyragget: O'Gorman House
Tel 056-8833377
St Mary's: Tel 056-7721253
Callan: Mount Carmel
Tel 056-7725301
Freshford: Prague House
Tel 056-8832281
Kilmacow: Rosedale
Tel 051-885125
Kilmoganny: St Joseph's
Tel 051-648091
Owning, Piltown: Lady Sue Ryder Home
Tel 051-643136
Rathdowney: Cuan Bhríde
Tel 0505-46521
Slieverue Parish: Tel 051-832773

L'Arche, Workshops and Accommodation for People with Learning Difficulties
Moorefield House, Kilmoganny,
Co Kilkenny
Tel 051-64809
An Siol: 42 West Street, Callan,
Co Kilkenny
Tel 056-7725230
Cluain Aoibhin: Fairgreen, Callan,
Co Kilkenny
Tel 056-7725628

Ossory Social Services
Social Service Centre,
Waterford Road, Kilkenny
Tel 056-7721685 Fax 056-7763636
Email kilkenss@iol.ie
Director: Rt Rev Mgr Kieron Kennedy

Local Social Services Centres:
Callan: Sr Cecilia Dowley
Tel 056-7725223
Castlecomer: Ms Bridget McLean
Tel 056-4441679
Ferrybank: Sr Constance O'Sullivan
Tel 051-832592
Freshford: Sr Brigid Lonergan
Tel 056-8832281
Moneenroe: Sr Anne Kearney
Tel 056-4442147
Rathdowney Cuan Bhríde
Sr Catherine O'Brien
Tel 0505-46521

SOS (Kilkenny) Ltd,
Sheltered Workshop and
Accommodation for People with
Learning Difficulties
SOS (Kilkenny) Ltd,
Callan Road, Kilkenny
Tel 056-7764000 Fax 056-7761212

Apostolic Work Society
Secretary: Mrs Nora Ryan
Ross, Rathdowney, Co Laois
Tel 0505-46524

St Joseph's Young Priests Society
Chairperson
Mrs Marie Hogan
Freshford, Co Kilkenny
Tel 056-8832125
Chaplain
Very Rev Seamus Canon Henry PP
Freshford, Co Kilkenny
Tel 056-88332146

DIOCESE OF RAPHOE

PATRON OF THE DIOCESE
ST EUNAN, 23 SEPTEMBER

INCLUDES THE GREATER PART OF COUNTY DONEGAL

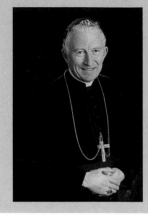

**Most Rev Philip Boyce
(OCD) DD**
Bishop of Raphoe;
born 25 January 1940;
ordained priest 17 April 1966;
ordained Bishop of Raphoe
1 October 1995

Residence: Ard Adhamhnáin,
Letterkenny, Co Donegal
Tel 074-9121208
Fax 074-9124872
Email
raphoediocese@eircom.net
Website www.raphoediocese.ie

ST EUNAN'S CATHEDRAL, LETTERKENNY

The old cathedral of Raphoe passed into Protestant hands at the Reformation. In the eighteenth century the Catholic bishops came to live in Letterkenny. A church was built circa 1820 and, having been extended by Bishop Patrick McGettigan, was used as a pro-cathedral. Bishop McDevitt (1871–1879) thought of building a new cathedral, and Lord Southwell promised a site, but it was not until 1891, when Bishop O'Donnell was in office, that actual building began. The cathedral was completed in 1901. Besides overseeing the cathedral project, Bishop O'Donnell had the task of providing a house for the bishop and priests of the cathedral parish.

The main benefactors were Fr J.D. McGarvey PP, Killygarvan, and Mr Neil Gillen of Airdrie. Various priests of the diocese spent considerable time fund-raising in Britain, the US and Canada. The style is Gothic, with some Hiberno-Romanesque features, and the building is of white Mountcharles sandstone. The cathedral dominates the Letterkenny skyline. Among the artistic features to be noted are the 'Drumceat' window, by Michael Healy (North Transept); the pulpit, by Messrs Pearse (Patrick Pearse's family); the Great Arch, with its St Columba and St Eunan columns; and, outside, the fine statue of Bishop O'Donnell, by Doyle of Chelsea.

Remodelling of the cathedral took place in 1985, with the addition of an altar table and chairs; great care was taken to preserve the style and materials of the original altar. Bishop Hegarty promoted this tasteful restoration work, which left intact the architectural character of the building.

Allianz (ⁱⁱⁱ)

CHAPTER

Dean: Very Rev Dean John Silke PE
Portnablagh
Archdeacon
Ven Archdeacon Patrick McShane PE
Donegal Town
Members
Very Rev Canon John Gallagher
Hospital Chaplain, Letterkenny
Very Rev Canon Austin Laverty PP
Ardara
Very Rev Canon William McMenamin PP
Drumoghill
Very Rev Canon John Silke PE
Portnablagh

ADMINISTRATION

Vicar General
Rt Rev Mgr Daniel Carr PP, VG
St Johnston, Lifford, Co Donegal
Tel 074-9148203

Diocesan Chancellor/Diocesan Secretary
Rev Michael McKeever
Diocesan Office, Ard Adhamhnáin,
Letterkenny, Co Donegal
Tel 074-9121208 Fax 074-9124872
Email raphoediocese@eircom.net

College of Consultors
Rt Rev Mgr Daniel Carr PP, VG
St Johnston
Very Rev Edward Gallagher PP
Kilcar, Co Donegal
Very Rev Canon Austin Laverty PP, VF
Adara
Very Rev Francis McLoone PP
Killymard
Very Rev Cathal O'Fearraí PP, VF
Ballyshannon
Very Rev Michael Sweeney PP, VF
Derrybeg

Vicars Forane
Rt Rev Mgr Daniel Carr PP, VG
St Johnston
Very Rev Canon Austin Laverty PP
Ardara
Very Rev Cathal O'Fearraí PP
Ballyshannon,
Very Rev Eamonn Kelly Adm
Letterkenny
Very Rev Michael Sweeney PP
Derrybeg
Very Rev James Friel PP
Tamney

Financial Administrators
Rt Rev Mgr Daniel Carr PP, VG
Rev Martin Timoney CC
Ard Adhamhnáin,
Letterkenny, Co Donegal

Finance Committee
Bishop Philip Boyce, Mgr Dan Carr,
Mr Noel O'Connell, Mrs Mary Foley,
Mr John McCreadie, Mr Peadar Murphy,
Rev Martin Timoney CC,
Ms Siobhan Logue, Mr Conal Boyle,
Rev Michael McKeever *(Secretary)*

Building Committee
Very Rev Canon Austin Laverty PP
Very Rev Canon John Gallagher

Diocesan Archives
Faíche Ó Dónaill Building
Ard Adhamhnáin, Letterkenny,
Co Donegal
Tel 074-9161109
Email raphoearchives@eircom.net

CATECHETICS EDUCATION

Religious Education in Primary Schools
Co-ordinator
Rev Aodhan Cannon
Ardara, Co Donegal
Tel 074-9541930

Religious Education in Secondary Schools
Resource Centre, 13a Lower Main Street,
Letterkenny, Co Donegal
Tel 074-9177388
Sr Susan Evangelist Taegue
Drumkeen, Co Donegal
Rev Philip Kemmy CC
Letterkenny
Tel 074-9121021

LITURGY

Perpetual Eucharistic Adoration
Diocesan Director: Rev Patrick Dunne
St Eunan's College, Letterkenny

PASTORAL

Accord
Letterkenny area: Pastoral Centre,
Monastery Ave, Letterkenny
Tel 074-9122218
Chairperson: Mr Pól Ó Curráin
Treasurer: Mrs Sheila Leeper
Secretary: Mrs Sheila Leeper
Chaplain: Rev Eamonn Kelly
Open Monday-Friday 10.00 am-1.00 pm
Donegal Town area:
Chairman: Mr Tom Lynch
Secretary: Ms Brenda Burke
Tel 073-9723944
Chaplain: Very Rev John McLoone PP
Frosses
LoCall 1850-201878

Child Protection Office
Pastoral Centre, Monastery Avenue,
Letterkenny, Co Donegal
Tel 074-9121394
Email cporaphoediocese@eircom.net

CURA
Tel 074-9123037
Thursday 5-7pm
National Helpline 1850-622626
Letterkenny
Spiritual Director
Rev Patrick Dunne

Diocesan Social Worker
Mr Seamus Gallagher
Secretary: Kathleen Kelly
The Pastoral Centre,
Monastery Avenue,
Letterkenny, Co Donegal
Tel 074-9122047 Fax 074-9128433

Ecumenism
Diocesan Director
Very Rev Francis McAteer PP
Carrick, Co Donegal
Tel 074-9739008

Family Ministry Centre
Director: Sr Mary O'Donovan (RSM)
The Pastoral Centre,
Letterkenny, Co Donegal
Tel 074-9121853 Fax 074-9128433

Fatima Pilgrimage
Director: Rev James Sweeney CC
Ardaghey, Co Donegal
Tel 074-9736007

Knock Pilgrimage
Director: Rev Michael McKeever
Churchill, Co Donegal
Tel 074-9137057

Laity Commission
Mr Peadar Murphy
'Matapos', Beechwood Avenue,
Letterkenny, Co Donegal

Lourdes Pilgrimage
Director: Rev Martin Chambers
Chaplain, Letterkenny General Hospital,
Co Donegal
Tel 074-9125888 *(hospital)* 074-9125090
(Lourdes office)

Marriage Tribunal
(See also Marriage Tribunals section)
Secretary: Kathleen Kelly
The Pastoral Centre, Letterkenny,
Co Donegal
Tel 074-9121853
Officialis: Vacant
Assistant: Rev Philip Daly CC
Kilclooney

Pioneer Total Abstinence Association
Diocesan Directors
Very Rev James Friel PP
Tamney, Co Donegal
Tel 074-9159015
Rev James Sweeney CC
Ardaghey, Co Donegal
Tel 074-9736007

Raphoe Diocesan Directory
Rev Michael McKeever
Ard Adhamhnáin, Letterkenny,
Co Donegal
Tel 074-9121208
Fax 074-9124872
Email raphoediocese@eircom.net

Religious Broadcasting
Diocesan Director: Rev Patrick Dunne
St Eunan's College, Letterkenny
Tel 074-9121143

Vocations
Directors: Rev Joseph O'Donnell CC
Church of the Irish Martyrs, Letterkenny
Tel 074-9122608
Rev Gerard Cunningham CC
Parochial House, Fintown
Tel 074-9546107
Rev Rory Brady
1 Cathedral Place,
Letterkenny, Co Donegal
Tel 074-9125182

World Missions Ireland
Diocesan Director
Very Rev Francis McAteer PP
Parochial House, Carrick, Co Donegal
Tel 074-9739008

PARISHES

The mensal parish is listed first. Other parishes follow alphabetically. Historical names are given in parentheses.

LETTERKENNY (CONWAL AND LECK)
Cathedral of St Eunan and St Columba
Very Rev Eamonn Kelly Adm
Rev Philip Kemmy CC
Rev William Bradley (CSSp) CC
Parochial House, Letterkenny, Co Donegal
Tel 074-9121021 Fax 074-9122707
Email steunanscathedral@eircom.net
Letterkenny General Hospital
Rev Martin Chambers
2 Chaplain's House, Knocknamona,
Letterkenny, Co Donegal
Tel 074-9125090
Canon John Gallagher
1 Chaplain's House, Knocknamona,
Letterkenny, Co Donegal
Tel (Hospital) 074-9125888

ANNAGRY
Very Rev Michael Herrity PP
Annagry, Co Donegal
Tel 074-9548111

ARDARA
Very Rev Canon Austin Laverty PP, VF
Ardara, Co Donegal
Tel 074-9541135
Rev Aodhan Cannon CC
Ardara, Co Donegal
Tel 074-9541930
Rev Philip Daly CC
Kilclooney, Co Donegal
Tel 074-9545114

AUGHANINSHIN
Very Rev Brian Quinn PP
Ballyraine, Letterkenny,
Co Donegal
Tel 074-9127600
Rev Joe O'Donnell CC
Carnamuggagh Lower,
Letterkenny, Co Donegal
Tel 074-9122608

BALLINTRA (DRUMHOLM)
Very Rev Seamus Dagens PP
Ballintra, Co Donegal
Tel 074-9734016

BALLYSHANNON (KILBARRON)
Very Rev Cathal Ó Fearraí PP, VF
Tel 071-9851295
Rev Dermot Burke PE

BRUCKLESS (KILLAGHTEE)
Very Rev Dermot McShane PP
Bruckless, Co Donegal
Tel 074-9737015

BURTONPORT (KINCASSLAGH)
Very Rev Pat Ward PP
Burtonport, Co Donegal
Tel 074-9542006
Rev John Joe Duffy CC
Arranmore Island, Co Donegal
Tel 074-9520504

CARRICK (GLENCOLMCILLE)
Very Rev Francis McAteer PP
Carrick, Co Donegal
Tel 074-9739008

CARRIGART (MEEVAGH)
Very Rev Charles Byrne PP
Carrigart, Co Donegal
Tel 074-9155154

CLOGHAN (KILTEEVOGUE)
Very Rev Lorcan Sharkey PP
Cloghan, Co Donegal
Tel 074-9133007

DONEGAL TOWN (TAWNAWILLY)
Very Rev William Peoples PP
Tel 074-9721026
Donegal Town, Co Donegal
Rev Danny McBrearty CC
Parochial House, Clar
Tel 074-9721093

DRUMOGHILL (RAYMOCHY)
Very Rev Canon William McMenamin PP
Drumoghill, Manorcunningham,
Co Donegal
Tel 074-9157169

DUNFANAGHY (CLONDAHORKEY)
Very Rev Martin Doohan PP
Dunfanaghy, Co Donegal
Tel 074-9136163
Rev Joseph Briody CC
Cleeslough, Co Donegal
Tel 074-9138011

DUNGLOE (TEMPLECRONE AND LETTERMACAWARD)
Very Rev Séamus Meehan PP
Tel 074-9521008
Rev Nigel Ó Galláchóir CC
Tel 074-9522194
Dungloe, Co Donegal
Rev Eamonn McLaughlin CC
Leitirmacaward, Co Donegal
Tel 074-9544102

FALCARRAGH
Very Rev Denis Quinn PP
Falcarragh, Co Donegal
Tel 074-9135196

GLENSWILLY (GLENSWILLY AND TEMPLEDOUGLAS)
Very Rev Hugh Sweeney PP
Glenswilly, New Mills, Letterkenny,
Co Donegal
Tel 074-9137020

GLENTIES (INISKEEL)
Very Rev Patrick Prendergast PP
Tel 074-9551117
Rev Shane Gallagher CC
Tel 074-9551136
Glenties, Co Donegal
Rev Gerard Cunningham CC
Fintown, Donegal Town,
Co Donegal
Tel 074-9546107

GORTAHORK (TORY ISLAND)
Very Rev Seán Ó Gallchóir PP
Tel 074-9135214
Rev Francis Ferry CC
Tory Island, Co Donegal
Tel 074-9135505

GWEEDORE
Very Rev Michael Sweeney PP, VF
Tel 074-9531310
Rev Padraig Ó Baoighill CC
Tel 074-9531308
Rev Brian O'Fearraigh CC
Derrybeg, Letterkenny
Tel 074-9531947
Rev Donnchadh Ó Baoill CC
Bun-a-leaca, Letterkenny, Co Donegal
Tel 074-9531155

INVER
Very Rev John McLoone PP
Frosses, Co Donegal
Tel 074-9736006
Rev James Sweeney CC
Ardaghey, Co Donegal
Tel 074-9736007
Rev Adrian Gavigan CC
Mountcharles, Co Donegal
Tel 074-9735009

KILCAR
Very Rev Edward Gallagher PP
Kilcar, Co Donegal
Tel 074-9738007

KILLYBEGS
Very Rev Colm O'Gallchoir PP
Killybegs, Co Donegal
Tel 074-9731030

KILLYMARD
Very Rev Francis McLoone PP
Killymard, Co Donegal
Tel 074-9721929

KILMACRENNAN
Very Rev Michael Conaghan PP
Kilmacrennan, Co Donegal
Tel 074-9139018
Rev John Boyce CC
Golan, Milford, Co Donegal
Tel 074-9153280

NEWTOWNCUNNINGHAM & KILLEA
Very Rev Seamus Gallagher PP
Parochial House,
Newtowncunningham,
Lifford, Co Donegal
Tel 074-9156138

RAMELTON (AUGHNISH)
Very Rev Michael Carney PP
Ramelton, Co Donegal
Tel 074-9151304

RAPHOE
Very Rev Denis McGettigan PP
Raphoe, Lifford, Co Donegal
Tel 074-9145647
Rev Paul Gallagher CC
Convoy, Lifford, Co Donegal
Tel 074-9147238
Rev Martin Timoney CC
Drumkeen, Ballybofey,
Co Donegal
Tel 074-9134005

RATHMULLAN (KILLYGARVAN AND TULLYFERN)
Very Rev Martin Collum PP
Rathmullan, Co Donegal
Tel 074-9158156
Rev James Gillespie CC
Milford, Co Donegal
Tel 074-9153236

ST JOHNSTON (TAUGHBOYNE)
Rt Rev Mgr Daniel Carr PP, VG
St Johnston, Lifford, Co Donegal
Tel 074-9148203

STRANORLAR
Very Rev Kieran McAteer PP
Parochial House, Ballybofey, Co Donegal
Tel 074-9131135
Rev Ciaran Harkin CC
Parochial House, Stranorlar,
Co Donegal
Tel 074-9131157

TAMNEY (CLONDAVADDOG)
Very Rev James Friel PP
Tamney, Letterkenny, Co Donegal
Tel 074-9159015
Rev Patrick McGarvey CC
Fanavolty, Kindrum,
Letterkenny, Co Donegal
Tel 074-9159007

TERMON (GARTAN AND TERMON)
Very Rev Patrick McHugh PP
Termon, Letterkenny, Co Donegal
Tel 074-9139016
Rev Michael McKeever CC
Church Hill, Letterkenny, Co Donegal
Tel 074-9137057
www.gartantermon.net

INSTITUTIONS AND THEIR CHAPLAINS

General Hospital
Letterkenny, Co Donegal
Tel 074-9125888
Rev Martin Chambers
c/o General Hospital, Letterkenny
or 2 Chaplain's House,
Knocknamona, Letterkenny
Canon John Gallagher
1 Chaplain's House,
Knocknamona, Letterkenny

Letterkenny Institute of Technology
Letterkenny, Co Donegal
Tel 074-9124888
Rev Rory Brady

St Conal's Hospital
Letterkenny, Co Donegal
Tel 074-9121022
Canon John Gallagher
Rev Martin Chambers

St Joseph's Hospital
Stranorlar, Co Donegal
Tel 074-9131038
Parochial clergy Stranorlar

PRIESTS OF THE DIOCESE ELSEWHERE

Rev Patrick Bonner
140 Willowood Drive, Wantagh,
New York, USA
Rev Niall Coll
St Mary's College, Belfast
Rev Martin Cunningham
c/o Diocesan Office, Letterkenny,
Co Donegal
Rev Paul M. Geehan
The Presbytery, 36 Victoria Grove,
Bridport, Dorset DT6 3AD
Tel 01308-422594
Rev Kevin Gillespie
Congregation for the Clergy, Rome
Rev Brendan McBride
St Philip's Church, 725 Diamond Street,
San Francisco, California, 94114
Rev Declan McCarron
c/o Diocesan Office, Letterkenny,
Co Donegal

RETIRED PRIESTS

Very Rev Canon Patrick McShane PE
Tully, Donegal Town, Co Donegal
Tel 074-9740150
Very Rev Connell Cunningham PE
Carrick, Co Donegal
Rev Thomas Curran
Glenview House, College Road,
Letterkenny, Co Donegal
Tel 074-9127617

Rev Anthony Griffith
Rushbrook, Laghey, Co Donegal
Tel 074-9734021
Rev Ernan McMullin DPhil
Mountcharles, Co Donegal
Very Rev Daniel O'Doherty PE
Ballyheerin, Fanad, Co Donegal
Very Rev John J. Silke PhD
'Stella Maris', Portnablagh,
Co Donegal
Tel 074-9136122
Very Rev Seamus L. Gallagher PE
Glenlee, Killybegs, Co Donegal
Tel 074-9732729
Very Rev Kevin O'Doherty PE
Falcarragh, Co Donegal
Tel 074-9165356
Very Rev Desmond Sweeney PE
Ramelton
Tel 074-9151085

RELIGIOUS ORDERS AND CONGREGATIONS

PRIESTS

CAPUCHINS (OFMCAP)
Capuchin Friary, Ard Mhuire,
Creeslough, Letterkenny,
Co Donegal
Tel 074-38005/38031
Fax 074-38371
Guardian
Rev Donal Sweeney (OFMCap)
Vicar
Rev Vianney Holmes (OFMCap)

FRANCISCANS (OFM)
Franciscan Friary, Rossnowlagh,
Co Donegal
Tel 072-9851342
Fax 072-9852206
Email franciscanfriary@eircom.net
Guardian
Rev Paschal McDonnell (OFM)

SISTERS

CONGREGATION OF THE SISTERS OF MERCY
Convent of Mercy, Donegal Town,
Co Donegal
Tel 074-9721175
Shared leadership
Community: 6

Convent of Mercy,
15 Blackrock Drive, Ballybofey,
Co Donegal
Tel 074-9132721
Leader: Sr Nuala Mullin
Community: 4

St Catherine's,
Ballyshannon, Co Donegal
Tel 071-9851268
Shared leadership: Sr Magdalene Moore
& Sr Goretti McGale
Community: 10

Bethany, 23 Ernedale Heights,
Ballyshannon, Co Donegal
Tel 071-9852186

Dia Linn, Gortnamucklagh,
Glenties, Co Donegal
Tel 074-9551125

Convent of Mercy, Carnmore Road,
Dungloe, Co Donegal
Tel 074-9521209

Sisters of Mercy,
Ceoil na Coille, Stranorlar,
Lifford, Co Donegal
Tel 074-9131245
Family Enrichment Centre
Dromboe Avenue, Stranorlar
Tel 074-9131245

Convent of Mercy, Windy Hall,
Letterkenny, Co Donegal
Tel 074-9122729
Community: 4

Sisters of Mercy,
St Anne's Convent,
Ballyshannon, Co Donegal
Tel 071-9852737
Community: 3

Sisters of Mercy,
Mount Carmel House of Prayer,
Drumkeen, Ballybofey,
Co Donegal
Tel 074-9134167
Contact: Sr Susan Evangelist Teague

Sisters of Mercy,
No. 1 McCloskey Close,
Glenties, Co Donegal
Tel 074-9551713

Sisters of Mercy,
15 Taobh na Cille,
Moville, Co Donegal
Tel 074-9385454

Sisters of Mercy, Glór na Mara,
West End, Bundoran, Co Donegal
Tel 071-9833899

18 Beinn Aoibhin,
Letterkenny, Co Donegal
Tel 074-9177837

LORETO (IBVM)
Loreto Community, Letterkenny,
Co Donegal
Tel 074-9122896
Superior: Sr Rosaleen O'Kane
Community: 13
Loreto Primary School
Tel 074-9122896
Loreto Secondary School
Tel 074-9124237

NEW FORMS OF CONSECRATED LIFE

THE SPIRITUAL FAMILY THE WORK OF CHRIST (FSO)
Bishop's House, Ard Adhamhnáin,
Letterkenny, Co Donegal
Tel 074-9124898
Fax 074-9128142
Email thework@catholic.org
Website www.thework-fso.org
Superior: Sr Nellie Baerts FSO
Community: 2

EDUCATIONAL INSTITUTIONS

Coláiste Ailigh
High Road, Letterkenny,
Co Donegal
Tel 074-9125943
Príomh-Óid
 Mr Michael Gibbons
Séiplineadh
Mr Séan Ó Gallchóir

Coláiste Cholmcille
Ballyshannon, Co Donegal
Tel 071-9858288/9851369/9852459
Principal: Mr Jimmy Keogh
Chaplain: Ms Pauline Kilfeather

Rosses Community School
Dungloe, Co Donegal
Tel 074-9521122
Principal: Mr John Gorman
Chaplain: Rev Nigel Ó Gallchóir CC

Comprehensive School
Glenties, Lifford,
Co Donegal
Tel 074-9551172
Fax 074-9551664
Principal: Mr Harry Reid
Chaplain: Rev Shane Gallagher CC

Institute of Technology, Letterkenny
Director: Mr Paul Hannigan
Tel 074-9124888
Chaplain: Rev Rory Brady

Loreto Convent Secondary School
Letterkenny, Co Donegal
Tel 074-9121850
Principal: Mrs Susan Kenny
Chaplain: Parish Clergy

Loreto Community School
Milford, Co Donegal
Tel 074-9153253
Fax 074-9153518
Principal: Mr Andrew Kelly
Tel 074-9153399
Chaplain: Mr John Lynch

Pobalscoil Chloich Cheannfhaola
Falcarragh, Letterkenny, Co Donegal
Tel 074-9135424/9135231
Fax 074-9135019
Príomh-Oide: Mr Patrick McVicar
Séiplineach: Rev Brian O'Fearraigh CC

Pobalscoil Ghaoth Dobhair
Derrybeg, Letterkenny, Co Donegal
Tel 074-9531040
Príomh-Oide: Mr Noel Ó Gallchóir
Séiplineach: Rev Padraig O'Baoill CC

Royal and Prior Comprehensive School
Raphoe, Co Donegal
Tel 074-9145389
Principal: Mr D. G. West
Chaplain: Rev Paul Gallagher CC

St Columba's College
Stranorlar, Co Donegal
Tel 074-9131246
Principal: Mr Gerry Bennett
Chaplain: Vacant

St Eunan's College
Letterkenny, Co Donegal
Tel 074-9121143
Principal: Mr Chris Darby
Chaplain: Rev Patrick Dunne

Vocational Schools
Arranmore Island, Co Donegal
Tel 074-9521747
Principal: Ms Poilín Ní Chomaic
Chaplain: Rev John Joe Duffy CC

Ballinamore, Co Donegal
Tel 074-9546133 Fax 074-9546256
Principal: Mrs Fiona Bonner
Chaplain: Rev Gerard Cunningham CC
Fintown, Donegal Town, Co Donegal

Carrick, Co Donegal
Tel 074-9739017 Fax 074-9739265
Principal: Mr Tony Bonner
Chaplain: Very Rev Eddie Gallagher PP
Kilcar, Co Donegal

Abbey Vocational School,
Donegal Town, Co Donegal
Tel 074-9721105 Fax 074-9722851
Principal: Mr Emmanuel McCormick
Chaplain: Rev Adrian Gavigan CC

Gairm Scoil Catríona,
Killybegs, Co Donegal
Tel/Fax 074-9731491
Principal: Ms Mary Anne Looby

Errigal College,
Letterkenny, Co Donegal
Tel 074-9121047/9121861
Fax 074-9121861
Principal: Ms Anne McHugh
Chaplain: Rev Eamonn Kelly Adm

Allianz (ⅱ)

Mulroy College,
Milford, Co Donegal
Tel 074-9153346
Principal: Ms Rita Gleeson
Chaplain: Rev James Gillespie CC
Milford, Co Donegal

Deele College,
Raphoe, Co Donegal
Tel 074-9145277
Principal: Mr P. J. McGowan
Chaplain: Very Rev Denis McGettigan PP

Finn Valley College,
Stranorlar, Co Donegal
Tel 074-9131355
Principal: Mr Frank Dooley

CHARITABLE AND OTHER SOCIETIES

Ards Friary Retreat and Conference Centre
Manager: Mr Benito Conangelo
Tel 074-9138909
Email info@ardsfriary.ie
Website www.ardsfriary.ie

Society of St Vincent de Paul
North West Region Council,
Meeting House Street,
Raphoe, Co Donegal
Tel/Fax 074-9173933
Email svpnorthwest@eircom.net

St Mura's Adoption Society
The Pastoral Centre, Monastery Avenue,
Letterkenny, Co Donegal
tel 074-9122047

Trócaire
Rev Aodhan Connor CC
Parochial House, Ardara,
Co Donegal
Tel 074-9541930

DIOCESE OF WATERFORD AND LISMORE

PATRONS OF THE DIOCESE
ST OTTERAN, 27 OCTOBER; ST CARTHAGE, 15 MAY;
ST DECLAN, 24 JULY

INCLUDES COUNTY WATERFORD
AND PART OF COUNTIES TIPPERARY AND CORK

Most Rev William Lee DD
Bishop of Waterford and Lismore; born 1941; ordained priest 19 June 1966; ordained Bishop of Waterford and Lismore 25 July 1993

Residence: Bishop's House, John's Hill, Waterford
Tel 051-874463
Fax 051-852703
Email
waterfordlismore@eircom.net

CATHEDRAL OF THE MOST HOLY TRINITY, WATERFORD

The Cathedral of the Most Holy Trinity, Barronstrand Street, Waterford is the oldest Roman Catholic cathedral in Ireland. The work began in 1793 with the Protestant Waterford man, John Roberts, as architect. Roberts also designed the Church of Ireland cathedral.

Over the years, additions and alterations have been made. Most of the present sanctuary was added in the 1830s; the apse and a main altar in 1854. The beautiful baldachin, which is supported by five Corinthian columns, was erected in 1881.

The carved oak Baroque pulpit, the chapter stalls and bishop's chair, designed by Goldie and Sons of London and carved by Buisine and Sons of Lille, were installed in 1883.
The stained-glass windows, mainly by Meyer of Munich, were installed between 1883 and 1888.

The Stations of the Cross, which are attached to the columns in the cathedral, are nineteenth-century paintings by Alcan of Paris. The cut-stone front was built in 1892–1893 for the centenary of the cathedral.

In 1977, a new wooden altar was placed in the redesigned sanctuary. The Belgian walnut panels of the base of the altar were originally part of the altar rails at St Carthage's Church, Lismore.

There are many plaques in the cathedral. One of them commemorates fourteen famous Waterford men: Luke Wadding OFM; Peter Lombard; Patrick Comerford OSA; James White; Michael Wadding SJ: Peter Wadding SJ; Thomas White; Paul Sherlock SJ; Ambrose Wadding SJ; Geoffrey Keating; Luke Wadding SJ; Stephen White SJ; Thomas White SJ and Bonaventure Barron OFM.

Ten Waterford Crystal chandeliers were presented by Waterford Crystal in 1979.

In 1993 the Bicentenary of the Cathedral was celebrated.

CHAPTER

Right Rev Mgr Dean John Shine AP
Tramore
Very Rev Nicholas Canon O'Mahony PP, VG
Tramore
Very Rev Gregory Power PE
St Mary's, Clonmel
Right Rev Mgr Michael Olden PE
Waterford
Very Rev Francis Hopkins AP
Ballybricken, Waterford
Very Rev Martin Slattery AP
Cathedral, Waterford
Very Rev Daniel O'Connor AP
Dungarvan
Very Rev Thomas Nugent AP
Lismore
Very Rev Nicholas Power AP
SS Peter & Paul's, Clonmel
Very Rev William Ryan PP
Dungarvan
Very Rev Paul Beecher PE, Cahir

College of Consultors

Very Rev Nicholas Canon O'Mahony PP, VG
Very Rev Raymond Liddane AP
Very Rev Patrick Cooney PP
Very Rev Patrick Fitzgerald PP
Rt Rev Mgr Michael Olden PE
Very Rev Liam Power Adm

ADMINISTRATION

Vicar General
Very Rev Nicholas Canon O'Mahony PP, VG
Parochial House, Tramore,
Co Waterford
Tel 051-381525

Chancellor
Rev Gerard Chestnutt CC
Sacred Heart Presbytery, The Folly,
Waterford
Tel 051-878429

Diocesan Development Committee
Right Rev Mgr John P. Shine AP
Very Rev Nicholas Canon O'Mahony PP, VG
Very Rev Michael Cullinan PP
Very Rev Matthew Cunningham PP
Very Rev Michael Guiry PP
Rev Richard O'Halloran CC

Diocesan Finance Committee
Very Rev Nicholas Canon O'Mahony PP, VG
Rt Rev Mgr Michael Olden PE
Mr Anthony Brophy
Rev Gerard Chestnutt CC
Very Rev Brendan Crowley PP
Mr Michael Holland
Very Rev Gerard Langford Adm
Sr Marie Murphy
Mrs Alice Pollard
Very Rev Gerard Purcell AP
Mr Sean Ryan
Mr Tim Walsh

Diocesan Financial Administrator
Rev Gerard Chestnutt CC
Sacred Heart Presbytery, The Folly,
Waterford
Tel 051-878429

Diocesan Building Projects Committee
Right Rev Mgr Michael Olden PE
Very Rev Richard Doherty AP
Very Rev Patrick Fitzgerald PP
Very Rev Thomas Flynn PP
Mr Michael J. Maguire BE, CEng, MIEI
Very Rev Michael F. Walsh PP

Diocesan Common Fund Committee
Very Rev Raymond Liddane AP
Very Rev Garret Desmond PP
Very Rev Joseph Flynn PP
Very Rev Martin Keogh PP
Very Rev William Ryan PP

Diocesan Retirement Fund Committee
Very Rev Nicholas Canon O'Mahony PP, VG
Rev Gerard Chestnutt CC
Very Rev Richard Doherty AP
Very Rev Patrick Cooney PP
Very Rev Martin Keogh PP
Very Rev Brendan Crowley PP
Rev Paul Waldron CC

Diocesan Secretary
Rev Gerard Chestnutt CC
Sacred Heart Presbytery, The Folly,
Waterford
Tel 051-878429

Episcopal Vicar for Retired Priests
Very Rev John Kiely PP
Cappoquin, Co Waterford
Tel 058-54216

CATECHETICS EDUCATION

Catechetics
Primary Schools Religious Education:
Sr Antoinette Dilworth
Mercy Convent, Military Road, Waterford
Tel 051-874199
Sr De Lourdes Breen
Presentation Sisters, 158 Larchville,
Waterford
Tel 051-355496
Rev Edmond Hassett CC
Portlaw, Co Waterford
Tel 051-387227
Rev Richard O'Halloran CC
41 Lismore Park, Waterford
Tel 051-354034
Rev Paul Waldron CC
The Presbytery, Dungarvan, Co Waterford
Tel 058-42384
*Director Post-Primary Schools Religious
Education:* Ms Roseanne Sinnott
St John's Pastoral Centre, John's Hill,
Waterford
Tel 051-874199

**Catholic Primary School Managers'
Association**
Secretary: Very Rev Patrick Cooney PP
30 Viewmount Park, Waterford
Tel 051-873073
Chairman: Mr Michael O'Shea
West Street, Lismore, Co Waterford

LITURGY

Assistant to Parishes
Ms Mary Dee
St John's Pastoral Centre,
John's Hill, Waterford
Tel 051-874199

Diocesan Liturgy Committee
Very Rev William Ryan PP
Very Rev William Meehan PP
Rev Paul Waldron CC
Mr Noel Casey
Ms Deirdre Moore
Ms Adrienne Dolphin
Ms Mary Dunphy
Ms Anna Fennessey

PASTORAL

Accord
Director: Very Rev Liam Power Adm
St John's Pastoral Centre, John's Hill
Waterford
Tel 051-874199
Rev Raymond Reidy CC
Church of the Resurrection,
Fethard Road, Clonmel, Co Tipperary
Tel 052-6123239

Charismatic Groups
Very Rev Matthew Cunningham AP
Grangemockler, Carrick-on-Suir,
Co Tipperary
Tel 051-647011

CURA
St John's Pastoral Centre, John's Hill,
Waterford
Tel 051-876452

Diocesan Archivist
Sr Rita Fennell
St John's Pastoral Centre,
John's Hill, Waterford
Tel 051-874199

Ecumenism
Director: Very Rev Edmond Cullinan PP
Parochial House, Chapel Street,
Carrick-on-Suir, Co Tipperary
Tel 051-640168

Emigrant Bureau
Director: Very Rev Michael Enright PE
Priest's Road, Tramore, Co Waterford
Tel 087-2371546

Family Ministry
Director: Ms Ann O'Farrell
Family Ministry Office,
St John's Pastoral Centre,
John's Hill, Waterford
Tel 051-874199/858772

Historic Churches Advisory Committee
Mr Eamonn McEneaney
Very Rev William Ryan
Very Rev Michael Walsh
Tel 051-874463

Marriage Tribunal
Diocesan Official. Rt Rev Mgr John Shine AP
Tramore, Co Waterford
Tel 051-381531
(See also Marriage Tribunals section)

Media Spokesperson
Very Rev Liam Power Adm
St John's Pastoral Centre, John's Hill
Waterford
Tel 051-874199

Ministry to Polish Community
Rev Emil Adler
St Anne's Presbytery, Convent Hill,
Waterford
Tel 087-4182223

Pastoral Development
Very Rev Liam Power Adm
St John's Pastoral Centre, John's Hill
Waterford
Tel 051-874199

Pilgrimage
Director: Very Rev Conor Kelly PP
Ring, Dungarvan, Co Waterford
Tel 058-46125

Pioneer Total Abstinence Association
Diocesan Director
Very Rev Kevin Mulcahy PE
No 3 The Carechoice, Burgery,
Dungarvan, Co Waterford
Tel 058-40253/087-6409622

Pontifical Mission Societies
Diocesan Director
Very Rev Sean O'Dwyer PP
Parochial House, Cahir, Co Tipperary
Tel 052-7441404

Senate of Priests
Chairperson
Very Rev Patrick Fitzgerald PP
Parochial House, Lisduggan, Waterford
Tel 051-372257
Secretary: Rev John Treacy CC
14 Heathervue Road, Riverview,
Knockboy, Waterford
Tel 051-843207

Travellers
Chaplain: Very Rev Paul Murphy PP
Butlerstown, Co Waterford
Tel 051-384192

Trócaire
Diocesan Director
Very Rev Conor Kelly PP
Ring, Dungarvan, Co Waterford
Tel 058-46125

Vocations
Director: Very Rev William Meehan PP
St Mary's, Irishtown, Clonmel, Co Tipperary
Tel 052-6122954

Youth Ministry
Edmund Rice Youth & Community
Centre, Manor Street,
Waterford
Tel 051-872710

PARISHES

City parishes are listed first. Other parishes follow alphabetically. Italics denote church titulars where they differ from parish names.

TRINITY WITHIN AND ST PATRICK'S
Holy Trinity Cathedral
Very Rev Gerard Langford Adm
Cathedral of the Most Holy Trinity,
Barronstrand Street, Waterford
Tel 051-392666
Very Rev Martin Slattery AP
18 John's Hill, Waterford
Tel 051-311561
Sacristy: Tel 051-875166

ST JOHN'S
Very Rev Liam Power Adm
Rev Thomas Burns
Rev Robert Grant CC
St John's Presbytery, New Street,
Waterford
Tel 051-874271
Sacristy: Tel 051-875849

SS JOSEPH AND BENILDUS
SS Joseph & Benildus, Newtown
St Mary, Ballygunner
Very Rev Patrick Cooney PP
30 Viewmount Park, Waterford
Tel 051-873073
Very Rev Raymond Liddane AP
Newtown, Waterford
Tel 051-874284
Rev John Treacy CC
14 Heathervue Road, Knockboy,
Waterford
Tel 051-843207
Sacristy: Tel 051-878977
Parish Pastoral Worker:
Ms Aoife McGrath
Tel 051-854690

BALLYBRICKEN
Holy Trinity Without
Very Rev Michael Mullins PP
Very Rev Francis Canon Hopkins AP
Rev Michael O'Brien
Rev Emil Adler
St Anne's Presbytery, Convent Hill,
Waterford
Tel 051-855819
Sacristy: Tel 051-874519

HOLY FAMILY
Very Rev Thomas Rogers PP
Tel 051-375274
Rev James Denmead CC
Tel 051-374720
Holy Family Presbytery,
Luke Wadding Street, Waterford

ST PAUL'S
Very Rev Patrick Fitzgerald PP
Parochial House, Lisduggan, Waterford
Tel 051-372257
Rev Richard O'Halloran CC
41 Lismore Park, Waterford
Tel 051-353938
Sacristy: Tel 051-378073

SACRED HEART
Very Rev Sean Melody PP
Sacred Heart Presbytery,
21 The Folly, Waterford
Tel 051-873759
Rev Gerard Chestnutt CC
The Presbytery, The Folly, Waterford
Tel 051-878429
Sacristy: Tel 051-873792

ST SAVIOUR'S
Very Rev Fergal Mac Eoinin (OP) PP
Rev Martin Crowe (OP) CC
Rev Richard Walsh (OP)
St Saviour's Priory, Kilbarry,
Waterford
Tel 051-376581

ABBEYSIDE
St Augustine, Abbeyside
St Laurence, Ballinroad
St Vincent de Paul, Garranbane
Very Rev Timothy O'Riordan PP
Abbeyside, Dungarvan, Co Waterford
Tel 058-42036
Very Rev Richard Doherty AP
Abbeyside, Dungarvan, Co Waterford
Tel 058-42379

AGLISH
Our Lady of the Assumption, Aglish
St James, Ballinameela
St Patrick, Mount Stuart
Very Rev Finbarr Lucey PP
Aglish, Cappoquin, Co Waterford
Tel 024-96287

ARDFINNAN
Holy Family, Ardfinnan
St Nicholas, Grange, Ballybacon Church
Very Rev Robert Power Adm
Ardfinnan, Clonmel, Co Tipperary
Tel 052-7466216

ARDMORE
St Declan, Ardmore
Our Lady of the Assumption, Grange
Very Rev Michael Guiry PP
Ardmore, Youghal, Co Waterford
Tel 024-94275

BALLYDUFF
St Michael
Very Rev Gerard McNamara PP
Ballyduff, Co Waterford
Tel 058-60227

BALLYLOOBY
Our Lady & St Kieran, Ballylooby
St John the Baptist, Duhill
Very Rev Michael F. Walsh PP
Ballylooby, Cahir, Co Tipperary
Tel 052-7441489

BALLYNEALE AND GRANGEMOCKLER
St Mary
Very Rev Patrick Gear PP
Ballyneale, Carrick-on-Suir, Co Tipperary
Tel 051-640148
St Mary
Very Rev Matthew Cunningham AP
Grangemockler, Carrick-on-Suir,
Co Tipperary
Tel 051-647011

BALLYPOREEN
Our Lady of the Assumption
Very Rev Joseph Flynn PP
Ballyporeen, Cahir, Co Tipperary
Tel 052-7467105

BUTLERSTOWN
St Mary
Very Rev Paul Murphy PP
Parochial House, Butlerstown,
Co Waterford
Tel 051-384192

CAHIR
St Mary
Very Rev Sean O'Dwyer PP
Parochial House, Cahir, Co Tipperary
Tel 052-7441404

CAPPOQUIN
St Mary's
Very Rev John Kiely PP
Tel 058-54216
Very Rev Robert Arthure AP
Tel 058-54221
Cappoquin, Co Waterford

CARRICKBEG
St Molleran, Carrickbeg
St Bartholomew, Windgap
Very Rev Thomas Flynn PP
Carrickbeg, Carrick-on-Suir, Co Tipperary
Tel 051-640340

CARRICK-ON-SUIR
St Nicholas, Carrick-on-Suir
St Patrick, Faugheen
Very Rev Edmond Cullinan PP, VF
Parochial House, Carrick-on-Suir,
Co Tipperary
Tel 051-640168
Rev Richard Geoghegan CC
The Presbytery, Carrick-on-Suir,
Co Tipperary
Tel 051-640080

CLASHMORE
St Cronan, Clashmore
St Bartholomew, Piltown
Very Rev Maurice O'Gorman PP
Clashmore, Co Waterford
Tel 024-96110

CLOGHEEN
St Mary, Clogheen
Our Lady of the Assumption, Burnecourt
Very Rev Patrick Butler PP
Parochial House, Clogheen, Cahir,
Co Tipperary
Tel 052-7465268

CLONMEL, ST MARY'S
St Mary
Very Rev William Meehan PP
Tel 052-6122954
Rev Patrick Hayes CC
Tel 052-6121952
St Mary's, Clonmel, Co Tipperary

CLONMEL, ST OLIVER PLUNKETT
St Oliver Plunkett
Very Rev Michael Hegarty (IC) PP
Rev Partolan O'Leary (IC) CC
Cooleens, Glenconnor, Clonmel,
Co Tipperary
Tel 052-6125679

CLONMEL, SS PETER AND PAUL'S
SS Peter and Paul's,
Church of the Resurrection
Very Rev Brendan Crowley PP, VF
SS Peter and Paul's, Clonmel,
Co Tipperary
Tel 052-6122138
Very Rev Canon Nicholas Power AP
Parochial House, SS Peter and Paul's,
Clonmel, Co Tipperary
Tel 052-6121932
Rev Raymond Reidy (SPS) CC
Church of the Resurrection,
Fethard Road, Clonmel, Co Tipperary
Tel 052-6122138

DUNGARVAN
St Mary
Very Rev William Ryan PP
Parochial House, Dungarvan,
Co Waterford
Tel 058-42374
Very Rev Canon Daniel O'Connor AP
Tel 058-42381
Rev Paul Waldron CC
Tel 058-42384
Rev Matthew Cooney (OSA)
The Presbytery, Dungarvan,
Co Waterford

DUNHILL
Sacred Heart, Dunhill
Immaculate Conception, Fenor
Very Rev Michael Kennedy PP
Dunhill, Co Waterford
Tel 051-396109
Very Rev Paul F. Murphy Adm
Ballynageeragh, Dunhill, Co Waterford
Tel 051-396616

KILGOBINET
St Gobnait, Kilgobinet
St Anne, Colligan
St Patrick, Kilbrian
Very Rev Michael Kennedy PP
Parochial House, Colligan, Dungarvan,
Co Waterford
Tel 058-41629

KILLEA (DUNMORE EAST)
Holy Cross, Killea
St John the Baptist, Crooke
St Nicholas, Faithlegg
Very Rev Brian Power PP
Dunmore East, Co Waterford
Tel 051-383127

KILROSSANTY
St Brigid, Kilrossanty
St Anne, Fews
Very Rev John Delaney PP
Parochial House, Kilrossanty,
Kilmacthomas, Co Waterford
Tel 051-291985

KILSHEELAN
St Mary, Gambonsfield
St John the Baptist, Kilcash
Very Rev William Carey PP
Tel 052-6133118
Rev James O'Donoghue CC
Tel 052-6133292
Kilsheelan, Clonmel, Co Tipperary

KNOCKANORE
Very Rev Patrick T. Condon PP
Knockanore, Tallow, Co Waterford
Tel 024-97140

LISMORE
St Carthage
Very Rev Michael Cullinane PP, VF
Parochial House,
Lismore, Co Waterford
Tel 058-54246
Very Rev Canon Thomas Nugent AP
The Presbytery,
Lismore, Co Waterford
Tel 058-54173

MODELIGO
Our Lady of the Assumption, Modeligo
St John the Baptist, Affane
Priest in charge:
Very Rev John Kiely
Cappoquin, Co Waterford
Tel 058-54216
Rev Gerard O'Connor CC
Chapel Road, Modeligo,
Cappagh, Co Waterford
Tel 058-68136

NEWCASTLE AND FOURMILEWATER
Our Lady of the Assumption, Newcastle
Our Lady & St Laurence, Fourmilewater
Very Rev Garrett Desmond PP
Newcastle, Clonmel, Co Tipperary
Tel 052-6136387

NEWTOWN
All Saints, Newtown
St Mary, Saleen, Kill Church
Very Rev Martin Keogh PP
Parochial House, Newtown,
Kilmacthomas, Co Waterford
Tel 051-294261
Very Rev William Callanan AP
Kill, Co Waterford
Tel 051-292212

PORTLAW
St Patrick, Portlaw
St Nicholas, Ballyduff
Very Rev Michael O'Byrne PP
Kilmeaden, Co Waterford
Tel 051-384117
Rev Edmond Hassett CC
Portlaw, Co Waterford
Tel 051-387227

POWERSTOWN
St John the Baptist, Powerstown
St John the Baptist, Lisronagh
Very Rev Peter Ahearne PP
Rathronan, Clonmel, Co Tipperary
Tel 052-6121891

RATHGORMACK
SS Quan & Broghan, Clonea
Sacred Heart, Rathgormack
Very Rev Michael Curran PP
Rathgormack, Carrick-on-Suir, Co Tipperary
Tel 051-646006

RING AND OLD PARISH
Nativity of the BVM
St Nicholas
Very Rev Conor Kelly PP
Ring, Dungarvan, Co Waterford
Tel 058-46125

STRADBALLY
Exaltation of the Holy Cross, Stradbally
St Anne, Ballylaneen, Faha Church
Very Rev Jeremiah Condon PP
Stradbally, Kilmacthomas, Co Waterford
Tel 051-293133

TALLOW
Immaculate Conception
Priest in Charge
Very Rev Gerard McNamara PP
Ballyduff Upper, Co Waterford
Tel 058-60227
Very Rev Michael Farrell AP
Parochial House, Tallow, Co Waterford
Tel 058-56117

TOURANEENA
St Mary, Touranleena, Nire Church
Very Rev Cornelius Kelleher PP
Tournaneena, Ballinamult,
Clonmel, Co Tipperary
Tel 058-47138

TRAMORE
Holy Cross, Tramore
Our Lady, Corbally
Very Rev Nicholas Canon O'Mahony PP, VG
Parochial House, Tramore, Co Waterford
Tel 051-381525
Rt Rev Mgr John Shine AP
Priest's Road, Tramore, Co Waterford
Tel 051-381531
Rev Michael Toomey CC
Priest's Road, Tramore, Co Waterford
Tel 051-386642

INSTITUTIONS AND THEIR CHAPLAINS

Bon Sauveur Services
Carriglea, Dungarvan, Co Waterford
Tel 058-41322 Fax 058-41432
Email bonsav@eircom.net

Little Sisters of the Poor
Manor Hill, Waterford
Tel 051-874480

Regional Hospital, Waterford
Tel 051-873321
Chaplains: Rev Art McCoy OFM
Rev Baptist O'Toole OFM
Rev Br Isidore Cronin OFM

South Tipperary General Hospital
Chaplain: Rev Matthew Gaffney (IC)
Tel 052-6177000

Waterford Institute of Technology
Chaplain: Rev David Keating
10 Claremont, Cork Road, Waterford
Tel 051-378878

PRIESTS OF THE DIOCESE ELSEWHERE

Rev David McGuinness
St Joseph's Catholic Church,
134 Prince Avenue, Athens,
Georgia 30601, USA
Very Rev Michael O'Connor
c/o St John's Pastoral Centre,
John's Hill, Waterford
Email mnoc@iol.ie
Rev Charles Scanlan
Ballinwillin, Lismore, Co Waterford
Tel 058-54282

RETIRED PRIESTS

Very Rev Canon Paul Beecher PE
Cahir, Co Tipperary
Tel 052-7443193
Very Rev John Boyle PE
Ardmore, Youghal, Co Cork
Tel 024-94177
Very Rev John Callanan PE
Kilmacthomas, Co Waterford
Tel 051-294266
Very Rev Eanna Condon PE
St Mary's, Clonmel, Co Tipperary
Tel 052-6127870
Rev James Curran
61 Tournane Court, Dungarvan,
Co Waterford
Tel 058-45177
Very Rev Michael Enright PE
Priest's Road, Tramore, Co Waterford
Tel 087-2371546
Very Rev Patrick Fitzgerald PE
Priest's House, Ballinameela,
Cappagh, Co Waterford
Tel 058-68021
Very Rev James Griffin PE
10 Woodbrook Manor, Tralee, Co Kerry
Very Rev Francis Lloyd PE
The Presbytery, Dungarvan,
Co Waterford
Very Rev Thomas Morrissey PE
Upper Mullough, Newcastle,
Clonmel,Co Tipperary
Tel 051-6136236
Very Rev James Mulcahy PE
St John's Pastoral Centre,
John's Hill, Waterford
Tel 051-858306
Very Rev Kevin Mulcahy PE
No 3 The Carechoice, Burgery,
Dungarvan, Co Waterford
Tel 058-43555
Very Rev Sean Nugent PE
6 James Street, Clonmel, Co Tipperary
Tel 052-6128815

Rt Rev Mgr Michael Olden PE
'Woodleigh', Summerville Avenue,
Waterford
Tel 051-874132
Rev John P. O'Callaghan
Mount Carmel, Carriglea,
Halfway House, Waterford
Tel 051-382919
Very Rev Gregory Power PE
St Mary's, Clonmel, Co Tipperary
Tel 052-6182690
Very Rev Gerard Purcell PE
Fenor, Co Waterford
Tel 051-396971
Very Rev Patrick Canon Quealy AP
Care Choice Dungarvan, The Burgery,
Dungarvan, Co Waterford
Tel 058-40200
Very Rev Michael J. Ryan PE
Clonmel Road, Cahir, Co Tipperary
Tel 052-7443004
Very Rev Edmond Tobin PE
Munroe, Rehill, Ballylooby,
Cahir, Co Tipperary
Tel 052-7441975

RELIGIOUS ORDERS AND CONGREGATIONS

PRIESTS

AUGUSTINIANS
St Augustine's Priory, Dungarvan,
Co Waterford
Tel 058-41136 Fax 058-44534
Prior: Rev Seamus Humphries (OSA)

St Augustine's College,
Abbeyside, Dungarvan,
Co Waterford
Tel 058-41140/41152 Fax 058-41152
Tel 058-41385 (Students)

Duckspool House (Retirement Community)
Abbeyside, Dungarvan, Co Waterford
Tel 058-23784
Prior: Rev Columba O'Donnell (OSA)

CISTERCIANS
Mount Melleray Abbey,
Cappoquin, Co Waterford
Tel 058-54404 Fax 058-52140
Email mountmellerayabbey@eircom.net
Superior: Rev Michael Ahern(OCSO)
Prior: Br Boniface McGinley (OCSO)

DOMINICANS
Bridge Street, Waterford
Tel 051-875061
Prior: Very Rev James Harris (OP)

Ballybeg, Waterford
Tel 051-376581
Prior and Parish Priest
Very Rev Fergal Mac Eoinin (OP) PP

FRANCISCANS
Franciscan Friary, Carrick-on-Suir,
Co Tipperary
Tel 051-640015 Fax 051-645359
Email hermitage@eircom.net

Franciscan Friary, Clonmel, Co Tipperary
Tel 052-6121378 Fax 052-6125806
Email clonmel@eircom.net
Vicar: Br Isoidore Cronin (OFM)

Franciscan Friary, Lady Lane, Waterford
Tel 051-874262 Fax 051-843062
Email waterfordfriary@eircom.net
Guardian: Rev Patrick Younge (OFM)

MISSIONARIES OF THE SACRED HEART
Grace Dieu,
Tramore Road, Waterford
Tel 051-374417 Fax 051-374536
Superior: Rev Michael Serrage (MSC)

ROSMINIANS
Rosminian House of Prayer,
Glencomeragh, Kilsheelan, Co Tipperary
Tel 052-33181
Rector: Rev Pat Pierce (IC)

St Joseph's Doire na hAbhann
Tickincor, Clonmel, Co Tipperary
Tel 052-26914Fax 052-26915
Rector: Rev P. J. Fegan (IC)
Residential centre for children in care

(See also under parishes – St Oliver
Plunkett)

BROTHERS

CHRISTIAN BROTHERS
Christian Brothers' House,
Brú na Cruinne, Carrick-on-Suir,
Co Tipperary
Tel 051-640335 Fax 051-642605
Email brunacruinne@eircom.net
Community: 5

Mount Sion, Waterford
Tel 051-879580 Fax 051-841578
Community: 5

Intrnational Heritage Centre & Chapel
Mount Sion, Barrack Street, Waterford
Tel 051-874390 Fax 051-841578
CEO: Br Pat Madigan

DE LA SALLE BROTHERS
De La Salle College, Newtown,
Waterford
Tel 051-875294 Fax 051-841321
Email delasall@iol.ie
Superior: Br Amedy Hayes
Community: 6
Secondary School
Headmaster: Br Damian Kellegher

De La Salle Brothers
25 Patrick Street, Waterford
Tel 051-874623
Community: 4
Superior: Br Martin Curran
St Stephen's Primary School
Principal: Br Martin Curran
Tel 051-871716

PRESENTATION BROTHERS
Glór na hAbhann, Ballinamona Lower,
Old Parish, Dungarvan, Co Waterford
Tel 058-46904
Contact: Br John Hunt

SISTERS

BON SAUVEUR SISTERS
Carriglea, Dungarvan, Co Waterford
Tel 058-45884 Fax 058-45891
Email lbscarriglea@eircom.net
Superior: Sr Mary Fitzgerald
Community: 6
Pastoral Ministry to Carriglea Cairde
Service – Residential and day care services
for persons with an intellectual disability

CARMELITES
St Joseph's Carmelite Monastery, Tallow,
Co Waterford
Tel 058-56205
Email carmeltallow@eircom.net
Superior: Sr Teresa Gibbons
Community: 10
Contemplatives

CISTERCIANS
St Mary's Abbey, Glencairn,
Co Waterford
Tel 058-56168 Fax 058-56616
Email glencairnabbey@eircom.net
Abbess: Sr Marie Fahy
Tel 058-56197
Email mbfahy@eircom.net
Community: 33
Monastic

CONGREGATION OF THE SISTERS OF MERCY
Convent of Mercy, Cahir, Co Tipperary
Tel 052-7441294
Leader: Srs Josephine O'Grady Walshe
and Teresa Kennedy
Primary School
Tel 052-7441950
Aiseiri Alcoholism Treatment Centre
Tel 052-7441166/7441192

Teach Bride, Convent Road,
Townspark, Cahir, Co Tipperary
Tel 052-7443809
Contact: Sr Eileen Fahey

St Mary's Mount Anglesby,
Clogheen, Co Tipperary
Tel 052-7465255

Greenhill, Carrick-on-Suir,
Co Tipperary
Tel 051-640059
Leader: Sr Joan McGrath

Springwell, Pill Road,
Carrick-on-Suir, Co Tipperary
Tel 051-642870

12 Comeragh View,
Carrick-on-Suir, Co Tipperary
Tel 051-645012

10 Ash Park, Carrick-on-Suir,
Co Tipperary
Tel 051-640814
Contact: Sr Regina Power

Apartment 1, William Street,
Carrick-on-Suir, Co Tipperary
Tel 051-642576
Contact: Sr Carmel Uwins

21 Heywood Heights,
Clonmel, Co Tipperary
Tel 052-6125235
Contact: Sr Mary Muckley

32 Willow Park,
Clonmel, Co Tipperary
Tel 052-6125809
Contact: Sr Brenda Gallagher

Convent of Mercy, Church Street,
Dungarvan, Co Waterford
Tel 058-41293/41337
Leader: Sr Eileen Troy
Primary School

7 Lisfennel Close, Dungarvan,
Co Waterford
Tel 058-24341
Contact: Sr Laura Uwins

8 Lisfennel Close, Dungarvan,
Co Waterford
Tel 058-43191

1 Park Lane Drive, Abbeyside,
Dungarvan, Co Waterford
Tel 058-48795

22 Blackrock Court, Youghal Road,
Dungarvan, Co Waterford
Tel 058-48286
Contact: Sr Assumpta Hackett

16 Blackrock Court, Youghal Road,
Dungarvan, Co Waterford
Tel 058-45713
Contact: Sr Monica O'Sullivan

17 Blackrock Court, Youghal Road,
Dungarvan, Co Waterford
Tel 058-44865
Contact: Sr Ita Phelan

Convent of Mercy,
Military Road, Waterford
Tel 051-74161/77909
Contact: Sr Magdalen Agar
Holy Family Primary
Our Lady of Mercy Primary

Coolock House,
Grange Park Road, Waterford
Tel 051-878710
Contact: Sr Josephine Walsh

17/18 Bromley Close,
Ardkeen Village, Waterford
Tel 051-857684

2 Chestnut Grove, Waterford
Tel 051-373542

93 Clonard Park,
Ballybeg, Waterford
Tel 051-379110

7 Aisling Court,
Hennessy's Road, Waterford
Tel 051-874592
Contact: Sr Patricia Condon

5 Cul Rua, Portlaw, Co Waterford
Tel 051-387125
Contact: Sr Margaret Hackett

GOOD SHEPHERD SISTERS
Virginia Crescent, Hennessy's Road,
Waterford
Tel 051-874294 Fax 051-855940
Email rgswat@eircom.net
Superior: Sr Bríd Mullins
Community: 19

St Mary's Residence, Virginia Crescent,
Hennessy's Road, Waterford
Tel 051-877156
and 1-6 Ashling Court, Hennessy's Road
Tel 051-855045
Oasis Night Shelter. Tel 051-870367

1 Glencarra, Ballybeg, Waterford
Tel 051-378508 Fax 051-378508
Email ballybegrgs@eircom.net
Community: 3
Parish social work; youth work

LITTLE COMPANY OF MARY
36 Willowbrook,
Tallow, Co Waterford
Tel 058-55962
Apostolic community: 1

LITTLE SISTERS OF THE POOR
Manor Hill, Waterford
Tel 051-374481
Superior: Sr Roseline
Community: 22
Nursing home for the elderly

LORETO (IBVM)
Loreto Secondary School,
Clonmel, Co Tipperary
Tel 052-21402
Community: 2

PRESENTATION SISTERS
Presentation Sisters, Chapel Street,
Carrick-on-Suir, Co Tipperary
Tel 051-40069
Contact: Sr Immaculata Buckley

Presentation Convent,
Clonmel, Co Tipperary
Tel 052-21538
Local Leader: Sr Marie Stella Mangan
Community: 20
Primary school, secondary school,
Maryville Home for sick and elderly
sisters

Presentation Convent, Dungarvan,
Co Waterford
Tel 058-41359
Local Leader: Sr Perpetua Gannon
Community: 9
Primary School

Presentation Sisters, 158 Larchville,
Waterford
Tel 051-55496
Contact: Sr de Lourdes Breen
Community: 3

Presentation Sisters, 81 Treacy Park,
Carrick-on-Suir,Co Tipperary
Contact: Sr Veronica Casey
Community: 2
Primary School

Presentation Sisters,
50 Cathal Brugha Place,
Dungarvan, Co Waterford
Tel 058-45582
Community: 3

11 Convent Lodge, Mitchell Street,
Dungarvan, Co Waterford
Contact: Sr Martina O'Callaghan

Apartment 3, The Cloisters,
John's Hill, Waterford
Contact: Sr Catherine Mooney

RELIGIOUS SISTERS OF CHARITY
Star of the Sea,
Tramore, Co Waterford
Tel 051-381308
Various apostolic ministries

Comeragh Lodge,
St Patrick's Road,
Silver Springs, Clonmel,
Co Tipperary
Tel 052-6121092
Various apostolic ministries

ROSMINIANS (SISTERS OF PROVIDENCE)
Rosminian Convent,
Killea, Dunmore East, Co Waterford
Tel 051-383491

ST JOHN OF GOD SISTERS
8 The Cloisters, John's Hill,
Waterford
Tel 051-874370
Resident Leader: Sr Una Guing
Community: 9
Primary School. Pupils: 344

St John of God Sisters,
41 Grange Cove, Waterford
Tel 051-374397
Community: 4

ST JOSEPH OF CLUNY SISTERS
Woodlock, Portlaw, Waterford
Tel 051-387216
Superior: Sr Josephine Glynn
Community: 15

URSULINES
Ursuline Convent, Waterford
Tel 051-874068
Email ursuline94@eircom.net
Local Leader: Sr Margaret Breen
Community: 14
Primary School
Tel 051 873788/852855 Fax 051-852855
Secondary School
Tel 051-876121 Fax 051-879022

18 Shannon Drive, Avondale, Waterford
Tel 051-854680
Email ursulinesisterswd@eircom.net
Community: 2

1 St Anne's, Ursuline Court, Waterford
Tel 051-857015
Email onestannes@eircom.net
Community: 2

EDUCATIONAL INSTITUTIONS

EDMUND RICE SCHOOLS TRUST
Christian Brothers School,
Carrick-on-Suir, Co Tipperary
Primary School
Tel 051-641333
Principal: Mr Pat Mansell
Secondary School
Tel 051-640512 Fax 051-640522
Email cbscus@eircom.net
Principal: Mr William O'Farrell

Christian Brothers High School,
Kickham Street, Clonmel, Co Tipperary
Tel 052-24459 Fax 052-25320
Email ardscoilnamb@eircom.net
Principal: Mr S. Bannon

Dungarvan, Co Waterford
Secondary School
Principal: Mr John Murphy
Tel 058-41185/41955 Fax 058-48512
Email gpower@cablesurf.com

Blackwater Community School
Tel 055-53620/54349 Fax 058-53813
Principal: Mr Denis Ring

Christian Brothers Secondary School,
Tramore, Co Waterford
Principal: Mr Pat McEvoy
Tel 051-386766/386560
Fax 051-3811492
Email office@cbstramore.com
Website www.cbstramore.com

Cnoc Síon Primary School,
Barrack Street, Waterford
Tel 051-377947 Fax 051-358304
Email cnocsion.ias@eircom.net
Principal: Mr Michael Walsh

Cnoc Síon Secondary School,
Barrack Street, Waterford
Tel 051-377378/376309 Fax 051-376468
Staff Tel 051-877456
Email mtsion.ias@eircom.net
Principal: Mr John McArdle

Waterpark College Secondary School
Park Road, Waterford
Tel 051-874445/893101 Fax 051-874040
Staff Tel 051-877456
Email waterparkcollege@eirccom.net
Website www.waterparkcollege.com
Principal: Mr T. Beecher

ST JOHN'S
PASTORAL CENTRE

St John's Pastoral Centre
John's Hill, Waterford
Tel 051-874199 Fax 051-843107
Email stjohnspastoralcentre@eircom.net
Administrator: Ms Mary Dee

CHARITABLE AND OTHER
SOCIETIES

Apostolic Work Society
President of Diocesan Council
Mrs Nancy Kenny
10 Powerstown Road, Clonmel,
Co Tipperary
Secretary: Sr Annunciata Butler
Ballyragget, Co Kilkenny
Centres at Dungarvan, Cappoquin,
Carrick-on-Suir, Kilmacthomas, Dunmore
East, Clogheen, Clonmel

Hostels
Men's Hostel, Ozanam House,
Lady Lane, Waterford
(St Vincent de Paul)

PERSONAL PRELATURES

Prelature of the Holy Cross and Opus Dei

Founded by Saint Josemaría Escrivá in 1928, it was erected as a Personal Prelature (cf CIC 294-297) in 1982, and is constituted by the Prelate (Bishop Javier Echevarría), incardinated clergy, and lay people. Members try to promote a deep consciousness of the universal call to holiness and apostolate in all sectors of society and, more specifically, an awareness of the sanctifying value of ordinary work.

Information Office:
10 Hume Street, Dublin 2
Tel 01-6614949

Website www.opusdei.ie
Email info@opusdei.ie

Vicar for Ireland
Rt Rev Robert Bucciarelli DD
Harvieston,
Cunningham Road, Dalkey,
Co Dublin
Tel 01-2859877
Fax 01-2305059

Archdiocese of Dublin
Harvieston, Cunningham Road,
Dalkey, Co Dublin
Tel 01-2859877
Rt Rev Robert Bucciarelli
Rev Gavan Jennings
Rev Patrick Gorevan
Rev Francis Planell

30 Knapton Road,
Dun Laoghaire, Co Dublin
Tel 01-2804353
Rev Daniel Cummings
Rev Thomas McGovern

Cleraun Study Centre, 90 Foster Avenue,
Mount Merrion, Co Dublin
Tel 01-2881734
Rev James Gavigan
Rev Martin Hannon

Nullamore, Richmond Avenue South,
Dublin 6
Tel 01-4971239
Rev Philip Griffin
Rev Donncha Ó hAodha

Ely University Centre
10 Hume Street, Dublin 2
Tel 01-6767420
Rev Thomas Dowd
Rev Brendan O'Connor

Archdiocese of Tuam
Ballyglunin Park Conference Centre,
Tuam, Co Galway
Tel 093-41423
Rev Walter Macken, Chaplain

Diocese of Galway
Gort Ard University Residence,
Rockbarton North, Galway
Tel 091-523846
Rev Walter Macken
Rev Oliver Powell

Diocese of Limerick
Castleville Study Centre,
Golf Links Road, Castletroy, Limerick
Tel 061-331223
Rev Brian McCarthy

Diocese of Meath
Lismullin Conference Centre
Navan, Co Meath
Tel 046-9026936
Rev James Gavigan, Chaplain

RELIGIOUS ORDERS AND CONGREGATIONS

MALE RELIGIOUS

AUGUSTINIANS (OSA)
Irish Province
www.augustinians.ie

Archdiocese of Dublin

St Augustine's
Taylor's Lane,
Ballyboden, Dublin 16
Tel 01-4241000
Fax 01-4939915

Provincial: Rev Gerry Horan
Tel 01-4241030
Fax 01-4932457
Email osaprov@eircom.net
Secretary: Tel 01-4241040
Email
hibprovsec@irishbroadband.net
Prior: Rev John Lyng
(Provincial Secretary)
Bursar: Rev Michael Brennock

Rev John Bresnan
Rev Andrew Caples
Rev Gervase Corcoran
Rev Gabriel Daly
Rev Pádraig Daly
(PP Ballyboden)
Rev John Doran
Rev Patrick Farrell
Rev Noel Hession
Rev Henry Leahy
Rev David Kelly
Rev Nicholas O'Brien
Rev John Williams

St John's Priory
Thomas Street, Dublin 8
Tel 01-6770393/0415/0601
Fax 01-6713102 (Mission Office)
Fax 01-6770423 (House)

Prior: Rev Tony Egan
Bursar: Rev Michael O'Sullivan
Sub-Prior: Rev Giles O'Halloran

Rev Declan Brennan (PP Meath St)
Rev Niall Coghlan (CC Meath St)
Rev Thomas Cooney
Rev Matthew Curran
Rev Finbarr Fortune
Rev Pat Gayer
Rev Peter Haughey
Rev John Hughes
Rev Nicholas Kearny
Rev Joseph Kirwan

Rev Kevin McManus
Rev Michael Mernagh
Rev Martin Nolan
Rev Louis O'Donnell
Rev Charles O'Reilly
Rev Brendan Quirke
Rev Bernard Twomey

Meath Street Parish
Dublin 8
Tel 01-4543356
Fax 01-4738303

No Resident Community

Augustinian Retreat Centre
Orlagh Retreat Centre,
Old Court Road, Dublin 16
Tel 01-4930932/4933315/
4931163 Fax 01-4930987
Email orlagh@augustinians.ie
www.augustinians.ie/orlagh

Prior: Rev John Byrne
Bursar: Rev Columba Higgins

Rev Jude King
Rev Kieran O'Mahony

Rivermount Parish
Parochial House,
5 St Helena's Drive, Dublin 11
Tel 01-8343444/8343722
Fax 01-8642192

Superior: Rev Noel Hession
Very Rev Seamus Ahearne PP
Bursar: Rev Paddy O'Reilly CC

Archdiocese of Armagh

St Augustine's Priory
Shop Street,
Drogheda, Co Louth
Tel 041-9838409
Fax 041-9831847

Prior: Rev Richard Goode
Sub-Prior:
Rev Malachy Loughran

Bursar:
Rev Ignatius O'Donovan

Archdiocese of Cashel and Diocese of Emly

The Abbey
Fethard, Co Tipperary
Tel 052-31273

Prior: Rev Martin Crean
Sub-Prior: Rev John Meagher

Rev Gerard Horan *(Provincial)*
Rev Timothy Walsh

Diocese of Cork & Ross

St Augustine's Priory
Washington Street, Cork
Tel 021-275398/270410
Fax 021-275381

Prior: Rev Pat Moran
Bursar: Rev Francis Aherne

Rev Michael Boyle
Rev Sean Dowling
Rev James Furlong
Rev Michael Leahy
Rev James Maguire
Rev Michael O'Regan
Rev John O'Sullivan

Diocese of Ferns

St Augustine's Priory
Grantstown, New Ross,
Co Wexford
Tel 051-561119

Rev Aidan O'Leary
Priest-in-residence

**St Augustine's Priory
(Residence)**
New Ross, Co Wexford
Tel 051-421237

Prior: Rev Michael Collender
Sub-Prior
Rev Vincent McCarthy
Bursar: Rev Philip Kelly
School Principal
Rev John Hennebry

Rev Michael Collender
Rev Seán Mac Gearailt
Rev Henry MacNamara
Rev Vincent McCarthy
Rev Ben O'Brien
Rev Aidan O'Leary
Rev John Power

Good Counsel College
New Ross, Co Wexford
Tel 051-421663/421909
Fax 051-421909

No Resident Community

Diocese of Galway

St Augustine's Priory
Galway
Tel 091-562524
Fax 091-564378

Prior: Rev Desmond Foley
Sub-Prior: Rev Richard Lyng PP

Rev John Whelan

Diocese of Limerick

St Augustine's Priory
O'Connell Street, Limerick
Tel 061-415374

Prior: Rev Frank Sexton
Bursar: Rev Jeremiah Hickey

Rev Michael Danaher
Rev Leo O'Sullivan
Rev William Prendiville
Rev Brendan Quirke
Rev Liam Ryan
Rev Frank Sexton

Diocese of Waterford & Lismore

St Augustine's College
Dungarvan, Co Waterford
Tel 058-41140/41152
Fax 058-41152

No Resident Community

Duckspool House
(Retirement Community)
Abbeyside, Dungarvan,
Co Waterford
Tel 058-23784

Prior: Rev Columba O'Donnell
Bursar: Rev Joseph Crean

Rev Patrick Lennon
Rev Kieran O'Brien
Rev Columba O'Connor
Rev John Walsh

St Augustine's Priory
Dungarvan, Co Waterford
Tel 058-41136 Fax 058-44534

Prior: Rev Seamus Humphries
Sub-Prior: Rev Finbar Spring
Bursar: Rev David Slater

Rev Matthew Cooney
Rev Flor O'Callaghan

Rome

St Patrick's College and Church
Via Piemonte 60,
00187 Rome, Italy
Tel 00396-4203121
Fax 00396-4231236
Email st.patricks@rm.nettuno.it

Prior: Rev James Downey
Sub-Prior: Vacant
Bursar & Church Rector
Rev Tony Finn

Rev Declan Deasy

The Irish Province also has missions in Ecuador, Kenya and Nigeria.

Irish Augustinian Personnel on Other Assignments

Rev Ailbe Brennan (San Bernardino, CA)
Rev David Crean (San Bernardino, CA)
Rev Paul Flynn (Orange, CA)
Rev Declan Fogarty (San Bernardino, CA)
Rev John Grace (Orange, CA)
Rev Greg Howard (Cork & Ross)
Rev Paul O'Brien (Canada)
Rev Brian O'Sullivan (Rome)

BENEDICTINES (OSB)

Archdiocese of Cashel and Diocese of Emly

Attached to the Benedictine Congregation of the Annunciation, Belgium.

Glenstal Abbey
Murroe, Co Limerick
Tel 061-386103
Fax 061-386328
Email monks@glenstal.org

Abbot: Right Rev Dom Mark Patrick Hederman
Abbot 1992-2008
Right Rev Dom Christopher Dillon
Abbot 1980-92
Right Rev Dom Celestine Cullen
Prior & Novice Master
Very Rev Brendan Coffey
Headmaster
Br Martin Browne
Guestmaster
Rev Christopher Dillon
Sub-Prior
Very Rev Senan Furlong

Director of Associates
Rev David Conlon

Rev Anselm Barry
Br Cuthbert Brennan
Rev Gregory Collins
Br Matthew Corkery
Rev Alan Crawford
Rev Bonaventure Dunne
Rev William Fennelly
Br Ciarán Forbes
Rev Basil Forde
Br Denis Hooper
Br Anselm Hurt
Br Anthony Keane
Br Cyprian Love
Rev Fintan Lyons
Rev Columba McCann
Rev Joseph McGilloway
Br Timothy McGrath
Rev Francis McHenry
Rev James McMahon

Rev Luke Macnamara
Rev Brian Murphy
Rev Placid Murray
Rev Paul Nash
Rev Andrew Nugent
Rev John O'Callaghan
Br Colmán Ó Clabaigh
Br Michael O'Connor
Br Cillian Ó Sé
Rev Henry O'Shea
Rev Simon Sleeman
Rev Mark Tierney
Rev Philip Tierney
Rev Ambrose Tinsley

Diocese of Dromore

Attached to the Benedictine congregation of St Mary of Monte Oliveto.

Benedictine Monks
Holy Cross Monastery,
119 Kilbroney Road,
Rostrevor, Co Down BT34 3BN
Tel 028-41739979
Fax 028-41739978
Email benedictinemonks@btinternet.com
Website www.benedictinemonks.co.uk

Superior
Very Rev Dom Mark-Ephrem M. Nolan

Rev D. Eric M. Loisel
Rev D. Thierry M. Marteaux
D. Benoît M. Charlet
D. Pascal M. Jouy
D. Joshua M. Domenzain Canul

BLESSED SACRAMENT CONGREGATION (SSS)

Provincial
Rev Patrick Costello
Blessed Sacrament Chapel
20 Bachelors Walk, Dublin 1
Tel 01-8724597
Fax 01-8724724
Email pjcostello@aol.com

Archdiocese of Dublin

Blessed Sacrament Chapel
20 Bachelors Walk, Dublin 1
Tel 01-8724597
Fax 01-8724724
Email sssdublin@eircom.net

Superior
Rev James Campbell

Rev Patrick Costello
Br Joseph Donegan
Rev Renato Esoy
Rev James Hegarty
Br Timothy McLoughlin
Br Andrew McTeigue
Rev Maurice Rouleau

CAMILLIANS (MI)
Order of St Camillus

Anglo-Irish Province

Archdiocese of Dublin

St Camillus
South Hill Avenue,
Blackrock, Co Dublin
Tel 01-2882873
Fax 01-2833380

Superior: Rev Denis Sandham
(Chaplain to Beaumont Hospital)

Br Gabriel Brady
Rev Sean Bredin
Rev Pat O'Brien *(Chaplain to St Luke's Hospital)*

St Camillus
4 St Vincent Street North,
Dublin 7
Tel 01-8300365 (residence)
Tel 01-8301122 (Mater Hospital)

Superior & Provincial
Rev Stephen Forster

Rev Martin Geraghty *(Chaplain to Connolly Memorial Hospital, Blanchardstown)*
Rev Stephen Forster
(Chaplain to Mater Hospital)

Diocese of Meath

St Camillus
Killucan, Co Westmeath
Tel 044-74196 (nursing centre)
Tel 044-74115 (community)
Fax 044-74309

Superior: Rev Frank Monks
Email frankmonks@eircom.ne

Rev Noel Carrigg
Rev Andrew Carroll
Rev Brendan Conway
Rev Nik Houlihan
Br Augustine McCormack
Rev P. McKenna
Br John O'Brien

CAPUCHINS (OFM Cap)

Province of Ireland

Includes ten friaries in Ireland, three friaries in South Korea and New Zealand and Vice-Provinces in South Africa and Zambia.

Archdiocese of Dublin

Provincial Office
12 Halston Street, Dublin 7
Tel 01-8733205
Fax 01-8730294
Email capcurirl@eircom.net

Provincial Minister
Very Rev Terence Harrington

Rev Anthony Boran
Rev Patrick Cleary
Rev Christopher Twomey

Capuchin Friary
Church Street, Dublin 7
Tel 01-8730599
Fax 01-8730250

Guardian: Rev Desmond McNaboe (PP, Halston Street Parish)
Vicar: Rev Bernard McAllister

Rev Leonard Coughlan
Rev Kevin Crowley
Rev Richard Hendrick (Curate, Halston Street Parish)
Rev Sean Kelly
Rev Paul Murphy
Rev Pádraig Ó Cuill
Rev Piaras Ó Dúill
Rev Bruno McKnight
Rev Alphonsus Ryan

Capuchin Friary
Station Road,
Raheny, Dublin 5
Tel 01-8313886
Fax 01-8511498

Guardian: Rev Sean Donohoe
Vicar: Rev Eustace McSweeney

Rev Oliver Brady
Rev Simeon Breen
Rev Adrian Curran
Rev Tom Forde
Rev Joe Gallagher

Capuchin Friary
Clonshaugh Drive,
Priorswood, Dublin 17
Tel 01-8474469
Fax 01-8487296

Guardian
Rev Angelus O'Neill (PP, St Francis of Assisi Parish)

Rev Patrick Flynn (Curate, St Francis of Assisi Parish)
Rev Dan Joe O'Mahony
Rev Bill Ryan
Rev Bryan Shortall

Diocese of Cork & Ross

Holy Trinity
Fr Mathew Quay, Cork
Tel 021-4270827
Fax 021-4270829

Guardian: Rev Dermot Lynch
Vicar: Rev Silvester O'Flynn

Rev Edwin Flynn
Rev Ronan Herlihy
Rev John Hickey
Rev Joe Nagle
Rev Edward Neville

Allianz (il)

Rev Brendan O'Mahony
Rev Kenneth Reynolds
Rev Carthage Ruth
Rev Aidan Vaughan

St Francis Capuchin Friary
Rochestown, Co Cork
Tel 021-4896244
Fax 021-4895915

Guardian: Rev Paul O'Donovan
Vicar: Rev Benjamin O'Connell

Rev Paul Barrett
Br Felix Carroll
Br Albert Cooney
Rev Hugh Davis
Rev Jeremy Heneghan
Rev Berchmans McCarthy
Rev Sylvius McCarthy
Rev Anthony O'Keeffe
Rev Jack Twomey

St Francis Capuchin Franciscan College
Rochestown, Co Cork
Tel 021-4891417
Fax 021-4361254

Principal
Mr Diarmaid Ó Mathúna

Capuchin Parochial House Parish of the Ascension
Gurranabraher, Cork
Tel 021-4303655
Fax 021-4303658

Guardian: Rev John Manley
Vicar: Rev Kevin Kiernan

Rev Kiran Shorten (PP)

Diocese of Kildare & Leighlin

St Anthony's Capuchin Friary
43 Dublin Street, Carlow
Tel 059-9142543
Fax 059-9142030

Guardian: Br John Wright
Vicar: Rev Michael Duffy

Rev Dominic S. Boland
Rev Alexius Healy
Rev Leo McAuliffe

Diocese of Ossory

Capuchin Friary
Friary Street, Kilkenny
Tel 056-7721439
Fax 056-7722025

Guardian
Rev Benignus Buckley
Vicar: Rev James Harrington

Rev Philip Connor
Rev Ignatius Galvin
Rev Flannan Lynch
Rev Paul Tapley
Rev Michael Tobin
Rev Philip Tobin

Diocese of Raphoe

Capuchin Friary
Ard Mhuire, Creeslough,
Letterkenny, Co Donegal
Tel 074-9138005
Fax 074-9138371

Guardian: Rev Donal Sweeney
Vicar: Rev Vianney Holmes

Rev Brian Browne
Rev Roch Bennett
Rev Mark Coyle
Rev Edward Dunne
Rev Michael Murphy
Rev Owen O'Sullivan
Rev James Ryan
Rev Charles Stewart

New Zealand

Holy Cross Friary & Vice-Provincial Residence
PO Box 21082, Henderson,
Auckland 8, New Zealand
Tel 0064-9-8388663
Fax 0064-9-8387114
Email capauck@ihug.co.nz

Korea

Capuchin Friars Minor
Hyochang-Dong 5-40,
Yong San-Gu, Seoul,
South Korea 140-120
Tel 0082-2-7015727
Fax 0082-2-7176128

Vice-Province of Zambia

Vice Provincialate
PO Box 33705,
Lusaka, Zambia
Tel 00260-1250205
Fax 00260-1252828

Vice-Province of South Africa

Vice-Provincialate
PO Box 118, Howard Place 7450,
South Africa
Tel 00272-16370026
Fax 00272-16370014

For further details concerning
the missions contact:
Capuchin Mission Office,
Church Street, Dublin 7
Tel 01-8731022
Fax 01-8740478

CARMELITES (OCARM)

Irish Province

Archdiocese of Dublin

Provincial Office and Carmelite Community
Gort Muire, Ballinteer,
Dublin 16
Tel 01-2984014
Fax 01-2987221

Provincial
Very Rev Martin Kilmurray
Email mkilmurray@eircom.net
Assistant Provincial
Rev Patrick Staunton
Email
pstaunton@gortmuire.com

Prior/Bursar: Rev Martin Baxter
Sub-Prior: Rev Simon Nolan

Rev Albert Breen
Rev Michael Cremin
Rev PJ Cunningham
David Eivers
Rev Liam Fennell
Rev Patrick Gallagher
Rev Dermot Kelly
Rev Brian Kiernan
Rev William Langan
Rev Paul McChrystal
Rev Anthony McKinney
Rev Joseph Mothersill
Neil Scott
David Twohig
Ged Walsh
Rev Edward Ward

Whitefriar Street Church
56 Aungier Street, Dublin 2
Tel 01-4758821
Fax 01-4758825
Email whitefriars@eircom.net

Prior: Rev David Weakliam
Sub-Prior: Rev Bernard Murphy
PP and Director of Whitefriar
Street Community Centre
Rev Charles Hoey

Rev Daniel Callaghan
Rev Christopher Conroy
Rev Sean Coughlan
Rev Christopher Crowley
Rev Patrick (Alan) Fitzpatrick
Rev Patrick Graham
Rev Thomas Higgins
Rev Paul Hughes
Rev Desmond Kelly CC
Rev Robert Manik
Rev Patick Mullins
Rev Jarlath O'Hea
Rev Fergus O'Loan

Terenure College
Terenure, Dublin 6W
Tel 01-4904621
Fax 01-4902403
Email admin@terenurecollege.ie

Prior/Manager
Rev Michael Troy
Sub-Prior: Rev Eoin Moore
Principal Senior School
Rev Eanna Ó hÓbáin
Principal Junior School
Rev Michael Troy

Rev P. J. Breen
Rev Richard Byrne
Rev Desmond Flanagan
Rev John Madden
Rev Benedict O'Callaghan
Rev Christopher O'Donnell

Parish of the Nativity of Our Lord
The Presbytery, Montrose Park,
Beaumont, Dublin 5
Tel 01-8477740/8476359
Fax 01-8473209
Email
beaumont@irishcarmelites.com

Parish Priest/Prior
Rev Francis O'Gara

Rev Donal Byrne CC
Rev Brian McKay
Rev Martin Parokkaran

St Colmcille's
The Presbytery, Idrone Avenue,
Knocklyon, Dublin 16
Tel 01-4941204/4944986
Fax 01-4946842
Email the presbytery@
knocklyonparish.com

Parish Priest/Prior
Rev James Murray

Rev Seán Ford CC
Rev Michael Morrissey CC

Diocese of Cork & Ross

Carmelite Friary
Kinsale, Co Cork
Tel 021-772138
Email
kinsale@irishcarmelites.com

Prior: Rev Míceál O'Neill
Bursar: Rev Frank McAleese

Rev Maurice Barry
Rev Phiip Brennan
Rev Stan Hession
Rev Mariusz Placek

Diocese of Kildare & Leighlin

Carmelite Priory
White Abbey, Co Kildare
Tel 045-521391 Fax 045-522318
Email whiteabbey@eircom.net

Prior: Rev Anthony McDonald
Bursar: Rev Frederick Lally

Rev John Lawler
Rev Aloysius Ryan
Rev Patrick Smyth

Diocese of Meath

Carmelite Priory
Moate, Co Westmeath
Tel 090-6481160/6481398
Fax 090-6481879
Email
carmelitemoate@eircom.net

Prior: Rev Martin Ryan
Sub-Prior
Rev Jaison Kuthanapillil
Bursar: Rev Brendan O'Reilly

Rev John Mulcahy
Rev Andrew O'Reilly

Diocese of Ossory

**Carmelite Priory
(Knocktopher/Ballyhale)**
Knocktopher, Co Kilkenny
Tel 056-7768675
Fax 056-7768237
Email knockcar@indigo.ie

Prior/Parish Priest
Rev Peter Kehoe
Bursar: Rev Laurence Lynch

Rev Fintan Burke
Rev Aidan McLoughlin

CARMELITES (OCD)

Anglo-Irish Province

The Province has five
communities in Ireland and
thirteen overseas including
five in Nigeria.

Provincial: Rev James Noonan
53 Marlborough Road,
Donnybrook, Dublin 4
Tel 01-6617163/6601832
Fax 01-6683752
Email jnoonan@ocd.ie
Website www.ocd.ie

Archdiocese of Dublin

St Teresa's
Clarendon Street, Dublin 2
Tel 01-6718466/6718127
Fax 01-6718462

Prior: Rev David Donnellan
Email stteresa@ocd.ie

Rev Michael Brown
Rev Michael Coen
Rev William Finn
Rev Joe Glynn
Rev Desmond McCaffrey
Rev Paul Sullivan
Br Patrick Walsh

Avila
Bloomfield Avenue,
Morehampton Road, Dublin 4
Tel 01-6430200
Fax 01-6430281
Email avila@ocd.ie

Prior
Rev Michael MacLaifeartaigh

Rev Joseph Birmingham
Rev Stanislaus Callanan
Rev Máirtín Ó Conaire
Rev Vincent O'Hara
Rev Stephen Ugwu

53/55 Marlborough Road,
Dublin 4
Tel 01-6601832

Prior: Rev Herman Doolan

Rev Terence Carey
Rev Liam S. Ó Bréartúin
Rev Nicholas Madden

St Joseph's
Berkeley Road, Dublin 7
Tel 01-8306356/8306336
Fax 01-8304681

Prior
Rev Christopher Clarke PP

Rev Peter Cryan
Rev Patrick Keenan CC
Br Noel O'Connor
Rev Richard Young

Diocese of Clonfert

The Abbey
Loughrea, Co Galway
Tel 091-841209
Fax 091-842343

Prior: Rev Liam Finnerty

Rev Patrick Beecher
Rev Bernard Cuffe
Rev Cronan Glynn
Rev Ambrose McNamee
Rev Finian Monahan
Rev Francis Quinn
Rev Tom Shanahan

Diocese of Derry

St Joseph's Carmelite
Retreat Centre
Termonbacca,
Derry BT48 9XE
Tel 028-71262512
Fax 028-71373589

Prior: Rev Jeremiah Fitzpatrick

Rev Sean Conlon
Rev Louis Gallagher
Rev Stephen McKeogh
Rev John McNamara

CISTERCIAN ORDER (OCSO)

The mother house of the
Cistercian Order is the Arch-
abbey of Cîteaux, Côte d'Or,
France.

Archdiocese of Armagh

Mellifont Abbey
Collon, Co Louth
Tel 041-9826103
Fax 041-9826713
Email
mellifontabbey@eircom.net

Abbot
Rt Rev Augustine McGregor
Prior
Rev Laurence McDermott
Sub-Prior
Br Joseph Ryan

Br Brian Berkeley
Rev Dom Bernard Boyle
Br Andrew Considine

Rev William Cullinan
Br Brendan Garry
Br Thomas Maher
Br Malachy Mallon
Rev Alphonsus O'Connor
Br Bernard Purcell
Rev Andrew Ward

Archdiocese of Dublin

Bolton Abbey
Moone, Co Kildare
Tel 059-8624102
Fax 059-8624309
Email info@boltonabbey.ie
Website www.boltonabbey.ie

Abbot
Rt Rev Dom Peter Garvey
Guestmaster
Rev Eoin de Bhaldraithe
Novice Director
Rev Ambrose Farrington

Br Christopher Burke
Rev Martin Garry
Br Alberic Turner
Br Anthony Jones
Br John O'Byrne
Br Brian O'Dowd
Br Francis McLean
Rev Michael Ryan

Diocese of Down & Connor

Our Lady of Bethlehem Abbey
11 Ballymena Road,
Portglenone, Ballymena,
Co Antrim BT44 8BL
Tel 028-25821211
Fax 028-25822795
Email kelly@unite.net
Website
www.bethlehem-abbey.org.uk

Abbot
Rt Rev Dom Celsus Kelly
Email kelly@unite.net

Retired Abbot
Rt Rev Dom Aengus Dunphy
Prior: Rev Martin Dowley
Sub-Prior: Rev Philip Scott

Rev Herman Hickey
Br Michael McCourt
Br Finbar McLoughlin
Rev Aelred Magee
Rev Francis Morgan
Br Brendan Murphy
Rev Chrysostom O'Connell
Br Veder O'Kane
Br Columba O'Neill
Rev Finnian Owens
Br Joseph Skehan

Diocese of Killaloe

Mount Saint Joseph Abbey
Roscrea, Co Tipperary
Tel 0505-25600
Fax 0505-25610
Email info@msjroscrea.ie

Abbot
Rt Rev Dom Richard Purcell
Prior
Rev Dom Laurence Walsh
Abbot Emeritus
Dom Colmcille O'Toole
Abbot Emeritus
Rt Rev Dom Kevin Daly

Rev Eanna Henderson
Rev Flannan Hogan
Rev Robert Kelly
Rev Nivard Kinsella
Br Niall Maguire
Rev Gabriel McCarthy
Br John McDonnell
Br Martin McDonnell
Rev Bonaventure Melvin
Br Laurence Molloy
Rev Anthony O'Brien
Rev Liam O'Connor
Rev Ciaran Ó Sabhaois
Br Malachy Thompson
Br Dominic Tobin
Rev Laserian Tobin
Br Oliver Tyrrell

Diocese of Waterford & Lismore

Mount Melleray Abbey
Cappoquin,
Co Waterford
Tel 058-54404
Fax 058-52140
Email mountmellerayabbey@
eircom.net

Superior: Rev Michael Ahern
Prior: Br Boniface McGinley
Sub-Prior: Rev Francis Carton

Br Camillus Canning
Br Peter Cassidy
Rev Denis Collins
Br Edmond Costin
Rev Bonaventure Cumiskey
Br Donal Davis
Br John Dineen
Rev Kevin Fogarty
Rev Ignatius Hahessy
Rev Columban Heaney
Rev Cornelius Justice
Br Denis Lynch
Rev Aodhán McDunphy
Br Declan Murphy
Rev Athanasius O'Brien
Rev Alphonsus O'Connell
Br Raphael Odukwe
Rev Denis Luke O Hanlon
Rev Celestine O'Leary
Rev Uinsean O Maidín
Rev Declan O'Rourke
Rev Patrick Ryan
Br Malachy Sutton

Allianz (ⅱ)

COMBONI MISSIONARIES (MCCJ)

Verona Fathers

Provincial: Rev Paul Felix
Comboni Missionaries,
London Road, Sunningdale,
Berks SL5 OJY, UK

Archdiocese of Dublin

8 Clontarf Road
Clontarf, Dublin 3
Tel/Fax 01-8330051
Email
combonimission@eircom.net

Superior
Awaiting appointment

Rev Antonio Benetti
Rev Patrick Burns

Congregation of the Sacred Hearts of Jesus and Mary (SSCC)

Sacred Hearts Community

Archdiocese of Dublin

Provincialate
Coudrin House,
27 Northbrook Road, Dublin 6
Tel 01-6604898 (Provincialate)
Email ssccdublin@eircom.net
Tel 01-6686584/01-6671513
(Community)
Fax 01-6608341
Website
www.sacredhearts.ie

Provincial
Very Rev Michael Ruddy
Email mikeruddy@eircom.net
Provincial Secretary
Sheila O'Dowd

Rev Patrick Bradley
Email pb2004@eircom.net
Most Rev Brendan Comiskey DD
Rev George Foley
Rev Michael F. Foley
Email
michaelffoley@eircom.net
Br Anthony McMorrow
Rev Andy Wafer
Email andywafer@eircom.net

Sacred Heart Presbytery
St John's Drive, Clondalkin,
Dublin 22
Tel 01-4570032

Rev Eamon Aylward
Email eamonmoz@yahoo.com
Very Rev Michael Ruddy
Email mikeruddy@eircom.net

Diocese of Clogher

Cootehill
Co Cavan
Tel 049-5552188

Br Harry O'Gara
Rev Jerry White
Email jerrysscc@eircom.net

St Mary's
Clontibret, Co Monaghan
Tel 047-80631

Rev Michael Gilsenan
Email gilsenaeve@eircom.net

DIVINE WORD MISSIONARIES (SVD)

Irish & British Province

The Irish and British Province
of the Society is independent.
When members are assigned
to work in the missions, they
automatically become
members of the territory to
which they are assigned and
are no longer members of the
Irish British Province.

Archdiocese of Dublin

3 Pembroke Road,
Dublin 4
Tel 01-6680904
Praeses: Rev Albert Escoto
Email
albert_escoto2000@yahoo.com

Rev Pat Claffey
Rev Shane FitzGerald
Rev Gaspard Habara

133 North Circular Road,
Dublin 7
Tel 01-8386743
Fax 01-8686257
Praeses: Rev John Feighery

Provincial: Rev Brian O'Reilly
Email
provincial@svdireland.com

Rev Henry Barlage
Rev Patrick Byrne
Rev Gerald Kennedy
Rev Patrick Lee
Rev John Owen
Rev Anthony O'Riordan
Rev Finbarr Tracey

City Quay
Immaculate Heart of Mary
City Quay, Dublin 2
Tel 01-6773073
Email
stjohnsp@gofree.indigo.ie

Rev Paul St John
(administrator)
Br Michael Ancheta

Maynooth
Co Kildare
Tel 01-6286391/2
Fax 01-6289184
Email rector@svdireland.com

Rector: Rev Peter Madden

Rev Brendan Casey
Rev Daniel Daly
Rev Liam Dunne
(Mission Procurator)
Rev Tadeusz Durajcyk
Rev Richard Flannagan
Br Paul Hurley
Rev Francis Kom
Rev George Millar
Br Patrick Murphy
Rev Anil Thekkedathu Paul
Rev Jega Susai
Rev Vincent Twomey
(Editor of Word Magazine)
Rev Jim Perry

Divine Word School of English
Tel 01-6290851 Fax 01-6289748
Email dwse@eircom.net

Director
Rev Richard Flannagan

Diocese of Elphin

Donamon Castle
Roscommon
Tel 090-6662222
Fax 090-6662511
Email gearoidmccarthy@o2.ie

Rector: Rev Gerard McCarthy
Provincial Treasurer
Rev Thomas Cahill

Rev Michael Barry
Rev Tony Coote
Rev Norman Davitt
Br Brendan Fahey
Rev Richard Flanagan
Rev Charles Guthrie
Rev Michael Joyce
Rev Kevin Keenan
Rev Richard Kelly
Rev Marek Kosciolek
Rev Gerry Lanigan
Rev Peter Maloney
Rev Francis Mansfield
Rev Michael Reddan
Rev Noel S. Ruane
Rev Krzysztof Sikora

British District

London
8 Teignmouth Road,
London, NW2 4HN
Tel 020-84528430

Praeses: Fr Michael Egan

Rev Kieran FitzHarris
Rev Martin McPake
Rev Kevin O'Toole
Rev Kazimierz Szalaj

Liverpool
St Gregory's House,
21 Halewood Road,
Liverpool 125 3PH
Tel 0151-4282860

Praeses: Rev Brian Gilmore

Rev Oliver O'Connor
Rev Thomas Morris

Bristol
Sr Mary-on-the-Quay
Presbytery, 20 Colston Street,
Bristol BS1 5AE
Tel 0117-9264702

Parish Priest
Rev Nikodemus Lobo Ratu

Rev John Bettison
Rev Rudy Montadas

DOMINICAN ORDER (OP)

Order of Preachers

Irish Province

Archdiocese of Dublin

Provincial Office
St Mary's, Tallaght,
Dublin 24
Tel 01-4048118/4048115
Fax 01-4515584
Email
provincialop@eircom.net

Provincial
Very Rev Pat Lucey
*Provincial Bursar and
Provincial Secretary*
Rev Gregory Carroll

Dominican Community
St Mary's Priory
Tallaght, Dublin 24
Tel 01-4048100
Parish 01-4048188
Fax 01-4596784
Email gerard.norton@
dominicanstallaght.org
Retreat House
Tel 01-4048189/8123/8191
Fax 01-4596080
Email domretreat@eircom.net

Prior
Very Rev Gerard Norton

Rev Peter Evans
Rev Wilfrid Harrington
Rev Gabriel Harty
Rev Thomas McInerney
Rev Hugh Fenning
Rev Joseph Kavanagh

Rev Philip Gleeson
Rev Leonard Perrem
Rev Donagh O'Shea
Rev Thomas O'Flynn
Rev Brian McKevitt
Br Martin Cogan
Rev Donal Roche
Br Eamonn Moran
Br Michael Neenan
Rev Marcin Lisak
Rev Dermot Brennan
Br James Ryan

St Saviour's
Upper Dorset Street,
Dublin 1
Tel 01-8897610
Fax 01-8734003
Email stsaviours@eircom.net

Prior
Very Rev Anthony Morris

Rev Clement Greenan
Rev Cyprian Candon
Rev Edward Foley
Rev Liam Walsh
Rev Diarmuid Clifford
Rev Thomas Jordan
Rev Martin Boyle
Very Rev Adrian Farrelly PP
Rev Nelson Medina
Rev Joseph Dineen
Rev John Harris
Rev Marek Grubka
Rev Bernard McCay-Morrissey
Rev Jaroslaw Krawiec
Br Maurice Colgan
Br Brian Doyle
Rev David Walker
Br Colm Mannion
Br Luuk Jansen
Br Matthew Martinez

Glasnevin
40 Iona Road, Dublin 9
Tel 01-8305880/8602790

Rev Gerard Dunne

47 Leeson Park
Dublin 6
Tel 01-6602427

Superior
Very Rev Bernard Treacy

Rev Patrick McGrath
Rev Cyril Ross
Rev Andrew Allen
Rev Joseph Cullen

St Aengus's
Tymon North, Balrothery,
Tallaght, Dublin 24
Tel 01-4513757

Superior
Very Rev Benedict Moran PP

Rev Albert Leonard CC

St Dominic's
St Dominic's Road,
Tallaght, Dublin 24
Tel 01-4510620 Fax 01-4623223

Superior:
Very Rev Laurence Collins Adm

Rev Declan Corish CC

St Dominic's
Athy, Co Kildare
Tel 0507-31573

Prior: Very Rev Joseph O'Brien

Rev Gerard O'Keeffe
Rev Andrew Kane
Rev Ross McCauley
Rev John Heffernan
Rev Dominic O'Connor

Archdiocese of Armagh

St Malachy's
Dundalk, Co Louth
Tel 042-9334179/9333714

Prior
Very Rev Bede McGregor

Rev Conor O'Riordan
Rev Edmund Murphy
Rev Anthony McMullan

St Magdalen's
Drogheda, Co Louth
Tel 041-9838271

Prior: Very Rev Ronan Cusack

Rev Humbert O'Brien
Rev Joseph Heffernan

Diocese of Cork & Ross

St Mary's
Pope Quay, Cork
Tel 021-4502267
Fax 021-4502307

Prior
Very Rev Edward Conway

Rev Robert Talty
Rev Finian Lynch
Rev Simon Roche
Rev Martin MacCarthy
Rev Donal Mehigan

St Dominic's Retreat House
Montenotte, Co Cork
Tel 021-4502520
Fax 021-4502712

Prior
Very Rev Benedict Hegarty

Br James Beausang
Br Thomas Casey
Rev Frank Downes
Rev Archie Byrne
Rev Denis Keating

Diocese of Dromore

St Catherine's
Newry, Co Down BT35 8BN
Tel 028-30262178
Tel 028-302252188

Prior
Very Rev Maurice Fearon

Br Mark McGreevy
Rev Raymond Watters
Rev Stephen Tumilty
Rev Noel McKeown

Diocese of Elphin

Holy Cross
Sligo, Co Sligo
Tel 071-42700 Fax 071-46533

Prior
Very Rev Timothy Mulcahy

Br Philip Kerrigan
Rev Sean Cunningham
Rev Thomas Monahan

Diocese of Galway

St Mary's
The Claddach, Co Galway
Tel 091-582884 Fax 091-581252

Prior: Very Rev Domhnall
MacSuibhne PP

Rev Peter Gaffney
Rev Terence McLoughlin
Rev John O'Reilly
Br Christopher O'Flaherty
Rev Walter Hegarty
Rev Denis Murphy

Diocese of Kerry

Holy Cross
Tralee, Co Kerry
Tel 066-21135/29185

Prior
Very Rev Joseph Bulman

Rev Placid Nolan
Rev James Duggan
Rev John O'Rourke
Rev Ambrose O'Farrell
Rev Krzysztof Kupczakiewicz

Diocese of Kildare & Leighlin

Newbridge College
Droichead Nua, Co Kildare
Tel 045-487200 Fax 045-487234
Secondary School for Boys

Prio:
Very Rev Stephen Hutchinson

Rev Bernard Casserly
Rev Raymond O'Donovan
Rev Brian Reynolds
Rev Michael Commane
Rev Benedict MacKenna
Rev Thomas McCarthy
Rev John Walsh

Diocese of Limerick

St Saviour's
Glentworth Street, Limerick
Tel 061-412333
Fax 061-311728

Prior
Very Rev James Donleavy PP

Rev Vincent Kennedy
Rev Brendan Clifford
Rev Thomas Brodie
Rev Philip McShane
Rev Ciaran Dougherty CC

Diocese of Ossory

Black Abbey
Kilkenny, Co Kilkenny
Tel 056-21279

Prior: Very Rev Louis Hughes

Rev Dominic Browne
Rev Finbar Kelly
Rev Stanislaus Foley
Rev Vincent Mercer

Diocese of Waterford & Lismore

St Saviour's
Bridge Street, Waterford
Tel 051-875061

Prior: Very Rev James Harris

Rev Anselm Ryan
Rev Raymond Collins
Rev Canice Murphy

St Saviour's
Ballybeg, Waterford
Tel 051-376581

Superior
Very Rev Fergal Mac Eoinin PP

Rev Martin Crowe CC
Rev Richard Walsh CC

FRANCISCAN ORDER (OFM)

Province of Ireland

Provincial Office, 'La Verna',
Gormanston, Co Meath
Tel 01-8020951 Fax 01-8020126

Provincial
Rev Caoimhín Ó Laoide
Email caoimhinofm@eircom.net

Vicar Provincial
Rev Hugh McKenna
Franciscan Friary,
Ennis, Co Clare
Tel 065-6828751
Fax 065-6822008
Secretary of Province
Rev Joseph MacMahon
Email jamacmahon@eircom.net

Guardian
Rev Joseph MacMahon
Vicar: Rev P. J. Brady

Archdiocese of Dublin

Adam & Eve's
4 Merchant's Quay, Dublin 8
Tel 01-6771128
Fax 01-6771000

Guardian: Rev Ulic Troy
Vicar: Rev James Hasson

Rev Angelus Lee
Rev Lomán MacAodha
Br Niall O'Connell
Rev Fintan O'Shea
(3 The Millhoue, Steelworks,
Foley Street, Dublin 1)
Rev Jude O'Riordan
Rev Columba Scanlon
Br Sebastian Tighe

Franciscan House of Studies
Dún Mhuire, Seafield Road,
Killiney, Co Dublin
Tel 01-2826760
Fax 01-2826993
Email dmkilliney@eircom.net

Guardian: Rev Kieran Cronin
Vicar: Rev Patrick Conlan

Rev Ronald Bennett
Rev Pádraig Coleman
Rev Francis Cotter
Rev John Dalton
(4 McSweeney House,
Berkeley Road, Dublin 7)
Rev Ignatius Fennessy
Rev Alexis King
Rev Simon O'Byrne
Rev Hugh O'Donnell
Rev Maelísa Ó Huallacháin
Rev Paschal Slevin

*Diocese of Ardagh &
Clonmacnois*

Franciscan Friary
Friary Lane, Athlone,
Co Westmeath
Tel 090-6472095
Fax 090-6424713
Email
athlonefriary@eircom.net

Guardian: Rev Michael Nicholas
Vicar: Rev Brian Allen

Rev Laurence Murphy
Rev John O'Brien
Rev Michael Holland
Rev Ralph Lawless

Diocese of Cork & Ross

Franciscan Friary
Liberty Street, Cork
Tel 021-4270302
Fax 021-4271841
Guardian: Rev Eugene Barrett
Vicar: Rev Brendan Scully

Rev Walter Crowley
Rev Iain Duggan
Rev Oswald Gill
Rev Seraphin Kennedy
Rev Larry Mulligan
Rev John Bosco O'Byrne
Rev Oscar O'Leary
Br Ambrose O'Mahony
Rev Christopher Regan

Diocese of Galway

The Abbey
8 Francis Street, Galway
Tel 091-562518 Fax 091-565663
Email galwayabbey@eircom.net

Guardian: Rev Gabriel Kinahan
Vicar, Parish Priest
Rev Pádraig Breheny

Rev Michael Bailey (Curate's
Residence, Monksfield,
Salthill, Galway)
Br Cathal Duddy
Rev Colin Garvey
(St Bonaventure College,
Makeni, PO Box 39312, Lusaka
10101, Zambia)
Br Patrick Lynch
Rev Mícheál MacCraith
Rev Peter O'Grady
Rev Hilary Steblecki CC
Br Martin Thompson

Diocese of Kerry

Franciscan Friary
Killarney, Co Kerry
Tel 064-6631334/6631066
Fax 064-6637510
Email friary@eircom.net

Guardian: Rev Philip Forker
Vicar: Rev Francis McGrath

Rev Christopher Connolly
Rev Philip Deane
Rev Marceli Gesla
(Chaplain to Polish Community)
Br Seán Murphy
Rev Declan Timmons

Diocese of Killaloe

Franciscan Friary
Ennis, Co Clare
Tel 065-6828751
Fax 065-6822008
Email friars.ennis@eircom.net
Guardian & Vicar Provincial
Rev Hugh McKenna
*Vicar, Provincial Definitor &
Director of Novitiate*
Rev Joseph Condren

Rev Séamus Donohoe
Rev Liam Kelly
Rev Feargus McEveney
Rev Cletus Noone
Br Elzear O'Brien

Diocese of Meath

Franciscan College
Gormanston, Co Meath
Tel 01-8412203 Fax 01-8412685
Email
friary@gormanstoncollege.ie

Guardian: Rev Malcolm Timothy
*Vicar, Provincial Definitor &
Rector:* Rev Brendan McGrath

Br Laurence Brady
Rev Edward Burke
Rev Seán Cassin
Rev Augustine Hughes
Br Philip Lane
Br Kevin McKenna
Rev Eamonn Newell
Rev Rory O'Leary
Rev Ailbe Ó Murchú
Br Gerard Phayer

Franciscan Abbey
Multyfarnham, Co Westmeath
Tel 044-9371114/9371137
Fax 044-9371387

Guardian: Rev Joseph Walsh
Vicar: Rev Richard Kelly

Rev John Kealy
Br Salvador Kenny

Diocese of Raphoe

Franciscan Friary
Rossnowlagh, Co Donegal
Tel 072-9851342
Fax 072-9852206
Email
franciscanfriary@eircom.net

Guardian
Rev Paschal McDonnell
Vicar: Rev Pius McLaughlin

Rev Florian Farrelly
Br Hugh Gallagher
Rev Seán Gildea
Rev Thomas Russell

*Diocese of Waterford &
Lismore*

Franciscan Friary
Clonmel, Co Tipperary
Tel 052-6121378
Fax 052-6125806
Email clonmel@eircom.net

Vicar: Br Isidore Cronin

Rev Richard Callanan
Rev Liam Costello
Rev John Harty
Rev Bernard Jones (Chaplain
WRH)
Rev Diarmaid O'Riain

Franciscan Friary
Lady Lane, Waterford
Tel 051-874262 Fax 051-843062
Email
waterfordfriary@eircom.net
Chaplaincy:
Tel 051-842244/8744188

Guardian
Rev Patrick Younge
Vicar: Rev Eamonn O'Driscoll

Rev Patrick Cogan
(15 Orchard Drive, Ursuline
Court, Waterford/
Tel 087-2360239/Respond!
Office Tel 051-876865)
Rev Ultan McCaffrey
Rev Art McCoy
Rev Edward O'Callaghan
Rev Peter Baptist O'Toole
Br Nicholas Shanahan
Br Bonaventure Ward

Other Individual Addresses

Rev Pádraig B. Coleman
Presbytery 2, Ballycullen Ave,
Firhouse, Dublin 24
Rev Bernardine Dore
Portiuncola Nursing Home,
Multyfarnham, Co Westmeath
Rev Bernard Hall
PO Box 7026, Katutura,
Windlock, Republic of Namibia
Rev William Hoyne
Hermanos Franciscanos, Iglesia
Parroquial 'Dios con Nostros',
1a Av, 5a-6a Calles, Monzana
10, Elmezquital,
Zana 12, 10102 Guatemala
City, Guatemala
Rev Patrick Hudson
Gymnázium sv. Frantiska
z Assisi v Ziline,
Vlica J.M. Hurbana 44,
01001 Ziline, Slovakia
Rev Crispin Keating
5225 North Himes Avenue,
Tampa, Fl 33614-6623, USA
Rev Matthew McDonald
Lawson House, Knockrathyle,
Glenbrien, Enniscorthy,
Co Wexford
Rev Aidan McGrath
Curia Generalizia dei Frati
Minoti, Via S. Maria Mediatrice
25, 00165 Roma, Italy
Most Rev Fiachra Ó Ceallaigh
'St Cecilia's', 19 St Anthony
Road, Rialto, Dublin 8
Rev Adrian Peelo
Br Giles Friary, 1920 7th Street,
Berkeley, CA 94710, USA

Franciscan Communities Abroad

St Anthony's Parish
(English-Speaking Chaplaincy)
23/25 Oudstrijderslaan,
1950 Kraainem, Belgium
Tel +32-2-7201970
Fax +32-2-7255810

Rev Patrick Power (PP)
Rev James Hynes (98 Bld de
Montpernasse, 95014 Paris,
France)
Rev Vincent Gallogley
(Associate Pastor)

Collegio S. Isidoro
Via degli Artisti 41,
00187 Roma, Italy
Tel +39-06-4885359
Fax +39-06-4884459
Email collegio_s_isidoro@libero.it

Rev Louis Brennan
Br Solanus Hughes
Rev John O'Keeffe

Franciscan Missionaries in
Zimbabwe
Custos: Rev Emmanuel Musara

Rev Nicholas Banhwa
Br Tawanda Chirigo
Rev Walter Gallahue
Rev Maxwell Jaya
Br Raymond Kondo
Br Francis Lembani
Rev Fanuel Magwidi
Rev Thomas Makamure
Br Naison Manjovha
Rev Liam McCarthy
Br Albert Mhari
Br Linous Mukumbuzi
Rev Xavier Mukupo
Br Salicio Mukuwe
Br Onward Murape
Rev Hosea Musengiwa
Br Juniper O'Brien
Br Stephen Office
Br Stephen O'Kane *(c/o*
Provincial Office, Gormanston)
Rev Joe O'Toole *(Province of the*
Immaculate Conception, UK)
Br Ndabaningi Sithole
Br Patience Tigere
Rev Alfigio Tunha
Br Clemence Wiziki

CONVENTUAL FRANCISCANS (OFMConv)

General Delegation Office
St Patrick's Friary
26 Cornwall Road, Waterloo,
London SE1 8TW, England
Tel 020-79288897

General Delegate
Very Rev James McCurry

Archdiocese of Dublin

Friary of the Visitation of the
BVM
Fairview Strand, Dublin 3
Tel 01-8376000
Fax 01-8376021

Rev Joseph Connick PP
Rev Ciprian Budu
Rev Patrick Griffin
Rev Antony Nallukunnel

HOLY SPIRIT CONGREGATION (CSSp)

Province of Ireland

Archdiocese of Dublin

Spiritan Provincialate
Temple Park, Richmond
Avenue South, Dublin 6
Tel 01-4975127/4977230
Fax 01-4975399
Email secretaryspiritan@
irishspiritans.ie

Provincial Superior
Rev Brian Starken
Assistants
Rev Peter Conaty
Rev Seán O'Leary
Provincial Bursar
Rev Conor Courtney
Provincial Secretary
Rev Eddie O'Farrell
Archivist: Br Ignatius Curry
House Bursar
Rev Francis Caffrey
Communications Manager
Mr Peter O'Mahony
Email communications@
irishspiritans.ie

Spiritan Education Office,
(Des Places Educational
Association Ltd)
Kimmage Manor, Dublin 12
Tel 01-4997610
Awareness Education Office
Rev Tony Byrne
Tel/Fax 01-8388888
Email
info@awarenesseducation.org

Spiritan Missionary College
Kimmage Manor, Dublin 12
Tel 01-4064300 Fax 01-4920062

Superior: Rev Michael Kilkenny

Rev James Adjei-Buor
Rev Enzo Agnoli
Rev Savino Agnoli
Rev Desmond Arigho
Rev Michael Begley
Rev John Brown
Br Albert Buckley
Rev Edward F. Buckley
Rev James Byrnes
Rev John Cahill
Rev Brian Carey
Rev Andrew Carroll
Rev Peter Casey
Bishop Michael J. Cleary
Rev John J. Coleman
Rev Martin J. Collins
Rev Frank Comerford
Rev Timothy Connolly
Rev Kevin Corrigan
Rev James Corry
Rev Conor Courtney
Rev Brian Cronin
Rev Patrick Cully
Rev Stephen Darcy

Rev Anthony Darragh
Rev James B. Devine
Rev Dermot Doran
Br Oliver Dowling
Rev Frank Duffy
Rev Colm Duggan
Rev James F. Duggan
Rev Bartholomew Egan
Rev John Egan
Rev Francis Toochukwu
Ekwomadu
Rev Hugh Fagan
Rev Anthony Farrell
Rev Matthew Farrelly
Rev James C. Foley
Rev Aengus C. Finucane
(Concern)
Rev John A. Finucane
(Concern)
Rev Aloysius P. Flood
Rev Anthony Geoghegan
Rev Reginald Gillooly
Rev Edward Grimes *(Director,*
Pontifical Mission Societies)
Rev Brendan Heeran
Rev Anthony Heerey
Rev John Hegarty
Rev Patrick Henehan
Rev John Hogan
Rev Gregory Iwuozor
Rev Michael Kane
Rev Martin J. Kelly
Rev Michael Kilkenny
Rev John Joe King
Rev John Laizer
Rev Jeremiah Lambe
Rev Owen Lambert
Rev Patrick Leddy *(Bursar)*
Rev Jude Lynch
Rev Liam Martin
Rev James Masterson
Rev Michael McCarthy
Rev Peter J. McEntire
Rev James McGann
Rev Laurence McHugh
Rev Brian McLaughlin
Rev Walter McNamara
Rev Linus Mbajo
Rev James F. Meade
Rev Thomas F. Meagher
Rev Henry Moloney
Rev John Moriarty
Rev James Morrow
Rev James Murphy
Rev Jack Nugent
Rev Brendan J. O'Brien
Rev Valentine O'Brien
Rev Thomas O'Byrne
Rev Vincent O'Connell
Rev David O'Connor
Rev Sean O'Donoghue
Rev Timothy O'Driscoll
Rev Hugh O'Reilly
Bishop John C. O'Riordan
Rev Sean O'Shaughnessy
Rev Desmond L. O'Sullivan
Rev John L. O'Sullivan
Rev Liam O'Sullivan
Rev Lorcan O'Toole
Rev Michael B. Reynolds
Rev Denis Rodgers
Rev Gerard Ryan

Rev Ciaran Shanley
Rev Joseph Sheehan
Br Senan Smith
Rev Michael P. Smyth
Rev Jim Stapleton
Rev Joseph M. Steele
Rev Marc Whelan
Rev Patrick A. Whelan

Kimmage Development
Studies Centre
Kimmage Manor, Dublin 12
Tel 01-4064386
Fax 01-4064388

Director: Mr Patrick Reilly

Kimmage Mission Institute at
Milltown
Milltown Park, Dublin 6
Tel 01-2776300
Fax 01-2692528

Rev Michael Kilkenny
Rev Denis Robinson
Rev Tom Whelan

Church of the Holy Spirit
Kimmage, Dublin 12
Tel 01-4558316

Very Rev Patrick Doody PP
Rev Austin Healy

Blackrock College
Blackrock, Co Dublin
Tel 01-2888681
Fax 01-2834267
Email
info@blackrockcollege.com

Superior: Rev Tom Nash
Principal: Alan MacGinty

Rev Kevin A. Browne
Rev Vincent Browne
Rev Sean Casey
Rev Patrick Devine
Rev Richard Eneji
Rev John (Seán) P. Farragher
Rev Thomas Farrelly
Rev Denis J. Gavin
Rev Brian M. Gogan
Rev Joseph A. Gough
Br Liam Kehoe
Rev Brian Kilbride
Rev Malachy Kilbride
Rev Francis Leahy
Rev Thomas McDonald
Rev James McDonnell
Rev Hyacinth Nwnkuna
Rev Cormac Ó Brolcháin
Rev Richard J. Thornton
Rev Enda Watters

Willow Park
Tel 01-2881651
Fax 01-2783353
Email
admin@willowparkschool.ie
Principal Senior School
Mr Donal Brennan
Principal Junior School
Mr Jim Casey

St Mary's College
Rathmines, Dublin 6
Community Tel 01-4062160
Fax 01-4972621
Junior School Tel 01-4062121
Email junsec@stmarys.ie
Senior School Tel 01-4062100
Fax 01-4972574
Email sensec@stmarys.ie

Superior: Rev Patrick B. Cleary
Principal, Secondary School
Mr Liam Naughton
Principal, Junior School
Ms Mary O'Donnell

Rev Michael J. Buckley
Br Ignatius Curry
Rev John P. Flavin
Rev Patrick J. Kelly
Rev Leo Layden
Rev James J. McNulty
Rev William Nugent
Rev Brian O'Toole

St Michael's College
Ailesbury Road, Dublin 4
Tel 01-2189400 Fax 01-2698862
Email stmcoll@indigo.ie
Community Tel 01-2189423
Fax 01-2600598

Superior: Rev Patrick Dundon
Principal: Mr Tim Kelleher
Principal, Junior School
Ms Lorna Heslin

Rev Michael Duggan
Rev Seamus Galvin
Rev Anthony G. Little
Rev Leo J. McGarry
Rev Patrick McGlynn
Rev Noel O'Meara
Rev Cyril Sheedy

Spiritan House
Spiritan Asylum Services
Initiative (SPIRASI)
213 North Circular Road,
Dublin 7
Tel 01-8389664/8683504
Fax 01-8686500

Mr Michael McMahon
(Director, SPIRASI)

Rev Brendan Carr
Rev Thomas Hogan
Rev William Jenkinson
Rev Patrick McNamara
Br Liam Sheridan

Templeogue College
Dublin 6W
Tel 01-4903909 Fax 01-4920903
Email
info@templeoguecollege.ie

Superior: Rev John Byrne
Principal: Ms Aoife O'Donnell

Rev Michael Kennedy
Rev Aidan Lehane
Rev Florence Lynch

Rev Frank Mulloy
Rev Thomas Raftery
Rev Noel Redmond
Rev Desmond Reid
Rev Patrick Reedy
Rev William A. Walsh

Church of the Holy Spirit
Greenhills, Dublin 12
Tel 01-4504040
www.holyspiritparish
greenshills.ie

Superior & Parish Priest
Very Rev Myles Healy PP

Rev Roderick Curran

Church of the Transfiguration
Presbytery, Bawnogue,
Clondalkin, Dublin 22
Tel 01-4592273/4519810
Fax 01-4670038

Superior & Parish Priest
Very Rev Joseph Beere PP

Rev Marino Nguekam

Newlands Institute for Counselling
2 Monastery Road, Clondalkin,
Dublin 22
Tel 01-4594573

Rev Ronan Grimshaw
Rev Patrick Coughlan

Parish of St Ronan's
Deansrath, Clondalkin,
Dublin 22
Tel/Fax 01-4570380

Rev Daithi Kenneally PP

Archdiocese of Cashel and
Diocese of Emly

Rockwell College
Cashel, Co Tipperary
Tel 062-61444 Fax 062-61661
www.rockwell-college.ie

Secondary Residential and Day
School

Superior: Rev John Meade
Principal: Mr Patrick O'Sullivan

Br Gerard Cummins
Rev Colm Cunningham
Rev Tom Cunningham
Rev Joseph D'ambrosio
Rev Patrick Downes
Rev Bernard M. Frawley
Rev Gerard Griffin
Rev Brendan Hally
Rev James Hurley
Rev William Kingston
Rev Matthew J. Knight
Rev Michael Moore
Rev Noel Murphy
(Promotions)

Rev William Murphy
Rev Sean O'Connell
Rev Edmond Purcell
Rev Peter Queally
Rev Peter J. Raftery

Diocese of Meath

Spiritan Missionaries
Ardbraccan, Navan, Co Meath
Tel 046-9021441
Fax 046-9021178

Superior: Br Conleth Tyrrell

Rev Phil Crowe
Rev Augustine G. Griffin
Rev Vincent McDevitt
Rev Brian Murtagh
Rev Edward Nealon
Rev Patrick O'Toole

Rome

Clivo di Cinna 195, 00136
Roma, Italy
Tel +39-06-3540461
Fax +39-06-35450676

Superior General
Most Rev Jean-Paul Hoch

JESUITS (SJ) SOCIETY OF JESUS

Irish Province

Archdiocese of Dublin

Jesuit Provincial Curia
IMI Centre, Sandyford Road,
Dublin 16
Tel 01-2932820 Fax 01-2934923
Email curia@jesuit.ie

Provincial: Rev John Dardis
Assistant Provincial
Rev Noel Barber

Jesuit Curia Community
33 Sandford Road, Ranelagh,
Dublin 6
Tel 01-4988004/5

Superior: Rev Noel Barber
Minister: Rev Piaras Jackson

Rev Peter Sexton
Rev Yong-su P. Kim

Applications for retreats to
Rev Finbarr Lynch SJ
Manresa House, Dollymount,
Dublin 3
Tel 01-8331352

Enquiries in respect of foreign
missions to Rev Director, Jesuit
Foreign Missions,
28 Upper Sherrard Street,
Dublin 1
Tel 01-8366509 Fax 01-8366510

St Francis Xavier's
Upper Gardiner Street,
Dublin 1
Tel 01-8363411 Fax 01-8555624
Email sfxcommunity@jesuit.ie
Parish church and residence

Superior
Rev Berenard McGuckian
Minister: Br Tom Phelan
Parish Priest
Very Rev Donal Neary PP

Rev Kieran Barry-Ryan
Rev Kevin Casey
Rev Derek Cassidy
Rev John B. Clear
Rev James Culliton
Br Eamonn Davis
Rev Paul Farquharson (Vice-
superior)
Rev John K. Guiney
Rev Brendan Kearney
Rev Frank Keenan
Rev Brian Lennon
Rev Mícheál Mac Gréil
Br Gerard Marks
Rev Liam McKenna
Rev John Moylan
Br Martin Murphy
Rev Proinsias Ó Fionnagáin
Rev John O'Holohan
Rev Frank O'Neill
Rev Anthony O'Riordan
Rev William Reynolds
Rev James Smyth
Rev Brendan Staunton

Belvedere College
Great Denmark Street,
Dublin 1
Community resides in SFX
Gardiner Street

Secondary day school
Tel 01-8586600 (College)
Fax 01-8744374
Rector: Rev Derek Cassidy
Headmaster: Mr Gerard Foley

35 Lower Leeson Street
Dublin 2
Tel 01-6761248 Fax 01-7758598
Residence

Superior: Rev Brian Grogan
Vice-Superior
Rev Edmond Grace

Rev Paul Andrews
Rev Gerard Bourke
Rev Richard Cremins
Rev John FitzGerald
Rev Philip Fogarty
Rev Michael O. Gallagher
Rev Kevin Laheen
Rev John Looby
Rev James Moran
Rev Fergus O'Donoghue
Rev Brian O'Leary
Br Joseph Osborne
Rev Frank Sammon

Jesuit Communication Centre

36 Lower Leeson Street,
Dublin 2
Tel 01-6768408 Fax 01-6629292
Email jcc@jesuit.ie

Manager: Ms Pat Coyle
Tel 01-7758514

Sacred Heart Messenger – a
Jesuit Publication
37 Lower Leeson Street,
Dublin 2
Tel 01-6767491
Editor: Rev John Looby
Manager: Ms Triona McKee
Email manager@messenger.ie

Sacred Space
Director: Rev Piaras Jackson
Website www.sacredspace.ie

Campion House Residence

28 Lower Hatch Street,
Dublin 2
Tel 01-6383990
Fax 01-6762805
Email campion@jesuit.ie

Superior: Rev John O'Keeffe
Provincial: Rev John Dardis

Rev Patrick Hume

Manresa House

Dollymount, Dublin 3
Tel 01-8331352 Fax 01-8331002
Email manresa@jesuit.ie
Retreat House

Rector: Rev Joseph Dargan
*Director of Retreat House/
Vice-Rector*
Rev Padraig Ó Cairbre
Plant Manager: Br Joseph Ward

Br Peter Doyle
Rev Patrick Greene
Rev Peter Hannan
Rev Finbarr Lynch
Rev Dermot Mansfield
Rev Thomas Morrissey
Rev Richard O'Dwyer
Rev Ciary Quirke
Rev Van de Poll

Dominic Collins' House Residence

129 Morehampton Road,
Dublin 4
Tel 01-2693075 Fax 01-2698462

Acting Superior
Rev David Coghlan

Rev Martin Curry
Rev Niall Leahy
Rev David Tuohy

Milltown Park

Sandford Road, Dublin 6
Tel 01-2698411/2698113
Fax 01-2600371
Email milltown@jesuit.ie

Rector
Rev Kevin O'Rourke
Vice-Rector
Rev Michael Drennan
Plant Manager
Br John Adams

Rev John Brady
Rev Fergal Brennan
Rev Liam Browne
Rev William Callanan
Rev Finbarr Clancy
Br Joseph Cleary
Rev Brendan Duddy
Br James Dunne
Br George Fallon
Rev Fabrice M. Fayana
Rev David Gaffney
Rev Henry Grant
Rev John Guiney
Rev Conor Harper
Rev Michael Hurley
Rev James Kelly
Rev Patrick Kelly
Rev Colm Lavelle
Br John Maguire
Rev William Mathews
Rev John McAuley
Br James McCabe
Rev Raymond Moloney
Rev Charles O'Connor
Rev Edmund O'Keefe
Rev Hugh O'Neill
Rev John Redmond
Rev Seamus Ward
Rev Brendan Woods

Lay Retreat Association of Saint Ignatius

Milltown Park, Dublin 6
Tel 01-2698411/2180274
Lay apostolate for the
promotion of retreats in
different locations

Spiritual Director
Rev Fergus O'Keefe
Tel 01-2951856

Milltown Institute of Theology and Philosophy

Milltown Park,
Sandford Road,
Dublin 6
Tel 01-2776300
Fax 01-2692528
Email
info@milltown-institute.ie

Acting President
Rev Cornelius Casey (CSsR)
Rector of Pontifical Athenaeum
Rev Finbarr G. Clancy (SJ)

Gonzaga College

Sandford Road, Dublin 6
Tel 01-4972943 (community)
Fax 01-4960849 (community)
Tel 01-4972931 (college)
Fax 01-4967769
Email
(Community) gonzaga@jesuit.ie
(College) office@gonzaga.ie

Rector: Rev Myles O'Reilly
Minister: Rev Kennedy O'Brien
Headmaster: Mr Kevin Whirdy

Rev Joseph Brennan
Rev John Callanan
Rev Frank Doyle
Rev Alan Mowbray
Rev Edward O'Donnell
Rev Desmond O'Grady
Br James Sutton
Rev Colin Warrack

John Sullivan House

56/56A Mulvey Park,
Dundrum, Dublin 14
Tel 01-2983978
Email sullivan@jesuit.ie
Residence for scholastics
attending universities

Rector: Rev Fergus O'Keefe
Tel 01-2986424
Minister
Rev Brendan Comerford

Rev Juan José Aguilar-Díez
Rev Albert In-young Cho
Rev Matthew Shen-yi Hssii
Ripox Rosario *(Scholastic)*

John Austin House

135 North Circular Road,
Dublin 7
Tel 01-8386768
Residence
Email m.osullivan@jesuit.ie

Superior
Rev Neil O'Driscoll
Vice-superior
Rev Dermot McKenna
Minister: Br Brendan Hyland

Rev John Dooley
Rev Michael O'Sullivan
Rev Stephen Redmond

Arrupe Community

127 Shangan Road,
Ballymun, Dublin 9
Tel/Fax 01-8625345
Email ballymun@jesuit.ie

217 Silloge Road, Ballymun,
Dublin 11
Tel 01-8420886

Superior
Rev Proinsias Mac Bradaigh

Rev Peter McVerry
Rev Kevin O'Higgins

25 Croftwood Park

Cherry Orchard, Dublin 10
Tel 01-6267413

Superior: Rev William Toner

Rev Gerard O'Hanlon

Jesuit Community

27 Leinster Road, Rathmines,
Dublin 6
Tel 01-4970250
Email leinster@jesuit.ie

Superior: Rev James Corkery
Minister: Rev Leon Ó Giolláin

Rev Gerard Clarke
Rev Jimenez A. Cristóbal
Rev Terence Howard
Rev Wojciech Kowalski
Rev Kizito Niyoyita

Jesuit Scholastics
Gellert Merza
Ripon Rosario

Archdiocese of Armagh

Iona
211 Churchill Park
Portadown, BT62 1EU
Tel 028-38330366
Fax 028-38338334
Email iona@jesuit.ie

Rev Brian Mac Cuarta
Rev Brendan MacPartlin
Rev Michael Bingham *(Prov
Brit)*
Br David Byrne

Diocese of Down & Connor

Peter Faber House
28 Brookvale Avenue
Belfast BT14 6BW
Tel 028-90757615
Fax 028-90747615
Email
peter_faber@lineone.net

Superior: Rev Alan McGuckian

Rev Patrick Davis
Rev Thomas Layden
Rev Joseph Palmisano
Rev Senan Timoney

Diocese of Galway

St Ignatius Community & Church
27 Raleigh Row, Salthill, Galway
Tel 091-523707
Email galway@jesuit.ie

Rector: Rev John Humphreys
Administrator
Rev Michael McGuckian

Rev Paul Brassil
Rev Dermot Cassidy
Rev Charles Davy
Rev Cathal Doherty
Rev Anthony Farren

Rev James Lynch
Rev Brendan McManus
Rev Enda O'Callaghan
Rev Conall Ó Cuinn
Rev Connla O Dulaine
Rev Paul Tonna
Rev Patrick Tyrrell

Coláiste Iognáid
24 Sea Road, Galway
College Tel 091-501550
Fax 091-501551
Email
colaisteiognaid@eircom.net

Secondary School Headmaster
Mr Bernard O'Connell
Scoil Iognaid (National School)
Principal: Maree Ui Chonaill
Tel 091-584491

Diocese of Kildare & Leighlin

Clongowes Wood College
Naas, Co Kildare
Tel 045-868663/868202
Fax 045-861042
Email *(College)*
reception@clongowes.net
(Community)
reception@clongowes.net
Secondary Boarding School

Rector: Rev Bruce Bradley
Headmaster
Rev Leonard Moloney
Email hm@clongowes.net
Minister: Rev Michael Sheil

Rev Joseph Brereton
Rev Eric Cantillon CC
Br Charles Connor
Rev Patrick Crowe
Rev Ronan Geary
Rev Patrick Lavery
Rev Vincent Murphy
Rev Laurence Murphy
Martin Benko (SVK)
(Scholastic)

Diocese of Limerick

Crescent College Comprehensive
Dooradoyle, Limerick
(Community)
Tel 061-480920 Fax 061-480927
Email dooradoyle@jesuit.ie
(College)
Tel 061-229655 Fax 061-229013
Email ccadmin.ias@eircom.net
Comprehensive Day School for
Boys and Girls

Superior: Rev Liam O'Connell
Minister: Rev James Maher
Headmaster
Mr Nicholas Cuddihy

Rev Hugh Duffy
Rev Rory Halpin
Rev Dermot Murray
Rev Niall O'Neill

Jesuits temporarily outside Ireland

Correspondence to
Jesuit Provincial Curia
IMI Centre,
Sandyford Road,
Dublin 16
Tel 01-2932820

Rev Brendan Carmody
Rev Thomas Casey
Rev Ashley Evans
Rev Michael P. Gallagher
Rev Donal Godfrey
Rev James Hayes
Rev Timothy Healy
Rev Patrick Heelan
Rev Bartholomew Kiely
Rev James Murphy
Rev Declan Murray
Rev Dermot O'Connor
Rev Patrick Riordan
Rev Patrick Sheary

LEGIONARIES OF CHRIST (LC)

Archdiocese of Dublin

Novitiate
Leopardstown Road, Foxrock
Dublin 18
Tel 01-2955902
Fax 01-2957773
Email ireland@legionaries.org

Superior & Novice Master
Rev Matthew Brackett
Vocations Director and Regnum Christi Lay Apostolate
Rev Michael Mullan
Email
mmullan@legionaries.org

Clonlost Retreat and Youth Centre
Killiney Road, Killiney,
Co Dublin
Tel 01-2350064
Day school retreats, pre-confirmation retreats, Creidim Leadership Programme

Chaplain: Rev Feargal O'Duill

Dublin Oak Academy
Kilcroney, Bray, Co Wicklow
Tel 01-2863290
Fax 01-2865315
Email
dublinoaksecretariat@arcol.org

Director
Rev Francisco Cepeda

Woodlands Academy
Wingfield House, Bray
Co Wicklow
Tel 01-2866323
Fax 01-2864918

Chaplain: Rev Michael Duffy

John Paul II Centre
Dal Riada House,
Avoca Avenue, Blackrock,
Co Dublin
Tel 01-2889317

Marriage Enrichment days,
Spiritual retreats, Evenings of
Reflection, Family days, Faith
development programmes
and personal spiritual
direction

Director: Rev Michael Mullan

MARIANISTS (SM) Society of Mary

Provincial Headquarters
4425 West Pine Boulevard,
St Louis, MO 63108-2301, USA
Tel 314-533-1207

Archdiocese of Dublin

St Columba's
Church Avenue, Ballybrack,
Co Dublin
Tel 01-2858301
Residence for religious and
candidates; religious centre

Director: Br James Contadino
Email
jimcontadino@yahoo.co.uk

Rev Michael Reaume
Br Fred Rech
Rev Neville O'Donohue
Br Gerry McAuley

St Laurence College
Loughlinstown, Shankill PO,
Co Dublin
Tel 01-2826930 Fax 01-2821878
Coeducational Secondary Day
School

Principal: Mr John Carr

MARISTS (SM) Society of Mary

Archdiocese of Dublin

Marist Regional Office
Mount St Mary's,
Dundrum Road, Milltown,
Dublin 14
Tel 01-2698100/087-9573973
Email corrigan@dna.ie

Regional Superior
Rev David Corrigan

Mount St Mary's, Milltown,
Dublin 14
Tel 01-2697322

Superior
Rev Brendan Bradshaw

Rev P. J. Byrne
Rev Liam Forde
Rev Frank Hennigan
Rev Des Hunt
Rev Tony Lambe
Rev Declan Marmion
Rev Ray Murray

St Brendan's Parish
Coolock Village, Dublin 5
Tel 01-8484799

Moderator and Superior
Rev John Hand

Rev P. G. Byrne
Rev John Harrington

Catholic University School
89 Lower Leeson Street,
Dublin 2
Tel 01-6762586

Headmaster: Rev Martin Daly

CUS Community
Tel 01-6760247

Superior
Rev Martin Daly

Rev Denis Green
Rev Sean Fagan
Rev Tony Malone
Rev Brendan Morrissey

Chanel College
Coolock, Dublin 5
Tel 01-8480655/8480896

Headmaster
Mr Declan Mowlds

Chanel Community
Tel 01-8477133

Superior
Rev Kieran Butler AP
St Brendan's Parish

Rev Thomas Butler
Rev Patrick Corcorcan
Rev David Corrigan

St Teresa's
Donore Avenue, Dublin 8
Tel 01-4542425/4531613

Parish Priest
Rev Edwin McCallion

Rev Tom Dalzell
Rev Bobby Kelly CC
Rev Sean McArdle

Archdiocese of Armagh

Cerdon
Marist Fathers, St Mary's Road,
Dundalk, Co Louth
Tel 042-9334019

Superior: Rev Kevin Cooney

Rev Jim Johnston
Rev James Kearney
Rev James McElroy
Rev Joseph McKenna
Rev Michael Maher
Rev Patrick Meehan
Rev John Mulligan

St Mary's College
Dundalk, Co Louth
Tel 042-9339984

Principal: Mr Con McGinley

Holy Family Parish
Parochial House,
Dundalk, Co Louth
Tel 042-9336301

Superior
Rev Jimmy O'Connell Adm

Rev Frank Corry
Rev Paddy Stanley

Marist Fathers elsewhere in Ireland

Armagh
Rev Barney King CC
Glassdrummond, Crossmaglen,
Newry, Co Down

Dublin
Rev Tom Dooley CC,
4 Greenmount Road, Terenure

Replacement Army Chaplain
Rev Tom Tuohy

Parish in Kildare & Leighlin
Rev Tom Bambrick CC,
Railway Road, Muinebheag,
Co Carlow

Tuam
Rev Joseph Jennings CC,
Inisheer Island, Aran Islands,
Co Galway

Ardagh & Clonmacnois
Rev Tim Kenny
Fermoyle, Lanesboro,
Co Longord

Marist Fathers outside Ireland

Rev Aidan Carvill, Australia
Rev Eddie Duffy, London
Rev Larry Duffy, Peru
Rev John Hannan, France
Rev Laurence Hannan, Fiji
Rev Niall Kernan,
Solomon Islands

Rev Patrick Muckian,
Philippines
Rev Paddy O'Hare, Japan
Archbishop Adrian Smith,
Honiara, Solomon Islands
Rev Paul Walsh, London
Rev Martin McAnaney,
London
Rev Roger McCarrick, Fiji
Rev Seamus McMahon,
Australia
Rev Cormac McNamara,
Mexico
Rev Rory Mulligan, Norway
Rv Joe Rooney, Philippines
Rev Jim Ross, Fiji
Rev Ray Staunton, France
Rev Tom Stokes, USA

MILL HILL MISSIONARIES (MHM)

Archdiocese of Dublin

St Joseph's House
50 Orwell Park,
Rathgar, Dublin 6
Tel 01-4127700 Fax 01-4127781
Email josephmhm@eircom.net

Regional Superior
Rev Maurice McGill
Tel 01-4127773/4127735
Email
millhillregional@eircom.net
Rector: Rev Patrick Molloy
Vice Rector
Rev Patrick O'Connell
Bursar: Rev Patrick Murray
Email millhill@iol.ie

Rev Patrick L. Bracken
Rev James Dolan
Rev Jeremiah Doona
Rev Matthew Dunne
Rev Lawrence English
Rv Christopher Fox
Rev Gerard Geraghty
Rev Martin Gillespie
Rev Denis Hartnett
Rev Bartholomew Hayes
Rev Ray Hogan
Rev Joseph Jones
Rev Thomas Keogan
Rev Roger McGorty
Rev Paddy Neville
Rev Sean O'Brien
Rev Christopher O'Connor
Rev Patrick J. Ryan
Rev John Slater
Rev Joseph Walsh
Rev Joseph P. Whelan

Diocese of Down & Connor

St Mary's Parish
25 Marquis Street,
Belfast BT1 1JJ
Tel 028-90320482

Rev James A. Boyle Adm
Rev John Nevin
Rev Jim O'Donoghue

Diocese of Ossory

St Joseph's
Freshford House, Kilkenny
Tel 056-7721482
Fax 056-7751490

Rector and Editor of Advocate: Rev Jim O'Connell
Email jimocmhm@eircom.net
Organising Secretary
Rev Maurice Crean

Rev Donal Harney
Rev Fachtna Staunton

Elsewhere in Ireland

Rev Noel Hanrahan
Rev Hugh Lee
Rev Anthony Murphy
Rev Edmund Prendergast
Rev Kevin Reynolds
Rev Thomas Sinnott

Generalate

Mill Hill Missionaries
1 Colby Gardens,
Cookham Road,
Maidenhead SL6 7GZ, England
Tel +44-1628-588401

Superior General
Very Rev Anthony Chantry

MISSIONARIES OF AFRICA (White Fathers)

Province of Europe
Irish Sector

Archdiocese of Dublin

Provincialate
Cypress Grove Road,
Templeogue, Dublin 6W
Tel 01-4055263 (House)
Tel 01-4992346 (Delegate Superior)
Tel 01-4992344 (Treasurer)
Email provirl@indigo.ie

Delegate Superior
Rev Ian Buckmaster
Provincial Treasurer
Rev Neil Loughrey

Cypress Grove
Templeogue, Dublin 6W
Tel 01-4055263/4055264
Tel 01-4055526 (Promotion)
Email provirl@indigo.ie
House of promotion/retired
priests and brothers/studies

Superior: Rev Andre Filion
Promotion Director
Rev Joseph McMenamin
Mite Boxes: Br Tim Murphy

Rev Cajethan Amaku MSP
Rev Thomas Bradley
Rev Henry Byamukama
Rev Bahlibi Desta
Rev Andre Filion

Rev James Fitzpatrick
Rev Gobezayehu Getachen
Rev Bonaventure Gubazire
Rev Eugene Lewis
Rev Stephen Dami Mamza
Rev Anselm Ngetwa
Rev Pierre Simson

Working in Provinces other than Africa

Rev James Greene
Br Raymond Leggett
Rev Michael O'Sullivan

Working in Dioceses in Ireland

Rev James Browne

MISSIONARIES OF THE SACRED HEART (MSC)

The Missionaries of the Sacred
Heart is a congregation of 16
provinces. Members of the
Irish Province work in
England, USA, South Africa,
Venezuela and Russia.

Archdiocese of Dublin

Provincialate
65 Terenure Road West,
Dublin 6W
Tel 01-4906622 Fax 01-4920148

Provincial Leader
Rev Patrick Courtney
Deputy-Leader, Provincial Secretary & Bursar
Rev Joseph McGee

Woodview House
Mount Merrion Avenue,
Blackrock, Co Dublin
Tel 01-2881644 (community)

Leader: Rev David Smith

Rev James Corbally
Rev John McCarthy
Rev Kevin McNamara
Rev Martin McNamara
Rev Tadhg Ó Dálaigh
Rev John O'Mahony
Rev John O'Sullivan
Rev Patrick Sheehan

Sacred Heart Parish
Killinarden,
Tallaght, Dublin 24
Tel 01-4522251
Rev Thomas Plower PP
Rev Desmond Farren

Diocese of Cork & Ross

MSC Mission Support Centre
PO Box 23,
Western Road, Cork
Tel 021-4545704
Fax 021-4343587
www.mscireland.com

Rev Michael O'Connell

Western Road
Cork
Tel 021-4804120
Fax 021-4543823

Leader: Rev John Fitzgerald
Parish Priest
Rev John Fitzgerald

Rev Allen Browne
Rev Michael Carrick
Rev John Kevin Fleming
Rev Donncha Mac Carthaigh
Rev Jim Mannix
Rev Michael O'Connell
Rev Dan O'Connor
Rev John Shanahan
Rev Patrick Walsh
Rev Michael Whelan

Carrignavar,
Co Cork
Tel 021-4884044

Leader: Rev Terence O'Brien

Rev Patrick Breen
Rev Jeremiah Murphy
Rev Liam O'Callaghan
Rev Daniel O'Neill
Rev Jerry O'Riordan

Coláiste an Chroí Naofa
Carraig na Bhfear, Co Chorcaí
Tel 021-4884104
Secondary School

Myross Wood Retreat House
Leap, Skibbereen, Co Cork
Tel 028-33118 Fax 028-33793

Leader & Director
Rev Michael Curran

Rev Michael Crowley
Rev Timothy Cullinane
Rev Dominic Duffy
Rev Brendan Hanley
Rev Edward McSweeney
Rev Thomas Mulcahy
Rev Daniel O'Brien

Castlehaven Parish
Parish House, Union Hall,
Skibbereen, Co Cork
Tel 028-34940

Parish Priest
Rev Christopher Coleman PP

Leap-Glandore Parish
Parish House, Leap,
Skibbereen, Co Cork
Tel 028-33177

Parish Priest
Áth Pádraig Ó Súilleabháin PP

Diocese of Galway

'Croí Nua'
Rosary Lane, Taylor's Hill,
Galway
Tel 091-520960 Fax 091-521168

Leader: Rev Michael Screene

Rev Daniel Cleary
Rev Eamon Donohoe
Rev Patrick Kelly
Rev Michael Smyth

Parish of the Resurrection
Ballinfoyle, Headford Road,
Galway
Tel 091-762883

Parish Priest
Rev Augustine O'Brien PP

Rev Gerard Thornton

Diocese of Waterford & Lismore

Grace Dieu Retreat House
Tramore Road, Waterford
Tel 051-374417/373372
Fax 051-874536

Leader & Director
Rev Michael Serrage

Rev John Bennett
Rev Donal McCarthy
Rev Con O'Connell

NORBERTINE CANONS (OPraem)

Diocese of Kilmore

Abbey of the Most Holy
Trinity and St Norbert
Kilnacrott,
Ballyjamesduff, Co Cavan
Tel 049-8544416
Fax 049-8544909
Email kilnacrottabbeytrust
@eircom.net

Prior: Rt Rev Oliver Martin

Rev Gerard Cusack
Rev Kilian Mitchell
Br Kevin O'Brien
Very Rev Kevin Smith
Rev Terry Smyth

Priests working elsewhere in Ireland
Rev Joseph O'Donohoe
Rev Pat Reilly
Rev Ray Riordan

OBLATES OF MARY IMMACULATE (OMI)

Archdiocese of Dublin

Provincial Residence
Oblates of Mary Immaculate
House of Retreat,
Tyrconnell Road, Inchicore,
Dublin 8
Tel 01-4541160/4541161
Fax 01-4541138
Email omisec@eircom.net

Provincial
Very Rev William Fitzpatrick
Provincial Treasurer
Rev Anthony Clancy

Oblate House of Retreat
Inchicore, Dublin 8
Tel 01-4534408/4541805
Fax 01-4543466

Superior: Rev Anthony Clancy
*Moderator of Pastoral Area of
Inchicore/Bluebell*
Very Rev Michael O'Connor

Rev Paul Byrne
Rev Edward Carolan
Rev Eugene Clerkin
Br John Delaney
Br Francis Flanagan
Br Patrick Flanagan
Rev Michael Guckian
Rev Richard Haslam
Rev Eoghan Haughey
Rev James Hyland
Br William Kelly
Rev Gerard Kenny
Rev Vincent Mulligan
Rev Denis O'Connell
Rev Desmond O'Donnell
Rev William O'Donovan
Rev Joseph O'Melia
Rev John Poole
Rev Eamon Reilly
Rev Thomas Scully

170 Merrion Road,
Ballsbridge, Dublin 4
Tel 01-2693658 Fax 01-2600597
Rev Charles O'Connor
Rev Sean Hynes

Oblate Scholasticate
St Anne's, Goldenbridge Walk,
Inchicore, Dublin 8
Tel 01-4540841/4542955
Fax 01-4731903

Rev Peter Clucas
Rev Thomas McCabe
Rev Kevin McLaughlin

Inchicore
St Michael's Parish
52a Bulfin Road,
Inchicore, Dublin 8
Tel 01-4531660 Fax 01-4548191

Rev M. Hughes
Rev D. Mills
Br M. Moore
Rev R. Warren

Bluebell Parish
Our Lady of the Wayside
118 Naas Road,
Bluebell, Dublin 12
Tel 01-4501040
olowbluebell@oceanfree.net

Very Rev Patrick Carolan

Darndale Parish
The Presbytery,
Darndale, Dublin 17
Tel 01-8474547 Fax 01-8479295
Email omiddale@eircom.net

Superior & Parish Priest
Very Rev Terence Murray PP

Rev Peter Daly CC

Archdiocese of Tuam

Robeen,
Hollymount, Co Mayo
Tel 094-9540026
Email patsheri@eircom.net

Rev Patrick Sheridan

The Presbytery,
Glenisland, Castlebar, Co Mayo
Tel 085-1086639
Email glenislandcc@eircom.net

Rev Martin O'Keeffe

Diocese of Kerry

Department of Chaplaincy,
Tralee General Hospital,
Tralee, Co Kerry
Tel 066-7126222

Rev Edward Barrett

PALLOTTINES (SAC) Society of the Catholic Apostolate

The Pallottine houses in
Ireland and Britain are united
in the Irish Province, as are the
houses in Kenya, Tanzania,
Rome, Argentina and the
USA.

Archdiocese of Dublin

Provincial House
'Homestead', Sandyford Road,
Dundrum, Dublin 16
Tel 01-2956180/2954170
Email pallotti@eircom.net

Provincial
Very Rev Eamon Monson
Rector: Rev John Kelly
Email pallotti@eircom.net
*Provincial Bursar/Secretary
for Missions:* Rev John Kelly
Email
pallbursar@oceanfree.net
Director of Formation
Rev Michael Irwin

Rev John Coen
Rev John Howlett
Rev Michael Kiely
Rev Donal McCarthy
Rev Ned O'Brien
Rev Louis Sisti
Br Tony Doherty

Attached to Provincial House
Rev Patrick Murray,
'Galilee', Stradbally Road,
Athy, Co Kildare
Tel 0507-31564

St Anne's
Rev John O'Connor PP
St Benin's, Dublin Road,
Shankill, Co Dublin
Tel 01-2824425

Rev Michael O'Dwyer CC
Rev Rory Hanly CC
9 Seaview Lawn, Shankill,
Co Dublin
Tel 01-2824381

St Patrick's
Corduff, Blanchardstown,
Dublin 15
Tel 01-8213596/8215930

Rev Liam McClarey PP
Rev Joseph McLoughlin CC

*Archdiocese of Cashel and
Diocese of Emly*

Pallottine College
Thurles, Co Tipperary
Tel 0504-21202

Rector: Rev Phil Barry

Rev Patrick Dwyer
Rev John Egan
Rev Aidan Maguire
Rev Roger Rafter
Rev John Bergin
Rev Matthew Shanka
Rev Emmet O'Hara

Attached to Pallotine College
Rev Vincent Kelly
18 Slivercourt,
Silversprings, Cork
Rev Joseph Campion
Freshford, Co Kilkenny

PASSIONISTS (CP)
Congregation of the Passion

Province of St Patrick: houses
in Ireland, Scotland and Paris;
missions in Africa.

Archdiocese of Dublin

St Paul's Retreat
Mount Argus, Dublin 6W
Tel 01-4992000 Fax 01-4992001
Email
passionistsmtargus@eircom.net
Provincial Office
Tel 01-4992050 Fax 01-4992055
passionistprov@eircom.net

Provincial: Rev Pat Duffy
Superior: Rev Bernard Lowe

Rev Kenneth Brady
Rev Fernando Carberry
Rev Ralph Egan
Rev Ambrose Fay
Rev Frank Keevins
Rev Anselm Keleghan
Rev Joseph Kennedy
Rev Brian Mulcahy
Rev Paul M. Madden

Br Vincent McCaughey
Rev Brendan McDermott
Rev Sylvias McGaughey
Rev Brendan McKeever
Rev Denis McLoughlin
Rev Herman Nolan
Rev Nicholas O'Grady
Rev Patrick Rogers
Rev James Sheridan
Rev Patrick Sheridan
Rev Osmund Slevin
Rev Ignatius Waters

Applications for missions and
retreats to Rev Superior of any
of our local Communities

Diocese of Clogher

St Gabriel's Retreat
The Graan, Enniskillen,
Co Fermanagh
Tel 028-66322272
Fax 028-66325201

Superior: Rev Brian D'Arcy
Bursar: Rev Anthony O'Leary

Rev Ailbe Delaney
Rev Marius Donnelly
Rev Myles Kavanagh
Br Mark O'Reilly

Diocese of Down & Connor

Passionist Retreat Centre
Tobar Mhuire, Crossgar,
Co Down BT30 9EA
Tel 028-44830242
Fax 028-44831382

Superior: Rev John Friel

Fr Mel Byrne

Holy Cross Retreat
Ardoyne, Belfast BT14 7GE
Tel 028-90748231
Fax 028-90740340

Superior: Rev Gary Donegan
Bursar: Rev Casimir Haran

Rev John Craven
Rev Salvian Maguire

Passionist Community
108 Salisbury Avenue,
Belfast BT15 5ED
Tel 028-90288306
Fax 028-90294085

Rev Pat Duffy
Rev John Friel
Rev Thomas Scanlon

Diocese of Galway

Passionist Community
35-36 Coill Tire, Doughiska,
Galway

Rev Ephrem Blake
Rev Charles Cross
Rev Victor Donnelly
Br Martin Deny

Scotland

St Mungo's Retreat
52 Parson Street,
Glasgow G4 ORX, Scotland
Tel 141-552-1823
Fax 141-553-1838

St Gabriel's Presbytery
Westloan, Prestonpans
EH32 9JX, Scotland
Tel 1875-810052
Fax 1875-814974

France

St Joseph's Church
50 Avenue Hoche, 75008 Paris
Tel 33-1-42272856
Fax 33-1-42278649

Botswana

Passionist Community
Forest Hill, PO Box 1216
Gaborone
Tel 267-3904382
Fax 267-3951693

Republic of South Africa

Passionist Community
PO Box 1395, Wingate 0153,
Republic of South Africa
Tel 27-11-3161852
Fax 27-11-3163763

REDEMPTORISTS (CSSR)
Congregation of the Most Holy Redeemer

The Irish Province of the
Redemptorists is a complete
province, with one dependent
Vice-Province in Brazil and
twenty-two other members
assigned to the Province of
CEBU/Philippines.

Archdiocese of Dublin

Liguori House
75 Orwell Road, Dublin 6
Tel 01-4067100 Fax 01-4922654
provincial@redemptorists.ie
Provincial administration

Provincial
Rev Michael G. Kelleher
Provincial Vicar: Rev Peter Burns
2nd Provincial Consultor
Rev Ciaran O'Callaghan
Provincial Treasurer
Mr Michael Dangerfield

Secretary to the Provincial
Ms Brid Raleigh
*Designated Officer, Child
Safeguarding:* Mr Phil Mortell
Tel 061-327184/087-2252415
*Delegate for the Proclamation
of the Word*
Rev Ciarán O'Callaghan
*Delegate for Youth/Young
Adult Ministry*
Ms Henrietta O'Meara

Human Resources Delegate
Mr Phil Mortell

Marianella/Liguori House
75 Orwell Road, Dublin 6
Tel 01-4067100 Fax 01-4929635
redemptorists@marianella.ie
Mission house and seminary

Superior: Rev Peter Burns
Vicar-Superior & Formator:
Rev Dan Baragry

Rev Con J. Casey
Rev John Casey
Rev John F. Corbett
Rev Frederick Dunne
Br Nicholas Healy
Rev Thomas Hogan
Br Brian Kelly
Rev Patrick Kelly Jnr
Rv Patrick Horgan
Br Michael McCloskey
Rev Brendan McConvery
Rev Robert McNamara
Rev Stanislaus Mellett
Rev Gerard Moloney
Rev Ciarán O'Callaghan
Rev Liam O'Connell
Rev Pat O'Connell
Rev Denis O'Connor
Br Jarlath O'Neill
Rev Alexander Reid
Rev Martin Ryan
Rev Patrick Scott
Rev Paud Sheils
Rev James Stanley
Rev George Wadding

Most Holy Sacrament Parish
Cherry Orchard, Dublin 10
Tel 01-6267930

Co-ordinator
Rev Gerry O'Connor
Rev Patrick Reynolds PP
Rev John Bermingham
Rev Brian Nolan

Redemptorist Communications
75 Orwell Road, Dublin 6
Tel 01-4922488

Editor: Rev Gerard Moloney

Archdiocese of Armagh

St Joseph's
Dundalk, Co Louth
Tel 042-9334042/9334762
Fax 042-9330893
Mission house and parish

Superior & PP
Rev Richard Delahunty
Vicar-Superior
Rev Eamonn Hoey

Rev Seán Bennett
Rev Finbarr Connolly
Rev Cathal Cumiskey
Rev Michael Dempsey
Br Patrick Doherty
Rev Louis Eustace
Rev Laurence Gallagher
Rev Patrick Kelly Snr

Br John Long
Rev Denis Luddy
Rev John McAlinden
Br Dermot McDonagh
Rev William McGettrick CC
Rev Brian McGrath
Rev Joseph Naughton
Rev Micheál O'Flatharta
Rev Tony Rice
Rev Ned Rocks
Rev Richard Tobin

Diocese of Clonfert

St Patrick's
Esker, Athenry, Co Galway
Tel 091-844549 Fax 091-845698
Mission house, retreat house
and Youth Village

Superior: Rev John Doherty
Vicar Superior
Rev Michael Cusack

Rev James Buckley
Br James Casey
Rev Gerald Crotty
Rev Fonsie Doran
Rev Patrick Egan
Br Thomas Farrell
Rev Anthony Flannery
Rev Peter Flannery
Rev Michael Flynn
Rev Brian Foley
Br Augustine Forrie
Rev Michael Heagney
Rev Philip Hearty
Rev Patrick Howell
Rev Vincent Kavanagh
Rev Edward Lynch
Rev Richard McMahon
Rev Sean Mullin
Rev Dermot O'Connor

Diocese of Cork & Ross

Scala
Bessboro, Blackrock, Cork
Tel 021-4358800
Fax 021-4359696
Co-ordinator: Rev Noel Kehoe

Rev Michael Forde
Rev Derek Meskell
Rev Brendan O'Rourke
Rev Paul Turley

Diocese of Down & Connor

Clonard Monastery
1 Clonard Gardens,
Belfast, BT13 2RL
Tel 028-90445950
Fax 028-90445988
Mission house

Superior: Rev Michael Murtagh
Vicar: Rev Pat O'Connor

Rev Kevin Browne
Rev Michael Browne
Rev Edmond Creamer
Rev Philip Dunlea
Br Michael Gilleece
Rev Brendan Keane
Rev Sean Keeney
Rev Clement MacManuis

Rev Sean Moore
Rev Patrick O'Donnell
Rev Patrick O'Keeffe
Rev Gerard Reynolds
Rev Derek Ryan
Br Thomas Walsh
Rev Peter Ward

St Gerard's
722 Antrim Road,
Newtownabbey,
Co Antrim BT36 7PG
Tel 028-90774833
Fax 028-90770923

Superior & PP: Rev Gerry Cassidy
Vicar Superior & Bursar
Rev Patrick Cunning

Rev Pat McLaughlin CC
Rev Brendan Mulhall CC

Diocese of Limerick

Mount Saint Alphonsus
Limerick
Tel 061-315099
Fax 061-315303 (Church)
Mission house

Superior: Rev Adrian Egan
Vicar Superior
Rev John P. O'Riordan

Rev Patrick Breen
Rev Peter Byrne
Rev Thomas Byrne
Br Seamus Campion
Br John Cashman
Rev Seamus Devitt
Rev Seán Duggan
Rev Seamus Enright
Rev John Goode
Rev John Hanna
Rev Tadhg Herbert
Rev Sean Lawlor
Rev John Lucey
Br Anthony McCrave
Rev David McNamara
Rev Joseph McLoughlin
Rev James Murphy
Rev James O'Connor
Rev Michael G. O'Connor
Rev John J. O'Riordáin
Rev Denis O'Sullivan
Rev Patrick O'Sullivan
Rev William Power
Rev Patrick Walsh

St Clement's College
Limerick
Tel 061-315878/318749 (staff)
Tel 061-310294 (students)
Fax 061-316640
Secondary School for Boys

Rev Seamus Devitt (Chaplain)

Province of Cebu (Philippines)

PO Box 280,
6000 Cebu City,
Philippine Islands
Tel +63-32-2553954

Provincial: Rev Ben Ma

Vice-Province of Fortaleza
(Brazil)

Missionarios Redentoristas
Caixa Postal 85
60,001-970 Fortaleza
Est. do Ceara, Brazil
Tel +55-8532232016

Vice-Provincial: Rev Brian Holmes

Mission in Luxembourg

European Parish
Communauté Des
Rédemptoristes, BP 354, L-
2013 Luxembourg
Tel +352-224880

Rev Eamonn Breslin

Mission in Rome

Via Merulana 31
CP 2458, 00100 Rome, Italy
Tel +39-06-494901
Rev Martin McKeever
*(President, Alphonsian
Academy)*
Rev Seán Cannon
(Alphonsian Academy)
Rev Raphael Gallagher
Rev Anthony Mulvey

Mission in Siberia

Redemptorysty
Ul. Ochotskaja – 81, 6530045
Prokopievsk, Kiemierovskaya
OBL, Rossia–Sibir'
Tel +7-3846-699103

Rev Anthony Branagan

ROSMINIANS (IC)
Institute of Charity

Irish Province

Archdiocese of Dublin

1 Grace Park Gardens
Drumcondra, Dublin 9
Tel 01-8378314/8368730
Fax 01-8368726

Provincial
Rev Joseph O'Reilly
Email joreilly@rosminians.ie
Vocations Director
Rev Joseph O'Reilly

Br Eamon Fitzpatrick
Rev Tom Griffin
Rev John Mullen
Rev Frank Quinn

Clonturk House
Ormond Road,
Drumcondra, Dublin 9
Tel 01-8374840
Home for blind adults

Rev Gerard Cassidy
Rev Dennis Sweeney

Cottrell Lodge
16A Ormond Road,
Drumcondra, Dublin 9
Tel 01-8572234

Rev Gerald Cunningham
Rev Thomas Hubbart
Rev Terence O'Donnell
Rev Joseph O'Reilly
Rev Donal Sullivan

Archdiocese of Armagh

Faughart Parish
St Brigid's, Kilcurry,
Dundalk, Co Louth
Tel 042-9334410

Rector & Parish Priest
Very Rev Christopher McElwee

Br James Kane
(Mission Secretary)
Rev Bernard Hughes

Diocese of Cork & Ross

St Patrick's
Upton, Innishannon, Co Cork
Residential centre for
mentally handicapped adults
Tel 021-4776268/4776923
Fax 021-4776268

Rector: Rev Seamus McKenna

Rev Matthew Corcoran
Rev Polachan Thettayil

*Diocese of Waterford &
Lismore*

St Joseph's
Doire na hAbhann, Tickincar,
Clonmel, Co Tipperary
Tel 052-26914 Fax 052-26915

Rector: Rev P. J. Fegan

Rev Tom Coffey
Rev Matthew Gaffney
Rev Thomas Marley

Rosminian House of Prayer
Glencomeragh House,
Kilsheelan, Co Tipperary
Tel 052-33181

Rector & Director
Rev Pat Pierce

Rev James Browne
Rev Martin Murphy

St Oliver Plunkett's Parish
Cooleens, Clonmel,
Co Tipperary
Tel 052-25679

Rev Michael Hegarty PP
Rev Partolan O'Leary CC

*Enquiries concerning the
missions to:* Br James Kane
No. 1 Gracepark Gardens,
Drumcondra, Dublin 9
Rev Frank Quinn
St Brigid's, Kilcurry,
Dundalk, Co Louth
Rev Thomas Marley
Doire na nAbhann, Tickincor,
Clonmel, Co Tipperary

SACRED HEART FATHERS (SCJ) Congregation of the Priests of the Sacred Heart of Jesus

British-Irish Province

Archdiocese of Dublin

Sacred Heart Fathers
Fairfield, 66 Inchicore Road,
Dublin 8
Tel 01-4538655
Email scjdublin@eircom.net

Superior & Formation Director
Rev John Kelly
Promotions Director
Rev James Lawless

Rev Andrew Ryder
Rev Owen Wynne
Rev Sunil Issac
Br Francis Murphy
Br Marek Skorski

Ardlea Parish
St John Vianney
Ardlea Road, Dublin 5
Tel 01-8474123/8474173
Email jvianney@indigo.ie

Rev Robert Mann *(Moderator)*
Rev David Marsden
Rev Liam Rooney
Rev Marian Szalwa

ST COLUMBAN'S MISSIONARY SOCIETY (SSC)

Maynooth Mission to China –
Ireland

Superior General
Rev Thomas Muphy
Suite 504, Tower 1, Silvercord,
30 Canton Road Tst, Kowloon,
Hong Kong SAR
Email columban@
columbangeneralcouncil.com
Vicar General: Rev Trevor Trotter
Email trevor@
columbangeneralcouncil.com
Councillors: Rev John Burger
Email John@
columbangeneralcouncil.com
Rev Eamon Sheridan
Email eamon@
columbangeneralcouncil.com
Procurator General
Padhraic O'Loughlin
Collegio San Colombano,
Corso Trieste 57, 00198 Roma
Email procol.roma@gmail.com
Bursar General
Rev Otto Imholte
St Columban's Dalgan Park,
Navan, Co Meath
Tel 046-9021525
Columban Intercom Editor
Rev John Colgan
St Columban's Dalgan Park,
Navan, Co Meath
Tel 046-9021525
Email intercom@columban.com

Research on JPIC Priorities
Rev Sean McDonagh
St Columban's Dalgan Park,
Navan, Co Meath
Tel 046-9021525
Email
seanmcdonagh10@gmail.com
Research on Mission and Culture: Rev Sean Dwan
48 Princess Margaret Road,
Homantin, Kowloon,
Hong Kong SAR

Archdiocese of Dublin

St Columban's
Grange Road,
Donaghmede, Dublin 13
Tel 01-8476647

Columban History Co-ordiantor
Rev Patrick Crowley
Society Archivist
Rev Michael Molloy
Columban Companions in Mission Co-ordinator (Office):
Ms Claire Carey
Email
info@columbancompanions.ie
Columban Lay Missionary Co-ordinator: Ms Serafina Ranadi
Email serafinarv@gmail.com

St Columban's
67-68 Castle Dawson,
Rathcoffey Road, Maynooth,
Co Kildare
Tel 01-6286036
Rev William Curry
(Priest in charge)

St Joseph's
Balcurris, Dublin 11
Tel 01-8423865
Rev Val Kyne PP
Rev John Chute
Rev Gerald French

Diocese of Meath

St Columban's
Dalgan Park, Navan, Co Meath
Tel 046-9021525
Email
regionaldirector@columban.ie

Regional Director
Rev Donal Hogan
Regional Vice-Director
Rev Patrick Raleigh
Email patraleigh@columban.com
Regional Secretary
Celine Tuite
Fax 046-9022799

Regional Council
Rev Noel Daly
Rev Padraig O'Donovan

Regional Offices
Fax 046-9071297
Email
missionoffice@columban.com
Regional Bursar
Rev David Kenneally
Email
regionalbursar@columban.ie

Assistant Bursar
Rev Desmond Quinn
Columban Companions in Mission: Claire Carey
Communications Co-ordinator
Rev Malachy Smyth
Justice & Peace/Ongoing Education: Rev Patrick Raleigh
Mission Education
Michael O'Sullivan
Lay Missionary Contact Person
Angie Escarsa
Vocations Contact Person
Rev Padraig O'Donovan
Regional Newsletter
Rev Michael A. Duffy
Office Manager: Rev Noel Daly
Far East Editor: Rev Cyril Lovett
Website Editor
Rev Charles Meagher
www.columban.com
Personnel Counsellor
Rev Patrick J. Smyth
Board of Reconciliation
Rev Patrick E. Fahey, Rev
Gerald French
Alcoholic Advisory Board
Rev Michael A. Duffy,
Rev Valentine Kyne
Apostolic Work Liaison
Rev Peadar O'Loughlin
Columban History
Rev Neil Collins
Librarian
Rev Patrick McManus
Staff
Rev Cornelius K. Campion
Rev Sean A. Dunne
Rev Seamus Egan
Rev Brendan MacHale

St Columban's
Dalgan Park, Navan, Co Meath
Tel 046-9021525
Fax 046-9022799

House Superior
Rev Peter O'Neill
Vice-Superior
Rev Patrick E. Fahey
Bursar: Rev Nicholas Murray
Fax 046-9098214
Assistant Bursar
Rev Frank Carr
Residents
Rev Sean Brazil
Rev Frank Carr
Rev Charles Coulter
Rev Noel Daly
Rev Joseph Dolan
Rev Noel Doyle
Rev Michael Duffy
Rev Seamus Egan
Rev Brendan Fahey
Rev Patrick Fahey
Rev Kevin Fleming
Rev John Gilmore
Rev Malachy Hanratty
Rev Donal Hogan
Rev Anthony Kelly
Rev David Kenneally
Rev Oliver Kennedy
Rev Cyril Lovett
Rev Gerard Markey
Rev Charles Meagher

Rev Martin Murphy
Rev Brendan Murray
Rev Nicholas Murray
Rev Brendan MacHale
Rev Sean McDonagh
Rev Joseph McDonnell
Rev Sean McGrath
Rev Austin McGuinness
Rev Patrick McManus
Rev Padraig O'Donovan
Rev Francis O'Kelly
Rev Owen O'Leary
Rev Peadar O'Loughlin
Rev Desmond Quinn
Rev Patrick Raleigh
Rev Matthew Reilly
Rev Eugene Ryan
Rev Malachy Smyth
Rev Patrick J. Smyth
Rev Bernard Steed

St Columban's Retirement Home
Dalgan Park, Navan, Co Meath
Tel 046-9021525

Director
Rev Bernard Mulkerins

Staff
Rev Sean Brazil
Rev Brendan Fahey
Rev Brendan Murray
Rev Daniel O'Gorman

Residents
Rev Dan Baragry
Rev Eamonn Byrne
Rev Loughlin Campion
Rev Daniel Canniffe
Rev Leo Clarke
Rev Patrick Clarke
Rev Kevin Connors
Rev Patrick Creaton
Rev Kevin Devine
Rev Sean A. Dunne
Rev Brendan Fahey
Rev Francis Gallagher
Rev John Vincent Gallagher
Rev Joseph Gallagher
Rev James Gavigan
Rev Eugene Griffin
Rev Gerald Griffin
Rev Donal Halliden
Rev Thomas Hanahoe
Rev Frederick Hanson
Rev Michael Healy
Rev Patrick Healy
Rev Sean Holloway
Rev Mark Kavanagh
Rev Sean McGrath
Rev Patrick Meehan
Rev John Molloy
Rev Francis Mullany
Rev James Murphy
Rev Thomas Parker
Rev Geoffrey Revatto
Rev Thomas Revatto
Rev Sean Ryle
Rev Michael Scully
Rev Patrick Scully
Rev Joseph Shiels
Rev Terence Twohig
Rev David Wall
Rev Vincent Walsh

Allianz (ⅼ)

Vocations & Promotion Work/Mission Awareness
Rev Bredan Hoban
Rev Joseph McDonnell
Rev Gerard Markey
Rev Padraig O'Donovan
Rev Pat O'Herlihy
Rev Bernard Steed
Angie Escarsa LM

Priests on Special Work
Rev Donal N. Bennett (Philippine Chaplaincy)
Rev Joseph Cahill
Rev P. Aloysius Connaughton (Myanmar/Burma)
Rev Patrick Donohoe (Columban Sisters, Magheramore, Co Wicklow)
Rev Patrick G. Dooher (Director, Mission Institute)
Rev Owen Doyle (Chaplain, St John of God, Louth)
Rev John Gilmore (Immigration Apostolate)
Rev E. Norman Jennings (CPE)
Rev Sean McDonagh (Research JPIC)
Rev Austin McGuinness (Chaplain, St Joseph's, Trim)
Rev Neil Magill (Myanmar/Burma)
Rev Patrick J. Smyth (Retreat Work)

Priests on diocesan work in Ireland
Rev Eamon Conaty (Elphin)
Rev Sean Connaughton (Ardagh & Clonmacnois)
Rev Patrick Conway (Killaloe)
Rev David Cribben (Galway)
Rev Daniel Fitzgerald (Killaloe)
Rev Kieran Heneghan
Rev John Hickey (Clonfert)
Rev Michael Irwin (Limerick)
Rev Noel Lynch (Clonfert)
Rev John McEvoy (Meath)
Rev Austin McGuinness (Meath)
Rev Jeremiah Murphy (Meath)
Rev Aidan Murray (Clonfert)
Rev Kevin O'Boyle (Killaloe)
Rev Patrick O'Connor (Ferns)
Rev Michael O'Loughlin (Killaloe)
Rev Seamus O'Neill (Derry)

Columban Lay Missionaries working in Ireland
Gracia Kibad
Angie Escarsa (Co-ordinator)
Lorelei Ocaya
Marife Padao
Marivic Quilab
Virgie Tanate
Lenette Toledo
All from the Philippines

ST PATRICK'S MISSIONARY SOCIETY (SPS)

Diocese of Kildare & Leighlin

St Patrick's
Kiltegan, Co Wicklow
Tel 059-6473600
Fax 059-6473622
Society Leader
Rev Seamus O'Neill
Assistant Society Leader
Rev David Walsh
Councillors
Rev Thomas McDonnell
Rev Martin Reilly
Fax *(Society Leader & Council)*
059-6473644
Email spsgen@iol.ie
Society Justice Co-ordinator
Mr Joseph Murray
House Leader – Rome
Rev Paddy O'Reilly
Bursar General
Rev Denis O'Rourke
Regional Leader for Ireland
Rev Liam Blayney
Assistant Regional Leader
Rev Joseph Cantwell
Tel 059-6473680
Fax 059-6473623
Email spsireland@iol.ie
Regional Bursar
Rev Kyran Murphy
Kiltegan Leader
Rev Patrick Connolly
Director of Promotion
Rev William Fulton
Fax 059-6473622
Email spsoff@iol.ie
Office Manager
Ms Joanne Fortune
Kiltegan House Manager
Ms Marie Hyland
Editors, Africa
Rev Martin Smith &
Rev Thomas Kiggins
Email africa@spms.org
Slí an Chroí
Rev Seamus Whitney
Tel 059-6473488

Rev Jim Birmingham
Rev John Brady
Rev Eugene Bree
Rev Michael Brennan
Rev Alfie Byrne
Rev Tom Cafferty
Rev John P. Carroll
Rev Michael Conroy
Rev Tony Cronin
Rev Jeremiah Curran
Rev Sean Dillon
Rev Martin Dwan
Most Rev Edmund Fitzgibbon
Rev Dermot Foley
Rev Leonard Forristal
Rev Michael Golden
Rev Ned Grace
Rev Tom Grealy
Rev Gary Howley
Rev Paddy Hyland
Rev Michael Kane
Rev Andy Keating

Rev Thomas Kiggins
Rev Michael Long
Rev Kevin Longworth
Rev Henry McCarney
Rev Francis McElhatton
Rev Des McKeever
Rev Sean McTiernan
Rev P. J. Melican
Rev Patrick Moore
Rev Joseph Mulcahy
Rev Tom O'Connor
Rev Joe O'Conor
Rev Bartie O'Doherty
Rev Kevin O'Doherty
Rev Sean O'Dowd
Rev Pádraig Ó Fatharta
Rev Eugene O'Reilly
Rev Paddy O'Reilly
Rev Leo O'Sullivan
Rev Tony Prunty
Rev Seamus Reihill
Rev Noel Ryan
Rev Liam V. Scanlan
Rev Tom Smith
Rev Donal Twomey
Rev T. T. Vaughan
Rev Nicky Walsh
Rev Seamus Whelan

Priests on promotion work
Rev Con Cronin

Archdiocese of Dublin

St Patrick's
21 Leeson Park, Dublin 6
Tel 01-4977897 Fax 01-4962812
House Leader: Rev Peter Coyle

Rev Donal Dorr
Rev Kieran Flynn
Rev Danny Gibbons
Rev Vincent MacNamara
Rev Padraig Ó Máille
Rev Denis O'Neill
Rev Declan Thompson

Archdiocese of Tuam

St Patricks
Main Street, Knock, Co Mayo
Tel 094-9388661
House Leader
Rev Donald McDonagh

Diocese of Cork & Ross

Kiltegan House
11 Douglas Road, Cork
Tel 021-4969371
House Leader: Rev Jim Barry

Diocese of Down & Connor

St Patrick's
21 Old Cavehill Road,
Belfast BT15 5GT
Tel 028-90778696

Priests on special ministries

Rev Michael Browne
Rev Joe Flynn
Rev Thomas Grenham
Rev Patrick Kelly

Rev Michael Rodgers
Tearmann Spirituality Centre,
Brockagh, Glendalough,
Co Wicklow
Tel 0404-45208

Priests on temporary diocesan work

Rev John Carroll
Rev Colm Clinton
Rev Stan Connolly
Rev Bernard Conway
Rev Eugene Drumm
Rev John Flanagan
Rev Padraig Flanagan
Rev Peter Gillooly
Rev Noel Hayes
Rev Laurence Kearney
Rev John Kearns
Rev Michael Kelly
Rv Thomas Leahy
Rev John McManus
Rev Patrick O'Brien
Rev Timothy O'Connor
Rev James Regan
Rev Ray Reidy
Rev Ted Smyth
Rev Joseph Spillane
Rev Martin Spillane

SALESIANS (SDB)

The Irish Province includes
Ireland, Malta and Tunisia.

Archdiocese of Dublin

Provincialate
Salesian House,
St Teresa's Road,
Crumlin, Dublin 12
Tel 01-4555787 Fax 01-4558781
Email (Secretary)
tsdun@gofree.indigo.ie
tdunnesdb@gmail.com

Provincial
Very Rev John Horan
Email ruanet@indigo.ie
jchoransdb@hotmail.com

Salesian House
45 St Teresa's Road,
Crumlin, Dublin 12
Tel 01-4555605
House of residence

Rector: Rev Michael Ross
Vice-Rector
Rev Peter Coffey CC
Provincial Secretary
Rev Thomas Dunne

Rev Pat Brewster CC
Rev James Cummins
Rev Darryl D'Souza
Rev John Finnegan
Rev John Foster CC
Rev P. J. Healy (CC Walkinstown)
Br Colum Maguire *(Bursar)*
Rev Florence McCarthy
Rev Michael Scott CC

Rinaldi House
72 Sean McDermott Street,
Dublin 1
Tel 01-8363358 Fax 01-8552320
Post-Novitiate, house of
formation

Rector: Rev Hugh O'Donnell
Vice-Rector: Rev John Quinn

Rev Charles Cunningham

Don Bosco Houses
57 Lower Drumcondra Road,
Dublin 1
Tel 01-8360696/8373449

12 Clontarf Road, Dublin 3
Tel 01-8336009/8337045

Priest-in-Charge: Rev Val Collier

Rev James O'Halloran

Our Lady of Lourdes Parish
Seán McDermott Street,
Dublin 1
Tel 01-8363554

Rev Michael Casey Adm
Rev Tomasz Grzegorzewski PC

Salesian College
Maynooth Road,
Celbridge, Co Kildare
Tel 01-6275058/60
Fax 01-6272208
Secondary School
Tel 01-6272166/6272200

Rector: Rev Patrick Hennessy
Vice Rector: Rev Daniel Carroll
Bursar: Rev A. McEvoy

Br Orzechowski Arkadiusz
Rev Hagos Berhane
Rev Michael Browne
Rev John Butler
Rev Pat Egan
Br Piskula Lukasz
Rev Eunan McDonnell
Rev Pat J. O'Connor
Rev Casimir Raj

Diocese of Limerick

Salesian College
Pallaskenry, Co Limerick
Tel 061-393313 Fax 061-393354
Secondary and agricultural
schools
Salesian Mission Office
Tel 061-393223 Fax 061-393021

Rector: Rev Martin Loftus
Vice-Rector & Bursar
Rev Raymond McIntyre
Mission Procurator
Rev Dan Devitt

Br Patrick Coye
Rev Patrick Donnellan
Br Dluzniak Grzegorz
Rev Thomas Ingoldsby
Br Padraig McDonald

Salesian House
Milford, Castletroy, Limerick
Tel 061-330268/330914
Student hostel and parish

Rector: Rev Koenraad Van Gucht
*(Chaplain, University of
Limerick)*
*Vice-Rector, Bursar and Parish
Priest:* Rev John Campion PP

Rev Vincent Diffley
Rev John Fagan
(Chaplain, Milford House)
Rev Joseph Harrington
Rev Bob Swinburne CC

Diocese of Meath

Salesian House
Warrenstown,
Drumree, Co Meath
Tel 01-8259761
Community 01-8259894
Fax 01-8240298

Rector: Rev P. J. Nyland
Vice-Rector: Rev Noel Burke
Bursar: Br James O'Hare

Rev David Cahill
Rev Thomas Kenny
Br Colm Kennedy
Rev George McCaughey
Rev Donal O'Mahony

Elsewhere in Ireland
Rev Desmond Campion
*(Chaplain Naval Service,
Haulbowline, Cobh, Cork)*
Rev Thomas Clowe CC
St Paul's, Ayrfield, Dublin 13
Rev G. Dowd *(Chaplain,
Custume Barracks, Athlone)*
Rev P. J. Healy CC
162 Walkinstown Road,
Dublin 12
Rev James Somers CC
Chapelizod
Rev Patrick J. Somers
*(Chaplain, The Curragh,
Co Kildare)*
Rev Joseph Whittle
Kilcullen Road,
Dunlavin, Co Wicklow
Rev Gerard O'Neill (Chaplain,
Collins Barracks, Cork)

SALVATORIANS (SDS)

Archdiocese of Dublin

Our Lady of Victories
Sallynoggin,
Dun Laoghaire, Co Dublin
Tel 01-2854667
Fax 01-2847024
Email
sallynogginparish@eircom.net

Superior: Rev Liam Talbot

Rev Eric Powell

SERVITES (OSM) Order of Friar Servants of Mary

Provincial
Very Rev Patrick Carroll
St Mary's Priory, 264 Fulham
Road, London SW10 9EL
Tel (+44) 20 779 52181

Assistant Provincial
Rev Chris O'Brien
Servite Priory, Benburb,
Co Tyrone BT71 7JZ
Northern Ireland
Tel 028-37548241

Province of the Isles

Archdiocese of Dublin

Servite Priory
St Peregrine, Kiltipper Road,
Tallaght, Dublin 24
Tel 01-4517115

Prior: Rev Tim Flynn

Rev Pat Carroll
Rev Jimmy Kelly

Servite Oratory
Rathfarnham
Shopping Centre, Dublin 14
Tel 01-4936300

Director: Rev Timothy Flynn

Church of the Divine Word
Marley Grange,
25-27 Hermitage Downs,
Rathfarnham, Dublin 16
Tel 01-4944295/4941064
Fax 01-4941069

Prior: Rev Liam Tracey

Very Rev Colm McGlynn PP
Rev Camillus McGrane CC

Archdiocese of Armagh

Servite Priory
Benburb, Dungannon,
Co Tyrone, BT71 7JZ
Tel 028-37548241
Tel 01861-548241/548533
Retreat, Conference Centre
and youth centre

Prior: Very Rev Chris O'Brien

Rev Sean Lennon
Rev Eamonn McCreave
Rev Colum McDonnell
Very Rev Raymond O'Connell
Rev Bernard Thorne
Br Eugene Traynor

Outside Ireland

Br Patrick Gethins (OSM)
Curia Generalizia,
Piazza S. Marcello, Al Corso 5,
00187 Roma, Italy
Tel 00396-699301

SOCIETY OF AFRICAN MISSIONS (SMA) Societas Missionum Ad Afros

Diocese of Cork & Ross

African Missions
Provincial House
Feltrim, Blackrock Road, Cork
Tel 021-4292871
Fax 021-4292873
Email provincial@sma.ie

Provincial
Rev Fachtna O'Driscoll
Vice Provincial
Rev John Dunne
Provincial Councillor
Rev Damian Bresnahan

African Missions
Blackrock Road, Cork
Tel 021-4292871

Superior
Rev Colum P. O'Shea
Vice-Superior
Rev Edward O'Connor
Bursar
Rev William O'Sullivan
Provincial Secretary
Rev Paul A. D'Arcy
Provincial Bursar
Rev Malachy Flanagan
Assistant Provincial Bursar
Rev Oscar Welsh
Provincial Archivist
Rev Edmund M. Hogan
*Provincial Development
Officer:* Rev Martin Kavanagh
Director of Communications
Rev Martin Kavanagh
JPIC Director
Rev Angelo Lafferty

Rev Liam Burke
Rev Anthony J. Butler
Rev Michael Cahill
Rev John Casey
Rev John Clancy
Rev Eugene Connolly
Rev Bernard Cotter
Rev Michael Darcy
Rev Thomas Faherty
Rev James Fegan
Br Thomas Fitzgerald
Rev Francis Furey
Rev William Ghent
Rev Gerard Hackett
Rev Hugh Harkin
Rev Jeremiah Healy
Rev Patrick Jennings
Rev James Kirstein
Rev Sean Lynch

Allianz (Ⅱ)

Rev Joseph Maguire
Rev Seán MacCarthy
Rev Michael McEgan
Rev Colm McKeogh
Rev Gregory McGovern
Rev H. McLoughlan
Rev Thomas Mullahy
Rev Daniel Murphy
Rev Fionnbarra O'Cuilleanáin
Rev Anthony O'Donnell
Rev Con O'Leary
Rev Eugene O'Riordan
Rev Robert O'Regan
Rev Bernard J. Raymond
Rev Desmond Smith

SMA House
Wilton, Cork
Tel 021-4541069/4541884

Superior
Rev Daniel Cashman
Bursar
Rev Terence Gunn

Rev Francis Coltsmann
Rev James Conlon
Rev William Foley
Rev Thomas Furlong
Rev Thomas Gorman
Rev John Horgan
Rev William Kennedy
Rev Angelo Lafferty
Rev Liam O'Callaghan
Rev James O'Hea
Rev Denis O'Sullivan
Rev John Quinlan
Br James Redmond
Rev Leo Silke

St Joseph's
African Missions Parish
Blackrock Road,
Cork
Tel 021-4293325
Email smapar@oceanfree.net

Rev Thomas Wade PP
Rev Eugene McLoughlin CC

St Joseph's Parish
Wilton, Cork
Tel 021-4341362
Fax 021-4343940

Rev Cormac Breathnach PP
Rev Denis Collins CC

Coís Tíne Pastoral
Outreach to Immigants
21 Victoria Avenue,
Cork
Tel 021-4316593
Email coistine@sma.ie

Director: Rev Angelo Lafferty

Archdiocese of Dublin

SMA House
82 Ranelagh Road,
Ranelagh, Dublin 6
Tel 01-4968162/3
Fax 01-4968164

Superior: Rev John O'Brien
Bursar: Rev Owen McKenna

Rev John Bowe
Rev Joseph Egan
Rev Seán Hayes
Rev Francis Meehan
Rev Kevin O'Gorman

Parish of St Peter the Apostle
Neilstown, Clondalkin,
Dublin 22
Tel 01-4573546

Very Rev Donal Toal PP
Rev Paul Monahan CC

Also in Dublin
Rev Sean Healy
Social Justice Ireland,
Arena House, Arena Road,
Sandyford, Dublin 18
Tel 01-2130724
www.socialjustice.ie

Diocese of Galway

SMA House
Claregalway, Co Galway
Tel 091-798880
Fax 091-798879
Email smafathers@eircom.net

Superior
Rev Seamus Nohilly
Bursar
Rev Patrick Whelan

Rev Martin Costello
Rev Brendan Dunning
Rev Thomas Fenlon
Rev Patrick McGovern
Rev Daniel O'Neill

Diocese of Dromore

Dromantine College
Dromantine, Newry,
Co Down BT34 1RH
Tel 028-30821224
Fax 028-30821704

Superior
Rev Noel O'Leary
Vice Superior and Bursar
Rev Peter Thompson
Vocations Ministry
Vacant

Rev Lee Cahill
Rev Edward Deeney
Rev Maurice Kelleher
Rev Hugh McKeown
Rev Kevin Mulhern
Rev Martin Nolan
Rev John Travers

Dromantine Retreat and Conference Centre
Dromatine College,
Newry, Co Down BT34 1RH
Tel 028-30821219
Fax 028-30821963
Email d.conferencecentre
@btopenworld.com

Director
Rev Desmond Corrrigan

Temporary diocesan work in Ireland

Rev Edward Casey
Rev John Dunleavy
Rev Thomas Kearney
Rev Michael Kidney
Rev Sean Kilbane
Rev Patrick Lynch
Rev John McCormack
Rev Kieran Morahan
Rev Michael Nohilly
Rev Martin O'Hare
Rev Hugh O'Kane
Rev Patrick O'Mahony
Rev Seán Ryan
Rev Gerard Sweeney

Retired in Ireland outside SMA houses

Rev Michael Boyle
Rev Eamonn Kelly
Rev Vincent Lawless
Rev Patrick Mackle

Church of Our Lady of the Rosary and St Patrick
61 Blackhorse Road,
Walthamstow,
London E17 7AS, England
Tel 20-85203647

Very Rev John Brown PP

Retired in Britain
Rev Donal O'Connor
Rev Martin Walsh

Rome
Generalate
Via della Nocetta 111,
00164 Rome, Italy
Tel 06-6616841 Fax 06-66168490
Email smaroma@smainter.org

Superior General
Very Rev Kieran O'Reilly
Anglophone Secretary
Rev Derek Kearney
Bursar General
Rev Jarlath Walsh

Further Studies
Rev Hugh Lagan, Maryland,
USA

Seconded to US Province
Rev Patrick Kelly

SOCIETY OF ST PAUL (SSP)

The Society of St Paul in
Ireland operates exclusively
through the mass media.

Archdiocese of Dublin

Society of St Paul
Moyglare Road,
Maynooth, Co Kildare
Tel 01-6285933 Fax 01-6289330
Email book@stpauls.ie

Superior: Rev Pius Nechikattil

Rev Alex Anadam
Rev John Echavarria
Br Pio Rizzo

Diocese of Meath

St Paul Book Centre
Castle Street,
Athlone, Co Westmeath
Tel/Fax 090-6492882
Email
saintpaul_books@yahoo.com

SONS OF DIVINE PROVIDENCE (FDP)

The Irish Foundation is part of
the Missionary English-
speaking Delegation of 'Mary
Mother of the Church'.

Regional Superior
Rev Philip Kehoe
c/o Don Orione 8, Rome, Italy
Local Co-ordinator
Rev Stephen Beale
25 Lower Teddington Road,
Kingston-on-Thames, Surrey
Tel 208-9775130

Archdiocese of Dublin

Sarsfield House
Sarsfield Road,
Ballyfermot, Dublin 10
Tel 01-6266193/6266233
Fax 01-6260303
Email don-orion@clubi.ie

Rev Roy Elikowski
Rev Michael Moss

VINCENTIANS (CM)

Vincentian communities of the
Irish Province are established
in Ireland and England.

Archdiocese of Dublin

Provincial Office
St Paul's, Sybil Hill,
Raheny, Dublin 5
Tel 01-8510840/8510842
Fax 01-8510846
Email cmdublin@iol.ie
www.vincentians.ie

Provincial: Very Rev Brian Moore

Allianz (ⁱⁱⁱ)

All Hallows Institute for Mission and Ministry
Drumcondra, Dublin 9
Tel 01-8373745/6
Fax 01-8377642
Email info@allhallows.ie

President
Very Rev Mark Noonan
Superior
Very Rev Joseph McCann

Seminary/Pastoral Ministry/Pastoral Leadership
Rev Desmond Beirne
Rev Eugene Curran
Rev Brian Nolan
Ministry to Priests, Missions and Retreats
Tel 01-8373745/6

Rev Thomas Lane
Rev Kevin Scallon

11 Iona Drive
Glasnevin, Dublin 9
Tel 01-8305238
Superior
Very Rev Stephen Monaghan

Rev Sean Farrell

St Paul's College
Raheny, Dublin 5
Tel 01-8314011/2 (college)
Tel 01-8318113 (community)
Fax 01-8316387
Secondary School
Superior
Very Rev Eamon Flanagan

Rev Anthony Clune
Rev Simon Clyne
Rev Michael Dunne
Rev Aidan Galvin
Rev Sean Johnston
Rev Richard McCullen
Rev Bernard Meade
Rev Brian Mullan
Rev Hugh Murnaghan
Rev Brendan Steen
Rev Thomas Woods

Phibsboro
St Peter's, Dublin 7
Tel 01-8389708/8389841
Email vinphibs@iol.ie
Superior
Very Rev Paschal Scallon

Rev Eamon Devlin
Rev Patrick Hughes
Rev Patrick Collins
Rev Joh Concannon
Rev Lazarus Iwueke
Rev Colm McAdam
Rev Andrew Spelman

St Joseph's
44 Stillorgan Park,
Blackrock, Co Dublin
Tel 01-2886961

Superior
Very Rev Joseph Cunningham

Rev Denis Collins
Rev Thomas Davitt
Rev Francis MacMorrow

St Vincent's College
Castleknock, Dublin 15
Tel 01-8213051
Secondary Day School for Boys

President/Superior
Very Rev Peter Slevin

Rev Stanislaus Brindley
Rev Roderic Crowley
Rev John Gallagher
Rev Desmond MacMorrow
Rev Michael McCullagh
Rev Henry Slowey

Diocese of Cork & Ross

St Vincent's
122 Sunday's Well Road,
Cork
Tel 021-4304070/4304529
Fax 021-4300103

Superior
Very Rev Jack Harris PP

Rev Timothy Casey CC
Rev Aidan McGing

Diocese of Down & Connor

99 Cliftonville Road
Belfast BT14 6JQ
Tel 028-90751771
Fax 028-90740547
Email cmbelfast@ntlworld.co.uk

Superior: Very Rev Peter Gildea

Rev Adrian Eastwood
Rev James Rafferty

COMMUNITIES OF RELIGIOUS BROTHERS

In this section, details of each community's main house are given, followed by a list of the dioceses in which the community is present. For more information on houses in particular dioceses, please see the entry for the appropriate diocese.

ALEXIAN BROTHERS (CFA)

Anglo-Irish Province

Regional Residence
Churchfield, Knock, Co Mayo
Tel 094-9376996
Email alexianbros@eircom.net

Regional Leader
Br Barry Butler

Dublin, Achonry

BROTHERS OF CHARITY

St Joseph's Region

Regional Office
Regional Administration
Kilcornan Centre,
Clarinbridge, Co Galway
Tel 091-796389/796413
Fax 091-796352
Email bronoelcorcoran@galway.brothersofcharity.ie

Regional Leader
Br Noel Corcoran

Cork & Ross, Galway,
Limerick, Ossory

CHRISTIAN BROTHERS (CFC)

European Province

Province Centre
Marino, Griffith Avenue,
Dublin 9

Leadership Team
Province Leader: Br J. K. Mullan
Deputy Leader: Br J. Burke

Br M. Reynolds
Br Edmund Garvey
Br M. O'Flaherty
Br E. Coupe
Br J. Donovan

Cashel & Emly, Dublin, Cork,
Derry, Down & Connor, Ferns,
Galway, Kildare & Leighlin,
Killaloe, Limerick, Meath,
Ossory, Waterford & Lismore

As of the 1 September 2008,
The Edmund Rice Schools Trust became Trustees of the 97 schools previously under the trusteeship of the Christian Brothers. The Company is established for the following charitable objects: to ensure and foster the advancement of education and to further the aims and purposes of Catholic Education in the Edmund Rice tradition in colleges, schools and other educational projects in Ireland owned or operated by the Company in accordance with the religion and education philosophy of the Company as stated in the Edmund Rice Schools Trust Charter, and so that they may continue to provide Catholic education in the spirit and tradition of Blessed Edmund Rice into the future for the people of Ireland.

DE LA SALLE BROTHERS (FSC)

Provincialate
121 Howth Road,
Dublin 3
Tel 01-8331815
Fax 01-8339130
Email province@iol.ie

Provincial
Br Stephen Deignan

Armagh, Dublin, Tuam,
Down & Connor, Kildare & Leighlin, Ossory, Waterford & Lismore

FRANCISCAN BROTHERS (OSF)

Franciscan Brothers of the Third Order Regular

A branch of the Regular Third Order of Penance of St Francis of Asissi, with communities in East Africa and the USA as well as Ireland.

Generalate
Mountbellew, Co Galway
Tel 090-9679295
Fax 090-9679687
Email franciscanbrs@eircom.net

Minister General
Br Peter Roddy
Assistant General
Br Michael Burke
Councillors
Br Sean Conway
Br Boniface Kyalo
Br Conal Thomas
Procurator General
Br Conal Thomas
Bursar General
Br Gerald Smith
Secretary General
Br Conal Thomas

Dublin, Tuam, Meath

MARIST BROTHERS (FMS)

The Marist Brothers in Ireland are part of the province of West Central Europe principally involved in education.

Provincialate
Sophiaweg 4
NL-6523 NJ Nijmegen
Netherlands
Email josmckee@maristen.nl

Provincial Superior
Br Joseph McKee

Dublin, Ardagh & Clonmacnois, Killala

PATRICIAN BROTHERS (FSP)

Brothers of St Patrick

Patrician Brothers' General Secretariat
Newbridge, Co Kildare
Tel 045-432357/087-2949504
Fax 045-432731
Email patriciangeneralate
@eircom.net

Superior General
Br Jerome Ellens
Vicar: Br Peter Ryan

Councillors
Br James O'Rourke
Br Edward McCarthy

Dublin, Kildare & Leighlin,
Clogher, Galway

PRESENTATION BROTHERS (FPM)

Generalate
Mount St Joseph,
Blarney Street, Cork
Tel 021-4392160
Fax 021-4398200
Email presgen@eircom.net

Congregation Leader
Br Martin Kenneally

Provincial House
3 Heatherton Park,
South Douglas Road, Cork
Tel 021-4361308
Fax 021-4364043
Email fpmoffice@ireland.com

Province Leader
Br Walter Hurley

Dublin, Cloyne, Cork & Ross,
Kerry, Killaloe, Waterford &
Lismore

ST JOHN OF GOD BROTHERS (OH)

The Hospitaller Order of
St John of God

The Irish Province has houses in
New Jersey, USA and Malawi.

Provincial Curia
Granada, Stillorgan, Co Dublin
Tel 01-2771495 Fax 01-2831274
Email provincial@sjog.ie

Provincial: Br Laurence Kearns

Provincial Administration
Hospitaller House,
Stillorgan, Co Dublin
Tel 01-2771500 Fax 01-2831257

Director
Email provincial@sjog.ie

Armagh, Dublin, Tuam, Down
& Connor, Kerry

COMMUNITIES OF RELIGIOUS SISTERS

*In this section, details of each
community's main house are
given, followed by a list of the
dioceses in which the
community is present. For
more information on houses
in particular dioceses, please
see the entry for the
appropriate diocese.*

ADORERS OF THE SACRED HEART OF JESUS OF MONTMARTRE (OSB)

St Benedict's Priory
The Mount, Cobh, Co Cork
Tel/Fax 021-4811354

Prioress
Mother Mary Vianney

Cloyne

AUGUSTINIAN SISTERS

'Villa Nova' Prayer House
Grangecon, Co Wicklow
Tel 045-403874

Contact: Sr Mary Bernard

Kildare & Leighlin

BENEDICTINE NUNS (OSB)

Kylemore Abbey
Kylemore, Connemara,
Co Galway
Tel 095-41146
Email info@kylemoreabbey.ie

Prioress Administrator
Sr Máire Hickey

Tuam

BLESSED SACRAMENT SISTERS

Blessed Sacrament Convent
High Street,
Tullamore, Co Offaly
Tel 057-9351371
Email rsstlm@eircom.net

Dublin, Meath

BON SAUVEUR SISTERS

Carriglea
Dungarvan, Co Waterford
Tel 058-45884 Fax 058-45891
Email lbscarriglea@eircom.net

Superior: Sr Mary Fitzgerald

Waterford & Lismore

BON SECOURS SISTERS (Paris)

Provincial House
College Road, Cork
Tel 021-4542416
Fax 021-4542533

Provincial
Sr Margaret Mary Hanafin
Email mhanafin@province.
bonsecours.ie

Dublin, Tuam, Cloyne, Cork &
Ross, Down & Connor, Galway,
Kerry

Sisters of the Irish Province are
also working in Peru and
Tanzania and South Africa

BON SECOURS SISTERS (Troyes)

St Paul's Home
Dooradoyle, Limerick
Tel 061-28209

Limerick

BRIGIDINE SISTERS Sisters of St Brigid

Brigidine Generalate
Unit 106, 678 Victoria Road,
Ryde, N.S.W. 2112, Australia

Congregational Leader
Sr Maree Marsh

Dublin, Galway, Kildare &
Leighlin

CARMELITE MONASTERIES

Archdiocese of Dublin

Carmelite Monastery of the Immaculate Conception
Roebuck, Dublin 14
Tel 01-2884732 Fax 01-2780145
Altar Breads Fax 01-2835037
Email
carmel@roebuckcarmel.com

Prioress: Sr Teresa Whelan

Carmelite Monastery of the Assumption
Firhouse, Dublin 24
Tel 01-4526320
Email
firhousecarmel@oceanfree.net

Prioress: Sr John Cunningham

Carmelite Monastery of the Immaculate Heart of Mary
Delgany, Co Wicklow
email prioress@carmelite
monasterydelgany.ie

Prioress: Sr Monica Lawless

Carmelite Monastery of the Incarnation
Hampton, Gracepark Road,
Drumcondra, Dublin 9
Email carmeliteshampton@
eircom.net

Prioress: Sr Brigid Murphy

Carmelite Monastery of St Joseph
Seapark, Malahide, Co Dublin
Email malahidecarmelites@
eircom.net

Prioress: Sr Rosalie Burke

Carmelite Monastery of St Joseph
Upper Kilmacud Road,
Stillorgan, Co Dublin
Email contact@kilmacudcarmel.ie

Prioress: Sr Carmel Breen

Archdiocese of Tuam

Carmelite Monastery
Tranquilla, Knock, Co Mayo
Email
tranquillacarmel@eircom.net

Prioress: Sr Catherine

Diocese of Clonfert

St Joseph's Monastery
Mount Carmel, Loughrea,
Co Galway
Email
theholychild1@eircom.net

Prioress
Sr M Catharina Murphy

Diocese of Dromore

Carmelite Monastery
42 Glenvale Road, Newry,
Co Down BT34 2RD
Fax 028/048-30252778
Email
nuns@carmelitesglenvale.org

Prioress: Sr M. Carmel Clarke

Diocese of Ferns

Mount Carmel Monastery
New Ross, Co Wexford

Prioress
Sr Margaret Mary Morris

Diocese of Waterford & Lismore

St Joseph's Carmelite Monastery
Tallow, Co Waterford
Tel 058-56205
Email
carmeltallow@eircom.net

Prioress: Sr Teresa Gibbons

Allianz (ⅼⅼⅼ)

CARMELITE SISTERS FOR THE AGED AND INFIRM

Our Lady's Manor
Bullock Castle,
Dalkey, Co Dublin
Tel 01-2806993 Fax 01-2844802
Email
ourladysmanor1@eircom.net

Superior
Sr Therese Eileen Mulvaney
Email sistereileen@eircom.net
Administrator
Sr Bernadette Murphy

Dublin

SISTERS OF CHARITY OF THE INCARNATE WORD

Carrigoran House
Newmarket-on-Fergus, Co Clare
Tel 061-368100 Fax 061-368170
Email
carrigoranhouse@eircom.net

Administrator
Sr Christina Murphy

Killaloe

CHARITY OF JESUS AND MARY SISTERS

Anglo-Irish Province
Moore Abbey
Monasterevin, Co Kildare
Tel 045-525327

Contact
Sr Mary-Anna Lonergan
Email maryannal@eircom.net
Provincial Superior
Sr Helen O'Brien
Email helen@scjm.org
108 Spring Road, Letchworth,
Hertfordshire SG6 3B
Tel 0462-675694

Dublin, Kildare & Leighlin,
Meath

CHARITY OF NEVERS SISTERS

76 Cherrywood,
Loughlinstown Drive,
Dun Laoghaire, Co Dublin
Tel 01-2720453

Dublin

SISTERS OF CHARITY OF OUR LADY MOTHER OF MERCY

St Andrews
3 Avonmore Road,
Raheen, Limerick
Tel 061-229935

Superior: Sr Clare Clifford

Limerick

CHARITY OF ST PAUL THE APOSTLE SISTERS

St Paul's Convent
Greenhills, Dublin 12
Tel 01-4505358
Fax 01-4505132

Superior: Sr Mary Lyons
Email
marylyons446@hotmail.com

Dublin, Limerick

CHRISTIAN RETREAT SISTERS

Holy Rosary Convent
Mountbellew, Ballinasloe,
Co Galway
Tel 090-9679311

Contact: Sr Margaret Buckley
Email
margaretmbuckley@eircom.net
Regional Superior
Sr Melanie Kingston

House of Prayer
35 Seymour Road,
East Molesey,
Surrey KT8 0PB, England
Tel 0044-2089412313

Tuam

CISTERCIANS

St Mary's Abbey
Glencairn,
Co Waterford
Tel 058-56168
Fax 058-56616
Email
glencairnabbey@eircom.net

Abbess: Sr Marie Fahy

Waterford & Lismore

CLARISSAN MISSIONARY SISTERS OF THE BLESSED SACRAMENT

**Our Lady of Guadalupe
Residence for Students**
28 Waltersland Road,
Stillorgan,
Co Dublin
Tel/Fax 01-2886600
Email
misclaridub@hotmail.com
www.guadaluperesidence.com

Superior
Sr Francisca Riera

Dublin

CONGREGATION OF THE SISTERS OF MERCY

The Congregation of the Sisters of Mercy is an International Congregation. It has 2498 members currently serving in Ireland, Britain, Brazil, Kenya, South Africa, Peru, Nigeria, Zambia and the US.

Congregational Leadership Team
Sr Coirle McCarthy
(Congregational Leader)
Sr Cáit O'Dwyer
Sr Susan DeGuide
Sr Kathy Rule
Sr Miriam Kerrisk

Congregational Offices
'Rachamim',
13/14 Moyle Park, Convent
Road, Clondalkin, Dublin 22
Tel 01-4673737 Fax 01-4673749
Email mercy@csm.ie
Website www.sistersofmercy.ie

The Northern Province
comprising the dioceses of
Raphoe, Derry, Down &
Connor, Armagh, Dromore,
Clogher, Kilmore, Meath and
the regions of Nigeria and
Zambia.

Provincial
Sr Nellie McLaughlin

Sr Joan Dunne
Sr Rose Marie Conlan
Sr Anne Lyng
Sr Winnie Lynott
Sr Eleanor Murphy

Provincial Office
74 Main Street, Clogher,
Co Tyrone BT76 0AA
Tel 028-85548127
Fax 028-85549459
Email mercy@mercynth.org

The Western Province
comprising the dioceses of
Killala, Achonry, Elphin,
Galway, Tuam, Clonfert,
Ardagh & Clonmacnois.

Provincial
Sr Elizabeth Manning

Sr Mary Walsh
Sr Martina Barrett
Sr Margaret Farrell
Sr Angela Forde

Provincial Office
Caoineas, Society Street,
Ballinasloe, Co Galway
Tel 090-9645202
Fax 090-9645203
Email caoineas@smwestprov.ie

The South Central Province
comprising the dioceses of
Dublin, Cashel & Emly, Kildare
& Leighlin, Killaloe and
Limerick.

Provincial: Sr Peggy Collins

Sr Thomasina Finn
Sr Therese Barry
Sr Breda Coman
Sr Anne Doyle
Sr Patricia O'Meara

Provincial Office, Oldtown,
Sallins Road, Naas, Co Kildare
Tel 045-876784 Fax 045-871509
Email provoffice@mercyscp.ie

The Southern Province
comprising the dioceses of
Cork & Ross, Cloyne, Kerry,
Ferns, Ossory, Waterford &
Lismore.

Provincial: Sr Liz Murphy

Sr Bernie Ryan
Sr Maria Goretti Comerford
Sr Veronica Mangan
Sr Monica Mohally

Provincial Office
Bishop Street, Cork
Tel 021-4975380
Fax 021-4915220
Email
provincialoffice@mercysouth.ie

CONGREGATION OF THE SISTERS OF SION

547 Ormeau Road,
Belfast BT7 3JA

Down & Connor

CROSS AND PASSION CONGREGATION

299 Boarshaw Road,
Middleton,
Manchester M24 2PF
Tel 0161-6553184
Fax 0161-6533666
Provincial: Sr Francis Cullen

Dublin, Down & Connor

DAUGHTERS OF CHARITY OF ST VINCENT DE PAUL

St Catherine's Provincial House
Dunardagh, Blackrock, Co Dublin
Tel 01-2882669/2882896/
2882660 Fax 01-2834485

Local Superior
Sr Carmel McArdle
Provincial Superior
Sr Catherine Prendergast

Armagh, Dublin, Tuam, Cork
& Ross, Down & Connor,
Ferns, Galway and Killaloe

DAUGHTERS OF THE CROSS OF LIÈGE

Daughters of the Cross
Beech Park, Stillorgan,
Co Dublin
Tel 01-2887401/2887315
Fax 01-2881499
Email beechpark@eircom.net

Superior: Sr Anne Kelly

Dublin

DAUGHTERS OF THE HEART OF MARY

St Joseph's
Tivoli Road, Dun Laoghaire,
Co Dublin
Tel 01-2801204

Dublin

DAUGHTERS OF THE HOLY SPIRIT

88 Foxfield Road
Raheny, Dublin 5
Tel 01-8312795

Contact person
Sr Teresa Buckley DHSp

Provincial Superior
Sr Dympna Connolly
Provincial House,
103 Harlestone Road,
Northhampton,
Norths NN5 7AQ, England

Dublin

DAUGHTERS OF JESUS

Ard Mhuire,
12 Shorelands, Greenisland,
Co Antrim BT38 8FB
Tel 02890-864759

Superior: Sr Teresa McMenamin

Provincial Superior
Sr Anne Thompson
55 Nightingale Road,
Rickmansworth,
Herts WD3 7BU, England
Tel 01923-897386

Dublin, Down & Connor

DAUGHTERS OF MARY AND JOSEPH

Leadership Team
Email
dmjirishregion@eircom.net

Dublin, Kerry, Kildare &
Leighlin, Ossory

DAUGHTERS OF OUR LADY OF THE SACRED HEART

Provincial House
14 Rossmore Avenue,
Templeogue, Dublin 6W
Tel 01-4903200
Tel/Fax 01-4903113
Email olshprov@eircom.net

Provincial: Sr Vianney Murray

Dublin, Clogher

DISCIPLES OF THE DIVINE MASTER

Newtownpark Avenue,
Blackrock, Co Dublin
Tel 01-2114949/2886414
Fax 01-2836935

Regional Superior
Sr Kathryn Williams
Email
kathrynwilliams@pddm.org
www.pddm.org/ireland

Dublin, Elphin

DOMINICAN CONTEMPLATIVES

Monastery of St Catherine of Siena
The Twenties, Drogheda,
Co Louth
Tel 041-9838524
Email siena@eircom.net

Prioress: Sr Mairéad Mullen

Armagh

DOMINICAN SISTERS (King William's Town)

Our Lady of Fatima Convent
Oakpark, Tralee, Co Kerry
Tel 066-7125641/066-7125900
Fax 066-7180834
Email teresamcevoy@
fatimahome.com

Contact: Sr Teresa McEvoy OP

Kerry

DOMINICAN SISTERS

Region House
Dominican Sisters, Mary
Bellew House, Navan Road,
Cabra, Dublin 7
Tel 01-8383716/8682335
Fax 01-8387828
Email dominica@indigo.ie

Region Prioress in capite
Sr Marie Cunningham

Dublin, Down & Connor,
Galway

FAITHFUL COMPANIONS OF JESUS

Provincial House
12 Priory Walk,
Whitehall Road, Dublin 12
Tel 01-4924114 Fax 01-4924093

Provincial Leader: Sr Maria Dunne
Email
mariadunne77@hotmail.com
Bursar: Sr Frances Leahy
Tel 01-4924044 Fax 01-4924093
Eamil francesleahy@eircom.net

Dublin, Ferns, Limerick

FAMILY OF ADORATION SISTERS

St Aidan's Monastery
Ferns, Co Wexford
Tel 053-9366634
Email staidansferns@eircom.net

Superior: Sr Dolores O'Brien

Ferns, Down & Connor

FRANCISCAN MISSIONARIES OF THE DIVINE MOTHERHOOD

Regional House
Assisi, Harbour Road,
Ballinasloe, Co Galway
Tel 090-9642320
Fax 090-9642648

Regional Leader
Sr Anne O'Brien
Email anne4@gofree.indigo.ie

Dublin, Armagh, Clonfert, and
Kerry

FRANCISCAN MISSIONARIES OF MARY

Provincial House
5 Vaughan Avenue,
London W6 0XS
Tel 020-87484077

Provincial Superior
Sr Joan Doyle
Email joanfmm@aol.com

Dublin, Galway, Limerick

FRANCISCAN MISSIONARIES OF OUR LADY

Ballinderry
Mullingar, Co Westmeath
Tel 044-41500

Regional Superior
Sr Cecilia Cody
Email
ccody@stfrancishospital.ie

Meath

FRANCISCAN MISSIONARIES OF ST JOSEPH

Prague House
Freshford, Co Kilkenny
Tel 056-8832281

Regional Superior
Sr Bridget Anne Lonergan

Dublin, Cork & Ross, Ossory

FRANCISCAN MISSIONARY SISTERS FOR AFRICA

Generalate
34a Gilford Road,
Sandymount, Dublin 4
Tel 01-2838376 Fax 01-2602049
Email fmsagen@iol.ie

Congregational Leader
Sr Miriam Duggan

Armagh, Dublin

FRANCISCAN SISTERS

6 Collinstown Grove
Neilstown, Dublin 22
Tel 01-4573049
Email
angela_oconnell@eircom.net

Dublin

FRANCISCAN SISTERS OF THE ATONEMENT

2 Clooneen Park
Manorhamilton, Co Leitrim
Tel 071-9856785
Email fsoa@eircom.net

Superior: Sr Ita Flynn

Kilmore

FRANCISCAN SISTERS OF THE IMMACULATE CONCEPTION

Franciscan Sisters,
97/99 Riverside Park,
Clonshaugh, Dublin 17
Tel 01-8474214

Contact person: Sr Patricia Coyle
Tel 01-8771778 Fax 01-8771731
Email pcoylefran@eircom.net

Dublin

FRANCISCAN SISTERS OF LITTLEHAMPTON

Eden
Knock, Co Mayo
Tel 094-9388302

Leader: Sr Stanislaus

Tuam

FRANCISCAN SISTERS MINORESS

St Anthony's Convent
1 Cabra Grove, Cabra, Dublin 7
Tel 01-8380185

Superior: Sr Barbara Flynn

Mother General
Sr Thomas More Roddy
Franciscan Convent,
Dalby Road, Melton Mowbray,
Leicestershire LE13 OBP,
England
Tel 0044-1664-562422

Dublin

GOOD SHEPHERD SISTERS

Good Shepherd Provincialate
245 Lower Kilmacud Road,
Goatstown, Dublin 14
Tel 01-2982699 Fax 01-2989033
Email rgsdublin@eircom.net

Provincial Superior
Sr Bernie McNally

Dublin, Cork & Ross, Derry,
Down & Connor, Limerick,
Galway, Waterford & Lismore

HANDMAIDS OF THE SACRED HEART OF JESUS

St Raphaela's
Upper Kilmacud Road,
Stillorgan, Co Dublin
Tel 01-2889963
Fax 01-2889536

Superior: Sr Mary Corr
Email maryecorr@eircom.net

Dublin

HOLY CHILD JESUS, SOCIETY OF THE

Provincial
Sr Pauline Darby
10 Holland Villas Road,
London W14 8BP
Tel 020-76032133
Email europoff@cs.com

Provincial Representative
Mary McManus
1 Stable Lane,
Harcourt Street, Dublin 2
Email
marybenmcmanus@eircom.net

Dublin

HOLY FAITH SISTERS

Generalate
Aylward House,
Glasnevin, Dublin 11
Tel 01-8371426 Fax 01-8377474
Email aylward@elrcom.net

General Leader
Sr Margo Delaney

Regional Leader
Sr Evelyn Greene
68 Iona Road, Dublin 9
Tel 01-8301404 Fax 01-8303530
Email ionahfs@eircom.net

Dublin, Meath

HOLY FAMILY OF BORDEAUX SISERS

'Sonas Chríost'
100 Moorefield Park,
Newbridge, Co Kildare
Tel/Fax 045-450125

Regional Superior
Sr Maureen Slamen

Armagh, Derry, Dublin,
Kildare & Leighlin, Ossory

HOLY FAMILY OF SAINT EMILIE DE RODAT

Holy Family of St Emilie de Rodat
Arden Road, Tullamore,
Co Offaly
Tel 057-9321577
Email mpe1809@eircom.net

Superior: Sr Mary-Paul English

Meath

INFANT JESUS SISTERS

Provincial House
56 St Lawrence Road,
Clontarf, Dublin 3
Tel 01-8338930 Fax 01-8530857

Provincial: Sr Rosemary Barter
Email rbarterijs@eircom.net

Dublin, Cloyne, Cork & Ross,
Kerry, Limerick

JESUS AND MARY, CONGREGATION OF

The sisters from the Irish
Province work in Haiti,
Cameroon, Ekpoma and
Lagos. The sisters are involved
in education, working with
the handicapped and in
formation, including a house
of formation in Nigeria.

Provincialate, 'Errew House'
110 Goatstown Road,
Dublin 14
Tel 01-2966059

Provincial Superior
Sr Mary Mulrooney
Tel 01-2993130
Email
mulrooney.mary@gmail.com
Local Superior: Sr Pauline Caffrey

Dublin, Galway, Killala

SISTERS OF LA RETRAITE

77 Grove Park
Rathmines, Dublin 6
Tel 01-491171

Contact: Sr Barbara Stafford
Email
barbarastaffordlr@eircom.net

Dublin, Cork & Ross, Galway

LA SAGESSE (DAUGHTERS OF WISDOM)

Cregg House
Sligo
Tel 071-9177229
Fax 071-9177439

Dublin, Elphin

LA SAINTE UNION DES SACRES COEURS

Provincial Office
53 Croftdown Road,
London NW5 1EL
Tel 020-74827225
Fax 020-72844760

Province leadership Team
Sr Una Burke
Sr Mary Patricia Daly
Sr Helen Randles

Dublin, Ardagh & Clonmacnois

LITTLE COMPANY OF MARY

Provincialate
Cnoc Mhuire, 29 Woodpark,
Ballinteer Avenue, Dublin 16
Tel 01-2987040
Fax 01-2961936
Email lcom@irishbroadband.net

Province Leader
Sr Celine Bourke

Dublin, Cloyne, Kerry,
Limerick, Ossory, Waterford &
Lismore

LITTLE SISTERS OF THE ASSUMPTION

Provincial House
42 Rathfarnham Road,
Terenure, Dublin 6W
Tel 01-4909850 Fax 01-4925740
Email pernet42@eircom.net

Provincial: Sr Mary Keenan

Dublin, Cork & Ross, Galway,
Limerick

LITTLE SISTERS OF THE POOR

Sacred Heart Residence
Sybil Hill Road,
Raheny, Dublin 5
Tel 01-8332308
Email pcedublin@aol.com

Provincial: Sr Christine Devlin

Dublin, Waterford & Lismore

LORETO (IBVM)

Provincialate
Loreto House, Beaufort,
Dublin 14
Tel 01-4933827
Email
lorprovbeaufort@eircom.net

Provincial: Sr Teresa MacPaul

Dublin, Cloyne, Derry, Ferns,
Kerry, Kilmore, Meath, Ossory,
Raphoe, Waterford & Lismore

MARIE AUXILIATRICE SISTERS

7 Florence Street,
Portobello, Dublin 8
Tel/Fax 01-4537622

Dublin

MARIE REPARATRICE SISTERS

Regional House,
29 Brackenstown Village,
Swords, Co Dublin
Tel 01-8406321
Email smrbtown@eircom.net

Regional Superior
Sr Eileen Carroll

Dublin, Cork & Ross, Limerick

MARIST SISTERS

Provincialate
51 Kenilworth Square, Dublin 6
Tel 01-4972196
Email secirl@eircom.net

Leader – Ireland
Sr Brigid M. McGuinness

Dublin, Achonry, Ardagh &
Clonmacnois, Armagh,
Down & Connor

MEDICAL MISSIONARIES OF MARY

Rosemount,
Rosemount Terrace,
Booterstown, Co Dublin
Tel 01-2882722 Fax 01-2834626
Email rcsmmm@eircom.net

Armagh, Dublin, Meath, Ossory

MISSIONARIES OF CHARITY

Gift of Love
223 South Circular Road,
Dublin 8
Tel 01-4534141

Regional Superior
Sr M. Lawrence
177 Bravington Road
London W9 3AR
Tel 0208-9602644

Armagh, Dublin, Cloyne, Elphin

MISSIONARY FRANCISCAN SISTERS OF THE IMMACULATE CONCEPTION

Franciscan Convent
Assisi House, Navan Road,
Dublin 7
Tel 01-8682216

Dublin

MISSIONARY SISTERS OF THE ASSUMPTION

Assumption Convent
34 Crossgar Road, Ballynahinch,
Co Down BT24 8EN
Tel 028-97561765
Fax 028-97565754

Superior: Sr Ursula Hinchion

Dromore

MISSIONARY SISTERS OF THE HOLY CROSS

86 Glen Road,
Belfast BT11 8BH
Tel 028-90614631
Fax 028-90614631
Email
mary@thcross.freeserve.co.uk

Superior
Sr M. Brigid McGuigan

Down & Connor

MISSIONARY SISTERS OF THE HOLY ROSARY

Regional House
Drumullac, 42 Westpark,
Artane, Dublin 5
Tel 01-8392070 Fax 01-8392025
Email mshrrege@eircom.net

*Regional Superior for Ireland,
England and Scotland*
Sr Conchita McDonnell

Dublin, Cork, Ferns, Kilmore,
Meath, Ardagh & Clonmacnois

MISSIONARY SISTERS OF OUR LADY OF APOSTLES

Provincialate
Ardfoyle Convent,
Ballintemple, Cork
Tel 021-4294076
Fax 021-4291105
Email prov@eircom.net

Provincial: Sr Mary Crowley

Dublin, Tuam, Cork & Ross,
Dromore

MISSIONARY SISTERS OF ST COLUMBAN

St Columban's Convent
Magheramore, Wicklow
Tel 0404-67348
Fax 0404-67002

Community Leader
Sr Ita McElwain

Dublin

MISSIONARY SISTERS OF ST PETER CLAVER

Our Lady of the Angels
81 Bushy Park Road,
PO Box 228,
Terenure, Dublin 6
Tel 01-4909360
Fax 01-4920918

Contact Person
Sr Lucyna Wisniowska
Email claver4@hotmail.com

Dublin

MISSIONARY SISTERS SERVANTS OF THE HOLY SPIRIT

Regional House,
143 Philipsburgh Avenue
Fairview, Dublin 3
Tel 01-8369383 Fax 01-8369912
Email sspsfairview@yahoo.com

Community Leader
Sr Carmen Lee

Dublin

NOTRE DAME DES MISSIONS
Our Lady of the Missions

Upper Churchtown Road,
Dublin 14
Tel 01-2983308/2989991

Armagh, Dublin, Down &
Connor, Ferns

OBLATES OF THE ASSUMPTION

1 Churchview Avenue
Johnstown, Killiney,
Co Dublin
Tel 01-2854572

Sister-in-Charge: Sr Monica

Dublin

OUR LADY OF THE CENACLE

3 Churchview Drive,
Killiney,
Co Dublin
Tel/Fax 01-2840175
Email
cenacledublin@eircom.net

Dublin, Cork & Ross

OUR LADY OF CHARITY SISTERS

Regional Administration
63 Lower Sean McDermott
Street, Dublin 1
Tel 01-8711109
Fax 01-8366526
Email regionaloffice@olc.ie

Regional Leader
Sr Sheila Murphy

Dublin

OUR LADY OF SION SISTERS

Provincial
Sr Brenda McCole
49 St Peter's Road,
Harborne,
Birmingham B17 0AU
Tel 0121-4266679
Email
brenda.mccole@btinternet.com

Dublin

PERPETUAL ADORATION SISTERS

Perpetual Adoration Convent
Wexford
Tel 053-9124134
Email
adoration44@eircom.net

Superior: Sr Peter Leech

Ferns

POOR CLARES

Archdiocese of Dublin

St Damian's
Simmonscourt Road,
Ballsbridge, Dublin 4
Fax 01-6685464
Email pccdamians@mac.com

Abbess: Sr M. Brigid

*Diocese of Ardagh &
Clonmacnois*

**Poor Clare Monastery of
Perpetual Adoration**
Drumshanbo, Co Leitrim

Abbess
Mother M. Angela McCabe

Diocese of Cork & Ross

**Poor Clare Colettine
Monastery**
College Road, Cork

Abbess: Sr Miriam Buckley

Diocese of Down & Connor

120 Cliftonville Road
Belfast BT14 6LA

Superior
Sr Immaculata Enderez OSC

Diocese of Galway

St Clare's Monastery
Nuns' Island, Galway

Abbess: Sr M. Colette Hayden

Diocese Kildare & Leighlin

**Poor Clare Colettine
Monastery**
Graiguecullen, Carlow

Abbess: Sr M. Francis O'Brien

Diocese of Killaloe

Poor Clare Monastery
St Francis Street,
Ennis, Co Clare

Abbess: Sr Bernardine Meskell
Email
bernardinemeskell@eircom.net

POOR SERVANTS OF THE MOTHER OF GOD

Generalate
Maryfield Convent,
Mount Angelus Road,
Roehampton SW15 4JA,
England
Tel 0208-7884351

General: Sr Mary Whelan

Local Leader (Dublin region)
Sr Margaret Cashman
Email margaretcashmansmg@
eircom.net
Local Leader (outside Dublin)
Sr Catherine Gleeson
Email cgleesonsmg1@eircom.net

Dublin, Cloyne, Limerick

CONGREGATION OF THE SISTERS OF NAZARETH

Nazareth House
Malahide Road, Dublin 3
Tel 01-8332024 Fax 01-8334988
Email
regionaldublin@hotmail.com

Regional Superior
Sr Cataldus Courtney

Dublin, Cloyne, Derry, Down
and Connor, Elphin

PRESENTATION SISTERS

Generalate
Monasterevin, Co Kildare
Tel 045-525335/525503
Fax 045-525209
Email
adminpresevin@eircom.net
Website www.
presentationsistersunion.org

Congregational Leader
Sr Terry Abraham

Armagh, Dublin, Cashel,
Tuam, Ardagh & Clonmacnois,
Cloyne, Cork and Ross, Derry,
Ferns, Galway, Kerry, Kildare
and Leighlin, Limerick, Meath,
Ossory, Waterford & Lismore

PRESENTATION OF MARY SISTERS

4 Lower John Street,
Sligo
Tel 071-9160740

Superior: Sr Elenita Baguio
Email elenitabaguio@yahoo.fr

Elphin

REDEMPTORISTINES

Monastery of St Alphonsus
St Alphonsus Road, Dublin 9

Superior: Sr Gabrielle
Email
gabrielle.fox@redemptorists.ie

Dublin

RELIGIOUS OF CHRISTIAN EDUCATION

Provincial Office
3 Bushy Park House,
Templeogue Road, Dublin 6W
Tel 01-4901668 Fax 01-4901101

Provincial Superior
Sr Rosemary O'Looney

Dublin

RELIGIOUS OF SACRED HEART OF MARY

13/14 Huntstown Wood,
Mulhuddart, Dublin 15
Tel 01-8214888

Dublin, Down & Connor,
Ossory

RELIGIOUS SISTERS OF CHARITY

Generalate
Caritas, 15 Gilford Road,
Sandymount, Dublin 4
Tel 01-2697833/2697935

Provincialate, Provincial House,
Our Lady's Mount,
Harold's Cross, Dublin 6W
Tel 01-4973177

Dublin, Cork & Ross, Galway,
Ossory, Waterford & Lismore

ROSMINIANS (SISTERS OF PROVIDENCE)

104a Griffith Court
Fairview, Dublin 3
Tel 01-8375021

Dublin, Down & Connor,
Waterford & Lismore

SACRED HEART SOCIETY

Provincial Administration Office
76 Home Farm Road,
Drumcondra, Dublin 9
Tel 01-8375412 Fax 01-8375542

Provincial Secretary
Email rscj@eircom.net
Provincial Superior
Sr Aideen Kinlen

Armagh, Dublin, Killaloe

SACRED HEARTS OF JESUS AND MARY (PICPUS)

Sector House
11 Northbrook Road
Ranelagh, Dublin 6
Tel 01-4910173 (Provincial)
Tel 01-4974831 (Community)
Fax 01-4965551

Contact
Sr Mary McCloskey SSCC

Dublin

SACRED HEARTS OF JESUS AND MARY

St Anne's
Sean Ross Abbey,
Roscrea, Co Tipperary
Tel 0505-21629
Fax 0505-22525
Email mdobbin@eircom.net

Community Leader
Sr Margaret Dobbin

Cork & Ross, Down & Connor,
Killaloe

SALESIAN SISTERS OF ST JOHN BOSCO

Provincialate
203 Lower Kilmacud Road,
Stillorgan, Co Dublin
Tel 01-2985188
Fax 01-2951572
Email prov@salsisdb.iol.ie

Provincial Superior
Sr Nora Ryan

Dublin, Limerick

SISTERS OF ST CLARE

St Clare's Convent
Generalate,
63 Harold's Cross Road,
Dublin 6W
Tel 01-4966880/4966791
Fax 01-4966388
Email progers3@eircom.net

Abbess General
Sr Patricia Rogers

Armagh, Dublin, Down &
Connor, Dromore, Kerry,
Kilmore

Regional Superior
Sr Sheila Ryan
St Clare's Convent,
75 Damolly Road,
Newry, Co Down BT34 1QW
Tel/Fax 028-30268471

ST JOHN OF GOD SISTERS

St John of God Congregational Centre
1 Summerhill Heights, Wexford
Tel 053-9142396
Fax 053-9141500
Email stjohnogoffice@eircom.net

Congregational Leader
Sr Bríd Ryan

Armagh, Dublin, Achonry,
Dromore, Ferns, Kildare &
Leighlin, Killaloe, Ossory,
Waterford & Lismore

ST JOSEPH OF ANNECY SISTERS

St Joseph's Convent
Killorglin, Co Kerry
Tel 066-9761809
Fax 066-9761127
Email
margaret.lyne@talk21.com

Superior: Sr Helena Lyne

Kerry

ST JOSEPH OF THE APPARITION SISTERS

St Joseph's Convent
Garden Hill, Sligo
Tel 071-9162649
Fax 071-915200
Email stjsligo@eircom.net

Elphin

SISTERS OF ST JOSEPH OF CHAMBERY

St Joseph's Convent
Springdale Road, Raheny,
Dublin 5
Tel 01-8478351 (Convent)
Fax 01-8485764 (Convent)
Email mpraleigh@eircom.net
Tel 01-8478433/8478008
(Hospital)

Superior: Sr Mary Peter Raleigh
Email mpraleigh@eircom.net

Dublin

ST JOSEPH OF CLUNY SISTERS

Mt Sackville Convent
Chapelizod, Dublin 20
Tel 01-8213134 Fax 01-8224002
Email clunyprov@sjc.ie
Website www.sjc.ie

Provincial Superior
Sr Maeve Guinan

Dublin, Ardagh & Clonmacnois,
Waterford & Lismore

ST JOSEPH OF LYON SISTERS

10 Kilbarrack Road,
Sutton, Dublin 5
Tel 01-8325896

Contact: Sr Marcelle

Dublin

ST JOSEPH OF PEACE SISTERS

Peace House
43 Kenilworth Park,
Harold's Cross, Dublin 6
Tel 01-4922011

Dublin

ST JOSEPH OF THE SACRED HEART SISTERS

Cranagh
Kilmallock, Co Limerick
Tel 061-399027

Regional Leader
Sr Margaret O'Sullivan

Dublin, Tuam, Achonry, Cloyne,
Killaloe, Limerick, Kerry

ST LOUIS SISTERS

St Louis Regional House
60 Ard Easmuinn,
Dundalk, Co Louth
Tel 042-9334752/9334753
Fax 042-9334651
Email regionalate@stlouisirl.ie

Regional Leader
Sr Anne Kavanagh

Armagh, Dublin, Achonry,
Clogher, Down & Connor, Ferns

ST LUCY FILIPPINI SISTERS

Mother of the ChurchConvent
Newport, Co Mayo
Tel 098-41248 Fax 098-41092
Email stlucynewport@eircom.net

Local Superior: Sr Joan Henry
Regional Superior
Sr Dorothy Di Cristofaro

Convent of St Lucy,
Medstead nr Alton,
Hants GU34 5LL, England

Tuam

ST MARY MADELEINE POSTEL SISTERS

Mount Carmel Nursing Home
Parkmore Convent, Abbey
Street, Roscrea, Co Tipperary
Tel 0505-21038/21146
Fax 0505-21542

Local Superior: Sr Marie Keegan

Dublin, Tuam, Killaloe

ST PAUL DE CHARTRES SISTERS

Queen of Peace Centre
Garville Avenue,
Rathgar, Dublin 6
Tel 01-4975381/4972366
Fax 01-4964084
Email spcqueen@eircom.net

Regional Superior
Sr Rose Margaret Nuval

Dublin

URSULINES

Ursuline Generalate
17 Trimleston Drive,
Booterstown, Co Dublin
Tel 01-2693503 Fax 01-2602748
Email angemer@eircom.net
Website www.ursulines.ie

Congregational Leader
Sr Kitty Kelly
Assistant: Sr Mary Gilbride

Dublin, Tuam, Cashel & Emly,
Cork & Ross, Elphin,
Waterford & Lismore

URSULINES OF JESUS

26 The Drive
Seatown Park,
Swords, Co Dublin
Tel 01-8404323

Provincial Superior
Sr Hilary Brown
St Ursula's Convent,
11 Amhurst Park, Stamford Hill,
London N16 5DH, England
Tel 020-88020256
Email supgb@dircon.co.uk

Dublin

VISITATION SISTERS

Monastery of the Visitation
Stamullen, Co Meath
Tel 01-8412533

Superior: Sr Paul Mary Supple
Email visitationstamulen
@gmail.com

Meath

INSTITUTES

LAY SECULAR INSTITUTES

Lay secular institutes come
under the jurisdiction of the
Sacred Congregation for
Religious Secular Institutes as
laid down by the Apostolic
Constitution, *Provida Mater
Ecclesia.*

Caritas Christi
Secular institute of pontifical
right founded in 1937 for
laywomen.

Priest Assistant
Rev Finian Lynch (OP)
St Mary's Priory,
Pope's Quay, Cork
Tel 021-4502267
Fax 021-4502307
Email simonrop@eircom.net

Columba Community
Private association of the
faithful involved in prayer,
Christian teaching, counsel,
reconciliation and healing and
rehabilitation from drugs and
alcohol.

Columba House,
11 Queen Street,
Derry BT48 7EG
Tel 028-71262407
Email columbacommunity@
hotmail.com
Website
www.columbacommunity.com

Spiritual Director
Rev Neal Carlin
Treasurer: Ms Kathleen Devlin
Contact: Tommy McCay

Missionaries of the Kingship
of Christ
Secular Institute (affiliated to
the Orders of Friars Minor) for
women applicants aged 21-40
years.

Ecclesiastical Assistant
Rev Joseph Walsh (OFM)
Tel 01232-775279

Servitium Christi
Secular Institute of the Blessed
Sacrament (affiliated to
Blessed Sacrament
Congregation) for women.

Enquiries: Mary Keane
58 Moyne Road,
Ranelagh, Dublin 6

Servite Secular Institute
Laymen and laywomen who
live in their own homes, have
their own occupations and
also live a vowed life of prayer
and service.

Society of Our Lady of the
Way
Founded in Austria in 1936 for
single or widowed laywomen;
membership worldwide.

Enquiries: Mary C. Peyton
18 Rock Road, Lisburn,
Co Antrim BT28 3SU
Tel Lisburn 92648244
Miss Helen Spellman
22 Avondale Road,
Highfield Park, Galway
Tel 091-521872

NEW FORMS OF CONSECRATED LIFE

Next to already existing
institutes of consecrated life
new forms of evangelical life
spring up, 'through which
God in his goodness enriches
the Church, enabling her to
follow her Lord in a constant
outpouring of generosity and
attentive to God's invitation
revealed through the signs of
the times' (John Paul II)
(Annuario Pontificio p1646).

The Spiritual Family
The Work of Christ Familia
Spiritualis Opus (FSO)
Family of consecrated life
pontifical right. Founded in
Belgium in 1938 by Julia
Verhaeghe. It consists of a
Priests' Community and of a
Sisters' Community of
Consecrated Women. The
nucleus of The Work is made
up of members in the strict
sense who are consecrated to
the Sacred Heart of Jesus in a
'Holy Covenant in the three
evangelical counsels'. They
strive to unite contemplation,
the apostolic life and the
sanctification of the world.
They follow above all the
example of St Paul, imitating
his love for Christ and his
body, the Church. They seek
to help with the new
evangelisation as spiritual
fathers and mothers in a spirit
of unity and respectful
complementarity. They are
joined by members in a wider
sense, and by lay faithful who
are spiritually associated with
the Work of Christ.

Enquiries
Sr Nellie Baerts FSO
Bishop's House,
Ard Adhamhnáin,
Letterkenny, Co Donegal
Tel 074-9124898
Fax 074-9128142
Email thework@catholic.org
www.thework-fso.org

Raphoe

SEMINARIES AND HOUSES OF STUDY

SEMINARIES

PONTIFICAL IRISH COLLEGE, ROME
Founded in 1628 the Irish National College in Rome provides formation to seminarians and priests for the diocesan priesthood in Ireland and beyond.
Via dei SS Quattro 1, 00184 Roma, Italy
Tel 003906-772631 Fax 003906-77263323
Email ufficio@irishcollege.org
www.irishcollege.org
Rector: Mgr Liam Bergin BSc, HDE, STD
Vice-Rector
Rev Albert McDonnell STL, MA, JCL
Spiritual Director
Rev Chris Hayden STL, PhD
Director of Formation
Rev William Swan BSc, BTh, STL

ST PATRICK'S COLLEGE, MAYNOOTH
Founded in 1795, the National Seminary for Ireland and Pontifical University, Maynooth, Co Kildare
Tel 01-7084700 Fax 01-6289063
Email presoff@may.ie
College Officers
President
Rt Rev Mgr Hugh Connolly BA, DD
Financial Officer: Ms Fidelma Madden ACA, AITI
Registrar and Supervisor of Examinations
Rev Dr Michael Mullaney
Directors of Formation
Rev Donal O'Neill, BSc, STL HDE
Rev Paul Prior
Dean of Faculty of Theology
Rev Dr Padraig Corkery BSc, STD (CUA), LSS, HDE
Dean of Faculty of Philosophy
Vacant
Librarian: Cathal McCauley
Archivist: Rt Rev Mgr Patrick J. Corish MA, DD, MRIA
Director of Human Resources: Brendan Baker

Pontifical University Courses:
Professors/Department Heads
Canon Law: Rev Dr Michael Mullaney
Dogmatic Theology
Rev Professor Brendan Leahy, BL, STD
Ecclesiastical History
Prof Salvador Ryan
Homiletics
Rev Professor T. Ronan Drury BA, BD
Liturgy: Rev Professor Liam Tracey (OSM) STB, SLD, DipMar, DipPastoral Theology
Moral Theology: Rev Dr Padraig Corkery, BSc, STD (CUA)
Sacred Scripture
Rev Dr Seamus O'Connell BSc, LSS
Faith and Culture
Rev Dr Michael A. Conway

MILLTOWN INSTITUTE OF THEOLOGY AND PHILOSOPHY
Milltown Park, Sandford Road, Ranelagh, Dublin 6
Tel 01-2776300
Fax 01-2692528
Email info@milltown-institute.ie
www.milltown-institute.ie
Founded in 1968. A Pontifical Athenaeum and a designated institution of HETAC.
Patron: Dr Diarmuid Martin Archbishop of Dublin
Chancellor: Adolfo Nicólas SJ
Vice-Chancellor: John Dardis SJ
Acting President: Dr Cornelius Casey CSsR
School of Undergraduate Studies
Dean of Theology
Dr Thomas R. Whelan CSSp
Dean of Philosophy
Prof Santiago Sia
School of Postgraduate Studies and Research
Head of School: Dr Anthony White
Head of Department: Scripture:
Dr Kieran O'Mahoney OSA
Head of Department: Systematic Theology and History
Dr Declan Marmion SM
Head of Department
Spirituality
Dr Denis Robinson CSSp
Acting Head of Department
Moral Theology and Canon Law
Dr Thomas R. Whelan CSSp
Head of Department: Pastoral Theology
Dr Thomas Grenham SPS
Head of Department
Mission Theology & Cultures
Dr Patrick Claffey SPS
Editor, Milltown Studies
Dr Joseph Egan SMA
Assistant to the President
Mr Philip FitzPatrick
Registrar: Dr Anthony White
Acting Librarian: Ms Mary Glennon
Financial Advisor: Mr Patrick Lally
Head of Student Services:
Mrs Dierdre Tallan
Chaplain: Mrs Bairbre De Burca
Contact Person: Registrar

KMI INSTITUTE OF THEOLOGY AND CULTURES
Tel 353-1-2776300 ext. 203
Fax 353-1-2692528
www.kmitc.ie
Email mission@milltown-institute.ie
Founded in 1991 to engage in theological studies with respect to issues of cross-cultural exchange and inter-faith dialogue. Designated college of HETAC.

Since September 2003 this institute has become the Department of Mission Theology and Cultures at Milltown Institute of Theology and Philosophy (see separate entry).
Head of Department
Dr Patrick Claffey SVD
Secretary of Department
Ms Bronia Kornas

ALL HALLOWS COLLEGE DUBLIN
Grace Park Road, Drumcondra, Dublin 9
Tel 01-8373745/8373746 Fax 01-8377642
Email info@allhallows.ie
www.allhallows.ie
Founded in 1842. Prepares students for priestly ministry and lay people for mission and ministry.
President
Very Rev Mark Noonan (CM), MA, BD
Vice-President: Rev John Joe Spring MA
Vice-President of Development
Rev Robert Whiteside, MA
Financial Manager
Mr Ian Baker, BBS, BA, FCA
Dean of Studies and Acting Registrar
Mr Ronan Tobin, BA, HDipEd, MA
Senior Office Administrator, Registry Office: Nina Sheil Mohitt
Director of Vocations
Rev John Joe Spring MA
Sr Dorothy Balfe (OP) MA
Ms Jean Cleary MA
Rev Eugene Curran CM, BA, BD, DMin
Sr Moya Curran (OP) MA
Rev Thomas Dalzell (SM) BA, STL, PhD
Rev Anthony Draper DD, BA, HDE
Kevin Egan STL, MS, DMin
Sr Madeleine Fitzpatrick (RSHM) MA
Maureen Gainey (LSU) BA, HDipEd, Dip Couns & Psychotherapy, MIACT
Sr Bernadette Flanagan BA (Th), HDE, DipIT, MA, PhD
Ms Kathleen Soden, MBCS, MA
Ms Carolanne Henry, BA
Sr Sheila O'Dea RSM, BAEd, DMin
Sr Patricia Holden (SHCJ) BMus, DipLit
Rev James McCormack (CM) PhD
Ms Jean Mullen MA
Rev James Murphy (CM) PhD
Rev Brian Nolan (CM) STD, LSS
Ms Rosemary Walton BA, HDipEd, MA, DipLibrarianship
Rev Joseph McCann, CM, PhD
Ms Margarita Synott, BA, MTh
Patrick Quinn, BA, BD, MA, PhD, HDE, DCG
Ms Anne Marie Lowry, MA
Ms Cora Lambert, MA
Ms Marjorie Fitzpatrick, MA

Purcell House
Retreat/Conference Centre
Tel 01-8373745 Fax 01-8571135
Director
Ms Mary McPhillips BA, HDip,
Grad.Dip.Past
Administrator
Ms Alicia Fitzgerald, Ms Mary Hayes
Ministry to Priests
Rev Kevin Scallon (CM) MA
Rev Tom Lane (CM) DD
Coordinator of Ember Mission Team
Ms Mary O'Broin, MA

HOUSES OF STUDY

*For details see Religious Orders and
Congregations Section*

Augustinians (OSA)
Prior: Rev John Lyng OSA
St Augustine's, Ballyboden, Dublin 16
Tel 01-4241000 Fax 01-4939915

Camillians (OSCam)
St Camillus, South Hill Avenue,
Blackrock, Co Dublin
Tel 01-2882873Fax 01-2833380

Capuchins (OFMCap)
Immaculate Heart of Mary, Raheny,
Dublin 5
Tel 01-8313886/8312805

Carmelites (OCarm)
Prior: Rev Martin Baxter
Gort Muire, Ballinteer, Dublin 16
Tel 01-2984014 Fax 01-2987221
Email gortmuire@gortmuire.com
Email mvjbaxter@eircom.net

Divine Word Missionaries (SVD)
Divine Word Missionaries,
Maynooth, Co Kildare
Tel 01-6286391/2
Fax 01-6289184
Email rector@svdireland.com

Dominicans (OP)
St Mary's Priory, Tallaght, Dublin 24
Tel 01-4048100 Fax 01-4596784
The Priory Institute
Tel 01-4048124 Fax 01-4626084
Email enquiries@prioryinstitute.com

St Saviour's Priory, Upper Dorset Street,
Dublin 1
Tel 01-8897610 Fax 01-8734003
Email stsaviours@eircom.net

Dominican Biblical Institute,
Upper Cecil Street, Limerick
Tel 061-490600 Fax 061-468604

Franciscans (OFM)
Dún Mhuire, Seafield Road,
Killiney, Co Dublin
Tel 01-2826760 Fax 01-2826993
Email dmkilliney@eircom.net

Legionaries of Christ (LC)
Leopardstown Road, Foxrock,
Dublin 18
Tel 01-2955985/2955902
Fax 01-2957773
Email ireland@legionaries.org

Mill Hill Missionaries (MHM)
St Joseph's House, 50 Orwell Park,
Rathgar, Dublin 6
Tel 01 4127700 Fax 01 4127781
Email josephmhm@eircom.net
Rector: Rev Patrick Molloy
Vice Rector: Rev Patrick O'Connell
Bursar Rev Patrick Murray MHM
Tel 01 4127774

Missionaries of Africa (White Fathers)
Cypress Grove, Templeogue, Dublin 6W
Tel 01-4055263
Contact Person: Fr Ian Buckmaster
Email provirl@indigo.ie

Oblates (OMI)
St Anne's, Goldenbridge Walk, Inchicore,
Dublin 8
Tel 01-4540841

Redemptorists (CSSR)
Marianella, 75 Orwell Road, Rathgar,
Dublin 6
Tel 01-4067100
Contact Person: Dan Baragry CSsR
(Director of Formation)

Salesians (SDB)
De Sales Language School,
St Catherine's, Maynooth, Co Kildare
Tel 01-6286111 Fax 01-6286268
Email sdbmaynooth@iol.ie
Members part of Celbridge community

SPECIAL INSTITUTES OF EDUCATION

Dominican Centre for Biblical Teaching & Research
Mary Immaculate College
University of Limerick
South Circular Road, Limerick
Tel 061-412333 (priory)
061-204396 (dept secretary)
Fax 061-311728

IMU Mission Institute
St Columba's, Dalgan Park, Navan,
Co Meath
Tel 046-9021525 Fax 046-9022799
Email imuinst@eircom.net
Director: P. Dooher (SSC)

Irish School of Ecumenics
Trinity College Dublin
Bea House, Milltown Park, Dublin 6
Contact: Professor Linda Hogan, Head of
School
Tel 01-2601144 Fax 01-2601158
Email isedir@tcd.ie
www.tcd.ie/ise

Irish School of Ecumenics
Trinity College Dublin
683 Antrim Road, Belfast BT15 4EG
Tel 028-90775010 Fax 028-90373986

Mater Dei Institute of Education
Clonliffe Road, Dublin 3
Tel 01-8086500 Fax 01-8370776
Email info@materdei.dcu.ie
www.materdei.ie

RETREAT AND PASTORAL CENTRES

RETREAT HOUSES

ANTRIM
Drumalis, Glenarm Road,
Larne, Co Antrim BT40 1DT
Tel 028-28272196/28276455
Fax 028-28277999
Email drumalis@btconnect.com
www.drumalis.co.uk
Retreat Team: Sr Margaret Rose
McSparran CP, Sr Anna Hainey CP
Acc: twin 37, doubles 13, singles 3, group 3
Cross & Passion Sisters
Parkview: self-catering cottage in
grounds, sleeps 5
Contact: Katrina Hartin, Coordinator of
Administration Services

CORK
Myross Wood House, Leap, Co Cork
Tel 028-33118 Fax 028-33793
Email mscmyross@eircom.net
Acc: singles 32, doubles 6
Offering preached, directed and themed
retreats throughout the year
Director/Contact person: Fr Michael
Curran (MSC)
Missionaries of the Sacred Heart

St Benedict's Priory Retreat House
The Mount, Cobh, Co Cork
Tel/Fax 021-4811354
Acc: 6 single rooms, 2 double rooms
available for private individual or group
retreats, private day retreats, opportunity
to share in the liturgical life of the Sisters –
Holy Mass, Liturgy of the Hours and
Eucharistic Adoration. Quiet peaceful
setting, Bible Garden, all meals supplied.
Contact for private retreats: Guest
Mistress

St Dominic's Retreat & Conference
Centre, Ennismore, Montenotte, Cork
Tel 021-4502520 Fax 021-4502712
Email ennismore@eircom.net
www.ennismore.ie
Contact person: Mary Smith
Acc: singles 36, doubles 2
Dominicans

DERRY
Carmelite Retreat Centre
Termonbacca, Derry BT48 9XE
Tel 028-71262512 Fax 028-71373589
Email ocdderry@hotmail.co.uk
www.ocd.ie
Contact person: Fr Sean Conlon (OCD)
Acc: singles 20, twin 20, ensuite rooms 5
Carmelites (OCD)

DONEGAL
St Anthony's Retreat Centre
Dundrean, Burnfoot, Co Donegal

Tel/Fax 074-9368370
Email columbacommunity@hotmail.com
or sarce@eircom.net
Acc: 5 hermitages, 1 double (3 en suite)
Director: Rev Neal Carlin
Spiritual direction available

DOWN
Dromantine Retreat and Conference
Centre, Newry, Co Down BT34 1RH
Tel 028-30821964 Fax 028-30821963
Email
admin@dromantineconference.com
www.dromatineconference.com
Contact: Rev Desmond Corrigan SMA
Accommodation: 40 single en suite
rooms, 30 double en suite rooms, 8
conference rooms

The Christian Renewal Centre –
A House of Prayer for Ireland
44 Shore Road, Rostrevor, Newry,
Co Down BT34 3ET   Tel 028-41738492
Email crc-rostrevor@lineone.net
Acc: singles 3, double/family 1, twin 5,
disabled 1
Contact: Harry Smith (Director)
www.crc-rostrevor.org

Passionist Retreat Centre,
Tobar Mhuire, Crossgar,
Downpatrick, Co Down BT30 9EA
Tel 028-44830242   Fax 028-44831382
Email tobarmhuire@googlemail.com
Acc: singles 10, twin 4, double 2

DUBLIN
Avila Carmelite Centre
Bloomfield Avenue
Morehampton Road, Dublin 4
Tel 01-6430200 Fax 01-6430281
Email avila@ocd.ie
Prior: Fr Michael Fitzgerald (OCD)
Carmelites (OCD)

Dominican Retreat and Pastoral Centre
Tallaght Village, Dublin 24
Tel 01-4048189 Fax 01-4596080
Email retreathouse@eircom.net
www.goodnews.ie
Secretary/Contact: Anita Kenny
Acc: singles 30, 1 large, 3 medium
conference rooms, oratory
Dominicans

Emmaus,
Lissenhall, Swords, Co Dublin
Tel 01-8700050 Fax 01-8408248
Email admin@emmauscentre.ie
www.emmauscentre.ie
Residential accommodation
63 ensuite bedrooms, 3 prayer rooms, 13
meeting rooms

Office Administrator: Nora Meenaghan
Christian Brothers, Holy Faith Sisters and
Oblate Fathers

Tallaght Rehabilitation Project
Kiltalown House, Jobstown,
Tallaght, Dublin 24
Tel 01-4597705 Fax 01-4148123
Email info@tallaghtrehabproject.ie
Co-ordinator: Marie Hayden

Manresa House
Dollymount, Dublin 3
Tel 01-8331352 Fax 01-8331002
Email manresa@jesuit.ie
Acc: singles 41
Director: Rev Patrick Carberry SJ
Contact: Eileen Toomey. Jesuits

Orlagh Retreat Centre
Old Court Road, Dublin 16
Tel 01-4933315/4958190 Fax 01-4930987
Email info@orlagh.ie www.orlagh.ie
Acc: singles 24, doubles 1; 1 large, 1
medium and 2 small conference rooms
Director: John Byrne (OSA)
Email john@orlagh.ie
Augustinians

Purcell House, All Hallows College
Drumcondra, Dublin 9
Tel 01-8520754 Fax 01-8571135
Email purcell_house@allhallows.ie
Acc: singles ensuite 50
Director: Mary McPhillips
Contact: Mary or Alicia

Stella Maris Retreat Centre
Carrickbrack Road, Baily,
Howth, Co Dublin
Est. 1893
Tel 01-8322228 Fax 01-8063469
Email stellamarisretreatcentre@gmail.com
http://stellamarisretreatcentre.
googlepages.com
In charge: Sr Phyllis Behan
Community: 6, Chaplains: Parish Clergy
Spirituality centre, centre for retreats,
meetings, days of prayer for groups, self-
catering hermitage.

GALWAY
Emmanuel House of Providence
Clonfert, Ballinasloe, Co Galway
Tel 0579-151552/51641 Fax 0579-152957
Email emmanuelclonfert@eircom.net
No Accommodation
Eddie and Lucy Stones
Catholic centre for prayer and
evangelisation. It is a new community of
Christ's faithful, a spiritual hospital where
people can experience the healing power
of God in spirit, mind and body.

Esker Retreat House and Youth Village
Athenry, Co Galway
Tel 091-844549 Fax 091-845698
Email eskerret@indigo.ie
www.eskercommunity.net
Acc: singles 17, doubles 26 in retreat
house, 70 in 2 dorms in youth village
Retreat House Co-ordinator: Fr Fonsie
Doran CSsR
Email rev_dorancssr@yahoo.com
Youth Village Co-ordinator: Fr Michael
Cusack CSsR
Contact: The Secretary

KERRY
Ardfert Retreat Centre
Ardfert, Co Kerry
Tel 066-7134276 Fax 066-7134867
Email ardfertretreat@eircom.net
Acc: 29 rooms
Contact Person: Sr Angela Kiely RSM
Kerry Diocese and Intercongregational
Team: Mercy/Presentation and Ursuline
Sisters

KILKENNY
Peace in Christ, Sion Road, Kilkenny
Tel 056-7721054 Fax 056-7770755
Email peaceinchrist@eircom.net
Acc: singles 26
Contact: Sr Margaret Moloney
Daughters of Mary and Joseph

LAOIS
La Salle Pastoral Centre, Castletown,
Portlaoise, Co Laois
Tel 057-8732442 Fax 057-8732925
Contact: Br Stephen Dignan
Acc: 40. De La Salle Brothers

Mount St Anne's Retreat and Conference
Centre, Killenard, Portarlington, Co Laois
Tel 057-8626153 Fax 057-8626700
Email msannes@eircom.net
http://www.mountstannes.com
Acc: singles 22, doubles 6
Director: Sr Róisín Gannon (PBVM)
roisingannon@eircom.net
Contact Person: Christine or Catherine

LIMERICK
Baile Mhuire, Foynes, Co Limerick
Tel 069-65181 (payphone on-site)
Limerick Diocese House of Welcome
for Young People
Acc: Hostel type; sleeping bags required
Contact: The Secretary, Limerick

Diocesan Pastoral Centre
St Michael's Courtyard,
Denmark Street, Limerick
Tel 061-400133 Fax 061-400601
Email ldpc@eircom.net
www.limerickdiocese.pastoralcentre.com
Director: Rev Éamonn Fitgibbon
Diocese of Limerick

LOUTH
Domenican Nuns
Monastery of St Catherine of Siena,
The Twenties, Drogheda, Co Louth
Tel 041-9838524
Email sienaretreat@eircom.net

In a quiet country setting – self-catering
Retreat House
Acc: singles en suite 4, conference room
to facilitate groups for day retreats and
an oratory
Opportunity to participate in sung
Monastic Liturgy and Eucharistic
Adoration with the Community
Contact: Sister in Charge (Retreat Rooms)

TIPPERARY
House of Prayer, Glencomeragh,
Kilsheelan, Co Tipperary
Tel 052-33181 Fax 052-33636
Email info@glencomeragh.ie
www.glencomeragh.ie
Contact: Rev Patrick Pierce (IC)
Acc: singles 18, doubles 8, twin 2
Available for preached, directed or
private retreats, groups or individuals,
lay, religious or priests, conferences and
seminars; 4 hermitages and self-catering
also available.
Rosminians. A recent addition to
grounds is the 'Glencomeragh
Labyrinth'.

TYRONE
Servite Priory, Benburb, Dungannon,
Co Tyrone BT71 7JZ
Tel 028-37548241/028-37548533
Fax 028-37548524
Email servitepriory@btinernet.com
www.servites-benburb.com
Open to all who wish to call
Contact: Programme Co-ordinator

WATERFORD
Grace Dieu Retreat House
Tramore Road, Waterford
Tel 051-374417 Fax 051-874536
Email gracedieu@ireland.com
http://homepage.eircom.net/~gracedieu
Acc: 26 twins, 2 doubles, 5 singles all
ensuite
Director: Rev Michael Serrage (MSC)
Situated on the Waterford/Tramore Road.
Available for individuals or groups of
clergy, religious or lay peple.
Missionaries of the Sacred Heart

WEXFORD
St John of God Sisters Retreat House
Ballyvaloo, Blackwater, Co Wexford
Tel 053-9137160
Email
ballyvalooretreatcentre1@eircom.net
Director: Sr Leonie Dobbyn
Acc: ensuite rooms 33

WICKLOW
Chrysalis Holistic Centre
Donard, Co Wicklow
Tel/Fax 045-404713
Email peace@chrysalis.ie
www.chrysalis.ie
Contact: Deirdre Ahern
Acc: 20
Full programme of retreats and
workshops.
Two secluded hermitages for individual
private retreats.

Catholic Youth Care
Teach Chaoimhín,
Glendasan, Glendalough, Co Wicklow
(Enquiries to CYC,
Arran Quay, Dublin 7)
Tel 01-8725055
Fax 01-8725010
Email info@cyc.ie
Acc: small dormitories,
22 bunk beds

Catholic Youth Care
Teach Lorcain, Glendasan,
Glendalough, Co Wicklow
(Enquiries to CYC,
Arran Quay, Dublin 7)
Tel 01-8725055
Fax 01-8725010
Email info@cyc.ie
Acc: small dormitories,
23 beds including bunks

PASTORAL CENTRES

CORK
Dominican Pastoral Centre
Popes Quay, Cork
Tel 021-4502067/021-4502267
Fax 021-4502307
Email dompc@eircom.net
Director: Rev Donagh O'Shea (OP)
Acc: 2 conference rooms, 1 hall
Non-residential

Nano Nagle Centre
Ballygriffin, Mallow,
Co Cork
Tel 022-26411
Email enquiries@nanonaglebirthplace.ie
www.nanonaglebirthplace.ie
Presentation Sisters
Ecology and spirituality centre with
opportunities to work with the earth.
Facilities for self-catering private/group
retreats conferences, workshops.

DONEGAL
Whiteoaks Rehabilitation Centre
Derryvane, Muff, Co Donegal
Tel 07493-84400
Fax 07493-84883
Email whiteoaksrehabcentre@hotmail.com
www.whiteoaksrehabcentre.com
Director
Mr Tony Brown
General Manager
Sharon McMullan
The purpose of White Oaks is to aid the
recovery of people suffering from
addictions. We offer a 30-day residential
treatment programme, for people
addicted to drugs, alcohol and gambling,
based on the 12-step model. There is a
two year aftercare programme.
We have established a long-term
residential aftercare service.

KERRY
John Paul II Centre
Rock Road, Killarney, Co Kerry
Tel 064-32644 Fax 064-31170
Email accordkillarney@eircom.net/
reledkerry@eircom.net/dprt3@eircom.net
Non-residential
Director: Rev George Hayes
Kerry Diocese

KILKENNY
Seville Lodge Trust, Callan Road,
Kilkenny
Tel/Fax 056-7721453
Conferences, retreats, courses
Acc: 30 beds
Contact: Dick Curtin (Manager)
Diocese of Ossory

LIMERICK
Limerick Diocesan Pastoral Centre
St Michael's Courtyard,
Denmark Street, Limerick
Tel 061-400133 Fax 061-400601
Email ldpc@eircom.net
www.pastoralcentre.limerickdiocese.org
Director: Rev Noel Kirwan

MEATH
Dowdstown House, Blowick Centre,
Dalgan Park, Navan, Co Meath
Tel 046-9021407 Fax 046-9073091
Email dowdstownhouse@eircom.net
www.dowdstownhouse.com
Acc: single 23, shared rooms 50
Director: Elma Peppard (RSM)
Meath Diocese

WATERFORD
St John's Pastoral Centre
John's Hill, Waterford
Tel 051-874199 Fax 051-843107
Administrator: Ms Mary Dee
Email stjohnspastoralcentre@eircom.net

PRIVATE RETREATS

ANTRIM
Adoration Sisters
63 Falls Road, Belfast BT12 4PD
Tel 02890 325668
www.adorationsisters.com
Altar Bread Suppliers
'Saint Joseph's House of Bread'
Tel 02890 247175
Contact: Sr Molly Caldwell

Our Lady of Bethlehem Abbey
11 Ballymena Road, Portglenone,
Co Antrim BT44 8BL
Tel 028-2582 1211 Fax 028-2582 2795
Email kelly@unite.net
www.bethlehem-abbey.org.uk
Contact: Rev Guestmaster
9.30am-5.00 pm, Monday-Saturday
Acc: 10 rooms: 8 singles/doubles, 2 singles
Cistercians

DERRY
Columba Community
Columba House of Prayer and
Reconciliation
11 Queen Street, Derry BT48 7EG
Tel 02871 262407
Email columbacommunity@hotmail.com
www.columbacommunity.com
Director: Rev Neal Carlin
Contact: Tommy McCay
Email columbacommunity@hotmail.com
A basic Christian community with 20
members offering opportunities for
private reflection and group worship.
Prayer and pastoral counselling available
on a one-to-one and group basis.
Blessed Sacrament Chapel open daily
9.30am-5.00pm
Monday to Friday: all welcome
Thursday 7.30pm Mass and Prayer for
Healing

DOWN
Holy Cross Monastery
119 Kilbroney Road, Rostrevor,
Co Down BT34 3BN
Tel 028-41739979 Fax 028-41739978
Email benedictinemonks@btinternet.com
www.benedictinemonks.co.uk
Contact: The Guestmaster
Accommodation: 8 singles/doubles
Benedictines

GALWAY
La Retraite Hermitage
2 Distillery Road, Newcastle, Galway
Tel 091-524548
Contact: The community
Self-catering, retreat direction available
La Retraite Sisters

LEITRIM
La Verna, Convent Avenue,
Drumshanbo, Co Leitrim
Tel 071-9641308
Contact: Sr Helen Keegan
Self-catering: 3 bedroom retreat house
Poor Clare Monastery of Perpetual
Adoration

LIMERICK
Glenstal Abbey, Monastic Guest House,
Murroe, Co Limerick
Tel 061-386103 Ext 225
Contact: Fr Christopher Dillon OSB
Email guestmaster@glenstal.org
Acc: 12
Benedictines

WEXFORD
St Aidan's Monastery of Adoration
Ferns, Co Wexford
Tel 053-9366634
Email staidansferns@eircom.net
Contact: Sr M. Dolores O'Brien
Acc: 2 singles, 7 hermitages, 1
wheelchair-friendly, 2 for couples.
House: sleeps 5 – 1 twin, 1 double, 1
single room. Suitable for small groups.

ORGANISATIONS, SOCIETIES AND RELIGIOUS PERIODICALS

ORGANISATIONS AND SOCIETIES

Accord Catholic Marriage Care Service
President: Most Rev William Walsh
Vice-President: Most Rev Raymond Field
National Director: Ms Ruth Barror
National Chaplain: Rev Peter Murphy
Central Office: Columba Centre,
Maynooth, Co Kildare
Tel 01-5053112 Fax 01-6016410
Email admin@accord.ie
www.accord.ie
For details, see Departments of the Irish Episcopal Conference.

Adoption Contact Register
Administrator: Dr M. A. Tierney
Grange Clare, Kilmeague, Naas, Co Kildare

No longer operating by mail or phone but all helpful information for adopted people and birth mothers can be found at http://www.myhelppage2.homestead.com/adoptioncontact.html

Assists all Irish fostered/adopted persons to gain contact with their 'birth' relatives and also assists Irish mothers who, reluctantly, 'gave up' their children, when this is the wish of all parties concerned. Completely confidential service. No fee charged, although donations towards this work are greatly appreciated, since it enables us to help more people in the future. Adoption Contact Register Charity No CHY.11776.

Aid to the Church in Need
National Director: George Lynch
151 St Mobhi Road, Glasnevin, Dublin 9
Tel 01-8377516 Fax 01-8369189
Email churchinneed@eircom.net
www.kirche-in-not.org
Registered Charity No 9492

An association of Pontifical Right. The principal goal of the association is to support the Church pastorally, especially where she is persecuted and threatened. It also supports refugees and appeals to the faithful to assist in this work by prayers and donations. (See our advertisement, p. 306)

Alert
President: Rev Leonard Coughlan (OFMCap)
Chairman: Mr Shane Redmond
Secretary: Miss Colette Garvey
Office: 133 Church Street, Dublin 7
Tel 01-8722597

Educational and social movement, founded in 1990, to create a greater awareness of the dangers of drink and drugs.

Alpha Ireland
National Coordinator
Paddy Monaghan
72 Hillcourt Road,
Glenageary, Co Dublin
Tel 01-2369821 Fax 01-2369800
Email alphairel@eircom.net
www.alphacourse.ie

The 10-week Alpha Course explores some basic doctrines of the Christian faith – Who is Jesus? Why did Jesus die? This user-friendly course on Evangelisation is endorsed by Church leaders. It is aimed at those who do not attend church and it also helps church-goers renew their faith. Participants meet weekly. Talks are available on DVD. After Alpha, participants are encouraged to continue their spiritual journey often through parish cell groups, pastorates or *Lectio divina* groups. The Alpha Board includes Fr Pat Collins, David Quinn, Sr Brigid Dunne, Cork, Ger Gallagher, CYC, Fr Michael Hurley, Basil Good. Alpha has spread to all Christian Churches and 160 countries. Its success has led to Youth Alpha (used in schools), Alpha in the workplace (run at lunch times), Alpha in prisons and the Alpha Marriage Course. Email for details of conferences.

Apostolic Work Society
President: Mrs Anne Minihan
Abbey Road, Thurles
Secretary: Mrs Anna Maher
5 Bohernamona, Thurles
Contact: Thurles Parish Centre,
Cathedral Street, Thurles
Tel 0504-22229 Fax 0504-22414
Email parishcentre@thurlesparish.ie

Apostleship of Prayer
National Secretary: Rev John Looby (SJ)
37 Lower Leeson Street, Dublin 2
Tel 01-6767491 Fax 01-6611606
Email sales@messenger.ie
www.messenger.ie

A world-wide union of the faithful who, by the making of a daily offering and by praying for the Pope's intentions for the Church and the world, unite themselves with Christ in the Mass and with the prayers of his heart. The *Sacred Heart Messenger*, published monthly, is the official magazine. Messenger publications is a Jesuit Apostolate and publishes a range of religious booklets and calendars, as well as the *Sacred Heart Messenger*.

Apostleship of the Sea
Episcopal Promoter
Most Rev Fiachra Ó Ceallaigh,
19 St Anthony's Road,
Rialto, Dublin 8
Correspondence to President:
Ms Rose Kearney
Stella Maris Seafarers' Club,
3 Beresford Place, Dublin 1
Tel 01-8749061/8742428 (7pm to 10.30pm nightly)

Apostolate for Family Consecration
National Co-ordinator
Mr Cathal Magee
Corpus Christi Centre, Maynooth,
Co Kildare Tel/Fax 01-2692781
The Apostolate for Family Consecration was founded on 18 June during the Holy Year of 1975, and was officially approved by the Church on 3 October 1975. The Apostolate seeks to transform parishes and neighbourhoods into God centered communities by providing deeply spiritual multi-media programmes in the Eucharistic, Marian and family-centered spirit of Pope John Paul II.

Association for Church Archives Ireland
Chairperson: Dominique Horgan (OP)
Vice-Chairperson: Noelle Dowling
Treasurer: Marie Feely (OSC)
Editor of Newsletter: Teresa Delaney (RSM)
Committee members: David Kelly (OSA)
Paula Doolin (IBVM), Marie Coyle (FMDM)
Secretary: Sr Marie Bernadette O'Leary (RSC)
Sisters of Charity, Caritas,
Gilford Road, Sandymount, Dublin 4
Tel 01-2697833 Fax 01-2603085
Email archives@rsccaritas.com

Association of Irish Liturgists
Contact: Rev Hugh P. Kennedy
Cathedral Presbytery,
St Peter's Square, Belfast BT12 4BU
Tel 028-90327573

An informal association of people engaged in the study and teaching of liturgy.

Association of Papal Orders in Ireland
President: Donal Downes KSG (Galway)
Vice President: Gearóid O'Broin, GCPO
Secretary: Peter F. Durnin KC*SG (Armagh)
'Rosaire'. Crosslanes, Drogheda,
Co Louth, Republic of Ireland
Email peternora12281@eircom.net
Chaplain: Rev Fr Timothy Bartlett

The Association is open to all ladies and gentlemen resident in or native of Ireland who have recieved a Knighthood from the Holy Father. It meets twice yearly.

Allianz ⑪

Association of Primary Teaching Sisters
7/8 Lower Abbey Street, Dublin 1
President: Sr Mary Collins
Secretary/Treasurer: Sr Margaret Ivers
Tel 01-8781986 Fax 01-8781986
Email srmarycollins@eircom.net

Aims to unite its members through their religious consecration to share in the mission of the Church by ensuring Catholic education in schools and fostering the Christian message; to facilitate communication and liaison to improve the educational opportunity of children in primary schools.

Cardijn Association
Crumlin Road, Belfast 14, Northern Ireland
Tel 028-90807288 *Contact:* Mr Sean Cooney

The Cardijn Association consists of former members and chaplains of the YCW movement. They meet on a regular basis for retreat days and hold a special Mass for deceased members and chaplains each year.

Catholic Boy Scouts of Ireland (see Scouting Ireland)

Catholic Guides of Ireland
(Banóglaigh Catoilicí na hÉireann)
Chief Commissioner: Catherine Lenihan
Assistant Chief Commissioner
Dolores Farnan
National Treasurer: Cecilia Browne
National Chaplain
Rev Eamonn McCamley
National Office Coordinator
Laura Saunders
National Secretary: Martha McGrath
National Office: 12 Clanwilliam Terrace, Grand Canal Quay, Dublin 2
Tel 01-6619566 Fax 01-6765691
Email nat.office@girlguidesireland.ie
www.girlguidesireland.ie

The Catholic Guides of Ireland (CGI) is a voluntary nationwide association open to all girls and women. It is organised on a diocesan basis, providing challenging indoor and outdoor activities which encourage the overall development of the individual. CGI through the Council of Irish Guiding Associations (CIGA) is a member of the World Association of Girl Guides and Girl Scouts (WAGGGS). CGI's youth programmes are available for 5-18 year olds at local community level. There are also opportunities for volunteer adult leadership, who receive training and support for this role.

Catholic Nurses Guild of Ireland
National President: Ms Breda Murphy
Ballyshane, Inishtigue, Kilkenny
National Vice-President
Sr Brid Commins, 29 Green Road, Mullingar, Co Westmeath
National Secretary and Contact
Ms Therese McCormack White Hart House, Ballbriggan, Co Dublin

National Treasurer: Sr Margaret Vincent
Sisters of Charity, Ard Mhuire, Harold's Cross, Dublin 6
Headquarters: Central Catholic Library, 74 Merrion Square, Dublin 2
Tel 01-6761264

The Guild is a response to the Vatican's Decree on the Apostolate of the Laity. Its role is to promote the social, educational, professional and spiritual development of its members so as to help them to work effectively in the service of life. There are several branches of the Guild active throughout Ireland.

Catholic Communications Office
(Incorporating the Catholic Press and Information Office)
Irish Bishops' Conference,
St Patrick's College, Maynooth,
Co Kildare
Director: Mr Martin Long
Communications Officer
Ms Brenda Drumm
Tel 01-5053000 Fax 01-6016413
Email info@catholiccommunications.ie
www.catholiccommunications.ie

CatholicIreland.net
St Mary's, Bloomfield Avenue,
Donnybrook, Dublin 4
Tel 01-6680505 Fax 01-6319755
Email info@catholicireland.net
www.catholicireland.net;
www.getonline.ie; www.gettingmarried.ie
Chairman: Fr Alan McGuckian (SJ)
Chief Executive: Mr Tony Bolger
Patron: Cardinal Sean Brady

CatholicIreland.net is an organisation whose aim is to promote the Catholic faith using modern communications like the world wide web. The site is a dynamic and attractive internet portal, which gathers and disseminates a wealth of quality information and resources, including the times of all masses in Ireland and a daily news service, to support believers and to reach out to others, in Ireland and throughout the world. Catholic Ireland also designs and builds websites for dioceses, parishes, schools and other Church-related groups.

Catholic Primary School Managers' Association
7/8 Lower Abbey Street, Dublin 1
Tel 01-8742171/1850-407200
Fax 01-8747397
Email cpsma@indigo.ie
Chairman
Very Rev Canon Francis Kelly
General Secretary
Rt Rev Mgr Dan O'Connor
www.cpsma.ie
(For details, see Episcopal Commissions)

Catholic Historical Society of Ireland
Secretary: Dáire Keogh
Treasurer: Colm Lennon
Conference Secretary: Mary Ann Lyons
Editor (Contact): Dr Thomas O'Connor
Tel 01-7083926 Fax 01-7083314
Email thomas.oconnor@nuim.ie
www.archivium-hibernicum.ie

Founded in 1911, its annual journal *Archivium Hibernicum* publishes documents and studies dealing with Irish ecclesiastical history and Irish history in general.

Catholic Men and Women's Society of Ireland
Patron: Most Rev Donal Murray, Bishop of Limerick
President: Mr Eamon Hennessy
Tel 045-525165
Hon Secretary: Mr Ken Butterworth
Tel 087-1257132
Hon Treasurer: Ms Esther Brady
Tel 045-522094
National Chaplain: Vacant
Office: 2A Irishtown Road, Dublin 4

The Society strives for the personal development of its members through spiritual, intellectual, social and physical activities. The basic unit is called the branch. The society is organised at national level by the governing body, the National Council.

CEIST
Chairperson, Board of Directors
Mr Jack O'Brien
CEO: Ms Anne Kelleher
Director of Faith Development
Mr Ned Prendergast
Director of School Support Services
Ms Margaret O'Brien
Director of Finance: Mr Mike Higgins
IT Manager: Mr John Woods
First Floor, Block A,
Maynooth Business Campus,
Maynooth, Co Kildare
Tel 01-6510350 Fax 01-6510180
Email info@ceist.ie
www.ceist.ie

CEIST: Catholic Education – An Irish Schools Trust is a new collaborative trustee body for the voluntary secondary schools of the following congregations:
• Presentation Sisters
• Sisters of the Christian Retreat
• Congregation of the Sisters of Mercy
• Missionaries of the Sacred Heart
• Daughters of Charity
CEIST Ltd was incorporated in May 2007
Vision: A compasianate and just society inspired by the life and teachings of Jesus Christ

Mission Statement: To provide a holistic education in the Catholic tradition
Values: Promoting spiritual and human development, achieving quality in teaching and learning, showing respect for every person, creating community and being just and responsible.

Central Catholic Library

Chairman: Rev Noel Barber (SJ)
Correspondence to:
Librarian: Ms Teresa Whitington
74 Merrion Square, Dublin 2
Tel 01-6761264
Email catholiclibrary@imagine.ie
www.catholiclibrary.ie

Nationally important collection (founded 1922 by Fr Stephen Brown) of over 90,000 books with reference, research and lending departments. Emphasis on theology, scripture, spirituality, Church history, etc., but also on Irish history and culture (including Gaelic); literature and foreign languages (including important Dante collection), biography, history, travel; an extensive collection on art and architecture; and the philosophy, religion and sociology books of the old Central Students Library (for loan). Some pre-1800 titles. Runs of 400 journals (from 1814) in these areas. Audio and audio-visual materials. A voluntary subscription library, with an annual fee for borrowing rights; the reference and research departments are open to the public. Managed by an elected council, the library relies on public support for its continued existence and welcomes new members. Open: Mon-Fri 11.00-18.00; Saturday 11.00-17.50.

Charismatic Renewal Movement

Emmanuel, 3 Pembroke Park, Ballsbridge, Dublin 4

The Charismatic Renewal Movement seeks to foster spiritual renewal under the inspiration of the Holy Spirit and to promote Christian unity. There are over 450 prayer groups in Ireland which are open to all. The movement maintain an office at 'Emmanuel'. Tel 01-6670570 NSC, Box 2434, Dublin 4. All telephone messages will be returned. The office is manned on Tuesday and Thursday 10.30am to 12.30pm

Office of the National Service Committee for Catholic Charismatic Renewal in Ireland
Chairperson: Marie Beirne
Tel 071-9624404
Liaison Bishop to Charismatic Renewal:
Bishop Martin Drennan
Email nsc@iol.ie

Christian Life Communities

35/36 Lower Leeson Street, Dublin 2
Tel 01-6471096
Email clc@jesuit.ie
www.jesuit.ie/clc

CLC is a worldwide lay association which has special links with the Society of Jesus. Founded in 1563 as the 'Sodality of Our Lady', it has changed radically since the Second Vatican Council. Members of CLC are helped to integrate their faith and daily living through the carism of the Spiritual Exercises of St Ignatius of Loyola. They meet on a regular basis, in groups of between six

and ten, thereby getting support from each other. This form of spirituality, supported by the Group, leads to a sense of mission, which is rooted in the whole quality of presence which we bring to the world in which we live.

At present there are more than twenty thousand members in over 50 countries in every continent.

For more information, contact:
Fr Michael Gallagher (SJ)
Tel 01-7758596
Email mgallagher@jesuit.ie

Church Resources/Church Telecom/Staffroom.ie

St Mary's, Bloomfield Avenue, Donnybrook, Dublin 4
Tel 01-6680505 Fax 01-6319755
Email info@churchresources.ie
www.churchresources.ie
www.churchresources.co.uk
Chairman: Fr Alan McGuickan SJ
Chief Executive: Mr Tony Bolger

Church Resources exists to combine the purchasing power of church organisations, including parishes, schools, religious congregations, care facilities and all other ministries and Church-related groups, to achieve financial savings on their everyday essential purchases. The savings that each group makes can then be used to finance their ministry activity. In the process this activity attracts a small commission from each of Church Resources' suppliers, which is in turn used to finance the maintenance and expansion of Churchservices.tv

ChurchServices.tv

St Mary's, Bloomfield Avenue, Donnybrook, Dublin 4
Tel 01-6680505 Fax 01-6319755
Email info@churchservices.iv
www.churchservices.tv

ChurchServices.tv provides live video streaming from Cathedrals, Churches, or any other location via the internet. The video streaming can come from a permanent installation or from a one-off broadcast from a conference or any other single event. Video documentaries or other video material can also be streamed from ChurchServices.tv.

Communion and Liberation

Contact: Margaret Biondi
Tel 01-2987564
Email cldublin@eci.iewww.clonline.org

An international movement founded by Mgr Luigi Giussani in Italy in 1954 and approved by the Church. It is present in over seventy countries throughout the world. The essence of its charism is the announcement of the Incarnation of Christ who is present in the here and now and can be encountered in the unity of his people which is the Church.

Concern Worldwide

Office: Camden Street, Dublin 2
Tel 01-4177700
Fax 01-4757362
Email info@concern.net
www.concern.net
Chief Executive: Mr Tom Arnold
Chairperson: Jim Miley
Secretary: Frances O'Keefe

Concern Worldwide is an international humanitarian organisation dedicated to reducing suffering and ending extreme poverty. We work with the very poorest people in the world's poorest countries to help them bring about long-lasting change in their lives and realise their fundamental human rights; to food, to health, to education, and ultimately to a life of dignity. Together with local and international partners, and with poor people themselves, we respond to emergency situations and undertake long-term development work. We work across the world to promote a better understanding of extreme poverty and hunger, and we campaign for local and global action that will help to end them for good.

Conference of Religious of Ireland

Bloomfield Avenue, off Morehampton Road, Dublin 4, Tel 01-6677322 Fax 01-6689460
Email secretariat@cori.ie
www.cori.ie
Director General
Sr Marianne O'Connor (OSU)
President: Sr Conchita McDonnell (MSHR)
Vice-President: Br Martin Kenneally (FPM)
Offices: Child Protection 01-6677343, Education 01-6677346, Healthcare 01-6677349, Justice 01-6677363 Northern Ireland 028-90694443

The Conference is a voluntary coming together of religious. Among its objectives are: to promote the spiritual and religious welfare of the congregations of Irish religious; to foster an ever-increasing effectiveness in the apostolate of the congregations; to effect a closer co-operation between congregations and with all members of the Church; to provide appropriate and official representation with civil government and bishops.

Council of Irish Adoption Agencies

Chairperson: Ms Sheila Gallagher
St Attracta's Adoption Society, St Mary's Sligo
Tel 071-9143058
Email ciadoptionagencies@gmail.com
Vice Chairperson: Ms Marian Bennett
Social Worker, Health Centre, Coosan Road, Athlone, Co Westmeath
Tel 090-6483136
Email marian.bennett@hse.ie

Secretary: Margaret Comaskey
Adoption Service, St Mary's Hospital,
Dublin Road, Drogheda, Co Louth
Tel 041-9832963
Email margaret.comaskey@hse.ie
Treasurer: Laura O'Callaghan
St Catherine's Adoption Society,
Clarecare, Harmony Row, Ennis, Co Clare
Tel 065-6828178

The Council of Irish Adoption Agencies
represents statutory and voluntary
adoption agencies. The Council aims to
standardise adoption policy and practice,
highlight adoption issues, influence
policy, campaign for changes in adoption
leglisation, develop services for all those
with concerns in relation to adoption.

Council of Management of Catholic Secondary Schools
President: Mr Noel Merrick
Secretariat of Secondary Schools
Emmet House, Dundrum Road, Dublin 14
Tel 01-2838255 Fax 01-2695461
Email info@secretariat.ie
www.jmb.ie
CMCSS and AMCSS

The Council of Management of Catholic
Secondary Schools (CMCSS) was founded
in the 'sixties' and since 1972 has become
a national organisation which includes
representatives of the Irish Catholic
Hierarchy. The Council of Management
of Catholic Secondary Schools is the
governing body of the Secretariat of
Secondary Schools which is the
administrative centre of information,
research and action on behalf of the
schools. The Council of Management of
Catholic Secondary Schools maintains
contacts and interacts with other
national and international groups
interested in Catholic education.

CPRSI (See Cúnamh)

Cumann na Sagart
Uachtarán: An tAth Tadhg Ó Móráin
Corr na Móna, Co na Gaillimhe
Guthán 094-9548003
Email tomorain5@eircom.net
Rúnaí: An tAth Tadhg Furlong
Ceapach na bhFaoiteach,
Co Thiobraid Arann
Guthán 062-75427
Cathaoirleach
An tAth Seamus Ó hÉanaigh SP
Delvin, Co na hIarmhí
Guthán 044-9644127

Is é aidhm an Chumainn ná dúchas
creidimh na tíre a chothú, agus tacaíocht
a thabhairt do shagairt a bhfuil an
Ghaeilge in úsáid acu. Tugtar faoin
aidhm seo a chur i gcrích: (a) trí léachtaí
ag tionól bliantúil ina bpléitear gné
éigin den dúchas creidimh; (b) trí
fhoilseacháin liotúirge, scrioptúir,
diagachta agus cultúir dhúchais; (c) trí
chomhoibrú le pobal gach deoise tré
mhéan Ionadaí an Deoise, agus trí

imeachtaí éagsúla fríd an tír; (d) trí
chomhoibriú le heagrais eile chun
traidisiún dúchasach an phobail logánta
a chothú, go háirithe i gcomórtas *Ghlór
na nGael*. Tá suíomh idirlín ag Cumann
na Sagart www.cumannnasagart.ie

Cúnamh (formerly Catholic Protection and Rescue Society of Ireland) (CPRSI)
Secretary/Senior Social Worker
Julie Kerins, BSocSc, CQSW, MSocSC
Office: 30 South Anne Street, Dublin 2
Tel 01-6779664
Email info@cunamh.com
www.cunamh.com

Cúnamh is a registered adoption agency
providing pre- and post-natal counselling
for pregnant girls, their partners and
families; short-term foster care and
adoption. Cúnamh provides support and
advice for adoptive parents and an
information and trace service for adult
adoptees and birthparents.

CURA Pregnancy Counselling Service
President: Bishop John Fleming
National Co-ordinator: Ms Louise Graham
National Office: Columba Centre,
Maynooth, Co Kildare
Tel 01-5053040/1 Fax 01-6292364
Email curacares@cura.ie
www.cura.ie
National Helpline: 1850-622626

CURA is an agency of the Catholic
Church and was eastablished in 1977 as a
caring service for those whose pregnancy
is or has become a crisis. Services
provided include:

- Free pregnancy testing
- Crisis pregnancy counselling and
  support (phone Helpline and Face to
  Face)
- Information on social welfare and
  other rights and entitlements
- Making links with agencies providing
  accommodation and other support
  services as required
- Post-natal support
- Counselling after an abortion
- Crisis pregnancy counselling to baby's
  father and other family members
- School Awareness Programme.

Dialogue Ireland Trust
7/8 Lower Abbey Street, Dublin 1
Tel 01-8309384/087-2396229
Fax 01-8744913
Director: Mike Garde
Email info@dialogueireland.org
www.dialogueireland.org

The Dialogue Ireland Trust was
established to promote awareness and
understanding of 'cultist' New Religious
Movements (NRMs) and to assist with
advice and documentation. Dialogue
Ireland Trust is an independent
organisation at the service of Irish
Society. Our mission is to assist in the
protection of Religious freedom and to

alert the public to the challenge cults
pose to our mental health and our
democratic freedoms. A specific area
addressed is our schools programme
directed at 6th years at Secondary School
as a preparation for third level.

Eco-Congregation Ireland
Eco-Congragation aims to encourage
churches to celebrate the gift of Gods
creation, to recognise the
interdependence of allcreation and to
care for it in their life and mission and
through the members personal lifestyles
Communications Officer: Fiona Murdoch
Email fionam1840@oceanfree.net
Tel 01-4939387/086-1706923

The Emmaus Community
PO Box 53, Dun Laoghaire, Co Dublin
Tel 01-2859962
Email emmaus@iol.ie
www.emmaus.ie/
www.emmauscommunity.com
Community Director: Rónán Johnston
Community Leader: Ray Ekins

All Emmaus worship and liturgical music
available from PO Box above.

ERST – Edmund Rice School Trust
Chairperson, Board of Directors
Mr Pat Diggins
Chief Executive: Mr Gerry Bennet
Coordinator of Ethos: Mr Tony McCann
Coordinator of Governance
Ms Helen O'Brien
Finance/Property Officer
Ms Louise Callagahn
Meadow Vale, Clonkeen Road
Blackrock, Co Dublin
Tel 01-2897511 Fax 01-2897540
Email reception@erst.ie
www.erst.ie

The Edmund Rice Schools Trust, an
independent lay company based in
Dublin, ensure that the schools in the
former Christian Brother Network
(currently 97) will continue to provide a
Catholic education into the future, in the
spirit and tradition of Blessed Edmund
Rice, for the people of Ireland.
ERST was incorporated in May 2008.
Vision: Promoting full personal and
social development in caring Christian
communities of learning and teaching.
Mission Statement: To provide Catholic
Education in the Edmund Rice tradition.
The five keys elements of an Edmund
Rice Schools Trust School are:
- Nurturing faith, Christian spirituality
  and Gospel-based values;
- Promoting partnership in the school
  community;
- Excelling in teaching and learning;
- Creating a caring school community;
- Inspiring transformational leadership.

Allianz ⑪

Equestrian Order of the Holy Sepulchre of Jerusalem, Lieutenancy of Ireland
Lieutenant
HE Nicholas McKenna KSG, KCHS
'ByeWays', 27 Old Galgorm Road,
Ballymena, Co Antrim BTH IAL
Tel 048-25663401
Email
nicholas.mckenna@galgormgroup.com
Grand Prior: Cardinal Séan Brady
Archbishop of Armagh
Secretary: Peter F. Durnin KSG, GCHS
Rosarie, Moneymore, Drogheda,
Co Louth

The Lieutenancy of All Ireland of the Equestrian Order of the Holy Sepulchre of Jerusalem was established in July 1986. The venue for investitures is St Patrick's College, Maynooth, Co Kildare.

Evangelical Catholic Initiative
72 Hillcourt Road, Glenageary, Co Dublin
Tel 01-2369821 Fax 01-2369800
Email evancat@eircom.net
Secretary: Paddy Monaghan
60 Shore Road, Rostrevor,
Co Down BT34 3AA Tel/Fax 028-41738801
Email boylecb@aol.com
Secretary: Eugene Boyle

ECI is an initiative for a New Evangelisation, comprised of Catholic Christians who are evangelical by conviction and committed to a personal relationship with Jesus Christ. It seeks to promote the kingdom of God under the guidance and empowering of the Holy Spirit, through working for a Christ-centred, biblically based renewal in the Catholic Church, through fostering reconciliation and unity among Christians and through building up Jewish/Christian relationships.

Adventures in Reconciliation, with a foreword by Cardinal Cahal Daly, includes testmonies from 29 Catholics in Ireland all of whom are involved in bridge-building with Protestant Christians. Email for copy of book.

Family and Media Association
Chairman: Dr Ivo O'Sullivan PhD
Contact: Donal O'Sullivan, Executive
Development Officer
Alberione Media Centre, Newtownpark
Avenue, Blackrock, Co Dublin
Tel 01-2789288 Fax 01-2103834
Email info@fma.ie
www.familyandmedia.ie

Aims: to promote respect by the media for Christian values, especially those relating to the family; to seek high standards of honesty, decency, fairness and truthfulness in the media; to promote effective dialogue between the media and the public; to promote public understanding of the functioning and power of the media, and to assess and enhance the value of the media to the individual, the family and the community

The Family of God
The Oratory, Carroll Village,
Dundalk, Co Louth
Tel 042-9335566
Email fogoratory@eircom.net
Contact: Mr Teddy Lambe

The community was founded in Ireland in 1979. The community is non-residential and it is essentially a lay organisation although priests, religious and sisters are welcome to become associate members. The community is committed to a lifestyle of prayer, service and evangelisation. It is a registered charity in Ireland and Northern Ireland. The community has been recognised as a Private Association of the Faithful since July 1995 and it is a council member of the Catholic Fraternity, an international association of Catholic communities formally recognised by the Pontifical Council for the Laity.

Father Matthew Union
President: Most Rev Thomas A. Finnegan
Spiritual Director
Most Rev Francis McKiernan
Secretary: Rev Seán Moore CC
Parochial House, Carnmore Drive,
Newry, Co Down Tel 01693-68512

An organisation of priests interested in promotion of temperance. Its branches operate on a diocesan basis. The Union works in liaison with Catholic and interdenominational temperance groups, with Alcoholics Anonymous and with the Irish National Council on Alcoholism.

Focolare Movement
National Centre: Focolare Centre,
Curryhills, Prosperous, Co Kildare
Tel 045-840410 Fax 045-892997
Email focolare@focolare.ie,
czmdublin@eircom.net
Contact: Ms Juanita Majury/Mr David Hickey
Dublin Centres: 20 Ramleh Close,
Milltown, Dublin 6
Tel 01-2698081 Fax 01-2837705
Email ramleh@focolare.ie

Contact: Ms Paula Dowd
8 Clareville Road, Harold's Cross,
Dublin 6 Tel 01-4922709
Contact: Mr Declan O'Byrne
Email focmdublin@eircom.net
www.focolare.org

An international movement founded by Chiara Lubich in 1943, at Trent in Northern Italy. Subsequently approved by the Church, its principal aim is to help bring about the fulfilment of the prayer of Jesus 'That All may be One'.

Glencree Centre for Peace and Reconciliation
Glencree, Enniskerry, Co Wicklow
Tel 01-2829711 Fax 01-2766085
Email info@glencree.ie www.glencree.ie
Honorary President: Alfie Kane
Chief Executive: David Bloomfield
Chairperson: Peter Keenan
Contact, Programme Assistant:
Nicky Butler

A non-profit, non-governmental organisation committed to peacebuilding and reconciliation within and between communities. The centre provides facilities expressly devoted to peacebuilding issues in Ireland, North and South, Britain and beyond.

International Apostolate of Divine Mercy
Administator: Dr M. A. Tierney
Grange Clare, Kilmeague,
Naas, Co Kildare
Tel/Fax 045-860623
Email drmat@indigo.ie

Aimed at spreading devotion to Jesus' Divine Mercy throughout the world. Become an Apostle by sending your name and address and two Irish postage stamps. The Apostles Prayer and a small starter supply of leaflets to distribute will be sent to you by return post. Dr Tierney is promulgating the cause for beatification/ santification of Pope John Paul I, Albino Luciano. Please report favours to him.
www.myhelppage2.homestead.com

Irish Biblical Association
President: Fr Gerard Deighan
Email gdeighan@eircom.net
Vice President: Dr Kieran O'Mahony
Email komahony@milltown-institute.ie
Secretary: Tom Gillen
Email iba@iolfree.ie
Treasurer: Ms Anna O'Farrell
Email annof@gofree.indigo.ie
www.irish-biblical-association.com

The IBA was established in 1966. The aims of the association are to: (a) assist the Irish Church in its work of understanding and proclaiming the word of God; (b) promote the scientific study of the Bible and related branches of learning; (c) organise conferences, study groups and lectures on biblical subjects; (d) support the publication of scientific studies on the scripture; (e) contribute to articles on biblical matters which will be of assistance in promoting a general biblical apostolate.

The association publishes an annual periodical, the Proceedings of the Irish Biblical Association. The members of the Irish Biblical Association are engaged professionally with and/or take a personal interest in the Jewish and Christian Scriptures. The Irish Biblical Association welcomes new members. There are two kinds of membership, ordinary and associate. Associate members are those interested in supporting and taking part in the events arranged by the IBA. Ordinary membership is for people with a post-graduate qualification in biblical studies.

Membership is accepted at the annual AGM in the spring and in the meantime prospective members are, of course, welcome in our meetings and can be on our mailing list.

Allianz (ⓘ)

The Irish Chaplaincy in Britain
(For details, see Episcopal Commissions and Advisory Bodies and Chaplains)

Irish Church Music Association (Cumann Ceol Eaglasta na hÉireann)
National Centre for Liturgy,
St Patrick's College, Maynooth, Co Kildare
Chairperson: Fr Paul Kenny
St Nicholas of Myra, Francis Street,
Dublin 8 Tel 01-4542172
Secretary: Mrs Grace Lyons
134 Rialto Cottages, Dublin 8
Tel 01-4538750

An association for the promotion of church music. Activities include the publication of music, the organisation of regional meetings of church musicians and an annual summer school. A newsletter is issued regularly.

Irish College, Paris
Founded in 1578
5 Rue des Irlandais, 75005-Paris
Rector: Rt Rev Mgr Brendan P. Devlin
Communicating Secretary
Dr Thomas O'Connor
Maynooth College, Co Kildare
Tel 01-6285222
Email history.department@nuim.ie

The college is now vested in the Fondation Irlandaise, a trust for the education of Irish people and their accommodation in Paris. The college also hosts a full scale cultural centre. Visitors' rooms are periodically available to Irish people on application to the administrator, Ms Sheila Pratschke.
Tel 00-331-58 52 10 30
Resident Chaplain: Rev David Bracken
Tel 00-331-58 52 10 89

Irish Council of Churches
Inter-Church Centre,
48 Elmwood Avenue, Belfast BT9 6AZ
Tel 028-90663145 Fax 028-90664160
Email info@irishchurches.org
www.irishchurches.org
(For details, see General Information section)

Irish Episcopal Council for Emigrants
Columba Centre, Maynooth, Co Kildare
Tel 01-5053155 Fax 01-6016401
Chair: Most Rev Seámus Hegarty
Secretary: Ms Caroline Navagh
Email emigrants@iecon.ie

Irish Episcopal Commission for Liturgy
National Secretary: Rev Patrick Jones
National Centre for Liturgy
St Patrick's College, Maynooth, Co Kildare
Tel 01-7083478 Fax 01-7083477
Email liturgy@may.ie

IHCPT The Irish Pilgrimage Trust
Kilcuan, Clarenbridge, Co Galway
Tel 091-796622 Fax 091 796916
Email info@irishpilgrimagetrust.com
President: Most Rev Dermot O'Mahony
Chairman: John O'Reilly
Honorary Treasurer: James White

Contact: National Coordinator
Bernadette O'Connell (for further information and application forms)
Email boconnell@irishpilgrimagetrust.com

IHCPT Irish Pilgrimage Trust is a voluntary organisation which brings young people with special needs to Lourdes at Easter time. The helpers pay their own fares and raise the funds for the young people. The Irish Pilgrimage Trust has opened a holiday house, Kilcuan, in Clarenbridge, Co Galway, which caters for groups with special needs.
For further details contact
Pat Jordan, Kilcuan Manager
Tel 091-796900

Irish Hospitalité of Our Lady of Lourdes (Affiliated to Hospitalité Notre Dame de Lourdes)
Ely House, 8 Ely Place, Dublin 2
President: Ms Rosita McHugh
Secretary/Contact Person
Ms Deirdre O'Sullivan
26 Vernon Street, Dublin 8
Tel 01-6570138
Treasurer: Mr Gerard Bennett
Correspondence Address
26 Vernon Street, Dublin 8
Email deirdreosullivan@gmail.com

Founded in 1930, under the patronage of the Archbishop of Dublin. An organisation of people, from all walks of life, who are dedicated to working with the sick in Lourdes.

Irish Inter-Church Meeting
Inter-Church Centre, 48 Elmwood Avenue, Belfast BT9 6AZ
Tel 028-90663145 Fax 028-90664160
Email irish.churches@btconnect.com
Co-Presidents: Cardinal S. Brady
Rev A. D. Davidson
Joint Secretaries: Rev Professor T. Norris,
Bishop R. Clarke
Executive Secretary: Mr J. M. Earle
Administrator: Ms J. Fernandez
Treasurer: Mr Eamonn Fleming KCSG

Irish Inter-Church Meeting – Inter-Church Committee Social Issues
Chairperson: Mr R. Cochran

Irish Missionary Union (IMU)
Headquarters: St Pauls Retreat, Mount Argus, Lower Kimmage Road, Dublin 6W
Tel 01 4923326/4923325/4923337
Fax 01-4923316
Email executive@imu.ie
President, Executive Council
Sr Miriam Duggan (FMSA)
Vice President: Fr Fachtna O'Driscoll (SMA)
Executive Secretary
Fr Eamon Aylward (SSCC)
Contact Persons: Fr Eamon Aylward (SSCC)
Ms Anne Kelly

The Irish Missionary Union is a collaborative network of Missionary Groups that promotes the understanding, development and

sharing of Mission and strives to be a prophetic voice in society. It promotes the call of all Christians to Mission, and supports those sent to witness to the gospel of Jesus Christ and the reign of God in other cultures. The IMU runs: The IMU Mission Institute; The IMU Religion Formation Ministry Programme.

IMU Mission Institute
Director: Rev Patrick Dooher (SSC)
St Columban's, Dalgan Park, Navan
Tel 046-9021525 Ext 332
Fax 046-9073726/9022799
Email imuinst@eircom.net
www.imudalganpark.com

General renewal programme for priests and sisters. Centre for Theology and Ecology

Irish School of Ecumenics, Trinity College, Dublin
Ireland's Centre for Reconciliation Studies
Professor of Ecumenics and Head of School: Linda Hogan
Bea House, Milltown Park, Dublin 6
Tel 01-2601144 Fax 01-2601158
683 Antrim Road, Belfast BT15 4EG
Tel 028-90775010 Fax 028-90373986
Email isedir@tcd.ie
www.tcd.ie/ise

ISE is a multi-disciplinary, cross-border graduate school within Trinity College Dublin. It offers supervision of research (M. Litt. and Ph.D.) in a range of fields e.g. religion and politics; ecumenical theology; inter-religious dialogue; politics of peace and conflict; ethical globalisation; ethics in international affairs; trafficking and slavery; theologies of reconciliation; peacebuilding; international relations theory; religious fundamentalism. It also runs taught Masters programmes in Ecumenical Studies; International Peace Studies (Dublin); Reconciliation Studies (Belfast) and an evening Postgraduate Diploma in Conflict and Dispute Resolution Studies (Dublin). A one-term (ten week) non-degree programme is available and is suited for those on sabbatical, or for those who prefer a shorter study period. There is also the option of attending one course. ISE provides a broad-ranging Continuing Education programme on inter-church and cross-community topics, in Northern Ireland and the border counties.

Irish Theological Association
Secretary: Tony McNamara
66 Foxfield Avenue, Raheny, Dublin 5
Tel 087 2903493
Email ppkenny@iol.ie
Email mcnamaaa@tcd.ie
www.theology.ie

Founded in 1965, the object of the association is to promote theological studies, and for this purpose it organises conferences and meetings for discussion, lectures and the general exchange of ideas.

Jesuit Communication Centre
36 Lower Leeson Street, Dublin 2
Tel 01-6768408 Fax 01-6629292
Communications Manager: Ms Pat Coyle
Email jcc@jesuit.ie
www.jesuit.ie

Jesus Caritas Fraternity of Priests
National Responsible
Rev Joseph Deegan PP
Slane, Co Meath, Tel 041-9824249
Email jpdeegan@gmail.com

An international association of priests who, following the spirituality of Charles de Foucauld, try to help one another to live their priesthood through mutual support, in their presence to Jesus in daily Eucharistic adoration, in the Gospel and in his people. The National Responsible along with the four Regional Responsibles and the National Treasurer constitute the Irish Fraternity Council. Occasional meetings of the Council are held during each year.

Kairos Communications Ltd
Director: Fr Finbarr Tracey (SVD)
Tel 01-6286007 Fax 01-6286511
Email info@kairoscomms.ie

Kairos Communications Ltd, is the media arm of Divine Word Missionaries, Ireland. Established in 1973, Kairos is now one of the biggest Christian communications facilities in Europe. Equipped with its own studios and outside broadcast facilities, it produces masses/services for RTÉ television from all parts of the country on a monthly basis. Other religious productions for RTE television include the daily 'iWitness' and Angelus. On the education front Kairos works closely with St Patrick's College, Maynooth (Pontifical University), and the National University of Ireland, Maynooth (NUIM). Courses running at the moment include: Postgraduate Diploma in Christian Communications and Development (St PCM); Diploma in Communications (St PCM); BA in Media Studies (NUIM); MA in Radio and Television Production (NUIM), BA in Multimedia (NUIM).

Knights of St Columbanus
Supreme Secretary
Ely House, 8 Ely Place, Dublin 2
Tel 01-6761835 Fax 01-6762839
Email koc@iol.ie
www.knightsofstcolumbanus.ie

Organised into twelve Provincial Areas throughout Ireland. A member of Unum Omnes (International Federation of Catholic Men), based in Rome, since 1966. Foundation member of the International Alliance of Catholic Knights, which has 1.6 million members in Europe, Africa, Australasia and America.

Knock Shrine Pilgrimages
Promoting Knock Shrine, Co Mayo, as a place of pilgrimage. For details and dates of ceremonies and/or assistance in organising a pilgrimage or school tour to Knock, please contact:
Secretary: Knock Shrine Office, Knock, Co Mayo
Tel 094-9388100 Fax 094-9388295
Email info@knock-shrine.ie
www.knock-shrine.ie
Secretary: Knock Shrine Pilgrimages, Veritas Bookshop 7-8 Lower Abbey Street, Dublin 1 Tel/Fax 01-8733356
Email dublinoffice@knock-shrine.ie
Secretary: Knock Shrine Pilgrimages 76/77 Little Catherine Street, Limerick
Tel 061-419458 Fax 061-405178
Email limerickoffice@knock-shrine.ie
Secretary: Knock Shrine Pilgrimages 5 Bellevue Park, Newtownabbey, Co Antrim
Tel 02890-287690
Email knockshrinebelfast@gmail.com

Lay Fraternity of Blessed Charles de Foucauld
Enquiries: Seán Ryan
146 Norwood Park, Limerick
Tel 087-6157867

Composed of small groups of lay people, married or single, who, after the example of Charles de Foucauld, seek to follow the way of Jesus present to them in the Gospel, in the Eucharist, and in their fellow men and women.

Legion of Mary
President: Mr Tommy McCabe
Secretary: Mr Enda Dunleavy
Concilium Legionis Mariae, International Centre of the Legion of Mary, De Montfort House, Morning Star Avenue, Brunswick Street, Dublin 7
Tel 01-8723153/8725093 Fax 01-8726386
Email concilium@legion-of-mary.ie
www.legion-of-mary.ie

Catholic lay organisation for men and women. Its members are engaged in charitable and apostolic work.

Life in the Eucharist Team
Blessed Sacrament Chapel
20 Bachelors Walk, Dublin 1
Contact: Rev Jim Campbell (SSS)
Mr Enda Whelan
Tel 01-8724597 Fax 01-8724724
Mobile 086 3688080
Email sssdublin@eircom.net
www.blessedsacramentuki.org

A team of dedicated trained lay people under the direction of a priest who, through weekend or evening seminars, lead participants into a fuller awareness of the Eucharist as a living experience in daily life. It is a source of nourishment for new and existing ministers of the Eucharist and Adoration groups. Lay people interacting with lay people from personal experience.

Lough Derg
(For details, see Diocese of Clogher)

Marriage Encounter
Ecclesial Leadership Team
Tom and Madeline McCully
9 Kingsfort Crescent, Derry, N Ireland BT48 7TB
Tel 028-71350612
Email tomandmadelinemccully@gmail.com
Fr Otto Imholte, St Columban's, Navan, Co Meath
Email bursargeneral@columban.com
www.mariageencounter.ie

Worldwide Marriage Encounter is a movement dedicated to the renewal of Matrimony, Priesthood and Religious Life. It provides the opportunity for participants to reflect upon their vocation in a private and positive way. It is for those who are committed to living out their sacrament in a dedicated way. Weekends are held all over Ireland. The Marriage Encounter weekend is not a retreat or counselling workshop, rather it is an enriching experience based on deepening communication skills within the marriage relationship, within parishes and within religious communities.

Micah Community
Micah Coordinator: Stephanie Birk
St Peter's Church, Phibsboro, Dublin 7
Tel 01-8102573
Email hello@micah.ie
www.micah.ie

We are a parish-based ministry for young adults providing opportunity for friendship, faith information, and outreach to an international community of young people living in Ireland.

National Association of CBS Past Pupils Unions
National Officers
President Elect: Jim O'Connell
Aisling Lodge, Kilmurriheen, Togher, Cork
Secretary/Contact Person: John Cooley, 73 Lansdowne Road, Belfast BT15 4AD
Tel 028-90777491
Email johncooley50@hotmail.com
Treasurer: Richard Cruise
44 Granitefield, Cabinteely, Dublin 18

Established in 1976. There are 14 Unions affiliated in the two Christian Brothers' Provinces. The Association meets quarterly, generally in Dublin. Its aims include: co-operating with regional, national and international bodies of Past Pupils' Unions of Christian Brothers and with other organisations whose objectives and aims are similar in purpose and intent with those of the Association; promoting the cause of Blessed Edmund Rice with a view to canonisation; assisting the Christian Brothers in their efforts to ensure that the tradition of Christian education as maintained by the Brothers will not be lost, materially diluted or obscured; preserving and fostering the national heritage. The Association also fosters links with Christian Br PP unions in other countries, eg Australia.

National Association Executive of Primary Diocesan Advisors

Chairperson: Mr Joe Searson
Knocknahilla, Mullagh, Ennis, Co Clare
Tel 065-7087875/087-6762023
Email joesearson@eircom.net
Vice Chairperson: Rev Michael McGrath
Ballinamuck, Co Longford
Tel 043-24110/086-3871676
Email mcgrath94@yahoo.com
Secretary: Ms Maeve Mahon
Faith Development Services,
Cathedral Parish Centre,
College Street, Carlow
Tel 059-9164084
Email maeve.mahon@kandle.ie
Vice Secretary: Sr Noreen Quilter
c/o John Paul II Pastoral Centre,
Rock Road, Killarney, Co Kerry
Tel 064-30530
Email nquiter12@eircom.net
Treasurer: Rev Liam Enright
Tel 087-9603601
Email enright36@yahoo.com

The National Association of Primary Diocesan Advisors in Religious Education is a national organisation whose members support, educate and resource the partners in religious education at a primary school level in Ireland. Membership of the Association is open to all full-time or part-time primary Diocesan Advisers. Associate membership is open to others who work in the area of Religious Education in primary schools.

The association aims to:
- support individual members in their work.
- provide a forum for discussion and debate.
- offer further formation and education for the members.
- review nationally the work of religious education in the Primary School and to actively encourage continual evaluation of progress.
- liaise with other agencies involved in the field of Religious Education.
- articulate nationally the needs of Religious Education at primary level.
- foster co-operation between the three partners involved in Religious Education – home, school and parish.

The association holds an Annual Conference and a minimum of two other meetings during the year. It is represented and organised by an executive, which is elected by the membership and holds office for three years. Members of the Executive represent the Association at the Catholic Primary School Management Association, the Episcopal Commission on Catechetics, and the Consultation Group for the National Primary School Programme.

National Association of Healthcare Chaplains

Members of The NAHC Executive Committee 2009/2010
Chairperson: Ms Margo McKay, Chaplain, The Blackrock Hospice, Blackrock, Co Dublin Tel 01-2084000
Vice Chairperson: Mr Jim Owens
Secretary: Sr Marie Gribbon
Treasurer: Ms Phil O'Neill

Republic of Ireland Members
HSE Dublin/Mid-Leinster
Ms Phil O'Neill, Sr Margaret Nulcaire, Ms Margo McKay
HSE Western: Mr Raymond Gately, Sr Mary Kelly, Ms Joyce O'Sullivan
HSE Dublin/North-Eastern
Mr Jim Owens, Ms Margaret Sleator, Sr Mary Gribbon
HSE Southern
Rev Daniel Nuzum

Northern Ireland Members
Southern H&SS Board: Vacant
Eastern H&SS Board: Vacant
Western H&SS Board: Vacant

Hierarchy Representative
Most Rev Raymond Field DD
Secretary to the Executive
Danielle Browne
NAHC, PO Box 10858, Blackrock, Co Dublin
Tel/Fax 01-2782693
Email nahc@eircom.net
Website www.nahc.ie
National Association of Healthcare Chaplains is a support organisation for Chaplains working in hospitals and healthcare facilities. The Executive is composed of representatives from each of the HSE areas.

National Centre for Liturgy

St Patrick's College, Maynooth, Co Kildare
Tel 01-7083478 Fax 01-7083477
Email liturgy@may.ie
www.liturgy-ireland.ie
(For details, see Episcopal Commissions and Advisory Bodies)

National Chaplaincy for Deaf People

40 Lower Drumcondra Road, Dublin 9
Tel 01-8305744 Fax 01-8600284
Email office@ncdp.ie
www.ncdp.ie
Fr Gerard Tyrrell, Director of the National Chaplaincy for Deaf People
Email gerard@ncdp.ie
Ms Frankie Berry, National Chaplain
Email frankie@ncpd.ie
Ms Veronica White, Chaplain in Cork and Kerry
Lay Chaplain: Ms Denise Flack
Northern Ireland Tel 0044 78 77643961

The Chaplaincy gives a sacramental and pastoral service to the deaf community, seeks to increase awareness among priests and the wider church community of the pastoral needs of the deaf community and to promote an interest in the apostolate at diocesan level.

National Mission Council of Ireland

IMU, St Paul's Retreat,
Mount Argus, Lower Kimmage Road,
Dublin 6W
Tel 01-4923326, 4923325 Fax 01-4923316
Email executive@imu.ie
(For details, see Episcopal Commissions)

Order of Malta, Ireland

Services provided include

First Aid Training Services

Courses in Occupational First Aid, Basic First Aid, Manual Handling, Defibrillation Training (AED) and Refresher courses can be provided at your premises, a local venue or at our Training Centre in Ballsbridge, Dublin 4

Malta Services Drogheda

Provision of education and training to people with physical and learning disabilities on a daily basis. The service is run in partnership with the Health Service Executive.

Malta-Share, Lisnaskea, Co Fermanagh, N Ireland

Holidays for older people, respite care facilities for people with disabilities.

General Community Care activities

include:
Day care, supper clubs for the elderly. Pilgrimages to Knock and Lourdes and an International Camp for Young People with disabilities.

International

Many Order of Malta projects are supported particularly the Holy Family Maternity Hospital, Bethlehem, Palestine.

President: Adrian FitzGerald
Chancellor: John Graeme Igoe
Communications Officer: Rosita McHugh
St John's House,
32 Clyde Road, Ballsbridge, Dublin 4
Tel 01-6140031 Fax 01-6685288
Email chancellery@orderofmalta.ie
www.orderofmalta.ie

Order of Malta Ambulance Corps

Provides a range of first aid, ambulance and emergency care services at major national and local level events in most of the principal cities and towns throughout the island of Ireland. As part of the major emergency plans it provides assistance to the statutory services, drawing on its fleet of over 150 ambulances and vehicles, ranging from minibuses, 4WD support vehicles to full accident and emergency ambulances. It also provides youth development services through Order of Malta Cadets – a National Youth Organisation.

National Director: Comdr Winifred Maye
St John's House, 32 Clyde Road, Dublin 4
Tel 01-6140033/6 Fax 01-6685288
Email info@orderofmalta.ie
www.orderofmalta.ie

Pax Christi – International Catholic Movement for Peace (Irish Section)
National President
Most Rev Raymond Field
Chairperson: Mr John Harkin
Vice-Chairperson: Mr Peadar O'Neill
Treasurer: Mr Fintan Mullally
Headquarters: 52 Lower Rathmines Road, Dublin 6
Tel 01-4965293 Fax 01-4965492
Email info@paxchrist.ie
Contact: Mr Tony D'Costa
General Secretary

Pax Christi is an international Catholic peace movement, with national sections in four continents. Its international office is in Belgium. Its activities are mainly related to the issues of security and disarmament; human rights; East-West contacts; North-South relations; peace education; peace spirituality; non-violence; faith, dialogue and reconciliation. Pax Christi has consultative status at the United Nations, UNESCO and the Council of Europe.

People's Eucharistic League
Blessed Sacrament Chapel
20 Bachelors Walk, Dublin 1
Contact: Br Timothy McLoughlin

An association of men and women with special devotion to the Holy Eucharist. Founded by St Peter Julian Eymard, members are associated with the apostolate of the Congregation of the blessed Sacrament. Members undertake to spend one hour per month in prayer before the Blessed Sacrament.

Perpetual Eucharistic Adoration Apostolate
National Co-ordinator: Mr Cathal Magee
Corpus Christi Centre, Maynooth, Co Kildare Tel/Fax 01-2692781

A Pontifical Association of the faithful dedicated to promoting and spreading Eucharistic worship and devotion in parishes whereby Jesus in the Blessed Sacrament is worshipped and adored on a continual basis through a commitment of one weekly hour of adoration given by the people.

Pioneer Total Abstinence Association of the Sacred Heart
Chief Executive Officer Mr Padraig Brady
Information Officer: Ms Róisín Fulham
Central Spiritual Director
Rev Bernard J. McGuckian (SJ)
27 Upper Sherrard Street, Dublin 1
Tel 01-8749464 Fax 01-8748485
Email pioneer@jesuit.ie
www.pioneerassociation.ie

The Association has as its chief aim the promotion of temperance and sobriety, and prayer and self-sacrifice as its principal means. The members use their independence of alcohol to engage in good work and the organisation of counter-attractions to drinking.
(For details of spiritual directors see dioceses)

The Radharc Trust
Trustees: Mr Peter Dunn, Ms Philomena Donnelly
Acting Director: Mr Peter Dunn
18 Newbridge Ave, Sandymount, Dublin 4
Tel 01-2755909/087-2520158
Email peter@radharc.ie
www.radharc.ie

Promoting the Radharc Archive of over 400 television documentaries from 75 different countries. Promoting and sponsoring activities in television, radio and the press that reflect the ethos of Radharc.

Regnum Christi
Contact: Ms Helena Shekelton
Dal Riada Centre, Avoca Avenue, Blackrock, Co Dublin
Tel 01-2889317
Email hshekelton@arcol.org

The Regnum Christi Movement, founded in 1949 by Fr Marcial Maciel LC, is an apostolic movement open to all those (married, single men and women and diocesan priests) who want to live their baptismal commitments with a heightened awareness fulfilling, by word and personal witness, the command of our Lord Jesus Christ to work to extend the Kingdom of Heaven among people from all sectors of society. It pursues this goal through apostolates which, in communion with the magisterium of the Church, promote the integral formation of the human person (schools, recreational and cultural clubs, retreat centres, family centres, schools of faith.)

Religious Press Association
Chairperson and Public Relations Consultant: Garry O'Sullivan, Journalist, c/o 36 Lower Leeson Street, Dublin 2
Email garryos@yahoo.ie
Treasurer: Lillian Webb 66 Roseville, Naas, Co Kildare Tel 045-866160

Association of editors of religious papers and magazines in Ireland. Seeks to improve the quality of and develop the influence of the religious press.

Retreats Ireland
President: Sr Anna Hainey
Drumalis, 47 Glenarm Road, Larne, Co Antrim BT40 1DT
Tel 028-28276455
Email anna@drumalis.co.uk
Treasurer: Rev Michael Cusak
Esker Retreat House, St Patrick's, Esker, Athenry, Co Galway
Tel 091-844007
Email bishcus@yahoo.co.uk
Secretary: Sr Brenda Ahearn
Tearmann Spirituality Centre, Brockagh, Glendalough, Co Wicklow
Tel 0404-45639
Email bredaahearn@eircom.net
Benito Colangelo, Ards Friary, Creeslough, Letterkenny, Co Donegal
Tel 074-9138909
Email info@ardsfriary.ie

Catherine Coleman, Star of the Sea Retreat & Conference Centre, Mullaghmore, Co Sligo
Tel 071-9176722
Email catherinecolemanrsm@eircom.net
Eileen Egan, St John of God Retreat Centre, Ballyvaloo, Blackwater, Co Wexford
Tel 053-9137160
Email eganejog@eircom.net
Rose Fitzsimons
Emmaus Retreat and Conference Centre, Lissenhall, Swords, Co Dublin
Tel 01-8700050
Email rfitzsimons@osfphila.org
Una Lount
23 Glenshesk Road, Ballycastle, Co Antrim, BT54 6PA
Tel 028-20762907 Email unalount@googlemail.com
Vera Magee
Emmaus Retreat and Conference Centre, Lissenhall, Swords, Co Dublin
Tel 01-8700050
Email vtmagee@yahoo.co.uk
Richard Mohan
Lough Derg Pettigo, Co Donegal
Tel 071 9861518
Email rmohan@loughderg.org
Helena Rabbitte
Fr Peyton Avenue, Attymass, Ballina, Co Mayo
Tel 096-45544

The aim of Retreats Ireland is to promote retreat work, to provide an information service, to offer training programmes, to encourage mutual support and co-operation in the context of retreat and pastoral centres in Ireland.

RNN (Religious News Network)
36 Lower Leeson Street, Dublin 2
Tel 01-7758515 Fax 01-6767493
Email info@rnn.ie
Director: Eileen Good Tel 01-7758516
Email eileengood@rnn.ie
Production Administrator: Jeanann Cox
Tel 01-7758515
Email jeanann@rnn.ie
Editor: Miriam Gormally
Email miriam@rnn.ie
www.rnn.ie

RNN is a new syndication service of religious and social affairs, supplying more than 30 local, community and hospital radio stations throughout Ireland with live and recorded news, reaction stories and features. The service is funded by the religious congregations (CoRI) and the Church of Ireland.

Saint Joseph's Young Priests Society
President: Mrs Marie Hogan
23 Merrion Square, Dublin 2
Tel 01-6762593 Fax 01-6762549
Email sjyps@eircom.net

An Irish lay organisation founded in 1895 with branches in every diocese in Ireland. Its members promote vocations to the priesthood and religious life and assist some students financially, at home and abroad.

School Chaplains Association (Cumann na Seiplineach Scoile)
Chairperson: Ms Cora Guinnane
St Caimin's Community School, Shannon,
Co Clare Tel 061-364211
Email coraguinnane@gmail.com
Secretary: Mr Seán Mallon
Mount Anville Secondary School,
Mount Anville, Dublin 14
Tel 01-2885313
Treasurer: Ms Aoife Daly, Boyne
Community School, Trim, Co Meath

Scouting Ireland
Chief Scout: Michael John Shinnick
National Secretary: Mr Mick Devins
National Treasurer: Mr Niall Walsh
Communications Commissioner:
Mr Joe Boland
CEO: Mr Eamonn Lynch
Administration and Resource Centre,
Larch Hill, Dublin 16
Tel 01-4956300 Fax 01-4956301
www.scouts.ie

The aim of Scouting Ireland is to
encourage the physical, intellectual,
character, emotional, social and
spiritual development of young people
so they may achieve their full potential
and, as responsible citizens, to improve
society.

Scouting Ireland has a 32-county
membership of 40,000 including 60,000
adult volunteers. It provides young
people with opportunities to take part
and lead a progressive programme
through fun, friendship and challenge.

Secular Franciscan Order
National President: John Murray, Cork
National Headquarters
C/o Mary Tiernan SFO
3 St Mary's Terrace, Chapelizod, Dublin
Tel 01-6262264
Email sfohq@eircom.net
Contact: Mary Tiernan

An Order of lay people who seek to
follow Christ in their everyday life in the
footsteps of St Francis of Assisi (going
from gospel to life and life to gospel).

Society of St Vincent de Paul – National Office
National President: Ms Mairead Bushnell
Contact: Kieran Murphy
Headquarters: SVP House,
91-92 Sean MacDermott Street, Dublin 1
Tel 01-8386990
Email info@svp.ie
www.svp.ie

An international lay organisation, which
endeavours to alleviate need and redress
situations which cause it. Its principal
work is visiting people in their homes,
but it also provides holidays, hostels for
the homeless, youth clubs, housing for
the elderly, and good-as-new shops.

Teams of Our Lady (Equipes Notre-Dame)
Moyra and Brendan Bunting
Rev Gerard Cassidy (CSsR)
Email ireland@teams-transatlantic.org
www.equipes-notre-dame.com

An international movement of
spirituality for married couples which has
received official recognition from the
Pontifical Council for the Laity. A team
consists of five or six couples and a
priest, and meets once a month. United
by the sacrament of marriage, the
couples seek, by deepening their
spirituality, to strengthen their faith and
increase their love. Informal evenings are
arranged for couples wishing to know
more about the movement.

The Teresian Association
St Patrick's College,
21 Beaufield Park, Stillorgan,
Co Dublin Tel 01-2056937
Email irelandta@eircom.net

The Teresian Association is an
International Association of the Faithful
for lay Christians, present today in 30
countries. It was started in 1911 by Saint
Pedro Poveda, a Spanish diocesan priest,
canonised by Pope John Paul II in Madrid
on 4 May 2003. It aims to help transform
society through education and culture in
the light of the Gospel. Its members are
women and men who, according to their
specific calling, live out their vocation of
Christian lay people in society, working
in educational, cultural and professional
areas. They witness to Gospel values in
all they do and are involved in a wide
variety of areas across society. Their
particular focus, however, is education at
all levels and in its broadest sense.
Members do this through the way they
live their professional, occupational and
family lives. The Association supports
and sustains a number of non-
governmental organisations and
collaborates with Church programmes
and other institutions. It also runs a
number of educational centres in
different countries, including the
Teresian School in Dublin.

The Teresian School, (Pre-School,
Kindergarten, Junior and Secondary School)
12 Stillorgan Road, Dublin 4
Tel 01-2691376 Fax 01-2602878
Email school@teresian.iol.ie

Trócaire
Lenten Campaigns Organiser
Claire Whelan
Press & Communications
Emer Mullins, Maynooth, Co Kildare
Tel 01-6293333 Fax 01-6290661
Offices and Resource Centres
12 Cathedral Street, Dublin 1
9 Cook Street, Cork
50 King Street, Belfast BT1 6AD
(For details, see Episcopal Commissions)

Veritas Communications
Veritas House,
7–8 Lower Abbey Street, Dublin 1
Tel 01-8788177 Fax 01-8786507
(For details, see Episcopal Commissions)

Veritas Company Ltd
Veritas House,
7–8 Lower Abbey Street, Dublin 1
Tel 01-8788177 Fax 01-8744913
(For details, see Episcopal Commissions)

Veritas Publications
Veritas House,
7–8 Lower Abbey Street, Dublin 1
Tel 01-8788177 Fax 01-8786507
(For details, see Episcopal Commissions)

Viatores Christi
8 New Cabra Road, Phibsboro, Dublin 7
Tel 01-8689986 Fax 01-8689891
Email info@viatoreschristi.com
www.viatoreschristi.com

A voluntary Catholic lay missionary
association. Recruits, prepares and
facilitates the placement of people who
wish to work overseas, for one year or
more, in areas of need such as Africa,
South America, Asia and parts of
Canada, USA and Europe. Viatores Christi
offers a 6 month part-time preparation
programme.

Vocations Ireland
Bloomfield Ave (off Morehampton
Road), Donnybrook, Dublin 4
Director: Sr Eileen Linehan, IBVM
Tel 01-6689954
Email info@vocationsireland.com

Vocations Ireland presents Religious life
as a creative opportunity to live the
mission of Christ in today's world. It
provides information about missionary
and religious life as well as support,
resources and in-service opportunities
for those in vocation ministry. It also
provides personal accompaniment and
discernment programmes for prospective
candidates.

Volunteer Missionary Movement
VMM, 'All Hallows', Gracepark Road,
Drumcondra, Dublin 9
Tel 01-8376565 Fax 01-8367112
Email mission@vmm.ie
www.vmm.ie
Contact: Dr Vincent Kenny, Director
VMM (Europe)

The VMM is an international lay,
missionary organisation, founded in
1969. VMM currently have 65
professional volunteers currently
working in East Africa and Central
America. Following completion of their
overseas contract. They are enouraged
to maintain their Christian commitment
through working for change within their
home community.

Allianz (ⁱⁱ)

World Missions, Ireland
National Director
Rev Edward Grimes (CSSp)
64 Lower Rathmines Road, Dublin 6
Tel 01-4972035/4972422 Fax 01-4960140
Email director@wmi.ie
www.wmi.ie
Registered Charity Number: CHY 2318

The Pontifical Mission Societies form one institution with four branches:

Society for the Propagation of the Faith
Purpose: supports over 1,100 mission dioceses throughout the world. Each year the Society endeavours to increase clerical, religious and laity awareness of mission work. The Society is responsible for organising the Church's annual universal celebration of mission – Mission Sunday – encouraging spiritual and material support for Catholic missions worldwide.

Society of St Peter Apostle
Purpose: invites spiritual and finanancial support to assist young mission Churches in the training of their own priests, brothers and sisters.

Society of Missionary Children
Purpose: encourages Irish children to connect with children in mission lands through the sharing of prayer and material gifts. The Society's motto – 'Children Helping Children' – illustrates how Irish children of primary school age can make small gestures which will help to improve the lives of other children who experience war, famine, poverty and suffering.

Missionary Union of Priests and Religious
Purpose: unites clergy, religious, seminarians and catechists in helping the missionary activity of the Church by the sanctity of their lives and prayer. The Society promotes mission awareness among those involved in the pastoral ministry of the Church.

Young Christian Workers (Saotharaithe Ógra Críostaí)
National Co-ordinator: Ms Vicky Rattigan
email vicky@ycw.ie
National Chaplain: Rev Eoin McCrystal
YCW National Office, 11 Talbot Street, Dublin 1
Tel/Fax 01-8780291
Email info@ycw.ie
www.ycw.ie
Webmaster: Ms Melanie Gutman
Email melanie@ycw.ie

The Young Christian Workers is an international youth movement which values the dignity and worth of each young person. It enables its members to challenge social exclusion and take action to bring about change in their home, their workplace and their social life. Many useful skills are acquired through attendance at weekly meetings, socials, international exchanges and training weekends. YCW IMPACT! 'Change through Action' Programme is aimed at young people in the 16-18 age group. A starter pack for working with young people aged 18 plus and a media resource complete with accompanying DVD are also available at our national office. For further details on retreats and events check our website: www.ycw.ie.

RELIGIOUS PERIODICALS

PUBLICATION OF THE IRISH CATHOLIC BISHOPS' CONFERENCE

Intercom
Editor: Mr Francis Cousins
Email fcousins@catholicbishops.ie
Columba Centre, St Patrick's College
Maynooth, Co Kildare
A pastoral and liturgical resource for people in ministry, published by the Veritas Group, an agency of the Irish Catholic Bishops' Conference.
Subscriptions: Ross Delmar
7-8 Lower Abbey Street, Dublin 1
Tel 01-8788177 Fax 01-8786507
Email ross.delmar@veritas.ie

OTHER RELIGIOUS PERIODICALS

Africa
Editors: Rev Tom Kiggins (SPS), Rev Martin Smith (SPS)
Email africa@spms.org
Circulation Manager
Rev William Fulton (SPS)
Tel 059-6473600Fax 059-6473622
Email spsoff@iol.ie
International family mission magazine with topical articles on Christianity today; Bible reflections; youth and children's features. Nine issues per year. Published by St Patrick's Missionary Society, Kiltegan, Co Wicklow

African Missionary
Editor: Rev Tomás Walsh SMA
Newsletter Presentation of Missionary News and Profiles of the Lives and activities of SMA and OLA members in Africa and elsewhere,Three issues per year (including Calendar issue). Published by the Society of African Missions, Blackrock Road, Cork
Tel 021-4616318 Fax 027-4616393
Email amnewsletter@sma.ie
www.sma.ie

Alive!
Editor: Rev Brian McKevitt (OP)
Free 16-page Catholic tabloid paper with news, features, interviews. Available free for distribution by parishes, churches, shops, praesidia, etc. nationwide. Circulation: 385,000.
Published monthly from St Mary's Priory, Tallaght, Dublin 24
Contact: Breda
Tel 01-4048187 Fax 01-4596784
Email alivepaper@gmail.com

Being One
Editor: Rev Brendan Leahy
Focolare Centre, Prosperous, Co Kildare
Tel 045-840430
Email beingone@eircom.net
Published three times a year.

Bulletin of St Vincent de Paul
Editor: Tom MacSweeney
Published quarterly by the
Society of St Vincent de Paul
in Ireland at National Office, SVP House,
91-92 Sean MacDermot Street, Dublin 1
Tel 01-8386990 Fax 018387355
Email bulletin@svp.ie
www.svp.ie

Catholic Voice Newspaper
Editor: Anthony Murphy
PO Box 11559, Dublin 1
Tel 059-8627268
Email editor@catholicvoice.ie
Tabloid 28 pages. Rrp €1/£1

Church of Ireland Gazette
Editor: Rev Canon Ian Ellis
Office: 3 Wallace Avenue, Lisburn,
Co Antrim BT27 4AA
Tel Lisburn 9267 5743
Email gazette@ireland.anglican.org
The Church of Ireland Gazette is an
editorially independent weekly
newspaper.

Daystar
Editor: Sr Ann McColl
Email annca7349@yahoo.co.uk
Contact: Sr Nora Bergin
Published bi-annually by the Franciscan
Missionary Sisters for Africa
Mount Oliver, Dundalk, Co Louth
Tel 042-9371123 Fax 042-9371159
Email fmsamto@gofree.indigo.ie
Regional Leader: Sr Jeanette Watters (FMSA)
Franciscan Missionary Sisters of Africa
142 Raheny Road, Raheny, Dublin 5
Tel (01) 8473140 Fax (01) 8481428
Email fmsanar@iol.ie
www.iol.ie/~fmsanar

Doctrine and Life
Editor: Rev Bernard Treacy (OP)
Published ten times a year by Dominican
Publications, 42 Parnell Square, Dublin 1
Tel 01-8721611 Fax 01-8731760
Email
subscriptions@dominicanpublications.com

Face to Face
Editor: Rev Patrick Dunne
The National Journal of the Apostolate
of Perpetual Eucharistic Adoration,
published on behalf of the apostolate by
Face to Face Publications, St Eunan's
College, Letterkenny, Co Donegal

Face Up
Editor: Gerard Moloney (CSsR)
For teens who want something Deeper,
published ten times a year by
Redemptorist Communications,
75 Orwell Road, Rathgar, Dublin 6
Tel 01-4922488/4067100
Fax 01-4927999/4922654
Email info@faceup.ie
www.faceup.ie

The Far East
Editor: Rev Cyril Lovett (SSC)
Full colour, emphasis on Christian mission
and related topics.
Circulation: 100,000 in Ireland and
Britain. Published eight times a year by
the Missionary Society of St Columban,
St Columban's, Navan, Co Meath
Tel 046-9098272 Fax 046-9071297
Email editorfareast@columban.com
www.columban.com
Manager: Rev Noel Daly

Foundations
Editor: Fr Sean Fennelly
Cashel and Emly diocesan magazine
Hospital, Co Limerick
Tel 061-383565
Email foundations@cashel-emly.com

The Furrow
Editor: Rev Ronan Drury
Published monthly by
The Furrow Trust, St Patrick's College,
Maynooth, Co Kildare
Tel 01-7083741 Fax 01-7083908
Email furrow.office@may.ie
www.thefurrow.ie

Hallel
Editor: Vacant
A review of monastic spirituality and
liturgy published twice a year for the
Region of the Isles of the Order of
Cistercians of the Strict Observance at
Mount Saint Joseph Abbey, Roscrea.
Tel 0505-21711 Fax 0505-21198
Email hallel@msjroscrea.ie

Irish Catholic
Managing Editor: Mr Garry O'Sullivan
Published weekly by The Agricultural
Trust, The Irish Catholic is Ireland's
largest and best selling Catholic
Newspaper since 1888
Irish Farm Centre, Blubell, Dublin 12
Tel 01-4276400 Fax 01-4276450
Email news@irishcatholic.ie,
advertising@irishcatholic.ie

Irish Theological Quarterly
Editor-in-Chief: Rev Michael A. Conway
Secretary: Prof Salvador Ryan
Review Editor: Rev Liam Tracey
Business Manager: Ms Fidelma Madden
Published by members of the Faculty of
Theology, St Patrick's College, Maynooth,
Co Kildare
Tel 01-7083496 Fax 01-6289063
Email itq.editor@may.ie

Maria Legionis
(Journal published quarterly by the
Legion of Mary)
Presentata House,
263 North Circular Road, Dublin 7
Tel 01-8387770
Email marialegionis@eircom.net

Medical Missionaries of Mary
Editor: Sr Isabelle Smyth (MMM)
A yearbook on *Healing & Development*
published in December, with
supplementary newsletters in Spring and
Autumn, available from MMM
Communications, Rosemount Terrace,
Booterstown, Co Dublin
Tel 01-2887180 Mobile 087-9701891
Fax 01-2834626
Email mmm@iol.ie
www.mmmworldwide.org

Milltown Studies
Editor: Dr Joseph Egan (SMA)
Review Editor: Dr Gesa E. Thiessen
Milltown Institute of Theology and
Philosophy, Milltown Park, Dublin 6
Tel 01-2776311 Fax 01-2692528
Email mseditor@milltown-institute.ie

New Liturgy
Editor: Rev Patrick Jones
Bulletin of the National Secretariat, Irish
Episcopal Commission for Liturgy,
published quarterly at the National
Centre for Liturgy, St Patrick's College,
Maynooth, Co Kildare
Tel 01-7083478 Fax 01-7083477
Email liturgy@may.ie
www.liturgy-ireland.ie

Non-Subscribing Presbyterian Magazine
Editor: Rev Dr A. D. G. Steers
223 Upper Lisburn Road,
Belfast BT10 0LL
Tel 028-90947850
Email nspresb@hotmail.com

Oblate Missionary Record and Lourdes Messenger
Editor: Rev Tom McCabe (OMI)
Secretary: Ms Mary Gaynor
Tel 01-4542417/4540841 Fax 01-4731903
Email tmccabe@eircom.net
Published four times a year by Oblate
Fathers, Inchicore, Dublin 8

Outlook (Mission Outlook)
Editor: Ms Mary Rieke Murphy
Published bi-monthly by Holy Ghost
Missions from Kimmage Manor,
Whitehall Road, Dublin 12
Tel 01-4928519
Email editoroutlook@eircom.net

Pioneer
Editor: Fr Bernard J. McGuckian (SJ)
Sub-editor: Ms Róisín Fulham
Published monthly by Pioneer Total
Abstinence Association, 27 Upper
Sherrard Street, Dublin 1
Tel 01-8749464 Fax 01-8748485
Email pioneer@jesuit.ie
www.pioneerassociation.ie

Presbyterian Herald
Editor: Stephen Lynas
Published monthly by Presbyterian
Church in Ireland, Church House,
Fisherwick Place, Belfast BT1 6DW
Tel 028-90322284 Fax 028-90417307
Email herald@presbyterianireland.org
www.presbyterianireland.org

Proceedings of the Irish Biblical Association
Published by IBA Publications Comm.
Contact: Tom Gillen
141 Weston Park, Dundrum,
Dublin 14
Email iba@iolfree.ie

Reality
Editor: Rev Gerard R. Moloney (CSsR)
Marketing: Paul Copeland
Published monthly by Redemptorist
Communications, 75 Orwell Road,
Rathgar, Dublin 6 (€1.70)
Tel 01-4922488/4067271
Fax 01-4927999/4922654
Email
info@redemptoristcommunications.com
www.redemptoristcommunications.com

Religious Life Review
Editor: Rev Thomas McCarthy (OP)
Published six times a year by
Dominican Publications,
42 Parnell Square, Dublin 1
Tel 01-8587103 Fax 01-8731760
Email dompubs@iol.ie

Sacred Heart Messenger
Editor: Rev John Looby (SJ)
Official publication of the Apostleship of
Prayer, published monthly by Messenger
Publications at, 37 Lower Leeson Street,
Dublin 2, Tel 01-6767491
Fax 01-6611606 Email sales@messenger.ie
www.messenger.ie

An Sagart
Eagarthóir:
An Mgr Pádraig Ó Fiannachta
Foilsítear ceithre uair sa bhliain ag
An Sagart, An Díseart, An Daingean,
Trá Lí, Co Chiarraí
Tel 066-915000
Ephost pof@diseart.ie
www.ansagart.ie
Símtiús Bliana €15

The Salesian Bulletin
Editor: Rev Pat Egan (SDB)
Salesian College, Celbridge, Co Kildare
Tel 01-6275060 Fax 01-6303601
Email frpegan@iol.ie
homepage.eircom.net/~sdbmedia
Subscriptions
Rev Dan Devitt (SDB)
Salesian Missions, PO Box 50,
Pallaskenry, Co Limerick
Tel 061-393223 Fax 061-393354
Published quarterly for the Salesians of
Don Bosco by Salesian Bulletin.

Scripture in Church
Editor in Chief
Rev Martin McNamara (MSC)
Published quarterly by Dominican
Publications, 42 Parnell Square, Dublin 1
Tel 01-8721611 Fax 01-8731760
Email
subscriptions@dominicanpublications.com

The Sheaf
formerly *St Joseph's Sheaf*
Editor: Dominic Dowling FCII KCHS
St Joseph's Young Priests Society
23 Merrion Square, Dublin 2
Tel 01-6762593 Fax 01-6762549
Email sjyps@eircom.net
and jddowling@iname.com
Its purpose is twofold
(a) to foster vocations to priesthood and
religious life
(b) to promote the vocation of the laity
www.thesheaf.vpweb.ie

Spirituality
Editor: Rev Tom Jordan (OP)
Published six times a year by
Dominican Publications,
42 Parnell Square, Dublin 1
Tel 01-8721611 Fax 01-8731760
Email
tom.jordan@dominicanpublications.com
www.dominicanpublications.com

The St Anthony Brief
Editor: Ulic Troy (OFM)
Published every two months by the
Franciscan Missionary Union,
8 Merchant's Quay, Dublin 8
Tel 01-6777651 Fax 01-6777293
Email ulic@eircom.net

St Joseph's Advocate
Editor: Fr Jim O'Connell (MHM)
Tel 056-7753631
Published quarterly by Mill Hill Missionaries,
St Joseph's, Waterford Road, Kilkenny
Tel 056-7721482 Fax 056-7751490
Email jimocmhm@eircom.net

St Martin Magazine
Editor: Rev Diarmuid Clifford (OP)
Published monthly by St Martin
Apostolate,42 Parnell Square, Dublin 1
Tel 01-8745464/8730147 Fax 01-8731989
From UK 00-353-1-8745465
Email stmartin@iol.ie
Personal Email dcop@eircom.net

Studies – An Irish Quarterly Review
Editor: Rev Fergus O'Donoghue (SJ)
Published by the Irish Jesuits,
35 Lower Leeson Street, Dublin 2
Tel 01-6766785 Fax 01-6767493
Email studies@jesuit.ie
www.studiesirishreview.com

Timire an Chroí Naofa
Bunaíodh 1911
Eagarthóir Feidhmitheach
An tAth Alan MacEochagán (SJ)
Eagarthóir: Caitríona Uí Chatháin
37 Sr Líosáin Íocht, Baile Átha Cliath 2
Ephost timire@jesuit.ie
Bainistíocht: Coiste an Timire,
Teach Manresa SJ, Baile na gCorr,
Cluain Tarbh, Baile Áth Cliath 3
Fón 01-8325138

Traces
Subscriptions: Lee Sorensen
PO Box 7060, Dublin 6
Tel 01-4973361 Fax 01-4975008
Email cldublin@eci.ie
Traces is the monthly publication of
Communion and Liberation, the
international Catholic Movement
founded by Luigi Giussani. It expresses
the life and viewpoint of people in this
movement which is now a living reality in
the Church's social and ecclesial horizon.

The Universe Catholic Weekly
Editor: Joseph Kelly
Gabriel Communications Ltd
St James' Buildings, Oxford Street,
Manchester M1 6FP Tel 0161 236 8856
Email joseph.kelly@totalcatholic.com

MARRIAGE TRIBUNALS

By Decree dated 24 March 1975, the Irish Episcopal Conference decided to establish four Regional Marriage Tribunals of first instance to be located at Armagh, Dublin, Cork and Galway. This decree was formally approved by the Supreme Tribunal of the Apostolic Signatur on 6 May 1975. In accordance with the terms of the Roman rescript, the Episcopal Conference, in a decision of 30 September 1975, determined the Regional Tribunals would come into effect on 1 January 1976. From that date they replaced all previous diocesan marriage tribunals.

By the same process which established in Ireland Regional Marriage Tribunals of first instance, the Episcopal Conference set up a sole Appeal Tribunal, located in Dublin, to hear cases on appeal from each of the four Regional Tribunals. It also came into effect on 1 January 1976. Its personnel and administration are wholly distinct from the Dublin Regional Marriage Tribunal.

NATIONAL MARRIAGE APPEAL TRIBUNAL

Columba Centre, Maynooth, Co Kildare
Tel 01 5053119 Fax 01-5053122
Email brian.flynn@iecon.ie
Judicial Vicar:
Rev Michael Smyth (MSC), STL, JUD
Administrator: Mrs Stephanie Walpole
Vice Presiding Judge: Right Rev Mgr Francis Donnelly (Armagh)
Associate Judges: Very Rev Canon Eugene Mangan PP (Kerry), Very Rev Gerard McNamara PP (Limerick), Rt Rev Mgr John Shine BD, LCL, LPh, PP, (Waterford and Lismore), Very Rev Patrick Gill, AP, Very Rev John Canon O'Boyle BA, Very Rev Patrick Williams AP, Very Rev S.J. Clyne PP, VF, Rev Patrick Connolly DCL, Rev Brendan Kilcoyne LCL, Rev Michael Mullaney DCL, Rev William Dalton, Sr Máirín McDonagh SJM, Rev John Whelan (OSA), Mr Michael V. O'Mahony, Most Rev Laurence Forristal, Rev Seán O'Neill, Very Rev Francis Maher PP, Rev Lorcan Moran, Rt Rev Mgr Joseph Donnelly, PP, VF, Rt Rev Mgr Gerard Dolan, PP, LCL
Defenders of the Bond
Rev Brian Flynn, Rev Michael Bannon
Correspondence to: Vacant

REGIONAL MARRIAGE TRIBUNALS

ARMAGH REGIONAL MARRIAGE TRIBUNAL

Regional Office: 15 College Street, Armagh BT61 9BT
Tel 028-37524537 Fax 028-37528763
Email armthq@btconnect.com
Judicial Vicar: Rev Eugene D. O'Hagan JCL
Email armt@dnet.co.uk
Administrator: Rev James McGrory JCD
Presiding Judges: Rev Francis Bradley JCL, Rev James McGrory JCD, Sr Carmel Maguire JCL, Rev Joseph Rooney JCL, Rev Michael Toner JCL
Contact Person for Constituent Dioceses:
Armagh: Rev Michael Toner JCL, Rev John McKeever
Clogher: Sr Elizabeth Fee
Derry: Rev Francis Bradley JCL
Down & Connor:
Rev Eugene D. O'Hagan JCL
Dromore: Rev Peter C. McNeill
Kilmore: Mrs Rosaleen Howard
Raphoe: Rev Philip Daly

DUBLIN REGIONAL MARRIAGE TRIBUNAL

Diocesan Offices, Archbishop's House, Dublin 9
Tel 01-8379253 Fax 01-8368309
Email dublinrmt@eircom.net
Judicial Vicar
Vacant
Associate Judicial Vicar
Rev Paul Churchill
Judges
Rev Kilian Byrne LCL (Kildare and Leighlin)
Rev Kevin Cahill DCL (Ferns)
Rev Paul Churchill DCL (Dublin)
Sr Mary Grennan LCL (PBVM)
Rev Francis Herron STL (Dublin)
Rev Aidan McGrath DCL (OFM)
Rev William Richardson LCL (Dublin)
Defenders of the Bond
Mr Eugene Boland
Very Rev Laurence Collins (OP)
Rev William Stuart (IC)
Promoter of Justice
Rev Kevin Cahill DCL (Ferns)
Tribunal Assistants
Cathy Barry, Maeve Cotter, Collette Nugent, Jane O'Donoghue, Mary O'Kane, Edna Powell, Grace Murray, Pamela van de Poll
Correspondence to: The Rev Judicial Vicar
Constituent Dioceses: Dublin, Ferns, Kildare and Leighlin, Meath, Ossory

CORK REGIONAL MARRIAGE TRIBUNAL

Tribunal Offices, The Lough, Cork
Tel 021-4963653 Fax 021-4314149
Email crmt@iol.ie
Judicial Vicar
Very Rev Gerard Garrett LCL, MCL, LLM
Associate Judicial Vicar
Vacant
Judge: Very Rev Seamus McKenna BA, HDE, LCL
Constituent Dioceses
Cashel, Cloyne, Cork and Ross, Kerry, Limerick, Waterford and Lismore
Correspondence to : Mrs Marlies Ferriter, Administrator

GALWAY REGIONAL MARRIAGE TRIBUNAL

7 Waterside, Woodquay, Galway
Tel 091-565179 Fax 091-563512
Email 7waterside@eircom.net
Judicial Vicar: Very Rev Michael Byrnes BA JCL
Rev Barry Horan JCL
Sr Mary Lyons JCD
Mairéad Uí Mhurchadha
Correspondence to the Administrator: Nicola Burke
Constituent Dioceses: Tuam, Achonry, Ardagh and Clonmacnois, Clonfert, Elphin, Galway,Killala, Killaloe

CHAPLAINS

THE DEFENCE FORCES CHAPLAINCY SERVICE

Head Chaplain
Rt Rev Mgr Eoin Thynne HCF
Email eointhynne@eircom.net
Administration Secretary
Sgt. John Kellett
Department of Defence,
Colaiste Chaoimhín,
Mobhi Road, Glasnevin, Dublin 9
Tel 01-8042271 Fax 01-8379915
Email john.kellett@defenceforces.ie

Aiken Barracks
Dundalk, Co Louth
Tel 042-9331759
Rev Bernard McCay-Morrissey CF
Email bernardmm@eircom.net

Casement Aerodrome
Baldonnel, Co Dublin
Tel 01-4037536
Rev Jeremiah Carroll CF
Email jerryzulu@eircom.net

Cathal Brugha Barracks
Rathmines, Dublin 6
Tel 01-8046484
Rev David Tyndall CF
Email davidtyndall@yahoo.ie

Collins Barracks (Cork)
Tel 021-4502734
Rev Gerard O'Neill CF
Email frgerryoneill@eircom.net

Curragh Camp
Co Kildare
Rt Rev Mgr John McDonald CF
Tel 045-441369
Rev P.J. Somers CF
Tel 045-441277
Email spj40@hotmail.com

Custume Barracks
Athlone, Co Westmeath
Tel 0902-21277
Rev Gerard Dowd CF
Email gerard.dowd@yahoo.co.uk

Dún Uí Néill Barracks
Cavan
Rev Sean McDermott CF
Tel 049-4361632
Email jlmcdermott@vodofone.ie

Finner Camp
Bundoran, Co Donegal
Tel 071-9842294
Email awcf@hotmail.com
Rev Alan Ward CF

Gormanston Camp
Co Meath
Tel 01-8413990
Rev Robert McCabe CF
Email robert@militarychaplaincy.ie

McKee Barracks
Dublin 7
Tel 01-8046268
Rev Patrick Mernagh CF
Email pat.mernagh@defenceforces.ie

The Naval Base
Haulbowline,
Co Cork
Tel 021-4378046
Rev Desmond Campion (SDB) CF
Email campiond@eircom.net

Renmore Barracks
Galway
Tel 091-701055
Rev Tom Brady CF
Email bradt56@hotmail.com

Saint Bricin's Hospital
Infirmary Road,
Dublin 7
Tel 01-8042270
Rt Rev Mgr Eoin Thynne HCF

Sarsfield Barracks
Limerick
Tel 061-316817
Rev Seamus Madigan CF
Email seamusmadigan@hotmail.com
Mobile 086 8441609

James Stephens Barracks
Kilkenny
Tel 056-7761852
Rev Dan McCarthy CF
Tel 086-8575155
Email danielmaccarthy@eircom.net

International Military Pilgrimage to Lourdes (Pèlerinage Militaire International)
Director: Rt Rev Mgr Eoin Thynne HCF
Dept. of Defence,
Colaiste Chaoimhín,
Mobhi Road, Glasnevin, Dublin 9
Tel 01-8042270

PRISONS AND PLACES OF DETENTION IN IRELAND

There are fourteen prisons or places of detention in the Republic of Ireland

Liason Bishop between Prison Chaplains and the Bishops' Conference
Bishop Eamonn Walsh
'Naomh Brid,' Blessington Road
Tallaght, Dublin 24
Tel 01-4598032
Email elmham@eircom.net

National Coordinator of Prison Chaplains in the Republic of Ireland
Sr Eithne Corcoran IBVM
Mountjoy Prison
North Circular Rd, Dublin 7
Tel 01-8062846
Email emcorcoran@irishprisons.ie

Arbour Hill Prison
Ard na Gaoithe, Arbour Hill, Dublin 7
Rev Ciaran Enright Tel 01-6770901
Email ccenright@irishprisons.ie
Prison General Office Tel 01-6732990

Castlerea Prison
Castlerea, Co Roscommon
Margaret Connaughton Tel 094-9625278
Email maconnaugh@irishprisons.ie
Prison General Office Tel 094-9625213

Cloverhill Remand Prison
Cloverhill Road, Clondalkin, Dublin 22
Rev John O'Sullivan (MSC) Tel 01-6304586
Email jjosullivan@irishprisons.ie
Sr Carmel Miley CP Tel 01-6304585
Email cjmiley@irishprisons.ie
Sr Margaret O'Donovan DC
Tel 01-6304584
Email mmodonovan@irishprisons.ie
Prison General Office Tel 01-6304531/2

Cork Prison
Rathmore Road, Cork
Rev Fr Michael Kidney (SMA)
Tel 021-4518892
email mjkidney@irishprisons.ie
Sr Mary Jo Sheehy RSM
Tel 021-4518891 (part-time)
Email mjsheehy@irishprisons.ie
Prison General Office Tel 021-4503277

Dóchas Centre Mountjoy Women's Prison
North Circular Road, Dublin 7
Sr Mary Mullins Tel 01-8858920
Email mtmullins@irishprisons.ie
Prison General Office 01-8858987

Limerick Prison
Mulgrave Street, Limerick
Rev John Walsh Tel 061-204714
Mount David House,
North Circular Road, Limerick,
Email jawalsh@irishprisons.ie
Prison General Office Tel 061-204700

Loughan House
Blacklion, Co Cavan
Fr John McMahon PP (w) Tel 071-9853020
Main St Manorhamilton, Co Leitrum
(h) Tel 071-9856987
General Office Tel 071-9853020
Email manorhamilton@kilmorediocese.ie

Midlands Prison
Dublin Road, Portlaoise, Co Laois
Mrs Janet Finlay Tel 057-8672221 (part-time)
Email janpfinlay@irishprisons.ie
Michael Loughnane (part-time)
Tel 057-8672221
Email mjloughnane@irishprisons.ie
Vera Mc Hugh Tel 057-8672221
Email vamchugh@irishprisons.ie
Fr Tom Sinnott (MHM) Tel 057-8672222
Email tgsinnott@irishprisons.ie
Prison General Office 057-8672100

Mountjoy Prison
North Circular Road, Dublin 7
Ruth Breen (part-time) Tel 01-8062843
Email rabreen@irishprisons.ie
Sr Eithne Corcoran (IBVM) Tel 01-8062843
Email emcorcoran@irishprisons.ie
Mark Davis (part-time) Tel 01-8062843
Email mcdavis@irishprisons.ie
Sr Gráinne Haslam (RSM) Tel 01-8062846
Fr Jimmy Kelly OSM Tel 01-8062843
Email jjkelly@irishprisons.ie
Prison General Office 01-8062800

Portlaoise Prison
Dublin Road, Portlaoise, Co Laois
Fr Eugene Drumm Tel 057-8621318
Email eadrum@irishprisons.ie
General Office Tel 057-8621318

Saint Patrick's Institution
North Circular Road, Dublin 7
Miss Ruth Comerford Tel 01-8858945
Email rmcomerford@irishprisons.ie
Sr Eileen Crowley (SHC) (part-time)
Tel 01-8062894
Email eccrowley@irishprisons.ie
General Office Tel 01-8062906

Shelton Abbey
Arklow, Co Wicklow
Sr Patricia Egan (RSCJ) (part-time)
Tel 040-242321
Email pxegan@irishprisons.ie
General Office Tel 040-242300

Training Unit
Glengarrif Parade, Dublin 7
Sr Mairead Gahan LCM Tel 01-8309612
Email mxgahan@irishprisons.ie
Prison General Office Tel 01-8062881

Wheatfield Prison
Cloverhill Road, Clondalkin, Dublin 22
Sr Joan Kane (OSU) Tel 01-6209446
Email jakane@irishprisons.ie
Sr Esther Murphy (RSM) Tel 01-6209447
Email esmurphy@irishprisons.ie
Sr Kathleen Cunningham (part-time)
Email ktcunningh@irishprisons.ie
Tel 01-6209446/7
Sr Imelda Wickham (PBVM) Tel 01-6209466
Email imwickham@irishprisons.ie
Prison General Office Tel 01-6209400

There are three Prisons and Places of Detention in Northern Ireland, administered by the Northern Ireland Office (Use prefix (048) from Republic)

HMP Maghaberry
Old Road, Ballinderry Upper,
Lisburn, Co Antrim, BT28 2TP
Tel 028-92614825
Pastoral Team
Rev Michael Bingham, Br Brian Monaghan
Sr Angela Burke, Sr Rosaleen McMahon

HMP Magilligan
Point Road, Magilligan,
Limavaddy BT49 OLR, Co Derry
Fr Francis O'Hagan
Email www.frohagan@aol.com
Prison General Office Tel 028-77763311

Hydebank Young Offenders' Centre
Hydebank Wood, Hospital Road,
Belfast BT8 8NA, Co Antrim
Tel 028-90253666
Pastoral Team
Rev Stephen McBrearty
Sr Oonah Hanrahan

BRITAIN

The Irish Chaplaincy in Britain
Director: Ms Philomena Cullen
50-52 Camden Square, London NW1 9XB
Tel 0044-2074825528 Fax 0044-2074824815
Direct Line: 020-74828964
Email philomena.cullen@irishchaplaincy.
org.uk
Board of Trustees: Mr John Walsh (Chair),
Mgr Canon Tom Egan (Hon. Treasurer),
Sr Raymunda Jordan (OP), Mr John
Higgins KSG, Ms Nicola O'Regan, Mr
Stephen Hargrave, Ms Kathleen Walsh
and Rev Gerry McFlynn
Email steph.dardis@irishchaplaincy.org.uk
PA/Administrator: Stephanie Dardis

PARISH APOSTOLATES

Northampton Diocese

Luton
Rev John Daly,Holy Ghost, Beech Hill,
33 Westbourne Road, Luton,
Beds LU4 8JD, Tel 00-44-1582728849

SPECIALISED APOSTOLATES

Alcohol Recovery Project
Br Barry Butler (CFA) and Paula Bruce
28 Delancey Street, London NW1 7NH
Tel 0207-8370100

Homeless
Sr Eileen O'Mahony (DC)
Sr Antoinette McGrath (OSC)
Sr Maureen Coen (DC)
Luton Day Centre for the Homeless,
141 Park Street, London LU1 3HG
Tel 01582-728416/482029
Fax 01582-486757

Irish Prisoners Project
Irish Council for Prisoners Overseas (ICPO)
Project Manager: Conor McGinn
50-52 Camden Square, London NW1 9XB
Tel 0044-2074824148
Fax 0044-2074824815
Email conor.mcginn@irishchaplaincy.org.uk
Admin Assistant: Elizabeth Power

Irish Travellers Project
Project Manager: Rev Joseph Browne
50-52 Camden Square, London NW1 9XB
Tel 0044-2074825525 Fax-0044-2074824815
Email joebrowne@irishchaplaincy.org.uk

Older Persons Programme
Project Manager: Paul Raymond
50-52 Camden Square, London NW1 9XB
Tel 0044-2074823274
Fax 0044-207482825
Email
paul.raymond@irishchaplaincy.org.uk

HOSTELS

St Louise's (Female)
Sister in Charge,
33 Medway Street, London SW1P 2BE
Tel 0171-2222071/2226588

COMMUNITY CARE/ ADVICE CENTRES

Irish Welfare and Information Centre
Director: Mr Hugh Tibbs
45 Alcester St, Deritend, Birmingham B12
0PY
Tel 0044-1216046111
Fax 0044-1216046662
Email irishwelfare@icbirmingham.co.uk
Email bridie@iwic.org.uk

Camden London Irish Centre
Director: Peter Hammond
50-52 Camden Square,
London NW19 XB
Tel 0044-2079162222
Fax 0044-2079162638
Email director@irishcentre.org
Coordinator: Jeff Moore,
Irish Welfare Services
Tel 0044-2079162222
Fax 0044-2079162638
Missing Persons: Anne Slevin
missingpersons@irishcentre.org
(Fridays after 4.30 pm)

Manchester Irish Centre
Rose Morris, 89 Cheetham Hill Road,
Manchester, M8 0SN
Tel 0044-1612059105
www.iccmanchester.org.uk
Email iccmanchester.org.uk

Hammersmith Irish Support & Advice Service
Mike McGing, Blacks Road,
Hammersmith, W6 9DT
Tel 0044-2087410466 Fax 0044-2085630712

Allianz (ⅲ)

EUROPE

Brussels
Rev Vincent Gallogley (OFM)
23/25 Ave des Anciens Combattants,
1950 Kraainem, Belgium
Tel 0032-2-7201970 Fax 0032-2-7255810

Copenhagen
Rev Patrick Shiels (CSSR)
Skt Annae Kirke, Hans Bogbinders Alle 2,
2300 Copenhagen S, Denmark
Tel 0045-31-582102

Lisbon
Rev Gus Champion
St Mary's, Rua do Murtal 368
San Pedro do Estoril
2765 Estoril, Portugal
Tel 00-351-1-4673771 (Residence)
Tel 00-351-1-4681676 (Parish)

Luxembourg
Rev Eamonn Breslin
European Parish, 34 Rue des Capucins,
Luxembourg BP 175
Tel 00352-470039 Fax 00352-220859

Munich
Rev Chetus Cohace
Landsberger Strasse 39,
80399 Munich, Germany
Email englischsprachige-
mission.muenchen@erzbistum-
muenchen.de
Tel 0049-89-5003580 Fax 0049-89-
50035826
www.englishspeking-mission-munic.de

Paris
Rev Tom Scanlon (CP)
Rev Anthony Behan (CP)
St Joseph's Church,
50 Avenue Hoche, 75008 Paris, France
Tel 0033-1-42272856
Fax 0033-1-42278649
Rev Declan Hurley
Irish College, Paris, 5 Rue des Irlandais,
75005 Paris, France
Tel 0033-1-58521030 (College)
Email dechurley@eircom.net

Rome
Rev Raphael Gallagher (CSSR)
Redentoristi, Via Merulana 31,
CP2458, Rome, Italy Tel 0039-6-494932
Email rgallagher@alfonsiana.edu

AUSTRALIA

Sydney
Rev Tom Devereux OMI
Parish of St Patrick's,
2 Wellington St, Bondi, NSW 2026
Tel 0061-02-93651195
Fax 0061-02-93654002
Mobile 0061-04-07347301
Email stpatbon@bigpond.net.au

UNITED STATES OF AMERICA

Director
Rev Brendan McBride
Irish Immigration Pastoral Centre
5340 Geary Boulevard #206,
San Francisco, CA 94121
Tel 001-4157526006
Fax 001-4157526910
Email nationaloffice@usairish.org
Cellphone 001-4157609818

Administrator
Ms Geri M. Garvey
Irish Apostolate USA
1005 Downs Drive,
Silver Spring, MD 20904
Tel/Fax 001-3013843375
Email administrator@usairish.org

Boston
Irish Pastoral Centre
Executive Director: Sr Marguerite Kelly
953 Hancock Street,
Quincy, MA 02170
Tel 001-617-4797404
Fax 001-617-4790541
Email ipcboston@yahoo.com
Chaplain: Rev John McCarthy
15 Rita Road, Dorchester, MA 02124
Tel 001-617-4797404
Fax 001-617-4790541
Cellphone 001-617-4121331
Email jmccarthyipc@yahoo.com

Chicago
Chicago Irish Immigrant Support
Chaplain: Rev Michael Leonard
3525 S. Lake Park Avenue,
Chicago, IL 60653
Tel 312-5348445
Fax 312-5348446
Email irishoverhere@sbcglobal.net
www.ci-is.com

Ocean City, Maryland
(Open June–September)
Irish Student Outreach
Coordinator: William Ferguson
13701 Sailing Rd, Ocean City, MD 21842
Tel 001-410-2500362 and
001-443-7837893
Email wfergus4@aol.com

Milwaukee
Irish Immigrant Service of Milwaukee
John Gleeson, 2133 Wisconsin Ave,
Milwaukee, WI 53233-1910
Tel 001-414-3458800
Email gleeson@uwm.edu
www.ichc.net

New York
Project Irish Outreach
Coordinator: Patricia O'Callaghan
1011 First Avenue, New York NY 10022
Tel 001-212-3171011
Fax 001-212-7551526
Email patricia.ocallaghan@archny.org

Aisling Irish Community Centre
990 McLean Avenue, Yonkers, NY 10704
Chaplain: Sr Christine Hennessey
Tel 001-914-2375121 Fax 001-914-
2375172
Email Sr.Christine.Hennessy@archny.org,
aislingirishcc@mindspring.com
www.aislingirishcenter.org

Philadelphia
Philadelphia Immigration Resource Centre
Executive Director: Siobhan Lyons
7 South Cedar Lane
Upper Darby, PA 19082 2816
Tel 001-610-7896355 Fax 001-7896352
Email irishimmigration@aol.com
www.irishimmigrants.org

San Diego
Irish Outreach San Diego Inc.
Bernadette Cashmann
2725 Congress Street 2G,
San Diego, CA 92110
Tel 001-619-2911630
Email irishsd@sbcglobal.net
www.irishoutreachsd.org

San Francisco
Irish Immigration Pastoral Centre
Celine Kennelly
5340 Geary Boulevard #206,
San Francisco, CA 94121
Tel 001-415-7526006
Fax 001-415-7526910
Email iipc@pacbell.net
www.sfiipc.org
Cellphone 001-415-7605762

Seattle
Seattle Immigration Support Group
Chairman: James Cummins
5819 St Andrews Drive, Mukileto,
WA 98275
Tel 001-425-2445147
Email siisg@irishclub.org

GENERAL INFORMATION

OBITUARY LIST

Beata mortui qui in Domino moriuntur
Rv 14:13

PRIESTS AND BROTHERS

Boylan, John (SPS) 2 January 2009
Bradley, Joseph (SSC) 28 October 2008
Bransfield, Michael (SM) 4 August 2009
Bray, Daniel (CSsR) 11 June 2009
Breen, Sean (Dublin) 15 January 2009
Brennan, Cornelius (Dublin) 19 May 2009
Burke, Gus (CFC) 17 February 2009
Burke, Martin (Meath) 31 December 2008
Byrne, Paul (SSS) 14 February 2009
Cahalane, Timothy (MSC) July 2009
Campion, Neil (Killaloe) 25 July 2009
Carr, James, (SM) 31 October 2008
Carroll, Patrick (SMA) 28 January 2009
Casey, Henry (Down & Connor) 6 February 2009
Casey, Henry (Harry) (SMA) 6 February 2009
Clancy, Michael (CSsR) 6 May 2009
Clarkson, William (MSC) March 2009
Cleary, Michael (SVD) 28 October 2008
Clifford, Michael (OSA) 8 March 2009
Collins, Gerard (Cork & Ross) 3 May 2009
Comerford, Thomas (SSC) 18 February 2009
Conlon, Eugene (Meath) 14 July 2009
Conway, Joseph (Down & Connor) 8 December 2008
Corkery, Seamus (Cloyne) 25 March 2009
Cowan, Eamonn (CM) 2 January 2009
Crean, Thomas Francis (CSSp) 31 August 2009
Creaven, John A. (SMA) 2 December 2008
Cronin, Philbert (FSC) 17 March 2009
Crotty, Gerry (CFC) 9 April 2009
Crowley, William (CSSp) 16 November 2008
Culhane, Michael (Limerick) 3 July 2009
Curran, Killian (OCD) 17 September 2008
Curran, Patrick (Tuam) 2 July 2008
Curry, John (SSC) 26 December 2008
Curtin, Maurice (CSSp) 2 September 2009
✠ Daly, Cahal B (Armagh) 31 December 2009
Dennehy, John (SSC) 1 July 2009
Devine, James Bernard (CSSp) 3 May 2009
Diskin, Bill (Tuam) 29 December 2008
Donegan, Benignus (OCSO) 15 November 2008
Donohue, Michael (SSC) 18 October 2008
Donovan, John (SJ) 1 October 2008
Doogan, Michael (CP) 15 December 2008
Doohan, John (SSC) 24 January 2009
Doyle, Francis (Ardagh & Clonmacnois) 11 September 2009
Doyle, Liam (SPS) 2 June 2009
Doyle, Patrick (SJ) 14 September 2008
Duggan, Patrick Joseph (CSSp) 2 June 2009

Dunne, John A. (SJ) 27 December 2008
Dunne, Patrick Joseph (CSSp) 5 May 2009
Dunne, Timothy (FSP) 2 February 2009
Egan, David (OSCam) 27 February 2009
Egan, Francis Martin (CSSp) 19 February 2009
Fahey, Desmond (Tuam) 9 October 2009
Fallon, John P. (CSSp) 29 September 2008
Fitzgerald, Michael (OCD) 8 July 2009
Fitzgibbon, John (CFC) 4 August 2009
Flaherty, Colman (Richard) (CSSp) 23 December 2008
Flanagan, Brian (OMI) 20 December 2008
Flanagan, Brian (SPS) 9 September 2009
Gordon, Declan (Clonfert) 26 February 2009
Greene, Timothy (Limerick) 9 September 2009
Guidera, John (SCA) 27 March 2009
Hallahan, Declan (CFC) 25 December 2008
Harrold, James (SMA) 30 August 2009
Hassett, Michael (Dublin) 17 April 2009
Hayden, John (Kildare & Leighlin) 11 April 2009
Healy, Patrick (Elphin) 22 November 2009
Higgins, Tom (Tuam) 22 February 2009
Hogan, Kevin (Killaloe) 3 January 2009
Horkin, Leo Paul (CSSp) 6 March 2009
Hudner, James (Limerick) 25 August 2009
Johnson, Dominic (OSB) 12 December 2008
Kandemiiri, Tonderai (OFM) 1 July 2009
Keane, Barry (Cork & Ross) 30 October 2008
Keane, Tony (CFC) 16 February 2009
Keenan, Brian (SM) 14 August 2009
Kelly, Anthony (Dublin) 17 March 2009
Kelly, Francis (Ardagh & Clonmacnois) 9 January 2009
Kelly, Joseph (Galway) 23 January 2009
Kelly, Joseph (SJ) 5 December 2008
Kelly, Richard (Kildare & Leighlin) 17 February 2009
Kennedy, Sean (Cashel & Emly) 21 October 2009
Keohane, Gerard (Cork & Ross) 23 April 2009
Kerr, Norbert (FSC) 16 April 2009
Lee, Cornelius (Dublin) 14 March 2009
Loughlin, Eugene (Kilmore) 29 September 2009
Loughrey, Fergus (CP) 17 August 2009
Ludden, Stephen (Tuam) 31 July 2008
Lynch, Philip (CSSp) 10 April 2009
Lyons, Frank (Dromore) 12 February 2009
Lyons, Michael (Tuam) 1 February 2009
Lyons, Redmond (CSSp) 11 April 2009
MacMahon, Thomas (SJ) 24 January 2009
MacSorley, Fred (Down & Connor) 8 February 2009
Maguire, Bernard (Clogher) 2 April 2009
Maguire, Joseph (Down & Connor) 20 January 2009
Maher, Richard (Dublin) 29 August 2009
Marlow, Celestine (Peter) (CSSp) 10 August 2009

McBride, Charles Henry (CSSp) 9 November 2008
McCabe, Patrick (Dublin) 11 May 2009
McCaffrey, Macartan, (OH) 27 August 2009
McCarthy, Desmond (Dublin) 15 August 2009
McCarthy, Michael (Cork & Ross) 15 August 2009
McCartny, James (SMA) 13 October 2008
McCaughan, Ernest (Down & Connor) 18 January 2009
McCaughey, Patrick (Clogher) 29 March 2009
McClure, Hugo (SVD)
McGlynn, Peter (Raphoe) 16 January 2009
McHugh, Adrian (MSC) June 2009
McIldowney, Hugh (Down & Connor) 6 July 2009
McInerney, Rory (Killaloe) 30 June 2009
McNamara, Michael (Killaloe) 25 July 2009
McNamara, Tom (CFC) 20 July 2009
McSweeny, Patrick (OFM) 8 April 2009
Montes De Ola, Vincent (CSSp) 7 March 2009
Morris, Joseph (Derry) 27 November 2009
Morris, Vincent (Clogher) 23 July 2009
Mulcahy, Richard (Opus Dei) 23 April 2009
Mulvany, Peter (Meath) 2 October 2009
Mulvany, Thomas (OFM) 14 December 2008
Murphy, Joseph (OFM Cap) 21 May 2009
Murray, Hubert (Clonfert) 4 December 2008
Murray, Michael Canice (CSSp) 22 August 2009
Nagle, Fridolin (FSC) 29 June 2009
Ó Fatharta, Micheál 1 September 2009
O'Brien, Colm (Waterford & Lismore) 16 September 2009
O'Brien, Philip (OCarm) 7 October 2008
O'Brien, Timothy (Cashel & Emly) 24 July 2009
O'Connell, Fidelis (FSP) 2 March 2009
O'Connell, James (SMA) 4 August 2009
O'Connell, Richard (Dromore) 26 December 2008
O'Connor, Denis (Cloyne) 24 March 2009
O'Doherty, John (SSC) 14 November 2008
O'Donovan, John (Cork & Ross) 6 January 2009
O'Donovan, Patrick (SSC) 2 February 2009
O'Hanlon, Jerome (MSC) June 2009
O'Kelly, Pádraig (Armagh) 27 December 2008
O'Mahony, John (SMA) 12 November 2008
O'Mahony, Liam (Cork & Ross) 27 August 2009
O'Malley, Thomas Gerard (CSSp) 11 June 2009
O'Meara, James (Cashel & Emly) 14 March 2009

IRISH COUNCIL OF CHURCHES

Irish Council of Churches
President: Rev A. D. Davidson
Vice-President: Bishop R. Clarke

Inter-Church Centre
48 Elmwood Avenue, Belfast BT9 6AZ
Tel 028-90663145 Fax 028-90664160
Email info@irishchurches.org
Website www.irishchurches.org
General Secretary: Mr J. M. Earle

Member Churches of Council
Antiochian Orthodox Church in Ireland;
Church of Ireland; Greek Orthodox
Church in Ireland; Lifelink Network of
Churches; Lutheran Church in Ireland;
Methodist Church in Ireland; Moravian
Church, Irish District; Non-Subscribing
Presbyterian Church in Ireland;
Presbyterian Church in Ireland; Religious
Society of Friends; Cherubim and
Seraphim Church; Romanian Orthodox
Church in Ireland; Russian Orthodox
Church in Ireland; Salvation Army
(Ireland Division)

Leaders of Member Churches
Antiochan Orthodox Church in Ireland
Rev Fr Irenaeus Du Plessis
Antiochian Orthodox Church,
8 Wheatfield Gardens, Belfast BT14 7HU
Tel 028-90712523
Email irenaeus@btinternet.com

Church of Ireland
Most Rev A. E. T. Harper
Archbishop of Armagh, Primate of All
Ireland, Diocesan Office, Church House,
46 Abbey Street, Armagh BT61 7DZ
Tel 028-37522851 (H), 028-37527144 (O)
Fax 028-37510596
Email archbishop@armagh.anglican.org

Greek Orthodox Church
Church of the Annunciation
46 Arbour Hill, Dublin 7
Tel 01-6779020
Rev Dr Ireneu Ioan Craciun PP
38 Ardmore Crescent, Artane, Dublin 5
Tel/Fax 01-8474956
Email i.craciun@iolfree.ie
Fr Tom Carroll, Assistant Priest
133 Whitefields, Portarlington, Co Laois
Tel 057-8645069/086-2394539
Email fr.tomcarroll@gmail.com
Contact Person
Mrs Toulla Efthimiou Conran
103 Walkinstown Avenue, Dublin 12
Tel 01-4566509

Lifelink Newtork of Churches
Pastor Paul Reid
Christian Fellowship Church,
10 Belmont Road, Belfast BT4 2AN
Tel 028-90671838
Email paul@cfc-net.org

Lutheran Church in Ireland
Pastors C. & J. Diestelkamp, Luther House,
24 Adelaide Road, Dublin 2
Tel 01-6766548 Fax 01-6766548
Email info@lutheran-ireland.org
www.lutheran-ireland.org

Methodist Church in Ireland
President: Rev Donald P. Ker
1 Fountainville Avenue, Belfast BT9 6AN
Tel 028-90324554 Fax 028-90239467
Secretary: Rev Donald P. Ker
1 Fountainville Avenue, Belfast BT9 6AN
Tel 028-90324554 Fax 028-90239467
President-Designate:
Rev Paul Kingston (C)
Adare, Co Limerick
Tel 061-396236

Moravian Church, Irish District
Rev Kathryn Woolford, Chairperson
Moravian Church, Irish District,
5 Locksley Lane, Finaghy, Belfast BT10 0AR
Tel 028-90619755
Email woolford.moravian@ukgateway.net

Non-Subscribing Presbyterian Church
Moderator: Right Rev R.A. McKee
30 Comber Road, Killinchy,
Newtownards, Co Down BT23 6PB
Tel 028-97541329
Email ramck@talk21.com
Contact Person: Rev N. Hutton
(Clerk of General Synod)
25 Weavers Meadow, Banbridge,
Co Down BT32 4RL
Email norman.hutton3@btinternet.com
Tel 028-40626902
Rev Dr A.D.G. Steers *(Editor, Non-
Subscribing Presbyterian Magazine)*
223 Upper Lisburn Road, Belfast BT10 0LL
Tel 028-90947850
Email nspresb@hotmail.com
Clerk of the Presbytery of Antrim
Rev Dr J. W. Nelson
102 Carrickfergus Road,
Larne, Co Antrim BT40 3JX
Tel 028-28272600
Clerk of the Presbytery of Bangor
Rev I. Gilpin
15 Windmill Hill, Comber,
Co Down BT23 5WH
Tel 028-91872265
Clerk of the Synod of Munster
Mr F. Spengeman
12 Knocknasuff, Waterloo,
Blarney, Co Cork
Tel 087-8101943

Presbyterian Church in Ireland
Right Rev Dr Stafford Carson
Moderator, c/o Church House, Fisherwick
Place, Belfast BT1 6DW
Tel 028-90322284 Fax 028-90417301
Email moderator@presbyterianireland.org
Rev Dr Donald Watts, Clerk
Church House, Belfast BT1 6DW
Tel 028-90417208 Fax 028-90417301
Email clerk@presbyterianireland.org

Religious Society of Friends
Alan C. Plm
Clerk of Yearly Meeting
Clonfadda, Fenor, Co Waterford
For information contact
National Administrative Office,
Quaker House Dublin,
Stocking Lane, Dublin 16
Tel 01-4956889
Email office@quakers-in-ireland.ie

Rock of Ages Cherubim & Seraphim Church in Ireland
Rev Mother Agnes O. Aderanti
Rock of Ages Cherubim & Seraphim
Church, 46 Priory Gate, Athboy, Co Meath
Tel 046-9487977/086-8134747
Email rockofagescs@hotmail.com
Website rockofagescs@hotmail.com

Romanian Orthodox Church in Ireland
Romanian Orthodox Parish of the
Exaltation of the Holy Cross,
Christ Church, Leeson Park, Dublin 6
Parish Priest: Fr Calin Florea
18 Portersgate Green, Clonsilla, Dublin 15
Tel 087-6148140
Email revcalin.florea@gmail. com
Assistant Priest: Fr Godfrey O'Donnell
5 Cherry Park, Rathingle, Swords, Co Dublin
Tel 01-8404302/087-6780150
Email godo@eircom.net

Russian Orthodox Church in Ireland
Russian Orthodox Church St Peter-St Paul,
Moscow Patriarchate Representation,
Harold's Cross Road, Dublin 6W
Tel 01-4969038
Dean: Very Rev Fr Michael Gogoleff
Tel 0044-1225-858792 Fax 0044-1225-852211
Deputy: Fr Nikolai Evseev
Tel 086-1009531
Affiliated Parishes: Cork, Galway,
Waterford, Stradbally, Belfast
Services
Saturday Vespers – Matins: 6.00 pm
Sunday Liturgy: 10.00 am
Feast Days Liturgy: 10.00 am
Wednesday Pastoral Talks: 7.00 pm
Church Shop: religious books, candles, icons
Languages: Services in English and
Slavonic

Salvation Army
Major Alan Watters
Divisional Commander,
Divisional Headquarters, 12 Station Mews,
Sydenham, Belfast BT4 1TL
Tel 028-90675000 Fax 028-90675011
Email alan.watters@salvationarmy.org.uk
Captain James Wadsorth
Dublin City Corps
Tel 01-8481690
Email
james.wadsworth@salvationarmy.org.uk
Captain Marcus Mylechreest
Dublin South
Tel 01- 4126494
Email marcus.mylechreest@salvationarmy.ie

Allianz (ⅰⅼ)

CHURCH OF IRELAND ARCHBISHOPS AND BISHOPS

Armagh
Most Rev A. E. T. Harper, OBE, BA
Archbishop of Armagh, Primate of All
Ireland and Metropolitan,
Diocesan Office, Church House,
46 Abbey Street, Armagh BT61 7DZ
Tel 028-37522851 (H), 028-37527144 (O)
Fax 028-37510596
Email archbishop@armagh.anglican.org
Diocesan Secretary: Mrs J. Leighton
Church House, 46 Abbey Street,
Armagh BT61 7DZ
Tel 028-37522858 Fax 028-37510596
Email secretary@armagh.anglican.org

Dublin
Most Rev J. R. W. Neill MA, LLD
Archbishop of Dublin, Bishop of
Glendalough, Primate of Ireland and
Metropolitan, The See House,
17 Temple Road, Dartry, Dublin 6
Tel 01-4977849 Fax 01-4976355
Email archibishop@dublin.anglican.org
Diocesan Secretary: Mr K. Dungan PC
Diocesan Office, Church of Ireland House,
Church Avenue, Rathmines, Dublin 6
Tel 01-4966981/086-3117803
Fax 01-4972865

Meath and Kildare
Most Rev R. L. Clarke MA, BD, PhD
Bishop of Meath and Kildare,
Bishop's House, Moyglare,
Maynooth, Co Kildare
Tel 01-6289354 Fax 01-6292153
Email bishop@meath.anglican.org
Diocesan Secretary: Mrs K. Seaman
Meath & Kildare Diocesan Centre
Moyglare, Maynooth, Co Kildare
Tel 01-6292163
Email office@meath.anglican.org

Cashel and Ossory
Right Rev M. A. J. Burrows MA, MLitt,
Prof.Dip.Th
Bishop of Cashel, Waterford, Lismore,
Ossory, Ferns and Leighlin,
Bishop's House, Troysgate, Kilkenny
Tel 056-7786633
Email cashelossorybishop@eircom.net
Diocesan Secretary: Mrs D. Hughes
Diocesan Office, St Canice's Library,
Kilkenny
Tel 056-61910/27248 Fax 056-51813
Mon-Wed 9.30 am-1.00 pm
Email office@cashel.anglican.org

Ferns
Diocesan Secretary: Mrs G. Rothwell
Ballyeaton, Glynn,
Enniscorthy, Co Wexford
Tel 053-9128114
Email office@ferns.anglican.org

Down and Dromore
Right Rev H. C. Miller MA, BA (Hons), DPS
Bishop of Down and Dromore,
The See House, 32 Knockdene Park South,
Belfast BT5 7AB
Tel 028-90471973 Fax 028-90231902
Email bishop@down.anglican.org

Diocesan Secretary: Mr T. N. Wilson
Diocesan Office, Church of Ireland House,
61-67 Donegall Street, Belfast BT1 2QH
Tel 028-90322268/90323188
Fax 028-90321635
Email office@diocoff-belfast.org

Derry and Raphoe
Rt Rev K. R. Good BA (Hons), MEd,
HDipEd, DPS
Bishop of Derry and Raphoe,
The See House, 112 Culmore Road,
Londonderry BT48 8JF
Tel 028-71351206/028-71262440
Fax 028-71352554
Email bishop@derry.anglican.org
Diocesan Secretary: Mr G. Kelly
Diocesan Office, 24 London Street,
Londonderry BT48 6RQ
Tel 028-71262440 Fax 028-71372100
Email office.derry@btconnect.com

Limerick and Killaloe
Right Rev T. R. Williams BA, BA, DPs
Bishop of Limerick, Ardfert, Aghadoe,
Killaloe, Kilfenora, Clonfert,
Kilmacduagh and Emly,
Rien Roe, Adare, Co Limerick
Tel 061-396244
Email bishop@limerick.anglican.org
Diocesan Secretary: Rev Canon R. Warren
St John's Rectory, Tralee, Co Kerry
Tel 066-7122245 Fax 066-7129004
Email secretary@limerick.anglican.org

Tuam
Right Rev R.C.A. Henderson MA, DPhil,
DipTh, DPs
Bishop of Tuam, Killala and Achonry,
Bishop's House, Knockglass, Crossmolina,
Co Mayo
Tel 096-31317 Fax 096-31775
Email bptuam@iol.ie
Diocesan Secretary: Mrs H. Sherlock
Stonehall House, Ballisodare, Co Sligo
Tel 071-9167280 Fax 071-9130264
Email hsherlock@iolfree.ie

Clogher
Right Rev M.G.St. A. Jackson MA, PhD,
DPhil
Bishop of Clogher, The See House,
Fivemilestown, Co Tyrone BT75 0QP
Tel 028-89522475
Email bishop@clogher.anglican.org
Diocesan Secretary: Mr G. M. T. Moore
Clogher Diocesan Office,
St Macartan's Cathedral Hall,
Hall's Lane, Enniskillen,
Co Fermanagh BT74 7DR
Tel/Fax 028-66347879
Email secretary@clogher.anglican.org

Cork
Right Rev W. P. Colton BCL, DipTh, MPhil,
LL.M
Bishop of Cork, Cloyne and Ross,
The Palace, Bishop Street, Cork
Tel 021-4316114
Email bishop@ccrd.ie
Diocesan Secretary: Mr W. F. Baker
St Nicholas House, 14 Cove Street, Cork
Tel 021-5005080 Fax 021-4320960
Email secretary@cork.anglican.org

Kilmore
Right Rev K. H. Clarke BA
Bishop of Kilmore, Elphin and Ardagh,
48 Carrickfern, Cavan, Co Cavan
Tel 049-4372759
Email bishop@kilmore.anglican.org
Diocesan Secretary: Miss M. Cunningham
Kilmore Diocesan Office,
Whitestar Complex, Market Street,
Cootehill, Co Cavan
Tel 049-5559954 Fax 049-5559954
Email secretary@kilmore.anglican.org

Elphin and Ardagh
Diocesan Secretary: Mrs B. Barrett
The Rectory, Riverstown, Co Sligo
Tel 071-9165368
Email diosecea@eircom.net

Connor
Right Rev A. F. Abernethy
Bishop of Connor, c/o Church of Ireland
House, 61-67 Donegall Street,
Belfast BT1 2QH
Tel 028-90661942 (Home)
Email bishop@connor.anglican.org
Diocesan Secretary: Mr T. N. Wilson
The Diocesan Office,
Church of Ireland House,
61-67 Donegall Street, Belfast BT1 2QH
Tel 028-90322268 Fax 028-90321635
Email office@diocoff-belfast.org

GREEK ORTHODOX CHURCH IN IRELAND

Greek Orthodox Church of the
Annunciation, 46 Arbour Hill, Dublin 7
Tel 01-6779020
Rev Dr Ireneu Ioan Craciun PP
38 Ardmore Crescent, Artane, Dublin 5
Tel/Fax 01-8474956
Email i.craciun@iolfree.ie
Fr Tom Carroll, Assistant Priest
133 Whitefields, Portarlington, Co Laois
Tel 057-8645069/086-2394539
Email fr.tomcarroll@gmail.com
Contact Person: Mrs Toulla Efthimiou Conran
103 Walkinstown Avenue, Dublin 12
Tel 01-4566509

METHODIST CHURCH IN IRELAND

District Superintendents
Dublin: Rev Dr John Stephens
9 Finsbury Park, Churchtown, Dublin 14
Midlands and Southern:
Rev Brian D. Griffin
The Manse, Roscrea, Co Tipperary
Tel 0505-21670
Enniskillen and Sligo:
Rev Kenneth J. Robinson
'Aldersgate', 47 Chyanterhill Road,
Enniskillen, Co Fermanagh BT4 6DE
Tel 028-66322244
North West: Rev T. H. Samuel McGuffin
11 Clearwater, Clooney Road,
Londonderry BT47 6BE
Tel 028-71342644
North East: Rev Andrew N. Boucher
35a Rathcoole Drive, Newtownabbey,
Co Antrim BT37 9AQ
Tel 028-90852546

Allianz (ili)

Belfast: Rev William A. Davison
10 Locksley Park, Belfast BT10 0AR
Tel 028-90611741
Down: Rev Robert Cooper
'Epworth', 16 Brooklands Road,
Newtownards, Co Down BT23 4TL
Tel 028-91815959
Portadown: Rev David G. Clements
28 Margretta Park, Portadown,
Co Armagh BT63 5DF
Tel 028-38332616

PRESBYTERIES OF THE PRESBYTERIAN CHURCH

Ards
Rev Dr R.A. Russell
46 Dunover Road, Ballywalter, BT22 2LE
Tel 028-42758788
Email arussell@presbyterianireland.org

Armagh
Rev Colin Harris
14 Mullabrack Road, Gilford BT63 6BW
Tel 028-38830775
Email charris@presbyterianireland.org

Ballymena
Rev J. J. Andrews
1 Forthill Park, Ballymena BT42 2HI
Tel 028-25645544
Email jandrews@presbyterianireland.org

East Belfast
Mr Douglas Cowan
16 Ferndene Gardens,
Dundonald BT16 2EP
Tel 028-90481292
Email dcowan@presbyterianireland.org

North Belfast
Rev T. C. Morrison
39 Old Cavehill Road, Belfast BT15 5FH
Tel 028 9077 0301
Email cmorrison@presbyterianireland.org

South Belfast
Mr Cecil Graham
97 Orby Drive, Belfast BT5 6AG
Tel 028-90289702
Email cgraham@presbyterianireland.org

Carrickfergus
Rev Morris Gault
50 Harwood Gardens,
Carrickfergus BT38 7US
Tel 028-93367875
Email mgault@presbyterianireland.org

Coleraine and Limavady
Rev W. I. Hunter
8 Ballywatt Road, Coleraine BT52 2LT
Tel 028-20731310
Email ihunter@presbyterianireland.org

Derry and Donegal
Rev Stanley Stewart
35 Glencosh Road, Donemana,
Strabane BT52 0LY
Tel 028-71397186
Email sstewart@presbyterianireland.org

Down
Rev Dr Brian Black
Ballygowan Church Office,
Church Hill, Ballygowan
Tel 028-97521096
Email bblack@presbyterianireland.org

Dromore
Rev J. I. Davey
2 Lisburn Road, Hillsborough BT26 6AA
Tel 028-92683696
Email jdavey@presbyterianireland.org

Dublin and Munster
Rev C. J. Gamble
15 Hillside Drive, Naas, Co Kildare
Tel 045-898522
Email cgamble@presbyterianireland.org

Iveagh
Rev I. J. Patterson
19 Shimna Road, Newcastle BT33 0AT
Tel 028-43723455
Email
ipatterson@presbyterianireland.org

Monaghan
Rev Sam Anketell
Corglass Manse, Bailieborough
Tel 042-9665745
Email sanketell@presbyterianireland.org

Newry
Rev S. A. Finlay
156 Glassdrumman Road, Annalong,
Newry BT34 4QL
Tel 028-43768232
Email sfinlay@presbyterianireland.org

Omagh
Rev Robert Herron
10 Mullaghmenagh Avenue,
Omagh BT78 5QH
Tel 028-82243776
Email rherron@presbyterianireland.org

Route
Rev Noel McClean
Kilraughts Manse, 24 Topp Road,
Ballymoney BT53 8LT
Tel 028-27667618
Email nmcclean@presbyterianireland.org

Templepatrick
Rev John Murdock
50 Killead Road, Aldergrove,
Crumlin BT29 4EN
Tel 028-94422436
Email jmurdock@presbyterianireland.org

Tyrone
Rev T. J. Conway
74 Ballymacilcurr Road,
Upperlands BT46 5TT
Tel 028-79642278
Email tconway@presbyterianireland.org

IRELAND'S CARDINALS

Since 1866, when Ireland received its first residential cardinal, to the present, nine Irish bishops have been elected to the Sacred College. By 'Irish bishops' is meant those who, while exercising actual pastoral government, were cardinals; not included are those Irish prelates who were made cardinals but whose ministry was spent overseas (e.g. Cardinal Glennon), or in the service of the Roman Curia (e.g. Cardinal Browne), or those who, having been territorial bishops in Ireland, were elevated to the Sacred College while exercising pastoral government in a diocese overseas (e.g. Cardinal Moran).

Paul Cullen (1803-78)
Ordained Archbishop of Armagh (1850); translated to Dublin (1852); created Cardinal (22 June 1866) by Pius IX.

Edward McCabe (1816-85)
Ordained Bishop of Gadara and appointed auxiliary to the Archbishop of Dublin, Cardinal Cullen (1877); appointed Archbishop of Dublin, following Cardinal Cullen's death (1879); created Cardinal (27 March 1882) by Leo XIII.

Michael Logue (1840-1924)
Ordained Bishop of Raphoe (1879); translated to be Co-adjutor to Archbishop Daniel McGettigan of Armagh (March 1887), whom he succeeded (December 1887); created Cardinal (16 January 1893) by Leo XIII.

Patrick O'Donnell (1856-1927)
Ordained Bishop of Raphoe (1888); translated to be Co-adjutor to Cardinal Logue (1922), whom he succeeded as Archbishop of Armagh (1924); created Cardinal (14 December 1925) by Pius XI.

Joseph MacRory (1861-1945)
Ordained Bishop of Down and Connor (1915); translated to Armagh as Archbishop in succession to Cardinal O'Donnell (1928); created Cardinal (12 December 1929) by Pius XI.

John D'Alton (1882-1963)
Ordained Bishop of Binda and appointed Co-adjutor to the Bishop of Meath (1942), whom he succeeded (1943); translated to Armagh in succession to Cardinal MacRory (1946); created Cardinal (12 January 1953) by Pius XII.

William Conway (1913-77)
Ordained Bishop of Neve and appointed auxiliary to the Archbishop of Armagh, Cardinal D'Alton (1958), whom he succeeded (1963); created Cardinal (22 February 1965) by Paul VI.

Tomás Ó Fiaich (1923-90)
Ordained Archbishop of Armagh (1977) and created Cardinal (30 June 1979) by John Paul II.

Cahal Brendan Daly (1917-2009)
ordained priest 22 June 1941; ordained Bishop of Ardagh and Clonmacnois 16 July 1967; installed Bishop of Down and Connor 17 October 1982; installed Archbishop of Armagh 16 December 1990; created Cardinal 28 June 1991 by John Paul II; retired 1 October 1996.

The tenth Irish Cardinal is the Archbishop of Dublin, H. E. **Cardinal Desmond Connell** *(see Diocese of Dublin)*

The eleventh Irish Cardinal is the Archbishop of Armagh, H. E. **Cardinal Seán Brady** *(see Diocese of Armagh)*

STATISTICS

TABLE 1: CATHOLIC CHURCH PERSONNEL 2006

	Number
Diocesan	3,078
Clerical Religious Orders	3,278
Sisters' Orders	8,891
Brothers' Orders	697
TOTAL	15,944

Source: Council for Research and Development 2007

TABLE 2: VOCATIONS 2006

	Entrants
Diocesan	28
Clerical Religious Orders	15
Sisters' Orders	9
Brothers' Orders	1
TOTAL	53

Source: Council for Research and Development 2007

TABLE 3: NULLITY OF MARRIAGE

Year	Applications	Decrees of Nullity
1999	505	432
2000	484	477
2001	421	489
2002	406	386
2003	402	295
2004	499	272
2005	434	395
2006	391	701
2007	332	517
2008	309	314

EXPLANATORY NOTES:

1. The above figures relate to the 32 counties.
2. Only a minority of applications persist beyond the preliminary stages. About 40% are found to have no *prima facie* case for nullity and do not reach the stage of formal investigation; a further third are withdrawn by the applicants.
3. In about 75–80% of cases ending with a nullity decree, a veto – technically called a *vetitum* – on marriage in the Church is imposed on one or both parties. This is because the defect which caused the nullity is judged to be still present, putting at risk the validity of a future marriage. The *vetitum* may be lifted by the local bishop only if he is satisfied, after investigation, of the person's fitness for marriage in all essential respects. The purpose of the *vetitum* is to prevent the sacrament of marriage being brought into disrepute and to protect the genuine interests of any future spouse.
4. Before a decree is granted a) a case must be judged independently by two tribunals – in Ireland, first, by a regional tribunal and then by the National Appeals Tribunal; b) it must be established with moral certainty – probability alone is not enough – that nullity exists in a particular case; that is, that, because of fundamental defect of capacity for, or consent to, that marriage, established to have been present at the time of marriage, there was in fact, no valid marriage. The tribunal starts with the presumption that the marriage is valid; the onus is on the applicants to provide convincing evidence that it is not.
5. COST OF THE PROCEDURE: The costs involved for the applicant are kept as low as possible and are, in fact, very modest. Applicants are expected to pay if they can afford it. However, each applicant is formally told that the progress of the case or its outcome does not in any way depend on the ability or willingness to pay any or all of these expenses. If they genuinely cannot pay, the Church will come to their aid. In practice, only a minority pay the full case fee. Over half pay nothing.

Allianz (ⅱ)

TABLE 4: CATHOLICS 2009				TABLE 5: CATHOLIC SCHOOLS 2009			
	Parishes	Catholic Population	Churches	Schools (no)		School Population	
				Primary	Secondary[1]	Primary	Secondary[1]
Armagh[2]	61	213,030	152	145	24	24,867	17,309
Dublin	199	1,162,000	247	477	184	127,634	88,760
Cashel[2]	46	82,135	84	121	21	10,125	8,432
Tuam	56	122,397	131	195	18	15,324	8,564
Achonry[2]	23	34,826	47	53	10	3,780	3,969
Ardagh[2]	41	71,806	80	86	20	11,256	7,857
Clogher	37	86,047	85	96	18	11,743	9,401
Clonfert[2]	24	36,000	47	50	7	6,800	3,200
Cloyne	46	165,067	107	125	28	17,604	11,360
Cork & Ross	68	220,000	124	184	48	n/a	n/a
Derry	51	242,260	104	135	26	21,673	16,064
Down & Connor	88	336,462	151	163	41	31,976	26,385
Dromore[2]	23	63,400	48	51	14	10,270	11,524
Elphin	38	70,800	90	120	19	10,125	4,120
Ferns	49	100,227	101	96	20	15,287	10,682
Galway	39	115,487	71	85	20	13,614	6,565
Kerry[2]	54	127,850	105	168	33	17,200	12,400
Kildare & Leighlin[2]	56	205,185	117	172	43	30,864	17,707
Killala	22	40,432	48	68	11	5,610	3,392
Killaloe	58	122,746	133	150	21	15,885	11,500
Kilmore[2]	36	57,024	95	84	14	7,823	5,357
Limerick	60	184,340	94	109	22	22,000	20,000
Meath[2]	69	250,000	149	198	36	30,000	24,000
Ossory	42	88,549	89	86	16	10,782	6,626
Raphoe[2]	33	81,250	71	101	20	10,662	13,151
Waterford & Lismore[2]	45	146,206	85	98	24	16,368	12,132
Totals[3]	1,365	4,338,587	2,646	3,434	767	369,536	272,831

Notes:
1. Includes voluntary secondary schools and state schools.
Source: Diocesan returns

2. Data unchanged from 2008.
3. Total estimates only.

TABLE 6: NUMBER OF PRIESTS AND RELIGIOUS

	Active in Diocese[1]	Others[2]	RELIGIOUS ORDERS		
			Clerical	Brothers	Sisters
Armagh	101	37	55	31	362
Dublin	291	157	862	324	2,749
Cashel	86	11	20	8	153
Tuam	94	26	8	17	234
Achonry	36	9	1	0	75
Ardagh	59	14	5	9	190
Clogher	74	10	4	3	140
Clonfert	39	5	18	0	95
Cloyne	103	32	0	5	209
Cork & Ross[3]	119	30	141	36	580
Derry	96	19	5	4	102
Down & Connor	139	41	38	9	233
Dromore	33	21	26	11	156
Elphin	54	15	11	1	114
Ferns	98	25	10	6	164
Galway	55	21	43	20	213
Kerry[3]	84	25	10	5	292
Kildare & Leighlin[3]	106	17	93	54	380
Killala	47	18	4	3	54
Killaloe	104	19	19	8	180
Kilmore	72	18	7	1	54
Limerick	95	30	59	14	317
Meath[3]	113	19	102	20	163
Ossory[3]	63	16	17	52	211
Raphoe	66	17	12	5	53
Waterford & Lismore[3]	68	24	52	40	321
Totals[4]	2,536	555	1,651	686	7,796

Notes:
1. Diocesan priests only.
2. Priests of the diocese retired, sick, on study leave or working in other dioceses in Ireland and abroad. Details are listed under the diocese.
3. Data unchanged from 2008.
4. Totals estimates only.
Source: Diocesan returns

CATHOLIC ARCHBISHOPS AND BISHOPS OF BRITAIN

APOSTOLIC NUNCIO

Most Rev Faustino Sainz Muñoz
54 Parkside, London SW19 5NF
Tel 020-89447189
Fax 020-89472494

ENGLAND AND WALES

PROVINCE OF WESTMINSTER

Most Rv Vincent Nichols
Archbishop of Westminister

Auxiliaries
Right Rev George Stack
Rt Rev Bernard Longley
Rt Rev Alan Hopes
Rt Rev John Arnold

Suffragans
Right Rev Thomas McMahon
Bishop of Brentwood
Right Rev Malcolm MacMahon
Bishop of Nottingham
Right Rev Michael Evans
Bishop of East Anglia
Right Rev Peter Doyle
Bishop of Northhampton

PROVINCE OF BIRMINGHAM

Sede Vacante
Archbishop of Birmingham

Auxilary
Right Rev Philip Pargeter
Rt Rev David McGough
Rt Rev William Kenney, Diocesan
Administator

Suffragans
Right Rev Brian Noble
Bishop of Shrewsbury
Right Rev Declan Lang
Bishop of Clifton

PROVINCE OF LIVERPOOL

Most Rev Patrick Kelly
Archbishop of Liverpool

Auxilary
Right Rev Thomas Williams

Suffragans
Right Rev Patrick O'Donoghue
Diocese of Lancaster
Right Rev Terence Brain
Bishop of Salford
Right Rev Arthur Roche
Bishop of Leeds
Right Rev John Rawsthorne
Bishop of Hallam
Right Rev Terence Drainey
Bishop of Middlesbrough
Right Rev Seamus Cunningham
Bishop of Hexham and Newcastle
Right Rev Michael Campbell
Bishop of Lancaster

PROVINCE OF CARDIFF

Most Rev Peter Smith
Archbishop of Cardiff

Suffragans
Right Rev Tom Burns
Bishop of Menevia
Right Rev Edwin Regan
Bishop of Wrexham

PROVINCE OF SOUTHWARK

Most Rev Kevin McDonald
Archbishop of Southwark

Auxiliaries
Right Rev John Hine, Rt Rev Patrick
Lynch, Rt Rev Paul Hendricks

Suffragans
Right Rev Christopher Budd
Bishop of Plymouth
Right Rev Kieran Conry
Bishop of Arundel and Brighton
Right Rev Crispian Hollis
Bishop of Portsmouth

Bishop of the Forces
Right Rev Richard Moth

BISHOPS' CONFERENCE OF ENGLAND AND WALES

Bishop's Conference
39 Eccleston Square, London SW1V 1BX
Tel 020-76308220 Fax 020-79014821
Email secretariat@cbcew.org.uk

Most Rev Vincent Nichols
Archbishop's House, Ambrosden Avenue,
London SW1P 1QJ
Tel 020-77989033 Fax 020-77989077

Right Rev Declan Lang
Bishop of Clifton, St Ambrose, North
Road, Leigh Woods, Bristol BS8 3PW
Tel 0117-9733027 Fax 0117 9735913

Most Rev Kevin McDonald
Archbishop of Southwark,
Archbishop's House, St George's Road,
Southwark, London SE1 6HX
Tel 020 79282495 Fax 020 79287833

Right Rev Michael Campbell
Bishop of Lancaster,
Bishop's Office, Balmoral Road,
Lancaster LA1 3BT
Tel 01524-596050

Right Rev Christopher Budd
Bishop of Plymouth,
31 Wyndham Street West, Plymouth,
Devon PL1 5RZ
Tel 01752-224414 Fax 01752-223750

Right Rev Michael Evans
The White House, 21 Upgate,
Poringland, Norwich, Norfolk NR14 7SH
Tel 01586-2202/3956 Fax 01586-5358

Sede Vacante
Archbishop of Birmingham,
8 Shadwell Street, Birmingham B4 6EY
Tel 0121-2369090 Fax 0121-2120171

Right Rev George Stack
Auxiliary Bishop of Westminster
Archbishop's House, Ambrosden Avenue,
London SW1P IQJ
Tel 020-77989033 Fax 020-77989077

Right Rev Brian Noble
Bishop of Shrewsbury,
Laburnum Cottage, 97 Barnston Road,
Barnston, Wirral LG1 1BW
Tel 0151-6480623 Fax 0151 6480624

Right Rev Edwin Regan
Bishop of Wrexham, Bishop's House,
Sontley Road, Wrexham,
Clwyd LL13 7EW
Tel 01978-262726 Fax 01978-354257

Right Rev Terence Drainey
Bishop of Middlesbrough,
Bishop's House, 16 Cambridge Road,
Middlesbrough, Cleveland TS5 5NN
Tel 01642-818253 Fax 01642-850548

Right Rev John Hine
Auxiliary in Southwark, The Hermitage,
More Park, West Malling,
Kent ME19 6NH
Tel 01732-845486 Fax 01732-845888

Right Rev Crispian Hollis
Bishop of Portsmouth, Bishop's House,
Edinburgh Road, Portsmouth PO1 3HG
Tel 01705-820894 Fax 01705-863086

Right Rev Terence Brain
Bishop of Salford, Wardley Hall, Worsley,
Manchester M28 5ND
Tel 0161-7942825 Fax 0161-7278592

Right Rev Arthur Roche
Bishop of Leeds, Bishop's House,
13 North Grange Road, Headingley,
Leeds LS6 2BR
Tel 01532-304533 Fax 01532-789890

Right Rev Seamus Cunningham
Bishop of Hexham and Newcastle,
Bishop's House,
East Denton Hall, 800 West Road,
Newcastle Upon Tyne NE5 2BJ
Tel 0191-2280003 Fax 0191-2740432

Right Rev Peter Doyle
Bishop of Northampton,
Bishop's House, Marriott Street,
Northhampton NN2 6AW
Tel 01604-715635 Fax 01604-792186

Right Rev Malcolm MacMahon
Bishop of Nottingham, Bishop's House,
27 Cavendish Road East, The Park,
Nottingham NG7 1BB
Tel 01602-474786 Fax 01602-475235

Right Rev Thomas McMahon
Bishop of Brentwood, Bishop's House,
Stock, Ingatestone, Essex CM4 9BU
Tel 01277-232266 Fax 01277-214060

Right Rev Bernard Longley
Auxiliary Bishop of Westminster
Archbishop's House,
Ambrosden Avenue, London SWIP IQJ
Tel 020-7798 9033 Fax 020-7798 9077

Right Rev Alan Hopes
Auxiliary Bishop of Westminster
Archbishop's House,
Ambrosden Avenue, London SWIP IQJ
Tel 020-7798 9033 Fax 020-7798 9077

Right Rev John Rawsthorne
Bishop of Hallam, Bishop's House
75 Norfolk Road, Sheffield 52 2SZ
Tel 0114 278 7988 Fax 0114 278 7988

Right Rev Tom Burns
Bishop of Menevia,
79 Walter Road, Swansea SA1 4PS
Tel 01792-650534 Fax 01792-458641

Right Rev Kieran Conry
Bishop of Arundel and Brighton
St Joseph's Hall, Greyfriars Lane,
Storrington, Pulborough,
West Sussex RH20 4HE
Tel 01903-742172 Fax 01903-746336

Right Rev Richard Moth
Bishop of the Forces, Bishop's Oak,
26 The Crescent, Farnborough Park,
Farnborough, Hants GU14 7AS
Tel 01252-543649 Fax 01252-373748

Most Rev Peter Smith
Archbishop of Cardiff, Archbishop's
House, 42-43 Cathedral Road, Cardiff CF1
9HD, Tel 01222-20411 Fax 01222-345950

Most Rev Patrick Kelly
Archbishop of Liverpool,
Archbishop's House, Lowood,
Carnatic Road, Liverpool L18 8BY
Tel 0151-7246398 Fax 0151-7246405

Right Rev Thomas Williams
14 Hope Place, Liverpool L1 9BG
Tel 0151-7030109 Fax 0151-7030267

Rt Rev John Arnold
Auxiliary Bishop of Westminster
Archbishop's House, Ambrosden Avenue,
London SWIP IQJ
Tel 020-77989033 Fax 020-77989077

Rt Rev Paul Hendricks
Auxiliary Bishop of Southwark,
95 Carshalton Road, Sutton,
Surrey SMI 4LL
Tel 020-86438007

Rt Rev Patrick Lynch
Auxiliary Bishop of Southwark,
68 Crooms Hill, Greenwich SE10 8HG
Tel 020-82931238

Rt Rev David McGough
Auxiliary Bishop of Birmingham,
160 Draycott Road, Tean,
Stoke on Trent ST10 4JT
Tel 01538-722433 Fax 01538-722433

Rt Rev William Kenney
Auxiliary Bishop of Birmingham,
St Hugh's House, 27 Hensington Road,
Woodstock, Oxfordshire OX20 1JH
Tel/Fax 01993-812234

UKRAINIAN APOSTOLIC EXARCH

Right Rev Hlib Lonchyna
Apostolic Administrator
90 Binney Street, London W1Y 1YN
Tel 0171-6291534

RETIRED BISHOPS IN ENGLAND AND WALES

Right Rev Mervyn Alexander
Emeritus Bishop of Clifton
St Joseph's, Camp Road
Weston-Super-Mare BS23 2EN

Right Rev Frederick Hall (MHM)
former Bishop of Kisumu,
Herbert House, 41 Victoria Road,
Freshfield, Liverpool L37 1LW

Right Rev Patrick Kalilombe (WF)
former Bishop of Lilongwe,
Malawi, 31 Westholme Croft,
Birmingham B30 1TR

Right Rev Leo McCartie
Emeritus Bishop of Northampton
Aston Hall, Aston by Stone
Staffordshire ST1S OBJ

Right Rev Daniel Joseph Mullins
Emeritus Bishop of Menevia
79 Walter Road, Swansea SA1 4PS

Right Rev John Jukes (OFMConv)
Former Auxiliary in Southwark
St Margaret's, 30 Chapel Street,
Huntly, Aberdeenshire AB54 5BS

Right Rev Francis Walmsley
Bishop of the Forces, Emeritus,
St John's Convent, Linden Hill Lane,
Reading RG10 9XP

Most Rev Michael Bowen
Emeritus Archbishop of Southwark
54 Parkside, Vanbrugh Park,
London SE3 7QF

Right Rev Ambrose Griffiths
Emeritus Bishop of Hexham and
Newcastle
St Mary, Broadfield Walk
Leyland, Preston PRS IPD

Right Rev Howard Tripp
Former Auxiliary in Southwark
67 Haynt Walk, London SW20 9NY
Right Rev John Crowley
Emeritus Bishop of Middlesbrough
c/o Bishop's House, 16 Cambridge Road,
Middlesbrough TS5 5NN

Right Rev Patrick O'Donoghue
Emeritus Bishop of Lancaster,
c/o Cathedral House,
Balmoral Road, Lancaster LA1 3BT

Right Rev Philip Pargeter
Auxiliary in Birmingham, Grove House,
90 College Road, Sutton Coldfield,
West Midlands B73 5AH

Right Rev Mark Jabalé
Emeritus Bishop of Menevia,
Holy Trinity Presbytery, London Road,
Chipping Norton, Oxon OX7 5AX

THE HIERARCHY OF SCOTLAND

PROVINCE OF ST ANDREWS AND EDINBURGH

His Eminence Keith Patrick
Cardinal O'Brien
Archbishop of St Andrews and
Edinburgh, 42 Greenhill Gardens,
Edinburgh EH10 4BJ
Tel 0131-4473337
Fax 0131-4470816

Suffragans
Right Rev Peter A. Moran
Bishop of Aberdeen, Bishop's House,
3 Queen's Cross, Aberdeen AB9 2NL
Tel 01224-319154 Fax 01224-325570

Right Rev Vincent Logan
Bishop of Dunkeld, Bishop's House,
29 Roseangle, Dundee DD1 4LX
Tel 01382-225453
Fax 01382-204585

Right Rev Joseph A. Toal
Bishop of Argyll and The Isles
Bishop's House, Esplanade, Oban,
Argyll PA34 5AB
Tel 01631-571395
Fax 01631-564930

Right Rev John Cunningham
Bishop of Galloway, Candida Casa,
8 Corsehill Road, Ayr KA7 2ST
Tel 01292-266750
Fax 01292-289888

PROVINCE OF GLASGOW

Most Rev Mario Joseph Conti
Archbishop of Glasgow
40 Newlands Road, Glasgow G43 2JD
Tel 0141-2265898
Fax 0141-2252600

Suffragans
Right Rev Joseph Devine
Bishop of Motherwell,
9 Bothwell Park Road, Glasgow G71 8AQ
Tel 01698-854125 Fax 01698-850390
Right Rev Philip Tartaglia
Bishop of Paisley, Bishop's House,
107 Corsebar Road, Paisley,
Renfrewshire PA2 9PY
Tel 0141-8897200 Fax 0141-8496053

BISHOPS' CONFERENCE OF SCOTLAND

General Secretary: Rev Paul M. Conroy
General Secretariat,
64 Aitken Street, Airdrie,
Lanarkshire ML6 6LT
Tel 01236-764061 Fax 01236-762489
Email gensec@bpsconfscot.com
www.bpsconfscot.com

RETIRED BISHOPS IN SCOTLAND

Right Rev Maurice Taylor
Bishop Emeritus (Galloway Diocese)
41 Overmills Road,
Ayr KA7 3LH

Right Rev John A. Mone
Bishop Emeritus (Paisley Diocese)
Carnmore, 30 Esplande,
Greenock PA16 7RU

Right Rev Ian Murray
Bishop Emeritus (Argyll and The Isles)
St Columba's, 9 Upper Gray Street,
Edinburgh EH9 1SN

FORMS OF ECCLESIASTICAL ADDRESS

These notes should be understood as a guide to present-day practice in Ireland, rather than as 'prescriptive' rules. Forms of address – for example, whether someone is 'Very Rev', 'Right Rev', or 'Most Rev' – vary from country to country and language to language. The aim here has been to reflect Irish usage. These conventions are not static but are subject to gradual change. Some of the more involved forms of address have disappeared, and a dual standard of formality has emerged. For instance, 'Canon John Nonnullus' has in recent years tended to replace 'John Canon Nonnullus'. Where the older form is still found, the norm of normal address is given with the older form in parentheses ( ) as the more formal form of address. Since the form used is often a matter of preference of the person addressed, or the customary usage of a particular diocese or religious order, where this is known it should be followed. This directory uses what is considered to be the normal Irish form.

THE HIERARCHY

The Apostolic Nuncio
Written address: His Excellency Most Rev Dr John Nonnullus
Spoken address: same
In conversation: Your Excellency.
Reference to: 'The Nuncio said...'
('His Excellency said...')

Cardinals
Written address: His Eminence Cardinal John Nonnullus (H.E. John Cardinal Nonnullus)
Spoken address: Cardinal John Nunnullus (the more formal address is either of the written forms)
In conversation: Cardinal (Your Eminence)
Reference to: 'The Cardinal said...'
('His Eminence said...')

Note: The majority of cardinals are bishops, and they are divided into three groups, a small number known as the 'cardinal bishops', another small group who are the 'cardinal deacons', and the majority, who are called 'cardinal priests'. From this has arisen the form 'Cardinal-Archbishop of ...' or 'the cardinal-archbishop said', sometimes used in the media for emphasis. There is no category of 'cardinal-archbishops'; rather there are bishops and archbishops who are also cardinals. If one wishes to refer to a cardinal and also to draw attention to the see of which he is bishop, the following form should be used: 'Cardinal John Nunnullus, the Archbishop of Nusquam'.

Archbishops
Written address: The Most Rev John Nonnullus
Spoken address: Archbishop Nonnullus (His Grace the Archbishop of Nusquam)
In conversation: Your Grace
Reference to: 'The Archbishop said...'
('His Grace said...')

Bishops
Written address: The Most Rev John Nonnullus
Spoken address: Dr John Nonnullus, Bishop of Nusquam (His Lordship Dr...)
In conversation: Doctor (My Lord)
Reference to: 'The Bishop said...'

Note: The practice of using the word 'Bishop' in spoken address (e.g. Bishop John Nonnullus of Nusquam) and in conversation (e.g. 'Bishop, I am pleased to meet you') is becoming increasingly common.

CLERGY

Secular:
Monsignor
Written: Right Rev Mgr
Spoken: Monsignor

Capitular Dignitaries:
Archdeacon
Written: The Venerable John Nonnullus, Archdeacon of Nusquam
Spoken: Archdeacon

Dean
Written: The Very Rev Dean Nonnullus
Spoken: Dean

Canon
Written: The Very Rev Canon John Nonnullus (John Canon Nonnullus)
Spoken: Canon

Others
Those holding other capitular offices (e.g. precentor) are addressed as canons.

Parish Priest
Written: The Very Rev John Nonnullus PP
Spoken: Father

Curates
Written: The Very Rev John Nonnullus CC
Spoken: Father

Other Priests
Secular priests not included above:
Written: Rev John Nonnullus
Spoken: Father
Priests using academic titles are referred to by these titles, and in writing these are prefixed by 'Rev', e.g. Rev Prof John Nonnullus

Deacons
Written: Rev John Nonnullus
Spoken: Mister (Rev Mister)

Regular
The conventional protocol varies with religious orders, many of whom preserve forms of address peculiar to themselves. A general rule is that priests are addressed as found under Other priests above, and superiors (of houses or provinces) are addressed in writing as 'The Very Rev'.

Abbots
Written: 'The Right Rev' is placed before the conventional form of address of a member of that community.

NON-CLERICAL RELIGIOUS

Men
Non-clerical religious orders of men and non-clerical members of clerical religious orders are referred to as 'Br John Nonnullus' on writing, and `Brother' in speech.

Note 1. The use of Christian name or surname (e.g. 'Br John' or 'Br Nonnullus') depends on the usage of the order.

Note 2. Some orders have traditional ways of referring to their non-clerical members other than 'Brother'.

Women
Members of religious orders of women are referred to as 'Sr' in writing and 'Sister' in speech, irrespective of the position they hold in their institute.
Note 1. The form 'Reverend Mother' is obsolete and its use does not arise.
Note 2. The use of Christian name, name in religion, or surname, or the prefixing of the forename with 'M' (Mary) depends on the usage of the order.
Note 3. Some orders, in particular monastic and enclosed orders, use titles derived from their own traditions (e.g. abbess and prioress). There is no consistent usage with regard to these titles (e.g. it may be `Mother Abbess' or 'Sr Mary, the Abbess') and the usage depends on the order or the house.

THE ROMAN PONTIFFS

Information includes the name of the Pope, in many cases his name before becoming Pope, his birth-place or country of origin, the date of accession to the Papacy, and the date of the end of reign which, in all but a few cases, was the date of death. Double dates record the day of election and coronation.
Source: *Annuario Pontificio*

St Peter (Simon Bar-Jona) of Bethsaida, in Galilee, Prince of the Apostles, who received from Jesus Christ supreme pontifical power to be transmitted to his successors, resided first at Antioch, then at Rome, where he was martyred in the year 64 or 67, having governed the Church from that city for twenty-five years.
St Linus, Tuscany, 67-76
St Anacletus (Cletus), Rome 76-88
St Clement, Rome 88-97
St Evaristus, Greece, 97-105
St Alexander I, Rome, 105-25
St Sixtus I, Rome, 115-25
St Telesphorus, Greece, 125-36
St Hyginus, Greece, 136-40
St Pius I, Aquilea, 140-55
St Anictus, Syria, 155-66
St Soter, Campania, 166-75
St Eleutheius, Nicopolis in Epirus, 175-89

Up to the time of St Eleutherius, the years indicated for the beginning and end of pontificates are not certain. Also, up to the middle of the eleventh century, there are some doubts about the exact days and months given in chronological tables.

St Victor I, Africa, 189-99
St Zephyrinus, Rome, 199-217
St Callistus I, Rome, 217-22
St Urban I, Rome, 222-30
St Pontian, Rome, 21 July 230 to 28 Sept 235
St Anterus, Greece, 21 Nov 235 to 3 Jan 236
St Fabian, Rome, 10 Jan 236 to 20 Jan 250
St Cornelius, Rome, Mar 251 to June 253
St Lucius I, Rome, 12 May 254 to 2 Aug 254
St Stephen I, Rome, 12 May 254 to 2 Aug 257
St Sixtus II, Greece, 30 Aug 257 to 6 Aug 258
St Dionysius, birthplace unknown, 22 July 259 to 26 Dec 268
St Felix I, Rome, 5 Jan 269 to 30 Dec 274
St Eutychian, Luni, 4 Jan 275 to 7 Dec 283
St Caius, Dalmatia, 17 Dec 283 to 22 Apr 296
St Marcellinus, Rome, 30 June 296 to 25 Oct 304
St Marcellus I, Rome, 27 May 308 or 26 June 308 to 16 Jan 309
St Eusebius, Greece, 18 Apr 309 or 310 to 17 Aug 309 or 310
St Melchiades (Miltiades), Africa, 2 July 311 to 11 Jan 314
St Sylvester I, Rome, 31 Jan 314 to 31 Dec 335

Most of the popes before St Sylvester I were martyrs.

St Marcus, Rome, 18 Jan 336 to 7 Oct 336
St Julius I, Rome, 6 Feb 337 to 12 Apr 352
Liberius, Rome, 17 May 352 to 24 Sept 366
St Damasus I, Spain, 1 Oct 366 to 11 Dec 384
St Siricius, Rome, 15 or 22 or 29 Dec 384 to 26 Nov 399
St Anastasius I, Rome, 27 Nov 399 to 19 Dec 401
St Innocent I, Albano, 22 Dec 401 to 12 Mar 417
St Zozimus, Greece, 18 Mar 417 to 26 Dec 418
St Boniface I, Rome, 28 or 29 Dec 418 to 4 Sept 422
St Celestine I, Campania, 10 Sept 422 to 27 July 432
St Sixtus III, Rome, 31 July 432 to 19 Aug 440
St Leo I (the Grant), Tuscany, 29 Sept 440 to 10 Nov 461
St Hilary, Sardinia, 19 Nov 461 to 29 Feb 468
St Simplicius, Tivoli, 3 Mar 468 to 10 Mar 483
St Felix III (II), Rome, 13 Mar 483 to 1 Mar 492

He should be called Felix II, and his successors of the same name should be numbered accordingly. The discrepancy in the numerical designation of popes named Felix was caused by the erroneous insertion in some lists of the name of St Felix of Rome, a martyr.

St Gelasius I, Africa, 1 Mar 492 to 21 Nov 496
Anastasius II, Rome, 24 Nov 496 to 19 Nov 498
St Symmachus, Sardinia, 22 Nov 498 to 19 July 514
St Hormisdas, Frosinone, 20 July 514 to 6 Aug 523
St John I, Martyr, Tuscany, 13 Aug 523 to 18 May 526
St Felix IV (III), Samnium, 12 July 526 to 22 Sept 530
Boniface II, Rome, 22 Sept 530 to 17 Oct 532
John II, Rome, 2 Jan 533 to 8 May 535

John II was the first pope to change his name. His given name was Mercury.

St Agapitus I, Rome, 13 May 535 to 22 Apr 536
St Silverius, Martyr, Campania, 1 or 8 June 536 to 11 Nov 537 (d. 2 Dec 537)

St Silverius was violently deposed in March 537 and abdicated on 11 Nov 537. His successor, Vigilius, was not recognised as pope by all the Roman clergy until his abdication.

Vigilius, Rome, 29 Mar 537 to 7 June 555

Pelagius I, Rome, 16 Apr 556 to 4 Mar 561
John III, Rome, 17 July 561 to 13 July 574
Benedict I, Rome, 2 June 575 to 30 July 579
Pelagius II, Rome, 26 Nov 579 to 7 Feb 590
St Gregory I (the Great), Rome, 3 Sept 590 to 12 Mar 604
Sabinian, Blera in Tuscany, 13 Sept 604 to 22 Feb 606
Bonifcace III, Rome, 19 Feb 607 to 12 Nov 607
St Boniface IV, Abruzzi, 25 Aug 608 to 8 May 615
St Deusdedit (Adeodatus I), Rome, 19 Oct 615 to 8 Nov 618
Boniface V, Naples, 23 Dec 619 to 25 Oct 625
Honorius I, Campania, 27 Oct 625 to 12 Oct 638
Severinus, Rome, 28 May 640 to 2 Aug 640
John IV, Dalmatia, 24 Dec 640 to 12 Oct 642
Theodore I, Greece, 24 Nov 642 to 14 May 649
St Martin I, Martyr, Todi, July 649 to 16 Sept 655 (in exile from 17 June 653)
St Eugene I, Rome, 10 Aug 654 to 2 June 657

St Eugene I was elected during the exile of St Martin I, who is believed to have endorsed him as pope.

St Vitalian, Segni, 30 July 657 to 27 Jan 672
Adeodatus II, Rome, 11 Apr 672 to 17 June 676
Donus, Rome, 2 Nov 676 to 11 Apr 678
St Agatho, Sicily, 27 June 678 to 10 Jan 681
St Leo II, Sicily, 17 Aug 682 to 3 July 683
St Benedict II, Rome, 26 June 684 to 8 May 685
John V, Syria, 23 July 685 to 2 Aug 686
Conon, birthplace unkown, 21 Oct 686 to 21 Sept 687
St Sergius I, Syria, 15 Dec 687 to 8 Sept 701
John VI, Greece, 30 Oct 701 to 11 Jan 705
John VII, Greece, 1 Mar 705 to 18 Oct 707
Sisinnius, Syria, 15 Jan 708 to 4 Feb 708
Constantine, Syria, 25 Mar 708 to 9 Apr 715
St Gregory II, Rome, 19 May 715 to 11 Feb 731
St Gregory II, Syria, 18 May 731 to Nov 741
St Zachary, Greece, 10 Dec 741 to 22 Mar 752

Stephen II (III), Rome, 26 Mar 752 to 26 Apr 757

After the death of St Zachary, a Roman priest named Stephen was elected but died (four days later) before his consecration as Bishop of Rome, which would have marked the beginning of his pontificate. Another Stephen was elected to succeed Zachary as Stephen II. (The first pope with this name was St Stephen 254-7). The ordinal III appears in parentheses after the name of Stephen II because the name of the earlier elected but deceased priest was included in some lists. Other Stephens have double numbers.

St Paul I, Rome, Apr (29 May) 757 to 28 June 767
Stephen III (IV), Sicily, 1 (7) Aug 768 to 24 Jan 772
Adrian I, Rome, 1 (9) Feb 772 to 25 Dec 795
St Leo III, Rome, 26 (27) Dec 795 to 12 June 816
Stephen IV (V), Rome, 22 June 816 to 24 Jan 817
St Paschal I, Rome, 25 Jan 817 to 11 Feb 824
Eugene II, Rome, Feb (May) 824 to Aug 827
Valentine, Rome, Aug 827 to Sept 827
Gregory IV, Rome, 827 to Jan 844
Sergius II, Rome, Jan 844 to 27 Jan 847
St Leo IV, Rome, Jan (10 Apr) 847 to 17 Jan 855
Benedict III, Rome, July (29 Sept) 855 to 17 Apr 858
St Nicholas I (the Great), Rome, 24 Apr 858 to 13 Nov 867
Adrian II, Rome, 14 Dec 867 to 14 Dec 872
John VIII, Rome, 14 Dec 872 to 16 Dec 882
Marinus I, Gallese, 16 Dec 882 to 15 May 884
St Adrian III, Rome, 17 May 884 to Sept 885
Stephen V (VI), Rome, Sept 885 to 14 Sept 891
Formosus, Portus, 6 Oct 891 to 4 Apr 896
Boniface VI, Rome, Apr 896 to Apr 896
Stephen VI (VII), Rome, May 896 to Aug 897
Romanus, Gallese, Aug 897 to Nov 897
Theodore II, Rome, Dec 897 to Dec 897
John IX, Tivoli, Jan 898 to Jan 900
Benedict IV, Rome, Jan (Feb) 900 to July 903
Leo V, Ardea, July 903 to Sept 903
Sergius III, Rome, 29 Jan 904 to 14 Apr 911
Anastasius III, Rome, Apr 911 to June 913
Landus, Sabina, July 913 to Feb 914
John X, Tossignano (Imola), Mar 914 to May 928
Leo VI, Rome, May 928 to Dec 928
Stephen VII (VIII), Rome, Dec 928 to Feb 931
John XI, Rome, Feb (Mar) 931 to Dec 935
Leo VII, Rome, 3 Jan 936 to 13 July 939
Stephen VIII (IX), Rome, 14 July 939 to Oct 942

Marinus II, Rome, 30 Oct 942 to May 946
Agapitus II, Rome, 10 May 946 to Dec 955
John XII (Octavius), Tusculum, 16 Dec 955 to 14 May 964 (date of his death)
Leo VIII, Rome, 4 (6) Dec 963 to 1 Mar 965
Benedict V, Rome, 22 May 964 to 4 July 966

Confusion exists concerning the legitamcy of claims to the pontificate by Leo VII and Benedict V. John XII was deposed on 4 Dec 963 by a Roman council. If this deposition was invalid, Leo was an antipope. If the deposition of John was valid, Leo was the legitimate pope and Benedict was an antipope.

John XIII, Rome, 1 Oct 965 to 6 Sept 972
Benedict VI, Rome, 19 Jan 973 to June 974
Benedict VIII, Rome, Oct 974 to 10 July 983
John XIV (Peter Campenora), Pavia, Dec 983 to 20 Aug 984
John XV, Rome, Aug 985 to Mar 996
Gregory V (Bruno of Carinthia), Saxony, 3 May 996 to 18 Feb 999
Sylvester II (Gerbert), Auvergne, 2 Apr 999 to 12 May 1003
John XVII (Siccone), Rome, June 1003 to Dec 1003
John XVIII (Phasianus), Rome, Jan 1004 to July 1009
Sergius IV (Peter), Rome, 31 July 1009 to 12 May 1012

The custom of changing one's name on election to the papacy is generally considered to date from the time of Sergius IV. Before his time, several popes had changed their names. After his time, this became a regular practice, with few exceptions, e.g. Adrian VI and Marcellus II.

Benedict VIII (Theophylactus), Tusculum, 18 May 1012 to 9 Apr 1024
John XIX (Rosmanus), Tusculum, Apr (May) 1024 to 1032
Benedict IX (Theophylactus), Tusculum, 1032-44
Sylvester III (John), Rome, 20 Jan 1045 to 10 Feb 1045

Sylvester III was an antipope if the forcible removal of Benedict IX in 1044 was not legitimate.

Benedict IX (second time), 10 Apr 1045 to 1 May 1045
Gregory VI (John Gratian), Rome, 5 May 1045 to 20 Dec 1046
Clement II (Suitger, Lord of Morsleben and Homburg), Saxony, 24 (25) Dec 1046 to 9 Oct 1047

If the resignation of Benedict IX in 1045 and his removal at the December 1046 synod were not legitimate, Gregory VI and Clement II were antipopes.

Benedict IX (third time), 8 Nov 1047 to 17 July 1028 (d. c.1055)
Damasus II (Poppo), Bavaria, 17 July 1028 to 9 Aug 1028

St Leo IX (Bruno), Alsace 12 Feb 1049 to 19 Apr 1054
Victor II (Gebhard), Swabia, 16 Apr 1055 to 28 July 1057
Stephen IX (X) (Frederick), Lorraine, 3 Aug 1057 to 29 Mar 1058
Nicholas II (Gerard), Burgundy, 24 Jan 1059 to 27 July 1061
Alexander II (Anselmo da Baggio), Milan, 1 Oct 1061 to 21 Apr 1073
St Gregory VII (Hildebrand), Tuscany, 22 Apr (30 June) 1073 to 25 May 1085
Bl Victor III (Dauferius; Desiderius), Benevento, 24 May 1086 to 15 Sept 1087
Bl Urban II (Otto di Lagery), France, 12 Mar 1088 to 29 July 1099
Paschall II (Raniero), Ravenna, 13 (14) Aug 1099 to 21 Jan 1118
Gelasius II (Giovanni Caetani), Gaeta, 24 Jan (10 Mar) 1118 to 28 Jan 1119
Callistus II (Guido of Burgundy), Burgundy, 2 (9) Feb 1119 to 13 Dec 1124
Honorius II (Lamberto), Fiagnano (Imola), 15 (21) Dec 1124 to 13 Feb 1130
Innocent II (Gregorio Paperschi), Rome, 14 (23) Feb 1130 to 24 Sept 1143
Celestine II (Guido), Città di Castello, 26 Sept (3 Oct) 1143 to 8 Mar 1144
Lucius II (Gerardo Caccianemici), Bologna, 12 Mar 1144 to 15 Feb 1145
Bl Eugene III (Bernardo Paganelli di Montemagno), Pisa, 15 (18) Feb 1145 to 8 July 1153
Anastasius IV (Corrado), Rome, 12 July 1153 to 3 Dec 1154
Adrian IV (Nicholas Breakspear), England, 4 (5) Dec 1154 to 1 Sept 1159
Alexander III (Rolando Bandinelli), Siena, 7 (20) Sept 1159 to 30 Aug 1181
Lucius III (Ubaldo Allucingoli), Lucca, 1 (6) Sept 1181 to 25 Sept 1185
Urban III (Uberto Crivelli), Millan, 25 Nov (1 Dec) 1185 to 20 Oct 1187
Gregory VIII (Alberto de Morra), Benevento, 21 (25) Oct 1187 to 17 Dec 1187
Clement III (Paolo Scolari), Rome, 19 (20) Dec 1187 to Mar 1191
Celestine III (Giacinto Bobone), Rome, 30 Mar (14 Apr) 1191 to 8 Jan 1198
Innocent III (Lotario dei Conti di Segni), Anagni, 8 Jan (22 Feb) 1198 to 16 July 1216
Honorius III (Cencio Savelli), Rome, 18 (24) July 1216 to 18 Mar 1227
Gregory IX (Ugolino, Count of Segni), Anagni, 19 (21) Mar 1227 to 22 Aug 1241
Celestine IV (Goffredo Castiglioni), Milan, 25 (28) Oct 1241 to 10 Nov 1241
Innocent IV (Sinibaldo Fieschi), Genoa, 25 (28) June 1243 to 7 Dec 1254
Alexander IV (Rinaldo, Count of Segni) Anagni, 12 (20) Dec 1254 to 25 May 1261
Urban IV (Jacques Pantaléon), Troyes, 29 Aug (4 Sept) 1261 to 2 Oct 1264
Clement IV (Guy Foulques or Guido le Gros), France, 5 (15) Feb 1265 to 29 Nov 1268
Bl Gregory X (Teobaldo Visconti), Piacenza, 1 Sept 1271 (27 Mar 1272) to 10 Jan 1276
Bl Innocent V (Peter of Tarentaise), Savoy, 21 Jan (22 Feb) 1276 to 22 June 1276
Adrian V (Ottobono Fieschi), Genoa, 11 July 1276 to 18 Aug 1276

John XXI (Petrus Juliani or Petrus Hispanus), Portugal, 8 (20) Sept 1276 to 20 May 1277

Elimination was made of the name of John XX in an effort to rectify the numerical designation of popes named John. The error dates back to the time of John XV.

Nicholas III (Giovanni Gaetano Orsini), Rome, 25 Nov (26 Dec) 1277 to 22 Aug 1280
Martin IV (Simon de Brie), France, 22 Feb (23 Mar) 1281 to 28 Mar 1285

The names of Marinus I (882-4) and Marinus II (942-6) were construed as Martin. In view of these two pontificates and the earlier reign of St Martin I (649-55), this pope was called Martin IV.

Honorius IV (Giacomo Savelli), Rome, 2 Apr (20 May) 1285 to 3 Apr 1287
Nicholas IV (Girolamo Masci), Ascoli, 22 Feb 1288 to 4 Apr 1292
St Celestine V (Pietro del Murrone), Isernia, 5 July (29 Aug) 1294 to 13 Dec 1294; d. 1296. Canonised 5 May 1313
Boniface VIII (Benedetto Caetani), Anagni, 24 Dec 1294 (23 Jan 1295) to 11 Oct 1303
Bl Benedict XI (Niccolo Boccasini), Treviso, 22 (27) Oct 1303 to 7 July 1304
Clement V (Bertrand de Got), France, 5 June (14 Nov) 1305 to 20 Apr 1314 (first of Avignon popes)

From 1309 to 1377 Avignon was the residence of a series of French popes during a period of power struggles between the rulers of France, Bavaria and England and the Church. Despite some positive achievments it was the prologue to the Western Schism which began in 1378.

John XXII (Jacques d'Euse), Cahors, 7 Aug (5 Sept) 1316 to 4 Dec 1334
Benedict XII (Jacques Fournier), France, 20 Dec 1334 (8 Jan 1335) to 25 Apr 1342
Clement VI (Pierre Roger), France, 7 (19) May 1342 to 6 Dec 1352
Innocent VI (Etienne Aubert), France, 18 (30) Dec 1352 to 12 Sept 1362
Bl Urban V (Guillaume de Grimoard), France, 28 Sept (6 Nov) 1362 to 19 Dec 1370
Gregory XI (Pierre Roger de Beaufort), France, 30 Dec 1370 (5 Jan 1371) to 26 Mar 1378 (last of Avignon popes)
Urban VI (Bartolomeo Prignano), Naples, 8 (18) Apr 1378 to 15 Oct 1389
Boniface IX (Pietro Tomacelli), Naples, 2 (9) Nov 1389 to 1 Oct 1404
Innocent VII (Cosma Migliorati), Sulmona, 17 Oct (11 Nov) 1404 to 6 Nov 1406
Gregory XII (Angelo Correr), Venice, 30 Nov (19 Dec)1406 to 4 July 1415 when he voluntarily resigned from the papacy to permit the election of his successor.

This brought to an end in the Council of Constance the Western Schism which had divided Christendom into two and then three papal obediences from 1370 to 1417. Gregory XII died on 18 Oct 1417.

Martin V (Oddone Colonna), Rome, 11 (21) Nov 1417 to 20 Feb 1431
Eugene IV (Gabriel Condulmer), Venice, 3 (11) Mar 1431 to 23 Feb 1447
Nicholas V (Tommaso Parentucelli), Sarzana, 6 (19) Mar 1447 to 24 Mar 1455
Callistus III (Alfonso Borgia), Jativa (Valencia), 8 (20) Apr 1455 to 6 Aug 1458
Pius II (Enea Silvio Piccolomini), Siena, 19 Aug (3 Sept) 1458 to 14 Aug 1464
Paul II (Pietro Barbo), Venice, 30 Aug (16 Sept) 1464 to 26 July 1471
Sixtus IV (Francesco della Rovere), Savona, 9 (25) Aug 1471 to 12 Aug 1484
Innocent VIII (Giovanni Battista Cibo), Genoa, 29 Aug (12 Sept) 1484 to 25 July 1492
Alexander VI (Rodrigo Borgia), Jativa (Valencia), 11 (26) Aug 1492 to 18 Aug 1503
Pius III (Francesco Todeschini-Piccolomini), Siena, 22 Sept (1, 8 Oct) 1503 to 18 Oct 1503
Julius II (Guiliano della Rovere), Savona, 31 Oct (26 Nov) 1503 to 21 Feb 1513
Leo X (Giovanni de' Medici), Florence, 9 (19) Mar 1513 to 1 Dec 1521
Adrian VI (Adrian Florensz), Utrecht, 9 Jan (31 Aug) 1522 to 14 Sept 1523
Clement VII (Giulio de' Medici), Florence, 19 (26) Nov 1523 to 25 Sept 1534
Paul III (Alessandro Farnese), Rome, 13 Oct (3 Nov) 1534 to 10 Nov 1549
Julius III (Giovanni Maria Ciocchi del Monte), Rome, 7 (22) Feb 1550 to 23 Mar 1555
Marcellus II (Marcello Cervini), Montepulciano, 9 (10) Apr 1555 to 1 May 1555
Paul IV (Gian Pietro Carafa), Naples, 23 (26) May 1555 to 18 Aug 1559
Pius IV (Giovan Angelo de' Medici), Milan, 25 Dec 1559 (6 Jan 1560) to 9 Dec 1565
St Pius V (Antonio-Michele Ghislieri), Bosco (Alexandria), 7 (17) Jan 1566 to 1 May 1572. Canonised 22 May 1712
Gregory XIII (Ugo Buoncompagni), Bologna, 13 (25) May 1572 to 10 Apr 1585
Sixtus V (Felice Peretti), Grottammare (Ripatransone), 24 Apr (1 May) 1585 to 27 Aug 1590
Urban VII (Giovanni Battista Castagna), Rome, 15 Sept 1590 to 27 Sept 1590
Gregoryy XIV (Niccolo Sfondrati), Cremona, 5 (8) Dec 1590 to 16 Oct 1591
Innocent IX (Giovanni Antonio Facchinetti), Bologna, 19 Oct (3 Nov) 1591 to 30 Dec 1591
Clement VIII (Ippolito Aldobrandini), Florence, 30 Jan (9 Feb) 1592 to 3 Mar 1605
Leo XI (Alessandro de' Medici), Florence, 1 (10) Apr 1605 to 27 Apr 1605
Paul V (Camillo Borghese), Rome, 16 (29) May 1605 to 28 Jan 1621
Gregory XV (Alessandro Ludovisi), Bologna, 9 (14) Feb 1621 to 8 July 1623
Urban VIII (Maffeo Barberini), Florence, 6 Aug (29 Sept) 1623 to 29 July 1644

Innocent X (Giovanni Battista Pamfili), Rome, 15 Sept (4 Oct) 1644 to 7 Jan 1655
Alexander VII (Fabio Chigi), Siena, 7 (18) Apr 1655 to 22 May 1667
Clement IX (Giulio Rospigliosi), Pistoia, 20 (26) June 1667 to 9 Dec 1669
Clement X (Emilio Altieri), Rome, 29 Apr (11 May) 1670 to 22 July 1676
Bl Innocent XI (Benedetto Odescalchi), Como, 21 Sept (4 Oct) 1676 to 12 Aug 1689. Beatified 7 Oct 1956
Alexander VIII (Pietro Ottoboni), Venice, 6 (16) Oct 1689 to 1 Feb 1691
Innocent XII (Antonio Pignatelli), Spinazzola, 12 (15) July 1691 to 27 Sept 1700
Clement XI (Giovanni Francesco Albani), Urbino, 23, 30 Nov (8 Dec) 1700 to 19 Mar 1721
Innocent XIII (Michelangelo dei Conti), Rome, 8 (18) May 1721 to 7 Mar 1724
Benedict XIII (Pietro Francesco [in religion Vincenzo Maria] Orsini), Gravina (Bari), 29 May (4 June) 1724 to 21 Feb 1730
Clement XII (Lorenzo Corsini), Florence, 12 (16) July 1730 to 6 Feb 1740
Benedict XIV (Prospero Lambertini), Bologna, 17 (22) Aug 1740 to 3 May 1758
Clement XIII (Carlo Rezzonico), Venice, 6 (16) July 1758 to 2 Feb 1769
Clement XIV (Giovanni Vincenzo Antonio [in religion Lorenzo] Gaganelli), Rimini, 19, 28 May (4 June) 1769 to 22 Sept 1774
Pius VI (Giovanni Angelo Braschi), Cesena, 15 (22 Feb) 1775 to 29 Aug 1799
Pius VII (Barnabà [in religion Gregirio] Chiaramonti, Cesena, 14 (21) Mar 1800 to 20 Aug 1823
Leo XII (Annibale della Genga), Genga (Fabriano), 28 Sept (5 Oct) 1823 to 10 Feb 1829
Pius VIII (Francesco Saverio Castiglioni), Cingoli, 31 Mar (5 Apr) 1829 to 30 Nov 1830
Gregory XVI (Bartolomeo Alberto [in relgion Mauro] Cappellari), Belluno, 2 (6) Feb 1831 to 1 June 1846
Pius IX (Giovanni M. Mastai-Ferretti), Senigallia, 16 (21) June 1846 to Feb 1878
Leo XIII (Gioacchino Pecci), Carpineto (Anagni), 20 Feb (3 Mar) 1878 to 20 July 1903
St Pius X (Giuseppe Sarto), Riese (Treviso), 4 (9) Aug 1903 to 20 Aug 1914. Canonised 29 May 1954
Benedict XV (Giacomo della Chiesa), Genoa, 3 (6) Sept 1914 to 22 Jan 1922
Pius XI (Achille Ratti), Desio (Milan), 6 (12) Feb 1922 to 10 Feb 1939
Pius XII (Eugenio Pacelli), Rome, 2 (12) Mar 1939 to 9 Oct 1958
John XXIII (Angelo Giuseppe Roncalli), Sotto il Monte (Bergamo), 28 Oct (4 Nov) 1958 to 3 June 1963
Paul VI (Giovanni Battista Montini), Concessio (Brescia, 21 (30) June 1963 to 6 Aug 1978
John Paul I (Albino Luciani), Forno di Canale (Belluno), 26 Aug (3 Sept) 1978 to 28 Sept 1978
John Paul II (Karol Wojtyla), Wadowice, Poland, 16 (22) Oct 1978 to 2 April 2005
Benedict XVI (Joseph Ratzinger), Germany, April 2005A

Winner 'Irish Printer of the Year Award 2008'

Specialising in promotional literature and marketing material
Fully automated Heidelberg CTP system
State of the art Heidelberg printing presses
Operating 24 hours a day, 5 days a week
High quality and competitive prices

HUDSON KILLEEN

Over 25 years of excellence

Unit B14 Ballycoolin Business Park Blanchardstown Dublin 15
T. +353 1 829 3450 F. +353 1 829 3451 E. print@hudsonkilleen.ie W. www.hudsonkilleen.ie

ROBERT J. KIDNEY & CO.
CHARTERED ACCOUNTANTS

We provide an expert audit, accounting and tax service
to many religious organisations.

Call
Christopher Kidney

11 Adelaide Road
Dublin 2
Tel (01) 476 0410 • Fax (01) 478 0555
Email christopher@rjkidney.com

EMMAUS

Welcome to Tranquillity

Emmaus retreat & Conference Centre, Ennis Lane, Lissenhall, Swords, Co Dublin
Telephone (01) 8700050 • Fax (01) 8408248 • Email emmauscentre@emmauscentre.ie

The Emmaus Centre provides an excellent location
for both Adult & School Retreat Programmes.

Emmaus hosts a comprehensive range of Seminars,
Workshops, Chapters and Parish Renewal days. We also offer a quality,
relaxed and peaceful setting for Jubilee and Private Celebrations.

Our facilities include 62 en-suite guest rooms, 13 meeting rooms,
Private chapel, 2 prayer rooms, private dining rooms and extensive grounds for quiet reflection,
and all Located close to the M1 & Dublin International Airport.

For up to date information on all our Retreats/Seminars call us on 01-870005
Or log onto our website for a complete listing of seminars on www.emmauscentre.ie
Email emmauscentre@emmauscentre.ie

THE NATIONAL BIBLE SOCIETY
OF IRELAND
And Bestseller Bookshop

The widest possible effective distribution of the Holy Scriptures

'Bestseller', the Society's bookshop, will meet all your needs for religious books and special orders
with discounts for members. Mail Order welcome. All major credit cards accepted.

Special grants available for Scripture Resources for parish initiatives. Training courses are also
available. Individuals and parishes may support the work by becoming members of the Society.

BRIATHAR DÉ NOCHTAITHE DO CHÁCH
GOD'S WORD OPEN FOR ALL

Contact: Ms Judith Wilkinson, Chief Executive
41 Dawson Street, Dublin 2
Tel (01) 677 3272 Fax (01) 671 0040
Email nbsi@natbibsoc.iol.ie
Website www.biblesociety.ie
Charity No. CHY1592

Serving All Irish Churches with the Holy Scriptures
Under the patronage of Most Rev Diarmuid Martin, Archbishop of Dublin, and other Church leaders.

Creating a gateway to hope with your support

**"All the believers were one in heart and mind.
No one claimed that any of their possessions was their own, but they shared everything they had."**

(Acts of the Apostles 4: 32)

Photo: A young boy from Ethiopia

Today, almost half of the world's population live in extreme poverty, often with little or no access to resources such as land to grow food, clean water, credit or advice. However, your support through Trócaire, delivered to thousands of men, women and children in the developing world, is creating a vital gateway to hope and bringing positive and lasting change for the better.

Trócaire is deeply grateful for the support we receive every year from parishes and religious communities throughout the country. Together, as Church, we are working for and towards a just world.

TRÓCAIRE
Working for a Just World

MAYNOOTH, Co. Kildare
Tel: (01) 6293333

12 CATHEDRAL STREET, Dublin 1
Tel: (01) 874 3875

9 COOK STREET, Cork
Tel: (021) 4275622

50 KING STREET, Belfast, BT1 6AD
Tel: (028) 90808030

www.trocaire.org

In giving, we receive!

In recent years the world experienced some of its greatest disasters, starting with the Tsunami; Hurricanes in USA and Central America, Earthquakes in Pakistan and Peru; conflicts in Congo, Darfur, Iraq; famine in Niger. As is always the case, the poor and the weak suffer the most!

Throughout these affected areas the Church, through its priests and religious are forever present – they are the pastors, medics, social workers, teachers and leaders all rolled into one – bringing the light of Christ to all.

Aid to the Church in Need is dedicated to providing a lifeline to these heroes of the Church.

You can help them

You can express your love of God for all the blessings received in your life by sharing in the suffering of these unfortunate Christians through your support for Aid to the Church in Need. A legacy or a donation can make it possible to respond to so many cries for help.

Reflection

All the goods you have collected in your life, you will lose them when you die, but all the goods you have given to whoever in need, you will find them again in the hands of the Lord.

See our website for more information

www.acnirl.org

 Aid to the Church in Need

"St.Joseph's", 151 St. Mobhi Road, Dublin 9

TEL 01 837 7516   **EMAIL** churchinneed@eircom.net

Aid to the Church in Need is approved as an 'Elligible Charity' under section 45, Finance Act 2001 and qualifies for Tax Relief.

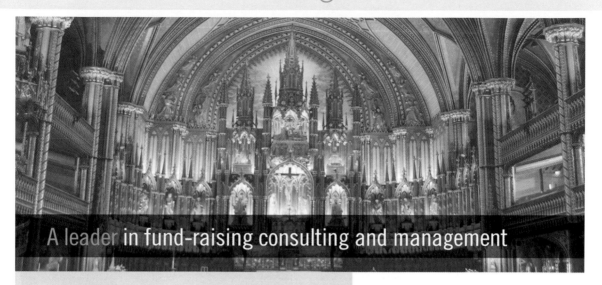

A leader in fund-raising consulting and management

A selection of current and recent clients

American Cathedral in Paris
American Church in Paris
Archdiocese of Armagh
Archdiocese of Glasgow
Archdiocese of Westminster (Harrow Deanery)
Christian Aid
Clongowes Wood College SJ
Daniel O'Connell Memorial Church of the Holy Cross
Diocese of Achonry
Diocese of Down & Connor
Diocese of Leeds
Diocese of Northampton
Diocese of Portsmouth
Habitat for Humanity
International Crisis Group
Lions Clubs International
Royal College of Physicians of Ireland
Royal College of Surgeons in Ireland
Trócaire
University of Liverpool
University of Manchester
Women for Women International

Community Counselling Service (CCS) is the most widely recommended fund-raising firm to faith-based and other institutions worldwide.

Established in 1947, CCS provides fund-raising counsel, development services, and strategic consulting to arch/dioceses, parishes, secondary schools, colleges and universities, hospitals, and religious communities.

CCS
Fund Raising · Development Services · Strategic Consulting

To learn more about CCS, contact

Derval Costello
Vice President
c/o Mazars
Harcourt Centre, Block 3
Harcourt Road
Dublin 2 Ireland
01.676.0041
ccsireland@ccsfundraising.com
www.ccsfundraising.com

Helping extraordinary people champion inspirational causes

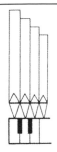

Paul Neiland & Associates
Organ Builders and Restorers
Newtown, Killinick, Wexford, Ireland
Tel ++ (053) 915 8622 • Fax ++ (053) 915 8574
www.neilandorgans.com

We have been responsible for the restoration of some very fine pipe organs throughout Ireland from Wexford in the South East, to Portsalon, Co Donegal and Schull in West Cork. We have recently completed the restoration of the 1809 Hugh Russell organ at St John the Baptist Church, Kinsale and the 1870s Forster & Andrews organ at Christ Church, Gorey. Following 20 years trading our business goes from strength to strength.

St John the Baptist Church, Kinsale

St Fachna's Cathedral, Roscarberry, Co Cork

Carmelite Convent, Tallow, Co Waterford

St Patrick's Church, Newport, Co Mayo

ST KIERAN'S COLLEGE KILKENNY
(founded 1782)

St Kieran's is a Catholic Diocesan College under the patronage of the Bishop of Ossory

It has two objectives:

To provide a well-rounded education at second level and to further ongoing formation and education for mature students.

The College has three departments on one campus:

1. A **secondary day school** which offers a complete programme at second level to 660 pupils, with a wide range of sporting and extracurricular activities.

2. A service for adults which offers courses designed to promote the ongoing formation and education of people in the diocese and region.

3. **The National University of Ireland, Maynooth** which offers an off campus degree course (BA in Local and Community Studies) and a range of other initiatives for mature students.

For further information apply to
The President, St Kieran's College, Kilkenny
Telephone: 056-7721086 • Fax: 056-7770001
Email skc1782@iol.ie

CHURCH GOODS

CHURCH VESTMENTS • TABERNACLES

CHALICES • MASS KITS • ALTAR LINENS

UNIQUE RELIGIOUS ART PIECES FOR HOMES

BANNERS MADE TO ORDER

STATUES AND CRIBS

Liturgical Centre

pddm

8 Castle Street, Athlone
Tel (090) 6492278 • Fax (090) 6492649

Newtownpark Avenue, Stillorgan, Dublin
Tel (01) 288 6414 • Fax (01) 283 6935

Email pddmdublin@eircom.net
Website www.pddm.org/ireland

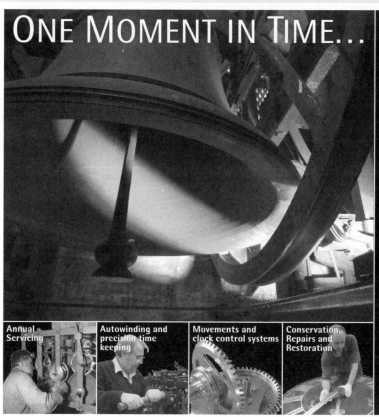

STONE MAD LIMITED
REGISTERED HERITAGE CONTRACTOR
STONEWORK AND ARCHITECTURAL RESTORATION

SERVICES

STONE SUPPLY AND INSTALLATION
(LIMESTONE, GRANITE, SANDSTONE AND MARBLE)

MASONRY RESTORATION AND REPAIR

STONEWORK REPOINTING

STONEWORK CONSERVATION

STONE CLEANING

SURVEYS OF BUILDING FAÇADES, GUTTERS, ROOFS, SPIRES AND BELFRYS

SPIRE AND STEEPLE RESTORATION

COMPLETED CONTRACTS INCLUDE:

ST PATRICK'S HOSPITAL ENTRANCE – DUBLIN
ST PETER & ST PAUL'S CHURCH, KILMALLOCK – CO LIMERICK
SLIGO TOWN HALL – SLIGO CORPORATION
TAIT CLOCK – LIMERICK CORPORATION
OLD WALLED MUSEUM – LIMERICK CORPORATION
FOTA HOUSE, CO CORK – OFFICE OF PUBLIC WORKS
ST MARY'S CHURCH, INNISHANNON, CO CORK
ELIZABETH FORT, BARRACK STREET, CORK – OFFICE OF PUBLIC WORKS
BLACKROCK CASTLE – CORK CITY COUNCIL
CHURCH OF ST ANNE, SHANDON – CORK
ST FINBARRE'S CATHEDRAL – CORK
DONERAILE HOUSE – OPW
HERITAGE COUNCIL HQ, THE PALACE, KILKENNY
BROSNA CHURCH, CO KERRY

CONTACT
JOSEPH COSTELLO, MD, RAILWAY ROAD, KILMALLOCK, CO LIMERICK
Tel (063) 20880 • Mobile (087) 2663580 • Fax (063) 20880
Website www.stonemadltd.ie • Email stonemad@iol.ie

Pioneer Total Abstinence Association of the Sacred Heart

The Association has as its chief aim the promotion of temperance and sobriety; with prayer and self-sacrifice as its principal means.
The members use their independence of alcohol to engage in good works and the organisation of counter attractions to drinking.

Central Spiritual Director:
Father Bernard McGuckian SJ

Monthly publication:
The Pioneer magazine

Dublin address:
The Secretary
Pioneer Association
27 Upper Sherrard Street
Dublin 1
Tel: (01) 874 9464
Fax: (01) 874 8485
Email: pioneer@jesuit.ie
website: http://www.pioneerassociation.ie

PONTIFICAL UNIVERSITY
St Patrick's College Maynooth

Undergraduate Degree Programmes
- Baccalaureate in Divinity (BD)
- Baccalaureate in Theology & Arts (BATh)
  CAO code MU001
- Baccalaureate in Theology (BTh)
  CAO code MU002

Northern Ireland applicants are eligible to apply for a student loan for the above programmes.

The latter two programmes qualify for the Higher Education Grants Scheme where applicable.

Mature students are very welcome to apply to all of the above programmes.

BTh/BD Add-On Modes: Students holding a Diploma in Theology or the equivalent may be admitted to the BTh or BD Add-on mode. The minimum duration of these programmes will be one academic year, and in the case of the BD, must be full-time. For further information, please contact the Theology Office 00353 (1) 7084772/3391/3892.

Postgraduate Programmes
- Doctoral Degree in Divinity (DD)
- Doctoral Degree in Theology (PhD)
- Licentiate in Divinity (STL)
- Master's Degree in Theology (MTh)
- Master's Degree in Pastoral Studies (MPS)
- Postgraduate Diploma in Christian Communication & Development
- Higher Diploma in Pastoral Liturgy
- Higher Diploma in Theological Studies

The Higher Diploma in Theological Studies is a one-year part-time evening course.

It is recognised by the Department of Education and Science as entitling teachers holding Department-recognised degrees and teacher-training qualifications to teach up to 15 hours Religious Education per week in a voluntary secondary school.

Some Postgraduate programmes qualify for the Higher Education Grants scheme and tax relief where applicable.

Information on other courses may be obtained from:
The Admissions Office,
Pontifical University,
St Patrick's College,
Maynooth, Co Kildare
Tel +353-1-708 4772/3391/3892
Fax +353-1-708 3441
Email theology.office@may.ie
Website www.maynoothcollege.ie

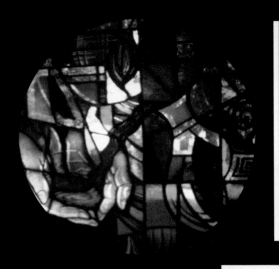

C.B.C. DISTRIBUTORS

COMPREHENSIVE SELECTION OF CHURCH FURNISHINGS AND SUPPLIES

CHURCH CANDLES - ALTAR WINE - INCENSE & CHARCOAL - MASS KITS - PRIEST'S SICK CALL SETS
INDOOR & OUTDOOR STATUARY - VESTMENTS - STATIONS OF THE CROSS - LECTERNS - PRIEDIEUX
TABERNACLES - PAPAL BLESSINGS - CHALICES - CIBORIA

Greenbank - Newry - Co. Down BT34 2JP
Tel: (028) 3026 5216   Fax: (028) 3026 3927

If dialing from Irish Republic
Tel: (042) 93 32321/2   Fax: (042) 93 37248

E.Mail: sales@cbcdistributors.co.uk

Guaranteed Craftsmanship in Church Organs

Church Organ building is a proud tradition enjoyed and preserved by the present firm of R. E. Meates & Son Ltd, through many generations in this country since 1830. We are pleased to announce the firm's steady progress in maintaining the highest standard in the art of building and restoring CHURCH ORGANS.

R. E. MEATES & SON LTD
ORGAN BUILDERS

Enquiries are invited for NEW ORGANS, RENOVATIONS and CLEANING REPAIRS and TUNINGS in any part of the country.

41 Foxrock Park, Foxrock, Dublin 18
Telephone (01) 289 3186

Works: 8/9 Erne Terrace, Dublin 2

ARIA STAINED GLASS

RESTORATION AND CONSERVATION

DESIGNED BY VICKI CROWLEY 2008

CONSERVATION, RESTORATION

CONSULTATION, NEW COMMISSIONS

Phone/Fax 091 793366 • 087 2375789

Email ariastainedglass@eircom.net

Contact: Richard Kimball

R.P.D. LIMITED
(Incorporating Rosario Press)

SPECIALISTS IN
CHURCH OFFERING ENVELOPES AND GENERAL PRINTING

- Calendars
- Christmas Cards
- Stationery
- Special Collection Envelopes
- 'Lotto' Envelopes

Let RPD Ltd provide you with everything you need to run a successful Fundraising Campaign from sets of collection envelopes to receipt books and 'thank you' cards

**Unit 25/26 Tolka Valley Business Park,
Ballyboggan Road, Glasnevin, Dublin 11
Telephone (01) 860 3088/860 3089 • Fax (01) 860 3092
Email tom@rpd.ie**

FEELYSTONE
SINCE 1780
CRAFTSMEN IN MARBLE

Ballinlough Church - 2007

Boyle
Co. Roscommon

Tel: 071 9662066   Fax: 071 9662894

Email: info@feelystone.ie

Website: www.feelystone.ie

✦ Altar Specialists ✦

✦ Large selection of old Altars in stock suitable for reconstruction ✦

✦ Marble Statues ✦ Celtic Memorials ✦

Specialists in Bells and Clocks, Belltower Structural Solutions
Installed Sound Systems and Radio Communications

BELLS & CLOCKS

- Bells – Automation, Restoration & Re-hanging
- Survey, Maintenance and Replacement of Bell Support Structures
- Digital Electronic Bells & Carillons via speakers – (1000 hymns/peals)
- Tower Clocks – Hour Ringing – Westminster Chime
- Liturgical Calendar Event Programming

COMMUNICATIONS

- The Parish Radio Link System
- Parish Video Links
- Sound & PA Amplification, Radio Microphones etc
- Audio Induction Loops for the Deaf
- Church Music Systems & Radio Remote Control

ENGINEERING & BUILDING MAINTENANCE

- Bell Support Structure installation and restoration
- Water ingress protection. Guttering & drains – cleaning – repair
- Pointing and sealing of stone. Roofing slates, tiles & flashing repairs
- Stone surface cleaning & restoration
- Lightning Protection: Dynasphere 3000 & Traditional systems
- Automation – Control of Heating, Lighting, Door opening etc
- Height Access for Surveys & Engineering reports
- Hoist Access to 75 mtrs – competitively priced

Installations by our Experienced, Highly Qualified and
Fully Insured Technical Team
Full Guarantees & After Sales Support
Contact Jim Doyle or Leo Brophy

Head Office: Dunleary House
83 Dublin Road, Sutton, Dublin 13
Tel/Fax 01-8392220 • Mobile 087-2538916
Email belltron@infatron.com • Website www.belltron.ie

 **MESSENGER PUBLICATIONS**

For all your publishing needs

Offering a fully integrated design and print management solution

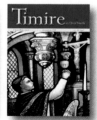 

For a quotation on design, print, and print management solutions please contact Triona McKee:
01~6767491
email: manager@messenger.ie

www.messenger.ie
01~6767491
sales@messenger.ie

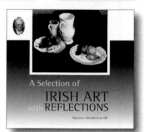  

Wynn's Hotel, Dublin

35/39 Lower Abbey Street, Dublin 1 • Tel 874 5131 • Fax 874 1556
Email info@wynnshotel.ie • Website www.wynnshotel.ie

Renowned for its Clerical clientele, Wynn's Hotel has catered for many religious orders from home and abroad since it opened its doors in 1845. Our proximity to Busaras, Heuston and Connolly Stations has been further enhanced by the Luas stop on our door step. We are within walking distance from Dublin's famous St Mary's Pro-Cathedral which has hosted many historic Church and State occasions as the 'mother church of the Archdiocese of Dublin, affectionately known as the PRO'.

After a €5 million euro renovation, Wynn's Hotel offers newly refurbished restaurant, lobby bar, function facilities to cater for seminars, conferences and parties up to 150 people. Our 70 bedrooms are a mixture of Standard and Deluxe rooms. All rooms are ensuite and feature multi-channel flat screen TV, tea/coffee making facilities, hair dryer, safe, iron and ironing board. In addition a 24 hour room service is available.

Our famous Ristorante Tomasso, has returned to a natural home from home style of cooking using mostly Irish and organic produce. Elegant and airy surroundings compliment a fabulous mouth watering menu.

Contact the hotel direct for various Special Offers throughout the year or log onto www.wynnshotel.ie.

Wynn's Hotel is the perfect blend of hospitality, historic splendour and modern comfort.
We look forward to welcoming you next time you're in town.

THE TABLET

stands where faith and modern culture meet

Each week *The Tablet*, the international Catholic weekly, informs and entertains on religion, politics, social and ethical issues, literature and the arts.

Our exclusive Letter from Rome - from our reporter at the Vatican - is combined with world Church news and practical advice on the parish. But writers are drawn from across the denominational spectrum, as we debate issues from ecumenism to the environment, as well as undertaking interviews with important religious figures.

Enjoy a prize crossword and sudoku, in-depth book reviews and regular articles on wine, racing and etymology.

Subscribe Today
and save €21 off the cover price
Call +44 20 8748 8484

Please open a 6 month (25 issues) subscription for €64.50

Name...

Address...

....

....

I enclose payment by ☐ credit card ☐ cheque (payable to *The Tablet*)

Credit Card Number..

Expiry Date......................... Signature...................

**Please return to 'LCI09 Offer', The Tablet,
1 King St Cloisters, Clifton Walk, London W6 0QZ, UK
Fax: +44 (0)20 8563 7644 Email: subscribe@thetablet.co.uk**

www.thetablet.co.uk

FINNS
Heritage & Restoration Division

Specialist nationwide Conservation Contractors with 5 decades of experience renovating heritage and church structures.

All types of conservation and maintenance contracts undertaken.

→ Inspections and survey reports
→ Lighting Conductor installation and testing
→ Roofs
→ Timber repair, treatment and preservation
→ Specialist steeplejack access
→ Bespoke scaffolding
→ Flagstaffs and weather vanes installed
→ Stone Masonry
→ Gilding and ironwork
→ Rainwater goods restoration
→ Protective coatings
→ Stone cleaning and anti-graffiti treatment
→ Heritage Funding Consultancy – ask about our Grant Application Pack
→ All works fully insured and compliant with latest Heritage Guidance from Department of Environment, Heritage and Local Government

sales@finns.ie • www.finns.ie
Tel 046 9430219 • Fax 046 9430082
Finns (Addinstown) Ltd, Addinstown, Devlin, Co Westmeath

NICHOLAS FORDE

Ballymakeera, Macroom, Co Cork

STATUE RESTORATION

Cleaning, Re-Painting and Repairs of Statues and Crib Sets

Handcrafted figures also supplied

All Statues Collected and Delivered

All Statues in Need of make Over, Please Contact me @
Tel 026-45465 or 087-0693473

Fáilte Roimh aon Fiosrúcháin

St Martin Apostolate

42 PARNELL SQUARE, DUBLIN 1

Religious Goods Supplies

Liturgical & Religious Goods

- *Mass Kits • Sick Call Sets and Pyxes*
- *Chalices • Ciboria • Communion Bowls*
- *Holy Water Containers and Sprinklers*
- *Thuribles*
- *Tabernacles suitable for Oratories or Prayer Rooms*
- *Statues*

The St Martin Apostolate are the agents for the
Slabbinck Vestment Company of Belgium.
Chasubles, overlay stoles, albs, altar cloths, etc.
A selection of Slabbinck Vestments are on display in our showrooms.
Catalogue available on request.

Visit our Showroom

(HOURS: MONDAY-THURSDAY 10.00 AM-4.00 PM • LUNCH: 12.30 PM-2.15 PM)
PLEASE PHONE, WRITE OR FAX FOR DETAILS:
Telephone (01) 874 5465/873 0147 • Fax (01) 873 1989
Email stmartin@iol.ie • Tel from UK 00353 1 8745465

ALL HALLOWS COLLEGE

UNDERGRADUATE PROGRAMMES:

BA in Theology & Philosophy
BA in Theology & Psychology
BA in Theology & English Literature
Four year BA programme; Mature applicants welcome

BA in Pastoral Theology (In-Service)
A one year part-time programme for those who have already
completed the equivalent of a three-year cycle in Theology and
related subjects

Adult Learning BA
New, unique, flexible degree programme for adult learners

POSTGRADUATE PROGRAMMES:
(Also available at Diploma level)
MA in Leadership & Pastoral Care
Holistic approach for those in Management
One year full-time or two years part-time

MA in Management for Community and
Voluntary Services
For Managers of non-profit organisations
Integrative & strategic approach to organisation and
decision-making
One year full-time or two years part-time

MA in Social Justice & Public Policy
For those seeking to make a difference in terms of equity &
justice
Focus on social analysis, public policy, advocacy, human rights
and strategic planning
Two years part-time

Research Masters and Doctoral Degrees
The research aims to explore subjects related to culture, religion
and society today.

SCHOOL OF ADULT & COMMUNITY LEARNING

Renewal for Ministry Sabbatical Programmes
Three month programmes:Spring, Post-Easter, Autumn
Renewal & Personal Reflection for those in Pastoral Ministry

Pathways: Exploring Faith & Ministry
To prepare people to respond to the needs of the Church in their
own environment;One night per week over two years, Sept-May

Continuing Education programme
A range of course, workshops, seminars and events throughout
the year including Developing Parish seminar and Facilitation

The Registrar, All Hallows College,
Drumcondra, Dublin 9.
T: 01 837 3745 E:info@allhallows.ie
www.allhallows.ie

Michael McGowan

CHURCH SUPPLIES

DROMOD • CO. LEITRIM
TEL (071) 9638357 • FAX (071) 9638528
MOBILE (086) 256 1023
Email churchsupplies@eircom.net

Suppliers of
Votive Lights • Shrine Candles • Sanctuary Candles
Altar Candles • Oil Candles • Altar Wines

Vestments • Albs • Cruets • Silverware • Brassware
Charcoal • Incense • etc.

Mass Kits • Statues • Crib Sets

Restoration of all Brassware

Contractors for Furniture and Kneeler Padding

Agent for
**Lalor, Boramic and Duffy & Scott Church
Candles**

Fast – Free Delivery

KENNETH JONES AND ASSOCIATES

DESIGNERS, MAKERS AND RESTORERS OF PIPE ORGANS

For more than 30 years we have been
designing, making, restoring and tuning pipe
organs. Our work is found in cathedrals,
churches and concert halls in Ireland and
across the globe.

Our current project is an organ of
3 manuals and pedal for Carlow Cathedral
for completion Easter 2010.

For all enquiries, including tuning and repairs,
please contact us:

Kenneth Jones Pipe Organs Ltd
7 Woodstock Business Park, Kilcoole, Co Wicklow
Tel: (01) 2018665   Fax: (01) 2811966
Email: organws@eircom.net

SKYLINE STEEPLEJACKS LTD

Mill Road, Greystones, Co. Wicklow
Phone: 01 287 4024 • Fax: 01 287 4321 • Mobile: 087 274 2033
Email skylinesteeplejacks1@eircom.net

" The Steeplejack Professionals"

- **Full Steeplejack Service**
- **Specialists in Stone Cleaning,**
  Restoration and Pointing Works
- **Roofing Repairs**
- **Lighting Conductor Engineers**
  New systems supplied and fitted
  Existing systems upgraded
- **All works to B.S. EN623052006**
- **Fully Insured • Nationwide Service**

SOUND SYSTEMS BY

PHONE
094 9659022

JOE O'NEILL LIMITED
GLENAMADDY
CO GALWAY

EMAIL
joe@joeoneill.ie

Official sound contractors
for Knock Shrine

Church Organs: Single manuals from €3,200, double manual from €4,400.
Public Address Systems: Amplifiers, speakers, portable amplifiers c/w radio microphone, latest microphone technology.
Induction Loop: For the hard of hearing. When looking at a congregation, people wearing spectables are obvious, a similar number have hearing defects.
Angelus Systems: Automated systems to ring mass, funeral, angelus bell and play hymns.
Candlelabra/Shrines: We offer expert advice, high quality work, emergency call out and guarantee satisfaction.

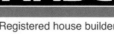

VERITAS GALLERY

Art for Churches, Parish Centres, Parish Groups & Schools

To view our extended portfolio
contact Mary Kelly Flynn
Veritas, 16–18 Park Street,
Monaghan
Tel. (047) 84077
monaghanshop@veritas.ie
or visit www.veritas.ie

VERITAS
www.veritas.ie

INTERCOM

A PASTORAL AND LITURGICAL RESOURCE

PUBLISHED MONTHLY, INTERCOM IS A PASTORAL AND LITURGICAL RESOURCE OF THE IRISH BISHOPS' CONFERENCE

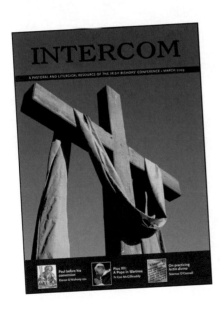
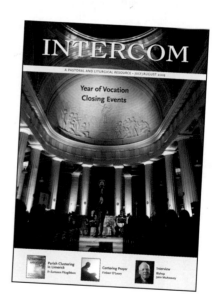

Annual subscription:

Ireland:	€50.00	Each additional copy	€17.50
Airmail:	€65.00	Each additional copy	€27.50
UK:	stg£40.00	Each additional copy	stg£15.00

(Prices correct at time of going to print)

Subscriptions to: Ross Delmar, Membership Secretary
7/8 Lower Abbey Street, Dublin 1 • Tel (01) 878 8177 • Fax (01) 878 6507
Email ross.delmar@veritas.ie

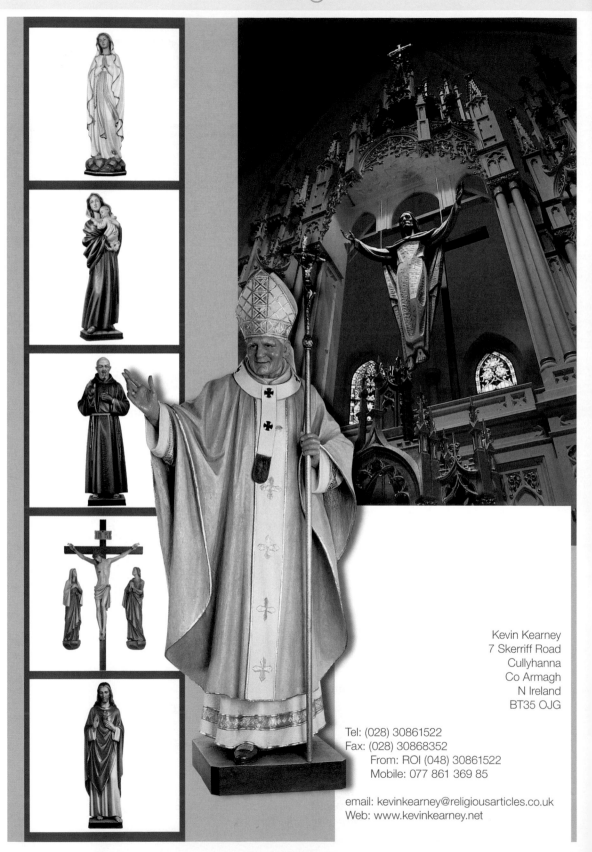

Kevin Kearney
7 Skerriff Road
Cullyhanna
Co Armagh
N Ireland
BT35 OJG

Tel: (028) 30861522
Fax: (028) 30868352
From: ROI (048) 30861522
Mobile: 077 861 369 85

email: kevinkearney@religiousarticles.co.uk
Web: www.kevinkearney.net

K N O C K

OUR LADY'S SHRINE, KNOCK, CO. MAYO
Phone (094) 9388100   Fax (094) 9388295
www.knock-shrine.ie   Email: info@knock-shrine.ie

Programme of Ceremonies and Devotions 2010

SUNDAYS AND HOLYDAYS
April 25 to October 10 (inclusive)
Masses: 8, 9.30, 10.30 am, 12 noon, 3 & 7 pm
(Eve of Sundays and Holydays: 7.30 pm)

Confessions: Continuously from 11 am to 7 pm

Public Ceremonies:
2.30 pm   Anointing of the Sick
3.00 pm   Concelebrated Mass followed by
                 the Solemn Blessing of the Sick.
                 Benediction of the Blessed
                 Sacrament, Rosary Procession to
                 the Shrine and the blessing of Pious
                 objects.

ALL WEEKDAYS
April 26 to October 09 (inclusive)
Masses: 9, 11 am, 12 noon, 3, 5 & 7.30 pm
Confessions: Continuously from 11 am to 5 pm
Public Ceremonies:
2.00 pm   Stations of the Cross and Rosary Procession
3.00 pm   Concelebrated Mass with Anointing of
          the Sick.

NATIONAL PUBLIC NOVENA
August 14 to 22 (inclusive) Ceremonies Twice daily:
3.00 pm Mass in the Basilica. Eucharistic Blessing
         of the Sick and Rosary Procession.
8.30 pm Mass in the Basilica. Eucharistic Blessing of
         the Sick and Candlelight Rosary Procession

SPECIAL PROGRAMME FOR SCHOOLS
- Retreats
- Faith Development Programmes
- Youth Liturgies
- Use of Audio Visual Facilities
- Further details: Phone (094) 9388100

KNOCK MUSEUM
Captures the compelling story of the Knock
Apparition of 1879
Opening Hours: May - October 10 - 6 p.m. daily
November - April 12 - 4 p.m. daily
Email: museum@knock-shrine.ie Phone:(094) 9375034

Pilgrims Guides, Knock Posters and details of main pilgrimage dates on request.
For assistance in organising your pilgrimage, please contact the above office or:

Knock Shrine Office, Veritas House,
7/8 Lower Abbey Street, Dublin 1
Tel/Fax: (01) 873 3356
Email: dublinoffice@knock-shrine.ie

Knock Shrine Pilgrimages, 5 Bellevue Park,
Newtownabbey, Co. Antrim, BT36 7QD
Tel/Fax: (028) 9028 7690
Email: knockshrinebelfast@gmail.com

Knock Shrine Office & Bookshop,
76/77 Little Catherine Street, Limerick
Tel: (061) 419 458   Fax: (061) 405 178
Email: limerickoffice@knock-shrine.ie

Knock Shrine Office & Bookshop,
101, Deansgate, Manchester, M3 2BQ, England
Tel: (0161) 8192558   Fax: (0161) 8340744
Email: knockshrineoffice@btconnect.com

KNOCK SHRINE BOOKSCENTRE
Knock Shrine, Knock, Co. Mayo
Tel: (094) 9375030 Fax: (094) 9375031
Email: bookshop@knock-shrine.ie

FOR A WIDE RANGE OF
RELIGIOUS BOOKS & SOUVENIRS YOU CAN
NOW SHOP ONLINE AT,
www.knock-shrine.ie/shop

KNOCK HOUSE HOTEL *
Beside Shrine Grounds, Groups Welcome
150 Seater Conference Centre
Four Seasons Restaurant, Open all Year
Tel: 094 93 88088   Fax: 094 93 88044
Email: info@knockhousehotel.ie
Web: www.knockhousehotel.ie

KNOCK CARAVAN & CAMPING PARK *
AA Recommended, Caravan Club Site,
Tourers Welcome, Mobile homes for hire
Open March to October
Tel: 094 9388100   Fax: 094 9388295
Email: caravanpark@knock-shrine.ie
Web: www.knock-shrine.ie/caravanpark

ST PAULS

Missalettes — Parish Bulletins
Yearly Sunday Missal
Bibles — Spiritual Books
St Pauls Publications

Moyglare Road, Maynooth, Co Kildare
Tel (01) 6285933 • Fax (01) 6289330
e-mail: sales@stpauls.ie / books@stpauls.ie
website: www.stpauls.ie

* * * * * *

ST PAULS

Castle Street, Athlone, Co Westmeath
Tel (090) 6492882 • Fax (090) 6492882
e-mail: saintpaul_books@hotmail.com

ST PAULS is an activity of the priests and brothers of the
Society of St Paul who proclaim the Gospel through the media
of social communication.

Rainey
· STEEPLEJACKS ·

Award Winning Church Restorers
Est. 1913

Lightning Protection Specialists

• *Stone Cleaning & Restoration*

• *Roofing & Guttering Maintenance*

• *Fully Insured all Heights Contracts*

ALL IRELAND COVERAGE

BALHEARY ROAD, SWORDS, CO DUBLIN
Tel (01) 840 1515/840 7099 • Fax (01) 840 2919

Email info@jrainey.com • Website www.jrainey.com

DUBLIN STAINED GLASS

SPECIALISTS
IN ECCLESIASTICAL WORK

Dublin Stained Glass with many
years experience specializing in
the conservation and restoration
of stained glass. Our Studio use
traditional techniques to create
stained glass windows for church.
We also provide a comprehensive
storm glazing system and
manufacture of brass ventilators.

Our skilled team of artists and
craftsmen can provide
a professional examination and
recommendation of each
individual ecclesiastical work

- Conservation
- Restoration
- Design
- Manufacture
- Storm glazing
- Bronze ventilators
- Doubleglazing

Contact Peter: Mobile: (085) 143 5404
e-mail: peter@dublinstainedglass.ie / www.dublinstainedglass.ie
Address: 283 Killinarden Estate, Tallaght, Dublin 24

International Missionary Benefits Society

Health Solidarity in Church

The I.M.S. is a mutual-aid association based on a mutual system, created 45 years ago. It offers health coverage based on the principle of solidarity for the care of medical expenses of missionaries, priests and religious.

✓ An answer to deficiencies of national health systems for missionaries and local people 23 000 members in 147 countries covering the costs of care from the first Euro.

✓ An associative network of 7 offices administered by Episcopal Conferences or Religious congregations
Managing claims in multiple currencies (Paris, Brussels, Abidjan, Nairobi, Antananarivo, Fortaleza / Brazil).

✓ Appropriate contributions to mission countries and the mobility of members
5 options from 50 euros to 990 euros per year.

Contact :

Entraide Missionnaire Internationale
Mr Stéphane PUECHBERTY
3 rue Duguay-Trouin
75280 PARIS Cedex 06 - FRANCE
Tél : (33) 01 42 22 91 29
Fax : (33) 01 45 48 53 90
Mail : puechberty@saintmartin.com.fr

More information :
http://www.entraide-missionnaire.com

SACRISTY REGISTER
Now Available from Veritas

SACRISTY REGISTER

Available from your local Veritas branch:

Abbey Street & Blanchardstown, Dublin · Belfast · Cork · Derry Ennis · Letterkenny · Monaghan Naas · Sligo

Or log on to www.veritas.ie
T: (01) 8788177

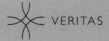

Call +353-1-6625810 to book your PRMS.

Parish Records Management System

A Simple Computer Solution for your parish records

PRMS

We provide:

✔ Scanning of your Parish Registers for future preservation

✔ PRMS software for searching your records and printing certificates

✔ Old records entry: Baptism/Confirmation/Marriage/Death

✔ Importing your existing data into PRMS

✔ Install & support PRMS to manage your daily parish needs

✔ Development of a new or existing Parish Website

✔ Publish parish news updates directly to your Website

e-Celtic Ltd., 40 Lower Leeson Street, Dublin 2, Ireland | info@prms.ie | www.prms.ie.

TREVOR CROWE LTD

Pipe Organ Specialists

Cleaning, Restoration, Rebuilding, Revoicing, Tuning, Maintenance & Advisory Service Nationwide

Upper Hodgestown,
Donadea, Co Kildare
Tel (045) 863768/(087) 2319988
Fax (045) 863558

BORAMIC
CANDLEMAKERS

Makers of all Church Candles

Votive Lights 2 & 4 Hours
Sanctuary Candles
Paschal Candles
Beeswax Altar Candles
Night Lights
Shrine Candles
Baptismal Candles
Altar Oil Lights
Advent Candles
Decorative Candles
Dinner Candles
Baton Candles

Stockists of Altar Wine, Charcoal, Incense and Tapers

Borris, Co Carlow, Ireland
Tel : + 353 5997 73161   Fax: + 353 5997 73548
Email: boramic@iol.ie
www.boramiccandles.com

ALTAR BREAD SUPPLIES LTD

ST FINBARRS, FARRANFERRIS,
REDEMPTION ROAD, CORK
TEL (021) 4300227
FAX (021) 4228199

Office Hours: 9.00 am to 5.00 pm
Answering Service after hours
Collection and postal services available

Index of Advertisers

ALPHABETICAL LIST OF CLERGY IN IRELAND

DIOCESAN, RELIGIOUS AND MISSIONARY

Irish Diocesan clergy working or studying abroad are also listed.
Telephone numbers are included in this list.
For all other forms of telephonic or electrical communications, including mobiles, faxes, email addresses and websites,
please refer to the main entries in this directory.

A

Adjei-Buor, James (CSSp)
Holy Ghost Missionary
College, Kimmage Manor,
Dublin 12
Tel 01-4064300

Adler, Emil
Ministry to Polish
Community,
St Anne's Presbytery,
Convent Hill, Waterford
Tel 087-4182223/051-855819
(Waterford & L.)

Agnoli, Enzo (CSSp)
Holy Ghost Missionary
College, Kimmage Manor,
Dublin 12
Tel 01-4064300

Agnoli, Savino (CSSp)
Holy Ghost Missionary
College, Kimmage Manor,
Dublin 12
Tel 01-4064300

Aguilar-Díez, Juan José (SJ)
John Sullivan House
56/56A Mulvey Park,
Dundrum,
Dublin 14
Tel 01-2983978

Ahearne, Peter, Very Rev, PP
Rathronan, Clonmel,
Co Tipperary
Tel 052-6121891
(Powerstown, Waterford &
L.)

Ahearne, Seamus (OSA), Very
Rev, PP
The Presbytery,
60 Glenties Park,
Finglas South, Dublin 11
Tel 01-8343722/087-6782746
(Rivermount, Dublin)

Ahern, Gerard, Very Rev, PP
Abbeyleix, Co Laois
Tel 057-8731135
(Abbeyleix, Kildare & L.)

Ahern, Michael (OCSO)
Superior,
Mount Melleray Abbey,
Cappoquin, Co Waterford
Tel 058-54404

Ahern, Niall, Very Rev Canon,
PP
Strandhill, Co Sligo
Tel 071-9168147
(Strandhill/Ransboro, Elphin)

Ahern, P.
St John's Parish Centre,
Castle Street, Tralee,
Co Kerry
(Kerry, retired)

Aherne, Francis (OSA)
St Augustine's Priory,
Washington Street,
Cork
Tel 021-2753982

Aherne, John, Very Rev
Canon, PE
Aghada, Co Cork
Tel 021-4661239
(Cloyne, retired)

Alexander, Anthony, Very
Rev, PP
824 Shore Road,
Newtownabbey,
Co Antrim BT36 7DG
Tel 028-90370845
(Greencastle, Down & C.)

Alexander, Paul, Very Rev, PP
St Vincent de Paul
Presbytery,
169 Ligoniel Road,
Belfast BT14 8DP
Tel 028-90713401
(St Vincent de Paul, Down &
C.)

Allen, Andrew (OP)
47 Leeson Park, Dublin 6
Tel 01-6602427

Allen, Brian (OFM)
Vicar, Franciscan Friary,
Friary Lane, Athlone,
Co Westmeath
Tel 090-6472095

Allman, Colm, Very Rev, BA,
HDE
President,
St Joseph's College,
Garbally Park, Ballinasloe,
Co Galway
Tel 090-9642504/9642254
(Clonfert)

Alwill, Gerard, Very Rev, PP
Drumkeerin, Co Leitrim
Tel 071-9648025
Visiting Chaplain,
Lough Allen College,
Drumkeerin, Co Leitrim
Tel 071-9648017
(Drumkeerin, Kilmore)

Amaku, Cajethan, MSP (White
Fathers)
Cypress Grove, Templeogue,
Dublin 6W
Tel 01-4055263/4055264

Ambrose, James, Very Rev
Canon, PP
Dromcollogher, Charleville,
Co Limerick
Tel 087-7740753
(Dromcollogher/Broadford,
Limerick)

Anadam, Alex (SSP)
Society of St Paul,
Moyglare Road,
Maynooth, Co Kildare
Tel 01-6285933

Andrews, Paul (SJ)
35 Lower Leeson Street,
Dublin 2
Tel 01-6761248

Anih, John (MSP), CC
St Patrick's Presbytery,
Roden Place, Dundalk,
Co Louth
Tel 042-9334648
(Dundalk, St Patrick's,
Armagh)

AnNguyen, Dan, CC
The Presbytery, Blacklion,
Greystones, Co Wicklow
Tel 01-2877036
(Blacklion, Dublin)

Arigho, Desmond (CSSp)
Holy Ghost Missionary
College, Kimmage Manor,
Dublin 12
Tel 01-4064300

Arkinson, Patrick, PP
Sessiaghoneill, Ballybofey,
Co Donegal
Tel 074-9131149
(Killygordon, Derry)

Armstrong, Paul, Very Rev, PP
28 Willowbank Park,
Belfast BT6 0LL
Tel 028-90793023
(St Bernadette's, Down & C.)

Arthure, Robert, Very Rev, AP
Cappoquin, Co Waterford
Tel 058-54221
(Cappoquin, Waterford & L.)

Asare, Anthony, PC
St Andrew's, Westland Row,
Dublin 2
Tel 01-6765517
(Westland Row, Dublin)

Audley, Padraic, Very Rev, PP
Carraroe, Co Galway
Tel 091-595452
(Carraroe (Kileen), Tuam)

Aughney, Edward, Very Rev,
PP
Glynn, St Mullins via
Kilkenny
Tel 051-424563
(St Mullins, Kildare & L.)

Aylward, Eamon (SSCC), CC
Sacred Hearts Presbytery,
St Johns Drive, Sruleen,
Dublin 22
Tel 01-4570032
(Sruleen, Dublin)

B

Bailey, Michael (OFM), CC
Curate's Residence,
Monksfield, Salthill, Galway
Tel 091-526006
(Salthill, Galway)

Baker, Eugene, CC
Greenhill, Fermoy, Co Cork
Tel 025-33507
(Fermoy, Cloyne)

Baker, Patrick, CC
157 Glen Road, Maghera,
Co Derry BT46 5JN
Tel 028-79642359
(Maghera, Derry)

Balfe, George, Very Rev, PP
Ardagh, Co Longford
Tel 043-75006
(Ardagh and Moydow,
Ardagh & Cl.)

Bambrick, Thomas (SM), CC
Railway Road, Muinebheag,
Co Carlow
Tel 059-9721154
(*Muinebheag/
Bagenalstown*, Kildare & L.)

Bane, John, Very Rev, PP
Broadford, Co Clare
Tel 061-473123/086-8246555
(*Broadford*, Killaloe)

Bannon, Michael, Very Rev, PP
St Mary's, Drumlish,
Co Longford
Tel 043-3324132
(*Drumlish*, Ardagh & Cl.)

Bannon, Gabriel (OSM) PP
Parochial House,
11 Benburb Road,
Moy, Dungannon,
Co Tyrone BT71 7SQ
Tel 028-87784262
(Armagh)

Bannon, Patrick, Very Rev, PP
Bunnoe, Co Cavan
Tel 049-5553035
(*Kilsherdany and Drung*,
Kilmore)

Banville, Patrick, CC
St Leonard's, Saltmills,
New Ross, Co Wexford
Tel 051-562135
(*Ballycullane*, Ferns)

Baragry, Dan (CSsR)
Vicar-Superior,
Marianella/Ligouri House,
75 Orwell Road, Dublin 6
Tel 01-4067100

Baragry, Dan (SSC)
St Columban's Retirement
Home, Dalgan Park,
Navan, Co Meath
Tel 046-9021525

Barber, Noel (SJ)
Assistant Provincial, Jesuit
Provincial Curia, IMI Centre,
Sandyford Road, Dublin 16
Tel 01-2932820

Barden, Thomas, PIC
Kenagh, Co Longford
Tel 043-3322127
(*Kilcommoc*, Ardagh & Cl.)

Barlage, Henry (SVD)
133 North Circular Road,
Dublin 7
Tel 01-8386743

Barrett, Edward (OMI)
Department of Chaplaincy,
Tralee General Hospital,
Tralee, Co Kerry
Tel 066-7126222

Barrett, Eugene (OFM)
Guardian, Franciscan Friary,
Liberty Street, Cork
Tel 021-4270302

Barrett, Martin
Saint Paul University,
223 Main Street,
Ottawa, Ontario,
Canada KIS 1CU
(Killala)

Barrett, Paul (OFMCap)
St Francis Capuchin Friary.
Rochestown, Co Cork
Tel 021-4896244

Barron, Liam, Very Rev, PP
Mullinavat, via Waterford,
Co Kilkenny
Tel 051-898108/087-2722824
(*Mullinavat*, Ossory)

Barros, Gabriel, IVE
Kilmyshall, Enniscorthy,
Co Wexford
Tel 053-9377188
(*Bunclody*, Ferns)

Barry, Anselm (OSB)
Glenstal Abbey, Murroe,
Co Limerick
Tel 061-386103

Barry, Eamonn,
Facilitator for Prayer and
Retreat Ministries
(*in residence*)
St Colman's College,
Fermoy, Co Cork
Tel 025-31622
(Cloyne)

Barry, Edward, CC
The Presbytery, Ashford,
Co Wicklow
Tel 0404-40224
(*Ashford*, Dublin)

Barry, Jim (SPS)
House Leader,
Kiltegan House,
11 Douglas Road, Cork
Tel 021-4969371

Barry, Maurice (OCarm)
Carmelite Friary, Kinsale,
Co Cork
Tel 021-772138

Barry, Michael (SVD)
Donamon Castle,
Roscommon
Tel 090-6662222

Barry, Michael, CC
Borrisoleigh, Thurles,
Co Tipperary
Tel 0504-51275
(*Borrisoleigh*, Cashel & E.)

Barry, Phil (SAC)
Rector, Pallottine College,
Thurles, Co Tipperary
Tel 0504-21202

Barry-Ryan, Kieran (SJ)
St Francis Xavier's,
Upper Gardiner Street,
Dublin 1
Tel 01-8363411

Bartlett, Timothy
Irish Bishops' Conference,
Columba Centre,
St Patrick's College,
Maynooth, Co Kildare
Tel 01-5053000
(Down & C.)

Bartley, Kevin, CC
8 Greenfield Road, Sutton,
Dublin 13
Tel 01-8322396
(*Sutton*, Dublin)

Battelle, John, Very Rev
Canon, PE
14 Pine Valley, Grange
Road, Dublin 16
(Dublin, retired)

Battelle, Patrick, Very Rev, PE
14 Pine Valley,
Grange Road, Rathfarnham,
Dublin 16
Tel 01-4935962
(*Ballinteer*, Dublin)

Battelle, Sean, Very Rev
Canon, PE
14 Pine Valley,
Grange Road, Dublin 16
(Dublin)

Baxter, Martin (OCarm)
Prior, Gort Muire,
Ballinteer, Dublin 16
Tel 01-2984014

Baxter, Turlough, CC
St Mary's, Carrick-on-
Shannon, Co Leitrim
Tel 071-9620054
(Ardagh & Cl.)

Beagon, Brendan, Very Rev,
CC
1 Christine Road,
Newtownabbey,
Co Antrim BT36 6TG
Tel 028-90841507
(*St Mary's on the Hill*, Down
& C.)

Beale, Stephen (FDP)
Local Co-ordinator,
25 Lower Teddington Road,
Kingston-on-Thames,
Surrey
Tel 208-9775130

Beatty, John, Very Rev, PP
Anacarty, Co Tipperary
Tel 062-71104
(*Anacarty*, Cashel & E.)

Beecher, Patrick (OCD)
The Abbey, Loughrea,
Co Galway
Tel 091-841209

Beecher, Paul, Very Rev
Canon, PE
Cahir, Co Tipperary
Tel 052-7443193
(Waterford & L., retired)

Beere, Joseph (CSSp), Very
Rev, PP
Presbytery, Bawnogue,
Clondalkin, Dublin 22
Tel 01-4592273/4519810
(*Bawnogue*, Dublin)

Beggan, Tiernach, Very Rev,
PP
Belleek, Enniskillen,
Co Fermanagh BT93 3FJ
Tel 028-68658229
(*Belleek-Garrison*, Clogher)

Beglan, Peter, Very Rev, PE
12 Pairc na-hAbhainn,
Edgeworthstown,
Co Longford
(Ardagh & Cl., retired)

Begley, George, CC
The Presbytery, Herbert
Road, Bray, Co Wicklow
Tel 01-2868413 (w)/
2862955 (h)
(*Bray*, Dublin)

Begley, Joseph, Very Rev, PP
Kilcummin, Killarney,
Co Kerry
Tel 064-6643176
(*Kilcummin*, Kerry)

Begley, Michael (CSSp)
Spiritan Missionary College,
Kimmage Manor,
Dublin 12
Tel 01-4064300

Behan, Laurence, CC
The Presbytery,
Booterstown Avenue,
Blackrock, Co Dublin
Tel 01-2882162
(*Booterstown*, Dublin)

Behan, Richard M., Very Rev,
VF
Presbytery No 1,
Ballinteer Avenue,
Dublin 16
Tel 01-4944448
(*Ballinteer*, Dublin)

Beirne, Desmond (CM)
All Hallows Institute for
Mission and Ministry,
Drumcondra, Dublin 9
Tel 01-8373745/6

Beirne, Francis, Very Rev, PP
Four Roads, Roscommon
Tel 090-6623313
(*Ballyforan*, Elphin)

Beirne, Seán, CC
Kilteevan, Roscommon
Tel 090-6626374
(*Roscommon,* Elphin)

Beirne, Thomas, Very Rev, CC
Newbridge,
Ballinasloe, Co Galway
Tel 090-6660018
(*Ballygar*, Elphin)

Belton, Liam, Very Rev, PP, VF
Parochial House, Kilquade,
Co Wicklow
Tel 01-2819252
(Dublin)

Benetti, Antonio (MCCJ)
8 Clontarf Road, Clontarf,
Dublin 3
Tel 01-8330051

Benko, Marticn (SVK)
Scholastic,
Clongowes Wood College,
Naas, Co Kildare
Tel 045-868663/868202

Bennett, Donal N. (SSC)
Philippine Chaplaincy

Bennett, John (MSC)
Grace Dieu Retreat House,
Tramore Road, Waterford
Tel 051-374417/373372

Bennett, Mark, CC
St Mary's, Athlone,
Co Westmeath
Tel 090-6472088
(Athlone, Ardagh & Cl.)

Bennett, Paul, CC
2 Church Cross, Coolmona,
Donoughmore, Co Cork
Tel 021-7437728
(Cloyne)

Bennett, Roch (OFMCap)
Capuchin Friary,
Ard Mhuire, Creeslough,
Letterkenny, Co Donegal
Tel 074-9138005

Bennett, Ronald (OFM)
Franciscan House of Studies,
Dun Mhuire, Seafield Road,
Killiney, Co Dublin
Tel 01-2826760

Bennett, Seán (CSsR)
St Joseph's, Dundalk,
Co Louth
Tel 042-9334042/9334762

Bennett, Terence (SSC)
St Columban's Retirement
Home, Dalgan Park,
Navan, Co Meath
Tel 046-9021525

Bergin, Denis T., Very Rev
76 Trintonville Road,
Sandymount, Dublin 4
(Dublin, retired)

Bergin, Francis, Very Rev, AP
Shinrone, Co Offaly
Tel 0505-47133
(Shinrone, Killaloe)

Bergin, John (SAC)
Pallottine College, Thurles,
Co Tipperary
Tel 0504-21202

Bergin, Liam, Very Rev
Rector,
Pontificio Collegio Irlandese,
via dei SS Quattro 1,
00184 Rome, Italy
Tel 003906-77263301
(Ossory)

Berhane, Hagos (SDB)
Salesian College,
Maynooth Road,
Celbridge, Co Kildare
Tel 01-6275058/60

Bermingham, John (CSsR)
Most Holy Sacrament Parish,
Cherry Orchard,
Dublin 10
Tel 01-6267930
(Dublin)

Bermingham, William, Very
Rev, PP
Parochial House, Balrney,
Co Cork
Tel 021-4385105
(Blarney, Cloyne)

Berney, Donal, CC
St Kevin's, Tinahely,
Co Wicklow
Tel 0402-38138
(Killaveney, Ferns)

Bingham, Michael (SJ)
Iona, 211 Churchill Park,
Portadown BT62 1EU
Tel 028-38330366

Birmingham, Jim (SPS)
St Patrick's, Kiltegan,
Co Wicklow
Tel 059-6473600

Birmingham, John (CSsR)
The Presbytery,
103 Cherry Orchard Avenue,
Dublin 10
Tel 01-6267930
(Cherry Orchard, Dublin)

Birmingham, Joseph (OCD)
Avila, Bloomfield Avenue,
Morehampton Road,
Dublin 4
Tel 01-6430200

Blake, Declan
Parochial House,
Sperrin Road, Dublin 12
Tel 01-4556103
(Mourne Road, Dublin)

Blake, Declan, Adm
Parochial House, 49 Seville
Place, Dublin 1
Tel 01-8741625
(North Wall-Seville Place,
Dublin)

Blake, Ephrem (CP)
Passionist Community,
35-36 Coill Tire,
Doughiska, Galway

Blake, Kieran, Very Rev, PP
Kilcolman, Sharavogue,
Birr, Co Offaly
Tel 0509-20812/087-9302214
(Kilcolman, Killaloe)

Blake, Kieran, Very Rev, PP
Kilronan, Aran Islands,
Co Galway
Tel 099-61221
(Aran Islands, Tuam)

Blake, Martin, CC
Cathedral Presbytery,
Ennis, Co Clare
Tel 065-6824043/
087-9033682
(Ennis, Killaloe)

Blake, Seán, Very Rev Canon,
AP
Clonberne, Ballinasloe,
Co Galway
Tel 093-45797
(Kilkerrin and Clonberne,
Tuam)

Blayney, Liam (SPS)
Regional Leader,
St Patrick's, Kiltegan,
Co Wicklow
Tel 059-6473680

Bluett, Garrett, Very Rev
Canon, PP
Manister, Croom,
Co Limerick
Tel 061-397335
(Manister, Limerick)

Bluett, Patrick, CC
Gortboy, Newcastle West,
Co Limerick
Tel 069-61881
(Newcastle West, Limerick)

Bluitt, Tobias, CC
Mallow, Co Cork
Tel 022-21259
(Cloyne)

Boggan, Matthew, CC
Galbally, Ballyhogue,
Enniscorthy, Co Wexford
Tel 053-9247814
(Bree, Ferns)

Bohan, Harry, Very Rev, PP
Director,
Pastoral Planning Office,
Westgate Business Park,
Ennis, Co Clare
Tel 065-6824094
(Killaloe)

Bohan, Seamus, Very Rev, PP
Tynagh, Loughrea,
Co Galway
Tel 090-9745113
(Clonfert)

Boland, Andrew P., Rt Rev
Mgr, Canon, PE
13 Griffith Avenue,
Dublin 9
(Dublin, retired)

Boland, Declan, PP
44 Barrack Street, Strabane,
Co Tyrone BT82 8HD
Tel 028-71883293
(Strabane, Derry)

Boland, Dominic S. (OFMCap)
St Anthony's Capuchin
Friary, 43 Dublin Street,
Carlow
Tel 059-9142543

Boland, Eugene, PP
14 Killyclogher Road,
Omagh,
Co Tyrone BT79 0AX
Tel 028-82243375
(Killyclogher, Derry)

Bollard, Daniel, Very Rev, PP
Chaplain,
St Columba's Hospital,
Thomastown, Co Kilkenny
Tel 056-7724279/
087-6644858
(Ossory)

Bonner, Patrick
140 Willowood Drive,
Wantagh, New York, USA
(Raphoe)

Boran, Anthony (OFMCap)
Provincial Office,
12 Halston Street,
Dublin 7
Tel 01-8733205

Bourke, Eamonn
Holy Cross College,
Clonliffe, Dublin 3
Tel 01-8379253/086-8346071
(Dublin)

Bourke, George, Very Rev, PP
Moycarkey, Thurles,
Co Tipperary
Tel 0504-44227
(Moycarkey, Cashel & E.)

Bourke, Gerard (SJ)
35 Lower Leeson Street,
Dublin 2
Tel 01-6761248

Bowe, John (SMA)
SMA House,
82 Ranelagh Road,
Ranelagh, Dublin 6
Tel 01-4968162/3

Bowen, Patrick, Very Rev, PP
Athea, Co Limerick
Tel 068-42116/087-6532842
(Athea, Limerick)

Boyce, Eugene, CC
14 Springfield Drive,
Dooradoyle
Tel 061-304508/086-2542517
(St Paul's, Limerick)

Boyce, John, CC
Golan, Milford, Co Donegal
Tel 074-9153280
(Kilmacrennan, Raphoe)

Boyce, Philip, Most Rev (OCD)
DD
Bishop of Raphoe,
Ard Adhamhnáin,
Letterkenny, Co Donegal
Tel 074-9121208
(Raphoe)

Boylan, Noel, CC
Knockraven, Enniskillen,
Co Fermanagh
Tel 028-67748266
Visiting Chaplain,
St Aidan's High School,
Derrylin, Co Fermanagh
Tel 028-67748337
(Derrylin, Kilmore)

Boyle, Bernard (OCSO), Dom
Mellifont Abbey,
Collon, Co Louth
Tel 041-9826103

Boyle, Brian
Ballyhooly, Co Cork
Tel 022-39148
(*Castletownroche*, Cloyne)

Boyle, Con, Very Rev, PP
Parochial House,
1 Craigstown Road,
Randalstown,
Co Antrim BT41 2AF
Tel 028-94472640
(*Randalstown*, Down & C.)

Boyle, Francis, Very Rev
Canon, PP
4 Shinn School Road,
Newry,
Co Down BT34 1PA
Tel 028-40630276
(*Saval*, Dromore)

Boyle, Gerry, Very Rev, PP
Parochial House,
Multyfarnham,
Co Westmeath
Tel 044-9371124
(*Multyfarnham*, Meath)

Boyle, James A. (MHM), Adm
St Mary's Parish,
25 Marquis Street,
Belfast BT1 1JJ
Tel 028-90320482
(*St Mary's*, Down & C.)

Boyle, John, Very Rev, PE
Ardmore, Youghal,
Co Cork
Tel 024-94177
(Waterford & L., retired)

Boyle, Lawrence, Very Rev, PP
'Glenshee', Dublin Road,
Newry, Co Down BT35 8DA
Tel 028-30262376
(*Middle Killeavy*, Armagh)

Boyle, Liam, Rt Rev
Knockaderry, Co Limerick
(Limerick, retired)

Boyle, Liam, Very Rev
9 Gargory Road, Ballyward,
Castlewellan,
Co Down BT31 9RN
Tel 028-40650234
(Dromore, retired)

Boyle, Martin (OP)
St Saviour's,
Upper Dorset Street,
Dublin 1
Tel 01-8897610

Boyle, Michael (OSA)
St Augustine's Priory,
Washington Street,
Cork
Tel 021-2753982

Boyle, Michael (SMA)
Retired in Ireland outside
SMA houses

Boyle, Paddy, CC
29 Glenayle Road,
Edenmore, Dublin 5
Tel 01-8481160/086-1011415
(*Edenmore*, Dublin)

Boyle, Ronnie, CC
Achill Sound, Achill,
Co Mayo
Tel 098-45109
(*Achill*, Tuam)

Bracken, John, CC
11 Foxrock Court, Foxrock,
Dublin 18
Tel 01-2895780
(*Foxrock*, Dublin)

Bracken, P. J., Very Rev, PP
Fahy, Eyrecourt, Ballinasloe,
Co Galway
Tel 090-9675116
(Clonfert)

Bracken, Patrick L. (MHM)
St Joseph's House,
50 Orwell Park, Rathgar,
Dublin 6
Tel 01-4127700

Brackett, Matthew (LC)
Superior & Novice Mater,
Novitiate,
Leopardstown Road,
Foxrock, Dublin 18
Tel 01-2955902

Bradley, Bruce (SJ)
Rector,
Clongowes Wood College,
Naas, Co Kildare
Tel 045-868663/868202

Bradley, David, Very Rev, PP
The Presbytery, Ballsgrove,
Drogheda, Co Louth
Tel 041-9831991
(*Drogheda, Holy Family*,
Meath)

Bradley, Francis
Director,
Diocesan Pastoral Centre,
164 Bishop Street,
Derry BT48 6UJ
Tel 028-71362475
The Presbytery,
11 Steelstown Road,
Derry BT48 8EU
Tel 028-71351718
(Our Lady of Lourdes,
Steelstown, Derry)

Bradley, John, Very Rev, PE
8 Killymeal Road,
Dungannon,
Co Tyrone BT71 6BE
Tel 028-87722183
(Armagh, retired)

Bradley, Manus
St Ignatius of Loyola,
4455 West Broadway,
Montreal,
Quebec H4B 2A7
(Derry)

Bradley, Patrick (SSCC), Very
Rev, PP
Coudrin House, 27
Northbrook Road, Dublin 6
Tel 01-6604898

Bradley, Thomas (White
Fathers)
Cypress Grove, Templeogue,
Dublin 6W
Tel 01-4055263/4055264

Bradley, William (CSSp) CC
Parochial House,
Letterkenny, Co Donegal
Tel 074-9121021
(*Letterkenny*, Raphoe)

Bradshaw, Brendan (SM)
Superior,
Mount St Mary's, Milltown,
Dublin 14
Tel 01-2697322

Brady, Bernard, Very Rev
Canon
61 Glasnevin Hill,
Dublin 9
(Dublin, retired)

Brady, Brian, PP
78 Ballerin Road, Garvagh,
Co Derry BT51 5EQ
Tel 028-29558251
(*Garvagh*, Derry)

Brady, Declan
Chaplain, Sligo Institute of
Technology
Tel 071-9155215
(Elphin)

Brady, Enda, CC
Ballina, Co Tipperary
Tel 061-376430
(*Ballina*, Cashel & E.)

Brady, Frank, (SJ), PC
The Presbytery,
Shangan Road, Ballymun,
Dublin 9
Tel 01-8421551
(*Ballymun*, Dublin)

Brady, Gerard, Very Rev, PP
Newtowncashel,
Co Longford
Tel 043-3325112
(*Newtowncashel*, Ardagh &
Cl.)

Brady, Harry, Very Rev, PP
Parochial House, Clarecastle,
Co Clare
Tel 065-6823011
(*Clarecastle*, Killaloe)

Brady, John (SJ)
Milltown Park,
Sandford Road,
Dublin 6
Tel 01-2698411/2698113

Brady, John (SPS)
St Patrick's, Kiltegan,
Co Wicklow
Tel 059-6473600

Brady, Kenneth (CP)
St Paul's Retreat,
Mount Argus, Dublin 6W
Tel 01-4992000

Brady, Kenneth (CP), AP
St Paul's Retreat,
Mount Argus, Dublin 6W
Tel 01-4992000
(*Mount Argus*, Dublin)

Brady, Macarten, Venerable
Archdeacon, PE
Sacred Heart Residence,
Sybil Hill Road, Killester,
Dublin 5
(Dublin, retired)

Brady, Oliver (OFMCap)
Capuchin Friary,
Station Road, Raheny,
Dublin 5
Tel 01-8313886

Brady, P. J. (OFM)
Provincial Office, La Verna,
Gormanston, Co Meath
Tel 01-8020951

Brady, Patrick V., Very Rev, VF
Drumkilly, Kilnaleck,
Co Cavan
Tel 049-4336120
(Kilmore)

Brady, Peter, Very Rev, PP
Lenamore, Co Longford
Tel 044-9357404
(*Legan and Ballycloghan*,
Ardagh & Cl.)

Brady, Philip, Very Rev
Laragh, Stradone,
Co Cavan
Tel 049-4330142
(*Laragh*, Kilmore)

Brady, Ray, Very Rev
c/o Bishop's House,
Mullingar
(Meath, retired)

Brady, Raymond, Very Rev, PP
Ballyhaise, Co Cavan
Tel 049-4338121
(*Castletara*, Kilmore)

Brady, Rory
1 Cathedral Place,
Letterkenny
Tel 074-9125182
Chaplain, Letterkenny
Institute of Technology,
Letterkenny, Co Donegal
Tel 074-9124888
(Raphoe)

Brady, Seán, His Eminence
Cardinal, DCL, DD
Archbishop of Armagh,
Ara Coeli,
Armagh BT61 7QY
Tel 028-37522045
(Armagh)

Brady, Thomas, CF
Chaplain, Dún Uí
Mhaoilíosa, Renmore,
Galway
Tel 091-701055
(Galway)

Branagan, Anthony (CSsR)
Mission in Siberia,
Redemptorysty,
UL Ochotskaja – 81,
6530045 Prokopievsk,
Kiemierovskaya OBL,
Rossia – Sibir
Tel 007-3846699103

Brankin, Aidan, Very Rev, PP
7 Culcrum Road,
Cloughmills BT44 9NH
Tel 028-27638267
(*Dunloy and Cloughmills*,
Down & C.)

Brassil, Paul (SJ)
St Ignatius Community &
Church, 27 Raleigh Row,
Salthill, Galway
Tel 091-523707

Brazil, Sean (SSC)
St Columban's, Dalgan Park,
Navan, Co Meath
Tel 046-9021525

Breathnach, Cormac, Very Rev
(SMA), PP
St Joseph's, Wilton, Cork
Tel 021-4341362
(*Wilton, St Joseph's*, Cork &
R.)

Bredin, Eamonn, CC
Arva, Co Cavan
Tel 049-4335246
(*Killeshandra*, Kilmore)

Bredin, Sean (MI)
St Camillus,
South Hill Avenue,
Blackrock, Co Dublin
Tel 01-2882873

Bree, Eugene (SPS)
St Patrick's, Kiltegan,
Co Wicklow
Tel 059-6473600

Breen, Albert (OCarm)
Gort Muire, Ballinteer,
Dublin 16
Tel 01-2984014

Breen, Daniel, Very Rev
2 St Mary's Court, Arklow,
Co Wicklow
(Dublin, retired)

Breen, Gerard, Very Rev, PP
Broadford, Co Kildare
Tel 046-9551203
(*Balyna*, Kildare & L.)

Breen, P. J. (OCarm)
Terenure College, Terenure,
Dublin 6W
Tel 01-4904621

Breen, Patrick (CSsR)
Mount Saint Alphonsus,
Limerick
Tel 061-315099

Breen, Patrick (MSC)
Carrignavar, Co Cork
Tel 021-4884044

Breen, Patrick, CC
Recess, Co Galway
Tel 095-34605
(*Roundstone*, Tuam)

Breen, Patrick, Very Rev, PE
Timahoe, Portlaoise,
Co Laois
Tel 057-8627023
(Kildare & L., retired)

Breen, Sean, Very Rev, PP
The Presbytery,
Ballymore Eustace,
Naas, Co Kildare
Tel 045-864114
(*Ballymore Eustace*, Dublin)

Breen, Simeon (OFMCap)
Capuchin Friary,
Station Road, Raheny,
Dublin 5
Tel 01-8313886

Breen, Thomas F., Very Rev
Canon, PP, VF
Fethard, Co Tipperary
Tel 052-31178
(*Fethard*, Cashel & E.)

Breen, Thomas J., Very Rev, PP
Holy Cross Abbey, Thurles,
Co Tipperary
Tel 0504-43124
(*Holy Cross*, Cashel & E.)

Breen, Thomas O., Very Rev,
PP
Ballingarry, Thurles,
Co Tipperary
Tel 052-9154115
(*Ballingarry*, Cashel & E.)

Breen, Thomas, Very Rev
Canon, PE
37 Esker Road,
Dromore, Omagh,
Co Tyrone BT78 3LE
Tel 028-82898216
(*Dromore*, Clogher)

Breheny, Pádraig (OFM), Very
Rev, PP
The Abbey,
St Francis Street, Galway
Tel 091-562518
(*St Francis*, Galway)

Brennan, Brian, Very Rev, PP
Ballinalee, Co Longford
Tel 043-3323110
(Ardagh & Cl.)

Brennan, David, Adm
Parochial House, Moynalvey,
Summerhill, Co Meath
Tel 046-9557031
(*Moynalvey*, Meath)

Brennan, Declan (OSA), CC
St Catherine's, Meath Street,
Dublin 8
Tel 01-4543356
(*Meath Street*, Dublin)

Brennan, Denis, Most Rev, DD
Bishop of Ferns,
Bishop's House, Summerhill,
Wexford
Tel 053-9122177
(Ferns)

Brennan, Dermot (OP)
St Mary's Priory, Tallaght,
Dublin 24
Tel 01-4048100

Brennan, Dermot J. (OP), Adm
St Mary's Priory, Tallaght,
Dublin 24
Tel 01-4048100
(*Tallaght, St Mary's*, Dublin)

Brennan, Fergal (SJ)
Milltown Park,
Sandford Road, Dublin 6
Tel 01-2698411/2698113

Brennan, Joseph (SJ)
Gonzaga College,
Sandford Road, Dublin 6
Tel 01-4972943

Brennan, Loughlin, CC
Upperchurch,
Thurles, Co Tipperary
Tel 0504-54492
(Cashel & E.)

Brennan, Louis (OFM)
Collegio S. Isidoro,
Via degli Artisti 41,
00187 Roma, Italy
Tel +39-06-4885359

Brennan, Michael (SPS)
St Patrick's, Kiltegan,
Co Wicklow
Tel 059-6473600

Brennan, Michael, Very Rev,
PP
Lettermore, Co Galway
Tel 091-551169
(*Lettermore*, Galway)

Brennan, Oliver, Very Rev, PP
Parochial House,
Grianán Mhuire,
Main Street, Blackrock,
Dundalk, Co Louth
Tel 042-9321621
(*Haggardstown and
Blackrock*, Armagh)

Brennan, Patrick, Very Rev
Canon
Gathabawn,
Via Thurles, Co Kilkenny
Tel 056-8832110
(Ossory, retired)

Brennan, Peter, CC
Ballinree, Boherlahan,
Cashel, Co Tipperary
Tel 0504-41215
(*Boherlahan and Dualla*,
Cashel & E.)

Brennan, Philip (OCarm)
Carmelite Friary,
Kinsale, Co Cork
Tel 021-772138

Brennan, Thomas
USA
(Ferns)

Brennock, Michael (OSA), CC
St Augustine's,
Taylor's Lane, Ballyboden,
Dublin 16
Tel 01-4944966
(*Ballyboden,* Dublin)

Brereton, Joseph (SJ)
Clongowes Wood College,
Naas, Co Kildare
Tel 045-868663/868202

Breslan, Oliver, Very Rev, PP
Parochial House,
Hanover Square,
Coagh, Cookstown,
Co Tyrone BT80 0EF
Tel 028-86737212
(*Coagh*, Armagh)

Breslan, Patrick, Very Rev, PP
Parochial House,
124 Eglish Road,
Dungannon,
Co Tyrone BT70 1LB
Tel 028-37548289
(*Eglish*, Armagh)

Breslin, Eamonn (CSsR)
European Parish,
Communauté Des
Rédemptoristes,
BP 354, L-2013 Luxembourg
Tel 00352-224880

Breslin, Michael, Very Rev, PP
Ballygar, Co Galway
Tel 090-6624637
(Elphin)

Bresnahan, Damian (SMA)
Provincial Councillor,
African Missions,
Provincial House, Feltrim,
Blackrock Road, Cork
Tel 021-4292871

Bresnan, John (OSA)
St Augustine's,
Taylor's Lane,
Balyboden, Dublin 16
Tel 01-4241000

Brewster, Patrick (SDB)
Salesian House,
45 St Teresa's Road,
Crumlin, Dublin 12
Tel 01-4555605
(*Crumlin*, Dublin)

Brick, Maurice, Very Rev, PP
Irremore, Listowel,
Co Kerry
Tel 066-7132111
(*Lixnaw*, Kerry)

Brickley, John, CC
Chapel Lane, Sallins Road,
Naas, Co Kildare
Tel 045-897260
(Kildare & L.)

Brilley, Joseph, Very Rev, PP
Drumraney,
Athlone, Co Westmeath
Tel 044-9356207
(*Drumraney*, Meath)

Brindley, Stanislaus (CM)
St Vincent's College,
Castleknock, Dublin 15
Tel 01-8213051

Briody, Joseph, CC
Cleeslough,
Co Donegal
Tel 074-9138011
(*Dunfanaghy*, Raphoe)

Briscoe, Peter, Rt Rev Mgr, PP
Stella Maris, Oswald Road,
Sandymount, Dublin 4
Tel 01-6684265
(*Sandymount*, Dublin)

Broaders, Brian, Very Rev,
Adm
The Presbytery,
Templeshannon,
Enniscorthy, Co Wexford
Tel 053-9237611
(*St Senan's, Enniscorthy*,
Ferns)

Broderick, Daniel, Very Rev,
PP
St Mary's, Tarbert, Co Kerry
Tel 068-36111
(*Tarbert*, Kerry)

Broderick, Donal, Very Rev, PP
Glanworth, Co Cork
Tel 025-38123
(*Glanworth and
Ballindangan*, Cloyne)

Broderick, John, Very Rev, PP
Killeagh, Co Cork
Tel 024-95133
(*Killeagh*, Cloyne)

Brodie, Thomas (OP)
St Saviour's,
Glentworth Street, Limerick
Tel 061-412333

Brogan, John, Very Rev, PP
Parochial House, Kilskyre,
Kells, Co Meath
Tel 046-9243623
(*Kilskyre*, Meath)

Brophy, Joseph, CC
Kiltegan, Co Wicklow
Tel 059-6473211
(*Rathvilly*, Kildare & L.)

Brophy, Robert, Very Rev, PP
The Presbytery,
Bantry, Co Cork
Tel 027-50096
(*Bantry*, Cork & R.)

Brouder, Jeremiah, CC
Crecora, Patrickswell,
Co Limerick
Tel 061-355148
(*Mungret/Crecora*, Limerick)

Brough, David, Very Rev, PP
Parochial House,
Bohernabreena, Tallaght,
Dublin 24
Tel 01-4627080
(*Bohernabreena*, Dublin)

Brown, Brian, Very Rev, PP
25 Bottier Road,
Moira, Craigavon,
Co Armagh BT67 0PE
Tel 028-92611347
(*Magheralin*, Dromore)

Brown, Francis, Very Rev
Canon, Adm
Cathedral Presbytery,
38 Hill Street,
Newry BT34 1AT
Tel 028-30262586
(*Newry*, Dromore)

Brown, John (CSSp)
Spiritan Missionary College,
Kimmage Manor,
Dublin 12
Tel 01-4064300

Brown, John (SMA), Very Rev,
PP
Church of Our Lady of the
Rosary and St Patrick,
61 Blackhorse Road,
Walthamstow,
London E17 7AS, England
Tel 20-85203647

Brown, Michael (OCD)
St Teresa's,
Clarendon Street, Dublin 2
Tel 01-6718466/6718127

Browne, Allen (MSC)
Western Road, Cork
Tel 021-4804120

Browne, Brian (OFMCap)
Capuchin Friary,
Ard Mhuire, Creeslough,
Letterkenny, Co Donegal
Tel 074-9138005

Browne, Colm, CC
Cathedral House, Mullingar,
Co Westmeath
Tel 044-9348338/9340126
(*Mullingar*, Meath)

Browne, David, Very Rev
Parochial House,
Ardpatrick, Co Limerick
Tel 063-91015
(Limerick, retired)

Browne, Denis
Brazil
(Ferns)

Browne, Denis, Very Rev
Canon
Kilmallock, Co Limerick
(Limerick, retired)

Browne, Dominic (OP)
Black Abbey, Kilkenny,
Co Kilkenny
Tel 056-21279

Browne, James (IC)
Rosminian House of Prayer,
Glencomeragh House,
Kilsheelan, Co Tipperary
Tel 052-33181

Browne, James (WF), CC
Gneeveguilla, Rathmore,
Co Kerry
Tel 064-56188
(*Rathmore*, Kerry)

Browne, James (White
Fathers)

Browne, Joseph
The Presbytery,
St Mellitus Church,
Tollington Park,
London N4 3AG
Tel 0171-2723415
(Cashel & E.)

Browne, Kevin (CSsR)
Clonard Monastery,
1 Clonard Gardens,
Belfast, BT13 2RL
Tel 028-90445950

Browne, Kevin A. (CSSp)
Blackrock College,
Blackrock, Co Dublin
Tel 01-2888681

Browne, Liam (SJ)
Milltown Park,
Sandford Road, Dublin 6
Tel 01-2698411/2698113

Browne, Michael (CSsR)
Clonard Monastery,
1 Clonard Gardens,
Belfast, BT13 2RL
Tel 028-90445950

Browne, Michael (SDB)
Salesian College,
Maynooth Road, Celbridge,
Co Kildare
Tel 01-6275058/60

Browne, Michael (SPS)
Tearmann Spirituality
Centre, Brockagh,
Glendalough, Co Wicklow
Tel 0404-45208

Browne, Patrick, CC
The Presbytery,
Templeshannon,
Enniscorthy, Co Wexford
Tel 053-9237611
(*St Senan's, Enniscorthy*,
Ferns)

Browne, Raymond A., Very
Rev, PP
Ballagh, Kilrooskey,
Roscommon
Tel 090-6626273
(*Ballagh*, Elphin)

Browne, Raymond, Very Rev,
PP
Fourmilehouse,
Roscommon
Tel 090-6629518
(*Fourmilehouse*, Elphin)

Browne, Richard, Very Rev, PP
Cappamore, Co Limerick
Tel 061-381288
(*Cappamore*, Cashel & E.)

Browne, Richard, Very Rev, PP
Kilnamartyra, Macroom,
Co Cork
Tel 026-40013
(*Kilnamartyra*, Cloyne)

Browne, Thomas, Very Rev
Canon, PP
South Abbey, Youghal,
Co Cork
Tel 024-92336
(*Youghal*, Cloyne)

Browne, Vincent (CSSp)
Blackrock College,
Blackrock, Co Dublin
Tel 01-2888681

Bryson, Bernard, PEm
Anniscliff House,
141 Moneysharvin Road,
Maghera, Co Derry
(Derry, retired)

Bucciarelli, Robert, Rt Rev, DD
Vicar for Ireland,
Harvieston,
Cunningham Road, Dalkey,
Co Dublin
Tel 01-2859877
(Opus Dei)

Buckley, Benignus (OFMCap)
Guardian, Capuchin Friary,
Friary Street, Kilkenny
Tel 056-7721439

Buckley, Con, CC
Knocknagree, Mallow,
Co Cork
Tel 064-56029
(*Rathmore*, Kerry)

Buckley, David, Very Rev, PE,
CC
Dromina, Charleville,
Co Cork
Tel 063-70207
(*Shandrum*, Cloyne)

Buckley, Edward F. (CSSp)
Holy Ghost Missionary
College, Kimmage Manor,
Dublin 12
Tel 01-4064300

Buckley, James (CSsR)
St Patrick's, Esker, Athenry,
Co Galway
Tel 091-844549

Buckley, John, Most Rev, DD
Bishop of Cork and Ross,
Cork and Ross Offices,
Redemption Road, Cork
Tel 021-4301717
(Cork & R.)

Buckley, John, Very Rev, PP
Annascaul, Co Kerry
Tel 066-9157103
(*Annascaul*, Kerry)

Buckley, Michael J. (CSSp)
St Mary's College,
Rathmines, Dublin 6
Tel 01-4062160

Buckley, Patrick, Very Rev, PP
Dromahane, Mallow,
Co Cork
Tel 022-21244
(Cloyne)

Buckmaster, Ian (White
Fathers)
Delegate Superior,
Provincialate,
Cypress Grove Road,
Templeogue, Dublin 6W
Tel 01-4992346

Budau, Ciprian (OFMConv), CC
Friary of the Visitation,
Fairview Strand, Dublin 3
Tel 01-8376000
(*Fairview*, Dublin)

Bulman, Joseph (OP), Very
Rev
Prior, Holy Cross,
Tralee, Co Kerry
Tel 066-21135/29185

Burger, John (SSC)
St Columban's,
Grange Road,
Donaghmede, Dublin 13
Tel 01-8476647

Burke, Alan
Chaplain, University
Hospital, Galway
Tel 091-524222
(Galway)

Burke, Christopher (CSSp)
Chaplain,
National Rehab Hospital,
Rochestown Avenue,
Dun Laoghaire, Co Dublin
Tel 01-2355272/2355287

Burke, Colm, Very Rev, AP
Barnacarroll, Claremorris,
Co Mayo
Tel 094-9388189
(Claremorris (Kilcolman),
Tuam)

Burke, Dermot, PE
Ballyshannon, Raphoe
(Ballyshannon, Raphoe)

Burke, Edward (OFM)
Franciscan College,
Gormanston, Co Meath
Tel 01-8412203

Burke, Enda, Very Rev, AP
Cloughjordan, Co Tipperary
Tel 0505-42120
(Cloughjordan, Killaloe)

Burke, Fintan (OCarm)
Carmelite Priory,
Knocktopher,
Co Kilkenny
Tel 056-7768675

Burke, Gabriel, CC
Macroom, Co Cork
Tel 026-41247
(Macroom, Cloyne)

Burke, Kieran, CC
Leenane, Co Galway
Tel 095-42251
(Ballyhaunis (Annagh),
Tuam)

Burke, Liam (SMA)
African Missions,
Blackrock Road, Cork
Tel 021-4292871

Burke, Noel (SDB)
Vice-Rector, Salesian House,
Warrenstown, Drumree,
Co Meath
Tel 01-8259894

Burke, Patrick
Hospital Chaplain, Castlebar,
Co Mayo
(Castlebar, Tuam)

Burke, Peter, Very Rev, PP
Drumshanbo, Co Leitrim
Tel 071-9641010
(Drumshanbo, Ardagh & Cl.)

Burke, Sean, CC
Ballintogher, Co Sligo
Tel 071-9164154
(Killenummery and
Ballintogher, Ardagh & Cl.)

Burke, Tom
Ruan, Co Clare and
c/o Carrigoran House,
Newmarket-on-Fergus,
Co Clare
Tel 061-368100
(Killaloe, retired)

Burns, Daniel, PE
Parochial House, Belgooly,
Co Cork
(Cork & R., retired)

Burns, Dermot, Very Rev, PP
Straide, Foxford,
Co Mayo
Tel 094-9031029
(Achonry)

Burns, Edward, CC
Maudabawn, Cootehill,
Co Cavan
Tel 049-5552508
(Cootehill, Kilmore)

Burns, Gerard, Very Rev, PP
The Parochial House,
Letterfrack, Connemara,
Co Galway
Tel 095-41053/087-2408171
(Letterfrack (Ballinakill),
Tuam)

Burns, John, CC
5 Plater's Hill, Coalisland,
Co Tyrone BT71 4JZ
Tel 028-87740302
(Coalisland, Armagh)

Burns, John, CC
Parochial House,
Ballycraigy Road, Craigyhill,
Larne, Co Antrim BT40 2LE
Tel 028-28260130
(Larne, Down & C.)

Burns, Karl, Very Rev, Adm
Parke, Castlebar,
Co Mayo
Tel 094-9031314
(Parke (Turlough), Tuam)

Burns, Pat, CC
Pallasgreen, Co Limerick
Tel 061-384114
(Cashel & E.)

Burns, Patrick (MCCJ)
8 Clontarf Road,
Clontarf, Dublin 3
Tel 01-8330051

Burns, Peter (CSsR)
Provincial Vicar,
Liguori House,
75 Orwell Road, Dublin 6
Tel 01-4067100

Burns, Thomas
St John's Presbytery,
New Street, Waterford
Tel 051-874271
(St John's, Waterford & L.)

Butler, Anthony J. (SMA)
African Missions,
Blackrock Road, Cork
Tel 021-4292871

Butler, Eamonn, Very Rev
10 Lynn Heights, Mullingar,
Co Westmeath
Tel 044-9344008
(Meath, retired)

Butler, James, CC
Ballygarrett, Gorey,
Co Wexford
Tel 053-9427330
(Ballygarrett, Ferns)

Butler, John (SDB)
Salesian College,
Maynooth Road, Celbridge,
Co Kildare
Tel 01-6275058/60

Butler, Kieran (SM), PC
The Presbytery,
Coolock Village, Dublin 5
Tel 01-8484799
Superior,
Chanel Community,
Coolock, Dublin 5
Tel 01-8477133
(Cookock, St Brendan's,
Dublin)

Butler, Patrick, Very Rev, PP
Parochial House,
Clogheen, Cahir,
Co Tipperary
Tel 052-7465268
(Clogheen, Waterford & L.)

Butler, Reuben, Very Rev
Canon, AP
Newmarket-on-Fergus,
Co Clare
Tel 061-368433
(Newmarket-on-Fergus,
Killaloe)

Butler, Robert, Very Rev, PP
Parochial House,
44 Lough Road,
Loughguile, Ballymena,
Co Antrim BT44 9JN
Tel 028-27641206
(Loughguile, Down & C.)

Butler, Thomas (SM)
Chanel Community,
Coolock, Dublin 5
Tel 01-8477133

Byamukama, Henry (White
Fathers)
Cypress Grove, Templeogue,
Dublin 6W
Tel 01-4055263/4055264

Byrne, Alfie (SPS)
St Patrick's, Kiltegan,
Co Wicklow
Tel 059-6473600

Byrne, Archie (OP)
St Dominic's Retreat House,
Montenotte, Co Cork
Tel 021-4502520

Byrne, Arthur, Very Rev
Castor's Bay Road, Lurgan
(Dromore, retired)

Byrne, Brendan, Rt Rev Mgr,
PP, VG
Tullow, Co Carlow
Tel 059-9152159
(Kildare & L.)

Byrne, Charles, Very Rev
Holy Family Convent,
Newbridge, Co Kildare
(Kildare & L., retired)

Byrne, Charles, Very Rev, Adm
Administrator
15 Chapel Hill,
Mayobridge, Newry,
Co Down BT34 2EX
Tel 028-30851225
Parish
84 Milltown Street,
Burren, Warrenpoint,
Co Down BT34 3PU
Tel 028-41772200
(Clonallon, St Mary's
(Burren), Dromore)

Byrne, Charles, Very Rev, PP
Carrigart, Co Donegal
Tel 074-9155154
(Carrigart, Raphoe)

Byrne, Conleth,
C/o 73 Somerton Road,
Belfast BT15 4DE
(Down & C., retired)

Byrne, Des (CSSp), CC
45 Woodford Drive,
Monastery Road,
Clondalkin, Dublin 22
Tel 01-4592323
(Clondalkin, Dublin)

Byrne, Diarmuid, Adm
18 St Anthony's Road,
Dublin 8
Tel 01-4534469
(Dolphin's Barn, Dublin)

Byrne, Donal (OCarm), CC
Presbytery, Montrose Park,
Beaumont, Dublin 5
Tel 01-8477740/8476359
(Beaumont, Dublin)

Byrne, Eamonn (SSC)
St Columban's Retirement
Home, Dalgan Park,
Navan, Co Meath
Tel 046-9021525

Byrne, Felix, Very Rev Canon,
CC
Monaseed, Gorey,
Co Wexford
Tel 053-9428207
(Craanford, Ferns)

Byrne, Gareth, PC
107 Mount Prospect Avenue,
Clontarf, Dublin 3
Tel 01-8339301
(Dollymount, Dublin)

Byrne, Gerald, Very Rev, PP
Parochial House,
Graignamanagh,
Co Kilkenny
Tel 059-9724973
(Graignamanagh, Kildare &
L.)

Allianz ⑪

Byrne, Gerard
Chaplain, Blackrock Clinic,
Dublin
Tel 01-2832222
(Dublin)

Byrne, James, Very Rev
Ballylannon,
Wellingtonbridge,
Co Wexford
(Ferns, retired)

Byrne, John (CSSp)
Superior,
Templeogue College,
Dublin 6W
Tel 01-4903909

Byrne, John, CC
Cathedral Presbytery,
38 Hill Street,
Newry BT34 1AT
Tel 028-30262586
(Dromore)

Byrne, John, CC
Monamolin, Gorey,
Co Wexford
Tel 053-9389223
(Kilmuckridge, Ferns)

Byrne, John (OSA)
Augustinian Retreat Centre,
Old Court Road,
Dublin 16
Tel 01-4930932

Byrne, John, Rt Rev Mgr, PP
Parochial House,
Dublin Road, Portlaoise,
Co Laois
Tel 057-8692153
(Kildare & L.)

Byrne, John, Very Rev, PP, VF
Parochial House, Kells,
Co Meath
Tel 046-9240213
(Meath)

Byrne, Martin, Very Rev, PP
Ballymore, Killinick,
Co Wexford
Tel 053-9158966
(Ballymore and Mayglass,
Ferns)

Byrne, Mel (CP)
Passionist Retreat Centre,
Tobar Mhuire, Crossgar,
Co Down BT30 9EA
Tel 028-44830242

Byrne, Michael, CC
Boolavogue, Ferns,
Wexford
Tel 053-9366282
(Monageer, Ferns)

Byrne, Michael, Very Rev, PP
Cushinstown, Foulksmills,
Co Wexford
Tel 051-428347
(Cushinstown, Ferns)

Byrne, P. G. (SM)
St Brendan's Parish,
Coolock Village, Dublin 5
Tel 01-8484799
(Coolock, St Brendan's,
Dublin)

Byrne, P. J. (SM)
Mount St Mary's,
Milltown, Dublin 14
Tel 01-2697322

Byrne, P. J., Very Rev, PP
Kilcock, Co Kildare
Tel 01-6287448
(Kilcock, Kildare & L.)

Byrne, Pat (SM), PC
The Presbytery,
Coolock Village, Dublin 5
Tel 01-8484799
(Coolock, Dublin)

Byrne, Pat (SVD)
133 North Circular Road,
Dublin 7
Tel 01-8386743

Byrne, Patrick, CC
Muinebheag, Co Carlow
Tel 059-9723886
(Muinebheag/
Bagenalstown, Kildare & L.)

Byrne, Paul (OMI)
Oblate House of Retreat,
Inchicore, Dublin 8
Tel 01-4534408/4541805

Byrne, Paul, CC
142 Carnmoney Road,
Newtownabbey,
Co Antrim BT36 6JU
Tel 028-90832488
(St Mary's on the Hill, Down
& C.)

Byrne, Paul, Very Rev, PP
Parochial House,
31 Brackaville Road,
Coalisland,
Co Tyrone BT71 4NH
Tel 028-87740221
(Coalisland, Armagh)

Byrne, Peter (CSsR)
Mount Saint Alphonsus,
Limerick
Tel 061-315099

Byrne, Richard (OCarm)
Terenure College, Terenure,
Dublin 6W
Tel 01-4904621

Byrne, Thomas (CSsR)
Mount Saint Alphonsus,
Limerick
Tel 061-315099

Byrne, Tony (CSSp)
Awareness Education Office,
3 Cabra Grove, Dublin 7
Tel 01-8388888

Byrne, William, CC
Coolfancy, Tinahely,
Co Wicklow
Tel 0402-34725
(Carnew, Ferns)

Byrne, William, CC
Newbridge, Co Kildare
Tel 045-433979
(Kildare & L.)

Byrne, Willie, CC
St Conleth's, Chapel Lane,
Droichead Nua, Co Kildare
Tel 045-433979
(Droichead Nua/Newbridge,
Kildare & L.)

Byrnes, James (CSSp)
Holy Ghost Missionary
College, Kimmage Manor,
Dublin 12
Tel 01-4064300

Byrnes, Michael
Galway Marriage Tribunal
(Clonfert)

Byrnes, Michael
Marriage Tribunal,
7 Waterside, Woodquay,
Galway
(Galway)

C

Cadam, Simon, Very Rev, PP,
VF
St Mary's, Granard,
Co Longford
Tel 043-6686550
(Ardagh & Cl.)

Cafferty, Tom (SPS)
St Patrick's, Kiltegan,
Co Wicklow
Tel 059-6473600

Caffrey, Francis (CSSp)
Spiritan Provincialate,
Temple Park,
Richmond Avenue South,
Dublin 6
Tel 01-4975127/4977230

Caffrey, James, Very Rev, PP
'Marmion', 87 Iona Road,
Dublin 9
Tel 01-8308257
(Iona Road, Dublin)

Cahill, David (SDB)
Salesian House,
Warrenstown, Drumree,
Co Meath
Tel 01-8259894

Cahill, Donal, Very Rev, Adm
Lisheen, Skibbereen,
Co Cork
Tel 028-38111
(Aughadown, Cork & R.)

Cahill, Éamann, Very Rev, PP
Parochial House,
Sandyford Village, Dublin 18
Tel 01-2956317
(Sandyford, Dublin)

Cahill, John (CSSp)
Holy Ghost Missionary
College, Kimmage Manor,
Dublin 12
Tel 01-4064300

Cahill, Joseph (SSC)
Bother na Sop, Ballina,
Co Mayo
Tel 096-22984

Cahill, Kevin (OCL) CC
Ballymitty, Co Wexford
Tel 051-561128/053-9165108
(Ferns)

Cahill, Lee (SMA)
Dromantine College,
Dromantine, Newry,
Co Down BT34 1RH
Tel 028-30821224

Cahill, Michael (SMA)
African Missions,
Blackrock Road, Cork
Tel 021-4292871

Cahill, Michael, Very Rev, PP
Parochial House, Kilbeg,
Kells, Co Meath
Tel 046-9246604
(Kilbeggan, Meath)

Cahill, Seán, Rt Rev Mgr, VG
6 Boyhill Road,
Maguiresbridge, Enniskillen
Co Fermanagh BT94 4LN
Tel 028-67721258
(Clogher)

Cahill, Sean, Very Rev, PP
Parochial House,
91 Main Street,
Castlewellan,
Co Down BT31 9DH
Tel 028-43778259
(Castlewellan (Kilmegan),
Down & C.)

Cahill, Thomas (SVD)
Donamon Castle,
Roscommon
Tel 090-6662222

Cahir, Anthony, Very Rev, PP
Birr, Co Offaly
Tel 057-9120097/086-
2612121
Chaplain, District Hospital,
Birr, Co Offaly
Tel 0509-20819
Chaplain, Welfare Home,
Birr, Co Offaly
Tel 0509-20248

Callaghan, Daniel (OCarm)
Whitefriar Street Church,
56 Aungier Street, Dublin 2
Tel 01-4758821

Callan, Paul, Very Rev Mgr
Archbishop's Secretary,
Archbishop's House,
Drumcondra, Dublin 9
Tel 01-8373732
(Dublin)

Callanan, John (SJ)
Gonzaga College,
Sandford Road, Dublin 6
Tel 01-4972943

Callanan, John, Very Rev, PE
Kilmacthomas,
Co Waterford
Tel 051-294266
(Waterford & L., retired)

Callanan, Patrick, Very Rev
Canon, PP
Kilbeacanty, Gort,
Co Galway
Tel 091-631691
(Galway)

Callanan, Richard (OFM)
Franciscan Friary, Clonmel,
Co Tipperary
Tel 052-6121378

Callanan, Stanislaus (OCD)
Avila, Bloomfield Avenue,
Morehampton Road,
Dublin 4
Tel 01-6430200

Callanan, William (SJ)
Milltown Park,
Sandford Road, Dublin 6
Tel 01-2698411/2698113

Callanan, William, Very Rev,
AP
Kill, Co Waterford
Tel 051-292212
(Newtown, Waterford & L.)

Campbell, Colm
20 Continental Avenue,
Apt 4D, Forest Hills,
New York 11375, USA
Tel 001-7185443304
(Down & C., retired)

Campbell, Garrett, CC
Parochial House,
3 Convent Road,
Cookstown,
Co Tyrone BT80 8QA
Tel 028-86763293
(Armagh)

Campbell, Gerard, Very Rev,
Adm, VF
St Patrick's Presbytery,
Roden Place, Dundalk,
Co Louth
Tel 042-9334648
(Dundalk, St Patrick's,
Armagh)

Campbell, James (SSS)
Superior,
Blessed Sacrament Chapel,
20 Bachelors Walk, Dublin 1
Tel 01-8724597

Campbell, Joseph, Very Rev,
PE
17 Lough Road,
Mullaghbawn, Newry,
Co Down BT35 9XP
(Armagh, retired)

Campbell, Michael, CC
Kilbrin, Kanturk, Co Cork
Tel 022-48169
(Ballyclough, Cloyne)

Campbell, Michael, Very Rev,
PP
Carra, Granard,
Co Longford
Tel 043-6686270
(Abbeylara, Ardagh & Cl.)

Campbell, Noel
Ballysmutton, Manor
Kilbride, Blessington,
Co Wicklow
(Dublin, retired)

Campion, Cornelius K. (SSC)
St Columban's, Dalgan Park,
Navan, Co Meath
Tel 046-9021525

Campion, Desmond (SDB)
Chaplain Naval Service,
Haulbowline, Cobh, Cork

Campion, John (SDB), Very
Rev, PP
Salesian House, Milford,
Castletroy, Limerick
Tel 061-330268
(Our Lady Help of Christians,
Limerick)

Campion, Joseph (SAC) CC
(Attached to Pallotine
College)
Freshford, Co Kilkenny
Tel 056-8832461/
086-1775172
(Freshford, Ossory)

Campion, Loughlin (SSC)
St Columban's Retirement
Home, Dalgan Park,
Navan, Co Meath
Tel 046-9021525

Canavan, Colm, Very Rev
Canon, AP
Tully, Ballinahown,
Co Galway
Tel 091-593142
(Spiddal, Tuam)

Candon, Cyprian (OP)
St Saviour's,
Upper Dorset Street,
Dublin 1
Tel 01-8897610

Canniffe, Daniel (SSC)
St Columban's Retirement
Home, Dalgan Park,
Navan, Co Meath
Tel 046-9021525

Canning, Gerald T.
35 Dun Emer Green, Lusk,
Co Dublin
(Dublin, retired)

Canning, Thomas, CC
50 Brook Street, Omagh,
Co Tyrone BT78 5HE
Tel 028-82242092
(Omagh, Derry)

Cannon, Aodhan, CC
Ardara, Co Donegal
Tel 074-9541930
(Ardara, Raphoe)

Cannon, Seán (CSsR)
Alphonsian Academy,
Via Merulana 31, CP 2458,
00100 Rome, Italy
Tel 49490-1

Canny, Bryan M., Rt Rev Mgr,
PP, VG
St Patrick's Presbytery,
Buncrana Road,
Derry BT48 7QL
Tel 028 71262360
(Derry)

Canny, Michael, Adm
Media Liaison Person,
PO Box 227, Bishop's House,
Derry BT48 9YG
Tel 028-71262302
Parochial House,
St Eugene's Cathedral,
Derry BT48 9AP
Tel 028-71262894/71365712
(Derry City, Derry)

Cantillon, Eric (SJ), CC
Clongowes Wood College,
Naas, Co Kildare
Tel 045-868663/868202

Cantwell, Brendan, Very Rev,
PP
Parochial House,
Castledermot, Co Kildare
Tel 059-9144164/
086-2528545
(Castledermot, Dublin)

Cantwell, Joe (SPS)
Assistant Regional Leader,
St Patrick's, Kiltegan,
Co Wicklow
Tel 059-6473600

Cantwell, Kieran, Very Rev, PP
Danesfort, Co Kilkenny
Tel 056-7727137/
087-2661228
(Danesfort, Ossory)

Caples, Andrew (OSA)
St Augustine's,
Taylor's Lane,
Balyboden, Dublin 16
Tel 01-4241000

Caraher, Laurence, Very Rev,
PP
Parochial House, Tullyallen,
Drogheda, Co Louth
Tel 041-9838520
(Mellifont, Armagh)

Carberry, Fernando (CP)
St Paul's Retreat,
Mount Argus, Dublin 6W
Tel 01-4992000

Carbery, Aidrian, Very Rev, PP
26 Beech Grove, Kildare
Tel 045-521900
(Kildare & L.)

Carbery, Brendan F., Very Rev
Canon
5 Griffith Avenue, Marino,
Dublin 9
(Dublin, retired)

Carey, Brian (CSSp)
Holy Ghost Missionary
College, Kimmage Manor,
Dublin 12
Tel 01-4064300

Carey, Jerry, Very Rev, Adm
3 The Woods, Cappahard,
Tulla Road,
Ennis, Co Clare
Tel 065-6822225/086-
2508444
(Doora, Killaloe)

Carey, John, CC
The Presbytery, Oldtown,
Co Dublin
Tel 01-8433133
(Rolestown, Dublin)

Carey, Michael, Very Rev,
Adm
151 Swords Road,
Whitehall, Dublin 9
Tel 01-8374887
(Larkhill-Whitehall-Santry,
Dublin)

Carey, Patrick
Errill, Portlaoise, Co Laois
Tel 0505-44973/087-2599087
(Ossory)

Carey, Terence (OCD)
53/55 Marlborough Road,
Dublin 4
Tel 01-6601832

Carey, William, Very Rev, PP
Kilsheelan, Clonmel,
Co Tipperary
Tel 052-6133118
(Kilsheelan, Waterford & L.)

Cargan, John, PP
The Presbytery,
11 Steelstown Road,
Derry BT48 8EU
Tel 028-71351718
(Our Lady of Lourdes,
Steelstown, Derry)

Carley, Martin, CC
St Mary's, Drogheda,
Co Louth
Tel 041-9834958
(Drogheda, St Mary's,
Meath)

Carlin, Harry, Very Rev
5 Fortwilliam Court,
Belfast BT15 4DS
Tel 028-90772376
(Down & C., retired)

Carlin, Neal
St Anthony's, Dundrean,
Burnfoot, Co Donegal
Tel 074-9368370
(Derry)

Carlin, Peter, Very Rev, PP
St Michael's Presbytery,
206 Finaghy Road North,
Belfast BT11 9EG
Tel 028-90913761
(St Michael's, Down & C.)

Carmody, Brendan (SJ)
c/o Jesuit Provincial Curia,
IMI Centre, Sandyford Road,
Dublin 16
Tel 01-2932820

Carmody, Patrick, Very Rev,
AP
Cooraclare, Co Clare
Tel 065-9059010
(*Cooraclare*, Killaloe)
Carmody, Patrick, Very Rev,
PP
Parochial House,
Main Street, Celbridge,
Co Kildare
Tel 01-6288827
(*Celbridge*, Dublin)
Carney, Denis, Very Rev
Balla, Co Mayo
Tel 094-9365025
(*Balla and Manulla*, Tuam)
Carney, Michael, PE
c/o Diocesan Office,
The Cathedral, Galway
Tel 091-563566
(Galway, retired)
Carney, Michael, Very Rev, PP
Ramelton, Co Donegal
Tel 074-9151304
(*Ramelton,* Raphoe)
Carolan, Edward (OMI)
Oblate House of Retreat,
Inchicore, Dublin 8
Tel 01-4534408/4541805
Carolan, Loughlain
15 Lisdarn Heights, Cavan
(Kilmore)
Carolan, Patrick (OMI), Very
Rev
Parochial House,
118 Naas Road, Dublin 8
Tel 01-4501040/087-2900468
(*Bluebell*, Dublin)
Carolan, Walter, PEm
100 Altinure Road Park,
Claudy, Co Derry BY47 4DE
(Derry, retired)
Carr, Brendan (CSSp)
SPIRASI, Spiritan House,
213 North Circular Road,
Dublin 7
Tel 01-8389664/8683504
Carr, Daniel, Rt Rev Mgr, PP,
VG
St Johnston, Lifford,
Co Donegal
Tel 074-9148203
Ard Adhamhnáin,
Letterkenny, Co Donegal
(Raphoe)
Carr, Frank (SSC)
St Columban's, Dalgan Park,
Navan, Co Meath
Tel 046-9021525
Carrick, Michael (MSC)
Western Road, Cork
Tel 021-4804120
Carrigan, James, Very Rev
Canon
Ballacolla, Portlaoise,
Co Laois
Tel 0502-34016
(Ossory, retired)

Carrig, Noel (MI)
St Camillus, Killucan,
Co Westmeath
Tel 044-74115
Carrigy, Colman
Clonee, Killoe, Co Longford
(Ardagh & Cl.)
Carroll, Aidan, CC
'Carraig Donn', 23
Glenageary Woods, Dun
Laoghaire,
Co Dublin
Tel 01-28072233
(*Dun Laoghaire,* Dublin)
Carroll, Andrew (CSSp)
Holy Ghost Missionary
College, Kimmage Manor,
Dublin 12
Tel 01-4064300
Carroll, Andrew (MI)
St Camillus, Killucan,
Co Westmeath
Tel 044-74115
Carroll, Daniel (SDB)
Salesian College,
Maynooth Road,
Celbridge, Co Kildare
Tel 01-627/5058/60
Carroll, Daniel, Very Rev, PP
St Fiacre's Gardens,
Bohernatounish Road,
Loughboy, Kilkenny
Tel 056-7764400/
087-9077769
(Ossory)
Carroll, David
Birr, Co Offaly
Tel 057-9120098/
086-2367909
(Birr, Killaloe)
Carroll, Declan, Very Rev, CC
Mulrany, Co Mayo
Tel 098-36107
(Newport (Burrishoole),
Tuam)
Carroll, Denis
85 Hillcrest Drive,
Lucan, Co Dublin
Tel 01-6280948
(Dublin, retired)
Carroll, Gerard
Ballinalee Road,
Longford
(Ardagh & Cl.)
Carroll, Gregory (OP)
Provincial Secretary,
Provincial Office,
St Mary's, Tallaght,
Dublin 24
Tel 01-4048118/4048115
Carroll, J.
Chaplain,
Sligo General Hospital
Tel 071-9171111
(Elphin)

Carroll, James, Very Rev
Canon, PP, VF
Parochial House,
9 Fair Street, Drogheda,
Co Louth
Tel 041-9838537
(*Drogheda*, Armagh)
Carroll, Jeremiah
Study Leave
Archdiocese of
Dublin/Defence Forces
(Clogher)
Carroll, Jerry
Casement Aerodrome,
Baldonnell, Co Dublin
Tel 01-4592497
(Dublin)
Carroll, John P. (SPS)
St Patrick's, Kiltegan,
Co Wicklow
Tel 059-6473600
Carroll, John, CC
Diocesan Secretary,
PO Box 40, Bishop's House,
Summerhill, Wexford
Tel 053-9124368
Diocesan Secretary,
Barntown, Co Wexford
Tel 053-9120853
(*Glynn*, Ferns)
Carroll, Patrick (OSM)
Provincial, St Mary's Priory,
264 Fulham Road,
London SW10 9EL
Tel 0044-2077952181
Carroll, Patrick, Very Rev, PP
124 New Cabra Road,
Dublin 7
Tel 01-8385244
(Dublin)
Carroll, Thomas, Very Rev, PP
Parteen, Co Clare
Tel 061-345613
(Limerick)
Carter, Seamus, Very Rev
Abbeybreaffey Nursing
Home, Dublin Road,
Castlebar, Co Mayo
(Tuam, retired)
Carton, Francis (OCSO)
Mount Melleray Abbey,
Cappoquin, Co Waterford
Tel 058-54404
Carvill, Gregory, CC
Parochial House,
17 Carnmore Drive, Newry,
Co Down BT35 8SB
Tel 028-30269047
(*Middle Killeavy*, Armagh)
Carvill, Aidan (SM)
Australia
Carvill, Andrew, CC
Monument Hill, Fermoy,
Co Cork
Tel 025-32212
(*Fermoy*, Cloyne)

Casey, Aquin, Very Rev, Adm
The Presbytery,
Ravenswood, Fermoy,
Co Cork
Tel 025-31414
(*Fermoy*, Cloyne)
Casey, Brendan (SVD)
Maynooth, Co Kildare
Tel 01-6286391/2
Casey, Con J. (CSsR)
Liguori House,
75 Orwell Road, Dublin 6
Tel 01-4067100
Casey, Cornelius (CSsR)
Acting President,
Milltown Institute of
Theology and Philosophy,
Milltown Park,
Sandford Road, Dublin 6
Tel 01-2776300
Casey, Eamonn, Most Rev, DD
Shanaglish, Gort,
Co Galway
(Galway, retired)
Casey, Edward (SMA), CC
Kinvara, Co Galway
Tel 091-637283
(*Kinvara*, Galway)
Casey, Gerard, Very Rev
Canon, PP, VF
Doneraile, Co Cork
Tel 022-24156
(Cloyne)
Casey, John (CSsR)
28 Broadway Road,
Blanchardstown,
Dublin 15
Tel 01-8213716
(*Blanchardstown*, Dublin)
Casey, John (CSsR)
Marianella, 75 Orwell Road,
Dublin 6
Tel 01-4067100
Casey, John (SMA)
African Missions,
Blackrock Road, Cork
Tel 021-4292871
Casey, Kevin (SJ)
St Francis Xavier's, Upper
Gardiner Street, Dublin 1
Tel 01-8363411
Casey, Martin, Very Rev, PP
Woolgreen, Carnew,
Co Wicklow
Tel 053-9426888
(*Carnew*, Ferns)
Casey, Michael (SDB), Very
Rev, Adm
24 Killarney Street,
Dublin 1
Tel 01-8363554/086-8382631
(*Sean McDermott Street*,
Dublin)

Casey, Michael, Very Rev, PP
Cross, Kilrush,
Co Clare
Tel 065-9058008/
086-0842216
(*Carrigaholt and* Cross,
Killaloe)
Casey, Patrick, Very Rev
St Mary's Terrace,
Bishopsgate Street,
Mullingar, Co Westmeath
Tel 044-9342746
(Meath, retired)
Casey, Paul, CC
Cootehill, Co Cavan
Tel 049-5552163
(*Lavey*, Kilmore)
Casey, Peter (CSSp)
Spiritan Missionary College,
Kimmage Manor,
Dublin 12
Tel 01-4064300
Casey, Peter, Very Rev, PP
Ballinagh, Co Cavan
Tel 049-4337232
(*Kilmore*, Kilmore)
Casey, Seamus
11 Auburn Heights,
Athlone, Co Westmeath
Tel 090-6478318
(Ardagh & Cl.)
Casey, Sean (CSSp)
Blackrock College,
Blackrock, Co Dublin
Tel 01-2888681
Casey, Sean, Very Rev, PP
Ennybegs, Longford
Tel 043-3323119
(*Killoe*, Ardagh & Cl.)
Casey, Thomas (SJ)
c/o Jesuit Provincial Curia,
IMI Centre, Sandyford Road,
Dublin 16
Tel 01-2932820
Casey, Timothy (CM), CC
122 Sunday's Well Road,
Cork
Tel 021-4304070
(*St Vincent's, Sunday's Well*,
Cork & R.)
Casey, Tony
Padres de San Columbano,
Apartado 39-073/074,
Lima 39, Peru
(Killaloe)
Cashman, Daniel (SMA)
Superior, SMA House,
Wilton, Cork
Tel 021-4541069/4541884
Cashman, Denis, Very Rev, PP
Parochial House,
Watergrasshill, Co Cork
Tel 021-4889103
(*Watergrasshill*, Cork & R.)
Cashman, James
1 Pinewood, Wexford
(Ferns)

Casserly, Bernard (OP)
Newbridge College,
Droichead Nua, Co Kildare
Tel 045-487200
Cassidy, Derek (SJ)
St Francis Xavier's, Upper
Gardiner Street, Dublin 1
Tel 01-8363411
Cassidy, Dermot (SJ)
St Ignatius Community &
Church, 27 Raleigh Row,
Salthill, Galway
Tel 091-523707
Cassidy, Eoin, PC
The Presbytery,
Haddington Road, Dublin 4
Tel 01-6600075
(*Haddington Road*, Dublin)
Cassidy, Gerard (IC)
Clonturk House,
Ormond Road, Drumcondra,
Dublin 9
Tel 01-8374840
Cassidy, Gerard, Very Rev
(CSsR), PP
722 Antrim Road,
Newtownabbey,
Co Antrim BT36 7PG
Tel 028-90774833/4
(*St Gerard's*, Down & C.)
Cassidy, Gerard
Sabbatical
C/o Bishop's House, Cullies,
Cavan, Co Cavan
(Kilmore)
Cassidy, Joseph, Most Rev,
DD, PP
Retired Archbishop of
Tuam,
1 Kilgarve Court, Creagh,
Ballinasloe, Co Galway
(Tuam, retired)
Cassidy, Seamus, Very Rev, PP
Parochial House,
199 Navan Road, Dublin 7
Tel 01-8389482
(*Navan Road*, Dublin)
Cassin, James, Rt Rev Mgr
St Patrick's College,
Maynooth, Co Kildare
Tel 01-6285222/086-2380984
(Ossory)
Cassin, Liam, Very Rev, PP
Hugginstown, Co Kilkenny
Tel 087-2312354/
056-7768678
(Ossory)
Cassin, Seán (OFM)
Franciscan College,
Gormanston, Co Meath
Tel 01-8412203
Caulfield, Joseph, Very Rev,
PP
Gurteen, Ballymote,
Co Sligo
Tel 071-9182551
(*Gurteen,* Achonry)

Cavanagh, Daniel, Very Rev,
PP
Rosbercon, New Ross,
Co Wexford
Tel 051-421515/087-2335432
(*Rosbercon*, Ossory)
Cawley, Farrell, Very Rev
Ballinacarrow, Co Sligo
Tel 086-0864347
(Achonry, retired)
Cawley, Michael, Very Rev
Sick leave
(Killala)
Cepeda, Francisco (LC)
Director,
Dublin Oak Academy,
Kilcroney, Bray, Co Wicklow
Tel 01-2863290
Chalissery, Johnson, CC
Church of the Most Precious
Blood, Clogheen, Co Cork
Tel 021-4392122
(*Clogheen (Kerry Pike)*, Cork
& R.)
Chambers, Martin, PP
2 Chaplain's House,
Knocknamona,
Letterkenny, Co Donegal
Tel 074-9125090
(*Letterkenny*, Raphoe)
Charles, Nigel, CC
The Presbytery, Longford
Tel 043-3346465
(Ardagh & Cl.)
Chester, John, CC
St Joseph's Presbytery,
Park Street, Monaghan
Tel 047-81220
(Clogher)
Chestnutt, Gerard, CC
Sacred Heart Presbytery,
The Folly, Waterford
Tel 051-878429
(*Sacred Heart,* Waterford &
L.)
Chisholm, John (CSSp)
135 The Stiles Road,
Clontarf, Dublin 3
Tel 01-8339025
Christy, Myles
Elmhurst Nursing Home,
Hampstead Avenue,
Glasnevin, Dublin 9
(Dublin, retired)
Chute, John (SSC), Very Rev,
CC
The Presbytery,
St Joseph's, Balcurris,
Ballymun, Dublin 11
Tel 01-8423865
(*Balcurris*, Dublin)
Claffey, Pat (SVD)
3 Pembroke Road, Dublin 4
Tel 01-6680904

Clancy, Anthony (OMI)
Provincial Treasurer,
Provincial Residence,
Oblates of Mary Immaculate
House of Retreat,
Tyrconnell Road, Inchicore,
Dublin 8
Tel 01-4541160/4541161
Superior,
Oblate House of Retreat,
Inchicore, Dublin 8
Tel 01-4534408/4541805
Clancy, Finbarr G. (SJ)
Rector of Pontifical
Athenaeum, Milltown
Institute of Theology and
Philosophy, Milltown Park,
Sandford Road, Dublin 6
Tel 01-2776300
Clancy, John (SMA)
African Missions,
Blackrock Road, Cork
Tel 021-4292871
Clancy, Peter, CC
75 Newtown Park, Leixlip,
Co Kildare
Tel 01-6243533
(*Confey*, Dublin)
Clancy, Tom, Very Rev, AP
Woodlawn,
Model Farm Road,
Ballineaspaig, Cork
Tel 021-4348588
(*Ballineaspaig*, Cork & R.)
Clarke, Christopher (OCD),
Very Rev, PP
The Presbytery,
Berkeley Road, Dublin 7
Tel 01-8306356/8306336
(*Berkeley Road*, Dublin)
Clarke, Dermot, Very Rev
Mgr, PP
Parochial House,
34 Aughrim Street, Dublin 7
Tel 01-8386571
(*Aughrim Street*, Dublin)
Clarke, Eamonn, CC
The Presbytery, Kilcoole,
Co Wicklow
Tel 01-2876207
(*Kilquade*, Dublin)
Clarke, Eugene
5 Brookside, Farnham Road,
Cavan
Tel 049-4331755
(Kilmore, retired)
Clarke, Gerard (SJ)
Jesuit Community, 27
Leinster Road, Rathmines,
Dublin 6
Tel 01-4970250
Clarke, Joseph, Very Rev, PP
Kilnadeema, Loughrea,
Co Galway
Tel 091-841201
(*Kilnadeema and Aille*,
Clonfert)

Clarke, Leo (SSC)
St Columban's Retirement
Home, Dalgan Park,
Navan, Co Meath
Tel 046-9021525

Clarke, Martin, Very Rev, PP
Church of the Sacred Heart,
Donnybrook, Dublin 4
(*Donnybrook*, Dublin)

Clarke, Patrick (SSC)
St Columban's Retirement
Home, Dalgan Park,
Navan, Co Meath
Tel 046-9021525

Clarke, Peter, Very Rev, PP
Parochial House,
Tallanstown, Dundalk,
Co Louth
Tel 042-9374197
(*Tallanstown*, Armagh)

Clavin, Joseph, Very Rev, PP,
VF
Parochial House,
Dunshaughlin, Co Meath
Tel 01-8259114
(Meath)

Clayton-Lea, Paul, Very Rev,
PP, VF
Parochial House,
Clogherhead, Drogheda,
Co Louth
Tel 041-9822438
(*Clogherhead*, Armagh)

Clear, John B. (SJ)
St Francis Xavier's, Upper
Gardiner Street, Dublin 1
Tel 01-8363411

Cleary, Brendan, Very Rev, AP
17 Churchfield, Clonlara,
Co Clare
Tel 061-354028/
086-8484550
(*Clonlara*, Killaloe)

Cleary, Daniel (MSC)
'Croí Nua', Rosary Lane,
Taylor's Hill, Galway
Tel 091-520960

Cleary, Edward, CC
Knockinrawley, Tipperary
Tel 062-51242
(*Tipperary*, Cashel & E.)

Cleary, Lorenzo, Very Rev
The Stables, Hayestown,
Wexford
(Ferns)

Cleary, Matthew L., Very Rev
The Stables, Bridgetown,
Co Wexford
(Ferns, retired)

Cleary, Michael J. (CSSp), Most
Rev
Holy Ghost Missionary
College, Kimmage Manor,
Dublin 12
Tel 01-4064300

Cleary, Patrick (OFMCap)
Provincial Office,
12 Halston Street, Dublin 7
Tel 01-8733205

Cleary, Patrick B. (CSSp)
Superior, St Mary's College,
Rathmines, Dublin 6
Tel 01-4062160

Cleary, William, Rt Rev Mgr,
PE
Curate's Residence,
Mornington, Co Meath
Tel 041-9827384
(*Laytown-Mornington*,
Meath)

Cleere, Martin, Very Rev, PP
Windgap, Co Kilkenny
Tel 051-648111/087-2954010
(*Windgap*, Ossory)

Clerkin, Colum, Very Rev, PP
55 St Patrick's Street,
Draperstown, Magherafelt,
Co Derry BT45 7AJ
Tel 028-79628248
(Derry)

Clerkin, Eugene (OMI)
Oblate House of Retreat,
Inchicore, Dublin 8
Tel 01-4534408/4541805

Clerkin, Sean, Very Rev
Canon, PE
Tydavnet, Co Monaghan
Tel 047-89402
(*Tydavnet*, Clogher)

Clifford, Brendan (OP)
St Saviour's, Glentworth
Street, Limerick
Tel 061-412333

Clifford, Dermot, Most Rev,
PhD, DD
Archbishop of Cashel and
Emly, Archbishop's House,
Thurles, Co Tipperary
Tel 0504-21512
(Cashel & E.)

Clifford, Diarmuid (OP)
St Saviour's,
Upper Dorset Street,
Dublin 1
Tel 01-8897610

Clifford, Gerard, Most Rev,
DD
Titular Bishop of Geron and
Auxiliary Bishop to the
Archbishop of Armagh,
Annaskeagh, Ravensdale,
Dundalk, Co Louth
Tel 042-9371012
(Armagh)

Clifford, Hugh
Pontifical Irish College,
Via dei Quattro 1,
00184 Rome, Italy
Tel 003906-77263301
(Galway)

Clinton, Colm (SPS)
(Adm protem)
New Quay, Co Clare
Tel 065-7078026
(*Carron and New Quay*,
Galway)

Clowe, Tom (SDB), CC
8 Slademore Close, Ard-na-
Greine, Dublin 13
(*Ayrfield,* Dublin)

Clucas, Peter (OMI)
Oblate Scholasticate,
St Anne's,
Goldenbridge Walk,
Inchicore, Dublin 8
Tel 01-4540841/4542955

Clune, Anthony (CM)
St Paul's College, Raheny,
Dublin 5
Tel 01-8318113

Clyne, S. James, Very Rev, PE,
AP
Mountain Lodge,
134 Dublin Road, Newry,
Co Down BT35 8QT
Tel 028-30262053
(*Cloghogue (Killeavy
Upper),* Armagh)

Clyne, Simon (CM)
St Paul's College, Raheny,
Dublin 5
Tel 01-8318113

Coady, Michael, Very Rev, PP
Parochial House,
Carrickbrennan Road,
Monkstown,
Co Dublin
Tel 01-2802130
(*Monkstown*, Dublin)

Coakley, Donal, Very Rev, PP
4 Upper Woodlands,
Cloghroe, Co Cork
Tel 021-4385311
(*Inniscarra*, Cloyne)

Coen, John (SAC)
Provincial House,
'Homestead',
Sandyford Road, Dundrum,
Dublin 16
Tel 01-2956180/2954170

Coen, Michael (OCD)
St Teresa's, Clarendon
Street, Dublin 2
Tel 01-6718466/6718127

Coffey, Brendan (OSB), Very
Rev
Glenstal Abbey, Murroe,
Co Limerick
Tel 061-386103

Coffey, Patrick
Lisgaugh, Doon,
Co Limerick
Tel 061-380247
(Cashel & E.)

Coffey, Peter (SDB), Co-PP
Salesian House, St Teresa's
Road, Crumlin, Dublin 12
Tel 01-4555605
(*Crumlin*, Dublin)

Coffey, Robert
37 Gouldavoher Estate,
Dooradoyle, Limerick
Tel 061-482437/087-6540908
(Limerick)

Coffey, Thomas, Very Rev, PE
Corcaghan, Monaghan
Tel 042-9744806
(*Corcaghan*, Clogher)

Coffey, Tom (IC)
St Joseph's,
Doire na hAbhann,
Tickincar, Clonmel,
Co Tipperary
Tel 052-26914

Cogan, John, Very Rev, PP
Castlemartyr, Co Cork
Tel 021-4667133
(*Imogeela (Castlemartyr)*,
Cloyne)

Cogan, Micheál, Very Rev, PE,
CC
Glantane, Mallow,
Co Cork
Tel 022-47158
(*Glantane*, Cloyne)

Cogan, Patrick (OFM)
15 Orchard Drive,
Ursuline Court, Waterford
Tel 087-2360239/Respond!
Office Tel 051-876865

Coghlan, David (SJ)
Acting Superior, Dominic
Collins' House Residence,
129 Morehampton Road,
Dublin 4
Tel 01-2693075

Coghlan, Kieran, Very Rev, PP
The Presbytery,
Chapel Green, Rush,
Co Dublin
Tel 01-8437208
(*Rush*, Dublin)

Coghlan, Niall (OSA), PP
St Catherine's, Meath Street,
Dublin 8
Tel 01-4543356
(*Meath Street*, Dublin)

Cogley, James, CC
Kilmore Quay, Co Wexford
Tel 053-9129638
(*Kilmore*, Ferns)

Colclough, Robert, CC
St Mary's, Sandyford,
Dublin 18
Tel 01-2958933
(*Sandyford*, Dublin)

Coleman, Christopher, Very
Rev (MSC), PP
Parish House, Union Hall,
Skibbereen, Co Cork
Tel 028-34940
(*Castlehaven*, Cork & R.)

Coleman, Gerard, CC
Callas, Berrings, Co Cork
Tel 021-7332155
(*Inniscarra*, Cloyne)

Coleman, Gerard, Very Rev,
PP
Castlelyons, Fermoy,
Co Cork
Tel 025-36372
(*Castlelyons*, Cloyne)

Coleman, John J. (CSSp)
Holy Ghost Missionary
College, Kimmage Manor,
Dublin 12
Tel 01-4064300

Coleman, Pádraig B. (OFM)
Franciscan House of Studies,
Dun Mhuire, Seafield Road,
Killiney, Co Dublin
Tel 01-2826760

Coleman, William, CC
St Mary's, Navan,
Co Meath
Tel 046-9027518/9027414
(Navan, Meath)

Colgan, John (SSC)
Columban Intercom,
St Columban's, Dalgan Park,
Navan, Co Meath
Tel 046-9021525

Colhoun, Roland, Adm
St Columba's Presbytery,
6 Victoria Place,
Derry BT48 6TJ
Tel 028-71262301
(St Columba's, Long Tower
(Templemore), Derry)

Coll, Francis, CC
Our Lady of Lourdes
Presbytery,
Hardman's Gardens,
Drogheda, Co Louth
(Armagh)

Coll, Niall
St Mary's College, Belfast
(Raphoe)

Collender, Michael (OSA)
St Augustine's Priory
(Residence),
New Ross, Co Wexford
Tel 051421237

Colleran, Martin G.
Our Lady's Manor,
Bulloch Castle, Dalkey,
Co Dublin
(Dublin, retired)

Collery, Seamus
Curry, Ballymote, Co Sligo
(Curry, Achonry)

Collier, Val (SDB)
Priest-in-Charge,
Don Bosco Houses,
57 Lower Drumcondra Road,
Dublin 1
Tel 01-8360696/8373449
12 Clontarf Road, Dublin 3
Tel 01-8336009/8337045

Collins, Cornelius
Patrickswell, Co Limerick
(Limerick, retired)

Collins, Denis (CM)
St Joseph's,
44 Stillorgan Park,
Blackrock, Co Dublin
Tel 01-2886961

Collins, Denis (OCSO)
Mount Melleray Abbey,
Cappoquin, Co Waterford
Tel 058-54404

Collins, Denis (SMA), CC
St Joseph's, Wilton, Cork
Tel 021-4341362
(Wilton, St Joseph's, Cork &
R.)

Collins, Edward J., CC
The Presbytery, Clonakilty,
Co Cork
Tel 023-33100
(Clonakilty and Darrara,
Cork & R.)

Collins, Gregory (OSB)
Glenstal Abbey, Murroe,
Co Limerick
Tel 061-386103

Collins, John, Very Rev, PP
Carraig na bhFear, Co Cork
Tel 021-4884119
(Carraig na bhFear, Cork &
R.)

Collins, John, Very Rev
The Presbytery,
James' Street, Dublin 8
Tel 01-4531143
(James's Street, Dublin)

Collins, Laurence (OP), Very
Rev, Adm
Presbytery,
St Dominic's Road, Tallaght,
Dublin 24
Tel 01-4510620
(Tallaght, Dodder, Dublin)

Collins, Martin J. (CSSp)
Holy Ghost Missionary
College, Kimmage Manor,
Dublin 12
Tel 01-4064300

Collins, Michael E., CC
O'Gorman Street, Kilrush,
Co Clare
Tel 065-9051016/087-
6389847
(Killimer and Kilrush,
Killaloe)

Collins, Michael, PP
119 Irish Green Street,
Limavady,
Co Derry BT49 9AB
Tel 028-77765649
(Limavady, Derry)

Collins, Michael, Very Rev, PP
Quin, Co Clare
Tel 065-6825430/
086-3475085
(Quin, Killaloe)

Collins, Michael
24 Barclay Court, Blackrock,
Co Dublin
Tel 01-2832302
(Blackrock, Dublin)

Collins, Neil (SSC)
St Columban's, Dalgan Park,
Navan, Co Meath
Tel 046-9021525

Collins, Owen, Very Rev, PP
Cootehill, Co Cavan
Tel 049-5552120
(Cootehill, Kilmore)

Collins, P. Gerard, Very Rev
The Presbytery, Passage
West, Co Cork
(Cork & R., retired)

Collins, Patrick (CM)
St Peter's, Phibsboro,
Dublin 7
Tel 01-8389708

Collins, Raymond (OP)
St Saviour's, Bridge Street,
Waterford
Tel 051-875061

Collins, Timothy, Very Rev, PP
The Presbytery,
Dunmanway, Co Cork
Tel 023-8845000
(Dunmanway, Cork & R.)

Collum, Martin, Very Rev, PP
Rathmullan, Co Donegal
Tel 074-9158156
(Rathmullan, Raphoe)

Colreavy, Tom, Very Rev, PP
28 Glentworth Park,
Ard na Gréine, Dublin 13
Tel 01-8484836
(Ayrfield, Dublin)

Coltsmann, Francis (SMA)
SMA House, Wilton, Cork
Tel 021-4541069/4541884

Comer, Liam, Very Rev, PP, VF
Dromagh, Mallow, Co Cork
Tel 029-78096
(Dromtariffe, Kerry)

Comer, Miceál, Very Rev, PP,
VF
St Anne's Strand Road,
Portmarnock, Co Dublin
Tel 01-8461081
(Dublin)

Comerford, Brendan (SJ)
Minister,
John Sullivan House,
56/56A Mulvey Park,
Dundrum, Dublin 14
Tel 01-2983978

Comerford, Frank (CSSp)
Holy Ghost Missionary
College, Kimmage Manor,
Dublin 12
Tel 01-4064300

Comerford, Patrick, Very Rev,
PP
Slieverue, via Waterford,
Co Kilkenny
Tel/Fax 051-832773/086-
1038430
(Slieverue, Ossory)

Comiskey, Brendan (SSCC),
Most Rev, DD
Coudrin House, 27
Northbrook Road, Dublin 6
Tel 01-6686584/01-6671513

Comiskey, Brendan, Most Rev,
DD
Retired Bishop of Ferns,
PO Box 40, Summerhill,
Wexford
(Ferns, retired)

Comiskey, Gerard, CC
Kill, Cootehill, Co Cavan
Tel 049-5553218
Chaplain, Cavan Institute,
Cathedral Road, Cavan
Tel 049-4332334
(Kilsherdany and Drung,
Kilmore)

Commane, Michael (OP)
Newbridge College,
Droichead Nua, Co Kildare
Tel 045-487200

Commins, Thomas, CC
Kilkerrin, Ballinasloe,
Co Galway
Tel 094-9659212
(Kilkerren and Clonberne,
Tuam)

Conaghan, Michael, Very Rev,
PP
Kilmacrennan, Co Donegal
Tel 074-9139018
(Kilmacrennan, Raphoe)

Conaty, Eamonn, (SSC), CC
Rooskey, Carrick-on-
Shannon, Co Roscommon
Tel 071-9638014
(Kilglass and Rooskey,
Elphin)

Conaty, Peter (CSSp)
Provincial Assistant,
Spiritan Provincialate,
Temple Park,
Richmond Avenue South,
Dublin 6
Tel 01-4975127/4977230

Concannon, Eamonn, Very
Rev Canon, PE
Balleyhowley, Knock,
Co Mayo
(Tuam, retired)

Concannon, John (CM)
St Peter's, Phibsboro,
Dublin 7
Tel 01-8389708

Condon, Eanna, Very Rev, PE
St Mary's, Clonmel,
Co Tipperary
Tel 052-6127870
(Waterford & L., retired)

Condon, Gerard, CC
Shanballymore, Doneraile,
Co Cork
Tel 022-25197
(Cloyne)

Condon, Jeremiah, Very Rev,
PP
Stradbally, Kilmacthomas,
Co Waterford
Tel 051-293133
(Stradbally, Waterford & L.)

Condon, John, CC
Templeorum, Piltown,
Co Kilkenny
Tel 051-643124/086-8394615
(Templeorum, Ossory)

Corkery, Sean
St Patrick's College,
Maynooth, Co Kildare
Tel 01-7084700
(Cloyne)

Corkery, Jackie, Very Rev
Canon, PP, VF
Kanturk, Co Cork
Tel 029-50192
(*Kanturk*, Cloyne)

Corkery, James (SJ)
Superior, Jesuit Community,
27 Leinster Road,
Rathmines, Dublin 6
Tel 01-4970250

Corkery, Michael, Very Rev, PP
Aghinagh, Coachford,
Co Cork
Tel 026-48037
(*Aghinagh*, Cloyne)

Corkery, Pádraig, Dr
St Patrick's College,
Maynooth, Co Kildare
Tel 01-7083639
(Cork & R.)

Corkery, Patrick, CC
Inch, Killeagh, Co Cork
Tel 024-95148
(*Killeagh*, Cloyne)

Cormac, Pierce
Chaplain, Mercy University
Hospital, Cork
Tel 021-4271971
(Cork & R.)

Cormican, Gregory, Very Rev,
PP
72 Nursery Avenue,
Coleraine,
Co Derry BT52 1LR
Tel 028-70343156
(*Coleraine*, Down & C.)

Corr, Anthony, CC
100 Dromore Street,
Banbridge,
Co Down BT32 4DW
Tel 028-40622274
(Seapatrick (Banbridge),
Dromore)

Corr, Sean (SSC)
38 Washingbay Road,
Coalisland,
Co Tyrone BT71 4PU

Corridan, Edward
No. 2 Cathedral Place,
Killarney, Co Kerry
(Kerry, retired)

Corrigan, Brendan, Very Rev,
PP
5 The Gallops, Kilbeggan,
Co Westmeath
Tel 057-9332155
(*Kilbeg*, Meath)

Corrigan, David (SM)
Regional Superior,
Marist Regional Office,
Mount St Mary's,
Dundrum Road, Milltown,
Dublin 14
Tel 01-2698100/087-9573973

Corrigan, Desmond (SMA)
Director, Dromantine
Retreat and Conference
Centre, Dromantine College,
Newry, Co Down BT34 1RH
Tel 028-30821219

Corrigan, Desmond
c/o Ara Coeli,
Armagh BT61 7QY
(Armagh, retired)

Corrigan, Kevin (CSSp)
Holy Ghost Missionary
College, Kimmage Manor,
Dublin 12
Tel 01-4064300

Corrigan, Patrick J., Rev
Canon
Fairgreen, Belturbet,
Co Cavan
Tel 049-9522151
(*Belturbet*, Kilmore)

Corrigan, Peter, Very Rev, PP
Shanco, Newbliss,
Co Monaghan
Tel 047-54011
(*Killeevan*, Clogher)

Corry, Edward
Presbytery No. 2,
Treepark Road,
Kilnamanagh, Dublin 24
(Dublin, retired)

Corry, Francis (SM), CC
Holy Family Parish, Dundalk,
Co Louth
Tel 042-9336301
(*Dundalk, Holy Family*,
Armagh)

Corry, Frank (SM)
Holy Family Parish,
Parochial House, Dundalk,
Co Louth
Tel 042-9336301
(*Holy Family*, Armagh)

Corry, James (CSSp)
Holy Ghost Missionary
College, Kimmage Manor,
Dublin 12
Tel 01-4064300

Cosgrave, William, Very Rev,
PP
Monageer, Ferns,
Enniscorthy, Co Wexford
Tel 053-9233530
(*Monageer*, Ferns)

Cosgrove, John, Very Rev
Canon, PP, VF
Castlebar, Co Mayo
Tel 094-9021274
(Tuam)

Cosgrove, Martin, Very Rev,
PP
Parochial House, Arklow,
Co Wicklow
Tel 0402-32294
(*Arklow*, Dublin)

Costello, Aidan, CC
The Presbytery, Loughrea,
Co Galway
Tel 091-841212
(*Loughrea, St Brendan's
Cathedral*, Clonfert)

Costello, Bernard
Creagh, Ballinasloe,
Co Galway
(Clonfert)

Costello, David
c/o The Missionary Society
of St James the Apostle,
24 Clark Street, Boston,
MA 02109, USA
(Limerick)

Costello, Denis, Very Rev
Fatima Home, Oakpark,
Tralee, Co Kerry
(Kerry, retired)

Costello, James, Very Rev
Canon, PP, VF
Bruff, Kilmallock,
Co Limerick
Tel 061-382555
(*Bruff/Meanus/Grange*,
Limerick)

Costello, Liam (OFM)
Franciscan Friary, Clonmel,
Co Tipperary
Tel 052-6121378

Costello, Martin (SMA)
SMA House, Claregalway,
Co Galway
Tel 091-798880

Costello, Maurice
Main Street, Rathkeale,
Co Limerick
Tel 069-63452
(Limerick, retired)

Costello, Pádraig, Very Rev, PP
Foxford, Co Mayo
Tel 094-9256131
(*Foxford*, Achonry)

Costello, Patrick (SSS)
Provincial, Blessed
Sacrament Chapel,
20 Bachelors Walk, Dublin 1
Tel 01-8724597

Costello, Patrick, Very Rev
51 Ashgrove, Mountbellew,
Co Galway
(Tuam, retired)

Costelloe, Morgan
21 Cullenswood Gardens,
Dublin 6
Tel 01-4975201
(Dublin, retired)

Cotter, Bernard (SMA)
African Missions,
Blackrock Road, Cork
Tel 021-4292871

Cotter, Bernard, Very Rev, PP
Ballingeary, Co Cork
Tel 086-3684164
(*Uibh Laoire*, Cork & R.)

Cotter, Donal, Very Rev, Adm
Skibbereen, Co Cork
Tel 028-22877
(*St Patrick's Cathedral,
Skibbereen*, Cork & R.)

Cotter, Francis (OFM)
Franciscan House of Studies,
Dun Mhuire, Seafield Road,
Killiney, Co Dublin
Tel 01-2826760

Cotter, John, Very Rev, PE
The Presbytery,
Lower Road, Cork
Tel 021-4551503
(*St Patrick's*, Cork & R.)

Cotter, Pat
c/o Killaloe Diocesan Office
(Killaloe)

Cotter, Sean, Very Rev Canon,
Adm, (*Pro tem*)
Shandrum, Charleville,
Co Cork
Tel 063-70207
(Cloyne)

Coughlan, John, CC
Deerpark Road, Athlone,
Co Westmeath
Tel 090-6490575
(*Athlone, SS Peter and
Paul's*, Elphin)

Coughlan, Leonard (OFMCap)
Capuchin Friary,
Church Street, Dublin 7
Tel 01-8730599

Coughlan, Patrick (CSSp)
Newlands Institute for
Counselling,
2 Monastery Road,
Clondalkin, Dublin 22
Tel 01-4594573

Coughlan, Sean (OCarm)
Whitefriar Street Church,
56 Aungier Street, Dublin 2
Tel 01-4758821

Coughlan, Thomas, Very Rev,
PP
Effin, Kilmallock,
Co Limerick
Tel 063-71314
(*Effin/Garrienderk*, Limerick)

Coughlan, Thomas
The Presbytery, Avoca,
Co Wicklow
Tel 0402-35204
(*Avoca*, Dublin)

Coulter, Charles (SSC)
St Columban's, Dalgan Park,
Navan, Co Meath
Tel 046-9021525

Courtney, Conor (CSSp)
Holy Ghost Missionary
College, Kimmage Manor,
Dublin 12
Tel 01-4064300
Provincial Bursar, Spiritan
Provincialate,
Temple Park,
Richmond Avenue South,
Dublin 6
Tel 01-4975127/4977230

Courtney, Patrick (MSC)
Provincial Leader,
Provincialate,
65 Terenure Road West,
Dublin 6W
Tel 01-4906622

Coveney, Patrick, Most Rev,
AP
Crosshaven, Co Cork
Tel 021-4831218
(Crosshaven, Cork & R.)

Cox, Seamus, Very Rev
Ballyleague, Co Roscommon
(Elphin, retired)

Cox, Tom, CC
Ferbane, Co Offaly
Tel 090-6454309
(Ardagh & Cl.)

Coyle, Harry
(in residence)
Lisieux, 99 Loup Road,
Ballynenagh, Moneymore,
Co Derry BT45 7ST
Tel 028-79418235
(Moneymore (Ardtrea),
Armagh)

Coyle, Mark (OFMCap)
Capuchin Friary,
Ard Mhuire, Creeslough,
Letterkenny, Co Donegal
Tel 074-9138005

Coyle, Paul, CC
The Presbytery, Maynooth,
Co Kildare
Tel 01-6290553
(Maynooth, Dublin)

Coyle, Peter (SPS)
House Leader, St Patrick's,
21 Leeson Park, Dublin 6
Tel 01-4977897

Coyle, Rory, CC
Parochial House,
42 Abbey Street,
Armagh BT61 7DZ
Tel 028-37522802
(Armagh, Armagh)

Coyle, Thomas, Very Rev, PP
Galmoy, Crosspatrick,
via Thurles, Co Kilkenny
Tel 056-8831227/
087-7668969
(Galmoy, Ossory)

Coyne, Joseph, Very Rev
Moderator,
Sacred Heart of Jesus,
Huntstown, Dublin 15

Coyne, P. J., CC
Kentstown, Navan,
Co Meath
Tel 041-9825276
(Beauparc, Meath)

Craven, John (CP), CC
Holy Cross Retreat,
432 Crumlin Road, Ardoyne,
Belfast BT14 7GE
Tel 028-90748231/2
(Holy Cross, Down & C.)

Crawford, Alan (OSB)
Glenstal Abbey, Murroe,
Co Limerick
Tel 061-386103

Crawford, Thomas, Very Rev,
PP
Glin, Co Limerick
Tel 068-26897
(Limerick)

Crawley, Michael, Very Rev
Canon, PP, VF
Parochial House,
34 Madden Row, Keady,
Co Armagh BT60 3RW
Tel 028-37531242
(Keady (Derrynoose),
Armagh)

Creamer, Edmond (CSsR)
Clonard Monastery,
1 Clonard Gardens,
Belfast BT13 2RL
Tel 028-90445950

Crean, Joseph (OSA)
Duckspool House
(Retirement Community),
Abbeyside, Dungarvan,
Co Waterford
Tel 058-23784

Crean, Martin (OSA)
The Abbey, Fethard,
Co Tipperary
Tel 052-31273

Crean, Maurice (MHM)
Organising Secretary,
St Joseph's,
Freshford House, Kilkenny
Tel 056-7721482

Crean, Thomas, Venerable
Archdeacon PP, VF
Kenmare, Co Kerry
Tel 064-41352
(Kenmare, Kerry)

Crean, William, Very Rev
Canon, PP, VF
Cahirciveen, Co Kerry
Tel 066-9472210
(Cahirciveen, Kerry)

Crean-Lynch, Pat, Very Rev
The Presbytery,
Ballymacelligott, Tralee,
Co Kerry
Tel 066-7137118
(Kerry)

Creaton, James, Very Rev, PC
Fairymount, Castlerea,
Co Roscommon
Tel 094-9870243
(Fairymount, Elphin)

Creaton, Patrick (SSC)
St Columban's Retirement
Home, Dalgan Park, Navan,
Co Meath
Tel 046-9021525

Cremin, Aidan, CC
Cork Road, Carrigaline,
Co Cork
Tel 021-4372229
(Carrigaline, Cork & R.)

Cremin, Gerard
Pontifical Irish College,
Rome
Tel 003906-772631
(Cloyne)

Cremin, Jeremiah, Very Rev,
PP
Parochial House, Tirelton,
Macroom, Co Cork
Tel 026-46012/086-2578065
(Kilmichael, Cork & R.)

Cremin, Michael (OCarm)
Gort Muire, Ballinteer,
Dublin 16
Tel 01-2984014

Cremins, Richard (SJ)
35 Lower Leeson Street,
Dublin 2
Tel 01-6761248

Cribben, J. J., Very Rev, PP
Milltown, Co Galway
Tel 093-51609
(Milltown (Addergole and
Liskeevey), Tuam)

Cribbin, David
Chaplain, University
Hospital, Galway
Tel 091-524222
(Galway)

Cribbin, James, CC
Glenhest, Newport,
Co Mayo
Tel 098-41170
(Lahardane, Killala)

Cribbin, Peter, Very Rev
c/o Bishop's House, Dublin
Road, Carlow
(Kildare & L.)

Crilly, Oliver, PP
230b Mayogall Road, Clady,
Portglenone,
Co Derry BT44 8NN
Tel 028-25821190
(Greenlough, Derry)

Cristóbal, Jimenez A. (SJ)
Jesuit Community,
27 Leinster Road,
Rathmines, Dublin 6
Tel 01-4970250

Crossan, Stephen, CC
68 North Street, Lurgan,
Co Armagh BT67 9AH
Tel 028-38323161
(Shankill, St Peter's,
Dromore)

Crofton, James
'Vinea Mea', Via S.
Francesco, 4,
Lappiano, 50064 Incisa (FI),
Italy
(Meath)

Crombie, Shane, CC
Parochial House, Tullamore,
Co Offaly
Tel 057-9321587
(Meath)

Cronin, Anthony, Very Rev, PE
Newmarket, Co Cork
Tel 029-60605
(Cloyne, retired)

Cronin, Brian (CSSp)
Spiritan Missionary College,
Kimmage Manor,
Dublin 12
Tel 01-4064300

Cronin, Kieran (OFM)
Guardian, Franciscan House
of Studies, Dún Mhuire,
Seafield Road, Killiney,
Co Dublin
Tel 01-2826760

Cronin, Tony (SPS)
St Patrick's, Kiltegan,
Co Wicklow
Tel 059-6473600

Crosbie, Paul, CC
Cathedral House, Mullingar,
Co Westmeath
Tel 044-9348338/9340126
(Mullingar, Meath)

Crosby, Denis, Very Rev, PP
Liscannor, Co Clare
Tel 065-7081248
(Liscannor, Galway)

Crosby, Edward, PP
Parochial House, Kilfenora,
Co Clare
Tel 065-7088006
(Kilfenora, Galway)

Crosby, Michael, Very Rev, PP
Shrule, Galway
Tel 093-31262
(Shrule, Galway)

Cross, Charles (CP)
Passionist Community,
35-36 Coill Tire,
Doughiska, Galway

Crossey, Colin, CC
120 Cavehill Road, Belfast
BT15 5BU
Tel 028-90714892
(Holy Family, Down & C.)

Crosson, Eamonn, Very Rev,
PP
Parochial House, Avoca,
Co Wicklow
Tel 0402-35156
(Avoca, Dublin)

Crotty, Gerald (CSsR)
St Patrick's, Esker, Athenry,
Co Galway
Tel 091-844549

Crotty, James, Very Rev, PP
Ferrybank, Waterford
Tel 051-832787/087-8317711
(Ossory)

Crotty, Michael, Rt Rev Mgr,
DD
Secretariat of State,
Vatican City
(Cloyne)

Crotty, Oliver, CC
Parochial House,
Glendalough, Co Wicklow
Tel 0404-45140
(Glendalough, Dublin)

Crowe, Martin (OP), CC
St Saviour's Priory, Kilbarry,
Waterford
Tel 051-376581
(St Saviour's, Waterford &
L.)

Crowe, Patrick (SJ)
Clongowes Wood College,
Naas, Co Kildare
Tel 045-868663/868202

Crowe, Phil (CSSp)
Spiritan Missionaries,
Ardbraccan, Navan,
Co Meath
Tel 046-9021441

Crowe, Philip (CSSp), CC
Drumgossatt,
Carrickmacross,
Co Monaghan
Tel 042-9661388
(Magheracloone, Clogher)

Crowe, Richard, CC
10 Mayorstone, Park,
Limerick
Tel 061-452952
(St Munchin's and St Lelia's,
Limerick)

Crowley, Adrian
Instituto de Idiomas
Maryknoll Padres,
Casilla 550, Cochabamba,
Bolivia
(Dublin)

Crowley, Aidan, CC
Ballycotton, Midleton,
Co Cork
Tel 021-4646726
(Cloyne, Cloyne)

Crowley, Brendan, CC
Malin Head, Co Donegal
Tel 074-9370134
(Malin, Derry)

Crowley, Brendan, Very Rev,
PP, VF
SS Peter and Paul's,
Clonmel, Co Tipperary
Tel 052-6122138
(Clonmel, SS Peter and
Paul's, Waterford & L.)

Crowley, Christopher (OCarm)
Whitefriar Street Church, 56
Aungier Street, Dublin 2
Tel 01-4758821

Crowley, Dan, Very Rev
Canon, PP
The Presbytery,
Lower Road, Cork
Tel 021-4502696
(St Patrick's, Cork & R.)

Crowley, Finbarr, Adm
Farnivane, Bandon, Co Cork
Tel 023-8820861
(Murragh and
Templemartin, Cork & R.)

Crowley, James, Very Rev, PE
Parochial House,
60 Aughnagar Road,
Ballygawley, Dungannon,
Co Tyrone BT70 2HP
Tel 028-85568399
(Armagh, retired)

Crowley, Kevin (OFMCap)
Capuchin Friary,
Church Street, Dublin 7
Tel 01-8730599

Crowley, Michael (MSC)
Myross Wood Retreat
House, Leap, Skibbereen,
Co Cork
Tel 028-33118

Crowley, Michael, Very Rev
Canon, AP
Ballinlough, Cork
Tel 021-4292684
(Ballinlough, Cork & R.)

Crowley, Michael, Very Rev
Canon, PE
The Lough Presbytery,
St Finbarr's West, Cork
Tel 021-4322633
(The Lough, Cork & R.)

Crowley, Patrick (SSC)
St Columban's, Grange
Road, Donaghmede,
Dublin 13
Tel 01-8476647

Crowley, Roderic (CM)
St Vincent's College,
Castleknock, Dublin 15
Tel 01-8213051

Crowley, Walter (OFM)
Franciscan Friary,
Liberty Street, Cork
Tel 021-4270302

Crudden, Jim, Very Rev, PP
Corpus Christi Presbytery,
4-6 Springhill Grove
Belfast BT12 7SL
Tel 028-90246857
(Corpus Christi, Down & C.)

Cryan, Gerard, BA, HDE, STB,
L Eccl Hist
(in residence)
St Mary's, Sligo
Tel 071-9162670/9162769
College of the Immaculate
Conception, Summerhill,
Sligo
Tel 071-9160311
(Elphin)

Cryan, Peter (OCD), CC
The Presbytery,
Berkeley Road, Dublin 7
Tel 01-8306356/8306336
(Berkeley Road, Dublin)

Cuffe, Bernard (OCD)
The Abbey, Loughrea,
Co Galway
Tel 091-841209

Cuffe, Liam
Chaplain,
St Vincent's Hospital,
Elm Park, Dublin 4
Tel 01-2094325
(Ardagh & Cl.)

Culhane, Patrick J., Very Rev
138 Lucan Road,
Chapelizod, Dublin 20
(Dublin, retired)

Cullen, Celestine (OSB), Rt Rev
Dom
Glenstal Abbey, Murroe,
Co Limerick
Tel 061-386103

Cullen, John, Very Rev, PP
Kiltoom, Athlone,
Co Roscommon
Tel 090-6489105
(Kiltoom, Elphin)

Cullen, Joseph (OP)
47 Leeson Park, Dublin 6
Tel 01-6602427

Cullen, Kevin, Very Rev, PP, VF
Parochial House,
Tullinavall Road,
Cullyhanna, Newry,
Co Down BT35 OPZ
Tel 028-30861235
(Cullyhanna (Creggan
Lower), Armagh)

Cullen, Laurence, Very Rev, PP
Geevagh, Boyle,
Co Roscommon
Tel 071-9647107
(Geevagh, Elphin)

Cullen, Michael, Very Rev, PP
The Presbytery,
Church Grounds,
Castleknock, Dublin 15
Tel 01-8208144
(Laurel Lodge-
Carpenterstown, Dublin)

Cullen, Seamus
2 Ceol Na Mara,
Lower Main Street,
Rush, Co Dublin
Tel 01-8438024
(Dublin, retired)

Culligan, Patrick, Very Rev
Carrigaholt, Co Clare
Tel 065-9058043/
087-9863865
(Carrigaholt and Cross,
Killaloe)

Cullinan, Alphonsus
142 Mayorstone Park,
Limerick
Tel 061-327836/208302
(Limerick)

Cullinan, Edmond, Very Rev,
PP
Parochial House, Chapel
Street, Carrick-on-Suir,
Co Tipperary
Tel 051-640168
(Waterford & L.)

Cullinan, William (OCSO)
Mellifont Abbey,
Collon, Co Louth
Tel 041-9826103

Cullinane, Michael, Very Rev,
PP, VF
Parochial House, Lismore,
Co Waterford
Tel 058-54246
(Lismore, Waterford & L.)

Cullinane, Timothy (MSC)
Myross Wood Retreat
House, Leap, Skibbereen,
Co Cork
Tel 028-33118

Culliton, James (SJ)
St Francis Xavier's,
Upper Gardiner Street,
Dublin 1
Tel 01-8363411

Cully, Patrick (CSSp)
Holy Ghost Missionary
College, Kimmage Manor,
Dublin 12
Tel 01-4064300

Cumiskey, Bonaventure
(OCSO)
Mount Melleray Abbey,
Cappoquin, Co Waterford
Tel 058-54404

Cumiskey, Cathal (CSsR)
St Joseph's, Dundalk,
Co Louth
Tel 042-9334042/9334762

Cummings, Daniel
30 Knapton Road,
Dun Laoghaire, Co Dublin
Tel 01-2804353
(Opus Dei)

Cummins, Anthony
Ballinderry NH, Kilconnell,
Ballinasloe, Co Galway
(Clonfert, retired)

Cummins, James (SDB)
Salesian House,
45 St Teresa's Road,
Crumlin, Dublin 12
Tel 01-4555605

Cummins, John, Adm
The Presbytery,
Dublin Road, Carlow
Tel 059-9131227
(Kildare & L.)

Cummins, William, Very Rev,
PP
Mervue, Galway
Tel 091-751721
(Mervue, Galway)

Cunnane, Fergal, CC
Castlebar, Co Mayo
Tel 094-901253/21844
(*Castlebar (Aglish,
Ballyheane and Breaghwy),*
Tuam)

Cunnane, Seamus, Very Rev
Grove House, Tuam,
Co Galway
(Tuam)

Cunning, Patrick (CSsR), CC
Vicar Superior & Bursar,
St Gerard's,
722 Antrim Road,
Newtownabbey,
Co Antrim BT36 7PG
Tel 028-90774833
(*St Gerard's*, Down & C.)

Cunningham, Charles (SDB)
Rinaldi House,
72 Sean McDermott Street,
Dublin 1
Tel 01-8363358

Cunningham, Colm (CSSp)
Rockwell College, Cashel,
Co Tipperary
Tel 062-61444

Cunningham, Connell, Very
Rev, PE
Carrick, Co Donegal
(Raphoe, retired)

Cunningham, Conor, CC
Galilee House, Monksfield,
Salthill, Galway
Tel 091-585693
(Galway)

Cunningham, Donal, Very
Rev, PP
Upperchurch, Thurles,
Co Tipperary
Tel 0504-54181
(*Upperchurch*, Cashel & E.)

Cunningham, Enda, Very Rev
Nativity of BVM Parochial
House, Saggart,
Co Dublin
Tel 087-1380695
(*Saggart*, Dublin)

Cunningham, Gerald (IC)
Cottrell Lodge,
16A Ormond Road,
Drumcondra, Dublin 9
Tel 01-8572234

Cunningham, Gerard, CC
Fintown, Donegal Town,
Co Donegal
Tel 074-9546107
(*Glenties*, Raphoe)

Cunningham, John Joe, Very
Rev
Newcastle, Co Down
(Dromore, retired)

Cunningham, John, (OP), CC
Batterstown, Dunboyne,
Co Meath
Tel 01-8259267
(*Kilcloon*, Meath)

Cunningham, Joseph (CM),
Very Rev
Superior, St Joseph's,
44 Stillorgan Park,
Blackrock, Co Dublin
Tel 01-2886961

Cunningham, Joseph, Very
Rev Canon
Our Lady's Home,
68 Ardnava Road,
Belfast BT12 6FF
(Down & C., retired)

Cunningham, Martin
c/o Diocesan Office,
Letterkenny, Co Donegal
(Raphoe)

Cunningham, Matthew, Very
Rev, AP
Grangemockler,
Carrick-on-Suir,
Co Tipperary
Tel 051-647011
(*Ballyneale and
Grangemockler*, Waterford
& L.)

Cunningham, PJ (OCarm)
Gort Muire, Ballinteer,
Dublin 16
Tel 01-2984014

Cunningham, Sean (OP)
Holy Cross, Sligo, Co Sligo
Tel 071-42700

Cunningham, Seán
The Presbytery, Tuam,
Co Galway
Tel 093-24250
(Tuam)

Cunningham, Tom (CSSp)
Rockwell College,
Cashel, Co Tipperary
Tel 062-61444

Curran, Adrian (OFMCap)
Capuchin Friary,
Station Road, Raheny,
Dublin 5
Tel 01-8313886

Curran, Anthony, Very Rev,
PP, VF
St Malachy's Presbytery,
24 Alfred Street,
Belfast BT2 8EN
Tel 028-90321713
(*St Malachy's*, Down & C.)

Curran, Colum, Very Rev, PP
4 Irish Street, Killyleagh,
Co Down BT30 9QS
Tel 028-44828211
(*Killyleagh*, Down & C.)

Curran, Eugene (CM), Very
Rev
All Hallows Institute for
Mission and Ministry,
Drumcondra, Dublin 9
Tel 01-8373745/6

Curran, James
61 Tournane Court,
Dungarvan, Co Waterford
Tel 058-45177
(Waterford & L., retired)

Curran, Jeremiah (SPS)
St Patrick's, Kiltegan,
Co Wicklow
Tel 059-6473600

Curran, Matthew (OSA)
St John's Priory,
Thomas Street, Dublin 8
Tel 01-6770393

Curran, Michael (MSC)
Leader & Director, Myross
Wood Retreat House, Leap,
Skibbereen, Co Cork
Tel 028-33118
Parish House, Union Hall,
Skibbereen, Co Cork
Tel 028-34940
(*Castlehaven*, Cork & R.)

Curran, Michael, Very Rev, PP
Rathgormack,
Carrick-on-Suir,
Co Tipperary
Tel 051-646006
(*Rathgormack*, Waterford &
L.)

Curran, Philip, Very Rev, PP
Presbytery No 1,
Kilnamanagh, Tallaght,
Dublin 24
Tel 01-4523805/086-2408188
(*Kilnamanagh*, Dublin)

Curran, Roddy (CSSp), CC
104 St Joseph's Road,
Greenhills, Dublin 12
Tel 01-4506617
(*Greenhills*, Dublin)

Curran, Roderick (CSSp)
Church of the Holy Spirit,
Greenhills, Dublin 12
Tel 01-4504040
(*Greenhills*, Dublin)

Curran, Thomas
Glenview House,
College Road, Letterkenny,
Co Donegal
Tel 074-9127617
(Raphoe, retired)

Currivan, Patrick, Very Rev, PP
Caherconlish, Co Limerick
Tel 061-351248
(*Caherconlish*, Cashel & E.)

Curry, Colum, Very Rev Dean,
PP, VG
Parochial House,
4 Circular Road,
Dungannon, Co Tyrone
BT71 6BE
Tel 028-87722775
(Armagh)

Curry, Martin (SJ)
Dominic Collins' House
Residence,
129 Morehampton Road,
Dublin 4
Tel 01-2693075

Curry, William (SSC)
Priest in charge,
St Columban's,
67-68 Castle Dawson,
Rathcoffey Road,
Maynooth, Co Kildare
Tel 01-6286036

Curtin, Jerome, Rt Rev Mgr,
PE
Holy Family Residence,
Roebuck, Dundrum,
Dublin 14
(Dublin, retired)

Curtin, Tim
Chaplain, Coláiste Na
Trócaire, Rathkeale,
Co Limerick
Tel 069-63432
(Limerick)

Curtis, James B., Very Rev
Canon
Rathjarney, Drinagh,
Co Wexford
(Ferns, retired)

Curtis, James, Very Rev
3 Oldtown Court,
Clongreen, Foulksmills,
New Ross, Co Wexford
(Ferns, retired)

Curtis, Thomas, Very Rev
Canon
2 The Hollows, Lugduff,
Tinahely, Co Wicklow
(Ferns, retired)

Cusack, Gerard (OPraem), Rt
Rev
Abbey of the Most Holy
Trinity and St Norbert,
Kilnacrott,
Ballyjamesduff, Co Cavan
Tel 049-8544416

Cusack, John, Very Rev, PP
Virginia, Co Cavan
Tel 049-8547063
(*Virginia*, Kilmore)

Cusack, Michael (CSsR)
Vicar Superior, St Patrick's,
Esker, Athenry, Co Galway
Tel 091-844549

Cusack, Ronan (OP), Very Rev
Prior, St Magdalen's,
Drogheda, Co Louth
Tel 041-9838271

Cushen, Bernard, Very Rev, PP
Ramsgrange,
New Ross, Co Wexford
Tel 051-389148
(*Ramsgrange*, Ferns)

Cushen, Patrick, Very Rev, PP,
VF
Ferns, Enniscorthy,
Co Wexford
Tel 053-9366152
(*Ferns*, Ferns)

Allianz (ⅲ)

Cushenan, Jarlath, Very Rev,
PP
17 Castlewellan Road,
Hilltown, Newry BT34 5UY
Tel 028-40630206
(Dromore)
Cushnahan, Vincent, CC
The Presbytery, Bell Steel
Road, Poleglass, Belfast
BT17 0PB
Tel 028-90625739
(The Nativity, Down & C.)
Cussen, Joseph, CC
Glenfield Road, Killmallock,
Co Limerick
Tel 063-98061
(Kilmallock, Limerick)
Cussen, Michael, Very Rev, PP
Fedamore, Kilmallock,
Co Limerick
Tel 061-390112/087-1279015
(Fedamore, Limerick)

D

D'ambrosio, Joseph (CSSp)
Rockwell College,
Cashel, Co Tipperary
Tel 062-61444
D'Arcy, Aidan, CC
2 Knightswood, Coolock
Lane, Santry, Dublin 9
Tel 01-8428283
(Larkhill-Whitehall-Santry,
Dublin)
D'Arcy, Brian (CP)
Superior,
St Gabriel's Retreat,
The Graan, Enniskillen,
Co Fermanagh
Tel 028-66322272
D'Arcy, Paul A. (SMA)
Provincial Secretary,
African Missions,
Blackrock Road, Cork
Tel 021-4292871
Dabrowski, Mariusz, CC
470 Falls Road,
Belfast BT12 6EN
Tel 028-90321102
(St John's, Down & C.)
Dagens, Seamus, Very Rev, PP
Ballintra, Co Donegal
Tel 074-9734016
(Ballintra, Raphoe)
Dallat, Christopher, Very Rev
Leabank Nursing Home, 1
Beechwood Avenue,
Ballycastle BT54 6BL
(Down & C., retired)
Dallat, Ciaran, Very Rev, PP
Sacred Heart Presbytery,
1 Glenview Street,
Belfast BT14 7DP
Tel 028-90351851
(Sacred Heart, Down & C.)

Dalton, John (OFM)
4 McSweeney House,
Berkeley Road, Dublin 7
Dalton, Patrick, Very Rev
Canon, PP
Gowran, Co Kilkenny
Tel 056-7726128/
086-8283478
(Ossory)
Dalton, Thomas, Very Rev, PP
Rathangan, Duncormick,
Co Wexford
Tel 051-563104
(Rathangan and
Cleariestown, Ferns)
Dalton, William, Very Rev, PP
Callan, Co Kilkenny
Tel 056-7725287/
086-8506215
(Callan, Ossory)
Daly, Brian, Very Rev, PP, VF
28 Chapel Road, Cushendall,
Ballymena,
Co Antrim BT44 0RS
Tel 028-21771240
(Cushendall, Down & C.)
Daly, Daniel (SVD)
Maynooth, Co Kildare
Tel 01-6286391/2
Daly, Edward, Most Rev, DD
Retired Bishop of Derry,
9 Steelstown Road,
Derry BT48 8EU
Tel 028-71359809
(Derry)
Daly, Edward, Very Rev, PE
Mount Bolus, Tullamore,
Co Offaly
Tel 057-9354035
(Kilcormac, Meath)
Daly, Gabriel (OSA)
St Augustine's,
Taylor's Lane,
Balyboden, Dublin 16
Tel 01-4241000
Daly, Hugh, Very Rev, PE
St Mary's, 50 Cremore Road,
Glasnevin, Dublin 11
(Dublin, retired)
Daly, John, Very Rev, PP
St Mochta's, Porterstown,
Dublin 15
Tel 01-8213218
(Porterstown-Clonsilla,
Dublin)
Daly, John, Very Rev, PP
St Nicholas' Presbytery,
Westbury, Limerick
Tel 061-340614/087-8180815
(St Nicholas, Limerick)
Daly, Kevin (OCSO), Dom
Abbot Emeritus, Mount
Saint Joseph Abbey,
Roscrea, Co Tipperary
Tel 0505-25600

Daly, Martin (SM)
Superior, Catholic University
School,
89 Lower Leeson Street,
Dublin 2
Tel 01-6762586
Daly, Martin, Very Rev, PP
Parochial House,
Chapelizod, Dublin 20
Tel 01-6264645
(Chapelizod, Dublin)
Daly, Michael V., Very Rev
35 Herbert Place, Navan,
Co Meath
Tel 046-9093935
(Meath, retired)
Daly, Michael, Very Rev, PP
Broomfield, Castleblayney,
Co Monaghan
Tel 042-9743617
(Donaghmoyne, Clogher)
Daly, Noel (SSC)
St Columban's, Dalgan Park,
Navan, Co Meath
Tel 046-9021525
Daly, Pádraig (OSA), Very Rev,
PP
St Augustine's, Taylor's
Lane, Ballyboden, Dublin 16
Tel 01-4944966
(Ballyboden, Dublin)
Daly, Patrick, Very Rev, PP
Cooleragh, Coill Dubh,
Naas, Co Kildare
Tel 045-860281
(Cooleragh and
Staplestown, Kildare & L.)
Daly, Peter (OMI), CC
The Presbytery, Darndale,
Dublin 17
Tel 01-8474547
(Darndale, Dublin)
Daly, Philip, CC
Kilclooney, Co Donegal
Tel 074-9545114
(Ardara, Raphoe)
Daly, Thomas, Very Rev, PP
Parochial House,
Boicetown, Togher,
Drogheda, Co Louth
Tel 041-6852110
(Togher, Armagh)
Dalzell, Tony (SM)
St Teresa's, Donore Avenue,
Dublin 8
Tel 01-4542425/4531613
(Donore Avenue, St Teresa's,
Dublin)
Danaher, Michael (OSA)
St Augustine's Priory,
O'Connell Street,
Limerick
Tel 061-415374
Daniels, Iomar
Chaplaincy Department,
NUIG, St Declan's,
Distillery Road, Galway
Tel 091-492168
(Clonfert)

Darby, Derek, CC
54 Brookville, Ashbourne,
Co Meath
Tel 01-8350547
(Ashbourne-Donaghmore,
Meath)
Darby, Gary (MI), CC
41 Grangemore Grove,
Donaghmede, Dublin 13
Tel 01-8476392
(Donaghmede, Dublin)
Darcy, Michael (SMA)
African Missions,
Blackrock Road, Cork
Tel 021-4292871
Darcy, Stephen (CSSp)
Holy Ghost Missionary
College, Kimmage Manor,
Dublin 12
Tel 01-4064300
Dardis, John (SJ)
Provincial,
Campion House Residence,
28 Lower Hatch Street,
Dublin 2
Tel 01-6383990
Dargan, Joseph (SJ)
Rector, Manresa House,
Dollymount, Dublin 3
Tel 01-8331352
Dargan, Neil, Very Rev, PP
Kildysart, Co Clare
Tel 065-6832155/
087-7530209
(Kildysart, Killaloe)
Darragh, Anthony (CSSp)
Holy Ghost Missionary
College, Kimmage Manor,
Dublin 12
Tel 01-4064300
Darragh, Vincent, Very Rev,
PE
81 Mullinahoe Road,
Ardboe, Dungannon,
Co Tyrone BT71 5AU
Tel 028-86735774
(Armagh)
Daukszewicz, Tomasz
Polish Chaplain,
Cathedral Presbytery,
Ennis, Co Clare
Tel 065-6824043/087-
0515788
(Ennis, Killaloe)
Davern, Richard, CC
17 Alderwood Avenue,
Caherdavin Heights,
Limerick
Tel 061-453226
(Christ the King, Limerick)
Davey, Gerard, CC
Foxford, Co Mayo
Tel 094-9256401
(Foxford, Achonry)
Davies, Anthony, Very Rev
Canon
Killowen, Rostrevor
(Dromore, retired)

Davis, Hugh (OFMCap)
St Francis Capuchin Friary.
Rochestown, Co Cork
Tel 021-4896244

Davis, Patrick (SJ)
Peter Faber House,
28 Brookvale Avenue,
Belfast BT14 6BW
Tel 028-90757615

Davitt, Norman (SVD)
Donamon Castle,
Roscommon
Tel 090-6662222

Davitt, Thomas (CM)
St Joseph's,
44 Stillorgan Park,
Blackrock, Co Dublin
Tel 01-2886961

Davy, Charles (SJ)
St Ignatius Community &
Church, 27 Raleigh Row,
Salthill, Galway
Tel 091-523707

Dawson, Laurence, Very Rev
Canon, PP
Clogher,
Co Tyrone BT76 0TQ
Tel 028-85548600
(Clogher, Clogher)

de Bhaldraithe, Eoin (OCSO)
Guestmaster, Bolton Abbey,
Moone, Co Kildare
Tel 059-8624102

de Burca, Peadar, Very Rev
Kilmeedy, Co Limerick
Tel 063-87008
(Limerick, retired)

De Val, Seamus, Very Rev
1 Irish Street, Bunclody,
Co Wexford
Tel 053-9376140
(Ferns, retired)

Deane, Philip (OFM)
Franciscan Friary, Killarney,
Co Kerry
Tel 064-6631334/6631066

Deasy, Declan (OSA)
St Patrick's College and
Church,
Via Piemonte 60, 00187
Rome, Italy
Tel 00396-4203121

Deasy, John, Rt Rev Mgr,
Moderator
55 St Agnes' Road, Crumlin,
Dublin 12
Tel 01-4550955
(Crumlin, Dublin)

Deegan, Gerard
67 Ramleh Park, Milltown,
Dublin 6
Tel 01-2196600
(Milltown, Dublin)

Deegan, Joseph, Very Rev, PP
Parochial House, Slane,
Co Meath
Tel 041-9824249
(Slane, Meath)

Deegan, Stan, Very Rev, PP
Parochial House,
Rochfortbridge,
Co Westmeath
Tel 044-9222107
(Meath)

Deely, Pat
Toomevara, Co Tipperary
Tel 067-26010/086-8330225
(Toomevara, Killaloe)

Deeney, Edward (SMA)
Dromantine College,
Dromantine, Newry,
Co Down BT34 1RH
Tel 028-30821224

Deenihan, Thomas
Cork & Ross Offices,
Redemption Road, Cork
Tel 021-4301717
(Cork & R.)

Deery, Cathal, CC
Emyvale, Monaghan
Tel 047-87221
(Donagh, Clogher)

Deighan, Gerard, Adm
The Parochial House,
Harrington Street, Dublin 8
Tel 01-4751506/4760036
(Harrington Street, Dublin)

Delahunty, Richard (CSsR),
Very Rev, Adm
St Joseph's,
St Alphonsus Road,
Dundalk, Co Louth
Tel 042-9334042
(Dundalk, St Joseph's,
Armagh)

Delaney, Ailbe (CP)
St Gabriel's Retreat,
The Graan, Enniskillen,
Co Fermanagh
Tel 028-66322272

Delaney, Denis M., Very Rev,
Moderator
Parochial House, Naul,
Co Dublin
Tel 01-8412932
(Naul, Dublin)

Delaney, Joe
Chaplain's Office, Galway
Clinic, Doughiska, Galway
Tel 091-785000
(Galway)

Delaney, John, CC
Coon, Carlow
Tel 056-4443116/
086-8596321
(Muckalee, Ossory)

Delaney, John, Very Rev, PP
Parochial House, Kilrossanty,
Kilmacthomas,
Co Waterford
Tel 051-291985
(Kilrossanty, Waterford & L.)

Delaney, John, Very Rev, PP,
VF
137 Ballymun Road,
Dublin 9
Tel 01-8376347
(Dublin)

Delaney, Joseph, Very Rev
St Kieran's College,
Kilkenny
Tel 056-7721086/
086-8206730
(Ossory, retired)

Delaney, Joseph, Very Rev, PP
Clonbealy, Newport,
Co Tipperary
Tel 061-378126
(Newport, Cashel & E.)

Delaney, Martin, CC
St Canice's Presbytery,
Granges Road, Kilkenny
Tel 056-7752994/
086-2444594
(St Canice's, Ossory)

Delany, John, Very Rev, PP
137 Ballymun Road,
Dublin 11
Tel 01-8376347
(Ballymun Road, Dublin)

Delargy, David, Very Rev, PP
Parochial House,
23 Hannahstown Hill,
Belfast BT17 0LT
Tel 028-90614567
(Hannahstown, Down & C.)

Delargy, Patrick, Very Rev, PP
Parochial House,
4 Broughshane Road,
Ballymena,
Co Antrim BT43 7DX
Tel 028-25641515
(Ballymena (Kirkinriola),
Down & C.)

Delimat, Piotr, CC
Our Lady of Lourdes
Presbytery,
Hardman's Gardens,
Drogheda, Co Louth
Tel 041-9831899
(Drogheda, Armagh)

Dempsey, Joseph, Very Rev
Canon, PP, VF
Lower Main Street,
Rathkeale, Co Limerick
Tel 069-63133
(Rathkeale, Limerick)

Dempsey, Micahel (CSsR)
St Joseph's, Dundalk,
Co Louth
Tel 042-9334042/9334762

Dempsey, Michael V., Very
Rev, PP
Parochial House, Barndarrig,
Co Wicklow
Tel 0404-48130
(Kilbride and Barndarrig,
Dublin)

Dempsey, Paul
Two-Mile-House, Naas,
Co Kildare
Tel 045-876160
(Naas, Kildare & L.)

Dempsey, Raymond, CC
Ferrybank, Waterford
Tel 051-832577/087-2859682
(Ferrybank, Ossory)

Denmead, James, CC
Holy Family Presbytery,
Luke Wadding Street,
Waterford
Tel 051-374720
(Holy Family, Waterford &
L.)

Dennehy, Philip
4 Stanhope Place, Athy,
Co Kildare
(Dublin, retired)

Denny, Aidan, Very Rev
10 New Barnsley Green,
New Barnsley,
Belfast BT12 7HS
Tel 028-90328877
(Corpus Christi, Down & C.)

Dermody, Eamonn, Very Rev
Canon, PP
Clarinbridge, Co Galway
Tel 091-796208
(Clarinbridge, Galway)

Desmond, Bartholomew, CC
Carriganimma, Macroom,
Co Cork
Tel 026-44027
(Clondrohid, Cloyne)

Desmond, Con
c/o Westbourne, Ennis,
Co Clare
(Killaloe, retired)

Desmond, Diarmuid, Very Rev,
PP
Kilrane, Co Wexford
Tel 053-9133128
(Kilrane and St Patrick's,
Ferns)

Desmond, Garrett, Very Rev,
PP
Newcastle, Clonmel,
Co Tipperary
Tel 052-6136387
(Newcastle and
Fourmilewater, Waterford &
L.)

Desmond, Patrick
The Lodge, Mount Sackville,
Chapelizod, Dublin 20
Tel 01-8214004
(Dublin)

Desta, Bahlibi (White Fathers)
Cypress Grove, Templeogue,
Dublin 6W
Tel 01-4055263/4055264

Devaney, Owen, Very Rev, PP
Mullahoran,
Kilcogy via Longford,
Co Cavan
Tel 043-6683141
(*Mullahoran and Loughduff*,
Ardagh & Cl.)

Devereux, Sean
The Gambia, West Africa
(Ferns)

Devine, Arthur, Very Rev, PE
Rathbawn Road, Castlebar,
Co Mayo
(Tuam, retired)

Devine, James B. (CSSp)
Holy Ghost Missionary
College, Kimmage Manor,
Dublin 12
Tel 01-4064300

Devine, Kevin (SSC)
St Columban's Retirement
Home, Dalgan Park,
Navan, Co Meath
Tel 046-9021525

Devine, Liam, Very Rev
Canon, PP, VF
SS Peter and Paul, Athlone
Tel 090-6492171
(Elphin)

Devine, Oliver, Very Rev, PP
Parochial House, Ballivor,
Co Meath
Tel 046-9546488
(*Ballivor*, Meath)

Devine, Olvier J., Very Rev, PP
Parochial House,
Mountnugent, Co Cavan
Tel 049-8540123
(*Mountnugent*, Meath)

Devine, Patrick (CSSp)
Blackrock College,
Blackrock, Co Dublin
Tel 01-2888681

Devine, Robert
(*priest in residence*)
Crossroads, Killygordon,
Co Donegal
Tel 074-9149194
(*Killygordon*, Derry)

Devitt, Dan (SDB)
Mission Procurator,
Salesian College,
Pallaskenry, Co Limerick
Tel 061-393313

Devitt, Patrick, PC
128 Clonliffe Road, Dublin 3
Tel 01-8373869
(*North William Street*,
Dublin)

Devitt, Seamus (CSsR)
Mount Saint Alphonsus,
Limerick
Tel 061-315099

Devlin, Anthony, Very Rev, PP
St Paul's Presbytery,
125 Falls Road,
Belfast BT12 6AB
Tel 028-90325034
(*St Paul's*, Down & C.)

Devlin, Brendan, Rt Rev Mgr,
MA, DD
St Patrick's College,
Maynooth, Co Kildare
Tel 01-6285222
(Derry)

Devlin, Eamon (CM), CC
St Peter's, Phibsboro,
Dublin 7
Tel 01-8389708
(*Phibsboro*, Dublin)

Devlin, Kieran, PEm
Colon House,
21 Buncrana Road,
Derry BY48 8LA
(Derry, retired)

Devlin, Patrick, CC
Priest's House,
29 Killough Road,
Downpatrick,
Co Down BT30 6PX
Tel 028-44613430
(*Downpatrick*, Down & C.)

Devlin, Peter, PP
Orchard park, Murlog,
Lifford, Co Donegal
Tel 074-9142022
(Derry)

Diamond, Mark, Very Rev
Canon
Cathedral Close, Ballina,
Co Mayo
(Killala, retired)

Diffley, Vincent (SDB)
Salesian House, Milford,
Castletroy, Limerick
Tel 061-330268/330914

Diggin, Fintan, PP
Parochial House, Cleagh,
Clonmany, Co Donegal
Tel 074-9376264
(*Clonmany*, Derry)

Dillon, Christopher (OSB), Rt
Rev Dom
Glenstal Abbey, Murroe,
Co Limerick
Tel 061-386103

Dillon, Sean (SPS)
St Patrick's, Kiltegan,
Co Wicklow
Tel 059-6473600

Dillon, Sean, Very Rev, PP
Parochial House,
8 Minorca Place,
Carrickfergus,
Co Antrim BT38 8AU
Tel 028-93363269
(*Carrickfergus*, Down & C.)

Dillon, Thomas, Very Rev, PP
Baltinglass, Co Wicklow
Tel 059-6482768
(*Baltinglass*, Kildare & L.)

Dineen, Joseph (OP)
St Saviour's,
Upper Dorset Street,
Dublin 1
Tel 01-8897610

Dobbin, Séamus, CC
St Patrick's Presbytery,
Roden Place, Dundalk,
Co Louth
Tel 042-9334648
(*Dundalk, St Patrick's*,
Armagh)

Doherty, Brendan, PP
4 Garvagh Road, Kilrea,
Co Derry BT51 5QP
Tel 028-29540343
(*Kilrea*, Derry)

Doherty, Cathal (SJ)
St Ignatius Community &
Church, 27 Raleigh Row,
Salthill, Galway
Tel 091-523707

Doherty, George, CC
Glebe, Linsfort, Buncrana,
Co Donegal
Tel 074-9361126
(*Buncrana*, Derry)

Doherty, John (CSsR)
Superior, St Patrick's, Esker,
Athenry, Co Galway
Tel 091-844549

Doherty, John, PP
Parochial House, 447
Victoria Road,
Ballymagorry, Strabane,
Co Tyrone BT82 0AT
Tel 028-718802274
(*Leckpatrick*, Derry)

Doherty, John, Rt Rev Mgr
Priest-in-residence,
Charlestown, Co Mayo
Tel 094-9255793
(Achonry, retired)

Doherty, Joseph, PEm
Clarcarricknagun,
Donegal Town, Co Donegal
Tel 073-21259
(Derry, retired)

Doherty, Kevin, CC
97 Ballymun Road,
Dublin 11
Tel 01-8375440
(*Ballymun Road*, Dublin)

Doherty, Michael, PP
39 Melmount Road,
Strabane,
Co Tyrone BT82 9EF
Tel 028-71882648
(*Melmount*, Derry)

Doherty, Patrick, PP
Parochial House, 32 Chapel
Road, Waterside,
Derry BT47 2BB
Tel 028-71342303
(*Waterside*, Derry)

Doherty, Richard, Very Rev,
AP
Abbeyside, Dungarvan,
Co Waterford
Tel 058-42379
(*Abbeyside*, Waterford & L.)

Doherty, Sean (SSC)
St Columban's, Dalgan Park,
Navan, Co Meath
Tel 046-9021525

Dolan, Andrew, PP
25 Ballynease Road,
Bellaghy, Magherafelt,
Co Derry BT45 8JS
Tel 028-79386259
(*Bellaghy (Ballyscullion)*,
Derry)

Dolan, Denis, Very Rev, PP
Fivemiletown,
Co Tyrone BT75 OQP
Tel 028-89521291
(*Brookeboro*, Clogher)

Dolan, Gerard, Rt Rev Mgr,
PP, VG
St Columba's, Rosses Point,
Co Sligo
Tel 071-9177133
Diocesan Secretary,
St Mary's, Sligo
Tel 071-9162670/9162769
(Elphin)

Dolan, James (MHM)
St Joseph's House,
50 Orwell Park, Rathgar,
Dublin 6
Tel 01-4127700

Dolan, John, Rt Rev Mgr, LCL
The Chancellery,
Archbishop's House,
Dublin 9
Tel 01-8379253
(Dublin)

Dolan, Joseph (SSC)
St Columban's, Dalgan Park,
Navan, Co Meath
Tel 046-9021525

Dolan, Martin, CC
The Presbytery,
Francis Street, Dublin 8
Tel 01-4544861
(*Francis Street*, Dublin)

Dollard, James, Very Rev, PP
Conahy, Jenkinstown,
Co Kilkenny
Tel 056-7767657
(*Conahy*, Ossory)

Donaghy, John, Very Rev
Canon, PE
Ashbrook Private Nursing
Home, 50 Moor Road,
Coalisland,
Co Tyrone BT71 4QB
(Armagh, retired)

Donaghy, Kevin
(priest in residence)
Parochial House,
86 Maydown Road,
Artasooley, Tullysaran,
Benburb,
Co Armagh BT71 7LN
Tel 028-37548210
Headmaster,
St Patrick's Grammar School,
Armagh
Tel 028-37522018
(Armagh)

Donegan, Gary (CP)
Superior, Holy Cross Retreat,
Ardoyne, Belfast BT14 7GE
Tel 028-90748231

Donegan, Gary, Very Rev (CP),
PP
Holy Cross Retreat, 432
Crumlin Road, Ardoyne,
Belfast BT14 7GE
Tel 028-90748231/2
(Holy Cross, Down & C.)

Donleavy, James (OP), Very
Rev, PP
St Saviour's,
Glentworth Street, Limerick
Tel 061-412333
(St Saviour's, Limerick)

Donlon, Chris, CC
Dromore, Mallow, Co Cork
Tel 022-21198
(Glantane, Cloyne)

Donnellan, David (OCD)
Prior, St Teresa's,
Clarendon Street, Dublin 2
Tel 01-6718466/6718127

Donnellan, Patrick (SDB)
Salesian College,
Pallaskenry, Co Limerick
Tel 061-393313

Donnellan, Patrick, Very Rev,
PP
Islandeady, Castlebar,
Co Mayo
Tel 094-9024125
(Islandeady, Tuam)

Donnelly, Brian, Very Rev, PP
16 Castlefin Road,
Castlederg,
Co Tyrone BT81 7EB
Tel 028-81671393
(Derry)

Donnelly, Francis, Rt Rev
Archdeacon, PE
64 Meadow Grove, Dundalk,
Co Louth
Tel 042-9353264
(Armagh, retired)

Donnelly, Gerald, Very Rev
Canon
Ballygar, Co Galway
(Elphin, retired)

Donnelly, James
Bóthar na Naomh
Presbytery, Thurles,
Co Tipperary
Tel 0504-22042/22688
(Thurles, SS Joseph and
Brigid, Cashel & F)

Donnelly, John, Very Rev, AP
Rathcabbin, Roscrea,
Co Tipperary
Tel 0509-39072
(Lorrha and Dorrha,
Killaloe)

Donnelly, Joseph, Rt Rev Mgr,
PP, VF
52 Brook Street, Omagh,
Co Tyrone BT78 5HE
Tel 028-82243011
(Omagh, Derry)

Donnelly, Kevin, Venerable
Archdeacon
Parochial House,
4 Broughshane Road,
Ballymena,
Co Antrim BT43 7DX
Tel 028-25641515
(Ballymena (Kirkinriola),
Down & C.)

Donnelly, Liam, CC
20 Loughermore Road,
Ogill, Ballykelly,
Co Derry BT49 9PD
Tel 028-77762721
(Limavady, Derry)

Donnelly, Marius (CP)
St Gabriel's Retreat,
The Graan, Enniskillen,
Co Fermanagh
Tel 028-66322272

Donnelly, Michael, Very Rev,
PP
Maugherow, Ballinfull PO,
Co Sligo
Tel 071-9163102
(Drumcliff/Maugherow,
Elphin)

Donnelly, Mícheál, CC
Caltra, Ballinasloe,
Co Galway
Tel 090-9678125
Chaplain, St Cuan's College,
Castleblakeney, Ballinasloe,
Co Galway
Tel 090-9678127
(Elphin)

Donnelly, Patrick, CC
Parochial House, Ratoath,
Co Meath
Tel 01-8256207
(Meath)

Donnelly, Peter, Very Rev, PP
Parochial House,
130 Ballinderry Bridge Road,
Coagh, Cookstown,
Co Tyrone BT80 0AY
Tel 028-79418244
(Ballinderry, Armagh)

Donnelly, Peter, Very Rev, PP
Parochial House,
15 Drumaroad Hill,
Castlewellan,
Co Down BT31 9PD
Tel 028-44811474
(Drumaroad and
Clanvaraghan, Down & C.)

Donnelly, T. Phil, PEm
Nazareth House, Fahan,
Co Donegal
(Derry, retired)

Donnelly, Victor (CP)
Passionist Community,
35-36 Coill Tire,
Doughiska, Galway

Donohoe, Eamon (MSC)
'Croí Nua', Rosary Lane,
Taylor's Hill, Galway
Tel 091-520960

Donohoe, Kevin
Magheranure, Cootehill,
Co Cavan
Tel 049-5552155
(Kilmore)

Donohoe, Patrick (SSC)
Columban Sisters,
Magheramore, Co Wicklow

Donohoe, Seamus (OFM)
Franciscan Friary, Ennis,
Co Clare
Tel 065-6828751

Donohoe, Sean (OFMCap)
Guardian, Capuchin Friary,
Station Road, Raheny,
Dublin 5
Tel 01-8313886

Donovan, Bernard, Very Rev,
PP
Cloughdubh, Crookstown,
Co Cork
Tel 028-7336053
(Kilmurry, Cork & R.)

Donovan, Roy, CC
Caherconlish, Co Limerick
Tel 061-351213
(Cashel & E.)

Donworth, John, Very Rev, PP
Kildimo, Co Limerick
Tel 061-394134/087-2237501
(Kildimo and Pallaskenry,
Limerick)

Doocey, Colin, CC
The Presbytery,
Frankfield, Cork
Tel 021-4362377
(Frankfield-Grange, Cork &
R.)

Doody, Patrick (CSSp), Very
Rev, PP
66 Rockfield Avenue,
Dublin 12
Tel 01-4558316
(Kimmage Manor, Dublin)

Doohan, Martin, Very Rev, PP
Dunfanaghy, Co Donegal
Tel 074-9136163
(Dunfanaghy, Raphoe)

Dooher, Patrick G. (SSC)
St Columban's, Dalgan Park,
Navan, Co Meath
Tel 046-9021525

Doolan, Herman (OCD)
Prior,
53/55 Marlborough Road,
Dublin 4
Tel 01-6601832

Doolan, William, Very Rev
c/o Diocesan Office,
Social Service Centre,
Henry Street, Limerick
(Limerick, retired)

Dooley, Francis D., Very Rev,
PP
The Presbytery, Baldoyle,
Dublin 13
Tel 01-8322060
(Baldoyle, Dublin)

Dooley, John (SJ)
John Austin House, 135
North Circular Road,
Dublin 7
Tel 01-8386768

Dooley, Maurice, Rt Rev Mgr,
AP
Loughmore, Templemore,
Co Tipperary
Tel 0504-31375
(Loughmore, Cashel & E.)

Dooley, Seán, CC
Parochial House,
42 Abbey Street,
Co Armagh BT61 7D2
Tel 028-37522802
(Armagh)

Dooley, Thomas, Very Rev, PP
Portarlington, Co Laois
Tel 057-8643004
(Kildare & L.)

Dooley, Tom (SM), CC
4 Greenmount Road,
Dublin 6
Tel 01-4904959
(Terenure, Dublin)

Doona, Jeremiah (MHM)
St Joseph's House,
50 Orwell Park, Rathgar,
Dublin 6
Tel 01-4127700

Doran, Dermot (CSSp)
Spiritan Missionary College,
Kimmage Manor,
Dublin 12
Tel 01-4064300

Doran, Fonsie (CSsR)
St Patrick's, Esker, Athenry,
Co Galway
Tel 091-844549

Doran, John (OSA)
St Augustine's,
Taylor's Lane,
Balyboden, Dublin 16
Tel 01-4241000

Doran, Joseph
Presbytery No 1,
Church Grounds,
Lower Kilmacud Road,
Kilmacud, Co Dublin
Tel 01-2880595
(*Kilmacud-Stillorgan*,
Dublin)

Doran, Kevin
Holy Cross Diocesan Centre,
Clonliffe Road,
Dublin 3
Tel 01-8087531
(Dublin)

Dore, Bernardine (OFM)
Portiuncola Nursing Home,
Multyfarnham,
Co Westmeath

Dorgan, Michael, Very Rev, PP
Castlemagner, Mallow,
Co Cork
Tel 022-27600
(*Castlemagner*, Cloyne)

Dorr, Donal (SPS)
St Patrick's, 21 Leeson Park,
Dublin 6
Tel 01-4977897

Dougherty, Ciaran (OP), CC
St Saviour's,
Glentworth Street, Limerick
Tel 061-412333
(*St Saviour's*, Limerick)

Dowd, Eugene, Canon
51 Drumnavanagh,
Farnham Road, Cavan
Tel 049-4326821
(Kilmore, retired)

Dowd, G. (SDB)
Chaplain, Custume Barracks,
Athlone

Dowd, Gerard, CF
Chaplain, Custume Barracks,
Athlone, Co Westmeath
Tel 090-6421277
(Elphin)

Dowd, Thomas
Ely University Centre,
10 Hume Street, Dublin 2
Tel 01-6767420
(Opus Dei)

Dowley, Martin (OCSO)
Prior, Our Lady of
Bethlehem Abbey,
11 Ballymena Road,
Portglenone, Ballymena,
Co Antrim BT44 8BL
Tel 028-25821211

Dowling, Cornelius
St Anthony's, 13 Richmond
Grove, Monkstown,
Co Dublin
Tel 01-2800789
(Dublin, retired)

Dowling, Patrick, Canon
Holy Family Residence,
Roebuck Road,
Dundrum, Dublin 14
(Dublin)

Dowling, Seán (OSA)
St Augustine's Priory,
Washington Street,
Cork
Tel 021-275398
(Cork & R.)

Downes, Frank (OP)
St Dominic's Retreat House,
Montenotte, Co Cork
Tel 021-4502520

Downes, Patrick (CSSp)
Rockwell College, Cashel,
Co Tipperary
Tel 062-61444

Downes, Teddy, CC
The Presbytery, Cross,
Vallymount, Co Wicklow
Tel 045-867151
(*Valleymount*, Dublin)

Downey, James
Catherine McAuley Home,
Balloonagh, Tralee, Co Kerry
Tel 066-7129700
(Kerry, retired)

Downey, James (OSA)
St Patrick's College and
Church, Via Piemonte 60,
00187 Rome, Italy
Tel 00396-4203121

Downey, Jim
Cragg, Castleisland,
Co Kerry
(Kerry, retired)

Downey, John, CC
36 Moneyneena Road,
Draperstown, Magherafelt,
Co Derry BT45 7DZ
Tel 028-79628375
(Derry)

Downey, Martin, Very Rev, PP
24 Presentation Road,
Galway
Tel 091-562276
(Galway)

Downing, Mortimer, Very Rev,
PP
Ballyhea, Co Cork
Tel 063-81470
(*Ballyhea*, Cloyne)

Doyle, Andrew, Very Rev, PP
Durhamstown, Bohermeen,
Navan, Co Meath
Tel 046-9073805
(*Bohermeen*, Meath)

Doyle, Bernard
Kiltyclogher, Co Leitrim
Tel 071-9854302
(Kilmore, retired)

Doyle, Declan, Adm
56 Foxfield Saint John,
Dublin 5
Tel 01-8325871
(*Kilbarrack-Foxfield*, Dublin)

Doyle, Denis, PE, CC
77 Lakelands, Naas,
Co Kildare
Tel 045-897470
(*Naas*, Kildare & L.)

Doyle, Denis, Very Rev, PP
Kilmore, Co Wexford
Tel 053-9135181
(*Kilmore*, Ferns)

Doyle, Derek
C/o St Columban's,
Dalgan Park, Navan,
Co Meath
(Dublin)

Doyle, Des, CC
Chaplain's Residence,
Dublin Airport, Co Dublin
Tel 01-8144340
(*Swords*, Dublin)

Doyle, Frank (SJ)
Gonzaga College,
Sandford Road, Dublin 6
Tel 01-4972943

Doyle, Gerard, CC
68 Maplewood Road,
Springfield, Tallaght,
Dublin 24
Tel 01-2859212
(*Springfield*, Dublin)

Doyle, James, CC
Bunclody, Enniscorthy,
Co Wexford
Tel 053-9377264
(*Bunclody*, Ferns)

Doyle, James, CC
Chapel Lane, Sallins Road,
Naas, Co Kildare
Tel 045-897150
(*Naas*, Kildare & L.)

Doyle, Martin, CC
1 Clonard Park, Wexford
Tel 053-9147686
(*Clonard*, Ferns)

Doyle, Michael, CC (Tyler,
Texas)
Ballyfad, Gorey, Co Wexford
Tel 0402-37124
(*Kilanerin*, Ferns)

Doyle, Noel (SSC)
St Columban's, Dalgan Park,
Navan, Co Meath
Tel 046-9021525

Doyle, Oliver
Diocese of Great Falls,
Billings, Montana, USA
(Ferns)

Doyle, Owen (SSC)
St John of God Brothers,
St Mary's Drumcar,
Dunleer, Co Louth

Doyle, Rossa, CC
3 Hoskyn Bank, Bawn Road,
Rush, Co Dublin
Tel 01-8430973
(Rush, Dublin)

Doyle, Thaddeus
Shillelagh, Arklow,
Co Wicklow
Tel 053-9429926
(Ferns)

Doyle, Thomas, Very Rev, PP
Craanford, Gorey,
Co Wexford
Tel 053-9428163
(Ferns)

Draper, Anthony, DD
All Hallows College,
Drumcondra, Dublin 9
Tel 01-373745
(Meath)

Drennan, Martin, Most Rev,
DD
Bishop of Galway,
Mount Saint Mary's,
Taylor's Hill, Galway
Tel 091-563566
(Galway)

Drennan, Michael (SJ)
Vice-Rector, Milltown Park,
Sandford Road, Dublin 6
Tel 01-2698411/2698113

Drumgoole, Joseph, Very Rev,
PE
35 Grange Park Avenue,
Raheny, Dublin 5
Tel 01-8480244
(Dublin, retired)

Drumm, Eugene (SPS)
On temporary diocesan
work

Drumm, Michael, PC
47 Westbury Drive, Lucan,
Co Dublin
Tel 01-5031106
(*Esker-Doddsboro-
Adamstown*, Dublin)

Drumm, Michael, STL
Columba Centre, St Patrick's
College, Maynooth
(Elphin)

Drury, Ronan
St Patrick's College,
Maynooth, Co Kildare
Tel 01-6285222
(Meath)

D'Souza, Darryl (SDB)
Salesian House,
45 St Teresa's Road,
Crumlin, Dublin 12
Tel 01-4555605

Duddy, Brendan (SJ)
Milltown Park, Sandford
Road, Dublin 6
Tel 01-2698411/2698113

Duffy, Aquinas T., Very Rev,
PP
22 Wainsfort Park,
Terenure, Dublin 6W
Tel 01-4908288
(*Templeogue*, Dublin)

Duffy, Austin, Rt Rev Mgr,
PEm
28 Glenroe Park, Dungiven,
Co Derry BT47 4PE
Tel 028-77741811
(Derry, retired)

Duffy, Bernard, Very Rev, PE
20 Clonarkin Drive,
Oranmore, Co Galway
Tel 091-794552
(Galway, retired)

Duffy, Dominic (MSC)
Myross Wood Retreat
House, Leap, Skibbereen,
Co Cork
Tel 028-33118

Duffy, Eddie (SM)
London

Duffy, Eugene, DD
Mary Immaculate College,
South Circular Road,
Limerick
Tel 061-204968
(Achonry)

Duffy, Francis
Bishop's House, Cullies,
Co Cavan
Tel 049-4331496
(Kilmore)

Duffy, Frank (CSSp)
Holy Ghost Missionary
College, Kimmage Manor,
Dublin 12
Tel 01-4064300

Duffy, Hugh (SJ)
Crescent College
Comprehensive,
Dooradoyle, Limerick
Tel 061-480920

Duffy, James, Very Rev, VF
Ballinamore, Co Leitrim
Tel 071-9644050
(Ballinamore, Kilmore)

Duffy, John Joe, CC
Arranmore Island,
Co Donegal
Tel 074-9520504
Chaplain, Vocational School,
Arranmore Island,
Co Donegal
Tel 074-9521747
(Raphoe)

Duffy, Joseph, Most Rev, DD
Bishop of Clogher,
Bishop's House, Monaghan
Tel 047-81019
(Clogher)

Duffy, Kevin, CC
Castleblayney,
Co Monaghan
Tel 042-9740027
(Castleblayney, Clogher)

Duffy, Larry (SM)
Peru

Duffy, Larry, Very Rev Canon,
PP, VF
Clones, Co Monaghan
Tel 047-51048
(Clones, Clogher)

Duffy, Michael (LC)
Chaplain,
Woodlands Academy,
Wingfield House, Bray,
Co Wicklow
Tel 01-2866323

Duffy, Michael (OFMCap)
Vicar, St Anthony's
Capuchin Friary,
43 Dublin Street, Carlow
Tel 059-9142543

Duffy, Michael (SSC)
St Columban's, Dalgan Park,
Navan, Co Meath
Tel 046-9021525

Duffy, Michael A. (SSC)
St Columban's, Dalgan Park,
Navan, Co Meath
Tel 046-9021525

Duffy, Pat (CP)
Passionist Community,
108 Salisbury Avenue,
Belfast BT15 5ED
Tel 028-90288306

Duffy, Pat (CP)
Provincial, St Paul's Retreat,
Mount Argus, Dublin 6W
Tel 01-4992050

Duffy, Stephen, Very Rev, PP
Parochial House, Fieldstown,
Monasterboice, Drogheda,
Co Louth
Tel 041-9822839
(Monasterboice, Armagh)

Duggan, Colm (CSSp)
Holy Ghost Missionary
College, Kimmage Manor,
Dublin 12
Tel 01-4064300

Duggan, Frank
Parochial House No 2,
124 Greencastle Road,
Dublin 17
Tel 01-8485194
(Bonnybrook, Dublin)

Duggan, Iain (OFM)
Franciscan Friary,
Liberty Street, Cork
Tel 021-4270302

Duggan, James (OP)
Holy Cross, Tralee,
Co Kerry
Tel 066-21135/29185

Duggan, James F. (CSSp)
Holy Ghost Missionary
College, Kimmage Manor,
Dublin 12
Tel 01-4064300

Duggan, John
St John and Paul Church,
341 South Main Street,
Coventary RI R102816-5987,
USA
(Ossory)

Duggan, John, Very Rev, PP
Castlemahon, Co Limerick
Tel 069-72108/086-2600464
(Mahoonagh, Limerick)

Duggan, Michael (CSSp)
St Michael's College,
Ailesbury Road, Dublin 4
Tel 01-2189423

Duggan, Patrick, Very Rev
Canon, PP
Bennetsbridge, Co Kilkenny
Tel 056-7727140/
087-6644858
(Tullaherin, Ossory)

Duggan, Sean (CSsR)
Mount Saint Alphonsus,
Limerick
Tel 061-315099

Duhig, Frank, Very Rev
Canon, PP
St Ita's Presbytery,
Newcastle West, Co Limerick
Tel 069-62141/087-6380299
(Limerick)

Duignan, Michael, SThD
St Mary's, Sligo, Co Sligo
Tel 071-9162670
(Elphin)

Dullea, Gearóid, Dr
St Patrick's College,
Maynooth, Co Kildare
(Cork & R.)

Dundon, Patrick (CSSp)
Superior, St Michael's
College, Ailesbury Road,
Dublin 4
Tel 01-2189423

Dunican, Nicholas, Very Rev
Knightsbridge Nursing
Home, Trim, Co Meath
(Meath, retired)

Dunican, Séamus, Very Rev,
PP
Parochial House, Killina,
Rahan, Tullamore, Co Offaly
Tel 057-9355917
(Rahan, Meath)

Dunlea, Philip (CSsR)
Clonard Monastery,
1 Clonard Gardens,
Belfast BT13 2RL
Tel 028-90445950

Dunleavy, John (SMA)
Temporary diocesan work in
Ireland

Dunleavy, John, CC
Ballyconneely, Co Galway
Tel 095-23541
(Clifden (Omey and
Ballindoon), Tuam)

Dunne, Aidan, CC
Parochial House,
6 Circular Road,
Dungannon,
Co Tyrone BT71 6BE
Tel 028-87722631
(Dungannon (Drumglass,
Killyman and Tullyniskin),
Armagh)

Dunne, Bonaventure (OSB)
Glenstal Abbey, Murroe,
Co Limerick
Tel 061-386103

Dunne, Daniel, Very Rev, PP
Tullamoy, Stradbally,
Co Laois
Tel 059-8627123
(Ballyadams, Kildare & L.)

Dunne, Edward (OFMCap)
Capuchin Friary,
Ard Mhuire, Creeslough,
Letterkenny, Co Donegal
Tel 074-9138005

Dunne, Edward, Rt Rev Mgr
Ratoath, Co Meath
(Meath, retired)

Dunne, Frederick (CSsR)
Marianella, 75 Orwell Road,
Dublin 6
Tel 01-4067100

Dunne, Gerard (OP)
40 Iona Road, Glasnevin,
Dublin 9
Tel 01-8305880/8602790

Dunne, John (SMA)
Vice Provincial,
African Missions,
Provincial House, Feltrim,
Blackrock Road, Cork
Tel 021-4292871

Dunne, Liam (SVD)
(Mission Procurator)
Maynooth, Co Kildare
Tel 01-6286391/2

Dunne, Liam, Very Rev
The Forge, Martin's Lane,
Upper Main Street, Arklow,
Co Wicklow
Tel 0402-32779
(Ossory, retired)

Dunne, Matthew (MHM)
St Joseph's House,
50 Orwell Park, Rathgar,
Dublin 6
Tel 01-4127700

Dunne, Michael (CM)
St Paul's College, Raheny,
Dublin 5
Tel 01-8318113

Dunne, Patrick
Chaplain, St Eunan's
College, Letterkenny,
Co Donegal
Tel 074-9121143
(Raphoe)

Dunne, Paul
60 Grange Park Grove,
Raheny, Dublin 5
Tel 01-8480647/087-6902246
(Grange Park, Dublin)

Dunne, Sean A. (SSC)
St Columban's Retirement
Home, Dalgan Park, Navan,
Co Meath
Tel 046-9021525

Dunne, Thomas (SDB)
Provincial Secretary,
Salesian House,
45 St Teresa's Road,
Crumlin, Dublin 12
Tel 01-4555605

Dunne, Thomas, CC
Templemore, Co Tipperary
Tel 0504-32890
(Cashel & E.)

Dunning, Brendan (SMA)
SMA House, Claregalway,
Co Galway
Tel 091-798880

Dunny, Patrick, Very Rev
Wood Road,
Graignamanagh,
Co Kilkenny
Tel 059-9724518
(Kildare & L.)

Dunphy, Aengus (OCSO), Rt
Rev Dom
Retired Abbot,
Our Lady of Bethlehem
Abbey, 11 Ballymena Road,
Portglenone, Ballymena,
Co Antrim BT44 8BL
Tel 028-25821211

Dunphy, John, Adm
30 Wheatfields Close,
Clondalkin, Dublin 22
Tel 01-6263920/087-6165666
(Rowlagh, Dublin)

Dunphy, John, Very Rev, PP
Graiguecullen, Co Carlow
Tel 059-9141833
(Kildare & L.)

Dunphy, Laurence, Very Rev
Canon, PP
Urlingford, Co Kilkenny
Tel 056-8831121/
087-2300849
(Urlingford, Ossory)

Dunphy, Noel, Very Rev, PE,
CC
Mountmellick, Co Laois
Tel 057-8624141
(Mountmellick, Kildare & L.)

Dunphy, Paul
Two-Mile-House,
Naas, Co Kildare
Tel 045-876160
(Naas, Kildare & L.)

Durajcyk, Tadeusz (SVD)
Maynooth, Co Kildare
Tel 01-6286391/2

Durkan, John, Very Rev, PP
Killasser, Swinford, Co Mayo
Tel 094-9251431
(Killasser, Achonry)

Durkan, Sean, Very Rev
79 The Glebe, Ballina,
Co Mayo
(Killala, retired)

Durrajczyk, Tadeusz
Polish Chaplaincy,
60 College Orchard,
Newbridge, Co Kildare
Tel 086-2354320
(Kildare & L.)

Dwan, Martin (SPS)
St Patrick's, Kiltegan,
Co Wicklow
Tel 059-6473600

Dwan, Sean (SSC)
48 Princess Margaret Road,
Homantin, Kowlon,
Hong Kong SAR

Dwyer, Donal, CC
Castleconnell, Co Limerick
Tel 061-377126
(Castleconnell, Killaloe)

Dwyer, Patrick (SAC)
Pallottine College, Thurles,
Co Tipperary
Tel 0504-21202

E

Earley, Patrick, Rt Rev Mgr,
PP, VG
Rathowen, Co Westmeath
Tel 043-6676044
(Ardagh & Cl.)

Early, Brian, Very Rev, PP
Scotstown, Co Monaghan
Tel 047-89204
(Clogher)

Early, Kevin, Very Rev Canon,
PP
Frenchpark, Castlerea,
Co Roscommon
Tel 094-9870105
(Frenchpark, Elphin)

Early, Thomas
23 Estuary Road, Malahide,
Co Dublin
(Dublin, retired)

Eastwood, Adrian (CM)
99 Cliftonville Road,
Belfast BT14 6JQ
Tel 028-90751771

Echavarria, John (SSP)
Society of St Paul,
Moyglare Road,
Maynooth, Co Kildare
Tel 01-6285933

Edwards, Brian
10 Bearna Park, Sandyford,
Dublin 18
Tel 01-2956916
(Sandyford, Dublin)

Egan, Adrian (CSsR)
Superior,
Mount Saint Alphonsus,
Limerick
Tel 061-315099

Egan, Bartholomew (CSSp)
Holy Ghost Missionary
College, Kimmage Manor,
Dublin 12
Tel 01-4064300

Egan, James, Very Rev, PP
Knockavilla, Dundrum,
Co Tipperary
Tel 062-71168
(Knockavilla, Cashel & E.)

Egan, John (CSSp)
Holy Ghost Missionary
College, Kimmage Manor,
Dublin 12
Tel 01-4064300

Egan, John (SAC)
Pallottine College, Thurles,
Co Tipperary
Tel 0504-21202

Egan, John, Very Rev, PP
Lattin, Co Tipperary
Tel 062-55240
(Lattin and Cullen, Cashel &
E.)

Egan, Joseph (SMA)
SMA House, 82 Ranelagh
Road, Ranelagh, Dublin 6
Tel 01-4968162/3

Egan, Joseph, Very Rev, PP
Boherlahan, Cashel,
Co Tipperary
Tel 0504-41114
(Boherlahan and Dualla,
Cashel & E.)

Egan, Pat (SDB)
Salesian College,
Maynooth Road, Celbridge,
Co Kildare
Tel 01-6275058/60

Egan, Patrick (CSsR)
St Patrick's, Esker, Athenry,
Co Galway
Tel 091-844549

Egan, Ralph (CP), CC
St Paul's Retreat,
Mount Argus, Dublin 6W
Tel 01-4992000

Egan, Seamus (SSC)
St Columban's, Dalgan Park,
Navan, Co Meath
Tel 046-9021525

Egan, Sean, CC
The Presbytery, Loughrea,
Co Galway
Tel 091-841212
(Loughrea, St Brendan's
Cathedral, Clonfert)

Egan, Thomas F., Very Rev, AP
Clonoulty, Casheel,
Co Tipperary
Tel 0504-42494
(Clonoulty, Cashel & E.)

Egan, Tony (OSA)
St John's Priory,
Thomas Street, Dublin 8
Tel 01-6770393

Ekwomadu, Francis
Toochukwu (CSSp)
Holy Ghost Missionary
College, Kimmage Manor,
Dublin 12
Tel 01-4064300

Elikowski, Roy (FDP)
Sarsfield House,
Sarsfield Road, Ballyfermot,
Dublin 10
Tel 01-6266193/6266233

Emechebe, Anselm (MSP) CC
Parochial House,
Hale Street, Ardee, Co Louth
Tel 041-6860080
(Ardee & Collon, Armagh)

Emerson, Sean, Very Rev,
Adm, VF
Parochial House, 3 Oriel
Road, Antrim BT41 4HP
Tel 028-94428016
(Antrim, St Comgall's and St
Joseph's, Down & C.)

Eneji, Richard (CSSp)
Blackrock College,
Blackrock, Co Dublin
Tel 01-2888681

English, Lawrence (MHM)
St Joseph's House, 50 Orwell
Park, Rathgar, Dublin 6
Tel 01-4127700

English, Mark, CC
2 Orchard Court, Dunboyne,
Co Meath
Tel 01-8255342
(Dunboyne, Meath)

Ennis, John, CC
The Presbytery, Jobstown,
Tallaght, Dublin 24
Tel 01-4523595/4610277
(Jobstown, Dublin)

Enright, Ciaran
Chaplain, Arbour Hill Prison,
Ard na Gaoithe, Arbour Hill,
Dublin 7
Tel 01-6770901
(Dublin)

Enright, Liam
Church Road, Croom,
Co Limerick
Tel 061-397986
(Limerick)

Enright, Liam, Very Rev, PP
Cratloe, Co Clare
Tel 061-357196/087-2546335
(Limerick)

Enright, Michael, Very Rev, PE
Priest's Road, Tramore,
Co Waterford
Tel 087-2371546
(Waterford & L., retired)

Enright, Seamus (CSsR)
Mount Saint Alphonsus,
Limerick
Tel 061-315099

Escoto, Albert (SVD)
Praeses, 3 Pembroke Road,
Dublin 4
Tel 01-6680904

Esoy, Renato (SSS)
Blessed Sacrament Chapel,
20 Bachelors Walk,
Dublin 1
Tel 01-8724597

Eustace, Conal, Very Rev
Canon, PP, VF
The Parochial House,
Ballinrobe, Co Mayo
Tel 094-9541784
(Ballinrobe, Tuam)

Eustace, Louis (CSsR)
St Joseph's, Dundalk,
Co Louth
Tel 042-9334042/9334762

Eustace, Thomas, Very Rev
The Cools, Barntown,
Wexford
(Ferns, retired)

Evans, Ashley (SJ)
c/o Jesuit Provincial Curia,
IMI Centre, Sandyford Road,
Dublin 16
Tel 01-2932820

Evans, Ian
Chaplain, England
(Dublin)

Evans, Peter (OP)
St Mary's Priory, Tallaght,
Dublin 24
Tel 01-4048100

Everard, Eugene, Very Rev
Canon, PP
The Parochial House,
Templemore, Co Tipperary
Tel 0504-31684
(Cashel & E.)

Everard, Liam, Very Rev, PP
Borrisoleigh, Thurles,
Co Tipperary
Tel 0504-51259
(Borrisoleigh, Cashel & E.)

F

Fagan, Anthony, Very Rev
Killinkere, Virginia,
Co Cavan
Tel 049-8547307
(Kilmore)

Fagan, Hugh (CSSp)
Holy Ghost Missionary
College, Kimmage Manor,
Dublin 12
Tel 01-4064300

Fagan, John (SDB)
Chaplain, Milford House,
Salesian House, Milford,
Castletroy, Limerick
Tel 061-330268/330914

Fagan, Patrick, Very Rev
Canon, PE
The Presbytery,
Ballyboughal, Co Dublin
(Dublin, retired)

Fagan, Sean (SM)
CUS Community,
89 Lower Leeson Street,
Dublin 2
Tel 01-6762586

Faherty, Thomas (SMA)
African Missions,
Blackrock Road, Cork
Tel 021-4292871

Fahey, Brendan (SSC)
St Columban's, Dalgan Park,
Navan, Co Meath
Tel 046-9021525

Fahey, Francis, CC
Ballintubber Abbey,
Claremorris, Co Mayo
Tel 094-9030934
(Tuam)

Fahey, Patrick (SSC)
St Columban's, Dalgan Park,
Navan, Co Meath
Tel 046-9021525

Fahey, Patrick E. (SSC)
Vice-Superior,
St Columban's, Dalgan Park,
Navan, Co Meath
Tel 046-9021525

Fallon, John, Very Rev, PP
Kilmaine, Co Galway
Tel 093-33378
(Kilmaine, Tuam)

Fallon, Kevin, CC
Curate's Residence,
Roscommon
Tel 090-6626189
(Roscommon, Elphin)

Farnon, Damian, CC
St Cecilia's, New Road,
Clondalkin,
Dublin 22
Tel 01-4592665
(Clondalkin, Dublin)

Farquhar, Anthony, Most Rev,
DD
Titular Bishop of Ermiana
and Auxiliary Bishop of
Down and Connor,
24 Fruithill Park,
Belfast BT11 8GE
Tel 028-90624252
(Down & C.)

Farquharson, Paul (SJ)
Vice-Superior,
St Francis Xavier's,
Upper Gardiner Street,
Dublin 1
Tel 01-8363411

Farragher, John (Seán) P.
(CSSp)
Blackrock College,
Blackrock, Co Dublin
Tel 01-2888681

Farragher, Michael, CC
Castlebar, Co Mayo
Tel 094-901253/21844
(Castlebar (Aglish,
Ballyheane and Breaghwy),
Tuam)

Farragher, Patrick
Castlebar, Co Mayo
Tel 094-9035748
(Tuam)

Farragher, Stephen, Very Rev,
Adm
Tuam, Co Galway
Tel 093-24250
(Tuam)

Farrell, Andrew, Very Rev, PE
Parochial House, Trim,
Co Meath
Tel 046-9431251
(Trim, Meath)

Farrell, Anthony (CSSp)
Holy Ghost Missionary
College, Kimmage Manor,
Dublin 12
Tel 01-4064300

Farrell, Derek, Very Rev, PP
Ministry to the Travelling
People, St Laurence House,
6 New Cabra Road,
Phibsboro, Dublin 7
Tel 01-8388874/087-2573857
(Dublin)

Farrell, Dermot, Rt Rev Mgr,
PP, VG
Parochial House, Dunboyne,
Co Meath
Tel 01-8255342
(Dunboyne, Meath)

Farrell, Fergus
Mater Dei Institute of
Education, Clonliffe Road,
Dublin 3
Tel 01-8376027/086-0782066
(Ossory)

Farrell, Fergus, PC
St Laurence O'Toole's
Presbytery, 49 Seville Place,
Dublin 1
Tel 01-8740796
(North Wall-Seville Place,
Dublin)

Farrell, John, PEm
5 Ballyreagh Road, Portrush,
Co Antrim
(Derry, retired)

Farrell, Liam, CC
Moate, Co Westmeath
Tel 090-6481189
(Moate and Mount Temple,
Ardagh & Cl.)

Farrell, Michael, Very Rev, AP
Parochial House, Tallow,
Co Waterford
Tel 058-56117
(Tallow, Waterford & L.)

Farrell, Patrick (OSA)
St Augustine's,
Taylor's Lane,
Balyboden, Dublin 16
Tel 01-4241000

Farrell, Sean (CM)
11 Iona Drive, Glasnevin,
Dublin 9
Tel 01-8305238

Farrell, William, Very Rev, PP
Parochial House, St Joseph's,
Glasthule, Co Dublin
Tel 01-2801226
(Glasthule, Dublin)

Farrelly, Adrian (OP), Very
Rev, PP
St Saviour's,
Upper Dorset Street,
Dublin 1
Tel 01-8897610
(Dominick Street, Dublin)

Farrelly, Florian (OFM)
Franciscan Friary,
Rossnowlagh, Co Donegal
Tel 072-9851342

Farrelly, Matthew (CSSp)
Holy Ghost Missionary
College, Kimmage Manor,
Dublin 12
Tel 01-4064300

Farrelly, Pat, CC
Kildallan, Ballyconnell,
Co Cavan
Tel 049-9526252
(Kildallan and Tomregan,
Kilmore)

Farrelly, Peter, Very Rev, PP
Parochial House, Beauparc,
Navan, Co Meath
Tel 046-9024114
(Beauparc, Meath)

Farrelly, Thomas (CSSp)
Blackrock College,
Blackrock, Co Dublin
Tel 01-2888681

Farren, Anthony (SJ)
St Ignatius Community &
Church, 27 Raleigh Row,
Salthill, Galway
Tel 091-523707

Farren, Desmond (MSC), CC
Killinarden, Tallaght,
Dublin 24
Tel 01-4522251
(Killinarden, Dublin)

Farren, John, Very Rev, PP
Muff, Co Donegal
Tel 074-9384037
(Iskaheen, Derry)

Farren, Neil, PP
Parochial House,
32 Chapel Road, Waterside,
Derry BT47 2BB
Tel 028-71342303
(Derry)

Farren, Paul
21 Derry Road, Strabane,
Co Tyrone BT82 8DX
Tel 028-71883247
Director, Derry Diocesan
Catechetical Centre,
The Gate Lodge,
2 Francis Street,
Derry BT48 9DS
Tel 028-71264087
(Derry)

Farrington, Ambrose (OCSO)
Novice Director,
Bolton Abbey, Moone,
Co Kildare
Tel 059-8624102

Faughnan, Cathal, PP
Keadue, Boyle,
Co Roscommon
Tel 071-9647212
(Ardagh & Cl.)

Fay, Ambrose (CP)
St Paul's Retreat,
Mount Argus, Dublin 6W
Tel 01-4992000

Fay, Kevin, CC
Lavey, Ballyjamesduff,
Co Cavan
Tel 049-4330018
(*Cavan*, Kilmore)

Fay, Sean, Very Rev, PE
Parochial House,
Rathmolyon, Co Meath
Tel 046-9555212
(*Enfield*, Meath)

Fayana, Fabrice M. (SJ)
Milltown Park,
Sandford Road, Dublin 6
Tel 01-2698411/2698113

Fearon, Maurice (OP), Very
Rev
Prior, St Catherine's,
Newry, Co Down BT35 8BN
Tel 028-30262178

Fee, Benedict PP
Parochial House,
Magheralanfield,
140 Mountjoy Road,
Coalisland,
Co Tyrone BT71 5DY
Tel 028-87738381
(Armagh)

Fee, Ian, CC
Lisnaskea, Enniskillen,
Co Fermanagh BT92 0JE
Tel 028-67721324
(Clogher)

Feehan, James, Very Rev
1 Castle Court, Thurles,
Co Tipperary
Tel 0504-24935
(Cashel & E., retired)

Feeney, Ciaran, CC
191 Upper Newtownards
Road, Belfast BT 3JB
Tel 028-9065417
(*St Colmcille's*, Down & C.)

Feeney, Derek, Very Rev, PP
Ennistymon, Co Clare
Tel 065-7071063
(*Ennistymon*, Galway)

Feeney, Joseph, Very Rev, PP
Ballinlough, Co Roscommon
Tel 094-9640155
(*Ballinlough (Kiltullagh)*,
Tuam)

Fegan, James (SMA)
African Missions,
Blackrock Road, Cork
Tel 021-4292871

Fegan, James, Very Rev, Adm
The Presbytery,
12 School Street, Wexford
Tel 053-9122055
(*Wexford*, Ferns)

Fegan, P. J. (IC)
Rector, St Joseph's,
Doire na hAbhann,
Tickincar, Clonmel,
Co Tipperary
Tel 052-26914

Fehily, G. Thomas, Rt Rev
Mgr, PE
Hampstead Hospital,
Glasnevin, Dublin 11
(Dublin, retired)

Feighery, John (SVD)
Praeses,
133 North Circular Road,
Dublin 7
Tel 01-8386743

Fenlon, Thomas (SMA)
SMA House, Claregalway,
Co Galway
Tel 091-798880

Fennell, Liam (OCarm)
Gort Muire, Ballinteer,
Dublin 16
Tel 01-2984014

Fennelly, Sean
Barrysfarm, Hospital,
Co Limerick
Tel 061-383565
(*Knockainey*, Cashel & E.)

Fennelly, William (OSB)
Glenstal Abbey, Murroe,
Co Limerick
Tel 061-386103

Fennessy, Ignatius (OFM)
Franciscan House of Studies,
Dún Mhuire, Seafield Road,
Killiney, Co Dublin
Tel 01-2826760

Fenning, Hugh (OP)
St Mary's Priory, Tallaght,
Dublin 24
Tel 01-4048100

Fergus, Austin, Very Rev, PP
Mayo Abbey, Claremorris,
Co Mayo
Tel 094-9365086
(*Mayo Abbey (Mayo and
Rosslea)*, Tuam)

Ferguson, Chris, CC
Parochial House,
32 Chapel Road, Waterside,
Derry BT47 2BB
Tel 028-71342303
(Derry)

Ferguson, Gerard, Very Rev
Canon, PE
Rockcorry, Monaghan
Tel 042-9742243
(Rockcorry, Clogher)

Ferris, Brendan, CC
Tyrrellspass, Co Westmeath
Tel 044-9223115
(*Castletown-Geoghegan*,
Meath)

Ferris, John, CC
(priest in charge, Church of
Our Lady of the Visitation,
Drynam)
The Presbytery,
18 Aspen Road,
Kinsealy Court
Tel 01-8405948
(*Swords*, Dublin)

Ferris, Stephen, Very Rev, PP
91 Newry Road,
Barnmeen, Rathfriland,
Co Down BT34 5AP
Tel 028-40630306
(*Drumgath (Rathfriland)*,
Dromore)

Ferry, Francis, CC
Tory Island, Donegal
Tel 074-9135505
(*Gortahork (Tory Island)*,
Raphoe)

Field, Raymond, Most Rev,
DD, VG
Titular Bishop of Ard Mor
and Auxiliary
Bishop of Dublin,
3 Castleknock Road,
Blanchardstown, Dublin 15
Tel 01-8209191
(Dublin)

Filion, Andre (White Fathers)
Superior, Cypress Grove,
Templeogue, Dublin 6W
Tel 01-4055263/4055264

Finan, Andrew, BA, HDE
St Nathy's College,
Ballaghaderreen,
Co Roscommon
Tel 094-9860010
(Achonry)

Finan, James, Very Rev Canon,
PP
Keash, Ballymote, Co Sligo
Tel 071-9183334
(*Keash (Drumrat)*, Achonry)

Finan, Thomas
St Patrick's College,
Maynooth, Co Kildare
Tel 01-6285222
(Killala)

Fingleton, James
279 Howth Road, Raheny,
Dublin 5
(Dublin, retired)

Fingleton, John, Very Rev, PE
Graiguecullen, Carlow
Tel 059-9142132
(Kildare & L., retired)

Finn, James, Very Rev Canon
c/o 76 Corish Park, Wexford
(Ferns, retired)

Finn, James, Very Rev, PP
Crossabeg, Co Wexford
Tel 053-9159015
(Ferns)

Finn, John, Very Rev, PE
Parochial House, Grange,
Knockbridge, Dundalk,
Co Louth
Tel 042-9374792
(Armagh, retired)

Finn, Patrick, Very Rev Mgr,
PP
St Mary's, Haddington Road,
Dublin 4
Tel 01-6643295/086-3848432
(*Haddington Road*, Dublin)

Finn, Tony (OSA)
St Patrick's College and
Church,
Via Piemonte 60, 00187
Rome, Italy
Tel 00396-4203121

Finn, William (OCD)
St Teresa's,
Clarendon Street, Dublin 2
Tel 01-6718466/6718127

Finnegan, John (SDB)
Salesian House,
45 St Teresa's Road,
Crumlin, Dublin 12
Tel 01-4555605

Finnegan, John, Very Rev
Canon, PP
Arney, Enniskillen,
Co Fermanagh BT92 2AB
Tel 028-66348217
(*Arney (Cleenish)*, Clogher)

Finnegan, Thomas, Most Rev,
DD
Bishop Emeritus,
Carrowmore Lacken,
Ballina, Co Mayo
(Killala, retired)

Finnegan, Thomas, Very Rev,
PP
Liscarnan, Magheracloone,
Carrickmacross,
Co Monaghan
Tel 042-9663500
(*Magheracloone*, Clogher)

Finneran, Michael, Very Rev,
PP, VF
Clontuskert, Ballinasloe,
Co Galway
Tel 090-9642256
(*Clontuskert*, Clonfert)

Finnerty, Liam (OCD)
Prior, The Abbey, Loughrea,
Co Galway
Tel 091-841209

Finnerty, Paul
Diocesan Secretary,
Diocesan Office,
Social Service Centre,
Henry Street, Limerick
Tel 061-315856
(Limerick)

Finnerty, Peter, Very Rev, PP,
VF
2 Maypark, Malahide Road,
Dublin 5
Tel 01-8313722
(Dublin)

Finucane, Aengus C. (CSSp)
Holy Ghost Missionary
College, Kimmage Manor,
Dublin 12
Tel 01-4064300

Finucane, Gerard, Adm
(protem)
St John's Presbytery, Tralee,
Co Kerry
Tel 068-7122522
(*Tralee, St John's*, Kerry)

Finucane, John A. (CSSp)
Holy Ghost Missionary
College, Kimmage Manor,
Dublin 12
Tel 01-4064300

Fitzgerald, Brendan
c/o Diocesan Office,
Social Service Centre,
Henry Street, Limerick
(Limerick)

Fitzgerald, Christopher
1 The Presbytery,
Friar's Walk, Ballyphehane,
Cork
Tel 021-4537472
(Cork & R.)

Fitzgerald, Dan (SSC)
The Presbytery, Nenagh,
Co Tipperary
Tel 067-37132
(Nenagh, Killaloe)

Fitzgerald, Jack, Very Rev
St John's Pastoral Centre,
Castle Street, Tralee,
Co Kerry
Tel 066-7122280
(Kerry)

FitzGerald, John (SJ)
35 Lower Leeson Street,
Dublin 2
Tel 01-6761248

Fitzgerald, John, Very Rev
(MSC), PP
Sacred Heart Parish,
Western Road, Cork
Tel 021-4804120
(Sacred Heart, Cork & R.)

Fitzgerald, John, Very Rev
Canon, PE
7 Cunnane Place, The Gleve,
Tuam, Co Galway
(Tuam, retired)

Fitzgerald, John, Very Rev, PP
Abbeydorney, Co Kerry
Tel 066-7135146
(Abbeydorney, Kerry)

Fitzgerald, John, Very Rev, PP
Parish Administrator
Rockhill, Bruree,
Co Limerick
087-6522746
(Rockhill/Bruree, Limerick)

Fitzgerald, Joseph, Very Rev
Canon, PP, VF
Castlerea, Co Roscommon
Tel 094-9620040
(Castlerea, Elphin)

Fitzgerald, Michael, CC
Charleville, Co Cork
Tel 063-81437
(Charleville, Cloyne)

Fitzgerald, Michael, Very Rev,
PP
Mitchelstown, Co Cork
Tel 025-84090
(Cloyne)

Fitzgerald, Norman (CSSp)
66 Biscayne, Malahide,
Co Dublin
Tel 01-8451262

Fitzgerald, Patrick, Very Rev,
PP
Parochial House, Lisduggan,
Co Waterford
Tel 051-372257
(Waterford & L., retired)

Fitzgerald, Patrick, Very Rev,
PP
Parochial House, Lisduggan,
Waterford
Tel 051-372257
(St Paul's, Waterford & L.)

FitzGerald, Shane (SVD)
3 Pembroke Road, Dublin 4
Tel 01-6680904

Fitzgerald, Tadhg, Very Rev,
PP
Brosna, Co Kerry
Tel 068-44112
(Brosna, Kerry)

Fitzgibbon, Eamonn, Rt Rev,
VG
Ballyduane, Clarina,
Co Limerick
Tel 087-6921191
(Limerick)

Fitzgibbon, Edmund (SPS),
Most Rev
St Patrick's, Kiltegan,
Co Wicklow
Tel 059-6473600

Fitzgibbon, John, Very Rev
Canon, PE
St MacCullin's, Lusk,
Co Dublin
Tel 01-8438023
The Presbytery,
Chapel Road, Lusk,
Co Dublin
(Dublin, retired)

Fitzmaurice, William, Very Rev
Canon, PP, VF
Killmallock, Co Limerick
Tel 063-98287/086-2423728
(Kilmallock, Limerick)

Fitzpatrick, Bernard
Lagos, Nigeria
(Kilmore)

Fitzpatrick, Gerard, Very Rev
Cahercalla Community
Hospital, Ennis, Co Clare
Tel 065-6824388/
086-2311923
(Killaloe, retired)

Fitzpatrick, James (White
Fathers)
Cypress Grove, Templeogue,
Dublin 6W
Tel 01-4055263/4055264

Fitzpatrick, James, CC
Galbally, Curracloe,
Co Wexford
Tel 053-9137140
(Castlebridge, Ferns)

Fitzpatrick, Jeremiah (OCD)
St Joseph's Carmelite
Retreat Centre,
Termonbacca,
Derry BT48 9XE
Tel 028-71262512

Fitzpatrick, John, Rt Rev Mgr,
PP
Episcopal Vicar,
3 Glencarraig, Church Road,
Sutton, Co Dublin
Tel 01-8323147
(Dublin)

Fitzpatrick, John, Very Rev
116 Strangford Road,
Ardglass BT30 7SS
(Down & C., retired)

Fitzpatrick, John, Very Rev, PP
Carbury, Co Kildare
Tel 046-9553355
(Carbury, Kildare & L.)

Fitzpatrick, Patrick (Alan)
(OCarm)
Whitefriar Street Church,
56 Aungier Street, Dublin 2
Tel 01-4758821

Fitzpatrick, P.J., Very Rev, PP
Gowna, Co Cavan
Tel 043-6683120
(Lough Gowna and
Mullinalaghta, Ardagh &
Cl.)

Fitzpatrick, Paul, CC
St Mary's, Tower Hill,
Portlaoise, Co Laois
Tel 057-8621671
(Portlaoise, Kildare & L.)

Fitzpatrick, Tom, Very Rev, PP
Director, Ennis Accord Centre,
c/o Clarecare, Harmony Row,
Ennis, Co Clare
Tel 1850-585000
Chaplain, Carrigoran House,
Newmarket-on-Fergus,
Co Clare
Tel 061-471406
Newmarket-on-Fergus,
Co Clare
Tel 061-368127
(Newmarket-on-Fergus,
Killaloe)

Fitzpatrick, William (OMI),
Very Rev
Provincial, Provincial
Residence, Oblates of Mary
Immaculate House of
Retreat, Tyrconnell Road,
Inchicore, Dublin 8
Tel 01-4541160/4541161

Fitzsimons, Anthony, CC
Curates' Residence,
Massforth, 152 Newry Road,
Kilkeel, Co Down BT34 4ET
Tel 028-41762257
(Kilkeel (Upper Mourne),
Down & C.)

Fitzsimons, Patrick, Very Rev
Canon
Holy Family Residence,
Roebuck, Dundrum, Dublin
14
(Dublin, retired)

Fitzsimons, William, Very Rev,
PP
Parochial House, Milltown,
Rathconrath, Co Westmeath
Tel 044-9355106
(Milltown, Meath)

Flaherty, John, Very Rev
Canon, Adm
Pro-Cathedral House,
83 Marlborough Street,
Dublin 1
Tel 01-8745441
(Dublin)

Flaherty, Raymond, CC
The Presbytery, Tuam,
Co Galway
Tel 093-24250
(Tuam (Cathedral of the
Assumption), Tuam)

Flanagan, Benny, Very Rev, PP
Carrabane, Athenry,
Co Galway
Tel 091-841103
(Clostoken and Kilconieran,
Clonfert)

Flanagan, Desmond (OCarm)
Terenure College, Terenure,
Dublin 6W
Tel 01-4904621

Flanagan, Eamon (CM)
St Paul's College, Raheny,
Dublin 5
Tel 01-8318113

Flanagan, John (SPS), CC
Parochial House,
6 Tullydonnell Road,
Dungannon,
Co Tyrone BT70 3JE
Tel 028-87758224
(Cookstown (Desertcreight
and Derryloran), Armagh)

Flanagan, John, CC
Roslea, Enniskillen,
Co Fermanagh BT92 7LA
Tel 028-67751393
(Clogher)

Flanagan, Malachy (SMA)
Provincial Bursar,
African Missions,
Blackrock Road, Cork
Tel 021-4292871

Flanagan, Padraig, (SPS), CC
Cliffoney, Co Sligo
Tel 071-9166133
(Cliffoney, Elphin)

Flannagan, Richard (SVD)
Donamon Castle,
Roscommon
Tel 090-6662222

Flannery, Anthony (CSsR)
St Patrick's, Esker, Athenry,
Co Galway
Tel 091-844549

Flannery, John D., Very Rev
Canon, PE
Cartron, Milltown,
Co Galway
(Tuam, retired)
Flannery, Michael, Very Rev,
PP
Knock, Inverin, Co Galway
Tel 091-593122
(Spiddal, Tuam)
Flannery, Peter (CSsR)
St Patrick's, Esker, Athenry,
Co Galway
Tel 091-844549
Flannery, Paschal, Very Rev
Ballinderry, Nenagh,
Co Tipperary
Tel 067-22916/086-2225099
(Killaloe, retired)
Flavin, John P. (CSSp)
St Mary's College,
Rathmines, Dublin 6
Tel 01-4062160
Flavin, Nicholas, Very Rev, PP
Dunamaggan, Co Kilkenny
Tel 056-7728173/
087-2257498
(Dunamaggan, Ossory)
Fleck, Robert, Very Rev, PP
Parochial House, Ardglass,
Co Down BT30 7TU
Tel 028-44841208
(Ardglass (Dunsford), Down
& C.)
Fleming, David, CC
Parochial House,
Bohernabreena, Tallaght,
Dublin 24
Tel 01-4510986
(Bohernabreena, Dublin)
Fleming, Gerard (SAC), Very
Rev, CC
437 South Circular Road,
Dublin 8
Tel 01-4533490
(Dolphin's Barn, Dublin)
Fleming, John Kevin (MSC)
Western Road, Cork
Tel 021-4804120
Fleming, John, Most Rev, DD,
DCL
Bishop of Killala,
Bishop's House, Ballina,
Co Mayo
Tel 096-21518
(Killala)
Fleming, Joseph, Very Rev,
Adm
Clonegal, Enniscorthy,
Co Wexford
Tel 053-9377298
(Clonegal, Kildare & L.)
Fleming, Kevin (SSC)
St Columban's, Dalgan Park,
Navan, Co Meath
Tel 046-9021525

Fleming, Laurence, Very Rev,
PE
Teach Moling, Oak Park,
Carlow
Tel 059-9140944
(Kildare & L., retired)
Fleming, Michael, Very Rev
Canon, PP, VF
The Presbytery, Killorglin,
Co Kerry
Tel 066-9761172
(Kerry)
Fleming, Paul, BA, BD, STL
St Mary's University College,
191 Falls Road,
Belfast 12 6FE
Tel 028-90327678
(Down & C.)
Fleming, Seamus (CSSp)
Chaplain,
Cherry Orchard Hospital,
Ballyfermot, Dublin 10
Tel 01-6206000
Fletcher, Robert, CC
Dealginis, Garraun Upper,
Ballinahinch, Birdhill,
via Killaloe, Co Clare
Tel 086-1927455/061-379862
(Ballinahinch, Cashel & E.)
Flood, Aloysius P. (CSSp)
Holy Ghost Missionary
College, Kimmage Manor,
Dublin 12
Tel 01-4064300
Flynn, Brian
(in residence)
Tierworker, via Kells,
Co Meath
Tel 042-9665374
(Kilmainhamwood and
Moybologue, Kilmore)
Flynn, Brian
Administrator of the
National Marriage Appeal
Tribunal,
St Patrick's College,
Maynooth, Co Kildare
(Kilmore)
Flynn, Brian, Very Rev, PP
Kilmacow, via Waterford,
Co Kilkenny
Tel 051-885122/087-2828391
(Kilmacow, Ossory)
Flynn, Edward, Very Rev
Multyfarnham Retirement
Village, Co Westmeath
(Meath, retired)
Flynn, Edwin (OFMCap)
Holy Trinity,
Fr Mathew Quay, Cork
Tel 021-4270827
Flynn, Gabriel, DD, PC
1 Orchard Court, Dunboyne,
Co Meath
Tel 01-8255342
(Dunboyne, Meath)

Flynn, Joe (SPS)
Tearmann Spirituality
Centre, Brockagh,
Glendalough, Co Wicklow
Tel 0404-45208
Flynn, John, Very Rev Canon
Mount Falcon, Knockmore,
Ballina, Co Mayo
(Killala, retired)
Flynn, Joseph, Very Rev, PP
Ballyporeen, Cahir,
Co Tipperary
Tel 052-7467105
(Ballyporeen, Waterford &
L.)
Flynn, Kieran (SPS)
St Patrick's, 21 Leeson Park,
Dublin 6
Tel 01-4977897
Flynn, Laurence, Very Rev, PP
Ballybay, Co Monaghan
Tel 042-9741032
(Ballybay, Clogher)
Flynn, Michael (CSsR)
St Patrick's, Esker, Athenry,
Co Galway
Tel 091-844549
Flynn, Michael, Very Rev, PP
Parochial House,
Knockmore, Ballina,
Co Mayo
Tel 094-58108
(Killala)
Flynn, Nicholas, Very Rev,
Adm, VF
Killarney, Co Kerry
Tel 064-31014
(Killarney, Kerry)
Flynn, Patrick (OFMCap), CC
Capuchin Parochial Friary,
Clonshaugh Drive,
Priorswood, Dublin 17
Tel 01-8474469/8474538
(Priorswood, Dublin)
Flynn, Robert, Very Rev Dean
Ballymote, Co Sligo
Tel 071-9183312
(Achonry, retired)
Flynn, Thomas, CC
Granard, Co Longford
Tel 043-6686591
(Granard, Ardagh & Cl.)
Flynn, Thomas, Most Rev, DD
Bishop Emeritus of Achonry,
St Michael's,
Cathedral Grounds,
Ballaghaderreen,
Co Roscommon
Tel 094-9877808
(Achonry)
Flynn, Thomas, Very Rev, PP
Carrickbeg, Carrick-on-Suir,
Co Tipperary
Tel 051-640340
(Carrickbeg, Waterford & L.)

Flynn, Tim (OSM)
Prior, Servite Priory,
St Peregrine, Kiltipper Road,
Tallaght, Dublin 24
Tel 01-4517115
Flynn, Timothy (OSM)
Director, Servite Oratory,
Rathfarnham Shopping
Centre, Dublin 14
Tel 01-4936300
Flynn, Tomás, Very Rev, PP
Drumcong,
Carrick-on-Shannon,
Co Leitrim
Tel 071-9642021
(Kiltubrid, Ardagh & Cl.)
Flynn, William, CC
Glenbrien, Enniscorthy,
Co Wexford
Tel 053-9138112
(Oylegate, Ferns)
Fogarty, James, Very Rev, PP
Clonoulty, Cashel,
Co Tipperary
Tel 0504-42388
(Clonoulty, Cashel & E.)
Fogarty, Kevin (OCSO)
Mount Melleray Abbey,
Cappoquin, Co Waterford
Tel 058-54404
Fogarty, Pat, Very Rev, PP
The Presbytery,
Knocknaheeny, Cork
Tel 021-4392459
(Knocknaheeny/Hollyhill,
Cork & R.)
Fogarty, Philip (SJ)
35 Lower Leeson Street,
Dublin 2
Tel 01-6761248
Fogarty, Thomas, Very Rev
President,
St Patrick's College, Thurles,
Co Tipperary
Tel 0504-21201
(Cashel & E.)
Foley, Brian (CSsR)
St Patrick's, Esker, Athenry,
Co Galway
Tel 091-844549
Foley, Declan, Very Rev, PP
Bagenalstown, Co Carlow
Tel 059-9721154
(Kildare & L.)
Foley, Denis, Very Rev, PE
32 Walkinstown Road,
Dublin 12
Tel 01-4501350
(Dublin, retired)
Foley, Dermot (SPS)
St Patrick's, Kiltegan,
Co Wicklow
Tel 059-6473600
Foley, Desmond (OSA)
St Augustine's Priory,
Galway
Tel 091-562524

Allianz (ⅲ)

Foley, Eamon, Very Rev, PP
Rathdowney, Portlaoise,
Co Laois
Tel 0505-46282
(*Rathdowney*, Ossory)

Foley, Edward (OP)
St Saviour's,
Upper Dorset Street,
Dublin 1
Tel 01-8897610

Foley, George (SSCC)
Coudrin House,
27 Northbrook Road,
Dublin 6
Tel 01-6686584/01-6671513

Foley, James C. (CSSp)
Holy Ghost Missionary
College, Kimmage Manor,
Dublin 12
Tel 01-4064300

Foley, James, CC
St Michael's Street,
Tipperary Town,
Co Tipperary
Tel 062-51283
(*Tipperary*, Cashel & E.)

Foley, Joseph, Very Rev, CC
Bruff, Kilmallock,
Co Limerick
Tel 061-382290/087-2618412
(*Bruff/Meanus/Grange*,
Limerick)

Foley, Liam, CC
Kildorrery, Co Cork
Tel 022-25110
(*Kildorrery*, Cloyne)

Foley, Michael F. (SSCC)
Coudrin House,
27 Northbrook Road,
Dublin 6
Tel 01-6686584/01-6671513

Foley, Niall, BSc, BD, HDE
Vice-President,
St Joseph's College,
Garbally Park, Ballinasloe,
Co Galway
Tel 090-9642504/9642254
(Clonfert)

Foley, Stanislaus (OP)
Black Abbey, Kilkenny,
Co Kilkenny
Tel 056-21279

Foley, William (SMA)
SMA House, Wilton, Cork
Tel 021-4541069/4541884

Forbes, John, Very Rev, PP
Parochial House,
Gortin, Omagh,
Co Tyrone BT79 8PU
Tel 028-81648203
(*Gortin*, Derry)

Ford, Seán (OCarm), CC
The Presbytery,
Idrone Avenue, Knocklyon,
Dublin 16
Tel 01-4941204/4944986
(*Knocklyon*, Dublin)

Forde, Basil (OSB)
Glenstal Abbey, Murroe,
Co Limerick
Tel 061-386103

Forde, Denis, Very Rev
Tigh an tSagairt,
Clogheen, Cork
(Cork & R.)

Forde, Des, Very Rev, PP
Ballyvaughan, Co Clare
Tel 065-7077045
(Galway)

Forde, Liam (SM)
Mount St Mary's, Milltown,
Dublin 14
Tel 01-2697322

Forde, Michael (CSsR)
Scala, Bessboro, Blackrock,
Cork
Tel 021-4358800

Forde, Peter, Very Rev, PP
51 Bay Road, Carnlough,
Ballymena,
Co Antrim BT44 0HJ
Tel 028-28885220
(*Carnlough*, Down & C.)

Forde, Robert, Very Rev, PE
Fermoy, Co Cork
Tel 025-34022
(Cloyne, retired)

Ford, Sean (OCarm), CC
Carmelite Presbytery,
Idrone Avenue, Knocklyon,
Dublin 16
Tel 01-4941204
(Dublin)

Forde, Tom (OFMCap)
Capuchin Friary,
Station Road, Raheny,
Dublin 5
Tel 01-8313886

Forde, Walter, Very Rev, PP
Castlebridge, Co Wexford
Tel 053-9159769
(*Castlebridge*, Ferns)

Forker, Philip (OFM)
Guardian, Franciscan Friary,
Killarney, Co Kerry
Tel 064-6631334/6631066

Forrester, Gerald, Very Rev
62 Rathgannon,
Warrenpoinnt BT34 3TU
(Down & C., retired)

Forristal, Desmond, Very Rev
St Joseph's Centre,
Crinken Lane, Shankill,
Co Dublin
(Dublin, retired)

Forristal, James, CC
St Canice's Presbytery,
Granges Road, Kilkenny
Tel 056-7722150
(*St Canice's*, Ossory)

Forristal, Laurence, Most Rev,
DD
Retired Bishop of Ossory,
Molassy, Freshford Road,
Kilkenny
Tel 056-7777928/
087-2330369
(Ossory)

Forristal, Leonard (SPS)
St Patrick's, Kiltegan,
Co Wicklow
Tel 059-6473600

Forster, Stephen (MI)
Superior and Provincial,
St Camillus,
4 St Vincent Street North
Dublin 7
Tel 01-8300365

Forsythe, John, Very Rev, PP
81 Lagmore Grove,
Stewartstown Road,
Belfast BT17 0TD
Tel 028-90309011
(*Christ the Redeemer,
Lagmore*, Down & C.)

Fortune, Finbarr (OSA)
St John's Priory, Thomas
Street,
Dublin 8
Tel 01-6770393

Fortune, Karl CC
55 Wainsfort Manor
Crescent, Templeogue,
Dublin 6W
Tel 01-4928651
(*Templeogue*, Dublin)

Fortune, William, CC
32 Newtownpark Avenue,
Blackrock, Co Dublin
Tel 01-2100337
(*Newtownpark*, Dublin)

Foster, John (SDB), CC
Salesian House,
St Teresa's Road, Crumlin,
Dublin 12
Tel 01-4555605
(*Crumlin*, Dublin)

Fox, Christopher (MHM)
St Joseph's House,
50 Orwell Park, Rathgar,
Dublin 6
Tel 01-4127700

Fox, Gerard
201 Donegall Street,
Belfast BT1 2FL
Tel 028-90263473
(Down & C.)

Fox, John, Very Rev, PP
Parochial House,
153 Aughrim Road,
Toomebridge,
Antrim BT41 3SH
Tel 028-79468277
(*Newbridge*, Armagh)

Frawley, Bernard M. (CSSp)
Rockwell College, Cashel,
Co Tipperary
Tel 062-61444

Freeman, Seamus (SAC), Most
Rev, DD
Bishop of Ossory,
Tilbury Place, James's Street,
Kilkenny
Tel 056-7762448
(Ossory)

Freeney, Paul, Very Rev, PE
Parochial House,
43 Upper Beechwood
Avenue, Ranelagh, Dublin 6
Tel 01-4972687
(Dublin, retired)

French, Gerry (SSC)
The Presbytery,
St Joseph's, Balcurris,
Ballymun, Dublin 11
Tel 01-8423865
(*Balcurris*, Dublin)

French, John, Very Rev
Horeswood, New Ross,
Co Wexford
Tel 051-593196
(Ferns, retired)

Friel, James, Very Rev, PP
Tamney, Letterkenny,
Co Donegal
Tel 074-9159015
(*Tamney*, Raphoe)

Friel, John (CP)
Superior, Passionist Retreat
Centre, Tobar Mhuire,
Crossgar,
Co Down BT30 9EA
Tel 028-44830242

Fullerton, Robert, Very Rev
Canon
501 Ormeau Road,
Belfast BT7 3GR
Tel 028-90641064
(*Holy Rosary,* Down & C.)

Fulton, Raymond, Very Rev,
PP
10 St Patrick's Road,
Saul, Downpatrick,
Co Down BT30 7JG
Tel 028-44612525
(*Saul and Ballee,* Down & C.)

Fulton, William (SSC)
St Patrick's, Kiltegan,
Co Wicklow
Tel 059-6473600

Furey, Francis (SMA)
African Missions,
Blackrock Road, Cork
Tel 021-4292871

Furlong, James (OSA)
St Augustine's Priory,
Washington Street, Cork
Tel 021-2753982

Furlong, James, Very Rev, CC
Raheen, Clonroche,
Co Wexford
Tel 051-428328
(*Newbawn*, Ferns)

Furlong, Odhran, CC
Rathgarogue, New Ross,
Co Wexford
Tel 051-424521
(*Cushinstown*, Ferns)

Furlong, Senan (OSB), Very
Rev
Glenstal Abbey, Murroe,
Co Limerick
Tel 061-386103

Furlong, Tadgh, Very Rev, PP
Cappawhite, Co Tipperary
Tel 062-75427
(*Cappawhite*, Cashel & E.)

Furlong, Thomas (SMA)
SMA House, Wilton, Cork
Tel 021-4541069/4541884

G

Gaffney, David (SJ)
Milltown Park,
Sandford Road, Dublin 6
Tel 01-2698411/2698113

Gaffney, Matthew (IC)
St Joseph's,
Doire na hAbhann,
Tickincar, Clonmel,
Co Tipperary
Tel 052-26914

Gaffney, Peter (OP)
St Mary's, The Claddach,
Co Galway
Tel 091-582884

Gaffney, Philip, Very Rev,
Adm
Parochial House, Curraha,
Ashbourne, Co Meath
Tel 01-8350136
(*Curraha*, Meath)

Gaffney, Thomas W., Very Rev
Canon
Derrylin
Tel 028-66748921
(*Kilmore*, retired)

Gahan, Dermot, CC
The Ballagh, Wexford
Tel 053-9136200
(*Oulart*, Ferns)

Gahan, James, Very Rev, PP
Killinure, Tullow,
Co Carlow
Tel 059-9156111
(*Clonmore*, Kildare & L.)

Gahan, Raymond, Very Rev,
PP
Killaveney, Tinahely,
Co Wicklow
Tel 0402-38188
(*Killaveney*, Ferns)

Gallagher, Brendan, Very Rev,
PP
Ederney, Enniskillen,
Co Fermanagh BT93 0DG
Tel 028-68631315
(*Ederney*, Clogher)

Gallagher, Colm, PP
Historical Churches Advisory
Commission, Dublin
(Dublin)

Gallagher, Colm, Very Rev
Mgr
594 Howth Road, Raheny,
Dublin 5
(Dublin, retired)

Gallagher, Declan, CC
Assumption of the BVM,
Dalkey, Co Dublin
(*Dalkey*, Dublin)

Gallagher, Denis
'Shraheens', Achill South,
Achill, Co Mayo
(Tuam)

Gallagher, Eddie, Very Rev, PP
Kilcar, Co Donegal
(Raphoe)

Gallagher, Edward, CC
4 Scroggy Road, Limavady,
Co Derry BT49 0NA
Tel 028-77763944
(*Limavady*, Derry)

Gallagher, Edward, Very Rev,
PP
Kilcar, Co Donegal
Tel 074-9738007
(*Kilcar*, Raphoe)

Gallagher, Francis (SSC)
St Columban's Retirement
Home, Dalgan Park, Navan,
Co Meath
Tel 046-9021525

Gallagher, Francis, Very Rev,
PP
Ballinahinch, Birdhill,
Co Limerick
Tel 061-379111
(*Ballinahinch*, Cashel & E.)

Gallagher, Joe (OFMCap)
Capuchin Friary,
Station Road, Raheny,
Dublin 5
Tel 01-8313886

Gallagher, John (CM)
St Vincent's College,
Castleknock, Dublin 15
Tel 01-8213051r

Gallagher, John Vincent (SSC)
St Columban's Retirement
Home, Dalgan Park, Navan,
Co Meath
Tel 046-9021525

Gallagher, John, Canon
1 Chaplain's House,
Knocknamona,
Letterkenny, Co Donegal
(Raphoe)

Gallagher, Joseph (SSC)
St Columban's Retirement
Home, Dalgan Park, Navan,
Co Meath
Tel 046-9021525

Gallagher, Joseph, Very Rev,
PP
Parochial House, Kilcormac,
Co Offaly
Tel 057-9335013
(*Kilcormac*, Meath)

Gallagher, Laurence (CSsR)
St Joseph's, Dundalk,
Co Louth
Tel 042-9334042/9334762

Gallagher, Louis (OCD)
St Joseph's Carmelite
Retreat Centre,
Termonbacca,
Derry BT48 9XE
Tel 028-71262512

Gallagher, Michael O. (SJ)
35 Lower Leeson Street,
Dublin 2
Tel 01-6761248

Gallagher, Michael P. (SJ)
c/o Jesuit Provincial Curia,
IMI Centre, Sandyford Road,
Dublin 16
Tel 01-2932820

Gallagher, Patrick (OCarm)
Gort Muire, Ballinteer,
Dublin 16
Tel 01-2984014

Gallagher, Patrick, Rt Rev Mgr
Cathedral Close, Ballina,
Co Mayo
(Killala, retired)

Gallagher, Paul, CC
Convoy, Lifford, Co Donegal
Tel 074-9147238
Chaplain, Royal and Prior
Comprehensive School,
Raphoe, Co Donegal
Tel 074-9145389
(*Raphoe*, Raphoe)

Gallagher, Peter, Very Rev, PP
Lavagh, Ballymote,
Co Sligo
Tel 071-9184002
(*Achonry*, Achonry)

Gallagher, Raphael (CSsR)
(Alphonsian Academy)
Via Merulana 31, CP 2458,
00100 Rome, Italy
Tel 0039-06494901

Gallagher, Seamus L., Very
Rev, PE
Glenlee, Killybegs,
Co Donegal
Tel 074-9732729
(Raphoe, retired)

Gallagher, Seamus, Very Rev,
PP
Parochial House,
Newtowncunningham,
Lifford, Co Donegal
Tel 074-9156138
(*Newtowncunningham*,
Raphoe)

Gallagher, Shane, CC
Glenties, Co Donegal
Tel 074-9551136
(*Glenties*, Raphoe)

Gallagher, Thomas
Cloughmore, Achill,
Co Mayo
(Tuam)

Gallinagh, Padraic, Very Rev
'Polperro', 8 Beverley Close,
Newtownards BT23 7FN
(Down & C., retired)

Gallogley, Vincent (OFM)
Associate Pastor,
St Anthony's Parish (English-
Speaking Chaplaincy),
23/25 Oudstrijderslaan,
1950 Kraainem, Belgium
Tel +32-2-7201970

Galus, Piotr
Diocesan Chaplain to Polish
Community,
c/o St Augustine's,
Washington Street, Cork
Tel 021-4275390
(Cork & R.)

Galvin, Aidan (CM)
St Paul's College, Raheny,
Dublin 5
Tel 01-8318113

Galvin, Gerard, Very Rev, PP
Durrus, Co Cork
Tel 027-61013
(*Muintir Bhaire*, Cork & R.)

Galvin, Ignatius (OFMCap)
Capuchin Friary,
Friary Street, Kilkenny
Tel 056-7721439

Galvin, John, AP
Passage West, Co Cork
Tel 021-4841267
(*Monkstown*, Cork & R.)

Galvin, John, CC
60 Mountpleasant Avenue,
Dublin 6
Tel 01-4968969
(*Rathmines*, Dublin)

Galvin, Micheál, Very Rev
Catherine McAuley Home,
Balloonagh, Tralee, Co Kerry
(Kerry, retired)

Galvin, Seamus (CSSp)
St Michael's College,
Ailesbury Road, Dublin 4
Tel 01-2189423

Gannon, John J., Very Rev, PP
Elphin, Co Roscommon
Tel 071-9635058
(*Elphin*, Elphin)

Gannon, Peter, CC
The Presbytery, Claremorris,
Co Mayo
Tel 094-9362477
(*Claremorris (Kilcolman)*,
Tuam)

Gardiner, Seamus, Very Rev
Portroe, Nenagh,
Co Tipperary
Tel 067-23105/086-8392741
(*Portroe*, Killaloe)

Garland, Sean, Very Rev, PP
Parochial House,
Clonmellon, Navan,
Co Meath
Tel 046-9433124
(*Clonmellon*, Meath)

Garrett, Gerard, Very Rev, VJ
Cork Regional Marriage
Tribunal, The Lough, Cork
Tel 021-4963653
(*Limerick*)

Garry, Martin (OCSO)
Bolton Abbey, Moone,
Co Kildare
Tel 059-8624102

Garvey, Colin (OFM)
St Bonaventure College,
Makeni, PO Box 39312,
Lusaka 10101, Zambia

Garvey, Francis, Very Rev, PP,
VF
Carrick-on-Shannon,
Co Leitrim
Tel 071-9620118
(*Carrick-on-Shannon*,
Ardagh & Cl.)

Garvey, John, Very Rev, Adm
St Michael's, Creagh,
Ballinasloe, Co Galway
Tel 090-9643916
(*Clonfert*)

Garvey, John, Very Rev, PP
Carnacon, Claremorris,
Co Mayo
Tel 094-9360205
(*Burriscarra and
Ballintubber*, Tuam)

Garvey, Joseph, Very Rev, PE
Kilbrew Nursing Home,
Curaha, Ashbourne,
Co Meath
(Meath, retired)

Garvey, Peter (OCSO), Rt Rev
Dom
Abbot, Bolton Abbey,
Moone, Co Kildare
Tel 059-8624102

Garvey, Thomas
Kilconnell, Ballinasloe
(Elphin, retired)

Gates, John, Very Rev, PP, VF
Parochial House,
30 King Street, Magherafelt,
Co Derry BT45 6AS
Tel 028-79632439
(*Magherafelt and Ardtrea
North*, Armagh)

Gaughan, J. Anthony, Very
Rev, PE
56 Newtownpark Avenue,
Blackrock, Co Dublin
Tel 01-2833897
(Dublin, retired)

Gavigan, Adrian, CC
Mountcharles, Co Donegal
Tel 074-9735009
(*Inver*, Raphoe)

Gavigan, James
Cleraun Study Centre,
90 Foster Avenue,
Mount Merrion, Co Dublin
Tel 01-2881734
Chaplain, Lismullin
Conference Centre, Navan,
Co Meath
Tel 046-9026936
(Opus Dei)

Gavigan, James (SSC)
St Columban's Retirement
Home, Dalgan Park,
Navan, Co Meath
Tel 046-9021525

Gavigan, Joseph, Very Rev, PP
The Presbytery,
Ballaghaderreen,
Co Roscommon
Tel 094-9860011
(Achonry)

Gavin, Denis J. (CSSp)
Blackrock College,
Blackrock, Co Dublin
Tel 01-2888681

Gavin, Dwayne, CC
St Mary's, Navan, Co Meath
Tel 046-9027518/9027414
(*Navan*, Meath)

Gavin, John
c/o Archbishop's House,
Tuam
(Tuam)

Gavin, Thomas P., Very Rev,
PP
Parochial House,
Summerhill, Co Meath
Tel 046-9557021
(*Summerhill*, Meath)

Gavin, Tony, CC
Parochial House,
Rosemount, Co Westmeath
Tel 090-6436110
(Meath)

Gayer, Pat (OSA)
St John's Priory,
Thomas Street,
Dublin 8
Tel 01-6770393

Gaynor, Harry, CC
194 Navan Road, Dublin 7
Tel 01-8383313
(*Navan Road*, Dublin)

Gaynor, Patrick, Very Rev, PP
Walsh Island, Geashill,
Co Offaly
Tel 057-8649510
(*Clonbullogue*, Kildare & L.)

Geaney, Michael
3 Hillview Cross,
Douglas Road, Cork
(Dublin, retired)

Gear, Patrick, Very Rev, PP
Ballyneale, Carrick-on-Suir,
Co Tipperary
Tel 051-640148
(*Ballyneale and
Grangemockler*, Waterford
& L.)

Geary, Ronan (SJ)
Clongowes Wood College,
Naas, Co Kildare
Tel 045-868663/868202

Geehan, Paul M.
The Presbytery, 36 Victoria
Grove, Bridport,
Dorset DT6 3AD, UK
Tel 01308-422594
(Raphoe)

Geelan, John, Very Rev, PP
Parochial House,
Bonniconlon,
Ballina, Co Mayo
Tel 096-45016
(*Bonniconlon*, Achonry)

Geoghegan, Anthony (CSSp)
Holy Ghost Missionary
College, Kimmage Manor,
Dublin 12
Tel 01-4064300

Geoghegan, Brian
Tubber, Co Clare
Tel 091-633124/087-2387067
(*Tubber*, Killaloe)

Geoghegan, Richard, CC
The Presbytery,
Carrick-on-Suir, Co Tipperary
Tel 051-640080
(*Carrick-on-Suir*, Waterford
& L.)

Geraghty, Cathal, Very Rev
Mgr, VG
Chancellor, The Presbytery,
Barrack Street, Loughrea,
Co Galway
Tel 091-841212
(Clonfert)

Geraghty, Gerard (MHM)
St Joseph's House,
50 Orwell Park, Rathgar,
Dublin 6
Tel 01-4127700

Geraghty, Gerard, Very Rev,
PP
Aughrim, Ballinasloe,
Co Galway
Tel 090-9673724/090-
9686614
(*Aughrim and Kilconnell*,
Clonfert)

Geraghty, Martin (MI)
(Chaplain to Connolly
Memorial Hospital,
Blanchardstown)
St Camillus,
4 St Vincent Street North,
Dublin 7
Tel 01-8300365

Gesla, Marceli (OFM)
Chaplain to Polish
Community
Franciscan Friary, Killarney,
Co Kerry
Tel 064-6631334/6631066

Getachen, Gobezayehu
(White Fathers)
Cypress Grove, Templeogue,
Dublin 6W
Tel 01-4055263/4055264

Ghent, William (SMA)
African Missions,
Blackrock Road, Cork
Tel 021-4292871

Gibbons, Danny (SPS)
St Patrick's, 21 Leeson Park,
Dublin 6
Tel 01-4977897

Gibbons, Richard, CC
Knock, Co Mayo
Tel 094-9388100
(*Knock*, Tuam)

Gibson, David, Very Rev, Adm
'Brookhaven', Monagea,
Newcastle West,
Co Limerick
Tel 069-72743/087-2528738
(*Monagea*, Limerick)

Gilbert, Patrick
Chaplain, Birr, Co Offaly
Tel 057-9120098/
087-2431956
Chaplain, St Brendan's
Community School, Birr,
Co Offaly
Tel 0509-20510
(Killaloe)

Gilcreest, Martin
Chaplain, Cavan General
Hospital
Tel 049-4361399
(Kilmore)

Gildea, Peter (CM), Very Rev
Superior,
99 Cliftonville Road,
Belfast BT14 6JQ
Tel 028-90751771

Gildea, Seán (OFM)
Franciscan Friary,
Rossnowlagh, Co Donegal
Tel 072-9851342

Giles, Seamus, Very Rev, PP
Parochial House,
Castletown-Geoghegan,
Co Westmeath
Tel 044-9226118
(*Castletown-Geoghegan*,
Meath)

Gilhooly, John, Adm
Gatehouse, St patrick's
College, Cullies, Co Cavan
Tel 049-4371583
(*Cavan*, Kilmore)

Gill, Oswald (OFM)
Franciscan Friary,
Liberty Street, Cork
Tel 021-4270302

Gill, Patrick, Very Rev, AP
Lecanvey, Westport,
Co Mayo
Tel 098-64808
(*Westport (Aughaval)*,
Tuam)

Allianz (ⅱ)

Gillan, Hugh (OH)
St John of God Hospital
Stillorgan, Co Dublin
(Dublin)

Gillespie, Anthony, Very Rev,
PP
Moygownagh, Ballina,
Co Mayo
Tel 096-31288
(Killala)

Gillespie, Gerard, Very Rev, PP
Dromore West, Co Sligo
Tel 096-47012
(Dromore-West, Killala)

Gillespie, James, CC
Milford, Co Donegal
Tel 074-9153236
(Rathmullan, Raphoe)

Gillespie, Kevin
Congregation for the
Clergy, Rome
(Raphoe)

Gillespie, Martin (MHM)
St Joseph's House,
50 Orwell Park, Rathgar,
Dublin 6
Tel 01-4127700

Gilligan, John, Very Rev, Adm,
VF
47 Westland Row, Dublin 2
Tel 01-6765517
Director, Lourdes Pilgrimage
Office, Holy Cross College,
Clonliffe Road, Dublin 3
Tel 01-8376820
(Dublin)

Gilligan, Patrick, Very Rev, PP
Cong, Co Mayo
Tel 094-9546030
(Cong and Neale, Tuam)

Gillooly, Dominic, Very Rev,
PP
St Anne's, Sligo
Tel 071-9145028
(Sligo, St Anne's, Elphin)

Gillooly, Peter, (SPS), CC
Kilmurray, Castlerea,
Co Roscommon
Tel 094-9651018
(Tulsk, Elphin)

Gillooly, Reginald (CSSp)
Holy Ghost Missionary
College, Kimmage Manor,
Dublin 12
Tel 01-4064300

Gilmartin, Joseph, Very Rev
Churchfield Presbytery,
Knock, Co Mayo
(Elphin)

Gilmore, John (SSC)
St Columban's, Dalgan Park,
Navan, Co Meath
Tel 046-9021525

Gilmore, John, PP
11 Church Road,
Aghyaran, Castlederg,
Co Tyrone BT81 7XZ
Tel 028-81670728
(Aghyaran
(Termonamongan), Derry)

Gilmore, Sean, Very Rev, PP
Parochial House, 284
Glassdrumman Road,
Annalong,
Newry, Co Down BT34 4QN
Tel 028-43768208
(Lower Mourne, Down & C.)

Gilroy, Michael, Dr
Cathedral Close,
Ballina, Co Mayo
Tel 096-217464
(Ballina, Killala)

Gilroy, Thomas, Very Rev, PP
Parochial House, Kinnegad,
Co Westmeath
Tel 044-9379170
(Kinnegad, Meath)

Gilsenan, Michael (SSCC), CC
St Mary's, Clontibret,
Co Monaghan
Tel 047-80631
(Clontibret, Clogher)

Gilton, Michael, CC
48 Aughrim Street,
Dublin 7
Tel 01-8386176
(Aughrim Street, Dublin)

Ginnelly, Christopher, PP
Parochial House, Ballycroy,
Westport,
Co Mayo
Tel 098-49134
(Ballycroy, Killala)

Glavin, Finbar, Very Rev
Parochial House,
16 Ballykilbeg Road,
Downpatrick,
Co Down BT30 8HJ
Tel 028-44613203
(Downpatrick, Down & C.)

Gleeson, Joseph, Very Rev, PE
Rathfeigh, Tara, Co Meath
Tel 041-9825159
(Skryne, Meath)

Gleeson, Martin, Very Rev, AP
Belclare, Tuam, Co Galway
Tel 093-55429
(Cummer (Kilmoylan and
Cummer), Tuam)

Gleeson, Padraig
3 Maypark, Malahide Road,
Dublin 5
Tel 01-8329598
Chaplain, DIT,
Bolton Street, Dublin
Tel 01-4023618
(Dublin)

Gleeson, Patrick
48 Westland Row,
Dublin 2
Tel 01-6081260
(Dublin)

Gleeson, Philip (OP)
St Mary's Priory, Tallaght,
Dublin 24
Tel 01-4048100

Glennon, Francis, Very Rev, PP
Cams, Roscommon
Tel 090-6626275
(Cloverhill, Elphin)

Glover, Joseph M.
Star of the Sea Presbytery,
305 Shore Road,
Whitehouse,
Newtownabbey, Co Antrim
BT37 9RY
Tel 028-90365142
(Whitehouse, Down & C.)

Glynn, Cronan (OCD)
The Abbey, Loughrea,
Co Galway
Tel 091-841209

Glynn, Enda, Very Rev, PP
New Quay, Co Clare
Tel 065-7078026
(Carron and New Quay,
Galway)

Glynn, Joe (OCD)
St Teresa's,
Clarendon Street, Dublin 2
Tel 01-6718466/6718127

Glynn, John, Very Rev, PP
Parochial House,
Tourlestrane, Ballymote,
Co Sligo
Tel 071-9181105
(Tourlestrane (Kilmactigue),
Achonry)

Glynn, Martin, Very Rev, PP
129 Túr Uisce, Doughiska,
Galway
Tel 091-756823
(Good Shepherd, Galway)

Glynn, Matthias, Very Rev, PP
Tagoat, Co Wexford
Tel 053-9131139
(Tagoat, Ferns)

Glynn, Michael
Chaplain, Convent of Mercy,
Mullaghmore, Co Sligo
Tel 071-9166345
(Elphin)

Goaley, Michael, Very Rev
Canon
Glenamaddy, Co Galway
(Tuam, retired)

Godfrey, Donal (SJ)
c/o Jesuit Provincial Curia,
IMI Centre, Sandyford Road,
Dublin 16
Tel 01-2932820

Godley, Gearóid
John Paul II Pastoral Centre,
Rock Road, Killarney,
Co Kerry
Tel 064-6630535
(Kerry)

Gogan, Brian M. (CSSp)
Blackrock College,
Blackrock, Co Dublin
Tel 01-2888681

Golden, Michael (SPS)
St Patrick's, Kiltegan,
Co Wicklow
Tel 059-6473600

Gonoude, Anthony, CC
The Presbytery, Ballsgrove,
Drogheda, Co Louth
Tel 041-9836287
(Drogheda, Holy Family,
Meath)

Good, James
Park View, Church Street,
Douglas, Cork
Tel 021-4363913
(Cork & R., retired)

Goode, John (CSsR)
Mount Saint Alphonsus,
Limerick
Tel 061-315099

Goode, Richard (OSA)
St Augustine's Priory,
Shop Street,
Drogheda, Co Louth
Tel 041-9838409

Goold, Eamonn, Rt Rev Mgr,
PP, VG
Ballybutler, Midleton,
Co Cork
Tel 021-4631750
(Midleton, Cloyne)

Gorevan, Patrick
Harvieston,
Cunningham Road, Dalkey,
Co Dublin
Tel 01-2859877
(Opus Dei)

Gormally, Michael, Very Rev,
PP
Achill Sound, Achill,
Co Mayo
Tel 098-45288
(Achill, Tuam)

Gorman, Owen, CC
Aghadrumsee, Roslea,
Enniskillen,
Co Fermanagh BT92 7NQ
Tel 028-67751231
(Clones, Clogher)

Gorman, Seán, Very Rev, PP
Taghmon, Co Wexford
Tel 053-9134123
(Taghmon, Ferns)

Gorman, Thomas (SMA)
SMA House, Wilton, Cork
Tel 021-4541069/4541884

Gormley, Derek, CC
Swinford, Co Mayo
Tel 094-9253338
(Swinford (Kilconduff and
Meelick), Achonry)

Gormley, Joseph, CC
2 Station Road, Dungiven,
Derry BT47 4LN
Tel 028-77741256
(Dungiven, Derry)

Gough, Brian
  Chaplain, St James's
  Hospital, James's Street,
  Dublin 8
  Tel 01-4103659/4162023
  (Dublin)
Gough, Joseph A. (CSSp)
  Blackrock College,
  Blackrock, Co Dublin
  Tel 01-2888681
Gould, Daniel, Very Rev, PP
  Ballygriffin, Mallow,
  Co Cork
  Tel 022-26153
  (Killavullen, Cloyne)
Grace, Edmond (SJ)
  Vice-Superior,
  35 Lower Leeson Street,
  Dublin 2
  Tel 01-6761248
Grace, James, Very Rev, PP
  Killaloe, Co Clare
  Tel 061-376137/087-6843315
  (Killaloe, Killaloe)
Grace, Ned (SPS)
  St Patrick's, Kiltegan,
  Co Wicklow
  Tel 059-6473600
Grace, Patrick, Venerable
  Archdeacon
  Inistioge, Co Kilkenny
  Tel 056-7758429/
  086-8817628
  (Ossory, retired)
Graham, Eamon, PP
  42 Glenedra Road,
  Feeny, Dungiven,
  Co Derry BT47 4TW
  Tel 028-77781223
  (Derry)
Graham, Martin, CC
  St Malachy's Presbytery,
  24 Alfred Street,
  Belfast BT2 8EN
  Tel 028-90321713
  (St Malachy's, Down & C.)
Graham, Patrick (OCarm)
  Whitefriar Street Church,
  56 Aungier Street, Dublin 2
  Tel 01-4758821
Grant, Colin, MA, STL, PGCE
  St Malachy's College,
  Antrim Road,
  Belfast BT15 2AE
  Tel 028-90748285
  Aquinas College,
  518 Ravenhill Road,
  Belfast BT6 0BY
  Tel 028-90643939
  (Down & C.)
Grant, Henry (SJ)
  Milltown Park,
  Sandford Road, Dublin 6
  Tel 01-2698411/2698113
Grant, Patrick, Very Rev
  Canon, PE
  Ballyragget, Co Kilkenny
  Tel 056-8833120
  (Ossory, retired)

Grant, Robert, CC
  St John's Presbytery,
  New Street, Waterford
  Tel 051-874271
  (St John's, Waterford & L.)
Gray, Francis, Very Rev, PP
  Carrick, Finea,
  Mullingar, Co Westmeath
  Tel 043-6681129
  (Carrick-Finea, Ardagh & Cl.)
Grealy, Tom (SPS)
  St Patrick's,
  Kiltegan, Co Wicklow
  Tel 059-6473600
Greed, Pat, Very Rev, PP
  18 Churchfield,
  Clonlara, Co Clare
  Tel 061-354594/086-6067003
  (Clonlara, Killaloe)
Green, Denis (SM)
  CUS Community,
  89 Lower Leeson Street,
  Dublin 2
  Tel 01-6762586
Green, Gerard
  c/o Bishop's House
  (Dromore, retired)
Greenan, Clement (OP)
  St Saviour's,
  Upper Dorset Street,
  Dublin 1
  Tel 01-8897610
Greene, James (White
  Fathers)
Greene, James, CC
  Mitchelstown, Co Cork
  Tel 025-84077
  (Mitchelstown, Cloyne)
Greene, John, Very Rev, PP
  No 3 Presbytery,
  Dunmanus Court,
  Cabra West, Dublin 7
  (Cabra West, Dublin)
Greene, Patrick (SJ)
  Manresa House,
  Dollymount, Dublin 3
  Tel 01-8331352
Grenham, Thomas (SPS)
  Tearmann Spirituality
  Centre, Brockagh,
  Glendalough, Co Wicklow
  Tel 0404-45208
Griffin, Augustine G. (CSSp)
  Spiritan Missionaries,
  Ardbraccan, Navan,
  Co Meath
  Tel 046-9021441
Griffin, Edward, Very Rev, PP
  10 The Oaks,
  Loughlinstown Drive,
  Dun Laoghaire, Co Dublin
  Tel 086-2395706
  (Loughlinstown, Dublin)
Griffin, Eugene (SSC)
  St Columban's Retirement
  Home, Dalgan Park, Navan,
  Co Meath
  Tel 046-9021525

Griffin, Gerald (SSC)
  St Columban's Retirement
  Home, Dalgan Park, Navan,
  Co Meath
  Tel 046-9021525
Griffin, Gerard (CSSp)
  Rockwell College,
  Cashel, Co Tipperary
  Tel 062-61444
Griffin, James, Very Rev, PE
  10 Woodbrook Manor,
  Tralee, Co Kerry
  (Waterford & L., retired)
Griffin, Pat
  Ashborough Lodge, Lyre,
  Milltown,
  Co Kerry
  (Kerry, retired)
Griffin, Patrick (OFMConv), CC
  Friary of the Visitation,
  Fairview Strand, Dublin 3
  Tel 01-8376000
  (Fairview, Dublin)
Griffin, Philip
  Nullamore, Richmond
  Avenue South, Dublin 6
  Tel 01-4971239
  (Opus Dei)
Griffin, Tom (IC)
  1 Grace Park Gardens,
  Drumcondra, Dublin 9
  Tel 01-8378314/8368730
Griffith, Anthony
  Rushbrook, Laghey,
  Co Donegal
  Tel 074-9734021
  (Raphoe, retired)
Grimes, Edward (CSSp)
  Director, Pontifical Mission
  Societies,
  Holy Ghost Missionary
  College, Kimmage Manor,
  Dublin 12
  Tel 01-4064300
Grimes, James, Very Rev, PE
  61 Castlecaulfield Road,
  Donaghmore,
  Co Tyrone BT70 3HF
  Tel 028-87767727
  (Armagh, retired)
Grimshaw, Ronan (CSSp)
  Newlands Institute for
  Counselling,
  2 Monastery Road,
  Clondalkin, Dublin 22
  Tel 01-4594573
Grogan, Brian (SJ)
  Superior, 35 Lower Leeson
  Street, Dublin 2
  Tel 01-6761248
Grogan, Desmond, Very Rev
  Canon, PP
  Partry, Claremorris,
  Co Mayo
  Tel 094-9543013
  (Partry (Ballyovey), Tuam)

Grubka, Marek (OP), CC
  St Saviour's,
  Upper Dorset Street,
  Dublin 1
  Tel 01-8897610
  (Dominick Street, Dublin)
Grzegorzewski, Tomasz, PC
  24 Killarney Street,
  Dublin 1
  Tel 01-8363554
  (Sean McDermott Street,
  Dublin)
Gubazire, Bonaventure
  (White Fathers)
  Cypress Grove, Templeogue,
  Dublin 6W
  Tel 01-4055263/4055264
Guckian, Michael (OMI), CC
  Oblate House of Retreat,
  Inchicore, Dublin 8
  Tel 01-4534408/4541805
  (Inchicore, Mary
  Immaculate, Dublin)
Guckian, Patrick, CC
  44 Woodview Grove,
  Blanchardstown, Dublin 15
  Tel 01-8626799
  (Blanchardstown, Dublin)
Guilfoyle, Patrick, Very Rev,
  PP
  Tullaroan, Co Kilkenny
  Tel 056-7769141/
  087-6644858
  (Tullaroan, Ossory)
Guiney, John (SJ)
  Milltown Park,
  Sandford Road, Dublin 6
  Tel 01-2698411/2698113
Guiney, John K. (SJ)
  St Francis Xavier's, Upper
  Gardiner Street, Dublin 1
  Tel 01-8363411
Guiry, Michael, Very Rev, PP
  Ardmore, Youghal,
  Co Waterford
  Tel 024-94275
  (Ardmore, Waterford & L.)
Gunn, David, CC
  Cullen, Mallow. Co Cork
  Tel 029-79028
  (Millstreet, Kerry)
Gunn, Joseph, Very Rev, PP,
  VF
  St Comgall's Presbytery, 27
  Brunswick Road, Bangor,
  Co Down BT20 3DS
  Tel 028-91465522
  (Bangor, Down & C.)
Gunn, Terence (SMA)
  SMA House, Wilton, Cork
  Tel 021-4541069/4541884
Guthrie, Charles (SVD)
  Donamon Castle,
  Roscommon
  Tel 090-6662222

Allianz (ⅲ)

H

Haan, Karl, CC
33 Glen Road, Garvagh,
Co Derry BT51 5DB
Tel 028-29558342
(*Garvagh*, Derry)

Habara, Gaspar, CC
St Brigid's, Kildare
Tel 045-520347
(*Kildare*, Kildare & L.)

Habara, Gaspard (SVD)
3 Pembroke Road,
Dublin 4
Tel 01-6680904

Hackett, Brian, Very Rev, PE,
AP
Parochial House,
31 Church Street,
Ballygawley,
Co Tyrone BT70 2HA
Tel 028-85568219
(*Ballygawley (Errigal
Kieran),* Armagh)

Hackett, Gerard (SMA)
African Missions,
Blackrock Road, Cork
Tel 021-4292871

Hackett, Michael, Very Rev
Canon, PP
44 Church Street, Rostrevor,
Co Down BT34 3BB
Tel 028-41738277
(*Kilbroney (Rostrevor),*
Dromore)

Hahessy, Ignatius (OCSO)
Mount Melleray Abbey,
Cappoquin, Co Waterford
Tel 058-54404

Hajkowski, Stanislaw (SC), CC
Cathedral Presbytery,
38 Hill Street,
Newry BT34 1AT
Tel 028-30262586
(*Newry*, Dromore)

Hall, Bernard (OFM)
PO Box 7026, Katutura,
Windlock, Republic of
Namibia

Halliden, Donal (SSC)
St Columban's Retirement
Home, Dalgan Park,
Navan, Co Meath
Tel 046-9021525

Hallinan, Malachy, Rt Rev
Mgr, VG
The Presbytery, Seamus
Quirke Road, Galway
Tel 091-522713
(*Sacred Heart Church,*
Galway)

Hally, Brendan (CSSp)
Rockwell College, Cashel,
Co Tipperary
Tel 062-61444

Halpin, David
43 Chestnut Grove, Tallaght,
Dublin 24
Tel 01-4415001/087-2048898
(*Kilnamanagh,* Dublin)

Halpin, Lauri, Very Rev, PE
Parochial House, Kilbeggan,
Co Westmeath
Tel 057-9332155
(Meath, retired)

Halpin, Martin, Very Rev, PP
Parochial House,
Ballinabrackey, Kinnegad,
Co Westmeath
Tel 046-9739015
(*Ballinabrackey,* Meath)

Halpin, Rory (SJ)
Crescent College
Comprehensive,
Dooradoyle, Limerick
Tel 061-480920

Halton, John, Very Rev, PP
Tempo, Enniskillen,
Co Fermanagh BT94 3LY
Tel 028-89541344
(*Tempo,* Clogher)

Hamill, Aidan, Rt Rev Mgr, PP,
VG
Parochial House,
70 North Street, Lurgan,
Co Armagh BT67 9AH
Tel 028-38323161
(*Shankill St Peter's (Lurgan),*
Dromore)

Hamill, Thomas
'Shekinah',
25 Wynnes Terrace,
Dundalk, Co Louth
Tel 042-9331023
(Armagh)

Hammel, James, Very Rev, PP
Annacurra, Aughrim,
Co Wicklow
Tel 0402-36119
(*Annacurra,* Ferns)

Hampson, Paul, PC
3 Beechmount Drive,
Clonskeagh, Dublin 14
Tel 01-2697797
(*Clonskeagh,* Dublin)

Hanafin, Sean, Dean, PP, VF
St John's Presbytery, Tralee,
Co Kerry
Tel 066-7122522
(*Tralee, St John's,* Kerry)

Hanahoe, Thomas (SSC)
St Columban's Retirement
Home, Dalgan Park, Navan,
Co Meath
Tel 046-9021525

Hand, John (SM),
Superior, The Presbytery,
Coolock Village, Dublin 5
Tel 01-8484799
(*Coolock,* Dublin)

Hanley, Brendan (MSC)
Myross Wood Retreat
House, Leap, Skibbereen,
Co Cork
Tel 028-33118

Hanley, Brian, Very Rev
Ballyhard, Glenamaddy,
Co Galway
(Elphin)

Hanley, Michael, Very Rev, PP
Kilfinane, Co Limerick
Tel 063-91016/086-8595733
(*Kilfinane,* Limerick)

Hanlon, Joseph, Very Rev
(Assistant Priest)
St Mary's Presbytery,
Willbrook Road,
Rathfarnham, Dublin 14
Tel 01-4932390
(*Rathfarnham,* Dublin)

Hanly, Gerard, Very Rev
Canon, PP, VF
Boyle, Co Roscommon
Tel 071-9662218
(*Boyle,* Elphin)

Hanly, John, Rt Rev Mgr, PP
Parochial House, Carnaross,
Kells, Co Meath
Tel 046-9245904
(*Carnaross,* Meath)

Hanly, Rory (SAC), CC
St Benin's, Dublin Road,
Shankill,
Co Dublin
Tel 01-2824425
(*Shankill,* Dublin)

Hanna, John (CSsR)
Mount Saint Alphonsus,
Limerick
Tel 061-315099

Hannan, Greg, Very Rev, PP
Ballymote, Co Sligo
Tel 071-9183361
(*Ballymote (Emlefad and
Kilmorgan),* Achonry)

Hannan, John (SM)
France

Hannan, Laurence (SM)
Fiji

Hannan, Peter (SJ)
Manresa House,
Dollymount, Dublin 3
Tel 01-8331352

Hannigan, Patrick, Very Rev,
PP, VF
Parochial House,
65 Tullyallen Road,
Dungannon,
Co Tyrone BT70 3AF
Tel 028-87761211
(*Killeeshil,* Armagh)

Hannon, Donald, Very Rev,
PP, VF
Swanlinbar, Co Cavan
Tel 049-9521221/
087-2830145
(*Swanlinbar,* Kilmore)

Hannon, James
Chaplain, St Mary's Hospital,
Phoenix Park, Dublin 20
Tel 01-6778132
(Dublin)

Hannon, James
Sandhill Road, Ballybunion,
Co Kerry
(Cloyne, retired)

Hannon, Martin
Cleraun Study Centre,
90 Foster Avenue,
Mount Merrion, Co Dublin
Tel 01-2881734
(Opus Dei)

Hannon, Patrick, PC
Parochial House, Donabate,
Co Dublin
Tel 01-8434604
(*Donabate,* Dublin)

Hannon, Patrick, Dr
Emeritus Professor of
Theology,
St Patrick's College,
Maynooth, Co Kildare
Tel 01-6285222
(Cloyne, retired)

Hannon, Ray, CC
10 Farnham Drive,
Finglas West, Dublin 11
Tel 01-8341284
(*Finglas West,* Dublin)

Hannon, Tom, PP
Templemore Road,
Cloughjordan, Co Tipperary
Tel 0505-42266
(*Cloughjordan,* Killaloe)

Hanrahan, Noel (MHM)

Hanrahan, Paschal, Capt
2/2 Paul Gerhardt Strasse,
Sennelager,
33104 Paderborn, Germany
(Killaloe)

Hanratty, David
Tierhogar, Portarlington,
Co Laois
Tel 057-8645719
(Meath)

Hanratty, Malachy (SSC)
St Columban's, Dalgan Park,
Navan, Co Meath
Tel 046-9021525

Hanratty, Oliver
The Bungalow,
Crescent Road, Rogerstown,
Rush, Co Dublin
(Dublin, retired)

Hanson, Frederick (SSC)
St Columban's Retirement
Home, Dalgan Park, Navan,
Co Meath
Tel 046-9021525

Haran, Casimir (CP), CC
Holy Cross Retreat,
432 Crumlin Road, Ardoyne,
Belfast BT14 7GE
Tel 028-90748231/2
(*Holy Cross,* Down & C.)

Haran, Cyril, Very Rev
Grange, Co Sligo
(Elphin, retired)
Harding, Michael, CC
Templemore Road, Roscrea,
Co Tipperary
Tel 0505-21218
(*Roscrea*, Killaloe)
Hardy, Francis
58 Shelmartin Avenue,
Marino, Dublin 9
(Dublin, retired)
Harkin, Ciaran, CC
Parochial House, Stranorlar,
Co Donegal
Tel 074-9131157
(*Stranorlar*, Raphoe)
Harkin, Dermott, CC
St Brigid's, Carnhill, Derry
BT48 8HJ
Tel 028-71351261
(Derry)
Harkin, Hugh (SMA)
African Missions,
Blackrock Road, Cork
Tel 021-4292871
Harmon, Maurice
Chaplain, District Hospital,
Raheen, Tuamgraney,
Co Clare
Tel 061-923007
(Killaloe)
Harmon, Sean
Chaplain,
St Joseph's Hospital,
Limerick
Tel 061-414624
(Limerick)
Harmon, Seán, CC
Cathedral House,
Cathedral Place, Limerick
Tel 061-414624/087-2589279
(*St John's*, Limerick)
Harney, Donal (MHM)
St Joseph's,
Freshford House, Kilkenny
Tel 056-7721482
Harper, Conor, (SJ)
Clongowes Wood College,
Naas, Co Kildare
Tel 045-868663/868202
Harper, Frank, Very Rev
32 Bryansford Ave,
Newcastle BT33 0EQ
(Down & C., retired)
Harper, Conor (SJ)
Milltown Park,
Sandford Road, Dublin 6
Tel 01-2698411/2698113
Harrington, Brendan, Very
Rev, PP
Fossa, Killarney, Co Kerry
Tel 064-6631996
(*Fossa*, Kerry)

Harrington, Christopher, CC
1 Kilmorna Heights,
Ballyvolane, Cork
Tel 021-4550425
(*Blackpool/The Glen*, Cork &
R.)
Harrington, Denis, Very Rev,
PE, CC
Clane, Naas, Co Kildare
Tel 045-868224
(*Clane*, Kildare & L.)
Harrington, James (OFMCap)
Vicar, Capuchin Friary,
Friary Street, Kilkenny
Tel 056-7721439
Harrington, John (SM), PC
The Presbytery,
Coolock Village, Dublin 5
Tel 01-8484799
(*Coolock*, Dublin)
Harrington, Joseph (SDB)
Salesian House, Milford,
Castleroy, Limerick
Tel 061-330268
Harrington, Michael, Very Rev
Canon, PP
Buttevant, Co Cork
Tel 022-23195
(*Buttevant*, Cloyne)
Harrington, Terence
(OFMCap), Very Rev
Provincial Minister,
Provincial Office,
12 Halston Street, Dublin 7
Tel 01-8733205
Harrington, Wilfrid (OP)
St Mary's Priory, Tallaght,
Dublin 24
Tel 01-4048100
Harris, Derek (SSC)
44 Harbour View, Howth,
Co Dublin
Tel 01-8395161
Harris, James (OP), Very Rev
Prior, St Saviour's,
Bridge Street, Waterford
Tel 051-875061
Harris, John (OP)
St Saviour's,
Upper Dorset Street,
Dublin 1
Tel 01-8897610
Harris, Walter, Very Rev
Canon, PE
151 Clonsilla Road,
Blanchardstown, Dublin 15
(Dublin, retired)
Harrison, Michael, Very Rev,
PP
Binghamstown, Belmullet,
Co Sligo
Tel 097-82350
(Killala)

Harte, Martin, CC
Presbytery No 2,
Church Grounds,
Lower Kilmacud Road,
Kilmacud, Co Dublin
Tel 01-2882257
(*Kilmacud-Stillorgan*,
Dublin)
Hartley, Noel, Very Rev Canon
10 Donovan's Wharf,
Crescent Quay, Wexford
(Ferns, retired)
Hartnett, Denis (MHM)
St Joseph's House,
50 Orwell Park, Rathgar,
Dublin 6
Tel 01-4127700
Harty, Gabriel (OP)
St Mary's Priory, Tallaght,
Dublin 24
Tel 01-4048100
Harty, John (OFM)
Franciscan Friary, Clonmel,
Co Tipperary
Tel 052-6121378
Haslam, Richard (OMI)
Oblate House of Retreat,
Inchicore, Dublin 8
Tel 01-4534408/4541805
Hassett, Edmond, CC
Portlaw, Co Waterford
Tel 051-387227
(Waterford & L.)
Hassett, John, Moderator
127 Castlegate Way,
Adamstown, Lucan,
Co Dublin
Tel 01-6281018
(Dublin)
Hasson, Eugene, PP
164 Greencastle Road,
Omagh,
Co Tyrone BT79 7RU
Tel 028-81648474
(*Greencastle*, Derry)
Hasson, Gerald, CC
Parochial House, St Mary's,
Creggan, Derry BT48 9QE
Tel 028-71263152
(*St Mary's, Creggan*, Derry)
Hasson, James (OFM)
Vicar, Adam & Eve's,
4 Merchant's Quay, Dublin 8
Tel 01-6771128
Hastings, Mícheál, Very Rev
103 Mount Prospect Drive,
Dollymount, Dublin 3
Tel 01-8335255
(Dublin, retired)
Haugh, Joseph, Very Rev
Bealaha, Doonbeg,
Co Clare
Tel 065-9055022/
087-2603314
(*Doonbeg and Killard*,
Killaloe)

Haughey, Eoghan (OMI)
Oblate House of Retreat,
Inchicore, Dublin 8
Tel 01-4534408/4541805
Haughey, Peter (OSA)
St John's Priory,
Thomas Street, Dublin 8
Tel 01-6770393
Hawis, Jack (CM), Very Rev, PP
St Vincent's,
122 Sunday Well Road,
Cork
Tel 021-4304070/4304529
Hayden, Chris
Pontifical Irish College, Via
de SS Quattro 1,
Roma 00184, Italy
(Ferns)
Hayden, Desmond
Pontificio Collegio
Teutonico, Via della
Sagrestia 17, 00120 Rome,
Vatican City
(Dublin)
Hayes, Bartholomew (MHM)
St Joseph's House,
50 Orwell Park, Rathgar,
Dublin 6
Tel 01-4127700
Hayes, Colm, Very Rev
15 St Patrick's Terrace, Sligo
(Elphin, retired)
Hayes, Conor, Very Rev, CC
The Parochial House,
Kilteely, Co Limerick
Tel 061-384213
(*Kilteely*, Cashel & E.)
Hayes, George, Very Rev, Adm
Diocesan Secretary,
Bishop's House, Killarney,
Co Kerry
Tel 064-6631168
(Kerry)
Hayes, James (SJ)
c/o Jesuit Provincial Curia,
IMI Centre, Sandyford Road,
Dublin 16
Tel 01-2932820
Hayes, Martin, Very Rev, Adm
Cathedral Presbytery,
Thurles, Co Tipperary
Tel 0504-22229/22779
(*Thurles, Cathedral of the
Assumption*, Cashel & E.)
Hayes, Noel (SPS)
Bridgetown, Co Clare
Tel 061-377158
(*Killaloe*, Killaloe)
Hayes, Noel (SPS)
On temporary diocesan
work
Hayes, Patrick, CC
St Mary's, Clonmel,
Co Tipperary
Tel 052-6121952
(*Clonmel, St Mary's*,
Waterford & L.)

Hayes, Richard, Very Rev, PP
Clonroche, Enniscorthy,
Co Wexford
Tel 053-9244115
(*Cloughbawn*, Ferns)
Hayes, Seán (SMA)
SMA House,
82 Ranelagh Road,
Ranelagh, Dublin 6
Tel 01-4968162/3
Hayes, Tom
1 The Presbytery, Friar's
Walk, Ballyphehane, Cork
Tel 021-4537472
(Cork & R.)
Hazelwood, Timothy, CC
Blarney, Co Cork
Tel 021-4385229
(*Blarney*, Cloyne)
Heagney, John, Very Rev, PP
Parochial House,
Mullaghbawn, Newry,
Co Down BT35 9XN
Tel 028-30888286
(*Mullaghbawn (Forkhill)*,
Armagh)
Heagney, Michael (CSsR)
St Patrick's, Esker, Athenry,
Co Galway
Tel 091-844549
Healy, Alexius (OFMCap)
St Anthony's Capuchin
Friary, 43 Dublin Street,
Carlow
Tel 059-9142543
Healy, Austin (CSSp)
Church of the Holy Spirit,
Kimmage, Dublin 12
Tel 01-4558316
(*Kimmage*, Dublin)
Healy, Bernard, CC
Dingle, Co Kerry
Tel 066-9151208
(*Dingle*, Kerry)
Healy, Charles, CC
St Mary's, Athlone,
Co Westmeath
Tel 090-6472088
(*Athlone*, Ardagh & Cl.)
Healy, Jeremiah (SMA)
African Missions,
Blackrock Road, Cork
Tel 021-4292871
Healy, Michael (SSC)
St Columban's Retirement
Home, Dalgan Park, Navan,
Co Meath
Tel 046-9021525
Healy, Myles (CSSp) , Very
Rev, PP
55 Fernhill Road, Greenhills,
Dublin 12
Tel 01-4504040
(*Greenhills*, Dublin)
Healy, P. J. (SDB), CC
162 Walkinstown Road,
Dublin 12
Tel 01-4501372
(*Walkinstown*, Dublin)

Healy, Patrick (SSC)
St Columban's Retirement
Home, Dalgan Park, Navan,
Co Meath
Tel 046-9021525
Healy, Peter
3 Sweetmount Drive,
Dundrum, Dublin 14
Tel 01-2983557
(*Dundrum*, Dublin)
Healy, Sean (SMA)
Socail Justice Ireland, Arena
House
Arena Road, Sandyford,
Dublin 18
Tel 01-2130724
Healy, Thomas, Adm
The Presbytery, Longford
Tel 043-3346465
(*Ardagh & Cl.*)
Healy, Timothy (SJ)
c/o Jesuit Provincial Curia,
IMI Centre, Sandyford Road,
Dublin 16
Tel 01-2932820
Heaney, Columban (OCSO)
Mount Melleray Abbey,
Cappoquin, Co Waterford
Tel 058-54404
Heaney, Seamus, Very Rev, PP
Parochial House, Delvin,
Co Westmeath
Tel 044-9664127
(*Delvin*, Meath)
Heaney, Seán, Rt Rev Mgr, PP,
VG
Parochial House, Tullamore,
Co Offaly
Tel 057-9321587/057-
9351510
(Meath)
Hearne, Thomas, CC
Brittas, Boher, Co Limerick
Tel 061-352223
(Cashel & E.)
Hearty, Phil, Very Rev (CSsR),
Adm
Lusmagh, Banagher,
Co Offaly
Tel 0509-51358
(*Lusmagh*, Clonfert)
Hearty, Philip (CSsR)
St Patrick's, Esker, Athenry,
Co Galway
Tel 091-844549
Hederman, Mark Patrick
(OSB), Rt Rev Dom
Abbot, Glenstal Abbey,
Murroe, Co Limerick
Tel 061-386103
Heelan, Patrick (SJ)
c/o Jesuit Provincial Curia,
IMI Centre, Sandyford Road,
Dublin 16
Tel 01-2932820

Heeran, Brendan (CSSp)
Holy Ghost Missionary
College, Kimmage Manor,
Dublin 12
Tel 01-4064300
Heerey, Anthony (CSSp)
Spiritan Missionary College,
Kimmage Manor,
Dublin 12
Tel 01-4064300
Heerey, Charles, Very Rev, PP
Ballinamore, Co Leitrim
Tel 071-9644039
(*Ballinamore*, Kilmore)
Heffernan, John (OP)
St Dominic's, Athy,
Co Kildare
Tel 0507-31573
Heffernan, Joseph (OP)
St Magdalen's, Drogheda,
Co Louth
Tel 041-9838271
Heffernan, Martin, BA, BD,
HDE
St Colman's College,
Fermoy, Co Cork
Tel 025-31622
(Cloyne)
Hegarty, Benedict (OP), CC
Presbytery,
St Dominic's Road,
Tallaght, Dublin 24
Tel 01-4510620
(*Tallaght, Dodder*, Dublin)
Hegarty, Benedict (OP), Very
Rev
Prior,
St Dominic's Retreat House,
Montenotte, Co Cork
Tel 021-4502520
Hegarty, Ciaran
The Presbytery,
30A Deanby Gardens,
Belfast BT14 6NN
Tel 028-90745140
(*Sacred Heart*, Down & C.)
Hegarty, James (SSS)
Blessed Sacrament Chapel,
20 Bachelors Walk, Dublin 1
Tel 01-8724597
Hegarty, John (CSSp)
Holy Ghost Missionary
College, Kimmage Manor,
Dublin 12
Tel 01-4064300
Hegarty, John Paul, Very Rev,
PP
St Joseph's Presbytery,
Mayfield, Cork
Tel 021-4501861
(*St Joseph's (Mayfield)*, Cork
& R.)
Hegarty, Kevin
Carne, Belmullet, Co Mayo
Tel 097-81011
(*Kilmore-Erris*, Killala)

Hegarty, Martin, Very Rev, PP
Ballybunion, Co Kerry
Tel 068-27102
(*Ballybunion*, Kerry)
Hegarty, Michael (IC), Very
Rev, PP
Cooleens, Glenconnor,
Clonmel, Co Tipperary
Tel 052-6125679
(*Clonmel, St Oliver Plunkett*,
Waterford & L.)
Hegarty, Patrick, Very Rev
Canon, PP
Carrowmore, Ballina,
Co Mayo
Tel 096-34014
(*Lacken*, Killala)
Hegarty, Richard, Very Rev,
PE, CC
Killavullen, Co Cork
Tel 022-26125
(*Killavullen*, Cloyne)
Hegarty, Seamus, Most Rev,
DD
Bishop of Derry,
PO Box 227, Bishop's House,
Derry BT48 9YG
Tel 028-71262302
(Derry)
Hegarty, Seán, Very Rev, PP
Parochial House,
2 Tullynure Road,
Cookstown,
Co Tyrone BT80 9XH
Tel 028-86763674
(*Lissan*, Armagh)
Hegarty, Walter (OP)
St Mary's, The Claddach,
Co Galway
Tel 091-582884
Hehir, Mark, CC (Cloyne)
Cathedral Presbytery, Cork
Tel 021-4304325
(*Cathedral of St Mary & St
Anne*, Cork & R.)
Henderson, Eanna (OCSO)
Mount Saint Joseph Abbey,
Roscrea, Co Tipperary
Tel 0505-25600
Hendrick, Richard (OFMCap),
Very Rev, CC
Capuchin Parochial Friary,
Church Street, Dublin 7
Tel 01-8730599
(*Halston Street and Arran
Quay*, Dublin)
Heneghan, James (CSSp)
(Chaplain to Brazilian
Community)
12 Abbeyville, Roscommon
Tel 090-6627978
(*Roscommon*, Elphin)
Heneghan, Jeremy (OFMCap)
St Francis Capuchin Friary.
Rochestown, Co Cork
Tel 021-4896244
Heneghan, Kieran (SSC)
Knock, Co Mayo

Heneghan, Patrick, Very Rev
Canon, PE
5 Pine Grove, Moycullen,
Co Galway
Tel 091-556698
(Galway, retired)

Henehan, Patrick (CSSp)
Holy Ghost Missionary
College, Kimmage Manor,
Dublin 12
Tel 01-4064300

Hennessy, Declan, Very Rev,
PP
Mallow, Co Cork
Tel 022-21149
(Mallow, Cloyne)

Hennessy, Gerard, CC
Cathedral Prestybery,
Thurles, Co Tipperary
Tel 0504-22229/22779
(Cashel & E.)

Hennessy, Patrick (SDB)
Rector, Salesian College,
Maynooth Road, Celbridge,
Co Kildare
Tel 01-6275058/60

Hennessy, Patrick, Very Rev,
PP
Ballyfin, Portlaoise, Co Laois
Tel 057-8755227
(Mountrath, Kildare & L.)

Hennessy, William, Very Rev,
PP
Castletown, Portlaoise,
Co Laois
Tel 0502-32622/087-8736155
(Castletown, Ossory)

Hennessy, William, Very Rev,
PP
Knocklong, Co Limerick
Tel 062-53114
(Cashel & E.)

Hennigan, Frank (SM)
Mount St Mary's, Milltown,
Dublin 14
Tel 01-2697322

Henry, Denis, Co-PP
1A Ballydowd Grove, Lucan,
Co Dublin
Tel 01-2955541
(Lucan, Dublin)

Henry, Leo, BA, HDE
St Nathy's College,
Ballaghaderreen,
Co Roscommon
Tel 094-9860010
(Achonry)

Henry, Martin, CC
The Presbytery,
Ballaghaderreen,
Co Roscommon
Tel 094-9860011
(Achonry)

Henry, Martin
St Patrick's College,
Maynooth, Co Kildare
Tel 01-6285222
(Down & C.)

Henry, Maurice, Very Rev, PP,
Adm
Parochial House,
15 Moyle Road, Ballycastle,
Co Antrim BT54 6LB
Tel 028-20762223
(Ballycastle (Ramoan), Down
& C.)

Henry, Seamus, Very Rev
Canon, PP
Freshford, Co Kilkenny
Tel 056-8832146/086-
0879296
(Freshford, Ossory)

Henry, Seán, Very Rev, PP
Parochial House, Trim,
Co Meath
Tel 046-9431251
(Trim, Meath)

Heraty, Jarlath
Hillside, Westport
Co Mayo
(Tuam)

Herbert, Tadhg (CSsR)
Mount Saint Alphonsus,
Limerick
Tel 061-315099

Herlihy, David, Very Rev, PP
Newmarket, Co Cork
Tel 029-60999
(Cloyne)

Herlihy, Ronan (OFMCap)
Holy Trinity,
Fr Mathew Quay, Cork
Tel 021-4270827

Herrity, Michael, Very Rev, PP
Annagry, Co Donegal
Tel 074-9548111
(Annagry, Raphoe)

Herron, Frank, Very Rev, PP
68 Maplewood Road,
Springfield, Tallaght,
Dublin 24
Tel 01-4513109
(Springfield, Dublin)

Hession, Noel (OSA), CC
Parochial House, 5 St
Helena's Drive,
Dublin 11
Tel 01-8343444
(Rivermount, Dublin)

Hession, Stan (OCarm)
Carmelite Friary, Kinsale,
Co Cork
Tel 021-772138

Hever, Thomas, Very Rev
Canon, Adm, VF
St Mary's, Sligo
Tel 071-9162670/9162769
Sligo Social Services,
Charles Street, Sligo
Tel 071-9145682
(Sligo, St Mary's, Elphin)

Heverin, Seamus, Rt Rev Mgr
Enniscrone, Co Sligo
Tel 096-37802
(Killala, retired)

Hickey, Herman (OCSO)
Our Lady of Bethlehem
Abbey, 11 Ballymena Road,
Portglenone, Ballymena,
Co Antrim BT44 8BL
Tel 028-25821211

Hickey, Jeremiah (OSA)
St Augustine's Priory,
O'Connell Street, Limerick
Tel 061-415374

Hickey, John (OFMCap)
Holy Trinity,
Fr Mathew Quay, Cork
Tel 021-4270827

Hickey, John (SSC)
Catholic Rectory, Abbey,
Loughrea, Co Galway
Tel 0909-745217

Hickey, John, CC
Abbey, Loughrea,
Co Galway
Tel 090-9745217
(Duniry and Abbey,
Clonfert)

Hickey, Liam, Very Rev
St Ciaran's,
1 Cherryfield Park,
Hartstown, Dublin 15
Tel 01-8214863
(Dublin, retired)

Hickey, Michael (CSSp), CC
Parochial House, Tenure,
Dunleer, Co Louth
Tel 041-6851281
(Monasterboice, Armagh)

Hickey, Michael, Very Rev, PP
Bansha, Co Tipperary
Tel 062-54132
(Bansha and Kilmoyler,
Cashel & E.)

Hickland, Brendan, Very Rev,
PP
St Teresa's Presbytery,
Glen Road,
Belfast BT11 8BL
Tel 028-90612855
(St Teresa's, Down & C.)

Higgins, Columba (OSA)
Augustinian Retreat Centre,
Old Court Road,
Dublin 16
Tel 01-4930932

Higgins, John
Arus Vianney, Ard Mhuire,
Ballinasloe, Co Galway
Tel 090-9631076
(Clonfert, retired)

Higgins, Richard, Very Rev
Canon, PP
C/o Diocesan Office,
The Cathedral, Galway
Tel 091-563266
(Galway, retired)

Higgins, Thomas (OCarm)
Whitefriar Street Church,
56 Aungier Street, Dublin 2
Tel 01-4758821

Hillery, Des
Padre de San Columbano,
Apartado 39-073/074,
Lima 39, Peru
(Killaloe)

Hoban, Brendan (SSC)
St Columban's, Dalgan Park,
Navan, Co Meath
Tel 046-9021525

Hoban, Brendan, Very Rev,
PP, VF
Cathedral Presbytery,
Ballina, Co Mayo
Tel 096-71365
(Ballina, Killala)

Hoban, Patrick, Very Rev, PP
Killala, Co Mayo
Tel 096-32176
(Killala, Killala)

Hodnett, Vincent, Very Rev
Canon, PP
The Lough Presbytery,
St Finbarr's West, Cork
Tel 021-4273821
(The Lough, Cork & R.)

Hoey, Charles, Very Rev
(OCarm)
Our Lady of Mount Carmel,
Whitefriar Street,
Dublin 2
(Whitefriar Street, Dublin)

Hoey, Eamonn, (CSsR), CC
St Joseph's,
St Alphonsus Road,
Dundalk, Co Louth
Tel 042-9334042
(Dundalk, St Joseph's,
Armagh)

Hogan, Bernard, Very Rev, PP
Mohill, Co Leitrim
Tel 071-9631024
(Ardagh & Cl.)

Hogan, Colm
Casilla 09-01-5825,
Guayaquil, Ecuador
(Killaloe)

Hogan, Diarmuid
Chaplain, NUI, Galway
Tel 091-524853/495055
(Galway)

Hogan, Donal (SSC)
Regional Director,
St Columban's, Dalgan Park,
Navan, Co Meath
Tel 046-9021525

Hogan, Edmund M. (SMA)
African Missions,
Blackrock Road, Cork
Tel 021-4292871

Hogan, Flannan (OCSO)
Mount Saint Joseph Abbey,
Roscrea, Co Tipperary
Tel 0505-25600

Hogan, John (CSSp)
Holy Ghost Missionary
College, Kimmage Manor,
Dublin 12
Tel 01-4064300

Hogan, John F., Venerable
Archdeacon, AP
Ballycommon, Nenagh,
Co Tipperary
Tel 067-24153/087-7536526
(*Puckane*, Killaloe)

Hogan, John, CC
St Mary's, Drogheda,
Co Louth
Tel 041-9834958
(*Drogheda, St Mary's*,
Meath)

Hogan, Martin
187 Clontarf Road, Clontarf,
Dublin 3
Tel 01-8338575
(*Clontarf, St John's*, Dublin)

Hogan, Michael
c/o Killaloe Diocesan Office,
Westbourne, Ennis, Co Clare
(Killaloe)

Hogan, Patrick, Very Rev, PP
334 O'Malley Park, Southill,
Limerick
Tel 061-414248
(*Holy Family*, Limerick)

Hogan, Ray (MHM)
St Joseph's House,
50 Orwell Park, Rathgar,
Dublin 6
Tel 01-4127700

Hogan, Thomas (CSSp)
SPIRASI, Spiritan House,
213 North Circular Road,
Dublin 7
Tel 01-8389664/8683504

Hogan, Thomas (CSsR)
Marianella, 75 Orwell Road,
Dublin 6
Tel 01-4067100

Hogan, Tom, Very Rev
Cathedral Presbytery, Ennis,
Co Clare
Tel 065-6824043
(Killaloe)

Hogg, Barry, Very Rev
President, St Mary's College,
Galway
Tel 091-522458/524904
(Galway)

Holahan, Ciarán, Very Rev, PP
Parochial House, Foxrock,
Dublin 18
Tel 01-2893229
(*Foxrock*, Dublin)

Holland, Michael (OFM)
Franciscan Friary,
Friary Lane, Athlone,
Co Westmeath
Tel 090-6472095

Holleran, Patrick, Very Rev, PP
Coolaney, Co Sligo
Tel 071-9167745
(*Coolaney (Killoran)*,
Achonry)

Holloway, James, Very Rev, PP
Moymore, Pallasgreen,
Co Limerick
Tel 061-384111
(*Pallasgreen*, Cashel & E.)

Holloway, Sean (SSC)
St Columban's Retirement
Home, Dalgan Park, Navan,
Co Meath
Tel 046-9021525

Holmes, Brian (CSsR)
Vice-Provincial,
Missionarios Redentoristas,
Caixa Postal 85,
60,001-970 Fortaleza,
Est. do Ceara, Brazil
Tel 0055-85322232016

Holmes, Kieran, CC
Enniscrone, Ballina,
Co Mayo
Tel 096-36164
(*Kilglass*, Killala)

Holmes, Liam, Very Rev, PP
Knockaney, Hospital,
Co Limerick
Tel 061-383127
(*Knockaney*, Cashel & E.)

Holmes, Samuel, PP
Cloone, Co Leitrim
Tel 071-9636016
(*Aughavas and Cloone*,
Ardagh & Cl.)

Holmes, Vianney (OFMCap)
Vicar, Capuchin Friary,
Ard Mhuire, Creeslough,
Letterkenny, Co Donegal
Tel 074-9138005

Hopkins, Francis, Very Rev
Canon, AP
St Anne's Presbytery,
Convent Hill, Waterford
Tel 051-855819
(*Ballybricken*, Waterford &
L.)

Horan, Gerry (OSA)
St Augustine's,
Taylor's Lane,
Balyboden, Dublin 16
Tel 01-4241000

Horan, John (SDB), Very Rev
Provincial, Provincialate,
Salesian House,
St Teresa's Road, Crumlin,
Dublin 12
Tel 01-4555787

Horgan, John (SMA)
SMA House, Wilton, Cork
Tel 021-4541069/4541884

Horgan, Patrick (CSsR)
Clonard Monastery,
Clonard Gardens,
Belfast BT13 2RL
Tel 028-90445950
(*St Paul's*, Down & C.)

Horgan, Patrick, Very Rev
(*in residence*)
Killarney, Co Kerry
Tel 064-31014
(*Killarney*, Kerry)

Horgan, Seamus
Apostolic Nunciature, En
Suisse, Thunstrasse 60,
Case Pastale 259, 3000
Berne 6, Switzerland
(Killaloe)

Horneck, Noel, Very Rev, PP
Parochial House, Dunderry,
Navan, Co Meath
Tel 046-9431433
(*Dunderry*, Meath)

Hough, Martin
England
(Clonfert)

Houlihan, Brendan, Rt Rev
Mgr, PP
Parochial House,
Mount Saint Mary's,
Howth, Co Dublin
Tel 01-8322036
(*Howth*, Dublin)

Houlihan, Nik (MI)
St Camillus, Killucan,
Co Westmeath
Tel 044-74115

Houlihan, Seamus, Very Rev,
PP
Parochial House, Nobber,
Co Meath
Tel 046-9052197
(Meath)

Hourigan, Joseph, Very Rev,
PP
Lissycasey, Ennis,
Co Clare
Tel 065-6834145
(*Ballynacally*, Killaloe)

Howard, Brendan, CC
Curate's House, Clonegal,
Enniscorthy, Co Wexford
Tel 053-9377291
(*Myshall*, Kildare & L.)

Howard, Gregory (OSA), CC
Glounthaune, Co Cork
Tel 021-4353078
(*Glounthaune*, Cork & R.)

Howard, Niall, CC
Cahirciveen, Co Kerry
Tel 066-9472210
(*Cahirciveen*, Kerry)

Howard, Patrick, Very Rev
Athlacca, Kilmallock,
Co Limerick
Tel 063-90540
(Limerick, retired)

Howard, Terence (SJ)
Jesuit Community,
27 Leinster Road,
Rathmines, Dublin 6
Tel 01-4970250

Howell, Patrick (CSsR)
St Patrick's, Esker, Athenry,
Co Galway
Tel 091-844549

Howell, William, Very Rev, PP
St Michael's, Gorey,
Co Wexford
Tel 053-9421112
(*Gorey*, Ferns)

Howlett, John (SAC)
Provincial House,
'Homestead',
Sandyford Road, Dundrum,
Dublin 16
Tel 01-2956180/2954170

Howley, Enda, CC
Parochial House, Ryehill
Monivea, Galway
Tel 091-849019
(*Abbeyknockmoy*, Tuam)

Howley, Gary (SPS)
St Patrick's, Kiltegan,
Co Wicklow
Tel 059-6473600

Hoyne, Peter, Very Rev, PE
Newmarket, Hugginstown,
Co Kilkenny
Tel 056-7768678
(*Aghaviller*, Ossory)

Hoyne, William (OFM)
Hermanos Franciscanos,
Iglesia Parroquial 'Dios con
Nostros',
1a Av, 5a-6a Calles,
Manzana 10, Elmezquital,
Zana 12, 10102 Guatemala
City, Guatemala

Hubbart, Thomas (IC)
Cottrell Lodge,
16A Ormond Road,
Drumcondra, Dublin 9
Tel 01-8572234

Hudson, Patrick (OFM)
Gymnazium sv. Frantiska, z
Assisi v Ziline,
Vlica J.M. Hurbana 44,
01001 Ziline, Slovakia

Hughes, Augustine (OFM)
Franciscan College,
Gormanston, Co Meath
Tel 01-8412203

Hughes, Benedict
Kellystown, Coolderry Road,
Carrickmacross,
Co Monaghan
Tel 086-3864907
(Clogher)

Hughes, Bernard (IC), CC
St Brigid's, Kilcurry,
Dundalk, Co Louth
Tel 042-9334410
(*Faughart*, Armagh)

Hughes, Eoin
Chaplain,
Beaumont Hospital,
Beaumont Road, Dublin 9
Tel 01-8477573
(Dublin)

Hughes, John (OSA)
St John's Priory,
Thomas Street,
Dublin 8
Tel 01-6770393

Hughes, John, Very Rev, PC
Archibishop's House,
Drumcondra, Dublin 9
Tel 01-8373732
(Dublin)

Hughes, John, Very Rev, PE, CC
Parochial House,
Benburb Road,
Moy, Dungannon,
Co Tyrone BT71 7SQ
Tel 028-87784240
(*Moy (Clonfeacle),* Armagh)

Hughes, Liam, Very Rev, PE
Inniskeen, Dundalk,
Co Louth
Tel 042-9378338
(Clogher, retired)

Hughes, Louis (OP), Very Rev
Prior, Black Abbey,
Kilkenny, Co Kilkenny
Tel 056-21279

Hughes, M. (OMI)
St Michael's Parish,
52a Bulfin Road, Inchicore,
Dublin 8
Tel 01-4531660
(*Inchicore*, Dublin)

Hughes, Oliver, Very Rev
Canon, PP
Cummer, Tuam,
Co Galway
Tel 093-41427
(*Cummer (Kilmoylan and Cummer),* Tuam)

Hughes, P. J., CC
Mission to Equador
(Ardagh & Cl.)

Hughes, Pat, CC
St Conleth's, Chapel Lane,
Droichead Nua, Co Kildare
Tel 045-438036
(*Droichead Nua/Newbridge*, Kildare & L.)

Hughes, Patrick (CM)
St Peter's, Phibsboro,
Dublin 7
Tel 01-8389708

Hughes, Patrick, Very Rev, PP
Parochial House,
10 Cloughfin Road,
Kildress, Cookstown,
Co Tyrone BT80 9JB
Tel 028-86751206
(*Kildress*, Armagh)

Hughes, Paul (OCarm)
Whitefriar Street Church,
56 Aungier Street, Dublin 2
Tel 01-4758821

Hume, Patrick (SJ)
Campion House Residence,
28 Lower Hatch Street,
Dublin 2
Tel 01-6383990

Humphries, Seamus (OSA)
St Augustine's Priory,
Dungarvan,
Co Waterford
Tel 058-41136

Humphreys, John (SJ)
Rector, St Ignatius
Community & Church,
27 Raleigh Row, Salthill,
Galway
Tel 091-523707

Hunt, Anselm (OSB)
Abbot, Glenstal Abbey,
Murroe, Co Limerick
Tel 061-386103

Hunt, Des (SM)
Mount St Mary's, Milltown,
Dublin 14
Tel 01-2697322

Hurley, Colm, Very Rev
Canon, PP
Killeshandra, Co Cavan
Tel 049-4334155
(Kilmore)

Hurley, Declan, Very Rev, Adm
St Mary's, Navan, Co Meath
Tel 046-9027518/9027414
(*Navan*, Meath)

Hurley, James (CSSp)
Rockwell College, Cashel,
Co Tipperary
Tel 062-61444

Hurley, John
St Paul's, Bushmount,
Clonakilty, Co Cork
(Cork & R., retired)

Hurley, Michael (SJ)
Milltown Park,
Sandford Road, Dublin 6
Tel 01-2698411/2698113

Hurley, Michael C., Very Rev
Canon, PP, VF
Killeshandra, Co Cavan
Tel 049-4334155
(*Killeshandra*, Kilmore)

Hurley, Michael, Very Rev, PP
Parochial House, Old Hill,
Leixlip, Co Kildare
Tel 01-6245597
(*Leixlip*, Dublin)

Hurley, Richard, Very Rev, PP
South Presbytery,
Dunbar Street, Cork
Tel 021-4272989
(*St Finbarr's South*, Cork & R.)

Hurley, Thomas, Very Rev
Templeglantine,
Co Limerick
Tel 068-84021
(Limerick, retired)

Hussey, Michael, Very Rev, PP
St Michael's, Ballinskelligs,
Co Kerry
Tel 066-9479108
(*Ballinskelligs*, Kerry)

Hutchinson, Stephen (OP), Very Rev
Prior, Newbridge College,
Droichead Nua, Co Kildare
Tel 045-487200

Hutton, John, Very Rev
Apt 2, Ceara Court,
Windsor Avenue,
Belfast BT9 6EJ
Tel 028-90683002
(Down & C., retired)

Hyde, Jeremiah, Very Rev
The Presbytery, Kinsale,
Co Cork
(Cork & R., retired)

Hyland, James (OMI)
Oblate House of Retreat,
Inchicore, Dublin 8
Tel 01-4534408/4541805

Hyland, Paddy (SPS)
St Patrick's, Kiltegan,
Co Wicklow
Tel 059-6473600

Hyland, Richard, Very Rev, PP
42 Strand Street, Skerries,
Co Dublin
Tel 01-8491250
(*Skerries*, Dublin)

Hynes, James (OFM)
98 Bld de Montpernasse,
95014 Paris, France

Hynes, Sean (OMI)
170 Merrion Road,
Ballsbridge, Dublin 4
Tel 01-2693658

I

Imholte, Otto (SSC)
St Columban's, Dalgan Park,
Navan, Co Meath
Tel 046-9021525

Ingoldsby, Thomas (SDB)
Salesian College,
Pallaskenry, Co Limerick
Tel 061-393313

In-young Cho, Albert (SJ)
John Sullivan House
56/56A Mulvey Park,
Dundrum, Dublin 14
Tel 01-2983978

Irwin, Charles, Very Rev, BD, HDE
President,
St Munchin's College,
Corbally, Limerick
Tel 061-348922
(Limerick)

Irwin, Edwin, Very Rev, PP
St Patrick's, Dublin Road,
Limerick
Tel 061-415397/087-2547707
(*St Patrick's*, Limerick)

Irwin, John
Chaplain, Nazareth House,
Bishop Street,
Derry BT48 6UN
Tel 028-71261425
(Derry)

Irwin, Michael (SAC)
Provincial House,
'Homestead',
Sandyford Road, Dundrum,
Dublin 16
Tel 01-2956180/2954170

Irwin, Michael (SSC)
(*priest in residence*)
Kilcornan, Co Limerick
Tel 061-393113
(*Kilcornan*, Limerick)

Irwin, Nicholas J., CC
Diocesan Secretary/
Chancellor,
Archbishop's House,
Thurles, Co Tipperary
Tel 0504-21512
Parish
Borrisoleigh, Thurles,
Co Tipperary
Tel 0504-51230
(Cashel & E.)

Issac, Sunil (SCJ)
Sacred Heart Fathers,
Fairfield, 66 Inchicore Road,
Dublin 8
Tel 01-4538655

Iwueke, Lazarus (CM)
St Peter's, Phibsboro,
Dublin 7
Tel 01-8389708

Iwuozor, Gregory (CSSp)
Holy Ghost Missionary
College, Kimmage Manor,
Dublin 12
Tel 01-4064300

J

Jackson, Piaras (SJ)
Minister,
Jesuit Curia Community,
33 Sandford Road,
Ranelagh, Dublin 6
Tel 01-4988004/5

Jacob, John, Very Rev, Adm
12 Walkinstown Road,
Dublin 12
Tel 01-4502541
(*Walkinstown*, Dublin)

Januszewski, Rafal
2 Gortaugher, Lisnakelly,
Buncrana, Co Donegal
Tel 074-9363455
(Derry)

Jenkinson, William (CSSp)
Spiritan House,
213 North Circular Road,
Dublin 7
Tel 01-8389664/8683504

Jennings, E. Norman (SSC)
CPE, Mater Hospital,
Dublin

Jennings, Gavan
Harvieston,
Cunningham Road, Dalkey,
Co Dublin
Tel 01-2859877
(Opus Dei)

Jennings, Gerard
Chaplain, Daughters of Our
Lady of the Sacred Heart
Convent, Ballybay,
Co Monaghan
Tel 042-9741524
(Clogher)

Jennings, Gerard, Very Rev, PP
Salthill, Galway
Tel 091-523413
(Salthill, Galway)

Jennings, Joseph (SM), CC
Inishere, Aran Islands,
Co Galway
Tel 099-75003
(Aran Islands, Tuam)

Jennings, Martin, Very Rev, PP
Curry, Ballymote, Co Sligo
Tel 094-9254508
(Curry, Achonry)

Jennings, Norman (SSC)
St Columban's, Dalgan Park,
Navan, Co Meath
Tel 046-9021525

Jennings, Patrick (SMA)
African Missions,
Blackrock Road, Cork
Tel 021-4292871

Johnston, Andrew, Very Rev
Canon
C/o Sonas Care Centre,
Cloghanboy
Ballymahon Road, Athlone,
Co Westmeath
(Achonry, retired)

Johnston, Anthony, CC
8 Corrig Park, Dun
Laoghaire, Co Dublin
Tel 01-2805594
(Dublin)

Johnston, Jim (SM)
Cerdon, Marist Fathers,
St Mary's Road, Dundalk,
Co Louth
Tel 042-9334019

Johnston, Sean (CM)
St Paul's College, Raheny,
Dublin 5
Tel 01-8318113

Johnston, Thomas, Very Rev
Mgr, PP
Pastoral Centre,
Charlestown, Co Mayo
Tel 094-9254315
(Achonry)

Jones, Aidan G., Very Rev, PP
Bunclody, Enniscorthy,
Co Wexford
Tel 053-9377319
(Ferns)

Jones, Bernard (OFM)
Chaplain, WRH, Franciscan
Friary, Clonmel,
Co Tipperary
Tel 052-6121378

Jones, Christopher, Most Rev,
DD
Bishop of Elphin,
St Mary's, Sligo
Tel 071-9162670/9162769
(Elphin)

Jones, Joe
30 Willow Park Crescent,
Glasnevin, Dublin 11
(Dublin)

Jones, John, Very Rev, PP
Mountshannon, Co Clare
Tel 061-927213/086-1933479
(Mountshannon, Killaloe)

Jones, John, Very Rev, PP
Parochial House,
Blanchardstown, Dublin 15
Tel 01-8213660
(Blanchardstown, Dublin)

Jones, Joseph (MHM)
St Joseph's House,
50 Orwell Park, Rathgar,
Dublin 6
Tel 01-4127700

Jones, Patrick
Director, National Centre
for Liturgy,
St Patrick's College,
Maynooth, Co Kildare
Tel 01-7083478
(Dublin)

Jordan, Cathal, Very Rev
Canon, PP
6 Derrymacash Road,
Lurgan,
Co Armagh BT66 6LG
Tel 028-38341356
(Seagoe (Derrymacash),
Dromore)

Jordan, John, Very Rev, PP
Oulart, Gorey, Co Wexford
Tel 053-9136139
(Oulart, Ferns)

Jordan, Liam, Very Rev
C/o Bishop's House,
Co Wexford
(Ferns, retired)

Jordan, Michael, CC
St Joseph's, Carrickmacross,
Co Monaghan
Tel 042-9661231
(Clogher)

Jordan, Thomas (OP)
St Saviour's,
Upper Dorset Street,
Dublin 1
Tel 01-8897610

Joyce, Michael (SVD)
Donamon Castle,
Roscommon
Tel 090-6662222

Joyce, Michael, Very Rev
Canon
Bohola, Claremorris,
Co Mayo
Tel 094-9384115
(Achonry)

Joyce, Peter, CC
Maree, Oranmore,
Co Galway
Tel 091-794113
(Oranmore, Galway)

Joyce, Stephen
Kilnaclay, Threemilehouse,
Co Monaghan
Tel 047-57867
(Clogher)

Judge, Francis, Very Rev, PP,
VF
Belmullet, Co Mayo
Tel 097-81426
(Belmullet, Killala)

Judge, John, Very Rev, PP
Templeboy, Co Sligo
Tel 096-47103
(Templeboy, Killala)

Justice, Cornelius (OCSO)
Mount Melleray Abbey,
Cappoquin, Co Waterford
Tel 058-54404

K

Kakkadampallil, Vincent
Xavier (MI)
Chaplian, Mater Hospital
Eccles Street, Dublin 7
Tel 01-8301122
(Dublin)

Kane, Andrew (OP)
St Dominic's, Athy,
Co Kildare
Tel 0507-31573

Kane, Gerry, Very Rev, PP
213B Harold's Cross Road,
Dublin 6W
Tel 086-8220956
(Harold's Cross, Dublin)

Kane, Michael (CSSp)
Holy Ghost Missionary
College, Kimmage Manor,
Dublin 12
Tel 01-4064300

Kane, Michael (SPS)
St Patrick's, Kiltegan,
Co Wicklow
Tel 059-6473600

Kavanagh, Aidan, Very Rev,
PP
Bree, Enniscorthy,
Co Wexford
Tel 053-9247843
(Bree, Ferns)

Kavanagh, Brian, CC
15 Lowtown Manor,
Robertstown, Naas,
Co Kildare
Tel 045-890559
(Allen, Kildare & L.)

Kavanagh, Dermot (CSSp)
Ballybeg, Rathnew,
Co Wicklow
Tel 0404-69774

Kavanagh, Edward, CC
Mountmellick, Co Laois
Tel 057-8679302
(Mountmellick, Kildare & L.)

Kavanagh, Hugh, Very Rev, PP
No 1 Presbytery,
Brookfield Road, Tallaght,
Dublin 24
Tel 01-4525370
(Brookfield, Dublin)

Kavanagh, Joseph (OP)
St Mary's Priory, Tallaght,
Dublin 24
Tel 01-4048100

Kavanagh, Joseph, Very Rev,
PP
Camolin, Co Wexford
Tel 053-9383136
(Camolin, Ferns)

Kavanagh, Mark (SSC)
St Columban's Retirement
Home, Dalgan Park, Navan,
Co Meath
Tel 046-9021525

Kavanagh, Martin (SMA)
African Missions,
Blackrock Road, Cork
Tel 021-4292871

Kavanagh, Myles (CP), CC
St Gabriel's Retreat,
The Graan, Enniskillen,
Co Fermanagh
Tel 028-66322272

Kavanagh, Vincent (CSsR)
St Patrick's, Esker, Athenry,
Co Galway
Tel 091-844549

Kealy, John (OFM)
Franciscan Abbey,
Multyfarnham,
Co Westmeath
Tel 044-9371114/9371137

Keane, Brendan (CSsR)
Clonard Monastery,
1 Clonard Gardens,
Belfast, BT13 2RL
Tel 028-90445950

Keane, Jerry, CC
Kenmare, Co Kerry
Tel 064-6641352
(Kenmare, Kerry)

Keane, John
c/o Cloyne Diocesan Centre,
Cobh, Co Cork
Tel 021-4811430
(Cloyne)

Keane, John D., Very Rev
St Brigid's, Ballybane,
Galway
Tel 091-755381
(*Ballybane,* Galway)

Keane, Martin
Chaplain, Brothers of
Charity, Kilcornan,
Clarinbridge, Co Galway
Tel 091-796106
(Galway)

Keane, Matthew, Very Rev
Canon
Ashborough Lodge, Lyre,
Milltown, Co Kerry
(Kerry, retired)

Keane, Michael
Claremount Nursing Home,
Claremorris, Co Mayo
(Tuam)

Keane, Paul
Ballycrodick, Dunhill,
Co Waterford
(Tuam, retired)

Keane, Richard, CC
Gortboy, Newcastle West,
Co Limerick
Tel 069-77090/087-9552729
(*Newcastle West,* Limerick)

Keane, Stephen, PE
7 Garrai Sheann, Roscam,
Galway
Tel 091-767528
(Galway, retired)

Keaney, Charles, PP
Chapelfield,
59 Laurel Hill, Coleraine,
Co Derry BT51 3AY
Tel 028-70343130
(*Coleraine,* Derry)

Kearney, Brendan (SJ)
St Francis Xavier's, Upper
Gardiner Street, Dublin 1
Tel 01-8363411

Kearney, Derek (SMA)
Anglophone Secretary,
Generalate,
Via della Nocetta 111,
00164 Rome, Italy
Tel 06-6616841

Kearney, Francis, Very Rev, PP
17 Monteith Road,
Annaclone, Banbridge,
Co Down BT32 5AQ
Tel 028-40671201
(*Annaclone,* Dromore)

Kearney, James (SM)
Cerdon, Marist Fathers,
St Mary's Road, Dundalk,
Co Louth
Tel 042-9334019

Kearney, John, Very Rev
Canon, Adm, VF
Riverfields, Warrenpoint,
Co Down, BT34 3PU
Tel 028-41754684
(*Clonallon, St Peter's
(Warrenpoint),* Dromore)

Kearney, Laurence (SPS)
Derrada, Ballinamore,
Co Leitrim
Tel 071-9644067
(Kilmore, retired)

Kearney, Patrick, Very Rev, PP
Parochial House, Longwood,
Co Meath
Tel 046-9555009
(*Longwood,* Meath)

Kearney, Stephen, PP
41 Moyle Road,
Newtownstewart,
Co Tyrone BT78 4AP
Tel 028-81661445
(*Newtownstewart,* Derry)

Kearney, Thomas (SMA) CC
Keel, Achill, Co Mayo
Tel 098-43123
(*Achill,* Tuam)

Kearney, Thomas, CC
137 Shantalla Road,
Whitehall, Dublin 9
Tel 01-8420260
(*Larkhill-Whitehall-Santry,*
Dublin)

Kearns, Brendan, CC
14 Great George's Street,
Warrenpoint,
Co Down BT34 3PU
Tel 028-4177220
(*Clonallon, St Peter's
(Warrenpoint),* Dromore)

Kearns, Gerard M.
Director, Kilmore Diocesan
Pastoral Centre, Cullies,
Cavan
Tel 049-4375004
(Kilmore)

Kearns, Gerard, CC
Redhills, Co Cavan
Tel 047-55021
(*Belturbet,* Kilmore)

Kearns, John (SPS)
On temporary diocesan
work

Kearns, John, CC
Priests' House, Clones,
Co Monaghan
Tel/Fax 047-51064
(*Clones,* Clogher)

Kearny, Nicholas (OSA)
St John's Priory,
Thomas Street,
Dublin 8
Tel 01-6770393

Keary, Patrick, Very Rev, PP,
VF
Horseleap, Co Offaly
Tel 057-9335922
(Meath)

Keating, Andy (SPS)
St Patrick's, Kiltegan,
Co Wicklow
Tel 059-6473600

Keating, Augustine, Very Rev,
PP
Rossmore, Clonakilty,
Co Cork
Tel 023-8838630
(*Kilmeen and Castleventry,*
Cork & R.)

Keating, Crispin (OFM)
5225 North Himes Avenue,
Tampa, Fl 33614-6623, USA

Keating, David
Chaplain, Waterford
Institute of Technology,
10 Claremont, Cork Road,
Waterford
Tel 051-378878
(Waterford & L.)

Keating, Denis (OP)
St Dominic's Retreat House,
Montenotte, Co Cork
Tel 021-4502520

Keating, John, Very Rev, PP
Raheenagh, Ballagh,
Co Limerick
Tel 069-85014
(*Killeedy,* Limerick)

Keating, Patrick, Very Rev, PP
Ovens, Co Cork
Tel 021-4871180
(*Ovens,* Cork & R.)

Keaveny, Michael, CC
53 Brisland Road, Eglinton,
Co Derry BT47 3EA
Tel 028-71810234
(*Faughanvale,* Derry)

Keegan, John, Very Rev, PP
Parochial House, Rolestown,
Swords, Co Dublin
Tel 01-8401514
(*Rolestown-Oldtown,*
Dublin)

Keenan, Aidan, Very Rev, PP
St Matthew's Presbytery,
Bryson Street,
Newtownards Road, Belfast
BT5 4ES
Tel 028-90457626
(*Portglenone,* Down & C.)

Keenan, Brian (SM)
CUS Community, 89 Lower
Leeson Street, Dublin 2
Tel 01-6762586

Keenan, Frank (SJ)
St Francis Xavier's,
Upper Gardiner Street,
Dublin 1
Tel 01-8363411

Keenan, Kevin (SVD)
26 Cloonarkin Drive,
Oranmore, Co Galway
Tel 087-9905755
(*St John the Apostle,*
Galway)

Keenan, Kevin (SVD)
Donamon Castle,
Roscommon
Tel 090-6662222

Keenan, Pádraig, Very Rev,
Adm
Ard Easmuinn, Dundalk,
Co Louth
Tel 042-9334259
(*Dundalk, Holy Redeemer,*
Armagh)

Keenan, Patrick (OCD), CC
The Presbytery,
Berkeley Road, Dublin 7
Tel 01-8306356/8306336
(*Berkeley Road,* Dublin)

Keeney, Sean (CSsR)
Clonard Monastery,
1 Clonard Gardens,
Belfast, BT13 2RL
Tel 028-90445950

Keerins, Frank (CP), Very Rev,
PP
St Paul's Retreat,
Mount Argus, Dublin 6W
Tel 01-4992000
(*Mount Argus,* Dublin)

Kehoe, James, Very Rev, PP
Carrig-on-Bannow,
Wellington Bridge,
Co Wexford
Tel 051-561192
(*Bannow,* Ferns)

Kehoe, Joseph L., Rt Rev Mgr,
PA
13 Priory CT, Spawell Road,
Wexford
Tel 053-9180599
(Ferns, retired)

Kehoe, Noel (CSsR)
Co-ordinator, Scala,
Bessboro, Blackrock, Cork
Tel 021-4358800

Kehoe, Patrick, Very Rev, CC
Abbeyleix, Co Laois
Tel 057-8731181
(*Abbeyleix,* Kildare & L.)

Kehoe, Peter, (OCarm), Very
Rev, PP
Ballyhale, Co Kilkenny
Tel 056-7768686/086-
8252093
(Ballyhale, Ossory)

Kehoe, Philip (FDP)
Regional Superior,
c/o Don Orione 8, Rome,
Italy

Kehoe, Tomás
New Ross, Co Wexford
Tel 051-421214
(*New Ross,* Ferns)

Keleghan, Anselm (CP)
St Paul's Retreat,
Mount Argus, Dublin 6W
Tel 01-4992000

Kelleher, Cornelius, Very Rev,
PP
Tournaneena, Ballinamult,
Clonmel, Co Tipperary
Tel 058-47138
(*Touraneena,* Waterford &
L.)

Allianz (�)

Kelleher, Denis, Very Rev, PP
Church Road, Aghada,
Co Cork
Tel 021-4661298
(*Aghada*, Cloyne)

Kelleher, Eamonn, CC
Midleton, Co Cork
Tel 021-4631094
(*Midleton*, Cloyne)

Kelleher, Finbar, Very Rev
Canon, CC (pro tem)
Ballindangan, Mitchelstown,
Co Cork
Tel 025-85563
(*Glanworth and
Ballindangan*, Cloyne)

Kelleher, Francis
Chaplain,
Cork South Infirmary,
Old Blackroad, Cork
Tel 021-4966555
(Cork & R.)

Kelleher, Francis, Very Rev, PP
Knocktemple, Virginia,
Co Cavan
Tel 049-8547435
(*Castlerahan and
Munterconnaught*, Kilmore)

Kelleher, Liam, Very Rev, PP
Grenagh, Co Cork
Tel 021-4886128
(*Grenagh*, Cloyne)

Kelleher, Maurice (SMA)
Dromantine College,
Dromantine, Newry,
Co Down BT34 1RH
Tel 028-30821224

Kelleher, Michael G. (CSsR)
Provincial, Liguori House,
75 Orwell Road, Dublin 6
Tel 01-4067100

Kelleher, Michael, Very Rev,
PP
1 The Presbytery,
Holy Cross Church,
Mahon, Cork
Tel 021-4357394
(*Mahon*, Cork & R.)

Kelleher, Roger, Very Rev
9 Emmet's Terrace,
Killarney, Co Kerry
(Kerry, retired)

Kelleher, Thomas, Very Rev
Canon, PP
Ballinspittle, Co Cork
Tel 021-4778055
(*Courceys*, Cork & R.)

Kelleher, Tony, Very Rev, PP
Cloncagh, Ballingarry,
Co Limerick
Tel 069-83006
(*Knockaderry*, Limerick)

Kelliher, Padraig, CC
The Presbytery, Longford
Tel 043-3346432
(*Longford*, Ardagh & Cl.)

Kelly Jnr, Patrick (CSsR)
Marianella, 75 Orwell Road,
Dublin 6
Tel 01-4067100

Kelly Snr, Patrick (CSsR)
St Joseph's, Dundalk,
Co Louth
Tel 042-9334042/9334762

Kelly, Anthony (SSC)
St Columban's, Dalgan Park,
Navan, Co Meath
Tel 046-9021525

Kelly, Brendan, Most Rev, DD
Bishop of Achonry,
Bishop's House,
Edmondstown,
Ballaghaderreen,
Co Roscommon
Tel 094-9860021
(Achonry)

Kelly, Celsus (OCSO), Rt Rev
Dom
Abbot, Our Lady of
Bethlehem Abbey,
11 Ballymena Road,
Portglenone, Ballymena,
Co Antrim BT44 8BL
Tel 028-25821211

Kelly, Charles
Lurgan, Co Armagh
(Dromore, retired)

Kelly, Conor, Very Rev, PP
Ring, Dungarvan,
Co Waterford
Tel 058-46125
(*Ring*, Waterford & L.)

David, Kelly (OSA)
St Augustine's,
Taylor's Lane,
Balyboden, Dublin 16
Tel 01-4241000

Kelly, Declan, Adm
Killoran, Ballinasloe,
Co Galway
Tel 090-9627120
(*Kilmeen*, Tuam)

Kelly, Declan, Adm
St Andrew's Church, Leitrim,
Loughrea, Co Galway
Tel 091-841758
(Clonfert)

Kelly, Declan, Very Rev, PP
Preston Hill, Stamullen,
Co Meath
Tel 01-8418066
(*Stamullen*, Meath)

Kelly, Denis, Very Rev, Adm
St Aidan's, Enniscorthy,
Co Wexford
Tel 053-9235777
(*Enniscorthy, Cathedral of St
Aidan*, Ferns)

Kelly, Dermot (OCarm)
Gort Muire, Ballinteer,
Dublin 16
Tel 01-2984014

Kelly, Desmond (OCarm), CC
Carmelite Priory,
56 Aungier Street,
Dublin 2
Tel 01-4758821
(*Whitefriar Street*, Dublin)

Kelly, Desmond, Very Rev, PP
Corballa, Ballina,
Co Mayo
Tel 096-36266
(*Castleconnor*, Killala)

Kelly, Donal, Very Rev
7 Knocksinna Park,
Bray Road, Foxrock,
Dublin 18
Tel 01-2894170
(Down & C., retired)

Kelly, Eamonn (SMA)
Retired in Ireland outside
SMA houses

Kelly, Eamonn, Very Rev, Adm
Parochial House,
Letterkenny, Co Donegal
Tel 074-9121021
Chaplain, Errigal College,
Letterkenny, Co Donegal
Tel 074-9121047/9121861
(*Letterkenny*, Raphoe)

Kelly, Edward, Very Rev
Canon, PE
'Inchagill'
Ballinamana Road,
Clarinbridge, Co Galway
Tel 091-796095
(Galway, retired)

Kelly, Edward, Very Rev, PE
Rhode, Co Offaly
Tel 046-9737013
(Kildare & L., retired)

Kelly, Felim, Very Rev, CC
Castlerahan, Ballyjamesduff,
Co Cavan
Tel 049-8544150
(*Castlerahan and
Munterconnaught*, Kilmore)

Kelly, Finbar (OP)
Black Abbey, Kilkenny,
Co Kilkenny
Tel 056-21279

Kelly, Gabriel
Kinawley, Enniskillen,
Co Fermanagh
Tel 028-66348250
(Kilmore)

Kelly, Gilbert
Ballycarron House, Golden,
Co Tipperary
(Dublin, retired)

Kelly, James (SJ)
Milltown Park,
Sandford Road, Dublin 6
Tel 01-2698411/2698113

Kelly, James J., Very Rev, PE
Parochial House,
Clogher Road, Dublin 12
(Dublin, retired)

Kelly, James, Canon, AP
Tooreen, Ballyhaunis,
Co Mayo
Tel 094-9649002
(*Aghamore*, Tuam)

Kelly, Jimmy (OSM)
Servite Priory, St Peregrine,
Kiltipper Road, Tallaght,
Dublin 24
Tel 01-4517115

Kelly, Jimmy, Very Rev, PP
Raheen, Abbeyleix,
Co Laois
Tel 057-8731182
(*Raheen*, Kildare & L.)

Kelly, Joe, CC
5 Bayside Square East,
Sutton, Dublin 13
Tel 01-8322305
(*Bayside*, Dublin)

Kelly, John (SAC)
Rector, Provincial House,
'Homestead',
Sandyford Road, Dundrum,
Dublin 16
Tel 01-2956180/2954170

Kelly, John (SCJ)
Superior & Formation
Director,
Sacred Heart Fathers,
Fairfield, 66 Inchicore Road,
Dublin 8
Tel 01-4538655

Kelly, John
Chaplian, Adelaide and
Meath Hospital, Tallaght,
Dublin 24
Tel 01-4142000/4142480
(Dublin)

Kelly, John, Very Rev, PP
Labasheeda, Co Clare
Tel 065-6830126/
087-2439273
(*Kilmurry McMahon*,
Killaloe)

Kelly, Larry, Very Rev Canon,
PP
Rathmore, Co Kerry
Tel 064-58026
(*Rathmore*, Kerry)

Kelly, Lawrence, Very Rev
'Sunville', Kilgarvan,
Co Kerry
(Kerry, retired)

Kelly, Liam (OFM)
Franciscan Friary, Ennis,
Co Clare
Tel 065-6828751

Kelly, Liam, Very Rev, PP
Crosskeys, Co Cavan
Tel 049-4336102
(*Denn*, Kilmore)

Kelly, Martin J. (CSSp)
Holy Ghost Missionary
College, Kimmage Manor,
Dublin 12
Tel 01-4064300

Kelly, Martin, Very Rev, PP
Parochial House, 546
Saintfield Road,
Carryduff, Belfast BT8 8EU
Tel 028-90812238
(*Drumbo*, Down & C.)

Kelly, Matthew, Very Rev, PE,
CC
60 Hartwell Green, Kill,
Naas, Co Kildare
Tel 045-877880
(*Kill*, Kildare & L.)

Kelly, Michael
Rathvilly, Co Carlow
Tel 059-9161114
(*Rathvilly*, Kildare & L.)

Kelly, Michael (SPS)
On temporary diocesan
work

Kelly, Michael J., Very Rev
Canon
Church Street, Ballinamore,
Co Leitrim
Tel 071-9644580
(Kilmore, retired)

Kelly, Michael, Rt Rev Dean
St Catherine's Nursing
Home, Newcastle West,
Co Limerick
(Limerick, retired)

Kelly, Michael, Very Rev
Canon, PP, VF
Craughwell, Co Galway
Tel 091-846057
(*Craughwell*, Galway)

Kelly, Michael, Co-PP
94 Old County Road,
Crumlin Dublin 12
Tel 01-4542308
(*Crumlin*, Dublin)

Kelly, Oliver, Very Rev, PP, VF
Manorhamilton, Co Leitrim
Tel 071-9855042
(*Manorhamilton*, Kilmore)

Kelly, Patrick (MSC)
'Croí Nua', Rosary Lane,
Taylor's Hill, Galway
Tel 091-520960

Kelly, Patrick (SJ)
Milltown Park,
Sandford Road, Dublin 6
Tel 01-2698411/2698113

Kelly, Patrick (SMA)
Seconded to US Province

Kelly, Patrick (SPS)
Tearmann Spirituality
Centre, Brockagh,
Glendalough, Co Wicklow
Tel 0404-45208

Kelly, Patrick J. (CSSp)
St Mary's College,
Rathmines, Dublin 6
Tel 01-4062160

Kelly, Patrick, Very Rev
Canon, PE
Athea, Co Limerick
Tel 068-42107
(*Athea*, Limerick)

Kelly, Paul, Very Rev, PP
Parochial House,
Roundwood, Co Wicklow
Tel 01-2818149
(*Roundwood*, Dublin)

Kelly, Ray, Very Rev, PP
Parochial House, Oldcastle,
Co Meath
Tel 049-8541142
(*Oldcastle*, Meath)

Kelly, Richard (OFM)
Vicar, Franciscan Abbey,
Multyfarnham,
Co Westmeath
Tel 044-9371114/9371137

Kelly, Richard (SVD)
Donamon Castle,
Roscommon
Tel 090-6662222

Kelly, Richard, Very Rev, PP
Kilbehenny, Mitchelstown,
Co Cork
Tel 025-24040
(*Kilbehenny*, Cashel & E.)

Kelly, Robert (OCSO)
Mount Saint Joseph Abbey,
Roscrea, Co Tipperary
Tel 0505-25600

Kelly, Robert (SM), CC
The Presbytery,
Donore Avenue, Dublin 8
Tel 01-4542425
(*Donore Avenue*, Dublin)

Kelly, Seamus, Very Rev, PP,
VF
23 Thornhill Park, Culmore,
Derry BT48 4PB
Tel 028-71358519
(Derry)

Kelly, Sean (OFMCap)
Capuchin Friary,
Church Street, Dublin 7
Tel 01-8730599

Kelly, Seán, Very Rev, PE, CC
Stradbally, Co Laois
Tel 057-8625831
(*Stradbally*, Kildare & L.)

Kelly, Terence, Very Rev, PE
3 Cranagh, Ballinderry
Bridge Road, Coagh,
Cookstown,
Co Tyrone BT80 0AS
(Armagh, retired)

Kelly, Thomas V., Very Rev
Castlebar Road, Westport,
Co Mayo
(Dublin, retired)

Kelly, Vincent (SAC)
(Attached to Pallotine
College)
18 Silvercourt,
Silversprings, Cork

Kemmy, Bill
(in residence)
Arles, Ballickmoyler,
Carlow
Tel 059-9147637
(*Arles*, Kildare & L.)

Kemmy, Philip, CC
Parochial House,
Letterkenny, Co Donegal
Tel 074-9121021
(*Letterkenny*, Raphoe)

Kenneally, Daithi (CSSp), Very
Rev, PP
St Ronan's Presbytery,
Deansrath, Clondalkin,
Dublin 22
Tel 01-4570380
(*Deansrath*, Dublin)

Kenneally, David (SSC)
Regional Bursar
St Columban's, Dalgan Park,
Navan, Co Meath
Tel 046-9021525

Kennedy, Abe
St Molaise's, Portumna,
Co Galway
Tel 090-9741188
(Clonfert)

Kennedy, Bernard, MA, MSc,
Adm
67 Edenvale Road, Dublin 6
Tel 01-4972165
(*Beechwood Avenue*,
Dublin)

Kennedy, David, Very Rev
Clonlusk Doon, Co Limerick
(Limerick, retired)

Kennedy, Denis, (CSSp), CC
St Joseph's Presbytery,
Glasthule, Co Dublin
Tel 01-2800403
(*Glasthule*, Dublin)

Kennedy, Edmund, Very Rev,
AP
Newtown, Nenagh,
Co Tipperary
Tel 067-23103
(*Youghalarra*, Killaloe)

Kennedy, Eugene
7 Riverwood Vale,
Carpenterstown,
Castleknock, Dublin 15
(Dublin, retired)

Kennedy, Gerald (SVD)
133 North Circular Road,
Dublin 7
Tel 01-8386743

Kennedy, Hugh, Very Rev,
Adm
St Peter's Square,
Belfast BT12 4BU
Tel 028-90327573
(*The Cathedral (St Peter's)*,
Down & C.)

Kennedy, Ian, Very Rev, PC
The Parochial House,
Ballinafad, Boyle,
Co Roscommon
Tel 071-9666006
(*Ballinafad*, Elphin)

Kennedy, James, CC
St Michael Street,
Tipperary Town
Tel 062-51114
(*Tipperary*, Cashel & E.)

Kennedy, Joe, Very Rev, PP
Lorrha, Nenagh,
Co Tipperary
Tel 090-9747009
(*Lorrha and Dorrha*,
Killaloe)

Kennedy, John
(Congregation for the
Doctrine of the Faith)
Via del Mascherino 12,
00193 Roma, Italy
(Dublin)

Kennedy, Joseph (CP)
St Paul's Retreat,
Mount Argus, Dublin 6W
Tel 01-4992000

Kennedy, Joseph, Very Rev, PP
Croom, Co Limerick
Tel 061-397231/087-9217622
(*Croom*, Limerick)

Kennedy, Kieron, Rt Rev Mgr
President,
St Kiernan's College,
Kilkenny
Tel 056-7721086 Ext 118
(Ossory)

Kennedy, Michael
Emmanuel House of
Providence, Clonfert,
Ballinasloe, Co Galway
Tel 057-9151552
(Clonfert)

Kennedy, Michael (CSSp)
Templeogue College,
Dublin 6W
Tel 01-4903909

Kennedy, Michael, Very Rev,
PP
Dunhill, Co Waterford
Tel 051-396109
(*Dunhill*, Waterford & L.)

Kennedy, Michael, Very Rev,
PP
Parochial House, Colligan,
Dungarvan, Co Waterford
Tel 058-41629
(*Kilgobinet*, Waterford & L.)

Kennedy, Michael, Very Rev,
PP
The Parochial House, New
Inn, Cashel, Co Tipperary
Tel 052-7462395
(Cashel & E.)

Kennedy, Noel, Very Rev, PP
Bournea, Roscrea,
Co Tipperary
Tel 0505-43211/086-3576775
(*Bournea*, Killaloe)

Kennedy, Oliver (SSC)
St Columban's, Dalgan Park,
Navan, Co Meath
Tel 046-9021525

Kennedy, Oliver P.
68 Shore Road,
Toomebridge, Co Antrim
BT41 3NW
Tel 028-79650213/79650618
(Down & C., retired)

Kennedy, Sean, CC
Emly, Co Tipperary
Tel 062-57111
(*Emly*, Cashel & E.)
Kennedy, Stephen (OFM)
Franciscan Friary,
Liberty Street, Cork
Tel 021-4270302
Kennedy, Thomas, Co-PP
14 Roselawn, Lucan,
Co Dublin
Tel 01-6280205
(*Lucan*, Dublin)
Kennedy, Vincent (OP)
St Saviour's, Glentworth
Street, Limerick
Tel 061-412333
Kennedy, William (SMA)
SMA House, Wilton, Cork
Tel 021-4541069/4541884
Kennelly, John, Very Rev
24 Ferndene, Greenville,
Listowel, Co Kerry
(Kerry, retired)
Kennelly, Pádraig, PP
Glengarriff, Co Cork
Tel 027-63045
(*Glangarriff (Bonane)*, Kerry)
Kennelly, Séamus, Very Rev,
PP
Boherbue, Mallow, Co Cork
Tel 029-76038
(*Boherbue/Kiskeam*, Kerry)
Kenny, Colm, CC
The Presbytery,
2 St Canice's Church,
Finglas, Dublin 11
Tel 01-8341051
(*Finglas*, Dublin)
Kenny, Donald, Rt Rev Mgr
Chaplain,
Community School,
Ramsgrange
Tel 051-389211
Parish
Ballykelly, New Ross,
Co Wexford
Tel 051-422729
(*Horeswood*, Ferns)
Kenny, Gerard (OMI)
Oblate House of Retreat,
Inchicore, Dublin 8
Tel 01-4534408/4541805
Kenny, Gerard
Circular Road, Kilkee,
Co Clare
Tel 065-9056580/085-
7858344
(Killaloe)
Kenny, Jim, CC
The Presbytery, 5 St Mary's
Terrace,
Arklow, Co Wicklow
Tel 0402-32483
(*Arklow,* Dublin)
Kenny, John, Very Rev, PP, VF
Dunmore, Co Galway
Tel 093-38124
(Tuam)

Kenny, Lorcan
Chaplain, Community
School, Roscrea,
Co Tipperary
Tel 0505-21454
Chaplain, The Valley,
Roscrea, Co Tipperary
Tel 0505-23637/087-6553402
(*Roscrea*, Killaloe)
Kenny, Martin, Very Rev, PP
Parochial House,
Slane Road, Mell, Drogheda,
Co Louth
Tel 041-9838278
(*Mell*, Armagh)
Kenny, Merlyn
The Presbytery, Longford
Tel 043-46465
(*Longford*, Ardagh & Cl.)
Kenny, Michael, Very Rev, PP
Kilconly, Tuam, Co Galway
Tel 093-47613
(*Kilconly and Kilbannon*,
Tuam)
Kenny, Pat, Very Rev, PP
St Killian Church, Newinn,
Ballinasloe, Co Galway
Tel 090-9675819
(*New Inn and Bullaun*,
Clonfert)
Kenny, Paul, Very Rev, PP
Parochial House,
La Touche Road,
Greystones, Co Wicklow
Tel 01-2874278
(*Greystones*, Dublin)
Kenny, Thomas (SDB)
Salesian House,
Warrenstown, Drumree,
Co Meath
Tel 01-8259894
Kenny, Tim (SM)
Fermoyle, Lanesboro,
Co Longford
Keogan, Thomas (MHM)
St Joseph's House,
50 Orwell Park, Rathgar,
Dublin 6
Tel 01-4127700
Keogan, Thomas M., Very
Rev, PP
Kinlough, Co Leitrim
Tel 071-9841428
(*Kinlough and Glenade*,
Kilmore)
Keogh, Henry, Very Rev, PE
The Presbytery, Bushypark,
Galway
Tel 091-520300
(Galway, retired)
Keogh, Joseph, Very Rev
Canon, PE
Cregclare, Ardrahan,
Co Galway
Tel 091-635940
(Galway, retired)

Keogh, Martin, Very Rev, PP
Parochial House, Newtown,
Kilmacthomas,
Co Waterford
Tel 051-294261
(*Newtown*, Waterford & L.)
Keogh, Pádraig, Very Rev, PP
Milford, Charleville,
Co Cork
Tel 063-80038
(*Milford*, Cloyne)
Keohan, Edmund
The Bungalow, Turners
Cross, Cork
Tel 021-4320592
(Cork & R., retired)
Keohane, Martin, Very Rev,
PP
Parochial House,
Enniskeane, Co Cork
Tel 023-8847769
(*Enniskeane and
Desertserges*, Cork & R.)
Keohane, Michael, PIC
St Patrick's Presbytery,
Rochestown Road, Cork
Tel 021-4892363
(*Douglas*, Cork & R.)
Kerin, John, Very Rev, PP
Tel 066-9474495
(*Waterville*, Kerry)
Kernan, Niall (SM)
Solomon Islands
Kerr, Aidan, Very Rev, PP
Parochial House,
1 The Cloney,Glenarm,
Co Antrim BT44 0AB
Tel 028-28841246
(*Glenavy and Killead*, Down
& C.)
Kerr, Peter, Very Rev, PP
Parochial House,
Ballymacnab,
Armagh BT60 2QT
Tel 028-37531641
(*Killcluney*, Armagh)
Kerr, Samuel, Very Rev
Priest-in-residence
463 Shore Road,
Whiteabbey,
Newtownabbey,
Co Antrim BT37 0AE
Tel 028-90365773
(*Whiteabbey (St James's),*
Down & C.)
Kerrane, John, Very Rev, PE
'St Martin's', Culmullen,
Drumree, Co Meath
Tel 01-8241976
(*Dunshaughlin*, Meath)
Kett, Patrick J., Very Rev
27 Huntsgrove, Ashbourne,
Co Meath
(Dublin, retired)

Keveny, Martin, Very Rev
Paroquia Sao Sebastiao,
Caixa Postal 94,
CEP 77760-000,
Colinas Do Tocantins, Brazil
Tel 63-8311427
(Killala)
Kidney, Michael (SMA)
Temporary diocesan work in
Ireland
Kiely, Bartholomew (SJ)
c/o Jesuit Provincial Curia,
IMI Centre, Sandyford Road,
Dublin 16
Tel 01-2932820
Kiely, Charles, CC
The Presbytery,
Turner's Cross, Cork
Tel 021-4313103
(*Turner's Cross*, Cork & R.)
Kiely, Eugene, Very Rev, PP
Ballyferriter West, Tralee,
Co Kerry
Tel 066-9156131
(*Ballyferriter*, Kerry)
Kiely, John, Very Rev, PP
Cappoquin, Co Waterford
Tel 058-54216
(*Cappoquin*, Waterford & L.)
Kiely, Michael (SAC)
Provincial House,
'Homestead',
Sandyford Road, Dundrum,
Dublin 16
Tel 01-2956180/2954170
Kieran, Aidan, CC
59 Auburn Road,
Dun Laoghaire, Co Dublin
Tel 01-2852509
(*Johnstown-Killiney*, Dublin)
Kiernan, Brian (OCarm)
Gort Muire, Ballinteer,
Dublin 16
Tel 01-2984014
Kiernan, John, Very Rev
Holy Trinity Abbey,
Kilnacrott, Ballyjamesduff,
Co Cavan
(Meath, retired)
Kiernan, Kevin (OFMCap)
Vicar,
Capuchin Parochial House,
Gurranabraher, Cork
Tel 021-4303655
Kiernan, Kevin, (OFMCap), CC
Ascension Presbytery,
Gurranabraher, Cork
Tel 021-4303655
(*Gurranabraher*, Cork & R.)
Kiernan, Patrick, CC
Mount Temple, Moate,
Co Westmeath
Tel 090-6481239
(*Moate and Mount Temple*,
Ardagh & Cl.)
Kiggins, Thomas (SPS)
St Patrick's, Kiltegan,
Co Wicklow
Tel 059-6473600

Kilbane, Seán (SMA), Very
Rev, AP
Clonfad, Oldtown, Athlone,
Co Roscommon
Tel 090-9673527
(*Moore*, Tuam)

Kilbride, Brian (CSSp)
Blackrock College,
Blackrock, Co Dublin
Tel 01-2888681

Kilbride, Malachy (CSSp)
Blackrock College,
Blackrock, Co Dublin
Tel 01-2888681

Kilcoyne, Brendan, Very Rev
Canon
President, St Jarlath's
College, Tuam, Co Galway
Tel 093-24248
(Tuam)

Kilcoyne, Colm, Very Rev
Canon, PE
20 Rathbawn Drive,
Castlebar, Co Mayo
(Tuam, retired)

Kilcoyne, Patrick, Very Rev
Canon, PP
Kiltimagh, Co Mayo
Tel 094-9381198
(*Kiltimagh (Killedan)*,
Achonry)

Kilcoyne, Seán
Chaplain,
Bon Secours Hospital,
Renmore, Galway
Tel 091-751534/757711
(Galway)

Kilduff, Donal, CC
Ballyjamesduff, Co Cavan
Tel 049-8544410
(*Castlerahan and
Munterconnaught*, Kilmore)

Kilkelly, Christopher
c/o Archbishop's House,
Tuam, Co Galway
(Tuam, retired)

Kilkenny, Michael (CSSp)
Kimmage Mission Institute
at Milltown,
Milltown Park, Dublin 6
Tel 01-2776300

Killeen, James
3 Cathedral Terrace, Cobh,
Co Cork
Tel 021-4813601
Pastoral Coordinator
Cloyne Diocesan Centre,
Cobh, Co Cork
Tel 021-4811430
(Cloyne)

Killeen, John D., Very Rev, PP
20 Abbey Court,
Abbey Road, Blackrock,
Co Dublin
Tel 01-2802533
(*Kill-O'-The-Grange*, Dublin)

Killeen, Sean, Rt Rev Mgr, PP,
VF
Ballycastle, Co Mayo
Tel 096-43010
(Killala)

Killian, Michael
Mulross Nursing Home,
Carrick-on-Shannon,
Co Leitrim
(Ardagh & Cl., retired)

Kilmartin, Michael, CC
Cathedral House, Mullingar,
Co Westmeath
Tel 044-9348338/9340126
(*Mullingar*, Meath)

Kilmurray, Martin (OCarm)
Provincial, Provincial Office,
Gort Muire, Ballinteer,
Dublin 16
Tel 01-2984014

Kilpatrick, Edward, PP
Orchard Park, Murlog,
Lifford, Co Donegal
Tel 074-9142022
(Derry)

Kilroy, Peter, CC
74 Iona Road, Dublin 9
Tel 01-8305698
(*Iona Road*, Dublin)

Kim, Yong-su P. (SJ)
Jesuit Curia Community,
33 Sandford Road,
Ranelagh, Dublin 6
Tel 01-4988004/5

Kinahan, Gabriel (OFM)
Guardian, The Abbey,
8 Francis Street, Galway
Tel 091-562518

King, Alexis (OFM)
Franciscan House of Studies,
Dún Mhuire, Seafield Road,
Killiney, Co Dublin
Tel 01-2826760

King, Anthony, Very Rev
Canon, PP, VF
Athenry, Co Galway
Tel 091-844076
(*Athenry*, Tuam)

King, Bernard (SM), CC
Parochial House,
Glassdrummond,
Crossmaglen, Newry,
Co Down BT35 9DY
Tel 028-30861270
(*Crossmaglen (Creggan
Upper)*, Armagh)

King, John Joe (CSSp)
Holy Ghost Missionary
College, Kimmage Manor,
Dublin 12
Tel 01-4064300

King, Jude (OSA)
Augustinian Retreat Centre,
Old Court Road,
Dublin 16
Tel 01-4930932

King, Michael, Very Rev, PP
Newtownbutler, Enniskillen,
Co Fermanagh BT92 8JJ
Tel 028-67738229
(*Newtownbutler*, Clogher)

King, William, PP
23 Clare Road, Drumcondra,
Dublin 9
Tel 01-8378552
(*Drumcondra*, Dublin)

Kingston, John, Very Rev, PP
Innishannon, Co Cork
Tel 021-4775348
(*Innishannon*, Cork & R.)

Kingston, William (CSSp)
Rockwell College, Cashel,
Co Tipperary
Tel 062-61444

Kinsella, Nivard (OCSO)
Mount Saint Joseph Abbey,
Roscrea, Co Tipperary
Tel 0505-25600

Kinsella, Tobias, Very Rev, PP
Oylegate, Co Wexford
Tel 053-9138163
(*Oylegate*, Ferns)

Kirby, Brendan, Very Rev
Canon
9 Kilmartin Hill, Wicklow,
Co Wicklow
(Ferns, retired)

Kirby, John, Most Rev, DD
Bishop of Clonfert,
Coorheen, Loughrea,
Co Galway
Tel 091-841560
(Clonfert)

Kirstein, James (SMA)
African Missions,
Blackrock Road, Cork
Tel 021-4292871

Kirwan, Joseph (OSA)
St John's Priory,
Thomas Street,
Dublin 8
Tel 01-6770393

Kirwan, Noel, Very Rev
Limerick Diocesan Pastoral
Centre,
St Michael's Courtyard,
Denmark Street, Limerick
Tel 061-400133/087-2616843
(Limerick)

Kitching, Ciaran, Very Rev, PP
Killimor, Ballinasloe,
Co Galway
Tel 090-9676151
(Clonfert)

Kitt, Liam, Very Rev
Cleveland, Ohio
(Tuam)

Knight, Matthew J. (CSSp)
Rockwell College, Cashel,
Co Tipperary
Tel 062-61444

Knowles, Desmond, Very Rev
Canon
Newry, Co Down
(Dromore, retired)

Kom, Francis (SVD)
Maynooth, Co Kildare
Tel 01-6286391/2

Kosciolek, Marek
(Polish Chaplaincy)
St Mary's, Athlone,
Co Westmeath
Tel 090-6472088
(Athlone, Ardagh & Cl.)

Kosciolek, Marek (SVD)
Donamon Castle,
Roscommon
Tel 090-6662222

Kowalski, Stanislaw (SCHR) CC
Parochial House,
6 Circular Road,
Dungannon,
Co Tyrone BT71 6BE
Tel 028-87722631
(Armagh)

Kowalski, Wojciech (SJ)
Jesuit Community, 27
Leinster Road, Rathmines,
Dublin 6
Tel 01-4970250

Koxaczkowski, Andrzej, (SCHR)
27 Glenveagh Drive,
Belfast BT11 9HX
Tel 028-90615702
(*St Oliver Plunkett*, Down &
C.)

Krawiec, Jaroslaw (OP)
St Saviour's,
Upper Dorset Street,
Dublin 1
Tel 01-8897610

Kupczakiewicz, Krzysztof (OP)
Holy Cross, Tralee, Co Kerry
Tel 066-21135/29185

Kuthanapillil, Jaison (OCarm)
Carmelite Priory, Moate,
Co Westmeath
Tel 090-6481160/6481398

Kyne, Brendan, Very Rev, PP
Castleconnell, Co Limerick
Tel 061-377170
(*Castleconnell*, Killaloe)

Kyne, Thomas, Very Rev Dean,
AP
Réalt na Mara, Furbo,
Co Galway
Tel 091-592457
(*Barna*, Galway)

Kyne, Val (SSC), PP
The Presbytery, St Joseph's,
Balcurris, Ballymun, Dublin 11
Tel 01-8423865
(*Balcurris*, Dublin)

L

Lacey, Liam, Very Rev, PP
6 Allen Park Road,
Stillorgan, Co Dublin
Tel 01-2880545
(*Kilmacud-Stillorgan*,
Dublin)

Laffan, Sean, Very Rev, CC
Gusserane, Co Wexford
Tel 051-562111
(*Ballycullane*, Ferns)

Lafferty, Angelo (SMA)
African Missions,
Blackrock Road, Cork
Tel 021-4292871

Lagan, Francis, Most Rev, DD
Titular Bishop of Sidnacestre
and Auxiliary Bishop of
Derry, 9 Glen Road, Strabane,
Co Tyrone BT82 8BX
Tel 028-71884533
(Derry)

Lagan, Hugh (SMA)
Further studies, Maryland,
USA

Laheen, Kevin (SJ)
35 Lower Leeson Street,
Dublin 2
Tel 01-6761248

Laizer, John (CSSp)
Holy Ghost Missionary
College, Kimmage Manor,
Dublin 12
Tel 01-4064300

Lally, Fredrick (OCarm)
Bursar, Carmelite Priory,
White Abbey, Co Kildare
Tel 045-521391

Lalor, John, Very Rev, PP
Camross, Portlaoise,
Co Laois
Tel 0502-35122/087-6888711
(*Camross*, Ossory)

Lalor, Tom, Very Rev, PP
Leighlinbridge, Co Carlow
Tel 059-9721463
(Kildare & L.)

Lambe, Jeremiah (CSSp)
Holy Ghost Missionary
College, Kimmage Manor,
Dublin 12
Tel 01-4064300

Lambe, Michael, Very Rev, PE
The Bungalow Presbytery,
St Mary's Church Grounds,
Lucan
Tel 01-6280954
(*Lucan*, Dublin)

Lambe, Tony (SM)
Mount St Mary's, Milltown,
Dublin 14
Tel 01-2697322

Lambe, Tony, Very Rev, PP
Drangan, Thurles,
Co Tipperary
Tel 052-52103

Lambert, Owen (CSSp)
Holy Ghost Missionary
College, Kimmage Manor,
Dublin 12
Tel 01-4064300

Lane, Daniel, Very Rev, PP
Ballingarry, Co Limerick
Tel 069-68141/087-2533030
(*Ballingarry and Granagh*,
Limerick)

Lane, Dermot A., Very Rev, PP
162 Sandyford Road,
Dublin 16
Tel 01-2956165
(*Balally*, Dublin)

Lane, Michael, Rt Rev Mgr, VG
2 Meadowvale, Raheen,
Limerick
Tel 061-228761/087-2544450
(Limerick, retired)

Lane, Michael, Very Rev
Shrakovee, Clonlara, near
Limerick
(Limerick, retired)

Lane, Thomas (CM)
All Hallows Institute for
Mission and Ministry,
Drumcondra, Dublin 9
Tel 01-8373745/6

Lane, Thomas
Mount Saint Mary's
Seminary, 16300 Old
Emmitsburg Road,
Emmitsburg,
Maryland 21727-7797, USA
(Cloyne)

Langan, William (OCarm)
Gort Muire, Ballinteer,
Dublin 16
Tel 01-2984014

Langford, Gerard, Very Rev,
Adm
Cathedral of the Most Holy
Trinity, Barronstrand Street,
Waterford
Tel 051-392666
(*Trinity Within and St
Patrick's*, Waterford & L.)

Lanigan, Gerry (SVD)
Donamon Castle,
Roscommon
Tel 090-6662222

Lanigan-Ryan, Thomas, CC
Bóthar na Naomh
Presbytery, Thurles,
Co Tipperary
Tel 0504-22042/22688
(*Thurles, SS Joseph and
Brigid*, Cashel & E.)

Larkin, Aidan
c/o St Columban's,
Dalgan Park, Navan,
Co Meath
(Dublin)

Larkin, Barry, Very Rev, PP
Suncroft, Curragh,
Co Kildare
Tel 045-441586
(*Suncroft*, Kildare & L.)

Larkin, Francis, Very Rev
Canon, PP
Kinvara, Co Galway
Tel 091-637154
(*Kinvara*, Galway)

Larkin, Pat, Very Rev, PP
Mullagh, Co Clare
Tel 065-7087012/
087-2300627
(*Mullagh*, Killaloe)

Larkin, Patrick, Very Rev, PE,
AP
Parochial House,
Jenkinstown, Dundalk,
Co Louth
Tel 042-9371328
(*Lordship (and
Ballymascanlon)*, Armagh)

Larkin, Seamus, Very Rev, PP
Kilmuckridge, Gorey,
Co Wexford
Tel 053-9130116
(*Kilmuckridge*, Ferns)

Larkin, Seán, PP
Parochial House,
11 Chapel Road, Bessbrook,
Newry, Co Down BT35 7AU
Tel 028-30830206
(*Bessbrook (Killeavy Lower)*,
Armagh)

Lavelle, Colm (SJ)
Milltown Park,
Sandford Road, Dublin 6
Tel 01-2698411/2698113

Lavelle, Paul, Very Rev, PP
49 Rathgar Road, Dublin 6
Tel 01-4971058
(*Rathgar*, Dublin)

Laverty, Austin, Very Rev
Canon, PP, VF
Ardara, Co Donegal
Tel 074-9541135
(*Ardara*, Raphoe)

Laverty, Denis, PC
Pro-Cathedral House,
83 Marlborough Street,
Dublin 1
Tel 01-8745441
(*Pro-Cathedral*, Dublin)

Lavery, Patrick (SJ)
Clongowes Wood College,
Naas, Co Kildare
Tel 045-868663/868202

Lavin, Peadar, Very Rev
Canon, PP
Knockcroghery,
Co Roscommon
Tel 090-6661127
(Elphin)

Lawler, John (OCarm)
Carmelite Priory,
White Abbey, Co Kildare
Tel 045-521391

Lawless, Brendan, Very Rev,
PP
Dunkellin Tce, Portumna,
Co Galway
Tel 090-9741092
(Clonfert)

Lawless, Brian, Very Rev, Adm
Presbytery,
46 North William Street,
Dublin 1
Tel 01-8556474
(*North William Street*,
Dublin)

Lawless, James (SCI)
Promotions Director, Sacred
Heart Fathers, Fairfield,
66 Inchicore Road, Dublin 8
Tel 01-4538655

Lawless, Ralph (OFM)
Franciscan Friary,
Friary Lane, Athlone,
Co Westmeath
Tel 090-6472095

Lawless, Richard, CC
St Aidan's Cathedral,
Enniscorthy, Co Wexford
Tel 053-9235777
(Ferns)

Lawless, Vincent (SMA)
Retired in Ireland outside
SMA houses

Lawlor, Brendan, CC
2 Powerscourt, Tulla,
Co Clare
Tel 065-6835284/
087-9845417
(*Tulla*, Killaloe)

Lawlor, John, Very Rev, PP, VF
The Presbytery,
Ballydonoghue, Co Kerry
Tel 068-47103
(Kerry)

Lawlor, Sean (CSsR)
Mount Saint Alphonsus,
Limerick
Tel 061-315099

Lawton, Liam
Crossneen, Carlow
Tel 059-9134548
(Kildare & L.)

Lawton, Patrick, Very Rev, PP
Shandrum, Charleville,
Co Cork
Tel 063-70016
(*Shandrum*, Cloyne)

Layden, Leo (CSSp)
St Mary's College,
Rathmines, Dublin 6
Tel 01-4062160

Layden, Thomas (SJ)
Peter Faber House,
28 Brookvale Avenue,
Belfast BT14 6BW
Tel 028-90757615

Leader, Liam, Very Rev Canon,
AP
The Presbytery,
Lower Road, Cork
Tel 021-4500282
(*St Patrick's*, Cork & R.)

Leader, Micheál, CC
Mallow, Co Cork
Tel 022-21382
(*Mallow*, Cloyne)

Leahy, Andy, CC
Tullow, Co Carlow
Tel 059-9180641
(*Tullow*, Kildare & L.)

Leahy, Brendan
St Patrick's College,
Maynooth, Co Kildare
(Dublin)

Leahy, Denis, Very Rev, PP
Ardfert, Co Kerry
Tel 066-7134131
(*Ardfert*, Kerry)

Leahy, Donal, Very Rev, PP
Kilworth, Co Cork
Tel 025-27186
(*Kilworth*, Cloyne)

Leahy, Francis (CSSp)
Blackrock College,
Blackrock, Co Dublin
Tel 01-2888681

Leahy, Henry (OSA)
St Augustine's,
Taylor's Lane,
Balyboden, Dublin 16
Tel 01-4241000

Leahy, Michael (OSA)
St Augustine's Priory,
Washington Street, Cork
Tel 021-2753982

Leahy, Michael, Rt Rev Mgr
Fatima Home, Oak Park,
Tralee, Co Kerry
(Kerry, retired)

Leahy, Niall (SJ)
Dominic Collins' House
Residence,
129 Morehampton Road,
Dublin 4
Tel 01-2693075

Leahy, Thomas (SPS) CC
Ballinaheglish,
Co Roscommon
Tel 090-6662229
(*Cloverhill (Oran)*, Elphin)

Leamy, Michael, Very Rev,
Adm
Rushbrook, Cobh,
Co Cork
Tel 021-4813144
(Cloyne)

Leane, Thomas, Very Rev, PP
Ballyheigue, Tralee,
Co Kerry
Tel 066-7133110
(*Ballyheigue*, Kerry)

Leddy, Patrick (CSSp)
Holy Ghost Missionary
College, Kimmage Manor,
Dublin 12
Tel 01-4064300

Lee, Angelus (OFM)
Adam & Eve's,
4 Merchant's Quay, Dublin 8
Tel 01-6771128

Lee, Francis, PP
Barna, Co Galway
Tel 091-592173
(*Barna*, Galway)

Lee, Hugh (MHM), CC
Curraghboy, Athlone,
Co Roscommon
Tel 090-6488143
(*Kiltoom*, Elphin)

Lee, Patrick (SVD)
133 North Circular Road,
Dublin 7
Tel 01-8386743

Lee, William, Most Rev, DD
Bishop of Waterford and
Lismore, Bishop's House,
John's Hill, Waterford
Tel 051-874463
(Waterford & L.)

Lehane, Aidan (CSSp)
Templeogue College,
Dublin 6W
Tel 01-4903909

Lenihan, Jim, Adm
Allihies, Bantry, Co Cork
Tel 027-73024
(*Allihies*, Kerry)

Lennon, Brian (SJ)
St Francis Xavier's,
Upper Gardiner Street,
Dublin 1
Tel 01-8363411

Lennon, Denis, Very Rev, PP
39 Beechlawn, Wexford
Tel 053-9124417
(Ferns)

Lennon, James, CC
(Hexham & Newcastle)
Castledockrell, Ballycarney,
Enniscorthy, Co Wexford
Tel 053-9388569
(*Marshallstown*, Ferns)

Lennon, Moling, Very Rev, PE
364 Sundays Well, Naas,
Co Kildare
Tel 045-888667
(Kildare & L., retired)

Lennon, Pat, Parish
Administrator
Ardagh, Co Longford
Tel 043-6675006
(*Ardagh and Moydow*,
Ardagh & Cl.)

Lennon, Patrick (OSA)
Duckspool House
(Retirement Community),
Abbeyside, Dungarvan,
Co Waterford
Tel 058-23784

Lennon, Sean (OSM)
Servite Priory, Benburb,
Dungannon,
Co Tyrone, BT71 7JZ
Tel 028-37548241

Leogue, John, Very Rev, PP
Athleague, Co Roscommon
Tel 090-6663338
(*Athleague*, Elphin)

Leonard, Albert (OP), CC
Presbytery, St Aengus's,
Balrothery, Tallaght,
Dublin 24
Tel 01-4513757
(*Tallaght, Tymon North*,
Dublin)

Leonard, Derek
c/o The Missionary Society
of St James the Apostle,
24 Clark Street, Boston,
MA 02109, USA
(Limerick)

Leonard, John, Very Rev, PP,
VF
The Presbytery,
10 St Nessan's Park,
Dooradoyle, Limerick
Tel 061-302729
(*St Paul's*, Limerick)

Leonard, Michael
6020 West Ardmore
Avenue, Chicago, IL 60646,
USA
Tel 001-7736775341
(Killaloe)

Lewis, Eugene (White Fathers)
Cypress Grove, Templeogue,
Dublin 6W
Tel 01-4055263/4055264

Leycock, Dermot, Very Rev, PP
64 Newtownpark Avenue,
Blackrock, Co Dublin
Tel 01-2784860
(*Newtownpark,* Dublin)

Liddane, Raymond, Very Rev,
AP
Newtown, Waterford
Tel 051-874284
(*SS Joseph and Benildus*,
Waterford & L.)

Linehan, Diarmuid, Very Rev
Canon
2 Maglin View, Ballincollig,
Co Cork
Tel 021-4875857
(Cork & R., retired)

Linehan, Donal, Very Rev
Canon, PP
Ballinora, Waterfall, near
Cork
Tel 021-4873448
(*Ballinora*, Cork & R.)

Linehan, Patrick, CC
Kanturk, Co Cork
Tel 029-50061
(*Kanturk*, Cloyne)

Linnane, James, Very Rev
Canon, PP, VF
Listowel, Co Kerry
Tel 068-21188
(*Listowel*, Kerry)

Lisak, Marcin (OP)
St Mary's Priory, Tallaght,
Dublin 24
Tel 01-4048100

Liston, Mícheál, Very Rev
Canon, PP, VF
21 Sullane Crescent,
Raheen Heights, Limerick
(Limerick, retired)

Little, Anthony G. (CSSp)
St Michael's College,
Ailesbury Road, Dublin 4
Tel 01-2189423

Little, Thomas, Very Rev, PP
St Mary's,
Browneshill Avenue, Carlow
Tel 059-9131559
(*Bennekerry*, Kildare & L.)

Littleton, John
The Priory Institute, Tallaght
Village, Dublin 24
(Cashel & E.)

Littleton, Patrick, CC
St Luke's, Kilbarron Road,
Kilmore West, Dublin 5
Tel 01-8486806/087-2408188
(*Kilmore Road West*, Dublin)

Lloyd, Enda, Rt Rev Mgr, PP
The Presbytery,
Herbert Road, Bray,
Co Wicklow
(Dublin)

Lloyd, Francis, Very Rev, PE
The Presbytery, Dungarvan,
Co Waterford
(Waterford & L.)

Loftus, Hughie, Very Rev, PP
Corrandulla, Co Galway
Tel 091-791125
(*Corrandulla
(Annaghdown)*, Tuam)

Loftus, John, CC
Church Road, Belmullet,
Co Mayo
Tel 097-81087
(*Belmullet*, Killala)

Loftus, Kevin, Rt Rev Mgr, PP
Easkey, Co Sligo
Tel 096-49011
(Killala)

Loftus, Martin (SDB)
Rector, Salesian College,
Pallaskenry, Co Limerick
Tel 061-393313

Logue, Charles, CC
91 Drumgarner Road, Kilrea,
Co Derry BT51 5TE
Tel 028-29540528
(*Kilrea*, Derry)

Loisel, D. Eric M. (OSB)
Benedictine Monks,
Holy Cross Monastery,
119 Kilbroney Road,
Rostrevor,
Co Down BT34 3BN
Tel 028-41739979

Lomasney, Michael, CC
Cloghroe, Blarney, Co Cork
Tel 021-4385163
(*Inniscarra*, Cloyne)

Lombard, Patrick, CC
St Mary's, Sligo
Tel 071-9162670/9162769
(*Sligo, St Mary's*, Elphin)

Lonergan, Patrick, Very Rev
Canon, PE
Garrison, Enniskillen,
Co Fermanagh BT93 4AE
Tel 028-68658234
(*Belleek-Garrison*, Clogher)

Long, Leo
Templederry, Nenagh,
Co Tipperary
Tel 0504-52988/086-8353388
(*Killanave and Templederry*,
Killaloe)

Long, Martin, Very Rev, PP
Louisburgh, Co Mayo
Tel 098-66198
(*Louisburgh (Kilgeever)*,
Tuam)

Long, Michael (SPS)
St Patrick's, Kiltegan,
Co Wicklow
Tel 059-6473600

Longworth, Kevin (SPS)
St Patrick's, Kiltegan,
Co Wicklow
Tel 059-6473600

Looby, John (SJ)
35 Lower Leeson Street,
Dublin 2
Tel 01-6761248
Editor, Sacred Heart
Messenger,
37 Lower Lesson Street,
Dublin 2
Tel 01-6767491

Looney, Thomas, Very Rev
Canon, SP, VF
Dingle, Co Kerry
Tel 066-9151104
(Dingle, Kerry)

Loughran, Desmond, CC
Drumaness, Ballynahinch,
Co Down BT24 8NG
Tel 028-97561432
(*Magheradroll*
(*Ballynahinch*), Dromore)

Loughran, James, Very Rev
Canon, PE
Parochial House, Esker,
Lucan, Co Dublin
(Dublin, retired)

Loughran, Malachy (OSA)
St Augustine's Priory,
Shop Street,
Drogheda, Co Louth
Tel 041-9838409

Loughran, Terence
Parochial House, Cappagh,
Askeaton, Co Limerick
Tel 087-7524439
(*Cappagh*, Limerick)

Loughrey, Neil (White
Fathers)
Provincial Treasurer,
Provincialate,
Cypress Grove Road,
Templeogue, Dublin 6W
Tel 01-4992344

Loughrey, Vivian
St Gregory The Great Parish
200 Nr. University Drive,
Plantation,
FL 33324, USA
(Galway)

Lovell, Liam, CC
Kilmoyley, Ardfert, Co Kerry
Tel 066-7133169
Director, Retreat Centre,
Ardfert, Co Kerry
Tel 066-7134276
(Kerry)

Lovett, Cyril (SSC)
(Editor, Far East),
St Columban's, Dalgan Park,
Navan, Co Meath
Tel 046-9021525

Lowe, Bernard (CP)
Superior, St Paul's Retreat,
Mount Argus, Dublin 6W
Tel 01-4992000

Lucey, Finbarr, Very Rev, PP
Aglish, Cappoquin,
Co Waterford
Tel 024-96287
(*Aglish*, Waterford & L.)

Lucey, John (CSsR)
Mount Saint Alphonsus,
Limerick
Tel 061-315099

Lucey, Pat (OP), Very Rev
Provincial, Provincial Office,
St Mary's, Tallaght,
Dublin 24
Tel 01-4048118/4048115

Lucid, John, Very Rev, PP
Moyvane, Listowel,
Co Kerry
Tel 068-49308
(*Moyvane*, Kerry)

Luddy, Denis (CSsR)
St Joseph's, Dundalk,
Co Louth
Tel 042-9334042/9334762

Ludlow, Brendan, CC
St Mary's, Navan, Co Meath
Tel 046-9027518
(*Navan*, Meath)

Lumsden, David, Very Rev, PP
83 Tonlegee Drive,
Raheny, Dublin 5
Tel 01-8480917/087-2569873
(Dublin)

Lynch, Dermot (OFMCap)
Guardian, Holy Trinity,
Fr Mathew Quay, Cork
Tel 021-4270827

Lynch, Dominic
Gallen Nursing Home,
Ferbane, Co Offaly
(Ardagh & Cl., retired)

Lynch, Eamonn, Very Rev, PP
Ballyconnell, Co Cavan
Tel 049-9526291
(*Kildallan and Tomregan*,
Kilmore)

Lynch, Edward (CSsR)
St Patrick's, Esker, Athenry,
Co Galway
Tel 091-844549

Lynch, Finbarr (SJ)
Manresa House,
Dollymount, Dublin 3
Tel 01-8331352

Lynch, Finian (OP)
St Mary's, Pope Quay, Cork
Tel 021-4502267

Lynch, Flannan (OFMCap)
Capuchin Friary,
Friary Street, Kilkenny
Tel 056-7721439

Lynch, Flor (CSSp)
Assistant Priest
37 Palmerstown Drive,
Palmerstown, Dublin 20
Tel 01-6264642
(*Palmerstown*, Dublin)

Lynch, Florence (CSSp)
Templeogue College,
Dublin 6W
Tel 01-4903909

Lynch, James (SJ)
St Ignatius Community &
Church, 27 Raleigh Row,
Salthill, Galway
Tel 091-523707

Lynch, James, Very Rev, PP
Parochial House, Ashbourne,
Co Meath
Tel 01-8350406
(*Ashbourne-Donaghmore*,
Meath)

Lynch, John
2 Cooleen Avenue,
Beaumont, Dublin 9
(Dublin, retired)

Lynch, Jude (CSSp)
Holy Ghost Missionary
College, Kimmage Manor,
Dublin 12
Tel 01-4064300

Lynch, Laurence (OCarm)
Carmelite Priory,
Knocktopher, Co Kilkenny
Tel 056-7768675
(*Knocktopher/Ballyhale*,
Ossory)

Lynch, Lorcan, Very Rev PP
Derrygonnelly, Enniskillen,
Co Fermanagh BT93 6HW
Tel 028-68641207
(*Derrygonnelly*, Clogher)

Lynch, Noel, (SSC), CC
Tiranascragh, Ballinasloe,
Co Galway
Tel 090-9675238
(*Killimor and Tiranascragh*,
Clonfert)

Lynch, Owen, CC
The Presbytery,
Kilmacanogue, Bray,
Co Wicklow
Tel 01-2862110
(*Enniskerry*, Dublin)

Lynch, Patrick (SMA)
Temporary diocesan work in
Ireland

Lynch, Paddy, Very Rev
Deerpark, Clarecastle,
Co Clare
Tel 065-6822588
(Killaloe, retired)

Lynch, Patrick, Very Rev, PP
Tubbercurry, Co Sligo
Tel 071-9185049
(Achonry)

Lynch, Patsy, CC
St Brendan's, Tralee,
Co Kerry
Tel 066-7125932
(*Tralee, St Brendan's*, Kerry)

Lynch, Sean (SMA)
African Missions,
Blackrock Road, Cork
Tel 021-4292871

Lyng, John (OSA) CC
Prior, St Augustine's,
Taylor's Lane, Ballyboden,
Dublin 16
Tel 01-4944966
(*Ballyboden*, Dublin)

Lyng, Richard, Very Rev (OSA),
PP
St Augustine's Priory,
Galway
Tel 091-562524
(*St Augustine's*, Galway)

Lyon, Kevin, CC
Archdeacon of
Glendalough,
Parochial House,
Crosschapel, Blessington,
Co Wicklow
Tel 045-865215
(*Blessington*, Dublin)

Lyons, Enda, Dr
Bermingham Road, Tuam,
Co Galway
(Tuam, retired)

Lyons, Fintan (OSB)
Glenstal Abbey, Murroe,
Co Limerick
Tel 061-386103

Lyons, Gabriel, Very Rev, PP
119 Glenravel Road,
Martinstown, Ballymena,
Co Antrim BT43 6QL
Tel 028-21758217
(*Glenravel (Skerry)*, Down &
C.)

Lyons, Seán, Very Rev, PP
Duniry, Loughrea,
Co Galway
Tel 090-9745125
(*Duniry and Abbey*,
Clonfert)

Lyons, Thomas
Chaplain, Cork University
Hospital, Wilton, Cork
Tel 021-4546400/4922391
(Cork & R.)

Lyons, Thomas
Cork University Hospital,
Wilton, Cork
Tel 021-4546109
(Galway)

M

Ma, Ben (CSsR)
PO Box 280, 6000 Cebu City,
Philippine Islands
Tel 0063-322553954

Mac Bradaigh, Proinsias (SJ)
Superior, Arrupe
Community,
127 Shangan Road,
Ballymun, Dublin 9
Tel/Fax 01-8625345

Mac Carthaigh, Donncha
(MSC)
Western Road, Cork
Tel 021-4804120

Mac Cuarta, Brian (SJ)
Superior, Iona,
211 Churchill Park,
Portadown BT62 1EU
Tel 028-38330366

Mac Gréil, Mícheál (SJ)
St Francis Xavier's,
Upper Gardiner Street,
Dublin 1
Tel 01-8363411

MacAodh, Loman (OFM)
Adam & Eve's,
4 Merchant's Quay,
Dublin 8
Tel 01-6771128

MacAodh, Seán, PP
Teach an Sagairt,
An Spidéal, Co na Gaillimhe
Tel 091-553155
(An Spidéal, Galway)

MacAulay, Ambrose, Rt Rev
Mgr, PP
42 Derryvolgie Avenue,
Belfast BT9 6FP
Tel 028-90668053
(St Brigid's, Down & C.)

Macaulay, Jeremiah, Very Rev,
AP
Edgeworthstown,
Co Longford
Tel 043-6671159
(Ardagh & Cl.)

MacCarthaigh, Pádraig, Very
Rev, PP
Ballydesmond, Mallow,
Co Cork
Tel 064-51104
(Ballydesmond, Kerry)

MacCarthy, Martin (OP)
St Mary's, Pope Quay, Cork
Tel 021-4502267

MacCarthy, Seán (SMA)
African Missions,
Blackrock Road, Cork
Tel 021-4292871

MacCormack, Gerard, Very
Rev, PP
Parochial House, Kingscourt,
Co Cavan
Tel 042-9667314
(Kingscourt, Meath)

MacCourt, Aloysius, CC
Parochial House,
55 West Street,
Stewartstown, Dungannon,
Co Tyrone BT71 5HT
Tel 028-87738252
(Armagh)

MacCraith, Micheál (OFM)
The Abbey, 8 Francis Street,
Galway
Tel 091-562518

MacDaid, Liam S., Rt Rev Mgr,
Adm
Chancellor, Tyholland,
Monaghan
Tel 047-85385
(Clogher)

MacDonagh, Fergal, CC
St Mary's, Irishtown Road,
Dublin 4
Tel 01-6689854
(Ringsend, Dublin)

MacDonald, Cristoír, CC
The Presbytery,
Curraheen Road, Cork
Tel 021-4343535
(Curraheen Road, Cork & R.)

MacEntee, Patrick, Very Rev,
PP
Shanmullagh,
Dromore, Omagh,
Co Tyrone BT78 3DZ
Tel 028-82898641
(Dromore, Clogher)

MacEoinin, Fergal (OP), Very
Rev, PP
St Saviour's Priory, Kilbarry,
Waterford
Tel 051-376581
(St Saviour's, Waterford &
L.)

MacGiolla Catháin, Darach,
CC
St Luke's Presbytery,
Twinbrook Road, Dunmurry,
Co Antrim BT17 0RP
Tel 028-90619459
(St Luke's, Down & C.)

MacGiollarnath, Sean (OCarm)
Carmelite Presbytery, Idrone
Avenue, Knocklyon,
Dublin 16
Tel 014941204
(Knocklyon, Dublin)

MacGowan, Padraig, Very
Rev, PP
Ballymahon, Co Longford
Tel 090-6432253
(Ballymahon, Ardagh & Cl.)

MacGurnaghan, Joseph, Very
Rev
14 Presbytery Lane,
Dunloy, Ballymena,
Co Antrim BT44 9DZ
Tel 028-27657223
(Down & C., retired)

MacHale, Brendan (SSC)
St Columban's, Dalgan Park,
Navan, Co Meath
Tel 046-9021525

MacHale, John George, Very
Rev Canon, PP
Kilglass, Enniscrone, Ballina,
Co Mayo
Tel 096-36191
(Kilglass, Killala)

Macken, Walter
Gort Ard University
Residence, Rockbarton
North, Galway
Tel 091-523846
Chaplain, Ballyglunin Park
Conference Centre, Tuam,
Co Galway
Tel 093-41423
(Opus Dei)

MacKenna, Benedict (OP)
Newbridge College,
Droichead Nua, Co Kildare
Tel 045-487200

MacKeone, Kieran, Very Rev,
PE, AP
Parochial House,
132 Washing Bay Road,
Coalisland, Dungannon,
Co Tyrone BT71 4QZ
Tel 028-87740376
(Clonoe, Armagh)

Mackey, Niall, Very Rev, PP
Parochial House,
1 River Valley Heights,
Swords, Co Dublin
Tel 01-8403400
(River Valley, Dublin)

MacKiernan, James, CC
Boher, Ballycumber,
Co Offaly
Tel 057-9336119
(Ardagh & Cl.)

Mackin, Patrick A., Very Rev,
PP
Parochial House,
Bohermeen,
Kells, Co Meath
Tel 046-9240633
(Bohermeen, Meath)

Mackle, Patrick (SMA)
Retired in Ireland outside
SMA houses

MacLaifeartaigh, Michael
(OCD)
Avila, Bloomfield Avenue,
Morehampton Road,
Dublin 4
Tel 01-6430200

MacLochlainn, Piaras, CC
10 Finglaswood Road,
Finglas West, Dublin 11
Tel 01-8347041
(Finglas West, Dublin)

MacMahon, James Ardle, Rt
Rev Mgr, Canon
Queen of Peace Centre,
6 Garville Avenue, Rathgar,
Dublin 6
(Dublin, retired)

MacMahon, John, Very Rev
Canon, PE
Holy Family Residence,
Roebuck Road, Dundrum,
Dublin 14
(Dublin, retired)

MacMahon, Joseph (OFM)
Secretary of Province and
Guardian, Provincial Office,
La Verna, Gormanston,
Co Meath
Tel 01-8020951

MacManuis, Clement (CSsR)
Clonard Monastery,
1 Clonard Gardens,
Belfast, BT13 2RL
Tel 028-90445950

MacMorrow, Desmond (CM)
St Vincent's College,
Castleknock, Dublin 15
Tel 01-8213051

MacMorrow, Francis (CM)
St Joseph's,
44 Stillorgan Park,
Blackrock, Co Dublin
Tel 01-2886961

MacNamara, Francis, Very
Rev, PP, VF
Mountmellick, Co Laois
Tel 057-8624198
(Kildare & L.)

MacNamara, Luke (OSB)
Glenstal Abbey, Murroe,
Co Limerick
Tel 061-386103

MacNamara, Vincent (SPS)
St Patrick's, 21 Leeson Park,
Dublin 6
Tel 01-4977897

MacNamee, David, Very Rev
Canon
St Bernadette's,
13 Osmington Terrace,
Thomondgate, Limerick
(Limerick)

MacNeill, Arthur, Very Rev
14 Ballyholland Road,
Newry, Co Down
(Dromore, retired)

MacOscar, Kieran, Very Rev,
PE, AP
Parochial House,
10 Mullavilly Road,
Tandragee,
Co Armagh BT62 2LX
Tel 028-38840840
(Armagh, retired)

MacPartlin, Brendan (SJ)
Iona, 211 Churchill Park,
Portadown BT62 1EU
Tel 028-38330366

MacRaois, Brian, Very Rev, PP
Parochial House, Chapel Hill,
Carlingford, Co Louth
Tel 042-9373111
(Carlingford and Clogherny,
Armagh)

MacSuibhne, Domhnall (OP),
Very Rev, PP
Prior, St Mary's,
The Claddach, Co Galway
Tel 091-582884
(The Claddach, Galway)

MacSweeney, James, CC
64 Westcourt, Ballincollig,
Co Cork
Tel 021-4870434
(*Ballincollig*, Cork & R.)

Madden, Brendan, Very Rev,
PP
67 Anne Devlin Park,
Ballyroan, Dublin 14
Tel 01-4950444
(*Ballyroan*, Dublin)

Madden, Christopher J.,
Lisieux
196 Oakcourt Avenue,
Palmerstown, Dublin 20
(Dublin, retired)

Madden, John (OCarm)
Terenure College, Terenure,
Dublin 6W
Tel 01-4904621

Madden, Laurence, Very Rev,
PP
Ardagh, Co Limerick
Tel 069-76121/087-2286450
(*Ardagh and Carrickerry*,
Limerick)

Madden, Michael, Very Rev,
PE
Ballycrennane, Ballymacoda,
Co Cork
Tel 024-98840
(Cloyne, retired)

Madden, Nicholas (OCD)
53/55 Marlborough Road,
Dublin 4
Tel 01-6601832

Madden, Noel, Very Rev, PE
3 Rosemount,
Malahide Road, Dublin 5
Tel 01-8315207
(Dublin, retired)

Madden, Patrick, Very Rev,
PP, VF
Presbytery No 1,
Ballycullen Avenue,
Firhouse, Dublin 24
Tel 01-4599855
(Dublin)

Madden, Paul M. (CP)
St Paul's Retreat,
Mount Argus, Dublin 6W
Tel 01-4992000

Madden, P.J.
Graiguecullen, Carlow
Tel 059-9141833
(*Graiguecullen*, Kildare &
Leighlin)

Madden, Peter (SVD)
Rector, Maynooth,
Co Kildare
Tel 01-6286391/2

Madden, Peter, PP
50 Tobermore Road,
Desertmartin, Magherafelt,
Co Derry BT45 5LE
Tel 028-79632196
(*Desertmartin*, Derry)

Madigan, Martin, Very Rev
Hamilton's Terrace, Glin,
Co Limerick
Tel 087-9418568
(Limerick, retired)

Madigan, Seamus
Chaplain, Sarsfield Barracks,
Limerick
Tel 061-316817
(Limerick)

Magee, Aelred (OCSO)
Our Lady of Bethlehem
Abbey, 11 Ballymena Road,
Portglenone, Ballymena,
Co Antrim BT44 8BL
Tel 028-25821211

Magee, Bernard, Very Rev
Canon
41 Lower Square,
Castlewellan BT31 9DN
Tel 028-43770377
(*Castlewellan (Kilmegan)*,
Down & C.)

Magee, Gerard
Cistercian Monastery,
Portglenone
(Down & C.)

Magee, John, Most Rev, DD
Bishop of Cloyne,
Cloyne Diocesan Centre,
Cobh, Co Cork
Tel 021-4811430
(Cloyne)

Magennis, Feidlimidh, LSS
St Mary's University College,
Belfast
(Dromore)

Magill, Martin, Very Rev, PP
St Oliver Plunkett
Presbytery,
27 Glenveagh Drive,
Belfast BT11 9HX
Tel 028-90618180
(Down & C.)

Magill, Neil (SSC)
St Columban's, Dalgan Park,
Navan, Co Meath
Tel 046-9021525

Maginn, Michael, Very Rev, PP
Lisadell, 54 Francis Street,
Lurgan,
Co Armagh BT66 6DL
Tel 028-38327173
(*Shankill, St Paul's (Lurgan)*,
Dromore)

Magorian, Eamon, CC
Parochial House,
27 Chapel Hill, Lisburn,
Co Antrim BT28 1EP
Tel 028-92660206
(*Lisburn (Blaris)*, Down & C.)

Maguire, Aidan (SAC)
Pallottine College, Thurles,
Co Tipperary
Tel 0504-21202

Maguire, Bernard, Very Rev,
CC
Cross, Mullagh, Kells,
Co Meath
Tel 049-8547024
(*Mullagh*, Kilmore)

Maguire, Edmond, Very Rev,
PE
Donaghmoyne,
Carrickmacross,
Co Monaghan
Tel 042-9661586
(Clogher, retired)

Maguire, James (OSA)
St Augustine's Priory,
Washington Street, Cork
Tel 021-2753982

Maguire, Joseph (SMA)
African Missions,
Blackrock Road, Cork
Tel 021-4292871

Maguire, Salvian (CP)
Holy Cross Retreat, Ardoyne,
Belfast BT14 7GE
Tel 028-90748231

Maher, Francis, Very Rev, PP
Johnstown via Thurles,
Co Kilkenny
Tel 056-8831219/087-
2402487
(*Johnstown*, Ossory)

Maher, James (SJ)
Minister, Crescent College
Comprehensive,
Dooradoyle, Limerick
Tel 061-480920

Maher, Michael (SM)
Cerdon, Marist Fathers,
St Mary's Road, Dundalk,
Co Louth
Tel 042-9334019

Maher, Michael, Very Rev
11 Woodlawn, Listowel,
Co Kerry
(Kerry, retired)

Maher, Noel, Very Rev, PP
Clough, Ballacolla,
Portlaoise, Co Laois
Tel 057-878513
(*Aghaboe*, Ossory)

Maher, Oliver, Very Rev, Adm
St Mary's Cathedral,
Kilkenny
Tel 056-7721253 Ext
181/086-8323010
(*St Mary's*, Ossory)

Maher, Sean, CC
Baltinglass, Co Wicklow
Tel 059-6481123
(*Baltinglass*, Kildare & L.)

Maher, Thomas, Rt Rev Mgr
Archersrath Nursing Home,
Kilkenny
Tel 056-7790137
(Ossory, retired)

Mailey, Anthony, CC
Parochial House,
Quigley's Point, Co Donegal
Tel 074-9383008
(*Iskaheen*, Derry)

Mallon, Brendan
Mallow, Co Cork
Tel 022-20792
(*Mallow*, Cloyne)

Mallon, Dominic
13 Richview Heights, Keady,
Co Armagh BT60 3SW
(Armagh)

Mallon, Thomas, Very Rev, PE,
AP
Parochial House, 170
Loughmacrory Road,
Omagh, Co Tyrone BT79 9LG
Tel 028-80761230
(*Termonmaguirc
(Carrickmore, Loughmacrory
& Creggan)*, Armagh)

Malone, Douglan, Very Rev,
Adm
St Luke's, Kilbarron Road,
Kilmore West, Dublin 5
Tel 01-8475898
(*Kilmore Road West*, Dublin)

Malone, Laurence, Very Rev,
PP
Goresbridge, Co Kilkenny
Tel 059-9775180
(*Paulstown*, Kildare & L.)

Malone, Liam, CC
Parochial House, Kells,
Co Meath
Tel 046-9240213
(*Kells*, Meath)

Malone, Pat, Very Rev, PP
'Maryville', Church Road,
Nenagh, Co Tipperary
Tel 067-37130
Chaplain, County Hospital,
Nenagh, Co Tipperary
Tel 067-31491
Chaplain, Welfare Home,
Nenagh, Co Tipperary
Tel 067-31893
(Killaloe)

Malone, Tony (SM)
CUS Community, 89 Lower
Leeson Street, Dublin 2
Tel 01-6762586

Maloney, Dermot, Very Rev,
PP, VF
Parochial House,
40 The Village, Jonesboro,
Newry, Co Down BT35 8HP
Tel 028-3084945
(Armagh)

Maloney, John
Curate's House, Kikelly,
Co Mayo
Tel 094-9367031
(Achonry)

Maloney, Michael
c/o Parochial House,
Charlestown, Co Mayo

Maloney, Peter (SVD)
Donamon Castle,
Roscommon
Tel 090-6662222

Mamza, Stephen Dami (White Fathers)
Cypress Grove, Templeogue,
Dublin 6W
Tel 01-4055263/4055264

Mandi, Josephat
Parish Chaplain,
287 South Circular Road,
Dublin 8
Tel 01-4533490
(*Dolphin's Barn*, Dublin)

Mangan, Cyril, Very Rev, PP
5 Lissenhall Park,
Seatown Road, Swords,
Co Dublin
Tel 01-8403378
(*Swords*, Dublin)

Mangan, Eoin, Very Rev, PP
Diocesan Office, Bishop's House,
Killarney, Co Kerry
Tel 068-46107
(*Knocknagoshel*, Kerry)

Mangan, Patrick J., Very Rev
Dún Mhuire,
44 Beechwood Avenue
Upper, Dublin 6
Tel 01-4975180
(Dublin, retired)

Mangan, Thomas, Very Rev, Adm
'Naomh Joseph',
Lifford Avenue, Limerick
Tel 061-303777/087-2376032
(*St Joseph's*, Limerick)

Manik, Robert (OCarm)
Whitefriar Street Church,
56 Aungier Street, Dublin 2
Tel 01-4758821

Manley, John (OFMCap), CC
Ascension Presbytery,
Gurranabraher, Cork
Tel 021-4303655
(*Gurranabraher*, Cork & R.)

Mann, Robert (SCJ), Very Rev, Moderator
Parochial House,
St John Vianney,
Ardlea Road, Dublin 5
Tel 01-8474173/8474123
(*Ardlea*, Dublin)

Manning, Francis, CC
Macroom, Co Cork
Tel 026-41092
(*Macroom*, Cloyne)

Manning, Michael, Rt Rev Mgr, AP
Millstreet, Co Cork
Tel 029-70043
(*Millstreet*, Kerry)

Manning, Seán, Very Rev Canon
St Mary's College, Galway
(Galway)

Mannion, John, CC
Killoran, Ballinasloe,
Co Galway
Tel 090-9627120
(*Mullagh and Killoran*, Clonfert)

Mannion, Micheál, CC
Westport, Co Mayo
Tel 098-28871
(*Westport (Aughaval)*, Tuam)

Mannion, Thomas, Very Rev Canon, PP
The Presbytery, Claremorris,
Co Mayo
Tel 094-9362477
(*Claremorris (Kilcolman)*, Tuam)

Mannion, Tom, CC
Butlersbridge, Cavan
Tel 049-4365266
(*Cavan*, Kilmore)

Mannix, Jim (MSC)
Western Road, Cork
Tel 021-4804120

Mansfield, Declan, Very Rev, Adm
Cathedral Presbytery, Cork
Tel 021-4304325
(*Cathedral of St Mary & St Anne*, Cork & R.)

Mansfield, Dermot (SJ), PC
Maressa House, Dollymount,
Dublin 3
Tel 01-8339666
(*Dollymount*, Dublin)

Mansfield, Francis (SVD)
Donamon Castle,
Roscommon
Tel 090-6662222

Marken, Aodhan, CC
Chaplain/Counsellor,
St Peter's Diocesan College,
Wexford
Tel 053-9142071
Parish
The Presbytery,
12 School Street, Wexford
Tel 053-9122055
(*Wexford*, Ferns)

Markey, Gerard (SSC)
St Columban's, Dalgan Park,
Navan, Co Meath
Tel 046-9021525

Markuszewski, Robert, CC
139 Andersonstown Road,
Belfast BT11 9BW
Tel 028-90613724
(*St Agnes'*, Down & C.)

Marley, Thomas (IC)
St Joseph's, Doire na hAbhann, Tickincar,
Clonmel, Co Tipperary
Tel 052-26914

Marmion, Declan (SM)
Mount St Mary's,
Milltown, Dublin 14
Tel 01-2697322

Marrinan, Thomas, Very Rev, PP
Gort, Co Galway
Tel 091-631220
(*Gort/Beagh*, Galway)

Marron, Eamonn, Rt Rev Mgr, PE
Parochial House, Raharney,
Co Westmeath
Tel 044-9374271
(*Kinnegad*, Meath)

Marron, Patrick, Very Rev Canon, PE
Fintona, Omagh,
Co Tyrone BT78 2NS
Tel 028-82841239
(*Fintona*, Clogher)

Marron, Thomas, Very Rev Canon, PE
Trillick, Omagh,
Co Tyrone BT78 3RD
Tel 028-89561217
(*Trillick*, Clogher)

Marsden, David (SCJ)
Parochial House,
St John Vianney,
Ardlea Road, Dublin 5
Tel 01-8474173/8474123
(*Ardlea*, Dublin)

Marteaux, D. Thierry (OSB)
Benedictine Monks,
Holy Cross Monastery,
119 Kilbroney Road,
Rostrevor,
Co Down BT34 3BN
Tel 028-41739979

Martin, Diarmuid, Most Rev, DD
Archbishop of Dublin and Primate of Ireland,
Archbishop's House,
Drumcondra, Dublin 9
Tel 01-8373732
(Dublin)

Martin, Eamon, Very Rev
Exective Secretary, Irish Bishops' Conference
Secretariat, Columba Centre,
Maynooth, Co Kildare
Tel 00353-1-5053000
(Derry)

Martin, Hubert, Very Rev, PP
Glaslough, Monaghan
Tel 047-88120
(*Donagh*, Clogher)

Martin, Liam (CSSp)
Holy Ghost Missionary College, Kimmage Manor,
Dublin 12
Tel 01-4064300

Martin, Oliver (OPraem)
Prior, Abbey of the Most Holy Trinity and St Norbert,
Kilnacrott,
Ballyjamesduff, Co Cavan
Tel 049-8544416

Martin, Valentine, Very Rev, PP
The Presbytery, Jobstown,
Tallaght, Dublin 24
Tel 01-4523595
(*Jobstown*, Dublin)

Masterson, James (CSSp)
Holy Ghost Missionary College, Kimmage Manor,
Dublin 12
Tel 01-4064300

Mathews, Colm, CC
47 Old Court Manor,
Dublin 24
Tel 01-4525624
(*Bohernabreena*, Dublin)

Mathews, William (SJ)
Milltown Park,
Sandford Road, Dublin 6
Tel 01-2698411/2698113

Matthews, Richard, Very Rev, PP, VF
Parochial House, Killucan,
Co Westmeath
Tel 044-9374127
(*Killucan*, Meath)

Mawn, Sean
Ballinaglera,
Carrick-on-Shannon,
Co Leitrim
Tel 071-9643014
(Kilmore)

Maxwell, Barney
Empor, Ballymacargy,
Co Westmeath
(Meath, retired)

Mbajo, Linus (CSSp)
Holy Ghost Missionary College, Kimmage Manor,
Dublin 12
Tel 01-4064300

McAdam, Colm (CM), Very Rev, PP
122 Sunday's Well Road,
Cork
Tel 021-4304070
(*St Vincent's, Sunday's Well*, Cork & R.)

McAleer, Brendan, Very Rev, PP
Parochial House,
Garristown, Co Dublin
Tel 01-8354138
(*Garristown*, Dublin)

McAleer, Gerard, Very Rev, PP
Parochial House,
63 Castlecaulfield Road,
Donaghmore, Dungannon,
Co Tyrone BT70 3HF
Tel 028-87761327
(*Donaghmore*, Armagh)

McAleese, Frank (OCarm)
Carmelite Friary,
Kinsale, Co Cork
Tel 021-772138

McAlinden, John (CSsR)
St Joseph's, Dundalk,
Co Louth
Tel 042-9334042/9334762

McAlinden, John (CSsR), CC
Our Lady of Lourdes
Presbytery,
Hardman's Gardens,
Drogheda, Co Louth
Tel 041-98318998
(*Drogheda*, Armagh)

McAlinden, Martin, Very Rev,
PP, VF
The Presbytery,
11 Tullygally Road,
Legahory,
Craigavon BT65 5BL
Tel 028-38341901
(*Moyraverty (Craigavon)*,
Dromore)

McAllister, Bernard (OFMCap)
Vicar, Capuchin Friary,
Church Street, Dublin 7
Tel 01-8730599

McAnaney, Martin (SM)
London

McAnenly, Peter, CC
Parochial House,
6 Circular Road,
Dungannon,
Co Tyrone BT71 6BE
Tel 028-87722831
(Armagh)

McAnerney, Arthur, Very Rev,
PP
Parochial House,
Beragh, Omagh,
Co Tyrone BT79 0SY
Tel 028-80758206
(*Beragh*, Armagh)

McAnuff, Patrick, Very Rev
Canon
58 Armagh Road,
Newry, Co Down
(Dromore, retired)

McArdle, Martin, Very Rev, PP
Parochial House,
10 Springhill Road,
Moneymore, Magherafelt,
Co Derry BT45 7NG
Tel 028-86748242
(*Moneymore (Ardtrea)*,
Armagh)

McArdle, Sean (SM), Very Rev,
CC
The Presbytery, Donore
Avenue, Dublin 8
Tel 01-4542425
(*Donore Avenue*, Dublin)

McAreavey, John, Very Rev,
DD
Bishop of Dromore, Bishop's
House, 44 Armagh Road,
Newry, Co Down BT35 6PN
Tel 028-30262444
(Dromore)

McAteer, Brendan, Very Rev
Warrenpoint, Co Down
(Dromore, retired)

McAteer, Francis, Very Rev, PP
Parochial House, Carrick,
Co Donegal
Tel 074-9739008
(Raphoe)

McAteer, Gerard
124 Staffordstown Road,
Randalstown,
Co Antrim BT41 3LH
Tel 028-94478373
(Down & C., retired)

McAteer, Kieran, Very Rev, PP
Parochial House, Ballybofey,
Co Donegal
Tel 074-9131135
(*Stranorlar*, Raphoe)

McAteer, Tom, CC
15 Chapel Hill, Mayobridge,
Newry, Co Down BT34 2EX
Tel 028-30851225
(*Clonallon, St Patrick's
(Mayobridge)*, Dromore)

McAuley, John (SJ)
Milltown Park, Sandford
Road, Dublin 6
Tel 01-2698411/2698113

McAuliffe, David
Chaplain, University College,
Iona, College Road, Cork
Tel 021-4902704
(Cork & R.)

McAuliffe, Desmond, Very
Rev, Adm
Rockhill, Bruree,
Co Limerick
Tel 063-90515/087-6522746
(*Rockhill/Bruree*, Limerick)

McAuliffe, Leo (OFMCap)
St Anthony's Capuchin
Friary, 43 Dublin Street,
Carlow
Tel 059-9142543

McBrearty, Danny, CC
Parochial House, Clar,
Co Donegal
Tel 074-9721093
(*Donegal Town
(Tawnawilly)*, Raphoe)

McBrearty, Stephen, Very Rev,
PP
St Anthony's Presbytery,
4 Willowfield Crescent,
Belfast BT6 8HP
Tel 028-90253666
(*St Anthony's*, Down & C.)

McBride, Brendan
St Philip's Church,
725 Diamond Street,
San Francisco,
California, 94114
(Raphoe)

McBride, Colm, Very Rev, PP
Netherley Lodge, 130 Upper
Dunmurry Lane,
Belfast BT17 0EW
(*Our Lady Queen of Peace,
Kilwee*, Down & C.)

McCabe, John, Very Rev
Canon, PP, VF
Castleblayney,
Co Monaghan
Tel 042-9740051
(Clogher)

McCabe, Robert, CF
Gormanston Military Camp,
Gormanston, Co Meath
Tel 01-8413990
(*Stamullen*, Meath)

McCabe, Thomas (OMI)
Oblate Scholasticate,
St Anne's,
Goldenbridge Walk,
Inchicore, Dublin 8
Tel 01-4540841/4542955

McCafferty, Patrick
52 Lower Rathmines Road,
Dublin 6
(Down & C.)

McCafferty, Patrick, CC
52 Lower Rathmines Road,
Dublin 6
Tel 01-4976148
(*Rathmines*, Dublin)

McCafferty, Paul
Moderator of the Diocesan
Curia, PO Box 27,
Bishop's House,
Derry BT48 91G
Tel 028-71262302
(Derry)

McCaffrey, Desmond (OCD)
St Teresa's,
Clarendon Street, Dublin 2
Tel 01-6718466/6718127

McCaffrey, James (CSSp), CC
The Presbytery, St Mary's,
New Road, Clondalkin,
Dublin 22
Tel 01-4592311
(*Clondalkin*, Dublin)

McCaffrey, Ultan (OFM)
Franciscan Friary, Lady Lane,
Waterford
Tel 051-874262

McCague, Brendan, CC
Corduff, Carrickmacross,
Co Monaghan
Tel 042-9669456
(*Carrickmacross*, Clogher)

McCahery, Barney (CSsR), CC
6 Market Street, Ballycastle,
Co Antrim BT54 6DP
Tel 028-20762202
(*Ballycastle (Ramoan)*, Down
& C.)

McCallion, Edwin (SM), Very
Rev, PP
The Presbytery,
Donore Avenue, Dublin 8
Tel 01-4542425
(*Donore Avenue*, Dublin)

McCallion, John, CC
Parochial House,
18 Annaghmore Road,
Coalisland, Dungannon,
Co Tyrone BT71 4QZ
(*Clonoe*, Armagh)

McCamley, Eamonn, Very Rev,
PP
Parochial House, 17
Eagralougher Road,
Loughgall,
Co Armagh BT61 8LA
Tel 028-38891231
(*Loughgall*, Armagh)

McCann, Brian, CC
St Paul's Presbytery,
125 Falls Road,
Belfast BT12 6AB
Tel 028-90325034
(*St Paul's*, Down & C.)

McCann, Columba (OSB)
Glenstal Abbey, Murroe,
Co Limerick
Tel 061-386103

McCann, Henry, PP
St Mary's Presbytery, 12
Ballymena Road,
Portglenone,
Co Sntrim BT44 8BL
Tel 028-25821218
(*Portglenone*, Down & C.)

McCann, Joseph (CM)
All Hallows Institute for
Mission and Ministry,
Drumcondra, Dublin 9
Tel 01-8373745/6

McCanny, Bryan, Rt Rev Mgr,
PP, VG
St Patrick's, Buncrana Road,
Pennyburn, Derry BT48 7QL
Tel 028-71262360
(*The Three Patrons*, Derry)

McCarney, Eugene, Very Rev
Parochial House,
Castletown, Gorey,
Co Wexford
Tel 0402-37115
(Dublin, retired)

McCarney, Henry (SPS)
St Patrick's, Kiltegan,
Co Wicklow
Tel 059-6473600

McCarrick, Roger (SM)
Fiji

McCarron, Declan
c/o Diocesan Office,
Letterkenny, Co Donegal
(Raphoe)

McCarron, Peter, CC
The Presbytery,
2 River Valley Heights,
Swords, Co Dublin
Tel 01-8404162
(*River Valley*, Dublin)

McCartan, Sean
Parochial House,
St Patrick Street, Keady,
Co Armagh BT60 3TQ
Tel 028-37531246
(Armagh)

McCarthy, Berchmans
(OFMCap)
St Francis Capuchin Friary,
Rochestown, Co Cork
Tel 021-4896244

McCarthy, Brian
Castleville Study Centre,
Golf Links Road, Castletroy,
Limerick
Tel 061-331223
(Opus Dei)

McCarthy, Daniel (Cloyne)
Chaplain, Stephen's
Barracks, Kilkenny
Tel 056-7761852
(Ossory)

McCarthy, Dermod
RTÉ, Donnybrook, Dublin 4
Tel 01-2083237/087-2499719
(Dublin)

McCarthy, Donal (MSC)
Grace Dieu Retreat House,
Tramore Road, Waterford
Tel 051-374417/373372

McCarthy, Donal (SAC)
Provincial House,
'Homestead',
Sandyford Road, Dundrum,
Dublin 16
Tel 01-2956180/2954170

McCarthy, Eamonn, CC
Coachford, Co Cork
Tel 021-7334059
(Cloyne)

McCarthy, Eamonn, CC
The Presbytery, Donard,
Co Wicklow
Tel 045-404614
(Dunlavin, Dublin)

McCarthy, Eugene (CP), Very
Rev, PP
24 The Court,
Mulhuddart Wood,
Mulhuddart, Dublin 15
Tel 01-8202544
(Mulhuddart, Dublin)

McCarthy, Florence (SDB)
Salesian House,
45 St Teresa's Road,
Crumlin, Dublin 12
Tel 01-4555605

McCarthy, Francis, CC
Holycross House, Moyglass,
Fethard, Co Tipperary
Tel 052-6131343
(Killeanaule, Cashel & E.)

McCarthy, Gabriel (OCSO)
Mount Saint Joseph Abbey,
Roscrea, Co Tipperary
Tel 0505-25600

McCarthy, Gerard (SVD)
Kilbegnet, Creggs,
Co Galway,
(via Roscommon)
Tel 090-6621127
(Creggs (Glinsk and
Kilbegnet), Elphin)

McCarthy, John (MSC)
Woodview House,
Mount Merrion Avenue,
Blackrock, Co Dublin
Tel 01-2881644

McCarthy, John
Irish Pastoral Centre,
953 Hancock Street, Quincy,
Massachusetts CO2170, USA
Tel 001-617479740
(Limerick)

McCarthy, John, CC
Cobh, Co Cork
Tel 021-4815619
(Cobh, St Colman's
Cathedral, Cloyne)

McCarthy, John, Very Rev, PP
Rosscarbery, Co Cork
Tel 023-8848168
(Rosscarbery and Lissavaird,
Cork & R.)

McCarthy, John, Very Rev, PP
Roundstone, Co Galway
Tel 095-35846
(Roundstone, Tuam)

McCarthy, Michael (CSSp)
Holy Ghost Missionary
College, Kimmage Manor,
Dublin 12
Tel 01-4064300

McCarthy, Patrick A., Very
Rev, PP
35 Paul Street, Cork
Tel 021-4276573
(Ss Peter's and Paul's, Cork
& R.)

McCarthy, Patrick J., Very Rev,
Adm
Ardfield, Clonakilty,
Co Cork
Tel 023-8840649
(Ardfield and Rathbarry,
Cork & R.)

McCarthy, Patrick, CC
Mallow, Co Cork
Tel 086-3831621
(Mallow, Cloyne)

McCarthy, Sean, Very Rev
Canon
Loma, Newtown Road,
Wexford
(Ferns, retired)

McCarthy, Sylvius (OFMCap)
St Francis Capuchin Friary.
Rochestown, Co Cork
Tel 021-4896244

McCarthy, Thomas (OP)
Newbridge College,
Droichead Nua, Co Kildare
Tel 045-487200

McCarthy, Vincent (OSA)
St Augustine's Priory
(Residence),
New Ross, Co Wexford
Tel 051421237

McCartney, Sean, Very Rev, PP
25 Alt-Min Avenue,
Belfast BT8 6NJ
(Down & C., retired)

McCaughan, Aidan
(priest in residence)
Parochial House,
4 Broughshane Road,
Ballymena,
Co Antrim BT43 7DX
Tel 028-25641515
(Ballymena (Kirkinriola),
Down & C.)

McCaughan, Dermot, Very
Rev, PP
St Patrick's Presbytery,
29 Chapel Hill, Lisburn,
Co Antrim BT28 1EP
Tel 028-92662341
(Lisburn (Blaris), Down & C.)

McCaughey, George (SDB)
Salesian House,
Warrenstown, Drumree,
Co Meath
Tel 01-8240298

McCaughey, Hugh, Very Rev,
PE
St Mary's, Latnamard,
Smithboro, Co Monaghan
Tel 042-9744976
(Killeevan, Clogher)

McCaughey, Michael, CC
Parochial House,
32 Chapel Road, Waterside,
Derry BT47 2BB
Tel 028-71342303
(Waterside, Derry)

McCaughey, Shane, Very Rev,
BD
Manager, St Macartan's
College, Monaghan,
Co Monaghan
Tel 047-81642/83365/83367
(Clogher)

McCauley, John, Very Rev
40 Rathmore, Clonallon
Road, Warrenpoint,
Co Down
(Dromore, retired)

McCauley, Ross (OP)
St Dominic's, Athy,
Co Kildare
Tel 0507-31573

McCay-Morrissey, Bernard
(OP)
St Saviour's,
Upper Dorset Street,
Dublin 1
Tel 01-8897610

McChrystal, Paul (OCarm)
Gort Muire, Ballinteer,
Dublin 16
Tel 01-2984014

McClarey, Liam (SAC)
St Patrick's, Corduff,
Blanchardstown, Dublin 15
Tel 01-8213596

McCloskey, Gerard, Very Rev,
Adm
Holy Family Presbytery,
Newington Avenue,
Belfast BT15 2HP
Tel 028-90743119
(Holy Family, Down & C.)

McCluskey, Brian, Very Rev
Canon, PE
Apt 2, 2 Danesfort Park
North, Stranmillis Road,
Belfast BT9 5RB
Tel 028-90683544
(Clogher, retired)

McCluskey, Joseph, Very Rev,
PP
Threemilehouse, Monaghan
Tel 047-81501
(Corcaghan, Clogher)

McConnell, Noel, CC
Shantonagh, Castleblayney,
Co Monaghan
Tel 042-9745015
(Aughnamullen East,
Clogher)

McConvery, Brendan (CSsR)
Liguori House,
75 Orwell Road, Dublin 6
Tel 01-4067100

McConville, Conor, CC
Cathedral Presbytery,
38 Hill Street,
Newry BT34 1AT
Tel 028-30262586
(Newry, Dromore)

McConville, Gerard, Very Rev
68 Main Street,
Portglenone BT44 8HS
(Down & C., retired)

McConville, Matthew
c/o Bishop's House
(Dromore)

McCormack, Christy
Fohenagh, Ahascragh,
Ballinasloe, Co Galway
Tel 090-9688623
(Fohenagh and Killure,
Clonfert)

McCormack, Ignatius
St Flannan's College, Ennis,
Co Clare
Tel 065-6828019/
086-2777139
(Killaloe)

McCormack, James (MSC),
Adm
Hacketstown, Co Carlow
Tel 059-6471257
(Hacketstown, Kildare & L.)

McCormack, John (SMA), CC
Breaffy, Castlebar,
Co Mayo
Tel 094-9022799
(*Castlebar (Aglish,
Ballyheane and Breaghwy),*
Tuam)

McCormack, Martin (SDB)
Salesian College,
Pallaskenry, Co Limerick
Tel 061-393313

McCormack, William, Very
Rev, PP
Toomevara, Co Tipperary
Tel 067-26023/087-4168855
(*Toomevara,* Killaloe)

McCormick, Diarmuid, CC
Kilkishen, Co Clare
Tel 061-367193
(*O'Callaghan's Mills,*
Killaloe)

McCorry, Francis, Very Rev
212 Staffordstown Road,
Cargin, Toomebridge,
Co Antrim BT41 3QT
Tel 028-79650079
(*Duneane,* Down & C.)

McCoy, Art (OFM)
Franciscan Friary,
Lady Lane, Waterford
Tel 051-874262

McCrann, Christopher (LC), CC
Knocknahur, Sligo
Tel 071-9128470
(*Strandhill/Ransboro,* Elphin)

McCreave, Eamonn (OSM)
Parochial House,
54 St Patrick's Avenue,
Downpatrick,
Co Down BT30 6DN
Tel 028-44612443
(*Downpatrick,* Down & C.)

McCrory, Gerard, Very Rev
Canon, PP
Church Street, Ballynahinch,
Co Down BT24 8LP
Tel 028-97562410
(*Magheradroll
(Ballynahinch),* Dromore)

McCrory, James, PEm
124 Carrigans Road,
Knockmoyle, Omagh,
Co Tyrone BT79 7TW
(Derry, retired)

McCrory, Patrick, J., Very Rev,
PE
Parochial House,
Sixemilecross, Omagh,
Co Tyrone BT79 9NF
Tel 028-80758344
(Armagh, retired)

McCrystal, Eoin, Very Rev, PP
12 Grangemore Grove,
Dublin 13
Tel 01-8474652
(*Donaghmede,* Dublin)

McCullagh, John
Parochial House,
46 Barrack Street, Strabane,
Co Tyrone BT82 8HD
Tel 028-71882215
(*Strabane,* Derry)

McCullagh, Michael (CM),
Very Rev, PP
St Peter's, Phibsboro,
Dublin 7
Tel 01-8389708
(*Phibsboro,* Dublin)

McCullagh, Raymond
1 Seafield Park South,
Portstewart,
Co Derry BT55 7LH
Tel 028-70832066
(Down & C.)

McCullen, Richard (CM)
St Paul's College, Raheny,
Dublin 5
Tel 01-8318113

McCurry, James (OFMConv),
Very Rev
General Delegate, General
Delegation Office,
St Patrick's Friary,
26 Cornwall Road,
Waterloo, London SE1 8TW,
England
Tel 020-79288897

McDermott, Brendan (CP)
St Paul's Retreat,
Mount Argus, Dublin 6W
Tel 01-4992000

McDermott, Joseph, Very Rev,
PP
St Conleth's, Newbridge,
Co Kildare
Tel 045-431741
(Kildare & L.)

McDermott, Kieran
'Emmaus', Holy Cross,
Main Street, Dundrum,
Dublin 14
Tel 01-2984348
(*Dundrum,* Dublin)

McDermott, Laurence (OCSO)
Prior, Mellifont Abbey,
Collon, Co Louth
Tel 041-9826103

McDermott, Niall, CC
12 Blackberry Rise,
Portmarnock, Dublin
Tel 01-8461398
(*Portmarnock,* Dublin)

McDermott, Noel, CC
91 Ervey Road, Eglinton,
Co Derry BT47 3AU
Tel 028-71810235
(*Faughanvale,* Derry)

McDermott, Padraic, CC
The Presbytery, Manor
Kilbride, Blessington,
Co Wicklow
(*Blessington,* Dublin)

McDermott, Patrick, CC
St Mary's, Athlone,
Co Westmeath
Tel 090-6472088/6473358
(*Athlone,* Ardagh & Cl.)

McDermott, Sean
Chaplain, Cavan and
Monaghan Defence Forces,
Dun Ui Neill, Cavan
Tel 049-4361631/
087-8292333
(Kilmore)

McDermott, Thomas, CC
Churchtown, Mallow,
Co Cork
Tel 022-41916
(*Churchtown (Liscarroll),*
Cloyne)

McDevitt, Eamon, PP
78 Lisnaragh Road,
Dunamanagh, Strabane,
Co Tyrone BT82 0QN
Tel 028-71398212
(Derry)

McDevitt, John, CC
50 Brook Street, Omagh,
Co Tyrone BT78 5HE
Tel 028-82242092
Director,
Omagh Pastoral Centre,
Mount St Columba Pastoral
Centre, 48 Brooke Street,
Omagh,
Co Tyrone BT78 5HD
Tel 028-82242439
(Derry)

McDevitt, Vincent (CSSp)
Spiritan Missionaries,
Ardbraccan, Navan,
Co Meath
Tel 046-9021441

McDonagh, Brendan (SPS) CC
Lisacul, Castlerea, Co
Roscommon
Tel 094-9880068
(*Loughglyn,* Elphin)

McDonagh, Donald (SPS)
House Leader, St Patricks,
Main Street, Knock,
Co Mayo
Tel 094-9388661

McDonagh, Enda
St Patrick's College,
Maynooth, Co Kildare
Tel 01-6285222
(Tuam, retired)

McDonagh, James, CC
Ballymote, Co Sligo
Tel 071-9189778
(*Ballymote (Emlefad and
Kilmorgan),* Achonry)

McDonagh, John, Very Rev,
PP, VF
No 1 Presbytery,
Castle Street, Dalkey,
Co Dublin
Tel 01-2857773
(Dublin)

McDonagh, Martin, (CSSp) CC
Hunter's Hill, Gilford,
Co Armagh BT63 6AJ
Tel 028-38831256
(*Tullylish,* Dromore)

McDonagh, Oliver, Very Rev,
PP
Ballintubber, Castlerea,
Co Roscommon
Tel 094-9655226
(*Ballintubber,* Elphin)

McDonagh, Sean (SSC)
(Research JPIC)
St Columban's, Dalgan Park,
Navan, Co Meath
Tel 046-9021525

McDonald, Anthony (OCarm)
Prior, Carmelite Priory,
White Abbey, Co Kildare
Tel 045-521391

McDonald, Daniel, Very Rev,
PP
Marshallstown, Enniscorthy,
Co Wexford
Tel 053-9388521
(Marshallstown, Ferns)

McDonald, John, CC
3 Stanhope Place, Athy,
Co Kildare
Tel 059-8631698
(*Athy,* Dublin)

McDonald, John, Rt Rev Mgr,
PP
Curragh Camp, Co Kildare
Tel 045-441369
(Kildare & L.)

McDonald, Matthew (OFM)
Lawson House,
Knockrathkyle, Glenbrien,
Enniscorthy, Co Wexford

McDonald, Thomas (CSSp)
Blackrock College,
Blackrock, Co Dublin
Tel 01-2888681

McDonnell, Albert
Vice Rector,
Irish College,
Via dei SS Quattro 1,
00184 Roma, Italy
Tel 00-3906-772631
(Killaloe)

McDonnell, Charles
The Presbytery, New Line,
Athenry, Co Galway
Tel 091-844227
(Tuam)

McDonnell, Colum (OSM)
Servite Priory, Benburb,
Dungannon,
Co Tyrone BT71 7JZ
Tel 028-37548241

McDonnell, Eunan (SDB)
Salesian College,
Maynooth Road, Celbridge,
Co Kildare
Tel 01-6275058/60

McDonnell, Francis, Very Rev,
PP
Parochial House,
83 Terenure Road East,
Dublin 6
Tel 01-4905520
(*Terenure*, Dublin)

McDonnell, Fred, CC
The Presbytery, Meelick,
Co Clare
Tel 061-325556/087-7706023
(*Parteen/Meelick*, Limerick)

McDonnell, James (CSSp)
Blackrock College,
Blackrock, Co Dublin
Tel 01-2888681

McDonnell, Joseph (SSC)
St Columban's, Dalgan Park,
Navan, Co Meath
Tel 046-9021525

McDonnell, Leo, CC
Cathedral House,
Cathedral Place, Limerick
Tel 061-414624/087-2589279
(*St John's*, Limerick)

McDonnell, Paschal (OFM)
Guardian, Franciscan Friary,
Rossnowlagh, Co Donegal
Tel 072-9851342

McDonnell, Patrick, Very Rev
Canon, PE, AP
Our Lady of Lourdes
Presbytery, Hardman's
Gardens, Drogheda,
Co Louth
Tel 041-9831899
(*Drogheda*, Armagh)

McDonnell, Paudge, Very Rev,
PP
Annyalla, Castleblayney,
Co Monaghan
Tel 042-9740121
(*Clontibret*, Clogher)

McDonnell, Thomas (SPS)
St Patrick's, Kiltegan,
Co Wicklow
Tel 059-6473600

McDonnell, Thomas, Very Rev,
PP
Chapel Lane, Sallins Road,
Naas, Co Kildare
Tel 045-897150
(*Naas*, Kildare & L.)

McDunphy, Aodhán (OCSO)
Mount Melleray Abbey,
Cappoquin, Co Waterford
Tel 058-54404

McEgan, Michael (SMA)
African Missions,
Blackrock Road, Cork
Tel 021-4292871

McElhatton, Francis (SPS)
St Patrick's, Kiltegan,
Co Wicklow
Tel 059-6473600

McElhennon, Kevin, CC
5 Strathroy Road, Omagh,
Co Tyrone BT79 7DW
Tel 028-82251055
Director of Adult Education,
The Gate Lodge,
2 Francis Street,
Derry BT48 9DS
Tel 028-71264087
(Derry)

McElhill, Laurence, Very Rev,
PP
Parochial House,
5 Aghalee Road,
Aghagallon, Craigavon,
Co Armagh BT67 0AR
Tel 028-92651214
(*Aghagallon and
Ballinderry*, Down & C.)

McElhinney, Brian, Very Rev,
PP
Lavey, Stradone, Co Cavan
Tel 049-4330125
(*Lavey*, Kilmore)

McElligott, David, Very Rev
Catherine McAuley Home,
Balloonagh, Tralee, Co Kerry
Tel 066-7129700
(Kerry, retired)

McElroy, James (SM)
Cerdon, Marist Fathers,
St Mary's Road, Dundalk,
Co Louth
Tel 042-9334019

McElvaney, Terence
Church Square,
Co Monaghan
Tel 047-82255
(Clogher)

McElwee, Christopher (IC),
Very Rev, PP
Rector, St Brigid's, Kilcurry,
Dundalk, Co Louth
Tel 042-9334410
(*Faughart*, Armagh)

McEneaney, Owen J., Very
Rev, Adm
St Joseph's Presbytery,
Park Street, Monaghan
Tel 047-81220
(Clogher)

McEnroe, Patrick, Very Rev,
PP, VF
Darver, Readypenny,
Dundalk, Co Louth
Tel 042-9379147
(*Darver and Dromiskin*,
Armagh)

McEntegart, Liam, Rt Rev Mgr
Canon, PE, VG
10 Killymeal Road,
Dungannon,
Co Tyrone BT71 6DP
Tel 028-87722906
(Armagh, retired)

McEntire, Peter J. (CSSp)
Holy Ghost Missionary
College, Kimmage Manor,
Dublin 12
Tel 01-4064300

McErlean, Martin, Very Rev,
PP
Parochial House,
Castletown-Kilpatrick,
Navan, Co Meath
Tel 046-9055789
(*Castletown-Kilpatrick*,
Meath)

McEveney, Feargus (OFM)
Franciscan Friary, Ennis,
Co Clare
Tel 065-6828751

McEvoy, A. (SDB)
Bursar, Salesian College,
Maynooth Road, Celbridge,
Co Kildare
Tel 01-6275058/60

McEvoy, Francis, Very Rev, PP,
VF
Parochial House,
Crookstown, Athy,
Co Kildare
Tel 059-862154
(*Narraghmore*, Dublin)

McEvoy, James, Rev Prof
(Queen's University)
St Malachy's College,
Antrim Road,
Belfast BT15 2AE
Tel 028-90748285
(Down & C.)

McEvoy, John, (SSC), CC
Mucklagh, Tullamore,
Co Offaly
Tel 057-9321892
(*Rahan*, Meath)

McEvoy, John, Very Rev, PP
Tinryland, Carlow
Tel 059-9131212
(*Tinryland*, Kildare & L.)

McEvoy, Joseph, Very Rev, PP
Parochial House, Moynalty,
Kells, Co Meath
Tel 046-9244305
(Meath)

McEvoy, P. J., Very Rev, PP
Francis Street, Edenderry,
Co Offaly
Tel 046-9737010
(*Rhode*, Kildare & L.)

McEvoy, Seamus, Very Rev
Dean, PP
The Rower, Inistioge,
Co Kilkenny
Tel 051-423619/086-2634093
(*Inistioge*, Ossory)

McEvoy, Seán, Very Rev, PP
Parochial House,
19 Caledon Road,
Aughnacloy,
Co Tyrone BT69 6HX
Tel 028-85557212
(*Aughnacloy (Aghaloo)*,
Armagh)

McFaul, Daniel, CC
Parochial House,
St Eugene's Cathedral,
Derry BT48 9AP
Tel 028-71262894/71365712
(*Derry City*, Derry)

McFlynn, Gerard
18 Maresfield Gardens,
London NW3 5SX
(Down & C.)

McGahan, Noel, CC
4 Darling Street, Enniskillen,
Co Fermanagh BT74 7DP
Tel 028-66322075
(Clogher)

McGann, James (CSSp)
Holy Ghost Missionary
College, Kimmage Manor,
Dublin 12
Tel 01-4064300

McGarry, Leo J. (CSSp)
St Michael's College,
Ailesbury Road, Dublin 4
Tel 01-2189423

McGarvey, Patrick, CC
Fanavolty, Kindrum,
Letterkenny, Co Donegal
Tel 074-9159007
(*Tamney*, Raphoe)

McGaughey, Sylvius (CP)
St Paul's Retreat,
Mount Argus, Dublin 6W
Tel 01-4992000

McGauran, Francis, Very Rev,
PP
Ballinameen, Boyle,
Co Roscommon
Tel 071-9668104
(*Ballinameen*, Elphin)

McGee, Brendan, Dean
St Patrick's Presbytery,
199 Donegall Street,
Belfast BT1 2FL
Tel 028-90324597
(*St Patrick's*, Down & C.)

McGee, Edward
St Malachy's College,
36 Antrim Road,
Belfast BT15 2AE
Tel 078-11144268
(Down & C.)

McGee, Edward, BA, BD
St Mary's University College,
191 Falls Road,
Belfast 12 6FE
Tel 028-90327678
(Down & C.)

McGee, Joseph (MSC)
Deputy-Leader,
Provincial Secretary &
Bursar, Provincialate,
65 Terenure Road West,
Dublin 6W
Tel 01-4906622

McGeough, Thomas, Very Rev, PE, AP
Parochial House,
Hale Street, Ardee, Co Louth
Tel 041-6850920
(*Ardee & Collon*, Armagh)

McGettigan, Denis, Very Rev, PP
Raphoe, Lifford,
Co Donegal
Tel 074-9145647
Chaplain, Deele College,
Raphoe, Co Donegal
Tel 074-9145277
(*Raphoe*, Raphoe)

McGettrick, William (CSsR), CC
St Joseph's,
St Alphonsus Road,
Dundalk, Co Louth
Tel 042-9334042/9334762
(*Dundalk, St Joseph's*, Armagh)

McGill, Maurice (MHM)
Regional Superior,
St Joseph's House,
50 Orwell Park, Rathgar,
Dublin 6
Tel 01-4127773/4127735

McGillicuddy, Cornelius
33 Gracepark Road,
Drumcondra, Dublin 9
(Dublin, retired)

McGilloway, Joseph (OSB)
Glenstal Abbey, Murroe,
Co Limerick
Tel 061-386103

McGing, Aidan (CM)
122 Sunday's Well Road,
Cork
Tel 021-4304070

McGinley, Séamus, Very Rev, PP
Parochial House, Moortown,
Cookstown, Co Tyrone BT80 0HT
Tel 028-86737236
(*Ardboe*, Armagh)

McGinn, Emlyn
Parochial House, Barn Road,
Dunleer, Co Louth
Tel 041-6863822
Chaplain, Dundalk Institute of Technology, Dublin Road,
Dundalk, Co Louth
Tel 042-9370224
(Armagh)

McGinn, Patrick, CC
St Joseph's Presbytery,
Park Street, Monaghan
Tel 047-81220
(*Monaghan*, Clogher)

McGinnity, Gerard, Very Rev, PP
Parochial House,
Knockbridge, Dundalk,
Co Louth
Tel 042-9374125
(*Knockbridge*, Armagh)

McGinnity, Michael
Family Ministry Office,
Good Shepherd Centre,
511 Ormeau Road,
Belfast BT7 3GS
Tel 028-90492777
(Down & C.)

McGirr, Austin, Very Rev, PP, VF
Parochial House,
4 The Crescent, Portstewart,
Co Derry BT55 7AB
Tel 028-70832534
(*Portstewart*, Down & C.)

McGirr, Dermot, CC
St Joseph's, Fairview Road,
Galliagh, Derry BT48 8NJ
Tel 028-71352351
(*The Three Patrons*, Derry)

McGlinchey, James, PEm
'Mellifont', Grianan Park,
Buncrana, Co Donegal
Tel 074-9361465
(Derry, retired)

McGlynn, Colm (OSM), Very Rev, PP
25/27 Hermitage Downs,
Marley Grange,
Rathfarnham, Dublin 16
Tel 01-4944295
(*Marley Grange*, Dublin)

McGlynn, Fergus, (Team member)
197 Kylemore Road,
Ballyfermot, Dublin 10
Tel 01-6264881/6264646
(*Ballyfermot*, Dublin)

McGlynn, Patrick (CSSp)
St Michael's College,
Ailesbury Road, Dublin 4
Tel 01-2189423

McGlynn, Thomas
The Cathedral Presbytery,
St Peter's Square,
Belfast BT12 4BU
(Down & C.)

McGoldrick, Brian, PP
Doneyloop, Castlefin,
Lifford, Co Donegal
Tel 074-9146183
(*Doneyloop*, Derry)

McGoldrick, John
(in residence)
Parochial House,
56 Minterburn Road,
Laireakean, Caledon,
Co Tyrone BT68 4XH
Tel 028-37568288
(*Aughnacloy (Aghaloo)*, Armagh)

McGoldrick, Neil, PP
Parochial House, Fahan,
Lifford, Co Donegal
Tel 074-9360151

McGoldrick, Patrick, CC
Parochial House, Moville,
Co Donegal
Tel 074-9382102
(*Moville*, Derry)

McGonagle, Hugh, CC
7 Elm Park, Ballinode, Sligo
Tel 071-9143430
(Elphin)

McGonagle, James, PP
Parochial House, Culdaff,
Co Donegal
Tel 074-9379107
(*Culdaff*, Derry)

McGoohan, Ultan, CC
The Presbytery, Cavan
Tel 049-4331404/4332269
(*Cootehill*, Kilmore)

McGorty, Roger (MHM)
St Joseph's House,
50 Orwell Park, Rathgar,
Dublin 6
Tel 01-4127700

McGourty, Michael, Very Rev, PP
Irvinestown, Enniskillen,
Co Fermanagh BT94 1EY
Tel 028-68628600
(*Irvinestown*, Clogher)

McGovern, Ciaran, Very Rev, PP
Newtownforbes,
Co Longford
Tel 043-3346805
(*Newtownforbes*, Ardagh & Cl.)

McGovern, Felim
The Presbytery, Cavan
Tel 049-4331404
(*Kilmore*, retired)

McGovern, Gregory (SMA)
African Missions,
Blackrock Road, Cork
Tel 021-4292871

McGovern, John, Very Rev
St Joseph's Presbytery, 52 Kincora Park, Lifford
Ennis, Co Clare
Tel 065-6822166/086-3221210
(*Ennis*, Killaloe)

McGovern, Patrick (SMA)
SMA House, Claregalway,
Co Galway
Tel 091-798880

McGovern, Thomas
30 Knapton Road,
Dun Laoghaire, Co Dublin
Tel 01-2804353
(Opus Dei)

McGowan, Michael, PC
7 St Patrick's Crescent,
Rathcoole, Co Dublin
Tel 01-4589210
(*Saggart*, Dublin)

McGowan, Padraig, Very Rev
Parochial House,
Ballymahon, Co Longford
(Ardagh & Cl.)

McGrady, Colm, Very Rev, PP
Parochial House, 8 Shore Road, Strangford,
Co Down BT30 7NL
Tel 028-44881206
(*Kilclief and Strangford*, Down & C.)

McGrady, Fergal, Very Rev, PP
111 Queensway, Lambeg,
Lisburn BT27 4QS
Tel 028-92662896
(*Derriaghy*, Down & C.)

McGrane, Camillus (OSM), CC
25/27 Hermitage Downs,
Marley Grange,
Rathfarnham, Dublin 16
Tel 01-4944295
(*Marley Grange*, Dublin)

McGrath, Aidan (OFM)
Curia Generalizia dei Frati Minoti,
Via S. Maria Mediatrice 25,
00165 Roma, Italy

McGrath, Adrian
Chaplain, Galway/Mayo Insititute of Technology,
Dublin Road, Galway
Tel 091-753161/757298
(Galway)

McGrath, Brendan (OFM)
Vicar, Provincial Definitor & Rector, Franciscan College,
Gormanston, Co Meath
Tel 01-8412203

McGrath, Brian (CSsR)
St Joseph's, Dundalk,
Co Louth
Tel 042-9334042/9334762

McGrath, Francis (OFM)
Vicar, Franciscan Friary,
Killarney, Co Kerry
Tel 064-6631334/6631066

McGrath, John, Very Rev, PP
Mullinahone, Thurles,
Co Tipperary
Tel 052-53152
(*Mullinahone*, Cashel & E.)

McGrath, Joseph
Chaplain, Parochial House,
Boherquill, Lismacaffney,
Mullingar, Co Westmeath
(*Streete*, Ardagh & Cl.)

McGrath, Joseph, Very Rev, PP
New Ross, Co Wexford
Tel 051-421348
(Ferns)

McGrath, Matthew,
Venerable, PP, VG
St Michael Street,
Tipperary Town
Tel 062-51536
(Cashel & E.)

McGrath, Michael, CC
St Mary's,
Carrick-on-Shannon,
Co Leitrim
Tel 071-9620347
(*Carrick-on-Shannon*, Ardagh & Cl.)

McGrath, Patrick (OP)
47 Leeson Park, Dublin 6
Tel 01-6602427

McGrath, Sean (SSC)
St Columban's, Dalgan Park,
Navan, Co Meath
Tel 046-9021525

McGrath, Thomas, Very Rev,
PP
Newbawn, Co Wexford
Tel 051-428227
(Newbawn, Ferns)

McGree, Thomas, CC
Durrow, Portlaoise,
Co Laois
Tel 057-8736155/
087-7619235
(Durrow, Ossory)

McGreevy, Gerard, Very Rev
Canon, PE
Magherarney, Smithboro,
Co Monaghan
Tel 047-57011
(Clogher, retired)

McGregor, Augustine (OCSO),
Rt Rev
Abbot, Mellifont Abbey,
Collon, Co Louth
Tel 041-9826103

McGregor, Bede (OP), Very
Rev
Prior, St Malachy's, Dundalk,
Co Louth
Tel 042-9334179/9333714

McGroarty, Liam
Chaplain, Coláiste Mhuire
Marino, Griffith Ave,
Dublin 9
(Dublin)

McGrory, James
Armagh Regional Marriage
Tribunal, 15 College Street,
Armagh BT61 9BT
Tel 028-37524537
(Derry)

McGuane, Joseph, Very Rev
St Mary's, Church Street,
Youghal, Co Cork
Tel 024-93392
(Cloyne)

McGuckian, Alan, (SJ)
Superior, Peter Faber House,
28 Brookvale Avenue,
Belfast BT14 6BW
Tel 028-90757615

McGuckian, Bernard (SJ)
St Francis Xavier's, Upper
Gardiner Street, Dublin 1
Tel 01-8363411

McGuckian, Michael (SJ)
Administrator, St Ignatius
Community & Church,
27 Raleigh Row, Salthill,
Galway
Tel 091-523707

McGuckien, Kevin
St Patrick's Presbytery,
199 Donegall Street,
Belfast BT1 2FL
Tel 028-90324597
(Down & C.)

McGuckin, Felix, Very Rev
5 Oriel Road,
Antrim BT41 4HP
Tel 028-94428086
(Antrim, St Comgall's, Down
& C.)

McGuckin, Patrick, Very Rev,
PE, AP
Parochial House,
80 Dundalk Street,
Newtownhamilton, Newry,
Co Down BT35 OPE
Tel 028-30878232
(Cullyhanna (Creggan
Lower), Armagh)

McGuinness, Austin (SSC)
St Columban's, Dalgan Park,
Navan, Co Meath
Tel 046-9021525
Chaplain, St Joseph's, Trim

McGuinness, Brendan, PP
Williamstown, Co Galway
Tel 094-9643007
(Williamstown, Tuam)

McGuinness, David
St Joseph's Catholic Church,
134 Prince Avenue, Athens,
Georgia 30601, USA
(Waterford & L.)

McGuinness, Edward, CC
Cockhill, Buncrana,
Co Donegal
Tel 074-9363768
(Buncrana, Derry)

McGuinness, Joseph, Rt Rev
Mgr
1 Darling Street, Enniskillen,
Co Fermanagh BT74 7DP
Tel 028-66322627
(Clogher)

McGuinness, Peter, Very Rev
Canon, PE
3 Castleross Retirement
Village, Carrickmacross,
Co Monaghan
Tel 042-9690013
(Clogher, retired)

McGuinness, T. J.
South Africa
(Dromore, retired)

McGuire, Robert, CC
Poulpeasty, Clonroche,
Enniscorthy, Co Wexford
Tel 053-9244116
(Cloughbawn, Ferns)

McHale, Benny, CC
The Presbytery, Ballyhaunis,
Co Mayo
Tel 094-9630095
(Tuam)

McHenry, Francis (OSB)
Glenstal Abbey, Murroe,
Co Limerick
Tel 061-386103

McHugh, Adrian
Diocese of Rockville Centre,
St Patrick's, Huntington,
New York NY 11743
Tel +1-631-3853311
(Achonry)

McHugh, Anthony, Very Rev,
PP
Parochial House,
33 Crossgar Road, Saintfield,
Ballynahinch,
Co Down BT24 7JE
Tel 028-97510237
(Saintfield and
Carrickmannon, Down & C.)

McHugh, Brendan, Very Rev,
PE
Parochial House, Mullanhoe,
Ardboe, Dungannon,
Co Tyrone BT71 5AU
Tel 028-86737338
(Armagh, retired)

McHugh, Christopher, Very
Rev, PP
Chaplain,
Grange Vocational School,
Sligo
Tel 071-9163100
(Elphin)

McHugh, Dominic, Very Rev
Canon
79 Castle Street,
Ballymoney,
Co Antrim BT53 6JT
Tel 028-27662259
(Ballymoney and
Derrykeighan, Down & C.)

McHugh, Laurence (CSSp)
Holy Ghost Missionary
College, Kimmage Manor,
Dublin 12
Tel 01-4064300

McHugh, Patrick
3 Seafield Court,
60–64 Castle Avenue,
Clontarf, Dublin
(Kilmore, retired)

McHugh, Patrick
1 The Mall, Knock, Co Mayo
Tel 094-9376664
(Clogher)

McHugh, Patrick, Very Rev
22 Rosehill, Sligo
(Elphin, retired)

McHugh, Patrick, Very Rev, PP
Termon, Letterkenny,
Co Donegal
Tel 074-9139016
(Termon, Raphoe)

McHugh, Sean
Bohernasup, Ballina,
Co Mayo
(Killala, retired)

McHugh, Seán, PP
Spiddal, Co Galway
Tel 091-533155
(Galway)

McIldowney, Hugh
7 Riverdale Close,
Belfast BT11 9DH
Tel 028-90603042
(Down & C., retired)

McIlraith, Cormac
186 Clontarf Road, Dublin 3
Tel 01-8333394
(Clontarf, St Anthony's,
Dublin)

McInerney, Declan
Our Lady of Lourdes,
Creagh, Ballinasloe,
Co Galway
Tel 090-9645080
(Clonfert)

McInerney, Michael, Very Rev,
AP
Quin, Co Clare
Tel 065-6825649
(Killaloe)

McInerney, Thomas (OP)
St Mary's Priory, Tallaght,
Dublin 24
Tel 01-4048100

McIntyre, Raymond (SDB)
Vice-Rector & Bursar,
Salesian College,
Pallaskenry, Co Limerick
Tel 061-393313

McKay, Brian (OCarm)
Presbytery, Montrose Park,
Beaumont, Dublin 5
Tel 01-8477740/8476359
(Beaumont, Dublin)

McKay, Dermot, Very Rev, PP
Parochial House,
51 Victoria Road, Larne,
Co Antrim BT40 1LY
Tel 028-28273230/28273053
(Larne, Down & C.)

McKeever, Brendan (CP)
St Paul's Retreat,
Mount Argus, Dublin 6W
Tel 01-4992000

McKeever, Des (SPS)
St Patrick's, Kiltegan,
Co Wicklow
Tel 059-6473600

McKeever, John, CC
Parochial House,
42 Abbey Street,
Armagh BT61 7DZ
Tel 028-37522802
(Cooley, Armagh)

McKeever, Joseph, Very Rev,
PP
9 Newry Road, Crossmaglen,
Newry, Co Down BT35 9HH
Tel 028-30861208
(Armagh)

McKeever, Martin (CSsR)
President, Alphonsian Academy, Via Merulana 31, CP 2458, 00100 Rome, Italy
Tel 0039-06494901

McKeever, Michael, CC
Church Hill, Letterkenny, Co Donegal
Tel 074-9137057
Ard Adhamhnáin, Letterkenny, Co Donegal
Tel 074-9121208
(Termon, Raphoe)

McKenna, Dermot (SJ)
Vice-Superior, John Austin House, 135 North Circular Road, Dublin 7
Tel 01-8386768

McKenna, Hugh (OFM)
Guardian & Vicar Provincial, Franciscan Friary, Ennis, Co Clare
Tel 065-6828751

McKenna, John F., CC
19 Ballagh Road, Clogher, Co Tyrone BT76 0TQ
Tel 028-85548525
(Clogher, Clogher)

McKenna, John, Very Rev
Canon
Baile na Buaile, Daingean Ui Chuis, Co Chiarrai
(Kerry, retired)

McKenna, John, Very Rev
Canon, PP
Trillick, Omagh, Co Tyrone BT78 3RD
Tel 028-89561350
(Trillick, Clogher)

McKenna, Joseph (SM)
Cerdon, Marist Fathers, St Mary's Road, Dundalk, Co Louth
Tel 042-9334019

McKenna, Joseph
1 St Joseph's Villas, Church Road, Bundoran, Co Donegal
Tel 071-9841756
(Birmingham, retired)

McKenna, Kevin, PEm
24 Glenroe Park, Dungiven, Co Derry BT47 4PE
Tel 028-77743857
(Derry, retired)

McKenna, Liam (SJ)
St Francis Xavier's, Upper Gardiner Street, Dublin 1
Tel 01-8363411

McKenna, Owen (SMA)
SMA House, 82 Ranelagh Road, Ranelagh, Dublin 6
Tel 01-4968162/3

McKenna, P. (MI)
St Camillus, Killucan, Co Westmeath
Tel 044-74115

McKenna, Padraig, CC
St Joseph's, Carrickmacross, Co Monaghan
Tel 042-9661231
(Carrickmacross, Clogher)

McKenna, Patrick, CC
2 Drumnaconagher Road, Crossgar BT30 9AN
Tel 028-44830342
(Crossgar (Kilmore), Down & C.)

McKenna, Patrick, Very Rev, PP, VF
503 Ormeau Road, Belfast BT7 3GR
Tel 028-90642446
(Holy Rosary, Down & C.)

McKenna, Robert, Very Rev, PE, AP
Parochial House, 26 Newtown Road, Camlough, Newry, Co Down BT35 7JJ
Tel 028-30830237
(Bessbrook (Killeavy Lower), Armagh)

McKenna, Seamus (IC)
Rector, St Patrick's, Upton, Innishannon, Co Cork
Tel 021-4776268/4776923

McKenna, Seamus, BA, HDE
Cork Regional Marriage Tribunal, The Lough, Cork
Tel 021-4963653
(Kerry)

Lynch, Francis, PP
1 Aileach Road, Ballymagroarty, Derry BT48 0AZ
Tel 028-71267070
(Derry)

McKeogh, Colm (SMA)
African Missions, Blackrock Road, Cork
Tel 021-4292871

McKeogh, Stephen (OCD)
St Joseph's Carmelite Retreat Centre, Termonbacca, Derry BT48 9XE
Tel 028-71262512

McKeon, Austin, Very Rev, PP
Tulsk, Castlerea, Co Roscommon
Tel 071-9639005
(Elphin)

McKeon, Seamus, Very Rev, PP
Aughnacliffe, Co Longford
Tel 043-6684118
(Colmcille, Ardagh & Cl.)

McKeown, Donal, Most Rev, DD
Titular Bishop of Killossy and Auxiliary Bishop of Down and Connor, 96 Downview Park West, Belfast BT15 5HZ
Tel 028-90781642
(Down & C.)

McKeown, Hugh (SMA)
Dromantine College, Dromantine, Newry, Co Down BT34 1RH
Tel 028-30821224

McKeown, Noel (OP)
St Catherine's, Newry, Co Down BT35 8BN
Tel 028-30262178

McKeown, Phelim, CC
Parochial House, 9 Chapel Road, Bessbrook, Newry, Co Down BT35 7AU
Tel 028-30830272
(Bessbrook (Killeavy Lower), Armagh)

McKevitt, Brian (OP)
St Mary's Priory, Tallaght, Dublin 24
Tel 01-4048100

McKiernan, Fintan, Very Rev, PP
56 Mary Street, Derrylin, Co Fermanagh
Tel 028-67748315
(Derrylin, Kilmore)

McKiernan, Peter, Very Rev, PP
Knockbride, Bailieboro, Co Cavan
Tel 042-9660112
(Knockbride, Kilmore)

McKiernan, Tom, Very Rev, PP
Visiting Chaplain, St Mogue's College, Bawnboy, Co Cavan
Tel 049-9523112
(Kilmore)

McKinlay, Denis, Very Rev, PP
Parochial House, 121 Dublin Road, Kilcoo, Co Down BT34 5HP
Tel 028-40630314
(Kilcoo, Down & C.)

McKinley, Patrick, CC
1 Maypark, Malahide Road, Dublin 5
Tel 01-8313033
(Donnycarney, Dublin)

McKinney, Anthony (OCarm)
Gort Muire, Ballinteer, Dublin 16
Tel 01-2984014

McKinney, Liam, CC
Parochial House, 9a Newry Road, Crossmaglen, Newry, Co Down BT35 9HH
Tel 028-30868698
(Crossmaglen (Creggan Upper), Armagh)

McKinstry, Gordon
12 The Meadows, Randalstown, Co Antrim BT41 2JB
(Down & C., reitred)

McKittrick, Brian, CC
The Presbytery, Shangan Road, Ballymun, Dublin 9
Tel 01-8421551
(Ballymun, Dublin)

McKnight, Bruno (OFMCap)
Capuchin Friary, Church Street, Dublin 7
Tel 01-8730599

McLaughlin, Brian (CSSp)
Holy Ghost Missionary College, Kimmage Manor, Dublin 12
Tel 01-4064300

McLaughlin, Con, PP
Barrack Hill, Carndonagh, Lifford, Co Donegal
Tel 074-9374104
Director, Inishowen Pastoral Centre, Carndonagh, Co Donegal
Tel 074-9374103
(Derry)

McLaughlin, Eamonn, CC
Parochial House, Leitirmacaward, Co Donegal
Tel 074-9544102
(Dungloe, Raphoe)

McLaughlin, George
Chez Nous, Drumawier, Greencastle, Co Donegal
(Derry, retired)

McLaughlin, Kevin (OMI)
Oblate Scholasticate, St Anne's, Goldenbridge Walk, Inchicore, Dublin 8
Tel 01-4540841/4542955
52a/52b Bulfin Road, Dublin 8
Tel 01-4531660
(Inchicore, St Michael's, Dublin)

McLaughlin, Michael, Very Rev, PP
Airfield, Inch, Ennis, Co Clare
Tel 065-6839332
(Inch and Kilmaley, Killaloe)

McLaughlin, Pat (CSsR), CC
St Gerard's,
722 Antrim Road,
Newtownabbey,
Co Antrim BT36 7PG
Tel 028-90774833
(*St Gerard's*, Down & C.)

McLaughlin, Patrick, CC
65 Mayogall Road,
Knockloughrim,
Magherafelt,
Co Derry BT45 8PG
Tel 028-79642435
(*Lavey*, Derry)

McLaughlin, Peter, PP
143 Melmount Road,
Sion Mills, Strabane,
Co Tyrone BT82 9EX
Tel 028-81658264
(*Sion Mills*, Derry)

McLaughlin, Pius (OFM)
Vicar, Franciscan Friary,
Rossnowlagh, Co Donegal
Tel 072-9851342

McLaughlin, Stephen, PP
Parochial House,
St Mary's, Creggan,
Derry BT48 9QE
Tel 028-71263152
(*St Mary's, Creggan*, Derry)

McLaverty, Anthony, Very
Rev, CC
470 Falls Road,
Belfast BT12 6EN
Tel 028-90321102
(*St John's*, Down & C.)

McLaverty, George, Very Rev
518 Donegall Road,
Belfast BT12 6DY
(Down & C., retired)

McLoone, Francis, Very Rev,
PP
Killymard, Co Donegal
Tel 074-9721929
(Killymard, Raphoe)

McLoone, John, Very Rev, PP
Frosses, Co Donegal
Tel 074-9736006
(*Inver*, Raphoe)

McLoughlin, Aidan (OCarm)
Carmelite Priory,
Knocktopher, Co Kilkenny
Tel 056-7768675

McLoughlan, H. (SMA)
African Missions,
Blackrock Road, Cork
Tel 021-4292871

McLoughlin, Christopher, Very
Rev Canon
(Priest in residence,
Tourlestrane Parish)
Kilmactigue, Aclare,
Co Sligo
Tel 071-9181007
(Achonry, retired)

McLoughlin, Denis (CP)
St Paul's Retreat,
Mount Argus, Dublin 6W
Tel 01-4992000

McLoughlin, Eugene (SMA),
CC
St Joseph's,
Blackrock Road, Cork
Tel 021-4292871
(*St Joseph's (Blackrock
Road)*, Cork & R.)

McLoughlin, Eugene, Very Rev
Canon, PP, VF
Parochial House,
Roscommon
Tel 090-6626298
(*Roscommon*, Elphin)

McLoughlin, Joseph (CSsR)
Mount Saint Alphonsus,
Limerick
Tel 061-315099

McLoughlin, Joseph (SAC), CC
St Patrick's, Corduff,
Blanchardstown, Dublin 15
Tel 01-8213596/8215930
(*Corduff*, Dublin)

McLoughlin, Michael, Very
Rev, PP
Moycullen, Co Galway
Tel 091-555106
(*Moycullen*, Galway)

McLoughlin, Patrick (CSsR), CC
722 Antrim Road,
Newtownabbey,
Co Antrim BT36 7PG
Tel 028-90774833/4
(*St Gerard's*, Down & C.)

McLoughlin, Terence (OP)
St Mary's, The Claddach,
Co Galway
Tel 091-582884

McMahon, Andrew, CC
St Paul's Presbytery,
Old Portadown Road,
Lurgan,
Co Armagh BT66 8RG
Tel 028-38326883
(*Shankill, St Paul's (Lurgan)*,
Dromore)

McMahon, Anthony, CC
The Presbytery, Nenagh,
Co Tipperary
Tel 067-37134/086-8243801
(*Nenagh*, Killaloe)

McMahon, James (OSB)
Glenstal Abbey, Murroe,
Co Limerick
Tel 061-386103

McMahon, John, CC
Bridge Street,
Manorhamilton, Co Leitrim
Tel 071-9856987
(Kilmore)

McMahon, Joseph, BA, BD,
HDE
President,
St Flannan's College,
Co Clare
Tel 065-6828019
(Killaloe)

McMahon, Padraig, Very Rev,
Adm
Cathedral House, Mullingar,
Co Westmeath
Tel 044-9348338/9340126
(*Mullingar*, Meath)

McMahon, Richard (CSsR)
St Patrick's, Esker, Athenry,
Co Galway
Tel 091-844549

McMahon, Richard (CSsR), CC
Kiltulla, Athenry, Co Galway
Tel 091-848208
(*Kiltulla and Attymon*,
Clonfert)

McMahon, Seamus (SM)
Australia

McManus, Brendan (SJ)
St Ignatius Community &
Church, 27 Raleigh Row,
Salthill, Galway
Tel 091-523707

McManus, Frank, CC
Chaplain, The Rock Welfare
Home, Ballyshannon,
Co Donegal
Tel 071-9851221
(Clogher)

McManus, John, (SPS), CC
10 Ashford, Monksland,
Athlone, Co Westmeath
Tel 090-6493262
(*Athlone, SS Peter and
Paul's,* Elphin)

McManus, John, Very Rev
Lisbreen, 73 Somerton Road,
Belfast BT15 4DE
Tel 028-90776185
(Down & C.)

McManus, Kevin (OSA), PP
St John's Priory,
Thomas Street,
Dublin 8
Tel 01-6770393

McManus, Michael, CC
Castlerea, Co Roscommon
Tel 094-9620039
(*Castlerea*, Elphin)

McManus, Patrick (SSC)
St Columban's, Dalgan Park,
Navan, Co Meath
Tel 046-9021525

McManus, Thomas, Very Rev,
PP
Corlough, Belturbet,
Co Cavan
Tel 049-9523122
(*Corlough and Drumreilly*,
Kilmore)

McMenamin, Joseph (White
Fathers)
Promotion Director,
Cypress Grove, Templeogue,
Dublin 6W
Tel 01-4055526

McMenamin, William, Very
Rev Canon, PP
Drumoghill,
Manorcunningham,
Co Donegal
Tel 074-9157169
(*Drumoghill*, Raphoe)

McMorrow, Maurice, CC
Glenade, Kinlough,
Co Leitrim
Tel 071-9841461
(*Kinlough and Glenade*,
Kilmore)

McMullan, Alex, Very Rev
Canon, PP
4 Irish Street, Killyleagh,
Co Down BT30 9QS
Tel 028-44828211
(*Killyleagh*, Down & C.)

McMullan, Anthony (OP)
St Malachy's, Dundalk,
Co Louth
Tel 042-9334179/9333714

McMullan, Brendan, Very Rev
26 Willowbank Park,
Belfast BT6 0LL
(Down & C., retired)

McMullan, Kevin, Very Rev, PP
Parochial House, Crossgar,
Downpatrick,
Co Down BT30 9EA
Tel 028-44830229
(*Crossgar (Kilmore)*, Down &
C.)

McMullin, Ernan, DPhil
Mountcharles, Co Donegal
(Raphoe, retired)

McMyler, Francis, Very Rev, PP
Chaple Street, Louisburgh,
Co Mayo
(Tuam, retired)

McNaboe, Desmond
(OFMCap), Very Rev, PP
Capuchin Parochial Friary,
Church Street, Dublin 7
Tel 01-8730599
(*Halston Street and Arran
Quay*, Dublin)

McNally, Albert, Very Rev, PP,
VF
24 Downs Road, Newcastle,
Co Down BT33 0AG
Tel 028-43722401
(*Newcastle (Maghera)*,
Down & C.)

McNally, Andrew
(in residence)
24 Chapel Road, Killeavy,
Newry, Co Down BT35 8JY
Tel 028-30848222
(*Cloghogue (Killeavy
Upper)*, Armagh)

McNally, Andrew
Armagh Diocesan Pastoral
Centre, The Magnet,
The Demesne, Dundalk,
Co Louth
Tel 042-9336649
(Armagh)

McNally, Brendan, Very Rev, PE
Parochial House,
Reaghstown, Ardee,
Co Louth
Tel 041-6855117
(Armagh, retired)

McNally, James, Very Rev, PE
14 Derrygarve Road,
Castledawson,
Co Derry BT45 8HA
Tel 028-79649998
(Armagh, retired)

McNamara, Austin, Very Rev, Adm
Cathedral House,
Cathedral Place, Limerick
Tel 061-414624/087-2589279
(St John's, Limerick)

McNamara, Brian, Very Rev Canon, Adm
Derrylester, Enniskillen,
Co Fermanagh
Tel 028-66348224
(Killesher, Kilmore)

McNamara, Cormac (SM)
Mexico

McNamara, David (CSsR)
Mount Saint Alphonsus,
Limerick
Tel 061-315099

McNamara, Donal, Very Rev Canon, PP
St Munchin's, Clancy Strand,
Limerick
Tel 061-455635/087-2402518
(St Munchin's and St Lelia's, Limerick)

McNamara, Frank, Very Rev
Portiuncula Nursing Home,
Multyfarnham,
Co Westmeath
(Meath, retired)

McNamara, Gerard, Very Rev, PP
Ballyduff Upper,
Co Waterford
Tel 058-60227
(Ballyduff, Waterford & L.)

McNamara, Gerard, Very Rev, PP
Bulgaden, Kilmallock,
Co Limerick
Tel 063-88005/087-2408998
(Bulgaden/Martinstown, Limerick)

McNamara, John (OCD)
St Joseph's Carmelite Retreat Centre,
Termonbacca,
Derry BT48 9XE
Tel 028-71262512

McNamara, John, Very Rev, PP, VF
Parochial House,
Brackenstown Road,
Swords, Co Dublin
Tel 01-8401661
(Dublin)

McNamara, Kevin (MSC)
Woodview House,
Mount Merrion Avenue,
Blackrock, Co Dublin
Tel 01-2881644

McNamara, Kevin (MSC), CC (pro-tem)
Killarney, Co Kerry
Tel 064-31014
(Killarney, Kerry)

McNamara, Leslie
Columban Missionary Society, Dalgan Park,
Dublin Road, Navan,
Co Meath
(Limerick)

McNamara, Liam, Very Rev Canon, PP
Ballybricken, Grange,
Kilmallock, Co Limerick
Tel 061-351158
(Ballybricken, Cashel & E.)

McNamara, Martin (MSC)
Woodview House,
Mount Merrion Avenue,
Blackrock, Co Dublin
Tel 01-2881644

McNamara, Martin, Very Rev, PP
Kiltulla, Athenry,
Co Galway
Tel 091-848021
(Kiltulla and Attymon, Clonfert)

McNamara, Oliver, CC
Annaghdown, Co Galway
Tel 091-791142
(Corrandulla (Annaghdown), Tuam)

McNamara, Patrick (CSSp)
Spiritan House,
213 North Circular Road,
Dublin 7
Tel 01-8389664/8683504

McNamara, Robert (CSsR), CC
Curate's House,
Walter Macken Road,
Mervue, Galway
Tel 091-771662
(Mervue, Galway)

McNamara, Walter (CSSp)
Holy Ghost Missionary College, Kimmage Manor,
Dublin 12
Tel 01-4064300

McNamee, Ambrose (OCD)
The Abbey, Loughrea,
Co Galway
Tel 091-841209

McNamee, Paul
c/o Bishop's House,
Dublin Road, Carlow
(Kildare & L.)

McNeice, Damian
Diocesan Liturgical Resource Centre, Holy Cross College,
Clonliffe, Dublin 3
Tel 01-8379253 Ext 238
Chaplain, 149 Swords Road,
Whitehall, Dublin 9
Tel 01-8372521
(Dublin)

McNeill, Peter C., Adm
58 Ballydrumman Road,
Ballyward,
Castlewellan, Co Down
Tel 028-40650207
(Drumgooland and Dromara, Dromore)

McNelis, Denis, Very Rev, PP
Parochial House, Laytown,
Co Meath
Tel 041-9827258
(Meath)

McNerney, John
Chaplains' Residence,
St Stephen's, UCD, Belfield,
Dublin 4
Tel 01-2600715
(Dublin)

McNulty, James J. (CSSp)
St Mary's College,
Rathmines, Dublin 6
Tel 01-4062160

McNulty, Thomas, CC
Parochial House,
Grange, Carlingford,
Co Louth
Tel 042-9376577
(Armagh, Armagh)

McPadden, Charles
(in residence)
Glangevlin,
Via Carrick-on-Shannon,
Co Leitrim
Tel 071-9643104
(Killinagh and Glangevlin, Kilmore)

McParland, Peter, Very Rev, PP
Top Rath, Cooley,
Carlingford, Co Louth
Tel 042-9376105
(Cooley, Armagh)

McPartlan, Peter, Very Rev, PP
Ballintemple, Ballinagh,
Co Cavan
Tel 049-4337106
(Ballintemple, Kilmore)

McPhillips, James, CC
Killanny, Carrickmacross,
Co Monaghan
Tel 042-9661452
(Clogher)

McQuaid, Macartan, Very Rev Canon
Chaplain,
St Michael's College,
Enniskillen,
Co Fermanagh BT74 6DE
Tel 028-66322935
(Clogher)

McQuillan, Ignatius, Rt Rev Mgr
(priest in residence)
60 Glenmore Park,
Belt Road, Derry BT47 2JZ
Tel 028-91291758
(Ardmore, Derry)

McShane, Dermot, Very Rev, PP
Bruckless, Co Donegal
Tel 074-9737015
(Bruckless, Raphoe)

McShane, Patrick, Very Rev Canon, PE
Tully, Donegal Town,
Co Donegal
Tel 074-9740150
(Raphoe, retired)

McShane, Philip (OP)
St Saviour's,
Glentworth Street, Limerick
Tel 061-412333

McSorley, Gerard, Rt Rev Mgr, PE
Ballybay, Co Monaghan
Tel 042-9741031
(Ballybay, Clogher)

McSweeney, Anthony, CC
Fethard, Co Tipperary
Tel 052-6131187
(Fethard, Cashel & E.)

McSweeney, Edward (MSC)
Myross Wood Retreat House, Leap, Skibbereen,
Co Cork
Tel 028-33118

McSweeney, Eustace (OFMCap)
Vicar, Capuchin Friary,
Station Road, Raheny,
Dublin 5
Tel 01-8313886

McSweeney, Myles, CC
Bandon, Co Cork
Tel 023-8865067
(Bandon, Cork & R.)

McSweeney, Patrick T., Very Rev Canon, PE
Nazareth House, Mallow,
Co Cork
Tel 022-21561
(Cloyne, retired)

McTiernan, John, Very Rev, PP
Drumahaire, Co Leitrim
Tel 071-9164143
(Drumahaire and Killargue, Kilmore)

McTiernan, Sean (SPS)
St Patrick's, Kiltegan,
Co Wicklow
Tel 059-6473600

McVeigh, Joseph, CC
Loughside Road, Garrison,
Enniskillen,
Co Fermanagh BT93 4AE
Tel 028-68659747
(Belleek-Garrison, Clogher)

McVeigh, Martin, Very Rev, PP
Parochial House, 9
Cavanakeeran Road,
Pomeroy, Dungannon,
Co Tyrone BT70 2RD
Tel 028-87758329
(*Pomeroy*, Armagh)

McVeigh, Patrick, Very Rev
3 Broughshane Road,
Ballymena,
Co Antrim BT43 7DX
(Down & C., retired)

McVerry, Peter (SJ)
Arrupe Community,
127 Shangan Road,
Ballymun, Dublin 9
Tel/Fax 01-8625345

McWilliams, Luke, Very Rev,
PP
Parochial House,
59 Chapel Road,
Glenavy, Crumlin,
Co Antrim BT29 4LY
Tel 028-94422262
(*Glenavy and Killead*, Down
& C.)

McWilliams, Patrick, Very Rev,
PP
103 Roguery Road,
Moneyglass, Toomebridge,
Co Antrim BT41 3PT
Tel 028-79650225
(*Duneane*, Down & C.)

Meade, Bernard (CM)
St Paul's College, Raheny,
Dublin 5
Tel 01-8318113

Meade, James F. (CSSp)
Holy Ghost Missionary
College, Kimmage Manor,
Dublin 12
Tel 01-4064300

Meade, John (CSSp), CC
Superior, Rockwell College,
Cashel, Co Tipperary
Tel 062-61444/087-9450163

Meade, Michael, PP
Parochial House, Donore,
Drogheda, Co Louth
Tel 041-9823137
(*Donore*, Meath)

Meagher, Charles (SSC)
St Columban's, Dalgan Park,
Navan, Co Meath
Tel 046-9021525

Meagher, John (OSA)
The Abbey, Fethard,
Co Tipperary
Tel 052-31273

Meagher, Thomas F. (CSSp)
Holy Ghost Missionary
College, Kimmage Manor,
Dublin 12
Tel 01-4064300

Meaney, Anthony, CC
Parochial House,
Ballycruttle Road,
Downpatrick,
Co Down BT30 7EL
Tel 028-44841213
(*Saul and Ballee*, Down & C.)

Medina, Nelson (OP)
St Saviour's,
Upper Dorset Street,
Dublin 1
Tel 01-8897610

Meehan, Dermot, Very Rev,
PP
Swinford, Co Mayo
Tel 094-9252952
(Achonry)

Meehan, Francis (SMA)
SMA House,
82 Ranelagh Road,
Ranelagh, Dublin 6
Tel 01-4968162/3

Meehan, Frank, Very Rev, PP
Shinrone, Co Offaly
Tel 0505-47167/087-2302413
(*Shinrone*, Killaloe)

Meehan, Patrick (SM)
Cerdon, Marist Fathers,
St Mary's Road, Dundalk,
Co Louth
Tel 042-9334019

Meehan, Patrick (SSC)
St Columban's Retirement
Home, Dalgan Park, Navan,
Co Meath
Tel 046-9021525

Meehan, Séamus, Very Rev,
PP
Dungloe, Co Donegal
Tel 074-9521008
(*Dungloe*, Raphoe)

Meehan, William, Very Rev,
PP
St Mary's, Irishtown,
Clonmel, Co Tipperary
Tel 052-6122954
(Waterford & L.)

Mehigan, Donal (OP)
St Mary's, Pope Quay, Cork
Tel 021-4502267

Melican, P. J. (SPS)
St Patrick's, Kiltegan,
Co Wicklow
Tel 059-6473600

Mellett, Stanislaus (CSsR)
Marianella, 75 Orwell Road,
Rathgar,
Dublin 6
Tel 01-4922688
(Dublin)

Melody, Sean, Very Rev, PP
Sacred Heart Presbytery,
21 The Folly, Waterford
Tel 051-873759
(*Sacred Heart*, Waterford &
L.)

Melvin, Bonaventure (OCSO)
Mount Saint Joseph Abbey,
Roscrea, Co Tipperary
Tel 0505-25600

Mercer, Vincent (OP)
Black Abbey, Kilkenny,
Co Kilkenny
Tel 056-21279

Mernagh, Michael (OSA)
St John's Priory,
Thomas Street,
Dublin 8
Tel 01-6770393

Mernagh, Patrick, CF
McKee Barracks,
Blackhorse Avenue, Dublin 7
(Ferns)

Merrigan, Liam, Very Rev, PP
Drogheda Road,
Monasterevin, Co Kildare
Tel 045-525346
(Kildare & L.)

Meskell, Derek (CSsR)
Scala, Bessboro,
Blackrock, Cork
Tel 021-4358800

Mhamwa, Thaddeus, PC
128 Roselawn Road,
Blanchardstown, Dublin 15
Tel 01-8219014
(*Blanchardstown*, Dublin)

Millar, George (SVD)
Maynooth, Co Kildare
Tel 01-6286391/2

Mills, Dermot (OMI)
St Michael's Parish,
52a Bulfin Road, Inchicore,
Dublin 8
Tel 01-4531660
(*Inchicore*, Dublin)

Mills, Dermot, (OMI)
Parochial House,
118 Naas Road, Dublin 8
Tel 01-4501040
(Bluebell, Dublin)

Milton, Raymond, CC
Drum, Athlone,
Co Westmeath
Tel 090-6437125
(*Athlone, SS Peter and
Paul's,* Elphin)

Minniter, Anthony, Very Rev,
PP
Ballindereen, Kilcolgan,
Co Galway
Tel 091-796118
(*Ballindereen*, Galway)

Minogue, James, Very Rev, AP
Castleconnell, Co Limerick
Tel 061-377166/087-6228674
(*Castleconnell*, Killaloe)

Mitchell, Francis, Adm
The Presbytery, Westport,
Co Mayo
Tel 098-28871
(Tuam)

Mitchell, James, Rev Dr
11 St Mary's Terrace, Galway
Tel 091-524411
(Galway, retired)

Mitchell, Kilian (OPraem)
Abbey of the Most Holy
Trinity and St Norbert,
Kilnacrott, Ballyjamesduff,
Co Cavan
Tel 049-8544416

Mockler, John, CC
Study leave
C/o Diocesan Office, Social
Service Centre,
Henry Street, Limerick
(Limerick)

Mohan, Mark, CC
Parochial House, St Patrick's,
Trim, Co Meath
Tel 046-9431251
(*Trim*, Meath)

Mohan, Richard, Rt Rev Mgr
Adm
Pettigo, Co Donegal
Tel 071-9861666
(*Pettigo*, Clogher)

Moley, John, Very Rev
24 Mallard Road,
Downpatrick,
Co Down BT30 6DY
(Down & C., retired)

Mollin, Matthew, Very Rev
Maryfield Nursing Home,
Chapelizod, Co Dublin
(Meath, retired)

Molloy, Francis, Very Rev
Lurgan, Co Armagh
(Dromore, retired)

Molloy, John (SSC)
St Columban's Retirement
Home, Dalgan Park, Navan,
Co Meath
Tel 046-9021525

Molloy, John
Casa Central Santiago
Apostal,
Av. Pedro do Osma 428,
Lima, Peru
(Killaloe)

Molloy, Michael (SSC)
Society Archivist,
St Columban's,
Grange Road, Donaghmede,
Dublin 13
Tel 01-8476647

Molloy, Michael, Very Rev, PP
The Presbytery,
Ballydangan,
Athlone, Co Roscommon
Tel 090-9673539
(Moore, Tuam)

Molloy, Patrick (MHM)
Rector, St Joseph's House,
50 Orwell Park, Rathgar,
Dublin 6
Tel 01-4127700

Moloney, Bernard
Cahir Road, Cashel,
Co Tipperary
Tel 062-61443
(*Cashel*, Cashel & E.)

Moloney, Brendan, Very Rev, PP
Silvermines, Nenagh,
Co Tipperary
Tel 067-25864
(*Silvermines*, Killaloe)

Moloney, Dermot, Rt Rev Mgr, PP, VG
Crossboyne, Claremorris,
Co Mayo
Tel 094-9371824
(Tuam)

Moloney, Gerard (CSsR)
(Editor, Redemptorist Communications),
Liguori House,
75 Orwell Road, Dublin 6
Tel 01-4067100/4922488

Moloney, Henry (CSSp)
Holy Ghost Missionary College, Kimmage Manor,
Dublin 12
Tel 01-4064300

Moloney, John J., Rt Rev Mgr, PE
50 Rathgar Road, Dublin 6
(Dublin, retired)

Moloney, Joseph, Very Rev
Grove House, Vicar Street,
Tuam, Co Galway
(Tuam, retired)

Moloney, Leonard (SJ)
Headmaster,
Clongowes Wood College,
Naas, Co Kildare
Tel 045-868663/868202

Moloney, Michael
Daingean, Co Offaly
Tel 057-9362006
(Kildare & L.)

Moloney, Raymond (SJ)
Milltown Park,
Sandford Road, Dublin 6
Tel 01-2698411/2698113

Molony, Raymond T., Very Rev Canon
Presbytery No 2, Thormanby Road, Howth, Co Dublin
Tel 01-8222092
(Dublin, retired)

Monaghan, Stephen (CM), Very Rev
Superior, 11 Iona Drive,
Glasnevin, Dublin 9
Tel 01-8305238

Monahan, Finian (OCD)
The Abbey, Loughrea,
Co Galway
Tel 091-841209

Monahan, Fintan
Archbishop's House, Tuam,
Co Galway
Tel 093-24166
(Tuam)

Monahan, Patrick, CC
'Renvyle', Corrig Avenue,
Dun Laoghaire, Co Dublin
Tel 01-2802100
(*Dun Laoghaire*, Dublin)

Monahan, Paul (SMA), CC
The Presbytery, Neilstown,
Clondalkin, Dublin 22
Tel 01-4573546
(*Neilstown*, Dublin)

Monahan, Thomas (OP)
Holy Cross, Sligo, Co Sligo
Tel 071-42700

Mongan, Gerard, CC
St Columba's Presbytery,
6 Victoria Place,
Derry BT48 6TJ
Tel 028-71262301
(*St Columba's, Long Tower (Templemore)*, Derry)

Monks, Frank (MI)
Superior, St Camillus,
Killucan, Co Westmeath
Tel 044-74115

Monson, Eamon (SAC), Very Rev
Provincial, Provincial House,
'Homestead',
Sandyford Road, Dundrum,
Dublin 16
Tel 01-2956180/2954170

Montades, Rudy (SVD), CC
The Presbytery, City Quay,
Dublin 2
Tel 01-6773706
(*City Quay*, Dublin)

Montague, Paul, CC
6 Ard na Mara, Blackrock,
Dundalk, Co Louth
Tel 042-9322244
(*Haggardstown and Blackrock*, Armagh)

Mooney, Desmond, CC
The Presbytery,
13 Tullygally Road,
Legahory,
Craigavon BT65 5BY
Tel 028-38343297
(*Moyraverty (Craigavon)*, Dromore)

Mooney, Oliver, Very Rev
Newry, Co Down
(Dromore, retired)

Mooney, Patrick, Very Rev, PP
The Parochial House,
Glenamaddy, Co Galway
Tel 094-9659017
(Tuam)

Moore, Brian (CM), Very Rev
Provincial, Provincial Office,
St Paul's, Sybil Hill, Raheny,
Dublin 5
Tel 01-8510840/8510842

Moore, David, CC
Parochial House,
10 Aughrim Road,
Magherafelt,
Co Derry BT45 6AY
Tel 028-79632351
(*Magherafelt and Ardtrea North*, Armagh)

Moore, Edward, Very Rev, PP
Allen, Kilmeague, Naas,
Co Kildare
Tel 045-860135
(Allen, Kildare & L.)

Moore, Edward, Very Rev, PP
Aughrim, Hillstreet,
Carrick-on-Shannon,
Co Roscommon
Tel 071-9637010
(*Aughrim*, Elphin)

Moore, Eoin (OCarm)
Terenure College, Terenure,
Dublin 6W
Tel 01-4904621

Moore, Gerard, CC
The Presbytery,
Dublin Road, Balbriggan,
Co Dublin
Tel 01-8412116
(*Balbriggan*, Dublin)

Moore, James, CC
Jamesbrook, Midleton,
Co Cork
Tel 021-4652456
(Cloyne)

Moore, James, Very Rev, PP
Fintona, Omagh,
Co Tyrone BT78 2NS
Tel 028-82841907
(*Fintona*, Clogher)

Moore, Kevin, Very Rev
Moderator,
122 Greencastle Road,
Coolock, Dublin 17
Tel 01-8487657
(*Bonnybrook*, Dublin)

Moore, Michael (CSSp)
Rockwell College, Cashel,
Co Tipperary
Tel 062-61444

Moore, Paschal, Very Rev, PP
Piltown, Co Kilkenny
Tel 051-643112/087-2408078
(*Templeorum*, Ossory)

Moore, Patrick (SPS)
St Patrick's, Kiltegan,
Co Wicklow
Tel 059-6473600

Moore, Patrick B., Very Rev, PE
The Presbytery, Brittas Bay,
Co Wicklow
Tel 0404-47177
(Dublin, retired)

Moore, Patrick, Very Rev, PP
Duagh, Listowel, Co Kerry
Tel 068-45102
(*Duagh*, Kerry)

Moore, Patrick, Very Rev, PP, VF
Parochial House,
Castlepollard,
Co Westmeath
Tel 044-9661126
(Meath)

Moore, Seamus, Very Rev, PE
8 Herbert Avenue, Dublin 4
Tel 01-2692501
(Dublin, retired)

Moore, Sean (CSsR)
Clonard Monastery,
1 Clonard Gardens,
Belfast, BT13 2RL
Tel 028-90445950

Moore, Seán, Very Rev, PP
Parochial House,
290 Monaghan Road,
Middletown,
Co Armagh BT60 4HS
Tel 028-37568406
(*Middletown (Tynan)*, Armagh)

Moorhead, John, Very Rev, PP
Parochial House, Eglish,
Birr, Co Offaly
Tel 057-9133010
(*Eglish*, Meath)

Morahan, Kieran (SMA)
Temporary diocesan work in Ireland
C/o African Missions,
Provincial House, Feltrim,
Blackrock Road, Cork
Tel 021-4292871

Morahan, Leo, Very Rev, PE
2 The Beeches, Louisburg,
Co Mayo
Tel 098-66869
(Galway, retired)

Moran, Benedict (OP), Very Rev, PP, VF
St Aengus' Presbytery,
Balrothery, Tallaght,
Dublin 24
Tel 01-4513757
(Dublin)

Moran, James (SJ)
Vice-Superior,
35 Lower Leeson Street,
Dublin 2
Tel 01-6761248

Moran, John, CC
192 Navan Road, Dublin 7
Tel 01-8387902
(*Navan Road*, Dublin)

Moran, Joseph, Very Rev Canon
Abbeybreaffey Nursing Home, Dublin Road,
Castlebar, Co Mayo
(Tuam, retired)

Moran, Lorcan
Chaplain, St Luke's Hospital,
Kilkenny
Tel 056-7785000/7771815/086-8550521
(Ossory)

Moran, Martin, Very Rev, PP
Rosscahill, Co Galway
Tel 091-550106
(Galway)

Moran, Noel, Very Rev
Lahard, Milltown, Co Kerry
(Kerry, retired)

Moran, Paddy
Presbytery No. 1, Church of
the Ascension,
Balally, Dublin 16
Tel 01-2952869
(Balally, Dublin)

Moran, Pat (OSA)
St Augustine's Priory,
Washington Street,
Cork
Tel 021-2753982

Morgan, Francis (OCSO)
Our Lady of Bethlehem
Abbey, 11 Ballymena Road,
Portglenone, Ballymena,
Co Antrim BT44 8BL
Tel 028-25821211

Morgan, Liam, CC
Holy Family Presbytery,
Askea, Carlow
Tel 059-9143260
(Kildare & L.)

Moriarty, Frank, Very Rev
Adare, Co Limerick
Tel 061-396177
(Limerick, retired)

Moriarty, James, Most Rev,
DD
Bishop of Kildare and
Leighlin,
Bishop's House, Carlow
Tel 059-9176725
(Kildare & L.)

Moriarty, John (CSSp)
Holy Ghost Missionary
College, Kimmage Manor,
Dublin 12
Tel 01-4064300

Morris, Anthony (OP), Very
Rev
Prior, St Saviour's,
Upper Dorset Street,
Dublin 1
Tel 01-8897610

Morris, Colm, PEm
Muff, Co Donegal
Tel 074-9384407
(Derry, retired)

Morris, Donal, CC
St John's, Lecarrow,
Roscommon
Tel 090-6661115
(Knockcroghery, Elphin)

Morris, Fintan, CC
Kiltealy, Enniscorthy,
Co Wexford
Tel 053-9255124
(Ballindaggin, Ferns)

Morris, John, Very Rev, PP
Solohead, Co Limerick
Tel 062-47614
(Solohead, Cashel & E.)

Morrissey, Brendan (SM)
CUS Community,
89 Lower Leeson Street,
Dublin 2
Tel 01-6762586

Morrissey, Michael (OCarm)
CC
The Presbytery,
Idrone Avenue, Knocklyon,
Dublin 16
Tel 01-4941204/4944986
(Knocklyon, Dublin)

Morrissey, Robin, CC
1 Cathedral Terrace, Cobh,
Co Cork
Tel 021-4813951
(Cloyne)

Morrissey, Thomas (SJ)
Manresa House,
Dollymount, Dublin 3
Tel 01-8331352

Morrissey, Thomas, Very Rev,
PE
Upper Mullough, Newcastle,
Clonmel,Co Tipperary
Tel 051-6136236
(Waterford & L., retired)

Morrow, James (CSSp)
Holy Ghost Missionary
College, Kimmage Manor,
Dublin 12
Tel 01-4064300

Moss, Michael (FDP)
Sarsfield House,
Sarsfield Road, Ballyfermot,
Dublin 10
Tel 01-6266193/6266233

Mothersill, Joseph (OCarm)
Gort Muire, Ballinteer,
Dublin 16
Tel 01-2984014

Mowbray, Alan (SJ)
SS Columbanus and Gall,
Milltown, Dublin 6
Tel 01-2196740
(Milltown, Dublin)

Moylan, John (SJ)
St Francis Xavier's,
Upper Gardiner Street,
Dublin 1
Tel 01-8363411

Moynihan, James, CC
6 Meadowvale, Coolcotts,
Wexford
Tel 053-9143932
(Clonard, Ferns)

Moynihan, Michael
The Presbytery, Castleisland,
Co Kerry
Tel 066-7141241
(Kerry)

Muckian, Patrick (SM)
Philippines

Mulcahy, Brian (CP)
St Paul's Retreat,
Mount Argus, Dublin 6W
Tel 01-4992000

Mulcahy, James, Very Rev, PE
St John's Pastoral Centre,
John's Hill, Waterford
Tel 051-858306
(Waterford & L., retired)

Mulcahy, John (OCarm)
Carmelite Priory, Moate,
Co Westmeath
Tel 090-6481160/6481398

Mulcahy, Joseph (SPS)
St Patrick's, Kiltegan,
Co Wicklow
Tel 059-6473600

Mulcahy, Kevin, CC
Ballymacoda, Co Cork
Tel 024-98110
(Ballymacoda and
Ladysbridge, Cloyne)

Mulcahy, Kevin, Very Rev, PE
No 3 The Carechoice,
Burgery, Dungarvan,
Co Waterford
Tel 058-40253/087-6409622
(Waterford & L., retired)

Mulcahy, Pat, Very Rev, PP
Dunkerrin, Birr, Co Offaly
Tel 0505-45982/087-6329913
(Dunkerrin, Killaloe)

Mulcahy, Richard, Rt Rev
30 Knapton Road, Dun
Laoghaire, Co Dublin
Tel 01-2804353
(Opus Dei)

Mulcahy, Thomas (MSC)
Myross Wood Retreat
House, Leap, Skibbereen,
Co Cork
Tel 028-33118

Mulcahy, Timothy (OP), Very
Rev
Prior, Holy Cross, Sligo,
Co Sligo
Tel 071-42700

Muldowney, Peter, Very Rev,
PP
Seir Kieran, Clareen, Birr,
Co Offaly
Tel 0509-31080/086-8265955
(Seir Kieran, Ossory)

Mulhall, Brendan (CSsR), CC
St Gerard's,
722 Antrim Road,
Newtownabbey,
Co Antrim BT36 7PG
Tel 028-90774833
(St Gerard's, Down & C.)

Mulhern, Kevin (SMA)
Dromantine College,
Dromantine, Newry,
Co Down BT34 1RH
Tel 028-30821224

Mulholland, Patrick, Very Rev,
PP
Parochial House, Portaferry,
Co Down BT22 1RH
Tel 028-42728234
(Portaferry, Down & C.)

Mulkerins, Bernard (SSC)
Director, St Columban's
Retirement Home,
Dalgan Park, Navan,
Co Meath
Tel 046-9021525

Mulkerrins, Michael, Very Rev,
PP
Renmore Avenue,
Renmore, Galway
Tel 091-751707
(Renmore, Galway)

Mullahy, Thomas (SMA)
African Missions,
Blackrock Road, Cork
Tel 021-4292871

Mullan, Aidan, Rev, PP
19 Chapel Road, Dungiven,
Derry BT47 4RT
Tel 028-77741219
(Dungiven, Derry)

Mullan, Brian (CM)
St Paul's College, Raheny,
Dublin 5
Tel 01-8318113

Mullan, Joseph, Very Rev, PP
St MacCullin's, Lusk,
Co Dublin
Tel 01-8438421
(Lusk, Dublin)

Mullan, Kevin, PP
257 Dooish Road,
Drumquin, Omagh,
Co Tyrone BT78 4RA
Tel 028-82831225
(Drumquin, Derry)

Mullan, Michael (LC)
Director, John Paul II Centre,
Dal Riada House,
Avoca Avenue, Blackrock,
Co Dublin
Tel 01-2889317
Vocations Director and
Regnum Lay Apostolate,
Novitiate,
Leopardstown Road,
Foxrock, Dublin 18
Tel 01-2955902

Mullan, Michael, CC
300 Drumsurn Road,
Limavady,
Co Derry BT49 0PX
Tel 028-77762165
(Dungiven, Derry)

Mullan, Patrick, PP
Stella Maris House, Eglinton,
Co Derry BT47 3EA
Tel 028-71810240
(Faughanvale, Derry)

Mullane, Denis, Very Rev, PP
Kilcolman, Ardagh,
Co Limerick
Tel 069-60126
(Coolcappa, Limerick)

Mullane, Finbarr, CC
The Presbytery, Vevay Road,
Bray, Co Wicklow
Tel 01-2867303
(Dublin)

Mullaney, Michael
Ballycahill, Thurles,
Co Tipperary
Tel 0504-26080
(Cashel & E.)

Mullany, Francis (SSC)
St Columban's Retirement
Home, Dalgan Park, Navan,
Co Meath
Tel 046-9021525

Mullen, John (IC)
1 Grace Park Gardens,
Drumcondra, Dublin 9
Tel 01-8378314/8368730

Mulligan, Ben, Very Rev, PP
42 Corke Abbey, Little Bray,
Co Wicklow
Tel 01-2822204
(Bray, St Peter's, Dublin)

Mulligan, Declan, CC
24 Downs Road, Newcastle,
Co Down BT33 0AG
Tel 028-43722401
(Newcastle (Maghera),
Down & C.)

Mulligan, John (SM)
Cerdon, Marist Fathers,
St Mary's Road, Dundalk,
Co Louth
Tel 042-9334019

Mulligan, Larry (OFM)
Franciscan Friary,
Liberty Street, Cork
Tel 021-4270302

Mulligan, Rory (SM)
Norway

Mulligan, Thomas, Very Rev,
PP
Attymass, Ballina, Co Mayo
Tel 096-45095
(Attymass, Achonry)

Mulligan, Vincent (OMI)
Oblate House of Retreat,
Inchicore, Dublin 8
Tel 01-4534408/4541805

Mullin, Joseph, Very Rev
Canon, PP, VF
Lisoneill, Lisnaskea,
Enniskillen,
Co Fermanagh BT92 0JE
Tel 028-67721342
(Clogher)

Mullin, Noel, Very Rev Canon,
PP, VF
Claregalway, Co Galway
Tel 091-798104
(Claregalway, Galway)

Mullin, Seamus, Very Rev
Canon, AP
Miltown Malbay, Co Clare
Tel 065-7084003
(Miltown Malbay, Killaloe)

Mullin, Sean (CSsR)
St Patrick's, Esker, Athenry,
Co Galway
Tel 091-844549

Mullins, Anthony, Very Rev,
PP
Dromin, Kilmallock,
Co Limerick
Tel 063-31962
(Dromin & Athlacca,
Limerick)

Mullins, Melvyn
192 Sundrive Road,
Dublin 12
Tel 01-4540811
(Clogher Road, Dublin)

Mullins, Michael, Very Rev, PP
St Anne's Presbytery,
Convent Hill, Waterford
Tel 051-855819
(Ballybricken, Waterford &
L.)

Mullins, Patrick (OCarm)
Whitefriar Street Church,
56 Aungier Street, Dublin 2
Tel 01-4758821

Mullins, Patrick, Very Rev, PP
Bekan, Claremorris,
Co Mayo
Tel 094-9380203
(Bekan, Tuam)

Mulloy, Frank (CSSp)
Templeogue College,
Dublin 6W
Tel 01-4903909

Mulvaney, Martin, Very Rev,
PP
Drumlion,
Carrick-on-Shannon,
Co Roscommon
Tel 071-9620415
(Croghan, Elphin)

Mulvaney, Martin, Very Rev,
PP
Parochial House, Johnstown,
Navan, Co Meath
Tel 046-9021731
(Johnstown, Meath)

Mulvany, Seamus, Very Rev,
PP
Parochial House,
Tubberclaire-Glasson,
Athlone, Co Westmeath
Tel 090-6485103
(Glasson, Meath)

Mulvey, Anthony (CSsR)
Via Merulana 31, CP 2458,
00100 Rome, Italy
Tel 49490-1

Mulvey, Patrick, Very Rev
25 Thomastown Road,
Dun Laoghaire, Co Dublin
(Dublin, retired)

Mulvihill, Anthony, Very Rev,
PP
Croagh, Rathkeale,
Co Limerick
Tel 069-64185/087-9059348
(Croagh and Kilfinny,
Limerick)

Mulvihill, Eamonn, Very Rev,
PP
Eyeries, Co Cork
Tel 027-74008
(Eyeries, Kerry)

Mulvihill, William, CC
Parochial House, Collon,
Co Louth
Tel 041-9826106
(Ardee & Collon, Armagh)

Mundow, Sean, Very Rev, PP
77 Botanic Avenue,
Dublin 9
Tel 01-8373455
(Glasnevin, Dublin)

Munnelly, Alan, CC
Ardagh, Ballina, Co Mayo
Tel 096-31144
(Ardagh, Killala)

Munnelly, Patrick, Very Rev,
PP
Ardagh, Ballina, Co Mayo
Tel 096-31144
(Killala)

Munster, Ramon, Very Rev, PP
Bundoran, Co Donegal
Tel 071-9841290
(Bundoran, Clogher)

Murchan, Michael, Very Rev,
PE
Knightsbridge Nursing
Home, Trim, Co Meath
(Meath, retired)

Murnaghan, Hugh (CM)
St Paul's College, Raheny,
Dublin 5
Tel 01-8318113

Murney, Peadar, Very Rev, PP
56 Auburn Road, Killiney,
Co Dublin
Tel 01-2856660
(Johnstown-Killiney, Dublin)

Murphy O'Connor, Kerry, Ven
Archdeacon, PP
The Presbytery, Turner's
Cross, Cork
Tel 021-4312466
(Turner's Cross, Cork & R.)

Murphy, Aidan, Very Rev, PP
Parochial House,
Termonfechin, Drogheda,
Co Louth
Tel 041-9822121
(Termonfechin, Armagh)

Murphy, Anthony (MHM)
C/o St Joseph's House, 50
Orwell Park, Rathgar,
Dublin 6
Tel 01-4127700

Murphy, Alphonsus, Very Rev,
PE
Carbury, Co Kildare
Tel 046-9553020
(Kildare & L., retired)

Murphy, Barry
Commission for Sacred Art
and Architecture
(Dublin)

Murphy, Bernard (OCarm)
Whitefriar Street Church, 56
Aungier Street, Dublin 2
Tel 01-4758821

Murphy, Brendan, Very Rev,
PP
Feenagh, Kilmallock,
Co Limerick
Tel 063-85013/086-8094490
(Feenagh and Kilmeedy,
Limerick)

Murphy, Brian (OSB)
Glenstal Abbey, Murroe,
Co Limerick
Tel 061-386103

Murphy, Canice (OP)
St Saviour's, Bridge Street,
Waterford
Tel 051-875061

Murphy, Colm, Very Rev, PP
Clongeen, Foulksmills,
Co Wexford
Tel 051-565610
(Clongeen, Ferns)

Murphy, Daniel
(in residence)
Castlelyons, Fermoy,
Co Cork
Tel 025-36196
(Castlelyons, Cloyne)

Murphy, Daniel (SMA)
African Missions,
Blackrock Road, Cork
Tel 021-4292871

Murphy, David, CC
Caroreigh, Taghmon,
Co Wexford
Tel 053-9134113
(Ferns)

Murphy, David, CC
The Presbytery,
Seamus Quirke Road,
Galway
Tel 091-524751
(Sacred Heart Church,
Galway)

Murphy, Denis (OP), CC
St Mary's, The Claddagh,
Co Galway
Tel 091-582884

Murphy, Denis, Very Rev, PP
Tolerton, Ballickmoyler,
Carlow
Tel 056-4442126
(Doonane, Kildare & L.)

Murphy, Edmund (OP)
St Malachy's, Dundalk,
Co Louth
Tel 042-9334179/9333714

Murphy, Edward, Very Rev
Canon, PE
Newtownbutler, Enniskillen,
Co Fermanagh BT92 8JJ
Tel 028-67738640
(Newtownbutler, Clogher)

Murphy, Enda
Pontificio Collegio Irlandese,
Rome, Italy
(Kilmore)

Allianz ⑪

Murphy, Eoin
St Joseph's Church,
109 Linden Street,
Saint John's, MI48879, USA
(Dublin)

Murphy, Francis, CC
St Patrick's, Gorey,
Co Wexford
Tel 053-9421117
(Gorey, Ferns)

Murphy, Gabriel, CC
Kiltimagh, Co Mayo
Tel 094-9381492
(Achonry)

Murphy, George, Very Rev, PP
Minane Bridge, Co Cork
Tel 021-4887105
(Tracton Abbey, Cork & R.)

Murphy, James (CSSp)
Holy Ghost Missionary
College, Kimmage Manor,
Dublin 12
Tel 01-4064300

Murphy, James (CSsR)
Mount Saint Alphonsus,
Limerick
Tel 061-315099

Murphy, James (SJ)
c/o Jesuit Provincial Curia,
IMI Centre, Sandyford Road,
Dublin 16
Tel 01-2932820

Murphy, James (SSC)
St Columban's Retirement
Home, Dalgan Park, Navan,
Co Meath
Tel 046-9021525

Murphy, James, CC
St Brigid's, Rosslare,
Co Wexford
Tel 053-9132118
(Tagoat, Ferns)

Murphy, James, Very Rev, PP
St Canice's Presbytery,
Dean Street, Kilkenny
Tel 056-7752991/
087-2609545
(Ossory)

Murphy, Jason
Crosskeys, Co Cavan
Tel 049-4336563
(Denn, Kilmore)

Murphy, Jeremiah (MSC)
Carrignavar, Co Cork
Tel 021-4884044

Murphy, Jerry (SSC)
St Mary's, Tang,
Ballymahon,
Co Longford
Tel 0906-432214

Murphy, Jerry, CC
St Mary's, Tang,
Ballymahon, Co Longford
Tel 090-6432214
(Drumraney, Meath)

Murphy, John, Rt Rev Mgr
(in residence)
18 Rock Road, Lisburn,
Co Antrim BT28 3SU
Tel 028-92648244
(Hannahstown, Down & C.)

Murphy, John, Very Rev
Canon, PP, VF
Bailieboro, Co Cavan
Tel 042-9665117
(Bailieboro, Kilmore)

Murphy, John, Very Rev, PE
30 Moorehall Village,
Hale Street, Ardee, Co Louth
Tel 041-6871942
(Armagh, retired)

Murphy, John, Very Rev, PP
14 Rosemount Crescent,
Roebuck Road, Clonskeagh,
Dublin 14
Tel 01-2697754
(Clonskeagh, Dublin)

Murphy, Joseph (CSSp)
17 St Brigid's Park,
Blacklion, Greystones,
Co Wicklow
Tel 01-2874888

Murphy, Joseph (OFMCap)
Holy Trinity,
Fr Mathew Quay, Cork
Tel 021-4270827

Murphy, Joseph, Very Rev
Mgr
Secretariat of State, (Section
for Relations with States),
00120 Vatican City
Tel 0039-0669883193
(Cloyne)

Murphy, Kyran (SPS)
Regional Bursar,
St Patrick's, Kiltegan,
Co Wicklow
Tel 059-6473600

Murphy, Laurence (OFM)
Franciscan Friary,
Friary Lane, Athlone,
Co Westmeath
Tel 090-6472095

Murphy, Laurence (SJ)
Clongowes Wood College,
Naas, Co Kildare
Tel 045-868663/868202

Murphy, Malachy, CC
1a Rockstown Road,
Carrickmore, Omagh,
Co Tyrone BT79 9BE
Tel 028-80760853
(Termonmaguirc
(Carrickmore, Loughmacrory
& Creggan), Armagh)

Murphy, Malachy, Very Rev,
Canon, PP
56 Greystone Road,
Antrim BT41 1JZ
Tel 028-94429103
(Antrim, St Joseph's, Down
& C.)

Murphy, Martin (IC)
Rosminian House of Prayer,
Glencomeragh House,
Kilsheelan, Co Tipperary
Tel 052-33181

Murphy, Martin (SSC)
St Columban's, Dalgan Park,
Navan, Co Meath
Tel 046-9021525

Murphy, Martin, Very Rev, PP
Drom, Thurles, Co Tipperary
Tel 0504-51196
(Drom and Inch, Cashel & E.)

Murphy, Michael (OFMCap)
Capuchin Friary,
Ard Mhuire, Creeslough,
Letterkenny, Co Donegal
Tel 074-9138005

Murphy, Michael J., Venerable
Archdeacon
No 1 Cathedral Place,
Killarney, Co Kerry
(Kerry, retired)

Murphy, Michael
Youghal, Co Mayo
Tel 024-92336
(Youghal, Cloyne)

Murphy, Michael, CC
Roundfort, Hollymount,
Co Mayo
Tel 094-9540934
(Roundfort, Tuam)

Murphy, Michael, Very Rev
Canon, PP
Ballyphehane, Co Cork
Tel 021-4965560
(Ballyphehane, Cork & R.)

Murphy, Michael, Very Rev,
PP, VF
Parochial House, Kilcullen,
Co Kildare
Tel 045-481230
(Dublin)

Murphy, Mícheál, Very Rev
Rector, St Mary's,
Knockbeg College,
Knockbeg, Carlow
Tel 059-9142127
(Kildare & L.)

Murphy, Noel (CSSp)
Rockwell College, Cashel,
Co Tipperary
Tel 062-61444

Murphy, Pádraig, Very Rev, PP
Parochial House,
Ravensdale, Dundalk,
Co Louth
Tel 042-9371327
(Armagh)

Murphy, Patrick, PP, VF
St Mary's, Edgeworthstown,
Co Longford
Tel 043-6671046
(Ardagh & Cl.)

Murphy, Patrick, Very Rev, PP
Sneem, Co Kerry
Tel 064-45141
(Sneem, Kerry)

Murphy, Patrick, Very Rev, PP
Templetuohy, Thurles,
Co Tipperary
Tel 0504-53114
(Templetuohy, Cashel & E.)

Murphy, Paul (OFMCap)
Capuchin Friary,
Church Street, Dublin 7
Tel 01-8730599

Murphy, Paul F., Very Rev,
Adm
Ballynageeragh, Dunhill,
Co Waterford
Tel 051-396616
(Dunhill, Waterford & L.)

Murphy, Paul, Very Rev, PP
Parochial House,
Butlerstown, Co Waterford
Tel 051-384192
(Butlerstown, Waterford &
L.)

Murphy, Peadar, Very Rev, PP
Parochial House,
Aghabullogue, Co Cork
Tel 021-7334035
(Aghabullogue, Cloyne)

Murphy, Peter
National Chaplain, Accord
Catholic Marriage Care
Service, Columba Centre,
Maynooth, Co Kildare
Tel 01-5053107
(Dublin)

Murphy, Peter, Very Rev, PP,
VF
Parochial House,
Hale Street, Ardee,
Co Louth
Tel 041-6850920
(Ardee & Collon, Armagh)

Murphy, Pierce, Very Rev
(in residence)
Borris, Co Carlow via
Kilkenny
Tel 059-9773128
(Borris, Kildare & L.)

Murphy, Sean (OFM)
Franciscan Friary, Killarney,
Co Kerry
Tel 064-6631334/6631066

Murphy, Seán, Very Rev, PP
Miltown Malbay, Co Clare
Tel 065-7084129
(Miltown Malbay, Killaloe)

Murphy, Thomas (SSC)
Superior General, Suite 504,
Tower 1, Silvercord,
30 Canton Road Tst,
Kowloon, Hong Kong SAR

Murphy, Thomas, Very Rev
Canon, PP
Ballyragget, Co Kilkenny
Tel 056-8833123/
086-8130694
(Ossory)

Murphy, Tim, Very Rev, PP
The Presbytery, Main Street,
Blessington, Co Wicklow
Tel 045-865442
(*Blessington*, Dublin)

Murphy, Vincent (SJ)
Clongowes Wood College,
Naas, Co Kildare
Tel 045-868663/868202

Murphy, William (CSSp)
Rockwell College, Cashel,
Co Tipperary
Tel 062-61444

Murphy, William, Most Rev,
DD
Bishop of Kerry,
Bishop's House, Killarney,
Co Kerry
Tel 064-6631168
(Kerry)

Murray, Aidan
Temporary diocesan work in
Ireland
C/o St Columban's,
Dalgan Park,
Navan, Co Meath

Murray, Brendan (SSC)
St Columban's, Dalgan Park,
Navan, Co Meath
Tel 046-9021525

Murray, Brendan, Very Rev
Canon
St Thérèse's Presbytery,
71 Somerton Road,
Belfast BT15 4DE
Tel 028-90205041
(*Holy Family*, Down & C.)

Murray, Declan (SJ)
c/o Jesuit Provincial Curia,
IMI Centre, Sandyford Road,
Dublin 16
Tel 01-2932820

Murray, Denis, Very Rev, PP
Carrigallen, Co Leitrim,
via Cavan
Tel 049-4339610
(*Carrigallen*, Kilmore)

Murray, Dermot (SJ)
Crescent College
Comprehensive,
Dooradoyle, Limerick
Tel 061-480920

Murray, Donal, Most Rev, DD
Former Bishop of Limerick,
Diocesan Office, Social
Service Centre,
Henry Street, Limerick
Tel 061-315856
(Limerick)

Murray, Francis, CC
46 Knockmoyle Road,
Omagh, Co Tyrone BT79 7TB
Tel 028-82242793
(*Killyclogher*, Derry)

Murray, Francis, Very Rev, PP
Ferbane, Co Offaly
Tel 090-6454380
(*Ferbane High Street and
Boora*, Ardagh & Cl.)

Murray, James
9 Hillcrest Manor,
Templeogue, Dublin 6W
(Dublin, retired)

Murray, James, CC
Carraroe, Sligo, Co Sligo
Tel 071-9162136
(Elphin)

Murray, James (OCarm)
Carmelite Presbytery,
Idrone Avenue, Knocklyon,
Dublin 16
Tel 01-4941204

Murray, John, CC
Castlebar, Co Mayo
Tel 094-901253/21844
(*Castlebar (Aglish,
Ballyheane and Breaghwy)*,
Tuam)

Murray, John, Very Rev, PP
Parochial House,
9 Gortahor Road, Rasharkin,
Ballymena,
Co Antrim BT44 8SB
Tel 028-29571212
(*Rasharkin*, Down & C.)

Murray, John, Very Rev, PP
St Luke's Presbytery,
Twinbrook Road, Dunmurry,
Co Antrim BT1/ 0RP
Tel 028-90619459
(*St Luke's*, Down & C.)

Murray, Liam, Adm
St Mary's, Athlone,
Co Westmeath
Tel 090-6472088
(*Athlone*, Ardagh & Cl.)

Murray, Liam, Very Rev, AP
Whitegate, Co Clare
Tel 061-927009
(*Mountshannon*, Killaloe)

Murray, Michael, CC
Belcarra, Castlebar, Co Mayo
Tel 094-9032006
(*Balla and Manulla*, Tuam)

Murray, Michael, Very Rev, PP
Parochial House,
Greencastle Road, Kilkeel,
Co Down BT34 4DE
Tel 028-41762242
(*Kilkeel (Upper Mourne)*,
Down & C.)

Murray, Nicholas (SSC)
St Columban's, Dalgan Park,
Navan, Co Meath
Tel 046-9021525

Murray, P. J., Very Rev, PP
Maypole Hill, Dromore,
Co Down BT25 1BQ
Tel 028-92692218
(Dromore)

Murray, Patrick (MHM)
St Joseph's House,
50 Orwell Park, Rathgar,
Dublin 6
Tel 01-4127700

Murray, Patrick (SAC)
'Galilee', Stradbally Road,
Athy, Co Kildare
Tel 0507-31564

Murray, Patrick, Very Rev
Canon
27 Ardbrea Park, Baylough,
Athlone
(Elphin, retired)

Murray, Placid (OSB)
Glenstal Abbey, Murroe,
Co Limerick
Tel 061-386103

Murray, Ray (SM)
Mount St Mary's, Milltown,
Dublin 14
Tel 01-2697322

Murray, Raymond, Rt Rev
Mgr, PE
60 Glen Mhacaha,
Cathedral Road,
Armagh BT61 8AS
Tel 028-37510821
(Armagh, retired)

Murray, Senan (CSSp), CC
Askeaton, Co Limerick
Tel 061-392131
(*Askeaton and Ballysteen*,
Limerick)

Murray, Terence (OMI), Very
Rev, PP
Superior, The Presbytery,
Darndale, Dublin 17
Tel 01-8474547
(*Darndale*, Dublin)

Murray, Tom
Diocesan Offices,
St Michael's, Longford
Tel 043-3346432
(Ardagh & Cl.)

Murtagh, Brian (CSSp)
Spiritan Missionaries,
Ardbraccan, Navan,
Co Meath
Tel 046-9021441

Murtagh, Colm, Very Rev
Parochial House, Kildalkey,
Co Meath
Tel 046-9546488
(Meath, retired)

Murtagh, John
Warrenpoint, Co Down
(Dromore, retired)

Murtagh, Liam, Very Rev
167 Charlemont,
Griffith Avenue,
Dublin 9
(Dublin, reirted)

Murtagh, Michael (CSsR)
Superior,
Clonard Monastery,
1 Clonard Gardens,
Belfast, BT13 2RL
Tel 028-90445950

Murtagh, Michael, PP
Parochial House, Athy,
Co Kildare
Tel 059-8631781
(*Athy*, Dublin)

Murtagh, G. Michael, Very
Rev, PP
Parochial House, Old Chapel
Lane, Dunleer, Co Louth
Tel 041-6851278
(*Dunleer*, Armagh)

Murtagh, Ronan
Bishop's House,
Edmondstown,
Ballaghaderreen,
Co Roscommon
094-9860021
(Achonry)

Murtagh, William, Very Rev,
PE, AP
Parochial House,
Clogherhead, Drogheda,
Co Louth
Tel 041-9822224
(*Clogherhead*, Armagh)

N

Nagle, Joe (OFMCap)
Holy Trinity,
Fr Mathew Quay, Cork
Tel 021-4270827

Nallukkunnel, Antony (OFM
Conv), CC
Friary of the Visitation,
Fairview Strand, Dublin 3
Tel 01-8376000
(*Fairview*, Dublin)

Nallen, Michael
Aughoose, Ballina, Co Mayo
Tel 097-87990
(Killala)

Nally, John, Very Rev, PP
Parochial House,
Ballynacargy, Co Westmeath
Tel 044-9373932
(*Ballynacargy*, Meath)

Nash, Ger
Crusheen, Ennis, Clare
Tel 065-6827113
(*Crusheen*, Killaloe)

Nash, Paul (OSB)
Glenstal Abbey, Murroe,
Co Limerick
Tel 061-386103

Nash, Tom (CSSp)
Superior, Blackrock College,
Blackrock, Co Dublin
Tel 01-2888681

Naughten, Patrick
Woodford, Co Galway
Tel 090-9749010
(Clonfert, retired)

Naughton, John, Very Rev, PP
Eyrecourt, Ballinasloe,
Co Galway
Tel 090-9675148
(Clonfert)

Naughton, Joseph (CSsR)
St Joseph's, Dundalk,
Co Louth
Tel 042-9334042/9334762

Naughton, Richard, Very Rev, PP, VF
Mountain Lodge,
132 Dublin Road, Newry,
Co Down BT35 8QT
Tel 028-30262174
(*Cloghogue (Killeavy Upper)*, Armagh)

Naughton, Tom, CC
Midleton, Co Cork
Tel 021-4636704
(*Midleton*, Cloyne)

Navin, Charles, Very Rev
Tubber, Gort, Co Galway
Tel 091-63323
(Killaloe, retired)

Nawalaniec, Kaz
2 The Presbytery, Mahon,
Co Cork
Tel 021-4357665
(*Mahon,* Cork & R.)

Nealon, Edward (CSSp)
Spiritan Missionaries,
Ardbraccan, Navan,
Co Meath
Tel 046-9021441

Neary, Donal (SJ), Very Rev, PP
Presbytery,
Upper Gardiner Street,
Dublin 1
Tel 01-8363411
(*Gardiner Street*, Dublin)

Neary, Michael, Most Rev, DD
Archbishop of Tuam,
Archbishop's House, Tuam,
Co Galway
Tel 093-24166
(Tuam)

Nechikattil, Pius (SSP)
Superior, Society of St Paul,
Moyglare Road, Maynooth,
Co Kildare
Tel 01-6285933

Neenan, Daniel, Rt Rev Mgr, PP, VG
1 Trinity Court,
Monaleen Road, Monaleen,
Limerick
Tel 061-330974/087-2208547
(Limerick)

Neeson, Patrick, Very Rev, PP
46 Blackstaff Road,
Ballycranbeg, Kircubbin,
Newtownards,
Co Down BT22 1AG
Tel 028-42738294
(*Kircubbin (Ardkeen),* Down & C.)

Nellis, Christopher, Very Rev, PP
Parochial House, Armoy,
Ballymoney,
Co Antrim BT53 8RL
Tel 028-20751205
(*Armoy*, Down & C.)

Nestor, Dermot, Very Rev
Parochial House,
Nutgrove Avenue, Dublin 14
Tel 01-2985916
(*Churchtown*, Dublin)

Neville, Anthony, CC
Claddaghduff, Co Galway
Tel 095-44668
(*Inishbofin*, Tuam)

Neville, Edward (OFMCap)
Holy Trinity,
Fr Mathew Quay, Cork
Tel 021-4270827

Neville, James, Very Rev
Canon
Cedarville, Abbeyfeale,
Co Limerick
Tel 068-32884
(Limerick, retired)

Neville, Paddy (MHM)
St Joseph's House,
50 Orwell Park, Rathgar,
Dublin 6
Tel 01-4127700

Neville, Ronald, Very Rev, PE
213A Harold's Cross Road,
Dublin 6W
Tel 01-4974044
(Dublin, retired)

Nevin, John (MHM)
St Mary's Parish,
25 Marquis Street,
Belfast BT1 1JJ
Tel 028-90320482

Nevin, Michael G.
The Presbytery,
Harrington Street,
Dublin 8
Tel 01-4751506
(*Harrington Street,* Dublin)

Newell, Eamonn (OFM)
Franciscan College,
Gormanston, Co Meath
Tel 01-8412203

Newell, Martin, Very Rev
Canon, AP
Claran, Co Galway
Tel 093-35436
(*Headford (Killursa and Killower),* Tuam)

Newman, John, Very Rev, PP
Monkstown, Co Cork
Tel 021-4863267
(*Monkstown*, Cork & R.)

Neylon, Finbarr, CC
No 4 Presbytery,
Dunmanus Court, Cabra
West, Dublin 7
Tel 01-88384325
(*Cabra West*, Dublin)

Neylon, Sean, Very Rev, PP
Taghmaconnell, Ballinasloe,
Co Galway
Tel 090-9683929
(*Taghmaconnell*, Clonfert)

Ngetwa, Anselm (White Fathers)
Cypress Grove, Templeogue,
Dublin 6W
Tel 01-4055263/4055264

Nguekam, Marino (CSSp), CC
Church of the
Transfiguration, Presbytery,
Bawnogue, Clondalkin,
Dublin 22
Tel 01-4592273/4519810
(*Clondalkin, Bawnogue*, Dublin)

Niall, John (CSsR)
Liguori House,
75 Orwell Road, Dublin 6
Tel 01-4067100

Nicholas, Michael (OFM)
Guardian, Franciscan Friary,
Friary Lane, Athlone,
Co Westmeath
Tel 090-6472095

Niyoyita, Kizito (SJ)
Jesuit Community,
27 Leinster Road,
Rathmines, Dublin 6
Tel 01-4970250

Nohilly, Michael (SMA), CC
Moylough, Ballinasloe,
Co Galway
Tel 090-9679262
(*Moylough and Mountbellew*, Tuam)

Nohilly, Seamus (SMA)
Superior, SMA House,
Claregalway, Co Galway
Tel 091-798880

Nolan, Brendan, Very Rev, PP
Our Lady's Island,
Broadway, Co Wexford
Tel 053-9131167
(Ferns)

Nolan, Brian (CM)
All Hallows Institute for
Mission and Ministry,
Drumcondra, Dublin 9
Tel 01-8373745/6

Nolan, Brian (CSsR)
Most Holy Sacrament Parish,
Cherry Orchard, Dublin 10
Tel 01-6267930

Nolan, Bryan, PC
21 Wheatfield Grove,
Portmarnock, Dublin
Tel 01-8038970
(*Portmarnock*, Dublin)

Nolan, Damien
1a Laghtagoona, Corofin,
Co Clare
Tel 065-6837178/
086-8396636
(*Corofin*, Killaloe)

Nolan, Denis, CC
The Presbytery, Rathnew,
Co Wicklow
Tel 0404-67488/087-2389594
(*Wicklow*, Dublin)

Nolan, Francis
Institute of St Anselm,
51-59 Norfolk Road,
Cliftonvilee, Kent CT9 2EU,
UK
(Kerry)

Nolan, Herman (CP)
St Paul's Retreat,
Mount Argus, Dublin 6W
Tel 01-4992000

Nolan, J. Michael, Rt Rev Mgr
26 Harmony Avenue,
Donnybrook, Dublin 4
(Dublin, retired)

Nolan, J., Very Rev
36 Ashfield, Greenville,
Listowel, Co Kerry
(Kerry, retired)

Nolan, James, Very Rev, PP
Davidstown, Enniscorthy,
Co Wexford
Tel 053-9233382
(*Davidstown and Courtnacuddy*, Ferns)

Nolan, John P., Very Rev, PP
Duncannon, New Ross,
Co Wexford
Tel 051-389118
(*Duncannon*, Ferns)

Nolan, Mark-Ephrem M. (OSB), Very Rev Dom
Superior, Benedictine
Monks, Holy Cross
Monastery,
119 Kilbroney Road,
Rostrevor,
Co Down BT34 3BN
Tel 028-41739979

Nolan, Martin (OSA)
St John's Priory,
Thomas Street,
Dublin 8
Tel 01-6770393

Nolan, Martin (SMA)
Dromantine College,
Dromantine, Newry,
Co Down BT34 1RH
Tel 028-30821224

Nolan, Placid (OP)
Holy Cross, Tralee, Co Kerry
Tel 066-21135/29185

Nolan, Robert, Very Rev, PP
Adamstown, Enniscorthy,
Co Wexford
Tel 053-9240512
(*Adamstown*, Ferns)

Nolan, Rory, CC
1 Green Road, Carlow
Tel 059-9142632
(*Cathedral, Carlow*, Kildare & L.)

Nolan, Seán, Very Rev, PP
St Joseph's, Emyvale,
Monaghan
Tel 047-87152
(*Errigal Truagh*, Clogher)

O'Connor, Christopher (MHM)
St Joseph's House,
50 Orwell Park, Rathgar,
Dublin 6
Tel 01-4127700

O'Connor, Christopher, Very
Rev Dean, PE
Craughwell, Co Galway
Tel 091-846124
(Galway, retired)

O'Connor, Columba (OSA)
Duckspool House
(Retirement Community),
Abbeyside, Dungarvan,
Co Waterford
Tel 058-23784

O'Connor, Dan (MSC)
Western Road, Cork
Tel 021-4804120

O'Connor, Dan, Rt Rev Mgr,
PP, VF
4 Eblana Avenue, Dun
Laoghaire, Co Dublin
Tel 01-2804969
(Dun Laoghaire, Dublin)

O'Connor, Daniel, Very Rev
Canon, AP
The Presbytery, Dungarvan,
Co Waterford
Tel 058-42381
(Dungarvan, Waterford & L.)

O'Connor, David (CSSp)
Holy Ghost Missionary
College, Kimmage Manor,
Dublin 12
Tel 01-4064300

O'Connor, Declan, Rt Rev
Mgr, PP, VG
Millstreet, Co Cork
Tel 029-70043
(Kerry)

O'Connor, Denis (CSsR)
Marianella, 75 Orwell Road,
Dublin 6
Tel 01-4067100

O'Connor, Denis, CC
32 Auburn Drive, Dublin 15
Tel 01-8214003
(Castleknock, Dublin)

O'Connor, Denis, Very Rev
Dean, PE
2 Woodlawn,
Model Farm Road,
Ballineaspaig, Cork
Tel 021-4542972
(Cork & R., retired)

O'Connor, Dermot (CSsR)
St Patrick's, Esker, Athenry,
Co Galway
Tel 091-844549

O'Connor, Dermot (SJ)
c/o Jesuit Provincial Curia,
IMI Centre, Sandyford Road,
Dublin 16
Tel 01-2932820

O'Connor, Dominic (OP)
St Dominic's, Athy,
Co Kildare
Tel 0507-31573

O'Connor, Donal (SMA)
Retired in Britain

O'Connor, Donal, CC
Listowel, Co Kerry
Tel 068-21188
(Listowel, Kerry)

O'Connor, Eamonn, Very Rev,
PP
Rooskey, Carrick-on-
Shannon,
Co Roscommon
Tel 071-9638014
(Kilglass, Elphin)

O'Connor, Edward (SMA)
Vice-Superior,
African Missions,
Blackrock Road, Cork
Tel 021-4292871

O'Connor, Erill D., Very Rev
Canon
14 Clare Road, Drumcondra,
Dublin 9
(Dublin, retired)

O'Connor, Fergus, Very Rev,
(Opus Dei) PP
31 Herbert Avenue, Dublin 4
Tel 01-2692001
(Merrion Road, Dublin)

O'Connor, Frank
c/o Limerick Diocesan
Pastoral Centre,
St Michael's Courtyard,
Denmark Street, Limerick
Tel 061-400133
(Limerick)

O'Connor, Gerard, CC
Chapel Road, Modeligo,
Cappagh, Co Waterford
Tel 058-68136
(Modeligo, Waterford & L.)

O'Connor, Gerry (CSsR)
Most Holy Sacrament Parish,
Cherry Orchard,
Dublin 10
Tel 01-6267930

O'Connor, James (CSsR)
Mount Saint Alphonsus,
Limerick
Tel 061-315099

O'Connor, John (SAC), Very
Rev, PP
St Benin's, Dublin Road,
Shankill, Co Dublin
Tel 01-2824425
(Shankill, Dublin)

O'Connor, John C., Very Rev
Director, Our Lady's Home,
68 Ard Na Va Road,
Belfast BT12 6FF
Tel 028-90325731/90242429
(Down & C.)

O'Connor, Joseph, PP
Parochial House,
Plumbridge, Omagh,
Co Tyrone BT79 8EF
Tel 028-81648283
(Plumbridge, Derry)

O'Connor, Laurence, Very Rev,
PP
Ballycullane, New Ross,
Co Wexford
Tel 051-562123
(Ballycullane, Ferns)

O'Connor, Liam (OCSO)
Mount Saint Joseph Abbey,
Roscrea, Co Tipperary
Tel 0505-25600

O'Connor, Martin, Very Rev,
PE
Coral Haven Nursing Home,
Headford Road, Galway
Tel 091-762800
(Galway, retired)

O'Connor, Martin, Very Rev,
PP
Ballindine, Co Mayo
Tel 094-9364423
(Ballindine (Kilvine), Tuam)

O'Connor, Michael (CSSp), CC
Presbytery No 2,
Church Grounds,
Kill Avenue, Dun Laoghaire,
Co Dublin
Tel 01-2140863
(Kill-O'-The-Grange, Dublin)

O'Connor, Michael (OMI),
Very Rev
Moderator of Pastoral Area
of Inchicore/Bluebell,
Oblate House of Retreat,
Inchicore, Dublin 8
Tel 01-4534408/4541805
(Inchicore/Bluebell, Dublin)

O'Connor, Michael G. (CSsR)
Mount Saint Alphonsus,
Limerick
Tel 061-315099

O'Connor, Michael, Very Rev
c/o St John's Pastoral Centre,
John's Hill, Waterford
(Waterford & L.)

O'Connor, Muiris, Very Rev,
PP
Ballybrown, Clarina,
Co Limerick
Tel 061-353711/086-6075628
(Patrickswell/Ballybrown,
Limerick)

O'Connor, Padraig, Very Rev
Canon, PP
Mountbellew, Ballinasloe,
Co Galway
Tel 090-9679235
(Moylough and
Mountbellew, Tuam)

O'Connor, Pat (CSsR)
Vicar, Clonard Monastery,
1 Clonard Gardens,
Belfast, BT13 2RL
Tel 028-90445950

O'Connor, Pat J. (SDB)
Salesian College,
Maynooth Road, Celbridge,
Co Kildare
Tel 01-6275058/60

O'Connor, Patrick, Very Rev,
PP, VF
Parochial House, Athboy,
Co Meath
Tel 046-9432184
(Meath)

O'Connor, Peter
10 Cranfield Place, Dublin 4
(Ferns)

O'Connor, Peter, CC
10 Cranfield Place,
Sandymount, Dublin 4
Tel 01-6676438
(Sandymount, Dublin)

O'Connor, Peter, Very Rev, PP
12 Brookwood Grove,
Artane, Dublin 5
Tel 01-8312390
(Artane, Dublin)

O'Connor, Philip, Very Rev, PP
Parochial House, Dysart,
Mullingar, Co Westmeath
Tel 044-9226122
(Dysart, Meath)

O'Connor, Richard
C/o Diocesan Offices,
Killarney, Co Kerry
(Kerry)

O'Connor, Seamus (SSC)
St Columban's, Dalgan Park,
Navan, Co Meath
Tel 046-9021525

O'Connor, Sean
St Kieran's College, Kilkenny
Tel 086-3895911
(Ossory)

O'Connor, Thomas, DD
St Patrick's College,
Maynooth, Co Kildare
Tel 01-6285222
(Meath)

O'Connor, Tom (SPS)
St Patrick's, Kiltegan,
Co Wicklow
Tel 059-6473600

O'Connor, Timothy (SPS)
On temporary diocesan
work

O'Conor, Joe (SPS)
St Patrick's, Kiltegan,
Co Wicklow
Tel 059-6473600

O'Conor, Patrick (SSC), CC
Mulrankin, Co Wexford
Tel 053-9135166
(Kilmore, Ferns)

O'Cuilleanáin, Fionnbarra
(SMA)
African Missions,
Blackrock Road, Cork
Tel 021-4292871

O'Cuiv, Liam, Very Rev, PP
The Presbytery, Blakestown,
Dublin 15
Tel 01-8210874/086-2342170
(Mountview, Dublin)

O'Cuiv, Shan, PC
The Presbytery, Clonburris,
Clondalkin, Dublin 22
(*Clondalkin*, Dublin)

O'Dea, Francis, Very Rev, PP
134 Cosgrave Park, Moyross,
Limerick
Tel 061-451783/087-2443106
(*Corpus Christi*, Limerick)

O'Dea, Tom
Ballynacally, Co Clare
Tel 065-6838135/086-
8107475
(*Ballynacally*, Killaloe)

O'Doherty, Bartye (SPS)
St Patrick's, Kiltegan,
Co Wicklow
Tel 059-6473600

O'Doherty, Colm
7 Cloonty Road,
Drumquin, Omagh,
Co Tyrone BT78 7TG
Tel 028-81661475
(*Castlederg*, Derry)

O'Doherty, Daniel J., Very Rev
96 Knockmoyle, Tralee,
Co Kerry
(Kerry, retired)

O'Doherty, Daniel, Very Rev,
PE
Ballyheerin, Fanad,
Co Donegal
(Raphoe, retired)

O'Doherty, Donal, Very Rev
Mgr, PE
Holy Cross,
Upper Kilmacud Road,
Dundrum, Dublin 14
Tel 01-2985264
(Dublin, retired)

O'Doherty, Kevin (SPS)
St Patrick's, Kiltegan,
Co Wicklow
Tel 059-6473600

O'Doherty, Kevin, Very Rev,
PE
Falcarragh, Co Donegal
Tel 074-9165356
(Raphoe, retired)

O'Doherty, Kieran, Very Rev,
PP
34 Moneysharvin Road,
Swatragh, Maghera,
Co Derry BT46 5PY
Tel 028-79401236
(Derry)

O'Doherty, Michael, Very Rev
Canon
No 1 Lynch Heights,
Sun Hill, Killorglin,
Co Kerry
(Kerry, retired)

O'Doherty, Oliver, Very Rev
Church Road, Nenagh,
Co Tipperary
(Killaloe, retired)

O'Doherty, Seán, Very Rev
Canon, PP
Durrow, Portlaoise, Co Laois
Tel 057-8736156
(*Durrow*, Ossory)

O'Donnell, Anthony (SMA)
African Missions,
Blackrock Road, Cork
Tel 021-4292871

O'Donnell, Brian, PP
65 Mayogall Road,
Knockloughrim,
Magherafelt,
Co Derry BT45 8PG
Tel 028-79642458
(*Lavey*, Derry)

O'Donnell, Chris
Limerick Diocesan Pastoral
Centre,
St Michael's Courtyard,
Denmark Street, Limerick
Tel 061-400133
(Limerick)

O'Donnell, Christopher
(OCarm)
Terenure College, Terenure,
Dublin 6W
Tel 01-4904621

O'Donnell, Columba (OSA)
Duckspool House
(Retirement Community),
Abbeyside, Dungarvan,
Co Waterford
Tel 058-23784

O'Donnell, Cornelius, Very
Rev, PP
Rathcormac, Fermoy,
Co Cork
Tel 025-36286
(*Rathcormac*, Cloyne)

O'Donnell, Desmond (OMI)
Oblate House of Retreat,
Inchicore, Dublin 8
Tel 01-4534408/4541805

O'Donnell, Edward (SJ)
Gonzaga College,
Sandford Road, Dublin 6
Tel 01-4972943l

O'Donnell, Edward, Very Rev,
PP
St Anne's Parochial House,
Kingsway, Finaghy,
Belfast BT10 0NE
Tel 028-90610112
(*St Anne's*, Down & C.)

O'Donnell, Gerard, Very Rev,
PP
Geesla, Bangor, Ballina,
Co Mayo
Tel 097-86740
(*Kiltane*, Killala)

O'Donnell, Hugh (OFM)
Franciscan House of Studies,
Dun Mhuire, Seafield Road,
Killiney, Co Dublin
Tel 01-2826760

O'Donnell, Hugh (SDB)
Rector, Rinaldi House,
72 Sean McDermott Street,
Dublin 1
Tel 01-8363358

O'Donnell, James, CC
Bohermore, Cashel,
Co Tipperary
Tel 062-61409
(Cashel & E.)

O'Donnell, James, Rt Rev Mgr,
AP
Macroom, Co Cork
Tel 026-41042
(Cloyne)

O'Donnell, Joe, CC
Carnamuggagh Lower,
Letterkenny, Co Donegal
Tel 074-9122608
(*Aughaninshin*, Raphoe)

O'Donnell, John, Very Rev, PP
Blacklion, Co Cavan
Tel 071-9853012
(*Killinagh and Glangevlin*,
Kilmore)

O'Donnell, Louis (OSA)
St John's Priory,
Thomas Street,
Dublin 8
Tel 01-6770393

O'Donnell, Michael (MSC)
MSC Mission Support
Centre, PO Box 23,
Western Road, Cork
Tel 021-4545704

O'Donnell, Owen, Very Rev,
PE
Parochial House, Dunamore,
Cookstown, Co Tyrone
Tel 028-86751216
(Armagh, retired)

O'Donnell, P.J.
c/o Diocesan Office,
Social Service Centre,
Henry Street, Limerick
(Limerick, retired)

O'Donnell, Pat, Very Rev, PP
Milltown, Co Kerry
Tel 066-9767312
(*Milltown*, Kerry)

O'Donnell, Patrick (CSsR)
Clonard Monastery,
1 Clonard Gardens,
Belfast, BT13 2RL
Tel 028-90445950

O'Donnell, Terence (IC)
Cottrell Lodge,
16A Ormond Road,
Drumcondra, Dublin 9
Tel 01-8572234

O'Donoghue, Brendan, Very
Rev Canon, AP
12 Tullyglass Square,
Shannon, Co Clare
Tel 061-361257/086-8308153
(*Shannon*, Killaloe)

O'Donoghue, Fergus (SJ)
35 Lower Leeson Street,
Dublin 2
Tel 01-6761248

O'Donoghue, James (MHM),
CC
St Mary's, Marquis Street,
Belfast BT1 1JJ
Tel 028-90320482
(*St Mary's*, Down & C.)

O'Donoghue, James, CC
Kilsheelan, Clonmel,
Co Tipperary
Tel 052-6133292
(*Kilsheelan*, Waterford & L.)

O'Donoghue, James, CC
Holyford, Co Tipperary
Tel 062-71104
(*Kilcommon*, Cashel & E.)

O'Donoghue, Jim (MHM)
St Mary's Parish,
25 Marquis Street,
Belfast BT1 1JJ
Tel 028-90320482
(*St Mary's*, Down & C.)

O'Donoghue, Neville (SM)
St Columba's, Church
Avenue, Ballybrack,
Co Dublin
Tel 01-2858301

O'Donoghue, Patrick, CC
Pro-Cathedral House,
83 Marlborough Street,
Dublin 1
Tel 01-8745441
(*Pro-Cathedral*, Dublin)

O'Donoghue, Patrick, Most
Rev, AP
The Presbytery, Bantry,
Co Cork
Tel 027-50082
(*Bantry,* Cork and R.)

O'Donoghue, Paul, CC
Bandon, Co Cork
(Bandon, Cork & R.)

O'Donoghue, Sean (CSSp)
Holy Ghost Missionary
College, Kimmage Manor,
Dublin 12
Tel 01-4064300

O'Donohoe, Joseph
(OPraem)

O'Donohue, Neville (SM)
St Columba's, Church
Avenue, Ballybrack,
Co Dublin
Tel 01-2858301

O'Donohue, Vincent, Very Rev
Canon, PE
18 Kilcrea Park, Magazine
Road,
Co Cork
(Cloyne, retired)

O'Donovan, Chris, AP
Lissavaird, Rosscarbery,
Co Cork
Tel 023-8834334
(*Rosscarbery and Lissavaird*,
Cork & R.)

Allianz (ⓘ)

O'Donovan, Colman, Very Rev
Canon, PE
1 Youghal Road, Midleton,
Co Cork
Tel 021-4621617
(Cloyne, retired)

O'Donovan, Con, Very Rev, PE
16 Deer Park Avenue,
St Joseph's Road, Mallow,
Co Cork
Tel 022-51948
(Cloyne, retired)

O'Donovan, Dan
Creagh, Ballinasloe,
Co Galway
Tel 090-9645080
(Clonfert)

O'Donovan, Ignatius (OSA)
St Augustine's Priory, Shop
Street,
Drogheda, Co Louth
Tel 041-9838409

O'Donovan, James, Very Rev
Canon, PP
Ballinlough, Cork
Tel 021-4292296
(Ballinlough, Cork & R.)

O'Donovan, John, CC
The Presbytery,
Dunmanway, Co Cork
Tel 028-8845000
(Dunmanway, Cork & R.)

O'Donovan, John
PO Box 897, Oldsmar,
Florida 34677 USA
(Killaloe)

O'Donovan, John, Very Rev,
PP
Parochial House,
Hattons Alley, Blackpool,
Cork
Tel 021-4501022
(Blackpool/The Glen, Cork &
R.)

O'Donovan, Michael, Very
Rev, PP
The Presbytery, Caheragh,
Co Cork
Tel 028-31126
(Caheragh, Cork & R.)

O'Donovan, Padraig (SSC)
St Columban's, Dalgan Park,
Navan, Co Meath
Tel 046-9021525

O'Donovan, Pat, CC
Monkstown, Co Cork
Tel 021-4863267
(Monkstown, Cork & R.)

O'Donovan, Paul (OFMCap)
Guardian, St Francis
Capuchin Friary,
Rochestown, Co Cork
Tel 021-4896244

O'Donovan, Raymond (OP)
Newbridge College,
Droichead Nua, Co Kildare
Tel 045-487200

O'Donovan, Tadhg, CC
Whitechurch, Co Cork
Tel 021-4884111
(Blarney, Cloyne)

O'Donovan, William (OMI)
Oblate House of Retreat,
Inchicore, Dublin 8
Tel 01-4534408/4541805

O'Donovan, William, Very
Rev, PP
Conna, Mallow, Co Cork
Tel 058-59138
(Conna, Cloyne)

O'Dowd, Gabriel, CC
The Presbytery,
St Margaret's, Finglas,
Dublin 11
Tel 01-8341009
(Finglas, Dublin)

O'Dowd, Hugh, Very Rev, PP
Parochial House,
O'Callaghan's Mills,
Co Clare
Tel 065-6835148
(O'Callaghan's Mills,
Killaloe)

O'Dowd, Sean (SPS)
St Patrick's, Kiltegan,
Co Wicklow
Tel 059-6473600

O'Driscoll, Aidan, Very Rev, PP
The Presbytery,
Upper Mayfield, Cork
Tel 021-4503116
(Upper Mayfield, Cork & R.)

O'Driscoll, Eamonn (OFM)
Vicar, Franciscan Friary,
Lady Lane, Waterford
Tel 051-874262

O'Driscoll, Fachtna (SMA)
Provincial, African Missions,
Provincial House, Feltrim,
Blackrock Road, Cork
Tel 021-4292871

O'Driscoll, Kieron, PP
Barrett's Hill, Ballinhassig,
Co Cork
Tel 021-4885104
(Ballinhassig, Cork & R.)

O'Driscoll, Liam, Canon, Adm
Diocesan Offices,
Redemption Road, Cork
Tel 021-4301717
Administrator
Church of the Most Precious
Blood, Clogheen, Co Cork
Tel 021-4392122
(Cork & R.)

O'Driscoll, Martin, CC
North Street, Skibbereen,
Co Cork
Tel 028-22878
(St Patrick's Cathedral,
Skibbereen, Cork & R.)

O'Driscoll, Michael
Bushmount, Clonakilty,
Co Cork
Tel 023-33991
(Cork & R., retired)

O'Driscoll, Neil (SJ)
Superior,
John Austin House,
135 North Circular Road,
Dublin 7
Tel 01-8386768

O'Driscoll, P.J., CC
Monument Hill, Fermoy,
Co Cork
Tel 087-6490381
(Fermoy, Cloyne)

O'Driscoll, Paul, CC
The Presbytery,
2 St Mary's Terrace, Arklow,
Co Wicklow
Tel 0402-32196
(Arklow, Dublin)

O'Driscoll, Philip, CC
23 Barclay Court, Blackrock,
Co Dublin
Tel 01-2883329
(Blackrock, Dublin)

O'Driscoll, Sean, CC
Ballyphehane, Co Cork
Tel 021-4310835
(Ballyphehane, Cork & R.)

O'Driscoll, Timothy (CSSp)
Spiritan Missionary College,
Kimmage Manor, Dublin 12
Tel 01-4064300

O'Duill, Feargal (LC)
Chaplain, Clonlost Retreat
and Youth Centre,
Killiney Road, Killiney,
Co Dublin
Tel 01-2350064

O'Dwyer, Christy, Rt Rev Mgr,
PP, VG
Diocesan Archivist,
Bohermore, Cashel,
Co Tipperary
Tel 062-61127
(Cashel, Cashel & E.)

O'Dwyer, John, Very Rev
Canon, PP
Oranmore, Co Galway
Tel 091-794634
(Oranmore, Galway)

O'Dwyer, Michael (SAC), CC
St Benin's, Dublin Road,
Shankill, Co Dublin
Tel 01-2824425
(Shankill, Dublin)

O'Dwyer, Michael, Very Rev,
PP, VF
Parochial House,
15 Moy Road, Portadown,
Co Armagh BT62 1QL
Tel 028-38350610
(Portadown (Drumcree),
Armagh)

O'Dwyer, Richard (SJ)
Manresa House,
Dollymount, Dublin 3
Tel 01-8331352

O'Dwyer, Sean, Very Rev, PP
Parochial House, Cahir,
Co Tipperary
Tel 052-7441404
(Cahir, Waterford & L.)

O'Farrell, Ambrose (OP)
Holy Cross, Tralee, Co Kerry
Tel 066-21135/29185

O'Farrell, Eddie (CSSp)
Provincial Secretary,
Spiritan Provincialate,
Temple Park,
Richmond Avenue South,
Dublin 6
Tel 01-4975127/4977230

O'Farrell, Martin, Very Rev, PP
Aghadoe, Kinsaley Lane,
Malahide, Co Dublin
Tel 01-8461767
(Kinsealy, Dublin)

O'Farrell, Patrick, Very Rev, PP
Lisdowney, Ballyragget,
Co Kilkenny
Tel 056-8833138/
087-2353520
(Lisdowney, Ossory)

O'Farrell, Peter, CC
Cobh, Co Cork
Tel 021-4855983
(Cobh, St Colman's
Cathedral, Cloyne)

O'Fearraí, Cathal, Very Rev
PP, VF
Ballyshannon, Co Donegal
(Raphoe)

O'Fearraigh, Brian, CC
Derrybeg, Letterkenny
Tel 074-9531947
Séiplíneach, Pobalscoil
Chloich Cheannfhaola,
Falcarragh, Letterkenny,
Co Donegal
Tel 074-9135424/9135231
(Raphoe)

O'Flaherty, Michael
School of Law,
University of Nottingham,
University Park,
Nottingham NG7 2RD,
England
(Galway)

O'Flaherty, Séan, Rt Rev Mgr,
PP, VF
The Cathedral, Galway
Tel 091-563577
(Galway)

O'Flatharta, Micheál (CSsR)
St Joseph's, Dundalk,
Co Louth
Tel 042-9334042/9334762

O'Flynn, Finbarr, CC
Dungourney, Co Cork
Tel 021-4668406
(Imogeela (Castlemartyr),
Cloyne)

O'Flynn, Silvester (OFMCap)
Vicar, Holy Trinity,
Fr Mathew Quay, Cork
Tel 021-4270827

O'Flynn, Thomas (OP)
St Mary's Priory, Tallaght,
Dublin 24
Tel 01-4048100

O'Gara, Frank (OCarm), PP
Presbytery, Montrose Park,
Beaumont, Dublin 5
Tel 01-8477740/8476359
(*Beaumont*, Dublin)

O'Gorman, Charles, CC
Shercock, Co Cavan
Tel 042-9669127
(*Bailieboro*, Kilmore)

O'Gorman, Daniel (SSC)
St Columban's Retirement
Home, Dalgan Park, Navan,
Co Meath
Tel 046-9021525

O'Gorman, Daniel, CC
Herbertstown, Hospital,
Co Limerick
Tel 061-385104
(Cashel & E.)

O'Gorman, Eamonn, Very Rev,
PP
Mooncoin, Co Kilkenny
Tel/Fax 051-895123/
087-2236145
(*Mooncoin*, Ossory)

O'Gorman, John, Very Rev, PP
Menlough, Ballinasloe,
Co Galway
Tel 090-9684818
(*Menlough (Killascobe)*,
Tuam)

O'Gorman, Kevin (SMA)
SMA House,
82 Ranelagh Road,
Ranelagh, Dublin 6
Tel 01-4968162/3

O'Gorman, Maurice, Very Rev,
PP
Clashmore, Co Waterford
Tel 024-96110
(*Clashmore*, Waterford & L.)

O'Gorman, Patrick, Very Rev,
PP
Golden, Co Tipperary
Tel 062-72146
(*Golden*, Cashel & E.)

O'Gorman, Tom
Christ the King,
Cloughleigh, Ennis, Co Clare
Tel 065-6840715
(*Ennis*, Killaloe)

O'Gorman, William, Very Rev,
PP
Tournafulla, Co Limerick
Tel 069-81010/087-2580020
(Limerick)

O'Grady, Desmond (SJ)
Gonzaga College,
Sandford Road, Dublin 6
Tel 01-4972943

O'Grady, James, Very Rev, PP
Headford, Co Galway
Tel 093-35448
(*Headford (Killursa and
Killower)*, Tuam)

O'Grady, Nicholas (CP)
St Paul's Retreat,
Mount Argus, Dublin 6W
Tel 01-4992000

O'Grady, Peter (OFM)
The Abbey, 8 Francis Street,
Galway
Tel 091-562518

O'Hagan, Eugene, Very Rev,
Adm, JCL
Parochial House,
69 Doagh Road, Ballyclare,
Co Antrim BT39 9BG
Tel 028-93342226
The Good Shepherd Centre,
511 Ormeau Road,
Belfast BT7 3GS
Tel 028-90491990
(Down & C.)

O'Hagan, Francis, PP
71 Duncrun Road,
Bellarena, Limavady,
Co Derry BT49 0JD
Tel 028-77750226
(*Magilligan*, Derry)

O'Hagan, Hugh J., Very Rev,
PP
Parochial House,
31 Ballynafie Road,
Ahoghill BT42 1LF
Tel 028-25871351
(*Ahoghill*, Down & C.)

O'Hagan, Joseph, Very Rev
Canon
Cabra, Hilltown
(Dromore, retired)

O'Hagan, Mark, CC
St Patrick's Presbytery,
Roden Place, Dundalk,
Co Louth
Tel 042-9334648
(*Dundalk, St Patrick's*,
Armagh)

O'Hagan, Martin, Very Rev, PP
71 North Street,
Newtownards,
Co Down BT23 4JD
Tel 028-91812137
(*Newtownards*, Down & C.)

O'Hagan, Patrick, CC
41 Melmount Road,
Strabane,
Co Tyrone BT82 9EF
Tel 028-71882651
(*Melmount*, Derry)

O'Halloran, Giles (OSA)
St John's Priory,
Thomas Street,
Dublin 8
Tel 01-6770393

O'Halloran, J.A., Very Rev
Canon, PE
Creggana More, Oranmore,
Co Galway
Tel 091-794116
(Galway, retired)

O'Halloran, James (SDB)
Don Bosco Houses,
57 Lower Drumcondra Road,
Dublin 1
Tel 01-8360696/8373449
12 Clontarf Road, Dublin 3
Tel 01-8336009/8337045

O'Halloran, Richard, CC
41 Lismore Park, Waterford
Tel 051-354034
(*St Paul's*, Waterford & L.)

O'Halloran, Tom, Very Rev
Borrisokane, Co Tipperary
Tel 067-27105
(Killaloe)

O'Hanlon, David
Pontifico Colegio Portugues,
Via Nicolo V,
2-00165 Roma, Italy
(Meath)

O'Hanlon, Denis, CC
Carrigtwohill, Co Cork
Tel 021-4883867
(*Carrigtwohill*, Cloyne)

O'Hanlon, Francis, Very Rev,
PP
Shannonbridge, Athlone,
Co Westmeath
Tel 090-9674125
(*Shannonbridge*, Ardagh &
Cl.)

O'Hanlon, George, Very Rev
Canon
62 Coolkeeran Road,
Armoy, Ballymoney,
Co Antrim BT538XN
(Down & C.)

O'Hanlon, Gerard (SJ)
25 Croftwood Park,
Cherry Orchard, Dublin 10
Tel 01-6267413

O'Hara, Emmet (SAC)
Pallottine College, Thurles,
Co Tipperary
Tel 0504-21202

O'Hara, Vincent (OCD)
Avila, Bloomfield Avenue,
Morehampton Road,
Dublin 4
Tel 01-6430200

O'Hare, Martin (SMA), CC
The Presbytery, Togher,
Cork
Tel 021-4316800
(*Togher*, Cork & R.)

O'Hare, Paddy (SM)
Japan

O'Hare, Peter, Very Rev, PP
Parochial House,
22 Castle Street,
Killough,
Co Down BT30 7QQ
Tel 028-44841221
(*Killough (Bright)*, Down &
C.)

O'Hea, James (SMA)
SMA House, Wilton, Cork
Tel 021-4541069/4541884

O'Hea, Jarlath (OCarm)
Whitefriar Street Church,
56 Aungier Street, Dublin 2
Tel 01-4758821

O'Herlihy, Pat (SSC)
No. 2 Presbytery, Our Lady
Crowned Church,
Mayfield Upper, Cork
Tel 021-4508610/
087-2284284

O'Higgins, Kevin (SJ)
Arrupe Community,
127 Shangan Road,
Ballymun, Dublin 9
Tel/Fax 01-8625345

O'Holohan, John (SJ)
St Francis Xavier's, Upper
Gardiner Street, Dublin 1
Tel 01-8363411

O'Hora, Gerard, CC
St Patrick's Presbytery,
Ballina, Co Mayo
Tel 096-71360
(*Ballina*, Killala)

O'Horo, Michael, Very Rev, PP
Skreen, Co Sligo
Tel 071-9166629
(*Skreen and Dromard*,
Killala)

O'Kane, David, CC
9 Church Street, Claudy,
Derry BT47 4AA
Tel 028-71337727
(*Claudy*, Derry)

O'Kane, Hugh (SMA), CC
(priest in residence)
53 Ballinlea Road,
Ballycastle,
Co Antrim BT54 6JL
Tel 028-20762498
(*Ballintoy*, Down & C.)

O'Kane, James, Very Rev, PP
87 Cushendall Road,
Ballyvoy, Ballycastle,
Co Antrim BT54 6QY
Tel 028-20762248
(*Culfeightrin*, Down & C.)

O'Kane, Patrick, PP
Parochial House, Moville,
Co Donegal
Tel 074-9382057
(*Moville*, Derry)

O'Kane, Peter, CC
Pontificio Collegio Irlandese,
Via Dei SS Quattro 1,
00184 Roma, Italy
(Derry)

O'Kane, Peter, Very Rev, PP
2A My Lady's Mile,
Holywood,
Co Down BT18 9EW
Tel 028-90422167
(*Holywood*, Down & C.)

O'Kane, Seamus
12 Gortinure Road,
Maghera,
Co Derry BT46 5RB
Tel 07989-946344
(Derry)

O'Keefe, Edmund (SJ)
Milltown Park,
Sandford Road, Dublin 6
Tel 01-2698411/2698113

O'Keefe, Fergus (SJ)
Rector, John Sullivan House,
56/56A Mulvey Park,
Dundrum, Dublin 14
Tel 01-2983978
Spiritual Director, Lay
Retreat Association of Saint
Ignatius, Milltown Park,
Dublin 6
Tel 01-2951856

O'Keefe, John, CC
Birdhill, Killaloe,
Co Tipperary
Tel 061-379172
(Cashel & E.)

O'Keefe, Martin, CC
Glenisland, Castlebar,
Co Mayo
Tel 094-9024161
(Islandeady, Tuam)

O'Keeffe, Anthony (OFMCap)
St Francis Capuchin Friary,
Rochestown, Co Cork
Tel 021-4896244

O'Keeffe, Anthony, Very Rev
Canon, PP, VF
Shanagolden, Co Limerick
Tel 069-60112/087-4163401
(Limerick)

O'Keeffe, Gerard (OP)
St Dominic's, Athy,
Co Kildare
Tel 0507-31573

O'Keeffe, John (OFM)
Collegio S. Isidoro,
Via degli Artisti 41,
00187 Roma, Italy
Tel +39-06-4885359

O'Keeffe, John (SJ)
Superior,
Campion House Residence,
28 Lower Hatch Street,
Dublin 2
Tel 01-6383990

O'Keeffe, John, Very Rev
Cranny, Ennis, Co Clare
Tel 065-6832119
(Coolmeen, Killaloe)

O'Keeffe, Joseph
42 Nessan Court, Church
Road, Raheen, Limerick
Tel 061-309151/086-3333539
(Limerick)

O'Keeffe, Joseph, CC
Ballynoe, Mallow, Co Cork
Tel 058-59269
(Conna, Cloyne)

O'Keeffe, Laurence, Very Rev,
PP
Clifden Villa, Clifden,
Co Kilkenny
Tel 056-7726560/
087-2258443
(Clara, Ossory)

O'Keeffe, Martin (OMI)
The Presbytery, Glenisland,
Castlebar, Co Mayo
Tel 085-1086639

O'Keeffe, Patrick (CSsR)
Clonard Monastery,
1 Clonard Gardens,
Belfast, BT13 2RL
Tel 028-90445950

O'Keeffe, Philip, Very Rev, PE
Kiliphilbeen, Ballynoe,
Mallow, Co Cork
Tel 058-59526
(Cloyne, retired)

O'Keeffe, Thomas, Very Rev
20 Glen Avenue, The Park,
Cabinteely, Dublin 18
Tel 01-2853643
(Dublin, retired)

O'Keeffe, Tony
Chaplain, McKee Barracks,
Dublin 7
Tel 01-8388614
(Dublin)

O'Kelly, Francis (SSC)
St Columban's, Dalgan Park,
Navan, Co Meath
Tel 046-9021525

O'Kelly, Michael, (Moderator)
197 Kylemore Road,
Ballyfermot, Dublin 10
Tel 01-6264789
(Ballyfermot, Dublin)

O'Laoghaire, Sean, Very Rev,
PE
Paulstown, Gowran,
Co Kilkenny
Tel 059-9726104
(Kildare & L., retired)

O'Leary, Aidan (OSA)
St Augustine's Priory,
Grantstown, New Ross,
Co Wexford
Tel 051-561119

O'Leary, Alan, P
The Presbytery, Schull,
Co Cork
Tel 028-28171
(Schull, Cork & R.)

O'Leary, Anthony (CP)
St Gabriel's Retreat,
The Graan, Enniskillen,
Co Fermanagh
Tel 028-66322272

O'Leary, Brian (SJ)
35 Lower Leeson Street,
Dublin 2
Tel 01-6761248

O'Leary, Celestine (OCSO)
Mount Melleray Abbey,
Cappoquin, Co Waterford
Tel 058-54404

O'Leary, Con (SMA)
African Missions,
Blackrock Road, Cork
Tel 021-4292871

O'Leary, Denis J., Very Rev, PP
Bandon, Co Cork
Tel 023-8841728
(Bandon, Cork & R.)

O'Leary, Gerald, Very Rev, PP
Horeswood, Campile,
Co Wexford
Tel 051-388129
(Horeswood, Ferns)

O'Leary, Gerard, CC
Killarney, Co Kerry
Tel 064-6631014
(Killarney, Kerry)

O'Leary, Gerard, Very Rev,
Adm
Parochial House, Ballyhahill,
Co Limerick
Tel 069-82103/087-9378685
(Loughill/Ballyhahill,
Limerick)

O'Leary, John, Very Rev
175 Adams Street,
11E Brooklyn, NY 11208 USA
Tel 718-5107111
(Armagh)

O'Leary, Joseph
1-38-16 Ekoda, Nakanoku,
Tokyo, 16J0022 Japan
(Cork & R.)

O'Leary, Kevin, Very Rev
1 Clarmont Court,
Castlewellan,
Co Down BT31 9SE
(Down & C., retired)

O'Leary, Michael, AP
St John's Presbytery, Tralee,
Co Kerry
Tel 066-7122522
(Tralee, St John's, Kerry)

O'Leary, Noel (SMA)
Superior,
Dromantine College,
Dromantine, Newry,
Co Down BT34 1RH
Tel 028-30821224

O'Leary, Oscar (OFM)
Franciscan Friary,
Liberty Street, Cork
Tel 021-4270302

O'Leary, Owen (SSC)
St Columban's, Dalgan Park,
Navan, Co Meath
Tel 046-9021525

O'Leary, Partolan (IC), CC
Cooleens, Glenconnor,
Clonmel, Co Tipperary
Tel 052-6125679
(Clonmel, St Oliver Plunkett,
Waterford & L.)

O'Leary, Rory (OFM)
Franciscan College,
Gormanston, Co Meath
Tel 01-8412203

O'Leary, Sean (CSSp)
Provincial Assistant,
Spiritan Provincialate,
Temple Park,
Richmond Avenue South,
Dublin 6
Tel 01-4975127/4977230

O'Leary, Timothy, Very Rev
Canon, PE, CC, VF
Mitchelstown, Co Cork
Tel 025-84088
(Mitchelstown, Cloyne)

O'Leary, Timothy, Very Rev,
PP
Glenroe, Kilmallock,
Co Limerick
Tel 063-86040
(Glenroe and Ballyorgan,
Limerick)

O'Loan, Fergus (OCarm)
Whitefriar Street Church,
56 Aungier Street, Dublin 2
Tel 01-4758821

O'Loughlin, Declan
Parochial House, 30
Newline, Killeavy, Newry,
Co Down BT35 8TA
Tel 028-30889609
(Armagh)

O'Loughlin, Michael (SSC)
43 Moyland, Shanballa,
Loughville, Lahinch Road,
Ennis, Co Clare
Tel 065-6845321

O'Loughlin, Padhraic (SSC)
Collegio San Colombano,
Corso Trieste 57,
00198 Rome, Itlay

O'Loughlin, Peadar (SSC)
St Columban's, Dalgan Park,
Navan, Co Meath
Tel 046-9021525

O'Loughlin, Peter, Very Rev,
PP
Kilmihil, Co Clare
Tel 065-9050016/086-
8250016
(Kilmihil, Killaloe)

O'Mahony, Anthony, CC
The Presbytery, Bantry,
Co Cork
Tel 027-50193
(Bantry, Cork & R.)

O'Mahony, Bartholomew,
Very Rev, PP
Cork Road, Carrigaline,
Co Cork
Tel 021-4371684
(Carrigaline, Cork & R.)

O'Mahony, Brendan
(OFMCap)
Holy Trinity,
Fr Mathew Quay, Cork
Tel 021-4270827

O'Mahony, Damian, CC
1 Parochial House,
Blackrock, Cork
Tel 021-4358381
(Blackrock, Cork & R.)

O'Mahony, Dan Joe (OFMCap)
Chaplain, The Oratory,
Blanchardstown Shopping
Centre, Capuchin Parochial
Friary, Clonshaugh Drive,
Priorswood, Dublin 17
Tel 01-8474469/8474538
(*Priorswood*, Dublin)

O'Mahony, Dan, Very Rev, PP
Cloonacool, Tubbercurry,
Co Sligo
Tel 071-9185156
(*Tubbercurry*, Achonry)

O'Mahony, Denis, Very Rev
Canon
Killeagh, Farranfore,
Co Kerry
(Kerry, retired)

O'Mahony, Denis, Very Rev,
PP
Fenit, Tralee, Co Kerry
Tel 066-7136145
(Spa, Kerry)

O'Mahony, Dermot, Most Rev
DD
Titular Bishop of Tiava;
former Auxiliary Bishop of
Dublin, 19 Longlands,
Swords, Co Dublin
Tel 01-8401596
(Dublin)

O'Mahony, Donal (SDB)
Salesian House,
Warrenstown, Drumree,
Co Meath
Tel 01-8259894

O'Mahony, Donal, Very Rev
Canon, PP
Cloyne, Midleton, Co Cork
Tel 021-4652597
(*Cloyne*, Cloyne)

O'Mahony, George, Very Rev,
PP
Ballincollig, Co Cork
Tel 021-4871206
(*Ballincollig*, Cork & R.)

O'Mahony, John (MSC)
Woodview House,
Mount Merrion Avenue,
Blackrock, Co Dublin
Tel 01-2881644

O'Mahony, John K., Very Rev
Canon, AP
The Presbytery, Kinsale,
Co Cork
Tel 021-4773700
(*Kinsale*, Cork & R.)

O'Mahony, Joseph, CC
Buttevant, Co Cork
Tel 022-23716
(*Buttevant*, Cloyne)

O'Mahony, Kieran (OSA)
Augustinian Retreat Centre,
Old Court Road,
Dublin 16
Tel 01-4930932

O'Mahony, Michael, CC
8 The Meadows,
Classis Lake, Ballincollig,
Co Cork
Tel 021-4877161
(*Ballincollig*, Cork & R.)

O'Mahony, Nicholas, Very Rev
Canon, PP, VG
Parochial House, Tramore,
Co Waterford
Tel 051-381525
(*Tramore*, Waterford & L.)

O'Mahony, Pat (SMA), CC
The Presbytery, Upper
Mayfield, Cork
Tel 021-4500828
(*Upper Mayfield*, Cork & R.)

O'Mahony, Patrick (SMA)
Temporary diocesan work in
Ireland

O'Mahony, Stephen
Chaplain to school
Kiltimagh, Co Mayo
Tel 094-9381261
(*Kiltimagh (Killedan)*,
Achonry)

O'Mahony, Stephen, Very Rev,
PP
Liscarroll, Mallow, Co Cork
Tel 022-48128
(*Churchtown (Liscarroll)*,
Cloyne)

O'Mahony, Thomas, Very Rev,
PP
Parochial House, Skryne,
Tara, Co Meath
Tel 046-9025152
(*Skryne*, Meath)

O'Malley, Donough, Very Rev
Canon, PP
St Mary's,
Athlunkard Street, Limerick
Tel 061-414092
(*St Mary's*, Limerick)

O'Malley, Michael
c/o Archbishop's House,
Tuam
(Tuam)

O'Meara, Denis, Very Rev
Canon
Millbrae Lodge Nursing
Home,
Newport, Co Tipperary
(Cashel & E., retired)

O'Meara, Donagh
St Kevin's Catholic Church,
550 Stanford Road,
Windvogel, Port Elizabeth
6059, South Africa
(Killaloe)

O'Meara, Michael, Very Rev,
PP
Kinnity, Birr, Co Offaly
Tel 0509-37021/087-7735977
(*Kinnitty*, Killaloe)

O'Meara, Noel (CSSp)
St Michael's College,
Aylesbury Road, Dublin 4
Tel 01-2189423

O'Melia, Joseph (OMI)
Oblate House of Retreat,
Inchicore, Dublin 8
Tel 01-4534408/4541805

O'Moore, Maurice, Very Rev
Canon, PE
6 Richmond Avenue,
Monkstown, Co Dublin
Tel 01-2802186
(Dublin, retired)

O'Neill, Angelus (OFMCap),
Very Rev, Guardian
Capuchin Parochial Friary,
Clonshaugh Drive,
Priorswood, Dublin 17
Tel 01-8474469/8474538
(*Priorswood*, Dublin)

O'Neill, Arthur
1B Willow Court,
Druid Valley, Cabinteely,
Dublin 18
Tel 01-2814435/087-2597520
(*Cabinteely*, Dublin)

O'Neill, Charles
Colmanswell, Charleville,
Co Limerick
Tel 063-89459
(Limerick, retired)

O'Neill, Daniel (MSC)
Carrignavar, Co Cork
Tel 021-4884044

O'Neill, Daniel (SMA)
SMA House, Claregalway,
Co Galway
Tel 091-798880

O'Neill, Denis (SPS)
St Patrick's, 21 Leeson Park,
Dublin 6
Tel 01-4977897

O'Neill, Donal
St Patrick's College,
Maynooth, Co Kildare
(Kerry)

O'Neill, Eugene
4 Ballymacnab Road,
Armagh BT60 2QS
Tel 028-37531620
(Armagh)

O'Neill, Eugene, CC
40 Derryvolgie Avenue,
Belfast BT9 6FP
Tel 028-90665409
(*St Brigid's*, Down & C.)

O'Neill, Fergal
Cathedral Presbytery, Ennis,
Co Clare
Tel 087-6615975
(Killaloe)

O'Neill, Francis, Very Rev, PP
Ballyclough, Mallow,
Co Cork
Tel 022-27650
(Cloyne)

O'Neill, Frank (SJ)
St Francis Xavier's,
Upper Gardiner Street,
Dublin 1
Tel 01-8363411

O'Neill, Gerard (SDB)
Chaplain, Collins Barracks,
Cork

O'Neill, Hugh (SJ)
Milltown Park,
Sandford Road, Dublin 6
Tel 01-2698411/2698113

O'Neill, Ian
(in residence)
St Patrick's Presbytery,
Forster Street, Galway
Tel 091-563813
Diocesan Secretary,
Diocesan Office,
The Cathedral, Galway
Tel 091-563566
(Galway)

O'Neill, Joe, CC
Ballyfin Road, Portlaoise,
Co Laois
Tel 086-2354320
(*Portlaoise*, Kildare & L.)

O'Neill, John, Very Rev, PP
Ballylanders, Kilmallock,
Co Limerick
Tel 062-46705
(*Ballylanders*, Cashel & E.)

O'Neill, Kevin, Rt Rev Mgr,
BA, MSc Ed
President, Carlow College,
College Street, Carlow
Tel 059 9153200
(Kildare & L.)

O'Neill, Míceál (OCarm)
Prior, Carmelite Friary,
Kinsale, Co Cork
Tel 021-772138

O'Neill, Niall (SJ)
Crescent College
Comprehensive,
Dooradoyle, Limerick
Tel 061-480920

O'Neill, Pat
Ruan, Co Clare
Tel 065-6827799/086-
2612124
(*Dysart & Ruan*, Killaloe)

O'Neill, Peter (SSC)
House Superior,
St Columban's, Dalgan Park,
Navan, Co Meath
Tel 046-9021525

O'Neill, Roger, CC
New Ross, Co Wexford
Tel 051-421214
(*New Ross*, Ferns)

O'Neill, Seamus (SPS)
Society Leader, St Patrick's,
Kiltegan, Co Wicklow
Tel 059-6473600

O'Neill, Seamus (SSC)
20 Tobermore Road,
Moykeenan, Draperstown,
Co Derry BT45 7HG
Tel 048-79627206

Allianz (ⅼⅼ)

O'Neill, Sean, PP, VF
Parochial House,
1 Rockstown Road,
Carrickmore, Omagh,
Co Tyrone BT79 9BE
Tel 028-80761207
(*Termonmaguirc*
(Carrickmore, Loughmacrory
& Creggan), Armagh)

O'Neill, Sean, Very Rev, PE
'Iona', 3 St Colmcille's Park,
Swords, Co Dublin
(Dublin, retired)

O'Rahelly, Edmond V., Very
Rev, PP
Ballina, Co Tipperary
Tel 061-376178
(*Ballina,* Cashel & E.)

O'Regan, Kevin, CC
The Hill, Baltimore, Co Cork
Tel 028-20283
(*St Patrick's Cathedral,*
Skibbereen, Cork & R.)

O'Regan, Liam, Very Rev
Canon, AP
'Carraigin', Moneygourney,
Douglas, Cork
Tel 021-4363998
(*Douglas,* Cork & R.)

O'Regan, Michael (OSA)
St Augustine's Priory,
Washington Street,
Cork
Tel 021-2753982

O'Regan, Robert (SMA)
African Missions,
Blackrock Road, Cork
Tel 021-4292871

O'Reilly, Andrew (OCarm)
Carmelite Priory, Moate,
Co Westmeath
Tel 090-6481160/6481398

O'Reilly, Anthony
Newry, Co Armagh
(Kerry)

O'Reilly, Arthur P., CC
285 Foreglan Road,
Dungiven,
Co Derry BT47 4PJ
Tel 028-71338261
(*Banagher,* Derry)

O'Reilly, Brendan (OCarm)
Carmelite Priory, Moate,
Co Westmeath
Tel 090-6481160/6481398

O'Reilly, Brian (SVD)
Provincial, 133 North
Circular Road, Dublin 7
Tel 01-8386743

O'Reilly, Brian, Very Rev, PP
Parochial House, Rathdrum,
Co Wicklow
Tel 0404-46229
(*Rathdrum,* Dublin)

O'Reilly, Charles (OSA)
St John's Priory,
Thomas Street,
Dublin 8
Tel 01-6770393

O'Reilly, Colm, Most Rev, DD
Bishop of Ardagh and
Clonmacnois, St Michael's,
Longford, Co Longford
Tel 043-3346432
(Ardagh & Cl.)

O'Reilly, Damian, CC
Pro-Cathedral House,
83 Marlborough Street,
Dublin 1
Tel 01-8745441
(*Pro-Cathedral*, Dublin)

O'Reilly, Desmond
St Charles Borromeo Parish,
7584 Center Parkway,
Sacramento, California
95823, USA
(Dublin)

O'Reilly, Eugene (SPS)
St Patrick's, Kiltegan,
Co Wicklow
Tel 059-6473600

O'Reilly, F. X., Very Rev
Portiuncula Nursing Home,
Multyfarnham,
Co Westmeath
(Meath, retired)

O'Reilly, Hugh (CSSp)
Holy Ghost Missionary
College, Kimmage Manor,
Dublin 12
Tel 01-4064300

O'Reilly, John (OP), CC
St Mary's Priory,
The Claddagh, Galway
Tel 091-582884
(*St Mary's,* Galway)

O'Reilly, John, PP
Piercestown, Co Wexford
Tel 053-9158851
(*Piercestown and*
Murrintown, Ferns)

O'Reilly, Joseph (IC)
Cottrell Lodge,
16A Ormond Road,
Drumcondra, Dublin 9
Tel 01-8572234
Provincial,
1 Grace Park Gardens,
Drumcondra, Dublin 9
Tel 01-8378314/8368730

O'Reilly, Kieran (SMA), Very
Rev
Superior General,
Generalate,
Via della Nocetta 111,
00164 Rome, Italy
Tel 06-6616841

O'Reilly, Leo, Most Rev, DD
Bishop of Kilmore, Bishop's
House, Cullies, Co Cavan
Tel 049-4331496
(Kilmore)

O'Reilly, Martin, CC
4 Darling Street, Enniskillen,
Co Fermanagh BT74 7DP
Tel 028-66322075
(*Enniskillen*, Clogher)

O'Reilly, Myles (SJ)
Rector, Gonzaga College,
Sandford Road, Dublin 6
Tel 01-4972943

O'Reilly, Oliver, CC
Bailieboro, Co Cavan
Tel 042-9665364
(*Bailieboro,* Kilmore)

O'Reilly, Paddy (OSA), CC
Parochial House,
5 St Helena's Drive,
Dublin 11
Tel 01-8343444
(*Rivermount,* Dublin)

O'Reilly, Paddy (SPS)
St Patrick's, Kiltegan,
Co Wicklow
Tel 059-6473600

O'Reilly, Peter, Co-PP
231 Beech Park, Lucan,
Co Dublin
Tel 01-6281756
(*Lucan,* Dublin)

O'Reilly, Peter, Very Rev, PP
Parochial House, Roslea,
Co Fermanagh BT92 7LA
Tel 028-67751227
(Clogher)

O'Reilly, Thomas, Very Rev, PP
Clonaslee, Co Laois
Tel 057-8648030
(Kildare & L.)

O'Ríordan, John P. (CSsR)
Vicar Superior,
Mount Saint Alphonsus,
Limerick
Tel 061-315099

O'Riordan, Anthony (SJ)
St Francis Xavier's, Upper
Gardiner Street, Dublin 1
Tel 01-8363411

O'Riordan, Anthony (SVD)
133 North Circular Road,
Dublin 7
Tel 01-8386743

O'Riordan, Conor (OP)
St Malachy's, Dundalk,
Co Louth
Tel 042-9334179/9333714

O'Riordan, Daniel, Rt Rev
Mgr, PP, VG, VF
The Presbytery, Castleisland,
Co Kerry
Tel 066-7141241
(Kerry)

O'Riordan, David, Very Rev,
PP
Ladysbridge, Co Cork
Tel 021-4667173
(*Ballymacoda and*
Ladysbridge, Cloyne)

O'Riordan, Eugene (SMA)
African Missions,
Blackrock Road, Cork
Tel 021-4292871

O'Riordan, Jeremiah, Very
Rev, PP
Donoughmore, Co Cork
Tel 021-7337023
(*Donoughmore*, Cloyne)

O'Riordan, Jerry (MSC)
Carrignavar, Co Cork
Tel 021-4884044

O'Riordan, John C. (CSSp),
Most Rev
Holy Ghost Missionary
College, Kimmage Manor,
Dublin 12
Tel 01-4064300

O'Riordáin, John J. (CSsR)
Mount Saint Alphonsus,
Limerick
Tel 061-315099

O'Riordan, Jude (OFM)
Adam & Eve's,
4 Merchant's Quay, Dublin 8
Tel 01-6771128

O'Riordan, Martin
Lisgoold, Co Cork
Tel 021-4642343
(*Cloyne,* retired)

O'Riordan, Timothy, Very Rev,
PP
Abbeyside, Dungarvan,
Co Waterford
Tel 058-42036
(*Abbeyside*, Waterford & L.)

O'Rourke, Brendan (CSsR)
Scala, Bessboro, Blackrock,
Cork
Tel 021-4358800

O'Rourke, Declan (OCSO)
Mount Melleray Abbey,
Cappoquin, Co Waterford
Tel 058-54404

O'Rourke, Denis (SPS)
Bursar General, St Patrick's,
Kiltegan, Co Wicklow
Tel 059-6473600

O'Rourke, John (OP)
Holy Cross, Tralee, Co Kerry
Tel 066-21135/29185

O'Rourke, John, Very Rev, PP
Gortnahoe, Thurles,
Co Tipperary
Tel 056-8834128
(*Gortnahoe,* Cashel & E.)

O'Rourke, John, Very Rev, PP
Loughglynn, Castlerea,
Co Roscommon
Tel 094-9880007
(*Loughglynn,* Elphin)

O'Rourke, Kevin (SJ)
Rector, Milltown Park,
Sandford Road, Dublin 6
Tel 01-2698411/2698113

O'Rourke, Kieran, Very Rev,
PP
Looscaun, Woodford,
Co Galway
Tel 090-9749100
(*Woodford*, Clonfert)

O'Rourke, Pat, CC
24 Watermill Road, Raheny,
Dublin 5
Tel 01-8316219
(*Raheny*, Dublin)

O'Rourke, Sean
15 Seaview Park, Shankill,
Co Dublin
(Dublin, retired)

O'Rourke, Seán, Very Rev
Canon
Retreat Nursing Home,
Athlone, Co Westmeath
(Ardagh & Cl., retired)

O'Saorai, Padraig
12 Ashville, Athy, Co Kildare
(Dublin, retired)

O'Shaughnessy, Sean (CSSp)
Holy Ghost Missionary
College, Kimmage Manor,
Dublin 12
Tel 01-4064300

O'Shaughnessy, Tom, CC
73 Annamoe Road, Dublin 7
Tel 01-8685626
(*Cabra*, Dublin)

O'Shea, A. B., Very Rev, PP
Sooey, Coola, via Boyle,
Co Sligo
Tel 071-9165144
(*Riverstown*, Elphin)

O'Shea, Colum P. (SMA)
Superior, African Missions,
Blackrock Road, Cork
Tel 021-4292871

O'Shea, Donagh (OP)
St Mary's Priory, Tallaght,
Dublin 24
Tel 01-4048100

O'Shea, Fintan (OFM)
3 The Millhouse, Steelworks,
Foley Street, Dublin 1

O'Shea, Henry (OSB)
Glenstal Abbey, Murroe,
Co Limerick
Tel 061-386103

O'Shea, John, Very Rev
Canon, PP
Convent Street, Abbeyfeale,
Co Limerick
Tel 068-31157/087-9708282
(*Abbeyfeale*, Limerick)

O'Shea, Kieran
Ballycallan, Co Kilkenny
Tel 056-7769564/
086-8272828
(Ossory)

O'Shea, Martin, Rt Rev Mgr,
PP
5 St Assam's Road West,
Raheny, Dublin 5
Tel 01-8313806
(*Raheny*, Dublin)

O'Shea, Maurice, Very Rev, PP
6 Beechpark Lawn,
Castleknock, Dublin 15
Tel 01-8212967
(*Castleknock*, Dublin)

O'Shea, Michael, CC
9 Castletroy Heights,
Monaleen, Limerick
Tel 061-335764/087-9791432
(*Monaleen*, Limerick)

O'Shea, Michael, CC
The Presbytery,
12 School Street, Wexford
Tel 053-9122055
(*Wexford*, Ferns)

O'Shea, Philip, Very Rev, PP
Myshall, Co Carlow
Tel 059-9757635
(*Myshall*, Kildare & L.)

O'Shea, Thomas, Very Rev, PE
Ballylinan, Athy, Co Kildare
Tel 059-8625261
(*Arles*, Kildare & L.)

O'Sullivan, Andrew, CC
83 The Rise, Mount Merrion,
Co Dublin
Tel 01-2882556
(*Mount Merrion*, Dublin)

O'Sullivan, Anthony, Very Rev,
PP
Glenbeigh, Co Kerry
Tel 066-9768209
(*Glenbeigh*, Kerry)

O'Sullivan, Billy
(in residence)
c/o Parochial House,
Ballincollig, Co Cork
Tel 021-4371206
(*Ballincollig*, Cork & R.)

O'Sullivan, Brendan, CC
The Presbytery, Longford
Tel 043-46465
(*Longford*, Ardagh & Cl.)

O'Sullivan, Brian
The Cottage, Glengara Park,
Glenageary,
Dun Laoghaire, Co Dublin
(Dublin, retired)

O'Sullivan, Denis (CSsR)
Mount Saint Alphonsus,
Limerick
Tel 061-315099

O'Sullivan, Denis (SMA)
SMA House, Wilton, Cork
Tel 021-4541069/4541884

O'Sullivan, Denis, Very Rev, PE
Monasterevin, Co Kildare
Tel 045-525351
(Kildare & L., retired)

O'Sullivan, Desmond L. (CSSp)
Holy Ghost Missionary
College, Kimmage Manor,
Dublin 12
Tel 01-4064300

O'Sullivan, John L. (CSSp)
Spiritan Missionary College,
Kimmage Manor,
Dublin 12
Tel 01-4064300

O'Sullivan, John (MSC)
Woodview House,
Mount Merrion Avenue,
Blackrock, Co Dublin
Tel 01-2881644

O'Sullivan, John (OSA)
St Augustine's Priory,
Washington Street, Cork
Tel 021-2753982

O'Sullivan, John K.
97 Kincora Avenue,
Clontarf, Dublin 3
(Dublin, retired)

O'Sullivan, John L. (CSSp), CC
35 Paul Street, Cork
Tel 021-4276575
(*Ss Peter's and Paul's*, Cork
& R.)

O'Sullivan, John, Very Rev
6 Ferngrove Avenue,
Aghagallon,
Craigavon BT67 0HA
(Down & C., retired)

O'Sullivan, Kieran, Very Rev,
PP
Adrigole, Bantry, Co Cork
Tel 027-60006
(*Adrigole*, Kerry)

O'Sullivan, Leo (OSA)
St Augustine's Priory,
O'Connell Street,
Limerick
Tel 061-415374

O'Sullivan, Leo (SPS)
St Patrick's, Kiltegan,
Co Wicklow
Tel 059-6473600

O'Sullivan, Liam (CSSp)
Holy Ghost Missionary
College, Kimmage Manor,
Dublin 12
Tel 01-4064300

O'Sullivan, Louis
Our Lady's Manor, Bulloch
Castle, Dalkey, Co Dublin
(Dublin, retired)

O'Sullivan, Michael (SJ)
John Austin House,
135 North Circular Road,
Dublin 7
Tel 01-8386768

O'Sullivan, Michael (OSA)
St John's Priory,
Thomas Street,
Dublin 8
Tel 01-6770393

O'Sullivan, Michael (White
Fathers)

O'Sullivan, Noel, Very Rev Dr,
PP
Glanmire, Co Cork
Tel 021-4866307
(*Glanmire*, Cork & R.)

O'Sullivan, Owen (OFMCap)
Capuchin Friary,
Ard Mhuire, Creeslough,
Letterkenny, Co Donegal
Tel 074-9138005

O'Sullivan, Padraig, CC
The Presbytery,
Dublin Road, Balbriggan,
Co Dublin
Tel 01-8412116
(*Balbriggan*, Dublin)

O'Sullivan, Patrick (CSsR)
Mount Saint Alphonsus,
Limerick
Tel 061-315099

O'Sullivan, Patrick, Very Rev
(MSC), Adm
Leap, Co Cork
Tel 028-33177
(*Kilmacabea*, Cork & R.)

O'Sullivan, Patrick, Very Rev,
PP, Adm
'Elm View', Roxboro Road,
Limerick
Tel 061-410846/087-2237501
(Limerick)

O'Sullivan, Séan, AP
Lissarda, Crookstown, Cork
Tel 021-7336053
(*Kilmurry*, Cork & R.)

O'Sullivan, Teddy, Very Rev
Canon, PP
Parochial House, Douglas
Co Cork
Tel 021-4891265
(*Douglas*, Cork & R.)

O'Sullivan, William (SMA)
African Missions,
Blackrock Road, Cork
Tel 021-4292871

O'Toole, Brian (CSSp)
St Mary's College,
Rathmines, Dublin 6
Tel 01-4062160

O'Toole, Colm (OCSO), Dom
Abbot Emeritus,
Mount Saint Joseph Abbey,
Roscrea, Co Tipperary
Tel 0505-25600

O'Toole, Lorcan (CSSp)
Holy Ghost Missionary
College, Kimmage Manor,
Dublin 12
Tel 01-4064300

O'Toole, Patrick (CSSp)
Spiritan Missionaries,
Ardbraccan, Navan,
Co Meath
Tel 046-9021441

O'Toole, Peter Baptist (OFM)
Franciscan Friary, Lady Lane,
Waterford
Tel 051-874262

O'Toole, Sean
The Presbytery, Sea Road,
Arklow, Co Wicklow
(Dublin, retired)

O'Toole, Thomas, CC
Kilmacow, via Waterford,
Co Kilkenny
Tel 051-88529/087-2240787
(Ossory)

Olden, Michael, Rt Rev Mgr,
PE
'Woodleigh',
Summerville Avenue,
Waterford
Tel 051-874132
(Waterford & L., retired)

Olejnik, Krzysztof, CC
12 Tullygally Road,
Craigavon BT65 5BL
Tel 028-38311872

Orr, Thomas, CC
Ballycanew, Gorey,
Co Wexford
Tel 053-9427184
(Camolin, Ferns)

Owen, John (SVD)
133 North Circular Road,
Dublin 7
Tel 01-8386743

Owens, Finnian (OCSO)
Our Lady of Bethlehem
Abbey, 11 Ballymena Road,
Portglenone, Ballymena,
Co Antrim BT44 8BL
Tel 028-25821211

Owens, Peter, PP
143 Andersonstown Road,
Belfast BT11 9BW
Tel 028-90615702
(St Agnes', Down & C.)

P

Palmisano, Joseph (SJ)
Peter Faber House,
28 Brookvale Avenue,
Belfast BT14 6BW
Tel 028-90757615

Parker, Thomas (SSC)
St Columban's Retirement
Home, Dalgan Park, Navan,
Co Meath
Tel 046-9021525

Parokkaran, Martin (OCarm)
Presbytery, Montrose Park,
Beaumont, Dublin 5
Tel 01-8477740/8476359
(Beaumont, Dublin)

Patton, Gerard, Very Rev, PP
Parochial House,
Dundrum, Newcastle,
Co Down BT33 0LU
Tel 028-43751212
(Dundrum and Tyrella,
Down & C.)

Pazhayakalam, Tony (CST), PC
The Presbytery,
Brackenstown Road, Swords,
Co Dublin
Tel 01-8408926
(Brackenstown, Dublin)

Pecak Marek, CC
Priest-in-residence
Midleton, Co Cork
Tel 021-4634027
(Midleton, Cloyne)

Peelo, Adrian (OFM)
Br Giles Friary,
1920 7th Street, Berkeley,
CA 94710, USA

Pentony, Liam, Very Rev, CC
Parochial House, Dromiskin,
Dundalk, Co Louth
Tel 042-9382877
(Darver and Dromiskin,
Armagh)

Peoples, William, Very Rev, PP
Donegal Town, Co Donegal
Tel 074-9721026
(Donegal Town, Raphoe)

Pepper, Pierre, CC
Banagher, Co Offaly
Tel 090-6454309
(Cloghan and Banagher,
Ardagh & Cl.)

Perrem, Leonard (OP)
St Mary's Priory, Tallaght,
Dublin 24
Tel 01-4048100

Perry, Jim (SVD)
Maynooth, Co Kildare
Tel 01-6286391/2

Peyton, Patrick, Very Rev
Canon, PP
Parochial House, Collooney,
Co Sligo
Tel 071-9167235
(Achonry)

Phair, John, Very Rev, PP
Rossinver, Co Leitrim
Tel 071-9854022
(Ballaghameehan, Kilmore)

Phelan, Richard, Very Rev
Canon, PP
Kilmanagh, Co Kilkenny
Tel 056-7769116/
087-2843461
(Ballycallan, Ossory)

Pierce, Pat (IC)
Rector & Director,
Rosminian House of Prayer,
Glencomeragh House,
Kilsheelan, Co Tipperary
Tel 052-33181

Pierse, Thomas, Very Rev
32 Knockmoyle Estate,
Tralee, Co Kerry
(Kerry, retired)

Piert, John, Very Rev Canon,
PC
The Presbytery, Johnstown,
Co Wicklow
Tel 0402-31112
(Arklow, Dublin)

Placek, Mariusz (OCarm)
Carmelite Friary, Kinsale,
Co Cork
Tel 021-772138

Planell, Francis
Harvieston,
Cunningham Road, Dalkey,
Co Dublin
Tel 01-2859877
(Opus Dei)

Plower, Thomas (MSC), Very
Rev, PP
Sacred Heart Parish,
Killinarden, Tallaght,
Dublin 24
Tel 01-4522251
(Killinarden, Dublin)

Plunkett, Oliver, Very Rev, PP
Donaghmore, Co Limerick
Tel 061-313898/087-6593176
(Donaghmore/Knockea,
Limerick)

Poland, James, Very Rev
Rostrevor, Co Down
(Dromore, retired)

Polke, Desmond, CC
Parochial House, Castlefin,
Lifford, Co Donegal
Tel 074-9146251
(Doneyloop, Derry)

Poole, John (OMI)
Oblate House of Retreat,
Inchicore, Dublin 8
Tel 01-4534408/4541805

Porter, Michael, CC
Parochial House, Burt,
Lifford, Co Donegal
Tel 074-9368155
(Fahan, Derry)

Powell, Eric (SDS), CC
St Kevin's Presbytery,
Pearse Street, Sallynoggin,
Co Dublin
Tel 01-2854667
(Sallynoggin, Dublin)

Powell, Gerald, Very Rev, PP
4 Holymount Road, Gilford,
Craigavon,
Co Armagh BT63 6AT
Tel 028-40624236
(Tullylish, Dromore)

Powell, Oliver
Gort Ard University
Residence,
Rockbarton North, Galway
Tel 091-523846
(Opus Dei)

Power, Brian, Very Rev, PP
Dunmore East,
Co Waterford
Tel 051-383127
(Killea (Dunmore East),
Waterford & L.)

Power, Gregory, Very Rev, PE
St Mary's, Clonmel,
Co Tipperary
Tel 052-6182690
(Waterford & L., retired)

Power, Joe, Very Rev, PP
Kilrush, Bunclody,
Co Wexford
Tel 053-9377262
(Ferns)

Power, John (OSA)
St Augustine's Priory,
New Ross, Co Wexford
Tel 051-421237
(Ferns)

Power, Liam, STL
Carlow College,
College Street, Carlow
Tel 059-9153200
(Kildare & L.)

Power, Liam, Very Rev, Adm
St John's Presbytery,
New Street, Waterford
Tel 051-874271
Communications Office,
St John's Pastoral Centre,
John's Hill, Waterford
Tel 051-874199
(St John's, Waterford & L.)

Power, Nicholas, Very Rev
Canon
Moorfield, Rathaspeck,
Co Wexford
(Ferns, retired)

Power, Nicholas, Very Rev
Canon, AP
Parochial House,
SS Peter and Paul's,
Clonmel, Co Tipperary
Tel 052-6121932
(Clonmel, SS Peter and
Paul's, Waterford & L.)

Power, Patrick (OFM), PP
St Anthony's Parish (English-
Speaking Chaplaincy),
23/25 Oudstrijderslaan,
1950 Kraainem, Belgium
Tel +32-2-7201970

Power, Robert, Very Rev, Adm
Ardfinnan, Clonmel,
Co Tipperary
Tel 052-7466216
(Ardfinnan, Waterford & L.)

Power, Seamus, Very Rev, PE
'Sheen Lodge', Ennis Road,
Limerick
Tel 061-454841
(Limerick, retired)

Power, Tony, CC
112 Ballygall Road East,
Glasnevin, Dublin 11
Tel 01-8342248
(Ballygall, Dublin)

Power, William (CSsR)
Mount Saint Alphonsus,
Limerick
Tel 061-315099

Prendergast, Edmund (MHM),
CC
Kilglass, Co Roscommon
Tel 071-9638162
(Kilglass, Elphin)

Prendergast, Patrick, Very
Rev, PP
Glenties, Co Donegal
Tel 074-9551117
(Glenties, Raphoe)

Prendiville, James, CC
The Presbytery, Hollywood
(via Naas), Co Wicklow
Tel 045-864206
(Ballymore Eustace, Dublin)

Prendiville, William (OSA)
St Augustine's Priory,
O'Connell Street,
Limerick
Tel 061-415374

Price, Cathal, Very Rev, CC
54 Foxfield St John, Dublin 5
Tel 01-8323683
(*Kilbarrack-Foxfield*, Dublin)

Prior, Dermot
Virginia, Co Cavan
Tel 049-8547015
(*Virginia*, Kilmore)

Prior, Paul
Director of Formation,
St Patrick's College,
Maynooth, Co Kildare
(Kilmore)

Prunty, Tony (SPS)
St Patrick's, Kiltegan,
Co Wicklow
Tel 059-6473600

Purcell, Denis, CC
Cuffesgrange, Co Kilkenny
Tel 056-7729299/
087-1356687
(*Danesfort*, Ossory)

Purcell, Eamon
112 Hilltop,
St Patrick's Road, Limerick
Tel 061-413734
(*St Patrick's*, Limerick)

Purcell, Edmond (CSSp)
Rockwell College, Cashel,
Co Tipperary
Tel 062-61444

Purcell, Francis, Very Rev
St John's Presbytery,
Kilkenny
Tel 056-7721072/
086-6010001
(*St John's*, Ossory)

Purcell, Gerard, Very Rev, PE
Fenor, Co Waterford
Tel 051-396971
(*Waterford & L.*, retired)

Purcell, James, CC
Rosegreen, Cashel,
Co Tipperary
Tel 062-61713
(*Cashel*, Cashel & E.)

Purcell, Richard (OCSO), Rt
Rev Dom
Abbot, Mount Saint Joseph
Abbey, Roscrea,
Co Tipperary
Tel 0505-25600

Purcell, William, CC
Callan, Co Kilkenny
Tel 056-7725858/
087-6286858
(*Callan*, Ossory)

Pyburn, Daniel, PP
The Presbytery, Dromore,
Bantry, Co Cork
(*Bantry*, Cork & R.)

Q

Queally, Peter (CSSp)
Rockwell College, Cashel,
Co Tipperary
Tel 062-61444

Queally, Peter, AP
Oiléan Cléire, Baltimore,
Co Cork
Tel 028-39103
(*Rath and the Islands*, Cork
& R.)

Quealy, Patrick, Very Rev
Canon, AP
Care Choice Dungarvan,
The Burgery,
Dungarvan, Co Waterford
Tel 058-40200
(Waterford & L., retired)

Quigley, Seán, PC
48 Aughrim Street, Dublin 7
Tel 01-8386176
(*Aughrim Street*, Dublin)

Quigley, Thomas, Very Rev, PP
Latton, Castleblayney,
Co Monaghan
Tel 042-9742212
(*Latton*, Clogher)

Quinlan, Brendan, Very Rev,
PP
41 Cremore Heights,
St Canice's Road, Ballygall,
Dublin 11
Tel 01-8573776
(*Ballygall*, Dublin)

Quinlan, John (SMA)
SMA House, Wilton, Cork
Tel 021-4541069/4541884

Quinlan, John
C/o Diocesan Office,
Killarney, Co Kerry
(Kerry)

Quinlan, Leo, Very Rev
42A Strand Street, Skerries,
Co Dublin
(Dublin, retired)

Quinlivan, Brendan
Feakle, Co Clare
Tel 061-92403
(*Feakle*, Killaloe)

Quinn, Brian, Very Rev, PP
Ballyraine, Letterkenny,
Co Donegal
Tel 074-9127600
(*Aughaninshin*, Raphoe)

Quinn, Denis, CC
The Presbytery,
Kimberley Road, Greystones,
Co Wicklow
Tel 01-2877025
(*Greystones*, Dublin)

Quinn, Denis, Very Rev, PP
Falcarragh, Co Donegal
Tel 074-9135196
(*Falcarragh*, Raphoe)

Quinn, Desmond (SSC)
Assistant Bursar,
St Columban's, Dalgan Park,
Navan, Co Meath
Tel 046-9021525

Quinn, Francis (OCD)
The Abbey, Loughrea,
Co Galway
Tel 091-841209

Quinn, Frank (IC)
1 Grace Park Gardens,
Drumcondra, Dublin 9
Tel 01-8378314/8368730

Quinn, James, CC
Taugheen, Claremorris,
Co Mayo
Tel 094-9362500
(*Crossboyne and Taugheen*,
Tuam)

Quinn, John (SDB)
Vice-Rector, Rinaldi House,
72 Sean McDermott Street,
Dublin 1
Tel 01-8363358

Quinn, John, Very Rev, PP
Gortletteragh,
Carrick-on-Shannon,
Co Leitrim
Tel 071-9631074
(*Gortletteragh*, Ardagh &
Cl.)

Quinn, John, Very Rev, PP
Mullagh, via Kells, Co Meath
Tel 046-42208
(*Mullagh*, Kilmore)

Quinn, Joseph, Rt Rev Mgr, PP
Knock, Co Mayo
Tel 094-9388100
(Tuam)

Quinn, Ken
General Hospital,
Co Wexford
Tel 053-9142233
(Ferns)

Quinn, Michael, Very Rev, PP
Carracastle,
Ballaghaderreen,
Co Mayo
Tel 094-9254301
(*Carracastle*, Achonry)

Quinn, Michael, Very Rev, PP
Crosserlough, Co Cavan
Tel 049-4336122
(*Crosserlough*, Kilmore)

Quinn, Richard (CSSp)
11 Silchester Court,
Glenageary,
Co Dublin
Tel 01-2806375

Quinn, Seamus, CC
Scotshouse, Clones,
Co Monaghan
Tel 047-56016
(*Killeevan*, Clogher)

Quinn, Sean, Very Rev, PE, AP
Parochial House,
Dillonstown, Dunleer,
Co Louth
Tel 041-6863570
(*Togher*, Armagh)

Quinn, Seán, Very Rev, PP
Parochial House,
Louth Village, Dundalk,
Co Louth
Tel 042-9374285
(*Louth*, Armagh)

Quinn, Stephen
St Peter's Square,
Belfast BT12 4BU
Tel 028-90327573
(*The Cathedral*, Down & C.)

Quinn, Tadhg, Very Rev, PP
St John the Apostle,
Knocknacarra, Galway
Tel 091-590059
(*St John the Apostle*,
Galway)

Quirke, Brendan (OSA)
St John's Priory,
Thomas Street,
Dublin 8
Tel 01-6770393

Quirke, Ciary (SJ)
Manresa House,
Dollymount, Dublin 3
Tel 01-8331352

Quirke, Denis, Very Rev
Nicholas Place, Bridge
Street, Milltown,
Co Kerry
(Kerry, retired)

Quirke, Derry, CC
Lisvernane, Aherlow,
Co Tipperary
Tel 062-56155
(*Galbally*, Cashel & E.)

R

Rabbitte, Peter, Very Rev, PP,
VF
Lisdoonvarna, Co Clare
Tel 065-7074142
(*Lisdoonvarna and
Kilshanny*, Galway)

Radley, William, Very Rev, PP
St Agatha's Parish Centre,
Headford, Killarney,
Co Kerry
Tel 064-6654008
(Kerry)

Rafferty, Colm (SSC)
126 Grove Road, Swatragh,
Co Derry BT46 5Q2
Tel 028-79401209

Rafferty, James (CM)
99 Cliftonville Road,
Belfast BT14 6JQ
Tel 028-90751771

Rafferty, Terence, Very Rev, PP
10 Barr Hill, Newry,
Co Down BT34 1SY
Tel 028-38821252
(Dromore)

Rafter, Roger (SAC)
Pallottine College, Thurles,
Co Tipperary
Tel 0504-21202

Raftery, Gregory
An Der Tiefenriede 11, 3000,
Hanover 1, Germany
(Galway)

Raftery, Peter, CC
Parochial House, St Eugene's Cathedral,
Derry BT48 9AP
Tel 028-71262894/71365712
(Derry)

Raftery, Peter J. (CSSp)
Rockwell College, Cashel,
Co Tipperary
Tel 062-61444

Raftery, Thomas (CSSp)
Templeogue College,
Dublin 6W
Tel 01-4903909

Raftice, Robert, Very Rev Canon
Mount Carmel, Callan,
Co Kilkenny
Tel 056-7725301/7725553/
086-0614682
(Ossory, retired)

Rainey, Sean (SSC)
St Columban's, Dalgan Park,
Navan, Co Meath
Tel 046-9021525

Raj, Casimir (SDB)
Salesian College,
Maynooth Road, Celbridge,
Co Kildare
Tel 01-6275058/60

Raleigh, Patrick (SSC)
Regional Vice-Director,
St Columban's, Dalgan Park,
Navan, Co Meath
Tel 046-9021525

Ramsbottom, Pat, Very Rev, PE
Gorman's Cottage,
Cooleragh, Co Kildare
Tel 045-890744
(Kildare & L., retired)

Randles, James A., Very Rev Canon, PE
5 St Margaret's Road,
Malahide, Co Dublin
(Dublin, retired)

Raymond, Bernard J. (SMA)
African Missions,
Blackrock Road, Cork
Tel 021-4292871

Reaume, Michael (SM)
St Columba's,
Church Avenue, Ballybrack,
Co Dublin
Tel 01-2858301

Reburn, Frank, CC
11 Millview Court,
Malahide, Co Dublin
Tel 01-8451902
(Yellow Walls, Dublin)

Reddan, Michael (SVD)
5 Woodlands Park, Birr,
Co Offaly
Tel 057-9121757/
087-7599789
(Birr, Killaloe)

Reddan, Michael (SVD)
Donamon Castle,
Roscommon
Tel 090-6662222

Redmond, John (SJ)
Milltown Park,
Sandford Road, Dublin 6
Tel 01-2698411/2698113

Redmond, Noel (CSSp)
Templeogue College,
Dublin 6W
Tel 01-4903909

Redmond, Richard, CC
(Ballyduff) The Square,
Ferns, Enniscorthy,
Co Wexford
Tel 053-9366162
(Ferns, Ferns)

Redmond, Stephen (SJ)
John Austin House,
135 North Circular Road,
Dublin 7
Tel 01-8386768

Reedy, Patrick (CSSp)
Templeogue College,
Dublin 6W
Tel 01-4903909

Regan, Christopher (OFM)
Franciscan Friary,
Liberty Street, Cork
Tel 021-4270302

Regan, Henry
Presbytery No 1,
Church Grounds,
Kill Avenue, Dun Laoghaire,
Co Dublin
Tel 01-2800901
(Dublin, retired)

Regan, James (SPS)
On temporary diocesan work

Regan, Michael
Chaplain,
Mercy University Hospital,
Cork
Tel 021-4271971
(Cork & R.)

Reid, Alexander (CSsR)
Liguori House,
75 Orwell Road, Dublin 6
Tel 01-4067100

Reidy, Denis, Very Rev Mgr, PP
Carrigtwohill, Co Cork
Tel 021-4883236
(Carrigtwohill, Cloyne)

Reid, Desmond (CSSp)
Templeogue College,
Templeville Road,
Dublin 6W
Tel 01-4903909

Reidy, Raymond (SPS), CC
Church of the Resurrection,
Fethard Road, Clonmel,
Co Tipperary
Tel 052-6123239
(Clonmel, SS Peter & Paul,
Waterford & L.)

Reihill, Seamus (SPS)
St Patrick's, Kiltegan,
Co Wicklow
Tel 059-6473600

Reilly, Anthony, Very Rev, PP
Parochial House,
Palmerstown, Dublin 20
Tel 01-6266254
(Palmerstown, Dublin)

Reilly, Cyril, Very Rev
18 Whitehall Avenue,
Ballycastle,
Co Antrim BT54 6WA
(Down & C., retired)

Reilly, Eamon (OMI)
Oblate House of Retreat,
Inchicore, Dublin 8
Tel 01-4534408/4541805

Reilly, John, Very Rev, PP
Lahardane, Ballina, Co Mayo
Tel 096-51007
(Lahardane, Killala)

Reilly, Martin (SPS)
St Patrick's, Kiltegan,
Co Wicklow
Tel 059-6473600

Reilly, Matthew (SSC)
St Columban's, Dalgan Park,
Navan, Co Meath
Tel 046-9021525

Reilly, Michael, CC
Crossmolina, Ballina,
Co Mayo
Tel 096-31344
(Crossmolina, Killala)

Reilly, Michael, Very Rev, PP
Castlegar, Galway
Tel 091-751548
(Galway)

Reilly, Michael, Very Rev, PP
Lanesboro, Co Longford
Tel 043-3321166
(Lanesboro, Ardagh & Cl.)

Reilly, Michael, Very Rev, PP
Parochial House,
Bunninadden, Ballymote,
Co Sligo
Tel 071-9183232
(Bunninadden (Kilshalvey,
Kilturra and Cloonoghill),
Achonry)

Reilly, Patrick (OPraem), CC
Parochial House, Donabate,
Co Dublin
Tel 01-8436099
(Donabate, Dublin)

Reilly, Peter, Very Rev, PP
Parochial House, East Wall,
Dublin 3
Tel 01-8742320
(East Wall, Dublin)

Reilly, William
Casilla 09-01-5825,
Guayaquil, Ecuador
(Killala)

Reilly, William, Very Rev, PP
Clonbur, via Claremorris,
Co Galway
Tel 094-9546304
(Clonbur (Ross), Tuam)

Relihan, Patrick, CC
Youghal, Co Cork
Tel 024-92456
(Cloyne)

Revatto, Geoffrey (SSC)
St Columban's Retirement
Home, Dalgan Park, Navan,
Co Meath
Tel 046-9021525

Revatto, Thomas (SSC)
St Columban's Retirement
Home, Dalgan Park, Navan,
Co Meath
Tel 046-9021525

Reynolds, Brian (OP)
Newbridge College,
Droichead Nua, Co Kildare
Tel 045-487200

Reynolds, Gerard (CSsR)
Clonard Monastery,
1 Clonard Gardens,
Belfast BT13 2RL
Tel 028-90445950

Reynolds, Kenneth (OFMCap)
Holy Trinity,
Fr Mathew Quay, Cork
Tel 021-4270827

Reynolds, Kevin, (MHM), PC
Ahascragh, Ballinasloe,
Co Galway
Tel 090-9688617
(Ahascragh, Elphin)

Reynolds, Michael B. (CSSp)
Holy Ghost Missionary
College, Kimmage Manor,
Dublin 12
Tel 01-4064300

Reynolds, Patrick (CSsR)
The Presbytery,
103 Cherry Orchard Avenue,
Dublin 10
Tel 01-6267930
(Cherry Orchard, Dublin)

Reynolds, William (SJ), CC
Presbytery,
Upper Gardiner Street,
Dublin 1
Tel 01-8363411
(Gardiner Street, Dublin)

Rhatigan, Edward, Very Rev
Castletown, Portlaoise,
Co Laois
Tel 087-8732622
(Ossory, retired)

Rice, Gerard, Very Rev, PP
Parochial House, Kilcloon,
Co Meath
Tel 01-6286252
(*Kilcloon*, Meath)

Rice, Patrick, Very Rev Canon,
PE
Little Sisters of the Poor,
Holy Family Residence,
Roebuck Road, Dundrum,
Dublin 14
(Dublin, retired)

Rice, Seamus, Very Rev, PE, AP
Parochial House,
89 Derrynoose Road,
Derrynoose,
Co Armagh BT60 3EZ
Tel 028-37531222
(Armagh)

Rice, Tony (CSsR)
St Joseph's, Dundalk,
Co Louth
Tel 042-9334042/9334762

Rigney, Liam, Very Rev, PP
St Mary's, Maynooth,
Co Kildare
Tel 01-6286220
(*Maynooth*, Dublin)

Riordan, Michael, Very Rev,
PP
The Presbytery, Togher,
Cork
Tel 021-4316700
(*Togher*, Cork & R.)

Riordan, Patrick (SJ)
c/o Jesuit Provincial Curia,
IMI Centre, Sandyford Road,
Dublin 16
Tel 01-2932820

Riordan, Ray (OPraem)

Riordan, Thomas, Very Rev, PP
Kilbrittain, Co Cork
Tel 023-8849637
(*Kilbrittain*, Cork & R.)

Roban, Myles (SSC)
10 Belfield Springs,
Enniscorthy, Co Wexford
Tel 0539237770

Roberts, Donal, Very Rev, PP,
VF
Macroom, Co Cork
Tel 026-21068
(Macroom, Cloyne)

Robinson, Denis (CSSp)
Kimmage Mission Institute
at Milltown, Milltown Park,
Dublin 6
Tel 01-2776300

Robinson, Denis, CC
The Presbytery, Mourne
Road, Dublin 12
Tel 01-4556199
(*Mourne Road*, Dublin)

Robinson, John, Very Rev, PP
Borris-in-Ossory, Portlaoise,
Co Laois
Tel 0505-41148/087-2431412
(*Borris-in-Ossory*, Ossory)

Roche, Donal (OP)
St Mary's Priory, Tallaght,
Dublin 24
Tel 01-4048100

Roche, Donal, Very Rev, PP
Parochial House,
Foxdene Avenue, Lucan,
Co Dublin
Tel 01-4056858
(*Lucan South*, Dublin)

Roche, Joseph, Very Rev, PP
Parochial House, Kilchreest,
Loughrea, Co Galway
Tel 091-840859
(*Kilchreest/Castledaly*,
Galway)

Roche, Luke, Very Rev, PP
Castlemaine, Co Kerry
Tel 066-9767322
(Kerry)

Roche, Simon (OP)
St Mary's, Pope Quay, Cork
Tel 021-4502267

Rochford, Seamus, Very Rev,
PP
Emly, Co Tipperary
Tel 062-57103
(*Emly*, Cashel & E.)

Rocks, Ned (CSsR)
St Joseph's, Dundalk,
Co Louth
Tel 042-9334042/9334762

Rodgers, Denis (CSSp)
Holy Ghost Missionary
College, Kimmage Manor,
Dublin 12
Tel 01-4064300

Rodgers, J. J., CC
Borrisokane, Co Tipperary
Tel 067-27140
(*Borrisokane*, Killaloe)

Rodgers, Manus, Very Rev, AP
Silvermines, Nenagh,
Co Tipperary
Tel 067-25131
(*Silvermines*, Killaloe)

Rodgers, Michael (SPS)
Tearmann Spirituality
Centre, Brockagh,
Glendalough, Co Wicklow
Tel 0404-45208

Rogan, Edward, Very Rev
Inver, Barnatra, Ballina,
Co Mayo
Tel 097-84598
(*Kilcommon-Erris*, Killala)

Rogan, Sean, Very Rev Canon,
PP, VF
Parochial House,
54 St Patrick's Avenue,
Downpatrick, Co Down
BT30 6DN
Tel 028-44612443
(*Downpatrick*, Down & C.)

Rogers, Michael, Very Rev, PP
Parochial House,
25 Priestbush Road,
Whitecross,
Co Armagh BT60 2TP
Tel 028-37507214
(*Whitecross (Loughilly)*,
Armagh)

Rogers, Patrick (CP)
St Paul's Retreat,
Mount Argus, Dublin 6W
Tel 01-4992000

Rogers, Thomas, Very Rev, PP
Holy Family Presbytery,
Luke Wadding Street,
Waterford
Tel 051-37527
(*Holy Family*, Waterford &
L.)

Rohan, Joseph, CC
Rathcormac, Fermoy,
Co Cork
Tel 025-36858
(*Rathcormac*, Cloyne)

Ronayne, James, Very Rev, PP
Clifden, Co Galway
Tel 095-21251
(*Clifden (Omey and
Ballindoon)*, Tuam)

Rooney, Joe (SM)
Philippines

Rooney, Joseph
(in residence)
45 Ballyholme Esplanade,
Bangor, Co Down BT20 5NJ
Tel 028-91465425
(*Bangor*, Down & C.)

Rooney, Joseph, JCL
Office of the Armagh
Regional Marriage Tribunal,
511 Ormeau Road,
Belfast BT7 3GS
Tel 028-90491990
(Down & C.)

Rooney, Liam (SCJ)
Parochial House,
St John Vianney,
Ardlea Road, Dublin 5
Tel 01-8474173/8474123
(*Ardlea*, Dublin)

Rooney, Noel, Very Rev, PP
279 Sunset Drive,
Cartron Point, Sligo
Tel 071-9142422
Chaplain, Ballinode
Vocational School, Sligo
Tel 071-9147111
(Elphin)

Rosario, Ripon (SJ)
John Sullivan House
56/56A Mulvey Park,
Dundrum, Dublin 14
Tel 01-2983978

Rosbotham, Gabriel, CC
Cathedral Close, Ballina,
Co Mayo
Tel 096-71355
(*Ballina*, Killala)

Rosney, Arnold, CC
5 Drumgeely Avenue,
Shannon, Co Clare
Tel 061-471513/087-8598710
(*Shannon*, Killaloe)

Ross, Cyril (OP)
47 Leeson Park, Dublin 6
Tel 01-6602427

Ross, Jim (SM)
Fiji

Ross, Michael (SDB)
Rector, Salesian House,
45 St Teresa's Road,
Crumlin, Dublin 12
Tel 01-4555605

Rouleau, Maurice (SSS)
Blessed Sacrament Chapel,
20 Bachelors Walk, Dublin 1
Tel 01-8724597

Router, Michael
Castletara, Ballyhaise,
Co Cavan
Tel 049-4338146
(*Castletara*, Kilmore)

Rowan, Kevin, Adm
Parochial House, Ashford,
Co Wicklow
Tel 0404-40540
(*Ashford*, Dublin)

Ruane, Noel S. (SVD)
Donamon Castle,
Roscommon
Tel 090-6662222

Ruddy, Michael (SSCC), Very
Rev
Sacred Heart Presbytery,
St John's Drive, Clondalkin
Dublin 22
Tel 01-4570032

Rushe, Patrick, CC
Holy Redeemer Parochial
House, Ard Easmuinn,
Dundalk, Co Louth
Tel 042-9334259
(Armagh)

Russell, Thomas (OFM)
Franciscan Friary,
Rossnowlagh, Co Donegal
Tel 072-9851342

Russell, William, Adm
Enniscouch, Rathkeale,
Co Limerick
Tel 069-63490/087-2272825
(*Kilcornan*, Limerick)

Ruth, Carthage (OFMCap)
Holy Trinity,
Fr Mathew Quay, Cork
Tel 021-4270827

Ryan, Aidan, Very Rev, PP
Ballinahown, Athlone,
Co Westmeath
Tel 090-6430124
(Ardagh & Cl.)

Ryan, Aloysius (OCarm)
Carmelite Priory,
White Abbey, Co Kildare
Tel 045-521391

Ryan, Alphonsus (OFMCap)
Capuchin Friary,
Church Street, Dublin 7
Tel 01-8730599

Ryan, Anselm (OP)
St Saviour's, Bridge Street,
Waterford
Tel 051-875061

Ryan, Anthony, Very Rev, PP
Parochial House,
Church Grounds, Doon,
Co Limerick
Tel 061-380165
(Doon, Cashel & E.)

Ryan, Bill (OFMCap)
Chaplain, Bon Secours
Hospital
Capuchin Parochial Friary,
Clonshaugh Drive,
Priorswood, Dublin 17
Tel 01-8474469

Ryan, Conor, Very Rev Canon,
PP, VF
Castlefarm, Hospital,
Co Limerick
Tel 061-383108
(Hospital, Cashel & E.)

Ryan, Damian, PP
Lourdes House,
Childers Road, Limerick
Tel 061-301047/087-2274412
(Limerick)

Ryan, Daniel J.
c/o Archbishop's House,
Thurles, Co Tipperary
(Cashel & E.)

Ryan, Denis, Very Rev, PP, VF
Parochial House,
1 Rossmore Road,
Dublin 6W
Tel 01-4500785
(Willington, Dublin)

Ryan, Derek (CSsR)
Clonard Monastery,
1 Clonard Gardens,
Belfast, BT13 2RL
Tel 028-90445950

Ryan, Dermot
Mooncoin, Co Kilkenny
Tel 086-6097483
(Mooncoin, Ossory)

Ryan, Eugene (SSC)
St Columban's, Dalgan Park,
Navan, Co Meath
Tel 046-9021525

Ryan, Fergal, Very Rev, PP
Cahirdaniel, Co Kerry
Tel 066-9475111
(Cahirdaniel, Kerry)

Ryan, Gerard (CSSp)
Spiritan Missionary College,
Kimmage Manor, Dublin 12
Tel 01-4064300

Ryan, James (OFMCap)
Capuchin Friary,
Ard Mhuire, Creeslough,
Letterkenny, Co Donegal
Tel 074-9138005

Ryan, James, Rt Rev Mgr, AP
Bohermore, Cashel,
Co Tipperary
Tel 062-61353
(Cashel, Cashel & E.)

Ryan, James, Very Rev
(priest in residence)
Cleariestown, Co Wexford
Tel 053-9139110
(Ferns, retired)

Ryan, John J., Very Rev, AP
Garryspillane, Kilmallock,
Co Limerick
Tel 062-53189
(Knocklong, Cashel & E.)

Ryan, John, CC
Freemount, Charleville,
Co Cork
Tel 022-28788
(Milford, Cloyne)

Ryan, Joseph, CC (Cashel & E.)
11 Palmerstown Court,
Dublin 20
Tel 01-6268772
(Ballyfermot Upper, Dublin)

Ryan, Liam (OSA)
St Augustine's Priory,
O'Connell Street, Limerick
Tel 061-415374

Ryan, Liam, Very Rev Canon,
PP, VF
Moyglass, Fethard,
Co Tipperary
Tel 052-9156244
(Killenaule, Cashel & E.)

Ryan, Liam, Very Rev, DD
Cappamore, Co Tipperary
(Cashel & E., retired)

Ryan, Liam, Very Rev, PE
Mondaniel, Fermoy, Co Cork
(Cloyne, retired)

Ryan, Martin (CSsR)
Liguori House,
75 Orwell Road, Dublin 6
Tel 01-4067100

Ryan, Martin (OCarm)
Prior, Carmelite Priory,
Moate, Co Westmeath
Tel 090-6481160

Ryan, Michael (SSC)
112 The Sycamores,
Freshford Road, Kilkenny
Tel 086-8977569

Ryan, Michael (OCSO)
Bolton Abbey, Moone,
Co Kildare
Tel 059-8624102

Ryan, Michael J., Very Rev, PE
Clonmel Road, Cahir,
Co Tipperary
Tel 052-7443004
(Waterford & L., retired)

Ryan, Michael, Rt Rev Mgr,
PP, VG
Castlecomer, Co Kilkenny
Tel 056-4441262/
086-3693863
(Castlecomer, Ossory)

Ryan, Noel (SPS)
St Patrick's, Kiltegan,
Co Wicklow
Tel 059-6473600

Ryan, Patrick (CSSp), CC
The Presbytery, Kilcullen,
Co Kildare
Tel 045-481222
(Kilcullen, Dublin)

Ryan, Patrick (OCSO)
Mount Melleray Abbey,
Cappoquin, Co Waterford
Tel 058-54404

Ryan, Patrick J. (MHM)
St Joseph's House,
50 Orwell Park, Rathgar,
Dublin 6
Tel 01-4127700

Ryan, Patrick M. (CSSp)
Holy Ghost Missionary
College, Kimmage Manor,
Dublin 12
Tel 01-4064300

Ryan, Patrick, Very Rev, PP
The Presbytery, Eadestown,
Naas, Co Kildare
Tel 045-862187
(Eadestown, Dublin)

Ryan, Paul
c/o Killaloe Diocesan Office,
Westbourne, Ennis, Co Clare
(Killaloe)

Ryan, Seamus, Very Rev, PP
(Cashel & E.)
No 1 Presbytery,
Blackditch Road, Dublin 10
Tel 01-6265695
(Ballyfermot Upper, Dublin)

Ryan, Sean (SMA), CC
St Peter's Presbytery,
10 Fair Street, Drogheda,
Co Louth
Tel 041-9838239
(Drogheda, Armagh)

Ryan, Thomas J., Very Rev,
Canon PP, VF
Liscreagh, Co Limerick
Tel 061-386227
(Murroe and Boher, Cashel
& E.)

Ryan, Thomas, Very Rev, CC
Gleneden,
North Circular Road,
Limerick
Tel 061-329448
(Our Lady of the Rosary,
Limerick)

Ryan, Thomas, Very Rev, PP
5 Derravaragh Road,
Caherdavin Park, Limerick
Tel 061-452790
(Christ the King, Limerick)

Ryan, Tom, Very Rev, PP
4 Dun na Rí, Shannon,
Co Clare
Tel 061-364133/087-2349816
(Shannon, Killaloe)

Ryan, William, Very Rev, PP
Parochial House,
Dungarvan, Co Waterford
Tel 058-42374
(Dungarvan, Waterford & L.)

Ryder, Andrew (SCI)
Sacred Heart Fathers,
Fairfield, 66 Inchicore Road,
Dublin 8
Tel 01-4538655

Ryder, John, PEm
16 Whitehouse Park,
Duncrana Road, Derry
(Derry, retired)

Ryle, Sean (SSC)
St Columban's Retirement
Home, Dalgan Park, Navan,
Co Meath
Tel 046-9021525

Rynn, Olan
c/o Diocesan Office,
The Cathedral, Galway
Tel 091-563566
(Galway)

S

Sammon, Frank (SJ), CC
156 Rathgar Road, Dublin 6
Tel 01-4966042
35 Lower Leeson Street,
Dublin 2
Tel 01-6761248
(Rathgar, Dublin)

Sandham, Denis (MI)
(Chaplain to Beaumont
Hospital)
Superior, St Camillus, South
Hill Avenue, Blackrock,
Co Dublin
Tel 01-2882873

Scallon, Kevin (CM)
All Hallows Institute for
Mission and Ministry,
Drumcondra, Dublin 9
Tel 01-8373745/6

Scallon, Paschal (CM), Very
Rev, PP
Superior, St Peter's,
Phibsboro, Dublin 7
Tel 01-8389708
(Phibsboro, Dublin)

Scanlan, Charles
Ballinwillin, Lismore,
Co Waterford
Tel 058-54282
(Waterford & L.)

Scanlan, Liam V. (SPS)
St Patrick's, Kiltegan,
Co Wicklow
Tel 059-6473600

Scanlan, Patrick, Very Rev, PP
Castletownroche, Co Cork
Tel 022-26188
(Castletownroche, Cloyne)

Scanlon, Columba (OFM)
Adam & Eve's,
4 Merchant's Quay, Dublin 8
Tel 01-6771128

Scanlon, Michael, Very Rev, PP
Cloghan, Birr, Co Offaly
Tel 090-6457122
(Cloghan and Banagher,
Ardagh & Cl.)

Scanlon, Thomas (CP)
Passionist Community,
108 Salisbury Avenue,
Belfast BT15 5ED
Tel 028-90288306

Scott, Patrick (CSsR)
Marianella, 75 Orwell Road,
Dublin 6
Tel 01-4067100

Scott, Philip (OCSO)
Our Lady of Bethlehem
Abbey, 11 Ballymena Road,
Portglenone, Ballymena,
Co Antrim BT44 8BL
Tel 028-25821211

Screene, Michael (MSC)
Leader, 'Croí Nua',
Rosary Lane, Taylor's Hill,
Galway
Tel 091-520960

Scriven, Richard
St John's Presbytery,
Dublin Road, Kilkenny
Tel 056-7756889/
087-2420033
(Ossory)

Scully, Brendan (OFM)
Vicar, Franciscan Friary,
Liberty Street, Cork
Tel 021-4270302

Scully, Michael (SSC)
St Columban's Retirement
Home, Dalgan Park,
Navan, Co Meath
Tel 046-9021525

Scully, Patrick (SSC)
St Columban's Retirement
Home, Dalgan Park, Navan,
Co Meath
Tel 046-9021525

Scully, Thomas (OMI)
Oblate House of Retreat,
Inchicore, Dublin 8
Tel 01-4534408/4541805

Scully, Tony, CC
89 Ballybough Road,
Dublin 3
Tel 01-8363451
(North William Street,
Dublin)

Seaver, Patrick, CC
4 Glenview Terrace,
Farranshone, Limerick
Tel 061-328838
(St Munchin's and St Lelia's,
Limerick)

Seery, Michael, Very Rev, PP
Parochial House,
115 Omagh Road,
Ballygawley,
Co Tyrone BT70 2AG
Tel 028-85568208
(Ballygawley (Errigal
Kieran), Armagh)

Serrage, Michael (MSC)
Leader & Director, Grace
Dieu Retreat House,
Tramore Road, Waterford
Tel 051-374417/373372

Sexton, Frank (OSA)
St Augustine's Priory,
O'Connell Street,
Limerick
Tel 061-415374

Sexton, John
Chaplain, St Clare's
Comprehensive School,
Manorhamilton
Tel 071-9855060
(Kilmore)

Sexton, P. J.
Mater Dei Institute
(Kilmore)

Sexton, Pat, Very Rev, PP
Scariff, Co Clare
Tel 061-921013/087-2477814
(Scariff and Moynoe,
Killaloe)

Sexton, Peter (SJ)
House 27, Trinity College,
Dublin 2
Tel 01-8961260
(Dublin)

Sexton, Sean, Very Rev, PP,
BA, DipYLO
Ennis Youth Centre,
Carmody Street, Ennis,
Co Clare
Tel 065-6824137/6829507/
087-2621884
(Killaloe)

Seymour, Tom, Very Rev, AP
Church Road, Nenagh,
Co Tipperary
Tel 067-31381
(Nenagh, Killaloe)

Shanahan, John (MSC)
Western Road, Cork
Tel 021-4804120

Shanahan, John, Very Rev, PP
Valentia Island, Co Kerry
Tel 066-9476104
(Valentia, Kerry)

Shanahan, Tom (OCD)
The Abbey, Loughrea,
Co Galway
Tel 091-841209

Shanka, Matthew (SAC)
Pallottine College, Thurles,
Co Tipperary
Tel 0504-21202

Shanley, Ciaran (CSSp)
Holy Ghost Missionary
College, Kimmage Manor,
Dublin 12
Tel 01-4064300

Shannon, Declan, CC
St Mary's, Athlone,
Co Westmeath
Tel 090-6472088
(Athlone, Ardagh & Cl.)

Shannon, Richard, CC
42A Strand Street, Skerries,
Co Dublin
Tel 01-8494033
(Skerries, Dublin)

Sharkey, Liam
Ballyweelin, Rosses Point,
Co Sligo
(Elphin, retired)

Sharkey, Lorcan, Very Rev, PP
Cloghan, Co Donegal
Tel 074-9133007
(Cloghan, Raphoe)

Shaughnessy, Bernard, CC
Coolarne, Turloughmore,
Co Galway
Tel 091-797626
(Lackagh, Tuam)

Sheary, Patrick (SJ)
c/o Jesuit Provincial Curia,
IMI Centre, Sandyford Road,
Dublin 16
Tel 01-2932820

Sheedy, Cyril (CSSp)
St Michael's College,
Ailesbury Road, Dublin 4
Tel 01-2189423

Sheedy, Michael, Very Rev, PP
Toler Street, Kilrush,
Co Clare
Tel 065-9051093
(Kilrush, Killaloe)

Sheehan, Anthony, CC
Doneraile, Co Cork
Tel 022-24120
(Doneraile, Cloyne)

Sheehan, Joseph (CSSp)
Holy Ghost Missionary
College, Kimmage Manor,
Dublin 12
Tel 01-4064300

Sheehan, Martin, Very Rev,
Adm
St Joseph's, Lauragh,
Killarney, Co Kerry
Tel 064-83107
(Tuosist, Kerry)

Sheehan, Michael, CC
St Patrick's Presbytery,
Roden Place, Dundalk,
Co Louth
Tel 042-9334648
(Dundalk, St Patrick's,
Armagh)

Sheehan, Michael, Very Rev,
Adm
St Patrick's Presbytery,
199 Donegall Street,
Belfast BT1 2FL
Tel 028-90324597
(St Patrick's, Down & C.)

Sheehan, Niall, CC
Cathedral Presbytery,
38 Hill Street, Newry,
Co Down BT34 1AT
Tel 028-30262586
(Dromore)

Sheehan, Patrick (MSC)
Woodview House,
Mount Merrion Avenue,
Blackrock, Co Dublin
Tel 01-2881644

Sheehan, Patrick, Very Rev
Canon
'Shalom', Rossbeigh,
glenbeigh, Co Kerry
(Kerry, retired)

Sheehan, Patrick, Very Rev, PP
The Presbytery,
Bell Steel Road, Poleglass,
Belfast BT17 0PB
Tel 028-90625739
(The Nativity, Down & C.)

Sheehan, Rory, Very Rev, PP
Parochial House,
111 Causeway Street,
Portrush,
Co Antrim BT56 8JE
Tel 028-70823388
(Portrush, Down & C.)

Sheehan, Ted
Springhill, Glanmire,
Co Cork
Tel 021-4866306
(Glanmire, Cork & R.)

Sheehy, Richard, Very Rev, PP,
VF
54 Lower Rathmines Road,
Dublin 6
Tel 01-4969049
(Rathmines, Dublin)

Sheehy, Sean
Assistant Priest,
Castlegregory, Co Kerry
Tel 066-7139145
(Castlegregory, Kerry)

Sheeran, James, CC
16 Brookwood Grove,
Artane, Dublin 5
Tel 01-8187908
(Artane, Dublin)

Sheerin, Michael, Very Rev, PP
Parochial House,
Lobinstown, Navan,
Co Meath
Tel 046-9053155
(Lobinstown, Meath)

Sheil, Michael (SJ)
Minister, Clongowes Wood
College, Naas, Co Kildare
Tel 045-868663/868202

Sheils, Paud (CSsR)
Liguori House,
75 Orwell Road, Dublin 6
Tel 01-4067100

Shelley, Padraig, CC
The Presbytery, Carlow
Tel 059-9131227
(*Cathedral, Carlow*, Kildare & L.)

Shen-yi Hssii, Matthew (SJ)
John Sullivan House,
56/56A Mulvey Park,
Dundrum, Dublin 14
Tel 01-2983978

Sheppard, Jim, Very Rev
189 Carrigenagh Road,
Ballymartin, Kilkeel,
Co Down BT34 4GA
(Down & C., retired)

Sheridan, Christopher PC
Chaplain, Rotunda Hospital,
Parnell Street, Dublin 1
Tel 01-8745441
(Dublin)

Sheridan, Daniel, Very Rev, PP
Staghall, Belturbet,
Co Cavan
Tel 049-9522140
(*Drumlane*, Kilmore)

Sheridan, Eamon (SSC)
St Columban's,
Grange Road,
Donaghmede, Dublin 13
Tel 01-8476647

Sheridan, James (CP)
St Paul's Retreat,
Mount Argus, Dublin 6W
Tel 01-4992000

Sheridan, John Paul, CC
Blackwater, Enniscorthy,
Co Wexford
Tel 053-9129288
(Ferns)

Sheridan, Paddy, CC
Robeen, Hollymount,
Co Mayo
Tel 094-9540026
(*Robeen*, Tuam)

Sheridan, Patrick (CP)
St Paul's Retreat,
Mount Argus, Dublin 6W
Tel 01-4992000

Sheridan, Patrick (OMI)
Robeen, Hollymount,
Co Mayo
Tel 094-9540026

Sherlock, Vincent, Very Rev
Kilmovee, Ballaghadereen,
Co Roscommon
Tel 094-9649137
(Achonry)

Sherry, Brendan, CC
Ballinagare, Castlerea,
Co Roscommon
Tel 094-9870410
(*Frenchpark*, Elphin)

Sherry, Richard, Rt Rev Mgr, DD, PE
No 2 Presbytery,
Stillorgan Road,
Donnybrook, Dublin 4
Tel 01-2692102
(Dublin, retired)

Shevlin, James, Very Rev, PE, AP
Parochial House, Omeath,
Co Louth
Tel 042-9375198
(*Carlingford and Clogherny*, Armagh)

Shibanada, Julius
Church of the Sacred Heart,
Donnybrook, Dublin 4
(*Donnybrook,* Dublin)

Shiel, Patrick, Very Rev, PP
1 The Glebe,
Peamount Road, Newcastle,
Co Dublin
Tel 01-4589230
(*Newcastle*, Dublin)

Shields, Michael, Adm
Parochial House,
Francis Street, Dublin 8
Tel 01-4542109
(*Francis Street,* Dublin)

Shiels, Joseph (SSC)
St Columban's Retirement
Home, Dalgan Park, Navan,
Co Meath
Tel 046-9021525

Shiels, Michael, CC
C/o The Sacristy,
St Vincent De Paul,
Griffith Avenue, Dublin 9
Tel 01-8339756
(*Marino*, Dublin)

Shine, John, Rt Rev Mgr, AP
Priest's Road, Tramore,
Co Waterford
Tel 051-381531
(*Tramore*, Waterford & L.)

Shine, Larry, (CSSp), CC
Ballyleague, Lanesboro,
Co Longford
Tel 043-21171
(*Ballagh*, Elphin)

Shire, Joseph, Very Rev, PP
Ballyagran, Kilmallock,
Co Limerick
Tel 063-82028/087-6924563
(Limerick)

Shortall, Bryan (OFMCap)
Chaplain, Beaumont
Hospital
Capuchin Parochial Friary,
Clonshaugh Drive,
Priorswood, Dublin 17
Tel 01-8474469/8474538
(*Priorswood*, Dublin)

Shortall, Michael
(in residence)
Nativity of BVM, Saggart,
Co Dublin
Tel 087-2861765
(*Saggart*, Dublin)

Shorten, Kieran, Very Rev
(OFMCap), PP
Ascension Presbytery,
Gurranabraher, Cork
Tel 021-4303655
(*Gurranabraher*, Cork & R.)

Sikora, Krzysztof (SVD)
Donamon Castle,
Roscommon
Tel 090-6662222
Polish Chaplain,
Knock Shrine, Co Mayo
Tel 094-9388100
(Tuam)

Silke, John J., Very Rev Dean, PhD
'Stella Maris', Portnablagh,
Co Donegal
Tel 074-9136122
(Raphoe, retired)

Silke, Leo (SMA)
SMA House, Wilton, Cork
Tel 021-4541069/4541884

Simpson, Michael, CC
264 Howth Road, Killester,
Dublin 5
Tel 01-8339177
(*Killester*, Dublin)

Simson, Pierre (White Fathers)
Cypress Grove, Templeogue,
Dublin 6W
Tel 01-4055263/4055264

Sinnott, John, Very Rev, PP
Ballindaggin, Enniscorthy,
Co Wexford
Tel 053-9388559
(*Ballindaggin*, Ferns)

Sinnott, John, Very Rev, PP
Parochial House, Enniskerry,
Co Wicklow
Tel 01-2863506
(*Enniskerry*, Dublin)

Sinnott, Patrick, CC
St Aidan's, Enniscorthy,
Co Wexford
Tel 053-9235777
(*Enniscorthy, Cathedral of St Aidan*, Ferns)

Sinnott, Peter J., CC
No 3 Presbytery,
Castle Street, Dalkey,
Co Dublin
Tel 01-2859212
(*Dalkey*, Dublin)

Sinnott, Thomas (MHM)

Sinnott, Tom
Tel 057-8672222
(Kildare & L.)

Sisti, Louis (SAC)
Provincial House,
'Homestead',
Sandyford Road, Dundrum,
Dublin 16
Tel 01-2956180/2954170

Siwek, Rafal, CC
The Presbytery, Cavan
Tel 049-4331404/4332269
(*Cavan*, Kilmore)

Skelly, Oliver, Very Rev, PP
Parochial House, Coole,
Co Westmeath
Tel 044-9661191
(*Coole*, Meath)

Slater, Albert, CC
Keenagh, Ballina, Co Mayo
Tel 096-53018
(*Crossmolina*, Killala)

Slater, David (OSA)
St Augustine's Priory,
Dungarvan,
Co Waterford
Tel 058-41136

Slater, John (MHM)
St Joseph's House, 50 Orwell
Park, Rathgar, Dublin 6
Tel 01-4127700

Slattery, Gerard
c/o Diocesan Office,
Social Service Centre,
Henry Street, Limerick
(Limerick)

Slattery, John, Very Rev, PP
Puckane, Nenagh,
Co Tipperary
Tel 067-24105/087-2466078
(*Puckane*, Killaloe)

Slattery, Martin, Very Rev, AP
18 John's Hill, Waterford
Tel 051-311561
(*Trinity Within and St Patrick's*, Waterford & L.)

Slattery, Sean, Very Rev, PP
Ballymacward, Ballinasloe,
Co Galway
Tel 090-9687614
(*Ballymacward and Gurteen*, Clonfert)

Sleeman, Simon (OSB)
Glenstal Abbey, Murroe,
Co Limerick
Tel 061-386103

Slevin, Osmund (CP)
St Paul's Retreat,
Mount Argus, Dublin 6W
Tel 01-4992000

Slevin, Paschal (OFM)
Franciscan House of Studies,
Dún Mhuire, Seafield Road,
Killiney, Co Dublin
Tel 01-2826760

Slevin, Peter (CM), Very Rev
President/Superior,
St Vincent's College,
Castleknock, Dublin 15
Tel 01-8213051

Slowey, Henry (CM)
St Vincent's College,
Castleknock, Dublin 15
Tel 01-8213051

Smith, Adrian (SM), Most Rev
Archbishop
Honiara, Solomon Islands

Smith, David (MSC)
Leader, Woodview House,
Mount Merrion Avenue,
Blackrock, Co Dublin
Tel 01-2881644

Allianz (ill)

Smith, Declan, Very Rev, PP
Parochial House, Taghmon,
Mullingar, Co Westmeath
Tel 044-9372140
(*Taghmon*, Meath)

Smith, Desmond (SMA)
African Missions,
Blackrock Road, Cork
Tel 021-4292871

Smith, Kevin (OPraem), Very
Rev
Abbey of the Most Holy
Trinity and St Norbert,
Kilnacrott, Ballyjamesduff,
Co Cavan
Tel 049-8544416

Smith, Martin (SPS)
St Patrick's, Kiltegan,
Co Wicklow
Tel 059-6473600

Smith, Michael, Most Rev,
DCL, DD
Bishop of Meath,
Bishop's House,
Dublin Road, Mullingar,
Co Westmeath
Tel 044-9348841
(Meath)

Smith, Philip, Very Rev, PP
Parochial House, Ballymore,
Mullingar, Co Westmeath
Tel 044-9356212
(*Ballymore*, Meath)

Smith, Sean, CC
The Presbytery,
Newtownmountkennedy,
Co Wicklow
Tel 01-2819253
(*Kilquade*, Dublin)

Smith, Tom (SPS)
St Patrick's, Kiltegan,
Co Wicklow
Tel 059-6473600

Smyth, Brendan, CC
Parochial House,
Glenavy Road, Crumlin,
Co Antrim BT29 4LA
Tel 028-94422278
(*Glenavy and Killead*, Down
& C.)

Smyth, Derek, CC
2 Kill Lane, Foxrock,
Dublin 18
Tel 01-2894734
(*Foxrock*, Dublin)

Smyth, James (SJ)
St Francis Xavier's,
Upper Gardiner Street,
Dublin 1
Tel 01-8363411

Smyth, Malachy (SSC)
Communications
Coordinator, St Columban's,
Dalgan Park, Navan,
Co Meath
Tel 046-9021525

Smyth, Michael (MSC)
'Croí Nua', Rosary Lane,
Taylor's Hill, Galway
Tel 091-520960

Smyth, Michael P. (CSSp)
Holy Ghost Missionary
College, Kimmage Manor,
Dublin 12
Tel 01-4064300

Smyth, Patrick (OCarm)
Carmelite Priory,
White Abbey, Co Kildare
Tel 045-521391

Smyth, Patrick J. (SSC)
St Columban's, Dalgan Park,
Navan, Co Meath
Tel 046-9021525

Smyth, Ted (SPS)
On temporary diocesan
work

Smyth, Terry (OPraem)
Abbey of the Most Holy
Trinity and St Norbert,
Kilnacrott,
Ballyjamesduff, Co Cavan
Tel 049-8544416

Somers, James (SDB), CC
The Presbytery, Chapelizod,
Dublin 20
Tel 01-6264656
(*Chapelizod*, Dublin)

Somers, P. J. (SDB)
Curragh Camp, Co Kildare
Tel 045-441277
(*Curragh Camp*, Kildare &
L.)

Sorahan, Jim, CC
Ballinamuck, Co Longford
Tel 043-3324110
(*Drumlish*, Ardagh & Cl.)

Spelman, Andrew (CM)
St Peter's, Phibsboro,
Dublin 7
Tel 01-8389708

Spelman, Joseph, Rt Rev Mgr
(*Priest in residence*)
Collooney, Co Sligo
Tel 071-9167109
(Achonry, retired)

Spence, Michael, Very Rev
St Malachy's College,
36 Antrim Road,
Belfast BT15 2AE
Tel 028-90748285
(Down & C.)

Spillane, Joseph (SPS), CC
Ballydehob, Co Cork
Tel 028-3711
(*Schull*, Cork & R.)

Spillane, Martin (SPS)
On temporary diocesan
work

Spillane, Martin
Chaplain, Tralee General
Hospital, Co Kerry
Tel 066-7126222
(Kerry)

Spring, Finbar (OSA)
St Augustine's Priory,
Dungarvan,
Co Waterford
Tel 058-41136

Spring, Noel, Very Rev, PP
The Presbytery, Firies,
Co Kerry
Tel 066-9764122
(Kerry)

St John, Paul (SVD), Very Rev,
Adm
The Presbytery, City Quay,
Dublin 2
Tel 01-6673073
(*City Quay*, Dublin)

Stack, Thomas, Very Rev Mgr,
PE
Apt 4, Maple Hall (adjoining
church), SS Columbanus and
Gall, Milltown, Dublin 6
Tel 01-2697613
(Dublin, retired)

Stafford, Patrick, Very Rev, PP
Glynn, Enniscorthy,
Co Wexford
Tel 053-9128115
(*Glynn*, Ferns)

Standún, Pádraic, CC
Tourmakeady, Claremorris,
Co Mayo
Tel 094-9544037
(*Partry (Ballyovey)*, Tuam)

Stankard, Edward, Rt Rev
Mgr, PP, VG
Cappatagle, Ballinasloe,
Co Galway
Tel 091-843017
(Clonfert)

Stanley, Cathal
(Leave of Absence)
Portumna
(Clonfert)

Stanley, Gerard, Very Rev, PP
Parochial House, Rathkenny,
Co Meath
Tel 046-9054138
(*Rathkenny*, Meath)

Stanley, James (CSsR)
Marianella, 75 Orwell Road,
Dublin 6
Tel 01-4067100

Stanley, Paddy (SM), CC
Holy Family Parish,
Parochial House,
Dundalk, Co Louth
Tel 042-9336301
(*Dundalk, Holy Family*,
Armagh)

Stapleton, Christy
c/o Diocesan Office,
Balinalee Road, Longford
(Ardagh & Cl.)

Stapleton, Jim (CSSp)
Holy Ghost Missionary
College, Kimmage Manor,
Dublin 12
Tel 01-4064300

Stapleton, John, Very Rev, PP
Killeigh, Co Offaly
Tel 057-9344161
(*Killeigh*, Kildare & L.)

Starken, Brian (CSSp)
Provincial Superior,
Spiritan Provincialate,
Temple Park, Richmond
Avenue South, Dublin 6
Tel 01-4975127/4977230

Starkey, Hugh, Very Rev
Canon
Parochial House,
26 Tyrella Road, Ballykinlar,
Downpatrick BT30 8DF
Tel 028-44851221
(*Dundrum and Tyrella*,
Down & C.)

Staunton, Brendan (SJ)
St Francis Xavier's,
Upper Gardiner Street,
Dublin 1
Tel 01-8363411

Staunton, Fachtna (MHM)
St Joseph's, Freshford
House, Kilkenny
Tel 056-7721482

Staunton, Patrick (OCarm)
Assistant Provincial,
Provincial Office and
Carmelite Community,
Gort Muire, Ballinteer,
Dublin 16
Tel 01-2984014

Staunton, Ray (SM)
France

Steblecki, Hilary (OFM), CC
The Abbey, St Francis Street,
Galway
Tel 091-562518
(*St Francis*, Galway)

Steed, Bernard (SSC)
St Columban's, Dalgan Park,
Navan, Co Meath
Tel 046-9021525

Steele, Joseph M. (CSSp)
Holy Ghost Missionary
College, Kimmage Manor,
Dublin 12
Tel 01-4064300

Steen, Brendan (CM)
St Paul's College, Raheny,
Dublin 5
Tel 01-8318113

Stenson, Alex, Rt Rev Mgr, PP
126 Furry Park Road,
Dublin 5
Tel 01-8333793
(*Killester*, Dublin)

Stevenson, Liam, Very Rev
Canon, PP, VF
6 Scarva Road, Banbridge,
Co Down BT32 3AR
Tel 028-40662136
(*Seapatrick (Banbridge)*,
Dromore)

Stevenson, Pat, Very Rev, PP
The Presbytery, Goleen, Co
Cork
Tel 028-35188
(*Goleen*, Cork & R.)

Stewart, Charles (OFMCap)
Capuchin Friary,
Ard Mhuire, Creeslough,
Letterkenny, Co Donegal
Tel 074-9138005

Stewart, John, Very Rev
27F Windsor Avenue,
Belfast BT9 6EE
(Down & C., retired)

Stokes, John, Very Rev
44 Carlton Court, Swords,
Co Dublin
(Dublin, retired)

Stokes, Tom (SM)
USA

Strain, Paul
Co-ordinator, St Joseph's
Centre for the Deaf,
321 Grosvenor Road,
Belfast BT12 4LP
Tel 028-40448211
(Down & C.)

Strain, Paul, Very Rev, PP
470 Falls Road,
Belfast BT12 6EN
Tel 028-90321511
(*St John's*, Down & C.)

Stritch, Denis, Very Rev, PP
Meelin, Newmarket,
Co Cork
Tel 029-68007
(*Rockchapel and Meelin*,
Cloyne)

Stuart, Gerard, Very Rev, PP
Parochial House, Ratoath,
Co Meath
Tel 01-8256207
(Meath)

Sugrue, Patrick, Very Rev, PP
Killeentierna, Killarney,
Co Kerry
Tel 066-9764141
(*Killeentierna*, Kerry)

Sullivan, Donal (IC)
Cottrell Lodge,
16A Ormond Road,
Drumcondra, Dublin 9
Tel 01-8572234

Sullivan, Kevin
Chaplain, Tralee Institute of
Technology, Tralee,
Co Kerry
Tel 066-7145639/7135236
(Kerry)

Sullivan, Patrick, CC
Glencar, Manorhamilton,
Co Leitrim
Tel 071-9855433
(*Manorhamilton*, Kilmore)

Sullivan, Paul (OCD)
St Teresa's,
Clarendon Street, Dublin 2
Tel 01-6718466/6718127

Supple, Michael D., Very Rev
Canon
Apartment 8,
Giltown Lodge, Kilcullen,
Co Kildare
(Dublin, retired)

Surlis, Paul
1684 Albermarle Drive,
Crofton, Maryland 21114,
USA
Tel 001-410-4511459
(Achonry, retired)

Surlis, Tómas
Pontificio Collegio Irlandese,
Via dei SS Quattro 1,
00184, Roma
(Achonry)

Susai, Jega (SVD)
Maynooth, Co Kildare
Tel 01-6286391/2

Swan, Colum, Very Rev, PE
32 Cherrygrove, Naas,
Co Kildare
Tel 045-856274
(Kildare & L., retired)

Swan, William
Pontifical Irish College,
Via de SS Quattro 1,
00184 Roma, Italy
(Ferns)

Sweeney, Dennis (IC)
Clonturk House,
Ormond Road, Drumcondra,
Dublin 9
Tel 01-8374840

Sweeney, Desmond, Very Rev,
PE
Ramelton, Co Donegal
Tel 074-9151085
(Raphoe, retired)

Sweeney, Donal (OFMCap)
Ard Mhuire, Creeslough,
Letterkenny, Co Donegal
Tel 074-9138005

Sweeney, Eugene, Very Rev,
Adm
Parochial House,
42 Abbey Street,
Armagh BT61 7DZ
Tel 028-37522802
(*Armagh*, Armagh)

Sweeney, Gerard (SMA)
Temporary diocesan work in
Ireland

Sweeney, Gerard, CC
The Presbytery,
10b Trench Road,
Waterside,
Derry 028-71348856
Tel 028-71348856
(*Waterside*, Derry)

Sweeney, Hugh, Very Rev, PP
Glenswilly, New Mills,
Letterkenny, Co Donegal
Tel 074-9137020
(*Glenswilly*, Raphoe)

Sweeney, James, CC
Ardaghey, Co Donegal
Tel 074-9736007
(Raphoe)

Sweeney, Michael, Very Rev,
PP, VF
Derrybeg, Letterkenny,
Co Donegal
Tel 074-9531310
(Raphoe)

Sweeney, Oliver, Very Rev, PP
Poulfur, Fethard-on-Sea,
New Ross, Co Wexford
Tel 051-397048
(Ferns)

Sweeney, Owen, Rt Rev Mgr
54 Seabury,
Sudney Parade Avenue,
Dublin 4
Tel 01-2698878
(Dublin, retired)

Sweeney, Patrick, (Team
member)
77 Colepark Drive, Dublin 10
Tel 01-6264639
(*Ballyfermot*, Dublin)

Sweetman, John, Very Rev, PP
The Riverchapel,
Courtown Harbour, Gorey,
Co Wexford
Tel 053-9425241
(*The Riverchapel, Courtown
Harbour*, Ferns)

Swinburne, Robbie (SDB), CC
Salesian House, Milford,
Castletroy, Limerick
Tel 061-330268
(*Our Lady Help of Christians*,
Limerick)

Swords, Liam, Very Rev
56 Sandford Road,
Ranelagh, Dublin 6
Tel 01-4972503
(Achonry)

Symonds, Paul
2/4 Broughshane Road,
Ballymena,
Co Antrim BT43 7DX
Tel 028-25641515
(Down & C.)

Szalwa, Marian (SCJ)
Parochial House,
St John Vianney,
Ardlea Road, Dublin 5
Tel 01-8474173/8474123
(*Ardlea*, Dublin)

T

Taaffe, Eugene, Very Rev, PP,
VF
Parochial House, Balbriggan,
Co Dublin
Tel 01-8412116
(*Balbriggan*, Dublin)

Taaffe, Pat, AP
3 Cottage Garden,
Station Road, Ennis,
Co Clare
Tel 065-6891983/
086-1731070
(*Ennis*, Killaloe)

Talbot, Denis, Very Rev
Canon, PP, VF
Galbally, Co Tipperary
Tel 062-37929
(Cashel & E.)

Talbot, Liam (SDS), Very Rev,
PP
St Kevin's Presbytery,
Pearse Street, Sallynoggin,
Co Dublin
Tel 01-2854667
(*Sallynoggin*, Dublin)

Talty, Robert (OP)
St Mary's, Pope Quay, Cork
Tel 021-4502267

Tanham, Gerard, Very Rev, PP
12 The Warren, Malahide,
Co Dublin
Tel 01-8457950/087-2311947
(Dublin)

Tapley, Paul (OFMCap)
Capuchin Friary,
Friary Street, Kilkenny
Tel 056-7721439

Tarpey, Richard, Very Rev
Canon, AP
Ennistymon, Co Clare
Tel 065-7071346
(*Ennistymon*, Galway)

Tarrant, Joseph, CC
Asdee, Co Kerry
Tel 068-41152
(*Ballylongford*, Kerry)

Taylor, Liam
St Patrick's, Ormonde Road,
Kilkenny
Tel 056-7764400/
086-8180954
(*St Patrick's*, Ossory)

Taylor, Paul, CC
The Presbytery, Main Street,
Celbridge, Co Kildare
Tel 01-6275874/086-3524530
(*Celbridge*, Dublin)

Teehan, Willie, Very Rev, PP
Templederry, Nenagh,
Co Tipperary
Tel 067-25140/087-2347927
Director, Nenagh Centre,
Loretto House,
Kenyon Street, Nenagh,
Co Tipperary
Tel 067-31272
(*Killanave and Templederry*,
Killaloe)

Terry, John, Very Rev Canon,
PE
Terriville, Ballylanders,
Cloyne, Co Cork
Tel 021-4646779
(Cloyne, retired)

Thankachan Njaliath, Paul, CC
Parochial House,
Foxdene Avenue, Lucan,
Co Dublin
Tel 01-6212560
(*Lucan South*, Dublin)

Thekkedathu Paul, Anil (SVD)
Maynooth, Co Kildare
Tel 01-6286391/2

Thettayil, Polachan (IC)
St Patrick's, Upton,
Innishannon, Co Cork
Tel 021-4776268/4776923

Thompson, Declan (SPS)
St Patrick's, 21 Leeson Park,
Dublin 6
Tel 01-4977897

Thompson, Peter (SMA)
Vice Superior and Bursar,
Dromantine College,
Dromantine, Newry,
Co Down BT34 1RH
Tel 028-30821224

Thorne, Bernard (OSM)
Servite Priory, Benburb,
Dungannon,
Co Tyrone BT71 7JZ
Tel 028-37548241

Thornton, Gerard (MSC), CC
Church of the Resurrection,
Headford Road, Galway
Tel 091-762883
(*Tirellan*, Galway)

Thornton, Paul CC
146 Seapark, Malahide,
Co Dublin
Tel 01-8454172
(*Yellow Walls*, Dublin)

Thornton, Richard J. (CSSp)
Blackrock College,
Blackrock, Co Dublin
Tel 01-2888681

Threadgold, Jeremiah
Sacred Heart Residence,
Sybil Hill Road,
Raheny, Dublin 5
(Dublin, retired)

Thynne, Eoin, HCF
McKee Barracks and St
Bricin's Hospital, Dublin 7
Tel 6778502
(Dublin)

Tiernan, Peter, Very Rev, PP
Carrickedmond, Colehill,
Co Longford
Tel 044-9357442
(*Carrickedmond and
Abbeyshrule*, Ardagh & Cl.)

Tierney, Celsus, CC
Holy Cross Abbey,
Holy Cross, Thurles,
Co Tipperary
Tel 0504-43118
(Cashel & E.)

Tierney, Mark (OSB)
Glenstal Abbey, Murroe,
Co Limerick
Tel 061-386103

Tierney, Martin
Ballycotton North,
Liscannor, Co Clare
Tel 087-2780496
(Dublin, retired)

Tierney, Philip (OSB)
Glenstal Abbey, Murroe,
Co Limerick
Tel 061-386103

Tighe, James, Very Rev, CC
Elphin, Co Roscommon
Tel 071-9635131
(*Elphin*, Elphin)

Tighe, Paul, Rt Rev Mgr
Secretary of the Pontifical
Council for Social
Communications,
Vatican City.
(Dublin)

Timmons, Declan (OFM)
Franciscan Friary, Killarney,
Co Kerry
Tel 064-6631334/6631066

Timoney, Gerald, Very Rev
Canon, PE
Irvinestown, Enniskillen,
Co Fermanagh BT94 1GD
Tel 028-68621329
(*Irvinestown*, Clogher)

Timoney, Martin, CC
Drumkeen, Ballybofey,
Co Donegal
Tel 074-9134005
Ard Adhamhnáin,
Letterkenny, Co Donegal
(*Raphoe*, Raphoe)

Timoney, Pearse
The Presbytery, Ballygarvan,
Co Cork
Tel 021-4888971
(*Ballinhassig*, Cork & R.)

Timoney, Senan (SJ)
Peter Faber House,
28 Brookvale Avenue,
Belfast BT14 6BW
Tel 028-90757615

Timothy, Malcolm (OFM)
Guardian, Franciscan
College, Gormanston,
Co Meath
Tel 01-8412203

Tinsley, Ambrose (OSB)
Glenstal Abbey, Murroe,
Co Limerick
Tel 061-386103

Toal, Donal (SMA), Very Rev,
PP
The Presbytery, Neilstown,
Clondalkin, Dublin 22
Tel 01-4573546
(*Neilstown*, Dublin)

Tobin, Edmond, Very Rev, PE
Munroe, Rehill, Ballylooby,
Cahir, Co Tipperary
Tel 052-7441975
(Waterford & L., retired)

Tobin, Laserian (OCSO)
Mount Saint Joseph Abbey,
Roscrea, Co Tipperary
Tel 0505-25600

Tobin, Martin, Very Rev, PP
Clogh, Castlecomer,
Co Kilkenny
Tel 056-4442135/
086-2401278
(*Clogh*, Ossory)

Tobin, Michael (OFMCap)
Capuchin Friary,
Friary Street, Kilkenny
Tel 056-7721439

Tobin, Philip (OFMCap)
Capuchin Friary,
Friary Street, Kilkenny
Tel 056-7721439

Tobin, Richard (CSsR)
St Joseph's, Dundalk,
Co Louth
Tel 042-9334042/9334762

Toland, Liam, CC
Parochial House,
189 Carnlough Road,
Broughshane,
Co Antrim BT43 7DX
Tel 028-25684211
(*Braid*, Down & C.)

Toman, Gary
The Chaplaincy,
28 Elmwood Avenue,
Belfast BT9 6AY
Tel 028-90669737
(Down & C.)

Toner, Michael
Parochial House,
114 Battlehill Road,
Richhill,
Co Armagh BT61 8QJ
Tel 028-38871661
(*Kilmore*, Armagh)

Toner, Terence, Very Rev, PP
Parochial House, Kilmessan,
Co Meath
Tel 046-9025172
(*Kilmessan*, Meath)

Toner, Thomas, Rt Rev Mgr
43b Glen Road,
Belfast BT11 8BB
Tel 028-90613949
(*St Teresa's*, Down & C.)

Toner, William (SJ)
Superior,
25 Croftwood Park,
Cherry Orchard, Dublin 10
Tel 01-6267413

Tonge, Ivan, Very Rev, PP
St Patrick's,
2 Cambridge Road, Dublin 4
Tel 01-6684192
(*Ringsend*, Dublin)

Tonna, Paul (SJ)
St Ignatius Community &
Church, 27 Raleigh Row,
Salthill, Galway
Tel 091-523707

Toohey, Seamus, CC
7 Avondale Court,
Blackrock, Co Dublin
Tel 01-2884043
(*Newtownpark*, Dublin)

Toomey, Michael
Priest's Road, Tramore, C
Waterford
Tel 051-386642
(*Tramore*, Waterford & L.)

Torbitt, Hugh
c/o Diocesan Office,
St Michael's, Longford
(Ardagh & Cl.)

Tormey, James, CC
130 Churchview Road,
Ballybrack, Co Dublin
Tel 01-2851919
(*Ballybrack-Killiney*, Dublin)

Towey, Thomas, Very Rev, PP
Ballisodare, Co Sligo
Tel 071-9167467
(Achonry)

Townsend, Mark, CC
Mountrath, Co Kildare
Tel 057-8732234
(Kildare & L.)

Tracey, Finbarr (SVD)
133 North Circular Road,
Dublin 7
Tel 01-8386743

Tracey, Liam (OSM)
Prior, Church of the Divine
Word, Marley Grange,
25-27 Hermitage Downs,
Rathfarnham, Dublin 16
Tel 01-4944295/4941064

Travers, Charles, Rt Rev Mgr,
CC
1 Convent Court,
Roscommon
Tel 090-6628917
(*Roscommon*, Elphin)

Travers, John (SMA)
Dromantine College,
Dromantine, Newry,
Co Down BT34 1RH
Tel 028-30821224

Treacy, Bernard (OP), Very
Rev
Superior, 47 Leeson Park,
Dublin 6
Tel 01-6602427

Treacy, John, CC
14 Heathervue Road,
Riverview, Knockboy,
Waterford
Tel 051-843207
(*SS Joseph and Benildus*,
Waterford & L.)

Treacy, Pat, CC
Roscrea, Co Tipperary
Tel 0505-21370/087-9798643
(*Roscrea*, Killaloe)

Treanor, Eamon, Very Rev, PP
Parochial House, Kilsaran,
Castlebellingham, Dundalk,
Co Louth
Tel 042-9372255
(*Kilsaran*, Armagh)

Treanor, Martin, Very Rev, PP
Inniskeen, Dundalk,
Co Louth
Tel 042-9378105
(*Inniskeen*, Clogher)

Treanor, Noel, Most Rev, DD
Bishop of Down and
Connor, Lisbreen,
73 Somerton Road, Belfast,
Co Antrim BT15 4DE
Tel 028-90776185
(Down & C.)

Treanor, Oliver
St Patrick's College,
Maynooth, Co Kildare
Tel 01-6285222
(Down & C.)

Tremer, Gerard, Very Rev, PP,
VF
Parochial House,
1 Convent Road,
Cookstown,
Co Tyrone BT80 8QA
Tel 028-86763370
(Armagh)

Trotter, Trevor (SSC)
St Columban's,
Grange Road,
Donaghmede, Dublin 13
Tel 01-8476647

Troy, Michael (OCarm)
Prior, Terenure College,
Terenure, Dublin 6W
Tel 01-4904621

Troy, Ulic (OFM), Very Rev,
Guardian
Adam and Eve's,
4 Merchant's Quay, Dublin 8
Tel 01-6771128
(*Merchant's Quay*, Dublin)

Tuffy, Muredach, CC
Director, Newman Institute
Ireland, Centre for Pastoral
Care, Salmon Weir, Ballina,
Co Mayo
Tel 096-72066
Parish
Rathduff, Ballina, Co Mayo
Tel 096-21596
(Backs, Killala)

Tully, Andrew, CC
The Presbytery, Cavan
Tel 049-4331404/4332269
(*Cavan*, Kilmore)

Tumilty, Stephen (OP)
St Catherine's, Newry,
Co Down BT35 8BN
Tel 028-30262178

Tuohy, David (SJ)
Dominic Collins' House
Residence,
129 Morehampton Road,
Dublin 4
Tel 01-2693075

Tuohy, Timothy, Very Rev, AP
Mullagh, Co Clare
Tel 065-7087014
(*Mullagh*, Killaloe)

Tuohy, Tom (SM)
Replacement Army
Chaplain, Dublin

Turley, Paul (CSsR)
Scala, Bessboro, Blackrock,
Cork
Tel 021-4358800

Twohig, Terence (SSC)
St Columban's Retirement
Home, Dalgan Park, Navan,
Co Meath
Tel 046-9021525

Twohig, Vivian, Very Rev, PP
Mullagh, Loughrea,
Co Galway
Tel 091-843119
(*Mullagh and Killoran*,
Clonfert)

Twomey, Bernard (OSA)
St John's Priory,
Thomas Street, Dublin 8
Tel 01-6770393

Twomey, Christopher
(OFMCap)
Provincial Office,
12 Halston Street, Dublin 7
Tel 01-8733205

Twomey, Donal (SPS)
St Patrick's, Kiltegan,
Co Wicklow
Tel 059-6473600

Twomey, Jack (OFMCap)
St Francis Capuchin Friary.
Rochestown, Co Cork
Tel 021-4896244

Twomey, Kieran, Very Rev, PP
The Presbytery,
Farranree, Cork
Tel 021-4393815/4210111
(*Farranree*, Cork & R.)

Twomey, Patrick, Very Rev
Canon, PP
Kildorrery, Co Cork
Tel 022-25174
(*Kildorrery*, Cloyne)

Twomey, Vincent (SVD)
(Editor of Word Magazine)
Maynooth, Co Kildare
Tel 01-6286391/2

Tynan, Joseph, CC
Ballydavid, Littleton,
Thurles, Co Tipperary
Tel 0504-44317
(*Moycarkey*, Cashel & E.)

Tynan, Sean, Very Rev
Laurel Lodge Nursing Home,
Longford
(Ardagh & Cl., retired)

Tyndall, David
Cathal Brugha Barracks,
Rathmines, Dublin 6
Tel 8046493
(Dublin)

Tyrrell, Gerard
Chaplaincy for Deaf People,
40 Lower Drumcondra Road,
Dublin 9
Tel 01-8305744
(Dublin)

Tyrrell, Patrick (SJ)
St Ignatius Community &
Church, 27 Raleigh Row,
Salthill, Galway
Tel 091-523707

Tyrrell, Paul, CC
The Presbytery,
Haddington Road, Dublin 4
Tel 01-6600075
(*Haddington Road*, Dublin)

U

Ugwu, Stephen (OCD)
Avila, Bloomfield Avenue,
Morehampton Road,
Dublin 4
Tel 01-6430200

Uranowski, Mariusz (SCHR)
Parochial House,
51 Victoria Road, Larne,
Co Antrim BT40 1LY
Tel 028-28273230/28273053
(*Larne*, Down & C.)

Uwah, Innocent
The Presbytery,
12 Coarse Moor Park,
Straffan, Co Kildare
Tel 01-6012197/085-1404355
(*Calebridge*, Dublin)

Uzochukwu, Peter
African Chaplaincy,
Prebytery, Portlaoise,
Co Laois
Tel 087-7850862
(Kildare & L.)

V

Van de Poll, Jan (SJ)
Manresa House,
Dollymount, Dublin 3
Tel 01-8331352

Van Gucht, Koenraad (SDB)
Rector and Chaplain,
University of Limerick,
Salesian House, Milford,
Castletroy, Limerick
Tel 061-330268/330914

Vaughan, Aidan (OFMCap)
Holy Trinity,
Fr Mathew Quay, Cork
Tel 021-4270827

Vaughan, Denis
45 The Oaks,
Maryborough Ridge,
Douglas, Cork
(Cloyne, retired)

Vaughan, T. T. (SPS)
St Patrick's, Kiltegan,
Co Wicklow
Tel 059-6473600

W

Wadding, George (CSsR)
Liguori House,
75 Orwell Road, Dublin 6
Tel 01-4067100

Wade, Thomas, Very Rev
(SMA), PP
St Joseph's,
Blackrock Road, Cork
Tel 021-4292871
(*St Joseph's (Blackrock
Road)*, Cork & R.)

Wafer, Andy (SSCC)
Coudrin House,
27 Northbrook Road,
Dublin 6
Tel 01-6686584/01-6671513

Waldron, Kieran, Very Rev
Canon, PP, VF
Killererin, Barnderg, Tuam,
Co Galway
Tel 093-49222
(*Killererin*, Tuam)

Waldron, Paul, CC
The Presbytery, Dungarvan,
Co Waterford
Tel 058-42384
(*Dungarvan*, Waterford & L.)

Waldron, Peter, Very Rev
Canon, PP
Keelogues, Ballyvary,
Co Mayo
Tel 094-9031009
(*Keelogues*, Tuam)

Walker, David (OP)
St Saviour's,
Upper Dorset Street,
Dublin 1
Tel 01-8897610

Wall, David (SSC)
St Columban's Retirement
Home, Dalgan Park,
Navan, Co Meath
Tel 046-9021525

Wall, John, Very Rev, PP
Annaduff,
Carrick-on-Shannon,
Co Leitrim
Tel 071-9624093
(*Annaduff*, Ardagh & Cl.)

Wall, John, Very Rev, PP
St Columba Parish House,
New Road, Clondalkin,
Dublin 22
Tel 01-4640441
(*Clondalkin*, Dublin)

Wall, Michael
Sacred Heart Residence,
Sybil Hill Road,
Raheny, Dublin 5
(Dublin, retired)

Wall, Michael
Chaplain, Mary Immaculate
College of Education
Tel 061-204331
(Limerick)

Wallace, Laurence, Very Rev,
PP
Muckalee, Ballyfoyle,
Co Kilkenny
Tel 056-4441271/
087-2326807
(Ossory)

Wallace, Matthew, Very Rev,
PP
Holy Trinity Presbytery,
26 Norglen Gardens,
Belfast BT11 8EL
Tel 028-90590985/6
(Holy Trinity, Down & C.)

Walsh, Brendan, Very Rev, PP
Causeway, Co Kerry
Tel 066-7131118
(Causeway, Kerry)

Walsh, David (SPS)
Assistant Society Leader,
St Patrick's, Kiltegan,
Co Wicklow
Tel 059-6473600

Walsh, Des, Very Rev, PP
Turloughmore, Co Galway
Tel 091-797114
(Lackagh, Tuam)

Walsh, Donal, Very Rev
Tinnahinch,
Graiguenamanagh,
Co Kilkenny
Tel 059-9725550
(Ossory, retired)

Walsh, Eamonn, Most Rev,
DD, VG
Titular Bishop of Elmham
and Auxiliary Bishop of
Dublin, Naomh Brid,
Bessington Road, Tallaght,
Dublin 24
Tel 01-4598032
(Dublin)

Walsh, Gearóid, Very Rev, PP
Castletownbere, Co Cork
Tel 066-7131118
(Causeway, Kerry)

Walsh, James, Adm
Oughterard, Co Galway
Tel 091-552290
(Oughterard, Galway)

Walsh, James, Very Rev, PP
Kilmeena, Westport,
Co Mayo
Tel 098-41270
(Kilmeena, Tuam)

Walsh, Jarlath (SMA)
Bursar General, Generalate,
Via della Nocetta 111,
00164 Rome, Italy
Tel 06-6616841

Walsh, John (OP)
Newbridge College,
Droichead Nua, Co Kildare
Tel 045-487200

Walsh, John (OSA)
Duckspool House
(Retirement Community),
Abbeyside, Dungarvan,
Co Waterford
Tel 058-23784

Walsh, John R., PP
Parochial House, Buncrana,
Co Donegal
Tel 074-9361393
(Buncrana, Derry)

Walsh, John
Mountdavid House, North
Circular Road, Limerick
Tel 061-452063/087-2433488
(Limerick)

Walsh, John, Very Rev, PE
Rath, Portlaoise, Co Laois
Tel 057-8626401
(Kildare & L., retired)

Walsh, John, Very Rev, PP
Aghamore, Ballyhaunis,
Co Mayo
Tel 094-9367024
(Aghamore, Tuam)

Walsh, John, Very Rev, PP
The Presbytery,
Frankfield, Cork
Tel 021-4361711
(Frankfield-Grange, Cork &
R.)

Walsh, Joseph (MHM)
St Joseph's House,
50 Orwell Park, Rathgar,
Dublin 6
Tel 01-4127700

Walsh, Joseph (OFM)
Guardian, Franciscan Abbey,
Multyfarnham,
Co Westmeath
Tel 044-9371114/9371137

Walsh, Joseph, CC
Crabb, Gortnahoe,
Thurles, Co Tipperary
Tel 056-8834867
(Gortnahoe, Cashel & E.)

Walsh, Kevin, CC
Dublin Road, Portlaoise,
Co Laois
Tel 057-8622301
(Portlaoise, Kildare & L.)

Walsh, Laurence (OCSO), Dom
Prior, Mount Saint Joseph
Abbey, Roscrea,
Co Tipperary
Tel 0505-25600

Walsh, Liam (OP)
St Saviour's,
Upper Dorset Street,
Dublin 1
Tel 01-8897610

Walsh, Martin (SMA)
Retired in Britain

Walsh, Michael F., Very Rev,
PP
Ballylooby, Cahir,
Co Tipperary
Tel 052-7441489
(Ballylooby, Waterford & L.)

Walsh, Michael, Rt Rev Mgr
Aghamore, Ballyhaunis,
Co Mayo
(Tuam, retired)

Walsh, Michael, Very Rev, PP
Parochial House,
Collinstown, Co Westmeath
Tel 044-9666326
(Collinstown, Meath)

Walsh, Michael, Very Rev, PP
Springlawn, Tubber, Moate,
Co Westmeath
Tel 090-6481141
(Tubber, Meath)

Walsh, Nicky (SPS)
St Patrick's, Kiltegan,
Co Wicklow
Tel 059-6473600

Walsh, Pádraig, CC
St Brendan's, Tralee,
Co Kerry
Tel 066-7125932/
087-6362780
(Tralee, St Brendan's, Kerry)

Walsh, Pat
Priests House, Aliohill,
Enniskeane, Co Cork
(Cork & R., retired)

Walsh, Patrick (CSsR)
Mount Saint Alphonsus,
Limerick
Tel 061-315099

Walsh, Patrick (MSC)
Western Road, Cork
Tel 021-4804120

Walsh, Patrick J., Most Rev,
DD
Bishop Emeritus of Down
and Connor,
6 Waterloo Park North,
Belfast BT15 5HW
Tel 028-90778182
(Down & C.)

Walsh, Paul (SM)
London

Walsh, Pearse, Very Rev, PP
87A St Stephen's Green,
Dublin 2
Tel 01-4780616
(University Church, Dublin)

Walsh, Richard (OP), CC
St Saviour's Priory, Kilbarry,
Waterford
Tel 051-376581
(St Saviour's, Waterford &
L.)

Walsh, Timothy (OSA)
The Abbey, Fethard,
Co Tipperary
Tel 052-31273

Walsh, Vincent (SSC)
St Columban's Retirement
Home, Dalgan Park, Navan,
Co Meath
Tel 046-9021525

Walsh, William A. (CSSp)
Templeogue College,
Dublin 6W
Tel 01-4903909

Walsh, William, Most Rev, DD
Bishop of Killaloe,
Westbourne, Ennis, Co Clare
Tel 065-6828638
(Killaloe)

Walsh, William, Very Rev, PP
8 Merval Crescent,
Clareview, Limerick
Tel 061-453026
(Our Lady of the Rosary,
Limerick)

Walshe, Adrian, CC
Castleblayney,
Co Monaghan
Tel 042-9740027
(Castleblayney, Clogher)

Walshe, Stephen (CSSp), CC
St Anne's, Sligo
Tel 071-9145028
(Sligo, St Anne's, Elphin)

Walshe, Thomas, Very Rev, PP
Rosenallis, Portlaoise,
Co Laois
Tel 057-8628513
(Rosenallis, Kildare & L.)

Walton, James, CC
Templemore, Co Tipperary
Tel 0504-31225
(Templemore, Cashel & E.)

Ward, Alan, CF
Chaplain, Finner Army
Camp, Ballyshannon,
Co Donegal
Tel 071-9842294
(Clogher)

Ward, Andrew (OCSO)
Mellifont Abbey, Collon,
Co Louth
Tel 041-9826103

Ward, Edward (OCarm)
Gort Muire, Ballinteer,
Dublin 16
Tel 01-2984014

Ward, John M.
1 Chestnut Grove,
Ballymount Road, Dublin 24
(Dublin, retired)

Ward, Michael, Very Rev
Canon, PE
6 Augherainey Close,
Donaghmore, Dungannon,
Co Tyrone BT70 3HF
Tel 028-87761847
(Armagh, retired)

Ward, Pat, Very Rev, PP
Burtonport, Co Donegal
Tel 074-9542006
(*Burtonport*, Raphoe)

Ward, Paul, Very Rev, PP
Parochial House, Bayside
Square North, Sutton,
Dublin 13
Tel 01-8323150
(*Bayside*, Dublin)

Ward, Peter (CSsR)
Clonard Monastery,
1 Clonard Gardens,
Belfast BT13 2RL
Tel 028-90445950

Ward, Seamus (SJ)
Milltown Park,
Sandford Road, Dublin 6
Tel 01-2698411/2698113

Warrack, Colin (SJ)
Gonzaga College,
Sandford Road, Dublin 6
Tel 01-4972943

Warren, Ray (OMI)
St Michael's Parish,
52a Bulfin Road, Inchicore,
Dublin 8
Tel 01-4531660
(*Inchicore*, Dublin)

Waters, Ignatius (CP)
St Paul's Retreat,
Mount Argus, Dublin 6W
Tel 01-4992000

Watson, Noel, CC
No 1 Presbytery, 4 Old Hill,
Leixlip, Co Kildare
Tel 01-6243718
(*Leixlip*, Dublin)

Watters, Brian, CC
79 Ivanhoe Avenue,
Carryduff, Belfast BT8 8BW
Tel 028-90817410
(*Drumbo*, Down & C.)

Watters, Enda (CSSp)
Blackrock College,
Blackrock, Co Dublin
Tel 01-2888681

Watters, Raymond (OP)
St Catherine's, Newry,
Co Down BT35 8BN
Tel 028-30262178

Weakliam, David (OCarm),
Very Rev, PP
Prior,
Whitefriar Street Church,
56 Aungier Street, Dublin 2
Tel 01-4758821

Welsh, Oscar (SMA)
Assistant Provincial Bursar,
African Missions,
Blackrock Road, Cork
Tel 021-4292871

Whearty, Roderick
St Fiacre's Gardens,
Bohernatownish Road,
Loughboy, Kilkenny
Tel 056-77701730
(*St Patrick's*, Ossory)

Whelan, Brian, CC
The Presbytery,
12 School Street, Wexford
Tel 053-9122055
(*Wexford*, Ferns)

Whelan, Edward, PE, CC
Ballon, Co Carlow
Tel 059-9159329
(*Ballon*, Kildare & L.)

Whelan, John (OSA)
St Augustine's Priory,
Galway
Tel 091-562524

Whelan, Joseph P. (MHM)
St Joseph's House,
50 Orwell Park, Rathgar,
Dublin 6
Tel 01-4127700

Whelan, Joseph, Very Rev,
Adm
75 Ludford Drive, Dublin 16
Tel 01-2988746
(Meadowbrook, Dublin)

Whelan, Marc (CSSp)
Holy Ghost Missionary
College, Kimmage Manor,
Dublin 12
Tel 01-4064300

Whelan, Martin, CC
18 University Road, Galway
Tel 091-524875/563577
(Galway)

Whelan, Michael (MSC)
Western Road, Cork
Tel 021-4804120

Whelan, Michael
c/o Archbishop's House,
Tuam
(Tuam)

Whelan, Patrick (SMA)
SMA House, Claregalway,
Co Galway
Tel 091-798880

Whelan, Patrick A. (CSSp)
Holy Ghost Missionary
College, Kimmage Manor,
Dublin 12
Tel 01-4064300

Whelan, Patrick, Very Rev, PP
St Patrick's Presbytery,
Forster Street, Galway
Tel 091-567994
(*St Patrick's*, Galway)

Whelan, Seamus (SPS)
St Patrick's, Kiltegan,
Co Wicklow
Tel 059-6473600

Whelan, Tom (CSSp)
Kimmage Mission Institute
at Milltown, Milltown Park,
Dublin 6
Tel 01-2776300

Whelan, Tom, CC
The Presbytery, Nenagh,
Co Tipperary
Tel 067-37131/087-2730299
(*Nenagh*, Killaloe)

White, Brian, CC
Parochial House,
11 Moy Road, Portadown,
Co Armagh BT62 1QL
Tel 028-38332218
(*Portadown (Drumcree)*,
Armagh)

White, Cornelius, Very Rev
Nazareth Home,
Dromahane, Mallow,
Co Cork
Tel 022-50486
(Cork & R., retired)

White, David, Very Rev, PP
Parochial House,
182 Garron Road,
Glenariffe,
Co Antrim BT44 0RA
Tel 028-21771249
(*Glenariffe*, Down & C.)

White, Jerry (SSCC)
Cootehill, Co Cavan
Tel 049-5552188

White, Laurence, Very Rev, PP
Parochial House,
Putland Road, Bray,
Co Wicklow
Tel 01-2862346
(*Bray, Putland Road*, Dublin)

White, Patrick
Training and Development
Officer,
Youth Link Training Offices,
143 University Street,
Belfast BT7 1HP
Tel 028-90323217
(Down & C.)

White, Séamus, CC
Parochial House,
6 Circular Road,
Dungannon,
Co Tyrone BT71 6BE
Tel 028-87722631
(*Dungannon (Drumglass,
Killyman and Tullyniskin)*,
Armagh)

White, Thomas, Most Rev
6 Osborne Court, Seapoint
Avenue, Blackrock,
Co Dublin
Tel 01-2806609
(Ossory)

Whiteford, Kieran, Very Rev,
PP
Parochial House,
Loughinisland, Downpatrick,
Co Down BT30 8QH
Tel 028-44811661
(*Loughinisland*, Down & C.)

Whitmore, Fintan Brennan
(OH)
Chaplain, Our Lady's
Chilren's Hospital
Crumlin, Dublin 12
Tel 01-4096100
(Dublin)

Whitney, Ciaran, Very Rev, PP,
VF
Chaplain, Post-Primary
School, Strokestown,
Co Roscommon
Tel 071-9633041
Parish
Strokestown,
Co Roscommon
Tel 071-9633027
(Elphin)

Whittaker, Michael, Very Rev,
PP
The Presbytery, Enfield,
Co Meath
Tel 046-9541282
(*Enfield*, Meath)

Whittle, Joseph (SDB)
Kilcullen Road, Dunlavin,
Co Wicklow

Whooley, Eoin, Very Rev, PP
Lislevane, Bandon, Co Cork
Tel 023-8846914
(*Barryroe*, Cork & R.)

Whyte, Daniel, Very Rev, PP,
VF
Elmfield, 165 Antrim Road,
Glengormley,
Newtownabbey,
Co Antrim BT36 7QR
Tel 028-90832979
(*St Mary's on the Hill*, Down
& C.)

Wickham, Anthony, Very Rev,
PP
Clondrohid, Macroom,
Co Cork
Tel 026-41014
(*Clondrohid*, Cloyne)

Williams, John (OSA)
St Augustine's,
Taylor's Lane,
Balyboden, Dublin 16
Tel 01-4241000

Williams, Patrick, Venerable
Archdeacon, PE
Caherlohan, Tulla,
Co Clare
(Tuam, retired)

Wilson, Desmond
6 Springhill Close,
Belfast BT12 7SE
Tel 028-90326722
(Down & C., retired)

Winkle, Patrick, CC
Youghal, Co Cork
Tel 024-92270
(Cloyne)

Winter, William, Very Rev PP
Banteer, Co Cork
Tel 029-56010
(*Banteer (Clonmeen)*,
Cloyne)

Woods, Brendan (SJ)
Milltown Park,
Sandford Road, Dublin 6
Tel 01-2698411/2698113

Woods, Daniel, Very Rev, PP
Kilcommon, Co Tipperary
Tel 062-78103
(*Kilcommon*, Cashel & E.)

Woods, Michael, Very Rev, PP
Parochial House,
40 Market Street,
Tandagree,
Co Armagh BT62 2BW
Tel 028-38840442
(*Tandragee (Ballymore and Mullaghbrac)*, Armagh)

Woods, Thomas (CM)
St Paul's College, Raheny,
Dublin 5
Tel 01-8318113

Woods, Thomas, Rt Rev Mgr, DD
Newbrook Nursing Home,
Mullingar, Co Westmeath
(Meath, retired)

Woods, Thomas, Very Rev, PP
East Barrs, Glenfarne,
Co Leitrim
Tel 071-9855134
(*Glenfarne*, Kilmore)

Wright, Colum, Very Rev, PP
10 Oaklands,
Loughbrickland,
Co Down BT32 3NH
Tel 028-40623264
(*Aghaderg*, Dromore)

Wynne, Owen (SCI)
Sacred Heart Fathers,
Fairfield, 66 Inchicore Road,
Dublin 8
Tel 01-4538655

Y

Young, Gerard, CC
23 Oakdown Road,
Dublin 14
Tel 01-2981744
(*Churchtown*, Dublin)

Young, Joseph
21 Marian Avenue,
Janesboro, Limerick
Tel 061-405835
(Limerick)

Young, Patrick, Very Rev
Billis, Cavan
Tel 049-4372386
(Kilmore, retired)

Young, Richard (OCD)
St Joseph's, Berkeley Road,
Dublin 7
Tel 01-8306356/8306336
(*Berkeley Road*, Dublin)

Young, Robert, Very Rev, PP
The Presbytery, Kinsale,
Co Cork
Tel 021-4774019
(*Kinsale*, Cork & R.)

Younge, Patrick (OFM)
Guardian, Franciscan Friary,
Lady Lane, Waterford
Tel 051-874262

Z

Zuribo, Aloysius
16 Ashfield Drive,
Balbriggan,
Co Dublin
Tel 01-8020602
(*Balbriggan*, Dublin)

Allianz (ⅲ)

GENERAL INDEX

Allianz

WORLD MISSIONS IRELAND
SPIRITUAL & PRACTICAL SUPPORT WORLDWIDE

Spiritual and Practical Support Worldwide

2009 CONTRIBUTIONS

Society of Missionary Children Total €193,000

Ghana	€50,268	Gambia	€26,170
South Africa	€44,687	Zambia	€21,875
Malawi	€43,750	Djibouti	€6,250

Society for the Propagation of the Faith Total €2,100,000

South Africa	€790,606	Lesotho	€170,960
Liberia	€280,825	Gambia	€100,556
Nigeria	€231,102	Sierra Leone	€95,143
Namibia	€178,159	Swaziland	€80,359
Botswana	€172,290		

Society of St Peter Apostle Total €904,363

Nigeria	€287,800	Sierra Leone	€28,188
India	€216,601	Lesotho	€27,246
Malawi	€163,805	South Africa	€16,768
Philippines	€65,217	Bolivia	€15,290
Liberia	€35,652	Namibia	€14,394
Cameroun	€32,047	Gambia	€1,355

WHAT A GIFT CAN DO

- **€50** will pay one month's food and accommodation for training a priest in Nigeria
- **€250** will fund parish pastoral activities for four months in the Philippines
- **€400** will feed four children one meal every day for one year in Uganda
- **€1,000** will buy an anti-malaria mosquito bed net for one hundred children in Malawi
- **€2,500** will pay for the formation of a student to the priesthood in Sierra Leone
- **€5,000** will cover the annual running costs of an orphanage in India
- **€10,000** will build a mission church and train five catechists in Ecuador

---

WORLD MISSIONS, IRELAND IS THE WORKING TITLE OF THE PONTIFICAL MISSION SOCIETIES. THE ORGANISATION IS MADE UP OF FOUR SOCIETIES EACH WITH A SEPARATE MISSION ROLE.

SOCIETY FOR THE PROPAGATION OF THE FAITH supports over 1,100 mission dioceses throughout the world. Each year the Society endeavours to increase both clerical, religious and laity awareness of mission work.

The Society is responsible for organising the Churches annual universal celebration of mission – Mission Sunday – encouraging spiritual and material support for Catholic missions worldwide.

SOCIETY OF ST PETER APOSTLE invites spiritual and financial support to assist Young mission Churches in the training of their own priests, brothers and sisters.

The Society which was established in 1889, supported the training of 2,700 seminarians in its first year but has continued to grow and in 2008/2009 supported 26,792 seminarians in their journey of faith.